American Cities

FODOR'S TRAVEL PUBLICATIONS

are compiled, researched, and edited by an international team of travel writers, field correspondents, and editors. The series, which now almost covers the globe, was founded by Eugene Fodor in 1936.

OFFICES

New York & London

Fodor's American Cities

Editor: Alice Thompson
Area Editors: Stephen Allen, Barry Anderson, Hilda Anderson, Jeri Bostwick, Curtis W. Casewit, Cecelia Caso, Mary Cooper, Cecilia Dames, Joan Dames, Diane DeMarco, Joyce Eisenberg, Robert J. Farrell, Nancy Haston Foster, Harry E. Fuller, Jr., JoAnn Greco, Carol Guensburg, Shirley Rose Higgins, Judy Hohman, Teresa Hurst, Mareal Johnson, John R. Kemp, Candace Kumerfield, Carolyn R. Langdon, Linda Lampman, Jane Lasky, Judy Liberson, Ira Mayer, Maribeth Mellin, Pam Parks, Gary Smith Ruderman, Jan Ryan, William G. Scheller, William Schemmel, Catherine Connor Schlaich, Mike Schwanz, Robert Taylor, Judy Williamson, Steve Winston, Fred. W. Wright, Jr., Su Wright
Maps: Jon Bauch Design, Burmar, Pictograph
Cover Photograph: Francesco Ruggeri

Cover Design: Vignelli Associates

Fodor's 89

American Cities

FODOR'S TRAVEL PUBLICATIONS, INC.
New York & London

ISBN 0–679–01642–2

MANUFACTURED IN THE UNITED STATES OF AMERICA
10 9 8 7 6 5 4 3 2 1

CONTENTS

FOREWORD

The city is a magnet—it attracts us or it repels us, but it seldom can be ignored.

The ebb of domestic American travel is from urban area to mountain, forest, or shore, but the flood, both vacation and business, is from city to city or from hinterland to city—the pull of the city can't be denied. We flock to our cities because they *are* cities, and because each is in some way unique.

Whether they're talking about the Big Apple, Windy City, City by the Bay, or any of the more than two dozen other major American cities in this volume, Americans describe their cities with a collection of superlatives—"biggest," "best," "greatest," or "most."

Those words, in themselves, can be scary. We wonder if we'll have fun, if we'll be cheated, or if we'll spend ourselves into bankruptcy. The latter, perhaps, is our greatest fear.

This, then, is why we've published this cost-conscious travel guide: to guide you, to the best of our ability, through 30 great American cities, to help you enjoy your visit at a *reasonable* expense, but also with a certain degree of style.

Note well that word "reasonable." Although we've listed many inexpensive accommodations and restaurants and found free activities and events for each of our 30 American cities, we have not limited ourselves to what is free or nearly so. Few things in this world are ever *totally* free. Meals must be eaten, weary bodies must have rest, and even an outing to a free park or exhibit may require transportation.

Moreover, we've assumed that you don't want to limit yourself to just the bare necessities, whether you're on your vacation or traveling on business. So we've searched out the best values at reasonable prices and given you more than enough information to be able to decide how to spend your time well and stay within your budget.

While every care has been taken to ensure the accuracy of the information contained in this guide, the publishers cannot accept responsibility for any errors that may appear.

All prices quoted in this guide are based on those available to us at the time of writing. In a world of rapid change, however, the possibility of inaccurate or out-of-date information can never be totally eliminated. We trust, therefore, that you will take prices quoted as indicators only, and will double-check to be sure of the latest figures.

Similarly, be sure to check all opening times of museums and galleries. We have found that such times are liable to change without notice, and you could easily make a trip only to find a locked door.

When a hotel closes or a restaurant produces a disappointing meal, let us know, and we will investigate the establishment and the complaint. We are always ready to revise our entries for the following year's edition should the facts warrant it.

Send your letters to the editors of Fodor's Travel Publications, 201 E. 50th Street, New York, NY 10022, or 30–32 Bedford Square, London WC1B 3SG, England.

FACTS AT YOUR FINGERTIPS

FACTS AT YOUR FINGERTIPS

PLANNING YOUR TRIP. Careful planning will enhance your trip and help keep expenses down. This introductory chapter provides general information for planning a trip in the United States and more specific information applicable to many or all the cities covered in this guide. Particular facts for each city are included in the individual chapters.

The Practical Information section on each city discusses the major modes of travel *to* the city and provides lists of hotels (with full mailing addresses and phone numbers) and restaurants as well as detailed information on tours, local transportation, parks and gardens, free events and activities, sports, museums, historic sites, shopping, nightlife, and much more. Also included are specific sources for additional tourist information.

WHAT WILL IT COST? Your major expenses will probably be transportation, accommodations, and food. Count the cost of transportation to and from your city first and then work out a daily budget for accommodations and food. The price categories in the accommodation and dining out sections in each chapter should serve as useful guidelines. (Necessarily, they vary from chapter to chapter.) Remember to budget money for all the meals you usually eat in an active day. If you require a substantial breakfast before a day of sightseeing, take that into account. We have supplied as many prices as possible for all attractions and activities, so that you can estimate how much money you are likely to spend on the things you want to do in a particular city—and how much you can afford to do. Many of the events and attractions listed in this guide are free, so if you budget your accommodation and food expenses carefully—even without settling for the cheapest possibilities—you should be able to keep the cost of your vacation within reason.

TRAVEL AGENTS. The best feature of the travel agent's role is that he does all your arranging, leaving you free to use your precious time elsewhere. But what should not be overlooked is his or her value in suggesting tailor-made vacations. Experienced agents have seen many tourist attractions firsthand and can suggest ır you—your purse, your age, your needs, and your desires. It is ..st interest to help you avoid the problems or complexities of travel-

..s service, the travel agent does not charge you a fee. His fee is collected ..ansportation carriers and hotels as a commission for promoting and mak- ..e. Your only charge might be for extra phone calls, cables, or other special .. On package tours and groups, the agent's and organizer's services are in- .. in the total price. If an agent has to arrange a complex itinerary and perform ..ad services, he may charge you, and you should discuss his charges in advance. ..he *American Society of Travel Agents, Inc. (ASTA)* is the world's largest profes- ..onal travel trade association, composed of all elements of the travel business. ASTA was established in New York in 1931 to promote travel, to prevent unethical practices, and to provide a public forum for travel agents. It is the duty of every ASTA member agency to protect the public against any fraud, misrepresentation, or unethical practices. To avoid being victimized by fly-by-night operators who might claim better bargains, look for the ASTA member shield—the hallmark of dependable travel service. You'll find the shield on entrance doors, windows, and all office forms of the member agency you select.

ASTA membership indicates that the agent has been in business for at least three years and is officially approved by the Society to sell tickets on behalf of airlines and cruise ships. ASTA agents also will arrange bookings for trains, buses, or car rentals. For further information write ASTA, 1101 King St., Alexandria, VA 22314, or phone (703) 944–5727.

The volatility of the travel field in the last several years has led to the failure of some tour operators and to losses on the part of their clients. To avoid this, a number of leading tour operators have formed a bonding association. For a list of these agencies whose stability is protected, write to: *United States Tour Operators Association,* 211 E. 51st Street, Suite 12B, New York, NY 10022, or phone (212) 944–5727.

PACKAGE TOURS. Time, convenience, cost, and the type of travel that most interests you are the factors to consider when it comes to choosing an all-inclusive, fully escorted tour, a loose plan-your-own-itinerary package tour, or totally independent travel. In between are fly-drive deals that might include a few nights lodging, hotel-only packages, and hotel packages with certain added services. Package tours are the easiest to arrange and probably the most economical and efficient way for a first-time traveler to get an overview of the most famous sights. Even a simple two-hour orientation bus tour on a first visit to a city can be enormously helpful in getting your bearings. Among the general terms to check when considering any package are:

Does the price quoted cover air as well as land arrangements? If airfare is not included, does the tour operator have a special rate available?

How many meals are included?

Does the rate for an automobile included in the package carry an additional fee per mile or is mileage unlimited? Is the car in the base rate exactly what you need? For example, is air conditioning included?

What "extras"—usually hotel services such as a bottle of wine, first night cocktail, transportation to another part of town—are thrown in that you don't need? A package for similar accommodations but without these unwanted extras might help keep the price even more within reason.

DISCOUNT TRAVEL. If you have the flexibility, you can sometimes benefit from last-minute sales tour operators have in order to fill a plane or prebooked hotels. A number of brokers specializing in such discount sales have sprung up. All charge an annual membership fee, usually about $35 to $45. Among these are the following: *Stand-Buys Ltd.,* 311 West Superior St., Suite 404, Chicago, IL 60610 (312–943–5737); *Moments Notice,* 40 E. 49th St., New York, NY 10017 (212–486–0503); *Discount Travel International,* 114 Forrest Ave., Narberth, PA 19072 (215–668–2182); and *Worldwide Discount Travel Club,* 1674 Meridian Ave., Miami Beach, FL 33139 (305–534–2082).

INSURANCE. In planning your trip, think about three kinds of insurance: *property, medical,* and *automobile.* The best person to consult about insuring your household furnishings and personal property while you are away is your insurance agent. For Americans, he is also the person to consult about whatever special adjustments might be advisable in your medical coverage while traveling. Foreigners visiting the United States should bear in mind that medical expenses in this country may seem astronomical by comparison with those they are accustomed to at home, and that the kind of protection that some countries (Britain, for example) extend to their own nationals and foreigners alike does not exist here.

Every state has some sort of financial responsibility law establishing the minimum and maximum amounts for which you can be held liable in auto accidents. Most states require insurance to be offered, and 17 states require you to have it in order to register a car or get a license within their jurisdictions. In any case, it is almost essential to have at least third party coverage, or "liability insurance," as claims can run very high both for car repairs and medical treatment. Insurance premiums vary according to place and person; they are generally highest for males under 25, and for drivers who live in large urban areas.

One possibility is the *American Automobile Association* (AAA), which offers both group personal accident insurance ($3,000) and bail bond protection up to $5,000 as part of its annual membership (fee $36). The AAA can also arrange the validation of foreign driving permits for use in the United States. Foreigners should consider getting their insurance before leaving their own countries since short-term tourists will find it difficult and expensive to buy here. For the AAA, write to *AAA,* 8111 Gatehouse Rd., Falls Church, VA 22047, or phone (703) 222–2000. Persons over 50 who are members of NRTA/AARP may join that organization's motoring plan which offers, among other things, reimbursement for legal fees, hospital emergency room bonding, arrest bonding, and emergency breakdown service. Write to: *AARP Motoring Plan,* Box 9052, Des Moines, IA 50369, or phone (515) 278–8030.

Trip cancellation insurance is also available (usually from travel agents) to protect you against losing any advance payments should you have to cancel your trip at the last moment.

TIPS FOR BRITISH VISITORS. Passports. You will need a valid passport and a U.S. Visitor's Visa (which can only be put in a passport of the 10-year kind). You can obtain the visa either through your travel agent or airline, or directly from the *United States Embassy,* Visa and Immigration Department, 5 Upper Grosvenor St., London W1A 2JB (01–499–3443). Allow six weeks if applying to the Embassy by mail; if you apply in person, your visa can be obtained in about three hours.

No vaccinations are required for entry into the United States.

Customs. If you are 21 or over, you can take into the U.S.: 200 cigarettes, or 50 cigars, or 3 lbs. of tobacco; 1 U.S. quart of alcohol. Everyone is entitled to take into the United States duty-free gifts to a value of $100. Be careful not to try to take in meat or meat products, seeds, plants, fruits, etc. And avoid narcotics like the plague.

Returning to Britain, you may bring home (1) 200 cigarettes or 100 cigarillos or 50 cigars or 250 grams of tobacco; (2) two liters of table wine and, in addition, (a) one liter of alcohol over 22° proof (most spirits), (b) two liters of alcohol under 22° proof (fortified or sparkling wine), or (c) two more liters of table wine; (3) 50 grams of perfume and ¼ liter of toilet water; and (4) other goods up to a value of £32.

Insurance. We strongly recommend that you insure yourself to cover health and motoring mishaps. *Europ Assistance,* 252 High St., Croydon CRO INF (01–680–1234), offers an excellent service that is all the more valuable when you consider the possible costs of health care in the United States. It is also wise to take out insurance to cover loss of luggage (though check that this isn't already covered in any existing policies you may have) and trip cancelation, which is particularly important if you are traveling on APEX or charter flights. The *Association of British Insurers,* Aldermary House, Queen St., London EC4N 1TT (01–248–4477), will give comprehensive advice on all aspects of vacation insurance.

Tour operators. The price battle that has raged over transatlantic fares has meant that most tour operators now offer excellent budget packages to the U.S. Among those you might consider as you plan your trip are:

Albany Travel (Manchester) Ltd., 190 Deansgate, Manchester M3 3WD (061–833–0202).

American Airplan, Marlborough House, Churchfield Rd., Walton-on-Thames, Surrey KT12 2TS (0932–246166).

Cosmos Air Holidays Ltd., 1 Bromley Common, Bromley, Kent BR2 9LX (01–464–3400).

Pan Am Fly/Drive, 193 Piccadilly, London W1V OAD (01–409–3377).

Speedbird, 152 King St., London W6 OQU (01–741–8041).

Travellers Jetways, 93 Newman St., London W1A 3LE (01–637–5444).

Airfares. We suggest that you carefully explore the current scene for budget flights. Start hunting well in advance and be prepared to be flexible; if you are persistent you should find something to suit your pocketbook. Try the ever-popular *Virgin Atlantic Airways.* It is also worth checking out the APEX and other bargain tickets offered by the major airlines serving the United States; you may be lucky and find an unexpected bargain.

HINTS TO DISABLED TRAVELERS. One of the newest, and largest, groups to enter the travel scene is the disabled, literally millions of people who are in fact physically able to travel and who do so enthusiastically when they know that they can move about in safety and comfort. Generally their tours parallel those of the nondisabled traveler, but at a more leisurely pace, and with all the logistics carefully checked out in advance. Three important sources of information in this field are: 1) the book, *Access to the World: A Travel Guide for the Handicapped,* by Louise Weiss, published by Henry Holt and Co.; 2) the *Travel Information Center,* Moss Rehabilitation Hospital, 12th St. and Tabor Rd., Philadelphia, PA 19141 (215–329–5715); 3) *Information Center for Individuals with Disabilities,* 20 Park Plaza, Rm. 330, Boston, MA 02116 (617–727–5540). In Britain, there are *Mobility International,* 62 Union St., London SE1 1JX (01–403–5688); and *The Royal Association for Disability and Rehabilitation,* 25 Mortimer St., London W1 8AB (01–637–5400).

The President's Commission on Employment of the Handicapped, along with the Easter Seal Society, has put together a series of guide books for every major city in the United States and a special book called *Guide to the National Parks and Monuments.* Each book lists only those places that are reasonably accessible to the handicapped or are so well known that information is frequently requested. The Commission has also issued a guide to over 330 roadside rest-area facilities considered "barrier free" for the disabled. Write to the Commission at Washington, DC 20210.

Lists of commercial tour operators who arrange or conduct tours for the disabled are available from the *Society for the Advancement of Travel for the Handicapped,* International Office, 26 Court St, Brooklyn, NY 11242 (718–858–5483). The Greyhound Bus system has special assistance for disabled travelers. International Air Transport Association (IATA) publishes a free pamphlet entitled *Incapacitated Passengers' Air Travel Guide.* Write IATA, 200 Peel St., Montreal, Quebec H3A 2R4, or phone (514) 844–6311. For a copy of the *Handicapped Driver's Mobility Guide,* contact your local AAA club (95 cents, ask for Stock No. 3772).

STUDENT AND YOUTH TRAVEL. The *International Student Identity Card* is not as universally recognized in the U.S. as it is abroad, though it can sometimes be used in place of a high-school or college identification card. Apply to *Council On International Educational Exchange (CIEE),* 205 E. 42 St., New York, NY 10017 (212–661–1414) or 312 Sutter St., San Francisco, CA 94108 (415–421–3473). Their *Whole World Handbook* ($7.95 plus postage) is the best listing of both work and study possibilities. Canadian students should apply to the *Association of Student Councils,* 187 College St., Toronto, Ont. M5T 1P7 (416–979–2406).

Students might also find it worthwhile to contact *Educational Travel Center,* 438 N. Frances, Madison, WI 53703 (608–256–5551), and *American Youth Hostels* (AYH), Box 37613, Washington, DC 20013–7613 (202–783–6161). AYH members are eligible for entree to the worldwide network of youth hostels, which isn't as extensive in the U.S. as in Europe but is a substantial resource nonetheless. Despite its name, AYH is also open to travelers of all ages. The organization publishes an extensive directory.

Among the leading specialists in the field of youth travel are the following:

Arista Student Travel Assoc., Inc., 11 E. 44th St., New York, NY 10017 (212–687–5121). Student and young adult tours for 14–16- and 16–18-year-olds, including a 27-day jaunt in the Northwest.

Bailey Travel Service Inc., 123 E. Market St., York, PA 17401 (717–854–5511). School-group, escorted, and independent tours.

Campus Holidays, 242 Bellevue Ave., Upper Montclair, NJ 07043 (800–526–2915).

In Canada: *AOSC (Association of Student Councils),* 187 College St., Toronto, Ont. M5T 1P7 (416–979–2406) is a nonprofit student-service cooperative owned and operated by over 50 college and university student unions. Its travel bureau provides transportation, tours, and work camps worldwide. Try also *Tourbec,* 535 Ontario E, Montreal, Quebec H2L 1N8 (514–288–4455).

TRAVELING WITH CHILDREN. Some of the following chapters include sections on children's activities, but in many cases we felt that the listings under parks, zoos, sports, historical sites, and museums provide more than enough to appeal to a carful of kids, all with varying interests.

AMERICA BY PLANE. A network of thousands of airline flights a day means that even with the limited time most vacations allow, you can see a lot of this country by flying from place to place. Nine airlines link the major U.S. cities. These are called *trunk lines.* They are *American, Continental, Delta, Eastern, Northwest Orient, Trans World (TWA), United,* and *Western* (mainly west of Minnesota, but now flying out of some East Coast cities). However, deregulation has opened the airways to literally dozens of other lines, many of which had formerly been limited to regional runs. (Deregulation has also prompted several of the larger airlines to eliminate competition by buying up the smaller airlines.) Among the latter are *USAir,* in the Northeast; *Frontier,* Midwest and West except the West Coast; *Piedmont,* middle east, north to New York. Information on connecting flights between trunk and regional airlines is available from any of the airlines or your travel agent.

FLY-DRIVE VACATIONS. Among the many ways you can travel, the fly-drive package can be an economical way to visit American cities. Most airlines, in conjunction with car rental companies, offer these combination opportunities to most parts of the country all year round. Fly-drive package rates and flexibilities vary considerably from one to another. Generally, they cover one or more cities plus the use of a rented car for the specified number of days.

Car usage also varies from one to another. For example, with some you can drive an unlimited number of miles, free. On others you get a specified amount of mileage free, and then must pay an additional charge per mile for the overage. Gas, generally, is not included.

Some packages offer plans for small groups and a choice of hotel accommodations. Some even offer motor homes, if you're interested in roughing it. Check into special children's rates.

Before booking, though, you should check with your agent about where you pick up the car (whether at the airport or some other station), and about the time it will take you to arrive at your hotel to meet your reservation. If you are not going to pick up the car at the airport, you should check ahead on airport limousines and bus and taxi service to your hotel. These are important details that should be included in or provided for by any good package-tour combination.

AMERICA BY TRAIN. *Amtrak* is the semi-governmental corporation that has taken over passenger service on most of the nation's railroads. At present the system has some 26,000 miles of track linking over 500 cities and towns in 44 states (except Maine, New Hampshire, Oklahoma, South Dakota, Alaska, and Hawaii) and since mid-1979, under the pressure of soaring gasoline prices the number of passengers carried has risen sharply. Amtrak's equipment, at best, is among the most modern and comfortable anywhere in the world; not all of the equipment is up to this standard, however; and the condition of the tracks and the adequacy of the auxiliary services (stations, meals, punctuality, etc.) is highly uneven. In general the system seems to work best in the "Northeast Corridor," the Boston–New York–Philadelphia–Baltimore–Washington megalopolis, and in southern California, where distances are short and getting to and from airports is inconvenient and expensive. On medium and longer runs the advantages of rail travel are in the spaciousness of the cars (against the cramped immobility of bus and plane) and the chance to enjoy the changing American landscape.

The simplest train accommodation is the day coach. There you ride in reclining seats, which may be reserved, with ample leg room, never more than two abreast. Next up is the leg-rest coach with (of course) leg rests, head rests, and deeper cushioning for the simplest kind of long distance nighttime accommodation. Slumbercoaches have lounge seats that convert into either a single bed or upper berths at night. For more space and privacy, a roomette gives a sitting room by day and at night a sleeping room with a full-length bed, and private toilet facilities. Bedrooms have two separate sleeping berths and private washing and toilet facilities. Superliner cars, operating between Chicago and the West Coast, also have family bedrooms that can sleep up to two adults and two children. Other types of special cars include dining cars, of course, and tavern lounges—an informal setting for a quiet drink, a game of cards, or just conversation. Some trains, especially where the scenery is best, have dome lounge cars, which give a great view of the countryside through high glass domes.

The reservation system is computerized and operates nationwide. Call 800–USA–RAIL. Amtrak has about 75 different package tours in addition to its regularly scheduled service. The tours may include hotels, meals, sightseeing, even Broadway shows. Write to *Amtrak Dept.,* Western Folder Distribution Co., Box 7717, 1549 W. Glen Lake Ave., Itasca, IL 60143, for brochures on the package tours available in the part of the country to which you are traveling.

Senior citizens, handicapped travelers, and families should inquire about discounts.

AMERICA BY BUS. The most extensive and one of the less expensive means of travel in America is the motor coach—the bus; 1,050 intercity and suburban bus companies operate to about 15,000 cities, towns, and villages in the United States, 14,000 of which have no other kind of intercity public transportation. The network totals over 277,000 miles of routes, carrying 10,000 buses. The major national bus line is *Greyhound-Trailways.* It covers the entire country with regularly scheduled routes. America's intercity buses carry over 350,000,000 passengers a year, more than Amtrak and all the airlines combined.

With more than 8,000 coaches on the road daily, you can go almost anywhere with little delay at connecting points. Reservations can be made for only a few trips. "Open date" tickets, good for travel any day, any time, are the rule. So, you just get your ticket, choose the time you want to travel, and show up early enough to get your bags checked in (15 minutes ahead in small towns, 45 minutes in cities).

Bargain-rate passes for unlimited travel on any regularly scheduled route in the United States and Canada are sometimes available. These passes are available to both residents and visitors, so there are no restrictions about when and where you can buy them. If they are bought abroad, the period of validity begins on the first day of use in this country; if they are bought here, it begins on the day of purchase.

Long-distance buses carry about 45 passengers. They are air-conditioned in summer, heated in winter. Baggage goes underneath, so the passenger compartment is up high, providing a better view through the big, tinted windows. Seats are the lounge chair type, with reclining backs and adjustable head rests. Reading lamps are individually controlled. Almost all long-distance buses have rest rooms.

HINTS TO THE MOTORIST. If you plan to take your own car on your trip, the first precaution you should take is to have your car thoroughly checked by your regular dealer or service station to make sure that everything is in good shape. The *National Institute for Automotive Service Excellence,* 1920 Association Dr., Reston, VA 22091 (703–648–3838), tests and certifies the competence of auto mechanics.

Each chapter, in the Hints to Motorists section, provides information about traffic laws and driving and parking conditions.

RENTAL CARS. Perhaps you would prefer to rent a car at your destination. If so, keep in maind that most companies require that you be at least 25; some, under special conditions, will rent to those who are only 21. Most companies accept major credit cards for deposit and payment. Cash transactions will require an advance cash deposit upon rental, and usually an application must be filled out and verified—which may be difficult after regular business hours or on weekends.

Be sure to check into the rent-it-here-leave-it-there option, which allows you to rent the car in one place and drop it off at any other company location in the United States for a modest drop-off charge. Also check into special rates offered for different categories of cars and for weekends, holidays, and extended trips. Rates and conditions can vary enormously; this is one area in which comparison shopping will pay off.

Car rental companies generally charge substantial per-day fees for insurance coverage. You should check the company of your choice for specifics. Here again, the services of a travel agent can save you time, money, and trouble, as he will have on file the relevant data for the major rental firms so that you will not have to check them all one by one yourself.

In most cases, a valid driver's license issued by any state or possession of the United States, by any province of Canada, or by any country which ratified the 1949 Geneva Motoring Convention, is valid and is required to rent a car.

Some of the nationwide rental agencies that provide 24-hour toll-free information and rental service are *Hertz* (800–654–3131), *Avis* (800–331–1212), *National* (800–227–7368), *Dollar* (800–421–6868), *Thrifty* (800–331–4200), and *Budget* (800–527–0700). In many chapters we have listed the names and numbers of local agencies that rent older or smaller cars at rates considerably less than those of the national companies.

AUTO CLUBS. If you don't belong to an auto club, now is the time to join one, even if you don't plan to drive to your destination. The maps, suggested routes, and emergency road service they offer can be helpful to those who rent a car as well as to those who drive from home. The *American Automobile Association* (AAA), in addition to its information services, has a nationwide network of some 26,000 service stations which provide emergency repair service. Its offices are at 8111 Gatehouse Rd., Falls Church, VA 22047 (703–222–2000). If you plan the route yourself, make certain the map you get is dated for the current year. Some of the major oil companies will send maps and mark preferred routes on them if you tell them what you have in mind. Try: *AMOCO Motor Club,* Box 9014, Des Moines, IA 50306 (515–225–4000).

Maps. The tradition of free road maps at gasoline stations has almost totally disappeared in the United States today. However, many of the local tourist bureaus listed in each chapter will send maps of cities, and state travel departments provide excellent road maps. The auto clubs offer members many maps to help them get around U.S. metropolitan areas. Another alternative is, of course, a road atlas, purchased at a bookstore, and costing anywhere from $1.50 to $6.00. There are three major ones published in this country now: by Rand McNally, by Grossett, and by Hammond. Rand McNally also publishes a "Standard Reference Map and Guide" for each state individually. The Hagstrom Company is the country's leading publisher of city street maps.

ACCOMMODATIONS. In this guide we've listed accommodations in two categories, determined by price: *Reasonable* and *Very Economical.* The actual prices vary from chapter to chapter, as they do from city to city; they are given at the beginning of each accommodation section. All hotel rates are for two people in a room and, unless otherwise noted, for European plan—no meals included.

Don't take potluck for lodgings. You'll waste a lot of time hunting for a place and often you won't be happy with what you finally find. The hotels we've listed give good value for your money, and they represent the range of standard prices for reasonable and economical accommodations in a particular city. If you don't have reservations, start looking in the afternoon. Each chapter provides information about when reservations are necessary in the city you plan to visit, but it's probably a good idea to make reservations whenever your plans are firm enough to allow it.

If you do have reservations (but expect to arrive later than 5 or 6 P.M.), advise the hotel or motel in advance. Some places will not otherwise hold reservations after 6 P.M. A hotel or motel will also usually guarantee a room regardless of your arrival time if you book using a major credit card. Of course, if you don't end up using the room in such instances, you are still charged the full rate (unless you cancel by a specified time). And if you hope to get a room at the hotel's *minimum* rates, be sure to reserve ahead or arrive early.

Hotel and motel chains. Although these establishments may not offer much local charm, they do offer two important conveniences: nationwide, toll-free reservation services (in most cases) and fairly dependable standards of quality. If you've stayed in one hotel in a chain, you've stayed in them all. Also, there are a number of budget motel chains that can be a good way to keep expenses down—if luxurious accommodations are not high on your list of vacation necessities. The following are some national chains and their toll-free numbers:

Comfort Inns Quality Hotels (800–228–5050), *Days Inns* (800–325–2525), *Econo-Lodges* (800–446–6900), *Holiday Inns* (800–HOLIDAY), *Howard Johnson* (800–654–2000), *La Quinta* (800–531–5900), *Quality International* (800–228–5151), *Ramada* (800–228–9898), *Super 8 Motels* (800–843–1991), and *TraveLodge* (800–255–3050).

DINING OUT. Restaurants are listed in this guide under three categories, determined by price: *Reasonable, Very Economical,* and *Low Budget.* The actual prices represented by these categories vary from chapter to chapter, as they do from city to city. We have also included a "recommended splurge": a restaurant that may be more expensive than the others listed but that offers a really special experience and great value for the money.

Brunches can be an economical way to eat or a splurge in themselves. In chapters where it seemed appropriate, we've listed some of both kinds.

Although many of the less expensive restaurants do not require or accept reservations, it is probably a good idea to call and ask about dinner reservations—and even lunch reservations in the larger cities. It's a good idea to call anyway, because, although we've made every effort to ensure that the restaurant lists are up to date, restaurants come and go very suddenly.

TRAVELER'S CHECKS. We urge you to use traveler's checks rather than cash when on the road. Many banks offer traveler's checks free as a service to their customers, but even if you have to pay one percent of the amount purchased, this is a small expense for the assurance that the checks will be replaced if stolen or otherwise lost. Don't forget to record the check numbers and carry them separately from the checks themselves.

CREDIT CARDS. Credit cards are widely accepted at hotels and motels and at many restaurants. However, many restaurants and shops have a minimum amount below which they do not accept the cards. Also, some establishments listed in this book manage to stay in the budget category in part because they don't contend with the extra fees involved in processing credit-card purchases. We have done our best to indicate establishments that don't accept credit cards, but if you're short on cash, double check before sitting down for a meal.

TIPPING. Tipping is standard practice throughout the country. Fifteen percent of the food bill in restaurants is probably typical nationwide, though 20 percent is becoming increasingly common for better than average service in the bigger cities. Ditto for cabs. $1.50 or so per night for a stay in a hotel or motel is the going rate, depending on services. Baggage handlers (admittedly a dying breed) at airports, bus, and rail terminals never get less than $1 for a bag or two, another 50 cents for each additional bag.

TIME ZONES. There are four time zones as you cross the continental United States. From east to west they are: Eastern, Central, Mountain, and Pacific. Daylight saving time, whereby clocks are set back an hour in the fall and forward again in the spring, keeps the maximum of sunshine available during summer days. Alaska is one hour earlier than California, and Hawaii is one hour earlier than Alaska.

HOLIDAYS. Five major holidays are marked uniformly every year throughout the nation: New Year's Day, January 1; Independence Day, July 4; Labor Day, the first Monday in September; Thanksgiving Day, the fourth Thursday in November; and Christmas Day, December 25. Banks and stock exchanges are closed on all of these days and selectively on other national and state holidays; many stores and restaurants are closed on some of them. It is best to check local papers. Most other holidays, such as Washington's Birthday and Memorial Day, are celebrated on Mondays in order to provide three-day weekends.

BANK HOURS. Banks are usually open Mon.–Fri., 9 A.M.–3 or 4 P.M., though these times vary somewhat. Most are open at least one evening a week, and some have Saturday hours. Increasingly popular are the automated-teller machines that dispense cash 24 hours a day. Certain bank cards are good nationally; you may wish to find out if the one you use at home will be honored in the cities you will be visiting.

MAIL. Stamps can be purchased at any post office in the United States, often from your hotel desk, or from coin-operated vending machines located in transportation terminals, banks, and some shops (stationers and drugstores, for example). They cost more if you get them from a machine—you pay for packaging and convenience—so for the sake of economy you may wish to buy as many as you think you will need when you find a handy post office.

There is no separate air mail rate for letters or postcards posted in the United States for delivery within the country or to Canada. Mail for distant points is automatically airlifted. The following are the postal rates in effect as of mid-1988:

	Letters	*Postcards*
United States, Mexico, and Canada	25¢ 1st oz.	15¢
*Overseas		
Air to Europe	45¢ 1st ½ oz.	36¢
Surface to most foreign countries	40¢ 1st oz.	28¢

TELEPHONES. Coin-operated public telephones are available almost everywhere: in hotel lobbies, transportation terminals, drugstores, department stores, restaurants, gasoline filling stations, in sidewalk booths, and along the highway. To use the coin telephone, just follow the instructions on the phone box. Local calls usually cost 25 cents and can be dialed directly. If you don't reach your party, your money is refunded to you automatically when you hang up.

For long-distance calls, dial 0 (zero) and have plenty of coins available, or ask to have the call charged to your home telephone (U.S.A. only; someone must be home to accept the charges). The operator may ask for enough change to cover the initial time period before he or she connects you. Often a 1 must be dialed before the area code; check the directions on the phone. To place a call outside the United States, dial 0 and ask for the overseas operator.

In hotels, your switchboard operator will either place your outside call for you, or tell you how to dial directly from your room. The telephone charges will be added to your hotel bill (although many times local calls are free) and you will pay for them when you check out.

TELEGRAPH. To send a telegram to a destination anywhere within the United States, ask for assistance at your hotel, or go to the nearest *Western Union* telegraph office. You'll find it listed in the classified section (yellow pages) of the telephone directory under "Telegraph." Overseas cablegrams can also be dispatched by Western Union, or by any cable company (also listed under "Telegraph"). You can phone Western Union and have a telegram charged to your home telephone (U.S.A. only). Mailgrams are similar to telegrams only they are delivered with the following day's mail and cost less than half what is charged for regular telegrams.

LIQUOR LAWS. These vary from state to state, and sometimes from county to county. (For instance, note the difference between the laws in Kansas City, Kansas, and Kansas City, Missouri.) In general, you must be at least 21 years of age to buy or drink alcohol, although Wyoming permits those 18 or over to drink. Wines and hard liquor are rarely sold in package stores on Sundays, holidays, or after midnight any day. We've noted relevant regulations in the introductions to the Nightlife sections.

[illegible] Christmas [illegible] December [illegible] or these days [illegible] and [illegible] are closed [illegible] other holidays [illegible] as Washington's Birthday [illegible] Memorial Day [illegible] for regional [illegible]

BANK HOURS. [illegible] these times vary [illegible] Saturday hours [illegible] [illegible]

MAIL. Stamps can be purchased [illegible] office in the United States [illegible] from your hotel desk [illegible] vending machines [illegible] [illegible] will reach you [illegible]

There is no separate [illegible] States [illegible] mail [illegible] The following [illegible]

United States, Mexico [illegible]	[illegible]
[illegible]	[illegible]
Air to Europe	[illegible]
Surface to [illegible]	[illegible]

TELEPHONES. [illegible] are available almost [illegible] [illegible] hotel lobbies [illegible] gas stations [illegible] [illegible] the [illegible] numbers [illegible] paid call [illegible] operator [illegible] [illegible]

[illegible] long distance [illegible] phone [illegible] [illegible] the call charged [illegible] [illegible]

[illegible]

TELEGRAPH. To send a telegram [illegible] Western Union [illegible] [illegible]

LIQUOR LAWS. These vary from state to state and sometimes from county to county [illegible] [illegible] the Virgin Islands [illegible]

THE CITIES

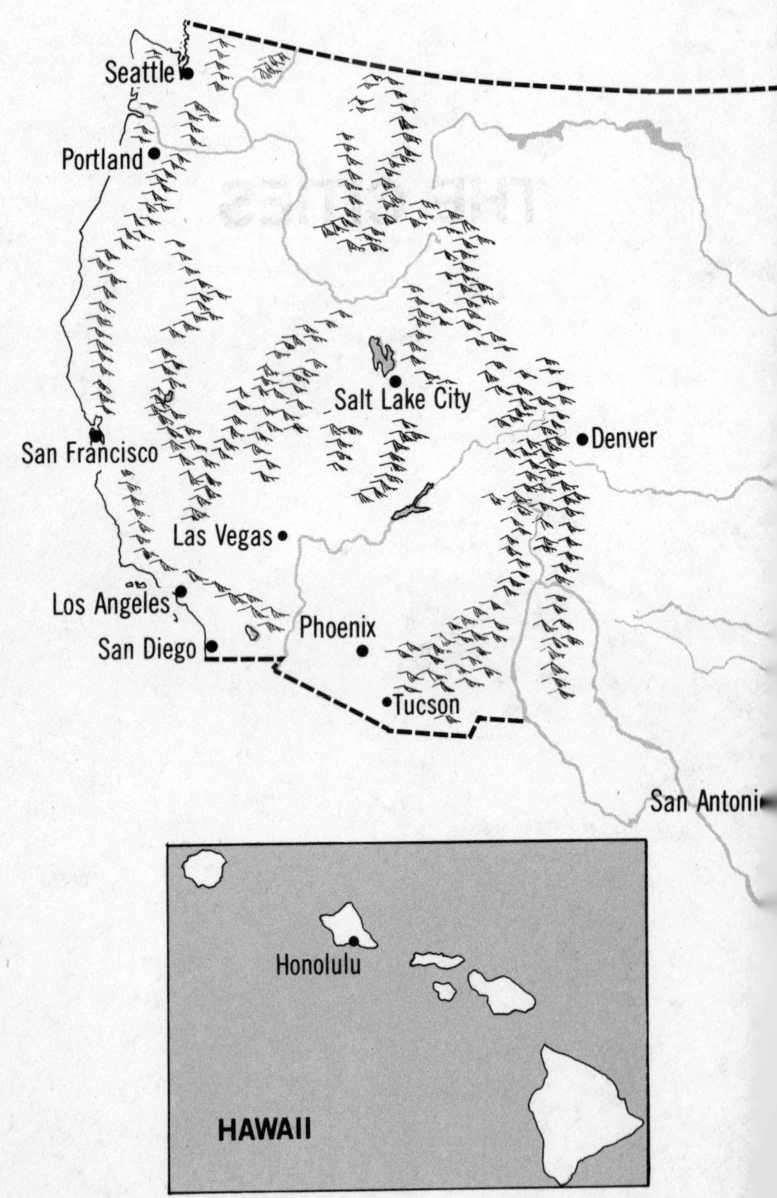
Seattle
Portland
San Francisco
Las Vegas
Los Angeles
San Diego
Salt Lake City
Denver
Phoenix
Tucson
San Antoni
Honolulu
HAWAII

Boston
St. Paul
Minneapolis
New York
Philadelphia
Atlantic City
Baltimore
Chicago
Washington, D.C.
St. Louis
Kansas City
Nashville
Atlanta
Dallas
Fort Worth
New Orleans
Tampa
Orlando
Houston
St. Petersburg
Miami

ATLANTA

by
William Schemmel

William Schemmel is a free-lance travel writer and photographer who lives in his hometown of Atlanta.

Even the most avid Atlantans admit that enjoying their city to the fullest requires patience, a reliable map, and advance reconnaissance. Physically akin to sprawling Los Angeles, Atlanta is a series of loosely defined neighborhoods strung together by freeways and a Rube Goldbergian street pattern. Aside from a few exceptional clusters downtown and in older neighborhoods, good restaurants, nightlife, museums, and attractions are scattered throughout the metropolitan area. Atlantans are hospitable and eager to show off their hometown to visitors. But even on your own, a little perseverance will soon bring it into focus.

Atlanta needn't be an expensive city. If one carefully selects accommodations and dining and takes advantage of public transportation and the discounts offered to students, senior citizens, and others, it can be enjoyed economically or even cheaply.

For a metropolitan area of 2 million, Atlanta has a relatively small **downtown** area. Running along the spine of Peachtree Street and its tributaries, downtown remains the center of banking and finance. Ballasted by the mammoth Georgia World Congress Center, it also forms the hub of the city's vital meetings industry. Among the many glamorous and expensive establishments catering to conventioneers and business travelers are many well-run hotels and motels tailored to budget travelers. There are also a variety of cafés and ethnic restaurants specializing in good food at reasonable prices.

By weekday, downtown bustles with office workers, shoppers, and out-of-town visitors. Except for hotels, the Congress Center, and a small selection of nonhotel restaurants and night places, most of the after-dark and weekend action is concentrated in close-in neighborhoods and far-flung suburbs.

Just north of downtown, Peachtree Street snakes into **Midtown.** Roughly bounded by Peachtree and Ponce de Leon Avenue, and extending north to about 19th Street, Midtown is a zesty neighborhood of handsomely restored 1920s bungalows and Victorians, eclectic and nonconventional life-styles, ethnic eateries, bars of all sorts, live theater, art galleries, small shops, and yeasty street life.

The Woodruff Arts Center at Peachtree and 15th streets is the home of the Atlanta Symphony Orchestra and Alliance Theatre. The dazzling new High Museum of Art is next door. Piedmont Park, off Piedmont Avenue between 10th and 14th streets, is the city's largest, a habitat for joggers, skaters, sunbathers, picnickers, and softball and tennis players; the setting for festivals and free concerts; and a forum for political and social activists.

From Midtown, Peachtree Street twists farther north, changes to Peachtree Road, and bisects the affluent **Buckhead** section. The area got its distinctive name from an 1830s tavern keeper who nailed a male deer's head to his door and called it the Buck's Head Tavern. Today, Buckhead boasts numerous "taverns" of all descriptions catering to young professionals and more sedate elders.

Many an aristocrat owes his mansion on Buckhead's Tuxedo, Habersham, and Blackland roads to wise investment in Coca-Cola stock way back when. Buckhead is also the retail capital of the southeastern Sunbelt, the rainbow's end for shoppers from all across the region.

While the city has been pushing to distant new suburbs, older close-in neighborhoods have been rediscovered. Just east of Piedmont Park, the Virginia-Highland neighborhood, around the corner of Virginia and N. Highland avenues, has witnessed a resurgence of residential prestige and a subsequent influx of moderately priced cafés, pubs, ice cream shops, and specialty stores tailored to largely young and upbeat new residents. More small cafés and whatnot shops are situated in the nearby Little Five Points neighborhood, around the corner of Euclid and Moreland avenues.

Atlanta's easygoing suburban life-style is symbolized by leafy new neighborhoods in Cobb, Gwinnett, northern DeKalb, and Fulton counties in the northern metropolitan area and Clayton and Fayette counties south of Hartsfield Airport. With all their trees, Atlantans feel close to the outdoors. Parks abound, and outdoor activities can be pursued most of the year.

The Chattahoochee River National Recreation Area offers scenic river rafting and woodland hiking within the metropolitan area; only an hour away, Lake Lanier and Lake Allatoona have hundreds of miles of shoreline for swimming, boating, and fishing. The mountains, lakes, and national forests of northern Georgia are just beyond, and the beaches of the Georgia, Florida, and South Carolina coasts can be reached within four to five hours by car.

PRACTICAL INFORMATION

WHEN TO GO. Atlanta is blessed with a moderate four-season climate. Spring is the ideal time for a visit. In late March and early April, millions of dogwoods and azaleas and other colorful flowers break into dazzling bloom. July and August are generally hot and humid, but a high altitude (1,050 ft.) precludes the suffocating

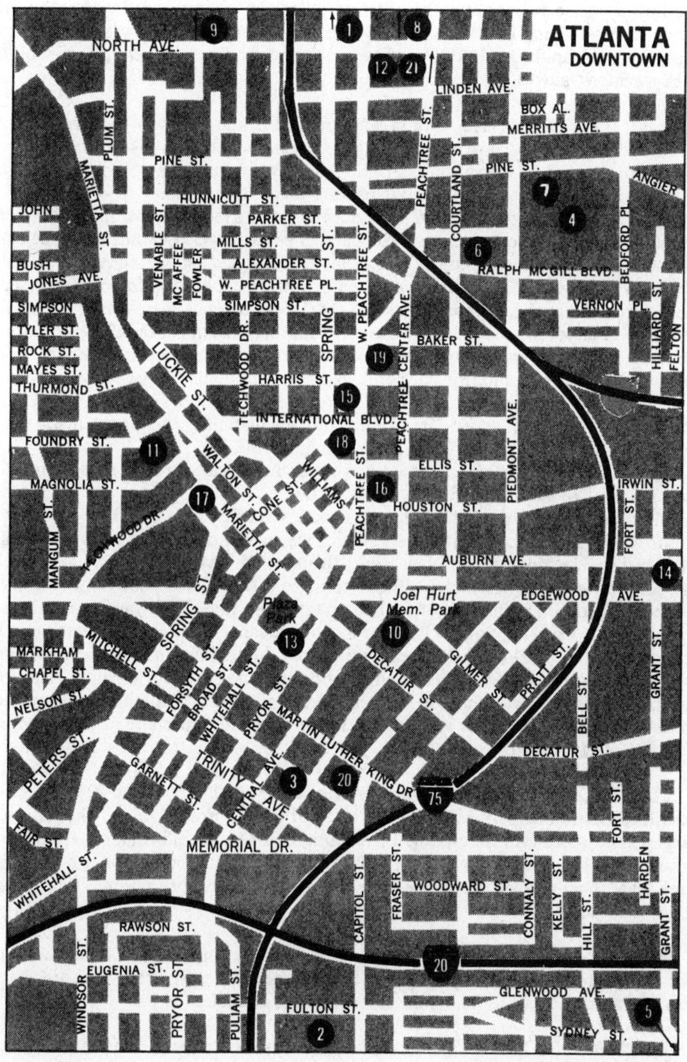

Points of Interest

1) Atlanta Historical Society
2) Atlanta Stadium
3) City Hall
4) Civic Center
5) Cyclorama
6) Marriott Marquis and Hilton hotels
7) Exhibition Hall
8) Fox Theater
9) Georgia Institute of Technology
10) Georgia State University
11) Georgia World Congress Center
12) High Museum of Art
13) Five Points Rapid Rail Station
14) Martin Luther King grave
15) Merchandise Mart
16) Georgia-Pacific Center
17) Omni Hotel and CNN Center
18) Peachtree Plaza Hotel
19) Hyatt Regency Atlanta Hotel
20) State Capitol
21) Woodruff Arts Center

humidity of the coastal Deep South and moderates temperatures at night. From middle to late October the city experiences a brilliant autumn foliage change and delightfully crisp temperatures. Winter weather can change rapidly from warm sunny days to biting cold and rain and occasional sleet and snow and then can change just as rapidly back to springlike temperatures. Thus, winter visitors should pack sweaters, gloves, and an overcoat.

HOW TO GET THERE. Atlanta was founded in the 1830s as the terminus of a railroad line into the northwest Georgia wilderness and today is the undisputed transportation hub of the southeastern Sunbelt. By air, bus, or automobile it's difficult to travel through Dixie without passing through Atlanta.

By air. *Hartsfield International Airport* is the world's largest jet terminal complex and currently the busiest in terms of the number of passengers (40 million annually). Major domestic airlines serving the city include *Delta, Eastern, American, TWA, United, Piedmont, USAir, Continental,* and *Northwest.* Nonstop international service is provided by *KLM* (Amsterdam), *Japan Air Lines* (Tokyo), *Swissair* (Geneva, Zurich), *Sabena* (Brussels), *Lufthansa* (Frankfurt), *Delta* (Frankfurt, London, Paris, and Nassau), and *Eastern* (Mexico, the Caribbean, and Latin America). Primarily a business hub and transfer point, and not an optional tourist mecca, Atlanta has traditionally been one of the nation's most expensive air destinations. However, recent inauguration of service by *Continental Airlines* and others have made dramatically discounted fares available for the first time.

By bus. *Greyhound-Trailways* has comprehensive service through modern terminals adjacent to each other in downtown Atlanta.

By train. A city born of the railroads is now served by only one daily passenger train. AMTRAK's "Crescent" offers service westward to New Orleans and northeastward to Washington and New York. Brookwood Station is at 1688 Peachtree St., 3 miles north of downtown. Phone toll-free 800–872–7245 for information.

By car. Atlanta is the hub of four interstate highways: I-85 running northeast to southwest, from the South Carolina to the Alabama borders; I-75, north-south from Tennessee to Florida; I-20, east-west from South Carolina to Alabama; and I-285, the Perimeter Highway, circling the metropolitan area for 65 miles. The entire metropolitan-area interstate system is undergoing a $2 billion expansion and modernization, and detours and delays can be expected, especially in the morning and late afternoon rush hours.

TELEPHONES. The area code for Atlanta and north Georgia is 404. The cost of a local telephone call is 25 cents. The local dialing area is one of the nation's largest, and there's no time limit. In Atlanta, dial 411 for information; from elsewhere, dial 404–555–1212. To dial long distance out of Atlanta, dial 1 before the area code. Dial 0 before the area code for operator assistance on credit card and long distance calls.

Emergency Telephone Numbers. In most of metropolitan Atlanta, including the city proper, dial 911 for the police and fire departments. Otherwise, dial 0 for the operator and ask to be connected with local agencies.

ACCOMMODATIONS. Atlanta is the third busiest convention and meeting center in the country, and it offers a broad range of accommodations, from the super deluxe to the economical. Hotel rates are based on double occupancy, EP. Categories, determined by price, are as follows: *Reasonable,* $55 to $75; *Very Economical,* $40 to $55.

Reasonable

American Hotel. 160 Spring St., Atlanta, GA 30303 (404–688–8600). Centrally located downtown, with restaurants, lounges, pool.

Days Inn Downtown. 300 Spring St., Atlanta, GA 30303 (404–523–1144). Deluxe member of the budget chain, adjacent to the Merchandise Mart and Apparel Mart. Full restaurant.

Habersham Hotel. 330 Peachtree St., Atlanta, GA 30303 (404–577–1980). Small hotel prides itself on personalized European service and refined accommodations.

Very Economical

Atlanta Cabana Hotel. 870 Peachtree St., Atlanta, GA 30308 (404–875–5511). Campy 1950s Miami Beach decor in the heart of a lively area of ethnic restaurants, bars, and street life.

Atlantan Hotel. 111 Luckie St., Atlanta, GA 30303 (404–524–7000). Recently refurbished old downtown hotel offers attractive rooms, good restaurant, and bar at moderate prices.

Barclay Hotel. 89 Luckie St., Atlanta, GA 30303 (404–524–7991). Quiet older downtown hotel popular with budget business travelers.

Cheshire Motor Inn. 1865 Cheshire Bridge Rd., Atlanta, GA 30324 (404–872–9628). Small, well-kept motel between downtown and Buckhead caters to business and budget travelers. Several inexpensive American and ethnic restaurants are nearby.

Days Inn-Peachtree. 683 Peachtree St., Atlanta, GA 30306 (404–874–9200). Small refurbished hotel across from the Fox Theatre; about 2 miles north of downtown.

Emory Pines Inn. 1650 Clifton Rd., Atlanta, GA 30307 (404–634–5152). Convenient to Emory University and Centers for Disease Control.

Red Carpet Midtown Inn. 1152 Spring St., Atlanta, GA 30303 (404–875–3511). Modern motor hotel with restaurant and bar; 2 miles north of downtown.

Budget Motel Chains. Virtually every national motel chain has multiple locations in the Atlanta area. Depending on the chain and the location, expect to pay from $30 to $50 for a double room.

Best Western. Numerous Atlanta-area locations with restaurants, lounges, and swimming pools. For reservations, phone toll-free 800–528–1234.

Days Inns of America. More than a dozen Atlanta-area Days Inns have moderately priced accommodations, family restaurants, gas stations, and swimming pools. Phone toll-free 800–325–2525 for reservations.

Fairfield Inns by Marriot. Marriott Hotels has opened two budget-category motels in the metro area: **Fairfield Inn-Northwest,** Delk Rd. at I-75, Marietta, GA 30067 (404–952–9863); and **Fairfield Inn-Atlanta Airport,** 2451 Old National Pkwy., College Park, GA 30349 (404–761–8371). Toll-free reservations: 800–228–2800. Both motels have swimming pools but not restaurants or bars. TVs; free morning coffee.

Holiday Inn. For information and reservations in metropolitan Atlanta, phone toll-free 800–465–4329.

Howard Johnson's. For information and reservations in metropolitan Atlanta, phone toll-free 800–654–2000.

LaQuinta Motor Inns. Phone toll-free 800–531–5900.

Ramada Inns. For information and reservations in metropolitan Atlanta, phone toll-free 800–228–2828.

Bed-and-Breakfast. Bed-and-Breakfast Atlanta. 1801 Piedmont Ave., Suite 208, Atlanta, GA 30324 (404–875–0525). Accommodations in lovely private homes, including full breakfast, private bath, and an opportunity to meet Atlantans on an informal basis. Rates from $24 to $48, with some exceptional accommodations up to $70 per night.

Beverly Hills Inn. 65 Sheridan Dr., Atlanta, GA 30305 (404–233–8520). European-style bed and breakfast, about 5 miles north of downtown, with 17 units decorated with period furnishings; Continental breakfast.

HOW TO GET AROUND. From the airport. Millions of travelers first glimpse Atlanta while descending toward Hartsfield International Airport. Moving sidewalks and a high-speed subway make negotiating the world's largest jet terminal complex a breeze. Reaching your hotel is also simple. *Atlanta Airport Shuttle* (766–5312) operates vans between the airport and downtown hotels ($7 one-way, $12 round-trip) and near-suburban locations such as Emory University ($10 one-way, $18 round-trip). *Northside Airport Express* buses (455–1600) run between the airport and seven suburban terminals ($9.75–$15 one way, $17–$25 round-trip).

Taxi fare downtown is fixed at $13.50, but taxis aren't Atlanta's strong suit. Many are mechanically faulty and run by drivers unfamiliar with the local terrain. Before setting off, make certain your driver has a lock on your destination.

By bus. The *Metropolitan Atlanta Rapid Transit Authority (MARTA)* operates a modern, efficient bus system. The fare is 75 cents, and exact change is required. For schedules and information, call 522–4711.

By subway. MARTA is good news for those baffled by Atlanta's street nonpattern. MARTA's clean, luxurious rapid rail-subway trains link downtown with such landmarks as the Memorial Arts Center, High Museum, Symphony Hall, Six Flags Over Georgia theme park, and the hotels, retail malls, dining, and entertainment in the uptown Buckhead–Lenox Square area. The rail system's two lines connect at the Five Points Station downtown. Trains run 5 A.M.–1:30 A.M., and parking (75 cents all day) can be found around most suburban stations. Stations have no rest rooms or concession stands. The fare is 75 cents one way, exact change required, including transfers valid for bus to train and vice versa. For schedules and information, call 522–4711.

By car. *Alamo Rent-A-Car,* at Hartsfield International Airport (768–8855, 800–327–9633), offers free unlimited mileage and corporate rates. *Budget Rent-A-Car,* also at the airport (530–3000, 800–527–0700), has weekend and vacation specials. *Hertz* (659–3000, 800–654–3131) gives special business, weekend, and vacation rates. *Ugly Duckling Rent-A-Car,* at the airport, (762–3000), has budget cars, trucks, and vans.

On foot. Pedestrians are advised that crosswalks are not a sanctuary from speeding motorists, who may or may not stop.

HINTS TO THE MOTORIST. Instead of being logically laid out in a neat grid of numbered streets and avenues, Atlanta's street "plan" more closely resembles a spilled platter of pasta. Narrow streets seem to meander over the landscape, colliding in maddening triangles and star-shaped chaos, changing names capriciously. Compounding the confusion, 32 thoroughfares have "Peachtree" as part of their names. You can begin to get a grip on things by orienting yourself to Peachtree *Street*—the main north-south thoroughfare that changes to Peachtree *Road* north of downtown—and casting a cautious eye on Peachtree Battle Avenue, Peachtree Memorial Drive, and the other pretenders.

Don't place much faith in numbered streets. The numbering system begins with Third St., proceeds northward along Peachtree St. to 19th St., loses 20th St. through 24th St. at triangular Pershing Point, picks up again at 25th St. and 26th St., forgets all about 27th St., and dies out completely at 28th St.

The entire metropolitan-area interstate highway is undergoing massive reconstruction, causing detours and delays at all hours. At the slightest hint of snow or ice, get off the streets. The city owns no snow-removal equipment, and even an inch can close down everything. At such times, motorists find out that this is a very hilly city.

TOURIST INFORMATION. Before arriving, write ahead for maps, brochures, and other free information to the *Atlanta Convention and Visitors Bureau,* 233 Peachtree St., Atlanta, GA 30303 (521–6600), and the *Georgia Department of Tourism,* 230 Peachtree St., Atlanta, GA 30303 (656–3590). The Atlanta Convention Bureau has information kiosks at Hartsfield International Airport, in the outdoor mall at Peachtree Center downtown, and inside the Lenox Square shopping mall. The *Atlanta Council for International Visitors,* Habersham Hotel, 330 Peachtree St., downtown (577–2248), offers foreign visitors assistance with translators and guides and puts them in touch with ethnic societies. Atlanta has more than 50 foreign consulates and trade and tourism offices listed in its telephone directory. For special problems, contact *Travelers Aid,* 40 Pryor St., downtown (527–7400).

Foreign Currency Exchange. *First National Bank of Atlanta,* Hartsfield International Airport (768–2856); and *Citizens & Southern National Bank,* Broad and Marietta streets, downtown (581–3424).

SENIOR-CITIZEN AND STUDENT DISCOUNTS. Students and senior citizens can take advantage of a variety of discounted services in metropolitan Atlanta. Students should be certain to carry college ID cards and ask about discounts at theaters, restaurants, museums, and transportation. Major colleges and universities in the area—Georgia Tech, Georgia State University, Emory University, Oglethorpe University, Atlanta University, Agnes Scott College, and Mercer University—have special films, lectures, concert series, and other events available to students and sometimes can supply short-term room rental for visiting students. Student cafeterias represent an inexpensive way to meet one's peers.

Special discounts are often available for senior citizens at sporting events, concerts, and tourist attractions. Seniors may travel for half fare on MARTA, the city's public transportation system, and most airlines and bus companies serving the city also offer special rates. By joining Days Inns' September Days Club (one year, $10), travelers over age 55 can receive discounts on rooms, meals, and gifts. The bed and breakfast lodgings in Atlanta homes (see the Bed-And-Breakfast section) represent another low-cost way for seniors to enjoy this sprawling, high-paced city.

HINTS TO DISABLED TRAVELERS. Atlanta has a number of special facilities and services for the disabled and the blind. On arrival at Hartsfield International Airport, the handicapped will find special ramps, elevators, rest rooms, and parking areas with the international handicapped symbol. MARTA has special lift buses on heavily traveled routes to assist wheelchair riders, and the parking lots and fare gates at MARTA rapid rail stations are designed to facilitate access for the handicapped. Many of the largest hotel and motel chains offer guest rooms especially equipped for disabled guests. Call in advance to Holiday Inns, Days Inns, Ramada Inns, Marriott, Sheraton, Omni International, and the Atlanta Hilton for information and rates.

At Atlanta Stadium, Atlanta Civic Center, Woodruff Arts Center, Fox Theatre, and the Omni Arena, special rows are available for wheelchair guests who phone ahead. The blind can receive information about special services and facilities by contacting the Atlanta Area Services for the Blind, 763 Peachtree St., Atlanta, GA 30303 (404–875–9011).

SEASONAL EVENTS. Atlanta's special events calendar is crowded year-round. **March:** *Saint Patrick's Day Parade,* downtown; *Virginia-Highlands Bungalow Tour* (522–4345). **April:** *Ansley Park Tour of Homes* (522–4345); *Atlanta Dogwood Festival* (892–0538), a major event with home and garden tours, free music, parades, and art shows; *Inman Park Festival* (681–2798), another major happening, with home tours, flea market, art, and music; *Midtown Tour of Homes* (522–4345). **July:** *Fantastic Fourth Celebration,* Stone Mountain Park, with symphony and country music, barbecue, and stage shows; *Peachtree Road Race,* with 25,000 runners in a 10-km classic; *Salute to America Parade,* downtown; *Atlanta Symphony* free concerts outdoors at Piedmont Park, Sunday evenings, July–Aug. **September:** *Arts Festival of Atlanta,* Piedmont Park (885–1125), one of the city's largest annual events, a week of outdoor music, drama, jugglers, mimes, hundreds of arts and crafts booths, and incomparable people watching. *Atlanta Greek Festival,* 2500 Clairmont Rd. (633–5870); *Grant Park Tour of Homes* (622–6366); *Powers Crossroads Country Fair,* huge Labor Day festival 50 miles south of Atlanta. **October:** *Scottish Festival and Highland Games,* Stone Mountain Park (498–5600); **December:** *Christmas at Callanwolde Fine Arts Center,* 980 Briarcliff Rd. (872–5338); *Nutcracker Ballet,* Fox Theatre (873–5811); *Peach Bowl* college football game, Atlanta Stadium.

TOURS. Guided tours of Atlanta and the surrounding areas are offered by *Gray Lines of Atlanta* (767–0594), and *Presenting Atlanta* (231–0200). *Atlanta Carriage Co.* has city tours by horsedrawn carriage; call 584–9960. *TourGals,* 262–7660, offers specially tailored tours with multilingual guides. Guided and self-guided tours of the city's historic areas are offered through the *Atlanta Preservation Center* (522–4345). For free guided tours of the *Martin Luther King Jr. National Historic Site,* call the U.S. Park Service at (331–3919).

PARKS AND GARDENS. Chattahoochee River National Recreation Area. U.S. 41 and I-75, about 12 miles north of downtown (394–8139). A popular area for rafting and inner-tubing over mild rapids, picnics and hiking. Open daily.

Grant Park. 800 Cherokee Ave. (624–1071). The highlight of the park, about 3 miles from downtown, is the Cyclorama, a dramatic circular painting, 50 ft. high by 400 ft. in circumference, depicting the most crucial hour in the 1864 Battle of Atlanta. Adults $3.50, senior citizens $2.50, children ages 6–12, $1.50. Open daily, 9:30–4:30. There is a museum, housing the locomotive "Texas," which took part in the Civil War's "Great Locomotive Chase," as well as photographs, uniforms, and other memorabilia. After a rash of bad publicity, the Atlanta Zoo in the same park has made some noticeable improvements.

Fernbank Science Center. 156 Heaton Park Dr., near Decatur (378–4311). A must-see for families. The large complex includes a planetarium with seasonal shows, natural history museum, greenhouses, botanical gardens, and nature trails. Admission fee only for planetarium shows ($2 adults, $1 students). Open Mon., 8:30 A.M.–5 P.M.; Tues.–Fri., 8:30 A.M.–10 P.M.; Sat., 10 A.M.–5 P.M.; Sun., 1–5 P.M.

Piedmont Park. Off Piedmont Ave., between 10th and 14th streets. Has softball fields, tennis courts, a swimming pool, picnic pavilions, jogging trails, and botanical gardens and greenhouses. Open daily, 6 A.M.–1 A.M. Small fee for some facilities.

Six Flags Over Georgia. Off I-20, 12 miles west of downtown (948–9290). An immaculately maintained theme park with something for every taste, from roller coasters to tame rides and live shows. All-inclusive $16.50 admission is valid for two days.

Stone Mountain Park. Off U.S. 78, 16 miles east of downtown (498–5600). Centerpiece is the granite monolith, 825 ft. high and 5 miles around, carved with images of three Confederate heroes. Other amusements include a Swiss skylift to the mountaintop, a steam locomotive ride, an antebellum plantation, an 18-hole golf course, swimming, fishing, camping, boating, and even ice skating. The park is 16 miles east of the city and served by MARTA buses from downtown. Admission $4 per car, with additional charges for rides and attractions. Gates open daily 6 A.M.–midnight, attractions 10 A.M.–5:30 P.M., in summer 10 A.M.–9 P.M.

PARTICIPANT SPORTS. With its temperate year-round climate, Atlanta offers golf, tennis, biking, skating, jogging, and other outdoor activities on all but a few bitterly cold winter days.

Bicycling. The *Southern Bicycle League* (294–1594) has regularly scheduled tours of the city and surrounding areas. At *Skate Escape,* 1086 Piedmont Ave., across from Piedmont Park (892–1292), bikes rent for $4.50 and $6.50 an hour, $15 and $18 all day; **roller skates** are $3 an hour, $6 all day.

Golf. The best courses are: *Stone Mountain Park* (498–5600), 18 holes; weekdays $16, weekends and holidays $18, closed Mon. *Chastain Park,* 216 W. Wieuca Rd. (255–0723), 18 holes; weekdays $9.45, weekends and holidays $10.50. *Sugar Creek,* 2706 Bouldercrest Rd. (241–7671), 18 holes; weekdays $10 non-residents, weekends and holidays $11, closed Tues. Carts and rental clubs are available at all three courses.

Running. Runners quickly learn that Atlanta is very hilly. *Piedmont Park,* Piedmont Ave., between 10th and 14th streets, is an excellent running area, 3 miles north of downtown. If you'd like to join 25,000 others in the annual *Peachtree Road Race,* contact the Atlanta Track Club, 3097 E. Shadowlawn Ave., Atlanta, GA 30305 (231–9064).

Tennis. *Bitsy Grant Tennis Center,* 2125 Northside Dr. (351–2774), is the area's nicest public facility. During the day hard courts are $1.50 per person per hour, clay courts $2.50; 25 cents higher after dark. *Piedmont Park,* Piedmont Ave. at 14th St. (872–1507), has hard courts only, $1.50 per person per hour.

Water Sports. Two mammoth man-made lakes are within an hour's drive. *Lake Sidney Lanier,* off I-85 northeast of the city, has a 550-mile shoreline for boating, fishing, swimming. Lake Lanier Islands, Box 605, Buford, GA 30518 (945–6701), is a state-operated recreational area with a sand beach, golf, tennis, horseback riding, rental cottages and a deluxe hotel. Similar facilities are available at Red Top Mountain State Park on *Lake Allatoona,* off I-75 northwest of the city (974–5182). Closer to the city, the *Chattahoochee River National Recreation Area,* U.S. 41 and I-75, 12 miles northwest of downtown (394–8139), is popular with summer rafters and picnickers. Sturdy 4-, 6-, and 8-man rafts are for rent at *Chattahoochee Outdoor Center,* Johnson Ferry Road bridge over the Chattahoochee (395–6851), for $25 to $45 for the entire day.

SPECTATOR SPORTS. Atlantans are intrepid fans of both spectator and participant sports. In spring and summer, **baseball's** Atlanta *Braves* meet National

League opponents at Atlanta-Fulton County Stadium just south of downtown. The Atlanta *Falcons* of the National **Football** League take over the stadium in fall. College football fans follow the fortunes of the *Georgia Tech Yellow Jackets* at Grant Field, north of downtown, and make the 60-mile pilgrimage to Athens to see the Georgia *Bulldogs.* The National **Basketball** Association's Atlanta *Hawks* play from fall through spring at the **Omni Arena** downtown, which is also the site of annual rodeos, tennis tournaments, circuses, and other events. Check local papers for times and schedules. More than 25,000 runners participate in the annual *Peachtree Road Race,* July 4, and several times that number line the route to cheer on their favorites.

CHILDREN'S ACTIVITIES. Children in your company will especially enjoy the Fernbank Science Center, Stone Mountain Park, the Six Flags Over Georgia theme park, the Children's Theatre at the Woodruff Arts Center, and the Center for Puppetry Arts; all are described in this chapter. They also can work off their energy on playgrounds in area parks—Playscapes in Piedmont Park is especially recommended—and let their imaginations run free at the High Museum's touch and feel "Sensations" exhibition. Punctuate your sight-seeing by eating at the *Varsity Drive-In,* 61 North Ave., at I-75 and I-85 (881–1706), having a barbecue sandwich at the *Old Hickory House* chain all over town, or enjoying ice cream from one of the many national chains or Atlanta's own *Gorin's Ice Cream and Sandwiches,* in malls and neighborhood shopping areas, or *Tim's Homemade Ice Cream,* 1002 Virginia Ave. (874–5127).

HISTORIC SITES AND HOUSES. Atlanta's rich and varied array of attractions includes Civil War battlefields, historic homes, and magnificent residential neighborhoods.

Atlanta Historical Society, Swan House, and Tullie Smith Plantation. 3101 Andrews Dr.,(261–1837). Even jaded jet-setters gasp in astonishment as they drive past French châteaus, Spanish and Italian villas, Tudor manors, and white-columned Greek Revival mansions in the Buckhead section of northwest Atlanta, along West Paces Ferry, Habersham, Blackland, Andrews, and other tree-lined thoroughfares. For an inside peek at privilege, visit the Swan House, an Italianate villa filled with European and Oriental furnishings and antiques. Tullie Smith House, on the same grounds, is furnished in the simple style of an 1830s farmhouse. Admission to both houses and grounds is $4.50 adults, $4 students and seniors, $2 ages 7–12. Mon.–Sat. 9:30 A.M.–4:30 P.M., Sun. 12:30–4:30 P.M.

Fox Theatre. Peachtree St. at Ponce de Leon Ave. (881–1977). One of the last of the 1920s picture palaces, a fantasy of Moorish arches, minarets, and Egyptian hieroglyphics that now hosts Broadway shows, concerts, and special films. The Atlanta Preservation Society (522–4345) conducts guided tours.

The Georgia Governors Mansion. 391 W. Paces Ferry Rd. (261–1776). Near the Historical Society, a modern-day Greek Revival building with Federal period furnishings and antiques, open free of charge Tues.–Thurs. 10–11:30 A.M.

Georgia State Capitol. Downtown on Capitol Hill (656–2844). Gleams with a dome of north Georgia gold. Inside are state offices, Confederate Battle flags, and museums. There's an inexpensive underground restaurant across the street in Georgia Plaza Park. Guided tours Mon.–Fri. at 10 and 11 A.M., and at 1 and 2 P.M.

Kennesaw Mountain National Battlefield Park. Off I-75 near Marietta (427–4686). This area saw some of the fiercest fighting of the 1864 Battle of Atlanta campaign. Stop at the National Park Service Visitors Center and then hike or take a shuttle bus to the crest, view the earthworks, and have a picnic lunch. Free. **The Big Shanty Museum** in the nearby town of Kennesaw houses the locomotive "General," subject of a Civil War spy chase re-created in Disney's *The Great Locomotive Chase.* Adults, $2; children 9 to 16, 50 cents. Daily, 8:30 A.M.–5 P.M.

The Martin Luther King Jr. Memorial Historic District, near downtown, includes the civil rights leader's birthplace home, the Ebenezer Baptist Church where he preached, his tomb, museums, and memorials. There is no charge to see the tomb or to take a walking tour with National Park Service rangers. Phone 524–1956 for the center; phone the Park Service at 331–3919. Daily, 9 A.M.–5 P.M.

The Wren's Nest. 1050 Gordon St. (753–8535). The former home of author Joel Chandler Harris, filled with memorabilia of Br'er Fox, Br'er Rabbit, and others made famous in the Uncle Remus tales. Admission $3 adults, $2 seniors and teens, $1 ages 4–12. Mon.–Sat. 10 A.M.–5 P.M., Sun. 2–5 P.M.

MUSEUMS AND GALLERIES. Atlanta's importance as the visual arts center of the Southeast is reflected by the opening in 1983 of its spectacular new High Museum of Art and by the number and variety of galleries. The "Weekend" tabloid section of Saturday's Atlanta *Journal–Constitution* carries news about exhibitions and galleries.

Atlanta Museum. 537 Peachtree St. (872–8233), is for admirers of the offbeat. The eight-room Queen Anne-style brick mansion is filled with antiques and curiosities from around the world, including Hitler's hat and coat, Civil War artifacts, and Indian relics. Antiques are for sale in a separate area of the house. Adults, $2; children, $1. Open Mon.–Fri. 10 A.M.–5 P.M., Sat.–Sun. by appointment.

Carter Presidential Center. N. Highland and Cleburne aves. (331–3942). Contemporary complex houses documents, photos, gifts from Jimmy Carter's presidency, and many multimedia displays on the history of all our presidents. Adults $2.50, seniors $1.50, under 16 free. Mon.–Sat. 9 A.M.–4:45 P.M., Sun. noon–4:45 P.M.

The High Museum of Art. 1280 Peachtree St. (892–3600). Moved into its new home in 1983; along with permanent collections of European, American, and African paintings, sculpture, and decorative arts, it hosts a continuous schedule of important traveling exhibitions. Designed by world-famed architect Richard Meier, the museum is a dazzling high-tech masterpiece with a light-flooded central atrium. Admission $3 adults, $1 students, under 12 free. Tues. & Thurs.–Sat., 10 A.M.–5 P.M., Wed. 10 A.M.–9 P.M., Sun. noon–5 P.M. Closed Mon.

The Margaret Mitchell Collections at the Atlanta Public Library, downtown at Peachtree and Forsyth streets, will appeal to *Gone With the Wind* buffs who want to see displays of memorabilia of the movie and editions of the book in many languages. Mitchell is buried in Oakland Cemetery, a landmark in its own right, on Memorial Dr., near the state capitol. Loew's Grand Theatre, where the movie had its stupendous 1939 premiere, was on the site of the Georgia-Pacific Tower, downtown. Mon.–Sat., 9 A.M.–6 P.M.; Sun., 2–6 P.M.

Nexus Gallery. Glen Iris Dr. and Ralph McGill Blvd. (688–1970). Photography is displayed by a consortium of independent artists with studios in a former school building.

The Catherine Waddell Gallery. Trevor Arnett Library, Atlanta University (681–0251). Has one of the nation's largest collections of Afro-American paintings, sculpture, and graphics. Daily, 9 A.M.–5 P.M.

FILM. Most Atlanta movie houses offer discounts for senior citizens and cut-rate prices for all before 6 P.M. ($3 compared with the $5 full price). Second-run features are 99 cents at all times at **Franklin-3 Theaters,** 1033 Franklin Rd., Marietta (952–1712), and $1.50 at **Toco Hills Theater,** 2983 N. Druid Hills Rd. (636–1858). Film series at Emory University, Georgia State University, and Agnes Scott College are open to the public at small charge. The latest foreign films, experimentals, and offbeat works are shown at the **Ellis Theater,** Euclid and Moreland avenues (688–FILM); **Screening Room,** Lindbergh Plaza, 2581 Piedmont Rd. (231–1924); and **Ansley Cinema,** Ansley Mall, Piedmont Ave. and Monroe Dr. (881–9955). You can relax with a movie and beer, wine, and eats at the Ellis (above) and **Excelsior Mill,** 695 North Ave., (577–6455). During the summer, the **Fox Theatre's Film Festival** provides an opportunity, for $4.50, to see *Gone With the Wind, South Pacific,* and other classics with concerts on the world's largest theater organ, cartoons, and newsreels in the splendor of one of the last 1920s picture palaces. Located at Peachtree St. and Ponce de Leon Ave. (881–1977). *Gone With the Wind* plays continuously at CNN Cinema, CNN Center, downtown at Marietta St. and Techwood Dr. (577–6928).

MUSIC. The **Atlanta Symphony Orchestra** is the keystone of the city's cultural life. Regarded as one of the nation's leading symphonies, ASO performs its regular season at Woodruff Arts Center, 1280 Peachtree St. (892–2414), with outstanding artists as guest performers ($10–$20). In the summer the orchestra puts on a series of free concerts Sunday nights in Piedmont Park as well as pops concerts at Chastain Park. Other highlights of the ASO year include the Christmas concerts, winter pops series, and children's concerts.

Other organizations performing regularly include the **Atlanta Boys Choir** (378–0064), **Choral Guild of Atlanta** (435–6563), **Atlanta Chamber Players** (872–3360), and **Atlanta Virtuosi** (938–8611).

DANCE. Atlanta's dance scene is headed by the highly acclaimed **Atlanta Ballet** (873–5811). The 50-year-old company is nationally known for its presentations of classical works as well as highly innovative new programs. Most programs are at the Atlanta Civic Center. Other excellent companies include the **Callanwolde Dance Ensemble** (874–1039), the **Carl Ratcliff Dance Theatre** (266–0010), and the **Ruth Mitchell Dance Company** (237–8829), a 20-year-old group that performs originally choreographed ballet and jazz dancing. Ticket prices vary with the event, but rarely exceed $12 to $15.

STAGE. Regional theater is thriving in Atlanta, with nearly a score of professional companies presenting traditional, modern, and experimental plays. Several of the largest companies are on Peachtree St. between 10th and 15th streets, convenient to downtown hotels and public transportation. Most theaters offer discounts to senior citizens, students, and groups. For current offerings, check the "Weekend" tabloid section of Saturday's Atlanta *Journal–Constitution.*

Alliance Theater. Woodruff Arts Center, 1280 Peachtree St. (892–2414). Presents a balanced repertory of new and standard plays to one of the nation's largest season-ticket audiences. Also in the Woodruff Center, the **Studio Theater** presents new and experimental works, while the **Atlanta Children's Theatre** presents classic and contemporary plays for the younger set.

Academy Theater, 173 14th St. (892–0880), and **Theatrical Outfit,** 1012 Peachtree St. (872–0665), offer modern and older works.

The Center for Puppetry Arts. 1404 Spring St. (873–3391). Offers regularly scheduled plays with an all-puppet cast as well as a puppet museum and a school of puppetry. Museum admission $1; show prices vary.

Theater of the Stars, in the Atlanta Civic Center, presents touring musicals with big-name stars during the summer and, in winter, drama and comedy, often fresh from Broadway.

SHOPPING. Atlanta is Dixie's shopping center. The metropolitan big-name department stores, mammoth regional malls, specialty galleries, international markets, and discount outlets lure shoppers from all across the region. You can get almost anything you want here, seven days a week. Most downtown stores are closed on Sunday, but suburban malls are open all week, from mid-morning to about 9:30 every night.

Downtown, the major magnets are the flagships of the *Rich's* and *Macy's* (formerly *Davison's*) department store chains. Both stores display a vast array of merchandise and have large budget-clothing departments. Macy's Cellar is an attractive ensemble of boutiques offering cookware and gourmet foods. Shoppers at the Cellar can relax in the store's own P.J. Clarke's Pub. Rich's is a part of Federated Department Stores.

Also downtown, on Peachtree Street, you can make the big splurge at *Brooks Brothers* and such other high-fashion stores as *Muse's* and *H. Stockton.* The shopping gallery at *Peachtree Center* has a number of gift and specialty shops. For an authentic look at southern down-home shopping, take a stroll through the cavernous *Municipal Market,* 209 Edgewood Ave., where you'll see every part of the pig, fresh fish, mounds of strange greens, wigs, cut flowers, and rich social undercurrents.

The biggest selections of stores are grouped in the metropolitan area's **regional malls.** The largest are at major intersections off the I-285 Perimeter Highway: *South DeKalb Mall* at Candler Rd., *North DeKalb* at Lawrenceville Hwy., *Northlake* at LaVista Rd., *Perimeter* at Ashford-Dunwoody Rd., and *Cumberland* at U.S. 41 and I-75.

For many shoppers, the major destination is the intersection of Peachtree and Lenox roads 8 miles due north of downtown. You won't find many bargains, but your eyes will be dazzled at **Phipps Plaza,** a stylish enclosed mall anchored by *Saks Fifth Avenue, Lord & Taylor, Gucci, Tiffany, Abercrombie & Fitch,* and other elite merchandisers from Beverly Hills, Fifth Avenue, and Europe. Across Peachtree Road, **Lenox Square** has more than 300 department stores—headed by *Neiman-Marcus, Rich's,* and *Macy's*—specialty shops, high-quality and fast-food dining, movies, and services. Even more stores and restaurants are located at the smaller adjacent **Around Lenox.** The area is served from downtown by MARTA's North rail line and by the number 23 bus.

If you're visiting Stone Mountain Park, detour from the park and enjoy the old-fashioned ambience of the **Town of Stone Mountain's** Main Street. Numerous craft stores, antique shops, and cafés can be seen along the covered sidewalk. Equally charming is the small crossroads of **Vinings,** on Paces Ferry Road west of the Chattahoochee River, renowned for antique shops. The *Old Vinings Inn* in the center of the village serves excellent country-French cuisine at lunch and dinner.

The small town of *Chamblee* in the northeast metropolitan area also has a cluster of **antique shops** and flea markets. A big selection of flea markets, oddity shops, and "junque" emporiums can be found around the Peachtree Road/Broad Street intersection, a block north of MARTA's Chamblee rapid rail station.

If **"junking"** is your pleasure, nirvana awaits at **Little Five Points.** This revived old neighborhood, around the intersection of Moreland and Euclid avenues, 3 miles east of downtown, is loaded with vintage clothing stores, used-record stores and bookshops, antique stores, and stores that defy description. The neighborhood has been revitalized by a cross section of young Atlantans who throw a community festival in May to celebrate. When you're tuckered out from browsing, you'll find several pubs and cafés serving Italian, Ethiopian, Mexican, Indian, Cajun, vegetarian, and deli foods. The Point Lounge and Little Five Points Pub have live nighttime entertainment.

The nearby **Virginia–Highland neighborhood,** around the intersection of Virginia and North Highland avenues, is another fine locale for people watching and browsing through small one-of-a-kind shops. The pubs and small restaurants around the corner are a magnet for an upbeat young crowd and are excellent places for meeting the natives.

Atlanta has caught the **discount** craze in a big way. Entire malls—such as *Outlet Square,* Buford Hwy. and Clairmont Rd., and *Loehmann's Shopping Center,* U.S. 41 in Smyrna—cater to shoppers with champagne tastes and soda pop budgets.

DINING OUT. A thriving national and international melting pot, Atlanta offers a broad and tempting range of cuisines from exotic ethnic specialties and trendy pastas to American regional cooking and earthy southern favorites. Restaurant categories, determined by the price of a meal for one, without beverages, tax, or tip, are as follows: *Reasonable,* $12 to $20; *Very Economical,* $8 to $12; and *Low Budget,* under $8. Except where noted, all restaurants listed accept major credit cards. Every effort has been made to ensure that the list is up to date, but restaurants come and go so quickly that it is advisable to call first.

Reasonable

Camille's. 1186 N. Highland Ave. (872–7203). Bustling neighborhood Italian café draws wall-to-wall crowds for its outstanding pizza and richly sauced pasta, veal, and seafood dishes. Lunch, dinner daily.

Dailey's. 17 International Blvd. (681–3303). Charmingly restored brick warehouse features imaginative Continental dishes, sandwiches, burgers, salads. Popular with downtown workers, shoppers. Lunch, Mon.–Sat.; dinner daily.

Indigo Coastal Grill. 1397 N. Highland Ave. (876–0676). A campy Caribbean-Key West decor, and excellently prepared seafoods make Indigo one of the city's favorite neighborhood cafés. Dinner Tues.–Sat.

Longhorn Steaks Restaurants. 8 metro area locations, check yellow pages for nearest. Done up with barn wood and Lone Star flags, this popular, local chain specializes in hearty cuts of beef at moderate prices. Lunch Mon.–Fri., dinner nightly.

Partners Morningside Cafe. 1399 N. Highland Ave. (875–0202). Intimate little neighborhood café and bar renowned for homemade pastas, spicy Cajun-style blackened redfish, salads, desserts. Dinner, Mon.–Sat.

Pentimento. Woodruff Arts Center, Peachtree & 15th sts. (875–6665). Small, stylish café/bar is a popular venue for lunch, dinner, wines, cocktails before and after Arts Center performances and visits to the adjacent High Museum. Lunch, dinner daily except Mon.

Pilgreen's. 1081 Lee St. (758–4669). A favorite for 50 years, this old-fashioned steak house serves some of the best beef in town at the most reasonable prices. Don't miss the French-fried cauliflower and onion rings. Lunch, dinner Tues.–Sat.

The Pleasant Peasant. 555 Peachtree St. (874–3223). Charming bistro-style café is one of the city's favorites. A pacesetter in casually sophisticated style with a moderately priced Continental menu. Dinner daily.

Sierra Grill. 1529 Piedmont Rd. at Monroe Dr. (873–5630). Modern Southwestern cuisine. Dishes combine the color and flavors of Arizona and New Mexico with European subtlety and visual impact at this stylish midtown eatery and bar. Lunch Mon.–Fri., dinner Mon.–Sat.

Very Economical

The Colonnade. 1879 Cheshire Bridge Rd. (874–5642). Atlantans seeking honest southern and American cooking, cheerful service, and a modest tab have sworn by this unique establishment for more than 25 years. Consistently one of the area's best bets. Lunch, dinner daily. No credit cards.

East Village Grille. 248 Buckhead Ave. (233–3345). Grilled chicken, fresh vegetables, omelets, and pork chops are the fare an old Buckhead area firehouse-turned-café/bar. A major meeting and mingling place. Drink prices can take the total tab out of the very economical category, but the food is a bargain. Open from early morning to the wee hours every day.

Gojinka Japanese Restaurant. 5269 Buford Hwy. (458–0558). The city's most popular Japanese restaurant, with a large sushi bar, tempura, sukiyaki, and other specialties. Dinner only, Mon.–Sat.

Jagger's Restaurant & Tavern. 1577 N. Decatur Rd., across from Emory University (377–8888). Crowded, frenetic college hangout boasts some of the best pizza in town, along with juicy burgers, salads, sandwiches, cold beer, and drinks. Lunch, dinner daily.

Jonathan Lee's. 1799 Briarcliff Rd. at Clifton Rd. (897–1700). Contemporary decor and savory Thai and Chinese dishes make Jonathan's a popular destination for Emory University area adventurers. Lunch Tues.–Fri.; dinner Tues.–Sun.

King & I. 1510 Piedmont Ave., Ansley Square (892–7743), and 4058 Peachtree Rd. (262–7965). Spicy Thai dishes and cordial service have made these two small restaurants favorites with local food adventurers. Lunch, Mon.–Fri.; dinner daily.

Korea House. 831 Peachtree St. (876–5310). Authentic Korean dishes, friendly atmosphere. Lunch, dinner Mon.–Sat.

Niko's. 1803 Cheshire Bridge Rd. (872–1254). Family-owned taverna excels in moussaka, dolmades, beef Stifado, and other Greek delights. Lunch, dinner daily.

Rio Bravo Cantina. 3172 Roswell Rd. (262–7431). Live mariachi music, a convivial bar, and wonderful fajitas, quesadillas, and other Tex-Mex favorites keep this Buckhead area eatery packed day and night. Lunch, dinner daily.

R. Thomas' Deluxe Grill. 1812 Peachtree Rd. (872–2942). This breezy little café with an outdoor patio looks like a junk collector's closet to some, charming to others. Serves burgers, chili, shrimp-stuffed omelets, apple pie, and other eclectic fare. Open daily from early morning to the wee hours of the night.

Touch of India. 970 Peachtree St. (876–7777). One of Atlanta's most outstanding ethnic restaurants. Superb curries, tandooris, Indian breads, with cordial service. Lunch, dinner daily.

Low Budget

Annie Keith's Homecookin'. 649 Willoughby Way NE, just off Ralph McGill Blvd. (521–3651). The best soul food in town—fried chicken, greens, banana pudding, cornbread—plus ample southern-style breakfasts. There's no outside sign; just look for the red awning and the crowds. Breakfast, lunch Mon.–Fri. No credit cards.

Burton's Grill. 1029 Edgewood Ave., across from the Inman Park MARTA rail station (525–9439). Another temple of soul food delights that attracts equal numbers of downtown executives and blue-collar workers. Breakfast, lunch Mon.–Fri.

El Toro. A dozen locations all over town (321–9502). Tasty enchiladas, tacos, and other Tex-Mex favorites in *simpatico* surroundings.

Fellini's Pizza. 422 Seminole Ave. at Moreland Ave. (525–2530). Fun, funky, and a bit like a Fellini movie, this little place serves its pizza to an eclectic crowd in the Bohemian Little Five Points neighborhood. Lunch, dinner daily.

Harold's Barbecue. 171 McDonough Blvd. (627–9268). The governor of Georgia and most of the state legislature are regulars at this humble place that serves some of the best barbecue in the world. Lunch, dinner Mon.–Sat. No credit cards.

Mary Mac's Tea Room. 228 Ponce de Leon Ave. (875–4337). A maze of bustling dining rooms famous for fried chicken, southern-style vegetables, cornbread, and desserts without the phony plantation gimmicks. A bona fide Atlanta landmark. Lunch, dinner Mon.–Fri. No credit cards.

Mick's. Lenox Square mall, Peachtree and Lenox roads (262–6425), and 557 Peachtree St. (875–6425). Breezy, super trendy little cafés with pastas, mesquite-grilled chicken, and enormous ice cream sundaes. Lunch, dinner daily.

Morrison's Cafeterias. Numerous locations. Southern cafeteria chain serves well-prepared meats, vegetables, and desserts at modest prices. Most locations open 7 days.

The Varsity. 61 North Ave., near Georgia Tech (881–1706). When exiled Atlantans dream of home, they often envision the chili dogs, onion rings, frosted orange drinks, and fried apple and peach pies at this enormous drive-in. Open 24 hours every day. No credit cards.

Old Hickory House. Popular chain of barbecue restaurants, with numerous locations around the metropolitan area.

Recommended Splurge. La Grotta. 2637 Peachtree Rd. (231–1368). Many Atlantans regard this northern Italian restaurant as the city's very best, regardless of cuisine. Memorable pastas, veal, and seafood dishes, fabulous desserts, and European service add up to an extraordinary evening. Dinner, Tues.–Sat. With wine and tip, a full dinner for two will be about $85.

Brunches. Cafe de la Paix. Atlanta Hilton Hotel, downtown (659–2000). Huge, beautifully balanced Sunday buffet is among the best in town.

The Country Place. Colony Square, Peachtree and 14th streets (881–0144). The many innovative dishes on the Sat.–Sun. brunch menu make this a popular retreat for the smart in-town crowd.

The Crown Room. Colony Square Hotel, Peachtree and 14th streets (892–6000). Attractive spread of hot and cold entrees, salads, and desserts has made the "Brunch Over Atlanta" a Sunday standard for several years.

First China Restaurant. 5295 Buford Hwy. (457–6788). The exotic *dim sum* Chinese lunch is one of Atlanta's most interesting ethnic adventures. Sat.–Mon.

Murphy's. 1019 Los Angeles Ave. (872–0904). Join an upbeat eclectic crowd for inexpensive breakfasts, freshly baked croissants, sandwich plates, soups, salads, and desserts; a good place to rub elbows with the natives.

Northwest Atlanta Hilton Inn. I-75 N and Windy Hill Rd. (953–9300). Complimentary champagne comes with the ample Sunday buffet brunch.

St. Charles Deli. N. Highland and St. Charles avenues (876–3351). Bright and lively in-town deli features omelets, gourmet salads and sandwiches, and pastries; a great people-watching spot.

Cafés and Coffeehouses. Cafe Intermezzo. Park Place shopping center, 4505 Ashford-Dunwoody Rd., at I-285 (396–1344), and 1845 Peachtree Rd. (355–0411). Espresso, wines, beer, European pastries. Open daily.

The Dessert Place. Virginia and N. Highland avenues (892–8921), 279 E. Paces Ferry Rd., Buckhead (233–2331). Chic desserterie features a regalia of luxurious sweets and excellent people watching.

Maison Robert. Cherokee Plaza, 3867 Peachtree Rd. (237–3675). Homemade European pastries, chocolates, and croissants and an inexpensive daily plat du jour.

Maison Gourmet. Lindberg Plaza, 2581 Piedmont Rd. (231–8552). European bakery, café, gourmet food shop.

NIGHTLIFE AND BARS. This once-quiet town now rivals New Orleans as Dixie's nighttime capital. Most bars, lounges, and clubs are open 7 days until the wee hours. Those with live entertainment usually have a cover charge or drink minimum. For an up-to-date listing of clubs and entertainers, consult the "Weekend" tabloid in Saturday's Atlanta *Journal–Constitution* or *Creative Loafing*, a lively free weekly distributed all over town. No package beer, wine, or liquor is sold all day Sunday. Except where noted, the bars are all inexpensive, with no cover charge.

Bars and Pubs

Atkins Park. 794 N. Highland Ave. (876–7249). Friendly neighborhood bar with an outdoor beer garden. Good place to meet the locals.

Churchill Arms. 3223 Cains Hill Pl., Buckhead (233–5633). A sure-enough British pub. Patrons down pints of Bass ale, throw darts, sing along at the piano, and generally have a jolly good time.

County Cork Pub. 56 E. Andrews Dr., Buckhead, (262–2227). Guinness and Harp Ale on tap, competitive darts, and Irish balladeers add up to a wee bit of a good time.

Little Five Points Pub. 1174 Euclid Ave. (577–7767). Hub of the revived Little Five Points neighborhood, renowned for burgers, beer, and conversations that cover the sociopolitical spectrum.

Manuel's Tavern. 602 N. Highland Ave. (525–3447). Atlanta's favorite neighborhood tavern; a gathering place for journalists, politicians, students, and a cross section of in-towners.

O'Henry's. 230 Peachtree St. (524–5175). With its array of Victoriana and long mahogany bar, O'Henry's is a mainstay of downtown shoppers, office workers, and visitors.

Reggie's British Pub. CNN Center, downtown (525–1437). A smashing bit of old England where dashing proprietor Reggie Mitchell presides over a kingdom of ale, darts, and steak and kidney pie.

The Ritz-Carlton Buckhead Hotel. Peachtree and Lenox roads (237–2700). A bit of a splurge (the drinks are at premium prices), but it's lots of fun to dress up and sit at the bar of Atlanta's most fashionable hotel, watching the minks and diamonds go by.

Taco Mac. Corner of Virginia and N. Highland avenues (873–6529). A beer-lover's Eden, this noisy, crowded tavern with its overflowing outdoor patio serves 122 international brands to go with Mexican food and spicy Buffalo-style chicken wings.

Vickery's Crescent Ave. Bar & Grill. 1106 Crescent Ave. (881–1106). Converted house with an Art Deco flair draws an inner-city clientele as eclectic as its menu.

Zasu's. 1923 Peachtree Rd. (352–3052). Late-night crowds congregate around the piano at this chic Art Deco–style café and bistro. Breakfast is served daily until 3 A.M.

Singles Bars

Confetti. 3906 Roswell Rd. (237–4238). Colorful bar attracts some of the area's most beautiful young people for dancing, drinking, and mixing.

Carlos McGee's. 3360 Chamblee-Tucker Rd. (452–8880), 3035 Peachtree Rd., Buckhead (231–7979). Music, margaritas, and close hip-rubbing quarters put this at the top of the young swinger's list of landmarks.

élan. Park Place Mall, 4505 Ashford-Dunwoody Rd. at I-285 (393–1333). *Playboy* and *Esquire* have declared this sleek, dressy suburban watering hole one of America's top singles gathering places. The prices are moderate, more expensive if you eat.

Clubs

Blind Willie's. 828 N. Highland Ave. (873–2583). Very lively storefront bistro features pulsating New Orleans blues and Cajun food.

Blues Harbor. 3179 Peachtree Rd. (261–6717). Dixieland, blues, and jazz a la New Orleans keep this Buckhead spot jumping all night.

Dante's Down the Hatch. 3380 Peachtree Rd. near Lenox Square (266–1600). A splurge (dinner and drinks will be $25 to $30) but worth it for the top-notch jazz by the Paul Mitchell Trio and the unique sailing ship setting.

Harvestmoon Saloon. 2423 Piedmont Rd. (231–1877). All manner of pop, rock, folk, blues, and country groups play this popular storefront music hall located across from the Lindbergh MARTA rail station.

Jerry Farber's Club. 54 Pharr Rd. (237–5181). Congenial host Jerry Farber offers a mixed menu of comedy acts, jazz, blues, folk music, etc.

Johnny's Hideaway. 3771 Roswell Rd. (233–8026). A mostly over-40 crowd packs the Hideaway to dance to the big band music of the '30s and '40s.

The Point Lounge. 420 Moreland Ave., Little Five Points (577–6468). Convivial in-town bar has excellent jazz, good drinks, and light foods with moderate prices. Draws a big cross section of upbeat Atlantans. Cover usually $1 to $2.

The Punch Line. 280 Hildrebrand Dr., off Roswell Rd., Sandy Springs (252–LAFF). Locally and nationally known comedians keep 'em rolling in the aisles at this popular northside club. Cover varies.

Walter Mitty's Jazz Cafe. 816 N. Highland Ave. (876–7115). The hottest jazz in town.

Cabarets and Music Halls

Buckboard Country Music Showcase. 2080 Cobb Pky., Smyrna (955–7340). Local and nationally renowned country performers are the draw at this rollicking suburban music hall.

Club Rio. 195 Luckie St., downtown (525–7467). Up to 1,500 merrymakers can groove on live and taped music at this slick downtown complex of bars and dance floors.

Center Stage Theatre. 1374 West Peachtree St. (874–1511). This cozy theater-in-the-round features an eclectic repertoire of jazz, blues, country, and folk performers, dramas and revues.

Upstairs at Gene & Gabe's. 1578 Piedmont Rd., at Monroe Dr. (892–2261). Original cabaret shows and revues make this one of the city's best evenings out. Full evening about $25.

SECURITY. With its friendly populace and relaxed lifestyle, Atlanta often lulls visitors into a false sense of security. The same precautions should be taken here as in other large cities. When leaving your hotel room, place jewelry and other valuables in the hotel safe. The safety situation in the downtown area has improved in the past few years with additional police patrols, but it's still a good idea to go out with one or more companions after dark and to avoid nonbusy side streets. Peachtree Street south of the MARTA Five Points rail station and streets around the World Congress Center/Omni International should be approached with special caution after dark. Some incidents occur around MARTA rail station parking lots late at night, but the bus and rail systems can be used with little apprehension.

ATLANTIC CITY

by
Mike Schwanz

Mike Schwanz, a writer based in New York City, specializes in travel, sports, outdoor recreation, and entertainment. He has contributed to scores of magazines and newspapers as well as several books.

During the 1980s, Atlantic City became the most visited vacation destination in the United States. Today, about 30 million people a year come here, mainly because this is the only city on the East Coast with legalized gambling. Since the first casino opened in 1978, Atlantic City's growth has been phenomenal. There are currently 12 casino-hotels in operation, and another is under construction.

But gambling certainly isn't the town's only attraction. The casino-hotels attract the biggest names in show business: Frank Sinatra, Jackie Mason, Liza Minnelli, Kenny Rogers, Bob Hope, Donna Summer, Bill Cosby, and many other stars perform here regularly. Atlantic City is now giving New York City some stiff competition as the entertainment capital of the East Coast. In addition, Atlantic City still has the wide, sandy beach that led to its development as a seashore resort a century ago. This section of the Atlantic Ocean is usually warm and tranquil; the gentle slope of the ocean floor makes swimming a delight.

Finally, Atlantic City boasts the most famous boardwalk on the Jersey Shore. More than 5 miles long and 60 feet wide, this magnificent structure is a beehive of activity, with bike riders, kite fliers, runners, and lovers of all ages strolling and holding hands. In nice weather, jugglers, dancers, musicians, and other street entertainers perform. There's a complete assortment of fast-food stores, souvenir shops, arcades, ice cream and fudge shops, pizza parlors, and saltwater taffy stores.

Atlantic City covers about 16 square miles and is located on Absecon Island about two-thirds of the way down the New Jersey shore. It shares the island with the small towns of Ventnor, Margate, and Longport, which are south of it. One major reason for this city's immense popularity is its extremely desirable location. Atlantic City is close to all the major population centers of the East Coast. It's just an hour from Philadelphia, 2½ hours from New York, 2½ hours from Baltimore, and 3½ hours from Washington, D.C. In fact, 25 percent of the population of the country (about 60 million people) live within 300 miles of Atlantic City.

This is a small town, both geographically and in population (only 40,000). The center of town is Pacific Avenue, the main street running parallel to the Atlantic Ocean. About a block south of Pacific Avenue and parallel to it is the famous Boardwalk, only a few feet from the sea. Between the Boardwalk and Pacific Avenue are the great casino-hotels. The major east/west streets are named after major world oceans and seas: Pacific Avenue, Atlantic Avenue, Arctic Avenue, and Baltic Avenue. The cross streets are named after states. Along a two-mile stretch lie most of the casino-hotels, from the Bally's Grand on Providence Avenue to the Showboat on Delaware Avenue. Between these two hotels, the Boardwalk is lined with many other casino-hotels, the Convention Hall, and hundreds of small stores and arcades.

Visitors can get up and down the Boardwalk easily. If you stay near Convention Hall, you will be able to walk to most tourist attractions on the Boardwalk. In addition, motorized trams ($1) run up and down the Boardwalk, allowing one to get from one end to another in only a few minutes. Another alternative is a jitney. These unique minibuses run up and down Pacific Avenue continually, making it very easy to get from casino to casino.

Two other casino-hotels—Trump's Castle and Harrah's Marina—are located next to Farley State Marina at the northern tip of the city. This region is about a mile from the Boardwalk area, but it is where most of the action is taking place in terms of construction.

Incorporated in 1854, Atlantic City gained prominence in the middle to late 1800s as a vacation resort for well-heeled Philadelphians. By the early 1900s it had become one of the most popular vacation spots in the country. During its heyday, Atlantic City was responsible for many firsts in American culture. It developed the first Ferris wheel, the first picture postcards, the first saltwater taffy, and even the first Easter parade. In 1921, the first Miss America pageant was held here. By the 1930s, the town's streets had become the inspiration for the classic game "Monopoly."

But after World War II things changed for the worse. East Coast vacationers began to fly to other, more distant spots. Tourism dropped, and the city began decaying. By the early 1970s, the town was a shadow of its former self. Most of the population was elderly and poor, and unemployment was high. Then, on November 2, 1976, New Jersey citizens passed a referendum that legalized casino gambling in Atlantic City.

Since the opening of the first casino—Resorts International—in May 1978, the city's oceanfront has made a remarkable comeback. Today's skyline is virtually unrecognizable from that of ten years ago. Several huge, brightly lit, towering casino-hotels border the sea along Pacific Avenue. Construction continues up and down the strip, either additions to existing hotels or new ones. The new Showboat opened in spring, 1987; the second Resorts International facility—the gigantic Taj Mahal—is scheduled to open sometime in 1989. The resplendent red, orange, purple, and green signs of the casino-hotels can be seen for miles at night. Hotel entrances are lined with limousines bringing in the high rollers.

Visitors should keep one thing in mind: this is a town that fervently hopes its guests will spend—and lose—a lot of money. After all, it's possible to lose $1 million in a single hour here. If you are a true tightwad, you probably shouldn't come here in the first place. But if you are looking for a great time and are willing to spend a moderate amount of money, the following pages should help you out.

The very soul of the town is the Boardwalk, and you can enjoy most of its activities without spending a dime. Swimming in the ocean is free in Atlantic City; no beach passes are required. It costs nothing to run, fly a kite, or just watch the world go by for a few minutes. During mornings, you can rent a bike for about $4 an hour or bring your own. During the summer, there are many free concerts and craft fairs. The casino-hotels continually sponsor free events along the Boardwalk.

Everyone who comes here should at least walk through a casino. It's an experience you'll never forget. How many times can you watch somebody lose $5,000 in a baccarat hand, and not blink an eyelash? But, you have to be 21 years old to enter a casino, and this is strictly enforced. Casinos are open from 10 A.M. to 4 A.M. on weekdays and stay open to 6 A.M. on weekends.

Sports enthusiasts will enjoy themselves, especially people who like water sports: fishing, boating, sailing, wind surfing, swimming, and water skiing. Many casino-hotels have tennis courts, and there are public courts in neighboring towns. There are several good public golf courses nearby.

The nightlife is absolutely top-notch. Besides offering world-class entertainers, all the casino-hotels have lounges, piano bars, and cabarets. Several nightclubs in town stay open until 6 or 7 A.M. to accommodate the thousands of casino employees who work late shifts.

There are many other interesting sights within a 30-minute drive of town. The Edwin B. Forsythe National Wildlife Refuge, north of the city, is one of the finest bird-watching areas in the East. The beautiful 40-mile-long Ocean Drive, which runs from Atlantic City to Cape May, offers panoramic views of the sea.

Three historic villages will interest history buffs. Gardner's Basin—a replica of a seacoast village—is next to Farley State Marina at the northern border of the city. The Towne of Historic Smithville, with colonial-era shops, galleries, and restaurants, is located in Galloway Township, a few miles north. Batsto, an old ironworks town, dates back to the Revolutionary War. There are even a couple of good wineries that offer tours: D'Arcy and Renault.

Art lovers will enjoy the Atlantic City Art Center at Garden Pier on the northern end of the Boardwalk. It has rotating special exhibits plus photography, paintings, sculpture, and an Atlantic City historical museum.

Several other interesting museums are only a short drive away, including the Atlantic County Historical Museum in Somers Point, the Noyes Museum in Oceanville, and the Ocean City Arts Center in Ocean City.

All in all, this is one of the unique vacation spots in the United States. It's alive with activity and energy, and most people will have a great time here. But remember that the key to enjoying Atlantic City to the fullest is planning your trip far in advance. With 30 million visitors, the pressure on housing is intense. Make a hotel or motel reservation several weeks in advance, especially if you plan a summer trip. Also, ask the city's visitors bureau (see "Tourist Information") for a listing of major events during your stay, such as casino showroom acts, free concerts on the Boardwalk, and boxing matches.

Finally, keep in mind two dressing tips: There is almost always an ocean breeze, even in summer, so plan to bring a sweater or windbreaker for evenings. Also, men are asked to wear a sport coat in the fancier casino-hotel restaurants during the evening.

PRACTICAL INFORMATION

WHEN TO GO. Deciding when to visit Atlantic City is a two-sided proposition. If you are visiting the city primarily to enjoy the beach (for sunbathing, swimming, etc.), you should go during the summer. After all, Atlantic City was founded as a seashore vacation spot. During summer, there is much more to do here than at any other time of year, especially if you have children. Unfortunately, summer is also the season when the hotel rates are highest, and the beach, streets, restaurants, and stores are more crowded. However, if you are going primarily to gamble and want to save as much money as possible, go in January or February. The hotel rates are cheapest then, the casinos are much less crowded, and the personnel in the gambling halls tend to be more patient.

The best two weeks of the year to visit are the two weeks after Labor Day. The ocean water is warmest then (often over 70 degrees Fahrenheit); the air temperatures are usually in the seventies or low eighties, and the Labor Day crowds are gone. In addition, the room rates at many motels and hotels drop right after Labor Day. In fact, the daily temperatures are in the seventies from mid-May through mid-September, but the ocean is pretty cold (low sixties) until the Fourth of July or so. In winter, the ocean tends to keep the air milder than the surrounding inland areas; it seldom gets below freezing in Atlantic City.

HOW TO GET THERE. By air. There is good air service to Atlantic City via three major eastern cities: Philadelphia, Washington, and New York. People who intend to fly here from other regions should fly into one of these cities first. Two airports serve Atlantic City: *Bader Field* is on U.S. 40 (Albany Avenue) in the western part of the city. *Allegheny Commuter* (609–344–7104 or 800–428–4253) flies to Bader frequently from Philadelphia, New York (from both Kennedy and La Guardia airports), and Washington. Costs range from about $70 to $90 one way from New York or Washington. From Philadelphia, it's about $40 to $70 one way. The second airport is the *International Air Terminal* about a dozen miles away in Pomona, which mostly handles chartered aircraft. However, air service has improved tremendously in the past few months. In April 1988, *Piedmont* (215–568–3805 or 800–251–5720) started to fly to Pomona from Baltimore and Philadelphia. In May 1988, *USAir* (412–922–7500 or 800–428–4322) initiated nonstop flights from Pittsburgh. Bader Field, as well as Pomona, also handles scores of charter flights daily from all over the country. Taxis serve both airports.

Some visitors prefer to fly into *Philadelphia International Airport* and, rather than take a small plane to an Atlantic City airport, take a shuttle limousine to Atlantic City. For information, call *AA Limousine Service* (609–344–2444), *Airport Limousine Service* (609–345–3244), *Blue and White Airport Service* (609–848–0770), *Casino Limousine Service* (609–646–5555 or 800–452–1110), *May's Call-a-Cab* (609–646–7600), or *Rapid Rover Airport Shuttle* (609–344–0100).

By bus. Approximately 1,000 buses enter Atlantic City every day from points all along the East Coast and every other part of the country. Casino buses leave from several major Eastern cities many times a day. (The Sunday travel section of your daily paper usually is filled with ads from such carriers.) These casino buses are a terrific bargain. If you don't expect to drive much, consider taking one. In many cases they cost only $15 to $25 round trip from major Eastern cities. Once you arrive, you usually get at least $10 in quarters, a meal discount coupon worth $5 or so, and a travel voucher for a discount on a future trip. Bus companies that serve the town include *Greyhound-Trailways, Lincoln Transit,* and *New Jersey Transit.* Many other regional carriers come here, too. The *Municipal Bus Terminal* is only two blocks from Pacific Avenue and the casinos.

By car. Drivers coming from the north can take several major highways that connect with the Garden State Parkway southbound. The Atlantic City Expressway takes drivers from Philadelphia to Atlantic City in just an hour. From the south, take I-95 or U.S. 40 from Washington, D.C. Atlantic City is about a 2½-hour drive from New York and a 4½-hour drive from Washington.

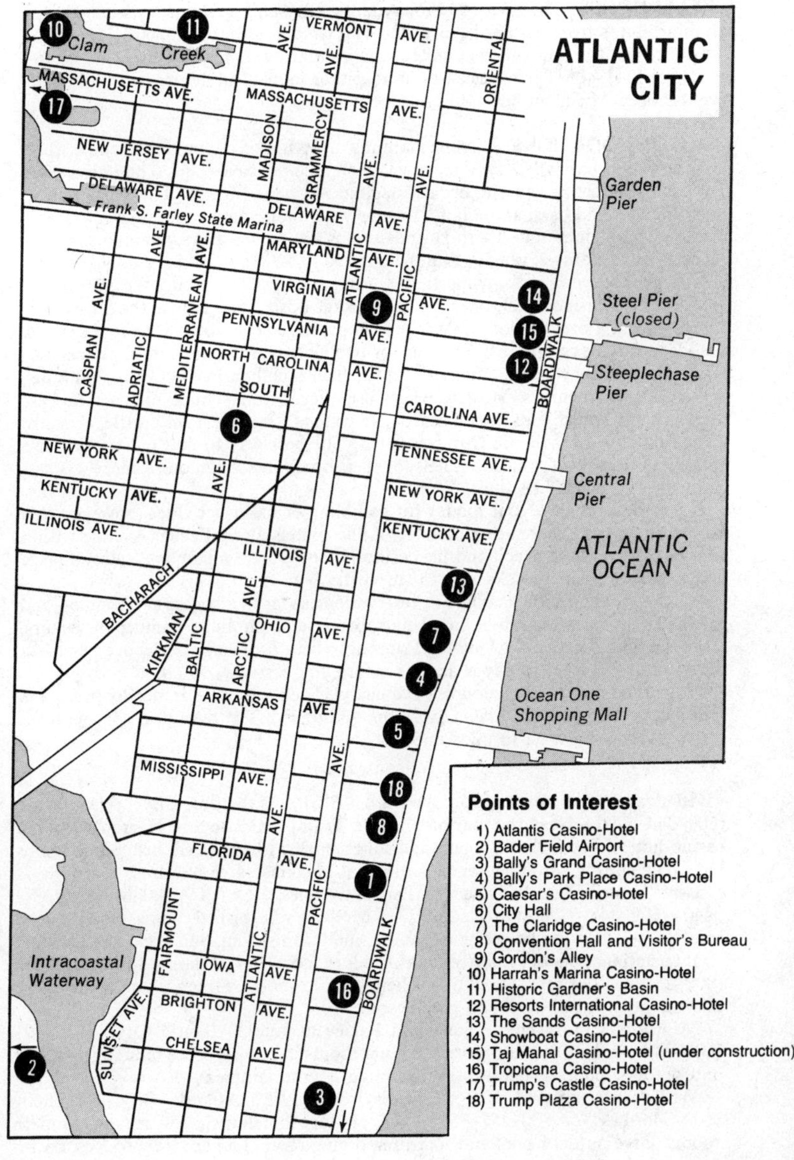
ATLANTIC CITY
Clam Creek
VERMONT AVE.
MASSACHUSETTS AVE.
NEW JERSEY AVE.
DELAWARE AVE.
Frank S. Farley State Marina
MARYLAND AVE.
VIRGINIA AVE.
PENNSYLVANIA AVE.
NORTH CAROLINA AVE.
SOUTH CAROLINA AVE.
TENNESSEE AVE.
NEW YORK AVE.
KENTUCKY AVE.
ILLINOIS AVE.
OHIO AVE.
ARKANSAS AVE.
MISSISSIPPI AVE.
FLORIDA AVE.
IOWA AVE.
BRIGHTON AVE.
CHELSEA AVE.
SUNSET AVE.
MADISON
GRAMMERCY
ATLANTIC AVE.
PACIFIC AVE.
ORIENTAL
CASPIAN AVE.
ADRIATIC AVE.
MEDITERRANEAN AVE.
BACHARACH
KIRKMAN
BALTIC
ARCTIC AVE.
FAIRMOUNT
BOARDWALK
Garden Pier
Steel Pier (closed)
Steeplechase Pier
Central Pier
ATLANTIC OCEAN
Ocean One Shopping Mall
Intracoastal Waterway
Points of Interest
1) Atlantis Casino-Hotel
2) Bader Field Airport
3) Bally's Grand Casino-Hotel
4) Bally's Park Place Casino-Hotel
5) Caesar's Casino-Hotel
6) City Hall
7) The Claridge Casino-Hotel
8) Convention Hall and Visitor's Bureau
9) Gordon's Alley
10) Harrah's Marina Casino-Hotel
11) Historic Gardner's Basin
12) Resorts International Casino-Hotel
13) The Sands Casino-Hotel
14) Showboat Casino-Hotel
15) Taj Mahal Casino-Hotel (under construction)
16) Tropicana Casino-Hotel
17) Trump's Castle Casino-Hotel
18) Trump Plaza Casino-Hotel

TELEPHONES. The area code for Atlantic City and nearby towns is 609. To call information from within the city, dial 411; from elsewhere, dial 609–555–1212. The police and fire **emergency number** is the standard 911. The Atlantic City Medical Center (344–4081) provides 24-hour hospital and medical services. It's at Pacific Ave. between Michigan and Ohio avenues.

ACCOMMODATIONS. Anyone planning a trip to this city must remember that Atlantic City is basically a two-tier town when it comes to lodging. The 12 magnificent casino-hotels provide luxurious lodging. All have three or four restaurants, many lounges and bars, and a large theater where top-name entertainers perform. Modern health clubs and superluxurious rooms are standard. As you might expect, the rates are expensive, ranging from about $90 to $200 a night for a double room. In summer the rates peak, while they are most reasonable during the winter.

Most of the casino-hotels offer special package deals (especially in the off-season) that represent a pretty good deal. A typical package costs from $225 to $250 and includes a double room for two people for two nights, at least one meal per person, admission to a showroom, admission to the health club, a free cocktail, and other souvenirs and amenities. Most packages are offered Sun.–Thurs. nights. The best packages are available in the off-season. If you want to live it up a little, they are a good bargain by Atlantic City standards. The best way to find out about these packages is to write the casino-hotels for their brochures. Each one's address is listed in the "Nightlife" section.

If you want to save your money for gambling or other activities, however, this can be done, too. There are a number of fine motels along Pacific Avenue within a block or two of the beach and the casino-hotels. Obtain a map and select a place that is near a casino-hotel you want to visit.

Whatever you decide, make your reservations as far in advance as possible—and get the room rates confirmed in writing. Because of the huge number of visitors, there is a high demand for lodging. Rates have been known to rise above what was stated orally. Expect to pay a deposit before you arrive.

Hotel rates are based on double occupancy. Categories, determined by price, are: *Reasonable,* $65 to $95, *Very Economical,* $35 to $65. The rates also vary with the season; they are lowest in midwinter.

Reasonable

Admiral's Quarters. 655 Absecon Blvd., Atlantic City, NJ 08401 (609–344–2201). Near the marina and the Trump's Castle and Harrah's Marina casino-hotels. There are 52 rooms and suites, each with a full kitchen. Some rooms have balconies. Complimentary Continental breakfast, free parking.

Best Western Inn. Indiana and Pacific avenues, Box 5309, Atlantic City, NJ 08404 (609–348–9175 or 800–528–1234). Modern, refurbished rooms. Good central location. All-weather heated pool, sauna, small game room. Sun deck, free parking.

International Motel. Boardwalk at Chelsea, Box 1904, Atlantic City, NJ 08401 (800–257–8612 or 609–344–7071). There are 125 rooms, dining room, coffee shop, all-year pool, health spa, and game room.

Midtown Motor Inn. Indiana and Pacific avenues, Atlantic City, NJ 08401 (609–348–3031). Contains more than 300 rooms in two separate buildings. Indoor and outdoor pool, restaurant, lounge, nightly entertainment.

World International. 110 S. Pennsylvania Ave., Atlantic City, NJ 08404 (609–344–1151 or 800–257–8522). An 11-story hotel with 250 rooms. Modern rooms, large outdoor pool and solarium, dining room, lounge. Next to Resorts International.

Very Economical

Acapulco Motel. 117 S. Kentucky Ave., Box 7128, Atlantic City, NJ 08401 (800–257–6223 or 609–344–9093). Has a pool and a restaurant that serves breakfast and lunch in summer. Located near Sands Casino. Free parking.

Aristocrat. 136 S. Pennsylvania Ave., Atlantic City, NJ 08401 (609–348–9115). Free parking, swimming pool; 55 units, color television, outdoor pool.

Baronet Motel. 3001 Pacific Ave., Atlantic City, NJ 08401 (609–344–2925). Free parking, air-conditioned rooms, sun deck, free cable TV, open year-round; 30 newly furnished rooms.

Dunes. 2819 Pacific Ave., Atlantic City, NJ 08401 (609–344–5271). Centrally located, 35 modern rooms. Wall-to-wall carpeting, color TV, individual room air-conditioning, free parking, sun deck, outdoor pool. Some efficiencies available.

Flamingo Motel. Chelsea and Pacific Aves., Atlantic City, NJ 08401 (609–344–3061). Dining room and cocktail lounge, open 24 hours. Air-conditioning, color TV, wall-to-wall carpeting, full-tile bath, free parking, three sun decks. Located between Tropicana and Golden Nugget casino-hotels.

Golden East Motel. 169 S. Kentucky Ave., Atlantic City, NJ 08401 (609–344–7001). Free parking, decent rooms. One block from three casinos.

Quality Inn. Pacific and South Carolina avenues, Atlantic City, NJ 08401 (609–345–7070). The first non-casino-hotel to be built in Atlantic City in 20 years. 206 rooms, coffee shop, cocktail lounge, game room, gift shop. Located near Resorts International. Open year-round.

Royal Inn. Park Place near Boardwalk, Atlantic City, NJ 08404 (609–344–7021). Athletic facility rights at Claridge Hotel next door ($5). Has an outdoor pool, restaurant, coffee shop; 150 guest rooms. Free parking.

Trinidad Motel. Tennessee Ave. near Boardwalk, Atlantic City, NJ 08401 (609–344–8956). Has 71 rooms, cocktail lounge, swimming pool. Some kitchen efficiencies available. Rooms have been refurbished. Free parking.

Village Motel. Boardwalk at Kentucky Ave., Atlantic City, NJ 08401 (609–345–8500). Coffee shop, free parking. Has 134 rooms.

World Tower. Beach Block, North Carolina Ave., Atlantic City, NJ 08404 (609–347–8000). Restaurant, cocktail lounge, coffee shop, rooftop swimming pool; 200 modern rooms. Free Parking.

HOW TO GET AROUND. From the airport. Taxis serve both local airports, but there is a considerable difference in the fare: from Bader Field a cab to downtown Atlantic City costs about $8, from the International Air Terminal in Pomona the ride costs about $25. Cab companies include *AA Limousine Service* (609–344–2444), *Airport Limousine Service* (609–345–3244), *Blue and White Airport Service* (609–848–0770), *Casino Limousine Service* (609–646–5555), *May's Call-a-Cab* (609–646–7600), and *Rapid Rover Airport Shuttle* (609–344–0100). Many hotels and casinos offer guests transportation from the airport.

By jitney. These little minibuses are great. They have only 13 seats or so, but they run continually and are very reliable. Their route takes them up and down Pacific Ave. 24 hours a day, from Gardner's Basin to Jackson Ave. Half of them also run to the Harrah's Marina and Trump's Castle from Park Place. Cost is 75 cents. Jitneys are especially useful on your first day; it's a very pleasant way to get oriented to all the casinos on Pacific Ave.

By tram. Another unique mode of transportation is the tram, which runs along the Atlantic City Boardwalk from Garden Pier to Albany Avenue. Hours are 10:00 A.M.–9:00 P.M. Sun.–Thurs., and 10:00 A.M.–2:00 A.M. Fri.–Sat. Adults, $1; senior citizens and children under 12, 75 cents; kids under 3 free.

By taxi. If you want to hire a taxi for an easy drive around the region, several are available. They usually are lined up at the major casino-hotels, or you can phone for one. Among the reliable companies are *Dial Cab Co.* (822–9422), *Mutual Cab* (345–6111), *Radio Cab* (345–1105), *Red Top Cab* (344–4104), and *Yellow Cab* (344–1221). A typical fare for a 2-mile trip is about $4.50.

By car. There are several major car rental companies. *Budget Rent-A-Car* has an office at Bader Field; call 609–345–0600 or 800–527–0700. Its rates are probably the cheapest: about $40 for an economy car, about $60 for a full-size car. The airport is also served by *Avis* (609–345–3350 or 800–331–1212), *Hertz* (609–646–1212 or 800–654–3131), and *National* (609–344–0441 or 800–328–4567). Their rates are somewhat higher.

HINTS TO THE MOTORIST. Before you leave for Atlantic City, ask yourself, Do I even want to be a motorist? If you are coming from New York, Philadelphia, or Washington, one of the many bus lines may be the answer if you basically intend to gamble and hang around the Boardwalk. Having a car can definitely be a hassle, especially in summer, because of the lack of parking. If you are staying at a casino-hotel or a large motel, you will probably get free parking. While making a hotel reservation, be sure to inquire about the parking policy. If you have to use a public lot, there are many on Pacific and Atlantic avenues. They usually charge $7 to $10 a day. There is metered parking on streets perpendicular to the beach, but most visitors won't want to put in a quarter every hour. Finding a free spot on a side street is very difficult unless you are far away from the Boardwalk and beach.

The traffic itself isn't too bad, except between 6 and 9 P.M. in the summer. Then Pacific Ave. can get quite congested. A few service stations stay open 24 hours to cater to the casino employees. Getting gas isn't a problem.

It should be mentioned that there are a lot of nice sights to see a few miles outside of town, and you do need a car to get to them. It's definitely worthwhile, for example, to drive through the Forsythe National Wildlife Refuge.

TOURIST INFORMATION. The major source of tourist information is the *Atlantic City Visitors Bureau,* Department of Public Relations, Convention Hall, Atlantic City, NJ 08401 (609–348–7044). For information about the entire southern Jersey Shore contact: *New Jersey Division of Travel and Tourism,* CN 826, Trenton NJ 08625 (609–292–2470). Both organizations supply brochures, maps, lists of events, and motel and restaurant guides. Scheduled events and performers appearing in Atlantic city are often listed or advertised in the entertainment sections of the major daily papers of nearby cities.

Once you arrive in town, pick up a current issue of *Atlantic City Magazine* ($2). It offers an excellent listing of the entertainment schedule of all the casinos plus a guide to restaurants, nightclubs, museums, and sporting activities. Brochures and local "shopper" papers that list current events are available at most motels and all casino-hotels.

SENIOR-CITIZEN DISCOUNTS. Atlantic City is fairly progressive when it comes to offering discounts to the senior citizens. Anyone 65 or older can get discounts throughout town. Many local merchants participate in a discount program for senior citizens. Simply look for a large green emblem in the store window and then go in and present a Medicare card. You will receive a 5 to 25 percent discount. The Atlantic County Office of Aging and Disabled, 1133 Atlantic Ave., Atlantic City, NJ 08401 (609–345–6700), offers a book of discount coupons if you visit the office personally and can prove you are 65. Senior citizens also can purchase discount tickets for the jitneys at many full-service banks in town. They cost only 30 cents instead of the usual 75 cents.

HINTS TO DISABLED TRAVELERS. Disabled people should consider staying at a new hotel. All the casino-hotels, for example, have excellent access for wheelchairs in accordance with state law. The Boardwalk is fairly easy to negotiate by wheelchair, and there are accessible points on the beach that lead right to the water. Handicapped people get a 50 percent reduction anywhere in New Jersey on full-sized buses. Some buses of the Atlantic City Transportation Company have wheelchair lifts. The jitneys do not. Most casino-hotels and major shopping centers offer parking for the handicapped. The directory of listings in *Atlantic City Magazine* indicates which restaurants, nightclubs, sight-seeing sites, etc., have wheelchair access. There are sidewalk ramps at 800 intersections in town, mostly along the most popular streets.

The Atlantic County Office of Aging and Disabled, 1133 Atlantic Ave., Atlantic City, NJ 08401 (609–345–6700), publishes many useful pamphlets for the handicapped.

FREE EVENTS. A wide number of free activities are held along the Boardwalk, nearly all of them in late spring, summer, and early fall. Many of them are fun.

The first big event of the year is the annual Easter Parade, which starts at noon on Easter Sunday at Virginia Ave. on the northern end of the Boardwalk. It then heads south along the Boardwalk to the Golden Nugget before returning to the Convention Hall.

Throughout the summer there are free concerts on the Boardwalk, and on summer weekends there are often art fairs. Other events include kite-flying contests and footraces. For a schedule of free events, stop by the *Atlantic City Visitors Bureau* in Convention Hall or call 609–348–7044. Local newspapers also list many free events.

It's safe to say that if you walk up and down the Boardwalk on any given day, you will find something free to keep you amused.

TOURS AND SPECIAL-INTEREST SIGHTSEEING. There are many interesting and inexpensive places to visit if you want to get away from the casinos. Most of these places are only a 30-minute drive from Pacific Ave.

Absecon Lighthouse. Rhode Island and Pacific avenues, Atlantic City. This 167-foot-high lighthouse was built in 1857 to warn ships of tricky rocks and reefs. It is a New Jersey state park.

Arthur Clauson's Fine Art Gallery. 2213–15 Arctic Ave. (345–8878). Shows posters, graphics, Oriental art prints. Mon.–Fri., 8 A.M.–5 P.M.; Sat., 8 A.M.–2 P.M.

Atlantic City Art Center. Garden Pier, Boardwalk and New Jersey Ave. (347–5844). Has rotating special exhibits plus photography, paintings, and sculpture. Open 9 A.M.–4 P.M. every day.

Atlantic City Convention Hall. 2300 Boardwalk (348–7044). One of largest such halls in country and worth a quick visit. Centrally located in middle of town, this is the site of the Miss America pageant and the world's largest pipe organ.

Atlantic County Historical Society. 907 Shore Road, Somers Point (927–5218). The Victorian Museum features a short slide show of early Atlantic City. There is also a genealogical research library and a maritime museum. Open year-round, Wed.–Sat., 10 A.M.–noon and 1–4 P.M. Free.

Basin Queen. Gardner's Basin, Atlantic City (348–2600). Offers an 80-minute tour of the Atlantic City coastline. Runs every day except Monday. Boats leave at noon, 2, 4, and 7:30 P.M. Adults, $6; children, $4.

Edwin B. Forsythe National Wildlife Refuge—Brigantine Division. Great Creek Road, off Route 9, Oceanville (652–1665). Has more than 20,000 acres of coastal marshland and woodlands. Motorists can enjoy a free 8-mile self-guided tour for bird-watching and wildlife photography. There are two walking trails about a half mile long. Open year-round. Office auditorium is open 8 A.M.–4:30 P.M. Plan 2 hours for a tour.

Lucy the Margate Elephant. 9200 Atlantic Ave., Margate, NJ 08402 (823–6473). This huge elephant, built as a real-estate promotion a century ago, is six stories high and weighs 90 tons. Children can walk through it. Lucy is open from May to Oct. on weekends, 10 A.M.–5 P.M. From late June to Labor Day, it is open daily 10 A.M.–8:30 P.M. Adults, $1.50; children, $1.

Ocean Drive. If you have the time, it's worthwhile to take the 40-mile Ocean Drive all the way down to Cape May at the southern tip of the state. There is a modest toll at a few bridges. Along the way you can stop and visit marinas and enjoy beautiful views of the sea.

Renault Winery. Bremen Ave., Egg Harbor (965–2111). Established in 1864, this is one of the East Coast's oldest wineries. There are guided tours Mon.–Sat., 10 A.M.–5 P.M.; Sun. and holidays, noon to 5 P.M. Adults, $1; children, free.

PARTICIPANT SPORTS. A wonderful variety of sporting activities are available to Atlantic City tourists, many of them inexpensive. As you might expect, many more outdoor sports are available in summer than in winter.

Bicycling. Few activities are as invigorating as an early morning bike ride down the 5-mile-long Boardwalk. It's open for bike riding 6–10 A.M. If you get up early enough, you can see the sun rise out of the sea! Bikes can be rented at several stores: *AAAA Bike Shop,* 5223 Ventnor Ave., Ventnor, NJ (487–0808). Open 9:00 A.M.–5:00 P.M. daily; $4 per hour. *H. Longo,* 1133 Boardwalk (344–8288). Large variety for $3.50 per person. Open 6 A.M.–5 P.M. *Margate Bike Shop,* 4 S. Douglas Ave., Margate (822–9415). $3 per hour. Mon.–Sat., 8 A.M.–5 P.M.; Sun., 8 A.M.–1 P.M.

There is also a local cycle club, *Shore Cycles.* Bikers gather at 8:00 A.M. on Saturday and Sunday in front of Beacon Pro Shop, 430 Tilton Rd., Northfield, for 20- to 40-mile rides. Call 641–9531 for information.

Jogging. Atlantic City is one of the best places in the country for running. Joggers used to the canyonlike sidewalks of New York or Philadelphia will find it especially enjoyable. As you run, you can watch the sea and gaze at the great casinos on the other side of the Boardwalk. This scenery will make any run go quickly.

Golf courses open to the public include the following: *Brigantine Country Club,* Roosevelt Blvd. and the bay, Brigantine (266–1388). *Mays Landing Country Club,*

Cates Road, McKee City (641–4411). *Ocean City Municipal Golf Course,* Ocean City (399–1315). *Pomona Golf and Country Club,* Moss Mill and Odessa roads, Pomona (965–3232). *Stone Harbor Golf Club,* Route 9, Cape May County (465–9270). Call for further information. Often green fees are discounted on afternoons or midweek.

Swimming. Unlike other communities along the shore, you don't need to buy a beach pass to enjoy Atlantic City's beaches. The water is usually calm, and the ocean floor slopes gradually so that it's fine for wading. Atlantic City beaches have lifeguards on duty from 9 A.M. to 6 P.M. during the summer. Cabanas and lounge chairs can be rented from each casino.

Fishing. This part of the Atlantic Ocean offers a wide variety of fishing, for such species as bluefish, striped bass, flounder, shark, and tuna. Party boats and charter boats can be hired at the Farley State Marina, South Carolina Ave. and Brigantine Blvd. (441–3600). It's located at the far northern tip of the island. Party boats are a good choice for budget-conscious fishers; they usually cost from $20 to $25 for a full day's outing. Rods, reels, tackle, and bait are on board; they usually can be rented for about $3.

Fishing outfitters include the following: *Angler's Roost—Pier IV,* 9401 Amherst Ave., Margate (822–2272). Charter boats and party boats for half-day and night fishing; tackle shop. *Atlantic City Fishing Center,* 433 N. Maryland Ave., Atlantic City, NJ 08401 (344–7442). *The Bricks 'n' Sticks,* Atlantic City Marina (266–0056 or 266–9118). Leaves every day at 7 A.M. The cost is $300 for a half day and $450 for a full day of bluefish fishing. *Captain Allen's Fishing Center,* 432 N. Rhode Island Ave., Atlantic City (345–0075). Charter boats, *Captain Andy's Marina,* 9317 Amherst Ave., Margate (822–0916). Has fleet of party boats, which carry up to 100 people. Rates vary. *Captain Applegate,* Farley State Marina, South Carolina and Brigantine Blvd. (345–4077 or 652–8184). All-day trips on party boat from 8 A.M. to 4 P.M. Adults, about $20; children under 12, $12. Night bluefishing from 7:30 P.M. to 3 A.M. is about $25. Rod rentals on board. Farley State Marina. Half-day party boat trips leave 8:15 A.M. and 1 P.M. *Horizon Sport Fishing,* Farley State Marina, 600 Huron Ave. (645–1214). Charter boats for up to 10 people, half day or full day.

Pier fishing is a great, inexpensive way to get in a few hours of fishing on a nice day. You can fish for free at the Sea Wall on Penrose Ave. in Atlantic City (near Gardner's Basin) and on the Maine Avenue jetty or, for a small charge, at Ventnor Fishing Pier, Cambridge Ave. and Boardwalk, Ventnor (823–4560), which is open from May to Nov., 6 A.M.–11 P.M.

SPECTATOR SPORTS. No professional or collegiate sports are played here. However, Atlantic City is now challenging its archrival, Las Vegas, as the **boxing** capital of the world. Nearly every month, a major championship fight is held at one of the casinos. For information, check the sports pages in your local newspaper, or contact the casino-hotels directly. They should have a list of major fights coming up in the near future.

The Atlantic City Race Course. Route 322 and Route 40, McKee City, Hamilton Township, NJ 08404 (641–2190). This is the site of thoroughbred horse racing from June to Sept. Races are held from 7 P.M. to midnight, every day except Tues. and Sun. Grandstand fee, $2; clubhouse admission, $3. There is a restaurant at the track.

Harrah's Marina sponsors one of the best polo teams in New Jersey. All matches are played at 1:30 P.M. at the Mattix Run Equestrian Center, Moss Mill Road, Smithville. Admission is $3. Call 609–441–5000 for information.

Bowling enthusiasts will want to visit the **Showboat,** which sponsors several major bowling tournaments annually. Every spring, a Professional Bowlers Association (PBA) event is held here. Call for exact dates.

Every August the LPGA (Ladies Professional Golf Association) runs a tournament at the Sands Country Club. Visitors have a chance to see the best women golfers in the world.

HISTORIC SITES AND HOUSES. Atlantic County Historical Society. 907 Shore Rd., Somers Point (927–5218). The Victorian Museum features a short slide show about early Atlantic City. There is also a genealogical research library and a maritime museum. It is open year-round, Wed.–Sat., 10 A.M. to noon and then 1–4 P.M. Free.

Historic Gardner's Basin. 800 N. New Hampshire Ave. (at the Inlet) (348–2880). This replica of a maritime village features historic vessels, a coastal museum, a marine mammal museum, a small aquarium, and a gift shop. There are films, boat rides, and a good restaurant. Free. Open May to Sept., 11 A.M.–4 P.M.

Towne of Historic Smithville. 12 miles from Atlantic City, north on Route 9 (652–7777). This beautiful little village—a replica of an 1800s colonial village—has cobblestoned paths, a little pond, and about 30 specialty shops. Open daily. Free.

Somers Mansion. Shore Road, Somers Point (927–2212). This is the oldest house in Atlantic County, built around 1725 and partially furnished with original pieces from that era. It has a fine view of Great Egg Harbor Bay. Open year-round, Wed.–Fri., 9 A.M. to noon and 1–6 P.M.; Sat., 10 A.M. to noon and 1–6 P.M.; Sun., 1–6 P.M. Free.

ARTS AND ENTERTAINMENT. Atlantic City has limited choices for **film** buffs. *Atlantic City Free Public Library,* Tennessee and Atlantic avenues (345–2269), shows free films every Wednesday at noon. *Atlantic Film Society,* Little Art Theater, Harbor Village Square, Zion Rd. and Ocean Heights Ave., Bargaintown (653–1626), specializes in foreign and revival movies. Admission $4.50; discounts for senior citizens.

There are a few first-run movie houses in neighboring towns a few miles away; *Margate Twin* in Margate (822–3817), *Point 4* in Somers Point (927–0131), *Towne 4* in Pleasantville (646–4700), *Twin Plaza* in Ventnor Heights (823–6641), *Twin Tilton 1 and 2* in Northfield (646–3147), and *Ventnor Twin* in Ventnor (822–4422).

Atlantic City is better suited to please lovers of contemporary **music** than classical or jazz enthusiasts. The casinos bring in the most popular performers in the world for shows throughout the year. For more information, contact the casinos directly or write to the Atlantic City Visitors Bureau for a list of coming attractions.

A few local **theaters** present well-known Broadway plays and musicals. Occasionally a casino, often Claridge's Palace Theater (340–3700), will present a musical with a big-name star. The *South Jersey Regional Theater,* Gateway Playhouse, Bay and Higbee avenues, Somers Point (653–0553), is the only Equity theater in Atlantic County and offers high-quality acting. It presents a regular assortment of dramatic plays and musicals. Tickets cost between $13 and $17. There is a 10 percent discount for senior citizens and a 50 percent discount for students.

DINING OUT. For several decades Atlantic City has been well known for its outstanding Italian and seafood restaurants. The opening of the casino-hotels in the late 1970s has made the dining better than ever. Each casino-hotel holds several eating establishments, ranging from modest coffee shops to elegant restaurants. There is intense competition between the casinos, and world-class chefs are being hired at all of them.

The dining boom has extended to the Boardwalk, where there are now more fast-food establishments and coffee shops than ever. In nice weather, it's extremely pleasant to sit in a little coffee shop, gaze at the sea, and watch the parade of people go by. It's also a great way to save money! Many budget-conscious visitors eat breakfast and lunch on the Boardwalk and then treat themselves to a nice dinner in a good restaurant.

Restaurant categories, determined by the price of a meal for one, without beverages, are as follows: *Reasonable,* $14 to $18; *Very Economical,* $10 to $14; and *Low Budget,* under $10. Unless noted otherwise, all accept some, if not all, major credit cards.

Reasonable

Dock's Oyster House. 2405 Atlantic Ave. (345–0092). One of the best seafood places in town, in business since the turn of century. Specializes in lobsters and salmon. Dinner from 5 P.M. Closed Mon. Reservations advised.

Orsatti's. 24 S. North Carolina Ave. (347–7667). One of newest and classiest restaurants in town. Specialties include veal, pasta, and seafood. Piano bar. Valet parking. Dinner 4–11:30 P.M. Tues.–Sat.

Peking Duck House. Iowa and Atlantic avenues (348–1313). Unusually good Chinese place. Peking duck is carved right at your table and served with green scallions and cucumbers julienne. Extensive Szechuan, Mandarin, and Cantonese menu. Reservations advised. Lunch noon–3 P.M. Mon.–Sat.; dinner 3–11 P.M. Mon.–Thurs., until midnight Fri. and Sat.; open 2–11 P.M. Sun.

Ristorante Alberto. Mississippi and Pacific avenues (344–7000). Features sumptuous Italian dishes. Specialty is veal. Dinner from 4 P.M. to midnight. Reservations advised.

Scannicchio's. 119 S. California Ave. (348–6378). Newly renovated. Serves outstanding dishes of both Italian seafood and pasta. Dinner from 4 P.M. to midnight. Late-evening snacks also served. Specialties are sausage, stuffed calamari, broccoli. Great dessert pastries. Reservations advised.

Very Economical

Angelo's Fairmount Tavern. 2300 Fairmount Ave. (344–2439). Serves outstanding Sicilian and Italian cuisine. Lunch and dinner. No credit cards. Lunch 11:30 A.M.–2 P.M.; dinner 5–10:30 P.M.

Aubrey's. Arkansas and Pacific avenues (344–1632). Features an outdoor café and patio. Seafood and salads are excellent. Excellent pastries for dessert. D, 4 P.M.–midnight. Late snacks served 'til 6 A.M.

Little Rock Cafe. 5214 Atlantic Ave., Ventnor (823–4411). A European-style quiet café with light food such as omelets, quiches, croissants, salads, and soups. Bring your own wine. Lunch, dinner, Sunday brunch. No credit cards.

Lobster Shack. 230 N. Adams Ave., Margate (823–8847). Delicious fresh seafood is the norm here. Located right on a bay, so diners get an outstanding waterfront view. Dinner and Sunday brunch. Reservations suggested.

Low Budget

Before listing restaurants in this category, it should be reiterated that there are several inexpensive coffee shops and fast-food establishments right on the Boardwalk. In addition, each casino-hotel has at least one good coffee shop or specialty food store that serves good, inexpensive meals. Most casinos also contain oyster bars and delis. Although it is probably not worthwhile to travel to sample these places, they are certainly worth investigating if you are already in a casino.

A.W. Shucks Oyster Bar and Beer. Ocean One, Arkansas Ave. at Boardwalk (344–3321). Conveniently located in the big shopping mall at center of boardwalk, this pleasant restaurant serves fresh oysters as well as clams, shrimp, mussels, crabs, and homemade chowders. Open daily 10 A.M.–11 P.M.

Flamingo Diner. 3101 Pacific Ave. (344–3061). Open 24 hours a day; diversified menu and excellent food.

Los Amigos. 1926 Atlantic Ave., Atlantic City (344–2293). Pleasant, informal restaurant, specializing in Mexican fare. Tacos, burritos, and Mexican pizza are specialties of the house. Great margaritas and many types of Mexican beer. Lunch 11:30 A.M.–4 P.M., Mon.–Fri.; dinner 4 P.M.–2 A.M., seven days. Late snacks served 2–6:30 A.M.

Lou's. 5011 Ventnor Ave., Ventnor (823–2733). Famous for homemade food. Corned beef, fresh roast turkey, waffles, steaks, salads, and fountain treats. Lunch, dinner. No credit cards.

White House Sub Shop. 2301 Arctic Ave. (345–1564). Currently performing show business celebrities often dash in here; it's known as one of the best submarine sandwich shops on the East Coast. If you are in the vicinity, it's definitely worth a visit.

Recommended Splurge. The **Knife and Fork Inn,** Albany and Pacific avenues (344–1133), is widely recognized as Atlantic City's finest restaurant. In business since 1927, it offers excellent seafood, steaks, fresh vegetables (many grown locally), and an extensive wine list. The seafood appetizers are terrific, as are the desserts. Dinner only is served. Reservations are accepted every day except Sat. A modest dress code is enforced (jackets for men). Plan to wait—but it's worth it. Dinner is served 5:30–10:30 P.M. Prices for seafood entrees average about $14 to $16. Steak entrees range from $17 to $19. Lobster entrees cost between $19 and $24. Parking is free for every day of the week except Sat., when it is $5. American Express cards are accepted.

NIGHTLIFE AND BARS. The name the City That Never Sleeps could be applied to Atlantic City as well as to its big brother up north, New York City. The casino-hotels, with their brilliantly lit marquees illuminating Pacific Ave., remain open until 4 A.M. on weekdays and 6 A.M. on weekends. (Remember, you must be 21 to enter a casino or drink in New Jersey.) All the casinos contain an official "showroom" theater where top-name entertainers perform. In addition, many casino-hotels have an additional auditorium or theater that offers a musical revue show. All the casino-hotels have numerous piano bars and lounges. Scores of taverns and discos cater to the locals as well as the 30 million visitors. Many stay open all night.

The Casinos

It is pretty easy to get tickets to casino acts. You don't have to be a guest. Tickets for headline engagements can be purchased at individual casino box offices or local Ticketron outlets or can be charged, with credit cards, through Teletron (northern New Jersey, 201–343–4200; southern New Jersey, 609–344–1770; New York, 212–947–5850; Pennsylvania, 215–627–0532). In all cases, try to reserve as early as possible.

Atlantis. Florida Ave. at Boardwalk, Atlantic City, NJ 08401 (609–344–4000, 800–257–8672). The Cabaret Theatre offers big-name stars. There is also entertainment at the Shangri-La Lounge and Le Club.

Bally's Grand. Boston and Pacific avenues, Atlantic City, NJ 08401 (609–347–7111, 800–257–8677). The Opera House Theater showcases big-name stars. Nightly entertainment is provided at Elaine's.

Bally's Park Place. Park Place and Boardwalk, Atlantic City, NJ 08401 (609–340–2000, 800–772–7777). The Park Place Cabaret features a musical revue. Billy's Pub offers nightly entertainment, as does Upstairs in the Park.

Caesars. Arkansas Ave. at Boardwalk, Atlantic City, NJ 08401 (609–348–4411, 800–257–8555). Circus Maximus Theatre has headliners. Other performers at Arena and Forum lounges.

Claridge. Indiana Ave. at Brighton Park, Atlantic City, NJ 08401 (609–340–3400, 800–257–8585). The Palace Theatre has old Broadway musicals plus occasional headliners. The Celebrity Cabaret features live entertainment, usually two shows a night.

Harrah's Marina. 1725 Brigantine Blvd., Atlantic City, NJ 08401 (609–441–5165, 800–2–HARRAHS). Broadway-by-the-Bay Theatre offers first-rate performers during most of the year. The Atrium Lounge, a beautiful garden bar with waterfalls, trees, and skylights, is a good setting for late-night drinks. The Bay Cabaret Theater has live music.

Resorts International. North Carolina Ave. at Boardwalk, Atlantic City, NJ 08401 (609–344–6000, 800–GET–RICH). Top-name performers entertain in the Superstar Theatre. The Carousel Cabaret offers musical revues, Las Vegas style. Other nightly entertainment can be found in the Camelot and Rendezvous lounges.

Sands. Indiana Ave. at Boardwalk, Atlantic City, NJ 08401 (609–441–4000, 800–257–8580). The Copa Room features nationally known stars. The Punch Bowl and Players lounges offer music.

Showboat. 800 Boardwalk, Box 840, Atlantic City, NJ 08404 (609–343–4000). Top show-biz performers appear in the 400-seat Mardi Gras Lounge, whose decor simulates New Orleans' famed Bourbon Street. The Hall of Fame Lounge is decorated with authentic sports memorabilia and features several televisions showing sporting events. The 11th Frame is the Bowling Center's Lounge.

Tropicana. Iowa Ave. at Boardwalk, Atlantic City, NJ 08401 (609–340–4000, 800–257–6227). The Tropicana Showroom features major show business headliners. The Top of the Trop lounge offers a great view of the ocean from the 21st floor; jazz is played there. The Comedy Stop features top-notch comedians.

Trump's Castle. Huron Ave. and Brigantine Blvd., Atlantic City, NJ 08401 (609–441–2000, 800–441–5551). King's Court Theatre is major showroom. Nightly entertainment in Viva's and the Casino Lounge.

Trump Plaza. Mississippi Ave. At Boardwalk, Atlantic City, NJ 08401 (609–441–6000, 800–2–HARRAHS). Trump Theater has headliners. Jezebel's is a nice piano bar. Swizzle's—a two-level bar—overlooks the casino.

Inexpensive Pubs and Taverns

Aubrey's. 2024 Pacific Ave. (344–1632). Next to Caesars, this bright, cheerful restaurant and bar has a wonderful enclosed sidewalk patio.

Irish Pub. St. James Place at Boardwalk (345–9613). Live entertainment featuring Irish music; light meals served 24 hours. Burgers and sandwiches are good.

Silver Dollar Saloon. 1719 Pacific Ave. (344–2202). Open 24 hours a day. One of few places left in town that serves $1 draft beer.

Quiet, Relaxed Bars

Brass Rail. 12 S. Mt. Vernon Ave. (348–0192). Has nice decor, and one of best jukeboxes in town. Working fireplace. Open 24 hours.

Dolley's Lounge. Madison House Hotel, 123 S. Illinois Ave. (345–1400). Cozy atmosphere in newly renovated hotel. Features happy hour with free hors d'oeuvres 5–7 P.M., Mon.–Fri. Open 4 P.M.–midnight Mon.–Thurs.; noon to 7 A.M. Fri. and Sat.

Herman's Place. 2 S. New York Ave. (344–1800). Resembles friendly local tavern, with great selection of domestic and imported beers. Open 8 A.M. to 4 A.M. Delicious chili and chicken wings.

Dancing Clubs

Bay Club. Monroe and Amherst aves., Margate (823–2121). One of the newest night spots in the area, with beautiful glassed-in patio overlooking the bay. Pleasant piano bar. Hours vary, call ahead.

Copa Club. Huge disco in the Sands. Indiana Ave. and Brighton Park, Atlantic City (441–4000). In late evening during weekends the main showroom of this casino-hotel becomes a dance club, open to 5 A.M.

Egos. 939 Bay Ave., Somers Point (653–4141). One of the most popular discos in town. A favorite of locals. This is a two-story club, complete with a disc jockey and light show. Dress code (no jeans) and cover.

Red's. 9217 Atlantic Ave., Margate (822–1539). Features three different sections: a pub, a dance club, and a video lounge.

Touché. 9300 Amherst Ave., Margate (823–2144). A sophisticated nightclub, complete with live dance revue, dancing bartenders and waitresses, and special nightly events. Happy hour buffets with unlimited free shrimp. Open 24 hours.

Upscale, Classy Bars

Friar Tuck's Tavern. 23 S. New Rd., Northfield (654–9400). On the mainland a few miles away, this is worth the drive. It has medieval decor plus good food and drinks. Open 11 A.M.–3 A.M.

Harbour Lights. 520 Bay Ave., Somers Point (653–0900). A favorite of local professionals who live here right off the marina.

Le Club. Enclave Condominiums, Lincoln Place and the Boardwalk (347–0400). One of newest—and best—jazz clubs in town, with great view of ocean. Open 5 P.M.–2 A.M., seven days.

Longport Inn. 31st and Atlantic avenues, Longport (922–5435). An elegant little bar that provides a great place for a quiet drink.

The Waterfront. Somers Point Circle, Somers Point (653–0099). A romantic bar overlooking the bay. This large nightclub's main attraction is its patio, where you can sip a drink and enjoy a nice view of the bay.

SECURITY. Generally speaking, the Boardwalk sections in front of all the casino-hotels are very well patrolled, even late at night. Pacific Avenue, the town's main drag, is also heavily patrolled by local police. The casinos themselves have outstanding security; you nearly always see a security guard somewhere.

Still, a few commonsense safety precautions should make your visit a safe, enjoyable one. There are a lot of professional pickpockets here, so guard your wallet or purse carefully, especially when you are gambling and your attention is diverted. Do not carry around a lot of cash. If you have a lot of valuables, put them in a hotel safe. Before going to a restaurant or nightclub outside the casino area, call the establishment and ask if they provide free parking—most do. Although the well-lit parking lots adjoining these restaurants are usually safe, sometimes the side streets are not. Try not to park your vehicle in a deserted, poorly lit area.

As a general rule, the farther west you get from Pacific Avenue, the less safe the neighborhood. If you stay in brightly lit, well-traveled areas, you will be fine.

BALTIMORE

by
Catherine Connor Schlaich

Catherine Connor Schlaich, a native of Baltimore, is an assistant vice president of the Barton-Gillet Company.

When out-of-towners think of Baltimore (and more and more people across the country *are* thinking about Baltimore), what comes to mind?

Harborplace, in capital letters, for one. James Rouse's renowned home for a thousand and one food and shopping delights, born in 1980, is perhaps the major tourist attraction. Recently the splendid, four-story Gallery of high-end shops and snacks was unveiled across from Harborplace.

Keep going. The National Aquarium in Baltimore, of course, also a national-headline grabber. (Some joke that the line to enter this seven-level sensation stretches to Washington, D.C. But the people in that line aren't laughing.) For gourmets, Baltimore means some of the best seafood anywhere. Taking a mallet to hot, spicy steamed crabs, piled high on newspaper, with a pitcher of frosty beer alongside, is *the* summer pastime. Sports fans know this town as home of the Preakness Stakes, the middle jewel in thoroughbred racing's Triple Crown, every May at Pimlico Race Track. We're also acknowledged as the unofficial capital of lacrosse, taken very seriously—especially at Johns Hopkins University, the setting for the International Lacrosse Tournament—in this pink-and-green alligator city.

But the backbone of Baltimore stretches far beyond the Inner Harbor waters. The myriad neighborhoods with which we began centuries ago form the support system that launched the port city's renaissance more than a decade ago and resurrected the economic center. Urban "homesteading" began here—and in the country—with Mayor-turned-Governor William Donald Schaefer's 1973 program, a huge success and boon to the city. More than five hundred abandoned properties were purchased for $1 each: Stirling Street's Federal-style row houses, nineteenth-century Ridgely's Delight houses, and refurbished Otterbein town homes dating to the 1700s. And historic Federal Hill, just south of the Inner Harbor, boasts beautifully renovated town houses with a stunning panoramic water view. Since the rebirth of these areas, neighborhood rehabilitation and conservation have been emphasized by the city government and residents.

The streets of Reservoir Hill, one of those delightful neighborhoods, are lined with turn-of-the-century brownstones. Mount Vernon Place, four parks surrounding the Washington Monument, is the setting for upscale nineteenth-century town houses and such cultural institutions as the Peabody Conservatory of Music and the Walters Art Gallery. You'll find sophisticated elegance in uptown's Bolton Hill, a neighborhood of Victorian dwellings.

Old, close-knit ethnic neighborhoods surround the Inner Harbor. A short walk to the east finds Little Italy, frequented for its exquisite restaurants and the gourmet finds in the charming family-owned groceries. Natives and descendants of Italy, Germany, Poland, Greece, and other countries make up Highlandtown, in East Baltimore, where the white marble steps glisten in front of the row houses, and many screen doors are painted with intricate landscapes and other scenes—a quaint folk art undergoing a revival. Little Lithuania, nestled west of the downtown area, sprouted in the 1880s and grew more during World War II.

Port-side Fells Point, Quaker Edward Fell's 1763 community, is about a mile east of the Inner Harbor. Home to comfortable bars, unique shops, a fine food market, and a number of superb hideaway eateries, the Point's prides are its more than three hundred original residential buildings. Luxury waterfront condos and town houses, complete with marina slips and other upscale amenities, are quickly revitalizing this long-forgotten end of town.

The language of development indeed is Baltimore's new tongue. After several steady, albeit snail's-paced, years, the central downtown area now is bursting with myriad major retail, office, and tourist accommodations projects in various stages of planning and construction. Among those updating Baltimore's image are the city's first world-class hotels, Peabody Court and Harbor Court; the Rouse Company's Gallery, topped by tony Stouffer's Hotel; The Brokerage at Market Place, an eclectic setting for offices, stores, eateries, and the city's first sports bar; the high-style Scarlett Place condo complex overlooking the Inner Harbor; and the glitzy courtyards and rental units of Waterloo Place. The ultramodern Provident Bank Tower, the Bank of Baltimore building of polished granite, and the crescent-shaped Brexton building are all beginning to sprout downtown. And, of course, the development venture on every Baltimorean's mind: the two new sports stadiums planned for Camden Yards.

It's clear that Baltimore is becoming a wealthier town in finances and offerings, but the cost of living—and visiting—here are East Coast bargains. The city's most expensive, first-rate restaurants and splurge guest facilities probably would fall in a New Yorker's moderate range. That makes the countless fine midprice bistros and tourist attractions seem double the savings.

There's another language in the city you'll recognize the minute you ask a Baltimorean for directions to a theater or ask a local salesclerk for assistance. It's a warm and friendly way of talking we have here, a willingness to help out a neighbor—or visiting neighbor—colored by a, well, interesting pronunciation style: Bawlamerese, our speech has been dubbed. At breakfast we drink *arnjuice* and a *cuppa* coffee. At lunch *cole race beef* is a favorite sandwich. Many of us work downtown in *bidness* offices or at the *Bethlum* steel mill. In summer Bawlamereans like to vacation on the beach *downey ayshin.* Our city boasts the *Beeno Railroad,* the zoo in *Droodle* Park, and several other attractions you and other *torsts prolly* will want to take a *cammer* and *fillum* to for some *pixtures.* If you don't *unnersteand* us, we may ask, *"Smar few?"* It's as though we have a *differnt* word for *everythink, idnit?*

PRACTICAL INFORMATION

WHEN TO GO. Baltimore overflows with tourists from early to midsummer, when the Inner Harbor attracts boaters on a stopover and the city is the site of myriad outdoor festivals. Temperatures hover in the mid-eighties until late summer, when hotter weather and the unbearable humidity for which the city is infamous take over. You'll miss the sticky air and be in time for the beginning of the arts season if you visit in mid-September or later. Expect high autumn temperatures in the sixties (with an October Indian summer hitting the eighties again for a short spell), lows in the forties, with a normal rainy season. Some recent Baltimore winters have been mild, in the thirties and forties with infrequent light snows; others have brought periods of frigid air and heavy snow or ice storms, paralyzing the city for a day or two. Occasional strong winds make 20-degree air feel subzero. The city also has seen frost—and sometimes snow—after the first day of spring. Be prepared.

HOW TO GET THERE. By air. *Baltimore/Washington International Airport* has increased its passenger traffic significantly during the past few years. The economical *Piedmont* has grown markedly since opening in 1983. Among international carriers added in recent years are *British Airways, Eastern Airlines, Air Jamaica, Icelandair,* and *World Airways, American, Delta, TWA, United,* and *USAir* are among the other major airlines. Shop around for discount rates for everything from limited seating to students to family members traveling together. Call 859–7035 for a free "BWI Flight Guide" pamphlet of schedules.

By bus. Hop a bus to Baltimore via *Greyhound-Trailways* (stations at the Baltimore Travel Plaza, 5625 O'Donnell St., 633–9200, and 210 W. Fayette St., 752–2115). Baltimore is an allowed stop on unlimited travel passes.

By train. The renovated *Pennsylvania Station,* 1515 N. Charles St., accommodates twenty-five *Amtrak* trains daily. You might consider a plane-train connection: Commuter and Amtrak trains are now available at the *BWI Rail Station* to and from Baltimore, Washington, D.C., Philadelphia, New York, and other cities in the northeast corridor and the south. A schedule is included in the "BWI Flight Guide," available free by calling 859–7035. Call the station for Amtrak information at 539–2112.

By car. There are four major routes to Baltimore. From points north take I-83. From the northeast and south I-95 connects to the Inner Harbor area via the I-395 extension. I-70, from the west, feeds into the Baltimore Beltway, I-695. From there take I-83 or I-395 straight downtown. (Expect I-83 delays due to renovation through this year.)

TELEPHONES. Maryland's area code is 301. Calls from Baltimore to some outlying counties require dialing 1 before the exchange. Directory assistance is 555–1212; 1–555–1212 for long distance information within the 301 area code; and 1 + an outside area code + 555–1212 outside the 301 area code. Call 1–800–555–1212 for toll-free 800 number assistance. To place a person-to-person or collect call, or to charge a call to a credit card, dial 0 + the number (including its area code if it's outside the 301 area code). A local call from a public telephone costs 25 cents. Area public phones compatible with some types of hearing aids are identified by a ring-type device attached to the cord at the base of the handset.

Emergency Telephone Numbers. The emergency number for Baltimore city fire, police, and ambulance is 911.

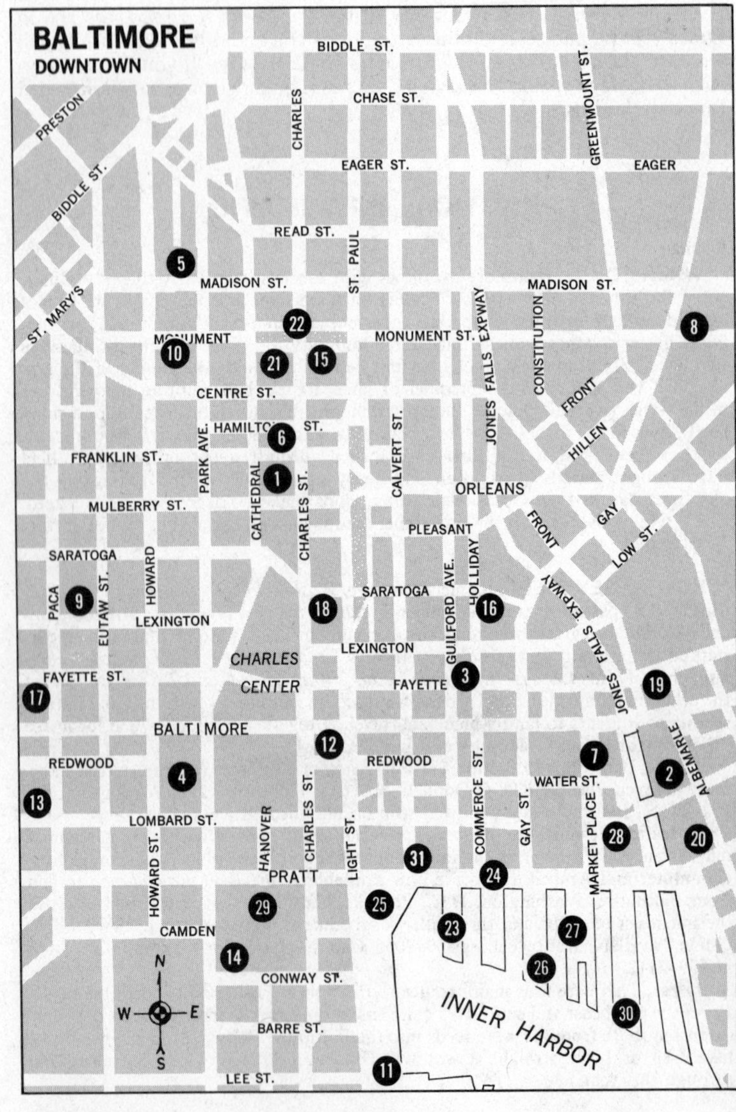

Points of Interest

1) Basilica of the Assumption
2) Carroll Mansion
3) City Hall
4) Baltimore Arena
5) First Presbyterian Church
6) First Unitarian Church
7) Market Place
8) Johns Hopkins Medical Center
9) Lexington Market
10) Maryland Historical Society
11) Maryland Science Center
12) Morris Mechanic Theater
13) Medical College (Univ. of Maryland)
14) Otterbein Church
15) Peabody Institute
16) Peale Museum
17) Edgar Allan Poe's Grave
18) Saint Paul's Rectory
19) Shot Tower
20) Star-Spangled Banner Flag House
21) Walters Art Gallery
22) Washington Monument
23) U.S. Frigate Constellation
24) World Trade Center
25) Harborplace
26) National Aquarium in Baltimore
27) U.S.S. Torsk and Light Ship Chesapeake
28) Baltimore Office of Promotion and Tourism
29) Convention Center and Festival Hall
30) Pier Six Concert Pavilion
31) The Gallery at Harborplace

ACCOMMODATIONS. A number of new hotels will more than double the number of rooms in Baltimore city alone in the latter half of the eighties. Several of the existing hotels charge for beyond the economy range, but when extra space is available, prices can plummet for a spell to fill rooms.

Hotel rates are based on double occupancy. Categories, determined by price, are: *Reasonable,* $65 to $85, and *Very Economical,* $50 to $65.

Reasonable

Days Inn. Lombard St. and Hopkins Place, Baltimore, MD 21201 (301–576–1000). Contemporary. Restaurant, greenhouse cafe, outdoor pool.

Holiday Inn. Howard and Lombard streets, Baltimore, MD 21201 (301–685–3500). Art deco and modern. Indoor pool, ballroom, restaurant, cocktail lounge.

Quality Inn. Baltimore Travel Plaza, 5625 O'Donnell St., Baltimore, MD 21224 (301–633–9500). New 200-room hotel. Contemporary. 24-hour restaurant; nightclub; dinner cabaret.

Very Economical

Comfort Inn. 24 W. Franklin St., Baltimore, MD 21201 (301–727–7200). Contemporary rooms, some with Jacuzzi, some with loft. Restaurant, small lounge.

Omni International Hotel Baltimore. 101 W. Fayette St., Baltimore, MD 21201 (301–752–1100). Traditional-modern mix. Restaurant; outdoor pool; exercise facility. Very economical upon availability.

Budget Motel Chains. These motels charge just under $50 for standardized accommodations.

Best Western Hallmark Hotel. 8 N. Howard St., Baltimore, MD 21201 (301–539–1188). Old World charm. Café.

Best Western—Harbor City Inn. 1710 Russell St., Baltimore, MD 21230 (301–727–3400). Contemporary. Restaurant, outdoor pool. Off-season discount plan.

Shoney's Inn. 1401 Bloomfield Ave., Baltimore, MD 21227 (301–646–1700). Contemporary. Restaurant, outdoor pool.

Bed-and-Breakfast. These old European-style accommodations are popping up in Baltimore—and folding here and there, too, so keeping a current list from month to month is nearly impossible. Presently there are a handful in the city, among which are the **Bolton Hill,** 1534 Bolton St., Baltimore, MD 21217 (301–669–5356), reserve a week in advance, up to $60; **Eagles Mere,** 102 E. Montgomery St., Baltimore, MD 21230 (301–332–1618), reserve two weeks in advance, up to $60; and **Inner Harbor,** 112 E. Montgomery St., Baltimore MD 21230 (301–528–8692), reserve two weeks in advance, up to $75, all year-round. Contact **Amanda's Bed and Breakfast,** 1428 Park Ave., Baltimore, MD 21217 (301–225–0001), a local reservations service, for information about and bookings with other metropolitan-area facilities.

Hostel. Baltimore International Youth Hostel. 17 W. Mulberry St., Baltimore, MD 21201 (301–576–8880). Bunk room facilities with pillow and blanket; sheets for rent. Large common room; no TVs or radios. Small kitchen for preparing breakfast or dinner during specified hours. 11 P.M. curfew. $13 a night, $10 for members, plus fifteen-minute chore.

HOW TO GET AROUND. From the airport. A ride downtown from Baltimore/Washington International Airport, ten miles, costs about $15 by taxi. Airport limo service to major hotels will put you back just $5. Go to the ground transportation desk on the lower level of the central terminal.

By bus. The Mass Transit Administration (539–5000) offers myriad convenient routes with frequent stops in the city. Many buses are new, with air conditioning, smoked-glass windows, and cushioned seats; be prepared, though, for an occasional older vehicle in disrepair. Initial bus fare is 90 cents, plus 10 cents for a transfer.

By subway. The MTA's young *Metro* subway offers travel from Owings Mills to Charles Center, with ten stations in between, every 7½ minutes during morning and afternoon rush hours and at ten-minute intervals during midday. Fare is 90 cents, plus zone fares; parking is available at most stations. The Metro recording number is 333–2700; call 539–5000 for more information.

By trolley. For just 25 cents, ride Charles Street, the Inner Harbor area, and South Baltimore San Francisco-style. Call Trolley Works (396–4259) for schedule.

By taxi. For transportation PDQ, hail a cab—$1.40 when you step in and 10 cents for each fraction of a mile. If you call ahead to order a taxi, the meter starts at $1.65. Cab companies servicing the downtown area include *Diamond Cab* (947–3333); *Royal Cab* (327–0330); and *Sun Cab* (235–0300);

By car. Contact one of these companies about car rental: *Avis* (685–6000; BWI, 1–800–331–1212); *Budget Rent-A-Car* (837–6955; BWI, 859–0850); *Hertz* (332–0015; BWI, 850–7400); *Sears Rent-A-Car* (685–0665; BWI, 859–0910); *Thrifty Rent-A-Car* (BWI, 768–4900). All companies request that you reserve at least 24 hours in advance. Rental cars can be picked up at the lower level of the airport terminal.

HINTS TO THE MOTORIST. Many of Baltimore's major attractions are centrally located within a short walk of each other; a bus to a gallery or a taxi to dinner are reliable, hassle-free, and economical alternatives to bringing your car downtown. If you're traveling in the city by car on weekdays, keep in mind that the majority of commuters and tourists arrive downtown between 9 and 11 A.M.; nearly half leave between 3 and 5 P.M.

As everywhere in the country, the top speed limit in Baltimore is 55 mph. Most city streets average 30 mph. Speed is checked by radar. Recently Baltimore and its surrounding counties have cracked down on drunk driving; you may be stopped at a random suburban checkpoint.

You may turn right on red after stopping in Baltimore; restrictions are posted by the traffic light. The Jones Falls Expressway (I-83) and the Fort McHenry Tunnel (I-95, $1 toll) are handy ribbons out of downtown, with hazardous traffic or weather conditions and suggestions for reduced speed posted overhead. (Expect I-83 delays due to renovation through this year; call JFX-INFO for alternate-route maps.)

The worst time to be looking for a **parking** space is weekdays noon–3 P.M. Red-painted curbs mark no-parking zones. Disabled parking spaces are clearly designated by sign and the wheelchair symbol painted on the space. Most downtown meters cost 75 cents–$1 an hour. Check the time limit before leaving your car: A meter with a red hood allows parking just 15–30 minutes; white stands for an hour; gray gets you two hours; four hours' parking is permitted at a meter with a blue hood; and a bronze head denotes eight- to ten-hour parking. Two city lots near the Inner Harbor offer the best deals: ten hours at meters for just 30 cents an hour. They're at the southwest corner of Pratt and Eutaw streets and at Pratt and Gay streets (the latter lot is reserved until 9 A.M. for ride-sharing participants). Most garages charge $7 or more for a day of parking; many offer greatly reduced rates on the weekend. Parking facilities are marked by a visible blue *P* sign.

Check with your insurance agent to make sure your car policy covers liability for out-of-state driving, because Maryland is not a "no-fault" state. Baltimore is well-outfitted with *AAA, Amoco,* and other major auto club repair facilities.

TOURIST INFORMATION. For city maps and special-interest brochures, turn to the *Baltimore Office of Promotion and Tourism,* 34 Market Place, Suite 310, Baltimore, MD 21202 (301–752–8632), Mon.–Fri., 9 A.M.–5 P.M., and the *Baltimore Convention Bureau,* 1 W. Pratt St., Baltimore, MD 21202 (301–659–7000), Mon.–Fri., 8:30 A.M.–5 P.M. The BPT's twenty-four-hour events hotline, updated daily, is 837–INFO. The *Visitors Information Center,* end of Pier 4 off Pratt St. (also 837–INFO), provides information guides, a variety of literature, and an audiovisual presentation of Baltimore's cultural and historical attractions. Hours are Mon.–Fri., 10 A.M.–6 P.M. The *International Visitors Center of Baltimore,* World Trade Center, Suite 1712, 401 E. Pratt St., Baltimore, MD 21202 (301–837–7150), Mon.–Fri., 9 A.M.–5 P.M., offers a list of area interpreters for foreigners' assistance.

Foreign Currency. *Ace Currency Exchange,* 230 Park Ave. (752–7451) and 212 E. Baltimore St. (752–7224). Mon.–Fri. 9:30 A.M.–5:30 P.M., Sat. 9:30 A.M.–1:30 P.M. *First National Bank,* 14 Light St., eleventh floor (244–4555). Mon.–Fri., 9 A.M.–2 P.M. *Mercantile Bank,* 2 Hopkins Plaza (237–5900). Mon.–Fri., 8:30 A.M.–4 P.M.

HINTS TO DISABLED TRAVELERS. All of Baltimore's major thoroughfares have cutaway curbs for wheelchair access. There are reserved parking spaces, marked by sign and painted symbol. The *Easter Seal Society of Central Maryland,* 3700 Fourth St., Baltimore, MD 21225 (301–355–0100), provides comprehensive accessibility information for Baltimore restaurants, hotels, attractions, and shopping facilities.

For current accessibility information, write or call *Maryland Information and Referral Service for the Handicapped,* Box 8717, BWI Airport, Baltimore, MD 21240 (301–383–6523). Write or call the *Baltimore League for the Handicapped,* 1111 E. Coldspring Le., Baltimore, MD 21239 (301–323–0500), about sports opportunities for the disabled.

The MTA's *Call-A-Lift Bus* service, daily, 8:30 A.M.–4:30 P.M., provides lift-equipped transit buses for anyone with impaired mobility on any bus route that MTA operates. Each bus can accommodate two wheelchair passengers. Order by 1 P.M. the day before you want to travel. Call MTA-LIFT and tell the operator where your trip will begin and end, what times you want to travel, and if possible which bus route you want to travel. Initial fare is 90 cents. The MTA *Metro* subway, with stations equipped with elevators, also is accessible for wheelchairs. Call 539–5000. For information about *Amtrak's* special rail facilities for the disabled and elderly, write for a free copy of *"Access Amtrak"* to Amtrak, National Railroad Passenger Corporation, 400 N. Capitol St. NW, Washington, DC 20001.

FREE EVENTS. Free festivals, street fairs, and holiday celebrations fill Baltimore's calendar. The Inner Harbor welcomes each year as host to a **New Year's Eve** fireworks display and concert, drawing thousands downtown despite the nippy air. February follows with a month of concerts, theater productions, lectures, films, and dance performances dedicated to **Black History Month.** Call the Enoch Pratt Free Library (396–5494), Morgan State University (444–3030), the Eubie Blake Cultural Center (396–1300), and the Baltimore Museum of Art (396–7101) for information about related activities. Watch regional Irish musicians, Mummers, and other performance groups in the March 17 **Saint Patrick's Day Parade,** which travels south on North Charles Street from Chase Street to Lombard Street beginning at 2 P.M.

Spring blooms in Baltimore with a 71-year-old city tradition, the Women's Civic League's **Flower Mart.** Flower-arranging demonstrations, gardening tips, a garden shop, booths of flowering plants, and entertainment and refreshments are among the treats that fill Mount Vernon Place the first week in May. May also brings **Preakness Festival Week,** leading up to the Preakness Stakes, the second jewel in the Triple Crown, at Pimlico Race Course. The celebration is filled with such free fun as the **Great Preakness Balloon Ascension and Race,** in Patterson Park, the **Preakness Parade,** downtown, the **Walters' Race,** the **Fastest Newstalker Contest,** and other crazy Inner Harbor contests. The breathtaking **Sailboat Regatta** is held in the harbor.

Baltimore kicks into high gear in summer. The city celebrates its myriad neighborhoods with **Showcase of Nations,** a series of Polish, Jewish, Italian, and other ethnic festivals, June-September, in Festival Hall. **Midtown Music** (837–INFO) hosts free jazz and pop lunchtime concerts, Mon., Wed., and Fri., June-Aug., at Hopkins Plaza. **Artscape,** on the third weekend in July in the Mount Royal corridor, near Chase and Howard streets, features oil paintings, video, music, dance, children's events, and more in a salute to local talent. Maritime displays and demonstrations are among the **Harbor Expo Celebration** highlights in summer in the Inner Harbor. For a taste of Baltimore spirit, visit September's **Baltimore City Fair,** a showcase of neighborhood displays, crafts, and ethnic foods at the city fairgrounds, Saratoga and Holliday streets.

The fun continues into autumn, with the **Fells Point Fun Festival** in October. The city's oldest festival offers family entertainment, crafts, and antiques. Then we're into the holidays, kicked off by the *Charles Street Thanksgiving Parade,* the weekend before Thanksgiving.

TOURS AND SPECIAL-INTEREST SIGHTSEEING. About Town Tours. 10 Fox Hill Ct., Perry Hall (592–7770). Historic and theme tours, Fri. 6:30–8 P.M.; $2.

Baltimore Defender and Guardian. Inner Harbor (685–4288). Daily round-trip narrated cruises to Fort McHenry or Fells Point Memorial Day-Labor Day, every half hour, 11 A.M.–5:30 P.M. (returns to Inner Harbor every half hour, 11:30 A.M.–6 P.M.). Adults, $3.85; children under 12, $2.50. Round-trip Inner Harbor-Fort McHenry-Fells Point cruises, $4.95; children under 12, $3.60.

Baltimore Patriot. Inner Harbor (685–4288). 1½-hr. round-trip narrated cruises to National Aquarium, Federal Hill, the submarine *Torsk,* Fells Point, Fort McHenry, grain and coal piers, commercial shipping, and Fort Carroll. Daily, Apr.-May, 11 A.M., 1 and 3 P.M.; June-Sept., hourly 11 A.M.–4 P.M. Adults, $5; children under 12, $2.50.

Footnotes. Meet at Hum Additi's, Pratt St. Pavilion, Harborplace (764–8067). 1½-hour walking tours of harbor, Tues.-Sun., 10:15 A.M.; and Little Italy, Thurs.-Sun., 5:30 P.M., with portable headsets. $5.

Minnie-V oyster dredge. Inner Harbor (522–4214). 1, 1½-, and 2-hr. cruises of old port section, including Federal Hill, Fells Point, Canton, and Locust Point. May-Sept. and holidays, Fri.-Sun., noon, 1:20, 3, 5, 7, and 9 P.M.; June-Sept., Tues.-Thurs., noon, 1:30, and 8 P.M. $5 to $10; children under 12, half price.

Port Welcome and Lady Baltimore. Inner Harbor (347–5552). *Port Welcome* cruises to Annapolis, St. Michaels, and also offers theme cruises. June-Sept., Wed.-Sat., 9 A.M.–5:30 P.M., 11:45 A.M.–2 P.M. in Annapolis. $14.30–$18.70. *Lady Baltimore* lunch and dinner Inner Harbor cruises year-round. Lunch daily, noon–2 P.M. Dinner daily, 7–10 P.M. $11–$27.

PARKS AND GARDENS. Carroll Park. Monroe St. and Washington Blvd. (685–8344). Surrounding the pre-Revolutionary *Mount Clare Mansion,* the park contains a golf course, tennis courts, and athletic fields. Dawn-dusk. Free.

Druid Hill Park. Druid Lake Dr., (396–0180). Besides the *Baltimore Zoo* and *Conservatory,* the six-hundred-acre park also offers pavilions, athletic fields, lakes, and picnic groves. Dawn-dusk. Free.

Federal Hill. Warren Ave. and Key Hwy. One of the best Inner Harbor views can be seen from this park, named for the celebration held here following the ratification of the Constitution. Dawn-dusk. Free.

Patterson Park. Eastern and Patterson Park avenues (396–9304). Many original nineteenth-century plantings and buildings remain, and the pagoda observatory provides a terrific city view. Tennis, biking, and ice skating are among the possible recreations. Open 24 hours. Free.

Robert E. Lee Park. Falls Rd. north of Lake Ave. (667–0123). Boat, fish, and picnic at *Lake Roland,* surrounded by woods, streams, and wetlands. More than forty species of birds reside there; the *Maryland Ornithological Society* conducts walks every spring Tues. and fall Thurs., 8–11 A.M. Park open dawn-dusk, year-round. Free.

Sherwood Gardens. Highfield Rd. and Greenway (366–2572). Mid-May is the peak season for the seven acres of tulips, azaleas, and flowering shrubs, originally privately owned. Dawn-dusk. Free.

Leakin-Gwynns Falls Park. 4900 Windsor Mill Rd., between Forest Park Ave., Windsor Mill Rd., Hilton Pkwy., and Franklintowne Rd. (396–0010). This is the second largest municipal park in the country. Much of it is virgin land, covered with trees dating from the eighteenth century. The Crimea, a nineteenth-century mansion of Russian-influence architecture; a wooden American chapel; and English gardens constitute the eclectic former estate of railroad magnate Thomas DeLay Winans, near the Forest Park Ave.-Windsor Mill Rd. intersection. Tennis courts, huge grills, forty movable picnic tables, and horses for trail rides ($7 an hour, 448–3225) are the featured attractions. Dawn-dusk, year-round. Free.

Cylburn Park. 4915 Greenspring Ave., (396–0180). About half of its 180 acres are pure wilderness. Hike the *Circle Trail* for bird-watching and tree, wildflower, and wildlife study. Formal gardens surround the *Tyson Mansion,* which houses a nature museum with almost four hundred species of stuffed birds among its collection. Dawn-dusk, year-round. Free.

ZOOS. Baltimore Zoo. Druid Hill Park, Druid Park Lake Dr. (396–7102). Rock Island, the country's largest colony of black-footed penguins, the natural African Plains exhibit of lions and giraffes, and a new three-acre elephant park are among the wonders at the 150 rolling acres that are home to more than a thousand animals. The Children's Zoo's highlights are baby animals for petting, the Zoo-Choo train that snakes through the park, a carousel, and a snack bar. Both zoos are open daily, year-round except Dec. 25, 10 A.M.–4:20 P.M., 11 A.M.–5:20 P.M. on summer Sundays. Adults, $2.50; senior citizens, and children 2–11, $1. Children are free on nonholiday Mondays. Sat., free until noon.

National Aquarium in Baltimore. Pier 3, 501 E. Pratt St. (576–3810). The seven levels house more than five thousand creatures in a hands-on Children's Cove, Amazon Rain Forest, Atlantic Coral Reef, and 220,000-gallon circular Open Ocean Tank of sharks and large game fish. Mid-Sept.-mid-May: daily 10 A.M.–5 P.M. Fri., 10 A.M.–8 P.M. Mid-May–mid-Sept.: Mon.–Thurs., 9 A.M.–5 P.M. Fri.-Sun., 9 A.M.–8 P.M. Adults, $6.75; senior citizens, students 12–18, and military personnel, $5; children 3–11, $3.75.

PARTICIPANT SPORTS. Biking. Serious bikers, pick up a copy of the *Baltimore Area Bike Map* ($2.50), which outlines local bike routes (rated for general safety) and the locations of repair shops, dangerous intersections, hills, bicycle lockers, and points of interest. Write to the *Regional Planning Council,* 2225 N. Charles St., Baltimore, MD 21218. The *Bicycle Hot Line* (333–1663) provides information Mon.-Fri. 8 A.M.–4 P.M.

Among Baltimore bike paths are paths at *Patterson Park* (Eastern and Patterson Park aves., 396–9304) and a two-mile circular path starting at the Harford Rd.–Argonne Dr. intersection, at *Herring Run Park,* and extending from the northern to the eastern city lines. Call the *Baltimore Bicycling Club* (486–7422) for information about group excursions. For route maps, contact the *Maryland Department of Transportation* (659–1140). Racing organizations include *Chesapeake Wheelman* (296–4236) and *Esquire Bicycle Club* (467–1123).

Fishing. *Middle Branch Park* (just south of the Hanover Street Bridge and adjacent to South Baltimore General Hospital) offers four fishing piers and a shoreline trail on 150 acres along the Middle Branch of the Patapsco River. You might make a catch at *Robert E. Lee Park* (Falls Road north of Lake Avenue, 667–0123), too.

Golf. Some public courses include *Mount Pleasant Golf Course* (6100 Hillen Rd., 254–5100), *Forest Park* (Hillsdale and Forest Park avenues, 448–4653), and *Pine Ridge Golf Course* (Dulaney Valley Road, Lutherville, Baltimore County, 252–1408).

Hiking and walking. The *Baltimore Environmental Center* (366–2070) and the *Mountain Club of Maryland* (377–6266) plan various hiking and outdoor activities. The *YWCA* (685–1460) offers brisk-walking tours in city neighborhoods in fall and spring. For other walking tours, see "Tours and Special-Interest Sightseeing."

Horseback riding. Trail rides are $7 an hour (which includes the mandatory guide) at the *Circle R Riding Academy* in *Leakin-Gwynns Falls Park* (4900 Windsor Mill Rd., 448–3225). The stables are behind the baseball fields at the Forest Park Ave.-Windsor Mill Rd. intersection. Lower rates are available for corral saunters, and there are horses and paths that cater to beginners and experts. Mon.–Fri., 2 P.M.–dusk; Sat.-Sun. 8 A.M.–dusk.

Ice skating. The outdoor bubble-enclosed rink at *Patterson Park* (Eastern and Patterson Park avenues, 396–9304) is open Nov.-Mar. Adults, $1.50; children under 11, $1. *Mount Pleasant* (Hillen Rd. and Northern Pkwy., 444–1888) and *Northwest* (5600 Cottonworth Ave., 433–2307), both indoor rinks, charge $3.50 per session.

Running. Call the *Marathon Commission* (882–5455) for marathon information and the *Baltimore Road Runners* (882–0438) about workshops and the many local races it sponsors. To take in all the Inner Harbor sites plus Federal Hill and Fort McHenry, begin your downtown run at McKeldin Fountain (Pratt and Light streets) and proceed south on Light Street. Turn left on Key Highway, right on Lawrence Street, and left on Fort Avenue. Enter the fort (open until dusk) and take a loop around the seawall. Return the same way for a six-mile, predominantly flat run.

Sailing. *Harbor Boating* (between the World Trade Center and Constellation Dock at the Inner Harbor, 547–0900) rents sailboats and paddleboats usually mid-Mar.-Nov. Its neighbor, *Trident Electric Boats* (539–1837), rents two-seaters for those who don't need the exercise.

Tennis. *Clifton Park* (Hillen Rd. north of 25th St.) boasts 11 hard courts and 16 clay courts. There are 4 hard-surface courts at *Leakin-Gwynns Falls Park* (4900 Windsor Mill Rd., 396–0010). Tennis courts can also be found at *Carroll Park* (Monroe St. and Washington Blvd., 685–8344), and *Patterson Park* (Eastern and Patterson Park avenues, 396–9304). *Johns Hopkins University* has 6 hard courts (3600 N. Charles St.) that you may use if no faculty members or students have signed up for them.

SPECTATOR SPORTS. The Baltimore *Orioles* (338–1300), the 1983 World Series **baseball** champs, garner the most local support of all the city's professional teams. The Baltimore *Blast* soccer team (347–2011) and the *Skipjacks* (727–0703), of the American **Hockey** League, play Oct.–Apr. in the Baltimore Arena, also host to the young *Baltimore Thunder* indoor lacrosse team (347–2010). Call 837–0900 for other events, including **boxing** and **wrestling** matches, at the Baltimore Arena. Although the official state sport is jousting, preppie Baltimore is the unofficial capitol of **lacrosse,** at local colleges Mar.–May. For games within the city limits, contact Johns Hopkins University *Blue Jays* (338–8197) and the Loyola College *Greyhounds* (323–1010). The **horse-racing** highlight in town is the May 20 *Preakness Stakes,* the middle jewel in the Triple Crown, at Pimlico Race Course (542–9400), where the gate's up starting at 1 P.M. Mid-Mar.–June 1, Mon.–Sat.

HISTORIC SITES AND HOUSES. Babe Ruth Birthplace and Orioles Museum. 216 Emory St. (727–1539). A life-size animated Babe Ruth figure and Baltimore Orioles exhibits. Adults, $2.50; senior citizens, $2; children under 13, $1.25. Daily, 10 A.M.–4 P.M.

Baltimore Maritime Museum. Pier 3, Pratt St. (396–5528). It's home to the submarine U.S.S. *Torsk,* which sank the last warship in World War II, and the lightship *Chesapeake,* a floating lighthouse built in 1930. Adults, $2.50; senior citizens, $2; children under 14, $1. Mon.–Thurs., 9 A.M.–5 P.M.; Fri.–Sun., 9 A.M.–7:30 P.M.

Baltimore and Ohio Railroad Museum. Pratt and Poppleton streets (237–2387). The Mount Clare Station was built in 1830 as the nation's first passenger and freight station. Adults, $2.50; children 6–12, $1.50; under 6, free. Wed.–Sun., 10 A.M.–4 P.M.

Carroll Mansion. 800 E. Lombard St. (396–3523). The mansion of Charles Carroll of Carrollton, the last surviving signer of the Declaration of Independence until his death in 1832, was built in 1812. Adults, $1.75; senior citizens and students, $1.25; children 6–18, 75 cents; under 6, free. Tues.–Sat., 10 A.M.–4 P.M.; Sun., noon–4 P.M. Guided tours.

Edgar Allan Poe House. 203 N. Amity St. (396–7932). This tiny house includes a garret where Poe wrote from 1832 to 1835. Wed.–Sat., noon–3:45 P.M. Adults, $1; children under 12, 50 cents. Poe, along with many other famous Marylanders, is buried at **Westminster Prebyterian Church Cemetery,** Fayette and Greene streets (528–2070). Beneath the church are unusual graves and crypts in catacombs. Tours, 1st and 3rd Fri. of the month and Sat. mornings. Adults, $3; children under 12 and senior citizens, $1.

1840 House. Lombard and Albemarle streets (396–3279). A re-creation of a Baltimore row house. Adults, $1.75; senior citizens and students, $1.25; children 6–18, 75 cents; under 6, free. Tues.–Sat., 10 A.M.–4 P.M.; Sun., noon–4 P.M.

Fort McHenry. End of E. Fort Ave. (962–4299). The star-shaped fort was the site of Baltimore's victory over the British in the War of 1812. The flag flying here inspired Francis Scott Key to write the "Star-Spangled Banner." Open daily, 8 A.M.–5 P.M.; in summer, 8 A.M.–8 P.M. Adults, $1; children under 12, free.

Mencken House. 1524 Hollins St. (396–7997). Renowned editor and critic H. L. Mencken lived and wrote for 70 years in this nineteenth-century row house overlooking Union Square. It has been furnished, restored, and equipped with audiovisual presentations to reflect Mencken's life and ideas. Wed.–Sun., 10 A.M.–5 P.M. Adults, $1.75; senior citizens and students, $1.25; children 6–18, 75 cents; under 6, free.

Mount Clare Mansion. Carroll Park, Monroe St. and Washington Blvd. (837–3262). One of the oldest pre-Revolutionary mansions in Baltimore, Mount Clare (built 1756–60 by the barrister Charles Carroll) still has many original furnishings. Tues.–Fri., 10 A.M.–4:30 P.M.; Sat.–Sun., noon–4:30 P.M. Adults, $3; senior citizens and students, $2; children 5–12, 50 cents; under 5, free.

Shot Tower. Fayette and Front Sts. (396–5894). A sound-and-light show tells the history of the tower, where from 1828 to 1892 shot was made by dropping molten lead from the top into tanks of water. Open daily, 9 A.M.–5 P.M. Free.

Washington Monument. N. Charles St. at Mount Vernon Place (539–9698). Completed in 1842, this 178-ft. column was the first architectural monument honoring George Washington. Climb 228 steps to the top for a spectacular view. Mon.–Tues., Fri.–Sun., 10 A.M.–4:30 P.M. 25 cents.

MUSEUMS AND GALLERIES. Baltimore Museum of Art. N. Charles and 32d streets (396–7100). At the edge of the venerable Johns Hopkins University campus, the museum, more than 70 years old, boasts the important Claribel and Etta Cone collection of impressionists and early modernists. Other permanent collections showcase, in the American Wing, period furniture, silver, and paintings; Old Masters; English sporting art; and arts of Africa, the Americas, and Oceania. Frequent gallery talks about permanent collections and special exhibits. The Museum Cafe offers sophisticated fare with a view to match: the Wurtzburger Sculpture Garden. Gift shop. Tues.–Fri., 10 A.M.–4 P.M.; Sat.–Sun., 11 A.M.–6 P.M., also Thurs.–Fri., 5–9 P.M. Adults, $2; free for those 21 and younger; no admission charge Thurs. all day and Fri. evening.

Baltimore Museum of Industry. 1415 Key Hwy. (727–4808). This national historic landmark takes visitors to bygone Baltimore with re-creations of old workplaces. On the water behind the museum, the historic S.S. *Baltimore* tugboat is under restoration. Thurs.–Sat., 10 A.M.–5 P.M.; Sun., noon–5 P.M. Adults, $2; senior citizens and students, $1; children under 6, free.

Baltimore Public Works Museum. 701 Eastern Ave. (396–5565). Housed inside the Sewerage Pumping Station, the two-level streetscape replicates what you'd find beneath city streets, including gas lines, underground pipes, and a telephone conduit. Tours are available. Wed.–Sun., 11 A.M.–5 P.M. Free.

Maryland Historical Society. 201 W. Monument St. (685–3750). This former residence of philanthropist Enoch Pratt stars Francis Scott Key's original manuscript of "The Star-Spangled Banner," along with period furnishings, clothing, and early Maryland artifacts. Gift shop. Tues.–Fri., 11 A.M.–4:30 P.M., Sat., 9 A.M.–4:30 P.M., Sun., 1–5 P.M. Tours 1 P.M. Adults, $2.50; senior citizens, $1; children under 16, 75 cents.

Maryland Science Center and Davis Planetarium. 601 Light St. (685–2370). Right on the Inner Harbor, the center holds three floors of hands-on activities and exhibits about the latest in technology, geology, evolution, the Chesapeake Bay, and more. Planetarium and IMAX big-screen theater with changing shows. Founded in 1797, in Baltimore, the Maryland Academy of Sciences is the second-oldest U.S. scientific institution. Gift shop. Sept.–June: Mon.–Fri., 10 A.M.–5 P.M.; Sat., 10 A.M.–6 P.M.; Sun., noon–6 P.M. Late June–Labor Day: daily, 10 A.M.–8 P.M. Adults, $6.50; senior citizens, military personnel, and children under 12, $5.50. Admission to the planetarium is $1 extra.

Peale Museum. 225 Holliday St. (396–1149). The oldest museum building in the country and the first City Hall, the Peale was founded as the Museum and Gallery of the Fine Arts by portrait painter Rembrandt Peale in 1814 and now contains an impressive collection of Baltimore photos, Peale family paintings, furniture, and other local items. "Row House: A Baltimore Style of Living," depicts the famous city structure. Tues.–Sat., 10 A.M.–5 P.M.; Sun., noon–5 P.M. Adults, $1.75; senior citizens and students, $1.25; children 6–18, 75 cents; under 6, free.

Walters Art Gallery. N. Charles and Centre streets (547–9000). One of the nation's most significant privately assembled general museums, spans Egyptian mummies, medieval manuscripts, and Art Nouveau. A 1931 gift to the city, the gallery is a reproduction of the sixteenth-century Palazzo Bianco, in Genoa; a major addition opened in 1974. Gift shop. Tues.–Sun., 11 A.M.–5 P.M. Adults, $2; senior citizens and students, $1; and free for those 18 and younger. No admission charged Wed.

FILM. The nine cinemas at the new **Movies At Harbor Park,** Lombard St. and Market Place (837–3500), feature first-run hits. For repertory and foreign films, visit the county's new **Towson Art Cinemas,** 512 York Rd. (823–2436), and the **Charles Theater,** 1711 N. Charles St. (727–FILM).

The **Baltimore Film Forum** (685–4170) hosts foreign and repertory retrospectives at the Baltimore Museum of Art, N. Charles and 32d streets, including the annual *Baltimore International Film Festival.*

Among other repertory hosts are the **Enoch Pratt Free Library,** 400 Cathedral St. (396–4616); **Johns Hopkins University,** 3400 N. Charles St. (338–8187); and **Walters Art Gallery,** 600 N. Charles St. (547–9000).

Major **first-run theaters** outside the city limits, a short trip by the Beltway, include: *Hillendale 1 and 2,* Taylor Ave. at Loch Raven Blvd. (823–4444); *Perring Plaza Cinema 1 and 2,* Beltway exit 30 (668–3111); *Security Mall Cinemas 1–8,* Beltway exit 17 (265–6911); *Timonium 3 Cinemas 1–3,* York Rd. opposite Timonium Fair Grounds (252–2202); *Westview Cinemas 1–8,* 6026 Baltimore National Pike (747–3800); and *Yorkridge 1–4,* York and Ridgely roads (252–2256).

MUSIC. The Baltimore music scene is diverse and exciting. Among the options are the new **Baltimore Chamber Orchestra** (366–8973) which performs Nov.–May; the **Baltimore Choral Arts Society** (523–7070); the **Baltimore Consort,** a fine early-music group in residence at the Walters Art Gallery (576–9276, 547–9000); and the **Baltimore Opera Company,** Lyric Opera House, 1404 Maryland Ave., and Miriam A. Friedberg Concert Hall, 1 E. Mount Vernon Place (685–0692), now in its 37th season. The **Baltimore Symphony Orchestra,** Joseph Meyerhoff Symphony Hall, 1212 Cathedral St. (783–8000), received its lavish new home largely from the late Baltimore philanthropist for whom the acoustically superior hall is named. Summertime outdoor recitals are offered in Baltimore County's *Oregon Ridge Park,* where picnicking is encouraged.

Cathedral of Mary Our Queen, 5200 N. Charles St. (433–8803), hosts concerts by pianists, choral groups, organists, jazz trios, and more, usually free (donations are requested) Sundays at 5:30 P.M., Sept.–May. **Chamber Music Society of Baltimore** (837–5691) is the area's best forum for contemporary works. **Handel Choir of Baltimore** (467–3053), a local pride, sings at various local venues. From Sept. to May, **Peabody Conservatory of Music,** Miriam A. Friedberg Concert Hall, 1 E. Mount Vernon Place (659–8124), offers concerts by its symphony orchestra, wind ensemble, opera theater, chamber orchestra, the Peabody-Hopkins Chorus, and guest artists.

Pro Musica Rara (358–5430), specializes in authentic performances of baroque repertoire. **Res Musica Baltimore** (889–3939) is dedicated to presenting works by living American composers, particularly those with native or professional ties to Baltimore or Maryland. Concerts at the Baltimore Museum of Art are free with museum admission. Johns Hopkins University's **Shriver Hall Concert Series** N. Charles and 34th streets (338–7164), hosts some of the world's greatest musicians every year, Oct.–April.

STAGE. Morris A. Mechanic Theater. Hopkins Plaza. Award-winners such as Neil Simon's *Biloxi Blues,* and, in the nearby Lyric Opera House, big-time Broadway musicals such as *Cats.* Tickets and information: telecharge, 625–1400.

Center Stage. 700 N. Calvert St. (332–0033). Locally cast and produced offerings—everything from Shakespeare to adventuresome and intellectually challenging contemporary plays.

Theater Project. 45 W. Preston St. (752–8558). Hosts international, avant-garde drama, performance art, comedy, and dance.

Arena Players. 801 McCulloh St. (728–6500). After more than 30 seasons, this is one of the country's oldest continuing community theaters. Comedies, dramas, and musicals, plus an annual Youtheatre production.

Baltimore Playwrights' Festival. (597–4709). Annual, June–Aug., showcase of local talent at such smaller theaters as **Cockpit in Court** (an Essex Community College summer theater, 522–1269), **Corner Theater** (366–7529), **Fells Point Theater** (732–2087), **Spotlighters Theater** (752–1225) and **Vagabond Theater** (563–9135). These downtown companies have regular season offerings, too.

DINING OUT. Maryland dining means Chesapeake Bay seafood: No Baltimorean *doesn't* like steamed crabs. Besides countless great seafood spots are myriad reasonably priced restaurants offering all types of cuisine, from Italian to French to Spanish to Szechuan, plus several light-fare eateries with trendy menus of spinach salads, innovative pasta creations, veggie dishes, and sushi. Unless otherwise stated, the following restaurants accept most, if not all, major credit cards. Restaurant categories are based on the price of a three-course meal for one, without beverage, tax, or tip. They are: *Reasonable,* $13 to $18; *Very Economical,* $10 to $13; and *Low Budget,* under $10. Maryland state food tax is 5 percent.

Reasonable

Bertha's. 734 Broadway, Fells Point (327–5795). Friendly, relaxed quarters for famous mussels, good paella, and other seafood dishes.

Haussner's. 3242 Eastern Ave. (327–8365). A crowded Baltimore landmark with wall-to-wall artwork. More than a hundred German and American entrees, including super sour beef. Don't miss the knockout strawberry pie.

Jean-Claude's Cafe. Light Street Pavilion, Harborplace (332–0950). Airy French bistro featuring lamb, veal, seafood, and omelets.

Little Italy, east of the Inner Harbor, boasts the best restaurants in town for pasta, veal, cannoli, and other delights. **Chiapparelli's,** 237 S. High St. (837–0309), serves the best house salad, in a warm, wood-paneled atmosphere. Comfortable and informal **DeNitti's,** 906 Trinity St. (685–5601), is proud of its dynamite pizza. A popular hangout for politicians, **Sabatino's,** 901 Fawn St. (727–9414), veal *francese* is exquisite. The elegant **Velleggia's,** 204 S. High St. (685–2620), hot tickets include superb lasagna and *brasciole.* Reservations on weekends.

Phillips Harborplace. Light Street Pavilion, Harborplace (685–6600). You might have to stand in line at this popular cousin of the Ocean City seafood restaurants, where crab cakes and an assortment of steamed or fried seafood entrees are on the menu.

P.J. Cricketts. 206 W. Pratt St. (244–8900). There are specialty sandwiches and barbecued ribs on the diverse menu at this hot singles spot, split into a downstairs pub and chic upstairs rooms.

Tandoor. Pratt Street Pavilion, Harborplace (547–0575). Indian menu of chicken, lamb, and vegetarian dishes. Reservations on weekends.

Tony Cheng's. 801 N. Charles St. (539–6666). Szechuan and Hunan cuisine are the mainstays in the plush surroundings, complete with an unusual aquarium. Reservations.

Very Economical

American Cafe. Light Street Pavilion, Harborplace (962–8800). Light gourmet food, croissant sandwiches, and notable homemade soups in a sleek high-tech dining area with harbor view. Reservations for five or more.

Bo Brooks Crab House. 5415 Belair Rd. (488–8144). *The* place for steamed crabs, also seafood platters, in an informal nautical setting.

Burke's. Light and Lombard streets (752–4189). Pan-fried chicken and incredible onion rings distinguish this dark and woody old-fashioned watering hole. No credit cards.

Great American Melting Pot. 904 N. Charles St. (837–9797). Lively afterhours spot with eclectic menu, including steak by the ounce, fondues, and ribs.

Ikaros. 4805 Eastern Ave. (633–3750). Lively restaurant with old-world flavor featuring authentic Greek favorites in generous portions. Reservations.

Kawasaki. 413 N. Charles St. (659–7600). Traditional Japanese food; sushi and sashimi. Reservations.

Pacifica. 326 N. Charles St. (727–8264). American cuisine grilled over wood chips; swordfish and daily pastas. Reservations.

Uncle Lee's Szechuan. 3313 Greenmount Ave. (366–3333). Superb Szechuan fare and Peking duck (with 24 hours' notice) in casual setting; Chinese groceries. Reservations.

Low Budget

Alley-Oop's. 1043 Marshall St. (962–8988). Fun eatery over saloon; sushi raw bar.

Connolly's. 705 E. Pratt St. (837–6400). Very informal; one of the biggest soft-shell crab sandwiches in town.

Harborplace. With a bite here and a taste there, you can have an inexpensive, international, full-course meal from the myriad stalls in the Light Street Pavilion. There are stand-up counters and tables and chairs throughout the building. In nice weather, pull up a bench, picnic harborside, or dine at the adjacent amphitheater and enjoy free music, juggling, or other entertainment.

Lexington Market. Lexington and Eutaw streets. The other place in town for a cheap walking meal, the 200-year-old market recently was expanded. There are several stand-up counters plus tables and chairs upstairs. Amid the countless meat, produce, dairy, seafood, and baked goods stalls are the makings of an ample, eclectic lunch or early dinner (the market closes at 6 P.M.).

Morning Edition. 153 N. Patterson Park Ave. (732–5133). Charming and whimsical; daily eclectic menu, from tenderloin with Brie to Persian pizza.

Red Sea. N. Charles and Madison sts. (547–8178). Comfortable setting for Ethiopian and vegetarian cuisine.

Sisson's. 36 E. Cross St. (539–2093). Neighborhood bar; light fare, Cajun dishes.

Szechuan. 1125 S. Charles St. (752–8409). Very popular, tiny, informal eatery for heaping portions of superhot *bon bon* chicken, Szechuan beef, and other Chinese fare.

Recommended Splurge. Tio Pepe. 10 E. Franklin St. (539–4675). Voted Baltimore's best restaurant for the nine years of *Baltimore* magazine's Reader Restaurant Poll, Chef-co-owner Pedro Sanz's charming Spanish bistro offers superb cuisine. Among the all-time favorites are shrimp in garlic, pheasant in green-grape sauce, roast suckling pig, and pine-nut roll cake. Because it's everyone's favorite, you'll need to make reservations several weeks in advance for prime weekend time. Plan on a late lunch or dinner after 9 on weeknights for a much better shot at a coveted table.

NIGHTLIFE AND BARS. You can swing, rock, or mellow out at night in Baltimore, depending on which of the numerous nightlife spots you visit. There are rock 'n' roll and new wave bars directed at the young set; loud, crowded happy-hour establishments for preppies and yuppies; and subdued piano bars for an intimate drink and chat. You must be 21 or older to drink alcoholic beverages in Baltimore.

Among the most exciting and popular sites on the after-hours scene is **Ethel's Place,** 1225 Cathedral (727–7077), a two-story cabaret opened by internationally renowned Baltimore jazz vocalist Ethel Ennis. Ennis and such jazz stars as pianist Ahmad Jamal, vocalist Joe Williams, and violinist Stephane Grappelli plus other contemporary and jazz local and national acts entertain; Mon. and Tues. are "fun nights," when anything from dancing to big-band music to local musicians playing classical or bluegrass can happen. Cover.

A thriving city attraction is the live music for business and post-theater crowds in the **Atrium Lobbibar,** 300 Light St., Hyatt Regency Hotel (528–1234). Hear jazz Thurs., 8 P.M.–midnight; Fri., 7:30–11:30 P.M., and big bands Fri., 5–7:30 P.M.

Cignel, 10 E. Lafayette Ave. (727–1003), is a one-of-a-kind members-only club that admits out-of-staters (with proof of residence) for $10. A DJ and a state-of-the-art sound and projection system are the usual stars; national acts perform about once a month. Friday is "new wave night." The unique hours are Fri.–Sat., midnight–6 A.M.

The wildest nightspot? The multilevel **P.T. Flaggs,** 601 E. Pratt St. (244–7327), with three packed dance areas: one with live rock, one with a laser show and dance troupe, and one with an oldies DJ. Dress code. Cover charge. A very young crowd frequents the hard-rocking **Hammerjacks,** 1101 S. Howard St. (752–3302), with seven bars and skylights. Baltimore's premiere gay disco is the **Hippopotamus,** 1 W. Eager St. (547–0069). Cover. For rockabilly and rhythm and blues, check out **8x10,** 10 E. Cross St. (837–8559). Cover. A light show and sunken dance floor are some of the highlights here, where a DJ spins Wed.–Sun.

A favorite gathering spot for many upscale professionals is the **13th Floor,** N. Charles and Chase streets, in the Belvedere (547–8220). Live piano, quiet standards and contemporary tunes are the offerings at this romantic lounge, with a spectacular city view. Jackets required. Pianists also perform at **Society Hill Hotel,** 58 W. Biddle St. (837–3630). **Mariner's Pier One,** Pratt Street Pavilion, Harborplace (962–5050), **Phillips Harborplace,** Light Street Pavilion, Harborplace (685–6600), **The Conservatory,** 612 Cathedral St., Peabody Court Hotel (727–7101), **Cafe des Artistes,** 1501 Sulgrave Ave., Mt. Washington (664–2200), and **Danny's,** 1201 N. Charles St. (539–1393).

For a change of pace, stop in at **Balls,** 200 W. Pratt St. (659–5844), a wonderland of electronics, including 19 televisions, for sports fans and the after-office crowd. **Charm City Comedy Club,** 102 Water St. (576–8558) draws hundreds a night for its local and national jokesters. Shows Fri., 8:30 and 10:30 P.M., and Sat., 7:30, 9:45 P.M., and midnight. Cover.

SECURITY. Like most northeastern cities, Baltimore has its share of urban criminal activity. However, all areas within a 5-block radius of the Inner Harbor are very active with business people on weekdays and well traveled almost every night until alcohol curfew (2 A.M.). The area bounded by Howard Street, Mount Royal Avenue, the Jones Falls Expressway, and the Federal Hill area, where the majority of the city's major attractions are located, is safe territory (although women should try not to walk alone there after dark). Almost all of the city is well lit, thanks to recently installed high-intensity lights. Keep an eye on your wallet or purse and packages at all times.

BOSTON

by
William G. Scheller

Mr. Scheller is the author of More Country Walks near Boston *and* Train Trips: Exploring America by Rail *as well as numerous articles on travel, conservation, and New England subjects.*

Boston is a walker's city. People who live here don't just say that for the benefit of outsiders; they actually do quite a bit of walking themselves. It's often the easiest way to get around in a city built on a small peninsula, where seventeenth-century cowpaths have grown to become downtown thoroughfares and one-way street patterns force taxicabs to take circuitous and expensive routes. The rapid-transit system, or "T" as it is called, is fine if you want to make a quick trip from, say, downtown to Cambridge, Jamaica Plain, Kenmore Square, or the airport, but central Boston's neighborhoods and the attractions they contain are so closely packed that shoe leather remains the best form of transportation. Unless you want to do some suburban sightseeing, there is absolutely no reason to rent a car; if you come with one, you may as well keep it garaged. There's no need to budget a large sum for local transportation when you visit Boston.

Boston was already 145 years old when the Revolution began. It was in this town that the political and intellectual foundations of American independence were laid and where the first serious acts of resistance to British rule took place. Boston's chief historic sites are among the most important in the nation. On your walks in Boston you may want to follow the self-guided **Freedom Trail,** which begins near Boston Common and is marked by a line of red brick or a painted stripe.

Boston Common is the heart of the old city, and the oldest public park in America. It has survived intact from the days when it was set aside as "common" ground on which the settlers could graze their cattle. That was in the 1630s, just after John Winthrop and the Puritans who sailed on the *Arbella* purchased the Shawmut peninsula from the Reverend William Blackstone, a reclusive scholar who had been living a solitary life on the slopes of **Beacon Hill.** The Hill was much higher and steeper in those days—higher, actually, than the present-day top of the State House dome. Beginning in the 1790s, when work commenced on Charles Bulfinch's magnificent State House, the hill was leveled to its present stature. Soil and rock from the summit was carried down by primitive, gravity-powered rail cars, and used as fill to create the dry land around what is now Charles Street.

This process of "making" land continued throughout the next century, and completely transformed the physical outline of Boston's cramped peninsula. The most ambitious filling job of all involved dumping thousands of cars of Needham gravel into the tidal flat known as the Back Bay, creating the residential neighborhood of the same name where before only a narrow peninsula had connected downtown Boston to the mainland.

At the head of Park Street stands the "new" State House, architect Bulfinch's crowning achievement and the seat of the Massachusetts government since Samuel Adams sat in the governor's chair. When you pause at the corner of Beacon and Park to take in the classical grandeur of the central structure (the nondescript wings were a later addition, as was a Victorian expansion out back), turn and take notice of the Robert Gould Shaw Memorial at the entrance to the Common. This detailed bronze bas-relief is the work of Augustus Saint-Gaudens, and commemorates a young Boston-Brahmin officer who died while leading black troops in the Civil War.

That phrase, "Boston Brahmin," was coined after the highest level caste system in India and came to mean the established Yankee aristocracy of Boston. (The best book on the subject is still Cleveland Amory's *The Proper Bostonians,* recently reissued by Parnassus Press.) At the beginning of the nineteenth century, when globe-circling Yankee traders were establishing the fortunes that ensured their families' security right up to the present day, a syndicate of local entrepreneurs began the development of the slopes of Beacon Hill. Most of the brick residential rows which we see on the Hill today are the product of that period. The "best" families moved here; many still remain. The rest of this choice housing stock, at least on this side of the Hill, is where some of the most upwardly mobile of Boston's young and old professionals reside. Dr. Oliver Wendell Holmes called Beacon Street "the sunny street that holds the sifted few," and little has changed in the twentieth century.

Beacon Hill's main shopping area is Charles Street, running perpendicular to Beacon on the "flat side" of the Hill. You'll find a dense concentration of antique shops on and around Charles, along with places selling books, second-hand ("vintage" in these parts) clothing, and Italian ice cream.

Boston's downtown **Government Center** is the result of a massive 1960s urban development program that wiped out the old West End and seedy Scollay Square. Its most prominent buildings are the twin-towered John F. Kennedy federal office complex, and Boston's new City Hall. There's no missing City Hall—it stands, like an upside-down ziggurat, amidst an eight-acre brick plaza frequently criticized for its starkness and lack of trees.

Government Center marks one corner of what Bostonians usually have in mind when they refer to their downtown district. **Downtown** is one of the older and more confusing quarters of the city; even natives often won't be able to give directions with any certainty. To make matters worse, this is where the city's high-rise "Manhattanization" is proceeding most intensively. What this means is that the streets are now not only narrow at the bottom, but at the top.

Still, there are some landmark streets and buildings that—along with a map—can help you keep your bearings. The nicely restored Old State House (1717), with its colorful lion and unicorn, still stands at the head of State Street, a name synonymous with Boston high finance. Just north of State Street (left, if the Old State House is behind you) and directly behind City Hall is Faneuil Hall and the three long, granite structures that make up Quincy Market. Faneuil Hall is renowned as the "Cradle of Liberty"; it was here that disgruntled colonists met as defiance to the Crown came to a head. Quincy Market was an 1826 design of Alexander Parris, built at the urging of then-mayor Josiah Quincy. Its original purpose was to expand the cramped market facilities centered in the ground floor of Faneuil Hall; for the past ten years, both have been joined as part of a project that has become the model for all big-city building recycling schemes. The 535-foot market buildings house dozens upon dozens of shops, food stalls, and restaurants.

The oldest (and maybe oddest) skyscraper in Boston stands on the south side of State Street down near the harbor. This is the Custom House Tower, built in 1915 as an addition to the original Greek Revival 1847 Custom House. Regardless of what you think of this architectural superimposition, it has a great 25th-floor observation deck, free and open weekdays, 10–3. (Forthcoming renovations may alter this schedule.)

The little warren of streets behind New Congress Street (opposite the rear of City Hall) is the threshold of the slowly-gentrifying but still heavily Italian **North End.** The North End was "proper" once, in the "Proper Bostonians" sense. That was 200 years ago and more, when this was the main residential and business district of a town that hadn't yet started building land to grow on. As the nineteenth century wore along, it became an immigrant quarter—Irish, Jews, and finally Italians. The Italians stayed. There must be thirty or forty Italian restaurants in the neighborhood, plus little bakeries, pizzerias, greengrocers, and shops selling fava beans and dried codfish. On weekends there's a busy pushcart market (fruit, vegetables, seafood) along Blackstone Street.

In the middle of it all are a handful of old colonial survivors, the most important of which are the Old North Church on Salem Street (1723), where Paul Revere's signal lanterns were hung and which has one of the most beautiful interiors of any church building in America, and Revere's own house in North Square. With its diamond-paned windows and second-floor overhang, it looks like a holdover from the Middle Ages, and it almost is. It was built around 1670, 100 years before Paul Revere bought it. When you visit the house, try to imagine this neighborhood when its winding streets were lined with similar structures.

If you plan to go to **Charlestown** on foot, you'll most likely be going by way of the Charlestown Bridge, which begins at the corner of North Washington and Commercial streets in the North End. (At Hull and Snowhill streets, just up the hill from Commercial Street, is the Copp's Hill Burying Ground, perhaps the most atmospheric of Boston's colonial graveyards.) As you cross the bridge, you'll see the Bunker Hill Monument—very much a smaller-scale version of the national capital's Washington Monument—standing before you. The Monument rises in a small park atop Breed's Hill, actual site of the misnamed battle, and is well worth a visit. The climb to the top is free, the views of the city are fine, and a series of dioramas at the base explain what happened here on June 17, 1775.

Charlestown's other big visitor attraction, a short walk from the Monument, is the Navy Yard National Historic Site, decommissioned a decade ago and since converted to museum and interpretive uses. Here you'll find the most famous vessel in the annals of American history, the USS *Constitution,* built in Boston in 1797 and the victor in every engagement in which she fought. "Old Ironsides," as she was dubbed because of the strength of her oaken hull, is still a commissioned ship of the U.S. Navy. A free tour takes visitors above and below decks, and offers a fascinating glimpse of what life was like aboard a sail-powered man-of-war. Also at the Navy Yard is the *Constitution* Museum; the former commandant's house; and the USS *Cassin Young,* a World War II destroyer typical of the ships built here during that conflict.

Along with Beacon Hill, the **Back Bay** is quintessential Old Boston. It's hard to imagine that just 140 years ago it didn't exist, except as a real bay. The landfill operation that made it into dry land was one of the most extensive public-works projects ever undertaken in an American city, and gave Boston an opportunity to create a planned neighborhood unlike any of the old, crooked-lane quarters of the city.

The Public Garden, just across Charles Street from the Commons, is a 12-acre jewel, with formal plantings, majestic old trees, and the lovely lagoon on which ducks paddle and the famous Swan Boats offer Boston's most relaxing ride. (The boats operate from May to Labor Day.) The Storrow Embankment is a grassy riverside oasis that extends all the way to Kenmore Square. It's connected to the Back Bay's streets by several elevated walkways that cross Storrow Drive; do not try to cross Storrow at ground level. If you bring children to either the Public Garden or the Embankment in spring or summer, bring along a bag of bread crumbs for the ducks.

The Back Bay was conceived as a residential neighborhood, and so it remains, with the exception of the retail blocks of Newbury and Boylston streets. The fact that most of the residences are now apartments and condominiums in no way diminishes the splendid brick and brownstone façades of the district's row houses. Virtually all of the formal Victorian styles are represented, yet there is an impressive unity of spirit in the overall streetscape. So much of Boston has an English appearance, but this is the part of town that reminds people of Paris—which indeed it should, since these streets were inspired by the rebuilding of that city in the mid-1800s. Commonwealth Avenue especially, with its 120-foot width and central pedestrian mall, is very much the Parisian boulevard.

The Back Bay is as noted for its religious and cultural buildings as for its stately row houses. Here are H. H. Richardson's 1872 First Baptist Church (Commonwealth and Clarendon), Richard Upjohn's 1867 Church of the Covenant (Berkeley at Newbury), and A. R. Estey's 1862 Emmanuel Episcopal Church (Newbury between Arlington and Berkeley). The grandest space in the Back Bay, though, and the site of two of America's finest works of architecture, is Copley Square. Facing each other across the square are Richardson's 1877 Trinity Church and the massive Renaissance pile of the Boston Public Library, designed by Charles McKim and opened in 1895. The exterior of **Trinity Church** is wonderful enough, with its massive Romanesque character, multicolored stonework, and great central tower. But you really should go indoors, since this church is not only the seat of an Episcopal congregation but a veritable three-dimensional catalogue of all that was best in artisanship and design in the last third of the nineteenth century. The paintings and stained glass are largely the work of John LaFarge, William Morris, and Edward Burne-Jones; LaFarge's brilliantly colored ornamentation of the vaulted ceilings is worth any crick in the neck you might get from gazing upward.

The **Boston Public Library** remains the "palace for the people" it was planned to be, with its sureness of balance and detail, rich interior stonework and mural paintings by Sargent and Puvis de Chavannes, and delightful inner courtyard, with fountains and flowers in season. A passage through the courtyard leads to the late twentieth century, in the form of Philip Johnson's library addition.

A walk through the **South End** will reveal some beautifully restored blocks of bowfront row houses (Union Park and Rutland Square are standouts) that resemble quiet districts in London. Some blocks are still a bit worn at the edges; this is a neighborhood in transition, with several community groups trying to preserve its multiclass, multiethnic character lest all of its streets wind up leading to Copley Place, the new indoor mall complex in which money talks as loudly as it does anywhere in Boston.

Cambridge, a city of over 100,000 on the opposite bank of the Charles, is often considered to be synonymous with a particular institution it happens to have played host to since 1636. That institution is, of course, Harvard University, centered around the square of the same name. Many residents quite naturally resent this attitude, since a good part of the city comes and goes without much involvement in the life of the Ivy League giant. The high-tech crowd might also point out that there is another school, down at the river end of Massachusetts Avenue: the Massachusetts Institute of Technology. MIT and Harvard loom large over Cambridge; they and their attendant cultural and scientific institutions are what bring most outsiders into town.

Central Square is the workaday downtown of Cambridge; outsiders are more often drawn to the shops, theaters, booksellers, and coffeehouses around Harvard Square. The Harvard Cooperative Society, or "Coop," has a tremendous selection of books and records; smaller bookstores in the area sell everything from feminist literature to volumes on architecture, from foreign titles to books on the occult. Also, despite the upward drift of Harvard Square rents, this is still a good place to find inexpensive ethnic restaurants.

Since Cambridge isn't all Harvard, take a stroll out Brattle Street from Harvard Square. This was the famous "Tory Row" of pre-Revolutionary days, magnificent with its country estates. Many of the houses are still here, in a setting only slightly urbanized; taken together they are one of the prime architectural treasures of the Boston area. Among them is the home of Henry Wadsworth Longfellow, now a National Historic Site.

Boston stretches out towards the west and south, incorporating residential neighborhoods such as Jamaica Plain, South Boston, Dorchester, and Roxbury, and nearly enveloping the separate town of Brookline. Anyone with more than a few days to spend in the area might consider trips to the Arnold Arboretum and Franklin Park in Jamaica Plain; both offer green, rolling expanses, and the Arboretum displays hundreds of species of labeled trees and shrubs. South Boston is the home of the Dorchester Heights National Historic Site, where Washington set up the guns that chased the British from Boston. On a peninsula in Dorchester Bay, just off Morrissey Boulevard, is the John F. Kennedy Library; on the other side of Boston, the late president's birthplace is preserved in Brookline.

If you have a car and wish to head farther out of town, there are several possibilities. **Lexington** and **Concord,** to the west via Route 2, contain the sites of the first battles of the War of Independence. Visitors to Concord can also see the houses of literary greats Ralph Waldo Emerson, Nathaniel Hawthorne, and Louisa May Alcott. At nearby Walden Pond, Henry David Thoreau built his cabin and wrote his account of the solitary life.

A drive along the **North Shore,** via Route 1A and side roads, leads to places like Salem, Marblehead, Gloucester, Ipswich, and Newburyport, rich in seafaring associations, mansions, and museums. The coastal scenery is sometimes rocky and sublime, sometimes marshy and tranquil, and always lovely. The old mill city of **Lowell,** reachable via Route 3, contains a National Historical Park that dramatically chronicles the history of the American industrial revolution. And to the south, at **Plymouth,** you can see the Rock where the Pilgrims landed, a floating replica of the Mayflower, and Plimoth Plantation, a working village modeled after the Pilgrims' first settlement.

And all New England lies beyond.

PRACTICAL INFORMATION

WHEN TO GO. You'll find the best Boston weather during late spring and the months of Sept. and Oct. Like other northeastern American cities, Boston can be uncomfortably hot and humid in high summer and freezing cold in the winter. The city is not without its pleasures in these seasons, though. In summer, there are Boston Pops concerts on the Esplanade, Red Sox games at Fenway Park, and inexpensive cruises to the Harbor Islands. In winter, the calendar is packed with musical and theatrical performances; many are held at local colleges and are either free or quite inexpensive.

Each Sept., Boston and Cambridge welcome thousands of returning students, along with the latest crop of freshmen. University life is a big part of the local atmosphere, and it begins to liven up considerably as the days grow shorter.

If you plan to visit the coastal or western suburbs, consider an off-season trip. You may not be able to take a dip in the Atlantic, but shore lodging rates are cheaper, the scenery is just as lovely, and traffic is generally lighter. Boston is a good take-off point for a fall foliage tour—but make your reservations well in advance if you plan to take advantage of low-cost guest houses and bed-and-breakfast inns.

HOW TO GET THERE. By air. Most of the major domestic and international carriers serve Logan Airport, which is just across the harbor from downtown Boston. *Continental, Eastern,* and *Pan Am* offer the most daily flights along the NY–Boston corridor; watch for periodic fare wars that bring ticket prices down.

By bus. *Peter Pan* and *Greyhound-Trailways* connect with other major U.S. and Canadian cities. The Greyhound station is on St. James Street, near Park Square (423–5810); Peter Pan is on Atlantic Avenue near South Station (426–7838). Regional bus companies share these facilities.

By train. *Amtrak* connects Boston's South Station with Providence, Hartford, New Haven, New York, and points south (transfer at New York for nationwide service), and with Albany, Buffalo, Cleveland, and Chicago via western routes. Call Amtrak (800–USA–RAIL) regarding schedules and "All America Fares" offering reduced-rate travel within specified zones.

By car. I–95 leads to Boston from New York and points south along the coastal route. The Massachusetts Turnpike (a toll road) begins at the Massachusetts–New York State border and ends at Boston. The main route from Montreal and northwest New England is I–89 to I–93.

TELEPHONES. The area code for Boston and environs is 617. You do not need to dial the area code if it is the same as the one from which you are dialing. Information is 411 in the immediate Boston area (including Cambridge and the nearer suburbs); 1–555–1212 if you are calling from Boston to outlying districts or vice versa; from U.S. points outside the 617 area, dial 617–555–1212. Dial 0 first for credit card, collect, and person-to-person calls. Pay telephones cost 10 cents in the Boston area.

Emergency Telephone Numbers. The universal emergency police, fire, and ambulance number is 911; the regular *Boston Police Department* number is 247–4200. Some other numbers: *Massachusetts State Police* (566–4500); *Rape Crisis Center* (492–7273); *24-hour pharmacy,* Phillips Drug Store, 155 Charles St., Boston (523–1028); *Massachusetts General Hospital,* Boston (726–2000); *Boston City Hospital* (424–5000).

ACCOMMODATIONS. As in most big cities, the visitor to Boston pays a premium for a hotel room in a convenient downtown location. With a couple of Back

Bay exceptions, lodgings in the central city are expensive, a fact which the recent Boston hotel building boom has done nothing to mitigate (the newer places are all in the top-dollar bracket). However, you can save a fair amount if you're willing to spend a small part of your day on buses or subways, "commuting" from less fancy accommodations in Cambridge or the outskirt neighborhoods of Boston. Hotel rates are based on double occupancy. Categories, determined by price, are: *Reasonable,* $50 to $100, and *Very Economical,* under $50. In addition, we've included two more expensive hotels with economical weekend packages.

Reasonable

Copley Square. 47 Huntington Ave., Boston, MA 02116 (617–536–9000). Conveniently located between Copley Square and Copley Place, right behind the library. Modest but clean; the economy rooms without private bath are a great bargain.

Eliot. 370 Commonwealth Ave., Boston, MA 02116 (617–267–1607). A sedate little hotel, recently renovated, at the west end of the Back Bay. A little pricier than most of the hotels in this bracket, but most of the rooms have kitchenettes, which can save you a bundle on breakfast alone. Weekly and monthly rates available.

Fenway Howard Johnson's. 1271 Boylston St., Boston, MA 02215 (617–267–8300, 800–654–2000). This member of the reliable chain is conveniently located near Fenway Park and the Museum of Fine Arts. Pool, restaurant and bar, free parking.

Harvard Motor House. 110 Mt. Auburn St., Cambridge, MA 02138 (617–864–5200). A small in-city motel, just a block from Harvard Square and the Red Line subway to Boston. On-site parking. Children under 16 free.

Howard Johnson's Fenway Commonwealth. 575 Commonwealth Ave., Boston, MA 02215 (617–267–3100, 800–654–2000). Yet another HoJo's, right near Kenmore Square. This is a good bet if you want to be near Boston University. Free parking, indoor pool, and a rooftop lounge with entertainment and great views.

Howard Johnson's. 5 Howard Johnson's Plaza, Boston, MA 02125 (617–288–3030, 800–654–2000). Located just off the Southeast Expressway, making a car worthwhile if you want to go into Boston (try to avoid rush hour). This HoJo's is convenient, however, to the new Bayside Expo Center and the JFK Library.

Howard Johnson's. 200 Stuart St., Boston, MA 02116 (617–482–1800, 800–654–2000). This is the expensive, upscale local member of the chain, but we've listed it here because the two-night weekend package (offered all year except Sept.–Oct.) is a good deal, including pool and sauna, and free parking—plus breakfast and dinner for both guests on one of the two days.

Lenox. 710 Boylston St., Boston, MA 02116 (617–536–5300, 800–225–7676). A small, pleasant hotel in the Back Bay, between Copley Place and Prudential Center. A restaurant and the popular Delmonico's Lounge are on the premises.

Parker House. 60 School St., Boston, MA 02107 (617–227–8600). This is Boston's oldest hotel (not in its original building), and perhaps its most centrally located. The regular tariff is in the deluxe bracket, but the weekend specials—two or three nights with breakfast (dinner can be added at extra cost)—are quite reasonable.

Quality Inn. 1651 Massachusetts Ave., Cambridge, MA 02138 (617–491–1000). Near Harvard Law School, a 10-min. walk from Harvard Square and on the bus line. Parking, restaurant, lounge.

Ramada Inn. 1234 Soldiers Field Rd., Brighton, MA 02135 (617–254–1234). Brighton is in Boston, but this motel is actually closer to Harvard Square. You'll probably be using your car if you stay here. Outdoor pool, restaurant, bar.

Terrace Motel. 1650 Commonwealth Ave., Brighton, MA 02135 (617–566–6260). This little motel stands on Beacon Street, a short ride on the Green Line from Boston. It's also handy to both Boston College and Boston University. All rooms have kitchenettes. Weekly rates available.

Very Economical

Susse Chalet. 211 Concord Turnpike (Rte. 2), Cambridge, MA 02140 (617–661–7800). About the lowest rates around, and now more convenient than before because of the recent completion of the Red Line station a short walk away.

Susse Chalet. 800 Morrissey Blvd., Dorchester, MA 02122 (617–287– 9100). This member of the budget chain is in Dorchester; it's convenient to the Bayside

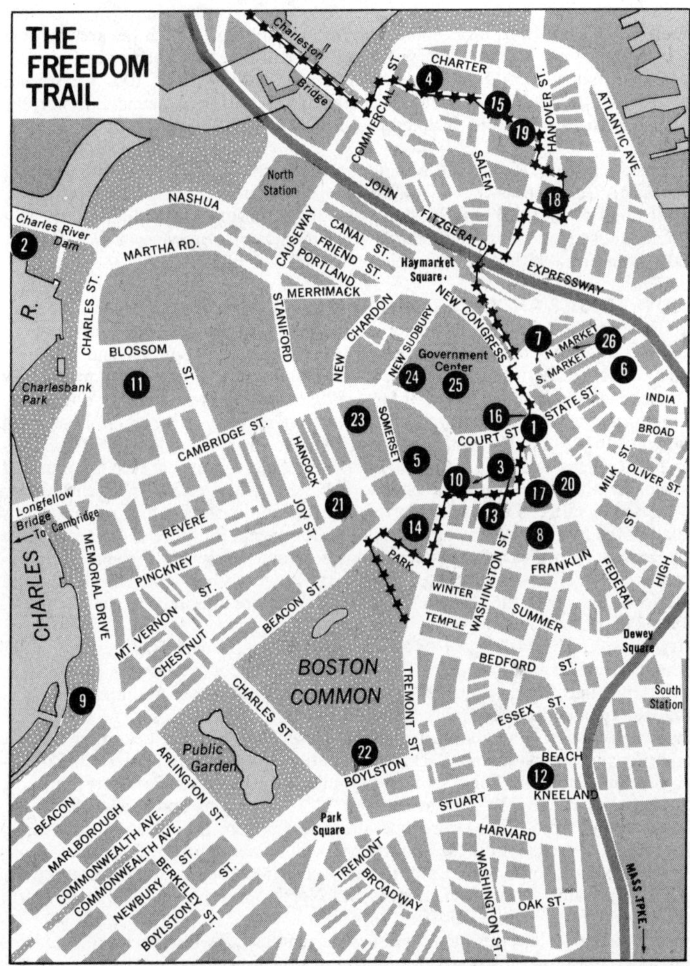

Points of Interest

1) Boston Massacre Site
2) Boston Museum of Science
3) Old City Hall
4) Copp's Hill Burying Ground
5) Court House
6) Custom House
7) Faneuil Hall
8) Franklin's Birthplace Site
9) Hatch Memorial Concert Shell
10) King's Chapel
11) Massachusetts General Hospital
12) Tufts New England Medical Center
13) Old Corner Book Store
14) Park Street Church and Old Granary Burying Ground
15) Old North Church (originally Christ Church)
16) Old State House
17) Old South Meeting House
18) Paul Revere's House
19) Paul Revere Statue
20) Post Office
21) State House
22) Central Burying Ground
23) State Office Building
24) John F. Kennedy Federal Building
25) New City Hall
26) Quincy Market

Expo Center and JFK Library, but you'll need to catch a bus or drive your car to get into town. Pool, play area.

Bed-and-Breakfast. B&B homes are proliferating throughout the greater Boston area; to reserve a room, you go through a central agency rather than contact the home's owners. Try **New England Bed and Breakfast, Inc.,** 1045 Centre St., Newton, MA 02168 (617–498–9819), or **Bed and Breakfast Areawide, Cambridge & Greater Boston,** Box 665, Cambridge, MA 02140 (617–576–1492).

Ys and Hostels. Berkeley Residence at the Boston **YMCA,** 140 Clarendon St., Boston, MA 02116 (617–482–8850), offers *women* visitors lodging at $29 per night. For information on the Youth Hostels operating in Boston, Brookline, and the rest of Massachusetts, contact the *Greater Boston Council, American Youth Hostels,* 1020B Commonwealth Ave., Brookline, MA 02146 (617–731–5430).

HOW TO GET AROUND. From the airport. Despite the proximity of Logan Airport to downtown, the harbor crossing can be a nuisance, especially at rush hour. For about $8, a *taxi* will take you into town via the Sumner and Callahan tunnels. One alternative is "Share-a-Cab" at about half the cost; look for specially marked phones at terminals or dial 569–4870, 3:30–11:30 P.M. Another alternative is *limousine* service to downtown hotels and bus depots; try *Airways Transportation Company* (267–2981). By far the cheapest way into town, though, is the *Massachusetts Bay Transportation Authority (MBTA) Blue Line;* the airport stop is connected to major terminals by shuttlebus. The fare is 60 cents (children 5–11, 25 cents; under 5, free; senior citizens ride subways for 10 cents and buses for half price) on this and all of the MBTA subway and surface routes, except for more distant extra-fare stops served by trolleys and suburban buses. From late spring through early autumn, there are ferries connecting Long Wharf, Rowe's Wharf, and Commonwealth Pier, downtown, with the airport. For schedule and fare information, dial 723–7800 or 328–0600.

By subway. The MBTA, or "T" as it is called, serves over 60 cities and towns in the metropolitan Boston area. The subway lines are *Red* (Alewife, Cambridge, to Mattapan and Braintree); *Blue* (Bowdoin Square, Boston, to Wonderland Racetrack, Revere); and *Orange* (Oak Grove, Malden, to Forest Hills). The *Green* line, consisting of below- and above-ground trolley service, connects Lechmere Square, Cambridge, and downtown's Park Street Station with Brighton, Brookline, Newton, and Jamaica Plain. For system maps and schedules, stop at Park Street Station. For information call 722–3200 weekdays, 722–5000 nights and weekends.

By bus and train. The T also operates a bus system (information, 722–3200) which extends farther into the suburbs, as well as commuter rail service. Trains for South Shore points and Framingham leave from South Station, Dewey Sq. (482–4400); trains for western suburbs and North Shore points leave from North Station, Causeway St. (227–5070).

By rental car. All of the major national car rental chains, along with several local companies, are represented at Logan Airport, downtown, and suburban locations. Here are some of the firms offering reasonable rates: *Budget Rent-a-Car,* 62 Eliot St. (617–426–2600) and at Logan Airport (617–569–4000). *Dollar Rent-a-Car,* Sheraton-Boston Hotel, 39 Dalton St. (617–523–5098) and at Logan Airport (617–569–5300). *National Car Rental,* 183 Dartmouth St. (617–426–6830, 800–328–4567) and at Logan Airport (617–569–6700).

HINTS TO THE MOTORIST. If you can manage to avoid driving in Boston, by all means do so. If you can't at least try to minimize frustrations by sticking to the main thoroughfares and by parking in lots—however expensive—rather than on the street. Some neighborhood streets have residents-only rules, with only a handful of two-hour visitors' spaces; others have meters at 25 cents for 15 minutes with a two-hour maximum. The meter maids are ruthless, and if you let too many tickets pile up police will clamp the "boot"—an immovable steel clamp—to one of your wheels. The more centrally located the parking lot, the more expensive it will be, with financial district parking costing the most. There is parking at the Prudential Center and under Boston Common, as well as at Copley Place; the least expensive garage is probably the big 8-story monster at Government Center.

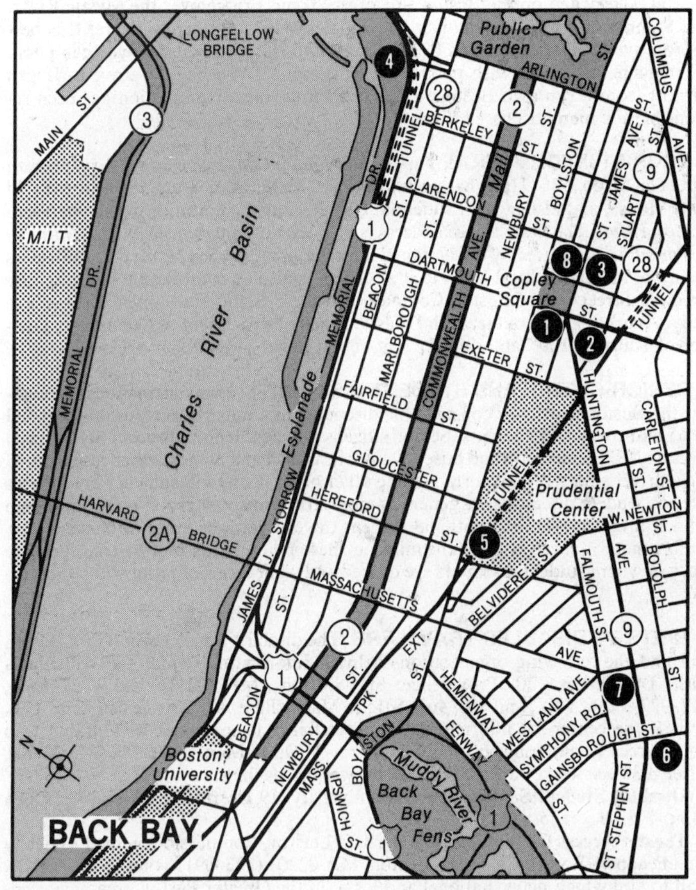

Points of Interest

1) Boston Public Library
2) Copley Place
3) Hancock Tower
4) Hatch Memorial Shell
5) Hynes Auditorium
6) New England Conservatory of Music (Jordan Hall)
7) Symphony Hall
8) Trinity Church

Boston drivers have a creative, devil-may-care approach that can scare the wits out of visitors. Street patterns and signposting practices add to the chaos; the faint-hearted need not apply. If you must drive, though, do it at the right time. The worst congestion occurs during weekday rush hours on the Southeast Expressway and Central Artery and on the Boston side of the Tobin Bridge over the Mystic River. The Sumner and Callahan tunnels can be sticky; so can Storrow Drive. It is best not to drive at all in downtown Boston or around Harvard Square if you can possibly manage on foot or with public transportation. If you have to drive to Logan Airport from downtown Boston, *allow extra time;* tunnel congestion has been responsible for many a missed flight.

TOURIST INFORMATION. The *Greater Boston Convention and Tourist Bureau* (800–858–0200, 536–4100) has an information center at 15 State St., near the Old State House, and also at the Prudential Center, near the entrance to the Sheraton-Boston Hotel. The State Street address is also the headquarters of *Boston National Historic Park,* operated by the National Park Service (242–5642), which administers the more important local historic sites. There is also an information booth on the Tremont Street side of Boston Common. All these facilities are open 9 A.M.–5 P.M. daily. Another good contact is the Massachusetts Department of Commerce, Division of Tourism, 100 Cambridge St., 13th floor, Boston, MA 02202 (617–727–3201).

SENIOR-CITIZEN AND STUDENT DISCOUNTS. Many attractions throughout the Boston area offer considerable discounts to senior citizens (usually defined as 65 and over) and students. Senior citizens are eligible for substantially reduced fares on MBTA subways and buses. On public transit and in most other cases, showing a driver's license, passport, or some other proof of age will suffice. Those places offering student discounts are generally more stringent about proof, requiring a high school or college ID, international student traveler card, or other evidence of age. Unfortunately, there is no uniformity on these matters; it's best to call ahead to learn of where student discounts are offered and what forms of proof will be accepted.

HINTS TO DISABLED TRAVELERS. The disabled traveler who visits Boston will find the following organizations helpful: **Information Center for Individuals with Disabilities.** 20 Providence St., Boston, MA 02116 (617–727–5540, 617–727–5236/TTY, and 800–462–5015 in Massachusetts). Anyone can write, call, or visit the center for information on accessibility to museums, restaurants, and hotels, recreation, transportation, and travel. Open Mon.–Fri., 9 A.M.–3:30 P.M. After 3:30 P.M. leave messages on an answering machine.

Disabled Student Services, Boston University, 19 Deerfield St, 2nd floor, Open Mon.–Fri., 9 A.M.–5 P.M.

Theater Access for the Deaf. c/o Barbara Levitov, Commission on the Physically Handicapped, Boston City Hall, Boston, MA 02201 (923–0911 voice/TTY–TDD). Call to find which plays, national and local, in the Greater Boston area have sign-language interpreted performances.

Museum of Science. (227–3235/TDD). The museum offers sign-language interpreted programs on the second Sat. of each month. Call for time and program topic.

The Adaptive Environments Center. Massachusetts College of Art, 621 Huntington Ave., Boston (739–0088). A design firm for disabled access with a library of travel and recreation information. Open Mon.–Fri., 9 A.M.–5 P.M.

FREE EVENTS. There aren't a great many out-and-out free events in Boston—maybe it goes against the Yankee grain—but because of the dozens of colleges and universities in the area there is a lot of low-priced entertainment, often even more low-priced if you have a student ID. Here are some useful numbers for information on what's going on at the major schools: *Boston University Campus Events,* 353–2169; *Harvard University,* general information, 495–1000; *MIT Campus Activities Center,* 253–4795; *Tufts University Student Activities,* 24-hour line, 381–3212.

During July, the **Boston Pops** (266–1492) gives 10 free outdoor concerts at the Hatch Memorial Shell on the Charles River Esplanade. The main event is the 4th of July concert (not always held on the 4th; check to make sure) featuring the Pops' trademark "Stars and Stripes Forever." In August, there are more free concerts featuring a variety of performers on Wed. evenings at City Hall Plaza, Government Center. For information, call 725–4006.

The **Lowell Institute** (523–1635), endowed in 1836 by John Lowell, sponsors dozens of free lectures on science, history, public affairs, and the arts throughout the fall, winter, and spring. Also contact the **Boston Public Library** (536–5400) for information on its series of free lectures and films.

Each Thurs., the Boston *Globe* publishes a handy tabloid insert, Calendar. It covers hundreds of events, exhibits, concerts, films, and gatherings of two people or more, many of them free or at nominal cost.

TOURS AND SPECIAL-INTEREST SIGHTSEEING. As we've already mentioned, central Boston is so compact that the easiest way to tour it is on foot. If this is inconvenient, however, there are a number of bus tours that include the main points of interest in their itineraries. The *Gray Line* (426–8805) offers a 3-hour tour that covers all Freedom Trail sites. Departure is from major downtown hotels. Other options include *Hub Bus Lines* (776–0630), *Boston Double Deckers* (629–2300), and *Trolley Tours* (269–7010). Adult fares for these tours average $9. Most lines limit off-season service to weekends. Call ahead for schedules.

There are also shorter, free tours limited to specific points of interest. **Massachusetts State House,** Beacon and Park streets (727–3676). Mon.–Fri., 10 A.M.–4 P.M. **Boston City Hall,** Government Center (725–4000). Mon.–Fri. 9 A.M.–5 P.M. by appointment. **Federal Reserve Bank,** 600 Atlantic Ave. (973–3451). Two Fridays a month, by appointment. A fascinating look at the production of a daily newspaper can be had at the **Boston Globe,** Morrissey Blvd., Dorchester (929–2000). Mon.–Thurs. at 9:30 and 11 A.M. and 2 P.M. A tour of the **Christian Science Center,** Huntington and Massachusetts avenues (450–2000), includes a walk inside the "Maparium," a huge glass model of the earth. Mon.–Sat., 10 A.M.–4 P.M.

In addition to the self-guided **Freedom Trail** tour (see "Historic Sites and Houses"), there are also guided walking tours of Boston that are well worth the modest fees charged. Try the varied itineraries of **Boston by Foot** (367–2345), which operates from May to Oct. About $5 for adults, $3 for children.

The multimedia presentation *Where's Boston,* at Sack Cinema, Copley Place, 100 Huntington Ave. (267–4949) keeps you in one place but provides a great introduction to the city. Hourly shows start at 10 A.M. Adults, $3.50; children under 12, $2.

You can tour the universities in Cambridge. You can join one of the guided tours of **Harvard** at the university's Holyoke Center (495–1573), or you can walk around on your own.

The best place to begin is in Harvard yard, behind the iron gates across the street from the subway station. The Widener Library, facing the yard, is the largest university library in the world; stop inside for a look at the late Harry Elkins Widener's own rare book collection. Nearby is Massachusetts Hall (1720), Holden Chapel (1744), Charles Bulfinch's University Hall (1815) and the 1878 Gothic Revival Memorial Hall, which contains the popular Sanders Theater. On the other side of the yard, Quincy Street leads to the Fogg and Sackler Art Museums, and on Kirkland Street is the Busch-Reisinger Museum of German and Central European Art. The University Museum complex on Oxford Street houses extensive archaeological, ethnographic, zoological, mineral, and botanical collections. Here are the famous "glass flowers," a collection of handcrafted, minutely detailed specimens executed in glass over a 65-year period.

Tours of the MIT campus, much of which was built 70 years ago in a serene classical style suggestive of reason and scientific order, leave from Building 7, 77 Massachusetts Ave. (the Hart Nautical Museum, a collection of ship models, is at the same address). Among the domes and pillars are some striking buildings by Le Corbusier, I. M. Pei, and Eero Saarinen.

Finally, you can see Boston from its upper stories at the following observatories: **John Hancock Tower Observatory,** St. James and Clarendon streets (247–1977). Mon.–Sat., 9 A.M.–10:15 P.M.; Sun., noon–10:15 P.M. Adults, $2.75; children and seniors, $2. **Prudential Skywalk,** Prudential Center (236–3318). Mon.–Sat., 10 A.M.–10 P.M.; Sun., noon–10 P.M. Adults, $2; children and seniors, $1. **Custom House Tower,** foot of State Street (233–6519). Weekdays, 10 A.M.–3 P.M. Free. (Forthcoming renovations may alter this schedule.)

PARKS AND GARDENS. Central Boston's municipal open spaces include **Boston Common,** America's oldest park, bounded by Beacon, Park, Boylston, Tremont, and Charles streets; the **Public Garden,** across Charles Street from the Common, with its formal plantings, lagoon, and Swan Boat rides; and the **Storrow Embankment,** in the Back Bay along the Charles River. The embankment is popular with runners and strollers, and is the home of the Hatch Concert Shell, where the Boston Pops play free summer concerts.

Farther from downtown, are **Franklin Park,** Blue Hill Ave. and Columbia Rd., Dorchester, an Olmsted gem of some 500 acres featuring a zoo, golf course, and horseback riding, and the **Arnold Arboretum,** on the Arborway, routes 1 and 203, Jamaica Plain (524–1717). The Arboretum is a Harvard University property containing hundreds of labeled specimens of trees, shrubs, and flowers. Maps are available at the Honeywell Building, on the grounds. Admission is free. Take the MBTA Green Line to Arborway or the Orange Line to Forest Hills.

All parks are open from dawn to dusk; the Common and Public Garden are frequented by pedestrians after dark, at least along the major walkways.

ZOOS. Boston's only zoo is the **Franklin Park Zoo,** located near the Blue Hill Avenue–Columbia Road entrance of Franklin Park in the city's Dorchester section. (442–2002). There is a good collection of mammals, an excellent aviary, and a children's petting zoo. Open daily year-round, except Christmas and New Year's Day, 10 A.M.–4 P.M. in winter; till 5 P.M. in summer. Free. Children's zoo open 9 A.M.–5 P.M.; admission $1.

The **New England Aquarium,** on Central Wharf right downtown (742–8870) abounds in seals, penguins, sharks, and other sea creatures (over 2,000 species in all), many of whom live in a 4-story, 200,000 gallon cylindrical tank—the largest of its kind in the world. Adjacent is the floating pavilion "Discovery," where dolphin and sea lion shows take place. Mon.–Thurs., 9 A.M.–5 P.M.; Fri. till 8 P.M.; weekends and holidays 9 A.M.–6 P.M. Adults, $6; children 4 to 15, $3.50; servicemen, senior citizens, and students with ID, $5. There is a dollar discount off all fees Fri. 4 P.M.–closing.

PARTICIPANT SPORTS. The physical fitness trend has caught on big in Boston, as you will notice when you start dodging runners and cyclists on city streets. Those are the two activities which should head any list of low-cost (actually no-cost, once you have the equipment) participant sports.

Running. The best places to run in the central metropolitan area are along the *Esplanade* and *Storrow Embankment* on the Boston side of the Charles, and the parklike embankment that lines the river on the Cambridge side. The Esplanade-Storrow route will take you from Beacon Hill to Boston University, a distance of about 2½ miles; to follow the Charles in Cambridge, head across the Longfellow Bridge from Beacon Hill and bear left for Harvard. The distance is a bit longer. Runners might also try the larger parks, particularly *Franklin Park* or the *Arnold Arboretum* (women should stay in pairs), or the Riverway and Jamaicaway to Jamaica Pond.

Bicycling. There are two designated bike paths in greater Boston. The *Dr. Paul Dudley White Bikeway* is approximately 18 miles long, running along both sides of the Charles River from Watertown Square to the Museum of Science. The *Stony Brook Reservation Bikeway* is a 4-mile route from River Street in Hyde Park to Washington Street, West Roxbury. Rent bikes ($12 a day) at *Community Bike Shop,* 490 Tremont St. (542–8623). Open daily, 10 A.M.–6 P.M.; till 8 P.M. Wed. and Fri.

Hiking. There are good footpaths for hikers at the 450-acre *Stony Brook Reservation* in Boston's Hyde Park and West Roxbury neighborhoods, and an even more extensive network of trails at the much larger and more rugged *Blue Hills Reservation,* off Randolph Avenue in south-suburban Milton.

Tennis. Free courts at *Charlesbank Park,* Charles St., Open Apr.–Nov., lighted until 11 P.M. A permit is required and can be picked up at the Metropolitan District Commission, Lee Pool Office, Charles St. (523–9746). Mon.–Fri. 10 A.M.–6:45 P.M.

Swimming. Although there are several neighborhood beaches in Dorchester and South Boston, the nicest swimming spots are on the Harbor Islands, now a state park. Try *Lovell's Island,* accessible in summer by free water taxi from George's Island, which is in turn accessible via a short, inexpensive boat ride from Long and Rowe's Wharves, Boston.

Ice skating. There are two outdoor spots right downtown: the lagoon in the *Public Garden,* and the Frog Pond in the *Common.* Or, try the Metropolitan District Commission's indoor rink on Commercial Street in the North End (523–9327). Adults $1; children and seniors, 50 cents.

SPECTATOR SPORTS. Boston, as you may have heard, is a gung-ho sports town. The big three **pro teams** are the Red Sox, baseball, the Bruins, hockey, and the Celtics, basketball. Here are the details: *Boston Red Sox,* American League, Fenway Park, Yawkey Way (267–8661). Baseball season early Apr.–early Oct. *Boston Celtics,* National Basketball Association, Boston Garden, Causeway St. (523–3030). Basketball season, Oct.–May. *Boston Bruins,* National Hockey League, Boston Garden (227–3200). Hockey season, Oct.–Apr.

College football: *Boston College Eagles,* Alumni Stadium, Chestnut Hill (552–3000). *Boston University Terriers,* Nickerson Field, off Commonwealth Ave. (353–3838). *Harvard University Crimson,* Harvard Stadium, North Harvard St. and Soldiers Field Rd., Allston (495–4848). College football season, Sept.–Dec., with bowl games played on New Year's Day.

College ice hockey and **basketball** are also popular, and less expensive than the pro games. Check the *Globe* or *Herald* sports sections for details of upcoming games.

CHILDREN'S ACTIVITIES. If your kids are interested in history, you've got no problem. Fortunately, most of Boston's historical legacy is easily accessible to youngsters. They can actually see where Paul Revere's lanterns were hung, or walk the decks of an undefeated man-of-war. See "Historic Sites," "Zoos," and "Museums" for attractions appealing to children.

The Children's Museum. 300 Congress St., Museum Wharf (426–8855). Well worth the admission price of $4.50 for adults, $3.50 for kids and seniors. Free Fri. evenings, 6–9 P.M.. The hands-on exhibits are designed with children in mind. A petting zoo, computers, video cameras, a model assembly line, and "Grandmother's Attic," where little visitors can dress up in old clothing. The Museum schedules a full calendar of special exhibits, crafts demonstrations, and live music and storytelling performances. Tues.–Sun., 10 A.M.–5 P.M.; Fri., till 9 P.M. Closed Mon., except during Boston school vacations and holidays.

The Swan Boats. (522–1966). These pedal-powered boats, piloted from the stern (passengers do no work), have been a fixture on the Public Garden lagoon since 1877. For 75 cents for adults and 50 cents for children it's the most pleasant ride in Boston. Boats run late May–late Sept. (from mid-Apr. on weekends, weather permitting). Bring a snack for the ducks.

Special Tours. Just as there are sightseeing tours geared for adults, several enterprising Boston organizations offer special tours for children. These include: *Make Way for Ducklings Tours* (426–1885), for children five years and older accompanied by adults, held on Sat. in late spring and on Fri. and Sat., July 4–Labor Day. The path begins at Boston Common and follows the same route taken by the ducks in Robert McCloskey's classic children's book, *Make Way for Ducklings.* The tour ends with a Swan Boat ride. $4 per person. *Boston by Little Feet* (367–2345) is a spin-off of the popular *Boston by Foot* tours; it includes interpretations of major local sites directed at children 6–12. Walks are scheduled weekly in late spring and summer. Cost, $3.

HISTORIC SITES AND HOUSES. Fortunately for travelers on a budget, most of Boston's premier historical attractions are either inexpensive or free. Two people can visit all of the places listed below for under $10, not counting lunch and transportation. Nearly all of the major historic sites in Boston are located along the **Freedom Trail,** a self-guiding route marked with either a line of red brick or a painted brick stripe. It begins on the Tremont Street side of Boston Common, where an information booth (open daily, 9 A.M.–5 P.M.) provides free maps, and runs to the Copp's Hill Burying Ground in the North End (an extension takes you across the Charlestown Bridge to Old Ironsides and the Bunker Hill Monument). Excluding the latter two sites, the whole trail can be covered in four or five hours. Most of that time will be spent visiting the sites, not walking; Boston, remember, is a very compact city. Here, then, are the major Freedom Trail sites, followed by several other recommended points of interest outside of the immediate downtown–North End area.

State House. Beacon Street, head of Park Street (727–3676; archives, 727–2816). This is the "new" state house, for which Charles Bulfinch provided the incomparable design and Samuel Adams laid the cornerstone, on July 4, 1795. It is not only one of the most beautiful works of classical architecture in America, but the seat of a state government which, for all its flaws, functions under the oldest written constitution in the world. Inside, tour the House and Senate chambers (for information on 45-minute tours, call 727–2356), see the famous "Sacred Cod," and visit Doric Hall and the Hall of Flags. The archives include the original colonial charter, original state constitution, witchcraft trial depositions, and even Paul Revere's expense account. Mon.–Fri., 10 A.M.–4 P.M.; archives 9 A.M.–5 P.M. Tours are free.

Park Street Church. Corner Tremont and Park streets (523–3383). Built in 1809 and designed by Peter Banner, the Park Street Church is the last major stand of Georgian architecture in Boston. Here, in 1829, William Lloyd Garrison began his public campaign for the abolition of slavery; here the hymn "America" was first sung, on July 4, 1832. Congregationalist services Sundays; open to visitors weekdays during the day.

Old Granary Burying Ground. Next door to the Park Street Church, this graveyard contains the remains of Paul Revere, Samuel Adams, John Hancock, and other colonial notables. An even older church, King's Chapel, and its burying ground are just one block to the north.

Old South Meeting House. 310 Washington St., at the corner of School St. (482–6439). Built in 1729, this is the second-oldest church building in Boston. It is most famous, though, for having been a meeting site for colonial dissidents. It was here, on Dec. 16, 1773, that Samuel Adams presided at a meeting that erupted into the Boston Tea Party. It is no longer used as a church, but the interior has been restored to its prerevolutionary state. Open daily; spring and fall, 10 A.M.–5 P.M.; summer till 5:45; winter till 4. 10-min. tours are given on the half hour. Adults, $1.25; senior citizens, 75 cents; children 6–16, free.

Old State House and Boston Massacre Site. 206 Washington St., at the corner of State St. (242–5655). This was the seat of colonial and, later, state government from 1713 to the turn of the nineteenth century, when the "new" state house was finished. Just outside, a circle of cobblestones marks the spot where British soldiers fired on a crowd, killing five men, on March 5, 1770—the Boston Massacre. Inside the building is the museum of the Bostonian Society, containing paintings, historical artifacts, and maritime memorabilia. Open 9:30 A.M.–5 P.M. in summer; till 4 P.M. the rest of the year. Adults $1.25; students and senior citizens, 75 cents; children over 6, 50 cents.

Faneuil Hall. Dock Sq. (523–3886). This was merchant Peter Faneuil's 1742 gift to the city, rebuilt to a Bulfinch design in 1805. The famous grasshopper weathervane is original. The Hall was a famous gathering place of patriots in the years before the Revolution; it remains a public meeting place. Open daily, 9 A.M.–4:30 P.M. Shops and eateries inside open 10 A.M.–9 P.M.

Paul Revere House. 19 North Sq. (523–2338). Built around 1670, this is the oldest house in Boston and was, from 1770 to 1780, the home of Paul Revere. It was from here that Revere set out on his famous "midnight ride." It was restored in 1905 to an approximation of its original seventeenth-century appearance. Although the clapboards, glass, and many other features are replicas, the beams are original. The interior furnishings represent both colonial centuries; a few pieces were Revere's. Open 9:30 A.M.–4:15 P.M., Tues.–Sun. Adults, $2; senior citizens and college students, $1.50; children under 17, 50 cents.

Old North Church. 193 Salem St. (523–6676). "One if by land, and two if by sea"—this is the place. The Old North was built as Christ Church in 1723 and is Boston's oldest church; 52 years later its steeple held Paul Revere's signal lanterns. The interior is one of the most graceful and lovely of Boston's spaces. Episcopal services Sun. and holidays; the church and adjacent museum are open daily, 9 A.M.–5 P.M. Tour guides are present weekdays; on Sundays visitors are welcome to services but may not walk about casually. Admission free; donation appreciated. From the church, the Freedom Trail leads to the **Copp's Hill Burying Ground,** bordered by Hull, Charles, and Snowhill streets. This is the most atmospheric of old Boston graveyards, and holds the remains of the famous Mather family of colonial ministers and educators.

Charlestown Navy Yard. Across the Charlestown Bridge from the North End (access by foot, or by bus from Haymarket Square) (426–1812). This sprawling navy yard is now a part of Boston National Historic Park and the home of a nautical museum and of the USS *Constitution.* "Old Ironsides," as she is called, is the oldest commissioned ship in the navy, a relic of the days of "wooden ships and iron men." She never lost a battle. Visit the ship from 9:30 A.M.–3:50 P.M. daily. Free. Museum open 10 A.M.–4 P.M. daily. Adults, $2; senior citizens, $1.50; children, $1; family admission, $5.

Bunker Hill Monument. Monument Sq., Charlestown. Just a few blocks from Old Ironsides. Yes, the battle actually took place on Breed's Hill, and that's where the monument stands. You can climb to the top for a fine view; admission is free for the monument, adjoining dioramas, and talks by ranger attendants. Open daily 9 A.M.–5 P.M. For a more detailed look at the battle, see the "Whites of Their Eyes" show at the Bunker Hill Pavilion, near the Navy Yard's Gate 1 on Constitution Avenue, every half-hour daily, 9:30 A.M.–4 P.M. Adults, $3; children, $1.50. Call 241–7575 for information.

Women's City Club of Boston. 40 Beacon St. (227–3550). The club is housed in one of the most stately of Beacon Hill's bowfronted row houses. It was built in 1814–15 for Nathan Appleton and Daniel Parker; the exterior is by Charles Bulfinch with interior detailing by the Greek Revival–master Alexander Parris. Windows in the structure contain what has become the very imprint of Beacon Hill authenticity: purple panes of glass. These panes were purchased abroad for installation in these and several other houses on the Hill; over the years, sunlight striking mineral imperfections within the glass created the distinctive tint. Call for information on tours (by appointment only).

Outside the immediate downtown area: *Fort Warren,* on Georges Island, is a monumental stone Civil War fort. Call Massachusetts Bay Line, 749–4500, for information on access. *Dorchester Heights National Historic Site* (269–4275), is the promontory in South Boston where Washington set up the cannons that routed the British from Boston. *John F. Kennedy Birthplace,* 83 Beals St., Brookline (566–7937). If you have an automobile, you'll also want to drive out to Concord to visit the *Minute Man National Historic Park,* site of the April 19, 1775, Battle of Concord and home of Daniel Chester French's heroic statue of a patriot farmer. Call 369–6993 or 484–6156 for information. Nearby is *Lexington Green,* where there is an annual dawn reenactment of the Battle of Lexington each year on Patriot's Day (the Monday nearest to Apr. 19).

MUSEUMS. Boston Tea Party Ship. Congress Street Bridge (338–1773). Moored here is the *Beaver II,* a faithful reproduction of one of the vessels boarded and looted of its tea cargo (which was thrown into the harbor) on that fateful night in 1773. An adjacent interpretive center explains the event. Open daily 9 A.M.–5 P.M. Adults, $3.25; children 5–14, $2.25.

Fogg Art Museum. 32 Quincy St., Cambridge (495–2387). Harvard's art collection includes European and American works; pre-Renaissance Italian holdings are strong. Revere silver. Open Tues.–Sat., 10 A.M.–5 P.M.; Sun., 1 P.M.–5 P.M. Adults, $3; under 18, free; Admission fee covers Fogg, Sackler (Oriental and Islamic), and Busch-Reisinger (German art) museums (Busch-Reisinger closed temporarily for renovation).

Isabella Stewart Gardner Museum. 280 The Fenway (734–1359). The personal collection of "Mrs. Jack" Gardner, in her Back Bay palazzo. Titian's "Rape of Europa," plus Matisse, Whistler, Sargent, Rubens—a very eclectic collection. Open Wed.–Sun., noon–5 P.M.; Tues., till 9 P.M. Admission free; $1 donation suggested.

Harvard University Museums. 24 Oxford St. and 11 Divinity Ave., Cambridge (495–1910). This rambling complex includes collections in botany, archaeology and ethnology (the Peabody Museum), comparative zoology, and mineralogy. The museums are free except for the highly recommended glass flowers, representing over 700 species (adults, $2; children 5–15, 50 cents; free Mon.). Open Mon.–Sat., 9 A.M.–4:30 P.M.; Sun. 1 P.M.–4:30 P.M.

Institute of Contemporary Art. 955 Boylston St. (266–5151). No permanent collection, but a continuing series of special exhibits—painting, sculpture, photography, video, you name it. Wed.–Sun., 11 A.M.–5 P.M. Adults, $3.50; students, $2; senior citizens and children, $1. Fri. 5–8 P.M., free.

Museum at the John F. Kennedy Library. Off Morrissey Blvd., Dorchester (929–4523; recorded information 929–4567). Adjoining the library containing JFK's papers, the museum offers a fine documentary film, a slide display, memorabilia from the Oval Office, interpretive displays, video excerpts, and a film on Robert Kennedy. Daily, 9 A.M.–5 P.M.; last film showing at 3:50. Adults, $2.50; senior citizens, $1.50; under 16, free.

Museum of Fine Arts. 465 Huntington Ave. (267–9300). The MFA is Boston's premier art museum, and one of the nation's best. Founded in 1870, it is especially strong in Impressionists (there are 43 Monets), including American members of the school. Other principal collections include American furniture and silver; Chinese porcelains; Egyptian, Greek, and Roman antiquities; and American paintings, from early folk art through abstract expressionists. Tues.–Sun., 10 A.M.–5 P.M.; Wed. till 10 P.M.; West Wing open Thurs. and Fri. till 10 P.M. Adults, $5; senior citizens, $4; under 16, free. Free to all Sat., 10 A.M.–noon.

Museum of Science and Charles Hayden Planetarium. Science Park, Charles River Dam (723–2500). Over 300 exhibits: astronomy, anthropology, medicine, computers, the earth sciences, and more. The adjacent planetarium offers a "Stars Tonight" show every day at 3 P.M., plus special shows. Tues.–Sun., 9 A.M.–5 P.M.; Fri., 9 A.M.–10 P.M.; Adults, $5; discount for seniors and children 4–14. Fri., 5–10 P.M., admission is half price; free to all Wed., Sept.–Mar. (See *Globe* Calendar section for planetarium schedules and admission fees.)

Museum of Transportation. 15 Newton St., Brookline (522–6140). Recently reopened, this museum recounts America's love affair with the automobile. A number of outstanding old cars are on display. There are also exhibits covering public transportation. Thurs.–Sun., 10 A.M.–5 P.M. Adults, $3; children and seniors, $2. Closed in winter.

ARTS AND ENTERTAINMENT. Boston's performing arts scene is rich and eclectic, representing virtually every category of price and professionalism. Since we couldn't possibly list all of the organizations and venues associated with music, dance, and theater in Boston, we should begin by mentioning two publications that come close: the Boston *Phoenix,* an independent weekly, and the Calendar, a pull-out section of the Boston *Globe* published every Thurs.

Anyone interested in keeping their Boston trip within a budget should remember that the area's wealth of colleges and universities are a source of high-quality performances at surprisingly reasonable prices. Tickets for student performances at **Harvard's Loeb Drama Center** (547–8300), for instance, seldom rise above $5; a downtown professional pre-Broadway or touring show might charge $25 or more for the best seats. Similar bargains are available to concert-goers. The **New England Conservatory of Music's Jordan Hall** (536–2412) and **Berklee College of Music's Berklee Performance Center** (266–7455) offer first-rate performances ranging from jazz to the classics. There are frequent free performances at the **Longy School of Music,** 1 Follen St., Cambridge (876–0956), and the **Gardner Museum,** 280 The Fenway (734–1359), and a free Bach cantata every Sunday morning at **Emmanuel Church,** 15 Newbury St. (536–3355). So, don't rule out the performing arts on a modestly budgeted trip to Boston; the weekly newspaper listings are always full of possibilities.

The established, big-name orchestras and performing companies will, of course, cost a bit more, but remember: you are paying for some of the highest standards in the U.S. and, in some cases, such as that of the Boston Symphony, in the world. Here are the major organizations:

Music. The **Boston Symphony Orchestra,** under Music Director Seiji Ozawa and guest conductors, plays at Symphony Hall, Massachusetts and Huntington avenues (266–1492), Oct.–Apr. The **Opera Company of Boston,** under the direction of Sarah Caldwell, performs a winter series of operas at the Savoy Theater, 539 Washington St. (426–5300). The **Handel and Haydn Society,** America's oldest choral group, performs at Symphony Hall and other locations (266–3605). The relatively new but highly acclaimed **Boston Philharmonic** gives concerts at Jordan Hall, opposite Symphony Hall, Huntington Ave., and Sanders Theater, Harvard (536–4001).

Dance. The **Boston Ballet** is the city's premier dance company, performing at the Wang Center, 268 Tremont St. (542–3945). (The Wang Center is also frequently booked for special performances by visiting singers, orchestras, and opera and dance companies.) Smaller dance companies, featuring modern, jazz, and classical repertoires, are proliferating; check weekly newspaper listings for their frequently inexpensive performances.

Stage. The three principal theaters in Boston are the **Colonial,** 106 Boylston St. (426–9366), **Wilbur,** 246 Tremont St. (423–4008), and **Shubert,** 265 Tremont St. (426–4520). Most plays presented at these major venues are either on their way to Broadway or hitting the road after successful New York runs. Less ambitious productions, with high standards but generally lower ticket prices, are mounted at smaller theaters such as the **Charles,** 76 Warrenton St. (426–6912), **Lyric Stage,** 54 Charles St. (742–8703), **Boston Shakespeare Company,** 17 Harcourt St. (267–5600), and Boston University's **Huntington Theater Company,** 264 Huntington Ave. (266–3913). At Harvard, Robert Brustein runs the **American Repertory Theater,** Loeb Drama Center, 64 Brattle St., Cambridge (547–8300).

Films. Small, first-run movie theaters have been worked into the development of new downtown Boston projects, particularly at Copley Place. Many of them are part of the USA Cinema chain, which offers a central information service (542–SACK). One local theatre popular with foreign and avant-garde film buffs is the *Nickelodeon,* 34 Cummington St. (424–1500). And here are three low-cost revival houses: *Coolidge Corner Theater,* 290 Harvard St., Brookline (734–2500); *Sommerville Theater,* Davis Square, Sommerville (625–1081); and *Brattle Theater,* 40 Brattle St., Cambridge (876–4226). Also, check the papers for film festivals and series at local colleges, where admission prices are always rock-bottom.

SHOPPING. The thrust of Boston's new mercantile image is definitely upscale, as witness the shops in Copley Place and Quincy Market. But the old Yankee tradition of good value for a dollar persists, especially in these local bastions: *Filene's Basement,* Washington and Franklin streets (357–2978), famous for its drastically reduced prices on designer men's and women's clothes. The longer stuff stays on the racks, the cheaper it gets. Prepare for chaos. For women's wear bargains in a less hectic environment, try *Browning's, Ltd.,* 2 Center Plaza (426–5700); *Tello's,* 364 Boylston St. (536–1565) and 417 Washington St. (426–9019); *Hit or Miss,* at 7 area locations, including 91 Franklin St., downtown (338–1208); and *The Limited,* 452 Boylston St. (247–0129), 431 Washington St. (426–6952), and Quincy Market (742–6837). Men looking for good prices on quality clothing should consider *Simon's,* 220 Clarendon St. (266–2345), *Joseph A. Bank,* 122 Newbury St. (536–5050), and the third floor Brooksgate shop, specializing in clothes for the younger man, at *Brooks Brothers,* 46 Newbury St. (267–2600).

For discounts on cameras, tape recorders, watches, small appliances, and luggage, the best bet is *Sherman's,* 11 Bromfield St. (482–9610). A wide assortment of tasteful, reasonably priced housewares is available at *Crate & Barrel,* 48 Brattle St., Cambridge (876–6300), and Quincy Market (742–6025). Also try *Conrans,* 26 Exeter St. (266–2836)

Finally, since so many people come to Boston to soak up the literary ambience, a word on books: the best prices on new and remaindered titles are at *Barnes & Noble,* 395 Washington St. (426–5502) and 603 Boylston St. (236–1308), opposite Trinity Church. For a terrific selection of old books, go to the *Brattle Bookstore,* 9 West St. (542–0210), or *Goodspeed's,* 2 Milk St. (523–5970), beneath the Old South Meeting House. On a rainy day, knowing these last two addresses beats having an umbrella.

DINING OUT. Boston took a long time to develop a reputation as a good restaurant town, and now that it's arrived it seems there's a new place opening every week. New trends in cookery appear in Boston about as fast as they do in New York or San Francisco. Admittedly, a lot of the star-quality cooking in this town has been commanding astronomical prices, but don't despair: virtually all of the culinary styles that make Boston such a good destination for the venturesome eater are available at a broad variety of prices. And don't forget the virtues of lunch: midday dining is an economical way to sample the offerings of even the more posh establishments.

Here, then, are some suggestions for worthwhile dining at reasonable prices without resorting to burger-chain standardization. Categories, based on the price of a dinner for one, without beverage, tax, or tip, are: *Reasonable,* $10 to $18; *Very Economical,* $6 to $10; and *Low Budget,* under $6. Except where noted, restaurants accept some if not all major credit cards.

Reasonable

Blazing Saddles. 940 Saratoga St., East Boston (569–2020). Recently renovated and located near Logan Airport, this is one of the best places around for baby-back ribs. Also steak, sirloin tips. Try the onion-ring loaf.

Blue Diner. 178 Kneeland St. (353–0554). A vintage diner updated with such touches as cloth napkins and a wine list. Recommended is the turkey, roasted fresh each day, and served with homemade cranberry sauce, old-fashioned gravy, and mashed potatoes. Open daily 7 A.M.–11 P.M., until midnight weekends.

Buteco Restaurant. 130 Jersey St. (247–9508). A fun Brazilian restaurant in the kind of animated atmosphere you would expect to find in a Rio café. Try the specialties *Feijoada* and *xim xim de galinha.*

The Cajun Yankee. 1193 Cambridge St., Cambridge (576–1971). The real thing—gumbos, jambalaya, blackened redfish, shrimp remoulade. The chef studied in New Orleans. No lunch; reserve well in advance for dinner. No credit cards.

Casablanca. 40 Brattle St., Cambridge (876–0999). Head down the alley and up the stairs to this intimate spot, decorated with murals of everyone's favorite movie. The menu ranges from steak au poivre to rich homemade soups to fettucine, and there are always daily specials.

Hampshire House. 84 Beacon St. (227–9600). Not the expensive second-floor restaurant or the cellar pub, but the main floor—the handsome paneled room with the fireplace and moose head, overlooking the Public Garden. It's quite reasonable at lunch; try the mussels, Caesar salad, onion soup, or a daily special.

Hilltop Steak House. Route 1, Saugus (233–7700). A bit of a Boston legend, this restaurant (popular with Celtic and Bruin players) serves huge slabs of beef with potato and vegetable, at very reasonable prices.

J.C. Hillary's. 793 Boylston St. (536–6300). The nineteenth-century mahogany, stained glass, and revolving ceiling fan motif are tastefully done. Sound basic cuisine—steaks, stew, seafood, good pasta.

Imperial Tea House. 70 Beach St. (426–8543). A Chinatown spot with a good repertoire of the standards, but the best reason for going is the lunchtime *dim sum,* an incredible assortment of three-bite snacks you order right off the cart.

Legal Seafoods. Park Plaza Hotel, 35 Columbus Ave., and several other locations in and around Boston. Legal has the widest variety of seafoods available in the Boston area. Depending on season, the menu may include shark, lemon sole, shad (and shad roe—in spring), monkfish, plus the usual favorites.

Peacock Restaurant. 5 Craigie Circle, Cambridge (661–4073). An intimate spot for delicious nouvelle American cuisine at very affordable prices.

Very Economical

Brandy Pete's. 82 Broad St. (482–4165). A weekday lunch and dinner spot in the financial district, Pete's serves the American basics—steaks, chops, roast turkey—at good working-class prices.

The Daily Catch. 323 Hanover St. (523–8567); branch at 261 Northern Ave. (423–6976), and One Kendall Sq., Cambridge (225–2300). Boston's only restaurants specializing in squid, the *calamari* of Italian cuisine. The little creatures don't have a pronounced flavor of their own, but they take nicely to frying and spicy sauces. Also other seafood dishes. No credit cards.

No-Name. 15½ Fish Pier, off Northern Ave. (338–7539). This used to be a joint frequented exclusively by working fishermen, and the original tiny room still has that salty ambience. It's been "discovered" and has expanded, but continues to serve good fish chowder and broiled and fried seafood specialties. It's probably the cheapest place in town for swordfish, when they're running. No credit cards.

Pat's Pushcart. 59 Endicott St. (523–9616). Not really a pushcart, this is a tiny spot featuring all the southern Italian basics. On a cold afternoon, stop in for sausage, peppers, and potatoes (order the vinegar peppers) or a plate of pasta. No credit cards.

Pentimento. 344 Huron Ave., Cambridge (661–3878). The Vermont-1970 decor is a nice break from the new-wave 1980s, and the home-style cooking is a welcome find in this quiet Cambridge neighborhood. The menu keeps changing, but includes things like chicken pot pie, vegetable burritos, and coconut almond bread pudding. No smoking. No credit cards.

Souper Salad. 119 Newbury St. (247–4983). Also three other Boston and Cambridge locations. Soups, sandwiches, quiche, a few hot specials, and a salad bar rated the best in Boston by the *Globe*.

Jacob Wirth's. 31 Stuart St. (338–8586). For well over a hundred years, Wirth's has been dispensing sausages, kraut, sandwiches, beer—and a conventional offering of American dishes—in quarters that are not calculatedly old-timey but just plain *old.* The waiters wear black jackets and long white aprons; the back bar is heavy with Victorian woodcarving. It's a real pre-Prohibition saloon.

Low Budget

Charlie's. 429 Columbus Ave. (536–7669). Many consider Charlie's to be the capital of the South End, a black–Latino–Yuppie–Asian–gay neighborhood with great architecture. This little luncheonette (breakfast and lunch only) excels in bacon and eggs, muffins, burgers, and sweet-potato pie.

Fill-a-Buster. 9 Park St. (523–8164). In the shadow of the State House, this popular breakfast and lunch spot does a good job with the luncheonette basics, but the real stars of the menu are the homemade Greek and Mideastern specialties—*hummus, felafel,* egg-lemon soup, spinach pie, and *souvlaki.* No credit cards.

Regina. 11½ Thatcher St. This North End pizzeria has spawned a score of downtown and suburban branches—forget about them, and head down to the original location for your pies. The line often stretches into the street, but it's worth it. No credit cards.

Victoria. 1024 Massachusetts Ave. (442–5965). The front looks like a diner, the back like a restaurant, and the seafood is usually a good bet. It's a little out of the way—down past City Hospital—but worth knowing about because it's open all night. No credit cards.

Recommended Splurges. Icarus. 3 Appleton St. (426–1790). An intimate and eclectically furnished restaurant in the South End, with an equally eclectic menu reflecting the tastes of the "New American" school of cuisine. Recently expanded to include pasta and salads. $20 and up per person.

Michela's. 245 First St. Cambridge (225–3366) This Italian restaurant opened with much acclaim, and has maintained its reputation and become an "in" place to eat. The dishes achieve Michela Larson's goal of "refined heartiness." Decor is very pink and "post-industrial." Reservations recommended. Entrees range in price from $17 to $24.

Brunches. Boston's fall from the grace of Puritan austerity is amply revealed by its embracing the New York custom of Sunday brunch. Lavish brunch buffets, starting around 11 A.M. or noon and ending as the last sections of the *Globe* (and the readers) fall to the floor, are a specialty of several area hotels. Hotel brunches aren't cheap—count on about $20 per person, plus drinks, for the two mentioned below—but when you figure that you won't be hungry again until Monday afternoon, the price looks good. Try Parker's Restaurant downtown at the **Parker House,** 60 School St., (227–8600). Settings are at 11:30 A.M. and 1:30 P.M.; take the latter if you like to linger. In Cambridge, it's the **Hyatt Regency,** 574 Memorial Dr. (492–1234). Reservations are suggested at both places, as is an appetite: you'll encounter roasts, smoked salmon, pâtés, eggs, sausages, breads and rolls, and plenty of rich desserts.

For a less extravagant but still ample brunch buffet at less than half the hotels' price, try an Irish bar called **The Black Rose,** 160 State St., near Quincy Market (742–2286). If you're tired of Bloody Marys, they have Guinness on tap. Brunch served 10:30 A.M.–2 P.M.

Cafés and Coffeehouses. Twenty-five years ago, Boston was the coffeehouse town where the folk-music boom took off. The greatest holdover from that era is the still-lively **Passim,** 47 Palmer St., Cambridge, near Harvard Square (492–7669). You can usually count on good folk music or maybe a poetry reading at Passim; check newspaper listings. Another Cambridge spot, with no music but plenty of atmosphere, is **Pamplona,** 12 Bow St., off Massachusetts Ave. near Harvard Square. The espresso, pastries, and chocolate mousse are good, as are the unusual summer drinks. There are a few outside tables in season, but it's the tiny whitewashed basement that will take you back to undergrad days. Open lunch–mid-afternoon and evenings.

Newbury Street, in Boston's Back Bay, has a couple of sidewalk cafés; try the **Florian** at number 85 (247–7603). Beer and wine; light meals. 8:30 A.M.–11:30 P.M. In the same neighborhood, at 190 Newbury, the **Harvard Bookstore Café** (536–0095) lets you peruse its literary wares while drinking wine, eating chocolate cake, or having a more substantial meal. Keep your fingers clean. 8 A.M.–11 P.M.

Finally, for some good North End color, try the **Cafe Pompeii,** 280 Hanover St. They've got espresso, *cannoli* and *sfogliatella,* a jukebox full of Italian hits, and a wraparound mural of the Bay of Naples. The pool table in the back room is not for you. Noon–1 or 2 A.M.

NIGHTLIFE AND BARS. Boston night spots tend to be concentrated in the major hotels, in and around Quincy Market, and—if rock music is what you're after—the clubs in Kenmore Square. A night spent bar-hopping in Boston can get pricey; promotional gimmicks such as happy hour, two-for-one drinks, and free food have been banned by the state legislature. The drinking age in Boston is 21.

You can pass a few hours without breaking the bank at **Delmonico's,** at the Hotel Lenox, 710 Boylston St. (536–5300), where piano sing-alongs are popular, or—for local Beacon Hill color—at **The Sevens,** 77 Charles St. (523–9074). In Cambridge, try **Ryle's,** 212 Hampshire St. (876–9330), for live jazz. **The Black Rose,** 160 State St., Boston, near Quincy Market (742–2286), features traditional Irish music.

For a big night out, head for the **Plaza Bar** at the Copley Plaza Hotel, Copley Plaza (267–5300), where jazz pianist Dave McKenna plays from September through June; the **Starlight Roof,** at the Howard Johnson's in Kenmore Square, 575 Commonwealth Ave., Boston (236–3100), considered Boston's premier jazz club; or the **Last Hurrah** in the Parker House, 60 School St., (227–8600) where the Winiker Orchestra plays big-band swing Sat. from 8 P.M., and Sun., 4 P.M.–8 P.M.

Over in Cambridge, they've been booking top jazz singers and instrumentalists into the **Regattabar** at the new Charles Hotel, 1 Bennett St. (864–1200).

SECURITY. Boston is not the most dangerous of American cities, but neither is it the safest. The neighborhoods described in this chapter are heavily used and quite safe by day; however, visitors to the more remote areas of larger parks, such as Franklin and the Arnold Arboretum, should always travel in pairs. At night, use common sense: try not to walk down deserted streets (stick to the middle if you do) and take a cab if you're uncertain of your route. Day or night, women should clutch handbags closely and avoid wearing flashy gold chains on the subway; they should try not to walk alone at night except on the busiest streets.

Keep your valuables in the hotel safe, rather than in your room. At night, use the deadbolt and chain on your hotel room door.

CHICAGO

by
Gary Smith Ruderman
and
Shirley Rose Higgins

Gary Smith Ruderman is a free-lance writer covering business and finance in the Midwest. His free-lance articles have appeared in Time *and* People *and in many newspapers here and abroad. Shirley Rose Higgins is a free-lance travel writer whose family has lived in Illinois since 1830. Her writing has won three Mark Twain Awards and a George Hedman Memorial Award. Her column covering international travel appeared in the Chicago* Tribune *for 14 years and is now syndicated nationally.*

What was known as the "stinking onion" when Chicago was just Fort Dearborn and a swamp is now the lusty beating heart of America's midsection. Chicago, with 3 million city dwellers speaking 54 languages, is the most ethnically and linguistically diverse city in the nation. Next to Warsaw, Chicago has the largest Polish-speaking community in the world. For years, neighborhoods were known as Greek or Swedish or Italian or Jewish. Today, ethnic lines have blurred.

While it is windy in Chicago, the "windy city" reputation comes from political hot air. Politics here is tough, with mayoral races likened to street fights. The Democratic Party "machine" ran the city and its patronage under the legendary Mayor Daley; today control of city jobs and the future direction of a half dozen major projects involve constant struggles between the mayor and the city council. But it is a city that works. The city (and state) voted to keep lights off Wrigley Field (although this may change by publication date); the parks are clean, the snow gets removed, and illegally parked cars get towed.

Chicagoans perceive themselves as honest, friendly, and hardworking, but don't expect a hometown "hi" as you're walking down Michigan Avenue. Life has a fast pace, without the treadmill existence of some large cities. To some, Chicago is the most racially segregated city in the country, with the white and Latino North Side and the predominantly black South and West sides. To others, Chicago is the birthplace of positive race relations and an exciting black business community. We see our city not as downtown or the skyscrapers but as the Chicago bungalow home and the six-flat apartment building; "My Kind of Town" is made up of neighbors and neighborhoods. A million people use one of the nation's widest reaching public transportation systems each day. The neighborhood aspect of Chicago is best seen at the back stairs and rooftop level from the elevated train track.

The city last had the strike-it-rich mentality at the turn of the century and settled down to a more get-along existence. Except for the Gold Coast (Lake Shore Drive from North Avenue to Oak Street) and gentrified pockets, Chicago is a blue-collar town; a real Chicagoan's speech is laced with "dis" and "dat," in reverence to "Hizzoner" the late Mayor Richard Daley. People work hard for their paychecks and expect to get their dollar's worth. Every neighbor has a cousin who's an insider, knowing exactly where the cheapest lumber or moderately priced Chippendale can be had. Someone in Chicago knows where to find virtually anything; just ask.

Getting to Know Chicago

Visitors may call it "downtown," but Chicagoans call it the Loop. The screeching cars of the elevated subway, known affectionately as the El, makes a loop around the business and financial district bounded on the west by Wells Street, on the east by Wabash Street, on the south by Jackson Street, and on the north by Lake Street. In common parlance, however, the Loop extends to Michigan Avenue and north to the Chicago River.

A Broad Sweep of Neighborhoods South of the Loop

Printers Row, just south of Congress Street, is an area of renovated warehouses and lofts now popular with singles. West a block or two is **Dearborn Park,** an expanse of new middle-income condominiums built in 1979 to revitalize the South Loop. The land was once warehouses, railroad bed, and tenements. West of the Loop on Jackson Street is **Greektown,** home of the city's first Greek immigrants, who later moved north to Lawrence Avenue. **Chinatown,** at Cermak Road, is the home of fine restaurants and the elegant Chinatown Merchants Association, a private organization dating back to the 1920s. Many older residents of Chinatown speak only Chinese. As in Manhattan, **Little Italy** abuts Chinatown, at Taylor Street. Along Halsted is the University of Illinois at Chicago with its jutting school of architecture and design; just a few blocks south is Maxwell Street, where peddlers hawk their wares and where the precinct station on the television program *Hill Street Blues* is located. The South Side remains Chicago's ethnic stronghold. Take Bridgeport (off Halsted near 30th), for example; it was the home of the late Mayor Richard Daley and remains a strongly Irish community.

Closer to the lake are South Shore and Hyde Park. **South Shore,** once the city's most affluent area of fine homes and elegant high-rises, underwent a racial change after World War II. Today, while known nationally among bankers for its community-development innovations, South Shore has yet to determine its direction. **Hyde Park,** on the other hand, is firmly set in rarefied heights near the University of Chicago and the Museum of Science and Industry.

Farther south and southwest are neighborhoods seldom seen by the majority of visitors. **Beverley** and **Morgan Park,** affluent areas still, have achieved a sense of racial cooperation, while **Marquette Park** still seethes with the kind of animosity that ignited in violence in 1978 and 1980. **East Chicago** is an old-line ethnic community built around the steel mills, Chicago's "rust belt."

A Broad Sweep of Neighborhoods North of the Loop

North of the river to Oak Street is considered the **Near North Side,** where you'll find N. Michigan Avenue and its fabulous stores. The Water Tower and Pumping Station at Chicago Avenue are survivors of the great fire in 1871. In the same area are the downtown campuses of Northwestern, DePaul, and Loyola universities. The **Gold Coast,** with its Lake Shore Drive high-rises and Astor Street mansions, lies north of Oak Street to North Avenue. Just west of the Gold Coast is Rush Street, scene of the city's nightlife. West of the Lake Shore Drive is **Old Town** along Wells Street. Once the home of artists and writers and of the hippies during the 1960s, Old Town is still known for its artsy quality and interesting homes. Just a mile west of the Lake Shore Drive affluence is Cabrini Green Housing Projects, a large gang-ridden housing project where former Mayor Jane Byrne once set up her home for two weeks.

Heading north, around Armitage Avenue and Lincoln Park West, are the **Lincoln Park, Lake View,** and **DePaul** neighborhoods. Here are the areas of greatest gentrification and recent rehabilitation in the city. Lincoln Avenue from Armitage to Belmont gives the walker or driver a good cross section and plenty of interesting shops, restaurants, and entertainment. Walk down the many side streets for a look at the changes; you're bound to see at least one house being restored. Amid the wall-to-wall homes and high-rises, turn east (toward the lake) from the corner of Clark and Arlington for a real hidden beauty, an overgrown Audubon Society bird sanctuary no larger than 75 by 100 feet.

New Town begins near Diversey and Broadway, extending to Irving Park where Uptown starts. New Town and **Uptown** are true areas in transition right now, struggling to keep up with new immigrants' demands for inexpensive housing and essential city services. By Foster Avenue, **Rogers Park** begins. East Rogers Park hugs the lake with large old homes and the campuses of Loyola University and Mundelein College. West of Ridge Avenue is West Rogers Park, a salt-and-pepper mixture of old homes and new apartment buildings. On both the west and the north, West Rogers Park is bounded by the city of Evanston, home of the historic Gross Point Lighthouse, the Women's Christian Temperance Union, and Northwestern University.

PRACTICAL INFORMATION

WHEN TO GO. Chicago is a year-round city; the lakefront is the city's country club in the summer and the place for restful solitude or cross-country skiing in the winter.

When you go is pretty much determined by what you want to do when you get there. The city's wealth of museums, entertainment, and excellent shopping possibilities lure many winter visitors. There is so much going on in the city at any time that it is up to travelers to decide whether they prefer a summer sightseeing boat trip on the lake or a winter view of that snowy shore from the comfort of a cozy rooftop dining room. Late May and June find the city in leafy bloom, and September and October are usually very pleasant. Weather patterns seem to be changing and

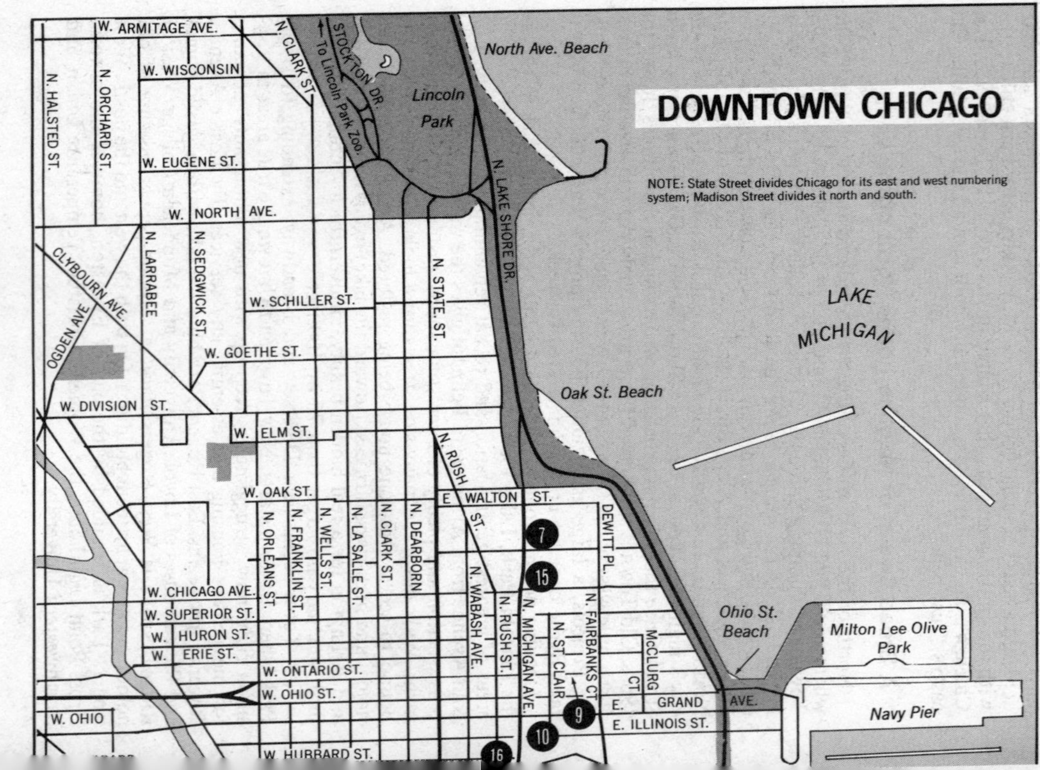

Points of Interest

1) Adler Planetarium
2) Art Institute and Goodman Theater
3) Buckingham Fountain
4) Civic Opera House
5) Field Museum
6) Greek Town
7) Hancock Center
8) Merchandise Mart
9) Museum of Contemporary Art
10) Pioneer Court
11) Sears Tower
12) Shedd Aquarium
13) Soldier Field
14) Union Station
15) Water Tower and Water Tower Place
16) Wrigley Building

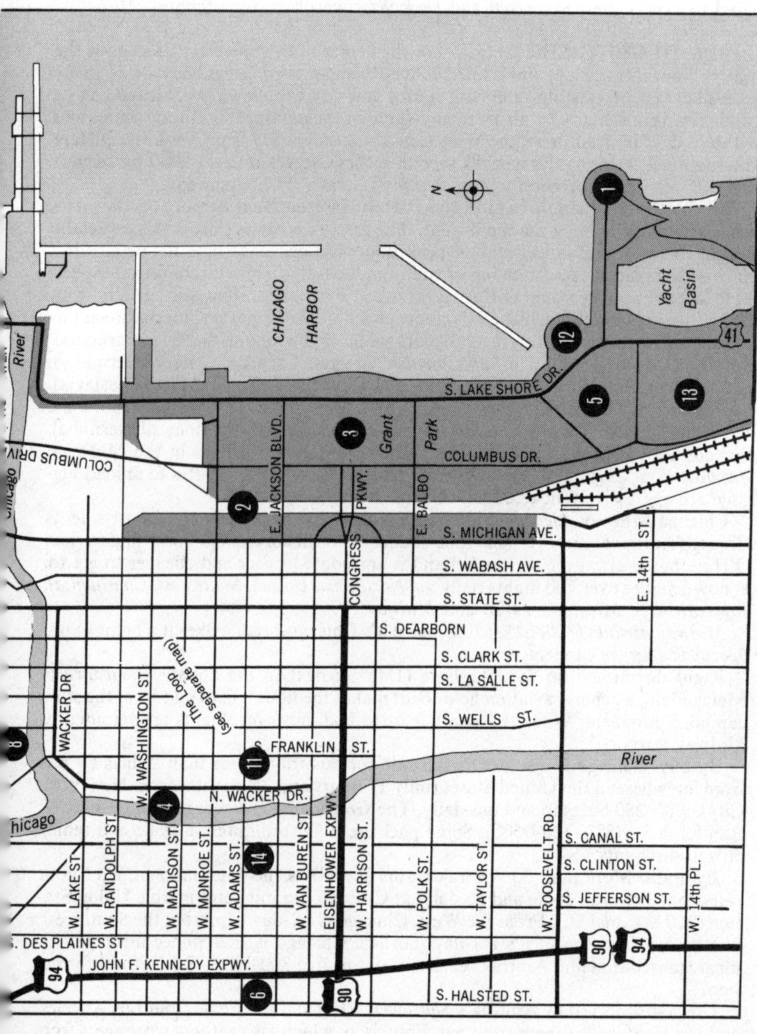
CHICAGO
HARBOR
Yacht
Basin
41
S. LAKE SHORE DR.
Grant
Park
COLUMBUS DR.
COLUMBUS DRIVE
E. JACKSON BLVD.
PKWY.
E. BALBO
S. MICHIGAN AVE.
CONGRESS
S. WABASH AVE.
S. STATE ST.
E. 14th ST.
S. DEARBORN
S. CLARK ST.
S. LA SALLE ST.
S. WELLS ST.
The Loop
(see separate map)
WACKER DR.
W. WASHINGTON ST.
S. FRANKLIN ST.
River
N. WACKER DR.
Chicago
W. LAKE ST.
W. RANDOLPH ST.
W. MADISON ST.
W. MONROE ST.
W. ADAMS ST.
W. VAN BUREN ST.
EISENHOWER EXPWY.
W. HARRISON ST.
W. POLK ST.
W. TAYLOR ST.
W. ROOSEVELT RD.
S. CANAL ST.
S. CLINTON ST.
S. JEFFERSON ST.
W. 14th PL.
S. DES PLAINES ST
94
JOHN F. KENNEDY EXPWY.
90
S. HALSTED ST.

there have been some cool Augusts, April heat waves, and mild winters, so be prepared to expect the unexpected and pack your wardrobe accordingly.

HOW TO GET THERE. Though not the center of the universe, Chicago is the hub of transportation in the United States. Almost every neighborhood is easily accessible via the existing interstate routes and city expressways. Chicago can be reached within 4 hours by air from anywhere in the continental United States and within 2 days by train from the West Coast and only a day from the East. O'Hare International Airport, the world's second busiest, serves over 115,000 passengers daily. Public transportation within the city operates 24 hours a day.

By air. Chicago has three airports; **O'Hare International Airport** on the city's far northwest side is by far the busiest. The airport is always crowded, especially during the morning and afternoon peak hours. Allow extra time for departures, since widespread construction has created chaotic traffic jams and confusion expected to last a few more years. O'Hare is served by most major domestic carriers, with *United Airlines* making Chicago its home and hub. A temporary international terminal will be in service for several years while a new one is under construction. *Air France, Alia* (Jordan), *Alitalia, British Airways, Cayman, Condor* (Germany), *Ecuatoriana* (Ecuador), *El Al, Iberia, Icelandic, Japan Airlines, JAT* (Yugoslavia), *Lufthansa, Mexicana, Philippine, Sabena, SAS,* and *Swissair* all serve Chicago, some as charter flights only. *Air Canada* serves Chicago through the domestic terminal. In addition to charters, O'Hare is served by commuter airlines in the Midwest: *America West, Britt,* and *Midstate.* Cars pausing even scant minutes to unload luggage are aggressively ticketed, so beware.

Chicago Midway Airport, 5700 S. Cicero, on the city's near southwest side, is Chicago's original airport. This mile-square bit of history offers fewer flights than O'Hare but is always less crowded and is considered easier and cheaper to get to. It now handles over 100 flights daily via *Northwest, United, Southwest, Continental, Iowa Airways, Midstate, TWA,* and *Midway.*

Midway Airlines (800–621–5700), since it's Chicago-bred, makes it a point to undercut the larger carriers.

Right downtown on the lakeshore (15th St. next to the Shedd Aquarium) is **Meigs Field,** a general aviation field. *Britt* makes the hour trip to and from the state capital, Springfield. When the weather turns bad, however, flights are rerouted to Midway Airport.

By bus. Chicago is also a national hub for bus travel: less than 2 days by bus from anywhere in the United States (only 17 hours and 25 minutes from New York City), with 280 buses in and out daily. The *Greyhound-Trailways* depot is at 70 W. Randolph St. (312–726–9500). Some packages offer unlimited mileage and senior citizen discounts.

By train. More than 50 Amtrak trains as well as the International, a 12-hour ride from Toronto, come and go daily at Chicago's granite and marble **Union Station** (210 S. Canal St.). From the West, Chicago is a 2-day trip; from the Southwest, South, and East Coast, it's a 1-day journey. Chicago is the connecting point for most transcontinental Amtrak service. Call toll-free 800–USA–RAIL for information.

Chicago is served by Amtrak's *Southwest Chief* and the *Eagle* from Los Angeles, and the *California Zephyr* from San Francisco, which also gathers passengers from Los Angeles, Oakland, and Portland. From the Northwest, the *Empire Builder* heads for the Midwest from Seattle and the Portland area. From the South, Chicago is an overnight ramble on the *City of New Orleans.* The song "Riding on the City of New Orleans" was written by the late Chicago folksinger Steve Goodman. From the East, it's a 22-hour trip from Boston aboard the *Lake Shore Limited,* offering lakefront views through Ohio. The *Broadway Limited* arrives from New York City and the *Capitol Limited* from Washington.

By car. I-80 (connecting to I-55) is the most direct route from Iowa on the west and (connecting with I-94) from Indiana and the eastern states. I-70 brings traffic from the south. I-90 and I-94 approach Chicago from Wisconsin and the north. I-57 is the major approach from Memphis and the south.

Chicago has five major expressways, all leading into downtown. From the south there are the Dan Ryan (I-94), the Eisenhower (I-290), and the Stevenson (I-55). Heading north from downtown are the Kennedy (I-94, which becomes I-90) and the Edens (I-94).

TELEPHONES. The area code for Chicago and suburbs is 312. You don't need to dial the area code if the number is in the Chicago area. Calls made by pay telephone to telephones in the city cost 25 cents for unlimited time. The telephone number for directory assistance for the city and suburbs is 411; the call is free from a coin phone. When you call the suburbs from a coin phone, an operator will tell you how much money to insert for the first 3 minutes. If you don't have exact change, the extra money will be credited for additional calling time.

To call outside the 312 area code, dial 1 before the area code. To charge a long-distance call to a credit card or to reverse the charges, dial 0 before the area code. In most instances after dialing a number with the 0, you'll hear a tone signaling you to punch in your credit card number. If you're not sure what to do or if nothing happens, dial 0 when the tone sounds.

Hotels can add whatever additional service charge they wish for directory assistance, in-city calls, and long-distance calls. Use the lobby pay phone whenever possible.

Emergency Telephone Numbers. 911 is the main emergency number for the police, fire department, ambulances, and paramedics. There are two 24-hour poison control numbers: 800–252–2022 and 942–5969.

ACCOMMODATIONS. Chicago is blessed with **hotels** ranging from glitz and gilt to plain and simple, from the aged beauties with great lobbies and small European-style hotels serving just *petit dejeuner* off small lobbies to run-of-the-mill motels. Because Chicago is a major business and convention town, March through June and Aug. through Nov. are the traditionally busy seasons. All hotels charge 10 percent room tax and 8 percent tax on food and beverage items.

Although rooms are plentiful, Chicago isn't cheap. Hotel rates are based on double occupancy. Categories, determined by price, are as follows: *Reasonable,* $65 to $95; *Very Economical,* under $60. Many of the larger, more expensive hotels offer attractive weekend rates in the range of $50 to $70. The *Chicago Hotel Association,* 100 W. Monroe, Chicago, IL 60603, will send free brochures outlining weekend specials.

Reasonable

Allerton Hotel. 701 N. Michigan Ave., Chicago, IL 60611 (312–440–1500 or 800–621–3211). An older, nicely renovated 450-room hotel, well placed in the city's most expensive district. Excellent dining at L'Escargot. Children under 16 free. Weekend rates are $60 Fri.–Sun. nights.

Bismarck. 171 W. Randolph, Chicago, IL 60601 (312–236–0123). Well-known older hotel with loyal following. Located across from County Building/City Hall. Good dollar value; some recent remodeling. Garage facilities. Rates fall to very economical on weekends.

Blackstone Hotel. 636 S. Michigan Ave., Chicago, IL 60605 (312–427–4300). Older hotel but a prime location for visits to the Art Institute and Grant Park. Weekend rate. Children free under 12, cribs free.

Comfort Inn of Chicago. 601 W. Diversey, Chicago, IL 60614 (312–348–2810). Although north of downtown, this renovated 100-room inn is in a prime location in the Lincoln Park neighborhood. Excellent jumping-off place for nearby neighborhoods. Free parking, complimentary Continental breakfast, children under 12 free.

Days Inn. 644 N. Lake Shore Dr., Chicago, IL 60611 (312–943–9200). The Fantasy Weekend package puts it in the "reasonable" category. Free champagne and food discount with package.

Essex Inn. 800 S. Michigan Ave., Chicago, IL 60605 (312–939–2800 or 800–621–6909). Though slightly away from the downtown bustle, this inn is convenient to the McCormick Place Convention Center. Cribs free, pets allowed, free parking. Delicatessen and restaurant.

Palmer House. 17 E. Monroe St., Chicago, IL 60690–1508, at State St. (312–726–7500). The best deal in the city takes place in this truly grand old hotel, now a Hilton property. The Mini-Vacation Value Package offers deluxe single or double occupancy with free parking and a 15 percent discount at Trader Vic's restaurant in the hotel. Package offered Fri. and Sat. nights. Children free if they sleep in the parents' room (no age limit). Pets allowed. Free health club facilities.

River North Hotel. 125 W. Ohio St., Chicago, IL 60610 (800–528–1234 Best Western toll-free, also 800–727–0800 and 312–467–0800). Free parking, easy access to major highways, indoor rooftop pool, saunas, fitness center, and fitness suites. Weekend packages.

Very Economical

Ascot House. 1100 S. Michigan Ave., Chicago, IL 60605 (312–922–2900 or 800–621–4196). A large motel 11 blocks south of the loop and the best jumping-off point for visits to the Alder Planetarium, the Field Museum, the Shedd Aquarium, and the McCormick Place Exposition Center. Outdoor heated pool, 14 cabana rooms, free parking, restaurant. Small pets allowed. Cribs free.

Belmont Hotel. 3170 N. Sheridan Rd., Chicago, IL 60657 (312–248–2100). Farther away from downtown in an excellent residential neighborhood known as Belmont Harbor. Excellent restaurants and gourmet cheese and wine store. A 15-minute cab or 30-minute bike ride away from Michigan Ave. and an easy drive for the out-of-towner. Suites have kitchens.

Hyde Park Hilton. 4900 S. Lake Shore Dr., Chicago, IL 60615 (312–288–5800). The weekend package makes this South Shore gem very economical. This very trendy enclave is the best base for visits to the Museum of Science and Industry and the University of Chicago's Oriental Institute. Free hourly shuttle bus to and from the Loop.

Lakeside Motel. 5440 N. Sheridan Rd., Chicago, IL 60640 (312–275–2700). While well away from downtown, it's two blocks from the public Bryn Mawr beach and a good jumping-off point for exploring the Rogers Park neighborhood and nearby Evanston. Free parking.

LaSalle Motor Lodge. 720 N. LaSalle St., Chicago, IL 60610 (312–664–8100). North of the Loop but just a few blocks from N. Michigan Ave. shopping areas. Restaurant and free parking. Children under 16 free, movie channel.

Ohio House. 600 N. LaSalle (Ohio, near the Merchandise Mart), Chicago, IL 60610 (312–943–6000). Two-story 50-room motel with coffee shop and free parking facilities near the heart of the city.

Sheridan Chase. 7300 N. Sheridan Rd., Chicago, IL 60626 (312–973–7440). Just before the Evanston border; this property isn't new, but it is clean. Across the street from the Lunt Street Beach in the up-and-coming Rogers Park neighborhood. Close to Loyola University and Mundelein College.

Bed-and-Breakfast. Bed & Breakfast–Chicago, Box 14088, Chicago, IL 60614–0088 (312–951–0085), is the reservation service for lodging in 100 private homes from Victorian city homes to high-rise condos. They're in the most desirable neighborhoods starting from south of the Loop in the Printers Row loft area to the North Side Victorian neighborhoods. Most recent prices were $45 for budget singles to $200 for a large condo, with most in the $45 to $75 range. Also self-catering furnished apartments with a minimum stay of 3 days. Rates vary by season. Hosts will accept American Express, MasterCard, Visa, or traveler's checks.

Ys and Youth Hostels. Lawson YMCA. 30 W. Chicago Ave., Chicago, IL 60610 (312–944–6211). 520-room Y. Close to N. Michigan Ave. and Rush St. entertainment. Reservations are recommended for the married couples' accommodations, $25 (no private baths). Booked up around the holidays. Use of athletic facilities included. Single $33. Parking nearby. Phones in the rooms. MasterCard and Visa. No children under 18.

The American Youth Hostel maintains two centers. The *International House,* 1414 E. 59th St., Chicago, IL 60637 (312–753–2270), at the University of Chicago is open June 1 to Sept. 9; $12 per night. On the city's far north side is their *Chicago International AYH,* 6318 N. Winthrop, Chicago, IL 60660 (312–262–1011). Located near Loyola University and Mundelein College, with excellent public transportation. It is open all year, with check in before 10 A.M. and after 4 P.M. Phone calls are answered after 4 P.M. Mostly dormitory-style rooms. Reserve ahead for limited number of private rooms. $9 for members (sheet rental $1.50), $10 nonmembers.

HOW TO GET AROUND. From the airport. The subway now connects downtown and O'Hare International Airport with fast (35 min.), cheap ($1.00), frequent (every 20 min.), and convenient service. Pick up the subway at Terminal 4, lower level. The stations at Lake and Clark streets are designed for the disabled; more will be accessible in the coming years. From the city, catch the "Airport" train at any Dearborn Street station or any of the hub stations in the neighborhoods.

From O'Hare to the Loop, the fastest way to make the 18-mile trip is the Kennedy Expressway (I-90 to I-94). Public transportation leaves from the lower (baggage claim) level. Many hotels and motels have telephones for courtesy bus service. The *Continental Air Transport* bus to downtown and Northside hotels costs $9 one way, $15 round-trip. Cabs cost $18 to $22. Limos cost $45 one way. Super Saver Shared Rides are $12 from lower level Terminal 3.

From Midway to the Loop, turn north on Cicero Ave. to I-55 and then I-94 north for the 11-mile trip. Bus service is available but slow. Taxis cost about $15 to $18 to downtown hotels; $8 one way via *Continental Air Transport.*

By public transportation. Virtually every Chicago neighborhood is within three blocks of a Chicago Transit Authority (CTA) bus stop or subway ("El") stop. The system operates 24 hours a day, although service is scaled back on weekends and after midnight. An information number (836–7000 or 800–972–7000) operates 24 hours a day, but it is best to call after 6 P.M. Tell the operator where you are and where you'd like to go. Bus and subway system maps are free and available at subway stations and public libraries.

Both buses and trains cost $1 for a ride anywhere in the city. A regular 25-cent transfer allows you to connect with another bus or spend an hour shopping or sightseeing before taking a ride back. On Sundays a Super Transfer (adults, $1.75; children and seniors, 85 cents) allows unlimited travel for the 24-hour period. During Sundays in the summer months, the CTA Culture Bus picks up passengers from the Art Institute and drops them off at one of 30 museums and cultural attractions before making a return trip. It operates 11 A.M.–5:15 P.M. Adults, $2.50; children, $1.25.

By taxi. Taxis currently charge $1 as the base fare, with 90 cents for each additional mile. Each additional rider adds 50 cents to the fare. No extra charge for seniors. Avoid the shared cab in downtown areas, but it's not a bad idea from the airports. The major cab companies are *Yellow and Checker* (829–4222) and *Flash Cab* (561–1444).

By rental car. There are usually rentals available from *Airways* (671–7070, 800–323–8515), *Avis* (694–5600), *Budget* (968–6661), *Dollar* (671–5100), *Hertz* (800–654–3131), and *National* (800–328–4567). Most have counters at the airports and downtown.

Suburban venturing: From Chicago, several unreserved commuter rail lines and a number of connecting suburban buses operate in all directions. The last train out of Chicago on most commuter lines is 12:30 A.M. The suburban buses run from about 6 A.M. to 11 P.M. Weekend service is very limited. For information, call 836–7000 or 800–972–7000.

HINTS TO THE MOTORIST. Chicago drivers are generally polite. The alert yet befuddled out-of-town drivers will see city drivers urging them to cut in or get across lanes of heavy traffic. Chicago drivers like to be thanked.

Luckily, most roads leading into Chicago tell you how to get there. In the city, the grid system applies. It begins downtown at the intersection of State and Madison, which is double zero. From this center, the numbers go up roughly 100 numbers a block. If you're looking for 2800 N. Halsted, for example, it's roughly 28 blocks north of the Loop (Diversey Ave.) and 8 blocks west of the lake (Halsted). Eight city blocks usually equals a mile. There are fewer than 10 streets in the entire city that confound even the most seasoned traveler. You can't get too lost heading east. The last road before heading into the chilly waters of Lake Michigan is either Lake Shore Drive or Sheridan Road. Chicago motorists know that Chicago streets and expressways have two seasons: winter (driving is slow and treacherous off the main roads) and under construction! Most Chicagoans avoid the Loop expressways around rush hour, opting instead for Lake Shore Drive (north and south) and main streets such as Western Avenue or even Halsted.

Morning rush hour going downtown starts at 6:30 A.M. from the southern expressways (Dan Ryan, Eisenhower, and Stevenson) and 7 A.M. from the northern (Kennedy and Edens). Traffic clears by 10:30 A.M. unless there's construction, as there will be on the Dan Ryan for a few years. The evening rush starts by 3:30 P.M. in both directions (earlier on Fridays). Don't be surprised if there is truck traffic all day. Street parking downtown is insane, but parking lots are plentiful. Parking lots slightly west of the Loop are cheaper and just a four- or five-block walk to the business district.

Right turns are allowed after a stop at a red light (unless posted), and U-turns are permitted in the middle of the block, not within 100 feet of an intersection. The maximum speed limit on city roads is 30 mph and 45 mph on Lake Shore Drive. Expressways vary between 45 mph (Kennedy downtown) and 50 mph. Overnight parking is banned on some major streets, and a two-in. snowfall on marked streets will close off more spaces. Few large streets have sufficient parking, so look for spots on smaller, predominantly residential, streets first.

If you're an AAA or CAA member, contact the **Chicago Motor Club** (312–372–1818; emergency road service, 390–7300) for 90 approved auto repair garages and routing information. Nonmembers can call for help in locating approved auto repairers. Check with European motor clubs for AAA reciprocity.

TOURIST INFORMATION. It's a good idea to get a picture of the city's offerings by requesting the free Chicago Visitors Guide and Map from the *Chicago Visitors Center,* Illinois Office of Tourism, 310 S. Michigan Ave., Suite 108, Chicago, IL 60604 (312–793–2094). *O'Hare Airport* has a multilingual service in Terminal 3 (686–2304). The *Chicago Visitor Information Center* is housed in the historic Water Tower (the sandstone tower that survived the Great Chicago Fire of 1871) at 806 N. Michigan; open 7 days a week, multilingual. Language problems can be overcome by the *International Visitors Center* at 520 N. Michigan (645–1836), *Travelers Aid* has offices at the Greyhound Bus station (435–4537), Union Train Station (435–4500), and O'Hare International Airport (686–7562). The *Illinois Travel Line* offers a 24-hour recorded list of events at 800–252–8987. For a free calendar of events call 800–223–0121. There are 60 foreign consulates in the city, and the list grows annually.

The best sources of information on what's going on in Chicago are newspapers and magazines. The *Sun Times* and *Tribune* are filled with enough offbeat and last-minute events to fill a whole week. The *Tribune's* weekend guide, published with the Friday newspaper, has a listing of the city's bar and restaurants along with interesting participant sport events (would you like to swim with the Polar Bear Club in frozen Lake Michigan?). Besides newspapers in Polish, Korean, and Spanish, the city has a number of free neighborhood weekly newspapers keyed to particular areas; the best for arts and entertainment is the *Chicago Reader,* free on Thursday afternoons after 1 P.M. at 11 E. Illinois St. or any of 100 merchants downtown and north. The *Reader* can give the visitor insight into not just theater and music but city politics and personalities, all from a liberal perspective.

Chicago magazine is literally the taste of the town, sampling many restaurants at least once and usually twice a year. Business people can get the inside scoop from *Crain's Chicago Business,* the weekly journal *Newsweek* magazine called the "country's preeminent local business newspaper." For up-to-the-minute news and traffic reports, tune in 780 (WBBM-AM) on the radio. For weather forecasts, dial 976–1212; time is 976–1616.

Foreign Currency. Best bet for exchanging foreign money is any downtown bank (Mon.–Thurs., 9 A.M.–3 P.M., Fri. 9 A.M.–5 P.M.). O'Hare International Airport, International Terminal, 8 A.M.–8 P.M., 7 days a week, does not offer the best rate, nor do hotels, where guests may need to cash small amounts in an emergency.

SENIOR-CITIZEN DISCOUNTS. Discount doors open for senior citizens who bring along proof of age and a small photo. Reduced-fare transportation identification cards for those 65 and older are available at no charge from 400 centers around the city. Call 800–252–6060 for the closest center and hours. The price of bus and subway rides drops about half with the card, and commuter rail tickets offer half-off prices to seniors. Numerous museums and attractions (including first-run movies) offer reduced prices to seniors also.

HINTS TO DISABLED TRAVELERS. Chicago's various private and public agencies offer art, culture, and a helping hand to the disabled visitor. *Silent Sounds* is a nonprofit arts organization that brings arts to all people through sign language. Their schedule from Box 8205, Chicago, IL 60680 or 778–0910 or teletype 381–1640. Rehabilitation Institute of Chicago, 345 E. Superior St., Chicago, IL 60611 (908–6071) can also offer helpful information. So can *Access Living* (226–5900), a private nonprofit agency with knowledge of everything from transportation to emergency wheelchair repair. The city of Chicago sponsors a referral service through their *Information and Referral Service for Persons with Disability,* 121 N. La Salle, Room 703, Chicago, IL 60602 (City Hall) (744–4016). It maintains a list of independent-living centers and an access directory of Chicago T.D.D. number 744–6777. The Chicago Hearing Society also maintains a teletype line at 427–2166. *CAST (Chicagoland Advocates for Signed Theatre),* 22 W. Monroe, Suite 806, Chicago, IL 60603 (341–6823), advises travelers where to find theatre interpreted in sign language for the hearing impaired. T.D.D. number 341–6823. Chicago Transit Authority's *Special Service Department* (664–7200) can arrange pickup in special vehicles at airports and train stations. Minimal fee. Several days' notice required, call and request application forms.

FREE EVENTS. Everyone in Chicago loves a parade and a party. And it seems there's at least one neighborhood or ethnic festival underway anytime during the year, and they're all free. The city and the Chicago Park District sponsor the major free music festivals from June through September. For complete information on all events and neighborhood festivals check with the City of Chicago Department of Special Events (744–5000 for activities information and 744–3315 for other questions).

At Christmas time, go caroling to the animals at the Lincoln Park Zoo (see Zoos). The Museum of Science and Industry (see Museums) has a free **Christmas around the world** exhibit showing how nations usher in the Yuletide. In February, when the weather is at its worst, the azalea and camellia **flower shows** bloom at the Lincoln Park Conservatory (at Stockton Drive near Fullerton Avenue, open year-round, 9 A.M.–5 P.M., free) and the Garfield Park Conservatory (300 N. Central Park Blvd., 533–1281, free). **Saint Patrick's Day** in March turns the Chicago River green while politicians with Polish and Italian names walk down the freshly painted green stripe down State Street. The **International Festival of Flowers and Gardens** brightens Navy Pier in May.

During the first half of June, even though the weather is balmy, Chicago is singing its own song—the blues—at the **Chicago Blues Festival,** Petrillo Music Shell, named after the longtime head of the musicians union. Call 744–3315 for information and times. Grant Park (Balboa and Columbus Dr.), surrounding the Music Shell, also hosts Saturday night concerts ranging from classical and opera to Broadway show tunes and concerts with the Grant Park Symphony Orchestra (294–2420). The **Old Town Art Fair** closes off 10 blocks of neighborhood streets for the best of Chicago's painters, printmakers, potters, and weavers. The second half of June brings **Sculpture in the Park,** a "monumental" fair, Saturdays, in and around Lincoln Park from North Ave. to Diversey Pkwy. Permanent and special exhibits of nineteenth- and twentieth-century sculpture, along with oratory, dance, open-air theater, and music to celebrate the park. An annual *Gospel Festival* in mid-June features the country's gospel greats. The Fourth of July weekend starts off with a **Taste of Chicago** on Columbus Dr. behind the Art Institute of Chicago. Chicago's best restaurants move their famous recipes to Grant Park to offer pricey morsels before, during, and after a week's worth of rock and folk concerts. Massive eyeball-to-eyeball crowds, long lines, and underage drinking have presented problems. The traditional **4th of July fireworks** and concert (featuring the *1812 Overture*) takes place on July 3. In mid-July, the skies over the lakeshore fill with aerial displays for the **Air and Water Show** (744–3315).

When mid-August brings steamy weather, spend the afternoon along the cool lakeshore flying a kite at the **Chinatown Summer Fair and Kite-Flying Contest** (744–3315). There's free bus service from Grant Park to Chinatown (22d and Wentworth) for food, live music, and lion dancers. The Field Museum opens its doors for a look at China's ancestral artifacts. People come from Wisconsin and Indiana for Chicago's oldest festival, **Venetian Nights** (744–3315). Free symphony and jazz concerts start in the afternoon at Petrillo Music Shell. At dusk, pick a spot on the grass along the lakeshore at Monroe St. to watch the city's parade of boats and floats.

When the temperature gets really hot, Chicago gets downright cool—5 nights of free concerts during the **Chicago Jazz Festival** (744–3315) in late August to early Sept. at the Petrillo Music Shell. The first Monday in Sept. brings the **Labor Day** concert in Grant Park, preceded by the Labor Day Parade down Michigan Ave. In mid-September, the late Mayor Daley's tribute to the city's diverse ethnic population gets under way at Donnelly Hall (Navy Pier) with the **International Folk Fair** (744–3315).

TOURS AND SPECIAL-INTEREST SIGHTSEEING. Chicago and nearby areas of interest are covered in tours offered by *Gray Line of Chicago,* 33 E. Monroe (346–9506) and *American Sightseeing Tours,* 530 S. Michigan Ave. (427–3100). Everything from Chinatown to plush suburbs and after-dark destinations. A large variety of half-day and full-day tours are offered year-round.

To get above the neighborhood sights for a big picture, try the world's tallest building at the **Sears Sky Deck,** 233 S. Wacker Dr. (875–9696), 9 A.M.–midnight, 7 days a week, for $3.75 ($2.50 for senior citizens) or the slightly shorter **John Hancock Center Observatory,** 875 N. Michigan (751–3681), for $3.50 adults, $2 seniors.

Both **Wendella Sightseeing Boats,** Michigan Ave. at Wacker Dr., Chicago, IL 60601 (337–1446), and **Mercury Sightseeing Boats,** Michigan at Wacker Dr., Chicago, IL 60601 (332–1353), leave on 1-, 1½-, and 2-hour cruises from beneath the Michigan Avenue Bridge at the Chicago River. In addition to a short cruise up (westward) the Chicago River, the ride takes the visitor through the locks at the river's mouth and out for a panoramic view. Prices begin at $5, with a $8 2-hour evening cruise. Reduced prices for children. Rides begin at 10 A.M.; call for schedules. **Shoreline Marine Sightseeing** offers numerous 1-hour lake cruises from 3 locations: Call 673–3399 for more information. The S.S. *Clipper,* now docked at Navy Pier, was built in 1905 to cruise the Great Lakes. Open May–Oct. for tours, cocktails, snacks. Call 329–1800 for information.

Year-round, the **Chicago Architecture Foundation,** 1800 S. Prairie, Chicago, IL 60616 (782–1776), offers at least four walking tours of 1 to 2 hours, showing off Chicago and Oak Park's wood and brick past and illuminating such names as Frank Lloyd Wright, Mies van der Rohe, and Louis Sullivan. Tours leave from various locations downtown and in Oak Park.

Railroad and sociology buffs can walk around America's first company town, **Pullman,** on 90-minute guided tours, the first Sunday of the month, May through Oct., for $3.50; student and senior discounts. Information at 1111 S. Forestville, Chicago, IL 60628 (785–8181). Or call the **20th-Century Railroad Club,** 509 W. Roosevelt Rd., Chicago, IL 60607 (829–4500), and arrange for a stop at their free library right in the Amtrak yards. By appointment.

PARKS AND GARDENS. Chicago overflows with more than 600 parks, including 8 verdant lakeshore expanses serving as summer resorts and winter playgrounds. Park hours are 6 A.M.–11 P.M. unless there is a special program.

Lincoln Park (294–4750), the largest park, extends from 5800 North to the Near North Side. In balmy months, joggers, bike riders, strollers, and picnickers populate the 20 miles coursing through Lincoln Park. There are innumerable paths, some crisscrossing at statues of Shakespeare, Goethe, and of course Abraham Lincoln. Some paths lead to attractions such as the Lincoln Park Zoo, a small farm, tennis courts, horseshoe pits, an archery and skeet range, an outdoor theater, baseball fields, golf courses, small boat harbors, and lagoons. The park also hosts three of the city's nicest gardens. The *Grandmother's Garden,* between Stockton Drive and Lincoln Park West, dates back to 1893 with old-fashioned flowers. The *Lincoln Park Conservatory* (294–4770) is a 3-acre Victorian masterpiece overflowing with tropical plants. A formal flower garden to the south surrounds Bates Fountain and the entrance to the Lincoln Park Zoo.

One neighborhood park of interest is **Oz Park** (787–3274) in the Lincoln Park neighborhood (2100 North). Author L. Frank Baum (1856–1919) lived in Chicago, and residents renamed the hilly, blocklong gathering place after his most famous novel, *The Wizard of Oz.*

Grant Park (294–2493), although missing a statue of General Ulysses S. Grant (it's in Lincoln Park), provides a grand respite along the lake just east of the Loop between Randolph St. and Roosevelt Rd. on the south. In addition to the city's largest public parking garage (underground), a yacht club, hidden tennis courts, and some fine gardens, Grant Park shelters some of the city's great showcases: the Buckingham Fountain, the Petrillo Music Shell at the south end of the park, the Monroe Street Harbor along the lake, the Field Museum, the Adler Planetarium, the Shedd Aquarium, and the Art Institute of Chicago.

Slightly west of the Loop is the 4.5-acre **Garfield Park Conservatory,** 300 N. Central Park Blvd., the world's largest conservatory under one roof. In addition to a 175,000 sq. ft. formal garden, the conservatory features a special garden for the blind. The Garfield Park Conservatory (3600 West, 300 North), is open daily 9 A.M.–5 P.M., free (533–1281). Later hours during special shows.

Burnham Park bridges Grant and the South Side's Jackson Park and the smaller Washington Park. Burnham was the site of the 1932–33 Century of Progress Exposition, a world's fair that left behind Soldier Field, home of the Chicago Bears. Farther south, starting at 5600 South, is **Jackson Park** (643–6363), site of the grand Columbian Exposition of 1893 and current home of the Museum of Science and Industry. Southwest of the lakeshore is the **Marquette Park Rose Garden,** sporting 4,000 fragrant beauties at 3540 W. 71st. Like parks in so many places of the world, most of these are best enjoyed in the daylight. It is not wise to wander around in them after dark.

ZOOS. Winter or summer, the **Lincoln Park Zoo,** 2200 N. Cannon Dr. (294–4660), is a favorite place for city kids. In addition to reptile, lion, small mammal, and ape houses, a baby animal nursery, and a petting zoo, there are outside natural environments. A favorite year-round is the polar bears' pond and seals' domain at the Lincoln Park entrance. An excellent place for lunch and picnicking. The 35-acre zoo also has a *Farm in the Zoo* where kids can pet cows, sheep, horses, and the other barnyard favorites. The Zoo Rookery is home to migrating birds and its own flock of North American ducks. Free; open year-round, 9 A.M.–5 P.M.

PARTICIPANT SPORTS. There are more than 20 miles of **jogging** paths along the lakeshore, from 5600 North to the Near South Side. There's plenty of company on the paths leading from the woods to the lakeshore. Between Fullerton and Belmont avenues there are wooden exercise spots, with advice to the runner and a 7-mile measured course. Be especially careful crossing streets at main intersections such as Fullerton Ave. There are plentiful water fountains during the summer months. In October, there's an increasingly competitive marathon, taking 12,000 runners through the Loop and Chicago neighborhoods. Write America's Marathon–Chicago, 223 W. Erie, Chicago, IL 60601 for information, or call 951–0660.

Tennis. There are outdoor public courts, open dawn–dusk, 7 days a week, literally anywhere there's a Chicago Park District park. Some charge nominal daily or hourly fees ($2 to $5); some are lighted at night. Get a court first thing in the morning or expect at least a 2-hour wait during the peak summer playing times. Oz Park, 2100 N. Burling, has free courts. The Daley Bicentennial Plaza, Randolph and Lake Shore Drive (294–4792), has 12 courts at $5 an hour; Reservations required. The Grant Park Tennis Courts, 9th and Columbus Drive (294–2307), at $2 a day, are downtown favorites. No reservations are necessary. *McFeteridge Sports Complex,* 3845 N. California (478–0210), has indoor courts. Open 7 A.M.–11 P.M. Weekdays, $6 an hour; nights and weekends, $13.

Bicycling. The lakefront offers 20-plus miles of well-marked bicycle paths. Although a determined cycler can peddle into the northern suburbs, be advised that the bicycle paths detour off the heavily trafficked and dangerous Sheridan Road. Bicycles can be rented in Lincoln Park at the intersection of Fullerton Ave. and Cannon Drive. $4 for the first hour, $3 for each additional hour; $25 deposit. Open 10 A.M., with last rental at 4:30 P.M. and return by 6:30 P.M. Season May–Labor Day, weekends in Apr., Sept., and Oct., and Mar., weather permitting. 935–6700.

Swimming. Chicago is blessed with wide sand beaches sloping gently into the chilly, fresh waters of Lake Michigan (60 to 70 degrees Fahrenheit at summer's peak). Hours are 9 A.M.–9:30 P.M. Lifeguards are on duty from Memorial Day to Labor Day. The most popular beach is the Oak Street Beach near the Gold Coast hotels and the North Avenue beaches (stretching to Fullerton Ave.). There are concession stands along the beachfront, picnic tables, grills at some beaches, and changing rooms at the North Avenue beach. The Chicago Park District's beach information number is 294–2333. Scuba diving, rafts, and even Frisbees are prohibited. Police also frown on the consumption of alcoholic beverages.

Fishing. Perch and Coho salmon are as abundant as the fishermen off the breakwaters at Farwell Ave. (6900 North), Montrose Ave. (4400 North), North Ave. (1600 North), 31st St. (3100 South), 59th St. (5900 South), and 63d St. (6300 South). Check with the Illinois Department of Conservation (917–2070) for license fees and seasons or the Chicago Sportfishing Association (922–1100) for the latest conditions. A word of warning: Lake Michigan often displays the temperament of the inland sea it is. Never venture out in a boat before checking weather predictions; sudden squalls are not uncommon. Call 298–1413 for extended forecast covering Lake Michigan wave and weather conditions.

Golf. The city has five, nine-hole golf courses ($4, Mon.–Fri.; $4.50 on weekends) with the *Waveland Golf Course* closest to the Loop (off Lake Shore Drive—Outer Drive—at 4000 N. Irving Park Rd.). The only 18-hole course is *Jackson Park* (E. 63d and Bennett, 493–1455, $6 during the week, $6.50 on weekends and $4 after 4 P.M.). You can easily get on all courses during the week but expect a four-hour wait on weekends without reserved times. For duffers unwilling to jaunt out to the links to make reservations, Ticketron (842–5387) sells reserved times ($2.25 service charge). For information on all courses call 294–2274.

Ice skating. *Waveland Field* has rentals, a warming house, and food in the winter. Off Lake Shore Drive (Outer Drive) at Irving Park Road (4000 North). Also McFeteridge Sports Complex, 3845 N. California, 478–0210, for indoor. Free skating 4–5:30 P.M., Wed.–Sun. Skate rental, $2.

Winter activities. Cross-country skiing and sledding are popular because there are no large hills in Chicago; riders of $30 Rosebud sleds or cardboard boxes and cross-country skiers make use of every incline. Lincoln Park at 2600 N. Wrightwood has one small hill, and there's a huge incline called Cricket's Hill in Lincoln Park farther north, between Montrose and Wilson avenues. Ski trails follow Lincoln Park's paths. Rent skis in Lincoln Park at the intersection of Fullerton Avenue and Cannon Drive. Winter hours vary.

Kite Flying. Even in the dead of winter, informal kite-flying clubs congregate at Cricket Hill in Lincoln Park between Montrose and Wilson avenues.

SPECTATOR SPORTS. The Chicago Bears play **football** at Soldier Field Sept. to Dec. Tickets are usually available (663–5408). There's college football at Northwestern University's Dyche Stadium in Evanston (491–7070). For **baseball** fans, the Chicago Cubs of the National League play daytime games only (because there are no lights) at Wrigley Field, 1060 W. Addison at N. Clark streets, Apr. through Oct. Unreserved bleacher seats are $4 (281–5050). The American League is represented on the South Side by the Chicago White Sox at Comiskey Park, 35th and Shields, off the Dan Ryan Expressway (924–1000). There are two NCAA college **basketball** teams to watch: Loyola, 274–3000, which plays on the North Side and DePaul, 341–8010, which plays at Rosemont Horizon Center, just a few minutes from O'Hare International Airport. In addition, the pro Chicago Bulls, playing Jan. through Apr. games at the Chicago Stadium, 1800 W. Madison (943–5800). **Hockey** is represented by the Chicago Blackhawks, also at the Chicago Stadium (733–5300); game time is 7:30 P.M.

CHILDREN'S ACTIVITIES. Kids' distractions that are free or have only a nominal ($2) cost include the following: The Art Institute Junior Museum, Michigan and Adams (443–3680), features do-together activities for parents and children. The Lincoln Park Zoo, 2200 N. Cannon Drive (294–4660), has a petting zoo and baby animals. The Chicago Public Library sponsors Puppets in the Park with a puppet show, games, and songs in Grant Park, Michigan at Washington (346–3278). The library's Cultural Center (78 E. Washington), features storytellers and exhibits for smaller folk Sat. at 11 A.M. For $3, Second City, 1616 N. Wells St. (929–6288), presents a children's show Sun. at 2:30 P.M. A mini-museum saying "please touch" can be found at the Field Museum of Natural History at Lake Shore Drive and Roosevelt Rd. (12th St.); weekdays, 1–3; Sat., 10 to noon; Sun., 1–3. Free admission to museum on Thurs.; normally $1 (922–9410). There's a children's show at the Adler Planetarium's Sky Show, 1300 S. Lake Shore Drive (322–0300), at 10 A.M. Sat. as kids under 6 are not normally allowed in; $1.50.

If you must have a **baby-sitter,** the American Registry of Nurses and Babysitters, 3921 N. Lincoln (248–8100), comes highly recommended and costly; $5 an hour, 4-hour minimum. Sitters are bonded and licensed.

HISTORIC SITES AND HOUSES. The city is awash in historic local and national landmarks. Many "interesting" buildings have informative plaques mounted by neighborhood associations, the city, or the National Society for Historic Preservation.

Probably nowhere else is the feeling of Chicago's many generations of immigrants more keenly represented than at **Hull House,** Jane Addams's social settlement house on the campus of the University of Illinois at Chicago, 800 S. Halsted St. (413–5353). Open Mon.–Fri. 10 A.M.–4 P.M. and Sun. at noon in the summer.

The Great Chicago Fire of 1871 left just a few buildings. Mrs. O'Leary's cow started the blaze by kicking over a lantern, or so the fable goes, at the scene of today's **Chicago Fire Department Academy,** at 558 W. DeKoven, on the near South Side. You can start your look at Chicago sights at the **Water Tower** at Michigan and Chicago avenues, one of the few structures to survive the inferno. It's also the Chicago Visitors Center. Across the street is the historic **pumping station** which today brings water into the city from Lake Michigan. Admission to the "*Here's Chicago*" show at the pumping station is $4.75 for adults, $3 for seniors and $2 kids; Family admission $10. Hours vary; tel. 467–7114.

Fort Dearborn, the original location of Chicago dating back to the 1700s, is depicted on bronze plaques on the bridge towers and sidewalks south of the Michigan Avenue Bridge at the Chicago River. To get a fuller history, stop by the **Chicago Historical Society,** Clark St. and North Ave. (642–4600), where there are exhibits on Chicago pioneer life, the Great Fire, Indians of Chicago and Illinois, and Abraham Lincoln. Mon.–Sat., 9:30 A.M.–4:30 P.M.; Sun., noon–5 P.M. Adults $1.50; children, 50 cents. Free on Mon. With its impressive Tiffany glass domes, grand staircases, and nineteenth-century Italian Renaissance palazzo, the **Chicago Public Library,** 78 E. Washington Blvd., at Michigan Ave. (269–2820) is a must-see. Mon.–Thurs., 9 A.M.–7 P.M.; Fri. until 6; Sat. until 5.

Prairie Avenue Historic District. Guided tours are available by the Chicago Architectural Foundation, 1800 S. Prairie (782–1776), through the 35-room Romanesque *Glessner House* and the *Widow Clarke House.* These are the surviving homes of the great opulence Chicago enjoyed as a "prairie" commercial center in the 1800s. Daily tours in winter and summer.

MUSEUMS AND GALLERIES. From peace to Picasso, African to Polish, impressionist to Oriental, the city's cultural, educational, and scientific communities maintain a wealth of free museums and galleries of world class. The listing is arranged here according to the days for which admission is free (regular admission is also listed).

Always Free

Adler Planetarium. 1300 S. Lake Shore Drive (322–0304). Located on a spit of land called Northerly Island Park on the lakefront. Antique astronomical items and space-age hardware mingle in this museum and working observatory. Mon.–Thurs., 9:30–4:30; Fri., 9:30–9; Sat., Sun., and holidays, 9:30–5. The sky show, a precursor to Star Wars, is $2.50, $1.50 for children over 6 (under 6 not permitted in the sky show). Christmas and holiday shows. Public meter parking.

International Museum of Surgical Sciences. 1542 N. Lake Shore Dr. (642–3555). Medicine from prehistoric times to the present; Indian medicine man's hat and healing herbs. Located in two impressive Lake Shore Drive mansions. Open Tues.–Sat., 10–4, Sun., 11–5. No parking nearby.

Museum of Science and Industry. Jackson Park at 57th St. (684–1414). As the name implies, this is a push-button and high-tech museum with most exhibits sponsored by Chicago or area companies in what was the Palace of Fine Arts during the 1893 Columbian Exposition. Many hands-on features plus the always popular World War II German submarine the U-505 and the coal mine, a simulated ride down into a mile-deep mine shaft. Special exhibits during the year; city favorite is Christmas Around the World with decorated trees, native dress, and traditions from around the world. Permanent collections include antique and space-age cars and a walk through a nineteenth-century street. Newly opened Space Center and Omnimax Theater. Restaurants and gift shops. Free parking. Open daily 9:30–5:30 in summer and 9:30–4 in winter.

Oriental Institute. University of Chicago, E. 58th St. and S. University Ave. (702–9521). Ancient history from 500 B.C. lives again in free tours (call for reservations); always free film on ancient civilizations. Pieces of the Dead Sea Scrolls and artifacts from archaeological digs in Egypt, Persia, Syria, Mesopotamia, Memphis, and Thebes. Tues.–Sat., 10–4; Sunday, noon–4.

Polish Museum of America. 984 N. Milwaukee (384–3352). Open noon–5 daily. Stained glass and paintings by Polish and American artists. Library and archives.

Ukrainian Institute of Modern Art. 2247 W. Chicago Ave. (227–5522). Tues.–Sun., noon to 4. Permanent collection of twentieth-century Ukrainian art, folk life, wood carving, national customs, and hand-decorated eggs.

Free on Mondays

Chicago Academy of Sciences. 2001 N. Clark (549–0606). Open daily 10–5. Oldest science museum in the Midwest features the natural history of the Midwest and current plant and animal ecology. Winter lecture series on Tues. and field trips to nearby Indiana dunes and state parks. Emphasis on children's exhibits. Normally $1 for adults, 50 cents for kids and seniors.

Free on Tuesdays

Art Institute. In the Loop at Michigan at Adams (443–3500). Also home of Art Institute School. Mon.–Fri., 10:30–4:30; Tues. until 8; Sat., 10–5, Sun. and holidays, noon–5. Stunning, world-renowned impressionist collection, Renaissance oils, Thorne miniature rooms, children's museum; garden restaurant, and gift shops. Permanent collection of works by masters such as Monet and Picasso, plus *American Gothic* by Grant Wood, Oriental art, sculpture, decorative arts, textiles, photography, primitives, Chinese pottery, windows by Marc Chagall. Daily free tours and lectures. Special exhibits are not free. Suggested donation is $4.50 for adults, $2.25 for seniors and kids. Parking at public meters on adjacent streets or in the underground city lot.

Museum of Contemporary Art. 237 E. Ontario (280–2660). Chicago artists' rooms and contemporary art exhibits from around the world; dance, theater, video library, music, German expressionism. Tues.–Sat., 10–5; Sun., noon–5. Gift shop. Normally $3 for adults, $2 for seniors and kids.

Free on Thursday

Du Sable Museum of African American Art. 740 E. 56th St. (947–0600). Mon.–Fri., 9–5; Sat.–Sun., 1–5. In February, this is a center of special exhibits for Black History Month. African and American art, African masks, photographs, library on Midwestern blacks, and documents pertaining to black history. Normally $2 adults, 50¢ seniors and children.

Field Museum of Natural History. Grant Park at 12th St. (922–9410). Daily, 9–5. Largest collection of natural history exhibits in the world, housed at the 1893 Columbian Exposition site. Huge dinosaurs and the 550-lb. stuffed gorilla Bushman (in life a longtime favorite at the Lincoln Park Zoo) to the smallest diamonds and precious stones make this an awesome spectacle. Excellent, lifelike exhibits on American Indian, Chinese, and Tibetan cultures. Normally $2 for adults, $1 for kids, 50 cents for seniors; family rate is $4. Restaurant and gift shop. Much free and public metered parking.

John Shedd Aquarium. Lake Shore Dr. at 12th St., across from Field Museum of Natural History (939–2438). Summer daily 9–5; other months vary. Adults, $2; children, $1; seniors, 50 cents. Special exhibits and regular population of 7,000 fish of more than 777 species. The 90,000-gallon Coral Reef, where divers feed the competitive (especially the tortoises) inhabitants daily at 11 and 2, is no goldfish bowl. Gift shop.

Free on Friday

Spertus Museum of Judaica. 618 S. Michigan Ave. (922–9012). Mon.–Thurs., 10–5; Fri., 10–3; Sun., 10–4. Seniors and students, $2; adults, $3.50. Modern art exhibits mixed with large private collection of Jewish artifacts, manuscripts, and ceremonial objects. Gift shop.

Always an Admission Fee

Balzekas Museum of Lithuanian Culture. 6500 S. Pulaski (582–6500). Daily, 10–4. Adults, $2; kids and seniors, $1.50. First Lithuanian museum in America; rare amber and armor, medieval weapons, household and farm items.

Peace Museum. 430 W. Erie (440–1860). Tues., Wed., Fri., and Sun., noon–5; Thurs., noon–8. Adults, $2; for children and seniors, 50 cents. Visual and performing arts examining the issues of war; photographic and textile exhibits.

ARTS AND ENTERTAINMENT. Films. With first-show-daily and weekend discounts (often half price), first-run films and even revivals are easily affordable. Neighborhood theaters cost as little as $1.75 for first-runs. The gilt-edged **Chicago Theater,** 175 N. State St. (236–4300), has undergone historic preservation and is definitely worth a visit. This dazzling collection of pillars and statuary is part Versailles, part Roman bath, and part Greek temple. Celebrities like Liza Minnelli, Red Skelton, and Frank Sinatra regularly appear on its opulent stage. November is **Chicago International Film Festival** month. The main revival house is the *Three Penny,* 2424 N. Lincoln (281–7200); neighborhood and street parking. Foreign and art films usually are shown at the famous *Biograph Theaters,* where John Dillinger met a fatal fusilade of gunfire, 2433 N. Lincoln (348–4123), with neighborhood and street parking; the *Fine Arts,* 418 S. Michigan (939–3700), parking at Grant Park underground; and the *Music Box,* 3733 N. Southport (871–6604), neighborhood and street parking.

The real gem of neighborhood theaters that feature $2-and-under seats on a regular basis is the *Davis,* 4614 N. Lincoln Ave. (784–0894), neighborhood parking. The theater's interior is a painted Italian village with small loges and twinkling stars overhead that make you wish they'd leave the lights on during the performance. Other off-price theaters are the *Lake Shore,* 3175 N. Broadway (327–4114), pay parking lot nearby and some street parking and the *Village,* Clark and North Ave. (642–2403), self-park pay lot nearby.

There are seven first-run theaters at the pricey Water Tower complex, 845 N. Michigan (649–5790), reduced-price yet expensive parking; and four screens at the *Chestnut Station,* a former post office, 830 N. Clark (337–7301), limited street parking.

Music. Whether it's the mournful blues, folk, or lyric opera, it beats here. Starting with the grand: *Chicago Symphony Orchestra* under the baton of Sir Georg Solti in the fall and winter at Orchestra Hall, 220 S. Michigan (435–8122); tickets $12 to $38. The symphony's string quartet breaks off for free concerts at the Public Library Cultural Center during the year (346–3278). The *Lyric Opera of Chicago,* 20 N. Wacker Dr. (346–0270), has a fall through New Year season of world-famous performers and, alas, one of the highest subscription rates. Single, upper balcony tickets are about $10. For a variety of classical and pop concerts, check with the *Auditorium Theater,* 70 E. Congress (922–2110), a gilt and granite fortress with unmatched acoustics.

Radio stations in Chicago cater to those aficionados who can't make the jazz and blues club dates. The best of local and top performers (including most of the Chicago Jazz Festival—see Free Events) are played on the city's three main jazz stations. For night owls, tune to WBEZ (FM 91.5) from 8 P.M.–5 A.M. (WBEZ is also the National Public Radio station in the city.) On the city's South Side is the all-jazz WBEE (AM 1570). Since WBEE is a low power, dawn to dusk station, it's heard mainly on the South Side. Northwestern University's WNUR (FM 89.3) features jazz, blues, and alternative rock but it's heard best only on the city's North Side.

Dance. The *Auditorium Theater,* 70 E. Congress (922–2110), has its share of visiting dance companies (Twyla Tharp). The downstairs show district's major attraction (with diversity and price) is the *Mo Ming Dance and Arts Center,* 1034 W. Barry (472–9894), which showcases Chicago artists and visiting ensembles. Resident companies without permanent homes include the *Gus Giordano Dance Company* (866–9442), and the ascending *Hubbard Street Dance Theater,* 218 S. Wabash (663–0853). (See Discount Tickets below.)

Stage. You'll find "names" and New York productions downtown at the remaining "Broadway" stage, the *Schubert,* 22 W. Monroe St., Chicago, IL 60603 (977–1700). Wed., Sat., and Sun. matinees. Blackstone, 636 S. Michigan (977–1700). Operating year-round is the Goodman Theater at the Art Institute's east entrance, 200 S. Columbus Dr. (443–3800). Excellent children's and American debut theater offering a fine package dinner and show. The Arie Crown Theater, at McCormick Place, 23d and the lake (791–6190), hosts a few Broadway shows during the year; underground city parking.

Don't miss Chicago's biting satire **Second City,** 1616 N. Wells (337–3992), lot parking, the original improvisational stage that brought out the late John Belushi, Mike Nichols, Elaine May, and Alan Arkin. If you're taking in Old Town and Wells St. on Tues., Thurs., or Sun. night, drop by at 11 P.M. for the free show; Sat. at 1 A.M.

The "off Loop" stage outshines and outprices (generally, $5 to $12.50) the Loop legit productions. Shakespeare is on some stage at all times, and famous Chicago playwrights (Pulitzer-Prize winner David Mamet) and unknown authors and actors keep the seats full. The city's best deal (free performance and usually front row center seats) is volunteering to usher. Call the day before and ask to usher; it's painless, fun, and well worth the $20 ticket saved. Neighborhood stages include the **Apollo Theater,** 2540 N. Lincoln (935–6100), neighborhood parking; **Steppenwolf,** 2851 N. Halsted (472–4141); **Wisdom Bridge,** 1559 W. Howard Street—Rogers Park (743–6442); **Victory Gardens** and **The Body Politic,** both at 2257 N. Lincoln Ave. (871–3000); **Absolute Theater Company,** first look at foreign works, Theater Building, 1225 W. Belmont (327–5252); **Court Theatre,** varied, University of Chicago, 5535 S. Ellis (753–4472); the **Organic Theater Co.,** new works, 3319 N. Clark (327–5588); and the **Chicago Theater Company,** varied, 500 E. 67th St. (493–1305). **Curtain Call** offers 24-hour information on performance schedules. Call 977–1755.

Discount Tickets. If the prospect of $20 tickets frightens you but $10 seems palatable for an evening or afternoon of theater, music, or dance at more than 40 theaters, half-price tickets for cash only are available at 11 A.M. the morning of a production through **Hot Tix,** 24 S. State St., Mon., noon–6; Tues.–Fri., 10–6; Sat., 10–5; locations in Oak Park and Evanston. Hot Tix also sells full-price advance seats. Call 977–1755 for 24-hour theater information, availability, prices, and times. You can charge full-price, advance-sale tickets on VISA, MasterCard, and American Express for a $1.65–$3 fee through **Theater Tix,** 10 A.M.–8 P.M. (853–0505).

SHOPPING. Chicago is the mail-order capital, what with Sears Roebuck & Co., Montgomery Ward & Co., Spiegel, and a host of smaller companies sending merchandise literally around the world. When it comes to bargains, Chicago has its share. Sales tax is 8 percent on all items except food and drugs.

Chicago has a good community of off-price and discount stores, including the now-sexy *Spiegel, Inc.,* fourth largest U.S. catalog retailer. The Chicago catalog outlet store, 1105 W. 35th near S. Ashland (890–9690), has designer-label men's, women's, and children's clothing at 40 to 60 percent off the store rack prices. Labels include Liz Claiborne, Vittadini, Norma Kamali, Laura Ashley home furnishings, Cardin, and Blass. *Chernin's Shoes,* 606 W. Roosevelt Rd. (922–4545), 9 A.M.–6 P.M. daily, has brand-name sport and dress footwear (9 West, Bally, Ferragamo, Adidas, and Nike) for 20 to 50 percent off. For the Ivy League boating or outdoor crowd, look into the *Land's End Outlet Store* for clothing overstocks, returned merchandise, and discontinued items at 10 to 60 percent off; it's located at 2241 N. Elston (276–2232). *Sears Catalog Supplies* at 5555 S. Archer (284–3200) offers surplus merchandise at 20 to 80 percent savings. *Clothing Clearance Center,* 1006 S. Michigan (663–4170), has men's designer suits at substantial savings. *Crate & Barrel Outlet,* 1510 N. Wells (787–4775), Mon., 10–7; Tues.–Sat., 10–6; Sun., noon–5, has a regular stock of closeouts and seconds on china, glassware, sheets, Marimekko, and gourmet items at 20 to 80 percent off. If the children become unbearable, take them to *Cut Rate Toys,* 2424 W. Devon (743–3822). *Obryan Bros.,* 4220 W. Belmont (283–3000), sells overstock and irregular nightgowns and lingerie.

For sheer city atmosphere, stop by *Maxwell Street* (20th and S. Halsted) market, where peddlers and hawkers "cheat you fair." It's an often unvisited four-block open market selling every type of merchandise from sunup to around 5 P.M. on Sat.

and Sun. Maxwell St. has a predominance of tires, automobile accessories, and tools, but the astute shopper can find bargains on books, clothing, an occasional antique, and general bric-a-brac. Expect high-pressure salesmen.

Heading the list of any shopping experience here is *Marshall Field & Company,* a prestige store synonymous with shopping in Chicago.

DINING OUT. Twenty-five years ago, when the Union Stock Yards were in full operation, Chicago was strictly a meat and potatoes town. When the center of beef packing moved west, Chicago's rich ethnic mix filled the gastronomic void, offering diverse and reasonable places for everything from deep-dish Chicago-style pizza to Polish or Ethiopian food. But if sushi or chimichangas aren't your plat du jour, you can still get that 2-inch steak. As in many cities, restaurants come and go. Even the best eatery has a bad night, but the following recommendations are known for their overall quality and consistent value. *Chicago* magazine is a good guide to what's in with its frequent tastings.

Restaurants come in all price ranges, but for this edition we've broken down three-course dining (appetizer, main course, and dessert—no tax, tip, or drinks) as follows: *Reasonable,* $16 to $20; *Very Economical,* $7 to $15; and *Low Budget,* $6 and under. It is not necessarily true that, just because a restaurant is listed as *Low Budget,* the service or the ambience is cheap (see Ed Debevic's). The tax on meals eaten in a restaurant or carried out is 8 percent. Unless indicated, all restaurants take at least traveler's checks, MasterCard, VISA, and American Express.

Reasonable

The Berghoff. 17 W. Adams (427–3170). Excellent German food makes this a Chicago institution. In addition to mandatory Wiener schnitzel and kassler rippschen, there's a complete menu with grilled meats, fresh and grilled seafood, and desserts of tortes, strudels, and Black Forest cake. Open since 1898.

Courtyards of Plaka. 340 S. Halsted St. (263–0767). Informality and hospitality are the charm of this unpretentious restaurant in the heart of Greek Town. All the usual Greek favorites plus some unusual selections.

L'Escargot. In the Allerton Hotel, 701 N. Michigan (337–1717). Bright and warm French. Friendly service and imaginative seasonal lunches or dinners for $20. Soups, casseroles, and desserts are the real standouts. Special menus for early and late diners. Fixed price Sunday brunch 11:30 A.M.–2 P.M., $16.50.

Santa Fe Cafe. 800 N. Dearborn Parkway (944–5722). This corner, fast-food restaurant is an example of Southwest-style cooking at its best and cheapest. Slabs of tangy barbecued ribs, meaty chili, grilled chicken.

Three Happiness No. 1. 209 W. Cermak, in Chinatown (842–1964). No credit cards. This is the original of Chicago's two Three Happiness restaurants. The mediocre fifties formica tables and chairs mislead the diner; the fabulous smells overcome the decor. Portions are fair sized. Chinese favorites are winter melon soup with pork strips, steaming pike; for lunch, an excellent *dim sum* is served from 9 A.M. to 2 P.M.

Very Economical

Ann Sather's. 929 W. Belmont (348–2378). Unpretentious, reliable restaurant, with limited selections but top-notch Swedish fare. Delicious fruit soup, Swedish meatballs, thin pancakes with tart lingonberry sauce.

Army & Lou's Soul Food. 422 E. 75th St. off King Dr. (483–6550). This landmark of the South Side will feed a family of three breakfast for under $15 and four people dinner for $25. Sunday morning breakfasts are a South Side tradition, starting at 9 A.M.

Catfish Digby's. 68 E. Cermak (842–7142). Just east of Chinatown and south of the Loop, this combination take-out and sit-down restaurant is an introduction to catfish chips or nuggets, with a dessert of peach cobbler, for $3.99.

Little Bucharest. 3001 N. Ashland (929–8640). Reservations suggested. A small Romanian restaurant behind a neighborhood bar. Roast duck and orange sauce, goulash like braised beef, stuffed peppers, and fried pork chops come with plenty of vegetables and dumplings to make this dinner almost too much to eat. Desserts are breathtaking multilayered masterpieces of walnut and chocolate.

Pizzeria Uno. 29 E. Ohio (321–1000). There's no stuffed or thin-crust pizza here. It's strictly thick, deep-dish Chicago-style pizza with real tomato and pieces of spicy sausage and cheese on slices that make a meal. Drinks come in pitchers, if necessary. Worth the wait. Limited to pizza, salads, and sandwiches. (Sister restaurant **Pizzeria Duo,** a block away at 619 N. Wabash; 943–2400.)

Rio's. 4611 N. Kedzie Ave. (588–7800). The only restaurant in Chicago specializing in the foods and wines of Portugal. Simple storefront setting, but nicely decorated; live entertainment weekends.

Schuliens. 2100 W. Irving Park Rd. (478–2100). This German restaurant has been in business for generations and was a speakeasy during Prohibition. Things are quieter now, but the Wienerschnitzel remains the same. Bartenders perform magic tricks and there are also guest magicians.

Low Budget

Athenian Room. 807 W. Webster (348–5155). No cards. This neighborhood lunch spot is packed by dinner; it is the place for lean gyros with garlicky yoghurt or spicy red sauce (red wine and barbeque combination), Greek lemon chicken, and souvlaki. Thick fries and Greek salads with oregano.

Bar Double R Ranch. 57 W. Randolph (263–8207). Gallons of every type of chili imaginable, plus Billy the Kid pork chops, served to live country and western music.

Ed Debevic's. 640 N. Wells (664–1707). No cards. Very trendy 1950s motif. You'll wonder why attendants are parking your car at this diner gone deluxe. Hot meat loaf, chicken fried steak, roast turkey, and other $5.25 and under platters come with potatoes, gravy and vegetables, bread, butter, and soup or slaw. Full roadside menu just like diners of yore. Simple American delicacies such as real chocolate pudding pie and homemade soups.

La Cocina Mexicana. 948 W. Webster (525–9793). No cards. So neighborhood that it's indistinguishable from the cleaners next door. Fewer than 10 tables. Chicken flautas, liver, and even the humble tacos and tostadas are memorable at one of the city's most low-key, consistently good, and low-priced Mexican restaurants.

Recommended Splurge. The Empire Room. Palmer House Hotel, State and Monroe (726–7500). This gilded beauty looks like a transplant from the Palace at Versailles and is a surprise setting for a live jazz brunch every Sunday between 11 A.M. and 2 P.M. $19.95 covers a complete brunch with hot and cold appetizers, such warm entrees as eggs Benedict, lavish desserts, and a glass of champagne. Daily lunch Mon.–Fri. from 11 A.M. to 2:30 P.M. One of Chicago's most beautiful rooms.

NIGHTLIFE AND BARS. Chicago swings through the dawn. Some bars serve the last round at 4 A.M. Many clubs have the musicians break, serve breakfast, and get on with the next jam. There's disco (still) on the South Side, along with the finest blues clubs in America. Out by Midway Airport there's a polka hall called the Baby Doll. The Loop is a beehive of bars, but it generally closes by 8 P.M. when the office crowd leaves. On N. Michigan Ave., the grand hotels offer subdued nightlife, while a block west, Rush St. and Division St. sizzle with the hustle of the singles crowd. Wells St. in Old Town attracts the local after-theater crowd, and N. Lincoln Ave. hosts the jazz and folk scene. Farther north on Lincoln and Clark the beat goes salsa.

The Secretary of State has taken a no-nonsense attitude toward drunk driving, so mind your P(int)s and Q(uart)s.

Like the musicians, music clubs come and go, often fading away as a result of changing neighborhoods or simple economics. But the blues, jazz, and folk scenes are such a part of Chicago that new locations for old names spring up. The music on the South Side is at its funky best. On the North Side, you can find whatever you're looking for on the Lincoln Ave. music strip, between Webster and Wrightwood, or on Halsted and Clark streets, between 2500 and 3500 North. The list includes clubs with little or no cover charge. Call for headliners. Latest phenomenon is the sports bar, catering to enthusiastic followers of baseball, football, basketball, etc., who tend to go off the deep end where sports are concerned. Like-minded visitors would enjoy the camaraderie among fans in some of these. Incidentally, there are over 6,000 liquor licenses in Chicago.

Blues

B.L.U.E.S. 2519 N. Halsted (528–1012). This is the logical start for a cozy, historic setting amid talent and audiences from around the world. Reasonable prices; arrive early for limited seating.

Kingston Mines. 2548 N. Halsted (477–4646). Presents dual stages and blues till sunrise. Open 7 days a week.

Jazz

The Bulls. 1916 N. Lincoln Park West (337–3000). Light jazz that takes its roots from the 1960s. A few sandwiches. Intimate cave like cellar level.

Lilly's. 2513 N. Lincoln (525–2422). Popular, comfortable tavern with large imported beer selection. No cover. Old-time favorites. Moderate prices.

Moosehead Bar & Grill. 163 W. Harrison (922–3640). A jazz club on the Loop's south end that gives the big bands a healthy serving with tasty lunches. Great for early evening jazz as the Moosehead begins weekdays at 5:30 P.M.

Sports Bars

Ditka's. 223 W. Ontario (280–1790). Chicago Bears coach Mike Ditka's place. Serves steak, chops, seafood, and lots of football talk.

Hunt Club Tavern and Grill. Racine & Clybourn (549–3020). Bears star Gary Fencik opened this popular spot and locals stop by hoping to see gridiron headliners.

McCuddy's. 35th St., across from Comiskey Park, home of Chicago White Sox. No phone, probably because noise level on game days is so loud that no one would hear it ring.

Ultimate Sports Bar & Grill. 354 W. Armitage (477–4630). Sportscasters broadcast from here. Has its own boxing ring and basketball hoop. Popular with Yuppie singles.

Others

Baby Doll Polka Club. 6201 S. Central Ave. (582–9706). The dance spot for the world's second largest Polish population. Big and friendly. Music starts at 9:30 P.M. on Fri. and Sat., Sun. at 5:00, when the polka music is broadcast live around the city. No cover or minimum. No credit cards.

Kitty O'Shea's. 720 S. Michigan (922–4400). Authentic Irish pub in Chicago Hilton and Towers. Gaelic atmosphere, good food, Irish entertainment.

Wild Hare & Singing Armadillo Frog Sanctuary. 3530 N. Clark (327–0800). Simple interior, laid-back atmosphere with great American reggae; two house bands and occasional international drop-ins.

Zanies. 1548 N. Wells (337–4027). Chicago's original comedy club. Reservations recommended.

SECURITY. Chicago is a big, racially mixed town with more than its share of mean streets and ethnic animosity. The city has the reputation, at least in Europe, of operating as it did in the days of Al Capone and the St. Valentine's Day Massacre. Although they're still a part of Chicago's past, today's mob and its violent doings are pretty well confined to their own circle. The cryptic initials and drawings on many subway platforms are the signatures of street gangs marking their territory. While neighborhood residents and police are trying to turn the gangs around, their brand of random violence sometimes takes in innocent victims. It is not impolite to ask in your hotel if the area is safe for walking or which blocks are best left alone.

Although N. Michigan Avenue from Oak Street to 12th Street is relatively safe for an evening walk, use prudence and caution when roaming new locations after dark; so-called good areas can change within a matter of blocks.

DALLAS–FORT WORTH

by
Judy Williamson

Judy Williamson, a journalism graduate of the University of Mississippi, is the travel writer for the Dallas Morning News *and has also served as staff writer for their* Guide *magazine, the weekly entertainment and leisure section.*

Symbolic of a dogged determination to make it and make it big, the city boom period that began in the late 1970s saw Dallas real estate developers engaging in endless battles to outdo the competition. Today, as a result, tall, glass-sheathed towers puncture the cornflower-blue Texas sky, rising like sparkling gems from a field of green.

After dark, visitors sit in the revolving restaurant atop the downtown Hyatt Regency's Reunion Tower and view the blinking lights that reach in every direction, particularly northward up and around Dallas Parkway into the burgeoning urban phenomenon known as Far North Dallas. From this northern vantage point, people in return see the blinking 50-story Reunion Tower. Dallas is growing so rapidly that the skyline changes almost weekly, with this one exception.

The level of affluence enjoyed by city residents has never been more apparent. Witness the centerpiece of the Far North Dallas area, the new Dallas Galleria, patterned after the highly successful Galleria in Houston. Set on 43 acres at one of the busiest intersections in the Lone Star State, the Galleria offers a glittering collection of shops—Saks Fifth Avenue, Marshall Field's, Cartier, and Tiffany's—in addition to fine restaurants, nightclubs, office towers, an ice rink, an athletic club, and the 21-story 440-room Westin Hotel.

Dallas offers perhaps the finest shopping in the Southwest, with local outposts of well-known retail names such as Lord & Taylor, Gump's, and Bloomingdale's. The hometown favorite, Neiman-Marcus, features stores all over town.

Despite the glitter and gloss, there are still parts of the city that are small-town. Mention Greenville Avenue to almost anyone living in the city, and the image that usually comes to mind is the singles strip stretching north from University to Meadow Road. But head south a mile or two—beyond the imaginary gates at Mockingbird—and the street changes. For those who live across these invisible tracks, Lower Greenville is "the neighborhood"—the kind that features home grocery delivery and shop owners who are on a first-name basis with their customers—a neighborhood that has undergone something of a renaissance during the last several years.

New restorations on Lower Greenville are similar to those already on McKinney Avenue and the West End Historic District downtown. Rickety old buildings are being reborn as chic restaurant-bars, and old storefronts are getting facelifts and new identities.

Cross busy Central Expressway and you come to Highland Park, one of the loveliest small towns in America today. It's incorporated but is very much a neighborhood and more still a state of mind. Southern Methodist University, the Park Cities YMCA, and the churches and synagogues dotting Preston Road echo the civic and social pride of its residents. A feeling of history pervades the town, from the tree-lined residential streets (Dallas's highest-priced real estate) to Highland Park Village on Preston at Mockingbird, where new shops are designed to blend with the old. Even the grocery store looks genteel.

Meanwhile, the central business district is experiencing a resurgence of sorts. The centerpiece is the new Dallas Museum of Art next door to the Fairmont Hotel. The museum, which opened in November 1984, will serve as the cornerstone of a 60-acre arts district, also to include a new symphony hall, located on the edge of downtown. A few blocks away, the West End Historical District (bounded by Woodall Rodgers Freeway, Commerce, and Lamar downtown) features 1920s warehouses and small factories being restored and converted for new uses, clubs, restaurants, and office space. Finally, downtown is in the midst of expanding a below-ground pedestrian walkway system called the Tunnel, linking downtown office buildings, banking facilities, restaurants, shops, and parking. Those who come up for air can view the city's beautiful open park Thanks-Giving Square, a downtown garden with trees, fountains, a lofty bell tower, and a chapel.

The good news for the traveler is that Dallas, unlike some other metropolises its size (1 million residents and counting), is affordable despite its Texas oil image. You'll soon learn that the inspiration for television's number one show has its fair share of real folks, too. J. R. Ewing is obviously more fiction than fact. Although the wheeler-dealer and cowboys-and-Indians stereotypes persist, no less than 80 percent of the state's population is centered in urban areas. Most Dallasites earn a livelihood not in the farm or the oil field but in business and industry, research, and space technology.

Within the state, Dallas is perhaps best known for its diversified economic, civic, and cultural interests. It's young, vivacious, urbane—and fun. There are few natural resources to boast of, nor any that brought about its fame. No mountains, lapping oceans, or mighty rivers. To use a whopping cliché, the greatest natural assets are its people: an alert, progressive, and friendly citizenry.

Most relics of Dallas's relatively short history are clustered in the west end of the thriving central business district. Here, perched on a concrete plaza, is the primitive log cabin that John Neeley Bryan built, putting the city on the map. Bryan allegedly chose this spot for its proximity to the Trinity River so that he could trade with Indians and the westbound wagon trains.

The name Dallas wasn't used until 1843, and its origin is still in question. Some say the city was named for George Mifflin Dallas, vice president of the United States. Others say it was named for a friend of Bryan's, one Joseph Dallas. The aggressive pioneer efforts that enabled the fledgling city to survive some rocky early days and to have "sprung without reason out of the prairie," as one local bank ad's civic campaign notes, have since been duplicated time after time. Successive generations, equally spirited, have attained their respective goals: making the town the center of the emerging highway network; digging a new channel for the unruly Trinity River, thus reclaiming 10,000 acres of land for the central business district; achieving a dominant position in the nation's burgeoning airline transportation system (the nation's largest, Dallas–Fort Worth airport is also its fourth busiest after Atlanta, O'Hare, and LAX); and implementing a series of farsighted master plans for the practical and aesthetic development of the city.

More simply stated, Dallas works. The area's economy is considered by many to be the brightest spot in the nation. Little wonder that more than 657 firms with a net worth of at least $1 million each have located their headquarters here, placing Dallas third in the nation. No fewer than 400 of *Fortune* magazine's Fortune 500 are rooted here. Dallas boasts more home offices of insurance companies than any other American metropolitan area.

The city holds its place as one of the nation's top three convention cities. Many of these conventions and trade and market shows are staged in the mammoth Convention Center as well as Trammel Crow's Market Center complex.

A new wing of the Loews Anatole and other new hotels were completed in time for the city to host the 1984 Republican national convention in August 1984. Developments such as these have made Dallas an entertainment, cultural, and sports mecca featuring a well-rounded roster of attractions and a full calendar of special events.

Fort Worth

Fort Worth, Dallas's sister city 30 miles down the road, is in some ways its polar opposite. Dallas is slick, savvy, and sophisticated; Fort Worth is the West in microcosm. Taken together, they have come to be known as Dallas–Fort Worth or the Metroplex. Between the two cities is a string of communities referred to in local jargon as the Mid-Cities, including, among others, Arlington, Irving, and Grand Prairie. First the stereotype. Fort Worth is positively chock-full of young Texans, posing, pouting, with jaws clenched (à la John Travolta's sullenly sensual Bud in *Urban Cowboy*), decked out in cowboy-stud silks and timeworn Levis, looking for a good time. But you'll also find well-dressed young businessmen, hollow-cheeked young ladies, and Izod-shirted students from local Texas Christian University in equal numbers.

Nicknamed Cowtown for the extensive cattle-trading operations that once thrived there, Fort Worth has some of the area's most impressive modern sights and museums and provides a real taste of the Old West. It was in fact once known as the "city where the West begins." A visitor should visit both old and new. Vestiges of the city that once served as the last major rest stop along the Chisholm Trail are clustered around Exchange Avenue, home to the old stockyards. The hub of activity for cattlemen from all over the west in the 1800s, now a major tourist attraction, the stockyards are home to the old (recently renovated) Stockyards Hotel,

Cowtown Coliseum, and boardwalk sidewalks lined with rough-tough cowboy bars.

But others visit Fort Worth for its world-class collection of museums, all within walking distance of each other at Montgomery, Lancaster, and Crestline roads. The Kimbell offers antique art; the Amon Carter, Remingtons and Russells; and the Fort Worth Art Museum, a contemporary collection. Dallasites regularly make the 40-minute drive to see these or the Water Gardens, a spectacular park in downtown Fort Worth featuring millions of gallons of water pushing over concrete elevations into a bubbling pool. A thousand steps take visitors below street level to its very heart. Welcome to Fort Worth.

PRACTICAL INFORMATION

WHEN TO GO. Average temperatures range from 56 to 35 degrees Fahrenheit in Jan. to 74 to 95 degrees Fahrenheit in July and Aug. Texas in the summer—roughly May through early Oct.—can be a killer. It can be blistering hot, with successive days seeing 100 and above. It also can be either thunderstorming or very dry, so wear cool, loose clothing and a hat and drink plenty of fluids to prevent sunstroke. Air-conditioning is a way of life in Texas, making all clothing comfortable indoors. Weather in the winter and spring months changes frequently. A blue norther in January can send temperatures in the sixties plummeting to the teens and lower twenties. Like a good Boy or Girl Scout, be prepared.

HOW TO GET THERE. By air. Most air travelers arrive at the nation's largest commercial airport, Dallas–Fort Worth International Airport, midway between Dallas and Fort Worth. Twenty major carriers serve the airport, the country's fourth busiest.

Southwest Airlines, a regional carrier serving Texas and surrounding states, operates out of Love Field near downtown Dallas. Southwest frequently offers the lowest rates.

The good news for the traveler is that at this writing industry analysts say that air fares will continue to decrease. Competition and more cost-efficient airline operations have contributed to the cost benefits for travelers. For example, the Ultimate Super Saver fares offered in Feb. 1988 by the major carriers represented up to a 70 percent reduction of the ticket price. Sample fare: New York to DFW, $99 each way. Restrictions apply, so call the carrier. Also, when making air reservations, check with local "discount travel" offices (see Accommodations) that specialize in tickets and packages offered close to departure, usually at a much lower rate.

By bus. *Greyhound-Trailways* bus lines provide regularly scheduled transcontinental service.

By train. *Amtrak,* the national passenger train, transports visitors to and from Dallas's Union Station and Fort Worth. There are several special rates: Excursion Fare (discounted round-trip ticket valid only on designated trains); Senior Citizen or Handicapped Fare, which provides a 25 percent discount on round-trip tickets (with some blackout periods); and Family Fare, for which the head of family pays full fare, spouse and all children 12 or over pay half fare, and children 2 to 11 pay 25 percent of the fare.

Amtrak also offers reduced-price package tours in conjunction with various hotels and tourism centers; Amtrak ticket necessary. For information about trains and programs, contact a travel agent or call Amtrak at 800–USA–RAIL.

TELEPHONES. The area code for Dallas is 214; the Fort Worth area code is 817. In order to place a long-distance call to any number within area code 214, it is necessary to dial 1 (or 0) and 214 and then the seven digit telephone number. A pay telephone call costs 25 cents. Local directory assistance in either city is 1–411. From elsewhere, Dallas directory assistance is 214–555–1212; Fort Worth, 817–555–1212. Ask the operator if the party you want to call has a Metro number that can be dialed free from anywhere in the Dallas–Fort Worth Metroplex.

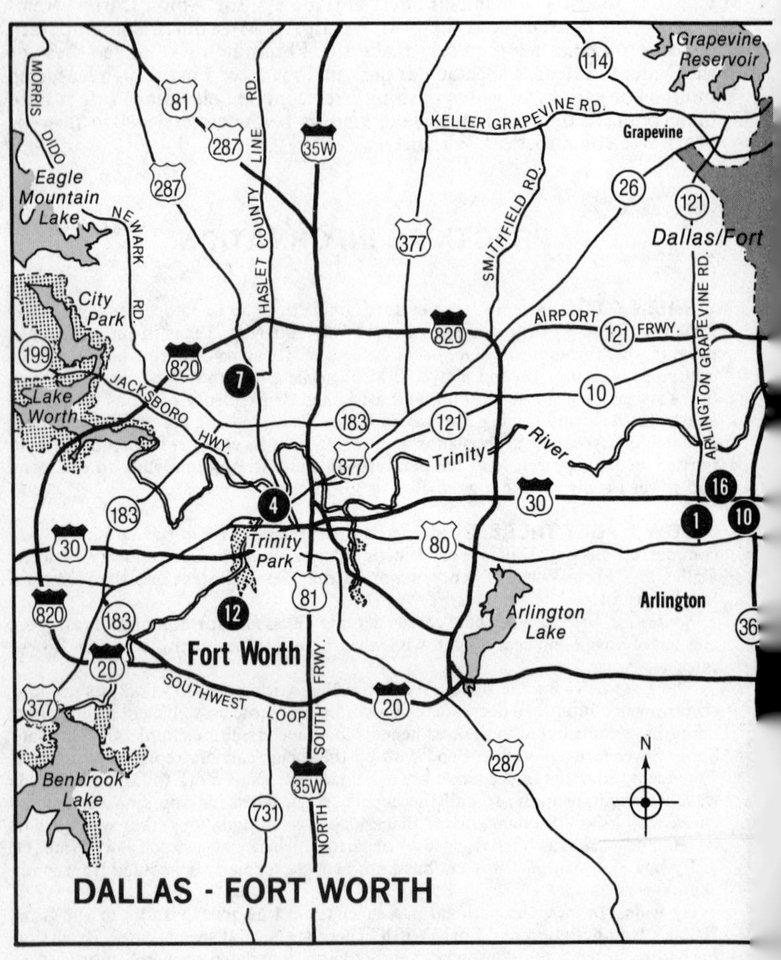

Points of Interest

Arlington Stadium, **1**
Dallas/Fort Worth Airport, **9**
Dallas Love Field, **2**
Downtown Dallas, **3**
Downtown Fort Worth, **4**
The Galleria, **5**
International Wildlife Park, **6**
Meacham Field Municipal Airport, **7**
Prestonwood Town Center, **8**

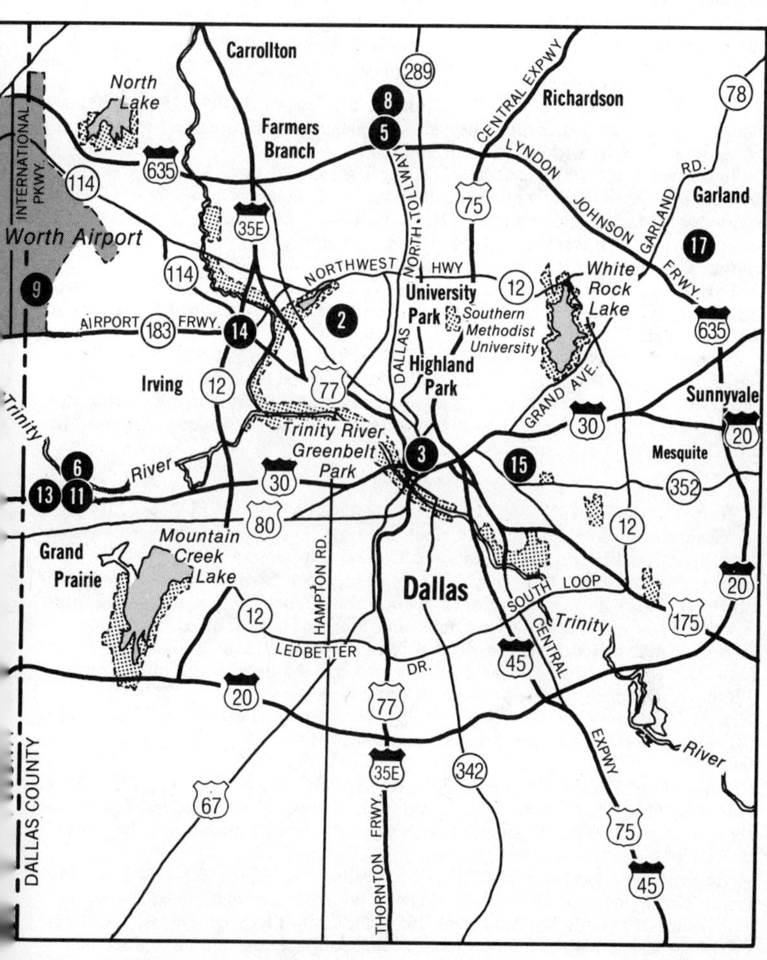

Six Flags Over Texas, **10**
Texas Christian University, **12**
Texas Sports Hall of Fame, **13**
Texas Stadium, **14**
Texas State Fair Grounds, **15**
Wax Museum of the Southwest, **11**
Wet 'n Wild, **16–17**

Emergency Telephone Numbers. The city of Dallas emergency number is 214–744–4444 (fire, police, and ambulance services).

ACCOMMODATIONS. Almost every budget chain in the U.S. is represented in Dallas and Fort Worth; call the toll-free reservation numbers for a favorite if it isn't listed below. Hotel rates are based on double occupancy. Categories, determined by price, are: *Reasonable,* $50 to $65; and *Very Economical,* $35 to $50.

Reasonable

Hampton Inn. 4555 Beltway Dr., Addison, TX 75244 (214–991–2800). 160 air-conditioned rooms, restaurants, heated pool, jogging track. Breakfast included in room rate. Located within blocks of Galleria.

LeBaron Hotel. 1055 Regal Row, Dallas, TX 75247 (214–634–8550). Centrally located with access to downtown Dallas, and to Trammell Crow's World Trade Center and Market Hall complex; Dallas–Fort Worth International Airport, and intersection of Airport Freeway and Texas Highway 114. 175 air-conditioned rooms, banquet rooms, and lower-level lounge.

Park Cities Inn. 6101 Hillcrest Ave., Dallas, TX 75205 (214–521–0330). Located directly opposite Southern Methodist University. 55 air-conditioned rooms, some with small refrigerators.

Stoneleigh Hotel. 2927 Maple Ave., Dallas, TX 75201 (214–871–7111). Renovated landmark 1927 hotel contains some of the original brass fixtures, marble columns, parquet flooring. Some kitchenettes, heated pool, lighted tennis courts, airport transportation, beauty and barber salons. Within walking distance of McKinney–Oak Lawn area.

Very Economical

Best Western Inn LBJ. 8051 LBJ Frwy., Dallas, TX 75251 (214–234–4231). 205 air-conditioned rooms, restaurants, pool. Centrally located at confluence of major thoroughfares: LBJ Freeway, Coit, and Central Expressway.

Best Western Raintree Inn. 2023 N. Industrial Blvd., Dallas, TX 75207 (214–741–5041). 96 air-conditioned rooms, restaurants. Across the street from Trammell Crow's World Trade Center and Market Hall complex.

Best Western Red Bird Inn. 4023 S. Walton Walker Blvd., Dallas, TX 75236 (214–339–3121). Motel is located off Cockrill Hill 9.5 miles south of downtown. 124 air-conditioned rooms, pool, small restaurant.

Best Western West Branch Inn. 7301 West Frwy., Fort Worth, TX 76116 (817–244–7444). 120 air-conditioned rooms, heated pool, access to golf and tennis facilities.

Days Inn Texas Stadium. 2200 E. Airport Frwy., Irving, TX 75062 (214–438–6666). 178 air-conditioned rooms, heated pool, valet services. Free shuttle to Dallas–Fort Worth International Airport. Located near Mid-Cities theme parks and across from Texas Stadium.

Forest Lane Days Inn. 2753 Forest Ln., Dallas, TX 75234 (800–325–2525). Far North Dallas location off the LBJ Freeway with 100 air-conditioned rooms.

Howard Johnson's North Central. 10333 N. Central Expwy., Dallas, TX 75231 (800–654–2000). 164 rooms, pool (and wading pool), bar, restaurant, lighted tennis courts.

Irving Inn. 909 W. Airport Hwy., Irving, TX 75062 (214–255–7108). In the Mid-Cities area about 20 minutes from Dallas. 100 air-conditioned rooms with kitchens, pool, restaurant.

La Quinta-North Central. 4440 N. Central Expwy., Dallas, TX 75206 (214–821–4220). Located 1½ blocks east of Central at the Knox-Henderson exit, minutes from downtown and Park Cities. Pool, adjacent 24-hour restaurant.

Non-Smoker's Inn. 9229 Carpenter Frwy., Dallas, TX 75247 (214–631–6633). Non-smokers only invited to stay in this 135-room inn. Heated pool, hot tubs.

Park Central Inn. 1010 Houston St., Fort Worth, TX 76102 (817–336–2011). 120 air-conditioned rooms, restaurants, pool, airport transportation. Adjacent to Fort Worth Convention Center.

Quality Inn South. 4201 South Frwy., Dallas, TX 76115 (817–923–8281). Four miles south of city at Seminole South exit. Fewer than 100 air-conditioned rooms, pool, restaurants, and bar with music for dancing.

Rodeway Inn Love Field. 3140 W. Mockingbird Ln., Dallas, TX 75235 (800–228–2000). Adjacent to Love Field airport. 42 air-conditioned rooms.

TraveLodge East. 6855 E. Lancaster Ave., Fort Worth, TX 76112 (817–457–1221 or 800–225–3050). 130 air-conditioned rooms, bar, restaurant, and Texas-shaped swimming pool.

Tropicana Inn. 3939 N. Central Expwy., Dallas, TX 75204 (214–526–8881). Fewer than 100 rooms, restaurants, and pool. Great location on Central Expressway, minutes from downtown.

Valley View Inn. 6101 LBJ Frwy., Dallas, TX 75240 (214–387–2525). 104 air-conditioned rooms. Located at Valley View Square shopping center, within walking distance of Valley View Shopping Mall.

Bed-and-Breakfast. If you like, you can stay in a private home and have breakfast the next morning. Bed-and-breakfast accommodations can range from large, spacious homes in the suburbs to small inner-city town houses. All listings in the bed-and-breakfast reservation agencies below should meet the basic needs for cleanliness and comfort. Rates for comfortable double rooms run from $25 to $40 and for exclusive double rooms run from $45 to $60. Write or call for an informative brochure and reservations request form. For Dallas and Fort Worth: **Bed & Breakfast Texas Style,** 4224 W. Red Bird Ln., Dallas, TX 75237 (214–298–5433).

HOW TO GET AROUND. From the airport. Surtran express coach service to and from Dallas–Fort Worth Airport is provided on a scheduled basis at a very reasonable rate. Taxis operate around the clock, but fares can be as much as $30 to the inner city.

By bus. Within the city, a municipally operated bus line (DART) operates a new modern fleet along a network of local, express, and crosstown routes. For routes, call 214–828–6700. For a trip from Dallas to Fort Worth, take one of three bus lines (Greyhound, Trailways, or Texas Bus Lines) for $4 to $5 one way, $8 to $9 round-trip.

For the convenience of the downtown shopper or sightseer, a better way to get around is on a Hop-A-Bus. The city's rabbit-eared Hop-A-Buses take visitors from one end of the downtown sector to the other for 25 cents. No way to miss these full-size city buses, which are painted Pepto Bismol pink from nose to tail, with protruding ears and fake whiskers. Bus stops are clearly marked.

In Fort Worth, stop by the Transportation Service Information Center, 1000 Throckmorton, at 10th St. (817–870–8070), for everything you might want to know about city buses, trains, and transportation to the airport.

By taxi. Service is supplied by three companies, with fares lower than many other American cities, though they still can be hefty.

By train. Amtrak makes the Dallas–Fort Worth trip Mon., Wed., and Sat. for $4.75 each way. Call 214–653–1101.

By rental car. All major car-rental agencies are represented in Dallas–Fort Worth: Alamo, Avis, Budget, Dollar, Hertz, and National. Before you go, call for specials, the best buys. Most have offices at the airport. Rent-A-Wreck, a nationwide discount auto rental chain, maintains a Fort Worth agency: 1500 W. 7th St., Fort Worth, TX 76103 (817–332–3137). Its motto: Yesterday's cars at yesterday's prices.

On foot. A special word to the wise when walking around downtown Dallas: Do not walk when corner traffic lights are flashing "do not walk." This violation is known as jaywalking and can result in a traffic ticket or citation. If a police officer approaches a violator, he or she is asked to show identification. Visitors are usually dismissed with a word of caution. Please respect this rule as it has been found to be a major factor of safety downtown.

HINTS TO THE MOTORIST. Dallas sits like a hub on seven spokes of the Interstate highway system branching out in all directions. Fourteen additional major highways lead motorists into Dallas, and the city is circled by two giant highway loops. As a result, driving isn't easy.

Dallas and Fort Worth roads are not laid out in a grid. In Dallas particularly, many major roads follow early trails and cattle paths that radiate from downtown. First-time visitors may want to pick up a copy of a *Mapsco,* a heavily detailed road handbook of the city available at most bookstores. The maximum speed limit is 55 mph; school zones (heavily enforced) are 20 mph. Central Expressway in Dallas should be avoided at peak traffic times, and a right turn on red is legal unless otherwise marked.

TOURIST INFORMATION. Pre-trip literature can be obtained from the Dallas Convention and Visitors Bureau, the Dallas Chamber, 1507 Pacific Ave. (214–954–1482). In Fort Worth: Fort Worth Chamber of Commerce, 700 Throckmorton at 6th St. (817–336–2491). Both stock pamphlets on area attractions, restaurants, and motels along with information on discounts. Both are open Mon.–Fri., 8:30 A.M.–5 P.M.

The Dallas Committee for Foreign Visitors, Union Station (214–747–2355) offers assistance, information, and translators in most languages for international visitors. Open Mon.–Sat., 10 A.M.–3 P.M. In Dallas, the chamber has a visitors' center at Love Field and Union Station downtown; Union Station itself is a free tourist attraction with fast-food kiosks upstairs at affordable prices. The fare: burgers, nachos, and salads.

Foreign currency. Foreign money can be exchanged for U.S. dollars at the *American Airlines Terminal,* DFW Airport (214–574–4754); *Deak-Perera,* 717 N. Harwood, Suite 111, Dallas (214–748–7403).

HINTS TO DISABLED TRAVELERS. In Fort Worth, the Transportation Service Information Center, 1000 Throckmorton at 10th St., downtown (817–870–8070), provides a van service for disabled and elderly people. In Dallas, an excellent publication lists city facilities and shows maps denoting curb cuts. Request *Access Dallas 82,* Texas Easter Seal Society, 4300 Beltway, Dallas, TX 75234 (214–934–9104). For city transport information, call the Dallas Transit System (214–828–6700) for routes on accessible buses and Care Car (214–651–7511) for pickup by appointment.

FREE EVENTS. Shakespeare Festival performances are held at no charge at Fair Park, Dallas, in the summer months. **Symphony in the Park** concerts are held all over town in the spring and summer at city parks. The Dallas Ballet presents **Ballet under the Stars,** locations vary, every spring. *Artsline* (214–385–1155) is a hotline detailing activities and events, many of them free, of over 50 Dallas cultural organizations.

TOURS AND SPECIAL-INTEREST SIGHTSEEING. You'll probably want to sample some of the tourist attractions. They're there even though the Metroplex has no French Quarter, no Chinatown, no Broadway, and no beach or mountains to boast of.

After Southfork, what else? Dallas has rich and historic architecture along with its glittery new skyscrapers, lovely parks, outstanding shopping institutions (Neiman-Marcus, of course, NorthPark Center, and the Galleria), and its fair share of history.

First, to **Southfork** (214–442–6536), fabled home of the *Dallas* series. Take Highway 75 north, exit Parker Rd., go east 6 miles, and then turn right on FM 2551. Tours conducted daily; gift shop, concession stands on the premises. Adults, $6.95; kids 4–12 $4.95; under 4, free.

Gray Line (214–824–2424 or 817–429–7563) offers a number of commercial bus tours. A typical morning tour includes the Kennedy Memorial, Thanks-Giving Square, the Swiss Avenue Historic District, White Rock Lake and the Hunt Mansion, the lovely homes in the Armstrong Parkway-Beverly Drive area, and a tour of McKinney Avenue, filled to its cobblestone curbs with antique stores, trendy restaurants, galleries, and bars. Another half-day tour takes in the Market Hall–Apparel Mart–World Trade Center complex, Old City Park, Southern Methodist University, and the new City Hall. Tours leave from many area hotels.

A **walking guide** to the downtown sights (Dallas City Hall, Dallas Public Library, Thanks-Giving Square, John F. Kennedy Memorial and John Neeley Bryan Cabin, Neiman-Marcus Museum, Farmers' Market, Dallas Museum of Art, the renovated West End,and Old City Park) is available from the visitor information centers.

Fort Worth sights, many free, include the museums, stockyards, Water Gardens, Japanese Gardens, Log Cabin Village, Omni Theater, the Western Company Museum, and Thistle Hill (see Historic Sights and Houses). Sundance Square is a restored area of brick streets designed for leisurely strolling and filled with shops and galleries. Begin at the Americana Hotel and then cross the street and visit the Sundance Gallery. For more serious art, take in the Hall Galleries upstairs. The Cowboy Culture has Western clothes for women and men. Also there: Red River Saloon, owned by Neiman-Marcus. Stay and have a bowl of the world's richest chili (in calories, not dollars) or a plate of prairie fire nachos.

PARKS AND GARDENS. The Metroplex possesses many lures, including its 250-plus parks. They're free! Pack a picnic lunch or just take the kids and enjoy nature at its best. The Dallas Parks and Recreation Department activity hotline number is 214–670–7070.

One of Dallas's most popular and largest parks is **White Rock Lake,** 830 E. Lawther (214–321–2125), with boating and fishing facilities, covered picnic pavilions, and a food concession. There is an 8-mile jogging and bicycling trail around the lake, and horseback riding is allowed on unmanicured areas. Overlooking the lake find the landscaped **DeGolyer Estate,** 8525 Garland (214–324–1401), renowned for the gardens, which are open to the public.

Bachman Lake, 2750 Bachman Blvd. (214–369–8451) is a second "inner-city" lake on Northwest Highway at Love Field. A 3-mile jogging path envelops the lake; boating and roller skate concessions are available. **Turtle Creek** is perhaps the loveliest area in town. The woodsy, landscaped area takes in Reverchon, Lee, and Turtle Creek parks as it stretches from Maple near Oaklawn Ave. northward along Turtle Creek Parkway through Highland Park. **Reverchon Park,** 3505 Maple Ave. (214–521–2690), is geared to the family: plenty of picnic tables and playground equipment plus one of the city's largest baseball facilities and recreation centers. **Lee Park,** 3400 Turtle Creek (214–369–8451), commemorates Robert E. Lee with a statue of the Confederate general overlooking the fountains and large azalea fields of Turtle Creek. Picnic tables are available. North of Lee Park along Turtle Creek is **Lakeside Park,** located along Lakeside Drive from Beverly to Wycliff, within the Highland Park city limits.

ZOOS. There are some spring days in Dallas when nothing has as much charm as a trip to the zoo and a box lunch in the special picnic area. Bears, tigers, leopards, primates, exotic birds, an outstanding reptile collection, and many rare and endangered species are on display in a parklike setting of flowers and greenery. Kids will enjoy a miniature train ride through the park. In the summer, the Children's Zoo gives kids a chance to see, hear, and touch animals. The zoo is located just minutes south of downtown on I-35 (take the Ewing exit). Call 214–946–5154. Daily, 9 A.M.–5 P.M. Adults, $2; kids 6–11, $1.25; children 5 and under free. Group rates available. Parking, $1.

Home to some 4,000 animals, the Fort Worth Zoological Park features an African diorama, reptiles, and an aquarium. Take I-30 and exit at University Drive South; the zoo is just past Trinity River. Call 817–870–7050. Mon.–Fri., 9 A.M.–5:30 P.M.; Sat., 9 A.M.–6 P.M.; Sun., 9 A.M.–6:30 P.M. Ages 18 and over, $2; ages 12–17, $1.50; ages 3–11, 25 cents; kids under 3 free.

PARTICIPANT SPORTS. Running. Joggers and runners head to the 3.8 miles of trails around *Bachman Lake,* 3500 W. Northwest Hwy., and 9 miles of trails around *White Rock Lake,* 8300 Garland. For information on both call 214–670–4029.

Swimming. For the best prices, the *Central YWCA,* 4621 Ross (214–827–5600), offers an indoor heated pool open daily for coed adult fitness swims, adult open swims, family swims, and classes. Showers and lockers available. Nonmembers, $2; youth nonmembers, $1. For a complete list of outdoor public pools, call Dallas Parks and Recreation Department (214–670–4100). The *Southern Methodist University pool,* Binkley at Bishop on campus (214–692–2864), allows visitors to swim in the 50-meter outdoor pool. Lap swim: Fri., noon–5 P.M.; Sat.–Sun., noon–6 P.M. Cost $2 a visit.

Tennis. For outdoor tennis court reservations and information, call 214–428–1501 Mon.–Fri., 8:15 A.M.–5:15 P.M. Private and clinic lessons are available at *Huffhines Tennis Center,* 1601 Syracuse (214–234–6697). Hours are Mon.–Sun., 7:30 A.M.– 10:30 P.M. Fees are $2.50 for 90 minutes. Reservations suggested. *The Garland Tennis Center,* 1010 W. Miller, has lighted courts; lessons are available. Reservations, 214–494–7101. Court fee, $1.50.

Bicycling. Marked bike trails are at *Bachman Lake,* 3500 W. Northwest Hwy.; *Crawford Park,* 8700 Elam; *Kiest Park,* 3000 S. Hampton; *Netherland Park,* 5700 Meaders Ln.; *Singing Hills Park,* 1010 Crough; and *White Rock Lake,* 8300 Garland. For information and maps of all, call 214–670–4029.

Golf. To arrange for some games on municipal courses, call the following parks: *Cedar Crest* (214–943–1004), *Grover C. Keaton* (214–388–4831), *L. B. Houston* (214–869–1778), *Plano* (214–423–5444), *Stevens* (214–946–5781), and *Tenison* (214–823–5350). Greens fee, $5 to $8.

Boating. For information about boating facilities, phone the following Dallas–Fort Worth area lakes: *Bachman Lake* (214–351–3990), *Lake Grapevine* (214–481–4549 or 817–488–9481), *Lake Lavon* (214–442–1143 or 214–331–1393), *Mountain Creek Lake* (214–331–5471), and *North Lake* (214–869–1633). *Scott's Boat Rentals,* Oak Grove Park north of Highway 121 near Dove Road (817–488–9481), offers various boats on Lake Grapevine. Sailboats about $15 for two hours. *Sue's Sailboats* (214–226–4954) on Lake Ray Hubbard at Captain's Cove, features sailboat rentals. Take Zion Road exit off I-30 East and continue on service road to Marina Drive, then go right. Sailboats about $20 for two hours.

Horseback riding. *Benbrook Ranch and Stables,* located west of Dallas off I-20 (817-249–4514), offers horseback riding at $10 an hour through wooded trails. *Diamond J Corral,* north of Dallas on Highway 380 and FM 1385 (214–733–4514), offers horse rentals and hayride. Rentals are $10 an hour.

SPECTATOR SPORTS. Texans lock horns over a number of issues, but they are nearly unanimous in their advocacy of sports, both as spectators and as participants.

Baseball. The Texas Rangers play at Arlington Stadium (about 15 miles west of Dallas in Arlington) Apr. through Sept. The cost is $2 to $8; group discounts and special reduced-rate nights. Information, 214–273–5222.

Basketball. The Dallas Mavericks play at Reunion Arena, Dallas (214–988–0117). Tickets cost $4 to $8.

Football. King Football finds ultimate expression in the venerable Dallas Cowboys, led by coach Tom Landry. From Aug. to Dec., the Cowboys hold forth at Texas Stadium, Irving (214–369–3211). Tickets cost $18 (no discounts available).

Golf. The Metroplex enjoys two stops on the Professional Golfers Association tour: The **Byron Nelson Classic** at Las Colinas in Irving (May) and the Colonial (the **National Invitational Tournament**) at Colonial Country Club in Fort Worth (May).

Rodeo. A vestige of the Old West, rodeo is an important local sporting event. The Mesquite Rodeo runs from Apr. through Sept. at Military Parkway at Scyene Road off LBJ Freeway in Mesquite (214–285–8777). The Southwestern Exposition and Fat Show features the biggest Professional Rodeo Cowboys Association–sanctioned rodeo in the area; it takes place in Fort Worth the last week of Jan. and the first week of Feb.

CHILDREN'S ACTIVITIES. International Wildlife Park. See exotic animals roaming free as you drive through park; also elephant and camel rides and shows. Wildlife Parkway, I-30 at Belt Line, Grand Prairie (214–263–2201). Open daily 9:30 A.M.–6 P.M. Try to visit on a weekday ($7.95) as the price jumps to $10.50 Sat. and Sun.; kids under 3 free, $1 discount for seniors.

Six Flags Over Texas. Large family amusement park features adventure rides (roller coasters and river ride), Pac-Man Land kids' section, live entertainment, and food and gift concessions. I-30 at Highway 360, Arlington (817–640–5050). Admission, $13.95; kids less than 42 inches high, $7.95; 2 and under free. Special discounts through the summer months. Watch the entertainment sections of daily papers.

Water Parks, featuring giant water slides, wave pool, rapids, body flumes, and more, plus picnic areas and food concessions, also offer occasional discounts; watch the daily papers. *Wet 'n' Wild,* off Highway 360 across I-30 from Six Flags, Arlington (214–265–3013), Sat.–Sun. 10 A.M.–6 P.M. Adults, $11.75; kids (3–12), $10.25; under 3, free; half price after 3 P.M.

HISTORIC SITES AND HOUSES. Judging from the number of Bermuda shorts, cameras, and shopping bags spotted here any day of the week, the city sightseeing tour must begin at **Dealey Plaza** downtown at the corner of Houston and Elm. Visitors gather there because Dealey Plaza, a swatch of grass, a fountain, and a statue of the Dallas *Morning News* founder George B. Dealey, overlooks the spot where President John F. Kennedy was killed on Oct. 22, 1963. You can walk across the park and view the Texas School Book Depository and the sixth-floor window where Lee Harvey Oswald aimed his rifle at the motorcade. Walk one block east (Main and Elm at Record) and see Dallas's memorial to the late president, an austere cream-colored concrete statueless monument.

Another history lesson is provided nearby by the one-room log cabin of John Neeley Bryan, founder of Dallas. Overlooking the simple cabin, which was built in 1841, is what is known locally as **Old Red,** the rust-colored castle-courthouse that was the seat of Dallas County government at the turn of the century. The two buildings are known collectively as the **Dallas County Historical Plaza** (bounded by Commerce, Elm, Market, and Houston; 214–651–1020). No tours of the courthouse are offered but those sites can be visited at any time of day. Free.

Old City Park, 1717 Gano St. (214–421–5141), near downtown Dallas, recreates the Dallas of a century ago. In the Brent House, one of more than 25 restored buildings, park docents in long gingham dresses serve country-style lunches. The park is open Tues.–Fri., 10 A.M.–4 P.M.; Sat.–Sun., 1:30–4:30 P.M. Adults, $4; senior citizens and children, $2.

Swiss Avenue Historic District (214–826–7402) conducts minitours ($3.50 for ½-day tours) of some of the restored homes in what formed Dallas's most prestigious neighborhood from 1911 to 1920. Call for special events and tour information.

Log Cabin Village, University at Colonial Pkwy. (817–926–5881), is the Fort Worth counterpart to Old City Park. Costumed docents demonstrate candlemaking, spinning, and more against a backdrop of several relocated 1850s log cabins. Mon–Fri., 8:30–4:30; Sat.–Sun, noon–4:30. Adults, $1; children, 50 cents.

Thistle Hill, 1509 Pennsylvania, Dallas (817–336–1212), is the Georgia Revival–style mansion built by Texas cattle-baron W. T. Waggoner. A gift shop sells western souvenirs. Mon.–Fri., 10–4; Sun., 1–5. Admission, $2.

MUSEUMS. The big news in the Dallas–Fort Worth museum scene is the new Dallas Museum of Art (formerly the Dallas Museum of Fine Art), which opened its doors on Jan. 29, 1984. Designed by Edward Larrabee Barnes, the museum is the catalyst and cornerstone of the new Dallas Arts District, a 60-acre community development located on the edge of the central business district. It is the largest such downtown development ever undertaken in the U.S.

Fortunately for the visitor, several of the other Dallas museums, including many fine examples of Art Deco architecture, are clustered together in Fair Park. Better known to some as home of the Cotton Bowl, the State Fair of Texas, and the annual Texas–Oklahoma clash, Fair Park was originally the grounds for the Texas Centennial Exposition of 1936. The museums contained there today include the Museum of Natural History, Garden Center, Aquarium, Dallas Historical Society Museum, the magnificent Hall of State, the Age of Steam Museum, and the Science Place. Also, the Fort Worth Art Museum, Kimbell, and the Amon Carter are conveniently located next to each other in Fort Worth. Southern Methodist University houses several art museums: the Owens Art Center, the Meadows Museum of Spanish Art, and the Meadows Sculpture Garden.

Biblical Arts Center. 7500 Park at Boedeker, across from NorthPark Shopping Mall (214–691–4661). Religious art museum features 124- by 120-foot oil painting depicting the reception of the Holy Spirit by the apostles. Tues.–Sat., 10 A.M.–5 P.M.; Sun., 1–5 P.M. Exhibition galleries free. "Miracle at Pentecost" admission: adults, $3.75; senior citizens, $3; children 6–12, $2.

Amon Carter Museum. Americana and Western art are showcased at the Fort Worth museum. The permanent collection features works of Charles Russell, Laura Gilpin, Peter and Thomas Moran, Seth Eastman, and others. Film series, classes, lectures, and other events. For information on interpreted tours for the deaf, call 817–232–2892. 3501 Camp Bowie, Fort Worth (817–738–1933). Tues.–Sat., 10 A.M.–5 P.M.; Sun., 1–5:30 P.M. Free.

Dallas Aquarium. Fair Park. (214–670–8441). Largest inland aquarium in U.S. with more than 300 species of marine, tropical, and freshwater fish. Regional exhibits include warm waters of Hawaiian islands, cool California coastal waters, and Asian fish. Call for information on guided tours, education programs, and volunteering. Mon.–Sat., 9 A.M.–5 P.M.; Sun. and holidays, noon–5 P.M. Free.

The Dallas Museum of Art. 1717 N. Harwood (214–922–0220). The permanent collection includes the new Decorative Arts Wing, pre-Columbian, Oriental, Old Masters, and modern American works. Special activities include films, music, lectures, tours, and classes. Lunch is served in the Gallery Buffet Tues.–Sat., 11:30 A.M.–2 P.M. Excellent museum shop. Tues.–Sat., 10 A.M.–5 P.M. (Thurs. till 9 P.M.); Sun. and holidays, noon–5 P.M. (closed Christmas). Free, except for the Decorative Arts Wing ($3 adults, $1 for children under 12).

Fort Worth Art Museum. 1309 Montgomery, Fort Worth (817–738–9215). Permanent collection features contemporary art including "American Art: 1900–1940." Tues., 10 A.M.–9 P.M.; Wed.–Sat., 10 A.M.–5 P.M.; Sun., 1–5 P.M. Free.

Fort Worth Museum of Science and History. 1501 Montgomery, Fort Worth (817–732–1631). Exhibits include Hall of Texas History, talking computers, and others tracing city's development since 1849. A Laser Magic show is held weekends in planetarium ($3). Mon.–Sat., 9 A.M.–5 P.M.; Sun., 1–5 P.M. Museum free. Regular Omni Theater shows: adults, $4; kids 12 and under and senior citizens 65 and older, $2.50; group rates.

Hall of State. Fair Park (214–421–5136). Centerpiece of Dallas Fair Park, the museum traces 400 years of Texas history. Mon.–Sat., 9 A.M.–5 P.M. Free.

Kimbell Art Museum. 3333 Camp Bowie, Fort Worth (214–654–1034 or 817–332–8451). The museum's collection covers prehistoric times to Picasso. In between find pre-Columbian sculpture, Oriental ceramics, and European paintings. Call for information on tours, lectures, and films. Museum buffet is available Tues.–Sat., 10 A.M.–5 P.M.; Sun. 1–5 P.M. (closed July 4, Thanksgiving, Christmas, and New Year's Day).

Meadows Museum. Southern Methodist University's Owen Fine Arts Center (214–692–2489). The permanent collection includes Spanish paintings, drawings, and prints of the sixteenth through twentieth centuries. Mon.–Sat., 10 A.M.–5 P.M.; Sunday, 1–5 P.M. Free.

Museum of African-American Life and Culture. Bishop College, 3837 Simpson-Stuart (214–372–8734). Works by and about blacks; African sculpture. Mon.–Fri., 10 A.M.–4 P.M.; Sat., noon–3 P.M.; Sun., 2–4 P.M. Free.

Old City Park. 1717 Gano (214–421–7800). Living history museum with authentic buildings depicting nineteenth-century Dallas. Tues.–Fri., 10 A.M.–4 P.M.; Sat.–Sun., 1:30–4:30 P.M. Free.

Wax Museum of the Southwest. 601 E. Safari Pkwy. (I-30 at Belt Line), Grand Prairie (214–263–2391). America's largest wax museum is located next to the Sports Hall of Fame. Features more than 274 figures. Food service on the premises. Mon.–Fri., 10 A.M.–5 P.M.; Sat.–Sun., 10 A.M.–6 P.M. Adults, $6.50; kids 4–12, $5.50. Free parking.

ARTS AND ENTERTAINMENT. The Frank Lloyd Wright–designed Dallas Theater Center, a symphony orchestra led by world-renowned conductor Eduardo Mata, and a first-class ballet company are a few of the things that make Dallas–Fort Worth a place with more to boast about than its namesake TV series.

Film. Most major theaters offer bargain matinees for shows before 6 P.M. (excluding holidays). The following theaters offer $1 shows at all times: *Northtown 6* (Webbs Chapel at LBJ), *Northwood 4* (Spring Valley at Coit), *Promenade* (Belt Line at Coit), *Big Town 4* (1400 Big Town Center), *Bruton 4* (Bruton east of Buckner), and *Lakewood* (Abrams at Gaston).

Music. The Dallas Symphony Orchestra, Music Hall at Fair Park (214–692–0203). Tickets $8.50 to $23.

Fort Worth Symphony, Tarrant Country Convention Center, 1111 Houston, Fort Worth (817–335–9000 or 429–1181). Tickets $9 to $25.

Fort Worth Civic Orchestra, 4401 Trail Lake Dr., Fort Worth (817–292–6071 or 738–6509). Tickets $5; students and seniors, $2.50.

Grapevine Opry (country-western family entertainment), 302 Main, Grapevine (214–481–7984). Adults, $6.50; kids, $3.75.

Dance. Dallas Ballet, Majestic Theatre, 1925 Elm (214–744–4430). At presstime, the ballet has temporarily suspended performances due to budget problems. Call the theater for an update.

Fort Worth Ballet Association. Tarrant County Convention Center, Fort Worth. Central Tickets, 214–429–1181. Tickets $7 to $23.

Theater. Dallas Theater Center. Frank Lloyd Wright Theater, 3636 Turtle Creek (214–526–8857 or 214–263–1709). Charge tickets at metro 265–0789. Previews, $9; others, $11 to $15; group discounts.

Majestic Theatre. 1925 Elm (Rainbow Ticketmaster 214–373–8000; charge at 214–787–2000 or 787–1500). $12 to $21.

New Arts Theatre. 702 Ross at Market (reservations at 214–761–9064). Previews, $5; shows, $8.50 to $12.50.

Theatre 3. 2800 Routh, in the Quadrangle (call for information on discounts and reservations at 214–871–3300). Tickets $11 to $13.50.

Hip Pocket Theatre. Fort Worth (817–332–8451, or charge at Rainbow Ticketmaster, 214–787–1500 or 787–2000). Adults, $7.50; students and senior citizens, $6; under 13, $4.

For information on **discounts,** contact these ticket agencies: Central Tickets, 214–429–1181; Rainbow Ticketmaster, 214–373–8000; Ticketron metro, 214–265–2646; Reunion Arena events line, 214–745–1540; and Texas Tickets, 214–696–8001.

SHOPPING. The bible for discount shoppers in the Metroplex (Dallas, Midcities, Fort Worth) is *The Underground Shopper,* SusAnn Publications, Dallas ($3.95). Updated annually, the paperback guide lists discount places for everything from antique armoires to full-length furs.

McKinney Square Outlets. U.S. 75 North at SH 380, McKinney. More than 20 fashion outlets, furniture outlets, and gift shops at savings up to 50 percent. McKinney itself is a charming small town 30–40 minutes north of downtown Dallas. Another major discount center, **Outlet Malls of America,** 1717 E. Springcreek, Plano (214–578–1591) is open Mon.–Sat., 10 A.M.–9 P.M.

There are discount stores in Dallas–Fort Worth as well, though not all grouped together. For boots, check out the *Justin Boot Co. Outlet,* 301 S. Jennings at Daggett, Fort Worth, which carries discontinued items (boots, belts, and the like) or slightly damaged stock. In Dallas, make it *Resistol Hats,* 6021 Marion Dr., Garland, where Resistol cowboy hats and other Western wear are marked way down. *Loehmann's,* 11411 E. Northwest Highway, offers ladies better wear of all kinds. Designer labels are cut away, as are the prices. The *Terry Costa Outlet,* on Inwood off Stemmons, sells Victor Costa cocktail dresses and ball gowns, as well as other labels, at heavily discounted prices. *Horchow Finale,* Inwood at Lovers, Dallas, and 5724 Locke near Camp Bowie, Fort Worth, offers luxury merchandise, slightly damaged, at a fraction of the original catalog cost. Clothes, jewelry, collectibles.

In 1985 voters revoked the long-standing Blue Law that required stores to close on Sundays. However, flea markets, originally opened to satisfy weekend shoppers, remain popular among residents. Several stand out: *The Antique Center,* 7429 E. Lancaster, Fort Worth (817–332–4574); *Big D Bazaar,* 3636 N. Buckner (214–328–6117); *Canton First Monday Trade Fair,* first weekend of the month, downtown Canton (214–567–6556); *Farmers' Market Bazaar,* indoors in an old warehouse adjacent to Farmer's Market at 901 S. Pearl (670–5880); and *Traders Village,* 2602 Mayfield, Grand Prairie (647–2331); $1.25 parking.

DINING OUT. How lucky for the budget-conscious tourist that Dallas–Fort Worth's most indigenous restaurants—those serving barbecue, Tex-Mex, and what has become known as "Texana"—are also its least expensive. Even local folks with money to burn frequently prefer a hole-in-the-wall Tex-Mex place or a cafeteria-style barbecue joint to a lavish and very expensive hotel dining room serving five-star French haute cuisine.

Rest assured, however, that Dallas-Fort Worth dining offers more than chicken-fried steak or barbecue brisket. The cities offer myriad dining experiences from Czech to Vietnamese, old and new, and there's not a bad one in the bunch. The following, although not a complete list, not only stand out in terms of quality of food and ambience, they're affordable.

Restaurant categories, determined by the price of a meal for one, without beverages, tax, or tip, are as follows: *Reasonable,* \$10 to \$15; *Very Economical,* \$5 to \$10; and *Low Budget,* under \$5. Unless otherwise noted, all restaurants accept some if not all, major credit cards. Traveler's checks are acceptable everywhere with identification. Restaurants open and close frequently; we have made every effort to ensure that this list is up to date.

Reasonable

Big Wong. 2121 Greenville at Richmond (214–821–4198). Chinese food; late-night service. Daily, 11 A.M.–4 A.M.

Campisi's Egyptian. 5610 E. Mockingbird (214–827–0355). Expect to wait in line for pizza and pasta during peak dining hours (no reservations accepted) at this Dallas institution. Pizzeria decor is part of the attraction; the clientele includes Dallas families and Southern Methodist University students from down the street. Mon.–Thurs., 11 A.M.–11:30 P.M.

Fang-Ti China I. 6752 Shady Brook (214–987–3877). Late-night Chinese food. Mon.–Thurs., 11:30 A.M.–4 A.M.; Fri., 11:30 A.M.–6 A.M.; Sat., 5 P.M.–6 A.M.

Joe T. Garcia's. 2201 N. Commerce (817–626–4356). A legendary Fort Worth restaurant; offers Tex-Mex food Open Mon.–Sat., 11 A.M.–3 P.M., 5–11 P.M.; Sun., 4–10 P.M.

A. J. Gonzales. 1701 Market (214–652–9507). Tex-Mex food in the West End Historical District. Enchiladas and pyromaniac's hot sauce recommended. Lunch, Mon.–Fri., 11 A.M.–3 P.M.; dinner, Mon.–Thurs., 5:30–10 P.M.; Fri. 5:30–11 P.M.; Sat., 11 A.M.–11 P.M.

Ninfa's, a member of the Houston chain, is popular with families and singles (expect to wait in line) for its low-calorie Tex-Mex specialties and festive decor. Couple of locations: 1515 Inwood (214–638–6865). Mon.–Fri., 11 A.M.–2 P.M.; Sat., noon–10 P.M.; Sun., noon–9 P.M. 2250 Belt Line (214–661–2671). Mon.–Fri., 11 A.M.–2 P.M.; Mon.–Thurs., 5:30–9 P.M.; Fri., 4:30–11 P.M.; Sat., noon–11 P.M.; Sun., noon–9 P.M.

Birra Poretti's. Caruth Plaza, 9100 North Central at Park (214–692–0565). Half casual and attractive Italian restaurant; half Irish bar geared to singles. Mon.–Sat., 11 A.M. –2 P.M.; Sun., noon–2 P.M.

Prego Pasta House. 4930 Greenville (214–363–9204). Menu emphasizes pizza and pasta dishes in rich, contemporary setting. Mon.–Thurs., 11 A.M.–11 P.M.; Fri.–Sat., 11 A.M.–midnight; Sun., noon–11 P.M.

Very Economical

Angelo's Barbecue. 2533 White Settlement, Fort Worth (817–332–0357). Ranks with Joe T. Garcia's as Fort Worth visitor attraction and good eating place. Beer doesn't come any colder or barbecue better. Mon.–Sat., 11 A.M.–10 P.M. No credit cards.

Chuck E. Cheese's Pizza Time Theater. 2095 Forest Ln. (214–243–0888). Kids will go wild here: There's larger-than-life stuffed animals, a rat named Mr. Cheese, and games. Beer and wine for Mom and Dad. No credit cards.

Dixie House offers home cooking, fresh vegetables served with homemade rolls, and cornbread. Locally popular; part of the appeal is its casualness. Three locations: 2822 McKinney (214–824–0891), Sun.–Thurs., 11 A.M.–11 P.M.; Fri.–Sat., 11 A.M.–11:30 P.M. 14925 Midway, Addison (214–239–5144), Sun.–Thurs., 11 A.M.–10 P.M.; Fri.–Sat., 11 A.M.–11 P.M. 3647 W. Northwest Hwy. (214–353–0769), Sun.–Thurs., 11 A.M.–11 P.M.; Fri.–Sat., 11 A.M.–11:30 P.M.

Fuddrucker's is a lively restaurant featuring industrial-size hamburgers, hot dogs, and other sandwiches. An on-premises bakery provides cookies. Two locations: 2614 McKinney (214–871–2068), Mon.–Thurs., 11 A.M.–10:30 P.M., Fri.–Sat., 11 A.M.–11:30 P.M., Sun., noon–10 P.M. 1520 NorthPark Center, (214-987–3733), Mon.–Sat., 11 A.M.–11 P.M., Sun., noon–10 P.M.

Judge Bean's. Tasty burgers, a lively bar, and a flavor of the Old West at three locations: 8214 Park at Greenville (214–363–8322); 14920 Midway, Addison (214–980–4400); and 1521 Northwest Hwy., Garland (214–271–4424). All Sun.–Mon., 11 A.M.–11 P.M.; Tues.–Sat., 11 A.M.–2 P.M.;

La Botica. 1900 N. Haskell at Munger (214–824–2005). Parties of at least 10 may be picked up at a hotel via a bright yellow school bus, transported to La Botica, and later brought back home again. The restaurant is carved out of an old drugstore;

endless margaritas and a piano player add to a dining experience that can only be described as funky chic. Lunch Mon.–Fri., 11 A.M.–2 P.M.; dinner Mon.–Sat., 5–10 P.M.

Mia's. 4322 Lemmon (214–526–1020). Inexpensive Mexican specialties at a mon-and-pop restaurant. Mon.–Fri., 11 A.M.–2 P.M., 5–10 P.M.; Sat., noon–10 P.M. No credit cards.

Primo's. 3039 McKinney (214–520–3303). Casual, trendy Tex-Mex restaurant. Good food and an inviting neighborhood bar atmosphere make this a popular stop on the McKinney strip. Grilled chicken entrees come highly recommended. Mon.–Sat. 11 A.M.–2 A.M., until midnight Sun.

Raphael's has a convivial atmosphere, lethal margaritas, and an admirable Tex-Mex fare (chicken and sour cream enchiladas). Best location: 3701 McKinney (214–521–9640). Mon.–Fri., 11:30 A.M.–10:30 P.M.; Sat., noon–10:30 P.M.

Snuffer's. 3526 Greenville (214–826–6950). This bar-restaurant on Lower Greenville offers a limited menu of munchie fare, great burgers, and sinful French fries. Mon.–Sat., 11:30 A.M.–2 P.M.; Sun., noon–2 P.M.

Low Budget

Aw Shucks. 3601 Greenville (214–821–9449). In good weather diners sit outside and enjoy boiled shrimp, oysters, and catfish while watching the world stroll by. Restaurant serves what is probably best fried catfish in the city. Mon.–Sat. 11 A.M.–11 P.M., Sun. noon–9 P.M.

Chili's, at its various locations, features, chili, burgers, and nachos served at Mexican tile-top tables and surrounded by chili-culture memorabilia. Locations: 7567 Greenville (214–361–4371); 4291 Belt Line (at Midway), Addison (214–233–0380); 924 Copeland, Arlington (214–261–3891). These three open Mon.–Thurs., 11 A.M.–11:30 P.M.; Fri.–Sat., 11 A.M.–1 A.M.; Sun., 11 A.M.–11 P.M. 1901 North Central, Plano, open Mon.–Sat., 11:30 A.M.–1 P.M.; Sun., 11:30 A.M.–1:30 P.M.

Gaylen's. 826 N. Collins, Arlington (817–275–9422). Located in the Mid-cities, this restaurant serves traditional barbecue and all the trimmings in a no-frills dining room. Mon.–Sat., 11 A.M.–10 P.M.

Sonny Bryan's. 2202 Inwood (214–357–7210). Noteworthy, in Dallas, for its ribs and barbecue served to patrons who eat at school desks. Mon.–Fri., 7 A.M.–5 P.M.; Sat., 7 A.M.–3 P.M.; Sun., 11 A.M.–2 P.M.

Terilli's. 2815 Greenville (214–827–3993). Interesting Italian-influenced food served in art deco surroundings. Live jazz some nights. Sun., 11 A.M.–2 A.M.; Mon.–Sat., 11:30 A.M.–2 A.M.

Recommended Splurge. Dinner at the **Mansion on Turtle Creek,** 2821 Turtle Creek (214–526–2121), can cost more than $100 for two, but Sunday brunch, at $20 per person, offers a relatively inexpensive way to enjoy the lavish setting as well as a gorgeous meal. The sheer physical grandeur and oasislike solitude of the Mansion on Turtle Creek set it apart from any other restaurant in town. It was converted several years ago from the former home of oil and cotton magnate Shepherd King into a hotel and restaurant.

Picnics. A big cost cutter is the picnic. The visitor who succumbs to picnic fever and decides to head to the nearest city park can supplement his or her basic jug of wine and loaf of bread with deli meats and cheese from the delicatessen in the major supermarkets (Tom Thumb, Kroger, Safeway, and Skaggs Alpha Beta stores offer extensive deli departments).

Al's Food Store, 8209 Park Ln. near Greenville, offers more of the same but with an Italian, Greek, and Lebanese flair.

Or pick up a bucket of fried chicken from one of the fast-food chicken franchises.

Brunches. Dalt's, 5100 Belt Line, Suite 410 (214–386–9078), serves brunch (ice cream drinks, and extensive menu including sandwiches, salads, snacks) in what can only be described as early soda-fountain decor. Daily 11 A.M.–2 P.M.

Andrew's serves a special brunch menu plus regular menu (burgers and black bean soup). Popular bar. Restaurant on McKinney is reminiscent of New Orleans, especially if you are having brunch out on brick courtyard. Locations: 3301 McKinney (214–521–6536), 14930 Midway (214–385–1613), and 7557 Greenville (214–363–1910). All open 11:15–2 A.M.; Sun. brunch, 11:15 A.M.–3 P.M.

NIGHTLIFE AND BARS. Dallas possesses an ever-changing after-dark scene. Although traditional happy hours have been affected by a recent state law prohibiting two-for-one drinks, some drink specials can still be had. Check the Friday weekend magazines in the two dailies, the Dallas *Morning News* and the Dallas *Times Herald.*

The 21st-story **Encounters,** at the top of the Doubletree, 8250 N. Central, Dallas (214–691–8700), offers a view of glittery Far North Dallas, one of the best happy hours in town, and live music (no cover charge) for dancing until closing. Mon.–Fri., 4:30 P.M.–2 A.M.; Sat., 7 P.M.–2 A.M.; Sun., 7 P.M.–midnight.

The revolving **Top of the Dome** at Reunion Tower, Hyatt Regency, 300 Reunion Blvd., Dallas (214–651–1234), offers a free elevator ride to the top for those who stay for a drink. The view is impressive—almost all the way to Fort Worth on clear day—and worth the cost of a Chablis, at least. Mon.–Fri., 2 P.M.–2 A.M.; Sat., noon–2 A.M.; Sun., 7 P.M.–midnight.

Dallas Alley, in the West End Marketplace (214–988–WEST) offers eight nightclubs under one roof, for one cover price. Free champagne is available on weekdays at happy hour. Call for times, which vary for each establishment. Two standouts: the Boiler Room and Alley Oops.

Chaise Lounge, near downtown at 3010 N. Henderson (214–823–1400) offers SRO crowds, a roadhouse menu, and dance music. Mon.–Wed., 4 P.M.–1 A.M.; Thurs.–Sat., 4P.M.–2 A.M.

Other watering spots with good happy hours, all popular with Dallas's young professionals: **Studebaker's,** N. Central at Park (214–696–2475). Mon.–Sat., 11 A.M.–2 A.M.; Sun., 4 P.M.–2 A.M. **Brio,** Old Town center, 5500 Greenville Ave. (214–361–9517). Mon.–Fri., 4:30 P.M.–2 A.M.; Sat. 8 P.M.–3 A.M.; Sun., 7 P.M.–2 A.M. **Copy Cats,** 5111 Greenville (214–692–9855). Sing-a-long piano bar. Tues.–Fri., 5 P.M.–2 A.M.; Sat.–Sun., 7 P.M.–2 A.M.

Finally, while mechanical bulls, ostrich-feather-bedecked Stetsons, and John Travolta look-alikes have long faded away, the country-western scene remains important to natives. At the **Longhorn Ballroom,** 216 Corinth (214–428–3128), 704122 you will find a larger-than-life steer out front, a parking lot that easily could be mistaken for a Western movie set, and cactus pillars inside. Wed.–Thurs., 7 P.M.–1 A.M.; Fri.–Sat., 7 P.M.–2 A.M.; Sun., 5 P.M.–midnight. The **Belle Starr,** 7724 N. Central at Southwestern (214–750–4787), is another Western favorite. Mon., 8 P.M.–2 A.M.; Tues.–Sat., 7 P.M.–2 A.M.; Sun., 4 P.M.–2 A.M. Cover charge for both, $2 to $5.

In Fort Worth you can see the real thing: In the historic Stockyards is the **White Elephant Saloon,** 106 E. Exchange, Fort Worth (817–624–1887), for longneck Lone Star beers and live entertainment by country-western performers (usually no cover charge). Mon.–Sun., 11 A.M.–2 A.M.

You might get a look at a local media star or a politican at **Louie's,** the town's official media hangout. It's a homey bar, serving pizzas and sandwiches, owned by Louis Canalakes, *D Magazine's* Best Bartender winner. Recorded music. On the edge of downtown, 1839 N. Henderson (214–826–0505). Mon.–Sat., 3 P.M.–2 A.M.

SECURITY Despite a reputation for cleanliness and a friendly Texas atmosphere, the Metroplex, Dallas in particular, is experiencing a rising crime rate. Visitors should use common sense at all times: Never leave cars unattended or with the keys in the ignition; keep purses snapped or zipped and close to the body; and avoid walking on deserted, dark streets.

DENVER

by
Curtis W. Casewit

Longtime Fodor's editor Curtis W. Casewit has resided in the Denver area for nearly 40 years, written 30 books, and garnered several "Best Book" awards from the Colorado Author's League. He writes travel features for 40 international newspapers as well as teaching journalism at the University of Colorado.

In 1858 Denver was a small Indian village with plenty of buffalo to hunt on the plains to the east and a variety of game and fish in the mountains to the west. The tranquility of the village was permanently changed when Green Russell, a Georgia prospector married to a Cherokee Indian, found small amounts of placer gold on the banks of Cherry Creek where Denver now stands. That same year gold was also discovered near Dry Creek, in what is now the Denver suburb of Englewood. Word of the find spread eastward, and some 150,000 people began the trek across the wide plains in wagons and on foot.

By 1859 the gold rush was in full swing. Denver soon had dry goods stores, blacksmith shops, real-estate agencies, doctors, and lawyers. Rich diggings were found, and the city continued to grow in size and culture. When the gold played out, silver replaced it. Railroads and the cattle industry guaranteed Denver's place as the hub of the West.

The city also owes much to General William Larimer, often credited as Denver's founder. His log cabin, built in 1858 at what has become the downtown intersection of 15th and Larimer streets, was one of the town's first. (Nearly everyone else lived in tents.) Although the front door was made of an old coffin lid, his place was Denver's first to have a genuine glass window. It was Larimer who jumped the claim of an older "town corporation" across the Platte River and named the resulting settlement "Denver City" in honor of the territorial governor, General James W. Denver.

Denver has been called the Queen City of the Plains, the Mile-High City (the elevation is 5820 feet), and the Climate Capital of the World. It has also been called a big cow town, an appellation which no longer holds true. The Denver of today is a far cry from the rowdy cattle country of a generation ago. Indeed, anyone who knew Denver even a decade or two ago wouldn't recognize it today. The growing city with a small-town ambience has become a sophisticated full-fledged metropolis.

Denver, as the center of finance and commerce for the Southwest, experienced enormous growth over the past 15 years. Its population swelled with arrivals from New York, Dallas, San Francisco, and other capitals. The new families have reclaimed dilapidated downtown neighborhoods, such as historic Capitol Hill, restored the old brick and frame homes, and have made the area thrive again.

The new Denverites have brought with them their favorite shopping, dining, and entertainment from around the world. City stores offer wares from antique clothing to Oriental jade, computers, even Greek and Thai groceries. There are restaurants that serve haute cuisine as well as those specializing in ethnic foods. Thanks to a more and more sophisticated public, the Colorado state capital also excels in its cultural life. There are numerous colleges and two big universities with their libraries and lectures. The Denver Symphony and the Denver Center Theater Company are at home in ultra-modern performance halls in the heart of downtown; the Denver Art Museum hosts top international exhibits. Foreign motion pictures garner large audiences. Denver is now rated among the more cosmopolitan cities in the United States.

The Queen City of the Plains has retained some of her Western flavor, however. Much of her heritage remains in the shape of historic buildings, fine museums, and old mansions. The analysis of a piece of quartz for mineral content, the tanning of leather, the hand-polishing of Indian silver still go on with great expertise. Denver is the ideal place to acquire western wear and saddles of all varieties. Many city parks contain statues of cowboys. The annual National Western Stockshow has been a popular event locally for more than 75 years. And the city boasts some of the finest buffalo and elk steaks to be found anywhere.

Because of its size, Colorado's capital offers many choices to visitors traveling on a budget. Hundreds of fine restaurants with reasonable prices dot the city; low-cost accommodations are equally varied. Many museums and galleries are free, and theaters often offer discounted tickets. The mild climate gives tourists ample opportunities to discover Denver's many parks and green belts. The city's tourist attractions are fortunately close together in or near the downtown area. Many points of interest can be handled on foot.

Denver is enhanced by a back country that provides scenery and sports, resort towns, sky-piercing peaks, wild flowers, idyllic picnic spots—in a word, pure vacation country. The charming city of **Boulder** is 22 miles away, about half-an-hour's drive on the (free) Denver-Boulder turnpike. The Flatirons, huge slabs of reddish flagstone lifted by the same geologic forces which caused the Rocky Mountains to be born, tower high above the city and are its trademark. Boulder is a blend of western down-to-earth life with a worldly and academic culture. From Boulder you can take a number of scenic drives into the Rockies. The most popular route goes west through Boulder Canyon on Colorado 119 to Nederland, then north on the Peak to Peak Highway, with its panoramic mountain views. Another fascinating spot is the famed town of **Central City,** 40 miles west of

Denver on U.S. 6 and Colorado 119. This old-time mining town, with its gingerbread Victorian houses, was once declared "the richest square mile on Earth," and is a popular tourist attraction.

Whether your time in Denver is spent discovering some of its theaters, museums, and shops or whether you use the city as a base for exploring Colorado's beautiful high-country, the Mile-High City is sure to long remain a fond memory.

PRACTICAL INFORMATION

WHEN TO GO. Whether you're at work or at play, the high, dry, sunny climate of colorful Colorado is most certainly one of the "Top-of-the-Nation's" outstanding assets. The Mile-High City boasts an average of 300 sunny days a year. The climate allows a choice of activities in any season. The summer weather seldom reaches the sweltering discomfort of America's more humid regions. Colorado's dry air permits one to stroll, jog, hike, or play tennis in relative comfort even as the mercury hits the eighties. Evenings can be cool, however, so bring a jacket.

Winters are also moderate. The average temperature is nearly 30 degrees Fahrenheit. Occasional snow in the city melts after a day or so; cold is more easily tolerated because of the dry air. The white flakes can be unpredictable, however. A storm may come before Thanksgiving or not until Christmas. Plan your late fall or spring visit as if snowfalls could be a part of it. Occasional blizzards still hit the Mile-High City in March.

HOW TO GET THERE. Because of its central location, Denver has always been a major transportation hub. Most airlines, bus companies, and trains serve the city, offering a large number of choices and range of prices. Generally, if you arrive from a long distance, flying is the least expensive way to go. For shorter trips and for travel within the state, buses have the edge.

By air. Denver's Stapleton Airport is the sixth busiest in the world and is served by most major carriers. Among these are: *American, Continental, Delta, Eastern, America West, TWA, United,* and *USAir.* Regional lines include *Air Midwest, NorthWest,* and *Midway.* Among the commuter carriers are *Centennial, Continental Express,* and *United Express.* Many international air carriers also serve Denver.

By bus. *Greyhound-Trailways* serves Colorado and has a terminal in downtown Denver at 1055 19th St. and an information number: 292–2291.

By train. Amtrak has service from Chicago, San Francisco, Seattle, Portland, and Los Angeles. Special regional fares are available. See a travel agent for up-to-date details, or call 800–872–7245.

By car. Main highways into Denver are I-25 from Wyoming in the north and New Mexico in the south, I-70 from Utah in the west and Kansas in the east, and I-80S from Nebraska in the northeast.

TELEPHONES. The area code for Denver and the northern region of Colorado is 303; the Southern region can be reached by dialing 719. It is necessary to dial 1 before the number for calls outside Denver but in the state. Directory assistance in Denver is 1–411; from outside the city, dial 303–555–1212. For information on toll-free numbers, call 800–555–1212. Dial 0 and the number you wish to reach for operator-assisted calls (collect and person-to-person). Pay phones cost 20 or 25 cents.

Emergency Telephone Numbers. In the metropolitan area, dial either 911 or 0 for ambulance, fire department, or police. The State Patrol number is 757–9475. The Poison Control Hotline can be reached at 629–1123. For road conditions, phone 639–1111.

ACCOMMODATIONS. Hotels and motels in Denver range from the old, world-famous, and high-priced Brown Palace to budget chains. The city's size ensures

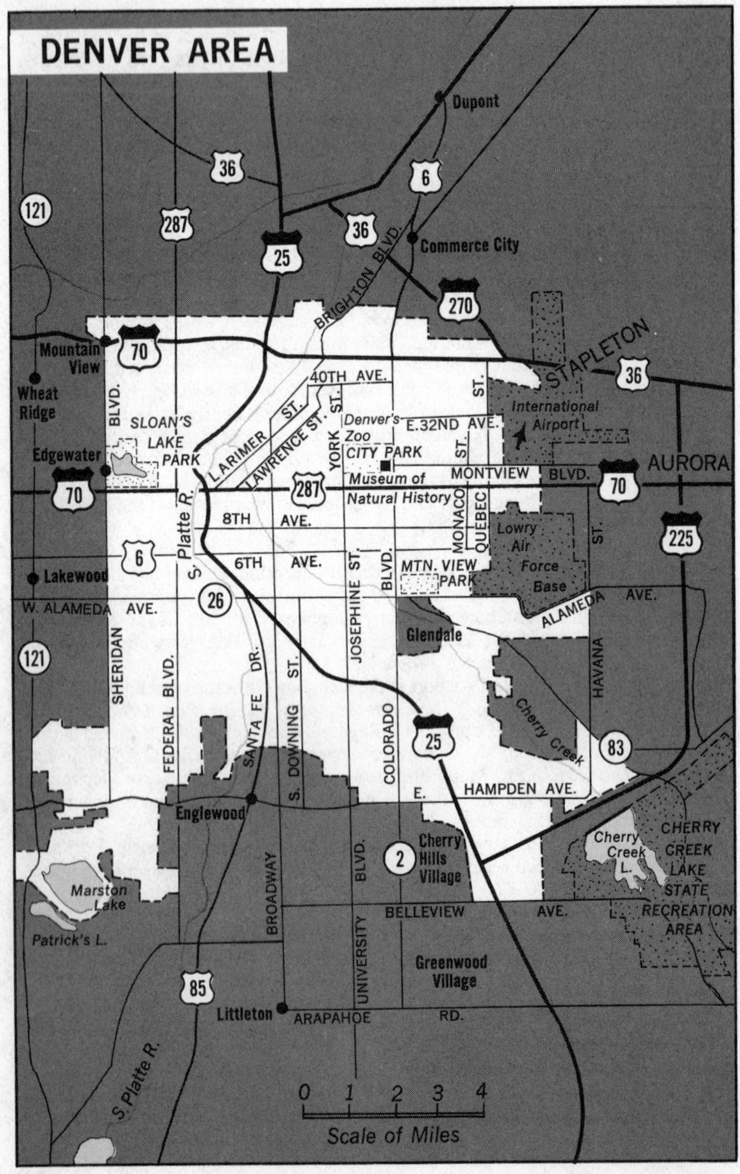
DENVER AREA
Dupont
Commerce City
Mountain View
Wheat Ridge
Edgewater
Lakewood
W. ALAMEDA AVE.
SLOAN'S LAKE PARK
40TH AVE.
LARIMER ST.
LAWRENCE ST.
YORK ST.
BRIGHTON BLVD.
Denver's Zoo
CITY PARK
E.32ND AVE.
Museum of Natural History
MONTVIEW BLVD.
STAPLETON International Airport
AURORA
8TH AVE.
6TH AVE.
MONACO
QUEBEC
Lowry Air Force Base
MTN. VIEW PARK
ALAMEDA AVE.
Glendale
Cherry Creek
HAVANA ST.
SHERIDAN BLVD.
FEDERAL BLVD.
S. Platte R.
SANTA FE DR.
S. DOWNING ST.
JOSEPHINE ST.
COLORADO BLVD.
E. HAMPDEN AVE.
Englewood
Cherry Hills Village
CHERRY CREEK LAKE STATE RECREATION AREA
Cherry Creek L.
Marston Lake
Patrick's L.
BROADWAY
UNIVERSITY BLVD.
BELLEVIEW AVE.
Greenwood Village
Littleton
ARAPAHOE RD.
S. Platte R.
0 1 2 3 4
Scale of Miles
36
6
121
287
25
270
70
225
26
83
2
85

that visitors will have many good and inexpensive places from which to choose. Generally, prices are lower during the winter, although regular rates may apply during the holiday season. Room taxes in the city and county of Denver are about 11.8 percent; in the suburbs, the rate varies but averages 7½ percent. All the suburban hotels and motels are within 15 miles of downtown.

Hotel rates are based on double occupancy. Categories, determined by price, are as follows: *Reasonable,* $30 to $40; *Very Economical,* $20 to $29.

Reasonable

American Family Lodge. 5888 Broadway, Denver, CO 80216 (303–296–3100). Four miles north at I-25, exit 215. Motel. Near Merchandise Mart.

American Family Lodge-West. 4735 Kipling St., Wheat Ridge, CO 80033 (303–423–0800). Eight miles west on I-70 on Wheat Ridge (exit 65). Heated pool; 24-hour café opposite.

Broadway Plaza. 1111 Broadway, Denver, CO 80203 (303–893–3501). Four blocks south of state capitol. Motel with 40 clean rooms, rooftop sun deck, free coffee. Cafés nearby.

Cameron Motel. 4500 E. Evans, Denver, CO 80222 (303–756–9431). Has 35 units, phones, and color TV.

Driftwood Motel. 1443 Oneida, Denver, CO 80220 (303–388–4261). Quiet motel near airport. Has heated pool, color TV.

Dunes Motel. 13000 E. Colfax, Denver, CO 80010 (303–344–3220). Pleasant motel with suites and kitchenettes. Near Fitzsimons Army Base.

Homestead Motel. 8837 W. Colfax, Lakewood, CO 80215 (303–232–8837). Clean, with heated pool. Close to restaurants.

Sands Motel. 13388 E. Colfax, Aurora, Co 80011 (303–366–3581). Waterbeds available. Some kitchens.

Very Economical

Anchor. 2323 S. Broadway, Denver, CO 80210 (303–744–3281). Four miles south on State 87. Small motel, free coffee, pets, sun deck; 24-hour café nearby. Good value.

Bar X Motel. 5001 W. Colfax, Denver, CO 80204 (303–534–7191). Quiet and clean; 15 units.

Biltmore Motel. 8900 E. Colfax, Aurora, CO 80010 (303–364–9286). Close to airport; offers courtesy car service. Restaurant nearby.

Rosedale Motel. 3901 Elati, Denver, CO 80216 (303–433–8345). Off I-25 at 38th Ave. A modest motel with basic rooms. Credit cards accepted.

Six Pence Inn. 9920 W. 49th Ave., Wheat Ridge, CO 80033 (303–424–0658). At I-70 and Kipling. Across from Furr's Cafeteria and Denny's.

Trails End Motel. 9025 W. Colfax, Lakewood, CO 80215 (303–237–5434). Nice rooms, some with waterbeds. Kitchens available. Pool.

Budget Motel Chains. The Mile High City has a list of chain motels almost a mile long. Prices are generally reasonable, and you get consistent standards and very often a toll-free telephone number for making reservations. Here are some of the better Denver chains.

Days Inn. Nicely furnished rooms, gift shops, and a restaurant are available in most Days Inns, as well as outdoor pools. For toll-free reservations phone 800–325–2525. Three Denver motels: *Denver North,* 36 E. 120th, Northglenn, CO 80233 (303–457–0688); *Denver West,* 15059 W. Colfax, Golden, CO 80401 (303–277–0200); *Denver East,* 9201 E. Arapahoe Rd., Englewood, CO 80111 (303–790–8220).

Denver 8 Motels. 620 N. Federal, Denver, CO 80204 (303–571–1715). Restaurant, color TV in rooms, swimming pool. Call toll-free 800–282–0711.

Friendship Inns. Each motel is independently owned, so rates vary. Call 800–453–4511 for reservations. Four Denver Inns: *Aristocrat Motor Hotel,* 4855 W. Colfax, Denver, CO 80204 (303–825–2755); *Kipling Inn,* 715 Kipling, Lakewood, CO 80215 (303–232–5000), located near a Coco's restaurant; *Mountain View Motel,* 14285 W. Colfax, Golden, CO 80401 (303–279–2526); *Red Coach Motor Inn,* 9201 E. Colfax, Aurora, CO 80010 (303–366–1586); several family restaurants close by.

Motel 6. Perhaps the best known budget chain. No toll-free number. Reserve in person early during the day. Televisions available at extra charge. Four area locations, each near a family restaurant: *Denver East,* 12020 E. 39th Ave., Denver, CO 80239 (303–371–1980); *Denver West,* 480 Wadsworth Blvd., Denver, CO 80226 (303–232–4924); *Denver North,* 6 W. 83d Place, Thornton, CO 80221 (303–429–1550); *Denver North West,* 10300 I-70 Frontage Rd., Wheat Ridge, CO 80033 (303–467–3172).

Regal 8 Inn. Free coffee, TV, comfortable rooms, and pools. Toll-free reservations at 800–851–8888. Two area motels: *Denver West,* 3050 W. 49th Ave., Denver, CO 80221 (303–455–8888); *Denver East,* 12033 E. 38th Ave., Denver CO 80239 (303–371–0740).

Relax Inn. 1680 Colorado Blvd., Denver, CO 80222 (303–691–2223, 800–661–9563). Canadian chain expanding into USA. Free HBO and Continental breakfast. Indoor pool and covered parking. Special weekend rates, senior discount.

Traveler's Inn. Three Denver units, all near family restaurants: the *airport area,* 3850 Peoria St., Denver, CO 80239 (303–371–0551); *Denver North,* 7333 Pecos, Denver, CO 80221 (303–427–9400); *Denver Southeast,* 14200 E. 6th Ave., Aurora, CO 80011 (303–366–7333).

Bed-and-Breakfast. Affectionately known as B&Bs, these guest homes provide the personal touch in accommodations and are becoming more popular every year. A B&B offers the warmth of sharing someone's house (in rooms set aside for that purpose), a delightful home-cooked breakfast, and the chance to get to know a local family. Rooms are infinitely varied, and you may have to head down the hall to the bathroom, but you often enjoy antique furniture or find fresh flowers on the bedside table. For a directory of guest homes in Denver, write to *Bed & Breakfast Colorado Ltd.,* Box 6061, Boulder, CO 80306. This service will assist you with reservations. B&Bs run $35–$100.

Ys and Hostels, located in most major cities, provide basic but economical alternatives for lodging. *YMCA,* 25 E. 16th Ave., Denver, CO 80202 (861–8300), downtown. Coffee shop in lobby; lobby open 24 hours. Check-in is between 11 A.M. and 10 P.M. on a first-come, first-served basis. Rooms are small but clean and have telephones. The YMCA has a separate floor for women. Cost for a double with bath is $31.25.

American Youth Hostels. 1452 Detroit St., Denver, CO 80206 (333–7672). Dormitory style, any age welcome. Three-night limit, communal kitchen. Bring sleeping bag or rent linens. Men and women on separate floors. Summer and winter rates for AYH members are $6. Nonmembers pay $8. Reservations with one-half deposit.

HOW TO GET AROUND. From the airport. Downtown is 7 miles from Stapleton International. Taxi service is readily available and costs from $8 to $10. Limousines to major hotels run $5 to city center, $7 to the southeast area (398–2284). City buses (50 to 75 cents) run every 30 minutes until 11:30 P.M. The last bus to downtown departs at 12:40 A.M. Cabs, limousines, and city buses leave from the lower level, doors 6–10.

By bus. The Denver Regional Transportation District (RTD) operates the city's buses. Buses run not only within Denver proper, but also out into the suburbs and to Boulder. Route and schedule information is available at 778–6000. Basic city fare, 50 cents; 75 cents at peak hours (6–9 A.M. and 4–6 P.M.); exact change required. Senior citizens, with ID, ride off-peak for only 10 cents. A free shuttle runs along the 16th Street Mall downtown. A first-time rider's kit with system maps, information, and two free passes can be obtained by writing RTD, Department of Marketing, 1600 Blake St., Denver, CO 80202.

By taxi. Cabs in Denver may be hailed or requested by phone. Taxis are usually plentiful in the city. Yellow Cab (292–1212) is one of the major operators, or call Metro Taxi (333–3333). Cabs operate on a "live meter" system, which means that in bad weather or heavy traffic rates change from by the mile to by the minute.

By rental car. All major agencies have offices in Denver, including airport booths. *Avis* and *Hertz*—the two most expensive—have toll-free numbers. Call *Avis* at 800–331–1212 and *Hertz* at 800–654–3131. The city has hundreds of rental offices. The least costly are often those which specialize in slightly older though mechanically sound vehicles. Best deals include the following: *Cheap Heaps* (393–0028), with free airport pick up; *Rent Rex-on-Wheels* (477–1635), with 20 free miles; *Rent-a-Lemon* (355–3666); and *Ugly Duckling* (722–8503 or 421–5600), with unlimited free in-state mileage.

HINTS TO THE MOTORIST. Two interstate highways intersect near downtown Denver. I-70 runs east-west; I-25, north-south. The Mile-High City's thoroughfares are simply arranged: north-south streets and east-west avenues from a grid. Street addresses start in both directions from Broadway, avenue addresses from Ellsworth. Street names fall in alphabetical order west of Broadway and east of Colorado Boulevard. Major east-west arteries include Colfax Avenue in the center of the metro area and Hampden Avenue to the south. North-south corridors include Wadsworth and Federal boulevards to the west and Colorado Boulevard to the east. In the heart of downtown Denver, thoroughfares are one-way and run diagonally to the normal grid. Numbered *streets* are in this section; in the balance of the city, *avenues* are numbered. (17th Street, for instance, is immediately downtown—17th Avenue is not.) It helps to remember that the mountains lie to the west.

The traffic usually flows smoothly, except during rush hours, generally 6:30–8:30 A.M. and 4–6 P.M., when it can be stop and go. (Most city AM radio stations provide traffic updates during the prime hours).

Parking downtown is hard to find and ranges from $1 a half hour to $6 a day. Parking is usually available in the suburbs. The Designated Snow Route signs around the city indicate on which streets parking is not allowed during a snowstorm. Unoccupied cars found on these roads during heavy storms will be towed. Parking for the disabled is indicated by blue and white signs.

The speed limit on highways is 55 mph except where marked. In the city, the limit is 25 mph, except where indicated. Right turns are permitted on a red light unless a sign indicates otherwise. Denver is hilly in some areas; if you park on an incline, remember to turn the front wheels into the curb when facing downhill, away from the curb when facing uphill. Children under 4 and those weighing under 40 lbs. must be strapped into an approved child-safety seat.

For advice on desert driving, see Hints to the Motorist in the Tucson chapter.

TOURIST INFORMATION. The *Denver Metro Convention and Visitors Bureau,* 225 W. Colfax Ave., Denver, CO 80202 (303–892–1112), provides an official visitors guide with a map and lists of attractions, events, and shopping. Winter hours, Mon.–Fri. 8 A.M.–5 P.M., Sat. 9 A.M.–1 P.M.; summer, Mon.–Fri. 8 A.M.–5 P.M., Sat. 9 A.M.–5 P.M. The bureau is just off the main business section and at the edge of the Civic Center Complex. The center is directly across from City Hall (distinguishable by the clock tower and chimes).

Foreign Currency. Foreign money can be exchanged for U.S. dollars at the airport, at the *United Bank Center,* 1700 Broadway (861–8811), and at *Deak Colorado, Inc.,* 1580 Court Pl., Denver, CO 80202 (571–0808).

HINTS TO HANDICAPPED TRAVELERS. Denver is becoming increasingly aware of the special needs of the handicapped, and public facilities are becoming more accessible. An excellent guide, *Access Denver,* describes the facilities at motels, restaurants, banks, churches, museums, stores, and theaters. Write the Sewall Rehabilitation Center, 1360 Vine St., Denver, CO 80206, to receive a copy. A donation is appreciated but not required. For information on wheelchair lifts on public buses, call RTD at 303–778–6000.

FREE EVENTS. Denver boasts the nation's second largest **Saint Patrick's Day Parade,** followed by an **Irish Pub Crawl** along Larimer Square downtown. Held the weekend closest to Saint Patrick's Day. **The Capitol Hill People's Fair,** held in June at Civic Center Park, downtown Denver, features free music, arts and crafts, food booths, and a merry party atmosphere. Fourth of July **fireworks displays** are numerous, and some are free. Local newspapers and newscasts have details. The *Drums Along the Rockies* competition is held at Mile High Stadium in July. **Festival of Mountain and Plain** on Labor Day offers music and low-cost samples from the culinary arts of about 30 local restaurants. It's held at Civic Center Park, downtown. Larimer Square gears up again the last two weekends in September and the first weekend in October with **Oktoberfest,** a lively German festival. A Dickens-style **Christmas walk** is held in Larimer Square every weekend from Thanksgiving to Christmas. The *Parade of Lights,* a beautiful nighttime event, is held downtown the first week of December.

The third Wed. of every month sees a **free concert** at lunchtime at the *Arvada Center for the Arts and Humanities,* 6901 Wadsworth Blvd. (422–8050). The *Denver Symphony Orchestra* offers four or five free concerts each year. Dates vary, call 572–1151 for information. In nice weather, music, entertainment, and exhibits abound on the downtown **Denver Mall,** especially during weekday lunch hours. Check local listings.

TOURS AND SPECIAL-INTEREST SIGHTSEEING. *Gray Line,* (289–2841), sells a deluxe, six-hour city and mountain tour which includes the main sights of Denver and the mountain parks. Children receive a discount. Write Box 38667, Denver,Co 80238. Tours depart from the Greyhound depot, 1055 19th St., downtown. *Historic Denver,* 1701 Wynkoop, Denver, CO 80202 (534–1858), offers two-hour van tours (adults, $10; seniors and children, $8) and walking tours (adults, $5; seniors and children, $4).

Denver Center for the Performing Arts. 14th St. and Curtis (893–4200). Free tours Wed. and Fri., 12:10 P.M. or by arrangement.

United States Mint. 320 Colfax (844–3322). You can see money being made on a free 25-minute tour. Mon.–Fri., 8:30 A.M.–3 P.M. at 30-minute intervals.

The Capitol Building, intersection of Broadway and Colfax, downtown (866–5000). Modeled after the U.S. Capitol in Washington, it has a gold dome and an elegant interior. Tours Mon.–Fri., 9 A.M.–4 P.M.

The Governor's Mansion. 8th Ave. and Pennsylvania (866–3682). Open for tours at announced times during the year. The house is surrounded by terraced gardens and ancient elms.

PARKS AND GARDENS. Over 150 parks attract city dwellers in droves on the weekend; the best time to go is on weekdays, particularly in the morning. Most of the parks have show-quality flower gardens, pools, picnic areas, and plenty of trees. Denver's parks are open from daylight to 11 P.M. For more information, call 575–2552.

Begin with Denver's largest, **City Park.** You reach it from downtown in 10 minutes of driving; enter through the gates at East 17th Ave. and York St. It's on the RTD bus line. The park is ideal for the economy-minded. Feed ducks at a small lake, take long walks on clean paths, and watch the children in a myriad of playgrounds. Active youngsters and exercise-seeking adults will welcome City Park's large lake, with its many paddle boats that work like bicycles. Denver's zoo is in the park (modest admission charged). In the zoo, a small train circles a lagoon and crosses tiny trestle bridges with a view of geese and swans; hours are 10–5 daily. Nearby you'll also view City Park's considerable tennis action. There are 15 hard surface courts, always available free on a first-come, first-served basis.

A weekday may be the best day to picnic and stroll through **Washington Park,** at S. Downing and E. Virginia, not far from E. Alameda Ave. Small creeks flow under willows and cottonwoods, students from nearby Denver University jog along the trails, elderly gentlemen enjoy a game of *boccie,* a soccer match draws crowds of cheering onlookers. On bus lines 3A and 12.

Four miles from downtown, on the drive to the mountains, is **Sloan's Lake Park,** at W. 26th and Sheridan (or enter from W. Colfax Ave.). On a clear day the view of the mountains is spectacular. Denverites use the park for sailing, motor boating, fishing, bicycling, tennis, or just walking around. It takes about an hour to circle the lake on foot. Also on the bus lines.

Denver Botanic Gardens, 1005 York St. (331–4010), offers outdoor gardens and a conservatory with beautiful arrangements of native and exotic plant life; 800 species of tropical and subtropical plants thrive year-round in the steel and glass conservatory. Daily, 9 A.M.–4:45 P.M. Adults, $3; seniors, $1.50; children 7 to 16, $1.

ZOOS. Denver's Zoological Gardens (331–4110) are located in City Park. Several thousand animals are housed in native habitats. The *children's zoo* sports a monkey island and cavorting seals. There are also several walk-through bird houses and a "Northern Shores" exhibit which features arctic animals. Daily, 10 A.M.–5 P.M. Adults, $4; children and seniors, $2.

PARTICIPANT SPORTS. With its 300 sunny days a year, Denver is a marvelous place for active people. Walk, bike, hike, ski, play tennis, swim—the Mile High City has it all. For **joggers,** there are paths in almost every city park. *City Park,* with its beautiful flower gardens, is especially nice. Or jog around *Sloan's Lake* at 26th Ave. and Sheridan. *Cheesman Park,* E. 8th Ave. and Franklin St., also has lovely scenery. Denver has an extensive network of **bike paths.** A map is available from the *Bicycle Racing Association of Colorado,* 1290 Williams St., Denver, CO 80218 (303–333–2453). Public **swimming pools** are located at *Congress Park,* E. 9th Ave. and University; *Eisenhower Park,* S. Colorado Blvd. and E. Dartmouth; and *Washington Park,* S. Downing and Exposition.

For **tennis buffs** there are numerous free courts. Try *City Park* at E. 23d Ave. and Josephine. *Washington Park,* S. Downing St. and E. Virginia Ave.; *Crestmoore,* First and Monaco; *Sloan's,* W. 26th Ave. and Tennyson St.; *Eisenhower Park,* S. Colorado Blvd. and E. Dartmouth Ave.; *Kunsmiller Junior High School,* W. Iliff Ave. and S. Quitman St.; *Bellevue Park,* E. 12th Ave. and Cherry St.; *Berkeley Park,* W. 46th Ave. and Tennyson St. Call 575–2552 for information.

For **racquetball,** try the *YMCA,* 25 E. 16th St., downtown. An $8 fee allows use of all facilities, including pool.

Golfers will find municipal courses at *City Park,* 2500 York (295–2585); *Kennedy,* 10500 E. Hampden Ave. (751–0311); *Overland Park,* S. Santa Fe Dr. and Jewell Ave. (777–7331); *Wellshire,* 3333 S. Colorado Blvd. (756–1352); and *Willis Case,* W. 50th and Vrain (575–2112). The fee for 18 holes is $12.

Fishing is permitted at all public lakes. A license is required and can be obtained at most sporting-goods stores. The cost is $7.25 for 2 days, $18.25 for 10 days. For a free map of area lakes, try *High Country Bass Pro Shop,* 1126 S. Sheridan (934–4156). If your enthusiasm leans toward **hiking,** exploring, and **mountain climbing,** consider the *Colorado Mountain Club.* This club trains for and organizes hikes and climbs—more than 500 adventures a year—both winter and summer. Guests are charged a fee per hike. The Colorado Mountain Club is located at 2530 W. Alameda (922–8315).

SPECTATOR SPORTS. The Denver area's auto race-tracks offer everything from Indianapolis-type formula cars to motorcycle competition. Nearest is *Lakeside Speedway* at the amusement park, W. 44th Ave. and Sheridan. The Sunday night programs run from early May through Labor Day. Call 477–1621. *Bandimere Speedway,* 3051 S. Rooney Rd. (697–6001), attracts drag racing fans to the foothills of the Rockies, April–September.

The 74,000 seats in *Mile High Stadium,* Federal Blvd, and 17th Ave., just west of downtown, are never enough to hold all the fans of the Denver *Broncos* **football** team. The team has improved greatly in recent years and is now a city-wide passion. Fans wait for years to get tickets; they brave traffic jams around the stadium at game times. Parking is usually adequate. Call 288–4653. Next to the stadium, the Denver *Nuggets* **basketball** team is based in McNichols Arena. The season runs Oct. to May. Tickets are $8 to $16; call 575–5833.

Ice hockey draws its following to use Denver University Arena to see the school's popular *Pioneers* play during the winter season. Call 871–2774 for game schedules.

If you have never seen a **dog race,** try the *Mile High Kennel Club* at Colorado Blvd. and E. 62d Ave. The greyhounds run six nights a week (closed Sun.), June–Aug., with matinees on Sat. Betting is legal for those 18 or over. Admission is 50 cents, programs cost $1, and parking is free. Phone 288–1591 for more information.

Each Jan., Denver hosts the week-long **National Western Stock Show** (297–1166), with a rodeo, cattle displays, and myriad contests. Rodeo tickets include admission to all grounds shows. For further information, write to National Western Stock Show, 1325 E. 46th Ave., Denver, CO 80216.

CHILDREN'S ACTIVITIES. A full day may easily be spent in **City Park** (see above) with its zoo, museum, and playgrounds. **Elitch Gardens,** 4620 W. 38th Ave. (455–4771), has a delightful kiddieland as well as the usual amusement-park attractions and beautiful flower gardens—at reasonable prices. The *Denver Public Library,* 1357 Broadway (571–2000), often features special children's programs. **The Children's Museum,** 2121 Crescent Dr. (433–7444), offers story hours, hands-on displays, health screening, and much more. Sun.–Fri., noon–5 P.M.; Sat., 10 A.M.–5 P.M. Adults and children, $2.25; seniors, $1.50.

HISTORIC SITES. The **Molly Brown House,** 1340 Pennsylvania Ave., (832–4092), home of the "unsinkable Molly Brown," recreates Denver's rich Victorian house in 1894. It has been beautifully restored. Tues.–Sat., 10 A.M.–3 P.M.; Sun., noon–3 P.M. Adults, $3; children 6 to 18, $1; those over 60, $1.50. Straight south of Molly's place, at 8th Avenue and Pennsylvania, is another famous residence, the **Colorado Governor's Mansion.** It's surrounded by terraced gardens and ancient elms. The house is open on summer Tuesdays; during the rest of the year special days are selected. Admission is free. Phone 866–3682. **Four Mile Historic Park,** 715 S. Forest, surrounds the oldest house in Denver. Tues.–Sun., 11 A.M.–5 P.M. Modest admission price.

MUSEUMS AND GALLERIES. Denver is a fast-growing city, and its museums and galleries reflect that growth. Here are some of the most notable: **Denver Museum of Natural History,** Montview and Colorado boulevards, in City Park (370–6363), features four floors of dinosaurs, Indian artifacts, insects, birds, and animals from around the world. Don't miss the moose and elk displays and the whale exhibit. Open daily 9 A.M.–5 P.M. Adults, $3.50; children and seniors, $1.50. **Gates Planetarium,** attached to the museum, offers laser-light concerts and trips through time and space projected onto an overhead 50-foot dome. Program information, 370–6351. The museum is also home to the *Imax Theater,* with its huge screen and elaborate sound system. Exciting shorts are featured. Call 370–6300 for show times.

The Colorado History Museum, 1300 Broadway (866–3682), houses artifacts and photos from Denver's early life, ancient Mesa Verde Indian pieces, and a fascinating diorama of Denver as it was in 1860. The center contains the treasures collected by the Colorado Historical Society, including many permanent exhibits.

The Denver Art Museum, 100 W. 14th Ave. Parkway (575–2793), houses a motley collection that includes U.S., Western, African, Oriental, and pre-Columbian items plus one or two masterpieces by Rembrandt, Picasso, Matisse, Renoir, Rubens, and others. There are also textiles, costumes, pottery, jewelry, period rooms, and antique furniture. Museum hours are Sun., 12–5 P.M.; Tues.–Sat., 9 A.M.–5 P.M.; closed Mon. Adults, $2.50; seniors, students, and children, $1.50.

The Museum of Western Art, at 1727 Tremont Place (296–1880), is outstanding and fits Denver's Western image. Open Tues. through Sat., 10 A.M.–4:30 P.M. Adults $3, children free.

The Buckhorn Exchange, 1000 Osage St., close to downtown (534–9505), is worth a visit just before lunchtime. Contents of this museum-in-a-restaurant include hundreds of historic photos, ancient western guns (including Sitting Bull's Colt .45), trophies and antlers of every description, Indian mementos, and paintings. There is no charge to view the collection, but visitors might wish to try the unusual western fare. Lunches are moderate; dinners, which include buffalo, quail, rabbit, and elk, are more expensive.

There are three interesting galleries in Golden, 10 miles west of Denver, **Foothills Art Center,** 809 15th St., Golden, CO 80401 (279–3922), built in 1892 and originally a Presbyterian church now houses regional arts and crafts. Open Mon.–Sat., 9 A.M.–4 P.M. Colorado School of Mine's **Geologic Museum** is nearby at 16th and Maple (273–3823). The 1940 structure displays mineral ore, fossils, mining equipment, meteorites, and even a replica of an old gold mine. The museum's hours are Mon.–Sat., 9 A.M.–4 P.M.; Sun., 1–4 P.M. Free. Also in Golden, **The Railroad Museum,** 17155 W. 44th Ave. (279–4591), has an 1880s style depot, historical exhibits, old narrow-gauge locomotives, and railroad and trolley cars. Daily, 9 A.M.–5 P.M. A family rate of $5.50 is offered.

FILM. Art and revival houses, featuring foreign films, oldies, and art flicks, include *The Ogden,* 935 E. Colfax (832–4500); *The Esquire,* 6th and Downing (733–5757); and the beautifully restored *Mayan,* 1st and Broadway (744–6796). Several chains, such as the *Thornton 3,* 761 E. 88th (287–9112); and *Brentwood 4,* Federal and Evans (935–4647) play second-run movies at very low prices. Most theaters offer reduced rates on twilight and matinee shows, and senior citizens get discounts. Check the listings in Denver's newspaper for times and locations.

Denver's first-run houses (charging adults $4.50 to $5.50 and children $2.50 to $3) include the *Continental,* S. Valley Highway at Hampden (758–2345); *Century 21,* 1370 S. Colorado Blvd. (759–0221); the *Cooper,* 960 S. Colorado Blvd., (757–7681); and *Trivoli 12,* 9th and Larimer (571–1000).

MUSIC. Denver has a variety of music, from bluegrass to opera. Check the entertainment sections of the Denver *Post* and the *Rocky Mountain News* for up-to-date music listings. Here are the major music groups in the city; **Avada Center for the Arts and Humanities,** 6901 Wadsworth Blvd., Arvada, CO 80003 (422–8050), offers everything from jazz to chamber music.

Denver Symphony Orchestra, Boettcher Concert Hall, 950 13th, Denver (592–7777), imports world-renowned conductors and musicians. The DSO also goes in for a jazz series, a pops series, and special outdoor concerts. The **Paramount Theater,** 1621 Glenarm Pl. (825–4904) showcases the Gibson Jazz Concerts and a variety of music. **Red Rocks Park,** near Morrison, is a 30-minute drive from Denver and well worth it for hard-rock enthusiasts. Concerts are performed in a natural amphitheater formed by jutting red sandstone formations. Call 575–2638 for concern information. Open June to Labor Day.

DANCE in Denver also takes many forms. **Ballet Denver,** 3955 Tennyson (455–4974), offers the quintessence of classical dance. Lecture-demonstrations and performances in schools around the city. **Colorado Contemporary Dance,** 1290 Williams, Denver, CO 80218 (321–6583), advertises performances by well-known companies several times each year. **Arvada Center for the Arts and Humanities,** 6901 Wadsworth Blvd., Arvada, CO 80003 (422–8052), brings nationally known troupes for its fall to spring programs. **New Dance Theater,** 2006 Lawrence St. (295–1759), is home to the Cleo Parker Robinson Dance Troupe, which stages ultra-modern dance performances at various times during the year.

STAGE. The Denver Center for the Performing Arts, 1050 13th St. (893–4000), offers playgoers several choices. The *Denver Center Company* performs in repertory Mon.–Sat., fall through spring. The Center also presents nationally known touring companies. *The Source,* a 158-seat theater, stages world premieres of locally written plays. Weeknight performances are less expensive than weekend shows, and during the first week of a production tickets sell at about half the regular price. **StageWest,** in the Galleria of the Denver Arts Center, offers professional off-Broadway-type productions in a 250-seat cabaret with bar; **Center Attractions** brings road tours of Broadway shows to the Auditorium Theater, in the same complex.

The Arvada Center, 6901 Wadsworth, Arvada, CO 80003 (422–8050), features a variety of attractions in fall and winter.

The Changing Scene, a small downtown theater, 1527½ Champa (893–5775), offers 20 original productions each year.

Opera Colorado runs several productions every year for a short season at the Denver Arts Center (893–4000).

Jack's Center for the Performing Arts, 1553 Platte St. (480–1219) is an intimate theater setting of only 95 seats. Various groups, such as *City Stage Ensemble,* offer musicals and drama here.

The Lowenstein Theatre, 2526 E. Colfax (322–7725), presents good actors from the community Sept. through June, with several children's shows. The Bonfils' BoBan's Cabaret presents mostly off-Broadway fare.

Heritage Square Opera House, Box D109, Golden (279–7881), offers a change of pace with live Western "melodrama." Open year-round.

SHOPPING. Downtown, retail shops line the 16th Street Mall from Court Place to Arapahoe St. Here you will find major department stores: *May D & F Company, Joslins,* and *Fashion Bar.* Try the basements for good bargains. *Loehmann's,* 7400 E. Hampden (779–6890), offers discounted designer clothes for women.

For the best deals on **skis** and other **sporting goods,** there is *Dave Cook,* 16th St. and Market, downtown (892–1929); and *Gart Brothers,* 1000 Broadway (861–1122). For **western wear,** *Miller Stockman,* 1409 15th St., carries a full array of authentic cowboy garb. *Kohlberg's* at 1720 Champa is the best place in the city to find **Indian crafts.** The store was opened in 1888 and still has its own Indian silversmith; the Kohlbergs are authorities on Pueblo pottery, turquoise, and all Native American arts. You can lose yourself browsing among the rugs, bracelets, and other items. *Robert Waxman Camera,* 913 15th St., is a stop for discount cameras, **photo supplies,** and advice.

DINING OUT. The restaurants of Denver and its large metropolitan area are often underestimated. There are approximately 2,000 restaurants, cafés, bistros, pizza places, franchises, taverns serving food, cafeterias, and other establishments where you can eat. You can find every type of fare in Denver, from haute cuisine to the simplest cowboy fare. Foreign restaurants proliferate, Western steak houses are abundant, and practically everywhere you can get excellent mountain trout.

Restaurant categories determined by the price of a meal for one person, without beverages, tip, or taxes, are as follows: *Reasonable,* $8.50–$13; *Very Economical,* $6–$8; and *Low Budget,* under $6. The restaurants, unless otherwise indicated, accept major credit cards.

Reasonable

Apple Tree Shanty. 8710 E. Colfax (333–3223). Takes no reservations but usually has enough room for families. Pit-prepared ribs a house specialty. Sizable dessert menu. Waitresses in Dutch-style garb.

Betty Rose. 1404 Larimer (623–0123). Downstairs restaurant with a Cajun accent: spicy shrimp, Cajun pork, garlic chicken, good seafood, and other dishes prepared by an innovative chef. Lively jazz club upstairs.

Hoffbrau Steaks. 13th and Santa Fe (629–1778). Large steaks; jukebox and bar.

Le Central. 112 E. 8th Ave. (863–8094). Genuine French restaurant at good prices. Lunch and dinner. Extremely busy. Many entrees, all excellent. French wines. No credit cards. Near downtown.

North Woods Inn. 6115 S. Santa Fe Dr., 12 miles southwest on U.S. 85 in Littleton (794–2112). This popular restaurant serves steak, beef stew, and logging-camp food with home-baked sourdough bread. The decor is north woods. Good value for big eaters.

Yuan Mongolian Barbeque. 7555 E. Arapahoe Rd. (771–6296). Mandarin, Cantonese, or Szechuan dishes, plus a Mongolian help-yourself barbecue.

Very Economical

Appleridge Cafe. 3790 Kipling (423–6800). Family-style. No credit cards.

Casa Bonita. 6715 W. Colfax (232–5115). Mexican food in a multitiered restaurant decorated with murals. Busy and entertaining. Mariachi music. Good for kids. "Mexican" restaurant for Americans.

Canton Landing. 6265 E. Evans (759–1228). Variety of Chinese cuisines under one roof. Luncheon buffet. Dinners daily until 10 P.M. Chinese beer.

Das Essen Haus Family Dining. Belmar Center, 1050 S. Wadsworth Blvd., Lakewood (936–7864). American version of German restaurant. Modest, bright, clean. No liquor.

The Egg Shell. 300 Josephine St., in Cherry Creek (322–1601). Extensive breakfast and lunch menu.

Harvest Restaurant and Bakery. 7730 E. Belleview (779–4111) and 430 S. Colorado Blvd. (399–6652). Natural foods.

Old Spaghetti Factory. 1215 18th Ave., downtown (295–1864). Pasta served in the old Denver Cable Car Company. Lively and crowded. A great value. No credit cards.

Swiss Bells. 7340 W. 38th Ave., Wheat Ridge (421–6622). Swiss cuisine, and some lighter "diet" dishes, served. No liquor served. No credit cards.

White Fence Farm. 6263 W. Jewell Ave. between S. Sheridan and Wadsworth boulevards (935–5945). In a meadow en route to mountains (car needed). Great American food with a southern accent and served by girls in historic colonial dress. Freshly baked goods. Liquor. Excellent-quality food. Mostly local clientele. Dinner only. Closed Mon. Senior discount.

Low Budget

King's Table. Buffet style. Eat all you want. Five locations: 6206 W. Alameda (935–6101), 11101 W. Colfax (238–8611), 12600 E. Colfax (341–5363), 10695 Melody Dr. (452–7547), and 7850 Sheridan (428–3662).

Recommended Splurge. Every budgeteer will jettison the best economy intentions at least once during a stay in a city like Denver, which boasts some 2,000 restaurants. Among the best choices in deluxe dining is **Chateau Pyrenees,** 6538 S. Yosemite Circle, Englewood (770–6660). Grandeur in furnishings, chandeliers, splendid French Chateau ambience, tuxedoed waiters and waitresses. Colorado's most elaborate menu, in French. Outstanding Swiss chef. Hors d'oeurves include escargots, lobster, and delicacies in champagne sauce. Entrees feature venison medallions, chateaubriand, roast rack of lamb, fish, and elegant fowl such as a baby poussaint and roast quail. All beautifully presented. Classical piano music, international wine list. Austrian proprietor Conrad Trinkaus is a perfectionist and always on the premises. Reservations essential.

Cafes and Coffeehouses. Hummel's Sidewalk Café. Cherry Creek Shopping Center, on 1st Ave. near University (322–4144). Outdoors in summer, indoors when it gets cold. Cheesecake, puddings, pastries, deli sandwiches. 10:30 A.M.–7 P.M., Mon.–Fri.; 9 A.M.–6 P.M. Sat.; closed Sun.

Racine's. 850 Bannock St. (595–0418). Their in-house bakery produces homemade pastries and pastas. Mon.–Fri. 7 A.M.–midnight; Sat. 8 A.M.–midnights; Sun. 8 A.M.–11 P.M.

NIGHTLIFE AND BARS. Denver's teeming nightlife can present a visitor—or even a resident—with many choices. Serious plays, "melodramas," opera, concerts, ballets, choirs, nightclubs, and "atmosphere" lounges abound. The drinking age in Colorado is 21; 18 for 3.2 beer. Liquor may only be purchased at liquor stores (closed Sun.), with the exception of 3.2 beer, available in supermarkets.

Rock and disco. The scene centers in Glendale, a nearby suburb that has been completely surrounded by Denver expansion. Leetsdale Dr. east from Colorado Blvd. is the main area for action; the places to try include *Bogart's,* 5231 Leetsdale Dr. (388–9393) has five bars and two dance floors. $1 cover charge; *NEO,* 350 S. Birch (320–0117); *Lauderdale's,* 2250 S. Monaco St. (756–4555), happy hour buffet. Big-name rockers appear regularly at *McNichols Arena,* and in the summer at *Red Rocks.*

Folk and Country.*Country Land,* at 7600 Highway 2 (288–9903). Features a live polka band and country-western music every night.

Comedy.*The Comedy Works,* 1226 15th (595–3637). Young, eager comedians, young crowd. *George Mc Kelvey's Comedy Club,* 7225 E. Hampden (758–5275), showcases improv groups and top-name comedians.

Dancing. *Park Hill Golf Club,* 35th Ave. and Colorado Blvd. (333–5411), puts on Sunday dances; *Bobby McGee's,* 2852 W. Bowles Ave. (730–0080), has a sunken dance floor, light show, and rock music.

Jazz. Try the Denver jazz-lovers' favorite, the *El-Chapultepec.,* Lower downtown at 19th and Market (295–9126). Very much worth visiting, in the popular North Cherry Creek area, is *The Bay Wolf,* 231 Milwaukee (388–9221). Live jazz seven nights a week, no cover charge (but drinks are on the expensive side). Open until 2 A.M. nightly except Sun., until midnight. Blackboard menu in bar. Formal dining room. Rated by *Esquire* magazine as one of the top 100 new nightclubs in the country in 1983, and still living up to its reputation.

Some nice bars. *Bonnie Brae Tavern,* 740 S. University (777–2262), is an old-style, neighborhood bar with good pizza. The lounge of *The Burnsley* hotel, 1000 Grant St. (830–1000), is plush, quiet, and intimate. *Ironworks,* 25 Larimer (825–4901), in a restored factory near Mile High Stadium, serves great hot Buffalo chicken wings. *Governor's Park,* 672 Logan (831–8605). Happy Hour, with free hors d'oeuvres, 4:30–6 P.M. Popular spot among Denver's young business crowd.

SECURITY. Denver and its suburbs are safe enough, if you know where to go at night, and which areas to avoid. On the positive side, the tourist is quite secure in the downtown area, meaning anywhere near the big hotels—the Westin, Hyatt Regency, Brown Palace, Oxford, and Radisson. Likewise, the well-lit 16th Street Mall and the famous Larimer Square Section—both downtown—do a big dinner and entertainment business until the late hours, and therefore present no problems.

A visitor can take a stroll along East Colfax Avenue between Broadway and Downing Street during the day when all kinds of boutiques, little bookstores and small cafés are busy. At night, however, it is wise to leave this East Colfax "Capitol Hill" area to some of its mixed denizens—the homeless and drunk, occasional prostitutes of both genders, drug addicts, and panhandlers.

There are few such folk in Denver's suburbs; nevertheless it's not a good idea to give a lift to *any* hitchhiker, young or old, male or female at any time of day or night. Denver's parks see lots of joggers, walkers, and picnickers during daytime, but are generally empty at night.

Many travelers arrive at Stapleton International Airport after dark, rent a car, and then head for their hotel. The airport hotels are easy to reach. But if you have a reservation downtown—perhaps at the Marriott or Brown Palace—you're best off to look for I-70 and then follow the signs for the downtown exits.

HONOLULU

by
Jeri Bostwick

Jeri Bostwick admits to a 20-year love affair with the Hawaiian Islands. She is presently Pacific bureau chief for TravelAge Magazines, and this is her third guidebook to the Sandwich Isles. Honolulu is her hometown.

The Hawaiian islands and their capital, Honolulu, only a 4½-hour flight from the West Coast, are a world apart from other American cities. They are exotic, romantic, and foreign but also familiar, with the incomparable comforts of American hotels and condominiums. At 20 degrees north latitude, in the middle of the Pacific, Hawaii is 2,000 miles from its nearest populated neighbors and is the youngest land group on earth. There are 122 islands in the Hawaiian chain, spreading 1,500 miles across the Pacific in a northwesterly direction from the volcanic hot spot that created them several million years ago. Most are truncated ocean-floor mountains, awash at high tide. Hawaii, the Big Island, whose constant molten lava flows add new land yearly, is the southernmost of the eight major islands of the archipelago. In order of size, they are Hawaii, Maui, Oahu—with its capital city of Honolulu—Kauai, Molokai, Lanai, Niihau, and Kahoolawe. Each has a personality and a loveliness all its own.

There's more to Oahu than Diamond Head. More than 210 miles of golden beaches spangled with sapphire-blue bays are strung around the 608 square miles of the island. The Waianae Mountains brooding in their blue haze edge the western shore, and the rest of the island is divided by the green velvet folds of the Koolau Mountains, sparkling with morning rain and arched by Oahu's frequent double rainbows. The spectacular Pali

Pass lookout and Pali Highway connect windward Oahu—with its banana groves, canefields, awesome surf at Banzai, Pipe Line and Sunset beaches, and neat suburbs—and bustling Honolulu—with historic Pearl Harbor, the peaceful Punchbowl National Cemetery, and that fabled beach and its surrounding resort, Waikiki.

Nicknamed "the Gathering Place," Oahu has more than 85 percent of the state's 1 million residents and dominates the other islands politically, economically, and culturally. As set up by the founding fathers in the 1800s, the city and county of Honolulu covers all of the island of Oahu.

Honolulu is an enchanting city of clean architecture, low and high rise, set between the Pacific and the green Koolaus in the narrow strip along the island's southern shore. From Koko Crater to Pearl Harbor, houses climb up all the steep hillsides and flowering trees line winding roadways. White sails and brightly colored spinnakers mark the outer edge of the protecting coral reef that produces the famous Hawaiian surf, ever breaking on the city's gold sand beaches. Its cosmopolitan people—a pleasing mélange of many cultures—make Honolulu unique. Everyone is a member of an ethnic minority, for no single racial group accounts for more than one-third of Oahu's population.

The first people to discover and settle the islands—a part of the South Pacific in the vast north Pacific—were Polynesians whose double-rigged voyaging canoes probably reached the island of Kauai between A.D. 200 and 400. The rest of the world did not learn of the islands until the English explorer Captain James Cook made landfall, also on Kauai, in 1778. Other explorers and traders soon followed. Local chiefs ruled each island as if their pagan, feudal society were a time capsule, until the powerful Kamehameha I (a contemporary of George Washington) united the islands into one kingdom in 1810.

Following Kamehameha the Great's death in 1819, his favorite queen, Kaahumanu, and Queen Keopuolani, mother of his heirs, were a potent force in turning the allegiance of Liholiho (Kamehameha II) away from the centuries-old worship of many gods and a structured system of taboos. Ancient idols were thrown down, and temples were destroyed. The fabric of Hawaiian life was ripped apart, and the young king turned to the lifestyle of the foreigners. Boston Congregational missionaries who arrived in 1820 assembled a written language for the Hawaiians. All the islands became literate and mostly Christian in the brief span of 50 years. Hawaii had leaped into the nineteenth century, and Hawaiian royalty was on a collision course with the English and Americans for control of the island kingdom.

Lord George Paulet forced the islands into a provisional cession to the British Empire in 1843, but the English backed out gracefully in a few months. In 1893, a large American proannexation group deposed Queen Liliuokalani and imprisoned her within Iolani Palace. The United States, however, was reluctant to actually annex the islands. Because the small Republic of Hawaii sorely needed a sugar reciprocity act, the government besieged President McKinley until he signed annexation papers in 1898. Hawaii became a U.S. territory in 1900 and the fiftieth U.S. state in 1959.

Honolulu, situated on the only deep-water harbor in the islands, was a Johnny-come-lately in the hierarchy of power. After the British Captain Brown discovered Honolulu harbor (the name means "sheltered bay") in 1794, trading ships began to seek its safety, and where the ships went, towns went. But Oahu still remained in the backwater of activity—whaling, missionary, and trading—until 1846, when Kamehameha III moved the capital from Lahaina, Maui, to Honolulu.

Pearl Harbor, made a major U.S. naval base in 1914, was used as a repair and coaling station in World War I. With regular steamer service between the West Coast and Honolulu, sugar traveled to California and cars and streetcars were sent to Honolulu. Sugar, the islands' major product, had already brought many new races to the islands as cane field workers. The first Chinese arrived in 1853, the Portuguese in 1878, the Japanese in 1884, and the Filipinos in 1906; since then Puerto Ricans, Koreans, and Samoans have arrived in rapid succession, to stay and make their homes.

The monarchy, the missionaries, and the legislature of the Territory of Hawaii bequeathed to modern Honolulu a not-too-shabby civic center and **downtown Honolulu.** There's a touch of France in Iolani Palace and its Royal Bandstand and a bit of England in St. Andrew's Cathedral, the Armory, and Washington Place, while the simple, austere mission houses and Kawaiahao Church trace their lineage to New England. Nor has the resurgence of Bishop and Fort streets and their environs since the mid-1960s spoiled the original. The strikingly handsome Dillingham, C. Brewer, and Alexander & Baldwin buildings are intact; the Stangenwald Building, First Federal Savings, Hawaii Times, First Interstate Bank, the Judiciary Building, and others have been artfully restored.

New Bishop Square, with its one-acre Tamarind Garden, far outshines the older building it replaced. The handsome and symbolic state capitol, open to the sky at its top level, depicts the state's volcanoes with cone-shaped, lava-block, inner buildings for the legislative houses; the slender columns with branching capitals supporting the main roofline are Hawaii's palm trees; and the large reflecting pools at their base represent the surrounding ocean. The square also has the stately Financial Plaza of the Pacific, Grosvenor Towers with their garden patio, and Amfac Towers with their triangle park and fountain. From South Street to River Street and from the harbor to Beretania Street the mix of buildings is gracious and the open space, trees, and fountains are a pleasure to contemplate. With the busy harbor at stage front and the Koolau Mountains as a backdrop, it's a joy to walk through beautiful downtown Honolulu.

Waikiki is the "action center" for all first-time visitors and is habit-forming for return travelers. The two-mile stretch of resorts along the beach between downtown Honolulu and suburban Honolulu has a hyperactive personality all its own.

Probably the first guidebook to the Hawaiian Islands was Captain Cook's popular ship's journal. But at the turn of the eighteenth century the islands did not yet represent everyone's dream vacation. Early tourists such as Mark Twain, Robert Louis Stevenson, Jack London, and Somerset Maugham wrote colorful, adjective-filled, flattering stories, and Hawaii was truly launched as a vacation spot.

With the twentieth century the first full-service hotel, the Moana, was opened at Waikiki, and in 1927 the Royal Hawaiian was built next door. The great white Matson ships plied faithfully across the sea. Until World War II most visitors arrived by steamer, with a few intrepid souls flying in on Pan American flying boats. By 1941 Waikiki had established itself as a resort of consequence. Then the shock wave of the Pearl Harbor bombing swept the islands and Honolulu to the forefront of world news. Once the Pacific was at peace again, the barbed wire was removed from the beaches and the hotels were refurbished. In 1959 Hawaii became the fiftieth state, and the first jet planes brought travelers from all over the world in only a few hours.

In the slender rectangle bordered by the Ala Wai Canal and the beach are most of the island's nightlife, all major restaurants, 32,000 hotel and condominium units, shopping centers, nightclubs, theaters, and 105 swimming pools. Three resorts not within Waikiki are at Kahala Beach, just east of landmark Diamond Head; Turtle Bay, on the North Shore; and Makaha Valley, on the Waianae Coast.

PRACTICAL INFORMATION

WHEN TO GO. The steady northeasterly trade winds that rustle the palm trees and billow the ubiquitous muumuus are the islands' natural air-conditioning, cooling the clean Hawaiian air, no matter how bright the sun. Because of the trade winds, Oahu has a windward, or rainy, side and a leeward, or dry, side—Waikiki.

Average midday temperatures range from 78 degrees Fahrenheit in the winter to 84 or 88 degrees in the summer at ocean level. A rise in altitude of 2,000 feet can lower the temperature 10 degrees.

Average ocean temperatures year-round are from 70 to 75 degrees, and there's an almost even 13 hours of daylight and 11 hours of dark. It rains daily on the mountaintops, and the prevailing winds blow the drops briefly over Waikiki; sometimes a whole cloud appears, and it rains briskly for several minutes. The rainy season is generally Dec. through Feb., but the storms seldom last more than a day.

Probably the most popular vacation time is Christmas through Easter—which is also the most expensive, high season—although summer runs a close second. Bargains are more apt to be found in May, Sept., and Nov. In this land of eternal spring, all activities, attractions, sports, festivals, scenic tours, and entertainment are available year-round.

HOW TO GET THERE. Unless you own a yacht comparable to Queen Elizabeth's *Britannia* or a TransPac sailing ketch, plan to arrive in Honolulu by air.

Honolulu International Airport is served by national carriers—*Air Micronesia, American Airlines, Continental Airlines, Delta Air Lines, Hawaiian Air, Northwest Orient, Trans World Airlines,* and *Total Air.* International carriers include *Air Nauru, Air New Zealand, Air Tungaru, China Air, Canadian Airlines International, Japan Air Lines, Korean Air Lines, Philippine Airlines, Qantas Airways, Singapore Airlines,* and *WardAir Canada.*

At press time, airline ticketing for coach fares to Hawaii held three possibilities: regular weekday fare, weekend fare (somewhat higher), and prior purchase fare (approximately $50 to $60 less). The best policy is to let your travel agent know your planned vacation dates as early as possible and keep an eye out for special discounts in that period. Probably the best price of all is a package vacation. Talk over with your agent the various packages of *Pleasant Hawaiian Holidays, Classic Hawaii, American Express, First Family of Travel, Cartan, Tauck Tours, Island Holidays, United Vacations,* and many more.

TELEPHONES. The area code for all of Hawaii is 808. To call another island from Honolulu, however, dial 1 first and then the number. Direct dialing is available to most of the world, but not from most hotels, where phones are operator assisted and there is an added hotel charge, except for charge-card calls. Local information is 1411; for other islands, 555–1212. Many toll-free 800 numbers are now available from Hawaii; dial 800–555–1212 for information.

Emergency Telephone Numbers. Honolulu's emergency number for ambulance, fire, police, and poison center is 911. A doctor on call in Waikiki can be reached 24 hours a day at 943–1111.

ACCOMMODATIONS. Waikiki's two-mile strip is the setting for 138 hotels and more than 40 condominium properties, enough to satisfy every taste and pocketbook. The budget hotels are invariably reliable and a good value, the moderate hotels offer more space and more amenities on the property, and the luxury hotels are some of the finest in the world. There are no motels, as the mainland knows them, in Hawaii.

Hotels. Reserve early is the byword. This is particularly true from the Christmas holidays until Easter (which is also a premium-rate period) as well as in the summer months.

Kitchenettes are a money saver, as are rooms on a lower floor or facing the mountains. Being on the ocean is most expensive, an ocean view slightly less. The most expensive hotels are along Kalakaua Ave., the main thoroughfare next to the beach. Less expensive hotels are found toward the mountains, on Kuhio Ave. and Ala Wai, and in a three-block area on Ala Moana past Fort DeRussy.

Hotel categories are based on double occupancy, and are determined by price as follows: *Reasonable,* \$50 to \$85; *Very Economical,* \$45 to \$70; *Budget,* \$25 to \$60. Air-conditioning is abbreviated A/C.

Reasonable

Ambassador Hotel. 2040 Kuhio Ave., Honolulu, HI 96815 (808–941–7777). A 225-room modern high rise, across from Ft. DeRussy and two blocks from beach. Pool, shops, coffee shop, A/C, color TV, some kitchens.

Breakers Hotel. 250 Beach Walk, Honolulu, HI 96815 (800–426–0494). Tropical garden and pool, 66 rooms with kitchenettes in a neat Oriental-style, two-story building tucked behind a high wall half a block from the ocean. A/C, color TV, wheelchair capabilities.

Coral Reef. 2299 Kuhio Ave., Honolulu, HI 96815 (800–92–ASTON, 800–922–7866). Has 279-room high rise adjoining International Market Place. Black Angus and Ferdinand restaurants. Comfortable, redecorated, refrigerators, pool, shops, A/C, color TV. One block to beach.

Hawaiiana Hotel. 260 Beach Walk, Honolulu, HI 96815 (800–367–5122). Pleasing small hotel, 95 studios with kitchenettes. Polynesian patio, pool, privacy, A/C. Half a block to beach.

Hawaii Dynasty. 1830 Ala Moana, Honolulu, HI 96815 (800–421–6662). Has 200 relatively spacious rooms, queen-size beds. Dynasty I is excellent Chinese-American restaurant. Pool, shops, color TV, A/C. A block to the beach.

Outrigger Malia. 2211 Kuhio Ave., Honolulu, HI 96815 (800–367–5170). Has 328 newly decorated rooms, a restaurant and cocktail lounge, tennis court, Jacuzzi, ramps for the disabled. Color TV, refrigerator, A/C. Two blocks to beach.

Outrigger Surf. 2280 Kuhio Ave., Honolulu, HI 96815 (800–367–5170). Has 251 A/C rooms with kitchenettes, twin beds, color TV. Pool, Rudy's Italian Restaurant. Two blocks to beach.

Outrigger West. 2330 Kuhio Ave., Honolulu, HI 96815 (800–367–5170). Has 660 rooms, most with kitchenettes, refurbished and with new baths, color TV, A/C. Two restaurants, bakery, shops, pool.

Queen Kapiolani. 150 Kapahulu Ave., Honolulu, HI 96815 (800–367–5004). Has 315 rooms, looking across Kapiolani Park to Diamond Head, turn-of-the-century Hawaiian. Peacock Room noted for lavish buffets, Garden Lanai for Hawaiian lunches. Pool, shops, cocktail lounges. A/C, color TV. Wheelchair capabilities.

Waikiki Mariana Hotel. 1956 Ala Moana, Honolulu, HI 96815 (800–367–6070). Has 323 A/C rooms with kitchenettes. Across from Ft. DeRussy Park, two blocks from DeRussy Beach. Color TV, pool, restaurant, cocktail lounge. Looks over park toward Diamond Head and beach.

Very Economical

Aloha Surf Hotel. 444 Kanekapolei, Honolulu, HI 96815 (800–423–4514). Has 204 A/C rooms on the edge of the Ala Wai. Rooms are small but pleasant, mostly twin beds, TV. Pool, shops, coffee shop. Three blocks from beach.

Continental Surf. 2426 Kuhio Ave., Honolulu, HI 96815 (800–3667–2303). 140 A/C rooms, color TV; some kitchenettes available. Outstanding Hy's Steak House next door. Two blocks from Kapiolani Park, tennis courts, and zoo; one block from shopping and Waikiki Beach.

Ilima Hotel. 445 Nahonani St., Honolulu, HI 96815 (800–367–5172). Has 100 studio and one-bedroom suites, all with kitchens, color TV, A/C, full hotel service. Sergio's Italian Restaurant, cocktail lounge, pool and sauna, sun decks. One-bedroom sleeps four at same price. Wheelchair capabilities.

Outrigger Edgewater Hotel. 2168 Kalia Rd., Honolulu, HI 96815 (800–367–5170). Has 185 A/C and recently renovated rooms, color TV; some kitchenettes are available. Pool with surrounding garden, recommended Trattoria restaurant and lounge, coffee and pastry shop. In the center of Waikiki stores and theaters; across the street from beach and DeRussy Park.

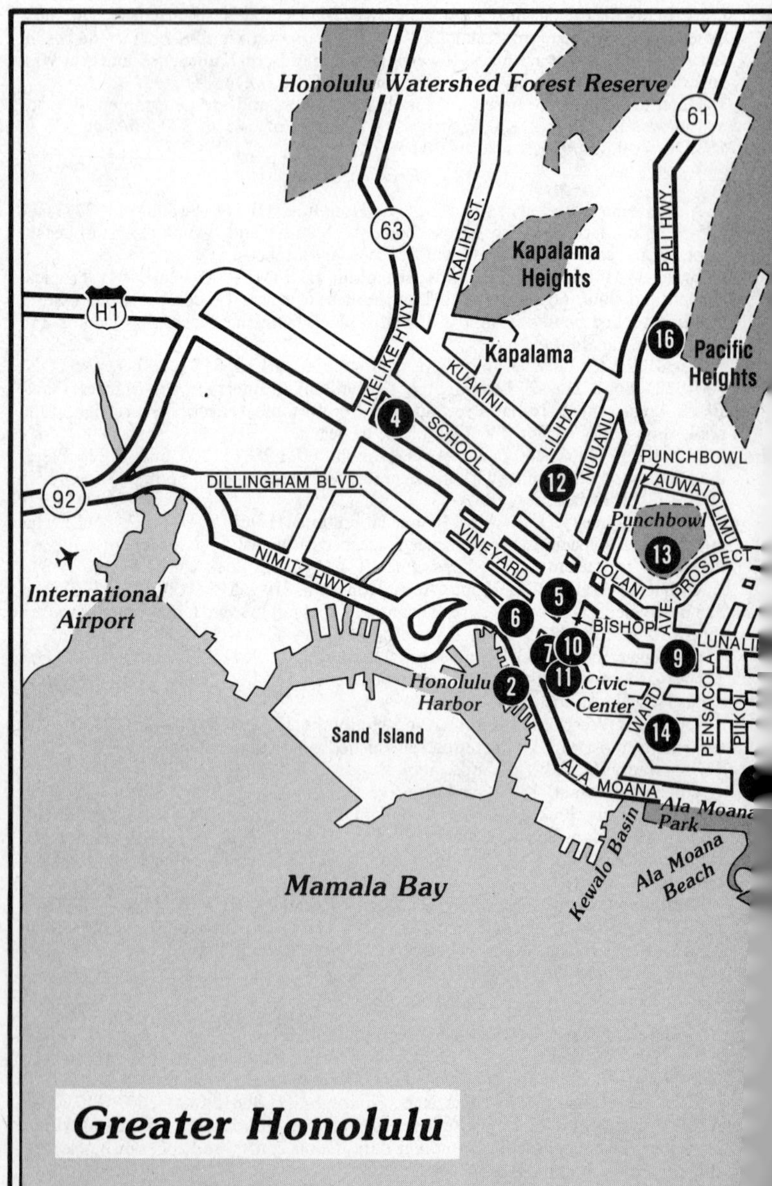

Points of Interest

1) Ala Moana Center
2) Aloha Tower
3) Aquarium
4) Bishop Museum
5) Chinatown
6) Cultural Plaza
7) Downtown
8) East West Center

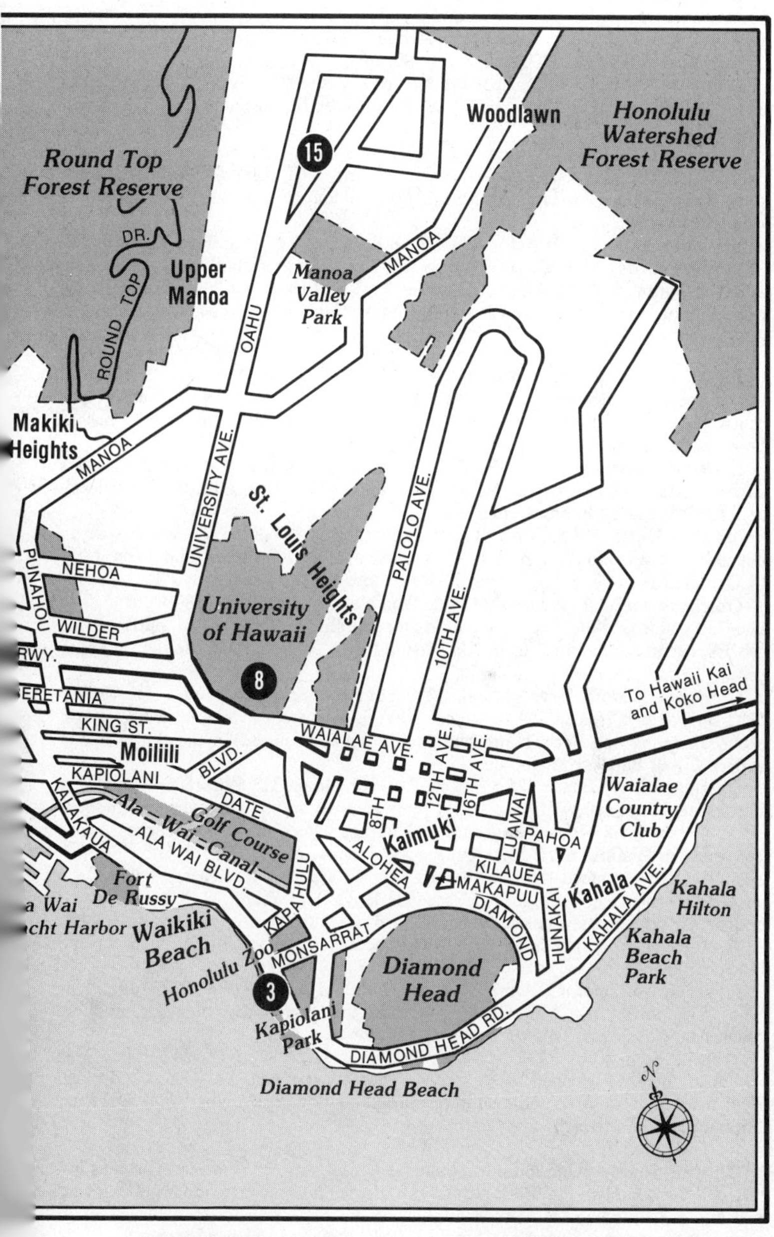

9) Honolulu Academy of Arts
10) Iolani Palace
11) Kamehameha Statue
12) Liliuokalani Gardens
13) National Memorial Cemetery
14) Neal Blaisdell Center
15) Paradise Park
16) Queen Emma Museum

Outrigger Royal Islander. 2164 Kalia Rd., Honolulu, HI 96815 (800–367–5170). 104 A/C rooms, color TV, refrigerator, coffee maker. Across street from beach. Restaurant, lounge, very reasonable penthouse. Nonsmoking floors.

Outrigger Waikiki Tower. 200 Lewers Rd., Honolulu, HI 96815 (800–367–5170). Has 440 recently renovated rooms, A/C, color TV, rooms to accommodate wheelchairs. Pool, shops, Waikiki Broiler restaurant and lounge. A half block from the beach.

Outrigger Waikiki Village. 240 Lewers Rd., Honolulu, HI 96815 (800–367–5170). Has 430 newly refurbished rooms, A/C, color TV; standard twins, some with kitchens. Two restaurants and cocktail lounge, pool, shops. A half block from the beach.

Waikiki Gateway Hotel. 1070 Kalakaua Ave., Honolulu, HI 96815 (800–92–ASTON). Has 200 A/C rooms with color TV in a small hotel shaped like a Mayan pyramid. At the edge of Gateway Park a block and a half from DeRussy Beach. Pool, coffee shop, award-winning Nick's Fishmarket restaurant, shops.

Budget

Big Surf Hotel. 1690 Ala Moana, Honolulu, HI 96815 (808–946–6525). 78 A/C rooms and one-bedroom apts., all with kitchens. Bright and cheery. Near restaurants, discos. Two blocks to famous Ala Moana Shopping Center, one block to Duke Kahanamoku lagoon and beach.

Driftwood Hotel. 1696 Ala Moana, Honolulu, HI 96815 (808–949–0061). Has 72 basic studio-lanai apartments, hot plate and refrigerator; 2 blocks from beach and Ala Moana Shopping Center.

Malihini Hotel. 217 Saratoga Rd., Honolulu, HI 96815 (808–923–9644). spartan but clean, comfortable rooms and 10 one-bedroom apts. both with kitchens. Next to DeRussy Park, one block from DeRussy Beach.

Outrigger Ala Wai Terrace. 1547 Ala Wai, Honolulu, HI 96815 (800–367–5170). Has 239 studio and one-bedroom condo units, kitchens fully supplied, partial A/C. No TV, no phones; a block from Ala Moana Beach Park and Ala Moana shopping center.

Outrigger Coral Seas Hotel. 250 Lewers St., Honolulu, HI 96815 (800–367–5170). Has 265 A/C rooms, TV; kitchenettes available. Pool, shops, House of Hong and Perry's Smorgy restaurants and lounge. In the center of the action, a half block from the beach.

Outrigger Reef Lanais. 225 Saratoga Rd., Honolulu, HI 96815 (800–367–5170). Has 110 A/C rooms, twin beds, newly renovated with color TV and some kitchenettes. Buzz's Steak House restaurant and lounge. One block from beach.

Outrigger Waikiki Surf. 2200 Kuhio Ave., Honolulu, HI 96815 (800–367–5170). Has 291 A/C standard twin-bed rooms, color TV, some kitchenettes, pool. Two sister hotels nearby, Waikiki Surf East, 422 Royal Hawaiian, has 102 A/C, twin-bedrooms, kitchenettes, color TV, pool. **Waikiki Surf West,** 412 Lewers St., has 110 two-bedroom family suites with full kitchen, color TV, partial A/C, pool. Two blocks from beach.

Royal Grove Hotel. 151 Uluniu Ave., Honolulu, HI 96815 (808–923–7691). Has 85 rooms, partial A/C, kitchenettes, comfortably furnished, color TV, pool. A block from the beach. Wheelchair capabilities.

Waikiki Sand Villa. 2375 Ala Wai, Honolulu, HI 96815 (800–247–1903). Has 223 A/C, nicely furnished small rooms, color TV, on Ala Wai Canal and park. Pool and sun deck, the Noodle Shop restaurant and lounge starring Frank DeLima. Four blocks from beach.

Condominiums. Condominiums can be divided into the same categories as hotels. All have kitchen facilities, although some can be split into one hotel unit and a studio with kitchen. Most of Waikiki's condos have full hotel amenities; maid service (sometimes on request), lobbies, pools, lounges, and restaurants.

Four Paddle. 2140 Kuhio Ave., Honolulu, HI 96815 (800–367–2321). Has 250 units, studio and one-bedroom, roomy apartments with full kitchen. A/C, color TV, pool, saunas. One-bedroom sleeps four. Some telephones, no maid service. Moderate.

Honolulu Prince. 415 Nahua St., Honolulu, HI 96815 (800–92–ASTON). Has 125 units, studios, one-bedrooms and two-bedrooms with kitchens, A/C, color TV, shops. One-bedroom sleeps four; two-bedroom, six or eight. Three blocks from beach. Full hotel service. Moderate.

Inn on the Park. 1920 Ala Moana, Honolulu, HI 96815 (800–225–1347). Has 238 studio units with kitchenette or refrigerator, coffee maker, A/C, color TV. Pool, shops, restaurant, cocktail lounge. Two blocks from DeRussy beach. Inexpensive.

Island Colony. 445 Seaside Ave., Honolulu, HI 96815 (800–92–ASTON). Has 700 studio and one-bedroom units with full kitchen, A/C, color TV, nicely furnished. Pool, shops, restaurant, cocktail lounge. On Ala Wai four blocks from beach. Full-service. One-bedroom sleeps four. Wheelchair capabilities. High moderate.

Royal Kuhio Condominium. 2240 Kuhio Ave., Honolulu, HI 96815 (800–367–5205). Has 385 one- and two-bedroom units with full kitchens, A/C, color TV, pool, paddle tennis. Wheelchair capabilities. Weekly maid service, some room telephone service. One-bedroom sleeps four; two-bedroom, six. High moderate.

Waikiki Grand Hotel. 134 Kapahulu Ave., Honolulu, HI 96815 (800–225–1347). Has 175 A/C units across from beach and Kapiolani Park. Studios with kitchenette, full hotel services, and color TV. Small rooms. Pool, shops, Zen Japanese restaurant. Reasonable.

Waikiki Shores Apartments. 2161 Kalia Rd., Honolulu, HI 96815 (800–367–2353). Has 150 beachfront studios and one- and two-bedroom apartments, full kitchens, washer-dryer, color TV, telephone, weekly maid service. Unobstructed view across DeRussy Beach. One-bedroom sleeps four; two-bedroom, six. Wheelchair capabilities. High moderate.

Ys and Hostels. YMCA Central Branch. 401 Atkinson Dr., Honolulu, HI 96814 (808–941–3344). At $22 per night, the cheapest hotel for men in Waikiki, and the tiny rooms come with use of the gym, restaurant, pool, and TV room. But the hotel is not coed and does not take advance reservations.

Honolulu International Youth Hostel. 2323 A Seaview Ave., Honolulu, HI 96822 (808–946–0591). This hostel on Oahu is in Manoa Valley, a block from the University of Hawaii and a half-hour bus ride from Waikiki. Dormitory-style separate quarters for men and women. Members $8, non-members $11 a night. Reservations can be made from 7 to 9 A.M. daily.

HOW TO GET AROUND. From the airport. Honolulu International Airport is 7 miles (20 to 25 minutes) from Waikiki. Taxi fare averages about $15, one way, without tip; a limousine, for five to seven people, is $30. The *GrayLine Airporter* has regularly scheduled service from and to the airport on comfortable air-conditioned motor coaches available to baggage claim areas. They will drop off and pick up passengers in Waikiki at 11 major hotels. Fare is $5 to or from airport to Waikiki, $9 round-trip ticket.

Two companies pick up at your hotel or condominium for transportation to the airport: *Airport Motor Coach* (926–4747) is $3.50 for adults, $2 for children; *Airport Shuttle* vans (533–7503) costs $4 for adults, $2 for children. Service is from 6 A.M. to 10 P.M., and reservations must be made at least one day ahead.

By bus. *The Bus,* Honolulu's municipal transportation covers all of the city of Honolulu and circles Oahu. Adult fare is 60 cents; children (6 to 18) pay 25 cents. Exact change is required. Transfers are free and good in one general direction. Monthly passes are $15 for adults and $7.50 for school students, kindergarten through high school, who may be asked for school activity cards. Call 531–1611 for routing and street information, any time of the day or night.

You can travel around the entire island for 60 cents—if you don't get off. Each time you exit TheBus to look at a pretty scene or visit an attraction, you must pay another fare to continue on the same line.

By rental car. Rental cars abound and add greatly to a stay on Oahu, at least for a couple of days of touring. A valid driver's license and a national credit card are required to rent a car. Rental cars are frequently a part of hotel and condominium packages—it's worth asking about.

There are more than 25 car-rental agencies in Honolulu, most with names familiar throughout the U.S.—*Alamo, American International, Avis, Budget, Dollar, Hertz, Holiday, National, Robert's Hawaii, Thrifty, Tropical,* and *United*—and rates are generally standardized. A compact with standard transmission rents at about $25 a day, and an automatic compact with air conditioning costs about $35, with no mileage charge. Insurance waiver extra. All the above agencies have airport pick-up vans to deliver you to your car and return you to the airport on departure. The cars are all 1988 or late 1987 models. *Budget* even adds a raft of free bonuses—show admissions, sunset dinner sails, luaus, jewelry, and dinners—to help cut your costs.

There are also several discount agencies in the Waikiki area that do not provide airport pickup or delivery but whose rates average around $10 per day, or $50 per week. The age and condition of these cars vary. You may want to check the following: *Honolulu Rent-a-Car,* 1865 Kalakaua, (808–941–9099); *Aloha Auto Leasing,* 829 S. King, (808–524–5770); *Waikiki Rent-A-Car,* 578 Ala Moana (808–545–2330) (which advertises free Waikiki and airport pickup); and better known *United Car Rental,* 234 Beach Walk (808–922–4605).

HINTS TO THE MOTORIST. It is easy to drive on the island. There are so few roads that it's impossible to get lost, and the highways are well marked. There are few driving hazards, no snow, no speed traps, and an island full of polite drivers. The few miles of freeway have a speed limit of 55 mph; limits on other highways are 50 mph and 45 mph; they are well posted.

Over some weekends and all major holidays the Honolulu Police Department sets up road safety blocks to remove intoxicated drivers from streets and highways.

TOURIST INFORMATION. An Oahu Drive Guide booklet with maps and information will come with a rental car; if not, ask for it. The Hawaii Visitors Bureau 2270 Kalahaua Ave., Ste. 801, Honolulu, HI 96815 (923–1811), staffs booths on the ground floor of Building A at the Royal Hawaiian Shopping Center and at the main terminal and Neighbor Island terminal at Honolulu International Airport. The bureau's muumuu-clad ladies have a large supply of *aloha,* information, and brochures of attractions, tours, and cruises to share with the traveling public.

Foreign Currency. *Bank of Hawaii,* 2220 Kalakaua Ave. (942–6222), is open 8:30 A.M.–3 P.M. Mon.–Thurs. and 8:30 A.M.–6 P.M. on Fri. The *A-1 Foreign Exchange Ltd.* (922–4761) on the ground floor of Building C, Royal Hawaiian Shopping Center, is open Mon.–Fri., 9 A.M.–4 P.M. *Citicorp* staffs a main office and three kiosks on the departure and arrival level of Honolulu International Airport. Open every day during plane arrival hours, from 7:30 A.M.–4:30 P.M. and 8 P.M.–3 A.M. (834–1099).

SENIOR-CITIZEN AND STUDENT DISCOUNTS. TheBus and local movie theaters have student prices, both requiring proof of age, generally a student activity card. Senior citizens also receive a movie discount, with a driver's license as proof. Those over 65 may apply for a free bus pass; however, it takes about a month and a half to process and thus is of no use for a short stay. From time to time restaurants have seniors' discounts that sometimes are listed in the discount sections of the tourist newspapers. The Hawaii Visitors Booth at the Royal Center may have such information as well.

HINTS TO DISABLED TRAVELERS. Each street corner curb in the Waikiki area has been built with a slanted ramp for easy wheelchair access, and all recent buildings have ramps and elevators large enough for wheelchairs and motorized chairs. Hawaii poses a special difficulty for blind or severely sight-impaired travelers. The Islands require a 120-day rabies quarantine for dogs, and seeing-eye dogs are not exempt, except dogs from totally rabies-free countries. Your travel agent will notify all flights reserved for your trip of the extent of your mobility impairment. Transportation will be provided at all airports, and your wheelchair will be tagged for "last-on, first-off" luggage. Hotels and condos with wheelchair capabilities have been noted in the Accommodations section.

The bus has not yet been modified to admit wheelchairs, but **Handi Cabs of the Pacific** (808–524–3866) is a taxi and tour company specifically for those in wheelchairs. The company performs as a taxi, requiring 24 hours' notice, and has city tours, Circle Island tours, Pearl Harbor cruises, and two sunset dinner cruises for mobility-impaired travelers. For an informative brochure write: Handi Cabs of the Pacific, Inc., Box 22428, Honolulu, HI 96822. **The Handi Van Service,** 1585 Kapiolani Blvd., #1554, Honolulu, HI 96814 (808–955–1717), also provides wheelchair transportation.

Melanie Chang, founder and director of Hawaii's **Why Not Travel Agency,** 1750 Kalakaua Ave., #188, Honolulu, HI 96826 (808–947–7044), specializes in tours (one or two persons or a full group) for the blind, paraplegics, elderly, retarded, deaf, and mobility-impaired. The agency will customize an entire trip or simply make recommendations and reserve hotels and tours.

The Aloha Guide to Accessibility on Oahu covers hotels, restaurants, shopping centers, beach parks, theaters, schools, and government buildings. To order, write: Aloha Guides, Commission on the Handicapped, 335 Merchant St., Room 215, Honolulu, HI 96813. Enclose $1 for the book and 50 cents for postage.

FREE EVENTS. There are a number of free tourist newspapers and magazines, available in the kiosks on Waikiki street corners that have complete listings of what's doing and what's new. Most also have a section (find it in the index) called variously "Freebies," "Discounts," "Coupons," or "Money Savers" that can include free sundaes and pizza, discount dinner prices, cruise tickets, admission to attractions, free transportation, free film, and more. The two Honolulu papers, the morning *Advertiser* and the evening *Star-Bulletin,* carry a large schedule of weekly coming events in their Friday editions. Among Honolulu's major attractions are a double dozen, at minimal cost or *manuahi* (free), including a broad variety of Hawaiiana:

Aloha Tower. Pier 9, at the foot of Fort Street Mall, downtown Honolulu. Ninth-floor Maritime Museum has nautical artifacts illustrating Hawaii's seafaring history. The harbor signaling tower was Honolulu's only skyscraper until 1961. Mon.–Fri., 9 A.M.–4 P.M.

U.S.S. Arizona Memorial. Take city bus 20 to Pearl Harbor Naval Base, National Park Service Visitor Center, Halawa Gate, on Kamehameha Hwy. (808–422–0561). Narrated historical movie of December 7, 1941, museum and tickets for shuttle boat ride to Memorial (children under 3 ft. 9 in. not allowed on shuttle). Tues.–Sun., 8 A.M.–3 P.M. It is best to arrive at 8, because on crowded days there can be a wait for a boat. Free.

Art Mart. Zoo Fence, Monsarrat Avenue, Kapiolani Park. Oil portraits, watercolor sunsets, pen and ink cartoons. Sat. and Sun., 10 A.M.–4 P.M. Free. Paintings are for sale.

Chado—The Way of Tea. 245 Saratoga Rd. Hanyoan, the Traditional Tea Ceremony, encompassing etiquette, philosophy, art. Wed. and Fri., 10 A.M.–noon. 923–3059. Free.

Coconut Leaf Weaving and Sculpture. Hilton Hawaiian Village. Demonstrations by Eric Poohina. Mon., 12:30–5 P.M., Princess Kaiulani Hotel, Wed., 8:30 A.M.–1 P.M.; Sheraton Waikiki Hotel, Fri., 8:30 A.M.–1 P.M. Free.

Fitness Exercise. Exercisers on vacation meet under the trees at Fort DeRussy Beach, Mon.–Sat., 9:30 A.M. Fitness for all ages. Free.

Hawaiian Aloha Activities. Hawaiian Regent Hotel, Garden Courtyard. 2552 Kalakaua Ave. Hawaiian songs, hula lessons, lei stringing, Mon., Wed., Fri., 10 A.M. Free.

Hawaiian Torchlight Ceremony. Ilikai Hotel Center Mall, 1777 Ala Moana. Temple drums, conch shells, and flaming torches signal a tropic evening of Hawaiian music. Daily, 6–8 P.M. Hula lessons, Mon., Wed., Fri., 10 A.M. Free.

Hilo Hattie's Fashion Tours. 700 Nimitz Hwy. Tour of Hawaii's islandwear in the making, plus refreshments. Visit the Fashion Center, T-Shirt factory, Macadamia Nut Chocolate Factory, and Dole Pineapple Cannery (newly renovated). With bus pickup from major hotels. Phone 537–2926 for schedule. Free.

Hyatt Regency Waikiki. 2424 Kalakaua Ave. The hotel's Great Hall has entertainment from 5 to 6 P.M. Tues. and Thurs., with Aunty Malia's Hawaiian entertainment Fri. at 5 P.M. and a special fashion show Wed. at 4 P.M. Free.

Kahala Hilton Dolphin Feeding. 5000 Kahala Ave. The hotel's waterfall lagoon and adjacent waterways are home to five big green sea turtles, two tropical penguins, a whole school of fish, and four playful and talented bottle-nosed dolphins. They put on shows daily at feeding time—11 A.M., 2 P.M., and 4 P.M.—when they hula, wear leis, jump through hoops, and show off. Turtles and penguins are fed about 15 minutes earlier. Free.

Kawaiahao Church. Across S. King St. from Iolani Palace, downtown Honolulu. Hawaii's focal church from missionary and monarchy days. Portraits of Hawaiian kings and queens, cemetery of royal and early missionary personages. Services in Hawaiian. Mon.–Sat., 8:30 A.M.–4 P.M. Sunday services at 10:30 A.M. All are welcome.

Kodak Hula Show. Waikiki Shell in Kapiolani Park, 2805 Monsarrat Ave. Delightful hula, music, and entertainment; popular photography show, first held in 1937. Tues.–Thurs., 10 A.M. (additional Fri. show in summer). Free.

Punchbowl National Cemetery of the Pacific. 2177 Puowaina Dr. In the peaceful green bowl of Punchbowl crater, this is the resting place of 26,000 American servicemen and women who served in the two world wars and the Korean and Vietnam wars, as well as a memorial to another 26,280 listed in the "Courts of Missing." Open daily, 8 A.M.–6:30 P.M.

Royal Hawaiian Band Concerts. Kapiolani Park Bandstand, near Kalakaua Ave. Includes Hawaiian, swing, jazz, musical comedy, and pop music. Every Sun. 2 P.M. Iolani Palace Bandstand, downtown, Fri., 12:15 P.M. Free.

Royal Hawaiian Shopping Center. In front of Royal Hawaiian Hotel. 2201 Kalakaua Ave. Presents interesting lessons and shows daily except Sun. in the Fountain Courtyard, second-floor bridgeway of Building B-C, and fourth floor Building B. From 10 A.M. to noon: hula lessons, lei making and quilt making lessons, Polynesian Cultural Center dancers, Hokule'a movie. 5–7 P.M. and 6–8 P.M., music and hulas. Free.

State Capitol. Beretania between Richards and Punchbowl streets, behind Iolani Palace. Open for visitors at any time. Brochure describing art, architecture, and statues available in governor's office. Free.

Under the Ukulele Tree. Beach in front of Reef Hotel, 2169 Kalia Rd., Waikiki. Hawaiian music and sing-along; Sun., 8 P.M. Free.

U.S. Army Museum. Fort DeRussy, Btry. Randolph Bldg., 2055 Kalia Rd., on Waikiki Beach. Displays and collections from most U.S. wars with emphasis on Pacific collections, artifacts, and artillery pieces. Tues.–Sun., 10 A.M.–4:30 P.M. Free.

Waikiki Aquarium. Oceanside, 2777 Kalakaua Ave. Third oldest aquarium in the U.S. More than 30 tanks and 300 marine species: sharks and octopus, starfish and squid, golden koi and performing seals, and many rare tropical species. Daily 9 A.M.–5 P.M. Adults, $1.50; children under 16 free.

Waikiki Calls. Fourth-floor showroom, Waikiki Shopping Plaza, 2270 Kalakaua Ave. Handsome cast of dancers and singers in a salute to Hawaii and the Pacific perform against a backdrop of ever-changing colorful scenes of Hawaii, past to present. Nightly except Sun., 6 and 7:15 P.M. Cocktail service available. Free.

TOURS AND SPECIAL-INTEREST SIGHTSEEING. Downtown Honolulu centers on Honolulu Harbor, halfway between Waikiki and Pearl Harbor, and is the site of the only royal palace on U.S. soil. Built by Hawaii's last monarch, King Kalakaua, in 1882, the small but exquisite **Iolani Palace** on King Street between Richard and Punchbowl streets (523–0141), is a wonderful mixture of European and Hawaiian stonework, beautiful woods, and etched glass. It has recently been restored and is being furnished as original furniture is found. Tours Wed.–Sat. every 15 minutes, 9 A.M.–2 P.M. Adults, $4; children, $1; under 5 not admitted. Reservation recommended.

Across King St. are handsome Kawaiahao Church, where services are still conducted in Hawaiian, and the Mission Houses Museum, displaying the well-preserved homes of the earliest missionaries. Near the palace are the modern state capitol built in 1968 and Washington Place, the home of Hawaii's last reigning monarch, Queen Liliuokalani and present home of the governor.

An interesting walking trip starts with the Mission Houses tour: $3.50, about 45 minutes. Then purchase the small 75-cent guidebook *Downtown Walking Tour of Historic Honolulu* in the Mission House gift shop and follow the directions.

A guided tour of Chinatown is conducted Tues. by the Chinese Chamber of Commerce. Visit open markets, herb shops, noodle factories, and chop houses, and the temple of Kuan Yin (goddess of mercy) with optional lunch at Wo Fat Chop Suey. Starts 9:30 A.M. at the Chamber offices 42 N. King (533–0697). Walk, $3; lunch, $4. Reservations needed.

Bus and van tours literally circle the island of Oahu, covering the areas and attractions described in this chapter. They cost about $20 for adults, less for children. Other popular, less expensive tours are "Historic City and Punchbowl Cemetery" and "Diamond Head, Sea Life Park, and Pali Lookout." Experienced bus companies are *Gray Line Hawaii* (834–1033), *Robert's Hawaii Tours* (947–3939) and *Trans Hawaiian Services* (735–6467). Van and minibus companies are *Akamai Tours* (922–6485) and *Polynesian Adventure Tours* (923–8687). All equipment is air-conditioned and tours pick-up and return to hotels.

PARKS, GARDENS, AND BEACHES. Foster Botanic Garden, 50 N. Vineyard Blvd., daily, 9 A.M.–4 P.M., is a major collection, on 15 acres, of rare Pacific Basin and tropical plants, flowers, and trees, started even before Hawaii became a territory. Adults $1; children free.

Paradise Park. 3737 Manoa Rd. Lush tropical setting deep in Manoa Valley. Botanical gardens, aviaries, rain-forest jungles, ponds, and streams. Daily bird shows, luaus, walking tours. Free shuttle bus from Waikiki; call 988–2141 for schedule. Daily, 9:30 A.M.–5 P.M. Adults, $7.50; juniors, $6.50; children, $3.75.

Castle Park. 4561 Salt Lake Blvd. (487–9941). Children's theme and amusement park, with midway rides, bumper boats, go-carts, miniature golf courses, medieval castle, and electronic arcade. Daily, 10 A.M.–10 P.M. All-day pass: adults, $6.50, children, $5. Golf and some ride fees extra.

Kapiolani Park (officially Queen Kapiolani Park) is 162 acres of grass and trees bounded by Kapahulu Ave., Kalakaua Ave., Leahi St., and the Pacific Ocean, at the foot of Diamond Head. It contains the Honolulu Zoo, Waikiki Aquarium, tennis courts, a golf driving range, and two busy entertainment centers. The *Waikiki Shell* is home to the Honolulu Symphony Summer Series, rock concerts, Aloha Week concerts, and holiday entertainment. The *Kapiolani Bandstand* and surrounding greensward has almost daily music concerts and activities. The park beach, *Queens Surf,* has a large grass area for picnicking.

Ala Moana Park and **Magic Island,** 1451 Ala Moana, bounds the opposite end of Waikiki. Its 77 acres contain one of the city's finest beaches; semi-attached Magic Island has another beach with good surfing waters in summer. There are two food concessions, McCoy Pavilion for music and entertainment concerts (mostly free), tennis courts, and a lawn bowling green. It is the favorite haunt of craft fairs and ethnic festivals.

Waimea Falls Park, in Sunset Beach Country on the North Shore, is a 1800-acre preserve of trees and flowers—some exist nowhere else in the world—centered around 45-foot Waimea Falls. There are ancient Hawaiian ruins, a minibus tour, cliff-diving shows and a restaurant. Open daily, 10 A.M.–5 P.M. Adults, $8.50; juniors, $5.25; children 4–6, $1.25.

Waikiki. Honolulu's beaches are all centered around Waikiki. The series starts at Kapiolani Park with *Sans Souci Beach* and *Queens Surf Beach,* which have good surfing in the summer months. Next, going west, is *Kuhio Beach Park,* a favorite spot for swimming, bodysurfing, and checkers under the hau trees. Then in front of the Moana, Surfrider, Outrigger, Royal Hawaiian, and Sheraton Waikiki hotels is the actual fabled *Waikiki Beach.* A people-beach for sunners, swimmers, surfers, as well as diners and drinkers in the beachside cafés. Next is tiny *Gray's Beach,* with excellent swimming. Fronting the fort, set beachside in the center of Waikiki, is *Fort DeRussy Beach,* with good swimming, some surfing, beach concessions, Sunday morning church services, and daily free morning excercise classes. Westernmost is *Kahanamoku Beach and Lagoon,* a broad pleasant beach with scattered palm trees offering shade, and a catamaran landing.

The full length of Waikiki Beach is open to the public, with walkways into the separate beaches along Kalakaua Avenue and Kalia Road. The series of beaches is less than three miles long and each section of beach has its own beach boys with canoes and catamarans to rent and its own team of lifeguards.

ZOOS. Honolulu Zoo, 151 Kapahulu Ave., edge of Kapiolani Park, is one of the major U.S. zoos. Forty-three landscaped acres are home to 1,200 animals. Open daily, 8:30 A.M.–4:15 P.M. Adults, $1; children under 12 free.

On the windward shore, 30 minutes from Waikiki, is **Sea Life Park** at Makapuu, a setting of wild ocean and soaring cliffs. The program includes porpoise and whale shows, seals and penguins, and baby booby birds. A huge man-made replica of reef life, placed in a massive plastic tank, has every fish, shark, squid, and sea urchin of any coral reef and an inclined ramp all the way around outside, from top to bottom for viewing the finny performers. Adults, $8.50; juniors, $6.50; children, $2.75.

PARTICIPANT SPORTS. Kapiolani Park bounds Waikiki on the Diamond Head side and draws a crowd from early morning to midnight. There's a 1.8-mile jogging track, 12 free city tennis courts, a soccer field, and a golf driving range as well as the Honolulu Zoo and the Waikiki Shell and bandstand. There is even good swimming and some surf on the beach side of the park.

At the Ewa, or townside end of Waikiki, is **Ala Moana Beach** and **Park** and the adjacent **Magic Island.** Joggers are out early and late on the nearly 2-mile path around Ala Moana Park and the 1-mile trail around Magic Island. Ten public tennis courts are always busy, and it's often a long wait for a free court. Showers, rest rooms, lifeguards on duty. Swimming is great. Note: Since the island of Oahu sits *kapakahi* (crooked) to the compass, directions are spoken of locally as *mauka* (toward the mountains) and *makai* (toward the ocean). The other two directions are Diamond Head (toward that landmark) and Ewa (pronounced "ev–ah") meaning toward a small town on the far western shore.

Bikes and mopeds can be rented at *Aloha Funway Rentals* in Waikiki. Phone 808–834–1016 for a free shuttle bus to their shop. *Odyssey Rentals* (808–947–8036) also has a free pickup. A snorkeling trip to breathtaking Hanauma Bay is only $6 with *Seahorse Snorkeling* (808–395–8947) or *Steve's Diving Adventures* (808–947–8900). Both include hotel pickup and return, mask, fins, snorkel, beach mats, corrective lenses, and fish food.

Oahu's 10 public **golf courses** circle the island from seaside to secluded valleys to pineapple fields and views of Pearl Harbor. Greens fees run $20 to $45; transportation to the course might be another $8. The *Ala Wai Golf Course* across the Ala Wai Canal from Waikiki, a city course, is the easiest to get to and the least expensive. Greens fees about $8, but so popular you must get your reserved tee time by 7 A.M.; call 732–7741.

SPECTATOR SPORTS. Except for the Honolulu pro baseball team, the Islanders, the most popular spectator sports are football, basketball, volleyball, and baseball, played at Aloha Stadium, the University of Hawaii, and the island high schools. Three major football games are played around Christmas—the **Aloha Bowl,** generally between Pac 10 and Big 10 colleges; the **Hula Bowl,** which is the annual, college all-star game; and the **Pro Bowl,** the annual professional all-star game. Tickets are available at the Sports Arena and Aloha Stadium.

The Hawaiian Open Golf Tournament, a PGA tournament with a $600,000 purse, featuring top professionals, is played at Waialae Country Club Golf Course the first week in Feb. Tickets available at the gate.

CHILDREN'S ACTIVITIES. In Hawaii, there seems little need to search for special children's activities. Most kids like the whole trip, especially the events listed in the Free Events section.

The Makiki Environmental and Education Center, 2131 Makiki Heights Dr. (call 942–0990 to make sure it's open). Has a museum with displays of birds, fish, insects, and plants indigenous to Hawaii. On the grounds are a taro patch, rice paddy, trees, and a charming, easy, woodsy path that wanders up into the rain forest with signs and markers.

Tours the whole family can enjoy are to **Shirokiya Department Store** in Ala Moana. Their third-floor Japanese food fair offers food preparation demonstrations and free samples. There's also an inexpensive little restaurant to complete the experience. On a trip to **Tamashiro Fish Market,** 802 N. King St., see the live fish, crabs, and lobsters and perhaps buy some star fruit, guava, or mountain apples, plus several kinds of kim chee for a new look at Hawaii. Also different and surprising is the **Ala Moana Farmers' Market,** with more than a dozen farmer's food stores and shops in the long red-and-white building at 1020 Auahi St. across from Ward Warehouse.

MUSEUMS. The Bishop Museum, 7 miles from Waikiki, in a marvelous 100-year-old building at 1355 Kalihi St., is the world's foremost repository of the arts, science, history, and artifacts of Hawaii, Polynesia, and Pacific Oceania. There is also a planetarium displaying Polynesian skies and the far reaches of space; two shows daily and four on Sat., as well as craft demonstrations, a restaurant, and an art and book shop. The Bus, "#2 School Street," departs frequently from locations along Kuhio Ave. to the Bishop Museum; 60 cents each way. Adults, $4.75; children, $2.50; children under 6 free. Admission free the first Sun. of every month.

Honolulu Academy of Arts. 900 S. Beretania (538–3693). Truly exceptional collection of Oriental art, paintings, and furniture from the European school and mainland and local masters in a beautiful setting. Tues.–Sat., 10 A.M.–4:30 P.M.; Sun., 2–5 P.M. Conducted tours Tues., Wed., Fri., Sat., 11 A.M.; Thurs. and Sun., 2 P.M. Free.

ARTS AND ENTERTAINMENT. Film. Seven movie theaters in Waikiki have the latest first-run films: *Waikiki #1* and *#2,* 333 Seaside (923–2394); *Waikiki #3,* 2284 Kalakaua, (923–5353); *Kuhio #1* and *#2,* 2095 Kuhio Ave. (941–4422); and *Royal Marina I* and *II,* 1765 Ala Moana (949–0018), Adults $4.50; children, $2. *The Empress Theatre,* 1190 Nuuanu Ave. (538–1035), shows kung fu and sword sagas for $3.25. *Hemenway Theater,* University of Hawaii (808–948–8855 or 808–948–8856), frequently shows silents and golden oldies for $2.50. *Honolulu Academy of Arts Academy Theatre,* 900 S. Beretania St. (538–3693), presents a full monthly schedule of art films, screen classics, and foreign award winners for $2.50; lectures, free or up to $3; and avant-garde musical concerts, $7.

Music. For such an isolated capital city, Honolulu has an active musical scene. The **Honolulu Symphony Orchestra** is more than 80 years old. It performs regularly, except for a brief hiatus from Apr. to July, after which the season begins again with the Starlight Series at the Waikiki Shell in Kapiolani Park. Its home base is the Concert Hall in the Neal Blaisdell Center. Contact Honolulu Symphony Society, 1000 Bishop St., #901, Honolulu, HI 96813 (537–6171; tickets, 537–6191). The **Hawaii Opera Theater,** also at the NBC Concert Hall, performs during Feb. and March in a season consisting of three or four operas. Hawaii Opera Theater, 987 Waimanu St., Honolulu, HI 96813 (521–6537).

The Blaisdell Sports Arena, Aloha Stadium, and Waikiki Shell are the venues for such well-known stars as Kenny Rogers, Dolly Parton, Menudo, Julio Iglesias, Lionel Ritchie, and John Denver.

Stage. Three amateur performing arts troupes present musicals, drama, and comedy at their own theaters: **Manoa Valley Theater and Hawaii Performing Arts Company,** 2833 E. Manoa Rd. (988–6131), and **Honolulu Community Theatre,** Ft. Ruger Theater, upper Diamond Head Rd. (734–0274), both have a year-round season. The **Honolulu Theatre for Youth,** 1100 Alakea, #333 (321–3487), is open only during the school year, with performances held at various schools. **Kennedy Theatre** at the University of Hawaii campus has an Oct.–May season of dance, drama, and Oriental theater (948–7655).

SHOPPING. There's more to shopping in Waikiki than just looking for a good buy or the right color. Shopping centers offer entertainment, including Hawaiian music, petting zoos, arts and crafts demonstrations, Hawaiian movies, and hula lessons. Finding bargains in the many malls is a matter of looking for what you like. Everybody maintains similar prices. The street stalls and alley byways dictate a sharp eye and a lot of questions—is it what they say it is?

Major shopping areas: *Ala Moana Shopping Center,* 1450 Ala Moana; *Eaton Square,* 444 Hobron Ln.; *International Market Place,* 2330 Kalakaua Ave.; *King's Village,* 131 Kaiulani Ave.; *Kuhio Mall,* 2301 Kuhio Ave.; *Royal Hawaiian Shopping Center,* 2201 Kalakaua Ave.; *Waikiki Shopping Plaza,* 2270 Kalakaua Ave.; *Ward Center,* 1200 Ala Moana; *Ward Warehouse,* 1050 Ala Moana.

There are one or two discount houses that have sun wear, sunglasses, T-shirts, and aloha shirts at about 50 percent off. *Surfsports Discount Store,* third floor, Building C, Royal Hawaiian Shopping Center, (923–3022), and *Hawaii Discount Mart,* ground level, Waikiki Shopping Plaza (922–0525). For the ladies, short and long muumuus for more than 50 percent off are to be found at *Island Muumuu Works*—whose designer is well known Hilda of Hawaii—660 Ala Moana (536–4475). The store is open only Thurs.–Sat., 9–5 P.M. Perhaps not as smart but still of good quality are the muumuus, aloha shirts, and kiddie wear (tiny to preteens) at *Muumuu Factory to You* in the Wailana, 1860 Ala Moana (942–2124), open 7 days a week from 8 A.M.–9 P.M. Actually, the store is around the corner on Ena Road. They even have a grass skirt, bra, and shell lei for $7.95.

Interesting for people watching as well as bargain hunting is the Aloha Stadium Sunday Swap Meet, 6 A.M.–3 P.M. Real bargains are to be found, but if it looks too good to be true, it probably is. Watch the *Advertiser* or *Star Bulletin* for white elephant sales by Temple Emanu-El, first week in Mar.; St. Andrews Cathedral, first weekend of Dec.; Greek Orthodox Church, mid-Aug. at McCoy Pavilion; Friends of the Library, first Sat. in Aug. for one week.

DINING OUT. Hawaiian dining accentuates the positive of Asian cuisines with a mélange of ethnic dishes that mirror the mix of Hawaii's racial backgrounds. There are outstanding restaurants featuring the foods of six different areas of China and Japan, Thailand, Indonesia, Vietnam, Malaysia, India, Portugal, Mexico, and the Philippine Islands as well as restaurants that mirror the best of France and Italy and the mainland U.S. Regional Hawaiian cuisine features the intoxicating freshness of tree-ripened papaya and avocado, sweet-tart pineapple and guava, Maui onions, Kohala tomatoes, Manoa lettuce, catch-of-the-day ono or opakapaka, and locally grown prawns.

Ten years ago Hawaii was not much of a gourmet's paradise, but the past decade has seen a burgeoning of great dining spots. Medium-priced restaurants hold their own with award-winning dining, and coffee shops and American fast-food outlets are available for the budget-minded. Otherwise, it's no place like home.

Restaurant categories, determined by the price of a meal for one, without beverages, tax, or tip, are as follows: *Reasonable,* $12 to $18; *Very Economical,* $7 to $12; and *Low Budget,* $6 and under. Abbreviations for meals are: breakfast, B; lunch, L; dinner, D. All restaurants accept some, at least, of the major credit cards; traveler's checks are acceptable everywhere with identification. What follows is a selection of good restaurants in Honolulu, not a complete list. Restaurants open and close frequently; we have made every effort to ensure that our list is up to date.

Reasonable

Compadres Bar & Grill. Ward Centre on Ala Moana (523–1307). Fajitas, chili rellenos, baby ribs, margaritas, Mexican beer. "In" spot for lunch and dinner, popular cocktail lanai, bright decor. Reservations.

Hau Tree Lanai. New Otani Kaimana Beach Hotel, 2863 Kalakaua Ave. (923–1555). Good food in glorious beachfront setting under a spreading hau tree. Seafood, curries, lamb, veal, salads. B,L,D. Reservations.

Keo's Thai Cuisine. 625 Kapahulu (737–8240). Tropical setting, orchids, and greenery. Best of Thai cuisine, spring rolls, satay with peanut sauce, evil jungle prince shrimp, chieng mai salad. L, Mon.–Fri., D nightly. Reservations.

Monterey Bay Canners. 2335 Kalakaua Ave., Outrigger Waikiki, (922–5761). A view over Waikiki Beach with Kiawe charcoal–broiled seafood specialties, fresh fish, oyster bar, cocktails. Dinner daily 5–10; entertainment, 8–12. Brunch selections 7 A.M.–2 P.M. Reservations.

Pagoda Floating Restaurant. 1525 Rycroft St., midtown Honolulu (941–6611). Japanese and American dishes, gourmet seafood. Glass-walled restaurant floating on fish ponds teeming with colorful *koi;* Japanese meditation garden and waterfall. Children love to watch the fish, especially at feeding time. L, D. Reservations.

Windows of Hawaii. 1441 Kapiolani Blvd. next to Ala Moana Center (941–9138). Flying saucer revolving restaurant 400 feet in the sky, 360-degree view of Honolulu every hour. New American cuisine. Some expensive dishes. New American cuisine. L, D daily. Brunch on Sat. and Sun., 11:30 A.M. to 3 P.M., with bountiful salad and dessert buffet and various entrees. Reservations.

Wo Fat Chop Suey. 115 N. Hotel St., downtown Honolulu (537–6260). Legendary, picturesque, Hawaii's oldest Chinese restaurant. Winter melon soup, steamed mullet, roast duck, and thousand-layer bun. L inexpensive, D moderate. Reservations.

Yacht Harbor Restaurant. Yacht Harbor Towers, 359 Atkinson Dr. (946–2177). Handsome, overlooks yacht harbor. Prime rib, seafood, roast chicken. L Mon.–Fri., D nightly. Happy hour 4–6 P.M., dinner music. Reservations.

Very Economical

The Cafe Regent. Hawaiian Regent Hotel, 2552 Kalakaua Ave. (922–6611). Parisian-style café in a delightful open-air setting. Fresh baked croissants and breakfast rolls, crisp salads, special soups, and desserts. Located in the hotel lobby; good people watching. B, L, and cocktails. No reservations.

Fisherman's Wharf. Kewalo Basin, 1009 Ala Moana (538–3808). Big, open rooms, overview of harbor. Seafood, chioppino, bookmaker soup, easygoing ambience. L, D. Reservations.

House of Hong. Upstairs at 260A Lewers St. in the heart of Waikiki (923–0202). Handsome Chinese restaurant, typical Cantonese dining. Noodles, pork, and seafood specialties. L, D from 11 A.M.–11 P.M. Takeout available. Entertainment in Red Chamber Bar. Reservations.

Orson's. Ward Warehouse, second level, 1050 Ala Moana (521–5681). View over Kewalo Basin or toward Koolaus, pleasing ambience. All fresh fish, specialty deep-fried scallops, oysters, clams, chowder with sourdough bread. L, D. Reservations.

Peacock Room. Queen Kapiolani Hotel, 150 Kapahulu Ave. (922–1941). Home of the lavish buffets. Hawaiian luau luncheon daily. Dinner buffets alternate Japanese, prime ribs, and Hawaiian; many special dishes. Bargain-priced Sun. brunch on Garden Lanai. L, D. Reservations.

Rudy's Italian Restaurant. 2280 Kuhio Ave. (923–5949). Warm, friendly; walls lined with photos of dining celebrities. Italian dinners, Genoan style. D. Reservations.

Shore Bird Beach Broiler. 2169 Kalia Rd. (922–2887). Beachfront in Reef Hotel. Complete dinner at the beach; local fish and meat favorites broiled to order. Reservations.

Tony Roma's A Place For Ribs. 1972 Kalakaua Ave. (942–2121). Wood paneling and greenery, closely placed tables, good service. Famous baby back ribs, onion ring loaves, steaks, chicken, brook trout. L, D. No reservations.

Tahitian Lanai. 1811 Ala Moana Blvd., Waikikian Hotel (946–6541). Casual indoor-outdoor restaurant under big umbrellas or in thatched huts; view over Kahanamoku Beach Lagoon. Famous banana muffins, eggs Benedict, Tahitienne shrimp. Happy hour 4–6 P.M. L, D. Reservations.

Trattoria. 2168 Kalia Rd. (923–8415). Fine Italian dishes, northern style. Special menu, one-third off for early diners 5:30–6:30 P.M. Busy, friendly. D. Reservations.

Low Budget

Columbia Inn. 645 Kapiolani Blvd., downtown Honolulu (531–3747). Everybody's favorite; menu changes daily, includes all Hawaii's ethnic cuisines. B,L,D. Children's menu. No reservations.

Eggs 'n' Things. 436 Ena Rd. (949–0820). Open from 11 P.M.–2 P.M. Breakfasts only, pancakes, waffles, omelets. Early and late riser's special, two eggs and fluffy pancakes, $1.99. No reservations.

Flamingo Chuckwagon. 1015 Kapiolani Blvd. (538–1161). Family-style, all-you-can-eat buffet. Specializes in roast beef, barbecue ribs, seafood, and big salads. Private rooms available. Daily L,D. Reservations.

King's Bakery Coffee Shop. Eaton Square, 444 Hobron Ln. (955–8899). Popular 24-hour restaurant with tasty local meals at local prices plus King's Portuguese bread and pastries. No reservations.

Perry's Smorgy. Kuhio at Kanekapolei (926–0184). Most beautiful restaurant in chain; great buffet for B,L,D. Six dinner entrees, five salads. No reservations.

Popo's Mexican Food. 2112 Kalakaua Ave. (923–7355). Traditional specials and combinations. Neat decor. Liters of margaritas specially priced Mon. and Thurs. L,D. No reservations.

Tops Canterbury Coffee Shop. 1910 Ala Moana (941–5277). 24-hour, snacks, hamburgers, salads, chicken teriyaki, steak. No reservations.

Wailana Coffee House. 1860 Ala Moana (955–1764). Features 24 hours of breakfasts, plate lunches, budget dinners. No reservations.

Yum Yum Tree. Ward Centre, ground level, 1200 Ala Moana (523–9333). Popular indoor-outdoor café, charming decor, low-priced, tasty B,L,D. Fabulous pies. No reservations.

Hawaiian Plate Lunch. For hungry sightseers Hawaii has its own special version of fast food—the plate lunch—never gourmet, always good, and a major bargain at $2 to $4.50. The firm paper plates are heaped to overflowing with barbecue beef, teriyaki chicken, beef curry, beef stew, or butterfish tempura; the meal includes bean sprouts, kim chee, or mixed green salad and two scoops of rice and one of macaroni club salad. Highly portable in plastic boxes or foil-wrapped, they are good for drives around the island.

Ono Hawaiian Foods. 726 Kapahulu (737–2275). A good spot for real Hawaiian food at any time; features Hawaiian plates of laulau, kalua pig, lomi salmon, haupia, and a bowl of poi for $4.50. Eat it there or take it out. **Rainbow Drive-In,** 3308 Kanaina Ave., corner of Kapahulu. Famous for teriyaki beef plates at $2.90. **Ala Moana Park Concession,** handy to the beach, has several selections at $2.90. At Kewalo Basin, a fascinating spot for children to watch the boats, **Yasuko Kando Lunchwagon,** open till 2:45 P.M., and **Kewalo Ships Galley,** open 5:30 A.M.–10 P.M., with a covered lanai and view of the harbor. Both have mixed plates for $2.60 to $3.50.

Recommended Splurge. The Maile Room, Kahala Hilton, 5000 Kahala Ave. (734–2211). A beautiful hotel to visit, dinner or not. Home away from home to Queen Elizabeth of England, King Juan Carlos of Spain, the late Prime Minister Indira Gandhi, and a host of television and cinema celebrities. The 30-foot ceilings of the lobby and open terrace hold two huge chandeliers with more than 300,000 squares and rectangles of Italian glass. There are orchids all over the place, even growing from the wall that leads down a circular staircase to the Maile Room. Elegant service, decor, and food. Roast duckling Waialae in brandy with bananas, peaches, lychee, and mandarin oranges or rack of lamb with herbs, champignons, and fiddleheads will run $38 each, plus wine, coffee, and desserts. But it's an elegant splurge. Jackets required for men.

NIGHTLIFE AND BARS. The drinking age in Hawaii is 21. Happy hours, some with nibbles, are held at the **The Chart House,** across from Ilikai, 4:30–7 P.M.; **Great Wok of China,** also at the Royal Hawaiian Center, third floor, 4–6:30 P.M.; **Benihana of Tokyo,** Hilton Hawaiian Village, 3:30–6:30 P.M.; **Princess Garden Court,** Royal Hawaiian Center, next to the fountain, from 4 P.M.; **Surfboard Lounge,** Waikiki Beachcomber Hotel, 4–7 P.M.; and **El Crab Catcher,** 1765 Ala Moana, 4–6 P.M.

After the sun sets on sand and sea and the "Honolulu City Lights" sparkle on, Waikiki offers a smorgasbord of diversions. Don Ho and Al Harrington, both seen on mainland television shows, may already be known to visitors. They perform, respectively, at the Hilton Hawaiian Village Dome, 2005 Kalia Rd., and the Polynesian Palace, 227 Lewers St. Other popular shows are the peppy, funny Society of Seven at the Waikiki Outrigger, 2335 Kalakaua Ave., the Brothers Cazimero at the Royal Hawaiian Hotel, and Danny Kalekini at the Kahala Hilton, 5000 Kahala Ave. Dinner shows are about $38 to $45. The bargain is cocktail-show packages (cover charge and a tropical or standard drink) at $16 to $18; children, $13.

Waikiki has an array of **Polynesian evenings**—songs and dances of the South Pacific, beautiful girls, handsome men, glorious costumes (what there is of them), and terrifying fire knife dances—on stage nightly at the Hula Hut Theater Restaurant, 286 Beachwalk; Princess Kaiulani Hotel, 120 Kaiulani Ave.; and Hilton Hawaiian Village, 2005 Kalia Rd. The same cocktail-show pricing applies.

Hawaiian **luaus** hold special interest for first-timers. Two are held on the leeward shore: **Germaine's Luau,** Campbell Estate, (941–3338), and **Paradise Cove Luau,** Campbell Estate, (945–3539). Both have bus pickups at Waikiki Hotels. A **Royal Luau** has been held on Waikiki Beach at the Royal Hawaiian Hotel, 2259 Kalakaua Ave. (923–7311), for 30 years. Least expensive on Waikiki Beach, the **Outrigger Waikiki,** 2335 Kalakaua Ave. (923–5726). Hawaiian and American food, leis, rum drinks, entertainment. All for $19.50. Others are $37 to $40. (Children's prices.)

Church- or school-sponsored local luaus will be $5 to $10 cheaper, with informal entertainment and authentic Hawaiian food. The best way to find these luaus as well as free musicales, street fairs, and current entertainment is in the Friday edition of the two Honolulu dailies, the *Advertiser* and *Star Bulletin.*

Waikiki Beach Press, one of the free tourist magazines, provides the best listing of discos and night spots with Dixieland, rock, country-western, jazz, and Hawaiian music for dancing and listening.

SECURITY. Honolulu is so hospitable and friendly that it diverts attention from the seamier side of a big city at a crossroads of the world. The Hawaiian Visitors Bureau has produced a small booklet for travelers, *The Happy Hawaii Visitor,* basically explaining sun safety, water safety, and care of money and valuables. Don't, they say, get too relaxed. Don't take valuables or airline tickets to the beach or leave cameras or radios visible in a locked car. Take only what you can carry with you, and *carry* it with you. If you plan to swim, leave valuables in the hotel safe. And to be sure you're safe, lock the door when you're in your room. Don't display large amounts of money in bars or street-side shops. Carry traveler's checks, and cash only what you need.

Relax and have fun, but be careful.

HOUSTON

by
Teresa Hurst

Teresa Hurst is a rare bird: a native Houstonian who still resides there. A former travel writer and magazine editor, she now writes for the petroleum industry.

Houston is a city in search of a personality. Oh, it used to have one. Thirty years ago, it was a friendly, slow-moving subtropical town. Unlike the rest of Texas, Houston was more truly southern than western, yet without the history and old-world charm of the Deep South. It was a little "country," but definitely not "cowboy." Where shopping malls and office buildings stand today, there were miles of green pastureland, marshes, and lush vegetation. Woods lining the bayous dripped with Spanish moss, and palm and banana trees decorated local yards. The weather was hot and muggy, but air-conditioning was still a luxury. Residents frequently slept with their windows open and their doors unlocked.

The turning point in Houston's modern development was the advent of affordable commercial and residential air-conditioning in the mid-1950s. No longer viewed as uninhabitable by those from colder climes, Houston emerged as the boom town of the 1960s and 1970s. It became the center of manned spacecraft activities, as well as a corporate center for more than 200 national and international companies. Most of the oil giants moved their headquarters to Houston, earning it the title of the "Energy Capital of America."

Hearing that the streets were paved with opportunity, people from all over the world swarmed into the city—thousands per day—hoping to make a fast buck or a fortune. Skyscrapers, apartment complexes, and housing developments sprang up daily to keep pace with the influx of newcomers. Houston became the fastest growing and fourth largest city in the nation.

Then came the recession and hard times for the oil industry. Many people packed their bags and returned whence they came, leaving thousands of homes, apartments, and offices empty. Builders stopped building, and the city stopped expanding. The boom didn't exactly go bust; it just fizzled out—at a propitious moment, when Houston was about to strangle on its own unbridled growth. Today the city is a mishmash of cultures and styles, a classic American melting pot. It has no distinct identity, but it's on the brink of forging one.

Perhaps it will become another great international metropolis like New York. In the past 30 years, Houston has developed into a truly cosmopolitan city, where the foreign influence is strongly felt. It's possible, for example, to take a turn around the mammoth Galleria shopping center without hearing English spoken once. The city certainly has picked up the rapid, stressful pace of New York and the traffic jams of Los Angeles. It also has acquired a new layer of sophistication, along with new money and power.

Visitors will note how clean and modern the city is. That's because most everything, including the downtown skyline, is only 20 years old. Aggressively future-oriented, Houston has scant respect for tradition or the past. The tendency is to tear down and build anew, rather than to preserve or restore. This is the most air-conditioned city in the world. Residents can get in their cars, drive to work or some other destination, and then arrive home again without once stepping outside into the heat and humidity. Connecting most of the buildings downtown is a vast underground tunnel system replete with restaurants and stores. (To take your own subterranean walking tour, pick up a map at one of the bank buildings along the route or at the Greater Houston Convention and Visitors Council.) Visitors will also note that Houstonians spend much of their day in the car, as traveling to virtually any destination in this spread-out city involves a long commute.

The freeway known as the Loop, Interstate-610, serves as both a geographical and figurative boundary. Inside its circle is the old, preboom Houston; outside is the new. Inside the Loop is what natives know as the real Houston. Here are the city's birth site, port, main business district, cultural attractions, and oldest and most gracious residential areas.

Houston began at Allen's Landing, where the Allen brothers landed in 1836, which is now a small municipal park downtown on Buffalo Bayou, bounded by Main, Commerce, and Travis streets. (The park does not have a great deal of sightseeing value.) The brothers named their new town after General Sam Houston, the hero of Texas independence. They paid about $1.40 per acre for 6,642 acres of coastal prairie near the headwaters of Buffalo Bayou, chosen because it was as close to Stephen F. Austin's central Texas colonies as shallow-draft boats could travel from the Gulf of Mexico.

The muddy, mosquito-infested settlement rapidly developed into a timber, cotton, and cattle-shipping town that served as capital of the Texas Republic from 1837 to 1840. Then, in 1901, the Spindletop discovery set off an oil boom that introduced the mainstay of Houston's economy for the twentieth century. The 1914 opening of the man-made Houston Ship Channel was the realization of the Allen brother's dream of Houston as a major port (today it is the nation's third largest) and the "City of the Future."

Little remains of the city's past except the area downtown around Old Market Square, bounded by Milam, Congress, Travis, and Preston streets. Market Square was once the site of cattle drives, ox caravans bringing cotton to waiting barges, saloons, gambling houses, and an opera house. Today the square is primarily a lunchtime-restaurant district catering to downtown office workers. The city's oldest commercial structure still stands here. Now a bar called La Carafe, it was built in the 1860s and served over the years as an Indian trading post, a stagecoach stop, and a brothel.

Other buildings of historical interest in the area are the Old Cotton Exchange at 2020 Travis, the Pillot Building at 1016 Congress, the Sweeny-Coombs-Fredericks Building at 301 Main, Christ Church Cathedral at 1117 Texas, and Sam Houston Park, bounded by Bagby, McKinney, and Dallas Streets.

These remnants of the past are dwarfed by the gleaming glass and steel skyscrapers of the present. A good vantage point to see many of Houston's new buildings is Tranquility Park (bounded by Smith, Walker, Bagby, and Rusk), which commemorates man's first landing on the moon. From there you can see the red granite Gothic spires of the Republic Bank Building; the white marble of One Shell Plaza, home of Shell Oil Company and at one time the tallest reinforced concrete building west of the Mississippi; the curving glass facade of Allied Bank Plaza; the top of the Texas Commerce Tower, which at 75 stories is the world's tallest composite tube tower; and the distinctive black glass Pennzoil Towers, which are twin trapezoids. You also can see both the old and new downtown branches of the public library, City Hall, Sam Houston Coliseum, Albert Thomas Convention and Exhibit Center, and the Music Hall, one of the city's main performance halls.

West of downtown, and bounded roughly by Bagby, U.S. 59 (the Southwest Freeway), Shepherd, and Allen Parkway, is the Montrose area. This is one of Houston's oldest neighborhoods and you'll see a curious mix: beautiful older houses sitting next door to virtual slums.

River Oaks, west of Montrose and bounded by the Loop, Westheimer, and Buffalo Bayou, is a bastion of the ultra-rich, Houston's version of Beverly Hills. You'll see fabulous mansions owned by oil men, politicians, celebrities, and even a few scions of European nobility.

Further south is another lovely older neighborhood, West University, named for its proximity to Rice University. This is a real-estate hot spot because it's inside the Loop and close to downtown; small brick cottages as well as mansions sell for a fortune. To see some of the nicest, take a drive down shady Sunset Boulevard.

Bordering Rice University on the east is a section of South Main Street that's Houston's version of the Champs Elysee. Lined with an archway of ancient oaks, this is the most attractively landscaped street in the city. At one end is the elegant Warwick Hotel, fronted by the circular Mecom Fountain. Across the street is the Museum of Fine Arts, and the Contemporary Arts Museum is another block over. There are also many art galleries in the immediate vicinity.

Continuing down South Main you'll come to the renowned Texas Medical Center, which was the home of the first successful artificial heart implant in the United States. The center consists of 29 colleges, schools, institutes, and hospitals, including the world famous M.D. Anderson Cancer Center.

The Astrodome, the world's first indoor, air-conditioned stadium is south of the Medical Center. It's home to major league baseball and football teams. Adjacent are the Astrohall and the Astro Arena, which house the Houston Livestock Show and various conventions. Across the street are AstroWorld, an amusement park, and Waterworld, an aquatic playground.

The Galleria, a lavish three-story mall with department stores, boutiques, restaurants, luxury hotels, movie theaters, and an ice-skating rink, lends its name to an area west of the Loop. The landmark for both mall and area is the Transco Tower, a spectacular skyscraper with a beacon on top, which dwarfs the surrounding office buildings and hotels. The Galleria offers the most expensive shopping in the city. Travelers on a budget will probably just want to browse. There's plenty to look at since the mall is a gathering spot on weekends for residents as well as international travelers.

The Galleria area, bounded by the Loop, the Southeast Freeway, Voss, and Woodway, is a choice business and residential neighborhood offering fine stores, restaurants, and clubs. If you're looking for nightlife, this is one of the best places to find it.

PRACTICAL INFORMATION

WHEN TO GO. Houston really only has two seasons, summer and winter. Blink, and you may miss the few days in Apr. and Nov., with temperatures in the mild 60s, that pass for spring and fall. Most of the time Houston is just plain hot or cold, and the humidity supplied by the nearby Gulf of Mexico makes the highs and lows feel more extreme than they really are. Whatever season you visit, be prepared for anything: Houston weather changes quickly.

The long sauna of a summer begins around the first of May and extends through Oct., with July and Aug. being the steamiest months. Temperatures usually range from the mid-80s to the high 90s. During hurricane season—June through Oct.—heavy rains frequently inundate the city, flooding streets and snarling traffic.

Winter hits about mid-Dec. and lasts through Mar. with normally moderate temperatures in the 40s and 50s. The thermometer can sometimes plunge below freezing, however, when cold winds called blue northers unexpectedly whip through town. Snow is a rare phenomenon, although sunbathing on Christmas Day is not unheard of.

HOW TO GET THERE. By air. Two airports serve the city, so confirm in advance which you will be using. Some airlines have flights into both.

W. P. Hobby Airport is about 9 miles southeast of downtown via I-45 and Broadway Boulevard. The airport has recently been remodeled to provide spacious parking. Commuter flights within Texas and from surrounding states mostly operate from here.

Houston Intercontinental Airport is about 16 miles north of downtown, accessible from either I-45 or U.S. 59 via the North Belt. The least expensive long-term parking ($2.50 per day) may be found in the City of Houston Satellite Parking lot, on the corner of Greens Road and Kennedy Boulevard. Courtesy buses transport passengers from the lot to the airport's three terminals.

Houston is served by most major domestic airlines including *American, Continental, Delta, Eastern, Northwest, Piedmont, Southwest United,* and *USAir.* Among the international airlines serving Houston are *Pan Am, TWA, Air Canada, Air France, Cayman Airways, KLM, Iberia,* and *British Caledonia. Aeromexico* and *Continental* offer the lowest priced flights into the Mexican interior, and *British Caledonia* and *Continental* offer reasonably priced nonstop flights to London.

For commuting within Texas, the best budget bets are *Southwest Airlines* and *Continental.*

By train. *Amtrak* passenger service connects Houston three times a week (Mon., Wed., and Sat.) with San Antonio, New Orleans, and Los Angeles. The station is downtown at 902 Washington Ave. and Bagby (713–224–1577). Reservations, 800–872–7245. Several different types of economical excursion fares are available.

By bus. Houston is served by *Greyhound-Trailways* bus lines, with terminals at 1410 Texas (713–222–1161) and 2121 Main (713–759–6500).

By car. Three major highways crisscross Houston, I-10 cuts through Texas from the Louisiana border on the east to the New Mexico border on the west. U.S. 59 runs northeast to southwest, and I-45 runs northwest to southeast.

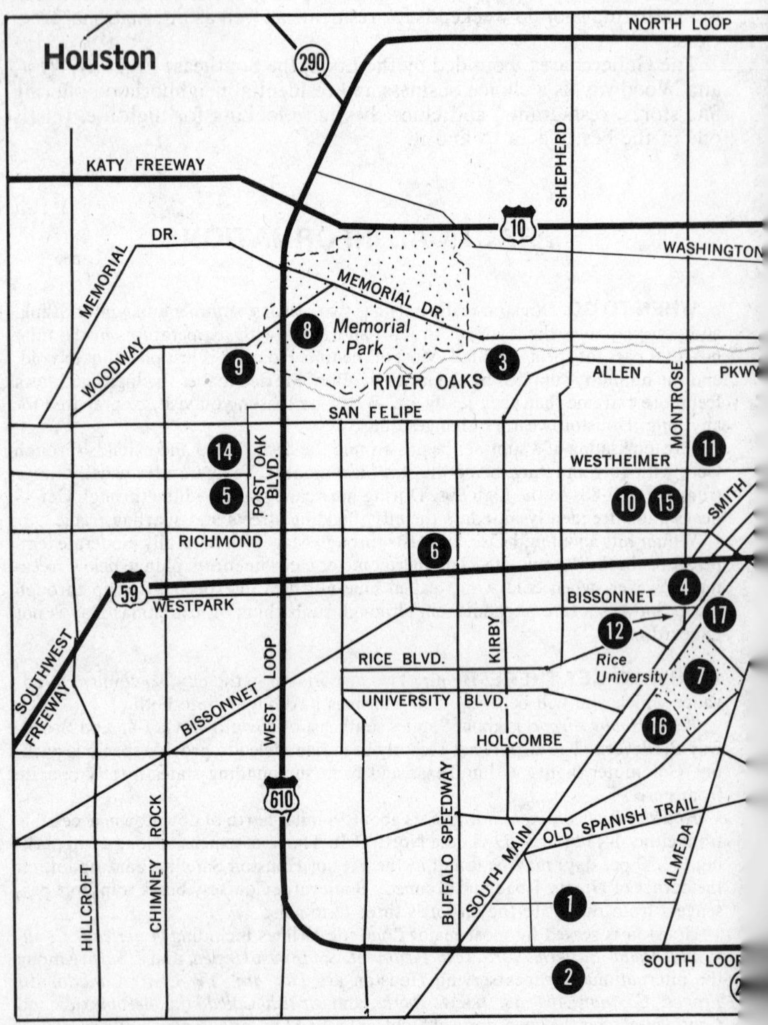

Points of Interest

1) Astrodome
2) Astroworld
3) Bayou Bend Branch, Museum of Fine Arts
4) Contemporary Arts Museum
5) Galleria
6) Greenway Plaza
7) Hermann Park, including the Museum of Medical Science, Museum of Natural Science, Hermann Park Zoo, and Hermann Park Garden Center

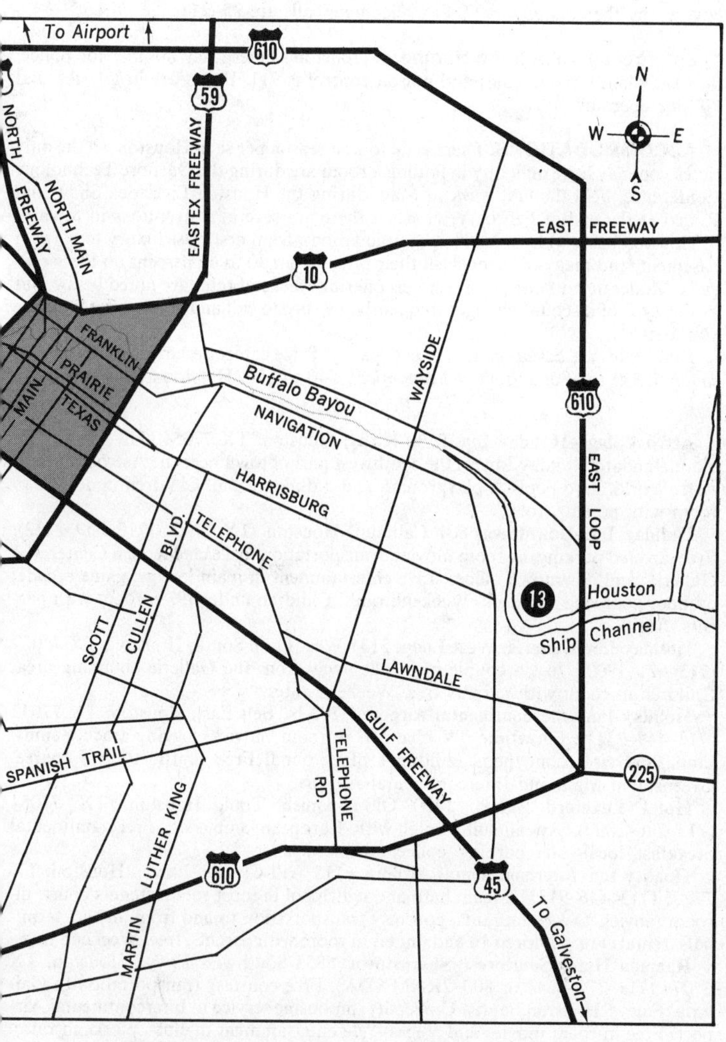

8) Houston Arboretum and Nature Center
9) Inn on the Park Hotel
10) Menil Collection
11) Montrose Neighborhood
12) Museum of Fine Arts
13) Port of Houston
14) Post Oak Shopping Sector
15) Rothko Chapel
16) Texas Medical Center
17) Warwick Hotel

TELEPHONES. The area code for the Houston metropolitan area is 713. You do not need to dial it within the area. Some 713 numbers in outlying areas, however, require that you dial 1 first, then the seven digit calling number. Nearby cities such as Galveston, Texas City, Sealy, Beaumont, and the Liberty-Daytona sectors are covered by the area code 409. Pay telephone calls are 25 cents.

Emergency Telephone Numbers. Houston's emergency number for police, fire, ambulance, paramedics and poison control is 911. If you are in a hotel, dial "0" for operator.

ACCOMMODATIONS. There is no tourist season per se in Houston, so the only times you may have difficulty in finding a room are during the Offshore Technology Conference, held the first week in May; during the Houston Livestock Show and Rodeo at the end of February; or when there are several conventions in town.

Houston has a wide range of accommodations, from first class luxury to bargain basement, and many of them slash their prices from 30 to 60 percent on the weekends. Moderate and inexpensive hotels offering weekend rates are noted below, but as this type of discount changes frequently, be sure to call and confirm rates before you arrive.

Hotel rates are based on double occupancy. Price categories are as follows: *Reasonable,* $50 to $80; and *Very Economical,* $40 to $50. Hotel tax is 14 percent.

Reasonable

Astro Village–Holiday Inn. 8500 Kirby, Houston, TX 77054 (713–799–1050). Your standard Holiday Inn on the southwest part of town near the Astrodome and AstroWorld. Two pools, a playground, and a dining room. Children under 12, in room with parents, free.

Holiday Inn–Downtown. 801 Calhoun, Houston, TX 77002 (713–659–2222). Free covered parking, in-room movies, transportation to Texas Medical Center, the Galleria, and downtown offices. Live entertainment in main lounge, game arcade, outdoor pool, and sun deck. Weekend rates. Children under 19, in room with parents, free.

Holiday Inn–Galleria/West Loop. 3131 West Loop South, Houston, TX 77027 (713–621–1900). Just a couple of blocks away from the Galleria shopping area. Children in room with parents free. Weekend rates.

Holiday Inn–Intercontinental Airport. 3702 N. Belt East, Houston, TX 77032 (713–449–2311). Showtime TV channel, in-room movies, jogging track, tennis, sauna, exercise room, pool, children's playground. Free shuttle to golf course. Greenspoint Mall, and Intercontinental Airport.

Hotel Luxeford Suites. 1400 Old Spanish Trail, Houston, TX 77054 (713–796–1000). An all-suite hotel with European ambience. Free continental breakfast, local calls, parking, coffee, and newspaper.

Quality Inn–Intercontinental Airport. 6115 Will Clayton Pkwy., Houston, TX 77205 (713–446–9131). Steam bath and whirlpool in most rooms, tennis court, in-room movies, two restaurants, courtesy transportation to and from airport terminals, rental cars. Children 16 and under, in room with parents, free. Weekend rates.

Ramada Hotel–Southwest/Sharpstown. 6855 Southwest Frwy., Houston, TX 77074 (713–771–0641 or 800–2RAMADA). Free courtesy transportation to Galleria, Foleys, Houston Baptist University; limousine service to Intercontinental Airport. Free in-room movies and Vegas-style entertainment in club. Weekend rates.

Ramada Inn–Hobby Airport East. 9005 Airport Blvd., Houston, TX 77061 (713–943–3300). In-room movies, airport courtesy car, seafood and steak restaurant, lounge with dancing. Weekend rates.

Residence Inn. 7710 South Main, Houston, TX 77030 (713–660–7993). One- and two-bedroom-suite hotel, and one mile from the Texas Medical Center and a quarter-mile from the Astrodome and Astroworld. Fully equipped kitchens, satellite TV, heated pool, spas. Continental breakfast and free van service to the Medical Center.

Texian Inn–Astrodome. 9911 Buffalo Speedway, Houston, TX 77054 (713–668–8082). Features complimentary Continental breakfast, satellite television, Water Pik showers, full-length mirrors, nonsmoking section, pool with hot tub. Children under 17, in room with parents, free.

Very Economical

Allen Park Inn. 2121 Allen Parkway, Houston TX 77019 (713–521–9321; 800–392–1499 in Texas, 800–231–6310 elsewhere). Comfortable rooms near downtown. Sauna-whirlpool, exercise room, barber shop, and 24-hour dining room.

Best Western Dome Royale. 3223 South Loop West, Houston, TX 77025 (713–664–6425). Near the Astrodome and Astroworld, with transportation to the Medical Center. Restaurant, lounge, in-house movies. Children under 12, in room with parents, free. Senior citizen discounts.

Galleria Oaks Corporate Inn. 5151 Richmond, Houston, TX 77056 (713–629–7120). An all-suite hotel located two blocks south of the Galleria shopping mall. Fully equipped kitchens, covered parking, and two pools.

Holiday Inn–Central. 4640 S. Main, Houston, TX 77002 (713–526–2811). Dining room, pool, wading pool, coin laundry. Suites available. Children under 18, in room with parents, free.

La Quinta Motor Inns. All offer weekend rates. Greenspoint area: 6 N. Belt East, Houston, TX 70060 (713–447–6888). Greenway Plaza area: 4015 Southwest Frwy., Houston, TX 77027 (713–623–4750). West of the Loop: 8017 Katy Frwy., Houston, TX 77024 (713–668–8941). Brookhollow area: 11002 Northwest Frwy., Houston, TX 77092 (713–688–2581). Sharpstown area: 8201 Southwest Frwy., Houston, TX 77074 (713–772–3626). Town and Country area: 11113 Katy Frwy., Houston, TX 77079 (713–932–0808).

Rodeway Inn. 5820 Katy Frwy., Houston, TX 77007 (713–869–9211). Near downtown. Complimentary coffee and doughnuts daily, HBO/cable TV, 24-hour restaurant, pool. Weekend rates.

Tides II Motor Inn. 6700 S. Main, Box 25006, Houston, TX 77005 (713–522–2811). Pool, restaurant, courtesy car to Texas Medical Center, jogging track at Rice University, limousine service to airport. Special medical rates available.

TraveLodge–Astrodome. 8700 S. Main, Houston, TX 77025 (713–666–0346). Pool, restaurant. Children under 17, in room with parents, free.

TraveLodge Viscount Club Hotel. 2828 Southwest Frwy., Houston, TX 77098 (713–526–4571 or 800–255–3050). Convenient to Greenway Plaza, the Galleria, and Rice University. Children under 17, in room with parents, free. Weekend rates.

Budget Motels. These are inexpensive chains or local motels that offer acceptable double rooms for less than $40.

Chief Motel. 9000 S. Main, Houston, TX 77025 (713–666–4151). Free courtesy bus to the Texas Medical Center and both airports. Children under 12, in room with parents, free.

Grant Motor Inn. 8200 S. Main, Houston, TX 77025 (713–668–8000). Near the Astrodome and Texas Medical Center. Covered reserved parking, pool, covered children's pool and playground. Free coffee and doughnuts in lobby. Special rates for medical, military and commercial personnel, and senior citizens.

Houston Villa Motor Hotel. 9604 S. Main, Houston, TX 77025 (713–666–1411). Pool, restaurant. Children under 16, in room with parents, free.

Regal 8 Inn–West. 9535 Katy Frwy., Houston, TX 77024 (713–467–4411 or 800–851–8888). National chain. Pool, color TV, restaurant. Children under 12, in room with parents, free.

Super 8 Motel–Crossroads Inn. 15350 J.F.K. Boulevard, Houston, TX 77025 (713–442–1830 or 800–843–1991). National chain near Intercontinental Airport, free airport shuttle. Complimentary Continental breakfast, pool, Jacuzzi, sauna, car rentals.

White House Motor Hotel. 9300 South Main, Houston, TX 77025 (713–666–2261). Restaurant, club, game room, Olympic-size pool. Free courtesy bus to Hobby Airport and Medical Center. Medical rates available.

Bed-and-Breakfast. The bed-and-breakfast craze has finally caught on in Houston, although there are not many in the city yet. Your best bet is to contact the **Bed and Breakfast Society of Houston,** 921 Heights Blvd., Houston, TX 77008 (713–868–4654). Affiliated with an international network of bed-and-breakfast associations, the society provides personalized overnight accommodations and accompanying benefits at a reasonable price. These accommodations, along with a hearty Texas breakfast, are available in private homes, guest houses, and town houses scattered throughout the city. Rates range from $35 to $50 for a double room. Hosts and guests are screened and matched up by the society staff. Advance reservations are required.

Ys and Hostels. Three branches of the Houston YMCA offer residence facilities for men. The best, and the one in the safest neighborhood, is the **Downtown Branch,** 1600 Louisiana, Houston, TX 77002 (713–659–8501). Rooms for one person are $15 per night or $65 per week. If all else fails, you can try one of the others: **Cossaboom East End Branch,** 7903 S. Loop East, Houston, TX 77012 (713–643–4396), $11.30 per night, $55.35 per week; and **South Central Branch,** 3531 Wheeler, Houston, TX 77004 (713–748–5405), $10.74 per night, $42–$52 per week. The YWCA has no residence facilities for women in Houston.

HOW TO GET AROUND. Like Los Angeles, Houston is the city of the automobile. Don't try to explore the area without one. Public transportation is improving, but you'll find it difficult to get from one end of this spread-out metropolis to another by bus.

From the airport. The *Houston Airport Express* (713–523–8888) provides shuttle service between Houston Intercontinental Airport and downtown passenger terminals for $7.70 one way. They leave the airport every 20 minutes from 5:40 A.M. to midnight, and intermittently throughout the late evening and early morning hours. The *Hobby Airport Limousine* (713–644–8359) provides a similar service for Hobby Airport at a cost of $5 one way. Shuttles from the airport begin at 5:30 A.M. and continue every 30–40 minutes until 11:30 P.M.

From Intercontinental, approximate taxi cab rates to the following areas are: downtown $24; Astrodome $28; Galleria $28; Greenway Plaza, $26. There is an additional $1 per person charge required by city ordinances on all trips originating from Intercontinental. As many as four persons can ride for the price of one. From Hobby, approximate prices are as follows: downtown, $16; Astrodome, $14; Galleria, $18; Greenway Plaza, $18.

At both Intercontinental and Hobby, shuttle services and taxis pick up passengers outside the airport terminals. Look for "Ground Transportation" signs to direct you to the appropriate doors.

By bus. The Metropolitan Transit Authority (Metro) operates a citywide bus system for a modest fare of 60 cents. Express fare is 85 cents. Two shopper specials, marked by red and blue flags, traverse the downtown area for a fare of 15 cents. In all cases, passengers must have exact change. Formerly infamous for its dismal service, Metro has made great improvements in terms of comfort and efficiency. However, if you plan to travel beyond the immediate vicinity of your lodgings, or if you're on a time schedule, rent a car. For routing and other information, call Metro at 713–635–4000.

By taxi. Several taxi companies operate in and around the city, among them: Yellow Cab (236–1111), Liberty Cab (695–6700), Sky Jack Cab (523–6080), and United Cab (699–0000). Although they are permitted to cruise and can be hailed from the street, most line up outside major hotels and airports. Rates begin at $2.45 for the first mile, add $1.05 cents for each additional mile.

By rental car. Houston has scores of car-rental companies scattered across the city, such as Hertz, Avis, National, Budget, and Dollar Rent-a-Car. They are well represented at various hotels and service locations in town and at or near the airports. Rates and conditions of rentals vary widely, although most of the major companies offer special low business or weekend rates. For the truly adventurous, two of the cheapest local agencies are *Rent A Heap Cheap,* 5722 Southwest Frwy., Houston, TX (977–7771), and *Rent A Wreck,* 2012 N. Shepherd (869–8144).

HINTS TO THE MOTORIST. If you intend to drive your own car in Houston, remember that Texas now has a seat-belt law. Also make sure you carry liability insurance; it's required by law for all drivers who reside in Texas. That law can extend to nonresidents as well, through an agreement that Texas has with several other states. If an uninsured out-of-stater causes an accident in Houston, the state of Texas can request the driver's home state to suspend his or her driver's license.

As a precaution, consult your insurance agent for the correct amount of liability coverage to purchase. Or consider joining an auto club that can provide you with insurance as well as trip planning information and emergency and repair service.

Even if it weren't a legal requirement, insurance would still be a must in Houston due to the erratic driving habits of many of its motorists. Native Houstonians attribute this problem to the massive influx of "foreigners" (meaning Yankees as well as people from outside the U.S.), who "don't know how to drive." Actually, it's simply the result of too many cars on too little pavement. Ask a Houstonian for his definition of hell, and he'll probably say it's the Southwest Freeway (U.S. 59) at 5 P.M. The city's unbounded growth has not been accompanied by an equal expansion in its highway system, either in areas served or in car capacity. If at all possible, avoid the freeways during Houston's dreaded rush hour. Peak traffic hours are 7–9 A.M. and 3:30–6 P.M. Visitors should know that during these hours, a contraflow system borrows one lane from the opposite side of the North Freeway (I-45 north of downtown) and the Katy Freeway (I-10 west of downtown). Limited to buses and passenger vans, these lanes are marked with concrete barricades, pylons on the road striping and with overhead warning lights.

On-street parking is limited, particularly downtown. Illegally parked cars get towed away and impounded until fines and storage charges are paid. It's best to use one of the many public garages.

Although spasmodically enforced, the freeway speed limit is 55 mph. The speed limit on surface roads is 30 mph, unless otherwise marked. School zones are 20 mph and are usually marked with flashing yellow lights. If you find yourself behind a loading or unloading school bus, it's illegal to pass or overtake it. There is no state requirement for posting warning signs on radar, mechanical, or electrical speed-checking devices. Radar detectors are not prohibited in the state of Texas.

TOURIST INFORMATION. The *Greater Houston Convention and Visitors Council* publishes free maps and an excellent series of multilingual brochures on local attractions, accommodations, downtown walking tours, shopping, restaurants, entertainment, and general public information. They also prepare a quarterly "Houston Public Events" brochure with a detailed schedule of sports, theater, and special events going on in the city and surrounding area.

Most of the brochures are available at the information booths in both airports, and "Houston Public Events" is widely distributed by restaurants, hotels, and businesses throughout the city. All are available by advance mail from the Greater Houston Convention and Visitors Council, 3300 Main, Houston, TX 77002 (call 523–5050 locally, 800–231–7722 in Texas, 800–231–7799 outside Texas). There also is a drive-up information booth with a multilingual staff at that location. It's open Mon.–Fri., 8:30 A.M.–5 P.M.; Sat., 9 A.M.–3 P.M.

Current happenings about town also are listed in *Texas Monthly* magazine, and weekly in both newspapers—the Houston *Post* and *Chronicle.*

Foreign currency exchange. The Airport Exchange (713–443–0070) in Houston Intercontinental Airport, has foreign-exchange booths in all three terminals, with varying hours of operation. The Texas Foreign Exchange Co., 1130 Travis, is open Mon.–Fri. from 8:30 A.M.–6 P.M., Sat. from 8:30 A.M.–5 P.M., and they will quote the current rate of exchange by telephone ,(713–654–0999). Other foreign currency exchanges around town include: Barri Remittance Corp., 7800 Bissonnet, (713–981–7671); International, 801 Travis (713–224–5796); and Monytron Inc., at several locations (713–926–8079 for information).

HINTS TO DISABLED TRAVELERS. All federal and state and most city office buildings, schools, and parks have instituted, or are in the process of establishing, special facilities for the disabled. More and more curbs, especially in the downtown area, have wheelchair ramps, as do newer shopping malls and restaurants. Most parking lots have reserved spaces, and public bathrooms have special stalls. The accommodations section of the "Houston Official Visitors' Guide" available at the Greater Houston Convention and Visitors Council (see Tourist Information, above) indicates which hotels and motels in town have facilities for handicapped travelers.

FREE AND ALMOST FREE EVENTS. Houston's calendar of free events is somewhat sparse, being confined primarily to festivals and parades. In mid-

February, trail riders from outlying areas ride into Houston, camp overnight in Memorial Park, and then parade through downtown to kick off the annual **Houston Livestock Show and Rodeo.** On this "Go Texan" day, most businesses allow employees to wear western duds to work, and it's one of the few times you'll see lawyers and bankers in the dressy downtown area decked out in cowboy boots and ten-gallon hats. A variety of other "Go Texan" celebrations also take place during the two weeks of rodeo and livestock competition.

In March, it's the wearin' of the green, as the city's lively Irish and would-be Irish sector congregate downtown for the annual Saint Patrick's Day Parade. Although not free, a number of Irish bars and restaurants across the city, notably **Birraporetti's** (the 1997 W. Gray location) and **Grif's Inn** (3416 Roseland) host several days of rowdy nonstop partying, featuring green beer and sometimes bagpipes. By mid-month, the **Houston Festival** begins. It is a two-week series of free outdoor celebrations, performances, and arts and crafts shows in downtown plazas and parks. The festival concludes with a Tardi Mardi Gras bash in Sam Houston Park. Also in Mar., the city is awash with the color of spring flowers, the most spectacular of which can be seen on the annual **Azalea Trail** winding through the mansions of River Oaks and Tanglewood. The impeccably manicured grounds of Bayou Bend also are included in this two-weekend show.

In early April, when bluebonnets and Indian paintbrush cover the Texas fields and roadways, it's a local spring custom to take a Sun. afternoon drive outside the city to see the wild flowers. Toward the end of the month, and again in October, 10 blocks of Westheimer in the Montrose area are closed to traffic for the biannual **Westheimer Colony Art Festival,** a street exhibition of arts and crafts.

A free summer series of plays, ballets, and concerts at **Miller Outdoor Theater** in Hermann Park begins in June. One concert, the Juneteenth Blues Festival, is a major celebration for the city's black population, to commemorate the delivery of the Emancipation Proclamation in Texas. Sam Houston Park and several shopping malls throughout the city are sites for Fourth of July celebrations and fireworks displays.

October brings Greek and Italian festivals, as well as the German Oktoberfest; all provide low-cost ethnic food and fun. In November, the annual **Foley's Thanksgiving Parade** marches through downtown, and in early December, the old homes in Sam Houston Park glow with free candlelight tours and resound with Christmas caroling.

TOURS AND SPECIAL-INTEREST SIGHTSEEING. Gray Line Tours, 602 Sampson (713–223–8800), offers four tours: a 4½-hour city tour including downtown, River Oaks, Rice University, Texas Medical Center, Hermann Park and a one-hour lecture tour of the Astrodome ($20); a 4½-hour tour of NASA including Mission Control ($20); a 7½-hour tour of Galveston ($35), and a 7-hour combination tour of the city, Port of Houston, and NASA ($35). Free pickup at major hotels is available upon request.

The **Astrodome,** the first indoor sports stadium in America, has tours that include a multimedia presentation at 11, 1, and 3 daily, unless there is a game. Admission is $2.75, children under 7 are admitted free. Parking costs $3. Call 713–799–9544 for information.

A Houston Walking Tour is presented by the **Greater Houston Preservation Alliance** on the third Wednesday of every month. The tour encompasses early commercial buildings dating from 1847 to 1915 in the Market Square–Main St. district, and emphasizes buildings of architectural or historical significance. It begins at noon on the corner of Milam and Preston and lasts about 45 minutes. A $1 donation is requested. For information call 713–236–5000.

The **Lyndon B. Johnson Space Center (NASA),** about 25 miles south of Houston via I-45, is the headquarters of the nation's manned space flight program. Visitors to the center will see rockets and spacecraft, lunar rocks, training labs and other examples of today's space technology. It's open daily from 9 A.M.–4 P.M. for free "green" self-guided tours of the buildings used for mission simulation and training, and space shuttle orbiter training. Free 35-minute "red" tours of Mission Control include a presentation on the history and future of space exploration. They are given every hour on a first-come-first-serve basis. Sign up for the next available tour at the information desk, Teague Visitor Center Building, Building 2. Allow about 3 hours in total for your NASA visit. Call 713–483–4321 for more information.

The **Port of Houston** offers free tours aboard the *Sam Houston,* an air-conditioned vessel that makes two-hour excursions at 10 A.M. and 2:30 P.M., Tues., Wed., Fri., and Sat. Only the 2:30 tour is available Thurs. and Sun., and no tours are given during the month of Sept. Tour reservations must be made well in advance. Visitors also are allowed on the observation deck, located at the turning basin, for pictures and sightseeing 8 A.M.–5 P.M. daily. For reservations and information, write the Port of Houston, Box 2562, Houston TX 77001, or call 713–225–4044.

Sam Houston Park features "memory tours" of four of the city's oldest homes, a church, and a log cabin, all within the shadow of downtown's gleaming skyscrapers. Mon.–Sat., 10 A.M.–4 P.M., and Sun. 1–5 P.M. Tours on the half hour. Admission is $2 for adults, 50 cents for students, and 35 cents for children under 11. Call 713–956–0480 for information. See "Parks and Gardens."

Volunteers from the **Assistance League of Houston** give free driving tours of the vast Texas Medical Center Mon.–Fri. at 10 A.M. Reservations are recommended and may be made by calling the Visitor Information Center, 1522 Braeswood, 713–790–1136 Mon.–Fri., 8 A.M.–5 P.M.

PARKS AND GARDENS. Encompassing 600 wooded acres southwest of downtown, **Hermann Park** is bordered by Rice University and the Texas Medical Center. At the main entrance of the park, near the Warwick Hotel and Mecom Fountain, is a statue of Sam Houston—Sam's hand points toward the San Jacinto battleground, where his army won Texas' independence from Mexico in 1836. The park has numerous picnic sites and playgrounds, as well as the Houston Zoological Gardens, Museum of Natural Science, Burke Baker Planetarium, Miller Outdoor Theater, a two-mile kiddie railroad and a golf course. Also within the park is the Houston Garden Center, 1500 Hermann Dr. (713–529–5371). The center features camellias; 3,000 rose bushes; and a fragrance garden for the blind. It's free and open Mon.–Fri., 8 A.M.–6 P.M.; Sat.–Sun., 10 A.M.–6 P.M.

A haven for joggers and picnickers, the 1,500 acres of woodland that comprise **Memorial Park** are bounded by Buffalo Bayou on the south, Loop 610 on the west and I-10 on the north. In addition to wilderness and picnic areas, it offers running, hiking, biking trails; a golf course; tennis center; archery range; polo grounds; and the 155-acre Houston Arboretum and Nature Center at 4501 Woodway Dr. An undisturbed sanctuary with numerous species of trees and shrubs native to Texas, the Arboretum has a botanical hall, nature trails, self-guiding maps, and hourly guided tours on Sun. beginning at 1:30 P.M. It's free and open Mon.–Sat. 9 A.M.–5 P.M., Sun. 1–5:30 P.M. For information call 713–681–8433.

The **Mercer Park Arboretum,** 22306 Aldine-Westfield Rd., 713–443–8731, offers natural woodlands with garden areas. Special tours are available. It's free and open 8 A.M.–5 P.M. daily.

The **Edith L. Moore Nature Sanctuary,** 12955 Memorial, 713–932–1392, is run by the Houston Audubon Society. It offers 17 acres of woodlands with nature trails bordering Rummel Creek. It's free and open daily from dawn to dusk. Parking is available at the nearby Memorial Drive Methodist Church (except Sun.).

Sam Houston Park, bounded by Bagby, McKinney, and Dallas streets downtown, is a small outdoor museum which preserves a few of the city's historical buildings in a shady green park. The only structure on its original site is the Kellum-Noble House (1847), the oldest brick house in the city. William Marsh Rice, the famous financier and founder of Rice University, once owned the Nichols-Rice-Cherry House (1850). The San Felipe Cottage typifies a Texas cottage of the 1870s, and the Pillot House (1868) features what is believed to be the first indoor kitchen in Houston. The Old Place (1824), a log cabin, is Harris County's oldest structure, and St. John's Church (1891) still has its original altar-pulpit and cypress plank pews. Entrance to the park is open and free, but tickets for guided tours are available in the Yesteryear Shop in the Long Row, a reconstruction of Houston's first stores. The Long Row also has a tea room which serves Mon.–Fri., 11 A.M.–1:30 P.M..

Less a park and more a monument is **Tranquility Park,** named after the Apollo XI flight landing on the Moon. Bounded by Bagby, Rusk, Smith, and Walker streets downtown, the park features a two-block-long, 32-level fountain, with five rising towers resembling rockets. There are bronze plaques in 15 languages at the entrances of the park, outlining the Apollo story, and assorted grassy knolls representing the earth, lunar mounds, and other celestial bodies.

South of Houston, via I-45, is the **Armand Bayou Nature Center,** 8600 Bay Area Blvd. (713–474–2551). It features more than 2,000 acres of preserved wilderness, which include a restored Indian village, a turn-of-the-century farm, nature trails, and exhibits. There are group hikes and classes, and you can explore the estuary by pontoon boat or canoe. It's free and open daily from 9 A.M.–5 P.M.

ZOO. The **Houston Zoological Gardens,** 1612 Zoo Circle in Hermann Park (523–5888 or 523–3211), is one of the few major zoos in the country that is free. The 42-acre center features thousands of animals in both natural outdoor settings and indoor cages. It includes a special 3-acre children's petting zoo, a walk-through aviary, and an aquarium. Children will enjoy feeding the ducks in the pond outside the entrance gates, and they can ride the park's kiddie train for 75 cents. Both the zoo and the train open daily, but their hours change with the season.

PARTICIPANT SPORTS. From Oct. through Apr. Houston's mild weather lends itself to all variety of outdoor sports. The summer heat can be killing, though, so it's best to confine your sports activities then to the early morning or evening.

A popular spot for **joggers** and runners is *Memorial Park,* which has a lighted jogging course at the tennis center. *Hermann Park* also has a jogging course, beginning at the Garden Center. Runners are partial to the jogging trails along the bayous, particularly along *Brays Bayou* on S. Braeswood, between Stella Link and Buffalo Speedway. An extensive system of **hike and bike trails** links many of the bayous, parks, and business centers. Free maps are available from the *Houston Parks and Recreation Dept.,* 2999 S. Wayside (641–4111). For listings of races and tournaments, check the Weekend section of the Thurs. Houston *Chronicle* or the Fri. *Post.* Also check *Inside Running,* a local magazine on newsstands.

For **tennis** players, there are scores of free small public courts scattered about the city. The City of Houston also operates three public facilities that charge $4 for 1½ hours of play: *MacGregor Tennis Center,* 5225 Calhoun (747–5466); *Memorial Drive Tennis Center,* Memorial Park (861–3765); *Southwest Tennis Center,* 9506 S. Gessner (772–0296).

The Houston area has 16 public **golf courses.** The cheapest of those are the six run by the city with greens fees of $5.50 during the week and $7.50 on weekends: *Brock Park Golf Course,* 8201 John Raulston Rd. (458–1350); *Glenbrook Park Golf Course,* 8205 Bayou (644–4081); *Gus Wortham Park Golf Course,* 7000 Capitol (921–3227); *Hermann Park Golf Course* (529–9788); *Memorial Park Golf Course* (862–4033); and *Sharpstown Park Golf Course,* 660 Harbortown (988–2099).

Swimmers have their choice of 47 free municipal pools. To find one near you call the city Parks and Recreation Department at 641–4111.

SPECTATOR SPORTS. There's always some type of sporting event going on in Houston. **Football** fans can watch the Houston Oilers play NFL football Sept.–Dec. Tickets may be purchased at the Astrodome (parking $3) or at the Oiler ticket office at 6910 Fannin in the lobby of the APC Building. The city also has two major college football teams playing Sept.–Dec. The **University of Houston Cougars** play in the Astrodome. Tickets may be obtained at the Hofheinz Pavilion on the university campus, or through Ticketron outlets around town. The **Rice University Owls** play in Rice Stadium. Obtain tickets at the campus ticket office in the Rice Gym.

The Houston Astros **baseball** team plays in the Astrodome Apr.–Oct. Purchase tickets there or through Ticketron outlets around town.

The Houston Rockets **basketball** team plays in the Summit Oct.–Apr. Purchase tickets there or at Ticketron and Ticket Master outlets. The University of Houston basketball team plays Nov.–Mar. at Hofheinz Pavilion on campus. Purchase tickets there or through Ticketron. The Rice University basketball team plays on campus at Autry Court. Purchase tickets at the gym.

The **Houston Livestock Show and Rodeo,** one of the largest in the country, is held in the Astrodome in mid-Feb. Purchase tickets there or through Ticketron.

There's **wrestling** at the Sam Houston Coliseum, downtown at 810 Bagby and Walker, every Fri. night. Purchase tickets at the Coliseum box office.

CHILDREN'S ACTIVITIES. In addition to the Hermann Park Zoo, the city's prime children's attraction is **AstroWorld,** a huge family entertainment center covering 75 acres. Across from the Astrodome on I-610, AstroWorld features more than 100 rides, shows, and attractions, including the Enchanted Kingdom—a magical land for younger children—and the futuristic-looking XLR-8 roller coaster, dubbed "the most unique roller coaster ride of the century." Open daily June–Aug., and on weekends only Mar.–May and Sept.–Nov. Admission is $16.95, although discount tickets frequently may be purchased at area banks, businesses, supermarkets, and through auto clubs. For the complex time schedule and other information call 713–799–1234.

WaterWorld, an aquatic theme park featuring a 300-foot water slide, a wave pool, a beach, a man-made river with rapids, and a children's water playground borders AstroWorld. Operating days and hours are the same. Admission is $11.50; children under 3 admitted free. For information call 713–799–1234.

Children's Museum, 3201 Allen Parkway, is an educational but fun hands-on museum for children ages 3–12. It features a Safeway minimart where younger children can go grocery shopping, a computer room with programs for all ages, a musical staircase for toddlers, a recycling center for artwork using recycled products, and a variety of changing exhibits. Admission is $2 for adults, $1 for children. Children must be accompanied by an adult. For hours and other information, call 522–1138.

The **Houston Public Library** downtown at 500 McKinney (224–5441) has a Children's Room that offers Storytime every Thurs. at 10 A.M. (ages 3–5) and Sat. at 11 A.M. (ages 3–8). Signed storytelling for the deaf is featured the second Sat. of each month. Free admission.

HISTORIC SITES AND HOUSES. Houston, a fairly young city, has few historic sites. In addition to Allen's Landing, Market Square, and Sam Houston Park downtown, the only other site of interest to history buffs is the **San Jacinto Battleground** where Texas won her independence from Mexico in 1836. About 21 miles from downtown Houston off State Highway 225, you'll find the *San Jacinto Monument,* a 570-foot obelisk which is the tallest masonry structure in the world. In its base is a free museum that traces the region's history, from the Indian civilization found by Cortez to the Civil War period. The displays include documents, maps, books, paintings, daguerreotypes, photographs, coins, costumes, and other memorabilia. The museum opens daily, 9 A.M.–6 P.M. Visitors also may ride the elevator to the top of the monument for a spectacular view of the area. The elevator ride is $2 for adults and 50 cents for children under 12. For information call 479–2421.

The *USS Texas* has been moored at the battleground since San Jacinto Day in 1948. This veteran of two world wars and many other campaigns is the only survivor of the dreadnought class of battleship. The entire ship serves as a museum as well as a monument to those in the U.S. military service. The ship opens daily from 10 A.M.–6 P.M., May–Aug., and 10 A.M.–5 P.M., Sept.–Apr. Admission is $2 for adults and $1 for children. For information call 479–2411.

MUSEUMS AND GALLERIES. As Houston grows more cosmopolitan, its cultural consciousness grows more sophisticated. Although the city as yet doesn't have any world-class museums or galleries, you're still bound to find one that suits your interests. Most of them are centered around the Hermann Park–Rice University–Montrose area. A listing of current special exhibits and traveling shows is published in *Texas Monthly,* and both Houston newspapers.

The **Houston Museum of Fine Arts.** 1001 Bissonnet (526–1361). Covers a vast range of art history, with 11,000 works ranging from antiquity to the modern era, from European and American to Oriental and pre-Columbian. Each year the museum features about 20 temporary exhibitions from major museums and collections throughout the world. Free ½-hr. "Gallery Talks," Wed. and Sun., 1:30 and 2 P.M. Sept.–May. The Hirsch Library, an art-history reference library, is open to the public, and the museum restaurant on the main level serves excellent and reasonably priced hot and cold lunches and snacks. Open Tues.–Sat., 10 A.M.–5 P.M.; Thurs. till 9 P.M.; Sunday 1–6 P.M. Admission is $2 for adults, $1 for students and senior citizens. Thursdays are free.

Across town in the River Oaks residential area is a branch of the Museum of Fine Arts called **Bayou Bend,** 1 Westcott St., off Memorial Dr. (529–8773). Formerly the home of one of the museum's most generous patrons, the late Ima Hogg,

Bayou Bend houses one of the country's finest collections of American arts from 1650 to 1870. The 14 acres of formal gardens surrounding the 28-room mansion are expertly maintained by the River Oaks Garden Club. Two-hour tours, by reservation only, Tues.–Fri., 10 A.M.–2:45 P.M.; Sat. 10 A.M.–11:45 P.M. Admission is $4 per person, $3 for senior citizens. The first floor of the classical revival mansion is open free to the public on the second Sun. of the month, except Mar. and Aug.

Across the street from the Museum of Fine Arts, at 5216 Montrose Blvd., is a gleaming wedge of aluminum known as the **Contemporary Arts Museum** (526–3129). It's the home of changing exhibits of various types of avant-garde work by local and nationally known artists. Free public tours, conducted by docents every Sun. at 2 and 4 P.M., begin at the upper gallery information desk. Open Tues.–Sat., 10 A.M.–5 P.M.; Sun., 1–6 P.M.

The newest addition to Houston's art scene is the nationally acclaimed **Menil Collection** near the University of St. Thomas at 1515 Sul Ross (525–9400). The museum houses antiquities, tribal art, and 20th-century works assembled by John and Dominique de Menil. Open Wed.–Sun. 11 A.M.–7 P.M. Free.

Near the University of St. Thomas, is the **Rothko Chapel,** 1409 Sul Ross at Yupon (524–9839), an interfaith chapel and place for meditation. This simple octagonal chapel houses 14 paintings by the late American abstract expressionist Mark Rothko. In the courtyard adjoining the chapel, Barnett Newman's steel sculpture, "The Broken Obelisk," stands in its own reflection pool. Dedicated to the late Martin Luther King, Jr., the obelisk has been hailed by art critics as one of the more important pieces of American contemporary sculpture. Open daily, 10 A.M.–6 P.M. Free.

Not far from the Rothko Chapel is the **Houston Center of Photography,** 1441 W. Alabama (529–4755), which offers a changing menu of photographic, video, and multimedia exhibitions. Wed.–Fri., 11 A.M.–5 P.M., Sat. & Sun., noon–5 P.M. Free.

The Houston Museum of Natural Science, Burke Baker Planetarium and the Museum of Medical Science share a wooded site in Hermann Park at the end of Caroline St. One of the largest of its kind in the country, the **Museum of Natural Science** offers 120,000 square feet of exhibits, displays, and animated models, including the Hall of Space Science, Hall of Petroleum Science, Farish Hall of Texas Wildlife, Indian artifacts and a 70-foot-long dinosaur skeleton. The main floor galleries often showcase important traveling exhibits. Upstairs is the **Museum of Medical Science,** which is maintained by the Harris County Medical Society. It features TAM, the transparent anatomical manikin, and other "talking" exhibits of human anatomy and physiology. Next to the Museum of Natural Science, **Burke Baker Planetarium** features a seasonal variety of educational programs. The Hall of Astronomy has telescopes and a heliostat, and offers additional programs in astronomy and space science. Hours for all three museums are Sun.–Mon. noon–5 P.M., Tues.–Sat. 9 A.M.–5 P.M. Admission is $2 for adults, $1 for children. Saturdays are free. Admission for the planetarium shows is $3 for adults and $1.50 for children under 12. For information call 526–4273.

The **Museum of Art of the American West** in One Houston Center, 1221 McKinney (650–3933), has changing exhibits of public and private collections of western art. Lectures, classes, and museum trips highlight its educational programs. Mon.–Fri., 10 A.M.–5 P.M. Free.

Houston also has a wide range of commercial art galleries scattered around town. To find one that suits your taste, pick up a free magazine, *Art Happenings in Houston,* that lists current exhibits. It's available at all the museums and galleries, and at most major hotels.

ARTS AND ENTERTAINMENT. The *Showtix* booth on the Rusk St. side of Tranquility Park downtown offers half-price tickets on the day of performance, as well as full price advance tickets, to most theatrical, dance, and musical performances. Hours are Tues.–Sat. 11 A.M.–5:30 P.M. For a list of tickets available, call 227–9292. Tickets to most performances also can be obtained from *Ticketron* (526–6557), *Rainbow Ticketmaster* (977–6200), and the *Downtown Ticket Center,* 1100 Milam (222–7469).

Film. The best movie bargains in town are Houston's dollar cinemas that feature films that have just left the first-run theaters. You may see this year's Academy

Award winner a month later than everyone else, but for an admission of only $1 for all shows, who cares? Some dollar cinemas are: *Briargrove 3,* 6100 Westheimer (780–1869); *Northshore 4,* 13311 E. Freeway, I-10, (453–2002); *Long Point 4,* 10016 Long Point (468–7948); *Parkview 2,* 3901 Spencer Hwy. (946–6168), and *Westminster 8,* 12121-B Westheimer (558–8827). Check local newspaper listings for others.

The *River Oaks Theater,* 2009 W. Gray (524–2175), offers an eclectic assortment of old classics, second-run movies, and occasional premieres of significant foreign or "art" films. The *Greenway 3,* at 5 Greenway Plaza East off U.S. 59 (626–0402), specializes in first-run foreign films. These two theaters sponsor the annual Houston Film Festival in Apr. The *Museum of Fine Arts,* 1001 Bissonnet (526–1361), has a film series that ranges from old favorites to the most esoteric of foreign films. Both Rice University and the University of Houston also offer their own film series. Movies are shown on campus at the Rice Media Center, entrance 7 at University Blvd. and Stockton (527–4853), and the U. of H. University Center, entrance 2 off Calhoun (749–1253).

Music. The **Houston Symphony Orchestra** (224–4240), conducted by Sergiu Comissiona, performs year-round in Jones Hall. Frequently with internationally known guest artists. The symphony also presents a series of free summer evening concerts in Miller Outdoor Theater.

The symphony musicians have formed two other professional groups: The **Houston Symphony Pops Orchestra** gives six to seven concerts Oct.–May in the Music Hall. The **Houston Symphony Chamber Orchestra** performs at special events. For information on both, call the Houston Symphony at 224–4240.

The acclaimed **Houston Grand Opera** (546–0200) stages six grand opera productions with internationally known stars in the Wortham Theater Center during its main season, Oct.–May. It also stages a free Spring Opera Festival in Miller Outdoor Theater.

The only year-round pops orchestra in the world is the **Houston Pops** (871–8300), conducted by Ned Battista. It performs six to eight times per year, in either Jones Hall or the Music Hall. The **Texas Chamber Orchestra** (529–5747) gives about eight concerts annually, many of them at St. John the Divine Episcopal Church at 2450 River Oaks Blvd.

The **Gilbert and Sullivan Society of Houston** (627–3570), performs in Jones Hall during the summer. The **Houston Symphony Chorale** (224–4240), gives concerts as well as accompanying the symphony, and the **Houston Chamber Singers** (627–3609), have a series featuring medieval to modern works.

Big-name rock and pop stars perform at **The Summit** sports arena, 10 Greenway Plaza on U.S. 59 (event information, 961–9003; ticket charge line, 627–9452). Nationally known rock and jazz groups also perform at two clubs: **Rockefeller's,** 3620 Washington (861–9365), and **Fitzgerald's,** 2706 White Oak (862–7580).

Dance. The **Houston Ballet** tours the U.S. and Europe and performs for hometown audiences in the Wortham Theater Center Sept.–June. The company traditionally dances *The Nutcracker* at Christmas each year, and presents at least one free summer performance in Miller Outdoor Theater in Hermann Park. For ticket information call 227–2787. The **Delia Stewart Dance Company** (522–6375), specializing in jazz, performs periodically at the Tower Theater at 1201 Westheimer. The **City Ballet of Houston** (468–4021), offers several performances each year, frequently showcasing new works by local and national choreographers. Other performing groups ranging from classical to modern are: **Southwest Jazz Ballet** (686–6299), **Discovery Dance Group** (667–3416), **Dancin'—The Company** (668–5166), **Academy Dancers** (497–4783), and the **Allegro Ballet** (496–4670).

Stage. Houston has a fine array of theatrical offerings ranging from touring Broadway shows that frequently play Jones Hall or the Music Hall, to local professional productions and amateur theatrics. The **Alley Theatre** (228–8421), one of the three original resident professional theaters in the country, features a balanced year-round bill—drama, comedy, classics, even some premieres of original works. Housed in a massive medieval-modernish building, the Alley company performs on two stages: A major production in the large 800-seat theater and a more intimate show in the 300-seat Arena theater often run simultaneously. Half-price tickets are often available at the Alley box office at 615 Texas noon–1 P.M. on the day of performance, as well as at the Showtix booth.

Theater Under the Stars (TUTS), 4235 San Felipe (622–1626), presents a free musical featuring imported Broadway talent as well as local professional performers each summer in Miller Outdoor Theater in Hermann Park. Either bring a picnic and sit on the grassy hill overlooking the theater, or drop by the theater box office at noon on the day of the performance and pick up free tickets for the covered reserved seating. TUTS also presents five indoor musicals Nov.–May in the Music Hall.

Stages, 3201 Allen Parkway (52–STAGE), annually in February presents a festival of new works by native or resident Texans. The theater features a variety of works throughout the rest of the year.

Offering plays and musicals ranging from classic to avant-garde are: **Chocolate Bayou Theater,** 4205 San Felipe (528–0119), **Country Playhouse,** 12802 Queensbury, Town and Country Village, (467–4497), **Main Street Theater,** 2540 Times Blvd. (524–7998), **The Ensemble,** 3535 Main (520–0055), and **Theater Suburbia,** 1410 W. 43d St. (682–3525).

DINING OUT. No one should leave Houston without sampling the four mainstays of the area: seafood, barbecue, Tex-Mex, and chicken-fried steak. That's not all the city has to offer, though. You can find everything from hot dogs to haute cuisine here, and there are a burgeoning number of ethnic restaurants. You may end up paying more for your meal than you expected, however. Many people labor under the misconception that Houston is an inexpensive town for dining. It may have been 10 years ago, but not anymore. Restaurant prices are about on par with most other major cities. It's still possible to obtain a good meal at a modest price, but you may have to do some driving to find it, as the better restaurants are scattered widely across more than 550 square miles.

Restaurant categories, based on the cost of an average meal for one person, without beverage, tax (8 percent), or tip, are *Reasonable,* \$10 to \$20; *Very Economical,* \$6 to \$10; and *Low Budget,* less than \$6. Unless otherwise noted, these restaurants accept some, if not all, major credit cards.

Reasonable

Atchafalaya River Cafe. 8816 Westheimer and Fondren (975–7873). Excellent Louisiana Cajun and Creole cooking served in a jovial Mardi Gras atmosphere. A few of the house specialties include spicy red beans and rice, BBQ shrimp and blackened soft-shelled crabs and redfish. Lunch and dinner daily.

Captain Benny's Half Shell. 7409 S. Main (795–9051). Other locations are listed in the phone book. This oyster bar in a boat serves some of the best fried seafood in the city. Lunch and dinner Mon.–Sat. No credit cards.

Dong Ting. 611 Stuart (527–0005). Delectable and unusual Hunan cuisine served in elegant surroundings. Lunch Mon.–Fri., dinner Mon.–Sat. Reservations suggested.

Ninfa's. 2704 Navigation (228–1175). Other locations listed in the phone book. The story of how widowed Mama Ninfa and her five children turned a struggling cantina into a statewide restaurant empire in less than 12 years is a local legend. Tacos al carbon, charbroiled beef wrapped in soft flour tortillas, made the place famous, but that's just the start of the extensive Mexican menu. Be sure to ask about off-the-menu specials. And beware of the potent but delicious Ninifaritas, their version of the margarita. Lunch and dinner daily. Reservations accepted but not required.

Nino's. 2817 W. Dallas (522–5120). There's no atmosphere—crowded formica tables in a wood-paneled dining room—but there's plenty of good Italian food ranging from your standard lasagne to more exotic items like crispy fried squid. The desserts are excellent. Lunch, Mon.–Fri., dinner Mon.–Sat. Reservations for parties of five or more.

Ouisie's. 1708 Sunset (528–2264). A casual but chic neighborhood restaurant that attracts the West University/Rice crowd. The eclectic and creative menu, featuring seasonal American and ethnic selections, changes daily. Lunch and dinner Tues.–Sat.

Pappasito's Cantina. 6445 Richmond (784–5253). It's one of the trendiest spots in town, so expect at least an hour's wait for dinner at prime time. The wait is worth it, though, for the enormous servings of Tex-Mex cooking and equally big drinks. Fantasy Mexican decor. Lunch and dinner daily.

Tila's Cantina and Taqueria. 616 Westheimer (520–6315). Yet another Mexican cantina, but this one serves Mexico City–style cuisine rather than the heavier Tex-Mex. The meats are grilled over mesquite. Ask for a window seat in the front art deco dining room and watch the Westheimer strip's wild and woolly goings-on. Lunch and dinner daily.

Very Economical

Austin's. 2732 Virginia (520–5666). It's Texas hill country cooking—grilled and country-fried steaks, fried catfish, chicken and dumplings, fresh vegetables, and other daily specials. Lunch and dinner daily.

Birraporetti's. 1997 W. Gray (529–9191). Other locations listed in the phone book. If you love pizza this eccentric Italian restaurant with an Irish bar is the place to go. The pizzas are great, but stay away from most of the pasta dishes. The bar specializes in piping hot Irish coffee. Lunch and dinner Mon.–Sun.

The Black-eyed Pea. 2048 W. Gray (523–0200). Other locations listed in the phone book. This chain serves up home cooking that's the next best thing to Mom's. The menu includes chicken-fried steak, meat loaf, fried catfish, black-eyed peas, fried okra, and peach cobbler. Lunch and dinner daily.

Butera's. 5019 Montrose (523–0722); 2946 S. Shepherd (528–1500). These museum-area delis are packed at lunch, but they can also provide a nice light supper. There are custom-made sandwiches, hearty soups, interesting salads and desserts. Lunch and dinner daily.

Goode Company Barbecue. 5109 Kirby (522–2530). Very good indeed, especially the barbecued chicken, beef, and sausage. Not to mention the stuffed baked potatoes and pecan pie. Lunch and dinner Mon.–Sat.

Hard Rock Cafe. 2801 Kirby (520–1134). Yet another offspring of the London original, complete with rock and roll memorabilia and tasty hamburgers and ribs. Lunch and dinner daily.

Otto's. 5502 Memorial (864–2573). This longtime favorite barbecue spot is patronized by Houston celebrities. Best bets are barbecued-beef plates and sandwiches. Lunch and dinner Mon.–Sat. No credit cards.

Treebeards. 315 Travis (225–2160). New Orleans-style food, especially red beans and rice with sausage. Only those with gargantuan appetites should order more than half a serving. Lunch Mon.–Fri. American Express only.

Low Budget

Antone's. 8111 S. Main (666–4191). Other locations listed in the phone book. Great po-boys, cheeses, Italian cold cuts, and wine at this ethnic grocery. Lunch and dinner Mon.–Sat. No credit cards.

The Avalon Drugstore. 2518 Kirby at Westheimer (524–2101). The "in" place to go for breakfast, particularly for the wealthy River Oaks crowd. And particularly on Sun., when you can sip your coffee and read the *New York Times.* Yes, this is a regular drugstore that sells toothpaste and prescription drugs, but the small restaurant also sells some famous pecan waffles, cheeseburgers, and malts. Breakfast and lunch daily; dinner Mon.–Fri.

Chapultepec Mexican Restaurant. 813 Richmond Ave. (522–2365). Decent and extremely inexpensive Tex-Mex. Each meal is served with free beet soup as an appetizer. Lunch and dinner Mon.–Sun.

Souper Salad. 5469 Weslayan (660–8950). Other locations. All the salad and homemade soup you can eat, plus sandwiches, corn bread, and gingerbread. Lunch and dinner Mon.–Sat. No credit cards.

Cafeterias. Cafeteria dining may not be a particularly enjoyable experience in other parts of the country, but Texas has several excellent cafeteria chains that provide good, well-balanced meals at dirt-cheap prices. **Luby's Cafeterias** has many locations; check the phone book. Others to try are **Allbritton's, Piccadilly,** and **Wyatt.** Most do not accept credit cards.

Recommended Splurge. Rainbow Lodge. 1 Birdsall, near Memorial Park (861–8666). It's more expensive than any of the above, but the atmosphere and food are worth the price. This fantasy hunting lodge, situated on the banks of Buffalo

Bayou, has some of the most romantic dining niches in Houston. The decor is Victorian, and the Continental menu includes wild game. Ask for a window table and enjoy a view of lush green woodlands. Lunch Tues.–Fri., dinner Tues.–Sun. Sun. brunch. Reservations required. Dinner entrees range from $10 to $18.

NIGHTLIFE. Since the *Urban Cowboy* fad passed, the number of "kicker" clubs in Houston has diminished considerably. Nevertheless, there still are a few country-western spots and enough genuine honkytonks—including the now world-famous Gilley's—to give visitors a sampling of real Texas culture. If you don't like country music, though, there are scores of clubs around town featuring rock and roll, jazz, disco, and even comedy. The areas with the highest concentration of nightlife activity are the Galleria, Montrose, and the southwest part of town.

The drinking age in Texas is 21. Remember that drinking establishments must stop serving alcohol at 2 A.M., and many close even earlier.

Music Clubs

Caribana. 8220 West Belfort (774–3454). It's an unlikely spot for reggae music, but that's what's featured in this slice-of-the-Caribbean club. Cover charge varies.

Cody's. 3400 Montrose (522–9747). The most beautiful view of Houston can be had from the rooftop patio of this classy club in the Montrose area. Inside, there's live jazz and fine dining. Dinner 6–10:30 P.M. Mon.–Thurs., and 6–midnight Fri.–Sat.

Fitzgerald's. 2706 White Oak, in the Heights (862–7580). This somewhat scruffy music hall features a variety of national and regional groups ranging from rhythm and blues to new wave. Cover charge varies, depending on who's playing.

Gilley's. 4500 Spencer Hwy., in Pasadena (941–7990). This is the airplane-hangar-sized honkytonk where John Travolta two-stepped with Debra Winger. Since the release of *Urban Cowboy,* the place has pretty much turned into a tourist trap. Many of the premovie regulars still hang out there, though, so there's some local color left. Take a ride on the mechanical bull or indulge in a mock shoot-out with paint pellets as bullets. Dance to the music of the house band, the Bayou City Beats, or national country stars, including the club's namesake, Mickey Gilley. The cover varies, depending on who's playing.

Kenneally's Irish Pub. 2111 S. Shepherd, near River Oaks (630–0486). This congenial saloon features national and regional Irish folk and traditional musicians. Irish coffee and 20 imported beers and ales (including Guinness Stout and Bass Ale on tap) are specialties. There's also moderately priced food.

Power Tools. 709 Franklin (225–2655). This dance club in a warehouse is the latest rage among New Wavers and yuppies alike. Every two weeks the club changes themes and everyone dresses accordingly. Some recent themes have included bigotry, religion, lingerie, and the *National Enquirer.* Attire is extremely casual and the cover is $5. Open Sat. night only.

Rockefeller's. 3620 Washington, in the Heights (861–9365). This music hall formerly was a bank. Today it's *the* place to go to hear nationally known touring musicians, ranging from jazz to punk to bluegrass.

Studebaker's. 2630 Augusta, near the Galleria (783–4208). A fun baby-boomer disco featuring music and decor from the fifties and sixties. During certain songs, the waitresses and bartenders hop up on the bars and perform choreographed dance routines. There's a red Studebaker at the back of the club, and lots of expensive foreign cars crowding the valet parking lot. Minimum age is 23 and there is a dress code.

Comedy Clubs

Comedy Workshop. 2105 San Felipe, in Montrose near River Oaks (524–7333). Full-fledged comedy reviews are presented at the Workshop, while the Comix Annex next door features stand-up comedians. The cover charge for both Workshop and Annex is $4 during the week and $7 on weekends.

The Laff Stop. 1952 W. Gray, in the River Oaks Shopping Center (524–2333). This club features nationally known, as well as up and coming, comedians. The cover charge varies depending on who's appearing.

Radio Music Theater. 1840 Westheimer (522–7722). This cabaret–revue theater features comedy and adventure scripts in the format of live studio performances from the golden age of radio. The cover charge is $8, Thurs.–Sat.

Bars

Grif's Inn. 3416 Roseland, in Montrose (528–9912). An Irish bar and the unofficial headquarters of Houston's most avid sports fans.

Inn on the Park Hotel. 4 Riverway, just north of the Galleria area (871–8181). If you want to enjoy a quiet drink in elegant surroundings, try this hotel lobby bar. Best in the early evening, when you can gaze at the swans on the lake outside while the pianist plays Gershwin.

La Carafe. 813 Congress, downtown in Market Square (229–9399). This quirky little bar in Houston's oldest commercial building offers beer and wine, with an interesting jukebox mix, ranging from Piaf to punk.

Marfreless. 2006 Peden, entrance on McDuffie (528–0083). Most businesses couldn't survive without putting up a sign outside. But Marfreless, of the famous unmarked door, thrives on anonymity. It's a favorite of classical music lovers, and just lovers in general, as it has all sorts of cozy couches and dark nooks.

Spindletop. 1200 Louisiana, downtown in the Hyatt Regency Hotel (654–1234). Want to take a turn around the city? Then have a drink in this revolving bar atop the Hyatt for a 360-degree, bird's-eye view of Houston.

SECURITY. Houston's phenomenal growth over the past 20 years has unfortunately spawned an equally phenomenal crime rate.

As a general rule of thumb, don't wander around by yourself after dark in any part of the city. One area to be particularly careful of at night is downtown, which is usually deserted after dark except for vagrants. During the day, the Market Square area and Main Street north of the downtown Foley's store attract street people and pickpockets, so watch your purse or wallet.

Although you might want to participate in the local custom of cruising the Westheimer strip in Montrose, don't walk around that area at night. Avoid Memorial Park after dark as well as Hermann Park, unless you're going to Miller Outdoor Theater or the Planetarium, and then don't go alone. The bars and restaurants along the Ship Channel attract a rough crowd, making them unsafe for tourists.

KANSAS CITY

by
Carolyn R. Langdon

Ms. Langdon lived on both coasts before settling in Kansas City fifteen years ago. Now a free-lance writer and regular contributor to Fodor's guides, she previously was a feature writer on the Kansas City Star.

Although visitors from the East are sometimes confused that a city containing the word "Kansas" is actually in Missouri, residents consider it a small inconvenience when they realize what the founding fathers contemplated naming the city. It seems that John Calvin McCoy, an early trader who lived in the area of Westport in 1838, banded together with 13 other investors and purchased 257 acres of land at the bend of the Missouri River at the foot of what is now Grand Avenue. They were planning to build a city, and colorful suggestions for a name included Possum Trot, Fort Fonda, and Rabbitville. Fortunately, banality won out, and they settled on "Town of Kansas" in honor of the Kanza Indians with whom McCoy had traded. The official name was changed to Kansas City in 1889.

Meanwhile, Westport, a bustling community dedicated to outfitting westward wagon trains, eventually got the upper hand on possums and rabbits. By the 1850s the streets were filled with covered wagons and the sidewalks were jammed with pedestrians as wave after wave of travelers prepared to embark on the Santa Fe Trail.

Today Westport is in the heart of Kansas City. The renovation in 1972 of the district turned it into a bustling four-square-mile community of retail shops, restaurants, and businesses. The area is bounded by Main Street and Southwest Trafficway on the east and west and by 39th and 44th streets on the north and south.

Kelly's Westport Inn at 500 Westport Road is in the city's oldest surviving building. The tavern, which has been in business nearly 50 years, draws a diverse crowd of all ages and is especially popular with singles.

Westport's prosperous outfitting trade during pioneer days was disturbed by border warfare in the late 1850s and the ensuing Civil War. But with peace came railroads and a boom that restored prosperity. Kansas City's location at the junction of the Kansas and Missouri rivers made it a natural hub of transportation and agriculture.

The booster spirit that was born in the early days has lived into the twentieth century. Today the city claims to have as many fountains as Rome and as many boulevards as Paris. In 1893 landscape architect George Kessler designed a network of public parks and boulevards that earned the town national acclaim. Andre Maurois described Kansas City as "one of the loveliest cities on earth."

The historical legacy Kansas City has inherited is mingled with an appreciation of the contemporary. Nowhere is the blending more apparent than in the stockyards district. Weathered wooden stalls and gangways are in the shadow of a steel and concrete complex that is the headquarters of the American Royal Livestock and Horseshow. One of the premier events of its kind, the American Royal has grown steadily since the first exposition was held in a tent in the stockyards in 1899. Although Kansas Citians are self-conscious and maybe a little defensive about the city's image as a cowtown, they are proud of the American Royal, and each November city slickers flock to the Kemper Arena for a close look at the horses and livestock. The modern arena is also used for sporting events and other entertainments, such as the circus.

As the city blossomed at the turn of the century, some cow pastures and swampland south of Westport were transformed into an elegant district of shops and homes, known as the Country Club district. The Country Club Plaza at 47th and Main streets is proudly claimed as America's first shopping center. It was created in the 1920s by the late J. C. Nichols. Moorish architecture, complete with minarets, courtyards, and fountains, is the hallmark of the Plaza. At Christmastime the buildings are outlined with thousands of colored lights, creating a magical spectacle.

Restaurants and fashionable shops line the Plaza's streets; even if you're not in the mood to buy, it is pleasant to stroll amid the tree-lined streets, statues, and fountains.

To savor the outdoor sculpture and art on the Plaza you may want to go on the Plaza Walking Art Tour that passes 31 artworks.

A magnificient edifice four blocks east of the Plaza is the Nelson Atkins Museum of Art, internationally renowned for its collection of Chinese art and sculpture. The gallery was built on the estate of William Rockhill Nelson, founder of the Kansas City *Star,* who also donated his art collection. The gallery now has art from every period and reconstructions of a medieval chapel, a Buddhist temple, and a Victorian drawing room. Admission is free on Sunday.

North of the Plaza downtown is the ultra-modern Crown Center complex, an 85-acre facility of specialty shops, apartments, hotels, and offices that includes the headquarters of Hallmark Cards. In 1919 Joyce Hall arrived in Kansas City from Nebraska with a shoebox of printed postcards. He parlayed his enterprise into the largest of its kind in the world. In the early 1960s, when other industries were leaving the center city, Hall decided to rebuild the area rather than retreat. The resulting Crown Center is a tribute to his genius.

The feeling downtown is quite different from that around the Plaza. A recent building boom of modern office complexes has kept the area in flux. When completed, these new buildings will contrast with those from another boom era in Kansas City: the 1930s. During that Art Deco period, architectural masterpieces such as the Municipal Auditorium and Music

Hall were constructed in sharp geometric lines. Kansas City's tallest building of that era, the Power and Light Building at 1330 Baltimore, is typical of the skyscrapers built in the 1930s. The top features a six-story shaft highlighted with prismatic glass and a lighting system that causes the tower to change colors at night.

For a different perspective on downtown, visit the south steps of city hall (414 E. 12th) at noon on a Friday during the summer. Bring your lunch and listen to a free brown bag concert sponsored by the Kansas City Parks and Recreation Department.

Generally, motorists find navigating in Kansas City fairly easy because of the basic north-south and east-west configuration of the streets. But some people are confused by the fact that there are actually two places called Kansas City. The larger, in Missouri, is descended from Westport. Across the Kaw or Kansas River is Kansas City, Kansas, settled around 1830 by Moses Grinter, who built a ferry across the river. Among his customers were the Wyandot Indians, and the county now bears the name Wyandotte.

The Shawnee Methodist Mission and Indian Manual Training School were founded in Wyandotte County and later moved south to the area now known as Johnson County, also in Kansas. The border between Johnson County and Missouri is a street called State Line.

There now are thirteen communities in northeast Johnson County. To simplify mail delivery, the U.S. Post Office created the unified postal district of Shawnee Mission. Thus, although there is no city of Shawnee Mission, nearly all residents of Northeast Johnson County receive mail with that designation.

PRACTICAL INFORMATION

WHEN TO GO. There's a popular saying here: If you don't like the weather today, stick around; it will be different tomorrow. Although the weather does fluctuate even within the same season (or the same day), you generally can count on hot, humid summer days with temperatures in the nineties, and cold, sometimes blustery winter days. That leaves spring and fall for those who prefer mildness. Although Mother Nature sometimes makes spring too short, it is so glorious that residents beg for more, no matter how long it lasts. May and June are usually bright, clear, and warm, perfect for picnicking or throwing a Frisbee after a long winter. Autumn in Kansas City produces azure skies, warm sun, and a kaleidoscope of colorful leaves. The average mean temperatures are 55 degrees Fahrenheit in spring, 79 in summer, 58 in fall, and 33 in winter.

HOW TO GET THERE. Kansas City's location in the "Heart of America" makes it easily accessible by many modes of transportation. I-70 runs through Kansas City from St. Louis to the east into Colorado on the west. Travelers from the south can take I-35 (the Kansas Turnpike) through Wichita and Topeka.

By air. Many major airlines serve Kansas City International Airport, a modern facility about 20 miles north of downtown. *Ozark Airlines* has service to other Missouri cities, including Joplin, St. Louis, and Columbia; *Air Midwest* is another large regional carrier. Travelers to Kansas City may be able to take advantage of the numerous price wars that periodically lower rates. These fares change constantly, so consult a travel agent for the latest data.

By bus. *Greyhound-Trailways* is the major carrier serving Kansas City.

By train. Kansas City is on the *Amtrak* line, with service from the Amtrak Building, 2200 Main St. (842–1416). Two eastbound trains daily originate in Kansas City, and westbound trains also depart twice daily. For information and reservations, call 800–USA–RAIL.

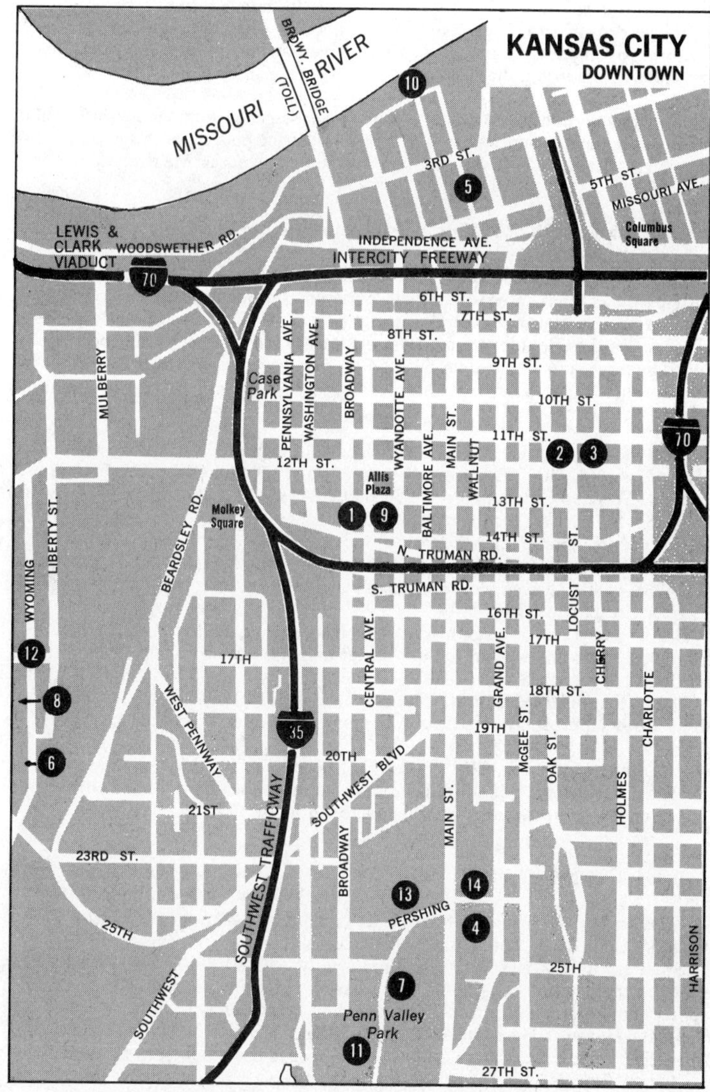

Points of Interest

1) H. Roe Bartle Exposition Hall
2) City Hall
3) Civic Center
4) Crown Center
5) Kansas City Market
6) R. Crosby Kemper Arena & American Royal Building
7) Liberty Memorial and Museum
8) Livestock Exchange
9) Municipal Auditorium
10) Municipal Wharf
11) Pioneer Mother Monument
12) Stock Yards
13) Union Station
14) Washington Monument

TELEPHONES. The area code for Kansas City, Missouri, and the surrounding counties is 816. In the Kansas counties bordering the city, the area code is 913. It is not a toll call to phone across the state line in the metropolitan area, and you do not need to dial the area code. The number for directory assistance is 1–411, 411 from pay phones. An operator will assist you on person-to-person, credit-card, and collect calls if you dial 0 first.

Emergency Telephone Numbers. The emergency number for fire, ambulance, police, and paramedics is 911. The number for poison control at Children's Mercy Hospital is 234–3000; at the University of Kansas Medical Center it is 588–6633.

ACCOMMODATIONS. Visitors on a limited budget have a wide selection of accommodations from which to choose. There are hotels downtown whose rates may be too pricey during the week but are lowered over the weekend; there are outlying motels that cater to families. What you opt for depends on your agenda and how much you want to spend. Listings here are for Kansas and Missouri. Hotel rates are based on double occupancy in the least expensive room. Categories, determined by price, are: *Reasonable,* $40 to $47; *Very economical,* under $40. Weekend packages are $65 to $77 per night.

Reasonable

Best Western Antioch Inn. 2620 N.E. 43, Kansas City North, MO 64117 (816–453–6550). Has 250 rooms. Restaurant and lounge. Color TV. Free cribs.

Best Western Flamingo. 4725 State Ave., Kansas City, KS 66102 (913–287–5511). Two blocks west of I-635 at the State Ave. exit. Some oversized beds. Free crib. Some kitchenettes.

Best Western Hallmark Inn. 3930 Rainbow, Kansas City, KS 66103 (913–236–6880). 15 even blocks south of I-35 at the 7th Street exit. Children under 12 free with parents. Free cribs.

Best Western Inn. 501 Southwest Blvd., Kansas City, KS 66103 (913–677–3060). 5 minutes to downtown convention center and the Country Club Plaza. 1 block south of I-35 at 7th St.

Drury Inn. 9009 W. 63d St., Merriam, KS 66202 (913–236–9200). Off I-35, in the Kansas suburbs. Oversized beds. Senior citizen rates; those under 18 free; free cribs.

La Quinta Motor Inn. 9461 Lenexa Dr., Lenexa, KS 66215 (913–492–5500). At the 95th St. exit off I-35., 15 miles southwest of Kansas City. Senior citizen rate. Those under 18 free; free cribs. Free coffee in lobby.

Very Economical

Belton Inn. 155 S. 71 Hwy. Belton, MO 64012 (816–331–6300). 20 miles southeast of Kansas City on I-70. 130 rooms, coin laundry. Children under 6 free.

Mission Inn. 7508 W. 63, Mission, KS 66202 (913–262–9600). 5 miles west of Country Club Plaza. Some queen-size beds.

Stadium Inn. 7901 E. 40 Hwy., Kansas City, MO 64129 (816–861–9400). This motel at the junction of I-70 and I-435 has an indoor heated pool. One mile from sports complex; 10 min. from Worlds of Fun or downtown.

White Haven. 8039 Metcalf, Overland Park, KS 66212 (913–649–8200). 11½ miles SW. Free coffee. Some kitchenettes. Always booked well in advance.

Weekend Packages

Allis Plaza Hotel. 200 W. 12th St., Kansas City, MO 64105 (816–421–6800). Downtown near convention facilities. Kansas City's newest hotel; modern, many amenities.

Embassy Suites Hotel. 220 W. 43, Kansas City, MO 64111 (913–756–1720). Two blocks north of Country Club Plaza. Package includes refrigerator in room, free made-to-order breakfast, free cocktails for two hours. All suites.

Westin Crown Center. 1 Pershing Rd. at Main, Kansas City, MO 64108 (816–474–4400). World-class hotel. Waterfall in lobby. Many facilities.

HOW TO GET AROUND. From the airport. Visitors arriving by air can take the KCI Express (a bus) to downtown or the Country Club Plaza for $11 one way,

$20 round-trip. Departs approximately every 30 min., 6:15 A.M. to 11:30 P.M. For information, call 816–243–5950. Cab fare is about $25 for the 30-minute ride downtown. *Yellow Cab* (471–5000) operates in the metropolitan area.

By bus. To navigate around the 300 or so square miles of Kansas City, most residents depend on private autos, although the Kansas City Area Transportation Authority does operate buses. Fare for the Metro, as the bus is called, starts at 60 cents. Call 221–0660 for information on routes. In Kansas City, KS, buses are operated by the Kansas City, Kansas Transportation Department; call 371–6402. Discount fares are offered to senior citizens and some students. Buses run from throughout the metropolitan area to the Chiefs and Royals games.

By rental car. Nearly every major car rental firm has an outlet in Kansas City. These include *Thrifty Rent-A-Car* (464–5670) and *Budget Rent-A-Car* (262–9090).

HINTS TO THE MOTORIST. A right turn on red is permitted in both Kansas and Missouri unless otherwise posted. In Missouri certain areas are designated snow emergency routes, and parking on those streets is forbidden during heavy snows. Some metered parking is available downtown, but check your watch closely, as the meters are closely monitored. Additional parking slots are available in lots, but these cost much more, often upwards of 95 cents an hour. Parking on the Plaza is free.

With a good street map, navigating around Kansas City should not be too confusing, because most of the streets are laid out in a true east-west or north-south pattern. In Missouri and Johnson County numbered streets generally run east-west, and named streets run north-south. You may cross into Kansas from Missouri or vice versa without even knowing it, and traffic laws generally are the same in both states. On the Kansas side lower speed limits are posted in school zones, which are carefully patrolled.

TOURIST INFORMATION. The Convention and Visitors Bureau of Greater Kansas City, 1100 Main (221–5242), is always eager to help travelers by providing maps and brochures. To find out what is currently happening, call the Visitor Information Phone at 474–9600, a 24-hour service that lists weekly happenings. Weekly listings of conventions, entertainment, and other events are contained in the "Sunday Arts" section of the *Kansas City Star.* For other information on restaurants, shops, etc., dial the information line at 764–1411. Foreign visitors can exchange their money for U.S. currency at any major bank in downtown Kansas City, MO.

HINTS TO DISABLED TRAVELERS. A directory giving detailed information about access to restaurants, public buildings, motels, bars, theaters, and other places is available from Whole Person, Inc., 6301 Rockhill Rd., Suite 305 E, Kansas City, MO 64131 (361–0304). Established in 1978, Whole Person is an authority on problems facing disabled persons. It conducts seminars, serves as an architectural consultant to those wanting to make their buildings accessible to the disabled, and studies legal action when rights have been violated.

FREE EVENTS. An abundance of free (and almost free) events exists in Kansas City, catering to a variety of interests from theater to horses. Here is a listing of some:

American Royal Parade. Downtown Kansas City. For years the Royal parade in Nov. has signaled the beginning of Royal Week in Kansas City. Many floats, saddle clubs, and marching bands strut their stuff.

DeAnn Rose Memorial Farmstead. Overland Park Community Park, 135th and Switzer (381–5252). Open daily 9 A.M.–8 P.M. during the warm months, the Farmstead offers a miniature barnyard setting with all sorts of animals, not just those found on a farm. Children are encouraged to pet and feed.

The **Governor's Exposition Building.** 1800 Genessee. During the American Royal Livestock and Horseshow (early–mid-Nov.) There is a small charge to enter the exhibition building, where the sheep, cattle, and pigs are housed. Tickets for the horse show are around $8.

Plaza Art Fair. Country Club Plaza. For the third weekend in September the streets on the Plaza are closed to motorists and are filled with artists from across the country displaying their wares. Music emanates from a bandstand while the crowds stroll amid the colorful art in the festive setting. For information, call 816–753–0100.

Plaza Lighting Ceremonies. Country Club Plaza. Since the 1920s it's been a tradition for the switch to be flipped on Thanksgiving night. The streets are jammed with spectators watching as the holiday lights turn the Plaza into a wonderland.

Saint Patrick's Day Parade. Downtown. This parade was started a few years ago by a local radio personality and has grown to the extent that participants now claim it is the third largest Saint Patrick's parade in the country.

The Spirit Festival. Downtown. Begun in 1984 by a coalition of civic leaders, this festival is an annual smashing success previously held on the Fourth of July. Beginning in 1988, the festival will be held in September. Wondrous fireworks and music by the Kansas City Symphony are the highlights. Small admission fee.

TOURS AND SPECIAL-INTEREST SIGHTSEEING. If you like to strike out on your own, there are numerous ways to see the city without spending a fortune. These self-guided tours also allow you to linger where you want and skip what doesn't interest you. Here are some:

Battle of Westport. Sponsored by the Westport Historical Society, 4000 Baltimore (561–1821). This is a driving tour with 25 stops that outlines the Battle of Westport in the Civil War. It begins at Westport Rd. and Pennsylvania and goes south to 96th and Wornall Rd. Free.

Downtown Walking Tour. The Historic Kansas City Foundation, 20 W. 9th (471–3391), sponsors this tour, which includes 31 points of interest such as the City Market and City Hall. A brochure guides you through the tour, which also may be done by car. Free.

Monuments. You will stroll down boulevards and through parks looking at markers, memorials, and statues on this tour sponsored by the Landmarks Commission, 26th floor, City Hall, 12th and Oak streets (274–2555). A booklet called *Kansas City: A Place in Time* ($6) directs you.

Plaza Walking Art Tour. The Plaza Merchants Assn., 4625 Wornall (753–0100), has an illustrated brochure and map that outlines the background on 31 pieces of outdoor art and sculpture on the Plaza.

Independence City Tour. The city Department of Tourism, 111 E. Maple, Independence (836–7111), furnishes a self-guided tour brochure that takes you around the area surrounding the Truman home and a map with other points of interest marked.

Heritage Hikes. Sponsored by the Historic Kansas City Foundation, 20 W. 9th (471–3391), these walks take you past older buildings and homes of historic significance.

Educational Tours Listing. The Convention and Visitors Bureau, 1100 Main (221–5242), has a listing of about 40 area firms and institutions that conduct educational tours for the public.

PARKS AND GARDENS. Kansas City likes to boast that it has as many fountains as Rome and as many boulevards as Paris. Enlightened city fathers created a park board in the 1890s and hired landscape architect George Kessler to design a unique network of free public parks connected by public boulevards. Many of those parks are still lovely today and have been joined by others. Here's a sampling:

Loose Park. 51st and Wornall, a few blocks south of Country Club Plaza. This park borders on some of the city's most exclusive residential neighborhoods. The park has open expanses of rolling terrain, a jogging path, a duck pond, tennis courts, and a renowned rose garden. Closes 10 P.M.

Swope Park. You could easily spend a day at this vast park at Swope Parkway and Meyer Blvd. (444–3113). This is the nation's third largest municipal park, with 1,769 acres, and it includes the Kansas City Zoo, two 18-hole golf courses, two fishing lakes, a nature center, 10 shelters, and numerous athletic fields. Always open.

Shawnee Mission Park. Covering more than 1,000 acres, this suburban facility at 79th and Renner Rd. in Lenexa, KS, is a favorite spot for picnicking, canoeing, and sailing. There are many trails; an added attraction in the summer is low-cost theater productions outdoors. Open 5 A.M.–11 P.M.

Minor Park. South Kansas City at Red Bridge and Holmes roads. This park's main attraction is an 18-hole golf course and tennis courts. Open 5:30 A.M.–9 P.M.

ZOOS. The **Kansas City Zoo** is tucked into Swope Park, a 1,769-acre stretch of land beginning at Swope Pkwy. and Meyer Blvd. in the southeast section of the city (333–7405). Access to the zoo is from 63d St. on the north, or Swope Parkway from the west.

Covering an expanse of some 80 acres, the zoo has varied terrain that makes it a suitable home for 700 animals representing 160 species. The biggest (literally) attraction is Casey, an African bull elephant. Weighing in at 6 tons and standing about 9 ft., he is the largest of his kind in the U.S. The zoo attracts the third largest crowd of any attraction in Kansas City (after the Royals baseball team and Worlds of Fun), with 500,000 visitors yearly. The reasonable admission fee ($3 for 12-year-olds and up; under 12, free) makes a zoo visit an inexpensive treat. Open 9 A.M.–5 P.M. daily except Christmas and New Year's.

PARTICIPANT SPORTS. Any time, day or night, during any weather, bitter cold or blistering hot, you are likely to see **runners** on the streets of Kansas City. In fact, some local communities have ordinances requiring joggers to wear reflective clothing at night as a safety measure. The jogging trail in picturesque Loose Park at 51st and Wornall Rd. is popular, as are parks with jogging trails on the Kansas side, such as Indian Trails Park, 87th and Greenway in Lenexa (492–8800), and South Lake Park, 86th and Valley View in Overland Park. Numerous other trails are tucked away here and there, such as the Parcourse at Shawnee Mission Medical Center (74th and Grandview in Merriam, KS), a 1-mile track with 18 exercise stations designed to keep heart, lungs, and muscles in tip-top shape. For those who like to run competitively several first-rate races are staged in Kansas City, most with registration in advance. These include *The Crown Center Hospital Hill Run,* first Sun. in June (write c/o Crown Center, 2440 Pershing Rd., Suite 500, Kansas City, MO 64108) (274–4039).

Bicycling buffs can pedal their way to fun in the Colonel's Bike Ride that departs at 2 P.M. from the Loose Park Tennis Courts, weather permitting, on Sun. from Mar. to Nov. There are no dues for this informal group, whose members ride the same scenic route through Johnson County each outing.

If **tennis** is your love check with the Kansas City Parks and Recreation Department (444–3113) for information about courts. Other communities also have courts. To obtain information, telephone the parks and recreation department in the particular city. Some of the larger ones are Johnson County, 831–3355; Kansas City, KS, 371–2000, ext. 236; and Overland Park, 381–5252.

For **golf** enthusiasts there are several public courses with fees under $10. These include Minor Park, Red Bridge and Holmes roads, South Kansas City, MO (942–9770); Swope Park, Swope Pkwy. and Meyer Blvd. (523–9770); Tomahawk Hills, 17501 Midland Dr., Lenexa (631–8000); Sunflower Hills, 122d and Riverview (721–2757); and St. Andrew's Golf Club, 11099 W. 135th St. (897–3804).

If you're visiting the city during a cold snap, some lakes may be frozen enough for **ice skating.** Phone the Kansas City Parks and Recreation Department at 444–3113 to learn which of the city's lakes and ponds are safe for skating. Otherwise, skaters can pay to glide at the Crown Center Ice Terrace.

SPECTATOR SPORTS. Make sure you bring the field glasses on your trip to Kansas City. You'll have a choice of professional baseball (the Royals), football (the Chiefs), and soccer (the Comets).

Baseball fever hits Kansas City with the first hint of warm weather. The World Series champs in 1985, the Royals are Kansas City's biggest summertime attraction when they hit the diamond at Royals Stadium at I-70 and Blue Ridge Cut-off (816–921–8000). Seats are snatched up quickly. Prices range from $6 to $10; general admission tickets, at $3, go on sale 90 minutes before game time.

Football is played in the adjoining Arrowhead Stadium (816–924–9300), where the Chiefs meet National Football League opponents in the autumn. Staunch fans still remember 1969, when the Chiefs won the Super Bowl, and are encouraged by a team that made the divisional playoffs in 1986. Ticket prices are $14 to $20; senior-citizen discounts available.

Soccer, the latest professional sport to locate in Kansas City, is played at Kemper Arena at 1800 Genessee in the Stockyards (816–421–7770). The Comets play in the Major Indoor Soccer League from Oct. through Apr. Advertisements claim "a hot summer's night" with the Comets, and fans seem to agree.

CHILDREN'S ACTIVITIES. There are lots of things to do with the kids in Kansas City, and the great thing is that parents enjoy many of them, too. Here's a sampling:

Benjamin Stables. I-435 and E. 87th St. (761–5055). Re-creation of early western town. Horseback ($15 per hour or $25 for 2 hours), pony rides, and hayrides ($5.00 per person, $60 minimum). Open 8 A.M.–9:15 P.M.

The Coterie at Crown Center. 2450 Grand Ave. (474–6552). This innovative theater company puts on original plays with good special effects for children.

Kaleidoscope. Crown Center, 25th and McGee (274–8300). Sponsored by Hallmark, this creative experience for young children challenges all the senses. It includes arts and crafts projects that the kids, aged 5 to 12, make to take home. Parents can leave their youngsters at Kaleidoscope for an hour while they shop or do something else. The parents are not allowed in, but can observe through one-way mirrors. Reservations required.

Oceans of Fun. Same exit as Worlds of Fun on adjoining grounds (454–4545). Features body surfing, waterslide, speed slide, waterskiing shows, adult pool, two children's pools, and playgrounds. Open 10 A.M., closing hour varies; closed in winter.

Theatre for Young America. 7201 W. 80th St., Overland Park, KS (648–4600). Plays aimed at the small fry are presented throughout the year. Tickets about $4.50; Tues.–Sun.; showtime varies.

Worlds of Fun. I-435 exit 54 between Parvin Rd. and NE 48 St. (454–4444). Lots of thrills in this park with internationally themed areas. One "passport" price, about $17, includes rides, shows, and attractions. Open 10 A.M., closing hour varies; closed in winter.

HISTORIC SITES AND HOUSES. Kansas City has a colorful history dating to frontier days, and many historic sites remain as testimony to the days of cowboys and Indians, the Civil War, and early statesmen.

1859 Jail-Museum. 217 N. Main, Independence, MO (252–1892). Near the square in Independence, this structure was used by both the North and the South during the Civil War, depending on which side controlled the area. Later, Frank James served time here. A one-room schoolhouse, marshal's office, and frontier museum are part of the complex. Open 9 A.M. to 4 P.M. Tues–Sat. Adults, $2; senior citizens, $1.50; children, 50 cents.

Fort Osage. U.S. 24 in Sibley, MO (795–8200). This restored fort and trading post was the first U.S. outpost in the Louisiana Purchase, dating to 1808. Open 9:30 A.M.–5 P.M. daily. Free.

Grinter House. K-32 Hwy. and S. 78th St., Kansas City, KS (299–0373). The first white settler in Wyandotte County, Moses Grinter, built this southern colonial home in 1857. The seven rooms contain furnishings from the period. Open 10 A.M.–5 P.M. Tues.–Sat., 1–5 Sun. Free.

Liberty Memorial. 100 W. 26th. (221–1918). Commemorates those who died in World War I. Outstanding murals and an extensive collection of World War I artifacts are included. The tower stands over 200 ft. tall and has an observation deck on top. Open 9:30 A.M.–4:30 P.M. Tues.–Sun.; closed Mon. Museum free; 50 cents to tower.

Shawnee Methodist Mission Museum. 53rd and Mission Rd., Fairway, KS (262–0867). The three brick buildings, recently renovated, were part of an Indian manual training school on the former Shawnee Indian Reserve. Rooms are on display, along with some objects made by the children. Open 10 A.M.–5 P.M. Tues.–Sat.; 1–5 P.M. Sun. Free.

Harry S. Truman Library and Museum. U.S. 24 at Delaware, Independence (833–1225). Located near the Truman home, the library has historical documents and relics of the Truman presidency. Open 9 A.M.–5 P.M. daily; closed holidays. Adults, $2; children free.

Union Station. Pershing Rd. and Main. The exterior of this Beaux-Arts design remains impressive. Built in 1914 of limestone and granite, it was the site of the infamous Union Station massacre involving Pretty Boy Floyd.

Westport Square. Westport Rd., from Pennsylvania to Broadway. This is where Kansas City began with a trading post in 1833. Today the area teems with nightlife, one of the favorite taverns being Kelly's, housed in Kansas City's oldest building. Specialty shops and good restaurants abound in the area.

MUSEUMS AND GALLERIES. You should not leave Kansas City without visiting the **Nelson-Atkins Museum of Art,** 4525 Oak (561–4000). It is one of the nation's top galleries and is internationally renowned for its Chinese collection, though it also has art from nearly every period. Open 10 A.M.–5 P.M. Tues.–Sat.; 1–5 Sun. Adults $3; under 19 and fulltime college students free. Free on Sun.

Kansas City Museum. 3218 Gladstone Blvd. (483–8300). This museum originally was the 70-room ornate home of lumber magnate R. A. Long. Among the exhibits of frontier life and early regional history are replicas of a trading post and store in Westport. Open 9:30 A.M.–4:30 P.M. Tues–Sat; noon–4:30 Sun. Suggested donation: $3 for adults, $2 for children and senior citizens.

The Miniature Museum. 5235 Oak (333–2055). It is housed in a grand turn-of-the-century mansion on the campus of the University of Missouri–Kansas City. Open 10 A.M.–4 P.M. Wed.–Sat.; 1–4 Sun. Adults $2.50; children $1.50; senior citizens $2.

FILM. Visitors on a budget should check the newspaper for movie theaters where all seats cost $1. Currently that includes the **Watts Mill** at 103d and State Line (942–8036). Twilight shows with a reduced rate before prime time also are advertised in the paper. Other good values include:

Fine Arts Theater. 5909 Johnson Dr., Mission, KS (262–0701). Old box office smashes are featured, and you can see two shows for the price of one. $3.50.

Free films. Nelson-Atkins Museum of Art, 45th and Oak (561–4000). A series of classical and foreign films is shown in the Atkins Auditorium.

MUSIC. Kansas City Symphony Orchestra, at Lyric Theatre, 1029 Central (471–4933). The orchestra has been delighting audiences since 1933, although it nearly went under several years ago. It was saved by community benefactors and is stronger than ever. Concerts Fri. and Sat. nights, Nov.–Mar. Ticket prices $10 to $22, $8 to $20 on Sun.

Conservatory of Music. University of Missouri–Kansas City, 4949 Cherry (363–4300). Programs include concerts, recitals, and workshops. Student events generally are free, but there may be a fee for professional performances.

Music in the Parks. Kansas City Parks and Recreation Department (444–3113). This has become a Sun. evening tradition in the summertime. Spectators jam the parks for these free events, often starring big-name groups such as the Tommy Dorsey Orchestra. The department also sponsors brown bag concerts on the steps of city hall during the summer.

Lyric Opera. 1029 Central (471–7344). Opera in English is featured here in Sept. and Apr. $5 to $25 Mon. and Wed.; $7.50 to $30 Fri. and Sat.

DANCE. The State Ballet of Missouri, at Lyric Theatre, 1029 Central (931–2232). This is a first-rate professional company that was started over 25 years ago. It is supported by dance patrons in the area. Season Oct.–May. Tickets $6 to $25.

Westport Ballet. 3936 Main (531–4330). This group was started in 1974 and now has its own semiprofessional company that performs each summer in Westport Square.

STAGE. Folly Theater. 300 W. 12th (474–4444). Opened at the turn of the century, this elegant old building has had many lives; after a major restoration in the early 1970s, it reopened as a showcase for dance, drama, and music.

Missouri Repertory Theatre. 50th and Cherry on campus of University of Missouri–Kansas City (276–2700). First-rate productions are staged by this professional resident company. Season July–Mar. $17 to $19 for evening performances; $14 for matinees.

Starlight Theater. Swope Park (333–9481). Enjoy an evening production in the large outdoor amphitheater, May–Sept. $3 to $20 for musicals; about $14 for concerts.

The Waldo Astoria. 7428 Washington, and **Tiffany's Attic,** 5028 Main (561–7529). These professional dinner theaters are under the same management. Buffet dinner is served before the show, generally a light comedy. $18 Sun.–Thurs. nights; $21 Fri. and Sat. nights; $16 Sun. matinees. Occasional Wed. matinees for senior citizens, $10.50.

DINING OUT. Kansas City is famous for its steaks, a reputation well deserved, as you will discover when cutting into a juicy, tender cut at an area restaurant. And you needn't spend a fortune; many steak dinners are a good value when you consider they come with salad, potato, and other fixings. Another local favorite is barbecue, whether it's beef, chicken, or pork. Purists insist that it is the sauce that makes the barbecue. Restaurant categories, determined by the price of a meal for one, without beverages, tip, or tax, are as follows: *Reasonable,* $12 to $15; *Very Economical,* $9 to $12; and *Low Budget,* less than $9. Every attempt has been made to ensure that this list is up to date, but restaurants come and go so quickly that it is advisable to call before you show up.

Reasonable

Golden Ox. 1600 Genessee (842–2866). Stockyards location with western motif. The place for steaks in the city.

Hereford House. 2 E. 20th (842–1080). Charcoal-broiled meats are the specialty. Western atmosphere.

Jess and Jim's Steak House. 135th and Locust (942–9909). Off the beaten path in Martin City. Gigantic portions. No-frills atmosphere. Display case lets patrons choose the cuts they prefer.

Very Economical

Annie's Santa Fe. 100 Ward Pkwy. (753–1621). South-of-the-border fare and decor. Good margaritas.

Gold Buffet. 503 E. 18th (221–4651). Feed the whole family from a large selection ranging from salads to desserts. Reduced prices for children.

Princess Garden. 8906 Wornall (444–3709). A favorite of locals; the variety of Oriental dishes is superb. Peking duck and walnut chicken are tops.

Whisker's in Westport. 1022 Westport Rd. (931–1448). Nightly specials are a good buy. Salad bar completes menu with prime rib, seafood, or steak. Old-time atmosphere.

Low Budget

Arthur Bryant's Barbecue. 1727 Brooklyn (231–1123). Even presidents have eaten the barbecue here. Heaping portions of ribs, gigantic sandwiches, and fries. Calvin Trillin raves about this place. Lunch is the best time to visit.

Fritz's. 250 N. 18th, Kansas City, KS (281–2777). Kids love the delivery system in this hamburger emporium. After you place order by telephone, the food arrives by way of a model train system that runs above tables.

Hayward's Pit Barbecue. 110th and Antioch, Overland Park, KS (649–8005). Another reason Kansas City is famous for barbecue. Contemporary atmosphere. Crowded nightly with Johnson Countians who savor the chicken, ribs, beef, and pork smoked on the premises.

John Francis Restaurant. One half block west of Metcalf on 80th, Overland Park. Family atmosphere with all ages of clientele. Reasonable smorgasbord, or select from menu of chicken, roast beef, chops, etc.

S.P. Ghetti's. 10300 Wornall Rd. (941–4808). Order spaghetti, topped with your favorite sauce at this casual eaterie in a converted railcar.

Recommended Splurge. Savoy Grill. 9th and Central (842–3890). A Kansas City landmark since 1903; you will step back in time as you dine on the house specialty of lobster. Elegant surroundings. Open daily; about $30 per person for full dinner.

NIGHTLIFE AND BARS. A distinctive style of jazz evolved in Kansas City in the 1930s, combining blues, folk, and ragtime. The area around 12th and Vine was where it all began, but the area today is not like it was then. Much of Kansas City's nightlife takes place around the Plaza or Westport areas or occasionally in a suburban hideaway. Check the arts section of the Sun. Kansas City *Star* for a list of current entertainment in the area.

The legal drinking age in Kansas is 21. Recently liquor-by-the-drink as a county option was passed by the state's voters.

In Missouri, the drinking age is 21, and any restaurant that is licensed may serve liquor. The following is a small selection of places in Kansas City, Missouri, where you can enjoy both good jazz and a cocktail:

City Light. 7425 Broadway (444–6969). Jazz is played here every night in one of Kansas City's earliest neighborhoods, Waldo.

Grand Emporium Saloon. 3832 Main (531–1504). Features a variety of bands in old, midtown building.

Parody Hall. 811 W. 39th (474–7070). Jazz and blues concerts.

Signboard Bar. Westin Crown Center Hotel, Pershing Rd. and Main (474–4400). Nostalgia decor depicting area in the 1930s. Mostly over-30 crowd comes to hear jazz or contemporary music.

Singles and Young Couples

Jimmy's Jigger. 1823 W. 39th (753–2444). A neighborhood hangout near the Kansas University Medical Center.

Kelly's Westport Inn. 500 Westport Rd. (753–9193). In Kansas City's oldest building. Casual denim crowd.

Fred P. Ott's. 4770 J.C. Nichols Pkwy. (753–2878). Often standing room only when the young crowd assembles here to imbibe. Burgers and appetizers for the hungry.

SECURITY. Kansas City generally is a safe city, yet it pays to be careful. Even on the fashionable Country Club Plaza there have been purse snatchings, mostly in the covered parking lots. Most would-be criminals in this area will be deterred if you have a firm clasp on your pocketbook, walk with a brisk and determined step, and have keys in hand as you approach the car. If you want to try the world-famous Bryant's barbecue, make it for lunch and avoid the area after dark. Another place to skip after sundown is Swope Park and the surrounding area, unless it's for a trip to the Starlight Theatre. Although downtown streets are generally safe for car traffic at night, it is not wise to stroll along them after dark, partially because they seem deserted.

Kansas City is a friendly city, and residents are willing to assist visitors to make their stay pleasant and memorable.

LAS VEGAS

by
Stephen Allen

Stephen Allen is a Las Vegas-based free-lance travel writer whose articles have been published in numerous national magazines and newspapers.

Las Vegas is known everywhere as the entertainment capital of the world because of the large number of superstars who appear in the lavish hotel-casinos along the 3½-mile Strip. But it also could be called the bargain capital of the world. The reason for this is simple: The hotels make so much money out of "gaming"—as they like to call it in Nevada—that they often can afford to offer other things to their guests and visitors at lower prices than can be found elsewhere.

To be sure, the good old days of Las Vegas, when you could see a show and enjoy a dinner for $3.50, are gone forever as more and more of the hotels are bought by corporations that want to see each room turn a profit. But even so, accommodations at a major luxury hotel—such as the Las Vegas Hilton—will cost you about half of what they would in other major capitals of the Western world. Other bargains are even more striking.

Las Vegas is not very old as an entertainment and gambling complex. Although some of the best restaurants in the United States can be found there now, not too long ago the idea of going out to dinner in Las Vegas meant a gopher going out the wrong hole and meeting a rattlesnake.

It all started in 1931, before which Las Vegas was little more than a dusty railroad stop on the mail route from Los Angeles to Salt Lake City. In that year two things happened that were to change the history of Las Vegas forever, and both for the same reason.

Along with the rest of the country, Nevada and Las Vegas were suffering from the effects of the Depression. There were just not enough ways to produce revenue in this mostly desert state. Thus, the Nevada legislature legalized gambling in the hopes of bringing more revenue and more visitors to the state. At around the same time the federal government began the construction of Hoover Dam just about 30 miles from Las Vegas. Construction of the dam, which took several years, brought an enormous amount of employment to the area, and the legalization of gambling offered the workers a way to spend all that money. Las Vegas began to exist.

But its growth was relatively slow until 1948, when the area caught the eye of mobster Benjamin "Bugsy" Siegel. Bugsy Siegel had a dream of building a gambling capital only 300 miles from Los Angeles. The dream was a good one, but Bugsy did not live to see its fruition. Obtaining money and materials from heaven knows where, he was able to build the Flamingo, the first luxury resort in Las Vegas. Financially, the Flamingo was a bust, and Bugsy was to die a short time later in typical gangland fashion, but his dream eventually would come to pass.

The Flamingo Hotel, much expanded and enlarged, is still in Las Vegas at the same location, but now it is owned by the Hilton Corporation and is called the Flamingo Hilton. The only reminder of Bugsy is his rose garden behind the hotel, where a sign informs visitors that never did the roses bloom so red as after Bugsy had recently lost a near and dear friend.

With the involvement of major corporations such as Hilton and MGM, Las Vegas began to lose some of its image as a gangster-ridden sin city, and today it is one of the major vacation and convention destinations of the nation.

Still, some of the old-timers feel a little of that sin city image should be preserved—otherwise, what's the point of coming to Las Vegas?

As the visitor will see, there are actually two Las Vegases. The more famous of the two is the 3½-mile Strip that runs roughly between Sahara Avenue (Sahara Hotel) and Tropicana Avenue (Tropicana Hotel). On this stretch, you will find the most lavish palaces of pleasure, such as Caesars Palace, Bally's-Las Vegas, the Desert Inn, the Frontier, the Stardust, and the Sands.

The other Las Vegas is the downtown area, along Fremont Street, just four blocks long from Las Vegas Boulevard to Main Street. This is the most photographed area of Las Vegas because it is so densely packed and brightly lighted; it has been used as the backdrop for the TV program *VEGA$* and a number of movies, including a James Bond film. There is so much light along this stretch that you can easily read a newspaper at 4 A.M!

The distance from the downtown area to the Strip is about 3½ miles.

Visitors to Las Vegas—particularly those who are flying in at night—will see that Las Vegas is a jeweled oasis in the middle of a black desert. The nearest cities are Los Angeles and Phoenix, both about 300 miles away. Flying into Las Vegas at night truly is an amazing sight.

Despite its isolation, Las Vegas also is a good jumping-off point for some other interesting sights. Hoover Dam is only 30 miles away, and interesting tours are offered down into the dam. Hoover Dam backs up Lake Mead, the largest man-made lake in the United States, offering boating, fishing, and swimming.

The Grand Canyon is only 300 miles away, and airlines in Las Vegas offer scenic flights over and through the canyon. Death Valley is just 165 miles to the northwest and is recommended in all but the heat of the summer.

Believe it or not, Las Vegas is also one of the few places in the country where, during January and February, you can go snow skiing in the morning at Mount Charleston, a ski resort about 30 miles from Las Vegas, return to the city for lunch, and then go waterskiing in the afternoon on Lake Mead, also about 30 miles away.

PRACTICAL INFORMATION

WHEN TO GO. Because of its sunny climate, in the heart of the Sunbelt, Las Vegas is nice almost any time of year, although it is quite hot during July and Aug. (temperatures up to 110 to 115 Fahrenheit). Locals say that since you are in the desert, the heat is dry and you do not feel it as much. But Las Vegas has the same problem that Palm Springs does: The increasing number of golf courses and swimming pools is making that heat less and less dry all the time.

Because of the increasing convention business, Las Vegas is a busy and exciting place almost all year. About the only time it slows down is during the first three weeks of Dec., as some of the hotels close their showrooms during that time. However, because of the empty hotel rooms, this is also the time of the year when the greatest bargains are to be found. How does a hotel room, single or double, right in the center of the Strip (Stardust) for just $14 a night sound? Shop around a little. Great bargains are to be found at this time of year.

HOW TO GET THERE. By air. The old days of "Jackpot" fares to Las Vegas seem to be gone, but you still can get some good buys if you shop around. The major airlines serving Las Vegas are *America West, American, Continental, Delta, Eastern, Hawaiian Air, Northwest, PSA, Pan Am, Southwest, TWA,* and *United.*

By bus. Las Vegas can be reached by *Greyhound-Trailways.* There are terminals conveniently located in the downtown area and on the Strip, next to the Stardust Hotel.

By train. Las Vegas has the only train station in the world that empties right into a casino. The Amtrak station is right in the back of the Union Plaza Hotel, in the heart of downtown, since the Union Plaza was built on the site of the former train station. The Amtrak route goes from Los Angeles through Las Vegas to Salt Lake City and from there beyond to Denver and Chicago.

By car. You can drive to Las Vegas on I-10 and I-15 from Los Angeles, on U.S. 95 from the east, and from U.S. 95–93 from the north. Las Vegas is about 5 hours from Los Angeles, 6 from San Diego, and about 8 from San Francisco.

TELEPHONES. The area code for the entire state of Nevada is 702. To get numbers in the state outside of Las Vegas, dial 1 first. Information is 555–1212. An operator will assist you on person-to-person, credit-card, and collect calls if you dial 0. From outside Las Vegas, directory information can be obtained by dialing 1, the area code, and then 555–1212. The price of a local call within Las Vegas is 25 cents.

Emergency Telephone Numbers. Las Vegas is now equipped with the "911" system. Just dial that for all emergencies. The Suicide Prevention Center can be reached at 731–2990, and the number for Poison Information is 385–1277.

ACCOMMODATIONS. In keeping with its designation as a resort and convention center and its image as the entertainment capital of the world, Las Vegas has more hotel and motel rooms for its size—over 50,000—than almost any other city in the world. They range from super-deluxe suites at Caesars Palace for $1,000 a day all the way down to $10-a-day motels. The only slow season in Las Vegas is Dec., when some of the greatest hotel bargains are to be found. At other times of the year, nearly all of the major hotels offer 2- to 3-day packages that can save you money. Room rates are based on double occupancy. Categories, based on price, are as follows: *Reasonable,* $40 to $60; *Very Economical,* under $40.

Reasonable

California. 12 Ogden Ave., Las Vegas, NV 89101 (702–385–1222). In the heart of the downtown area and not far from the train station.

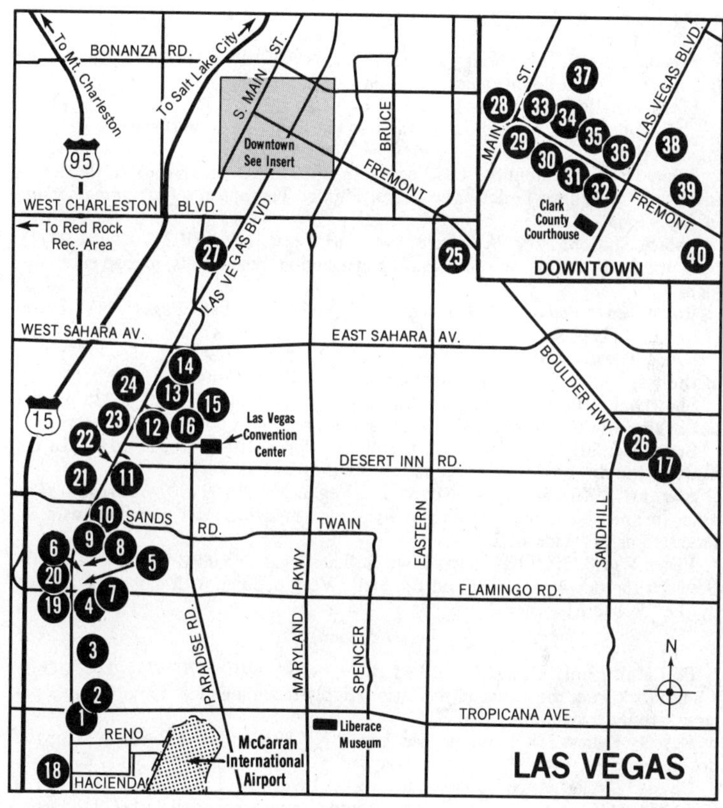

Resort Hotels and Casinos

1) Tropicana
2) Marina
3) Aladdin
4) Bally's-Las Vegas
5) Barbary Coast
6) Flamingo Hilton
7) Maxim
8) Imperial Palace
9) Harrah's Holiday Inn
10) Sands
11) Desert Inn
12) Riviera
13) El Rancho
14) Sahara
15) Las Vegas Hilton
16) Landmark
17) Nevada Palace
18) Haciẽnda
19) Dunes
20) Caesars Palace
21) Frontier
22) Silver Slipper
23) Stardust
24) Circus Circus
25) Showboat
26) Sam's Town

Downtown Hotels and Casinos

27) Vegas World
28) Union Plaza
29) Golden Gate Casino
30) Golden Nugget
31) Four Queens
32) Sundance
33) Las Vegas Club
34) Mint
35) Horseshoe
36) Fremont
37) California Hotel
38) Lady Luck Casino
39) El Cortez
40) Western Hotel

Continental. 4100 Paradise Rd., Las Vegas, NV 89109 (702–737–5555). Not far from the airport but too far to walk to the Strip.

Four Queens. 202 E. Fremont St., Las Vegas, NV 89101 (702–385–4011). Also in the downtown area, right on the Great White Way of Las Vegas. All rooms are the same price.

Fremont. 200 E. Freemont St., Las Vegas, NV 89101 (702–385–3232). Across the street from the Four Queens, also on Glitter Gulch.

Hacienda. 3950 Las Vegas Blvd. S., Las Vegas, NV 89119 (702–739–8911). At the tail end of the Strip and one of the two cheapest hotels on the Strip. Also has a camperland.

Mint. 100 E. Fremont St., Las Vegas, NV 89101 (702–387–6468). In the downtown area on Glitter Gulch. The site of Hunter Thompson's *Fear and Loathing in Las Vegas.*

Palace Station. 2411 W. Sahara Ave., Las Vegas, NV 89102 (702–367–2411). Near the Strip. Casino, in-room gaming instruction, restaurants, lounge entertainment.

Royal Las Vegas. 99 Convention Center Dr., Las Vegas, NV 89109 (702–735–6117). Near the Strip and the convention center.

Sam's Town. 5111 Boulder Hwy., Las Vegas, NV 89122 (702–456–7777). Out of the way but very popular with locals and tourists. Western theme.

Showboat. 2800 E. Fremont St., Las Vegas, NV 89104 (702–385–9123). A little out of the way but very popular with families and with bowlers (106 lanes).

Sundance. 301 E. Fremont St., Las Vegas, NV 89101 (702–382–6111). In the heart of the downtown area; the tallest building in Las Vegas.

Stardust. 3000 Las Vegas Blvd. S., Las Vegas, NV 89109 (702–732–6111). The other inexpensive hotel right on the Strip, with amazing rates during Christmastime. Home of "Lido de Paris."

Vegas World. 2000 Las Vegas Blvd. S., Las Vegas, NV 89109 (702–382–2000). Between the downtown area and the Strip. Very popular with gamblers. Owned by the "Polish Maverick."

Very Economical

Bali Hai. 336 E. Desert Inn Rd., Las Vegas, NV 89109 (702–734–2141). Only a half block from the center of the Strip. Highly recommended. Large rooms, spacious grounds, swimming pool.

Beverly Palms. 218 S. 6th St., Las Vegas, NV 89101 (702–387–9214). Near the downtown area.

Circus Circus Hotel. 2880 Las Vegas Blvd. S., Las Vegas, NV 89109 (702–734–0410). A great spot for families and circus lovers of all ages. On the strip. Free circus entertainment daily. 11 A.M.–midnight.

El Cid. 233 S. 6th St., Las Vegas, NV 89101 (384–4696). Near the downtown area. Clean and comfortable.

El Cortez. 600 E. Fremont St., Las Vegas, NV 89101 (702–385–5200). Right on Glitter Gulch, downtown. Oldest standing hotel in Las Vegas, but with a new tower.

Golden Gate. 111 S. Main St., Las Vegas, NV 89101 (702–382–3510). Near downtown and the bus stop.

Golden Inn. 120 Las Vegas Blvd. N., Las Vegas, NV 89101 (702–384–8204). Near downtown.

Lady Luck. 206 N. Third St., Las Vegas, NV 89101 (702–384–4680). Recently opened a brand new tower. One of the busiest casinos downtown.

Rainbow Vegas. 401 S. Casino Center, Las Vegas, NV 89101 (702–386–6166). Near the downtown area.

Budget Motel Chains. All of these are in the under-$45 category. Las Vegas has more motels than just about any city of its size in the world. Figure out first whether you want to be close to the Strip or close to downtown. The downtown area motels usually are cheaper.

Airport Inn. 5100 Paradise Rd., Las Vegas, NV 89119 (702–798–2777). Very near the airport.

Best Western. *Ambassador East,* 916 E. Fremont St., Las Vegas, NV 89101 (702–384–8281), downtown; *Mardi Gras Inn,* 3500 Paradise Rd., Las Vegas, NV

89109 (702–731–2020), near the airport; *Mariana Inn,* 1322 E. Fremont St., Las Vegas, NV 89101 (702–385–1150), near downtown; *Westwind,* 1150 Las Vegas Blvd. S., Las Vegas, NV 89104 (702–382–6001), near downtown.

Motel 6. 195 E. Tropicana Ave., Las Vegas, NV 89109 (702–736–4904). Near the Tropicana Hotel and the airport.

TraveLodge. *TraveLodge Downtown,* 2028 E. Fremont St., Las Vegas, NV 89101 (702–384–7540), near downtown; *TraveLodge Center Strip,* 3419 Las Vegas Blvd. S., Las Vegas, NV 89109 (702–734–6801), in the very heart of the Strip; *TraveLodge Strip,* 2830 Las Vegas Blvd. S., Las Vegas, NV 89109 (702–735–4222), across from Circus Circus Hotel.

Vagabond Inn. 3688 Las Vegas Blvd. S., Las Vegas, NV 89109 (702–736–0991). Next to the Dunes Hotel.

HOW TO GET AROUND. As with Los Angeles, Las Vegas is a city where everyone drives. However, for the visitor there are ample car rental agencies and taxis, and the bus service along the Strip to the downtown area is excellent. Since Las Vegas is a relatively small city, cab fares are not expensive; this is the cheapest and most convenient way to get around.

From the airport. McCarran International Airport is fairly close to downtown and the Strip. A cab ride to the Strip hotels will run $5 to $10; a trip to the downtown hotels will be $10 to $15. There also is a shuttle bus from the airport to the major Las Vegas hotels for just $3.50. Signs in the baggage area indicate the location of the cabs and shuttle bus.

By bus. The main bus route of interest to visitors is the one that runs along the Strip and goes to the downtown area. The cost is $1, and they run frequently. Operated by Las Vegas Transit (384–3540).

By taxi. Major companies are: *Checker* (873–2227), *Star* (873–2227), *Western* (382–7100), *Whittlesea* (384–6111) and *Yellow* (873–2227).

By rental car. There are plenty of car rental agencies right at the airport or along the Strip. Major ones are: *Abbey,* 3751 Las Vegas Blvd. S. (736–4988); *Airways,* 4920 Paradise Rd. (798–6100); *Allstate Dents* (cheap), 4034 Paradise Rd. (737–7277); *Avis,* airport (739–5595); *Budget,* near airport (735–9311); *Compacts,* downtown (386–6137); *Dollar,* near airport (739–8408); *National,* airport (739–5391); *Sav-Mor,* airport (736–1234); *Thrifty,* near airport (736–4706).

HINTS TO THE MOTORIST. Las Vegas is one of the worst cities in America to drive around for people who are not used to it. The reason is not that you can get lost: the city is small and is laid out simply. The reason is that Las Vegas has a collection of some of the most dangerous and reckless drivers in America. The explanation is simple: Las Vegas is a resort city where people carry on as they would not at home and, more important, there are no closing hours for the bars and no hours when liquor cannot be bought. Consequently, it is not uncommon to see a car weaving down the road at 6 A.M. Look out. Park your car, if you can, and use a cab. The speed limit is 55 mph on open highways, 35 mph in residential zones, and 25 mph in school zones. As with most western states, you can turn right on the red, but you are supposed to stop first. One great plus for the motorist is that it never snows in Las Vegas, and thus you can drive without worrying about snow tires or chains 365 days a year. However, the summer sun is rough on vinyl and rubber.

Most of the major hotels provide large, free self-parking lots, but many visitors also like to make use of the valet parking in front of the hotel. A $1 tip is expected.

For hints on desert driving, see the Tucson chapter.

TOURIST INFORMATION. Visitors can obtain information from the *Las Vegas Chamber of Commerce,* 2301 E. Sahara, Las Vegas, NV 89104 (702–457–4664), and from the *Las Vegas Convention and Visitors Authority,* 3150 Paradise Rd., Las Vegas, NV 89109 (702–733–2323). They can provide you with maps, lists of the hotels and their prices, general information on the city and outlying areas, and in some cases Fun Books for the casinos.

FOREIGN CURRENCY. *American Foreign Exchange of Nevada,* located in the Las Vegas Hilton (731–4155) and at 3025 Las Vegas Blvd. S., across from the Stardust Hotel (737–2096); and *Valley Bank,* 101 Convention Center Dr., is located between the Strip and the convention center (386–1417).

COUPON OR "FUN BOOKS." Many of the hotels, particularly the smaller ones, give out Fun Books that offer freebies on everything from beef stew to breakfast. They are worth having, but if you plan to use the entire book, you will find that you have to stay in one casino a long time, since the coupons can be used only so many per hour.

HINTS TO DISABLED TRAVELERS. Las Vegas is one of the best cities in America for the disabled, thanks to the many conventions that go there and demand such services. Most of the newer and bigger hotels, such as Bally's-Las Vegas and the Las Vegas Hilton, have excellent facilities for the disabled, including ramps and special rooms. You can get detailed information on these facilities by writing to the public relations director of the hotel in question.

FREE EVENTS. The famous **Mint 400 Off-Road Desert Race,** immortalized by Hunter S. Thompson, occurs in mid-May and is colorful and free to the public. Some of the convention displays at the Las Vegas Convention Center are open to the public. For updated information, consult the Las Vegas Chamber of Commerce, 2301 E. Sahara Ave. (702–457–4664).

TOURS AND SPECIAL-INTEREST SIGHTSEEING. Tours of Las Vegas and its nightlife as well as Hoover Dam, Death Valley, and the Grand Canyon are offered by *Ray & Ross Transport, Inc.,* 300 W. Owens Ave. (646–4661 or 800–338–8111); *Gray Line,* 1550 S. Industrial Rd. (384–1234); *Las Vegas Airlines* (647–3056); *Scenic Airlines,* (739–1900); and *Lake Mead Air, Inc.* (293–9906). *Cultural Focus,* 749 Veterans Memorial Dr. (382–7198), organizes tours that emphasize art galleries, media facilities, museums, parks, select homes, and historic sites. Advance reservations are suggested for all tours.

PARKS AND GARDENS. One of the nicest areas of Las Vegas in which to enjoy a little greenery in this desert environment is the campus of the **University of Nevada, Las Vegas,** 4505 S. Maryland Pkwy. Two other nice parks in the city are **Lorenzi Park,** 3333 W. Washington St., and **Sunset Park,** S. Eastern St. and Sunset Rd. Outside of town, the **Floyd Lamb State Park,** 10 miles north of Las Vegas off U.S. 95 is popular with picnickers and families.

Hoover Dam. This monument to engineering and human achievement was begun in the same year that gambling was legalized in the state of Nevada—1931—and brought a much-needed economic boost to the area. Hoover Dam is only 30 miles east of Las Vegas on Highway 93. The dam tamed the mighty Colorado and created Lake Mead, the largest man-made lake in the U.S., as well as supplying electrical energy to many western states. Interesting tours down into the dam are conducted 9 A.M.–4:30 P.M. daily; 7:30 A.M.–7:15 P.M. Memorial Day through Labor Day. Adults, $1; children under 17, free. Call 293–1081.

Valley of Fire. An open-air archaeological "museum" of early Indian civilization of the area. The ancient Indian petroglyphs on the rocks are said to date back to A.D. 1150. About an hour's drive through the desert and the Lake Mead area. Take Lake Mean Blvd. east from North Las Vegas. For additional information call 397–2088. $3 per vehicle.

PARTICIPANT SPORTS. With its nearly year-long sunny weather, Las Vegas is an ideal setting for both golf and tennis, and there are plenty of places to play both around the city.

Golf. The best courses are connected with the major hotels, and most of them are open to anyone for payment of the greens fees. They include the: *Tropicana Country Club, Dunes Country Club, Desert Inn Country Club,* and *Sahara Country Club.* Public courses are *Craig Ranch* in North Las Vegas (642–9700), *Las Vegas Golf Club,* on Washington Ave., one mile west of U.S. 95 (646–3003), and *Showboat Country Club* in nearby Henderson (451–2106).

Tennis. All the major hotels have lighted indoor or outdoor tennis courts, and some are open to the public or to guests of other hotels. Call the hotels for information.

Jogging and running. Las Vegas is not a good place to run during the summer. Dehydration or sunstroke can fell you quickly. But at other times of the year the best places to run are right down the Strip and out to the desert or on the track of the nearby University of Nevada–Las Vegas. One secret and wonderful place to run during the hot months is the air-conditioned Fashion Show Mall, right on the Strip at Spring Mountain Rd. They let runners use the mall before it opens at 10 A.M.

Bicycling. Las Vegas also is not the best town in America in which to bicycle. There are few provisions for those on two wheels, and there are a lot of reckless drivers. One excellent bicycle route leads out to the colorful Red Rock Canyon, on E. Charleston St. A 15-mile ride in one direction.

Sailing. Wonderful sailing is available on beautiful Lake Mead, just 25 miles from Las Vegas. Lake Mead is the largest man-made lake in the western hemisphere. Lake Mead also is the place to go for scuba diving, swimming (Boulder Beach on the Lake Shore Road), fishing, and waterskiing. No charge at Boulder Beach.

Bowling. Best lanes are at the *Showboat Hotel* (106 lanes), 2800 E. Fremont St. (385–9123), and *Sam's Town Hotel* (56 lanes), 5111 Boulder Hwy. (456–7777).

SPECTATOR SPORTS. The most popular spectator sport in Las Vegas probably is the basketball games played by Jerry Tarkanian's Runnin' Rebels at the University of Nevada–Las Vegas. Tickets average $10 to $15, and when available, can be obtained by calling the ticket office at the Thomas and Mack Center (739–3900). UNLV football games are played at the Silverdome, which is a few miles out of the city on Highway 95.

Other popular spectator sports are presented at Caesars Palace, such as boxing matches and gymnastic competitions. The biggest rodeo is the Helldorado, presented by the Elks Club in mid-May.

CHILDREN'S ACTIVITIES. As a "Disneyland for adults," Las Vegas has catered less to children than probably any resort in America. But as the entertainment capital of America becomes more and more a family resort as well, most of the major hotels are at least providing large video game rooms. The best are to be found at the Las Vegas Hilton and Bally's-Las Vegas and the Hilton even has its own children's hotel. Children also enjoy the live circus acts presented free day and night on the mezzanine of the Circus Circus Hotel and movies in the wraparound Omnimax Theater at Caesars Palace (just $3 and $4). The newest addition for young people is Wet 'n' Wild, (737–3819), a wet Disneyland. Not open in the winter. Kids also enjoy a free tour through the Ethel M Chocolate factory in nearby Henderson (458–8864).

MUSEUMS AND GALLERIES. Most of the few museums in Las Vegas are related to the history and topography of the desert Southwest. Many of the major hotels, such as Caesars Palace, Bally's-Las Vegas, and the Las Vegas Hilton, have important and attractive art galleries right in the hotel.

Gambling Museum. In the Stardust Hotel (732–6583). The world's largest collection of coin-operated machines.

Las Vegas Art Museum. 3333 W. Washington St. (647–4300). Regional artists.

Las Vegas Museum of Natural History. 3700 Las Vegas Blvd. S. (798–7977). Exhibits ranging from dinosaurs to present-day wildlife. Six animated "creatures" on display.

Liberace Museum. 1775 E. Tropicana Ave. (798–5595). The accumulated paraphernalia and pianos of a lifetime of this master Las Vegas showman.

Markus Galleries. In the Fashion Show Mall (737–7307). Features contemporary and modern masters, as well as emerging artists.

Nevada State Museum and Historical Society. 7009 Twin Lakes Dr. (385–0115). Four galleries display native plants and animals of southern Nevada.

Rozzi Western Art. 1041 Franklin Ave. (384–9786). Colorful interpretations of the Old West.

ARTS AND ENTERTAINMENT. There is more entertainment in this desert city than almost anyplace else you can find. Many of the options are listed below, under Nightlife.

Film. One of the largest movie theaters in the U.S. is right in Las Vegas: the *Red Rock Theaters,* with 11 movies under one roof. Call 870–1423 for information, or consult the daily newspaper.

One theater that shows first-run movies at less than normal prices is the *Huntridge,* 1250 E. Charleston Blvd. (382–3314). Tickets for a double-feature cost $1.99 all shows, every day.

An excellent bargain movie theater that many people are not aware of it in the shopping arcade of Bally's-Las Vegas. From the outside, the marquee looks like that of a little old 1930s movie palace, and they even show films like *Casablanca.* But on the inside the theater is designed to look like a Hollywood screening room, with big, soft, luxurious couches. Adults, $3.50; children, and seniors, $2. The theater shows classics from Hollywoods' golden era of the 1930s and 1940s.

The Clark County Library frequently shows movies free in its auditorium. Call 733–7810 for information.

The University of Nevada–Las Vegas hosts performances by the **Las Vegas Symphony** and the **Nevada Dance Theater** as well as by visiting guest artists and symphonies from around the country and the world (call 739–3801 for information). Plays are presented by the university and the **Clark County Community College** (643–6060).

SHOPPING. The best shopping in Las Vegas is to be found in its three big malls. *The Fashion Show Mall* is right on the Strip at Spring Mountain Rd. and includes stores such as Neiman-Marcus, Saks Fifth Avenue, Goldwater's, and Bullock's. The *Meadows Mall,* 4300 Meadows Ln., is several miles from the Strip but contains more than 140 stores. The *Boulevard Mall,* 3528 S. Maryland Pwky., is just a short distance from the Strip and boasts more than 80 stores.

Many of the major hotels, such as Bally's-Las Vegas, Las Vegas Hilton, and Caesars Palace, also feature lavish and luxurious stores in their shopping arcades. They offer the lucky gambler a way of spending his or her winnings.

Most stores in Las Vegas are open 10 A.M. to 9 P.M., although the ones in the hotels may stay open longer. The sales tax in Nevada is 6 percent.

DINING OUT. Because Las Vegas is the entertainment capital of the world and the bargain resort capital of America, you would expect there to be more restaurants of all types in this city than you can shake a credit card at—and you would be right. The restaurants range all the way from such $100-a-couple classic delights as the Palace Court and the Bacchanal Room, both in Caesars Palace, to the smaller hotel buffets where you can eat for less money than it would cost to cook at home. Categories, based on the price of a meal for one, with no beverage, tip, or tax, are as follows: *Reasonable,* $10 to $15; *Very Economical,* $5 to $10; and *Low Budget,* under $5. Except where noted, the following establishments accept some, if not all, major credit cards. We've tried to ensure that this list is up to date; still, since restaurants come and go so quickly, it's advisable to call first.

Reasonable

Alpine Village Rathskeller. 3003 Paradise Rd. (734–6888). Directly across the street from the Las Vegas Hilton and convention center. Good German-Swiss food and band.

Battista's Hole in the Wall. 4041 Audrie Dr. (732–1424). Directly across the street from Bally's-Las Vegas. Best Italian food in Las Vegas—and owned by an opera singer!

Cattleman's Steak House. 2635 S. Maryland Pkwy. (732–7726). One of the oldest restaurants in Las Vegas. Good steaks and drinks.

Cosmos Underground. 32 E. Fremont St. (382–0330). In the heart of downtown. Attractive decor and good Italian food.

Family Affair. 5006 S. Maryland Pkwy. (736–9200). Southern specialties like homemade gumbo, deep-fried catfish, black-eyed peas.

Great Wall. 2202 W. Charleston Ave. (385–2750). Excellent Chinese food in an out-of-the-way atmosphere.

Tillerman. 2245 E. Flamingo Rd. (731–4036). Excellent and relatively inexpensive seafood. Attractive atmosphere, friendly staff, good drinks.

The Vineyard. 3630 S. Maryland Pkwy., in the Boulevard Mall (731–1606). Italian food, an excellent value. Antipasto salad bar. Attractive decor.

Very Economical

Chicago Joe's. 820 S. 4th St. (382–5246). Near downtown. One of the city's oldest and best-loved Italian restaurants.

Fong's Garden. 2021 E. Charleston Blvd. (382–1644). Chinese. In Las Vegas since 1929. A little out of the way.

Ricardo's. 2380 E. Tropicana Ave. (798–4515). Easily the best Mexican food in Las Vegas. Large, wonderful atmosphere, terrific drinks, strolling guitar players.

Low Budget

Circus Circus Hotel. 2880 Las Vegas Blvd. S. (734–0410). The biggest buffet in town and, it's boasted, in the world.

Fremont Snack Bar. In the Fremont Hotel, 200 E. Fremont St., downtown (385–3232). Cheap eats.

Recommended Splurge. Palace Court. In Caesars Palace, 3570 Las Vegas Blvd. S. (731–7547). Easily the best restaurant in Las Vegas. Classical French in a setting of trees, shrubs, and flowers. When the weather is nice, the roof can be rolled back so that you can see the sky. Gold cutlery, white gloves, the works. Normally, dinner for two with a fairly good wine will run around $100, but you can cut the cost about 50 percent by going for lunch instead.

Brunches and Buffets. Nearly all of the major hotels have lavish brunches on weekends, as well as daily buffets. One of the best is at the **Dunes Hotel,** 3650 Las Vegas Blvd. S. (737–4110). It's called the International Buffet and is available weekends 7 A.M.–2 P.M., and 5–10 P.M.; weekends 9 A.M.–2 P.M. and 5–10 P.M.

NIGHTLIFE AND BARS. Quite simply, there is more nightlife in Las Vegas than in any other city on earth. All the major hotels have at least one huge extravagant show or an outstanding superstar. Some, such as Bally's-Las Vegas, have both. The price to see a superstar averages around $25–$50, and that may or may not include dinner. Show prices for major productions run $15 to $25, and the tariff for the smaller revues at the smaller hotels can go all the way down to $4.95.

There are actually two Las Vegases: the Strip, where most of the major entertainment is to be found, and the downtown area, where the lights are more congested but where entertainment is confined to only two hotels: the Golden Nugget and the Union Plaza.

In addition to the superstars who appear in Las Vegas, some of the hotels also offer the traditional Las Vegas "spectacular," with scores of beautiful and tall barebreasted girls, lavish costumes, exciting dancers, and special stage effects. The best of these long-running shows are "Jubilee!" at Bally's-Las Vegas, "Beyond Belief" with magicians Siegfried and Roy at the Frontier, "Folies Bergere" at the Tropicana, and "Lido de Paris" at the Stardust. These shows average $15 a person and include two cocktails. They are more representative of the "real" Las Vegas than the superstar entertainment.

Acts on their way up usually break into Las Vegas show business via the hotel lounges, where you often can see excellent performers for the price of two drinks. The Las Vegas hotel lounges are among the best entertainment bargains in the city.

The drinking age throughout the state of Nevada is 21, but Las Vegas and Reno are probably the only cities in America where there are no closing hours for drinking and no limit on when alcohol can be bought, so watch your step both as a pedestrian and as a driver.

Superstars

Bally's-Las Vegas. 3645 Las Vegas Blvd. S. (739–4111). Major international stars such as Frank Sinatra, Dean Martin, and Sammy Davis, Jr.

Caesars Palace. 3570 Las Vegas Blvd. S. (731–7333). Chuck Berry, the Pointer Sisters, and others.

Desert Inn. 3145 Las Vegas Blvd. S. (733–4444). Rich Little, Crystal Gayle.

Golden Nugget. 129 E. Fremont St. (385–7111). Dolly Parton, Kenny Rogers, Paul Anka.

Las Vegas Hilton. 3000 Paradise Rd. (732–5661). Bill Cosby, Wayne Newton, Suzanne Somers.

Production Shows

Bally's-Las Vegas. 3645 Las Vegas Blvd. S. (739–4111). "Jubilee!" a $10 million production that even features the sinking of the *Titanic!*

Flamingo Hilton. 3555 Las Vegas Blvd. S. (733–3111). "City Lites," a spectacular for the whole family.

Frontier. 3120 Las Vegas Blvd. S. (734–0240). "Beyond Belief" with superstar magicians Siegfried & Roy.

Riviera. 2901 Las Vegas Blvd. S. (734–5110). Five different shows.

Stardust. 3000 Las Vegas Blvd. S. (732–6111). "Lido de Paris."

Tropicana. 3801 Las Vegas Blvd. S. (739–2411). "Folies Bergere."

Smaller Revues

Harrah's Holiday Inn. 3475 Las Vegas Blvd. S. (369–5000).

Marina Hotel. 3805 Las Vegas Blvd. S. (739–1500).

Maxim. 160 E. Flamingo Rd. (731–4300).

Silver Slipper. 3100 Las Vegas Blvd. S. (734–1212).

Burlesque

Can Can Room. 3155 Industrial Rd., behind Stardust Hotel (737–1161). All nude, but no alcoholic beverages served. No cover charge, but a soft drink costs $10.

Palomino. 1848 Las Vegas Blvd. N. (642–2984). All nude; $10 cover charge plus two-drink minimum.

The Pussycat. 4416 Paradise Rd. (733–8666). Seminude; $10 cover charge.

Piano Bars

Cafe Michele. 1350 E. Flamingo Rd., in the Mission Shopping Center (735–8686). Casual atmosphere.

Play It Again Sam. 4120 Spring Mountain Rd. (876–1550). Also has excellent food.

Singles Bars

Beverly Hills Bar & Grill. 3550 S. Decatur Blvd. (876–8070). High-tech, high-energy bar.

Carlos Murphy's. 4770 S. Maryland Pkwy. (798–5541). Across from the university. Also serves good Mexican food.

Elephant Bar. 2797 S. Maryland Pkwy. (737–1586). Unusual decor, good drinks. Late-night dancing.

TGI Fridays. 1800 E. Flamingo Rd. (732–9905). Busy singles bar.

SECURITY. Las Vegas, because of the nature of the city, has a crime rate that is higher than that of most cities its size (about 570,000 population), but the figures are deceptive. Most of the crime is related to the gambling or to the types of drug deals that occur in every city. Since Las Vegas was developed as a resort and grew almost overnight, there are no actual slum areas. Consequently, it is one of the safest cities in America in which to walk around. The major hotel parking lots are all well lighted and well patrolled with security personnel. The safety of the visitor is of paramount concern. Still, that is no reason why you should open your hotel door when you don't know who is knocking on it. Internally, the hotels are well patrolled, but you should still take your own precautions. There is no actual area of the city that could be considered unsafe.

Also because of the nature of the city, Las Vegas has a high preponderance of prostitutes who ply the Strip, and some of the side streets. As with all ladies of this type, it is never a good idea to leave her and your wallet alone in the same room together; they may become fast friends. Nevada also happens to be the only state where brothels are legal; whatever one may say about their morality, they are safer than the hookers on the streets.

LOS ANGELES

by
Jane Lasky

Jane Lasky, a resident of Los Angeles, is the coauthor of The Women's Travel Guide: 25 American Cities. *She writes a weekly business travel column syndicated by the* San Francisco Chronicle *as well as articles for magazines such as* Esquire, Vogue, Connoisseur, *and* Los Angeles.

Many people, if they think of L.A., imagine surfers cruising to the beach in their convertibles while "California Girls" blares from the tapedeck. Or a group of shallow towheads soaking in a hot tub, sharing their space. Some think simply of movie stars, or of palm trees and shrinks, or of traffic and smog. Well, it's all true . . . to a point.

The Beach Boys do remain a perennial favorite out here. It's true that a surprising number of beautiful people call Los Angeles home. But, if you expect to run into a gorgeous sandy-haired surfer or sought-after movie star around every corner, you could be disappointed. Lots of everyday, average sorts live here, too.

As to the traffic, driving in the City of Angels *does* require a certain bold spirit, especially on the frenzied, crowded freeways. Still, a vast majority of Californians and visitors alike prefer the freedom of the car to any other mode of travel. Then there's the smog, a fact of Los Angeles life. But, if you visit some time other than the height of summer—and with the high temperatures, that's probably not the best choice anyway—you stand a good chance of seeing clear skies. Should the smog appear during your visit, be heartened by the fact that this smoky haze is responsible for some of L.A.'s most remarkable sunsets.

A common misconception is that this Southern California city lacks culture and variety. There's plenty, more than most give L.A. credit for: historic buildings, a multitude of important museums, and an array of stunning parks—all that along with the beaches, movie and television studios, and amusement parks visitors have no doubt heard about.

When Los Angeles was still in the hands of her Spanish founders, this was a farming community. That changed in the 1840s when the Gold Rush made L.A. the last leg of America's westward expansion. The railroad rolled in by the late 1870s, and as a result the area became one of the nation's leading orange exporters.

Yet another industrial boom era began in 1892 when oil was struck near what is now downtown. Motion pictures became big business in Hollywood after World War I, and, although much of the film production has moved into the neighboring San Fernando Valley, this general vicinity is still the entertainment world's production giant. Today the city makes much of its money in less glamorous industries as well, including auto parts, chemicals and shipping.

It's possible to get a feel for much of the history of Los Angeles even today. El Pueblo de Los Angeles is a state historic park. The missions San Gabriel and San Fernando are still active churches and open to visitors. Descanso Gardens was once part of one of the huge Mexican ranchos. You can enjoy some of the positive fruits of the era of the railroad barons by visiting the Huntington Library and Gardens, once the home of Henry E. Huntington. The J. Paul Getty Museum in Malibu is the legacy of the oil tycoon. The stars' footprints are still there on Hollywood Boulevard. As much as the motion-picture industry has changed, it's still here, and you can tour the studios.

You can get a good view of the city, for free, from the 27th floor of City Hall on Spring Street. This is a great picture spot—and photographs can provide better, and more inexpensive, souvenirs than any you can buy in the numerous Los Angeles tourist traps. When City Hall was built in the late 1920s, a city ban prohibited building any structure higher than 150 feet because of fear of earthquakes. The public voted to let City Hall exceed that limit, and it towered over the rest of the city until that restriction was lifted in 1957. Even in this spread-out city where almost no one goes anywhere on foot, downtown is one area where you can get that big-city feel and walking makes sense. (The best time to go is weekend days, when traffic and parking are less of a problem.)

You can't expect to see all of Los Angeles in a day, or even in one visit. Take your time and plan on coming back more than once, because there's plenty to do. Driving is definitely the preferred mode for sight-seeing in Los Angeles. Taxis are expensive, and public transportation may be difficult to negotiate in an area as large as the Greater Los Angeles Basin—464 square miles. You'll want to drive out Wilshire Boulevard, take a look around Hollywood and Beverly Hills, maybe tour the studios, try out the beaches, and quite possibly venture as far as Disneyland or the Huntington Library and Museum in San Marino.

Los Angeles isn't cheap. Accommodations and meals are more expensive than in many cities. But even if the admission fee at some of the major amusement parks is steep, you can get a very full day's pleasure for your money. Consider also that it costs nothing to walk up Sunset Strip or Hollywood Boulevard or to visit many of the area's fabulous parks. Many fine museums are very reasonably priced. In an area as culturally and ethnically diverse as L.A., there's a lot you can do and see and still stay on a budget.

PRACTICAL INFORMATION

WHEN TO GO. Los Angeles normally has a pleasant and mild climate year-round. In the summer the city's renowned smog will cause a problem for some who have respiratory ailments. Average summer temperature is 79.5 degrees Fahrenheit; the winter average is 69.3 degrees Fahrenheit. The rainy season usually runs from November through March, with the heaviest downpours in January; thunderstorms are infrequent. The coast may be overcast in late spring; summers are practically rainless. In fall, winter, and early spring, "Santa Ana" winds occasionally rage from the northeast, picking up a considerable amount of dust. These winds reach speeds of 35–50 mph and cause a heat cover to envelop the city and surrounding areas. The most discomfort occurs in the valley regions.

HOW TO GET THERE. By air. Three airports serve the Los Angeles area: Los Angeles International Airport (LAX) is the largest. The best way to get the lowest fare is to book through a good travel agent and to set up the trip as far in advance as possible. General information regarding the facilities at LAX and the airlines that fly into LAX is available by calling 213–646–5252.

Ontario International Airport, located 35 miles east of Los Angeles, serves the Riverside-San Bernardino area with the following airlines: *Alaska, American, American West, Continental, Delta, PSA, Southwest, TWA, United,* and four commuters. Most flights travel the western corridor. For further information, call 714–983–8282.

Burbank operates a smaller domestic terminal in the San Fernando Valley with some coast-to-coast flights as well as frequent short haul services. For further information on Burbank Airport call 818–840–8847.

By train. Los Angeles's Amtrak Union Station, one of the last grand railroad stations to be built in this country, is located at 800 N. Alameda Street. Trains operating out of this terminal link L.A. with most major cities in the U.S. Special fares like the Family-A-Fare and All Aboard America programs offer savings to the traveler; call Amtrak (800-USA-RAIL) or a travel agent for current prices.

By bus. Greyhound-Trailways bus routes provide a vast array of scheduled trips to or through Los Angeles. Contact a travel agent or a nearby Greyhound-Trailways office for information about rates and special tours.

TELEPHONES. There are three area codes in the Los Angeles area. The area code for Los Angeles proper is 213. Generally, outlying communities, including the San Fernando Valley, Glendale, Pasadena, and Burbank, are in the 818 area code. Anaheim, the rest of Orange County, and some nearby areas in L.A. County are in the 714 area code. Palm Springs is in the 619 area code. You do not need to dial the area code if it is the same as the one from which you are calling. Local directory assistance is 411. When trying to find a number, be aware of which section of the city you are seeking—Los Angeles has many different sections, each with individual telephone books. To make a long-distance call, dial 1 before the area code and the number itself. An operator will assist you on person-to-person, credit-card, and collect calls if you dial 0 first. Pay telephones start at 20 cents.

Emergency Telephone Numbers. In an emergency dial 911 or 0 and ask the operator to connect you immediately with the appropriate agency. Or dial direct yourself: Los Angeles police, 485–2121; state police, 620–4700; medical emergencies, 483–6721; fire and ambulance, 384–3131; poison control, 484–5151.

ACCOMMODATIONS. Selecting a Los Angeles hotel or motel should be done with care, not only with respect to the section of the city in which you plan to spend the majority of your time, but also with regard to the quality of the hotel or motel itself. The City of Angels offers quite a range, but the best known—the Beverly Wilshire, the Beverly Hills, the Bel Air—unfortunately fall into the deluxe category. It is possible, however, to obtain clean, decent accommodations at low-priced places

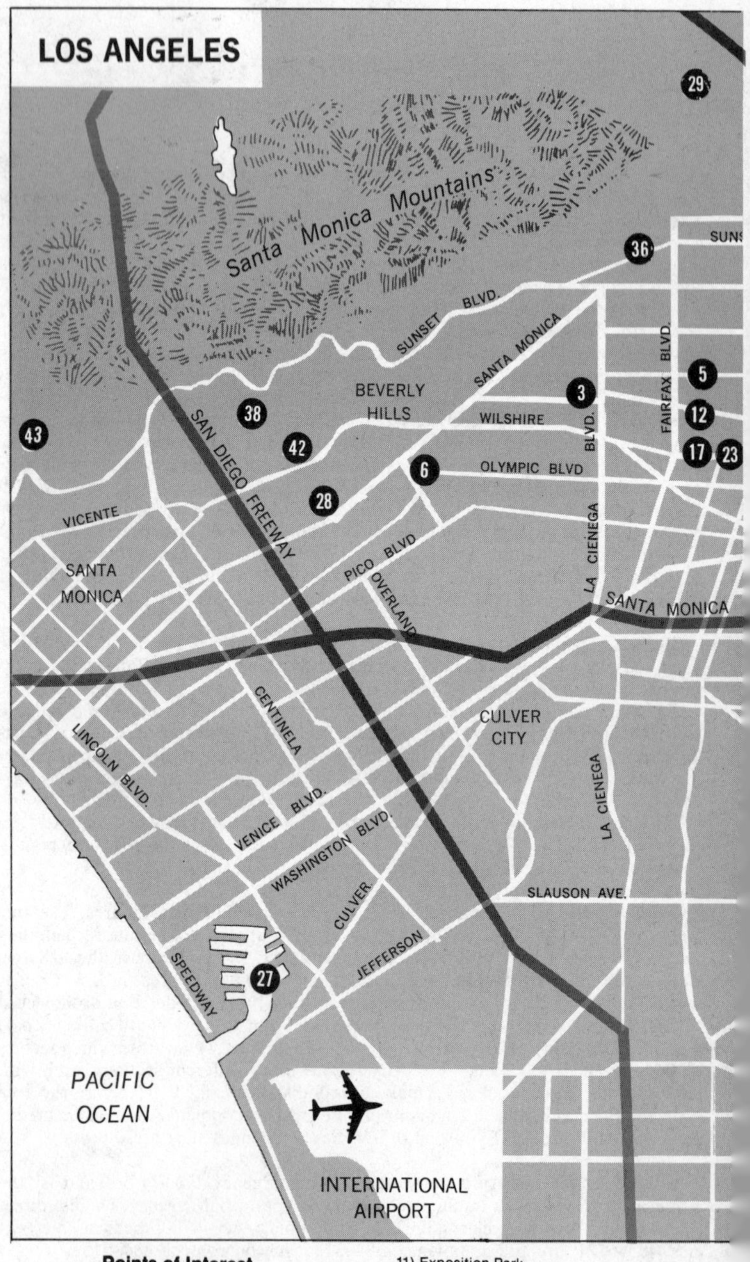

Points of Interest

1) Angelus Temple
2) Atlantic Richfield Plaza
3) Beverly Center
4) California Museum of Science and Industry
5) CBS Television
6) Century City, Shubert Theater
7) Chinatown
8) City Hall
9) Civic Center
10) Dodger Stadium
11) Exposition Park
12) Farmers' Market
13) Forest Lawn Memorial Park
14) Mann's Chinese Theater
15) Greek Theater
16) Griffith Park Zoo
17) Hancock Park
18) Hollywood Bowl
19) Hollywood Star Sidewalk
20) La Brea Tarpits, George C. Page Museum
21) Lawry's California Center
22) L.A. Convention Center

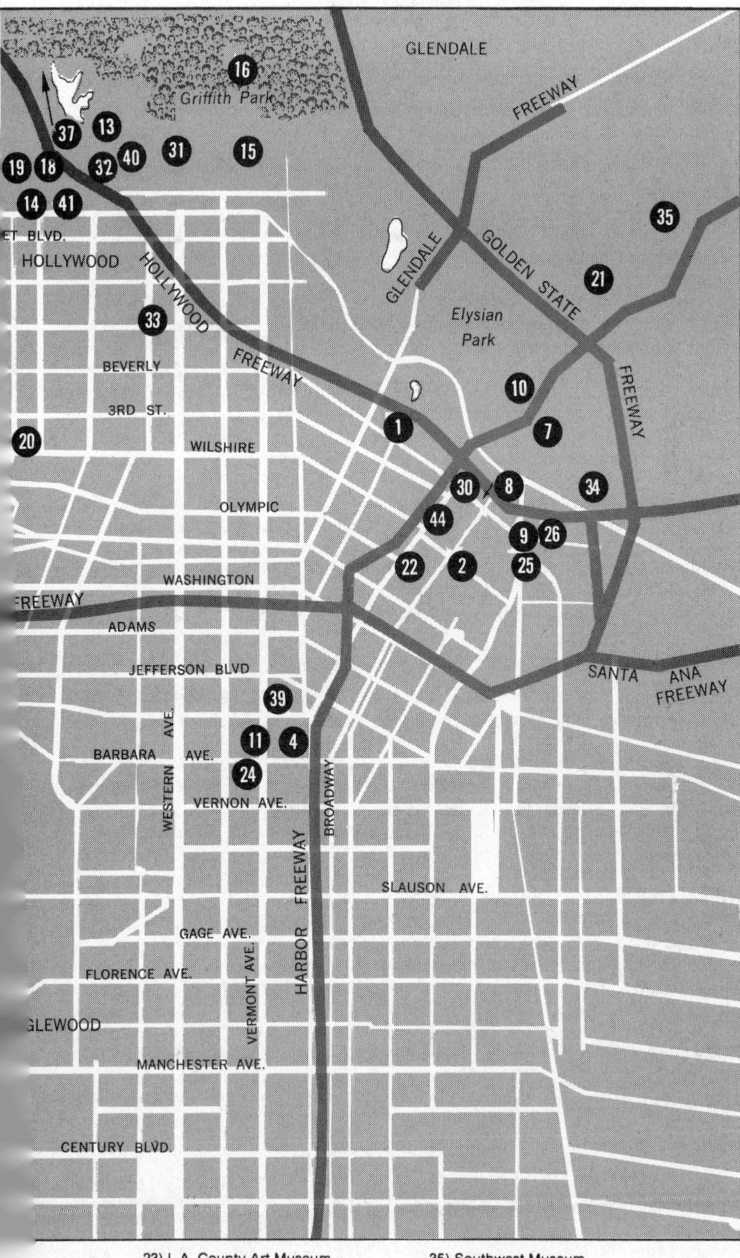

23) L.A. County Art Museum
24) L.A. Memorial Coliseum
25) L.A. Times
26) Little Tokyo/Museum of Contemporary Art
27) Marina del Rey
28) Mormon Temple
29) Mulholland Drive
30) Music Center
31) Observatory and Planetarium
32) Olvera Street
33) Paramount Studios
34) Pueblo de Los Angeles State Historical Park
35) Southwest Museum
36) Sunset Strip
37) Universal Studios
38) University of California
39) University of Southern California
40) Warner Brothers Studios (Burbank Studios)
41) Wax Museum
42) Westwood
43) Will Rodgers State Historic Park
44) World Trade Center

only a little distance from the city's mainstream. Hotels often offer special weekend rates, and many feature tickets to area amusement parks as a bonus. Prices can be lower in the winter. Los Angeles is a popular place in the spring and summer, especially around the holidays; it's best to make reservations. Below is a selection of recommended accommodations. Rates are based on double occupancy. Categories, determined by price, are *Reasonable,* $60 to $85; and *Very Economical,* under $60. A 10 percent room tax is added.

Downtown—Reasonable

Best Western Kent Inn. 920 S. Figueroa, L.A., CA 90015 (213–626–8701; 800–528–1234). Chinese restaurant, cocktail lounge, free parking. Two blocks from the Convention Center and near the famous Pantry Restaurant. Pool, free parking. Airport bus service.

Executive Motor Inn—Mariposa. 457 S. Mariposa, L.A., CA 90020 (213–380–6910). Relatively new Spanish-style hotel. Pool, sauna, refrigerators available. Spanish, Chinese staff.

Figueroa Hotel. 939 S. Figueroa, L.A., CA 90015 (213–627–8971, 800–421–9092, in California, 800–331–5151). This charming 55-year-old Spanish-style hotel is across the street from the historic Variety Arts Theater and one block from the Convention Center. 24-hour coffee shop, dining room, two bars, pool, Jacuzzi. On Gray Line sight-seeing tour route. Free parking. Airport service every hour.

Los Angeles Downtown Holiday Inn. 750 Garland Ave., L.A., CA 90017 (213–628–5242, 800–HOLIDAY). Restaurant, cocktail lounge, pool. Pets allowed. Plenty of free parking. Holiday Inn's usual professional staff.

Vagabond Olympic Hotel. 1904 W. Olympic, L.A., CA 90006 (213–380–9393; 800–854–2700; in California, 800–522–1555). Near the Convention Center, convenient to several area restaurants. On Gray Line sight-seeing tour route. Free parking.

Downtown—Very Economical

Beverly Hotel. 1330 S. Olive St., L.A., CA 90015 (213–745–9168). This 68-room hotel is convenient to airport bus service. Some units have kitchens for guest use. 24-hour security.

City Center Motel. 1135 W. 7th St., L.A., CA 90017 (213–628–7141, call collect for reservations). Quiet rooms, pool, parking. On Gray Line sightseeing tour route.

Los Angeles Huntington Hotel. 752 S. Main St., L.A., CA 90014 (213–627–3186). One block from main Greyhound Bus depot; not many services, but very clean. Vending machines off main lobby for 24-hour quick food. No parking.

Milner Hotel. 813 S. Flower, L.A., CA 90017 (213–627–6981). Across the street from the Broadway Plaza, and four blocks from the Convention Center. Very clean. Tour of Spanish L.A. available through hotel. Coffee shop, American-Mexican cuisine restaurant, popular bar decorated in old Hollywood theme.

Orchid Hotel. 819 S. Flower St., L.A., CA 90017 (213–624–5855). One of the smaller downtown hotels, the brick Orchid Hotel has no frills but is clean. Laundromat. No parking at hotel, but plenty of public lots close by. Low weekly rates.

Stillwell Hotel. 838 S. Grand, L.A., CA 90017 (213–627–1151). One of Los Angeles's oldest hotels, the Stillwell has kept its charm throughout the years. Indian and American restaurants. Low weekly rates. No parking at hotel, but plenty nearby.

Mid-Wilshire—Reasonable

Chancellor Hotel. 3191 W. 7th St., L.A., CA 90005 (213–383–1183, 800–421–8260). Near the Wilshire Center, this hotel provides an intimate atmosphere at a low price. Color television, air-conditioning, free parking, swimming pool.

Comfort Inn. 3400 W. 3d St., L.A., CA 90020 (213–385–0061). Centrally located between downtown L.A. and Hollywood, not on a busy boulevard. Coffee shop nearby, pool, free parking on premises.

Mid-Wilshire—Very Economical

Park Plaza Hotel. 607 S. Park View St., L.A., CA 90057 (213–384–5281). Plenty of amenities: weight room, heated pool, Jacuzzi, color television, self-service laundry, free parking, restaurant.

Wilshire Royale Hotel. 2619 Wilshire Blvd., L.A., CA 90057 (213–387–5311, 800–421–8072). Vintage 1920s hotel offers modern facilities, such as air-conditioning, a small Jacuzzi, self-service laundry, gift shop. Coffee shop open till 6 P.M. Small heated pool. Weekly and monthly rates.

Hollywood—Reasonable

Best Western Sunset Plaza Hotel. 8400 Sunset Blvd., Hollywood, CA 90069 (213–654–0750, 800–421–3652, in California, 800–252–0645). Located on the Sunset Strip, this is a favorite with show-business people. Rooms are modern in design, in the L.A. open-air style. Continental breakfast, heated pool. Free parking.

Farmer's Daughter Motel (Best Western). 115 S. Fairfax, Hollywood, CA 90036 (213–937–3930). Across the street from the fabulous Farmers Market shopping and CBS Television City. Good service, steak house, heated pool, free parking, refrigerator, color television. Cantor's 24-hour New York-style deli is down the street.

Franklin Motel. 1824 N. Beachwood Dr., Hollywood, CA 90028 (213–464–1824). Fairly new motel, immaculate, color television, movie rentals. Close to Bronson Canyon and Griffith Park. Weekly rates available for rooms with kitchenettes.

Hollywood Celebrity Hotel. 1775 Orchid Ave., Hollywood, CA 90028 (213–850–6464, 800–222–7090 in CA, 800–222–7017 outside CA). Recently renovated small art deco hotel in traditional Hollywood style. 32 rooms. Continental breakfast included in room price. Valet parking. Located around the corner from Mann's Chinese Theater and half a block from Hollywood Boulevard and the Walk of Fame.

Sunset Dunes Motel. 5625 Sunset Blvd., Hollywood, CA 90028 (213–467–5171). Across the street from two TV stations, so you'll find studio people around this hotel. Restaurant, cocktail lounge, free parking. Satellite television.

Hollywood—Very Economical

Hallmark House Motor Hotel. 7023 Sunset Blvd., Hollywood, CA 90028 (213–464–8344). This hotel offers free security parking, which is not easy to find in Hollywood. Pool, oriental restaurant.

Hollywood Highland Motel. 2051 N. Highland Ave., Hollywood, CA 90028 (213–851–3000). Here's something unusual—a free Continental breakfast. Just a few steps away from the Hollywood Bowl. Pool, laundry, free parking.

Hollywood Premier Hotel. 5333 Hollywood Blvd., Hollywood, CA 90027 (213–466–1691). Guests from this hotel often walk down the street to lounge in the sun in Ferndell, one of Griffith Park's loveliest spots. Peaceful, perfect place for a picnic. Room service available. Free parking.

Beverly Hills—Reasonable

Beverly House TraveLodge. 140 S. Lasky Dr., Beverly Hills, CA 90212 (213–271–2145). Small friendly establishment near Century City. 50 rooms. A bit higher priced than other hotels in this category, but great rate for the area.

Beverly Terrace Motor Hotel. 469 N. Doheny, Beverly Hills, CA 90210 (213–274–8141). Pentagon-shaped hotel with a roof terrace. International clientele. The Duke Restaurant. Pool, good security, free parking.

Beverly Hills—Very Economical

Crescent Hotel. 403 N. Crescent Dr., Beverly Hills, CA 90210 (213–274–7595). Just three blocks from Rodeo Drive boutiques, this hotel is European in style and modest in price: a steal in Beverly Hills. 44 rooms.

West Los Angeles—Reasonable

Best Western Royal Palace Hotel. 2528 S. Sepulveda Blvd., West L.A., CA 90064 (213–477–9066). Full-service hotel near Century City shopping and theater, tennis and golf facilities. Heated pool, self-service laundry, free parking.

West Los Angeles—Very Economical

St. Regis Hotel. 11955 Wilshire Blvd., West L.A., CA 90025 (213–477–6021). Convenient to UCLA and Westwood Village, many restaurants nearby. Pool, free parking for guests.

Santa Monica—Reasonable

Carmel Hotel. 201 Broadway, Santa Monica, CA 90401 (213–451–2469). Renovated in 1984, this charming four-story hotel was originally built in the 1920s. One block from the beach, shopping, theaters. Color TV, free parking, Mexican restaurant.

Santa Monica—Very Economical

Stardust Motor Hotel. 3202 Wilshire Blvd., Santa Monica, CA 90403 (213–828–4584). A ways from the beach, in the heart of the Santa Monica shopping area. Friendly, multilingual staff, room service, laundry facilities, free parking, pool.

Airport—Reasonable

Airport Century Inn. 5547 W. Century Blvd., L.A., CA 90045 (213–649–4000, 800–421–3939). A pink and blue hotel, designed for comfort, with a garden atmosphere. Restaurant, lounge, 24-hour coffee shop, pool, airport shuttle service. There are many personal touches in this friendly family inn—a true value.

Friendship Inn Manchester House Motel. 901 W. Manchester, L.A., CA 90301 (213–649–0800). Small, comfortable, and hospitable. Full limo service to and from airport. Heated pool, car rental arrangements, satellite television, restaurant. Suites for large families and interconnecting rooms.

Skyways Airport Hotel. 9250 Airport Blvd., L.A., CA 90045 (213–670–2900). Within minutes of LAX, free limo service to and from airport. Laundry, room service, coffee shop, free parking.

Airport—Very Economical

Capri Motel. 8620 Airport Blvd., L.A., CA 90045 (213–645–7700). Just a mile short of LAX, this 51-room property has many services: a heated pool, complimentary Continental breakfast, and babysitting among them.

Days Inn—Los Angeles Airport. 5101 Century Blvd., Inglewood, CA 90304 (213–419–1234, 800–325–2525). Clean, friendly, convenient. Heated pool. Restaurant serves breakfast, lunch, and dinner.

San Fernando Valley—Reasonable

Beverly Garland's Howard Johnson Resort Lodge. 4222 Vineland Ave., North Hollywood, CA 91602 (818–980–8000). Popular with business and entertainment types, this seven-story hotel has a country-club atmosphere. Private balcony patios. Swimming and wading pools, tennis courts, lounge. Free parking. Coffee shop.

Holiday Inn—Burbank. 150 E. Angeleno Ave., Burbank, CA 91502 (818–841–4770, 800–HOLIDAY; in California, 800–465–4329). Very large hotel near all major Burbank studios. Full service, restaurant, lounge, 45 banquet and meeting facilities, pool and sauna. Five-story parking lot, free.

Safari Inn. 1911 W. Olive, Burbank, CA 91506 (818–845–8586). Frequently used for location filming. Very good services, fine French restaurant, cable television, cocktail lounge, pool, Jacuzzi.

Sherman Oaks Inn. 12933 Ventura Blvd., Studio City, CA 91604 (818–788–2203). Clean and comfortable in lovely residential neighborhood. Plenty of reasonably priced restaurants within walking distance. Pool. Near freeway to Universal Studios and NBC.

San Gabriel Valley—Very Economical

El Dorado Motor Inn. 140 N. Azusa Ave., West Covina, CA 91791 (818–331–6371). Located just off I-10, this Spanish-style motel, with garden, has many luxuries. Therapy, swimming, and wading pools; nearby restaurants.

Holiday Inn—Montebello. 7709 E. Telegraph Rd., Montebello, CA 90640 (213–724–1400; 800–238–8000; in California, 800–465–4329). Conveniently located near the Santa Ana Freeway and next to the City of Commerce, this hotel caters to the business person as well as the tourist. Restaurant, pool, cocktail lounge, free parking.

Ramada Inn. 840 S. Indian Hill Blvd., Claremont, CA 91711 (714–621–4831). Off I-10. Reservations necessary during Los Angeles County Fair and the Ontario Races. Pool, eight tennis courts, Jacuzzi. Miyako Garden restaurant.

Bed-and-Breakfast. Although this rather new approach to visitor accommodations is very popular in the small coastal communities north of Los Angeles, this city is just now waking up to their potential. More and more bed-and-breakfast inns are opening every year in Los Angeles County. They are conservatively priced ($50 to $70), offer highly personalized service, and are generally very small—so reserve a room as far in advance of your trip as possible. Ambience in these hideaways usually leans toward the quaint, with special touches like Californian flowers, fluffy towels and homemade meals.

Reservation services for these charming hostelries are handled by the following agencies: **Bed and Breakfast of Los Angeles,** 32074 Waterside La., Westlake Village, CA 91361 (818–889–8870 or 889–7325), and **California Houseguests International Inc.,** 18653 Ventura Blvd., #190, Tarzana, CA 91356 (818–344–7878).

Ys and Hostels. All of the hostels and Ys in the L.A. area offer simple accommodations, in which dormitories are segregated by sex; some have private or double rooms. In season, it's wise to make reservations. Discounted rates are available to members of the organizations that sponsor many of these establishments. One good source of information is the *American Youth Hostel Association, Inc.,* 1332 L St. NW, 8th floor, Washington, D.C. 20005. If you join their association, you'll receive a copy of the hostel guide and handbook.

Below is a list of L.A.'s Ys and hostels, beginning with the Ys.

Pasadena YMCA. 235 E. Holly St., Pasadena, CA 91101 (818–793–3131). Has beds for 128 men in single rooms, at $55 to $75 a week. Must provide own linens. Hall showers. Kitchen and laundry facilities. Also offers the usual Y facilities such as gym, weight room, running track. No curfew; open all year. Best to make reservations "a couple of weeks ahead." MasterCard, Visa.

Hollywood YMCA. 1553 N. Hudson, Hollywood, CA 90028 (213–467–4161). Facilities for men at $27 for singles, $35 for doubles. Open all year. Restaurant on premises as well as pool, gym, weight room, handball courts, and running track. This is a popular place; reservations are recommended. Visa, MasterCard.

American Youth Hostels

Hollywood Hostel. 1553 N. Hudson, Hollywood, CA 90028 (213–467–4161). Shares same building with Hollywood YMCA; guests have access to the Y facilities. Houses up to 50 men and women at $8 per night for AYH members with passports, $10 for others. Memberships not sold on premises. Anywhere from two to 13 people in dorm-style rooms, segregated by sex. Bunk beds; must provide own linens or sleeping bag. Hall showers, restaurant, laundry facilities. A midnight curfew is "recommended." Open all year. No reservations; strictly first-come, first-served. Try checking in during the mornings, when other people are checking out. Visa, MasterCard.

Los Angeles International Hostel. Building 613, 3601 S. Gaffey, San Pedro, CA 90710 (213–831–8109). Has room for 60 people at $7.25 for members, $10.25 for nonmembers. Memberships sold here; cost is $20 for the calendar year. Maximum stay is five days for members, two days for others. Eight to 12 people per room in bunk beds. Pillows and linens can be rented. Kitchen and laundry facilities, recreation room. 10 P.M. curfew. Open all year; during spring and summer, it's a good idea to make reservations about two weeks ahead. Cash or traveler's checks only.

Bill Baker International Youth Hostel. 8015 S. Sepulveda, Westchester, CA 90045 (213–776–0922). Shares a building with the Westchester YMCA, although the Y has no lodgings. Beds for 25 men and 25 women at $6 for members, $7 for others (memberships not sold on premises). Three-night maximum stay. Men and women are housed in separate rooms with cots for sleeping; sheets and pillows can be rented for 25 cents. No kitchen or laundry; showers are at the YMCA gym. Swimming and other Y facilities are available for $7.50 extra. Cafe on premises. Guests must be out of their rooms 9 A.M.–8 P.M., and there is an 11 P.M. curfew. Open June–mid-Sept. Reservations not needed. No credit cards.

Huntington Beach Colonial Inn Hostel. 421 8th St., Huntington Beach, CA 92648 (714–536–3315). A three-story Victorian house, close to the beach, with room for 39 men and women. Rates are $7.50 for members, $9 for others. Memberships ($20) sold on premises. Two to four people per room; couples can share a room with two twin beds and a little privacy. Some bunk beds. Linens can be rented for $1.50. Hallway baths and showers. Kitchen and laundry facilities, TV room, balcony, barbecue pit. Doors lock at 11, but you can rent a key for $1 if you leave a $10 deposit. Open all year. Reservations recommended 3 to 4 weeks ahead. Cash or traveler's checks only.

Share-Tel International Hostel. 20 Brooks Ave., Venice Beach, CA 90291 (213–392–0325). Spanish-style house just steps away from the Pacific; not your run-of-the-mill hostel. Four-person bedrooms have fully equipped kitchens (pots, pans, and microwaves) and private baths. Linens, bunk beds; laundromat nearby. $15 a day or $105 a week in season, lower other times of the year. $30 deposit required. Passport or student ID required. Visa, MasterCard.

HOW TO GET AROUND. From the airport. From LAX to downtown is approximately 15 miles, but timing is essential as trip could vary from 25 minutes to more than an hour. If possible, avoid scheduling your arrival during rush hours between 7 A.M. and 9:30 A.M. and from 3 P.M. to 7:30 P.M. *The Super Shuttle,* 9625 Bellanca Ave., L.A., CA 90045 (213–777–8000), operating 24 hours and providing door-to-door service, is an economical method of traveling to and from the airport. After picking up baggage, use courtesy phone at terminal to call the shuttle at 213–417–8988; it will arrive within 15 minutes. Cost ranges between $5 and $25, depending on destination. If you take the shuttle to the airport, plan for at least a two-hour trip, since the shuttle picks up others along the way; give six hours or more advance notice for pickup at the airport. Cabs to and from LAX run from $15 upwards depending on time of travel and destination in L.A. Most areas, like Hollywood and downtown, are on the high end (around $30 and up) with Marina del Rey and Venice at the lower end. RTD has bus service to LAX aboard express bus #439 for $1.20. #42 operates from downtown for 85 cents; #560 operates from the San Fernando Valley for $1.55.

By bus. Many believe that a tourist in L.A. is helpless without a car but the Southern California Rapid Transit District (RTD) disagrees. Local buses cost 85 cents (senior citizens, 40 cents) and 10 cents for each transfer, so it's certainly a bargain considering distances that could be covered for that price. Routes are complicated, though, so write ahead for timetables (to RTD, Los Angeles, CA 90013) or call 213–626–4455.

By taxi. There's virtually no chance you're going to hail a cab on a Los Angeles street. About the only places you'll find them waiting are at the airports, train, bus stations, and at some of the major hotels. You must order a cab by phone. The rates are high because of the distance between points in L.A.

By car. Dozens of rental car companies, large and small, offer vehicles of all types in Los Angeles. The trick to renting a car in this city is to shop around. As a general rule, the larger companies like Avis (800–331–1212) and Budget (800–527–0700) offer the best deal, but smaller firms like Rent-A-Wreck (213–478–4393) and Bob Leech's (213–673–2727) at LAX are also worth considering. Renting a car in the end will probably be a money-saver since getting from point *A* to point *B* in this town can be costly in a cab and time-consuming on the bus.

HINTS TO THE MOTORIST. Motorists venturing out in Los Angeles should be aware that the basin takes up 464 square miles. Driving in L.A. is an experience in itself. The city is served by more than 30 freeways; eight radiate from the downtown freeway loop and, with the exception of the Golden State (I-5), are named for their major destinations. By traveling the freeways, you will familiarize yourself with metropolitan Los Angeles, but be sure to secure a good map before setting out. AAA has many maps to assist visitors, an exceptionally good one being *The Guide to Los Angeles Freeway System.* Take notes on how to get to and from each destination to avoid getting lost, and always travel with telephone numbers of the hotel concierge or friends so that they can talk you back to your original destination should you lose your way.

California speed limits comply with federal law: Outside L.A. proper, speed limits are 65 mph; otherwise, drivers must stay under 55 mph. Tops for cars hauling trailers is 50, but lower limits sometimes are posted. General speed limit for school zones and residential and business districts is 25, again except when posted. There's no state requirement for posting warning signs or radar or mechanical or electrical speed-checking devices. A right turn on a red light is allowed if you've stopped fully and there's no sign reading "no right on red." Los Angeles has alternate side of the street parking for street cleaning so look carefully to see what the situation is on the day you are there. In places this is a very hilly city. When parking downhill, turn your steering wheel away from the street, with the tires against the curb. Parking uphill, turn the steering wheel toward the street and brace the tires against the curb.

TOURIST INFORMATION. **The Greater Los Angeles Visitors and Convention Bureau** provides free information on attractions, public transportation, hotels, restaurants, and nightlife, bimonthly calendars of special events, climate and self-guided tours. **The Downtown Visitors Information Center** is at the Atlantic Richfield Plaza, B Level, 505 S. Flower St. (at 6th), L.A., CA 90071 (213–689–8822). Open Mon.–Fri., 8:30 A.M.–5 P.M. **Hollywood Visitors Information Center** is at 6541 Hollywood Blvd. (213–461–4213). Call for hours.

In addition, each community maintains either a tourism bureau or chamber of commerce with information for the traveler. Here's a sampling. **Beverly Hills Visitors and Convention Bureau,** Chamber of Commerce, 239 South Beverly Dr., Beverly Hills 90212. (213–271–8174). 8:30 A.M. to 5P.M., Monday through Friday. **Santa Monica Tourist Information Center,** Santa Monica Blvd., at Ocean Ave. in Palisades Park. 213–393–7593. 10 A.M. to 4 P.M., seven days. **Pasadena Convention and Visitors Bureau,** 171 S. Los Robles, south of the Pasadena Mall. 818–795–9311. 9 A.M.-5 P.M. Mon.–Fri., 10 A.M. to 4 P.M. Sat. For those areas not listed, consult directory assistance.

Telephone assistance is available for *beach* and *surfing conditions* (213–451–8761), *road conditions* (213–626–7231), and *weather* (213–554–1212).

Free newspapers with information on events, restaurants, shopping, and nightlife are the Los Angeles *Weekly* and the *Reader.* They can be found in many stores and neighborhood restaurants, bookstores, and theaters.

HINTS TO DISABLED TRAVELERS. As a result of a California law introduced in July, 1978, disabled people driving vehicles in Los Angeles that have been issued appropriate license plates are allowed special parking privileges. They are permitted to leave their cars in special blue-marked parking spaces, to park for unlimited periods in limited-time spaces and to park free in metered spaces. Blind persons ride RTD for free.

For a listing of what historic sites can accommodate wheelchair travelers in Los Angeles, write to the Junior League of Los Angeles, 3d and Fairfax streets, L.A., CA 90036. This organization will provide a free copy of *Round the Town with Ease.* Be sure to include a self-addressed, stamped envelope. Hotels and motels that can accommodate disabled visitors are numerous in this city. Check with the individual establishment.

FREE EVENTS. In Los Angeles, plenty of free activities, events and cultural attractions keep busy even those with limited budgets. **Free Music** is a frequent offering. Noontime concerts at the **Triforium** (213–485–2437), at the Los Angeles Mall, corner Temple and Main streets, are offered every day. The Chamber Series includes outdoor concerts held in the theater in **Barnsdall Park,** 4800 Hollywood Blvd., are held Sunday afternoons in the summer at 2 P.M. On Sun. evenings, July–Aug., Burbank's **Stough Park** is the site of free evening big band concerts at 7:30. Concerts in the Sky, on the pool deck of the **Westin Bonaventure Hotel,** 404 S. Figeroa, take place Mon., Wed., and Fri. at noon throughout the summer. Another concert series on Sun. afternoons, **The Watts Towers Jazz Concerts,** is at 1765 East 107th St. Because the schedule is a bit uneven, call 569–8181 for more information. In Santa Monica at **Lincoln Park** on 7th St. and Wilshire Blvd., afternoon concerts are held one Sunday a month; The outdoor summer band schedule features an array of music from marches to jazz (213–458–8323). The big band sound and jazz are among the musical entertainment heard on some Sunday afternoons in August at the **William Grant Still Community Arts Center** at 2520 West View St., L.A. (213–734–1164).

Free festivals abound in the City of Angels throughout the year. The Pasadena **Tournament of Roses Parade** is on the first of the year (but if you don't get there the night before you probably won't get anywhere near the event). March is **Nation-**

al Mime Week, celebrated in various areas of the city, with the closing celebration in Venice. **Cinco de Mayo** or the day of Mexican Independence is an especially Californian, or southwestern, celebration. All over town festivities occur, one of the largest at the El Pueblo de Los Angeles State Historical Park. **Nisei Week** is in Aug., a Japanese festival in Little Tokyo at 1st and San Pedro streets that offers tea ceremonies, dances, martial arts demonstrations and other Japanese traditions. Another Southern California festival takes place at the San Gabriel Mission in Sept.; at the **Community Fiesta** such traditions as blessing the animals are performed. The **Los Angeles Street Scene** takes place in late September on all the downtown streets around City Hall. Eleven stages are set up and the entertainment is nonstop. In Dec., **Christmas boat parades** fill the Los Angeles Harbor, Marina del Rey, Newport Harbor, and Dana Point.

Throughout the year communities open their streets to display the work of **local artists.** The Los Angeles *Times, Daily News,* and *Herald Examiner* as well as local free papers like the Los Angeles *Reader* and the Los Angeles *Weekly* have information on these shows as well as other free events. Art in progress is one of the attractions at the **Santa Monica Fine Art Festival** in Aug. at Palisades Park. The **Santa Monica Art Show** in Oct. takes place in the open air Santa Monica Mall. At Century City in Apr. the **Spring Festival** hosts an art exhibition for 4 days. And at the **Westwood Sidewalk Art and Craft Show** in May, strolling musicians serenade as visitors look at the art displayed throughout Westwood Village streets.

TOURS AND SPECIAL-INTEREST SIGHTSEEING. The largest of the sightseeing companies in L.A. is *Gray Line* (213–481–2121), which offers tours of Pasadena and the Huntington Library, Hollywood and Beverly Hills, and Universal Studios, among many others. Offices, branches, and travel desks are operated in hotels throughout Southern California. Tours make pickups at major hotels and then join other sightseers downtown, at 1207 W. 3d St., for a mass departure.

Other operators include *Hollywood Fantasy Tours,* 1721 N. Highland Ave., Hollywood (469–8184), with a streamlined double-decker bus and a guide who notes 160 different attractions. *Starline Sightseeing Tours,* 6822 Hollywood Blvd. (213–463–3131), goes to movie stars' homes in Beverly Hills and Universal Studios.

Entertainment Tours

Burbank Studios. 4000 Warner Blvd., Burbank (818–954–1008). The VIP Tour, a guided walking tour of the lot shared by Warner Brothers and Columbia Pictures, is limited to groups of 12 adults and costs $20. This fairly technical tour focuses more on the actual work of filmmaking than the tour at Universal. Visitors can make reservations to dine in the studio commissary, the Blue Room, after the tour.

Music Center. 135 N. Grand, downtown L.A. (213–972–7483). The Symphonians, a dedicated group of volunteers, conducts free tours of all three theaters (the Mark Taper Forum, the Dorothy Chandler Pavilion, and the Ahmanson Theater) during the week and focus on the Dorothy Chandler Pavilion on Saturday. No tours Mon., Fri., or Sun. Call for times and availability.

NBC Television Studios. 3000 W. Alameda Ave., Burbank (818–840–4444, 818–840–3537). Guided, 1½-hour tours of the largest color TV facilities in the U.S. The tour includes Studio One, where the *Tonight* show is filmed, and a huge prop warehouse as well as explanations of communication-satellite and videotape processes. 8:30 A.M.–4 P.M., Mon.–Fri.; 10A.M.–4 P.M., Sat.; 10 A.M.–2 P.M., Sun. Adults $6; children ages 5–14, $4.

Universal Studios. 100 Universal Pl., Universal City (818–508–9600 or 818–508–5444). The six-hour tour of the world's largest TV and movie studio includes the parting of the Red Sea, an avalanche, an attack by the terrifying giant King Kong, and sets such as a New England village, an aged European town, and a New York street. At the Entertainment Center visitors stroll around to enjoy various shows; they visit Castle Dracula and confront a variety of terrifying monsters; and at the Screen Test Theater visitors may find themselves being filmed as extras in films already released and now recut to include them. Summer hours: daily, 8 A.M.–6 P.M. Other seasons: Mon.–Fri., 10 A.M.–3:30 P.M.; Sat.–Sun., 9:30 A.M.–3:30 P.M. Admission: $16.95 adults; $11.95 children; $11.50 seniors.

University Tours

California Institute of Technology. 315 S. Hill, Pasadena (818–356–6328). One-hour walking tours feature an overview of the vast research done on the lovely CalTech campus. Mon., Thurs., Fri., 3 P.M.; Tues.–Wed., 11 A.M.

University of California, Los Angeles. 405 Hilgard Ave., Westwood (tour reservation, 213–206–8147, 213–825–4338). Many tours are offered, some self-guided. Of particular interest are the Japanese and botanical gardens, the many libraries on campus, and the Frederick Wight Art Gallery, Mon.–Fri., 10:30–1:30.

University of Southern California. Downtown L.A. (213–743–2983). Specially trained guides give 45-minute walking tours of the campus, including points reflecting USC's athletic fame; the Mudd Hall of Philosophy, seen in a number of films; and the multimillion-dollar performing-arts center, which was dedicated by George Lucas and Stephen Spielberg. Mon.–Fri., on the hour, 10 A.M.–2 P.M.

PARKS AND GARDENS. Los Angeles offers more than a city's share of parks and gardens, welcome oases from her myriad concrete freeways and urban sprawl. A visit to one will put the whole city in perspective and, in most cases, not cost a cent in the process. For additional information on locating and identifying the city park facilities, contact the Los Angeles Department of Parks and Recreation at 213–485–5555.

Barnsdall Park. 4800 Hollywood Blvd., L.A. Designed and built by Frank Lloyd Wright, the Hollyhock House overlooks Hollywood's hustle and bustle from a hillside olive grove. Picnicking on the premises and free house tours. Also here: A Junior Arts Center for arts and crafts and theater arts instruction and the Municipal Art Gallery with contemporary exhibits by local talent.

Descanso Gardens. 1418 Descanso Dr., La Canada (818–790–5571). Once part of the vast Spanish Rancho San Rafael that covered more than 30,000 acres, Descanso Gardens now encompasses 155 acres of native chaparral-covered slopes, with plantings of camelias, azaleas, and roses. The Tea House features pools, waterfalls, and a gift shop. Flower shows, including chrysanthemum, daffodil, camellia, and bonsai competitions, are held at various times of the year. Guided tours available; trams traverse the grounds. Daily, 9 A.M.–4:30 P.M. Tea House open Tues.–Sun., 11 A.M.–4 P.M. Adults, $3; seniors, $1.50; and students, 75 cents.

El Pueblo de Los Angeles State Historical Park. 420 N. Main St., L.A. Adjacent to Olvera St., the city's oldest thoroughfare, the park—known as the Old Plaza—is actually a cobblestone square with shops, restaurants, and entertainment, all with a Mexican village feel.

Elysian Park. Entrances on Academy Rd., Stadium Way, Scott Ave., L.A. Overlooking downtown and the San Gabriel Valley, this hilly 575-acre park is still wilderness. Ten acres of rare trees are set apart in a grove and labeled for identification. Rec center with volleyball, basketball. Children's play areas. Nature trails, nine picnic areas. Near Dodger Stadium.

Ernest E. Debs Park, 4235 Monterey Rd., L.A. 306 acres with 1½-acre lake for boating and fishing. Designated a bird sanctuary. Picnicking in the woods.

Exposition Park. Figueroa at Exposition Blvd., L.A. (213–749–5884). Site of the 1932 Olympics, this 114-acre park adjoins the University of Southern California and contains the California Museum of Science and Industry and the Natural History Museum, the Los Angeles Swimming Stadium (open in summer to the public) and Memorial Coliseum for college football and soccer. Picnic grounds. A sunken rose garden on Menlo Ave. near Exposition Blvd.

Forest Lawn Memorial Park. 1712 S. Glendale Ave., Glendale (213–254–3131). Open 8 A.M. to 5 P.M. This 300-acre cemetery, with marble statuary and art, including replica of da Vinci's *The Last Supper* erected of stained glass, was the setting for Evelyn Waugh's novel *The Loved One.* Crucifiction Resurrection shown daily on the half hour from 10 A.M. to 4 P.M. Walking trails. **Forest Lawn Memorial Park–Hollywood Hills.** 6300 Forest Lawn Dr. (213–254–3131), Hollywood. Just west of Griffith Park on Hollywood Hills' north slope, the theme of this 340-acre sister park to Forest Lawn Glendale is American liberty. *The Many Voices of Freedom* film is shown daily, Revolutionary War documents are on display, and bronze and marble statuary includes Thomas Ball's 60-foot Washington Memorial and a replica of the Liberty Bell. On site are reproductions of Boston's Old North Church and Longfellow's Church of the Hills.

Griffith Park. Entrances on Los Feliz Blvd. at Vermont, Western and Riverside Drive, and off Golden State Freeway at Los Feliz exit (213–665–5188). Donated to the city in 1896 by mining tycoon Griffith J. Griffith, this is the largest city park in the United States with 4,000 acres. Seemingly endless picnic areas, hiking and bridle trails, three public golf courses, driving range, tennis courts. Travel Town runs miniature railroad and pony riding. Across from park at Riverside is public swimming pool and soccer fields. Los Angeles Zoo on park's north side. On south side is Griffith Park Observatory and Planetarium. Western Avenue entrance is the location of Ferndell, a half-mile of paths that wind through shade past waterfalls, pools and thousands of ferns. Small nature museum there on fern species.

Hancock Park. Curson Ave. at Wilshire Blvd., L.A. Location of the **Los Angeles County Museum of Art** and the **La Brea Tar Pits,** where at the bubbling asphalt, replicas of prehistoric beasts recreate fateful ventures into tar. Discoveries from the pits and other park sites are in the George C. Page Museum. Summer visitors can watch ongoing excavations for fossilized animals.

Highland Park. 6150 Piedmont Ave., L.A. (213–256–0621). Suburban park with picnic space amid the sycamores.

Huntington Botanical Gardens. On the grounds of the Huntington Library, 1151 Oxford Road, San Marino (818–405–2275). The Huntington's 130-acre garden, formerly the grounds of rail-tycoon Henry E. Huntington's estate, includes a 12-acre desert garden, featuring the largest collection of mature cacti and other succulents in the world, and a Japanese garden with traditional Japanese plants, stone ornaments, a moon bridge, Japanese house, walled Zen garden, and bonsai court. The Ralph M. Parsons Botanical Center houses a botantical library, a herbarium, and a laboratory for research on plants. Tue.–Sun., 1–4:30 P.M. Sun. reservations (818–449–3901) required.

Lincoln Park. 3501 Valley Blvd., L.A. (213–225–2838). In Mexican-American neighborhood with bilingual activities plus basketball and tennis. Picnicking under trees.

Los Angeles State and County Arboretum. 301 N. Baldwin Ave., Arcadia (818–446–8251). 127 acres of native and exotic plants, in natural-habitat display, and flowers in bloom. The demonstration home gardens were designed to provided homeowners with ideas for gracious outdoor living. The begonia house features about 200 varieties, and the tropical greenhouse has orchids, bromiliads, and ferns in a rain-forest setting. The historical section displays buildings from different periods in California's colorful past, with appropriate flowers and plants. Lasca Lagoon, one of the few natural freshwater lakes in Southern California, may look familiar: It has been used as a jungle setting for movies and television series, including *Tarzan* and *Fantasy Island.* Daily tours. Adults, $3; seniors and students, $1.50 children 5–12. Third Tues. of the month, free for everyone.

Los Encinos State Historical Park. 16756 Moorpark, Encino. In San Fernando Valley, contains an early California dwelling furnished with historically accurate furniture, household goods, and tools. Tours Wed.–Sun.

MacArthur Park. 2230 W. 6th St., L.A. (213–383–0493). In the 1920s and 30s, a hangout for the elite underneath the majestic palms, now MacArthur Park suffers from urban blight. Gathering place for loiterers who have, however, been unable to diminish the park's beauty. Sunday afternoon impromptu jazz jams. Large lake with boating in summer.

North Hollywood Park. 11430 Chandler Blvd., North Hollywood (818–763–5361). Just off Hollywood Freeway at Magnolia, this vast park has baseball diamonds, swimming, tennis, and open space for picnics and volleyball. Spanish-style library with Amelia Earhart statue out front.

Palisades Park. 851 Alma Real Dr., Pacific Palisades (213–454–1412). Between W. L.A. and the Pacific Ocean, just off Sunset Blvd. Lush with palms and eucalyptus trees. Picnicking and hiking.

Plummer Park. 1200 N. Vista, L.A. Small 6-acre park in West Hollywood geared to the elderly. Senior citizen center with organized activities: Horseshoes, shuffleboard, checkers and croquet. Tennis, children's playground, bird sanctuary, historic Plummer House open for tours Sun. Picnicking.

The Virginia Robinson Gardens. In Beverly Hills. 6.2 acres of terraced gardens, with rare and exotic plants, surrounding the former estate of a member of the department-store clan. One-hour guided tours, 10 A.M. and 1 P.M., Tue.–Fri. Adults,

$3; children, students, and senior citizens, $2.25. Because the garden's administration is trying to avoid congestion, you must phone (213–276–5367) for reservations and the address.

Roxbury Park. 471 S. Roxbury Dr., Beverly Hills. Softball diamond, tennis courts and lawn bowling in the middle of Beverly Hills. Youth programs, with summer theater productions performed on a portable stage. Picnics on groomed grassy patches.

Silverlake Park. 1850 W. Silverlake, L.A. (213–669–9509). Adjacent to the reservoir for which this section of town is named, there's volleyball and basketball courts, tennis courts and room for soccer, jogging and picnicking.

South Coast Botanic Garden. 26300 Crenshaw Blvd., Palos Verdes (213–544–1847). A study in recycling, this 87-acre garden was built on landfill and now boasts a man-made lake, paths, plant identification exhibits, and small wildlife. Guided bird walks. Daily, 9 A.M.–5 P.M. Adults, $1.50; senior citizens and students, 75 cents; children under 5, free. Tram tours, $1.50. Third Tues. of the month, free for everybody.

Sycamore Park. 4702 N. Figueroa Ave., L.A. Near Highland Park, picnicking among the sycamores.

ZOOS. Los Angeles Zoo. Griffith Park, off Golden State Freeway (213–666–4090, 666–5133, or 666–4650; guided tours, 664–1100). This 113-acre compound holds more than 2,000 mammals, birds, amphibians and reptiles, grouped according to their natural geographical areas. The zoo is noted for its breeding of endangered species; an Indian rhinoceros was born as recently as 1982. Children's zoo has petting pen where you can walk among gentle animals like lambs, goats, and chickens, and an animal nursery where newborn mammals can be seen in incubators. Camel, elephant or Clydesdale horse rides ($1). Koala bears from Australia are housed in an area resembling their natural habitat, complete with eucalyptus trees. A walk-through bird exhibit features more than 50 species from around the world. A tram serves the perimeter of the zoo. Snack stands and picnic areas are on the grounds. In summer: daily, 10 A.M.–6 P.M.; other seasons: 10 A.M.–5 P.M. No one admitted an hour before closing. Adults, $4.50; children 2–12, $2; seniors, $3.50. Baby stroller and wheelchairs can be rented. Free parking.

PARTICIPANT SPORTS. Los Angeles's year-round sunshine, geographic variety and near-perfect climate combine to create the sport activist's heaven. Two resources are available for offering further ideas of what's available in L.A.: The City of Los Angeles Department of Recreation and Parks, 200 N. Main St., 13th floor, City Hall East, L.A. (213–485–5515) and Los Angeles County Parks and Recreation Department, 433 S. Vermont Ave., L.A.; 213–738–2961. Below are a sampling of affordable outdoor recreational facilities:

Golf. In Griffith Park, there are three public golf courses: *Harding Golf Course* (213–663–2555), an 18-hole course at the entrance on Los Feliz at Riverside Drive; *Wilson Golf Course* (213–663–2555), also 18 holes at the same entrance and *Roosevelt Golf Course* (213–665–2011), 9 holes at the Vermont Entrance. All three courses are quite hilly. Near Beverly Hills is the *Rancho Park Golf Course* (213–838–7373), 9 and 18 holes at 10460 W. Pico Blvd., L.A. Near the beach is *Penmar Golf Course* (213–396–6228), a flat 9-hole course at 1233 Rose Ave., Venice. All courses mentioned are municipally run and so greens fees are reasonable, $8 for the 18-hole courses and $4.50 for the 9-hole courses on weekdays, higher on weekends. Clubs can be rented for a nominal charge but electric carts are expensive to rent.

Tennis. Try the Racquet Center of Universal City. Charges are $10 and under, depending on when you choose to play. For reservations, call 818–760–2303. Most parks have courts for $4 an hour. Try the ones at Griffith Park. For additional information contact the *Southern California Tennis Association,* Los Angeles Tennis Center, 420 Circle Drive, West L.A., CA 90024 (213–208–3838).

Jogging. Angelenos jog everywhere: on sidewalks, along busy streets, in parks, or at high-school and college tracks. The best place is definitely the beach, where the air is less congested with smog. Redondo Beach maintains an area along the ocean called "the Strand," designated especially for runners. San Vicente Boulevard, from Brentwood to Santa Monica, has a wide, grassy meridian where runners jog under the shade of coral trees. This path ends at the Palisades, high above the Pacific Ocean; there are benches and lawns on which to rest. Griffith, Will Rogers, and Elysian parks are all good places to run unobstructed by most traffic. For information and updates on races, pick up a free copy of *City Sports* at many bookstores, coffee shops, and newsstands.

Volleyball. From Santa Monica to Marina Del Rey, volleyball nets line the beach. Just bring your own ball along. Even if you haven't a team assembled, there are always bystanders interested in getting involved. The best part is there's no fee and no reservations required.

Hiking. Most of the large city parks, such as *Griffith* (213-664-1191), *Elysian* (213–225–2044), and *Will Rogers* (213–454–8212), have wilderness paths. Remember that you may be hiking in dry areas with no water provided.

Placerita Canyon Park in Newhall (805–259–7721) is especially geared to the hiker, for it has well-marked trails of varying length for amateur and seasoned hikers. Information is available on wildlife and flora; rangers can answer questions. The park is in the dry, rocky terrain with live oaks typical of the San Gabriel Mountains.

Angeles National Forest (818–574–5200) has several hiking trails in dry, mountainous regions; drinking water is not available.

For further information on area hiking and outings, contact the *Sierra Club,* 2410 Beverly Blvd., 213–387–4287.

SPECTATOR SPORTS. Angelenos are well known for their enthusiasm for sports, both participant and spectator. Whether you like to try to follow the bouncing ball, hockey puck, or fast-moving thoroughbred, you'll always be able to find an arena showcasing your favorite sporting action. Reduced-priced tickets may be very hard to find. Good seats are almost always available through one of many ticket agencies, but these businesses charge more than face-value for their tickets. As a general rule in Los Angeles sports-going: A face-value ticket to a premier event is a good deal so get 'em while you can and enjoy!

Baseball. The National League Dodgers play at Dodger stadium in Chavez Ravine above downtown L.A. (213–224–1400). For American League fans, the California Angels have their home base just down the road in Anaheim (714–634–2000).

Golf. Professional golf tournaments in Southern California are the *L.A. Open* at Riviera Country Club in Pacific Palisades, in late Jan., and the *Bob Hope Desert Classic* in Palm Springs in early Feb. The Southern California Golf Association (818–980–3630) will provide details.

Thoroughbred racing can be enjoyed at *Santa Anita Park* in Arcadia (818–574–7223), late Dec.–Apr., culminating in the $500,000 Santa Anita Handicap. Races are run at *Hollywood Park* in Inglewood, near Los Angeles International Airport (213–419–1500), Apr.–July, Wed.–Sun., with many special promotions during the year. Post time is 2 P.M. Harness racing can be seen at *Los Alamitos* (213–431–4161).

Basketball. Los Angeles now has two NBA teams in residence. The Los Angeles Lakers play their home games at the Forum in Inglewood (213–673–1300), and the Los Angeles Clippers bang the boards at the Sports Arena, 3939 S. Figueroa. Information, 213–748–6131.

Auto racing. Every year in April the streets of Long Beach are stripped of every speed limit sign as Indy-car drivers come from around the world to compete in the *Long Beach Grand Prix.* There's always a celebrity race the day before, too, so make plans to enjoy three full days of racing in Long Beach. Information is available from Long Beach Grand Prix Ass'n., 110 W. Ocean, Suite A, Long Beach, CA 90802.

Football. The Los Angeles Raiders play their home games at the Memorial Coliseum (213–322–5901), Sept. through January, while at the same time the Rams occupy Anaheim Stadium (714–937–6767) just down the freeway in Orange County.

Collegiate athletics are not only big in Los Angeles, but offer visitors the chance to see top-flight teams in action; the Bruins of UCLA (213–UCLA101) and the Trojans of USC (213–743–2620) go virtually all year-round, fielding teams in various sports.

Boxing events are held at the Forum in Inglewood (information 213–673–1300). Check local newspaper listings. The Los Angeles Kings play **ice hockey,** also at the Forum. Marinas in Los Angeles County host all classes of **sailboat races** and, on special occasions, powerboat and wind-surfing contests.

CHILDREN'S ACTIVITIES. From the area's many amusement parks to the simple pleasures of a day swimming or playing in the sand at the beach to a trek to one of Los Angeles's excellent museums, this city will not fail to delight children. Not everything has to cost a fortune (a day at the beach, for instance, is free), just be selective. Below is a sampling:

Kidspace. 390 S. El Molino Ave., Pasadena (818–449–9143). Museum where kids can talk to robots, direct a radio or television show, or visit a medical clinic. Educational and fun. Open during the schoolyear, 11 A.M.–4 P.M., Sat.–Sun.; 2–5 P.M. Wed. Ages 2–64, $2.25; babies free.

Los Angeles Children's Museum. 310 Main St., L.A. (213–687–8800). A learning center where children participate in such adventures as crawling through mock manholes to discover what goes on beneath the pavement. Summer, Mon.–Fri., noon–5 P.M.; Sat.–Sun., 10 A.M.–5 P.M. Winter (beginning late Sept.), Wed.–Thurs., 2–4 P.M.; Sat.–Sun., 10 A.M.–5 P.M. Summer hours are observed during school vacations. Wed.–Thurs., free. Sat. and Sun., $4.

The Hollywood Studio Museum. 2100 N. Highland Ave., opposite the Hollywood Bowl (213–874–2276). A shrine to the movie pioneers of Hollywood in the old Lasky Barn, built in 1895 as a stable and then used a movie studio for Cecil B. DeMille. Film paraphernalia from the golden days will give kids an idea of what it was like way-back-when. Tues.–Sun. 10 A.M.–4 P.M. Adults, $2; seniors and students, $1.50; children under 12, $1.

Los Angeles Philharmonic Symphonies for Youth. Dorothy Chandler Pavilion, Music Center, 135 N. Grand Ave. (213–972–0703). Hour-long concerts with appearances by young guest artists, Jan.–Apr. Tickets are substantially below the normal cost to see performances of this caliber.

Disneyland. 1313 Harbor Blvd., Anaheim (714–999–4565). Although not the bargain of the century, there's good value per dollar spent here, and what kid can visit Southern California and face their friends back home if they haven't been to the Magic Kingdom? There's $200-million worth of magic in the park so the admission price (children 3–11, $16.50; adults $21.50) is well worth it. Mon.–Fri., 10 A.M.–6 P.M.; Sat., 9 A.M.–midnight; Sun., 9 A.M. midnight. Mid-June–mid-Sept.: 8 A.M.–1 A.M., daily.

Knott's Berry Farm. 8039 Beach Blvd., Buena Park (714–220–5200). Again not a real bargain but worth the extra bucks if you have them (choose Disneyland first, then this park if you must make a choice). Imax theater with real-life feel of thrill rides is a highlight. Adults, $16.95; children, $12.95. Free parking. Summer hours: Sun.–Fri., 9 A.M.–midnight; Sat., 9 A.M.–1 A.M. Winter hours: weekdays, 10 A.M.–7 P.M.; weekends, 10 A.M.–midnight. Closed Wed. and Thurs. during winter, except holidays and vacation periods. Major credit cards.

HISTORIC SITES AND HOUSES. Bradbury Building. 304 S. Broadway, L.A. Inside this Italian Renaissance building, built in 1893 and among the city's most remarkable architectural achievements, is a Victorian World of elaborate grillwork, French-made wrought-iron railings, and decorations with Belgian marble and Mexican tile.

El Pueblo de Los Angeles State Historical Park. 845 N. Alameda St., L.A. (213–628–7164). Site of the founding of the city in 1781, now the middle of today's modern L.A., this historic park, centered on the Old Plaza and Olvera Street, recalls the city's Mexican beginnings. Historic buildings include the Pelaconi House (now a restaurant), the Old Plaza Church, the Garnier Building, and the Merced, the city's first theater, which has a bicentennial exhibit inside. Avila Adobe, 14 Olvera St., built in 1818, is furnished with antiques. Free walking tours of the area every hour, 10 A.M.–1 P.M., Tues.–Sat., start at 130 Paseo de la Plaza.

Gamble House. 4 Westmoreland Place, Pasadena (818–793–3334). A noted Pasadena landmark built in 1908, this outstanding design by California architects Greene and Greene is a masterpiece of the turn-of-the century Arts and Crafts Movement. It displays exceptional woodwork. Open for one-hour guided tours, Tues. and Thurs., 10 A.M.–3 P.M.; Sun., noon–3 P.M.; closed on major holidays. Adults, $4; senior citizens, $3; college students, $2; those 18 and under, free.

Huntington-Sheraton Hotel. 1401 S. Oak Knoll (818–792–0266). Although all of the original buildings of this magnificent hotel were closed in 1986 due to an inability to conform to earthquake regulations, the edifice built in 1906 is still worth a visit. There are 23 acres of landscaped grounds featuring the Horseshow and the Japanese gardens and the Picture Bridge. Free.

Mission San Fernando Rey de Espana. 15151 San Fernando Mission Blvd., Mission Hills (818–361–0186). One of two missions in Los Angeles County, this one was established in 1797 and named in honor of the 13th-century King Ferdinand III of Spain. Restoration began in 1923. Today, as you walk through the mission's arched corridors, you may experience *déjà vu,* that feeling of having been here before—and you probably have, vicariously, through episodes of "Gunsmoke," "Dragnet," and dozens of movie epics. The two-story convent is the largest adobe structure in California today. The plaza consists of a grand fountain, lushly planted gardens, and a bell tower. Museum, gift shop. Daily, 9 A.M.–5 P.M. Adults, $1, children 7–15, 50 cents.

Mission San Gabriel Arcangel. 537 W. Mission Dr., San Gabriel (818–282–5191). The magnificent church and museum house mementos of the Franciscan fathers who founded the mission and early visitors to San Gabriel. The cemetery tells the history of the mission through the people who lived, died, and were buried there. The Court of Missions, established in 1921, has models of each of the twenty-one missions still standing today. Daily, 9:30 A.M.–4:15 P.M. Adults, $1; children, 50 cents.

Watts Tower. 1765 E. 107th St. From 1920 to 1954, without helpers, Simon Rodia, an Italian immigrant tile setter, erected three cement towers embellished with bits of colored glass, broken pottery, and assorted discards. Plans are underway to stabilize and protect this unique monument, often compared to 20th-century architectural wonders created by Barcelona's Antonio Gaudi.

Wrigley Mansion. 391 S. Orange Grove Blvd., Pasadena (818–449–4100). Free guided tours of the 18,500 sq. ft. mansion, now home of the Pasadena Tournaments of Roses Association, Wed., 2–4 P.M., Feb.–Sept. The surrounding gardens cover 4½ acres and are open to the public daily. Free parking on nearby streets.

MUSEUMS. It may be hard to come in from the sun to visit any of the Los Angeles museums, but you'll be glad you did. They reflect the great diversity of culture and ethnic background of Southern California that can be found once you scratch away that Hollywood veneer. And at just a few dollars each for a good day's sightseeing, they may be the best vacation value around. Two museums, the California Museum of Science and Industry and the J. Paul Getty Museum, are free. The private collections left by art collectors of the area disprove the notion that Los Angeles is a city interested only in the trends of the moment.

California Museum of Science and Industry. 700 State Dr., L.A. (213–744–7400). Located in the Exposition Park neighborhood, southeast of downtown. Hands-on computer exhibits; animal husbandry exhibits, with 150 chicks hatching daily; economic exhibits on labor, trade, and banking; exhibits on the human body; and an aerospace museum (in a separate building). The Imax Theater shows 3 films daily on a 3-story screen that makes you feel you're in the picture. Gift shop and McDonald's. Free tours, 10 A.M. and noon, Tues.–Fri. Open daily, 10 A.M.–5 P.M. Free.

Craft and Folk Art Museum. 5814 Wilshire Blvd., L.A. (213–937–5544). Continually changing exhibits of traditional and contemporary art from many parts of the world. Gift shop. The restaurant upstairs, The Egg and the Eye, serves a stunning variety of omelets. Tues.–Sun., 11 A.M.–5 P.M. Closed Mon. Adults, $1.50; students and senior citizens, $1; children, 75 cents.

The J. Paul Getty Museum. 17985 Pacific Coast Hwy., Malibu, CA 90265 (213–458–2003). This replica of a first-century Roman villa was completed in 1974, to house the collection (Greek and Roman antiquities, European paintings from the thirteenth to nineteenth centuries) that the famous oil magnate began in the thirties. Tues.–Sun., 10 A.M.–5 P.M. Free, but reservations required. Write or call a week (more in the summer) in advance.

The Huntington Gallery. 1151 Oxford Rd., San Marino (818–405–2275). This shares the grounds of the Huntington Library and Botanical Gardens (see "Parks and Gardens"). Eighteenth- and nineteenth-century British and European art are featured here, the perennial favorites being Gainsborough's *Blue Boy* and Lawrence's *Pinkie.* The *Virginia Steele Scott Gallery for American Art* (1740–1930) was added in 1984. Book and plant stores, snacks and sandwiches. Call in advance to find out about morning tours. Tues.–Sun., 1–4:30 P.M. Reservations required Sun. Free admission, $2 parking donation "requested."

Los Angeles County Museum of Art. 5905 Wilshire Blvd., L.A. (213–857–6211). Established in 1965, this museum is composed of three buildings: The Ahmanson Gallery (the permanent collection), the Frances and Armand Hammer Wing (for temporary exhibits), and the Leo S. Bing Theater. Two new additions in 1986 are the Robert S. Anderson Building, which holds the museum's modern art collection, and a pavilion for Japanese art. Gift shop, cafeteria. Tues.–Fri., 10 A.M.–5 P.M.; Sat.–Sun., 10 A.M.–6 P.M. Adults, $3; students, senior citizens, and children 5–17, $1.50. Second Tues. of the month, everyone free.

Museum of Contemporary Art (MoCA). 250 S. Grand Ave., L.A. (213–621–2766). A permanent collection of international scope representing modern art, 1940 to present. Painting, sculpture, environmental work, and a media and performing arts program are showcased at two major sites in downtown Bunker Hill's redevelopment area. The main facility, at California Plaza, is a red sandstone building designed by one of Japan's most renowned architects, Arata Isozaki. The Temporary Contemporary, 152 N. Central Ave. at First St., is a colorful warehouse space also used for the collection. Hours: Tue., Wed., Sat., and Sun., 11 A.M.–6 P.M.; Thurs., Fri., 11 A.M.–8 P.M.; closed Mon. Adults, $4; students and seniors, $2; children under 12, free. Thursday, 5–8 P.M., admission is free to everyone.

The Natural History Museum of Los Angeles County. 900 Exposition Blvd., L.A. (213–744–3466). Opened in 1913, this is a striking Spanish Renaissance building housing permanent and temporary exhibits, including some of the finest fossils discovered in the La Brea Tar Pits. Gift shop, bookstore, cafeteria. Tues.–Sun., 10 A.M.–5 P.M. Adults, $3; seniors and students, $1.50; children 5–17, 75 cents. Parking is free, except during events at the neighboring Coliseum, when the fee is a hefty $5.

Pacific Asia Museum. 46 N. Los Robles Dr., Pasadena (818–449–2742). Patterned after a Chinese imperial palace, this museum was built in the early 1920s to display Grace Nicholson's collection of Far Eastern art. The Gallery 8 East, besides displaying contemporary folk art and crafts, also serves tea and dessert. Bookstore; original art sold in Collectors Gallery. Wed.–Sun., noon–5 P.M. Tours, Sun., 2 P.M. Adults, $2; seniors and students, $1.50; children under 12, free.

George C. Page Museum of La Brea Discoveries. 5801 Wilshire Blvd., L.A. (213–936–2230). In front of the Page museum are the La Brea tar pits, where prehistoric animals became mired in the sticky asphalt while they were hunting or drinking. Inside are the remains of some of these animals, recovered from the pits: Reconstructed skeletons of the doomed saber-toothed cats, wolves, mammoths, and other creatures. Murals show the world as it was during those prehistoric times, and visitors can go by the Paleontological Laboratory to see how the newly found tar-pit specimens are handled. Two short educational films are shown continuously during the day. Gift shop. Tues.–Sun., 10 A.M.–5 P.M. Adults, $3; students and senior citizens and children, $1.50. Second Tues. of the month, free to all.

Norton Simon Museum. 411 W. Colorado Blvd., Pasadena (818–449–3730). Once the Pasadena Museum of Modern Art, this museum now displays art spanning more than 2,000 years. Gift shop. Thurs.–Sun., noon–6 P.M. Adults, $2; students and senior citizens, 75 cents; children under 12, free. Sun. admission, $3.

Will Rogers State Historic Park Art Collection. 14253 Sunset Blvd., Pacific Palisades (213–454–8212). The Wild West lives on in this 31-room ranch house, the former home of the late humorist Will Rogers. There are works here by Charles Bell, Howard Chandler Christy, and Ed Borein, as well as many Indian crafts and Rogers's own personal memorabilia. Self-guided tour. Daily, 10 A.M.–5 P.M. No admission charge to enter house, but $2 per car to enter park.

Southwest Museum. 234 Museum Dr., L.A. (213–221–2163). The building's design was inspired by southwestern Hispanic and pueblo architecture, appropriate to the work contained inside. American Indian art is the central theme, but the museum's definition of "America's earliest inhabitants" finds room for work by the Meso-American and pre-Columbian cultures as well. Gift shop. Tues.–Sat., 11 A.M.–5 P.M.; Sun., 1–5 P.M. Adults, $3; students, senior citizens, $1.50; and children 7–18, $1.

FILMS. As one might expect in the capital of movies, Los Angeles offers free film showings. To see free films try The Natural History Museum (213–744–3414), films shown the first Tuesday of every month at noon; the UCLA Meinitz Auditorium (213–206–8170), for offbeat films on Wednesday and Friday; the Norris Theater at USC (213–740–6089), for classics on Saturdays and Sundays.

Spending two hours in a movie while visiting Los Angeles is not, as one might think, taking time out from sight-seeing. Some of the most historic and architecturally interesting theaters in the country are found here. They host first-run and revival films worth seeing if only to visit the famed movie palaces. Perhaps the most celebrated movie theater in the world, **Mann's Chinese Theater,** 6925 Hollywood Blvd. (213–464–8111), preserves the legend of Hollywood in cement. Formerly owned by Sid Grauman, the Chinese pagoda structure still carries out the oldest of Hollywood traditions, the hand- and foot-printing ceremony. Mary Pickford and Douglas Fairbanks were the first to leave their mark at the entrance to the theater in 1927 and today everyone from Judy Garland and Burt Reynolds to Star Wars' robots C3PO and R2D2 have donated their imprints.

The **Egyptian Theater** down the street at 6712 Hollywood Blvd. (213–467–6167), was built in 1922. Also once owned by Sid Grauman, the lobby maintains the ornate Egyptian decor for which it was made famous.

A contrast to Grauman's theaters, the **Cinerama Dome** at 6360 Sunset Boulevard (213–466–3401), one block west of Gower Gulch, is a futuristic geodesic structure, the first theater designed specifically for Cinerama in the U.S. A bargain price of $4 is offered here for the first two shows of the day, Mon.–Fri.

Movies are listed in the Calendar section of the Los Angeles *Times* and the Style section of the *Herald Examiner.* Capsule reviews and schedules are also found in the L.A. *Weekly* and *Reader,* two free publications stacked in coffee shops and the entrances of book and record stores. The most common price of admission to first-run movies is $5.

MUSIC. Los Angeles is no doubt the focus of America's contemporary music scene. Hundreds of recording studios and over twenty record companies are headquartered here. Performers and songwriters from all over the world converge on the city seeking gold-record manna. As a result, the hills are quite literally alive with the sound of live music. There are helpful listings of inexpensive ways to hear the music in the free papers, the Los Angeles *Weekly* and *Reader.* Below are some ideas:

The Greek Theater. 2700 N. Vermont Ave., at the entrance to Griffith Park (213–642–4242). Popular and classical concerts under the stars, June–Oct. Doric columns evoke the amphitheaters of ancient Greece.

Hollywood Bowl. 2301 Highland Ave., Hollywood (213–850–2000). Nestled at the base of the Hollywood Hills, this is one of L.A.'s most venerable landmarks. It seats four times as many people as the Greek Theater does, which means around 17,000 picnickers.

L.A. Street Scene Festival (213–459–9724). Sponsored by the Joseph Schlitz Brewing Company, this event began in 1978 and is held the second week in Oct. Ten square blocks around City Hall in downtown L.A. are closed to traffic; stages are built; and the public is invited, for free. It's an event that features new talents, established performers, such as Chuck Berry and Helen Reddy, veteran ensembles, such as the Los Angeles Philharmonic. In addition, there are strolling mariachi bands, soul groups, and enough ethnic food to feed a United Nations picnic.

The Music Center. 135 N. Grand Ave., L.A. (213–972–7211). One of three theaters here, the Dorothy Chandler Pavilion, is the winter home (Nov.–Apr.) of the *Los Angeles Philharmonic.* (The Philharmonic performs at the Hollywood Bowl, July–Sept.)

Universal Amphitheater. Universal City (818–980–9421). A $20-million face-lift in 1982 (and an added roof) have transformed this venue into a spectacular state-of-the-art hall. Pop concerts, with a heavy emphasis on rock, make up 70 percent of the schedule; the remainder is ballet and legitimate theater. Beautiful fountains enhance the amphitheater's new look, which has to be seen to be appreciated.

DANCE. Despite the fact that the Los Angeles Ballet went bankrupt in 1984 the L.A. dance community has taken a grand jeté in the 1980s. In addition to Los

Angeles's own Bella Lewitsky, yearly visiting dance companies include the Joffrey, American Ballet Theater, Martha Graham, and Paul Taylor, to name a few.

The Music Center, 135 N. Grand (213–972–7211), is the western home of **Robert Joffrey's** bicoastal ballet company; Feb. and Sept. In March is the yearly **Folk Dance Festival.** The Shrine Auditorium, 649 W. Jefferson (800–472–2272) hosts the **American Ballet Theater** in March.

UCLA Center for the Arts, 650 Westwood Plaza (213–825–9261) attracts masters of modern, jazz, and ballet, including Martha Graham, Bella Lewitsky, Paul Taylor, Hubbard Street Dance Company and Béjart along with its own UCLA Dance Company. Rush $6 tickets are available on the night of performance for full-time students and senior citizens.

STAGE. It's said that Los Angeles has become "the Broadway of the West." San Franciscans may take issue with that statement, but the scope of theater here has seen some rapid growth in the past five years. Small theaters are blossoming all over town and the larger houses, despite price hikes that have accelerated to $40 a ticket, are full more often than not. To beat the big-city prices of the large productions around town, take a look in any of the city's newspapers and you're often told of special prices for special performances. Or give the theater a call directly; often they'll offer a good rate to people who don't mind buying the ticket at the last minute. An hour before curtain can often mean as much as a 50 percent savings. *Ticketmaster* (213–480–3232 or 213–480–1722) offers a half-price, same-day service. Theatergoers may purchase tickets at *May Company* stores located downtown in Citicorp Plaza, in the Westside Pavillion shopping galleria, and in the Sherman Oaks Galleria. *Sportmart* and *Music Plus* stores also offer this service. **Los Angeles Theater Center,** 1089 S. Spring St. (213–627–6500), offers all types of events, including free workshops and performances.

Below is a list (very incomplete) of some of the theaters in town. Again, the newspapers carry information about current productions.

John Anson Ford Theater. 2580 Cahuenga Blvd. E., L.A. (213–464–2130). This theater was built primarily to show pilgrimage plays, and the setting resembles the environment of Jerusalem. Today it is known for its Shakespeare productions and free summer jazz and ballet concerts.

James A. Doolittle Theatre. 1615 N. Vine St., Hollywood (213–462–6666; charge line, 851–9750). Centrally located in the heart of Hollywood, this house offers an intimate feeling despite its large (1,038-seat) capacity. New plays, dramas, comedies, and musicals throughout the year. $15 to $35.

The Henry Fonda Theatre. 6126 Hollywood Blvd., L.A. (213–410–1062). Major plays in a nice space refurbished in 1985.

Pantages. 6233 Hollywood Blvd., Hollywood (213–410–1062). Once the home of the Oscar telecast and big Hollywood premieres, this house is massive (2,300 seats) and elaborate. Musicals direct from Broadway, but the acoustics are less than perfect. $17 to $34.

Shubert Theater. 2020 Avenue of the Stars, Century City (213–556–3895). Broadway musicals are usually on stage here in this 1,824-seat house. $25 to $45.

Mark Taper Forum. 601 W. Temple, L.A. (213–972–7211; charge line, 972–7854). Part of the Music Center, this 742-seat house boasts excellent acoustics in an intimate setting. The theater, under Gordon Davidson, is committed to new works and to the development of a community of artists. Many plays, including *Children of a Lesser God,* have gone on to Broadway from the Mark Taper.

Westwood Playhouse. 10866 Le Conte Ave., Westwood (213–208–6500 or 213–208–5454). The basic architecture of this acoustically superior, 498-seat theater is Egyptian, with mosaics and columns decorating the walls. Sightlines are perfect anywhere in the house. New plays, primarily comedies and musicals in the summer; many come in from Broadway. Jason Robards and Nick Nolte both got their start at this theater. $20 to $28.50.

SHOPPING. Unlike New York with its Fifth Avenue and London with its Oxford Street, Los Angeles is a hodge-podge when it comes to shopping. Rodeo Drive comes to mind as the one recognizable shopping thoroughfare, but compared to the others, it is extremely short—and it's not the usual destination for someone headed for a bargain. The fact is there are dozens of sections about town in which to buy. As a rule, shopping should be done not by the area but rather by the item. Below are some places in which to unearth some real finds:

The Cooper Building. 860 S. Los Angeles St., downtown L.A. Nine floors of small clothing and shoe shops offer some of the most fantastic discounts in the city. For instance, Andrew Geller shoes are discounted at *Taburi Shoes* on the main floor, and, *Icarus Fashion Designs,* also on the main floor, is the place to shop for that dressy affair. *Le Club Handbag Co.* on the mezzanine has wallets, belts, and designer handbags sporting labels by Moskowitz, Anne Klein, and Christian Dior, with savings of 25 to 85 percent. Men who go along for the Cooper Building experience will be happy to run into *Outlook for Men* on the 11th floor for a large selection of famous brand sportswear at factory direct prices up to 70 percent off.

For those on a budget who just can't keep themselves away from Beverly Hills, there are some excellent bargains during traditional sale periods. When inventories must be cleared out prices may be slashed as much as 80 percent.

Those looking into thrift-shops (very popular in Los Angeles) should be warned that old clothes and furnishings go for a pretty penny in certain sections of town. Don't buy on Melrose Avenue, but visit anyway to experience our city's answer to Greenwich Village. Instead, look for vintage clothing, fifties dinnerware and pottery, turn-of-the-century jewelry and art deco furniture in Pasadena around Colorado and Fair Oaks, in Sherman Oaks on Ventura Blvd., or in Silverlake on Sunset Boulevard.

DINING OUT. It wasn't too many years ago that L.A. was considered a gastronomic wasteland, but today gourmets all over the country (and even the world) are waiting to see what's coming out of the Southland's restaurant kitchens next. For thrifty eating, visitors have more options than fast-food establishments. Many ethnic as well as American restaurants serve meals that cost less than they could be made for at home. Oriental cuisine, especially Thai, is a good choice for those on a budget. Not only are the entrees reasonably priced, but diners can share dishes and get a really exciting meal in the process. Those visitors who are dying to try some of the more famous L.A. bistros might want to order a couple of appetizers instead of a nine-course meal.

Restaurant categories, based on the price of a meal for one, without beverages, tax, or tip, are: *Reasonable,* $12 to $15; *Very Economical,* $8 to $12; and *Low Budget,* under $8. Unless otherwise noted, all accept at least some major credit cards. Every attempt has been made to ensure that the list is up to date, but it is always advisable to call ahead.

Reasonable

Angeli. 7274 Melrose Ave., W. Hollywood (213–936–9086). This upscale pizzeria's pesto pizza with fresh garlic and onions begins to rival the fare at Spago (see the Recommended Splurge, below). Atmosphere is definitely 1980s with tiny dough sculptures lining the walls. Mon.–Sat., noon–midnight; Sun., 6 P.M.–midnight. Make reservations if possible.

Bon-Appetit. 1601 Broxton Ave., Westwood (213–208–3830). Live jazz music permeates this romantic eatery on Fri. and Sat. evenings. Favorites are Duck L'Orange and boneless breast of chicken sauteed with artichokes and mushrooms. Fresh seafoods daily. Quiches, sandwiches, salads for lunch. Full bar. Mon.–Fri., 11 A.M.–1 A.M.; Sat., noon–1 A.M.; Sun., 5 P.M.–12 A.M. Reservations, very popular.

Canard de Bombay. 476 S. San Vicente Blvd., West L.A. (213–852–0095). An elegant ambience sets the stage for English-style Indian food. More than 130 curries are made to order, ranging in flavor from extremely mild to extremely hot. Dinner only, Wed.–Sun., 5:30 P.M.–11 P.M.; Closed Mon. Reservations.

El Morocco. 8222 Santa Monica Blvd., West Hollywood (213–654–9550). Where else in the country can you find a home-style Moroccan restaurant that offers a full seven-course feast at reasonable prices? Daily specials include stuffed prunes, spicy halibut, and chicken with Jeruselum artichokes. Mon.–Sun., 5 P.M.–11 P.M. Reservations.

Europa. 14929 Magnolia Blvd., Sherman Oaks (818–501–9175). The menu here roams the world. Great goulash, terrific teriyaki—and even great matzoh ball soup. Tiny and casual. Reservations a must as this is a community favorite. Dinner daily.

Great Greek. 13362 Ventura Blvd., Sherman Oaks (818–905–5250). Check your inhibitions at the door. This joint, where everyone joins in the fun, is jumping with

Greek music and Old World dancing. Food is a delight: Loukaniki (Greek sausages), butter-fried calamari, and two kinds of shish kabob. Valet parking. Daily: lunch, 11:30–4:00 P.M.; dinner, from 4:30 until the last person goes out the door. Reservations.

Kitty's. 10924 W. Pico, West L.A. (213–470–1255). Go Caribbean at this Jamaican eatery where the homeland is advertised on posters on the wall. Curried goat is on the menu, as are oxtail stew and changing specials. Lunch weekdays, dinner every night except Sun.

L.A. Nicola. 4326 Sunset Blvd., Hollywood (213–660–7217). Nouvelle cuisine with Californian accent served in a lively atmosphere where owner Larry Nicola makes everyone feel like part of the family. Imaginative, changing menu, plus standard favorites like potato skin appetizers and one of the best dinner salads in the city. Full bar adjoins restaurant, with fresh look complimenting the sleek eatery. Rotating exhibit by local artists. Weekday lunches and dinner nightly except Sun.

Lucy's El Adobe. 5536 Melrose Ave., Hollywood (213–462–9421). An intimate Mexican restaurant that is a music-industry hangout. Arroz con pollo, enchiladas rancheros, and enchiladas verdes are specialties. Lunch and dinner, Mon.–Sat.

Tommy Tang's. 7473 Melrose Ave., West Hollywood (213–651–1810). This bustling restaurant in the midst of new-wave Melrose Avenue is controlled by an innovative Thai chef who comes up with exciting entrees like crispy duck with ginger and plum sauce and a great mixed seafood platter. New wine cellar and sushi bar, fresh fruit daiquiris, and a variety of Asian beers. Mon.–Fri., 11:30 A.M.–midnight; Sat. and Sun., 5:30–midnight. Sushi is served until 1 A.M. on weekends. Reservations.

Tony Roma's. 100 Universal City Plaza, Universal City (818–777–3939). This is a fun place, divided into nine separate rooms, each named for popular vacation destinations in the West—Palm Springs, Beverly Hills, Las Vegas, etc.—and each is decorated with antique lighting fixtures, hooked rugs, and velvet draperies. The menu includes many barbecued items, ribs and chicken are the most popular. A great place to bring the family. Lunch and dinner daily 11 A.M.–2 A.M.; breakfast in the summer only.

Yanks. 262 S. Beverly Dr., Beverly Hills (213–859–2657). This restaurant serves regional American cuisine in a simple, elegant bistro setting. Some favorites on the eclectic menu include chicken pot pie and spicy Cajun meatloaf. Mon.–Fri., lunch, 12 P.M.–3 P.M., and dinner, 6–11 P.M.; Sat. and Sun., dinner only.

Very Economical

Canter's. 419 N. Fairfax Ave., L.A. (213–651–2030). The most renowned Los Angeles deli, located in the Fairfax district, close to Farmers Market. The food is not what it used to be, but the name still attracts customers. A hangout for entertainers late at night. Open 24 hours.

Chin Chin. 8618 Sunset Blvd., Hollywood (213–652–1818). Chinese restaurant with high-tech decor, in the midst of the Sunset Strip. Eat indoors or out in this great people-watching area. Order the shredded chicken salad or Cantonese duck. Beer and wine. Lunch and dinner, Sun.–Thurs., 11 A.M.–11 P.M.; Fri. and Sat., 11 A.M.–12 P.M. Reservations.

Diamonds the Rib Place. 20022 Ventura Blvd., Woodland Hills (818–710–8900). Very American restaurant offers baby-back ribs, onion rings, and large, juicy steaks. Lunch and dinner, Sun.–Thurs., 11 A.M.–10 P.M.; Fri.–Sat., 11 A.M.–11 P.M.

Gorky's. 536 E. Eighth St., L.A. (213–627–4060). Russian avant-garde restaurant with the atmosphere of an art-school cafeteria. Hangout for downtown artists and laborers. Kasha, borscht, and piroshkis appear on the menu with espresso, wine, and beer. Local art decorates the high walls. Blues and jazz performances most evenings. Mon.–Thurs., 6 A.M.–2 A.M.; Fri.–Sat., 24 hours. Cash only.

The Hard Rock Cafe. 8600 Beverly Blvd., West Hollywood (213–276–7605). A vintage '59 Cadillac juts out of the roof, "Happy Days" 's Fonzie's leather jacket hangs on the wall, along with Elvis's motorcycle, and the waitresses are dressed 1950s style. American favorites: burgers, baby-back ribs basted in watermelon barbecue sauce, and apple pie. The restaurant's message? Rock'n'roll is here to stay. Daily, lunch and dinner.

Larry Parker's Beverly Hills Diner. 206 S. Beverly Drive, Beverly Hills (213–274–5655). Eclectic menu consisting of more than 400 dishes from Mexico,

America, and the Orient: ribs, chicken, fish, salads, fresh croissants, espresso. Jukebox plays music 24 hours a day. No dress code. A fun place for families as well as singles. No reservations.

Walia Ethiopian Cuisine. 5881 W. Pico Blvd., L.A. (213–933–1215). The decor is African, dishes are served communal-style, and one eats with the aid of *injera,* the Ethiopian flat bread. *Sambusas* are crispy meat-filled turnovers, and entrees include spicy stewed beef in red-pepper sauce, chicken stew, raw chopped beef with hot peppers and spicy butter, and a combination vegetable platter. Order the honey wine; it's homemade with raisins, hops, and honey and tastes like the nectar of the gods. Lunch, Tues.–Fri.; dinner, Tues.–Sun.

Low Budget

El Tepeyac. 812 N. Evergreen Ave., East L.A. (213–267–8668). Home of the largest burritos in town. This Mexican restaurant that offers a plain, kitchen-like ambience and patio as well as indoor dining. Closed Tuesdays but open from 7 to 11:45 on weekdays and until 11 on weekends. Cash only.

Johnny Rockets. 7507 Melrose, West Hollywood (213–651–3361). Always fun and always lively, this '50s-style diner has loads of '80s flair. Only 20 seats, so be prepared to wait. Juicy burgers, great chili and fries. Lunch, dinner daily. No credit cards.

Mon Kee Live Fish & Seafood Restaurant. 679 N. Spring St., L.A. (213-628-6717). One of Chinatown's best seafood restaurants. Not upscale in ambience but in cuisine it's a winner: Try the platters of salt baked shrimp, steamed grouper in black bean sauce or the cuttlefish. Usually crowded but reservations are only accepted for parties of six or more. Open daily, lunch and dinner from 11:30.

Philippe's Original Sandwich Shop. 1001 N. Alameda St., L.A. (213–628–3781). A 76-year-old cafeteria close to Union Station. Thick, juicy roast-beef sandwiches, stew, soup, salads, and chili. Everyone eats together at long tables. Coffee is still 10 cents a cup! Breakfast, lunch, and dinner, daily 6 A.M.–10 P.M. No reservations, no credit cards.

Roscoe's House of Chicken and Waffles. 1514 N. Gower St., Hollywood (213–466–7453). This soul-food restaurant serves mostly breakfast, whatever the time of day. There are hot, fresh biscuits, chicken livers, and feather-light waffles made from Roscoe's own mix. Very good chicken "fried to the bone," is served in various combinations with eggs or waffles. Open daily, breakfast, lunch, and dinner. No credit cards.

Recommended Splurge. Spago. 1114 Horn Ave., just off Sunset Strip, West Hollywood (213–652–4025). Owner Wolfgang Puck is the "golden chef" of L.A.; his restaurant is innovative and unique. The menu features produce, poultry, and seafood native to California. Wood-burning ovens cook your meals right in the dining room as a bit of a show. Many unusual pizzas, Santa Barbara shrimp, homemade duck sausage, ravioli filled with lobster. The fresh fish is served pure, grilled in butter only. Decorated in beige, the restaurant has small tables, ice-cream-parlor chairs, and fine art on the walls. This is an establishment patronized by the elite; it's great for celebrity spotting; there are rows of Rolls-Royces and Mercedeses in the parking lot. Dinner nightly. There's only one hitch: This is such an in-spot that it's hard to get a reservation, so call even before you get to town. A three-course meal, without beverage, tax, or tip, costs $25 to $40.

Coffeehouses and Cafés. Between meal dining is an inexpensive way to fill up and relax in Los Angeles. The kinds of establishments that make this possible run the gamut, from converted warehouses to spiffy new eateries to down-home, set-a-spell sorts of places. Sip a cup of Columbian-Jamaican coffee or wash down a piece of chocolate cheesecake with a glass of fresh lemonade. There's something for every kind of appetite that needs filling during the off-meal hours. Below is a selection of economical places to rest your feet and nibble on a snack during a visit to Los Angeles. All accept major credit cards unless noted.

Downtown L.A. Café. 418 E. First St., L.A., (213–680–0445). Artists and theater patrons go for the innovative salads and wines-by-the-glass in this brightly furnished café around the corner from the Temporary Contemporary Museum and near the Music Center. Coffee is fresh and rich, and only 65 cents a cup. Make reservations if you're planning to try out the café after theater; otherwise it's probably safe to just drop in. Tues.–Fri., 11 A.M.–9 P.M., Sat. and Sun., 11 A.M.–7 P.M. Sun. brunch.

The Original Pantry Café. 877 S. Figueroa, L.A. (213–972–9279). Thirties-style waiters dressed in black tails do the honors at what may be the oldest café in L.A. It's been open for 60 years straight, offering a nostalgic charm unmatched in the city. There are no reservations taken here and always a line, so be prepared. But, once inside you'll appreciate the home-style cooking and unpretentious atmosphere. Open daily, 24 hours. Cash only.

Café de Paris. 821 S. Spring, downtown L.A. (213–623–7308). Opposite the California Mart, this tiny hole in the wall offers a big French experience for weary bargain shoppers. Freshly baked goods and rich coffee are available at more than reasonable prices. Mon.–Fri., 7:30 A.M.–4 P.M.

Pete's Pot-Pouri Café. 4908 Fountain Ave., Hollywood (213–669–9563). What? Stuffed cabbage at $5.95? A T-bone steak for less than $8? This Russian-style eatery is a real find and the service is warm and friendly, to boot. Dessert can get as exciting as crepe suzettes. Open 11 A.M.–11 P.M. daily.

Michel Richard. 310 Robertson, Beverly Hills (213–275–5707). Tables are set on the sidewalk just outside the busy bakery and restaurant. Aromatic coffees, and tasty, luscious pastries and croissants. Largely French clientele. Open Mon.–Sat., 8 A.M.–9 P.M.

Joe Allen. 8706 W. Third St., Beverly Hills (213–274–7144). The walls are lined with theater posters. The food is for the most part simple but ample. Fresh soups, chops, steaks, nightly specials. Usually draws a talkative crowd, including many folks in the Industry. Daily, 11:30 A.M.–12:30 A.M. Make reservations.

Café d'Etoile. 8941½ Santa Monica Blvd., West Hollywood (213–278–1011). Settle down in one of the cushy booths in this tiny café and order the beef stew if you're hungry, a glass of wine if you're not. Lunch and dinner daily. Sun.–Thurs., 11 A.M.–11 P.M.; Fri. and Sat., 11 A.M.–12 P.M.

The Rose Café & Market. 220 Rose Ave., Venice (213–399–0711). This industrial edifice has been transformed into a pleasant eatery with crisp white walls, exposed beams, skylight, pastry and salad counters, and specialty shop of imported coffee accompaniments like jugs, containers and, of course, an array of coffee beans. Fresh pasta and gourmet salads are the favorites. Wine and beer. Open daily. Sat. and Sun. brunch. Call for current hours.

Cafe 50's. 838 Lincoln Blvd., Venice (213–399–1955). Baby-boomers will thrive in this American-style coffee shop spiffed up by period decor. Fifties photos adorn the walls, as do old advertisements and movie posters. Blintzes are to die for and the "Leave It to Beaver" omelette is a treat. Music boxes at each table play tunes for a nickle. Stop by if only for a cherry coke or banana split. Sun.–Thurs., 7 A.M.–11 P.M. Fri.–Sat., until 1 A.M. No reservations taken. Cash only.

The Espresso Bar. 34 S. Raymond Ave., Pasadena (818–356–9095). High vaulted ceilings, Persian rugs, and a fireplace create a sophisticated European environment in this cafe. Great for espresso, cappucino, and pastries. Impromptu jazz is performed in the alcove, where the acoustics are "mind-blowing." Open daily.

NIGHTLIFE AND BARS. During the evening hours, Los Angeles offers whatever kind of entertainment the visitor wants. For the most part, this isn't a late-night sort of town (last drink is often called for at 1:30, and by 2 A.M. most jazz, rock, and disco clubs close for the night), but at certain establishments the candle does continue to burn until all hours.

On the **Sunset Strip,** running from West Hollywood to Beverly Hills, you'll find quite an assortment of nighttime diversions. Comedy clubs, restaurants with piano bars, cocktail lounges and hard-rock venues proliferate. **Gazzari's,** at 9039 Sunset, is a Sunset Strip landmark for rock'n'roll and casual dress. No credit cards here but the prices are fair. The **Le Mondrian Hotel,** on the Strip, has a lively piano bar and attracts many in the music business, so chances are you could be well entertained. **The Laugh Factory,** at 8001 Sunset, is inexpensive and there's no age limit for the comedy acts and improvisational floor shows.

In **Hollywood** proper, there's plenty to do, but watch for streetwalkers and muggers if you're out late at night. That's not the best time to stroll the streets. Go inside places like **Club Lingerie,** at 6507 Sunset. This Art Deco night spot offers everything from reggae to big-band and the door prices vary according to the attractions. Bar hoppers won't want to miss Wednesday Night at the **L.A. Nicola Bar,** 4326 Sunset, next door to the restaurant. That's martini night and the opening of a weekly art show. **The Improvisation,** at 8162 Melrose in West Hollywood, is a transplanted New York establishment and proving ground for such luminaries as Liza Minnelli and Richard Pryor. You'll get plenty of entertainment without going broke. Such famous comedians as Robin Williams and Steve Martin try out their stuff at **The Comedy Store,** at 8433 Sunset. Cover charges vary.

In **Westwood,** home of UCLA, college kids take over the town in the nighttime hours. The in-spot changes more regularly than we revise this book so just ask someone on the street, and if they're local and under 30, they'll know.

The chances are that for certain night-crawlers the in-spot will remain **Chippendales,** 3739 Overland Ave., West L.A., which is well known for its male exotic dancers and waiters who strip. Wed.–Sun. is for women only, and on Tues. rock videos debut. The cover varies but is usually moderate and there's an occasional free night for the ladies.

Downtown try the **New Otani Hotel and Garden,** at 120 S. Los Angeles St., where the Genji Bar of this Japanese-style hotel offers a sentimental vocalist in the evening hours. At the five-story Romanesque-style **Variety Arts Theater,** 940 S. Figueroa, is near nonstop entertainment: vaudevillians, singers, magicians and comics. Try the fourth floor W. C. Fields Bar, rescued from a San Pedro waterfront saloon. Enjoy a "martoonie," a martini with a kumquat, and dance to dreamy big-band sounds in the Roof Garden or kick back in Tin Pan Alley. Admission is $5 at night for dancing; no admission charged if you dine there.

At 5 P.M., the cocktail hour, stop by at **Rive Gauche,** in Sherman Oaks, where it's as lively as at Henry Africa's in San Francisco or Charley O's in Manhattan. The prices are reasonable, and the proprietors lay out a near-bacchanalian buffet. For entertainment nearby, the **Palomino Club** (6907 Lankershim Blvd., North Hollywood) has been a favorite for more than three decades. Once strictly offering country western fare, the club has now diversified to a wider variety with rock and blues, too. Dancing every night except Tuesday, which is amateur night—anyone who thinks he or she has talent can perform . . . and they do. Light fare is served.

For laughs there's the **L.A. Connection** at 13442 Ventura Blvd. (818–784–1868) in Sherman Oaks. Sawdust on the floor and big brisket sandwiches are the style of this inexpensive deli-turned-comedy-club. Thurs.–Sun. evenings.

SECURITY. Take a good look at a map before exploring L.A. This is an extremely seductive city, and looks safer than it really is. Some areas, in fact, should be avoided altogether, or at least after daylight hours. Stay away from south-central Los Angeles along Imperial Highway and around the Sports Arena and Coliseum in Watts unless absolutely necessary. When you must be in that part of town, ride with car doors locked and park in secured parking lots. Hollywood Boulevard, with all its neon and bright lights, is also a haven for pickpockets and street criminals. Although a stroll along the Walk of Stars shouldn't be discouraged, take caution. See the foot and handprints at Mann's Chinese Theatre during the day if possible.

Should trouble arise, no matter where you are in Los Angeles County, find a telephone and dial 911 to summon assistance.

MIAMI

by
Carol Guensburg

Carol Guensburg is a features reporter for the Miami News; *she also produces its travel section. A native of Wisconsin, she worked for several other papers before migrating south.*

Ever since Henry Flagler's railroad nosed into the pioneer settlement in 1896 at the behest of Julia Tuttle, tourists have been coming to Miami. They come—11 million strong each year—to frolic along the beaches fronting Biscayne Bay and the Atlantic, to revel in the tropical sun and, in recent decades, to sample the tastes, sights, and sounds of a cosmopolitan center with a pronounced Latin accent.

Almost 40 percent of metropolitan Dade County's 1.8 million residents are of Hispanic descent, joining Anglo and black Americans and those of Caribbean origin in a lilting mélange at the southeastern tip of the Sunshine State.

Tourism is heaviest in winter, when "snowbirds" flee the cold and flock south, filling hotels and motels and spilling into the golf courses, charter fishing boats, and restaurants and onto the beaches. Their influx drives hotel and motel prices to a premium from Nov. 1 through March, considered "the season." Reservations are recommended at least six weeks in advance.

The chief attraction, of course, is the water. The abundant marine life and lush tropical vegetation, plus the availability of fresh water, helped draw a succession of people to what is now Miami. Earliest were the Tequesta Indians, then the Spaniards. It's a paradox that although Florida was the point at which America was discovered, it is among the spots in the nation to be most recently developed.

For a solid understanding of the area's history, start at the Historical Museum of Southern Florida in downtown Miami in the $42-million Cultural Center designed by Philip Johnson. The museum, which opened in April 1984, features a permanent exhibit that chronicles the evolution from settlement to sophisticated port city. There you can trace the origins and growth of downtown Miami, Miami Beach, Coconut Grove, Coral Gables, and Key Biscayne—Greater Miami's most popular tourist destinations.

The museum rests in the heart of old Miami, near the Miami River and the spot once known as Fort Dallas. The settlement thrived when the Widow Tuttle, "the mother of Miami," convinced Flagler to extend his railroad farther south in exchange for land. Its arrival swelled the population from 1,500 in 1896 to 5,000 by 1910. A real-estate boom in the twenties, and Miami's establishment as a military training center in World War II, boosted its population to a quarter-million by 1950. In the sixties, Cubans fleeing Castro's regime came 200 miles north; refugees continue to arrive from the Caribbean, especially from Haiti and politically unstable spots in Central America.

From the museum, you can savor Greater Miami's offerings in almost any direction. The most popular tourist destination is **Miami Beach,** 2.5 miles east of the mainland across Biscayne Bay. In the early 1900s, Carl G. Fisher pumped sand from the bay and used elephants to plow down mangroves, in the hopes of establishing a coconut plantation. It failed, but years later the resort business here took off. In the 1930s, it was a ritzy retreat for the elite; in the fifties and sixties it went family-style. Tourism, though still considerable, has slowed since those golden days; hotels along the "concrete canyon" of Collins Avenue converted to condos and displaced visitors. The island measures ten miles long north to south, and its Atlantic side is almost entirely hotels and motels. The largest is the plush Fontainebleau Hilton, with 1,224 rooms contained in its sweeping glass curves. Even if you can't afford to stay here, you should look. The lobby of the hotel, designed by Morris Lapidus in the late 1950s, features his trademark woggles (amoeba-shaped holes into which the pillars disappear) and bow-tie-tiled floor. Outside, pass through a cave–dining nook to the lagoon-style swimming pool.

A new boardwalk stretches from just north of the Fontainebleau south to 21st Street, providing a fine vantage point for the 300-foot-wide beach recently restored by the Army Corps of Engineers at a cost of $64 million. The lighted boardwalk will be the focal point of the evolving, 45-foot-wide Beachfront Park. Beyond the southern end of the boardwalk is the Art Deco District, a 125-block area bounded by Sixth and 23rd streets, and the ocean and Jefferson Avenue. It was put on the National Register of Historic Places for its approximately 800 streamlined, pastel-painted structures built in the twenties and thirties.

With the old mingles the new. Now open is the $3.6-million, 17-acre South Pointe Park (with restaurants, amphitheater, recreational facilities, etc.); just completed is the Miami Beach Marina (300 Alton Road), with nautical boutiques, restaurants and 400 slips, making it the largest facility of its kind in South Florida.

At the north end of the beach, you'll find the high-stepping Bal Harbour Shops (Neiman-Marcus, Gucci and Saks Fifth Avenue are among them), and beyond that Haulover Beach and the Motel Row of Sunny Isles.

Key Biscayne, actually a community of two islands just south of Miami Beach, is linked to the mainland via the Rickenbacker Causeway. Planted between Biscayne Bay and the Atlantic, it boasts two major parks—Crandon and Bill Baggs Cape Florida—that draw hordes to their beaches on hot afternoons.

Southwest of downtown Miami, along the bay, is **Coconut Grove,** where Bahamian and white settlers made their homes in the mid-1800s. Today, it's the SoHo of the South, with art galleries and boutiques interspersed among elegant eateries and century-old landmarks such as the Barnacle, home of Commodore Ralph Munroe, who settled here in 1877. The Barnacle now is a state historic site and museum. Another point of interest is Peacock Park, site of the long-gone Peacock Inn. It was built by George Peacock as the first mainland hostelry, at a time when Key West was South Florida's most populous city.

West of downtown is **Coral Gables,** one of the nation's first planned cities. Its founder was George Merrick, who laid out the streets of the well-to-do, Mediterranean-style community. Today, Merrick's boyhood home, at 907 Coral Way, operates as a museum and historic site. In the 1920s, William Jennings Bryan sold real estate from the Venetian Pool. Other important attractions are the Biltmore Hotel, Fairchild Tropical Garden and the University of Miami, the largest private university in the Southeast, founded in 1925.

Little Havana, north of the Grove and west of downtown, is another important district. Here is where many Cubans settled after their exodus from the island in the 1960s. The district's main commercial strip is Calle Ocho (S.W. Eighth Street), an enclave of espresso stands, restaurants and varied stores. Businessmen here often forgo suits in favor of the guayabera, a loose-fitting, embroidered shirt.

PRACTICAL INFORMATION

WHEN TO GO. The bulk of tourists comes to Greater Miami between Nov. and Mar., considered "the season," when the balmy weather here provides an appreciable contrast to that of northern climes. The Gulf Stream is a moderating influence, with daytime temperatures averaging in the low seventies and nighttime temperatures in the low sixties. This is also the dry season, in which the humidity is comfortably low and the sky typically clear. The picture changes come Apr., when hotel and motel rates fall, temperatures and humidity rise and the clouds roll in. Expect temperatures in the mid to upper eighties during the day, and the low to mid seventies at night. The rainy season lasts from May through Oct. so count on carrying an umbrella for the brief but heavy showers. It's cheaper to visit off-season, when lodging prices often are substantially reduced.

HOW TO GET THERE. By air. Almost 20 million passengers come through *Miami International Airport* each year, served by its 21 domestic, 41 international, and many regional airlines (more than any other airport in the country). A travel agent will be able to help you find out what charter flights are available or determine discount rates on regularly scheduled flights. Regional airlines (including *Gull Air* and *Piedmont*) offer many scheduled flights between Miami and other Florida vacation spots.

By bus. *Greyhound-Trailways* routes connect Miami with points throughout the country and offers a range in schedules and destinations. This is the most time-consuming means of transportation, but it's also the cheapest. Unlimited passes—those that allow you to travel anywhere and at any time within a particular period—are especially advantageous to the traveler who wants to visit other distant points of Florida.

The main *Greyhound* bus terminal is in downtown Miami at 99 N.E. 4th St. (374–7222). Suburban terminals are located in Coral Gables, Hialeah–Miami Springs, Miami Beach, and North Miami Beach. The main *Trailways* terminal also is in downtown Miami at 99 N.E. Fourth St. (373–6561). Suburban terminals are in Coral Gables and in northwest Miami.

By train. Two *Amtrak* trains—the *Silver Meteor* and the *Silver Star*—travel the eastern corridor daily between New York and Miami, making the trip in just over

Points of Interest

1) Aventura Mall
2) Bass Museum of Art
3) Bayfront Park; Bayside Marketplace and the MGM Bounty Exhibit; Torch of Friendship
4) Biscayne Kennel Club
5) City Convention Complex
6) Coconut Grove Exposition Hall
7) Fairchild Tropical Garden
8) Flagler Dog Track
9) Hialeah Park Race Course
10) Hotel Fontainebleau Hilton
11) Jai-Alai Fronton
12) Japanese Gardens
13) Lincoln Road Mall
14) Lowe Gallery
15) Marine Stadium
16) Bayside Shopping and Entertainment Complex
17) Little Havana
18) Theater of the Performing Arts
19) Mayfair House/Shops
20) Museum of Science and Natural History, Planetarium
21) North Shore Open Space Park
22) Omni International Hotel
23) Orange Bowl
24) Parrot Jungle
25) Planet Ocean
26) Seaquarium
27) South Florida History Museum, Arts Center
28) University of Miami
29) Vizcaya Art Museum
30) Calder Race Track
31) Metrozoo

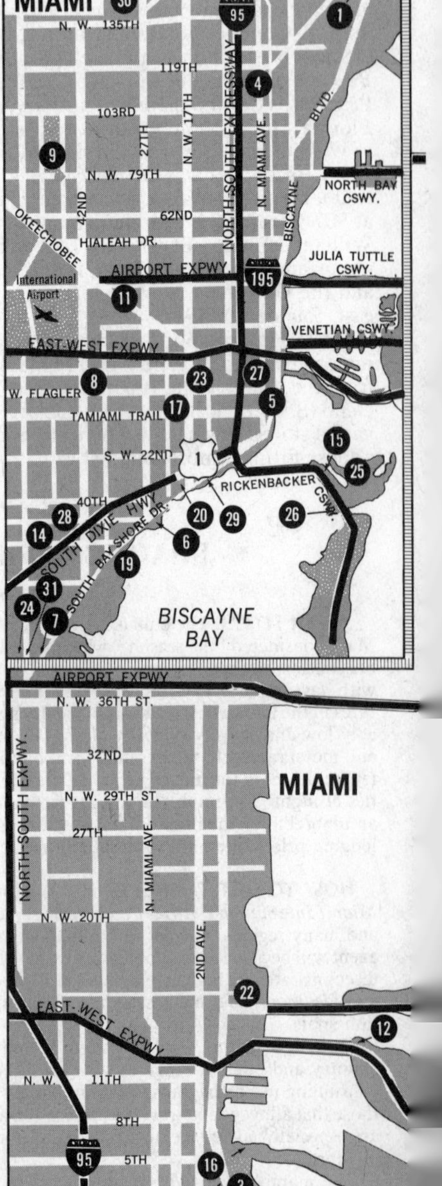

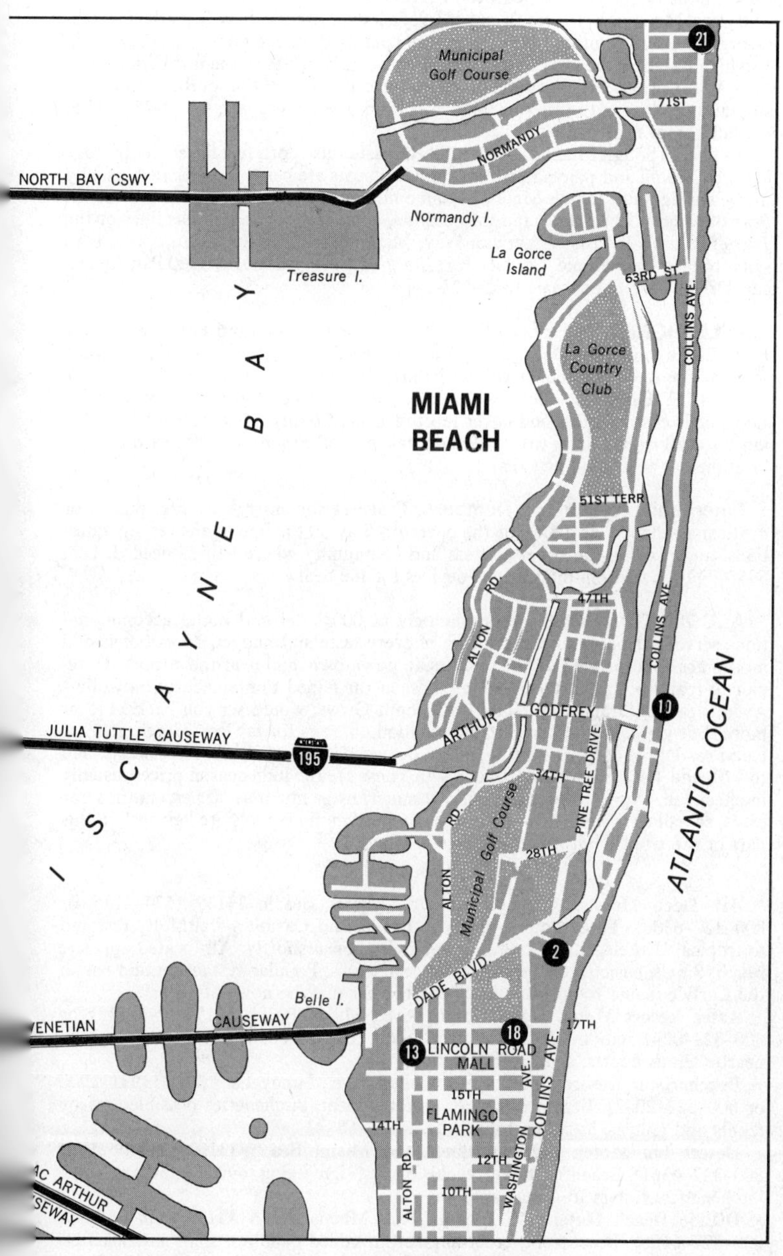
Municipal Golf Course
71ST
NORMANDY
NORTH BAY CSWY.
Normandy I.
La Gorce Island
Treasure I.
63RD ST.
COLLINS AVE.
La Gorce Country Club
MIAMI BEACH
B I S C A Y N E B A Y
51ST TERR
47TH
ALTON RD.
COLLINS AVE.
ATLANTIC OCEAN
GODFREY
10
JULIA TUTTLE CAUSEWAY
195
ARTHUR
34TH
PINE TREE DRIVE
ALTON RD.
Municipal Golf Course
28TH
2
DADE BLVD.
Belle I.
VENETIAN CAUSEWAY
18
17TH
13
LINCOLN ROAD MALL
15TH
FLAMINGO PARK
14TH
12TH
10TH
ALTON RD.
WASHINGTON AVE.
COLLINS AVE.
MAC ARTHUR CAUSEWAY
21

24 hours. Amtrak offers special round-trip fares and senior citizen discounts. For reservations or information, call toll-free 800–872–7245.

By car. Miami is at the south end of I-95, a long, 370-mile drive from the Florida-Georgia border. Another option, if you're coming from the north, is to take U.S. 1, which parallels the coast and passes scenic communities in the northern part of the state. However, it's a commercial strip through much of the southern half, with stop-and-go driving to test your patience. From the Gulf Coast, take I-75 or U.S. 41, both from near Naples.

By boat. Though Miami is the world's largest cruise port, few lines offer passage between Miami and points north except when boats are being repositioned, usually in the spring and the fall. Miami has nine lines and 20 ships based all year at the Port of Miami. For details and information, contact individual cruise lines or the *Port of Miami,* 1015 N. American Way, Miami (305–371–7678). An option is to sail into Fort Lauderdale. Contact *Port Everglades Port Authority,* 3360 Pan American Drive, Fort Lauderdale (305–523–3404).

TELEPHONES. The area code for all of Greater Miami (and Fort Lauderdale, Palm Beach, and Orlando) is 305. You don't need to dial the area code if it's the same as the one from which you're dialing. Information (directory assistance) is 1–555–1212. Dial 0 for operator assistance on person-to-person and collect calls. Local calls cost 25 cents and cover most of Dade County. However, it's long distance to call from Miami to Fort Lauderdale and other southern Broward County locations, so you must first dial 1.

Emergency Telephone Numbers. Dial 911 for emergency fire, police, or medical assistance, or dial 0 for the operator. Stay on the line to answer any questions, and provide the street address and community where help is needed. Dial 595–4749 for telecommunications devices for the deaf.

ACCOMMODATIONS. Approximately 60,000 hotel and motel accommodations serve metropolitan-area visitors of every taste and budget. Most hotels and motels are concentrated on the beaches, in downtown, and near the airport. To repair to really posh quarters, such as those at the famed Fontainebleau on Collins Avenue or the Grand Bay Hotel in Coconut Grove, would set you back $125 or more. But you can find comfortable vacation quarters for far less. Hotel rates are based on double occupancy. Categories, determined by price, are: *Reasonable,* $40 to $70, and *Very Economical,* under $40. These are the high-season prices, usually in effect Jan.–Apr. 1. Rates fall off in summer, by as much as 50 percent, in some cases, so call to inquire. Air-conditioning and swimming pools are "givens" in this part of the tropics. Other amenities are listed.

Reasonable

Art Deco Hotels. 1300 Ocean Dr., Miami Beach 33139 (534–2135 or 800–327–6306). Three hotels—**Carlyle, Leslie,** and **Cavalier**—faithfully restored to tropical '30s elegance. Several others due to open shortly. All located opposite beach. Small, basic rooms, some with ocean views. Popular restaurant and bar in the Carlyle (some rooms directly above the bar may be noisy at night).

Aztec Resort Motel. 15901 Collins Ave., Miami Beach 33154 (947–1481 or 800–327–0241 nationwide). Beachfront with coffee shop, entertainment nightly, nearby tennis courts, sight-seeing tours.

Beacharbour Resort Hotel. 18925 Collins Ave., Sunny Isles 33160 (931–8900 or 800–327–2042). Beachfront, with entertainment, kitchenettes possible, nearby tennis and golf, sight-seeing tours.

Desert Inn Motel. 17201 Collins Ave., Miami Beach 33160 (947–0621 or 800–327–6361). Beachfront, with tennis courts, sightseeing tours, restaurant, some kitchenettes. Caters to Canadians, too.

DiLido Beach Hotel. 155 Lincoln Rd., Miami Beach 33139 (538–0811 or 800–327–6105). Beachfront, entertainment, disabled facilities, some kitchenettes, Jacuzzi, sightseeing tours. Near Miami Beach Convention Center, Lincoln Road and more.

Dupont Plaza Hotel. 300 Biscayne Blvd. Way, Miami 33131 (358–2541). On the Miami River in downtown, near convention centers. Restaurant and bar, marina dock.

Golden Nugget Beach Resort. 18555 Collins Ave., Miami Beach 33160 (932–1445 or 800–327–0694). Coffee Shop, dining room, entertainment, disabled facilities, some kitchenettes. No charge for children under 15.

Hawaiian Isle Beach Resort. 17601 Collins Ave., Miami Beach 33160 (932–2121 or 800–327–5275). Kitchenettes available, cocktail lounge, sauna and Jacuzzi, tennis court, fitness facilities, sightseeing tours, Outrigger Lounge, children's playroom. On ocean.

Lifter's Waikiki Oceanfront Resort. 188th and Collins Avenue, Miami Beach 33160 (931–8600). Beachfront, entertainment, disabled facilities, kitchenettes available.

Monaco Resort. 17501 Collins Ave., Miami Beach 33160 (932–2100). On beach, with entertainment, disabled facilities, kitchenettes available, sightseeing tours, free HBO. Family-type atmosphere.

Riviera Courts. 5100 Riviera Drive, Coral Gables 33146 (665–3528). Near University of Miami. No restaurant or bar.

Sahara Best Western. 183 Street and Collins Avenue, Sunny Isles 33160 (931–8335 or 800–528–1234). On beach, with entertainment, disabled facilities, kitchenettes in half the rooms, no greens fees on local golf course, tennis courts. Family-oriented.

Suez Oceanfront Resort. 18215 Collins Ave., Miami Beach 33154 (932–0661 or 800–327–5278). On beach, with kitchenettes available, tennis courts, sightseeing tours. Daily activities program. German, French and Spanish spoken.

Tahiti Oceanfront Resort Motel. 16901 Collins Ave., Miami Beach 33160 (949–2255). Beachfront, entertainment, multilingual staff, kitchenettes available. Diners Club not accepted.

Very Economical

De Ville Inn–Downtown. 226 N.E. First Ave., Miami 33132 (374–7415). In downtown, paid parking, disabled facilities, cocktail lounge, easy access to retail and wholesale businesses and transportation systems.

Pier House Inn. 17451 Collins Ave., Miami Beach 33160 (931–7500). Beachfront, kitchenettes available, cocktail lounge, Tiki bar on beach, swimming pool with porthole. No American Express.

Budget Motel Chains. Days Inn. Two locations: *Miami Airport,* 3401 LeJeune Rd., Miami, FL 33142 (305–871–4221). *Miami–Civic Center–Downtown,* 1050 N.W. 14th St., Miami, FL 33136 (305–324–0200). The toll-free number for both is 800–325–2525. Gift shop, 24-hour restaurants, direct-dial phones.

Quality Inn. Two locations: *Quality Inn–South,* 14501 S. Dixie Hwy., Miami, FL 33176 (305–251–2000). *Quality Inn–Airport,* 1850 N.W. LeJeune Rd., Miami, FL 33126 (305–871–4350). The toll-free number for both is 800–228–5151. The south location has a Chinese restaurant (Chop Sticks); both have sun decks, game rooms, entertainment, laundromat, efficiencies, HBO.

Bed-and-Breakfast. Bed and Breakfast Co., Box 262, South Miami, FL 33243 (305–661–3270), coordinates lodging in approximately 35 homes in the Miami area, from oceanfront estates to island retreats to serene homes in nice residential areas. Rates are $32 to $65 in winter, $24 to $44 in summer, with the lower rates representing accommodations with shared bath. The price includes a Continental breakfast. Payment must be made in cash or by money order or traveler's checks.

Ys and Hostels. YMCAs in South Florida discontinued their lodging services in the late 1970s. Today, only one hostel operates in the area: **Clay Hotel and International Youth Hostel,** 1438 Washington Ave., Miami Beach, FL 33139 (305–534–2988). An affiliate of the International Youth Hostel Association, the hotel and hostel are located in a Mediterranean-style building spanning a block of Espanola Way, just a few blocks west of the beach. The hostel's rates are $8 for IYHA members and $10 for nonmembers; the price drops by $1, Apr. 1–Jan. 1. The hostel has a common kitchen and dining room. Rates at the hotel are $20 for double accommodations, $15 for a single. The surrounding streets have some of the most interesting Art Deco structures in the world, with literally hundreds of reminders of the Beach's glamorous old days. It's a spot beginning to emerge from a long slumber, as investors and yuppies are coming to see its potential for the future. However, certain side streets in this area are still rather run down, so exercise caution and travel with a friend at night. Reservations are recommended during the peak season.

HOW TO GET AROUND. From the airport. Miami International Airport is seven miles from downtown and roughly twice as far from Miami Beach; a trip via cab to the downtown area will cost about $10; to central Miami Beach, it will be approximately $15. Taxis are available on the ground level, just outside the baggage claim. *Metrobus* also serves the airport, with bus stops clearly marked on the ground level. The fare is 75 cents, plus 25 cents for transfers; exact change is required. Metrobus departs from the ground level every 30 to 60 minutes during the week and every hour on the weekends. For routing information and schedules, call 638–6700. *Red Top Sedan Service* provides 24-hour service aboard minibuses, with rates ranging from $6 to $9 a person, depending on destination. Go to the airport's Ground Transportation Centers or call 526–5764.

By bus. County-run Metrobus runs local and express buses throughout metropolitan Dade County. The fare is $1 in coins; transfers an additional 25 cents. Route maps and Metrobus information are available at the airport's ground-level waiting room or by calling 638–6700. If you have time, write in advance to *Maps by Mail,* 3300 N.W. 32nd Ave., Miami, FL 33152.

By Metrorail. The elevated rapid-transit system, which opened in May 1984, provides a panoramic view of the "Magic City" along its 20.5-mile route. Metrorail operates 6 A.M.–midnight daily. The fare is $1, and 25 cents more for a transfer to Metrobus. Exact change is required, though there are money-changing machines in the stations. For information, call 638–6700.

By taxi. Metropolitan Miami is served by more than 1,500 privately owned taxis. Rates are based on meter fares of $1 for the first one-third mile and 20 cents for each additional one-sixth mile. Each 48 seconds waiting costs 20 cents, and there's a $1 airport surcharge. Among the best bargains from airport to hotel is *Central Cab* (532–5555), which allows up to five people to ride for the price of one passenger. From the airport to Miami Beach, that would be about $14.50. Taxi services are listed in the yellow pages; among the major operators are *Checker Cab* and *Metro Taxi,* 1995 N.E. 142nd St., North Miami (888–8888), and *Yellow Cab,* 3775 N.W. 36th St., Miami (444–4444).

By rental car. Driving is the recommended mode of transportation here, even if you have to rent. Miami has some of the cheapest rates in any city, with many special offers available as part of packages. The area is served by all the major firms such as *Hertz, Avis,* and *National.* But you can reserve a car from a smaller agency, then take an airport limo to the rental lot to pick it up. Among the best deals are those offered by *A-Jiffy,* 16495 N.W. 27th Ave., (621–5566); *A-OK,* 2925 N.W. 36th St. (633–3313); *Alpha,* 2390 N.W. 39th Ave. (871–3432); *Budget,* 2601 N.W. 42nd Ave. (871–3053); *Chrysler Rental System,* 8455 S. Dixie Highway (667–5651). Rates range from $15 to $19, with weekly rates from $79 to $89. Be sure to inquire about insurance rates before you sign for the car.

HINTS TO THE MOTORIST. The intersection of Flagler Street and Miami Avenue in downtown Miami divides the city into quadrants. Miami Avenue divides east–west, and Flagler divides north–south. To get around, remember that "streets," "lanes" and "terraces" run east–west; "avenues," "courts" and "places" run north–south.

Heavy traffic clogs the main roads and thoroughfares during rush hour, 7–9 A.M. and 4–6 P.M. weekdays. It's best to take alternate routes or delay travel until less busy times. I-95 has a car-pool lane, marked by a diamond, for cars with at least two occupants during rush hour.

Parking isn't too much of a problem. There is metered parking throughout commercial sectors, with sufficient lots in the downtown area. However, be sure to check rates first. Private firms operate many lots, some of which charge as much as $20 per day. Two county-operated lots cost only $2 per day: the parking garage at the intersection of N.W. Second Avenue and Flagler Street, adjoining the Cultural Center, and another on N.W. Second Avenue between Third and Fourth streets. Elsewhere, street parking is allowed except along curbs painted yellow or where prohibitions are posted.

Florida speed limits comply with federal law: 55 mph on highways and freeways. In most city limits, the speed is restricted to 25 mph unless otherwise posted. Right turns on red generally are permitted.

The heavy, sudden showers typical in late spring and summer pose a hazard in drainage-poor Miami. When the rain begins, increase your following distance, turn on your headlights, and reduce your speed. When approaching standing water, reduce speed to a crawl to prevent splashing and stalling your engine. Out of the water, tap your brakes gently to dry the brake pads and to test the brakes' effectiveness. Good windshield wipers are essential.

TOURIST INFORMATION. More than 20 offices in the Greater Miami area, and most hotels, stock brochures detailing entertainment, attractions, and historic sites. The promotional material typically is in English and Spanish; sometimes in French. The *Greater Miami Convention & Visitors Bureau,* 4770 Biscayne Blvd., Penthouse A, Miami, FL 33137 (305–573–4300), has a wide range of maps, pamphlets, and information on special events and festivals. Other sources of information are the *Greater Miami Chamber of Commerce,* 1601 Biscayne Blvd, Miami, FL 33132 (305–350–7700); the *Greater Miami Hotel and Motel Association,* 300 Biscayne Blvd. Way, Suite 719, Miami, FL 33131 (305–371–2030); the *Coconut Grove Chamber of Commerce,* 2820 McFarlane Rd., Coconut Grove, FL 33133 (305–444–7270); the *Coral Gables Chamber of Commerce,* 50 Aragon Ave., Coral Gables, FL 33134 (305–446–1657); the *Key Biscayne Chamber of Commerce,* 95 W. McIntyre St., Key Biscayne, FL 33149 (305–361–5207); and *Sunny Isles Resort Association,* 17070 Collins Ave., Suite 257, Sunny Isles, FL 33160 (305–947–5826).

Foreign currency exchange. At least two institutions—BankAmerica and Barnett Bank—have offices at Miami International Airport. *BankAmerica* operates a 24-hour branch (526–5677) on the second level of Concourse E. There are no limits, and the branch also offers free travelers checks. *Barnett Bank*'s branch (883–2600) operates 9 A.M–4 P.M. weekdays and 9 A.M.–noon Sat. It's located on the second level, Concourse C, in front of Eastern. Barnett also exchanges currency at two other locations, in downtown Miami and Miami Beach, with weekday hours from 9 A.M.–5 P.M.: 150 W. Flagler St., Miami (789–3170) and at 420 Lincoln Rd., Miami Beach (674–6416). Other exchanges: *Bank of Miami,* 100 E. Flagler St., Miami (579–3027), 9 A.M.–3 P.M., Mon.–Thurs., and 9 A.M.–4 P.M., Fri. *Southeast Bank,* 101 S.E. Third St., Miami (375–7780), 8 A.M.–3 P.M. weekdays.

HINTS TO DISABLED TRAVELERS. Since 1974, all new buildings have been designed for easy access for the disabled. Elevators are coded in Braille, building entrances are gently sloped, and public restrooms have wider doors and special rails and stalls particularly suited to the wheelchair-bound visitor. Miami Beach's new boardwalk has wheelchair access at the 24th and 29th Street entrances, and at Crandon Park on Key Biscayne a ramp adjacent to the cabana area provides easy access. Metrorail, the rapid-transit system, has ramps and Braille; Metrobus is accessible to the visually handicapped.

Bird Drive Park and Therapeutic Campground, 3401 S.W. 72nd Ave. (665–5319), was specifically designed for the disabled. Its nature trails have rails for the visually impaired, and its solar-heated pool ($1 admission) has a hydraulic lift. The park also has overnight accommodations and special programs. **Country Gentleman Stables,** 15500 S.W. 200th St. (233–6615) offers a riding program for paraplegics. For details on provisions at other parks, call *Metro-Dade Parks and Recreation Department* (579–2676), the *City of Miami Park and Recreation Department* (579–6900) and the *Miami Beach Recreation Division* (673–7720).

Other resource centers for the disabled are the *City of Miami Information Office,* 174 E. Flagler St., Suite 1007, Miami, FL 33131 (305–579–6325); *Greater Miami Hotel & Motel Association Inc.,* 300 Biscayne Blvd. Way, Suite 718, Miami, FL 33131 (305–371–2030); the *Florida Restaurant Association,* 1065 N.E. 125th St., Suite 409, Miami, FL 33161 (305–891–1852); the *Citizens Information and Referral Service,* 600 Brickell Ave., Miami, FL 33131 (305–579–2200); and *Handicapped Opportunities,* 2501 Coral Way, Miami, FL 33145 (305–375–3566).

FREE EVENTS. South Florida's sunny, warm climate invites year-round festivals, outdoor events, and special tours. For complete up-to-the-minute listings, check the "Weekend" sections of The *Miami Herald* and The *Miami News.*

Ringing in the new year is the annual **Orange Bowl Festival,** Dec.–Feb. Among its highlights are the **King Orange Jamboree Parade** of bands and floats on downtown Biscayne Boulevard, immediately followed by the **Fiesta by the Bay,** a fling with international music, food, and fireworks in nearby Bayfront Park, leading up to the Orange Bowl Football Classic. Miami's Latin community stages its **Three Kings Parade** Jan. 6, along S.W. Eighth Street in Little Havana. Miami Beach pays tribute to streamlined structures of the 1930s and arts and crafts of the 1980s in its annual **Art Deco Weekend.** Celebrated in January, it draws crowds to Ocean Drive for a street fair replete with arts, international foods, and walking tours of the historic area. Late January brings the **Coral Gables Art Show,** an outdoor festival along Miracle Mile.

February highlights include the **Coconut Grove Annual Arts Festival,** South Florida's largest, with hundreds of displays and food booths lining Main Highway and Grand Avenue. The **Miami Film Festival** is a marathon showing of art and some commercial films, for which several free lectures usually are scheduled.

Carnaval Miami is the March highlight. The week-long celebration culminates in "Calle Ocho: Open House," a kaleidoscope of color and food and music unfurling in a glittering parade and booths.

April brings **Dade Heritage Days,** focusing on South Florida's history. Weekend events continue into May and are staged in various comunities.

May's major gala is the **Miami International Festival,** an annual celebration of the area's many cultures, sponsored by the City of Miami at the Coconut Grove Exhibition Center.

June's big event is the **Goombay Festival,** in which Junkanoo bands, steel drummers, and other performers strut down Coconut Grove's Grand Avenue in a celebration of the community's Bahamian roots.

July features an all-American celebration on Miami Beach's South Beach, marking **Independence Day** with music, foods and impressive fireworks. Later in the month, the **Miccosukee Indian Village** hosts an outdoor music festival.

October highlights include the **Columbus Day Regatta** at Coconut Grove's Dinner Key, and the **Hispanic Heritage Festival,** with special events including the "Hispanic Folklore Festivaland Festival" of the Americas, a two-day celebration at Tropical Park.

In November, there's South Miami's **Annual Arts Festival,** a street show of arts and crafts and foods; the **Miami Greek Festival** at St. Andrew's Greek Orthodox Church (595–1343), and a **Harvest Fair** at Tamiami Park. Call 251–7758 for dates.

TOURS AND SPECIAL-INTEREST SIGHTSEEING. By boat. Several companies operate sightseeing cruises on Biscayne Bay, with narrative in both English and Spanish on some cruises (call to confirm which times). *Nikko Gold Coast Cruises,* Haulover Park Marina, 10800 Collins Ave., Miami Beach (945–5461) offers four tours, from the two-hour, $6.50 cruise past the luxury estates of Millionaire's Row, to the $22 Gold Coast Special. *Island Queen,* 400 S.E. Second Ave. (behind the Hyatt Regency) (379–5119), cruises past the private islands of Biscayne Bay, Millionaire's Row, and the Port of Miami, with daily departures at 10:30 A.M., 1:30 and 4:30 P.M. Admission is $6 for adults, $3.50 for kids. You can simultaneously dine and sightsee on two three-hour cruises (Nov.–May only) offered by *Haulover Cruises,* Haulover Park Marina (947–6105). *Show Queen,* Crandon Park Marina, 4400 Rickenbacker Causeway, Key Biscayne (361–9418), offers nightly dinner cruises with a three-piece combo providing music.

By bus. *American Sightseeing Tours,* 4300 N.W. 14th St. (871–2370), offers a range of half- and full-day bus tours to the Everglades, Six Flags Atlantis, Metrozoo, Miccosukee Indian Village, Omni International, Parrot Jungle, Seaquarium, and Vizcaya ($10 to $24).

By foot. Birdwatchers can take to *Greynolds Park,* 17530 W. Dixie Hwy., North Miami (945–3425), for weekly tours Thurs. at 6 P.M.; extra walks Sat. mornings in spring and summer. Hikers with an interest in the past can take a *Historical Trail Walk* at *Arch Creek Park,* N.E. 135th St. and Biscayne Blvd. (944–6111), on Sat. afternoons, and learn about plant and animal life and the Tequesta Indians who once roamed the area. *Matheson Hammock Park,* 9610 Old Cutler Rd., Coral Gables (666–6979), offers exploration walks at 10 A.M. Sat., Nov.–Mar., and hosts a *Bayshore Walk* monthly except in winter. There are Sun. tours (1 and 3 P.M.) of the *Preston B. Bird and Mary Heinlein Fruit & Spice Park,* 24801 S.W. 187th Ave., Homestead (247–5727). $1.

The Miami Design Preservation League conducts weekend tours of the *Miami Beach National Historic District,* a premier collection of art deco architecture. For details, contact the League, 1236 Ocean Dr., Miami Beach (672–2014).

PARKS AND GARDENS. There are two major parks on Key Biscayne, the resort and residential island just south of Miami Beach, with access via the Rickenbacker Causeway ($1 toll). **Crandon Park** is Dade County's largest, attracting some 1.2 million visitors a year with its 2.5-mile public beach on the Atlantic and its 700-acre expanse. Entrance fee is $1 per car. Sunbathers can unfurl their towels on the beach or pay $12.50 for a cabana. The grounds also feature an 18-hole championship golf course, a marina (with sight-seeing tours of Biscayne Bay), bicycle trails and restaurants. **Bill Baggs Cape Florida State Park** (361–5811), at the tip of the key, is 406 acres dotted with picnic areas, bike paths, and a mile-long beach and seawall for fishing. A prime attraction is the historic Cape Florida Lighthouse and keeper's house, which was built in 1825, and is Dade County's oldest structure. Tours daily, except Tues., at 10:30 A.M., 1, 2:30, and 3:30 P.M. Lighthouse tours are 50 cents; park admission is $1 per car, 50 cents per passenger.

Besides Key Biscayne, beachcombers can turn to **Miami Beach's** 10.5 miles of restored Atlantic shoreline and 300-foot-wide public beach. A boardwalk that opened in 1984 stretches from 21st to 46th streets and is steadily being surrounded by a 45-foot, landscaped Beachfront Park. Ultimately, the boardwalk will extend the length of the beach.

Greater Miami's newest recreation center is **José Martí Park,** 351 S.W. Fourth St. (579–6959), which opened in 1985 and honors the Cuban patriot and poet. Its nearly ten acres, bordering the Miami River, feature Mediterranean-style buildings and sidewalks, a swimming pool with bathhouse, basketball and handball-racquetball courts, softball field, wading pool, playground, restaurant, and docking facilities.

Another popular retreat is **Matheson Hammock Park** in Coral Gables. The park has 560 acres and features picnic areas, boat ramp, bike paths, and marina. Its beach surrounds a salt-water lagoon, and fishing from the rock wall is popular.

Busiest of Metro-Dade's many parks is **Tropical,** 7900 S.W. Bird Road; 226–8315). Weekends, the 275-acre park's jogging trails, parcours stations, bike paths, and picnic areas are crowded with people reveling in the fresh air and sunshine. The park has two lakes for swimming, fishing and boating, soccer and softball fields, picnic areas (some with shelters), a boxing center, and an 18,500-seat stadium. Horse shows are held nearly every weekend at the Equestrian Center, and festivals are staged here periodically throughout the year.

The botanist—or virtually anyone interested in plants and gardens—should make a point to visit **Fairchild Tropical Garden,** 10901 Old Cutler Road, Miami (667–1651), the largest tropical botanical garden in the continental United States. The garden was founded in 1938 by Col. Robert H. Montgomery, and today boasts more than 5,000 species, including impressive collections of palms and cycads, orchids, tropical flowering plants, and bromeliads. Landscaping of the garden's 83 acres was done by William Lyman Phillips, a colleague of Frederick Law Olmstead. A guided tram tour ($1) provides an overview and information on the garden's history and collections; self-guided walking tours are also available. Open daily, 9:30 A.M.–4:30 P.M., with admission $3 for adults, free for kids 13 and younger.

Another stop recommended for the plant aficionado is **Preston B. Bird and Mary Heinlein Fruit & Spice Park,** 24801 S.W. 187th Ave., Homestead (247–5727). Its grounds feature more than 250 species of exotic fruit-, nut- and spice-producing plants, including oranges, mangoes, bananas, grapefruit, gourds and more; fruit and nuts that have fallen to the ground are yours. Guided tours are available Sun. 1 and 3 P.M.; they cost $1.

Orchid Jungle (26715 S.W. 157th Ave.; 247–4824) features orchids from every part of the world growing on huge oak trees in a jungle setting. It's open daily from 8:30 A.M.–5:30 P.M. Admission is $3.50 for adults, $2.80 for youths 12–17 and $1.25 for kids 6–12. The fee includes a free corsage for women.

ZOOS. In 1981, Metro-Dade moved its menagerie of tigers, deer, and other critters from its 40-year home in Key Biscayne's Crandon Park to its new **Metrozoo,**

at 12400 S.W. 152nd St., just west of the Florida Turnpike exit (251–0400), a cageless zoo on 225 acres far west of Miami proper. Today, the zoo showcases more than 100 species of animals, including a rare white Bengal tiger, gorillas, giraffes, zebras and elephants. A new attraction is the $1-million aviary "Wings of Asia," with more than 45 species and almost 400 birds in an open-air setting. An elevated, air-conditioned monorail provides a panoramic overview; is $2.90 for adults, $1.90 for children. Metrozoo has a petting zoo, and it stages an elephant show and "flying free" bird show several times daily. Elephant rides also are available. Adults, $4.50; children $2. Daily, 10 A.M.–5:30 P.M.

Kids usually go ape over **Monkey Jungle,** 14805 S.W. 216th St. (235–1611), a Miami tourist fixture in which the monkeys are "free" and the visitors are "caged." Hundreds of monkeys, gorillas, and trained chimpanzees make their homes here in a simulated rain forest. Daily, 9:30 A.M.–5 P.M. Adults, $5.50; children 5–12, $2.50.

A favorite of young and old alike is **Seaquarium,** on the Rickenbacker Causeway, Key Biscayne (361–5703), south Florida's largest tropical aquarium. The main building is built around a huge tank shared by thousands of fish and several wizened sea turtles. Daily, 9 A.M.–to 6:30 P.M. Adults, $8; seniors, $6.80; and children, $4.

Thousands of spectacular birds soar "free" at **Parrot Jungle,** 11000 S.W. 57th Ave., (666–7834), a tourist attraction that opened in 1936. You can see parrots skating, cockatoos driving miniature cars, and other feathered friends performing tricks in six daily shows at the Parrot Bowl. Parrots will perch on your head and shoulders in the photo area. The noise level is comparable to that of the Orange Bowl just after a Dolphin touchdown. Lush tropical vegetation lines the paths to the various cages or nesting areas, and the jungle gives way to a beautiful cactus garden with mosaic-tiled benches and striking stone towers. The coffee shop is a perfect place to relax and watch the birds and tourists. Daily, 9:30 A.M.–5 P.M. Adults, $6.75; children 6–12, $3.25.

PARTICIPANT SPORTS. Because of its climate and location, Greater Miami obviously is awash with opportunities for water sports. Most tourists have a choice of hotel pool or the ocean, but the ultimate freshwater **swimming** setting is *Venetian Pool,* 2701 Desoto Blvd., Coral Gables (442–6483). The pool and its caves were carved from coral rock; it also has a beach. Daily, 10 A.M.–4:45 P.M. Adults, $2.50; children 12 and younger, $1. Locker fee is $1.

If **sailing's** your thing, you can rent boats by the hour (approximately $18 and up for one that holds at least four), half-day ($70 and up) or full day ($125 and up). Call *Dinner Key Marina* in Coconut Grove (579–6980) or *Miami Beach Marina,* 300 Alton Rd. (673–6000). Powerboat rentals are available from *Crandon Park Marina* on Key Biscayne (361–5421); *Flamingo Lodge,* Marina and Outpost Everglades National Park (305–253–2241), *Miami Beach Marina* (673–6000), or *Pelican Harbor Marina,* 1275 79th St. Causeway (947–3525).

More than 2,000 species of saltwater and freshwater **fish** lure anglers to the Miami area. If you have a rod and reel, you can try your luck off the causeways, and there's no charge; consult a tackle shop to locate hot spots. *Haulover Fishing Pier,* 10501 Collins Ave., Miami Beach (947–6767), is open round-the-clock and charges $2 for adults and $1 for children; rod and reel rental is $5, with a $25 deposit. There's no charge, but no rental facility either at the *International Sunshine Pier* on the southeastern tip of Miami Beach. Numerous **party boats** cater to fishermen, and rates are low. At *Haulover Docks,* 10800 Collins Ave., Miami Beach (945–3801 or 949–1173), you'll find George Kelley's fleet of six party boats. Half-day trips cost $14 plus $3 rod and reel rental. Longer trips are available for $21 plus $3 rod and reel rental. The *Tiki,* 450 Sunny Isles Blvd., Sunny Isles (945–8571), has three trips daily for $12, plus $3 for rod and reel rental.

For **bicyclists,** 138 trails thread through Greater Miami. *Miami on Two Wheels a Day,* a brochure published by the Greater Miami Convention & Visitors Bureau, 4770 Biscayne Blvd., Penthouse A, Miami, FL 33137 (305–573–4300), lists 15 of the most popular ones. Among them are trails at *Crandon Park Beach* and *Bill Baggs Cape Florida Recreation Area,* both on Key Biscayne; *Matheson Hammock Park* in Coral Gables and *Tropical Park* on Bird Road. Bikes can be rented from cycle shops by the hour or by the day; consult the Yellow Pages.

Joggers find many paths and routes in this flat, flat area. They also find at least 20 Vita courses throughout the county. Favorites are those in *Margaret Pace Park,*

N. Bayshore Dr. and 17th Terrace, Miami, *Tropical Park,* 7900 Bird Rd., and *David Kennedy Park,* S. Bayshore Dr. and Kirk St., Coconut Grove.

Golfers can choose from about 20 public courses abundant with challenges and lush greens that stay that way 365 days a year. Among them are *Bayshore Golf Course,* 2301 Alton Rd., Miami Beach (532–3350), an 18-hole course. Just two blocks east of that is a par-three, nine hole course also operated by the City of Miami Beach. Other courses are the *Biltmore Golf Course* (1210 Anastasia Ave., Coral Gables (442–6485), the *Briar Bay,* nine holes, at 9373 S.W. 134th St. (235–6667), the *Country Club of Miami,* 6801 N.W. 186th St., North Miami (821–0111), the *Doral Country Club,* five courses, at 4400 N.W. 87th Ave., Miami (592–2030), *Key Biscayne* 6700 Crandon Blvd., Key Biscayne (361–9139), *Miami Springs,* 650 Curtiss Parkway, Miami Springs (888–4331) and *Normandy Shores Golf Course,* Biarritz Dr., Normandy Isle, Miami Beach (673–7775).

Public **tennis** courts are located in parks throughout Dade County. Among the best facilities are those at *Flamingo Park Tennis Center,* 1245 Michigan Ave., Miami Beach (673–7761), with 13 clay and four hard courts. Weekdays, 9 A.M.–9 P.M. weekends and holidays, 9 A.M.–6 P.M. Fees are $2 an hour during the day and $2.50 at night. *Key Biscayne Tennis Association,* 6702 Crandon Blvd., Key Biscayne (361–5263), operates five clay and five hard courts, open daily from 8 A.M.–10 P.M. Fees are $3 per hour; $5 an hour nights and weekends. *Tropical Park Tennis Center,* 7900 Bird Rd. (223–8710), has 12 hard courts open daily 9 A.M.–10 P.M. except Sun., when the hours are 9 A.M.–8 P.M. Fees are $1.25 per hour days, $1.85 at night. Among the other choices are *Coral Pine,* 6965 S.W. 104th St. (666–1797), *Salvadore Park Tennis Center,* 1120 Andalusia Ave., Coral Gables (442–6562) and *Surfside Tennis Center,* 8750 Collins Ave., Surfside (866–5176).

SPECTATOR SPORTS. Auto racing. The *Miami Grand Prix*'s $250,000 purse attracts the top racecar drivers from around the world to downtown Miami, where the streets are temporarily transformed into a track lined with concrete barricades and bleachers. The event usually is held in February. Contact the Greater Miami Chamber of Commerce (1601 Biscayne Blvd., Miami 33132; 350–7700). October brings *Championship Auto Racing Teams* (CART) to Tamiami Park (11201 S.W. 24th St.; 223–7070). *Stock-car racing* is scheduled every Saturday at 8 P.M. at the Hialeah Speedway, W. Okeechobee Road, Hialeah; 821–6644. Gates open at 6 P.M. Admission is $6 for adults ($5 for folks 64 or older, or with Medicare cards), $1 for kids 6–12.

Baseball. Teams in the "Grapefruit League" warm up here before the season starts in April. The Baltimore Orioles nest in Miami for spring training and play exhibition games at Bobby Maduro Miami Stadium (2301 N.W. 10th Ave.; 635–5395). Seats are $6 box, $4.50 reserved and $3.50 general admission. The Miami *Marlins,* Class A affiliates of the San Diego Padres, also play at Miami Stadium, mid-Apr.–Aug. Call 735–5395 for schedule and ticket information. The University of Miami Hurricanes, the top collegiate baseball team in 1982 and 1985, play in the cozy Mark Light Stadium on campus in fall and spring. Tickets are $4 general admission. Contact University of Miami Hecht Athletic Center, Coral Gables (284–3244).

Basketball. The University of Miami plays at the James L. Knight Center, 400 S.E. Second Ave., Miami; 372–0929; call 284–3244 for the U-M schedule. Florida International University plays at Sunblazer Arena on the main campus, on the Tamiami Trail (Rt. 41, at 117th Ave.). Phone 554–2900 for information.

Football. The Miami Dolphins, an NFL powerhouse team and two-time Super Bowl winners, play at the new Dolphin Stadium, in the suburbs about 15 miles north of downtown; 2269 N.W. 199th St.; 643–4700. Preseason begins in August and the regular season runs from Sept.–Dec. The University of Miami Hurricanes, national collegiate champions for the 1983 season, also play at the Orange Bowl. For schedules and game times, contact U-M at 284–3244.

Golf. Among the big tournaments is the *Doral-Eastern PGA Open* held in Feb. or Mar. on the "Blue Monster" course of the Doral Hotel & Country Club (4400 N.W. 86th Ave.; 592–2000).

Jai Alai, a handball-like Basque game in which players with curved baskets attached to their arms swat a hardball around a three-sided court, draws spectators to the *Miami Jai Alai Fronton* (3500 N.W. 37th Ave.; 633–6400). Mon.–Sat., 7:15

P.M., and Mon., Wed., and Sat. at noon. General admission is $1; parimutuel betting is permitted.

Greyhound racing is at two locations: *Biscayne Kennel Club,* 320 N.W. 115th St., Miami Shores (754–3484) late Oct.–Dec. and May–June. *Flagler Dog Track,* Miami (649–3000), has races late Apr.–June.

Thoroughbred racing. Three tracks—*Calder Race Course,* N.W. 27th Ave. and 210th St., (625–1311), *Gulfstream Race Track,* U.S. 1, Hallandale (944–1242), and *Hialeah Race Track,* 105 E. 21st St., Hialeah (885–8000)—rotate seasons among them. No one younger than 18 is allowed in the parimutuels, which are closed Sun.

Tennis. *Nastase Hamptons Invitational Tennis Tournament,* a Dec. event, is played at Turnberry Isle Yacht and Country Club, 20281 E. Country Club Dr. (935–0106). The *Junior International Tennis Championship,* also in Dec., is a feature of the Orange Bowl Festival and is open to 16- to 18-year-olds (previous contenders included John McEnroe, Jimmy Connors, Bjorn Borg and Jimmy Arias). The championship is at the Abel Holtz Tennis Stadium, Flamingo Park (1245 Michigan Ave., Miami Beach; 673–7760).

HISTORIC SITES AND HOUSES. Not to be missed is the art deco **Historic District** on Miami Beach, with more than 800 buildings (concentrated in a 125-block area bounded by 6th and 23rd streets and the ocean and Jefferson Avenue) identified for their pastel colors and Mediterranean, art deco, and streamline styles. Most of the buildings were constructed from 1920–1945, when Miami Beach was developing as a tropical resort. Guided walking tours are conducted at 10:30 A.M. Sat.; call 672–2014 for information on the starting point. The price is $4 per person. Special events include an art deco weekend every Jan.

Villa Vizcaya, an Italian Renaissance-style palace at 3251 S. Miami Ave. (579–2708), was built between 1914 and 1916 for James Deering of International Harvester and was used as his winter home. The 70-room palace is located on ten acres of formal gardens on Biscayne Bay. The villa contains a collection of fifteenth- to early nineteenth-century European decorative arts; occasionally, art exhibits are held in the gardens. The house and gardens are open daily, except Christmas, from 9:30 A.M.–5 P.M. Evening sound and light shows are scheduled periodically. The annual Shakespeare Festival and Italian Renaissance Faire is held in Feb. and Mar., with the bard's plays springing to life amid the food and merry-making. Regular admission to Vizcaya is $5 for adults, $3.50 for students and senior citizens.

The Spanish Monastery (16711 W. Dixie Highway, North Miami Beach; 945–1462). The Cloisters of the Monastery of St. Bernard originally were built in 1141 in Sacramenia, Spain. In 1925, newspaper baron William Randolph Hearst purchased the structure for his San Simeon estate. He had it dismantled and brought to the United States, where it remained in a New York warehouse for more than 20 years, until two businessmen purchased it in 1954, and had the giant jigsaw puzzle assembled at its present location. It now serves as an Episcopal church and houses works of art and antiques. Daily, 10 A.M. to 5 P.M. except Sun., noon–5 P.M. Admission is $3 for adults and 75 cents for children.

The Barnacle (3485 Main Highway, Coconut Grove) is the former estate of Commodore Ralph Munroe, a Coconut Grove pioneer. The 1891 residence and landscaped grounds have been restored and now operate as a State Historic Site and museum. Tours are conducted Wed.–Sun. at 9 and 10:30 A.M. and 1 and 2:30 P.M. Notable about this house is that the house once was jacked up to build a new ground floor.

Coral Gables House (907 Coral Way, Coral Gables; 442–6593) is the boyhood home of George Merrick, the founder and developer of the city of Coral Gables. The manor includes the original family home built of wood in 1898, now the back portion of the natural rock structure built between 1900 and 1906. Open Wed. 10 A.M.–4 P.M. and Sun. 1–4 P.M.; other times by appointment. Admission is $1 for adults and 50 cents for children.

Coral Castle (28655 U.S. 1, Homestead; 248–6344). With primitive hand tools and an obsession, Edward Leedskalnin built this complex in the 1920s and '30s in a vain attempt to regain a lost love who ditched him the day before their intended wedding. The commercial complex incorporates sculpted monolithic stones weighing up to 30 tons; how Leedskalnin single-handedly engineered this feat and precisely fitted these stones befuddles scientists today. The castle is open daily from 9 A.M.–9 P.M., with admission $5.50 for adults and $4 for youngsters 5–10.

MUSEUMS AND GALLERIES. The prestigious **Bass Museum** (2121 Park Ave., Miami Beach; 673–7530) hosts traveling exhibits, performing arts events, and lectures; its permanent exhibit features work from the thirteenth–twentieth centuries, including Oriental bronzes, and the art of masters Rubens and van Haarlem. The Rembrandt and El Greco schools are well-represented, too. The museum opened in April 1964, after a generous gift from John and Johanna Bass to the City of Miami Beach. It has galleries on two floors, and a gift shop with postcards and reproductions of art objects. Open Tues.–Sat. 10 A.M.–5 P.M.; Sunday 1 P.M.–5 P.M. Admission is $1 for adults and 50 cents for children; free on Tuesdays.

Black Archives (5400 N.W. 22nd Ave.; 638–5729) rely on photographs and writings to represent black history. Bahamian blacks were among Miami's earliest settlers. The museum also hosts traveling exhibits. Open weekdays, 8:30 A.M.–5 P.M.; Free.

The Cultural Center, which was designed by Philip Johnson and opened in April 1984, houses both the **Center for the Fine Arts** and the **Historical Museum of Southern Florida.** The Center (375–1700) shows traveling exhibits and loan collections in its two floors of galleries; it also has an auditorium and sculpture court. Across the large courtyard is the Museum (375-1492), which features a permanent exhibit on its second floor that traces 10,000 years of Florida history through slide shows, music, photographs and other memorabilia. The ground floor has a gallery devoted to traveling or temporary exhibits, plus a gift shop stocked with postcards, souvenirs, hand-made clothing from the nearby Miccosukee Indian Village, and arts and crafts from spots throughout the world. Both the Center and Museum open weekdays, 10 A.M.–6 P.M., except Thurs. 1–9 P.M.; 10 A.M.–5 P.M. Sat.; and Sun. noon–5 P.M. Adults, $3; children 6–12, $2. Mon. is contribution day.

Cuban Museum of Arts and Culture (1300 S.W. 12 Ave.; 858–8006) has exhibits of traditional and contemporary Hispanic artists, historic documents and memorabilia. Open weekends 10 A.M.–5 P.M. Donations are accepted.

The Lowe Art Museum (1301 Stanford Drive, Coral Gables; 284–3535). It's located on the University of Miami campus and is renowned for its collections of southwest American Indian art and textiles and its collection of Renaissance paintings. Tues.–Fri., noon–5 P.M.; Sat., 10A.M.–5 P.M.; Sun., 2–5 P.M. Suggested donation: adults, $1; children, 50 cents.

Metropolitan Museum & Art Center (1212 Anastasia Ave., Coral Gables; 442–1448) is located at the historic Biltmore Country Club planned by Coral Gables founder George Merrick in 1925. The museum's changing exhibits represent the multi-ethnic community; there are also films, lectures and concerts. Open Tues.–Sat. 10 A.M.–5 P.M.; Wed. 7 A.M.–10 P.M.; Sun. noon–5 P.M. Admission is $1 for adults, 50 cents for senior citizens and youngsters 12 to 18.

Museum of Science and Space Transit Planetarium (3280 S. Miami Ave; 854–4242) features more than 100 hands-on exhibits dealing with light, sound electronics, energy, biology, and ecology. Open Sun.–Thurs. 10 A.M.–6 P.M. Fri. and Sat. 10 A.M.–10 P.M. Admission is $3 for adults, $2.25 for senior citizens and kids 12 and younger. The planetarium (854–4242) is contained in a 65-foot dome in which star, solar-gazing, and laser shows are presented. Call the Cosmic Hotline (854–2222) for show times. Admission is $4 for adults and $2 for kids, except Mon. and Tues. evening shows, $1 a person.

North Miami Museum & Art Center (12340 N.E. Eighth Ave., North Miami; 893–6211) features changing exhibits of works of contemporary American artists, with special emphasis on state artists. Open weekdays 10 A.M.–4 P.M., Saturdays 1–3 P.M. Free.

FILMS. The Film Society of Miami, 7600 Red Rd., Suite 307, South Miami, FL 33143 (444–FILM), organizes the Feb. **Miami Film Festival,** a marathon showing of at least 30 independent and art films and premieres of Hollywood or pay-TV movies. The festival's heart is in downtown Miami's *Gusman Cultural Center* (174 E. Flagler St.), but films also are shown at art theaters: *Beaumont* (University of Miami, Coral Gables; 284–2173), *Miami-Dade Community College Auditorium* and *Knight Center Auditoriums.*

Several theaters offer second-run films at first-rate prices. Heading the list is the *Shores* (9806 N.E. Second Ave., Miami Shores; 756–6232), which charges 89 cents admission. Other bargains are the *Roxy* (1527 Washington Ave., Miami Beach; 531–6439) and the *Beaumont,* University of Miami (284–2173).

MUSIC. The **Greater Miami Opera Association** (1200 Coral Way, Miami; 854–1643), founded in 1941, now ranks among the top major opera companies in the country. It has four annual series: the International (original language) and the National (English) between Jan. and Mar., the "Pops on the Bay" summer concert series at Marine Stadium, and the American Musical Theater Series in Oct. and Nov. Call for performance times; prices range from $10 to $50, with discounts for students and senior citizens. Performances are at Dade County Auditorium in the spring and at Gusman Cultural Center in the fall.

The Miami Chamber Symphony (5690 N. Kendal Dr., Miami; 662–6600) brings in performers known world-wide.

P.A.C.E. (Performing Arts for Community Education, 2121 S.W. 27th Ave., Miami; 856–8836) hosts more than 1,000 concerts a year, most of them free at indoor and outdoor locations throughout Dade. Its largest event is the Big Orange Festival, the nation's only winter festival, which extends over several weeks. Call for dates and times. The P.A.C.E. Concertline, recorded listings, is 856–1966.

International Festival of the Americas (Box 248165, Coral Gables 33124; 284–3941) produces an Oct. series of concerts with jazz and Hispanic flavors, among others.

DANCE. Classical, modern, folk, and ethnic dance flourish here. The biggest news in dance these days is the **Miami City Ballet** (909 Lincoln Rd., Miami Beach, FL 33139; 532–4880), a new company directed by the renowned Edward Villella, which has won great acclaim. Among the other resident companies are: **Ballet Concerto** (3410 Coral Way; 446–7922). The company presents classic and new ballets with world-renowned guests. Greater Miami's oldest dance company is **Dance Miami** (7210 Red Rd.; 662–6953). The **Miami Ballet Company** (5818 S.W. 73rd St.; 667–5543) offers subscription concerts with internationally esteemed artists. **Momentum Dance Company** (12199 South Dixie Hwy.; 235–3047) presents new works of Florida choreographers. The **JND Concert Foundation** (c/o Temple Beth Sholom, 4141 Chase Ave., Miami Beach; 532–2207) also brings in internationally recognized performers. The **Dance Umbrella of Miami** (174 E. Flagler St., Miami; 371–2939) presents and promotes dance in the area.

STAGE. The **Coconut Grove Playhouse** (3500 Main Highway, Coconut Grove; 442–4000) is the area's leading resident professional theater, under the artistic direction of Arnold Mittelman. The historic playhouse, built in the late 1920s, has an Equity season Oct.–June, and stages Broadway and off-Broadway productions, including a few in Spanish. There are plans for an experimental stage as well. Tickets range from $7 to $22; all major credit cards accepted.

The Ring Theater (University of Miami, Coral Gables; 284–3355) stages six plays during the winter season and four in summer. Prices vary according to times and seat location; scripts include some new works.

The Ruth Foreman Theater (Bay Vista campus of Florida International University; 940–5902) is operated by the "First Lady of Florida theater," who has staged productions for more than 30 years. During the summer, Ruth Foreman's **Children's Theater** gives performances throughout the county. Dates and times vary. South Florida Theater Company (2522 Lincoln Ave.; 854–1983) stages Shakespearean plays on the grounds of Villa Vizcaya, an Italian Renaissance-style palace, in Feb. and Mar. **South End Alternative Theater** (561 N.W. 32 St. in the Bakehouse Art Complex; 887–3511), does experimental and avant-garde works.

Theater 24 (17996 S.W. 97th Ave.; 255–2206) offers new and experimental productions several times a year in a closet-sized theater named for its seating capacity (24). Reservations are essential.

Spanish theater. Three theaters—*Teatro Avante, Centro Dramático Antonin Artaud,* and *Teatro Bellas Artes*—present productions for Spanish-speaking audiences. Check the Miami *News* or *Herald* for listings.

SHOPPING. If you're trying to find items that are quintessentially Miami, you'll have to put in some footwork. Guayaberas, the multipocketed, loose-fitting shirts favored by Latin men, are available in shops along Flagler Street in downtown Miami and along Calle Ocho (S.W. Eighth Street). Hand-rolled cigars are found in shops throughout Little Havana; one in particular is Tobano Cigars (1444 W.

Flagler St.), which sells fresh stogies in 12 sizes. Patchwork clothing handmade by Miccosukee Indians is sold in the gift shop of the Historical Museum of Southern Florida in the downtown Cultural Center (375–1492), or direct from the Miccosukee Indian Village, 25 miles west of the city on U.S. 41 (223–8388).

As for foods, you can take back oranges available at stalls along Biscayne Boulevard from about 45th Street north to 79th Street. Buy here rather than at the airport, where prices escalate along with convenience. Supermarkets usually have Latin food sections where you can pick up a bag of dark-roast Cuban coffee.

Some of the most delightful shopping—though it's often pricy—is along Sunset Drive in South Miami; the funky boutiques wedged on and between Main Highway and Grand Avenue in Coconut Grove; and Miracle Mile (Coral Way) in Coral Gables, a four-block stretch of boutiques, art and jewelry stores. Or take a walk down memory lane on Miami Beach's Lincoln Road Mall, which is trying to dust itself off and regain the luster of the 1950s and '60s.

DINING OUT. It used to be that the preferred meals in Miami-area restaurants centered around seafood pulled fresh from the Atlantic or Biscayne Bay. In the early 1960s, though, the influx of Cubans added variety to the cooking pot as well as the melting pot. Most Hispanic restaurants congregate along Calle Ocho (S.W. Eighth Street).

Dade County's burgeoning population—1.8 million and counting—has given birth to countless other ethnic eateries representing cuisines throughout the world. Budget travelers should remember that portions are particularly generous at ethnic restaurants and Southern-style cafeterias. Casual attire will take you almost anywhere, though you should dress for dinner in fancy hotel restaurants and other spots. Inquire about the dress code if you're making reservations.

Restaurant categories, based on the price of a three-course meal for one, without beverage, tax, or tip, are: *Reasonable,* $10 to $15; *Very Economical,* $5 to $10; and *Low Budget,* under $5. Unless noted, all restaurants accept some, if not all, major credit cards. Every effort has been made to ensure that the list is up-to-date, but restaurants come and go so quickly that it is always advisable to call ahead.

Reasonable

Canton Too. 2614 Ponce de Leon Blvd., Coral Gables (448–3736). The name indicates only one cooking style; the quality restaurant also offers Mandarin and Szechwan. Honey chicken and Canton steak are the house specialties. The more diners in your party, the better, for you'll get to sample more. Lunch and dinner, daily.

Crab House. 1551 79th St. Causeway, North Bay Village (868–7085). Bring a hearty appetite, especially for the all-you-can-eat buffet featuring cold shrimp, clams on the half shell, oysters, etc. Don't let the parsleyed potatoes best you before you've gone back for seconds. Check out the early-bird special.

East Coast Fisheries. 360 W. Flagler St., Miami (373–5516). This fish warehouse on the Miami River has been around for decades, drawing patrons for its fine conch fritters, grouper, stone crabs, sea trout, seviche, crispy fries, and cole slaw. Ask for a balcony seat so you can watch the staff hustle at the fryers. You can get fresh fish to go, too.

Gino's Italian Restaurant. 1906 Collins Ave., Miami Beach (532–6426). The fettucine Alfredo is a find, but try one of the nine veal dishes, perhaps parmigiana. Dinner only, closed Monday.

Hungry Sailor. 3426 Main Highway, Coconut Grove (444–9359). Leave your high-falutin' fashions at the door; the dress is basic blue jeans. A cook works the grill at the front window, producing specialties such as swordfish or grouper. Come for lunch, when specials are posted on the blackboard.

Hy Vong. 3458 S.W. Eighth St., Miami (446–3674). This tiny dining room is perhaps the only South Florida spot in which Vietnamese food is served. Among the specialties are spicy chicken, snapper, lamb, and squid salad in ginger sauce with grated nuts. Dinner only, closed Sunday.

Sun Inn. 3045 Biscayne Blvd., Miami (576–1728). A range of Szechwan, Cantonese, and Mandarin entrees sate almost every taste. The mu shu pork is a must, with the thin pancakes providing a light wrapping for the delectable innards. Soong duck is crisp and tasty, or sample the cashew chicken. Lunch and dinner daily.

Very Economical

Ali Babba's Middle East Restaurant. 1764 S.W. Third Ave., Miami (446–5334). Tenting draped across the ceiling and candlelight flickering at the tables create an Arabian Nights atmosphere; belly dancing is the highlight. Among good choices from the Lebanese menu are the hummos (a chick-pea dish), stuffed grape leaves, or kibbeh (cracked wheat mixed with ground beef and lamb). Lunch and dinner daily; open late.

El Lechoncito. 5820 Bird Rd., Miami (662–1534). Plants and red tablecloths mask this former Lum's restaurant, but the food needs no disguising. Pork is the specialty; lobster creole, shrimp creole, palomilla steak, and baked chicken are favorites, too. Fried sweet-breads are another option. Moro rice is particularly good. Breakfast, lunch and dinner.

Granny Feelgoods. 9th-floor Plaza Venetia, 555 N.E. 15th St., Miami (371–2085). The blond wood and greenery is typical, but the food is fine. Huevos rancheros, a Tex-Mex dish of grilled corn tortillas with refried beans, eggs, salsa, sour cream, and cheese, is a good bet. Or accent a sandwich—chicken salad, cream cheese and pineapple, etc.—with a tossed salad or taboule (mideastern cracked-wheat salad) and fresh papaya, carrot, apple, grapefruit, or combination juice. Save room for the scrumptious carrot cake. Lunch and dinner weekdays, lunch Sat. Closed Sun.

La Rumba. 2008 Collins Ave., Miami Beach (538–8998). A guitarist and a bas relief of a carnival parade featuring Sammy Davis Jr., Jackie Gleason, and Carmen Miranda set the stage for pleasant, informal Cuban dining. The green salad is passable, but the snapper with green sauce, pork chunks and the arroz con pollo are enticing treats. Lunch and dinner daily.

Paesano's. 72nd St. and Harding Ave., Miami Beach (866–9618). This intimate, family-style eatery resembles a trattoria, with its tile floors, white-washed walls and trailing vines. The deluxe pizza is a delight, with thin, crisp crust and generous dollops of cheese, peppers, mushrooms, sausage, and olives. Eggplant parmigiana and baked manicotti are first-rate, too. Wide range of pasta dishes. Lunch and dinner daily.

Puerto Sagua. 700 Collins Ave., Miami Beach (673–9569). Plants add some dressing to this otherwise bare and informal restaurant. Choose from seafood, paella, arroz con pollo, shrimp in garlic sauce or other entrees with white rice and salad. For breakfast, you've got ham and eggs, grits, Cuban toast, cafe cubano. Breakfast, lunch and dinner. Open late.

Tropics International. In the Edison Hotel, 960 Ocean Dr., Miami Beach (531–5335). Airy, casual ambience, colorful clientele—beach veterans, yuppies, and jet-setters. Salads, sandwiches, interesting drinks, just off the sidewalk in a renovated art deco hotel, patrons can even laze around the hotel pool. Folk and popular music in the evenings. Lunch and dinner daily.

Tugboat Annie's. In Plaza Venetia building, 555 N.E. 15 St. (374–2814). Casual waterfront dining, indoors or out. Imaginative salads, chicken, fresh fish, Cajun dishes. Tall tropical drinks. Adjacent to marina filled with colorful boats. Lunch and dinner daily.

Wolfies. 2038 Collins Ave., Miami Beach (538–6626). This is the consummate Jewish deli, where kosher pickles, cole slaw and fresh rolls are whisked to your table. Save room for entrees including chicken cacciatore, liver and onions, a fish platter and more. Cash only. Breakfast, lunch and dinner daily.

Yeung's Mandarin Garden. 954 Arthur Godfrey Rd., Miami Beach (672–1144). The dining area is tiny, but the menu is large, including Cantonese specialties such as *fun see* (cellophane noodles with shredded pork, beef, or chicken). Hot and sour soup is a must. Lunch and dinner daily except Sun., dinner only.

Zum alten Fritz. 1840 N.E. Fourth Ave., Miami (374–7610). You can get the best "wurst" here; try the currywurst, a veal sausage topped with curry sauce and served with home fries. Or sample other German specialties: schnitzel, sauerbraten, Berlin-style onion soup, cold platters. Wash these down with a pilsner or hearty weiss beer. Lunch and dinner daily.

Low Budget

Aux Palmistes. The Palms, 6820 N.E. Second Ave., Miami (751–9189). This Little Haiti restaurant evokes the island's spirit with its thatched-roof, open-air cabana.

Griots (fried pork) served with a spicy sauce is the house favorite, but the fresh fish, oxtail or pigfeet stew is terrific, too. Served with plantains fried or boiled, lettuce salad, and massive portions of rice and red beans. Lunch and dinner daily. Live Caribbean music Fri. and Sat. nights. Open late. Cash only.

Biscayne Cafeteria. 147 Miracle Mile, Coral Gables (444–9005). Expect to stand in line for lunch and dinner at this venerable establishment of almost 40 years. Even Mom would be hard-pressed to top the beef brisket, meat loaf, or baked chicken. There's salmon, salad, macaroni and cheese, ribs, and other goodies, too. Fruit salads, greens, applesauce, and more tasty side dishes. Try the chocolate pudding, among the vast assortment of desserts. Cash only. Breakfast, lunch and dinner.

Davis Restaurant. 745 N.W. 62nd St., Miami (754–5921). This Liberty City eatery is a cinder-block refuge from hunger. Portraits of black greats like Martin Luther King, Jr., and Jesse Jackson stare down as diners, seated family-style, tackle generous helpings of soul food like pork chops, macaroni and cheese, greens, okra, and more. Breakfast, lunch and dinner daily except Sun. Closes at 5:30 P.M. Cash only.

Hot'Z Bar-B-Q. 1550 N.E. 164th St., North Miami Beach (940–RIBS). Wood benches, plants, and paintings warm up the atmosphere almost as much as the Cajun-style ribs heat up your mouth. The Buffalo chicken wings are tops, too. Homemade applesauce, corn on the cob, and fresh corn muffins please palates, southern or otherwise. Don't be embarrassed to ask for a doggy bag. The $4.95 early-bird special is a five-course meal offered from 3:00–6:30 P.M. daily. Lunch and dinner weekdays. Dinner only weekends.

Villa Deli. 1608 Alton Road, Miami Beach (538–4552). This venerable Beach eatery is divided into two sections: cafeteria-style and table service. Among the specialties are pepper steak with yellow rice, broiled chicken or fish, or liver and onions. Main courses are served with potatoes and a vegetable. Beer is available. Breakfast, lunch and dinner daily. Closed Sun. Cash only.

Recommended Splurge. Joe's Stone Crab. 227 Biscayne St., Miami Beach (673–0365). Owned and operated by the Weiss family since its inception in 1913, it has built an international reputation on its stone crabs served with drawn lemon butter. Near the southern tip of Miami Beach, this esteemed restaurant has other seafood on the menu, too. Expect long lines at this most popular place. No reservations. About $25.

Cafés and Coffeehouses. For some of the best coffee, stroll along **Calle Ocho** (S.W. Eighth St.) in Little Havana. Espresso stands line the route, dispensing conversation and the caffeine-rich cafe cubano through sidewalk windows. Coconut Grove is another good bet for people-watching, with pedestrians and fancy cars on parade from morning until the wee hours; try **La Petite Patisserie** (3045 Fuller St.; 442–9329), a pastry shop that specializes in croissants, quiches, and vegetable knishes.

NIGHTLIFE AND BARS. Once upon a time, Jackie Gleason and Arthur Godfrey showed American audiences the glitter and glamor that was Miami and Miami Beach in the 1950s and '60s. Celebrities flocked, and still do to a lesser degree, to some of the major Beach hotels and clubs. Typical of today's headliners are Buddy Hackett, Jackie Mason, and the Four Tops. But time has broadened the focus of the spotlight to points beyond Miami Beach. Especially hot with the younger set is Coconut Grove, which boasts the dancer's delight, Biscayne Baby, and the ritzy Regine's. The Latin beat or big-city pulse is prevalent in various revues and nightclubs. Club 1235 on Miami Beach, for instance, trips the light fantastic with its strobes, dry-ice mist and name acts. Clubs can stay open as late as 5 A.M.; the legal drinking age is 21.

General

Brass Menagerie. Radisson Mart Plaza Hotel, 711 N.W. 77th Ave., Miami (261–3800) features toucans on brass rings and a smart, stylish crowd around its bar. Intimate, open late.

Ciga Lounge. Grand Bay Hotel, 2669 S. Bayshore Dr., Coconut Grove (858–9600) is a top-scale, pricy place for a drink before or after Regine's, the exclusive club on the top floor. Talk here isn't cheap.

Coco Loco. Sheraton Brickell Point, 495 Brickell Ave., Miami (373–6000). Stylish, comfortable meeting and mixing place in newly purchased hotel property. Live music and dancing, good Happy Hour.

Cye's Rivergate. 444 Brickell Ave., Miami (358–9100) is a comfortable lounge-restaurant that draws a mixed crowd.

Sandbar. Silver Sands Motel, 301 Ocean Dr., Key Biscayne (361–5441) is the perfect place to gaze upon the moon over Miami and hear the waves wash the shore. It's crowded weekends, frequented by islanders and others favoring its informal atmosphere and inexpensive drinks.

700 Club. David William Hotel, 700 Biltmore Way, Coral Gables (445–7821), perched on the 12th floor, provides a panoramic view of the Mediterranean-style city. Dinner served, closed Sun. Moderate price.

Music Clubs

Current listings: call the *Blues Hotline* (666–6656) or the *Jazz Hotline* (382–3938).

Club Mystique. Miami Airport Hilton, 5101 Blue Lagoon Dr., Miami (262–1000) turns up the volume to a degree that you'll twist and shout to top-40s music live or recorded. Food is available, and there's a one-drink minimum.

Greenstreet's. Holiday Inn, 2051 LeJeune Road, Coral Gables (445–2131) plays live jazz and pop for an upscale crowd.

Monty Trainer's. 2560 S. Bayshore Dr., Coconut Grove (858–1431) brings a mixed crowd out back for open-air dining and dancing. Live reggae, calypso, pop, and rock keep the customers satisfied while they drink or down burgers, fried fish and french fries. Relatively cheap, very popular.

Rousseau's. Doral Country Club, 4400 N.W. 87th Ave., Miami (592–2000) appeals to the three-piece-suit set, offering disco and dancing in its elegant, circular room.

Tobacco Road. 626 S. Miami Ave., Miami (374–1198), a Miami fixture since 1913, has a speakeasy ambiance and live blues or rock bands playing simultaneously, one on each of its two floors. It's cheap and cozy, with free hors d'oeuvres and popcorn during happy hour. The grill operates late, too.

1235. 1235 Washington Ave., Miami Beach (531–1235). This old movie theater has been turned into a glamorous night spot where people go to see and be seen—if indeed they can be seen under their Viking helmets or their Arabic headdresses. The music blasts until the wee hours. Admission $5 to $15, depends on the night and whether there's a special event or act scheduled.

Revues

Marco Polo Hotel and Resort. 19201 Collins Ave., Miami Beach (932–2233). Offers musical revues of songs from the 1920s through the '80s in its locally produced productions. Shows Fri.–Sun.

Newport Beach Resort. 16701 Collins Ave., Miami Beach (949–1300). Often stages musical revues, along with road shows and name entertainment. Informal setting.

Sheraton Bal Harbour. 9701 Collins Ave., Miami Beach (865–7511). Stages lavish Las Vegas-type reviews in a nightclub setting.

Singles Bars

Biscayne Baby. 3336 Virginia St., Coconut Grove (445–3751). Trot out your blue suede shoes for fifties rock 'n' roll, often with oldies artists on stage. A diner adjoins the dance floor.

Fire and Ice. 3841 N.E. Second Ave., Miami (573–3473). A combination of big-screens video and outrageous new wave styles offers hi-tech hilarity. The music is mostly punk or new wave. Here, outrageous is in. Cover is $4, open late.

Strawberries. 755 E. Ninth St., Hialeah (888–3055). On the singles circuit for its disco and live bands. Ladies get free admission and free drinks on Wed. Food available.

Studebaker's. North Kendall Dr. at 117th Ave. (598–1021). One of the newest "in" spots, with fun and the fifties. Young singles and yuppie couples.

Sunday's on the Bay. 4000 Crandon Blvd., Key Biscayne (361–6777). A popular destination with the weekend beach crowd, but this bayside establishment hops with music every night 9 P.M.–3 A.M., live reggae Wed.–Sat. nights. Ladies night, 8 P.M.–closing Thurs.

Village Inn. 3131 Commodore Plaza, Coconut Grove (445–8721). This bar rocks until the wee hours; cover charge varies.

Supper Clubs

The Copacabana. 3600 S.W. Eighth St., Miami (443–3801). Dinner and a Latin-style revue will run you about $17. Dress for the occasion, as the Cubans do. Closed Mon.

Les Violins. 1751 Biscayne Blvd., Miami (371–8668). Havana-style club, offers two different floor shows each evening, with 30 opulently costumed performers. Shows are $7.50. The cuisine is Continental, with entrees starting at $9.50. The club opened in 1961, making it Miami's oldest Latin nightspot.

Ziegfield's. Holiday Inn Airport Lakes, 1101 N.W. 57th Ave., Miami (266–0000). Features American-style dining and dancing.

SECURITY. As in any urban area, Miami has its share of crime. Common sense is the best safeguard. If you have valuables, leave them in the hotel safe deposit box, not in your room. If possible, leave them at home. Do not keep valuable equipment—such as a camera—in your car, especially if it's exposed. At least put it in your trunk. Make sure the bulk of your money is in traveler's checks: Like cash, they're liquid. Unlike cash, they can be replaced if lost or stolen.

A swinging purse is an open invitation to crime. Metro-Dade police warn against wrapping the strap around wrist or shoulder, since you could be injured in a purse-snatching attempt. Instead, the department advises, keep the purse close to your body. Walk with a purpose, and be alert—you'll be far less vulnerable. If you're driving, be cautious while traveling through Liberty City or Overtown. Ask hotel personnel whether they advise against certain routes.

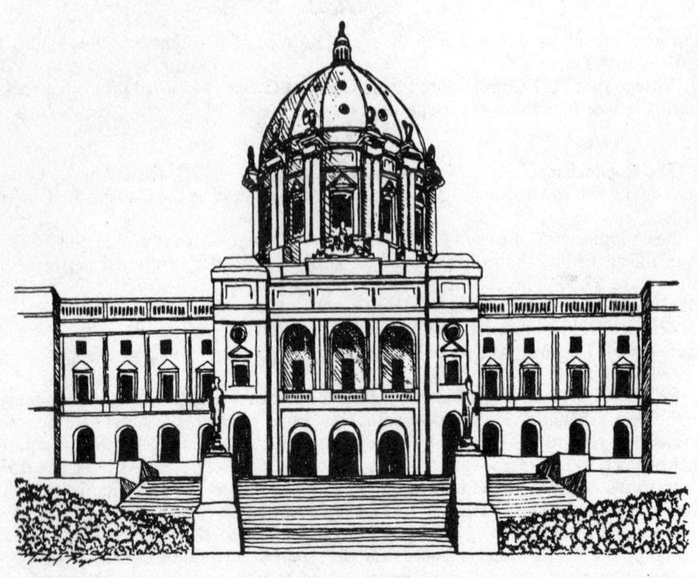

MINNEAPOLIS–ST. PAUL

by
Candace Kumerfield
and
Diane Nelsen DeMarco

Though certainly urban in character, the Twin Cities are frequently cast with a rural aura by those not well acquainted with their varied characters. Both geographical and historical attributes contribute to this image. Three major North American agricultural regions converge at the Twin Cities—the dairy belt from the east, the corn belt from the south, and the wheat lands from the west. From a historical perspective, the cities began as a fur-trading post, developed into a lumbering hub, then evolved as a flour-milling center.

Today Twin Cities manufacturers have added pacemakers and super computers to their top products, and this seven-county metropolitan area now boasts more major corporate headquarters and more artistic activity per capita than any city in the United States except New York City.

In addition, Twin Citians have developed a tradition of civic responsibility that permeates their life-styles. Business supports the arts, sports, and human services in equal measure. Several civic organizations promote research and dialogue that successfully generate greater cooperation between business and government.

All of this is centered in a natural setting dotted with nearly 1,000 lakes and 500 parks and crisscrossed with numerous hiking and biking trails, making it rich in urban possibilities while retaining its pristine character.

The Mississippi River runs diagonally through the Twin Cities from the northwest to the southeast, dividing Minneapolis on the west from St. Paul on the east. Traditionally, the cities have been characterized as anything but twins. Minneapolis, with its sleek towers of steel and glass, its upbeat nature, and its futuristic emphasis has been dubbed the more modern and progressive of the two—the "beginning of the West." St. Paul, by contrast, with its predominantly German and Irish ethnic roots, traditionally conservative attitude, and until recently a less than impressive list of new developments, has earned a reputation of being the less progressive and more traditional of the two—the "end of the East."

Recent years, however, have blurred the lines between the two reputations, as Minneapolis has blended futuristic developments with historic restorations and St. Paul has sought to divide its efforts between reviving old neighborhoods and transforming its skyline with the World Trade Center and modern shopping malls. Both cities are served by skyway systems—elevated, enclosed pedestrian walkways that link the majority of downtown buildings without requiring the visitor ever to leave their climate-controlled environments.

Today's visitor will find both cities excitingly eclectic. In St. Paul, you can grab breakfast at the art deco–style Mickey's Diner, marvel at the current showing at the technologically amazing 3M-Omnitheater where the screen engulfs you, relax through lunch at the restored and gracious St. Paul Hotel, spend the afternoon shopping in St. Paul Center: Town Square where shops encircle a central parklike atrium with cascading fountains, and Town Court where three levels of shops and restaurants surround a central courtyard that features a nine-foot waterfall. Later you can dine atop the Radisson St. Paul Hotel in its revolving Le Carrousel restaurant overlooking the Mississippi, and then select from an evening with the St. Paul Chamber Orchestra or Minnesota Opera at the European-style Ordway Music Theatre or a rock concert at the Civic Center.

In Minneapolis, you can start with a morning jog around Lake of the Isles, lined with turn-of-the-century mansions. Then catch a morning coffee concert at Orchestra Hall and enjoy lunch at one of the sidewalk cafés along Nicollet Mall. In the afternoon, shop in the myriad stores in City Center, the newly opened upscale Conservatory, or along Nicollet Mall or the many boutiques in nearby restored Butler Square, St. Anthony Main, or Riverplace. Afterwards relax for tea at the outdoor deck of Anthony's Wharf, at St. Anthony Main, where you can see views of St. Anthony Falls, the birthplace of Minneapolis. That evening either catch a first-run play downtown (ranging from Hennepin Center for the Arts, the Cricket Theatre on Nicollet, or several avant-garde theaters located in the "warehouse district"), or enjoy Vegas-style entertainment at hotels and restaurants downtown or in the suburbs.

In keeping with the slogan of its state, "Land of 10,000 Lakes" (which should read 15,000 lakes to be accurate), the Twin Cities have maintained or restored their downtown river and lake waterfronts to places of importance.

In the suburbs, visitors and natives alike share the campgrounds, boating facilities, playgrounds, picnic areas, and hiking, biking, and equestrian trails in the many county parks that dot the region. Of particular importance are two areas: the Lake Minnetonka area, west of the Cities, and the White Bear Lake region, north of St. Paul. Both began as resort centers. In fact, visitors from Chicago, St. Louis, and even New Orleans sought refuge from the summer heat on the long verandas of resort hotels and the breeze-cooled decks of over 90 paddlewheelers that once plied the waters of Lake Minnetonka in the late 1800s.

Shades of the past are still evident in several historic neighborhoods. A drive through Minneapolis's posh Kenwood district north of Lake of the Isles will route you by stately brick and stone mansions, including the home where Mary Tyler Moore "lived" at 2104 Kenwood Parkway. In St. Paul, the gracefully arching elm trees along Summit Avenue, known as the richest street in the world at the turn of the century, have fallen victim to disease and some of the old mansions have fallen victim to subdivision into apartments. Yet, the drive down this boulevard past the James J. Hill mansion and the smaller row house where F. Scott Fitzgerald once toiled in his third-floor alcove finishing the last pages of *This Side of Paradise* brings back the nostalgia of the era when lumber and milling magnates ruled both the commercial and social scenes.

If you like antiques, don't miss St. Paul's Grand Avenue, a stretch of shops and restaurants with a special eclectic flair and a neighborly atmosphere. In Minneapolis, an equally interesting collection of antique shops, punk-clothing shops, and trendy bar-restaurants—along with fascinating people-watching—can be found in the uptown area around the intersection of Hennepin Avenue and Lake Street.

Large enough to be a city within a city, the Twin Cities campus of the University of Minnesota has almost 50,000 students spread over three segments—East Bank (east of the Mississippi), West Bank (west of the Mississippi), and the St. Paul campus. As well as being a center of learning, it provides cultural and athletic events that attract many visitors each week. Theater abounds both on campus at Rarig Theater and near the campus, especially in what has been dubbed the West Bank Theatre District, where you might catch an Ibsen play or light satire. In the summer, you can even enjoy melodrama at the Minnesota Centennial Showboat, an actual paddle-wheel riverboat tied up below the Mississippi River bluffs on campus.

In Minneapolis, two cultural centers lie at opposite ends of Loring Greenway. On the east end is Orchestra Hall, where the Minnesota Orchestra alternates on stage with visiting symphonies and ensembles. On the west end is the Guthrie Theatre, a world-famous repertory theater, renowned for both classical plays and musicals, and Walker Art Center, an internationally famous modern art museum.

Lakes, rivers, parklands, museums, theaters, festivals, historic restorations, high-rise corporate towers, Germans, Scandinavians, and Irish—these are just a few of the things that the Twin Cities are made of and just a few of the reasons why so many visitors discover they wish they were residents.

PRACTICAL INFORMATION

WHEN TO GO. Frequently referred to as the "theater of seasons," the Twin Cities experience average temperatures ranging from the low teens in Jan. to the low seventies in July and August.

Although most people shudder at the thought of a Minnesota winter, the Twin Cities usually get hit with bitter subzero cold on only scattered days over a two- or three-week period in January or early February. Snowfall is relatively light, on the average about 42.5 inches per year. Expect the first freeze in early- to mid-October and the last freeze in very late April or early May.

Look for stormy springs with rain and snow mixing in March and traditional Apr. showers about every other afternoon. In summer, the extremes are again generally restricted to a two- to three-week period in July and August when both temperatures and humidity can climb well above the normal averages into the eighties and nineties. Yet, evening temperatures are generally comfortable, and two-thirds of the summer rain falls between 6 P.M. and 6 A.M., leaving most days generally sunny.

Vying for summer as the most popular season is Minnesota's fall, normally arriving by mid-September. Sometime between then and early November, Minnesota's "fifth season," or Indian summer, returns with a short reprieve of warmer days and cool nights.

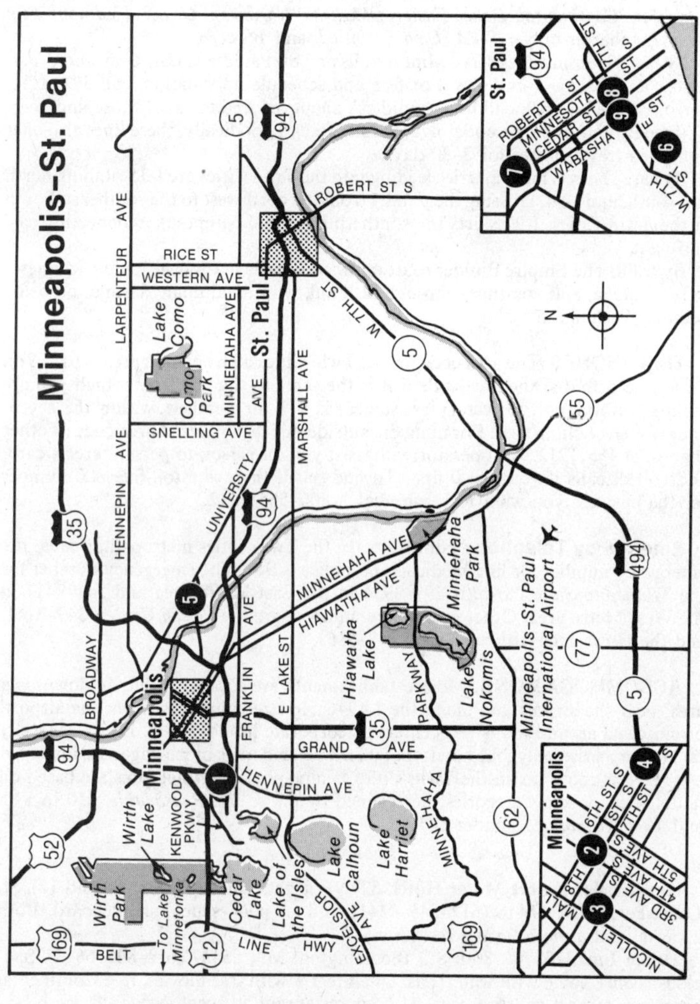

Points of Interest:

Minneapolis

1) Guthrie Theater
2) Hennepin County Government Center
3) IDS Center
4) Metrodome
5) University of Minnesota

St. Paul

6) Civic Center/Roy Wilkins Auditorium
7) State Capitol
8) Town Square
9) World Trade Center

HOW TO GET THERE. By air. The Minneapolis–St. Paul International Airport is located south of the Twin Cities, about 12 miles from downtown Minneapolis and 10 miles from downtown St. Paul. The major carriers serving the area are: *American, Continental, Delta, Eastern, Midway, Northwest, Ozark, Piedmont, Sun Country* (charter only), *TWA, USAir, United,* and *Western.*

By bus. Four bus lines serve Minneapolis and St. Paul: *Fourstar, Greyhound, Jefferson,* and *Zephyr Bus Lines.* For fare and schedule information, call 371–3311. Persons traveling with children should ask about reduced fares for those under age 12 (usually half-price) or under five (usually free). Periodically, these lines also offer unlimited travel passes for 7–30 days.

By car. The two main arteries leading into the Twin Cities are I-35 running north and south, and I-94, crossing diagonally from the northwest to the southeast. South of the Twin Cities, I-90 skirts the southern border of Minnesota, connecting east and west.

By train. The Empire Builder route of *Amtrak* starts in Chicago, enters Minnesota by Winona, and continues through St. Paul, with its ultimate destination being Seattle, Washington.

TELEPHONES. The area code for the Twin Cities metropolitan area is 612. You do not need to dial the area code if it is the same as the one from which you are dialing. Information (directory assistance) is 411 for numbers within the seven-county metropolitan area. For numbers outside this region, dial 1 area code (if other than 612) 555–1212. An operator will assist you on person-to-person, credit card, and collect calls if you dial 0 first. To find out if there is a toll-free 800 number for the business you want to reach, dial 1–800–555–1212.

Emergency Telephone Numbers. In the Twin Cities metropolitan area, the emergency number for fire, medical, and police is 911. The emergency number for the *Minnesota State Patrol* is 297–3934 in the East Metro area and 541–9411 in the West Metro area. Other emergency numbers are the *Poison Center,* 347–3141, and the *Crisis Intervention Center,* 347–3161.

ACCOMMODATIONS. Most establishments are located in either downtown area, near the airport and along the I-494 strip stretching west from the airport, or clustered around industrial centers or corporate headquarters. Prices generally do not vary seasonally, but hotels that offer weekend rates or packages are indicated by a P. The room tax in the Twin Cities is nine percent. Hotel rates are based on double occupancy. Categories, determined by price, are: *Reasonable,* $50 to $70; and *Very Economical,* under $45.

Reasonable

Ambassador Resort Motor Hotel. 5225 Wayzata Blvd. (Hwys. 100 and 12), St. Louis Park, MN 55416 (612–545–0441). Indoor pool, sauna, shuffleboard. Both a casual and a more formal restaurant. P.

Dillon Inn. 4201 W. 80th St., Bloomington, MN 55437 (612–835–6643). Spacious rooms, some with waterbeds. Satellite TV with free movies, free Continental breakfast, airport courtesy van, 24-hour restaurant adjacent.

Hopkins House (Best Western) Resort. 1501 Hwy. 7, Hopkins, MN 55343 (612–935–7711). Indoor pool, sauna, whirlpool, miniature golf. Two restaurants, two lounges, live entertainment. P.

Hotel Seville (Best Western). 8151 Bridge Rd. (Hwys. 494 and 100), Bloomington, MN 55437 (612–830–1300). Nice rooms, each with its own balcony. Indoor pool, whirlpool, sauna, game room, Cinemax in rooms. Restaurant and lounge. P.

McGuire's Inn. 1201 W. County Rd. E, at Lexington Ave. N., Arden Hills, MN 55112 (612–636–4123). Very nice rooms and suites. Well-known restaurant with Las Vegas-style entertainment and cocktail lounge with dancing. Indoor pool, sauna, whirlpool. P.

Normandy Motor Inn (Best Western). 405 S. 8th St., Minneapolis, MN 55404 (612–370–1400). Indoor pool, whirlpool, and sauna. Coffee shop, restaurant, cocktail lounge. Convenient to downtown, Metrodome and Minneapolis Auditorium and Convention Center. Free parking. P.

Quality Inn—Civic Center. 175 W. 7th St., St. Paul, MN 55102 (612–292–8929). Convenient to downtown, across from the Civic Center. Free parking. Nice rooms. Restaurant and bar.

Very Economical

Boulevard Motel. 5637 Lyndale Ave. S., Richfield, MN 55423 (612–861–6011). Heated outdoor pool, restaurant. Kitchenette units. Free coffee.

Fair Oaks Motor Hotel. 2335 3rd Ave. S., Minneapolis, MN 55404 (612–871–2000). Restaurant, free HBO, free airport shuttle. Across from the Minneapolis Institute of Arts.

Golden Steer Motor Hotel. 1010 S. Concord, South St. Paul, MN 55075 (612–455–8541). Outdoor pool, bar, and restaurant that serves Sun. brunch. P.

The Inn. 7640 Cedar Ave. (I-494 and Cedar), Richfield, MN 55423 (612–861–4491). Very nice rooms. German-American restaurant. Convenient to airport.

Red Roof Inn. 12920 Aldrich Ave. S. (I-35W and Burnsville Pkwy), Burnsville, MN 55337 (612–890–1420). Adjacent to several 24-hour restaurants. In-room movies, free morning coffee and paper.

Twins Motor Inn. 1975 Univ. Ave., St. Paul, MN 55104 (612–645–0311). Outdoor pool, free parking, dining room, lounge, satellite TV. Convenient, between Minneapolis and St. Paul.

Budget Motel Chains. The following chains operate establishments in the Twin Cities metropolitan area. Rates at the locations indicated generally range from $39–$49 for a double, EP.

Budgetel Inns. 7815 Nicollet Ave. S. (near the airport), Bloomington, MN 55420 (612–881–7311). 6415 N. James Circle, Brooklyn Center, MN 55430 (612–561–8400).

Days Inns. 13080 Aldrich Ave. S. (I-35W and Burnsville Pkwy.), Burnsville, MN 55337 (612–894–8280). 2955 Empire Ln. (I-494 and Hwy. 55), Plymouth, MN 55441 (612–559–2400). 8000 Bridge Rd., Bloomington, MN 55437 (612–831–9595). 6300 Wayzata Blvd., Golden Valley, MN 55416 (612–546–6277). 2550 Cleveland Ave. N. (I-35W and County Rd. C), Roseville, MN 55113 (612–636–6730). 285 Century Ave. N. (I-94 at Century Ave.), Maplewood, MN 55119 (612–738–1600). 2407 University Ave. SE (University & Washington Ave.), Minneapolis, MN 55414 (612–623–3999). Toll-free reservations: 800–622–3999; in Minnesota, 800–325–2525.

Exel Inns. 2701 E. 78th St. (I-494 & 24th Ave. exit), Bloomington, MN 55420 (612–854–7200). 1739 Old Hudson Rd., St. Paul, MN 55106 (612–771–5566). Toll-free reservations: 800–356–8013.

Imperial 400 Motel. 2500 University Ave. S.E., Minneapolis, MN 55414 (612–331–6000).

Super 8 Motels. 7800 2d Ave. S., Bloomington, MN 55420 (612–888–8800). 2401 Prior Ave. N., St. Paul, MN 55113 (612–636–8888). Toll-free reservations: (800–843–1991).

TraveLodge. 149 University Ave. E., St. Paul, MN 55101 (612–227–8801, 800–255–3050).

Bed-and-Breakfast. An alternative to the usual hotel or motel room is the bed-and-breakfast establishment, modeled after its European counterpart. Guests stay in rooms in private homes, with or without private bath, and are served breakfast and frequently an evening snack and wine in a common dining room or parlor. One of the easiest ways to book such accommodations in the Twin Cities is to contact the **Bed & Breakfast Registry,** 1519 Grantham St., St. Paul, MN 55108 (612–646–4238). Accommodations include: restored homes with Victorian antiques, condominiums overlooking the city and complete with health club facilities, waterfront homes and cottages with canoe or sailboat included, nearby farm homes, and even a mansion. Rates range from $30 up to $105 for a deluxe room or suite.

The Thorwood Bed and Breakfast, 649 W. 3d St., Hastings, MN 55033 (612–437–3297). In Hastings, just south of the Twin Cities, Dick and Pam Thorsen welcome you to their 1880 French Second Empire mansion listed on the National Register of Historic Places. Choose from five rooms, all with private baths. Rates range from $39 for the basic bedroom to $79 for their suite. Singles are $6 less.

Included are breakfast and an evening snack with wine. Antiques and local art are sold on the premises.

A brochure, "Explore Minnesota Bed and Breakfast and Historic Inns," is available from the Minnesota Office of Tourism, 375 Jackson St., Room 250, St. Paul, MN 55101 (612–296–5029, 800–652–9747 in Minnesota, 800–328–1461 nationwide).

HOW TO GET AROUND. Despite recurring media blitzes to increase bus ridership and annual renewal of interest in building either a subway or trolley system, the automobile remains the main means of transportation in the Twin Cities. Minneapolis streets generally follow in numerical or alphabetical order, but no such logical pattern exists in St. Paul. In fact, the address numbering system in St. Paul can be very misleading; addresses numerically close can be blocks apart.

From the airport. The Minneapolis–St. Paul International Airport is located south of the downtown districts, 12 miles from downtown Minneapolis and about 10 miles from downtown St. Paul, just off the I-494 beltline. Taxis to either downtown area cost approximately $15. Limousines to downtown Minneapolis cost $6.50 one-way or $9.50 round-trip. To St. Paul, shuttles cost $4.50 one-way, or $8.00 round-trip. Buses run periodically from the airport to downtown Minneapolis with transfers to downtown St. Paul; the fare ranges from 75 cents to $1.00. Updated information on both limousine and city bus service is available on the lower level of the airport terminal building. Both taxi service and limousines are available just outside the terminal's baggage claim area. To arrange reservations and complimentary transportation to many of the area's major hotels, use the free reservation telephones on the lower level.

By bus. The primary provider of public transportation in the seven-county metropolitan area is the *Metropolitan Transit Commission* (MTC). It operates approximately 1,100 buses on 120 routes, primarily in the downtown areas and on routes connecting the suburbs with the downtown districts. The basic fare is 60 cents. Trips between the cities or to suburbs cost up to $1.25. The surcharge for express buses is 10 cents; during rush hour, add 15 cents. The downtown shuttle is 10 cents. Children and senior citizens ride for less at specified times. Transfers are free and should be requested when boarding. Exact change is required. Call 827–7733 for information.

Two other bus lines operate in the suburbs: The *Medicine Lake Bus Co.* (545–1617) serves Golden Valley, New Hope, Crystal, Medina, Maple Grove, and portions of Minneapolis. The *North Suburban Lines* (784–7196) serve St. Paul and the northern suburbs. Limited Saturday service on the *Medicine Lake Bus Co.* only. Neither operates on Sundays.

By taxi. The base rate is $1.95 for the first mile and $1.10 per each additional mile. Although taxis can be found at cab stands in both downtown areas, they do not cruise in either city. Therefore, if you want a taxi, call for it. The number for *Yellow Cab* is 824–4444; for *Airport Taxi,* 721–6566; for *Blue and White Cabs,* 333–3331; for *Suburban Taxi,* 888–9199.

By rental car. Major rental car agencies provide both airport and downtown pick-up locations. Avis, Budget, Dollar, Hertz, National, and Thrifty serve the Twin Cities in addition to the less conventional Rent-a-Wreck or Ugly Duckling Rent-a-Car agencies that offer used cars at discount prices.

By skyway. Largely in response to Minnesota's winter months, both downtown Minneapolis and St. Paul have developed extensive skyway systems that connect several square blocks of downtown via climate-controlled walkways. Glass-enclosed bridges span streets, connecting second-story corridors that channel pedestrians through buildings. These corridors are lined with shops and restaurants. To reach them, take an escalator to the second floor of any of the connected buildings. In Minneapolis, the system's center is the Crystal Court in the IDS Center; in St. Paul, the hub is Town Square. Unfortunately, these systems are not fully accessible to wheelchairs.

HINTS TO THE MOTORIST. The metropolitan area is well-linked by a freeway system. The Beltline (I-494 in the south, I-694 in the north) encircles the Twin Cities, while I-35 bisects the metro area from north to south. Major north-south routes in the western suburbs are County Road 18 and Highway 100. Two common thoroughfares running west from downtown Minneapolis to the suburbs are highways 12 and 55. Highway 36 crosses the suburbs north of St. Paul, east to west. No tolls are charged on Twin Cities roads or bridges.

The speed limit on freeways complies with federal law—55 mph. On most main city thoroughfares, the limit drops to 30–45 mph. Right turns on red and left turns from a one-way to another one-way street are permitted except where prohibited by restriction signs. Seat belts are required for adults riding in the front seat, although there is no penalty for failing to do so; children under four years of age (residents only) must be secured in an approved child-restraint seat. In winter, check for parking restrictions on one side of the street, and during announced snow emergencies, do not park on any snow emergency route.

TOURIST INFORMATION. The **Minnesota Travel Information Center** publishes numerous pamphlets, all of which are free, on arts, attractions, and accommodations. Their *Minnesota Explorer* travel newspaper, published three times a year, includes information on attractions, facilities, events, campgrounds, restaurants, canoeing, hiking and backpacking, fishing, fall color driving routes, state parks, and historic sites. They also provide free highway maps, and regional brochures. Maps of canoeing and biking trails are available from the Minnesota Department of Natural Resources at a minimal cost. Stop by or write to: Minnesota Office of Tourism, 375 Jackson St., Rm 250, St. Paul, MN 55101 (296–5029, 800–652–9747 outside of the metro area, 800–328–1461 nationwide).

The **Chambers of Commerce** also maintain tourism centers in Minneapolis at 15 S. 5th St. (370–9132) or in the IDS Crystal Court, Nicollet Mall at 8th St., and in St. Paul at 600 N. Central Tower, 445 Minnesota St. (222–5561), or in Town Square, second level. In addition to offering maps and brochures of individual tourist attractions, they also have several brochures of interest to budget-minded travelers that list free tours and events. In downtown Minneapolis at 7 South 7th St., a shop called "Hello Minnesota" features several local guidebooks, cookbooks, maps, and handcrafted items made in Minnesota.

To find out what's going on, pick up one of the free weeklies available at stands throughout the cities: *Skyway News, City Pages,* and the *Twin Cities Reader.* They cover events, restaurants, reviews, and theaters. For the latest information regarding cultural events and exhibits, call or stop by the **Arts Resource and Information Center** at the Minneapolis Institute of Arts, 2400 3rd Ave. S. (870–3131). This clearinghouse provides information on current and upcoming art exhibits, theater, dance and music performances in the Twin Cities and throughout Minnesota. In the Crystal Court of the IDS Center in Minneapolis is the ticket reservation service, **Tickets-To-Go** (333–0159) and also available at Town Square in St. Paul. It provides performance information for over 50 organizations, advance ticket sales for many of these organizations and half-price day-of-performance tickets for some of the arts organizations.

Foreign Currency. Visitors may exchange foreign currencies at the *Norwest Banks,* 8th St. and Marquette Ave., Minneapolis, and 5th and Cedar, St. Paul; and the *First Banks,* 6th St. and 2nd Ave., Minneapolis, or 5th and Minnesota, St. Paul.

HINTS TO DISABLED TRAVELERS. Although state law requires any facility open to the public and built after November, 1976, to be wheelchair-accessible, not all events are held in such facilities. The *Minnesota Council on Disability* (296–6785) keeps a list of accessible programs and facilities and can help disabled individuals meet their particular needs. The Minnesota Department of Transportation sponsors *Metro Mobility* (349–7480), a transportation service for handicapped persons.

FREE EVENTS. Each year Twin Citians start off the new year with a **New Year's Eve** celebration along the Mississippi River at Minneapolis' Riverplace near where the city began. Ice skating, outdoor music, and fireworks cap off this free extravaganza. A month later, St. Paul answers with its **Winter Carnival,** complete with two parades (including an evening torchlight parade), ice sculpting, and competition in several winter sports. By Mar. 17, it's time for the Irish to reclaim the streets of St. Paul for the annual **St. Patrick's Day Parade.** With some 100,000 people participating each year, it has become the third-largest St. Patrick's Day parade in the nation.

Summer brings a plethora of arts and crafts fairs: In **June,** the **Edina Art Festival** attracts about 200 artists to the 50th and France district; the **Grand Old Day** along St. Paul's Grand Avenue includes a parade, food booths and bands as well as an art show; the **Minneapolis Art Fair** takes over Loring Park; the **CIL Festival** at the College of St. Catherine features a juried crafts show with approximately 150 top craftspersons, mixed with musicians, street players and other entertainment; the **Rose Fête** combines arts and crafts displays, family entertainment, and food and drink with free admission to the Minneapolis Institute of Arts where it is held; and **Svenskarnas Dag,** the traditional Swedish mid-summer festival, celebrates the longest day of the year with folk dancing, singing, a band contest, queen contest, and Swedish food specialties at Minnehaha Park in Minneapolis.

July is packed with several community celebrations: Bloomington's **Summer Fête;** Stillwater's **Lumberjack Days,** featuring a log-rolling event, parade, 100,000-meter footrace, barbershop chorus and quartets' jamboree, carnival and parade; and the biggest of all—Minneapolis' **Aquatennial,** the largest civic celebration in the United States, including some 250 family-oriented events, many of which are free, ranging from the Torchlight Parade to the milk carton boat race on Lake Calhoun. **Norway Day,** in Minneapolis' Minnehaha Park, includes a parade, demonstrations of Norwegian arts and crafts, and a queen coronation. On the Fourth of July, in addition to staging individual neighborhood events, all of Minnesota joins in the **Taste of Minnesota** celebration on the State Capitol Mall in St. Paul. The music and fireworks are free and tickets can be purchased for the food samples from Minnesota's favorite restaurants. In late July, **Riverfest,** on Harriet Island in St. Paul, along the banks of the Mississippi River, features eight days of music and entertainment with everything from national recording artists to regional arts and crafts fairs, children's programs to ethnic food booths. In August, one of the Midwest's largest art fairs, the **Uptown Art Fair,** attracts 600 artists and more than 150,000 people to the area around Lake Street and Hennepin Avenue.

TOURS AND SPECIAL-INTEREST SIGHTSEEING. City tour. *Gray Line* (349–7400) combines the best of Minneapolis and St. Paul in a 3½-hour tour, Tues.-Sat., the day after Memorial Day–October 2. Adults, $13; children, 14 and under, $6.50. Call 349–7400 for more information.

The Minneapolis Chamber of Commerce has a number of brochures on shopping, dining, arts and entertainment, and walking, jogging, and biking paths. Brochures and maps (some of which are free) describing tours of local businesses, buildings, and historic sites are also available.

Lake Harriet Trolley. W. Lake Harriet Blvd. and 42nd St. (348–2243). Climb aboard the restored streetcar for a two-mile, 20-minute round-trip between Lake Harriet and Lake Calhoun. Operates limited hours (usually afternoons and early evenings) during the summer and weekend afternoons in September and October. 50 cents.

Boat cruises. In the "Land of 10,000 Lakes," the Twin Cities also offers several excursions aboard their rivers and lakes. In St. Paul, regularly scheduled sightseeing cruises take you down the Mississippi River from downtown to Fort Snelling near the confluence of the Mississippi and Minnesota rivers. The paddlewheelers *Josiah Snelling* and *Jonathan Padelford* run Memorial Day through Labor Day. The regular cruise lasts 1 ¾ hours and leaves Harriet Island (take a right at the sign off S. Wabasha St. across the bridge from downtown) seven days a week at 10 A.M., noon, 2, and 4 P.M. Tickets can be picked up one-half hour before a cruise except for dinner cruises, which require reservations. For reservations, call 227–1100. A paddlewheeler departing from the Mississippi River on the Minneapolis side will begin during the summer of 1988.

On Minneapolis's Lake Harriet, the smaller *Queen of the Lakes* sternwheeler leaves the Lake Harriet bandstand area every 45 minutes, 1–8:15 P.M., seven days a week, June 15–Labor Day. Adults, $1; children, 50 cents. West of Minneapolis, for a 90-minute cruise on Lake Minnetonka, you can board the *Lady of the Lake* at Water and Lake streets, Excelsior, at 1 P.M. daily, Memorial Day–Labor Day. You can bring your own lunch. For more information, call 929–1209. Adults, $4; children, $3.

PARKS AND GARDENS. Approximately 50 parks, park reserves, gardens, and trail corridors covering 47,000 acres are maintained within the seven-county metropolitan area. Predictably lakes form the hub of many. In fact, approximately 950 lakes dot the metropolitan area, 25 of them within the city limits of Minneapolis and St. Paul. In warmer months, activities center around hiking, biking and jogging paths, swimming beaches, boat docks, fishing haunts, ballfields, and playgrounds. In winter, the focus switches to hockey and ice skating rinks, dogsled and cross-country ski trails, downhill ski runs, and bays known for their ice fishing. For a current schedule of special events call the *Minneapolis Park and Recreation Board* (348–2226), *St. Paul Parks and Recreation* (292–7400), the *Hennepin County Park Reserve District* (559–9000), and the *Ramsey County Parks Department* (777–1707).

In St. Paul, families have been spending Sunday afternoons at **Como Park** (on Lexington Pkwy.) for over a century. Golf, tennis, canoeing, paddle boats, a zoo, gardens, and—in winter—snowshoeing attract visitors. The **Como Park Conservatory,** open year-round, varies its floral displays by season. Free in summer, nominal charge in winter.

In south Minneapolis, a chain of four lakes—**Cedar, Lake of the Isles, Calhoun,** and **Harriet**—form the backbone of a popular park system. You can swim at one of seven beaches, rent canoes, rowboats, or sailboats, fish, bike, hike, ride the trolley from Lake Harriet to Lake Calhoun, or listen to a concert at the Lake Harriet bandstand. Twelve miles of continuous off-road trails are great for biking, hiking, roller-skating or jogging in the summer and skiing or snowshoeing in the winter. You can practice at the archery range or visit the Lake Harriet Rose Gardens with its more than 3,000 rosebushes plus annual and perennial flowers displayed in formal gardens at the northeast corner of Lake Harriet. Just north of the gardens is the **Thomas Sadler Robert Bird Sanctuary,** home of marshland birds. Both gardens and sanctuary are free.

In Minneapolis's **Minnehaha Park,** E. 48th St. and Minnehaha Ave., Minnehaha Creek winds into Minneapolis from the western suburbs, then plunges over the falls to the glen below. Hikers can follow the creek to where it flows into the Mississippi River. Two large picnic areas with pavilion and electric cooking equipment make this a popular place for family reunions. **Nokomis-Hiawatha Regional Park,** Cedar Ave. and Minnehaha Pkwy., Mpls., is named for its two lakes. The more active center is Nokomis with its two beaches, a 2½-mile fitness trail, bike and walking paths. At quieter Hiawatha, you can relax on the beach, enjoy the 18-hole golf course, canoe, sail, skate, or go ski touring.

West of downtown Minneapolis at the **Theodore Wirth Park,** Glenwood Ave. and Xerxes Ave. N., you can hike or bike over paved trails or drive through wooded areas. You can swim, canoe, sail, golf, ski, snowshoe, or visit the 20-acre Eloise Butler Wildflower Garden and Bird Sanctuary. A self-guided tour identifies the woodland, upland and bog flowers set on hilly terrain. The garden, open Apr.–Oct., is free.

Southwest of Minneapolis, in Bloomington and Eden Prairie, are three park reserves: **Hyland, Bush,** and **Bryant Lake.** Biking and hiking trails give visitors easy access to this nature center and picnic areas as well as to beaches, fishing and waterfowl observation sites. A two-acre Japanese garden is featured at **Normandale Community College,** 9700 France Ave., Bloomington, providing solace amid its lagoon, bridges. islands, waterfall, shrine, and beautiful trees and shrubs. Open year-round; admission free. Much larger is the **University of Minnesota Landscape Arboretum,** just off Hwy. 5 west of Chanhassen. Six miles of walking trails crisscross 675 acres of hills, lakes and marshland set with hundreds of trees and plants. In the winter, cross-country ski trails provide access to the area. On the grounds are also a conservatory with flowering plants, a tearoom, and a gift shop. Grounds are open 8 A.M.–sunset. Adults, $2; children, $1 (free when accompanied by parents). Seniors are free on the second and fourth Fridays of each month. Call 443–2460 for information.

In downtown Minneapolis, on the east bank of the Mississippi River near the Hennepin Avenue Bridge, you can enjoy free outdoor concerts in the summer and view the historic Stone Arch Railroad Bridge, the locks, and Nicollet Island. For concert schedule, call 348–2142 or 348–PARK. South of downtown St. Paul, along the Mississippi River, explore the **Lilydale–Harriet Island Regional Park** from which you can watch tugs, barges, and pleasure craft pass by on the Mississippi. Picnic on Cherokee Bluffs overlooking the river or explore for rocks and fossils in the clay pits. In summer, the boat launch is open and in winter, ski touring is popular.

ZOOS. In St. Paul, at Midway Parkway and Kaufman Dr., is the long-time favorite, **Como Park Zoo.** Recently upgraded, this collection features a large-cat building with Siberian tigers, cougars, and jaguars, and a marine animal building where you can watch polar bears swim underwater. In summer, seals perform and year-round you can watch the antics of the apes in the ape house. Parking and general admission are free, although some exhibit buildings charge 10 cents admission.

Newer and much larger is the **Minnesota Zoological Garden,** 12101 Johnny Cake Ridge Rd., Apple Valley, south of the Twin Cities. More than 1,700 animals roam their natural habitats, set on 485 acres. Visitors can explore by foot, skis or via monorail. As you enter, check the program board for the times of the dolphin feedings, theater programs, and live animal demonstrations. A children's petting zoo is popular with younger visitors. In the summer, picnic sites are available outside the zoo grounds. Open daily, except Christmas, 10 A.M.–6 P.M., summers, 10 A.M.–4 P.M., winters. Adults, $4; children 6–16, $1.50; seniors, $2. Parking, $1. Call 432–9000 for current hours and information.

PARTICIPANT SPORTS. Jogging and running fit in nicely with the Twin Cities landscape that includes so many parks, lakes, and suitable paths. For a complete list of popular runs in Minneapolis and St. Paul, including degree of difficulty, traffic, and aesthetics, pick up a copy of Gretchen Kreuter's book, *Running the Twin Cities.* As evidence of the popularity of the sport and the setting, the Twin Cities Marathon, held the first Sunday in October, has become one of the top-rated marathons in the country in the few years since its inception.

Both Minneapolis and St. Paul maintain several outdoor **tennis** facilities. For locations, call Minneapolis, 348–2226, or St. Paul, 292–7400. Private clubs that provide tennis for the general public include: in Minneapolis, *Nicollet Tennis Center,* 4005 Nicollet Ave., 825–6844; in St. Paul, *St. Paul Indoor Tennis Club,* 600 De Soto Ave. S., 774–2121.

Of the hundreds of miles of **bicycle** trails in the Twin Cities, one of the most enjoyable trails follows Minnehaha Creek. For bikes only, this trail runs from Minnehaha Park through south Minneapolis, encircling Lake Harriet, Lake Calhoun, and Lake of the Isles. The Minnesota Department of Transportation publishes *54 Minnesota Bikeways* maps, each including a road analysis and historical, social, and cultural attractions. To order, contact the Map Sales Office, Minnesota Dept. of Transportation, John Ireland Blvd., Rm. B-20, St. Paul 55155 (612–296–2216).

Canoes and rowboats may be rented at the *Lake Calhoun Boat House,* 3000 E. Calhoun Blvd., Minneapolis. In St. Paul, for information on canoes and sailboat rental call 776–9833.

Fishing is popular year-round. The only variation is that in summer you cast from shore, dock, or a boat; in winter you drill a hole in the ice. Lakes Calhoun, Harriet, and Lake of the Isles are good bass waters. Smallmouth bass and walleyes can be caught in the Mississippi River. West of downtown, in Lake Minnetonka and its connecting chain of lakes, you can land trophy largemouth bass, smallmouth bass, walleyes, northern pike and panfish. Across the northern tier of the metropolitan area, White Bear, Bald Eagle, and Forest Lakes, as well as the Rum River to the north and the St. Croix River to the east, teem with a variety of bass, pike, and panfish.

Approximately 50 **golf courses** are open to the public. Greens fees average $8 for nine holes; $12 for 18. Popular courses include: *Braemar,* 6364 Dewey Hill Rd., Edina (941–2072); *Dwan,* 3301 W. 110th St., Bloomington (887–9602); *Hiawatha,* 4553 Longfellow Ave. S., Minneapolis (724–7715); *University of Minnesota,* Larpenteur and Fulham avenues, Falcon Heights (par 3, 627–4002, long course, 627–4001); *Theodore Wirth,* Plymouth and Glenwood avenues, Minneapolis (par 3, 522–2818; long course, 522–4584) and the new *Edinburgh USA,* 8700 Edinbrook Crossing, Brooklyn Park (424–7060).

In winter, almost every major park maintains an outdoor **skating** rink and warming house. Year-round indoor skating is available at several arenas.

Cross-country skiers will find well-groomed trails in most major parks and reserves as well as at several golf courses and even the Minnesota Zoological Garden. A license is required on public trails. Fees are $5 for individuals; $7.50 for families. The major **downhill** areas are: *Afton Alps,* southeast of St. Paul off Hwy. 94E on County roads 20 and 21 (436–5245); *Buck Hill,* 15400 Buck Hill Rd., just off I-35 in Burnsville (435–7187); *Hyland Hills,* 8800 Chalet Rd., near I-494 and Hwy. 100 in Bloomington (835–4604); *Welch Village,* off U.S. 61 south of Hastings (222–7079 or 221–9145); and *Wild Mountain* in Taylor Falls, east of St. Paul (291–7980). Longest runs range from 2,000–4,000 feet with a 175- to 350-foot vertical drop.

SPECTATOR SPORTS. The Hubert H. Humphrey Metrodome, 900 S. 5th St., Minneapolis, is home to the 1987 World Champion Minnesota Twins (baseball), Vikings (football), and the University of Minnesota Gopher football team. The Minnesota North Stars (hockey) play at the Met Center in Bloomington, Oct.–Mar. Also at Met Center are the Minnesota Strikers, indoor soccer. The most recent addition is horse racing at Canterbury Downs, Shakopee. Coming soon will be professional basketball, with the Minnesota Timberwolves set to make their debut in 1989.

HISTORIC SITES AND HOUSES. Fort Snelling. Highways 5 and 55, Bloomington (726–9430). Perched on the bluffs at the confluence of the Mississippi and Minnesota rivers, the fort is a restored 1820s military outpost. Visitors are greeted by guides in period dress. The fort itself is open daily, May 1–Oct. 31, and the adjacent History Center is open year-round. Adults, $2.00, children 6–15, 50 cents.

Gibbs Farm Museum, 2097 W. Larpenteur Ave., St. Paul (646–8629) and the **Oliver H. Kelley Farm** on Hwy. 10, 2½ miles east of Elk River (441–6896), depict mid-nineteenth-century farm life. The Kelley Farm was the experimental farm of the founder of the national Grange movement and today is still a working, "living history" farm.

Murphy's Landing, Minnesota Valley Restoration Project (445–6900). Southwest of the Twin Cities, east of Shakopee on Hwy. 101 on the banks of the Minnesota River. This is a living history museum of the 1840s–1890s. Costumed interpreters in historic buildings tell the story of the Minnesota River. A working dressmaker, printer, and blacksmith, and boat rides are featured. Restaurants and gift shop. Memorial Day–Labor Day, Wed., Thurs., Fri., 11 A.M.–4 P.M.; weekends, noon–5 P.M. May, Sept., and Oct.: open weekdays by reservation (445–6900) and Nov. 27 and weekends through Dec. 20, and by reservation. 10 A.M.–4 P.M. Adults, $4; students and senior citizens, $3; children 5 and under, free.

Alexander Ramsey House. 265 S. Exchange St., St. Paul (296–0100). Home of Minnesota's first territorial governor. Many of the furnishings remain in the home, which is especially beautiful at Christmas. Open Apr.–Dec. Adults, $2; children 6–15 and senior citizens, $1; children 5 and under, free.

Henry Hastings Sibley House. 22 D St., Mendota (452–1596). Built in the 1830s and once the home of the first governor of Minnesota, this is the oldest private home in the state. The adjacent **Jean Faribault House,** home to an early fur trader and guide, is now a museum for Indian artifacts. Both houses are included in a 90-min. tour. Open May–Oct. Tues.–Sat., 10 A.M.–5 P.M.; Sun. and holidays, 1–6 P.M. Adults, $2; children, 50 cents.

Summit Avenue. This St. Paul street was once known as the richest street in the world. The James J. Hill mansion, the red sandstone home of Minnesota's railroad builder, is at 240 Summit. Open year-round, Wed., Thurs., and Sat., 10 A.M.–4 P.M. Adults, $2; children and senior citizens, $1. Farther west at 1006 Summit Ave. is the governor's residence built in 1910 by Horace Irvine, a prominent St. Paul lumberman. Reservations are required; 296–2881. At the eastern end of Summit rises the classical Renaissance St. Paul Cathedral at the intersection of Selby and Summit. North, across I-94, stands the State Capitol.

MUSEUMS. American Swedish Institute. 2600 Park Ave., Minneapolis (871–4907). Publisher Swan Turnblad built this turn-of-the-century 33-room mansion that now houses art and artifacts recalling the strong Swedish influence in Minnesota. Tues.–Sat., noon–5 P.M.; Sun., 1–5 P.M. Adults, $2; senior citizens and students under 21, $1.

Hennepin County Historical Society Museum. 2303 3d Ave. E., Minneapolis (870–1329). The museum's 30 rooms include a miniature village of the early 1900s. Tues.–Fri., 9 A.M.–4:30 P.M.; Sun. 1–5 P.M. Free.

Minnesota Historical Society. 690 Cedar, St. Paul (296–6126). Across the street from the Capitol; regularly changing exhibits graphically depict Minnesota's early history. Mon.–Sat., 8:30 A.M.–5 P.M., Sun 1–4 P.M. Free.

Minneapolis Institute of Arts. 2400 3d Ave. S., Minneapolis (870–3046). Renowned works by Rembrandt and Van Gogh share attention with the Pillsbury collection of ancient Chinese bronzes and exhibits by contemporary Minnesota artists. Daily public tours are offered and both wheelchairs and strollers are available. Adults, $2; students, $1; children under 12, seniors, and disabled veterans, free. Free on Thurs., 5–9 P.M. Closed Mon. Free ramp parking at 3rd Ave. S. and E. 25th St.

Minnesota Museum of Art. 305 St. Peter St., St. Paul (292–4355). The extensive permanent collection emphasizes early twentieth-century American art. Nearby at its **Landmark Center Galleries,** 75 W. Fifth St., the museum hosts changing exhibitions of regional and national importance. Both are free. Open Tues., Wed., and Fri., 10:30 A.M.–4:30 P.M.; Thurs., 10:30 A.M.–7:30 P.M.; Sat.–Sun., 1–4:30 P.M.

Science Museum of Minnesota. 505 Wabasha St., St. Paul (221–9488). The museum features hands-on experience and live demonstrations as well as the McKnight-3M Omnitheater. Tues.–Sat., 9:30 A.M.–9 P.M., Sun. 11 A.M.–9 P.M. Adults $4.50; children 12 and under, $3.50; additional $1 for omnitheater.

Walker Art Center. At Vineland Place, west of Loring Park, in Minneapolis (375–7600). Contemporary artists, including painters, sculptors, and photographers, are emphasized at one of the most famous museums in the nation. Free, except for special exhibitions. Lunch available in the Gallery 8 Restaurant; patio dining in the summer. Tues.–Sat., 10 A.M.–8 P.M., Sun. 11 A.M.–5 P.M.

FILMS. The major theaters showing current first-run movies are the *Cooper 1 and 2,* 5755 Wayzata Blvd. (Hwy. 55), St. Louis Park; *Skyway 5 Theatres,* 711 Hennepin Av., Mpls.; the *Southtown Theatre,* I-494 and Penn Ave. S., Bloomington; *St. Anthony Main,* 115 Main St. SE, Minneapolis; *Galtier,* 175 E. 5th St., St. Paul; and theaters at all major shopping centers in the suburban areas. Many offer discount tickets to showings before 5 P.M. or on Sunday afternoons. In addition, several organizations show classic, foreign, and experimental films not usually seen in local commercial movie theaters: **Film in the Cities.** Jerome Hill Theater, First Trust Center, 5th & Jackson, St. Paul (291–0801). New films by U.S. (including Minnesota) and foreign independent directors, film classics, and photography lectures and presentations. At the **Minneapolis Institute of Arts,** 2400 3d Ave. S., Minneapolis (870–3131), classics and movies relating to museum exhibits are shown on some evenings; family film festivals are scheduled on alternate weekends. Museum admission: Adults, $2; students, $1; children under 12, free. **University Film Society,** 122 Pleasant St. SE, Minneapolis (627-4431), shows foreign, experimental, popular current and classic films in the Bell Museum of Natural History Auditorium, University and 17th Ave. SE, Minneapolis. Occasionally international stars and critics appear as guest speakers. Admission is usually about $4. Each May the Society sponsors the Rivertown U.S.A. Film Festival. Current, historical, and experimental films run at the **Walker Art Center** (375–7600), usually in themed series. Some are followed by a presentation or discussion. Admission is approximately $3.

MUSIC. Under the direction of Edo de Waart, the **Minnesota Orchestra** (371–5656) performs at Orchestra Hall in downtown Minneapolis and O'Shaughnessy Auditorium at the College of St. Catherine in St. Paul, Sept. to May. Summer concerts include a Night at the Pops series, free concerts in the parks, and the Viennese Sommerfest. **The St. Paul Chamber Orchestra** performs music from Baroque to contemporary. This Grammy Award-winning, 34-member group performs in the new and highly acclaimed Ordway Music Theatre at Washington and E. 5th St., St. Paul (291–1144). The **Minnesota Opera Company** presents at least two classics and several contemporary operas, sung in English, or with English "supratitles" flashed above the stage; at the Ordway Music Theatre, St. Paul (221–0256).

Several free concerts are offered by numerous professional and semi-professional groups: the *Bloomington Symphony Orchestra* (881–4114), the *Civic Orchestra of Minneapolis* (929–8293), the *Kenwood Chamber Orchestra* (377–5095), the *Minnetonka Symphony Orchestra* (935–4615), the *St. Paul Civic Symphony* (696–6189), and the *Sylmar Chamber Ensemble* (331–3699). The Live from Landmark series presents a variety of free musical offerings, Sept.–May, at the Landmark Center, 75 W. 5th St., St. Paul. (292–3225). Free music in the parks has been a long-standing summer tradition in the Twin Cities parks. Call the Minneapolis (348–2226) and St. Paul (292–7400) Parks and Recreation departments for schedules. At the University of Minnesota, both outside on the mall and inside Northrop Auditorium, several free events feature blues to Dixieland in the Northrop Summer Series (624–2345).

DANCE. In addition to local professional companies that tour both regionally and nationally, several internationally renowned touring artists perform in the Twin Cities. The **NorthWest Ballet** (339–9150) performs classical and contemporary ballet. Modern dance is featured in the two concerts produced annually by the **Nancy Hauser Dance Company** (871–9077). The **Northrop Dance Season** (624–2345), scheduled at the University of Minnesota's Northrop Auditorium, brings to town such names as the Joffrey Ballet, Twyla Tharp, and Paul Taylor.

STAGE. The Guthrie Theater, Vineland Place, Minneapolis (377–2224), founded in 1963, places the Twin Cities in the hierarchy of theatrical cities. Although heavily committed to the classics, the schedule includes musicals and Dickens's *A Christmas Carol.* Tickets range from $6.95 to $20.95; public and student rush tickets offer substantial savings.

Children's Theater Company. 2400 3d Ave. S., Minneapolis (874–0400). Recognized as the nation's leading theater for families and young people, this theater brings to life classic and contemporary children's stories, folktales, and fantasies as well as original contemporary productions. $6.75–$15.75.

Dinner Theaters. Four separate productions are offered under one roof at the *Chanhassen Dinner Theatres* (934–1525). There is one stage for major musicals. In its pastoral setting in Excelsior, the *Old Log Theater* (474–5951) presents Broadway hits, mysteries, and British farces. Light comedies and musicals take center stage at the *Plymouth Playhouse,* at the Quality Inn, Plymouth, Hwy. 55 and I-494 (553–1155).

Community Theaters. The **Cricket Theatre** (871–3763), 9 W. 14th St., Minneapolis, produces new, critically acclaimed plays by modern, mostly American playwrights, at various area theaters. The **Great North American History Theatre** (292–4323), Landmark Center, St. Paul, produces original historical docudramas and musicals. **Actors Theatre** (227–0050), 28 W. 7th Place, St. Paul, presents classics and new plays by American playrights (including a one-act-play festival). **Park Square Theatre** (291–7005), Jemne Building, St. Paul, presents a variety of works. **The Theater 65** (647–5965), Brady Center-College of St. Thomas, St. Paul, produces plays featuring older actors (hence the name "65"). In summer, many area theater groups produce free summer performances as part of the Plays in the Parks. Call 348–2226 for their schedule.

West Bank Theater District. Named for its proximity to the University of Minnesota's West Bank Campus, this area has the highest concentration of theaters in Minneapolis, all of which are reasonably priced. In the early 1900s the West Bank combined a little of everything: vaudeville, music halls and bordellos, appealing to everyone from the resident Bohemians to local dignitaries. Today comedy and improvisation as well as contemporary and traditional plays are presented in several diverse neighborhood theaters.

The Southern Theater. 1420 Washington Ave. S. (340–0155). Home to several theaters: **At the Foot of the Mountain,** the oldest continuously producing women's theater in the country; **Theatre de la Jeune Lune,** performing innovative plays styled in the European tradition; plus **In the Heart of the Beast Puppet and Mask Theatre, Brass Tacks Theater,** and **Primary Vision.** Next door, **Dudley Riggs' E.T.C.,** 1430 Washington Ave. S., (332–6620), presents musical satire and stand-up comedy and has launched such new and original talents as the Flying Karamazov Brothers and "Saturday Night Live" performers Franken and Davis. Similar in nature, though located in south Minneapolis at 2605 Hennepin Ave. (332–6620), is the Dudley Riggs' **Brave New Workshop,** presenting satiric reviews on contemporary issues.

Also on the West Bank is Minneapolis's oldest community theater and one of its most renowned, **Theatre in the Round,** 245 Cedar (333–3010). Offering ten productions annually, the TRP schedule mixes classics with contemporary dramas and comedies. Nearby, one block west of Cedar and Riverside, in a famous old firehouse built in 1887, is the **Mixed Blood Theatre Company** (338–6131). It features original works, American premieres of new scripts, late-night musical revues, and contemporary classics cast multiracially. **The University Theatre,** at 4th St. and 21st Ave. S. (625–4001), completes the District's theaters. Famous graduates include Linda Kelsey, Loni Anderson, Peter Graves, and John Astin. Its program blends classics and contemporary theater as well as musicals. In the summer, they move down to the shores of the Mississippi to perform delightful melodrama aboard the Minnesota Centennial Showboat, an authentic sternwheel riverboat.

DINING OUT. If you've heard that dining experiences in the Twin Cities can be very inconsistent in quality, relax. Those critiques are directed primarily at establishments whose nouvelle cuisine can be delectable one night, detestable the next. In the less expensive categories, the fare is generally hearty, often home-cooked, ranging from hamburgers to shrimp toast.

Categories, based on the price of a three-course dinner for one, without beverage, tax (6 percent in Minnesota), or tip, are: *Reasonable,* $9 to $12; *Very Economical,* $6 to $8; and *Low Budget,* under $6. Except for the Ediner and Green Mill, no restaurant in the *Low Budget* or *Very Economical* categories accepts reservations or credit cards. Wheelchair-accessible establishments are noted by a W.

Reasonable

Black Forest Inn. 26th St. at Nicollet Ave., Minneapolis (872–0812). Rouladen, brats, apple strudel, and German beer on tap share space on the menu with standard American fare in a slightly Bohemian atmosphere where jeans and suits are equally acceptable. Beer garden open in the summer.

Ciatti's Italian Ristorante. 1346 LaSalle Ave., Minneapolis (339–7747); 850 Grand Ave., St. Paul (292–9942). Homemade pasta featured on a 30-plus item menu, including Italian hamburgers. Save room for the chocolate-almond torte. Classy, yet simple, surroundings. W.

Good Earth. Galleria, 3460 W. 70th St., Edina (925–1001); Bonaventure, Hwy. 12 and Plymouth Rd., Minnetonka (546–6432); and 1901 W. Hwy. 36, Roseville (636–0956). Not only good food but food that's good for you. No refined sugar here. Fresh fruits, vegetables, combined with poultry, seafood, and beef in imaginative dishes, including wok-cooked entrees and frozen-yogurt shakes. W.

Leeann Chin. Bonaventure, Hwy. 12 & Plymouth Rd., Minnetonka, (545–3600); International Center, 900 Second Ave. S., Minneapolis (338–8488); Union Depot, 214 E. 4th St., St. Paul (224–8814); Dayton's (take out only), 700 Nicollet Mall, Minneapolis (375–2763); and Norwest Center, 5th and Minnesota St., St. Paul (292–8776). Operated by popular cooking teacher and caterer-turned-restauranteur. Showcased museum artifacts and contemporary track lighting create an atypical setting for superb Chinese fare. No menu—you choose from a buffet that includes lemon chicken and shrimp toast. W.

Mancini's Char House. 531 W. 7th St., St. Paul (224–7345). A steak-lover's haven in informal setting (your party is paged over a loudspeaker). Expect a wait since reservations are accepted only for parties of 8 or more. W.

Market Bar-B-Que. 1414 Nicollet Ave. S., Minneapolis (333–1028 or 332–9980), and 15320 Wayzata Blvd., Minnetonka (475–1770). Black-and-white glossies of vaudeville's greats and more contemporary celebrities who have eaten here create the backdrop for diners diving into spareribs, chicken, and beef prepared on a wood-burning pit. W.

Nankin. 2 S. 7th St., Minneapolis (333–3303). A famous institution in its third location on 7th St., featuring more than 100 items on its Chinese-American menu. Popular with all ages. W.

Venetian Inn. 2814 Rice St., Little Canada (484–7215). Southern Italian specialties overseen by the now-famous Mama Vitale. Live music and dancing in the lounge Mon.–Sat. Closed Sun. W.

Very Economical

Annie's Parlour. 406 Cedar Ave., Minneapolis (339–6207); 313 14th Ave. SE, Minneapolis (379–0744); Lake St. & Hennepin Ave., Minneapolis (825–4455).

Great burger joint ice cream parlors. Fries sliced from fresh potatoes and thick, juicy burgers complemented by thick malts. W.

Convention Grill. 3912 Sunnyside Ave., Edina (920–6881). All the expected burgers, fries, and luscious malts, plus homemade chicken noodle soup, in a classic 1940s malt shop. W.

Malt Shop. 809 W. 50th St., Minneapolis (824–1352); Bandana Square, 1021 E. Bandana Blvd., St. Paul (645–4643); and St. Anthony Main, Second St. and Second Ave., Minneapolis (378–7251). Real fruit goes into the malts at this 1950s-style malt shop that specializes in vegetarian omelets and sandwiches. A homey, neighborhood atmosphere where local musicians perform. Phone ahead to have your name placed on a waiting list. W.

Low Budget

Al's Breakfast. 413 14th Ave. SE, Minneapolis (331–9991). A tradition near the University with counters running down the spine of one of the narrowest restaurants you'll encounter. Omelets, waffles, and the usual ham and eggs served up in a friendly atmosphere.

Byerly's. 1959 Suburban Ave., St. Paul (735–6340); 5725 Duluth St., Golden Valley (544–8846); 7171 France Ave. S., Edina (831–3601); 3777 Park Center Blvd. (Hwy. 100 at 36th St.), St. Louis Park, (929–2100); and 13081 Ridgedale Dr., Minnetonka (541–1414); and 401 W. 98th St., Bloomington (881–6294). Actually located in the most phenomenal "grocery stores" you've seen, these pleasant restaurants feature such homemade specialties as cinnamon rolls and wild rice soup as well as fresh seafood and daily specials ranging from salads to lamb. Open 24 hours a day, seven days a week. W.

Ediner. Galleria, 69th St. and France Ave. S., Edina (925–4008); and Calhoun Square, 3001 Hennepin Ave. Minneapolis (822–6011); Pavillion Place, 1655 W. City Rd., Roseville (636–2862); and Bonaventure, 1641 Plymouth Rd., Minnetonka (542–3060). Blue-plate specials are served up with authentic juke box music in this re-created 1940s-style diner. Great malts, homemade soups, sandwiches, salads, and desserts. W.

Green Mill. 57 Hamline Ave. S., St. Paul (698–0353); 2626 Hennepin Ave., Minneapolis (374–2131); 4501 France Ave. S., Edina (925–5400); and 5540 Brooklyn Blvd., Brooklyn Center (560–2500). Specialize in two inch thick deep-dish pizzas heaped with natural ingredients; sandwiches and seafood also available. A Twin Cities favorite. W.

Mickey's Diner. 36 W. 9th St., St. Paul (222–5633). You'll see everyone here from the bluest of blue collar to the (almost) bluest of bluebloods. Superb hash browns, omelets, and sandwiches served straight off a grill that is inches from you in this authentic 1930s dining car that was saved from urban renewal by being placed on the National Register of Historic Places.

Recommended Splurge. Willows. 1300 Nicollet Mall, Hyatt Regency Hotel, Minneapolis (370–1234, ext. 272 or 273). If you like fine food that comes with fine service (efficient and friendly, not stuffy) and a romantic atmosphere, this splurge will be well worth the $18-to-$20-dent in the pocketbook. If the superb duck doesn't win you over, the gourmet smorgasbord with both appetizers and entrees or the dessert bar with its sinfully rich selections will. Special touches such as chocolate curls and orange bits to add to your coffee and a rose delivered to each lady before you depart create a memorable evening (a bargain if you're really out to impress someone).

Cafés, Coffeehouses, and Alfresco Dining. Some of the best people-watching, as well as a satisfying cup of coffee, espresso or cool drink, can be enjoyed in one of three areas. In the West Bank District (in the vicinity of Washington, Cedar, and Riverside streets, adjacent to the University of Minnesota), you can relax amidst the casual European atmosphere of **Cafe Espresso,** 1430 Washington Ave. S., the Midwest's oldest espresso coffeehouse, featuring Viennese and Hungarian specialties. A short distance away at **The Extempore,** 416 Cedar Ave. S., you'll hear ballads, bluegrass, jazz, and blues mixed with songwriters and storytellers. For reservations, call 370–0004. A couple doors south is **The New Riverside Cafe,** at 1810 Riverside Ave., featuring a vegetarian menu and music from classical to reggae.

Minneapolis' Nicollet Mall is the second great place. Year-round you can relax in the Crystal Court of the IDS Center or at any of several restaurants that set up outdoor patios for the summer. West of the cities, on the shores of Lake Minnetonka, is the third (although not really budget) great spot where the "leisure class" gathers, complete with yachts. Stop by **Lord Fletcher's of the Lake,** 3746 Sunset Dr., Spring Park (471–8513); or **Mai Tai,** 687 Excelsior Blvd., Excelsior (474–1183); or **Sasha's Deli & Grill,** 294 E. Grove Lane (475–3354).

NIGHTLIFE AND BARS. Much of the night life in the Twin Cities is located on First and Hennepin avenues in downtown Minneapolis and along the I-494 strip in Bloomington, augmented by pockets of varying types scattered throughout the suburbs. Minnesota bars close at 1 A.M., Mon.–Sat.; midnight, on Sun. The legal drinking age is 21.

In downtown Minneapolis, Yuppies congregate at the **Loon Cafe and Bar,** 500 1st Ave. N. (332–8342), while **First Avenue,** 701-1st Ave. N. (332–1775), where musician Prince has played and filmed, attracts more of the "punk" crowd, who groove on its combination of music and videos. Cover charge varies according to the group playing. At the **Ha Ha Club** (formerly the **Comedy Cabaret**), 1414 W. 28th St. (872–0305), you'll hear stand-up comedians and skits by local talent. Other comedy clubs include **The Comedy Gallery** in three locations—Riverplace (331-JOKE), 65 Main St. SE; East (770–2811), Maplewood; South (888–8900), Bloomington **Rib Tickler Comedy & Magic Club** (339–9031), 716 N. 1st. St., Minneapolis; **Funny Bone Comedy Nite Club** (824–1981), 2911 Hennepin Ave.; and **That Comedy Place** (338–2424), 11th & LaSalle, Minneapolis.

Along the I-494 strip, every major hotel and several restaurants offer a choice of bars and live entertainment. At **Stonewings,** 8301 Normandale Blvd. (831–4811), and **Gregory's,** 7956 Lyndale Ave. S., (881–8611), bands play "Top 40s" and "easy listening" music for dancing and relaxing. Although **Bennigan's Tavern,** 1800 W. 80th St. (881–0013), has no live music, it's a lively meeting place.

Just beyond downtown Minneapolis, you can vary your selection from a quiet, Bohemian atmosphere at the **Black Forest Inn,** 1 E. 26th St. (872–0812), to polka music at the unpretentious **Mayslack's Polka Lounge,** 1428 NE 4th St. (789–9862) and live rock and blues at the **Cabooze on the West Bank,** 917 Cedar Ave. (338–6425). Out in the suburbs, your choice ranges from the nightclub atmosphere at **Rupert's,** 5410 Wayzata Blvd., St. Louis Park (544–4993), where a no-jeans dress code and $5 cover charge limit the clientele, to the zany atmosphere at **George is in Fridley,** 3720 E. River Rd., Fridley (781–3377), a Greek restaurant with Greek music and a belly dancer who frequently invites members of the audience to join in the fun. At the **Emporium of Jazz,** 1351 Sibley Memorial Hwy., Mendota (452–1868), New Orleans–style jazz sets the pace.

Ballroom dancing is alive and well at several Twin Cities ballrooms: **Bel-Rae,** Hwy. 10, Mounds View (786–4630); **Majestic,** 9165 S. Point Douglas Dr. (Hwys. 10 and 61), Cottage Grove (459–3457); **Medina,** 500 Hwy. 55, Hamel (478–6661). Cover charges vary by band and only Medina accepts credit cards.

SECURITY. The Twin Cities fortunately has few very "seedy" areas. However, at night you should avoid downtown Hennepin Avenue as well as Franklin Avenue and Lake Street east of Nicollet, and be cautious in any parking ramp. Parks such as Loring, although frequented by all ages during the day, should be avoided at night.

NASHVILLE

by
Randy Hilman and Jan Ryan

Randy Hilman is a reporter for the Tennessean. *He came to Music City as a professional bass player in the early 1970s. Jan Ryan is a television news journalist who has worked as a reporter and anchor in Atlanta, Los Angeles, and Nashville. Together they publish* Nashville Restaurants: Menus & Recipes *and similar volumes for Cincinnati and Memphis.*

Ask people what comes to mind when they think of Nashville, and the response is likely to be country music and the Grand Ole Opry. Music undeniably has had much to do with Nashville's mystique and growing prosperity. Most of the country records produced in America today come from the recording studios on Music Row. Many country music superstars live here, and dozens of others seeking stardom show up at the city's doorstep every year. Country music and its legendary showcase, the Grand Ole Opry, have elevated Nashville to world prominence as the capital of country music, and many of the city's more than seven million visitors each year are dyed-in-the-wool fans who trek from all parts of the globe to pay homage to hillbilly fortune and fame. Small wonder that one of Nashville's many names is Music City U.S.A.

Yet with a rich heritage and dynamic growth, Nashville has much more to offer. Nashvillians (noted for their unbridled optimism and sunny hospitality) have worked long and hard to build a broader image on the rhinestone bedrock of their community. And they are succeeding. It comes as no surprise to locals that Nashville is rated among the top ten vacation spots in the country or that it has become known as one of the Cinderella cities of the Southeast.

Nashville is the state capital. It has diverse economics, a temperate climate, and a central location that is easily accessible from all parts of the country. The tourist who wants to explore beyond the highly visible music attractions can find in Nashville's nooks and crannies a wealth of interesting and affordable gems. An abundance of lakes and parks provide excellent opportunities for boating, camping, hiking, fishing, golf, and tennis. Civil War history is well represented in Nashville and Middle Tennessee, and Nashville's preserved plantation homes provide a striking contrast between the old and the new South. Although Nashville has exploded with growth in the last decade, its downtown business district remains small and easily manageable for walkers. Points of interest outside the city generally are within a 30-minute drive from the downtown area.

The city is fast reaching critical mass as a cosmopolitan business and cultural center, with new corporations, entrepreneurs, and artists coming from all over the country. A renaissance of the central business district and inlying historic neighborhoods is under way to complement the suburban office parks and residential neighborhoods that have characterized its suburban sprawl. To bolster confidence in a revitalized downtown, the city has launched an active program to upgrade commercial districts with brick streets, attractive plantings, and new lighting. People have responded. Downtown streets, once empty after dark, now teem with life. Riverfront Park, an open-air music theater, and the redevelopment of historic Second Avenue have helped fuel a return to the **downtown** area for leisure-time activities.

The changes would astonish Colonel James Robertson, who led a small band of North Carolinians across the Cumberland River to found **Fort Nashborough** at Cedar Bluffs on Christmas Day 1779. Their small fort, named after Revolutionary War hero General Francis Nash, served as protection from hostile Indians. Today a replica on the waterfront, just a few hundred yards from the original site, vividly illustrates the city's evolution. Nashborough became Nashville in 1784. Tennessee became a state 12 years later, and Nashville was selected as its permanent capital in 1843.

Today Metropolitan Nashville has a population of 509,000, and the city limits have grown from the scant acre of the Fort Nashboro settlement to 531 square miles, encompassing all of Davidson County. The tremendous expanse of territory is the result of the nation's first merger of city and county governments. The consolidation in 1963 produced a strong, unified form of government with an improved tax base and streamlined city services. Consolidation set the stage for a pattern of new economic growth, and 20 years later the list of developments under construction seems endless. Population for the greater metropolitan area has grown to 1 million.

The **central business district** has not strayed much from the site of the earliest riverbank settlement. The Tennessee state capitol building is here, as is Riverfront Park, a compact open-air music theater at the foot of Broadway. Unfortunately, vast vacant areas to the north and south of downtown are unpleasant reminders of urban renewal programs. Developers, however, are becoming interested in new residential, cultural, and commercial projects that may turn around the once blighted areas north and south of Capitol Hill. The beautifully restored Hermitage Hotel and historic Union Station Hotel are elegant examples of increased interest in the downtown area. Already the urban pioneers have helped stabilize the inlying residential districts and stimulate new interest in the downtown area by restoring deteriorated houses to their former elegance. Restorations in Germantown to the north, Rutledge Hill to the south, the Second Avenue warehouse district downtown, and parts of East Nashville across the Cumberland are a few examples.

The long rows of multistoried, nineteenth-century Victorian buildings adjacent to the waterfront make up the historic **warehouse district,** which runs three blocks to the west of the river and north and south from Broadway to the Metro Courthouse, once the center of the old city square. The buildings along First Avenue once were offloading houses for the shipping industry. **Historic Second Avenue,** a block of buildings that back up to First Avenue, is being renovated into upscale space for shops, restaurants, and offices.

Visitors seeking information on Nashville history should contact the offices downtown of Historic Nashville Inc., Box 2785, Nashville, TN 37219 (244–7835). The five block stretch of Broadway made famous when the **Grand Ole Opry** was headquartered at the Ryman Auditorium is still home for the Ernest Tubb Record Shop and Tootsie's Orchard Lounge.

The Opry is now east of the city, at the Opryland Showpark, but the legendary **Ryman Auditorium** still stands as an impressive monument to Nashville's country music roots. Built by born-again riverboat captain Tom Ryman as a tabernacle, the auditorium became home to the WSM Grand Ole Opry in 1943 and remained its residence until 1974, when the nation's longest-running live radio show moved to its new home in the multimillion-dollar Opryland complex. Although no longer used on a regular basis, the auditorium remains open to the public. In recent years it has been used as a set for several movies, including *Coal Miner's Daughter,* the story of Loretta Lynn. When you walk through the Ryman today, you can almost hear country music legend Roy Acuff singing "The Wabash Cannonball" and see him balancing a fiddle bow on his nose.

Sandwiched between Third and Fourth avenues North, and Church and Union streets is **Printer's Alley,** so named because the saloons located there in the nineteenth century were frequented by workers in Nashville's large printing industry, which once was concentrated in the area. The saloons have given way to the downtown row of nightclubs, and the alley has been upgraded with plantings and cobbled walkways.

Just two miles southwest of downtown is **Music Row,** headquarters for Nashville's music industry. Its fountainhead is at Division Street and 16th Avenue, South, site of the Country Music Hall of Fame. The Row runs along 16th, 17th, 18th, and 19th avenues South. Nearly every major record label has offices on the row.

PRACTICAL INFORMATION

WHEN TO GO. Nashville has a temperate climate year-round. Spring and fall are the most pleasant times of year. The summer months, especially July and Aug., can be very hot and humid. Winters usually are not severe, but Jan. and early Feb. can produce bone-rattling cold and enough snow to shut down the city. The primary tourist season runs Apr. 1–Oct. 30, but Nashville's second season offers many of the same attractions without the multitudes.

HOW TO GET THERE. Nashville's central location in the Southeast makes it a convenient destination for travel from all parts of the country. It is about 750 miles from Washington, D.C., 450 miles from Chicago, and 250 miles from Atlanta. Nashville is a popular stopover for midwesterners heading south for the Florida Gulf, which is about 10 hours away by car. Many of the commercial airlines have expanded service to include stops in Nashville, and with the recent $120 million Metro Airport expansion, service is constantly expanding.

By air. Airline deregulation and the tremendous growth in the convention and tourist business have opened up a major network of U.S. routes with connections to Nashville. Most major U.S. carriers service the city. Nashville has achieved the status of a gateway city, meaning that it is eligible for the heavily discounted fares

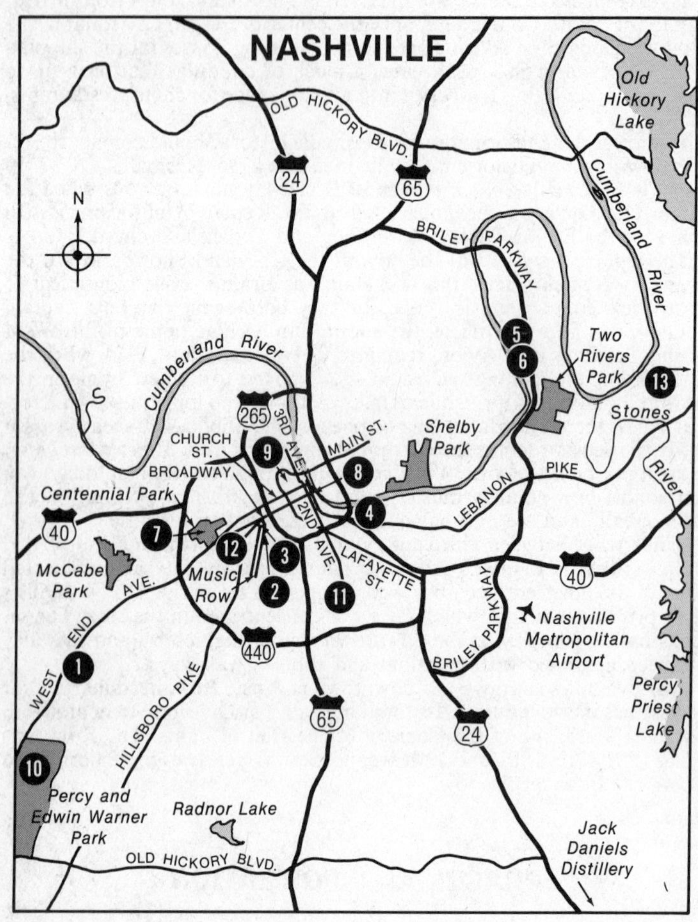

Points of Interest

1) Belle Meade Mansion
2) Country Music Hall of Fame Museum
3) Elvis Presley Memorial
4) Fort Nashborough
5) Grand Ole Opry
6) Opryland U.S.A.
7) Parthenon
8) Riverfront Park
9) State Capitol
10) Tennessee Botanical Gardens at Cheekwood
11) State Fairgrounds
12) Vanderbilt University
13) The Hermitage

that are accorded to cities with high-volume traffic. The Metro Nashville airport is conveniently located off Interstate 40, about eight miles southeast of the downtown area. The airport is served currently by nine major carriers (*American, Delta, Eastern, Northwest, Pan Am, Piedmont, United, TWA, US Air*), four regional carriers (*American Eagle, Allegheny Commuter, Branniff, ComAir*), and one national carrier (*Southwest Airlines*).

By bus. *Greyhound-Trailways* (in Nashville, 255–1691 for tickets, 256–6141 for information) travels to Nashville from nearly all states in the continental U.S. Also, a number of regional bus lines specialize in tours, which may include sightseeing, nightlife, entertainment packages, fly and drive packages, ground transportation, and other custom features. Check with your travel agent for current specialty tours and prices.

By car. A network of three interstate systems converges on Nashville, linking cities north and south of the Interstate 65 route and east and west of Interstates 24 and 40. Tennessee highways are in very good condition and well maintained unless you are unlucky enough to arrive during one of the two or three snowstorms that hit most winters.

TELEPHONES. The area code for Metro Nashville is 615. Local directory assistance is 411; for long distance within the area code, call 555–1212. An operator will assist on person-to-person, credit-card, and collect calls if you dial 0 before the number. Local pay telephone calls are 25 cents, no time limit. The front of the telephone book provides information on prefixes that fall within the toll-free local area.

EMERGENCY TELEPHONE NUMBERS. In any emergency, the number for police, fire, and ambulance is 911. For other police assistance, call 385–8600. The Poison Control Center is at 322–6435. Crisis Call Center, for personal and domestic crises, is at 244–7444.

ACCOMMODATIONS. Peak tourist season runs from May to September. During special events such as the Country Music Fan Fair, finding a room at any price can be difficult, and advance reservations are a must. Otherwise, accommodations generally can be found at one of the many hotels near Opryland, the airport, or downtown, although advance booking is helpful for securing the best discounts. Most hotels allow children under 12 to stay free.

Most hotels and motels maintain the same rates during the peak and so-called second seasons. Some raise rates slightly for the summer months. A few of the nicest hotels downtown offer special Fri.–Mon. weekend family rates on a limited number of rooms, first come, first serve. The special offerings make rates at the finer hotels comparable to those of the budget motels. Tennessee has a hotel-motel tax of 4 percent. An additional 7.75 percent is charged as sales tax. Rates are based on double occupancy. Categories, determined by price, are as follows: *Reasonable,* $50 to $70; *Very Economical,* under $50.

Reasonable

Best Western. Ten locations (all independently owned) throughout Nashville-Davidson County (800–528–1234). All are modern inns, some with restaurants and swimming pools. Some have cocktail lounges. Rates for children vary with location, ranging from no charge for children under 12 to special family plans for up to five people per room.

Fiddlers Inn, North. 2410 Music Valley Drive, Nashville, TN 37214 (615–885–1440). Modern hotel with restaurant, pool, and nightly entertainment in the lounge.

Hampton Inns. Four locations in Nashville (800–HAMPTON). Nearest to downtown: 1919 West End Ave., Nashville, TN 37203. Modern inns with free continental breakfast. Children under 18 stay free.

Holiday Inn. (800–465–4329). Six locations in and around Nashville, all with pools and restaurants. With the exception of the Nashville South location at I-65 in Franklin, TN, all have lounges, most with nightly live entertainment.

Shoney's Inn. 1521 Demonbreun St., Nashville, TN 37203 (615–255–9977 or 800–222–2222). Modern three-story motel with pool and popular family restaurant. Within walking distance of Music Row attractions. Children under 18 stay free.

Very Economical

Days Inn. (615–327–0922). Several independently owned locations, with pools. Children under 18, $1 or free depending on location. Nearest to downtown with a pool: Days Inn–**Vanderbilt,** 1800 West End Ave., Nashville, TN 37203.

Fiddlers Inn, South. I-40 at Briley Pkwy., Nashville, TN 37217 (615–367–9202). Modern hotel with restaurant and pool. Near the airport.

Walking Horse Hotel. Fifty miles southeast of Nashville, Box 266, Wartrace, TN 37182 (615–389–6407). Refurbished turn-of-the-century railroad stop inn in Tennessee Walking Horse country. A must for those who prefer quaint, secluded settings untouched by progress. A good base for the annual August Walking Horse Celebration in Shelbyville and glorious quilt and other crafts festivals in nearby Bell Buckle. Has 12 rooms with private bath and 13 rooms with shared bath. Traditional country cooking featured in dining room. Walking Horse stables.

Special Family Accommodations at Expensive Hotels. The Residence Inn. 2300 Elm Hill Pike, Nashville, TN 37210 (615–889–8600). Residence-style inn with lodging available on a per-night basis. All units have fully equipped kitchens. Several have wood-burning fireplaces. Any number of occupants in a one-bedroom unit (one king-size bed or double beds with sofa sleeper), $74; two-bedroom unit (king and queen-size beds, two full baths), $94.

Hyatt Regency Hotel. 623 Union St., downtown, Nashville, TN 37219 (615–259–1234 or 800–228–9000). Well appointed with a limited number of rooms at special family rates available Fri.–Sun. night and holidays. Children under 18 free; maximum four adults per room. Features include 28-story atrium lobby, glass bullet elevators, and plenty of greenery. Mezzanine lounge has evening pianist and munchies. Spectacular city view from revolving Polaris lounge at the top. Gourmet restaurant and comfortable coffee shop, $59 per night, two double beds.

Vanderbilt Plaza Hotel. 2100 West End Ave., Nashville, TN 37203 (615–320–1700). Sophisticated beauty marks this new, contemporary hotel near Centennial Park. Fri.–Sun. nights, up to four adults per room, children under 18 free. Moderately priced French café, afternoon tea and desserts in the lobby lounge; live entertainment in Snaffles lounge; gourmet dining room. $49 per night, two double or king-size beds.

Bed-and-Breakfast. Nashville has a growing network of private homes that are open to visitors. In the best tradition of southern hospitality, all homes are carefully screened for comfort and cleanliness. They are available in the city and out in the country. A continental breakfast is included in reasonable double occupancy rates: $40 to $60 with private bath, $60 to $120 for special one-of-a-kind quarters. Kitchen facilities available at some locations. For information and reservations call Bed & Breakfast of Middle Tennessee (297–0883) or Bed & Breakfast Host Homes of Tennessee/B&B Hospitality International (331–5244, or 800–727–733, dial tone, then 270).

HOW TO GET AROUND. From the airport. A taxi from Metro Nashville Airport to downtown costs $11.50–$13. Cabs run 24 hours a day and are always available at the airport. Shuttle service via *Downtown Airport Express* (275–1180), to downtown hotels only, $8; via *Airport Shuttle* (275–2555) to anywhere in Metro, rates vary by location. Most major hotels offer regular courtesy van service from the airport to the hotel, some free of charge. An automated dialing system near the entrances to the baggage claim level and the ground level connects you with the hotel for ride schedule information. Reservations for return trips should be made at one of the participating hotels. Opryland Hotel operates its own courtesy van dispatched from a separate airport counter. Limos and vans depart from a designated passenger pickup area.

By bus. Metropolitan Transit Authority buses cover the entire Davidson County area daily. Most routes begin 4 A.M. to 5 A.M. and run until 11:15 P.M. The fare is 75 cents within the central downtown zone and 5 cents for each additional zone traveled up to $1.05. Popular old-style trolleys operate daily within the central business district; the fare is 25 cents. Correct change is required. For Schedule information, call 242–4433.

By taxi. Cabs run 24 hours a day. Regulated fares have ceilings of $1.50 for entry and $1.50 per mile. Checker Cab (254–5031) and Yellow Cab (256–0101) start at $1.50 plus $1.10 per mile and 20 cents for each additional passenger. Hailing a cab from downtown is not impossible, but there are so few unoccupied taxis roaming around that it's best to phone for cab service.

By rental car. Most major car rental firms (Hertz, Avis, Budget, Dollar, Alamo, and National) have leasing desks both at the airport and downtown. It's best to make reservations to avoid the shortages that can occur on busy tourist weekends. Hertz has discounts for AAA members, and all offer discount weekend rates of $20 to $25 a day Thurs.–Mon. for subcompact and compact cars, with 100 to 200 free miles and 30 cents for each additional mile. The numbers, local and toll-free, for these agencies are as follows: *Hertz,* 275–2600, 800–654–3131; *Avis,* 361–1212, 800–331–1212; *Budget,* 366–0800, 800–527–0700; *Dollar,* 366–0449, 800–421–6868; and *National,* 361–7467, 800–328–4567.

HINTS TO THE MOTORIST. Nashville's streets and highways are easy to get around except at peak morning (7:30–8:30 A.M.) and evening (4:30–5:30 P.M.). The Interstate system (I-40, I-65, I-24, I-440) crisscrosses and encircles the metropolitan area, delivering motorists within a few miles of any destination. Nashville's primary streets are laid out in a spoke pattern leading out from the downtown area. Other major roads, such as Old Hickory Boulevard and Briley Parkway, cover vast arcs around the city. The names of Nashville streets, in tribute, apparently, to its many prominent citizens, can change within short distances. The direction can, too. A good road map and careful instructions can be invaluable.

Traffic laws contain no unusual prohibitions. Right turns on red are permitted after stopping except where marked. Coins are required for parking meters, Mon.–Fri., 8 A.M.–6 P.M. and Sat. until noon. Holidays and Sundays are exempt. The overtime parking law prohibits meter feeding, or parking for periods of time that exceed the meter's limit. Speed limits in the city are clearly posted.

The **AAA** office is within one mile of downtown at 1121 Church Street (244–8889).

A word of caution to motorists who drink and drive: Tennessee has a tough drunken driving law, with mandatory jail and fine penalties on conviction. For first offenders, the jail time and fine is a minimum two days and $250. Metro police occasionally set up roadblocks to screen drivers for intoxication. If they suspect you've been drinking, you'll be asked to pull off the road and take a breath test. You have the right to refuse, but that gives the police probable cause to believe that you are intoxicated. They can and will charge you with DWI.

TOURIST INFORMATION. The Nashville Area Chamber of Commerce publishes an annual travel guide packet complete with maps, sightseeing information, and up-to-date prices for events and accommodations, all free. Inquiries should be addressed to the *Nashville Area Chamber of Commerce,* 161 Fourth Avenue, N., Nashville, TN 37219 (615–259–3900).

Newcomers to Nashville should stop first at the *Tourist Information Center* (242–5606), also operated by the Chamber of Commerce. The center downtown is located just off Interstate 40 at the James Robertson Parkway exit. Look for the big green sign with the white question mark. The center is open seven days a week, year-round, during daylight hours. It is staffed by courteous and knowledgeable chamber employees. Free maps and brochures are available. Tennessee's welcome centers provide helpful maps and tourist and sightseeing brochures to motorists entering the state at 10 interstate locations. Centers are operated and staffed by the State Department of Tourist Development 24 hours a day, seven days a week, year-round.

HINTS TO DISABLED TRAVELERS. Much work has been accomplished to accommodate disabled people. Residents are issued special license plates allowing parking privileges in designated spaces nearest the entrances to virtually all public facilities. Park here without special tags and you will be subject to the city's tow-in ordinance. Additionally, curbs downtown and in many suburban areas have ramps to facilitate street crossings near public buildings, and most public rest rooms also accommodate wheelchairs. For the blind, many elevators are equipped with Braille floor indicators.

The Metro Office for Handicapped Persons publishes "Accessibility Guidebook," detailing accommodations for the disabled at restaurants, hotels, amusements, churches, and other facilities. For a free copy, write the *Office for Handicapped Persons,* 214 Stahlman Building, Nashville, TN 37201 (615–259–6676).

FREE EVENTS. Music City is the place to see country music stars perform, and Tennessee is the place to sample a wealth of traditional American music, arts, and crafts. Some events are free, and others charge a nominal admission. Many of the crafts shows benefit local charities.

Nashville Now, produced for The Nashville Network cable television system. Showcase of country music performers; big names and new talent. Taping from the Nashville Network Studio in Opryland Park takes place Mon.–Fri. nights year-round. Reservations required. Program is free except during peak summer months. June through August, when admission to Opryland Park is required. Call 883–7000 for reservations and information. **Fandango, You Can Be A Star, New Country, Country Kitchen** tapings, all produced for TNN, are scheduled throughout the year. No charge, tickets on first come first served basis; call 883–7000 for reservations and information. **Hee Haw,** the nationally syndicated country music and cornball humor review, is taped in Nashville June and October. No charge, except admission to Opryland (in summer). Call Opryland Information Center, 889–6611, for information on how to attend.

Summer Concerts. Sunday afternoons at the bandshells in Centennial and Hadley parks offer free classical, pop, and jazz performances from late May to late July. There are chamber music performances Fri. night in the Centennial Arts Center courtyard. At Riverfront Park downtown, June through Aug. Thurs. nights bring a wide variety of musical performances, and Sat. nights in June and July there is a big band dance under the stars. For information on all free concerts, call 259–5176.

Many seasonal events are also free.

SEASONAL EVENTS. The good things in Nashville life are not always free, but they are well worth the price of admission. Art and music festivals bring together some of the finest traditional artisans and musicians.

Heart of Country, American antique show, late Jan.–early Feb. at the Opryland Hotel (889–1000, ask for Convention Services).

A must for visitors is the Tennessee Crafts Fair, Fri.-Sun. during the first full weekend of May. Some 165 professional Tennessee craftsmen set up booths outdoors at Centennial Park. Items for sale, crafts demonstrations, food, live music, and children's "hands on" crafts; call 383–2502. Free.

Nashville Summer Lights Festival, late May to early June, is held in downtown Nashville between Legislative Plaza and Metro Courthouse. A free four-day festival to showcase excellence in the arts and entertainment. Includes arts market, Cabaret stage, children's activities, continuous music, dance, and theater on five stages, sidewalk cafés, and urban tours. Free; call 259–6374 for information.

Country Music Fan Fair, held in mid-June, is a country music extravaganza sponsored by the Grand Ole Opry and the Country Music Association. Weeklong festivities around the city attracted more than 20,000 fans. Record labels showcase big names and new talent, plenty of autograph sessions, and fan club booths. All-American Country Games feature major country artists in track-and-field events to benefit TN Special Olympics. $60 for a week-long pass good for all events and concerts. Expensive but a must for the hardcore country music fan. Call 889–7503 for information.

American Artisan Crafts Fair, held on Father's Day weekend (in June), Fri.-Sun. Over 150 professional fine artists and craftsmen from Tennessee and the nation sell their works from outdoor booths at Centennial Park. Exhibits, demonstrations, strolling musicians, and special art booths with instruction for children. Call 298–4691.

Italian Street Fair, on Labor Day weekend (Fri.–Mon.) in downtown Nashville, is a fundraiser for the Nashville Symphony. Family-oriented, it features a wide variety of Italian food, over 50 arts and crafts exhibitors, children's games, flea market, carnival, symphony performances, strolling musicians, and bands. Adults, $3; children, $1. Call 329–3033 for information.

Tennessee State Fair, mid-September at the fairgrounds. Traditional state fair with agriculture and livestock competitions, midway rides, and entertainment. Admission, $3; children 6–12, $1; under 6, free. Call 255–6441 for information and ticket discounts.

A Taste of Our Town: Food and Art Fair, Sat.–Sun., third weekend in Aug. at the Koger Center in Brentwood. Booths include 30 restaurants and 100 craftsmen plus musical performers. Admission, $3.50. Call 255–5656 for information.

Tennessee Grass Roots Days, a worthwhile annual gathering of blues and folk music artists and craftsmen in the traditional of Tennessee working people. Performances, exhibits, demonstrations, and crafts. Takes place in Centennial Park Sat.–Sun., last weekend in Sept. Call 331–0203.

The first weekend in Oct., **Market Street Festival,** on Historic Second Avenue, celebrates the revitalization of the downtown warehouse district with arts, crafts, and food. $2 donation to Historic Nashville, Inc., requested at the gate. Call 244–7835.

Oktoberfest, second Sat. in Oct., in restored Germantown, just north of the downtown area. Features arts and crafts booths, canned goods, and homemade foods for sale. A tour of historic Germantown homes usually coincides with Oktoberfest. Home tour tickets cost $5. Call 320–7914.

Tennessee Fall Crafts Fair in mid-Nov. at the Nashville Convention Center, Fri.–Sun. Features over 165 professional craftsmen from across the country. Adults, $3.50; senior citizens, $3; children under 12, free. Call 383–2502 for information.

Christmas Village, Fri.–Sun., early in November at the state fairgrounds. Fabulous arts, crafts, and hobby fair emphasizing handmade Christmas decorations, ornaments, clothing, toys, gifts, and food. Adults, $3; children, 6–12, $1; under 6, free. For information, call 255–6441.

Nashville's Country Holidays, Thanksgiving to New Year's Day. A five week, citywide celebration of the season featuring southern and international traditions. Call 259–3900 for scheduled events.

International Trees of Christmas. The Horticultural Society at Cheekwood Botanical Gardens presents an exhibition of Christmas trees decorated in international themes is throughout December. Adults, $2.50, students, 7 to 17, $1; children, 50 cents. Call 356–3308.

TOURS AND SPECIAL-INTEREST SIGHTSEEING. Nashville has a wealth of bus tours offered by several large sightseeing companies. They cover virtually everything you could want to see in Nashville, from the stars' homes, the Grand Ole Opry, and Music Row to President Andrew Jackson's Hermitage. Most tours last 3–4 hours and cost $13 to $24 for adults and half price for children. Most run daily; a few are closed Sun. and Mon. Call for times and reservations.

The major tour companies are: *Country & Western Roundup Tours, Inc.,* 2416 Music Valley Dr., Nashville, TN 37214 (883–5555); *American Sightseeing/Custom Tours,* 1000 4th Ave. North, Nashville, TN 37219 (227–5200); *Grand Ole Opry Tours,* 2810 Opryland Dr., Nashville, TN 37214 (889–9490); *Gray Line Tours,* 314 Hermitage Ave., Nashville, TN 37210 (244–7330 or 800–255–6940); *Johnny Walker Tours,* 97 Wallace Rd., Nashville, TN 37211 (834–8585); *Nashville Tours,* 2626 Music Valley Dr., Nashville, TN 37214 (889–4646); and *Stardust Tours,* 1504 Demonbreun St., Nashville, TN 37203 (244–2335).

Belle Carol Riverboat Co. offers sightseeing and dinner entertainment cruises on the Cumberland River. 106 First Ave. South, Nashville, TN 37201. (356–4120). Dinner and entertainment cruises, $25 to $35. Sightseeing cruises, $9 up.

Downtown Walking Tours are outlined in a free brochure prepared by the Historical Commission of Metropolitan Nashville and Davidson County, in the Customs House, 701 Broadway, Nashville, TN 37203 (259–5027).

Historic home tours. Features elegantly refurbished late nineteenth-century and early twentieth-century homes in renovation districts near downtown. Scheduled on occasional weekends throughout the summer and fall. Admission $2 to $5. For dates, call the Metro Historical Commission at 259–5027.

Self-guided driving tours also are outlined in a free brochure entitled *The Civil War Battle of Nashville.* This covers the major points of battle between Union and Confederate troops. Brochures are available at the Metro Historical Commission at 259–5027.

Jack Daniels Distillery is 65 miles southeast of Nashville but is easily accessible by I-24, East. A free one-hour tour of the facility is offered seven days a week year-round, except major holidays. See the making of the world-famous brand of Tennessee sour mash whiskey. Write Jack Daniels Distillery, Lynchburg, TN 37352. (759–4221), For lunch, Miss Mary Bobo's Boarding House in Lynchburg serves home-cooked fried chicken and vegetables, family style, Mon.–Sat. at 1 P.M. Reservations required. Adults, $9; children under 12, $4. Call 759–7394.

PARKS AND GARDENS. Metro Nashville has 70 public parks, in keeping with the tradition of spending time outdoors from early spring until late fall. The parks department maintains an active schedule of sports and entertainment events as well as gyms, game rooms, art classes, summer concerts, and outdoor art shows. For information regarding all parks activities, call 259–6399.

Riverfront Park, downtown, where Broadway meets the Cumberland River, is the concrete crown jewel of the park system. It offers a quiet waterfront setting for downtown brown bag lunches who want to watch the barges move along the Cumberland River. During summer months, there's a steady schedule of free concerts and dances (see Free Events).

Centennial Park, near downtown, on West End Ave. (259–6399), is home for the Parthenon replica (see Historic Sites). Lush acreage, shady, grassy, and beautifully landscaped with elaborate floral designs and ponds. Summer bandshell events and festivals. A great place to take the children for scheduled activities ranging from kite flying to outdoor theater.

Percy Warner and **Edwin Warner parks,** 7311 Hwy. 100 (352–6299), with 2665 acres, are Nashville's largest. Rolling hills, woods, and picnic areas are ideal for nature lovers. The adjacent Warner parks have a nature center, gardens, and nature trails with self-guided tours (booklets available at the nature center) or guided tours by reservation; call 352–6299. They also include picnic shelters, soccer fields, and playground equipment. Everything is free with the exception of the picnic shelters (call 259–5218 for reservations and fees) and the two golf courses. The parks are open year-round from daybreak until 11 P.M.

The **Tennessee Botanical Gardens and Fine Arts Center** at Cheekwood, Forest Park Dr., is the former home of the Leslie Cheek family. The grounds consist of nearly 55 acres of artfully manicured and landscaped gardens. Botanic Hall (356–3306) features botanical art exhibits adjacent to four public greenhouses and wild flower, herb, and Japanese gardens. (Fine Arts Center, see Museums and Galleries. Open Tues.–Sat., 9 A.M.–5 P.M.; Sun., 1–5 P.M.; closed Mon. and major holidays. Adults, $2.50; students, $1; children under 7 free. Group rates available. Call 352–5310.

Other parks and wildlife preserves that offer excellent scenic and sporting opportunities (see Participant Sports) include **Old Hickory Lake,** at the Old Hickory Dam on the Cumberland River (822–4846); **Center Hill Lake,** at the Center Hill Dam on the Caney Fork River (1–858–3125); **Percy Priest Lake** (several federal parks), picnics and sailboat races on Sun. (259–6735); and **Radnor Lake,** a state natural area with "Turtle's Eye View" guided nature trips by canoe, Sat.–Sun. in the fall and spring. Also free weekend guided walking tours during fall and spring. For reservations, call 377–1281.

PARTICIPANT SPORTS. Nashville is made to order for the outdoor enthusiast. With long, mild spring and autumn seasons, hilly and scenic terrain, plenty of lakes, and public tennis courts and golf courses, there's lots to do.

Jogging maintains its hold as one of the more popular outdoor pastimes, and Nashvillians have discovered a number of beautiful jogging sites, including Centennial Park, Vanderbilt University running track, Percy and Edwin Warner parks, and Radnor Lake. *The Nashville Striders Club,* affiliated with the downtown YMCA, can recommend choice sports and provide information on the many races that take place during the summer, such as their own weekly fun runs in area parks; call 254–0631.

Many of the places that provide joggers with running room also give **bicyclers** plenty of space for serious workouts or leisurely pedaling amid scenic backdrops. Most notable perhaps are the Percy Warner and Edwin Warner parks, easily accessible from Highway 100 and Belle Meade Boulevard. Miles of paved roads wind around beautiful hills, past remote picnic settings, and through dense woods.

Nashville has seven public **golf courses,** six of which are open year-round. Fees are $8.50 for 18 holes, $4.25 for 9 holes at the following courses: *Harpeth Hills,* an 18-hole, par-72 layout, 2424 Old Hickory Blvd. (373–8202); *McCabe,* 27 holes, pars 35, 35, and 36, 46th Ave., North, and Murphy Rd. (297–9138); *Percy Warner,* 9 holes, par 34, Forrest Park Dr., (352–9958); *Rhodes,* 9 holes, par 36, 2400 Metro Center Blvd. (242–2336); *Shelby,* 18-hole hangout for big money players, par 72, South 20th and Fatherland streets (227–9973); and *Two Rivers,* the newest 18-hole, par 72 course, McGavock Pike and Briley Parkway, (889–9748). Tee times may be required on weekends. Starters will help the lone golfer hook up with other players. *Nashboro Village,* 2250 Murfreesboro Road (361–3970), has a challenging 18-hole, par-72 golf course (367–2311). Fee for 18 holes is $13.

Many of Nashville's public parks have outdoor **tennis** courts, some of which are lighted. All are free to the public with the exception of the *Centennial Park Tennis Center,* which charges a nominal fee. For locations, check the blue pages of the telephone book under Metro Parks and Recreation or call 259–6314.

Several indoor **roller skating** rinks located in suburban areas include the *Rivergate Skate Center* (868–7655) and *Brentwood Skate Center* (373–1827). Call for times and charges (generally $2 to $4.50). Skate rentals are available. Other rinks are listed in the yellow pages under "Skating Rinks."

For **ice skating,** *Metro Ice Centennial* indoor rink at Centennial Park operates Sept. through May except major holidays. Adults, $3; children, $2.25; skate rental, $1. Call 320–1401 for information.

From Memorial Day to Labor Day, **swimming** is popular at Metro's *Wave Country,* on Two Rivers Pkwy. at Briley Pkwy., a wave action swimming pool with water slide (885–1902). Adults, $4; children, $3. Daily, 10 A.M.–8 P.M. Half price after 4 P.M.

Fishing and boating. A wide variety of outdoor water activities are available at the many lakes in and around Nashville and Middle Tennessee. At *Old Hickory Lake,* Old Hickory Dam on the Cumberland River (822–4846), there's a boat ramp for sailboats and motor-powered craft. No rentals. At *Center Hill Lake,* between Nashville and Cookeville (858–3125), launching ramps are provided, and houseboats, small fishing boats, and pontoon boats can be rented from *Cave Hollow Boat Dock* (548–4315). These and other lakes also host summertime weekend sailboat races. Old Hickory, Percy Priest, and Center Hill lakes are operated by the U.S. Army Corps of Engineers. For maps and information on these and other waterways ($1.50 to $8 fees), write Natural Resources Management Branch, U.S. Army Corps of Engineers, Box 1070, Nashville, TN 37202.

SPECTATOR SPORTS. Baseball. The Cincinnati Red's AAA farm team, the Nashville Sounds, plays at Greer Stadium from April through early Sept. The stadium is located at 534 Chestnut St. Tickets available from Sounds, Box 23290, Nashville, TN 37202 (242–4371). Adults, $3 to $5.50; children under 12, $1 off ticket price.

Football. The Vanderbilt University Commodores football team, in the Southeastern Conference, plays from early Sept. through late Nov. at Dudley Field on Vanderbilt's campus. Tickets cost $16.

Basketball. Vanderbilt's Commodores play basketball from late Nov. through early March in Memorial Gym on the campus. Tickets $10, no discounts. Contact Vanderbilt Ticket Office, Box 120158, Nashville, TN 37212 (322–3544).

Iroquois Steeplechase. Second Saturday in May, free, or $4 to $5 for preferred seating. People bring picnic baskets to the grassy slopes overlooking the racing grounds in Percy Warner Park. Tailgate and limited RV space available. Call 322–7450.

Longhorn Rodeo is a world championship indoors competition at Nashville Municipal Auditorium in July and Aug. Tickets, $7 to $10; children and senior citizens pay half price for Sun. matinees. Call 876–1016.

Walking Horse Celebration. This 10-day event, ending the Saturday prior to Labor Day, brings 250,000 visitors to the quaint town of Shelbyville to watch high-strutting Tennessee Walking Horses compete. Tickets $3.75 to $10. Call 684–5915.

CHILDREN'S ACTIVITIES. Cumberland Science Museum, 800 Ridley Blvd., Nashville, TN 37203 (259–6099). Adventures in discovery for the entire family.

Exhibits on natural and physical science, world cultures, astronomy, and human health plus visiting exhibits. The museum has a 40-foot planetarium, live animals, monthly science programs, and special local exhibits suited to children and adults. Museum is open Tues.–Sat, 9:30 A.M. to 5 P.M.; and Sun., 12:30 P.M. to 5:30 P.M.; closed Mon. and major holidays. Adults, $3; children 3 to 12, $2; children under 3, free; senior citizens, $2.

Nashville Academy Theater, 724 Second Ave., S., Nashville, TN 37210 (254–9103). Professional theater company stages plays for young audiences year-round. Morning shows Mon.–Fri., Sat. or Sun. mornings and matinees. Tickets $3.50 at the door.

Theater Tree, Centennial Park (259–5176). Offers plays for children, June–July, Sat. mornings at 11 A.M.

Metro Parks and Recreation Department schedules many summertime activities for children. Call 259–6399.

HISTORIC SITES AND HOUSES. Belle Meade Mansion. 110 Leake Ave., Nashville, TN 37205 (356–0501). A taste of the grand old South is evident in this early nineteenth-century "Queen of the Tennessee Plantations" mansion built by General William G. Harding on what was then a 5,300-acre farm and famous thoroughbred nursery. Open with guided tours Mon.–Sat., 9 A.M.–5 P.M.; Sun., 1 P.M.–5 P.M. Closed major holidays. Adults, $3.50; students 14 and over and tour group members, $2.50; children 6–13, $1.50; under 6, free.

Fort Nashborough. Adjacent to Riverfront Park, 170 First Ave. N. (255–8192). Five reconstructed log cabins, with costumed staff depicting late eighteenth-century frontier life. Colonel James Robertson and a band of settlers built the original Fort Nashborough in 1779, just a few hundred yards north of the current site, on the limestone bluff overlooking the river. Tues.–Sat., 9 A.M.–4 P.M. Closed Sun., Mon., and all legal holidays. Admission free.

The Hermitage. 4580 Rachel's Lane, Hermitage, TN 37076, 12 miles east of Nashville (889–2941). Well-informed tour guides take visitors through the estate of President Andrew Jackson. Features include original cabins, furnishings, and gardens. Visitor center with museum, theater, and tearoom; gift shop on the premises. Open daily 9 A.M.–5 P.M. Closed Thanksgiving and Christmas. Adults, $4.75; children, $1.25; under 6 and servicemen on active duty, free.

James K. Polk Residence. 301 W. Seventh St., Columbia, TN 38401, about 40 miles south of Nashville (388–2354). Ancestrial home of the eleventh president of the U.S. Original furnishings, clothing, china, and crystal used in the White House. Adults, $2.50; seniors, $2; children 6–12, $1; group rates available.

Ryman Auditorium. 116 Opry Pl. (Fifth Ave., North), Nashville, TN 37219 (254–1445). Built by riverboat captain Tom Ryman as a tabernacle, the auditorium was home for the WSM Grand Ole Opry from 1943 to 1974. The building is the sacred fount of Nashville's country music industry. Open daily, 8:30 A.M.–4:30 P.M., except Thanksgiving and Christmas. Adults $1.50; children 6–12, 75 cents; under 6, free.

The Parthenon. Centennial Park, West End Ave. (at 25th Ave. N.) Nashville, TN 37203 (259–6358). The world's only exact-size replica of the Greek Parthenon. It was completed in 1931 to replace a temporary structure built for the Tennessee Centennial Exposition in 1897. Casts of original Greek sculpture fragments line the interior. Changing art exhibits in the gallery level. Major restoration scheduled for completion in late 1988. Call for hours and admission charges.

Tennessee State Capital. Downtown on Charlotte between Fifth and Seventh avenues. Designed by Philadelphia architect William Strickland. Free guided tours conducted 7 days a week, except major holidays, every hour, 9 A.M.–3 P.M. Call the Curator of Education, 741–0830, for tour information.

MUSEUMS AND GALLERIES. Carl Van Vechten Gallery of Fine Arts at Fisk University (329–8543). Open 10 A.M.–5 P.M. Tues.–Fri., 1 P.M.–5 P.M. Sat.–Sun.; closed Monday. Adults, $2.50; 18 and under, free. Restored gallery is the permanent home for the Alfred Stieglitz collection donated to the historic black university by Stieglitz's widow, Georgia O'Keeffe. The collection features 101 pieces of nineteenth- and twentieth-century European and American art, including paintings, watercolors, drawings, lithographs, photographs, bronze sculpture, and African sculpture. A second gallery features changing exhibits. Also on campus is the Rinold Reiss permanent collection in the Fisk Library. The school administration building houses the Cyrus Leroy Baldridge permanent collection, and murals painted by Aaron Douglas. Administration building and Jubilee Hall hours vary. Free. Call 329–8500 or 329–8536.

The Country Music Hall of Fame and Museum, 4 Music Square E., offers the old and new in country music, instruments, costumes, and photos. Memorable special exhibits. Two theaters show movie clips. Gift shop. Daily, 9 A.M.–5 P.M.; June–Aug., 8 A.M.–8 P.M. Closed on Christmas, New Year's, and Thanksgiving. Adults, $6; children 6 to 11, $1.75; under 6 free. Call 256–1639.

Cumberland Gallery. 4107 Hillsboro Circle (297–0296). Free visiting exhibits of contemporary painting, sculpture, drawings, and prints. Tue.–Sat., 10 A.M.–5 P.M.

The Fine Arts Center at Cheekwood (Tennessee Botanical Gardens) hosts permanent collections of nineteenth- and twentieth-century American art, particularly the work of leading southern artists, Worcester porcelain, and Old Sheffield silver plate, shown in the exquisitely adapted Cheek mansion. Admission to Gardens and art center: adults, $2.50; students, $1; children under 7 free. Open Tues.–Sat., 9 A.M.–5 P.M.; Sun., 1 P.M.–5 P.M. Closed Mon. and major holidays. Call 352–8632.

Nashville Artist Guild. 100 Second Ave. N., at Broadway in the Silver Dollar Saloon (242–5002). Exhibits by artist guild members plus special exhibits of guest artists. Tues.–Sat. 12–4 P.M.; Sun. 1–4 P.M.

Tennessee State Museum. 505 Deadrick St. (741–2692). Exhibits depicting life in Tennessee, art gallery, visiting exhibits. Mon.–Sat., 10 A.M.–5 P.M.; Sun., 1–5 P.M. Across the street in the 1925 War Memorial Building, the museum's military branch illustrates Tennessee's role in wars; Mon.–Sat.; 1–4 P.M. Sun. 10 A.M.–4 P.M. Both museums free.

Zimmerman Saturn Gallery. 131 Second Avenue N., features emerging American artists. Original, contemporary works in two and three dimensions. Exhibits change monthly; openings are marked by artist's reception. All free. Call 255–8895. Mon.–Fri. 10 A.M.–5:30 P.M., Sat. 11 A.M.–5 P.M.

FILM. First-run movie theaters tend to be clustered in or near major shopping centers on the periphery of the city. Most offer half-price matinees on nearly all films, seven days a week, for showings before 5 P.M. Newspaper listings specify times and exceptions. **Sinking Creek Film Celebration,** Vanderbilt University (322–2471), is a week-long festival in mid-June of independent film productions, including art and experimental cinema, workshops, and lectures ($2 to $4). *Sarratt Cinema,* also on campus, shows classics, cult, art, and international movies most nights for $2.50–$3. Call 322–2425.

MUSIC. Some of the best country, bluegrass, and spiritual music is played in Nashville. The musical choices are steadily broadening to include credible jazz, pop, and rock as well. Local symphony performances are better than acceptable and are improving. Andrew Jackson Hall in the Tennessee Performing Arts Center (TPAC) hosts special performances by a growing number of touring symphonies, orchestras, singers, and dance and opera companies. For clubs presenting live music, see Nightlife.

Blair School of Music/Blair Ballet Center. Vanderbilt University campus (322–7651). Offers music and dance performances by faculty members during the academic year, Sept.–April. Concerts include performances by the Blair String Quartet and Chamber Players. Also included is Fiddle and Banjo Showcase. Fri., 8 P.M.; Sun., 2:30 P.M. Adults, $5; students and seniors, $2.50. Recitals given frequently at 8 P.M. by faculty and guest faculty. Free.

Fisk University Fine Arts Festival. (329–8536). Runs the first week in April. Visual and performing arts focus on black culture. Music by faculty members and students includes performances by the world-famous Fisk Jubilee Singers, and various musical ensembles. Other worthwhile musical performances are scheduled throughout the school year.

Friends of Music Series. (269–4129). Offers chamber music and occasional dance or marionette events. Oct.–May at the Polk Theater in TPAC. Write Friends of Music, Box 23593, Nashville, TN 37202. Tickets through Ticketmaster. Tickets $10 to $14.

The Great Performance Series. Sarratt Student Center, Vanderbilt campus (322–2471). Brings famous performers to Nashville for chamber music, dance, mime, and theater. Most performances are at Langford Auditorium Sept.–April. Tickets $6 to $20; some student discounts available for New Artists Series and Special Events Series.

Nashville Symphony Orchestra performs its subscription classical music series Sept.–May in Andrew Jackson Hall, featuring internationally renowned guest conductors and solo artists. Symphony also performs a six-concert pops series during the season. For information (no ticket orders), call 329–3033 or write Nashville Symphony, 208 23rd Ave. N., Nashville, TN 37203. Tickets available from Ticketmaster. Concert tickets, $8 to $20.

Starwood Amphitheater. The biggest names in rock, pop, jazz, and country perform in the outdoor amphitheater. Covered seating for 5,000; seating on grassy slopes for 12,000. Ten minutes southeast of downtown Nashville. Tickets average $14 and are available at Box Office, 793–7500, or Ticketmaster, 741–2787. Open May to Oct.

OPRYLAND U.S.A. Opryland is a musical show park for families that is in a class by itself. The theme park features 21 rides, 12 stage shows ranging from musical reviews to fully staged musical productions, strolling musicians and singers, mimes, and clowns. One-day ticket, $17.95; three-day tickets, $20.95; children under 4 free. Opryland U.S.A. Passport, $51.51, includes 3-day Opryland ticket, Grand Ole Opry matinee, day cruise aboard the *General Jackson* riverboat, sightseeing tours, and ticket to "Music, Music, Music" theater show. Open 7 days and evenings a week from Memorial Day through Labor Day weekends. Open weekends April, May, Sept., and Oct. Call 889–6611.

Grand Ole Opry. Legendary showcase of country music greats and new rising stars performed in the Grand Ole Opry House at Opryland U.S.A. Fri. and Sat. nights year-round. Special Tues., Thurs., Sat., and Sun. matinees in summer months. Prices $8 to $11.50. For weekly roster, consult Fri. and Sat. morning "Arts and Leisure" section of the *Tennessean.* Reservations recommended; call 889–6611.

General Jackson riverboat. A new 272-foot paddle wheel showboat with four decks, three lounges, snack bar, and Victorian dinner theater cruises the Cumberland River from Opryland to Nashville's Riverfront Park. Morning and mid-day cruises. Adults, $11.95; children under 4 free. Optional meal service available. Dinner dance and theater cruises about $33 per person, $26 ages 4 to 11. Call 889–6600.

DANCE. In Nashville, you can see dance recitals as part of the Great Performance and Friends of Music series and at the Blair School of Music. See the "Music" listings. **Nashville Ballet,** 1203-B Church St., Nashville, TN 37203 (244–7233), is a professional company with a growing schedule of performances and lecture demonstrations. Tickets $14 to $17, available at Ticketmaster; discounts for students, seniors, and groups.

STAGE. Nashville's **Tennessee Performing Arts Center** (TPAC). 505 Deaderick St., Nashville, TN 37219 (741–7975). Has created grand opportunities for exposure to the best in performing arts. Its three theaters—Andrew Jackson Hall, James K. Polk, and Andrew Johnson—have a combined seating of 3,800 and accommodate elaborate to intimate stage, musical, and dance performances. Current activities are featured in the Sunday "Showcase" section of the *Tennessean,* Nashville's morning newspaper. Phone orders for tickets are accepted with American Express, Visa, or Mastercard (sales are final) or through Ticketmaster Box Office (741–2787), Box 3406, Nashville, TN 37219 ($1.75 handling charge per ticket for mail and phone orders). Tennessee students, children under 12, and TenneSenior cardholders receive a $2 discount for many events.

Tennessee Repertory Theater. The resident professional theater company at TPAC performs in the Polk Theater September to May. Features international and American classics, musicals, current Broadway successes and original plays. Call 244–4878 for schedule information. Tickets through Ticketmaster Box Office (741–2787); $13 to $20, with $2 discount for students, seniors, and groups of 15 or more.

Actors' Playhouse. 2318 West End Ave., Nashville, TN 37203 (327–0049). A community theater specializing in contemporary off-Broadway hits. An intimate setting; seats 66. Tickets $6.50 to $8.50, available through the box office, or Ticketmaster, 741–2787.

SHOPPING. The best prices on prized handmade jewelry, pottery, fabrics, baskets, furniture, ceramics, etc., are to be found at the many crafts fairs and festivals for which Nashville is famous. (See "Seasonal and Free Events.") Antique hunting is also especially enjoyable in Nashville and surrounding areas. Major credit cards are accepted almost universally, even among merchants who set up temporary shops during the fairs and festivals.

The most exciting new shopping arena is *Fountain Square,* a $20 million festival marketplace featuring a wide variety of fashion retailers amid restaurants, open-air live entertainment, and film theaters. 5 minutes north of downtown Nashville at Metro Center (256–SHOP).

Many antique dealers congregate in little malls around the city to share storefront space. Some of the better locations are *Goodlettsville Antique Mall,* 213 North Main St. (859–7002), and *Madison Antique Mall,* 400 block of Gallatin Road, S. (865–4677). Eighth Avenue, South, near Wedgewood Ave., is home for nearly a dozen storefront and house malls and shops between the 2000 and 2110 blocks. A few of these businesses are *Antique Exchange Mall* (269–9638) and *Antique Associates Mall* (297–5514). Some of the best bargains for collectibles, antiques, furnishings, and whatnots are at the *Flea Market* at the Tennessee State Fairgrounds on the fourth weekend of every month.

Lakewood, a small city about 10 miles northeast of Nashville, accessible by I-65 North or I-40 East, has a row of interesting antique shops. Call Lakewood City Hall (847–3711), during business hours.

Historic Franklin, 16 miles southwest of Nashville, has several shops and malls featuring good antiques and new handmade solid cherry country furniture. The square also features an exceptional collection of shops housed in restored turn-of-the-century storefronts. For information, call the Heritage Foundation (790–0378), Mon.–Fri.

For produce, the **Farmers' Market** at the corner of Eighth Ave., North, and Jefferson St., is the place to go. Area farmers line open stalls to sell crops during warm-weather months.

DINING OUT. Nashville features a fully satisfying variety of all that is best in southern traditional cooking: inexpensive, casual, and housed in little hideaways where generous platefuls of home-style favorites are served. Nashvillians thrive on the "meat and three's" plate (daily specials of a meat and three veggies chosen from a list of offerings), fried catfish, fried and baked chicken, salty country ham, homemade buttermilk biscuits and jam, barbecue, and rich sugary cakes and pies that are the specialty of every southern mom. But although Nashville is famous for this kind of eatery, it boasts many other kinds as well. There are four Mobile Four Star dining rooms setting the standard for gourmet food and a growing number of more moderately priced gourmet continental and ethnic restaurants, especially Oriental. As more and more people migrate to Nashville from other parts of the country and the world, new choices in cuisine and setting continue to mount. There is no shortage of places to go if dressing up is what you have in mind, but Nashville's particular flair for the casual brings a relaxed manner and dress code to most restaurants. Reservations usually are required only for the most haute dining rooms, although it is always best to check ahead, especially when with groups.

Restaurant categories, based on the cost of an average three-course dinner for one, not including beverage, tax, or tip, are as follows: *Reasonable,* $14 to $22; *Very Economical,* $10 to $14; and *Low Budget,* less than $10. Unless otherwise noted, all restaurants listed accepted most if not all major credit cards. Every attempt has been made to ensure that this list is current, but restaurants come and go so frequently that it is advisable to call before going.

Reasonable

Cakewalk Cafe. 3001 West End Ave. (corner of 29th Ave. S.) (320–7778). Lots of original, contemporary art for sale, making this small eatery a colorful setting for casual lunches and dinners. Well-prepared, eclectic mix of international and American dishes. Seafood, poultry, pastas, stews, meat pies. Very inexpensive for lunch.

Faison's. 2000 Belcourt Ave. (298–2112). Renovated bungalow is a charming setting for a loyal following of media types and young executives. An especially imaginative lunch and dinner menu with daily specials. Veal, chicken, seafood, beef, and pastas. Inexpensive for lunch.

Giuseppe's. 936 Gallatin Rd. (865–1062). Guiseppe is showman and chef of his dining room, a proud Italian who concocts tasty dishes from old family recipes. Makes his own pasta, sauces, breads, sausage, and desserts.

Mere Bulles Restaurant and Wine Bar. 152 Second Ave. N. (256–1946). Elaborate restoration transformed this nineteenth-century warehouse into an elegant setting for candlelit dinners and quiet lunches. Continental-style seafood, poultry, beef, and pasta dishes.

Peking Garden. 1923 Division St. (327–2020). A long-standing establishment on restaurant row. An exceptional variety of dishes among the regional styles. Lunch is inexpensive, and the Sunday all-you-can-eat brunch features a buffet table of diverse dishes at a bargain price.

Tennessee Walking Horse Hotel. Wartrace, TN (389–6407). A renovated railroad stop inn and dining room with nineteenth-century decor and exceptional southern home cooking in the traditional style. Menu offers poultry, beef, seafood, fresh vegetables in season, and luscious homemade desserts. They light the taper candles on the breakfast table here. Inexpensive for lunch and breakfast. Located 55 miles southeast of downtown Nashville.

Third Coast. 913 20th Ave. S. (327–1115). A casual, contemporary setting near Music Row with cozy nooks and outdoor patio dining in warm weather make this a popular lunch and dinner spot for music industry types. Creative dishes of fish and fowl; sandwiches, daily specials.

Very Economical

Ciraco's. 212 21st Ave., S. (329–0036). Casual trattoria serving generous platefuls of pasta, pizza, veal, superb homemade bread, and Italian sausage. Vineyard Room in the rear is more expensive gourmet. Cantina lounge is comfortable bar with food and a large-screen TV. Outdoor tables. Free delivery service.

Daisy's. 4029 Hillsboro Rd. (269–5354). A traditional-contemporary mix of southern dishes served in a colonial Williamsburg setting. Imaginative casseroles and meats with stuffings and sauces. Inexpensive for lunch.

Ginza. 109 Second Ave. N. (244–8716). Intimate little Japanese café serving sushi, sukiyaki, shabu-shabu, and tempura. Complete meals include soup, salad, fruit, rice, and ample entrees.

Granite Falls. 2000 Broadway (327–9250). Smart California-style setting for lunch and dinner. Features ample salads, poultry, and seafood with a variety of sauces, and some beef. White paper tablecloths with crayons provided. Patio for outdoor dining in warm months.

Low Budget

Amanda Sue. 2201 Bandywood Dr. (297–1993). A bright café specializing in gourmet deli items, salads, sandwiches, soups, and hot lunches. Also an excellent and reasonably priced gourmet carry-out for dinners and parties. Exceptional desserts.

The Bluebird Cafe. 4104 Hillsboro Rd. (383–1461). A casual coffeehouse featuring a menu of appetizers, meal-sized salads and sandwiches, and rich homemade desserts. The eatery becomes a favorite music showcase spot in the evening.

Cawthon's Famous Bar-B-Que. 4121 Hillsboro Road (292–9311). Takeout. Smoked, hand-pulled pork barbecue with zesty mild and hot sauces, cornbread and pies. No credit cards.

Country Life Natural Foods. 1919 Division St. (327–3695). Rustic setting for vegetarian buffet and salad bar, with items changing frequently. No credit cards.

Elliston Place Soda Shop. 2111 Elliston Pl. (327–1090). A throwback to a simpler time; sports an old-fashioned soda bar, booths, and tableside jukebox selections. One of Nashville's more popular "meat and three's" for lunch and dinner. Breakfast also served. No credit cards.

Los Cunados. 1910 Belcourt Ave. (383–8920). Stuccoed hacienda with cozy dining rooms. Specializes in Tex-Mex. Ample servings and a wide variety.

Loveless Motel & Cafe. Route 5, Highway 100 (646–9700). Renowned for fresh-out-of-the-oven buttermilk biscuits, homemade jam, pan-fried country ham, and fried chicken. A favorite with film, television, and music personalities for Sat. and Sun. breakfast. About 20 miles southwest of downtown. No credit cards.

Obie's Flying Tomato Pan Pizza. 2217 Elliston Pl. (327–4772). Classic college pizza parlor. Located near the Vanderbilt campus. Initials are carved into tables. Serves authentic deep-dish Sicilian, thin-crust American, and whole wheat pizza. No credit cards.

Pancake Pantry. 1724 21st Ave. S. (383–9333). Nashville's oldest continuously operating restaurant, a no-nonsense room that serves as a neighborhood gathering spot. Menu includes a variety of pancakes and waffles, eggs, country ham, sandwiches, and salads.

San Antonio Taco. Two locations: 208 Commerce St. (downtown) (259–4413); and 416 21st Ave. S. (Vanderbilt campus) (312–4322). Lively restaurant that have made a big hit with traditional Tex-Mex dishes served fast-food-style. No credit cards.

12th & Porter. 114 12th Ave. N. (at Porter) (254–7236). Casual bistro setting in a restored warehouse, featuring a variety of pastas, pizzas, and deliciously unusual medleys of cheeses, seafood, and fowl.

Uncle Bud's. 1214 Lakeview Dr., Franklin, TN (790–1234). Well known among locals for all-you-can-eat fried chicken, catfish, or frog legs, served with all the fixings. Tucked away in a rustic house about 12 miles south of downtown Nashville. No credit cards.

Inexpensive for Lunch Only

Helma's Soup Kettle. 423 Union St. (242–9428). A cheery luncheonette that offers a variety of credible fresh soups with complimentary refills and a daily hot dish special. No credit cards.

Le Bon Vivant. 231 Franklin Rd., Brentwood, (377–1058). A French bakery and café offers salads, sandwiches, quiches, soups, fresh bread, and elaborate pastries. No credit cards.

The Pineapple Room at Cheekwood. Forrest Park Dr. (352–4859). A contemporary garden setting with a wall of windows that brings to each table an impressive view of the Tennessee Botanical Gardens and the Cheek mansion. Salads and sandwiches.

Satsuma Tea Room. 417 Union St. (256–5211). The menu changes daily at this downtown luncheon spot. Makes a great break from a downtown walking tour. Home-style hot lunches, sandwiches, and salads. No credit cards.

Recommended Splurges. Vanderbilt Plaza Hotel. 2100 West End Ave. (320–1700). Sunday champagne brunch buffet in the nicely appointed, comfortable Impressions French-style café. Omelets and pastas made to order; exceptional desserts. Live entertainment, often piano jazz. $14.95, reservations recommended.

Opryland Hotel. 2800 Opryland Dr. (889–1000). This luxurious hotel, at the hub of the famed Opryland convention center and theme park complex, serves a lavish Sunday buffet brunch. A wide assortment of breakfast dishes, hot entrees, fruits, cheeses, and pastries from the hotel's award winning chefs. Adults $14, children 12–5, $7; 4 and under free.

NIGHTLIFE AND BARS. With a few exceptions, Nashville nightlife bargains exist outside the central business district, either near downtown or in suburban locations. With a rekindled interest in nighttime activities downtown comes the promise of a new variety of eating and drinking establishments. Lounges in established hotels offer entertainment possibilities, but Printer's Alley between Third and Fourth avenues, North, and Church and Union streets remains the undisputed center of downtown nightclub activity. It is expensive and mostly overrun with tourists. The Alley offers floor shows, house bands, and exotic strippers. Established recording giants and songwriters have been known to show up in the Alley and even give impromptu performances. Dozens of established night spots exist outside downtown in no particular district. Many out-of-the-way places have worthwhile live entertainment, and those cherished by the locals feature some of Music City's best songwriters, musicians, and singers. Under Tennessee law, clubs that serve liquor by the drink are required to serve food. Beer-only taverns are not subject to this law. Drinks cannot be served past 2 A.M., and glasses must be off the table by 3 A.M. The drinking age is 21.

Nashville's talented musicians, singers, and songwriters seek exposure as well as income. An abundant talent pool lends itself nicely to bars and lounges in need of live entertainment. Several establishments showcase a variety of musical styles. The best overview of the music and entertainment scene from week to week is the "Showcase" section of the Sunday *Tennessean* newspaper. Cover charges at the un-touristy places generally are nominal ($2 to $7) but are considerably higher if a big name is booked for performances. Dress is casual, but patrons are comfortable in anything from jeans to jackets and ties. Some clubs do not allow jeans, so ask before arriving.

The Bluebird Cafe. 4104 Hillsboro Rd. (383–1461). A variety of music styles, occasionally by name talent, offered seven nights a week in a cozy café atmosphere. Sunday night is songwriter's night for established and amateur writers. Sun. no cover; Mon.–Sat., $2 to $5.

Bogey's. 5133 Harding Rd., (Belle Meade Galleria) (352–2447). A variety of live entertainment by established local talent. Tues.–Sun., $3 to $5 cover, no cover Mon. night.

Bullpen Lounge. Second Ave., North, and Stockyard Blvd. (255–6464). A big basement lounge beneath the popular Stockyard Restaurant seats 500 for country music entertainment. Special name acts are featured occasionally, and country music stars have been known to show up and sit in with the house band. A convicial setting in the renovated cattle stockyard building. Mon.–Thurs. usually no cover. Fri.–Sat. $2.00, or free with dinner. $5 to $10 cover for special acts.

Nashville Palace. 2400 Music Valley Drive (885–1540). Nightclub-style show-case for country entertainment. Located very near the Opryland Hotel and Park. Cover: $3 without dinner, $1 with dinner.

Printer's Alley. Between Third and Fourth avenues, North, and Church and Union streets. A descendant of Nashville's nineteenth-century saloon district. The cobbled alley is lined with restaurants and clubs that feature country and pop enter-tainment: Brass Rail Stables, Captain's Table, Boots Randolph's, Western Room, Embers Showcase, and others. Ideal location for club hopping. Dinner reservations may be required at some establishments. Dinners are expensive, although entertain-ment covers are moderate (about $5). Clubs are closed Sun.

The Station Inn. 402 12th Ave., S. (255–3307). A lively no-frills hideaway where some of Nashville's best down-home bluegrass is played and sung. Bluegrass jam sessions on Sun. bring together some of the genre's best talents. Opens at 7 P.M. Tues.–Sat. Music begins at 9 P.M. Cover, $4 to $6.

Zanie's. 2025 Eighth Ave., S. (269–0221). Stand-up comedy is the attraction at this stop on the national circuit. Professional talent performs Tues.-Sun. nights at 8:30 P.M. Late shows begin at 10:15 P.M. Fri., 10:45 P.M. Sat. Menu includes hamburg-ers, sandwiches, basket dinners, fried fish and chicken, and munchies. Admission varies.

SECURITY. When the Grand Ole Opry was downtown on Fifth Avenue, the immediate area around it was a seamy but lively and safe night spot. After the Opry's move in 1974, the Historic Broadway tavern district deteriorated into a peep show and red light district. The 1987 opening of Nashville's Convention Center on Lower Broadway has brought an increase in night street traffic and security pa-trols; however caution is still recommended. By day, Lower Broadway is a safe and well-traveled walkway, which the city has upgraded with plantings and brick side-walks in anticipation of redevelopment. Walking police patrol the area. Sections north of Church Street (hotel district) generally are safe for night walking, especial-ly near the performing arts center and Legislative Plaza, but the usual precautions should be taken to avoid wandering into areas that are poorly lit or underpopulated. The Church Street area between Fourth and Eighth avenues is a retail business dis-trict by day but is devoid of pedestrian traffic by night, save for a few prostitutes.

Riverfront Park and Historic Second Avenue, from Broadway north to the Metro Courthouse, have become safe areas with the help of police and the presence of nighttime pedestrian activity. Printer's Alley is a pocket of relative safety, but prostitutes have been known to lurk in the wings. In midtown and the suburbs, many restaurant proprietors have beefed up their own parking lot security by hiring off-duty police officers.

NEW ORLEANS

by
John R. Kemp

Mr. Kemp, columnist for New Orleans Magazine *and former staff writer for the New Orleans* The Times-Picayune, *is a New Orleans-area free-lance writer and director of publications at Southeastern Louisiana University. His* New Orleans: An Illustrated History *is one of five books about his native city and South.*

New Orleans is a great city and a fun place to visit where you can have a great time on a limited budget. New Orleans, known to generations as the "Crescent City" and more recently as the "Big Easy," is a city whose magical names conjure up images of a Gallic-Hispanic and Caribbean heritage in a predominantly Anglo-Saxon culture. It is an amalgamation of cultures from many parts of the world blending to form a unique city and people. It was founded by the French on the banks of the Mississippi River in 1718, taken over by the Spanish in 1762, regained by Napoleon in 1800, and sold to the U.S. in 1803.

During its more than 250-year history, New Orleans has survived yellow fever and cholera epidemics, Indian wars, slave uprisings, economic depressions, revolts, conspiracies, hurricanes, floods, the American and French revolutions, the Civil War and Reconstruction, racial riots, and political corruption. Today, its jazz, *Vieux Carré* (French Quarter), cuisine, Mardi Gras, and port are known worldwide.

It is a city where one never runs out of things to see and do. There are nightclubs, restaurants, museums, historic houses, jazz, blues, opera, symphony, amateur and professional sports, and theater. Dining out is a hallowed tradition.

It is a city whose mystique has captured the imagination of generations of writers and motion picture and television producers. New Orleans is a city of tourists, *beignets* (New Orleans French doughnuts), Creoles, aboveground cemetery tombs, William Faulkner's French Quarter, Tennessee Williams's *Streetcar Named Desire,* Walker Percy's *Moviegoer,* and John Kennedy Toole's *Confederacy of Dunces.*

As San Francisco is often called the most Asian of Occidental cities, New Orleans could be considered the most northern Caribbean city. Perhaps journalist A. J. Liebling best characterized the city when he described New Orleans as a cross between Port-au-Prince and Paterson, New Jersey, with a culture not unlike that of Genoa, Marseilles, Beirut, or Egyptian Alexandria. Colonial New Orleans was very much a part of the economic, political, and social milieu of the French and Spanish Caribbean. The city's earliest population consisted of lesser French and Spanish gentry, tradesmen, merchants, prostitutes, criminals, clergy, farmers from the fields of France and Germany, Acadians from Canada, Canary Islanders, Indians, Africans, Englishmen, Irishmen, and English-Americans. Italians, Greeks, Cubans, Vietnamese, and others from the earth's four corners came later.

A visitor may be shocked to hear a Brooklyn-style accent spoken in one section of the city while hearing an interesting blend of New England and southern accents in another part of town. Tune your ear for the familiar "choich" for church and "zink" for sink, and particularly for the "downtown" greeting, "Where y'at!" New Orleans's southern accent has a lot less magnolia and mint julep than a Mississippi or South Carolina accent.

New Orleans is a city of both the old and the new South with characteristics common to most American port cities. There are beautiful tree-shaded and azalea-lined streets and avenues, charming gingerbread-draped Victorian cottages, and drab ghettos, sprawling suburbs, and skyscrapers. There is prosperity and poverty, gracefulness and garishness, altruism and callousness. Above all, it is a place where the pursuit of pleasure is a full-time business. New Orleans perhaps has more churches and barrooms per capita than any other American city, and its citizens enjoy a political scandal almost as much as a Mardi Gras parade, a professional football game, or a sack of salty raw oysters.

Perhaps much of New Orleans's special flavor has been preserved by its relative isolation from the rest of the nation. It stands like a curious island of Roman Catholicism of the Mediterranean variety in a southern sea of hard-shell Protestantism that looks upon New Orleans as "Sin City." Novelist Walker Percy, who now lives in Covington, Louisiana, across Lake Pontchartrain from the city, writes that the arriving tourist will find New Orleans a "proper enough American city, and yet within the next few hours, the tourist is apt to see more nuns and naked women than he ever saw before."

Mardi Gras is the city's annual big bash and a time dedicated to fun. Despite the millions of people milling about the streets, it is perhaps the safest time of the year to visit the city. Everyone has a good time regardless of social status. Parades begin about two weeks before Mardi Gras Day, or Shrove Tuesday (40 days before Easter). It is a wonderfully silly time devoted to the old silk-stocking carnival balls (by invitation only), the newer and more egalitarian carnival organizations, street bands, marching groups, masquers, parties, balls, and over 60 parades. When the parades pass, highbrow and lowbrow alike shout the familiar call, "Throw me somethin', Mister!" and scramble on the ground, fighting over trinkets and doubloons thrown from the floats. St. Charles Avenue, Canal Street, and Bourbon Street form a single river of glowing humanity on Mardi Gras Day, with the number of people in the streets reaching over a million. But midnight Tuesday it all comes to an abrupt end, and the Lenten season begins the next morning on Ash Wednesday. Sparser lines queue at local churches for the traditional ashes on the forehead.

Like every other city, New Orleans is divided into a number of sections and neighborhoods. Each has its own flavor. New Orleans includes the French Quarter (the original city, also called the Vieux Carré), Central Business District, Faubourgs (suburbs) Marigny and Trémé, Garden District, Irish Channel, University Section, Carrollton, Lakefront, Gentilly, Bywater, and the parishes (counties) of Jefferson, Saint Bernard, and Saint Tammany.

Most of New Orleans is divided into Uptown and Downtown, with the streets running north and south from Canal Street. Uptown usually refers to a section of the city that includes the Garden District, Irish Channel, University Section, and Carrollton. Downtown can mean the Central Business District or most of New Orleans downriver (the Mississippi River, that is) from Canal Street. Canal Street is the dividing line between Uptown and Downtown. The closer you get to Canal Street, driving on streets designated north or south, the lower the block number. Downtown includes the French Quarter, Faubourg Marigny, Faubourg Trémé, and Tidewater.

The heart of old New Orleans is the **French Quarter,** which is bounded by Canal Street, North Rampart Street, Esplanade Avenue, and the river. The **Vieux Carré,** laid out in 1718 by the French, has all the charm and mystique of a historical community. But most visitors and some local real estate promoters forget that the French Quarter is a city where people live, work, and play. The buildings are not props in some historical reenactment. The aromas of age, garlic, and roasted coffee hang heavy in the damp, humid air. The streets and alleys are often dirty, yet this shabbiness adds to the area's charm. Overhanging galleries and balconies block both sun and rain.

A visit to the French Quarter should begin very early in the morning, before the midday sun burns off the morning river fog. The air is fragrant, and the aged colors of the centuries-old buildings are more vivid in the soft golden sunlight. You can see the Quarter come alive with people bustling off to work, sidewalk artists pulling their carts off to Jackson Square and Pirates Alley, and merchants bringing their produce to the farmer's market in the French Market. Also, you will probably discover a few people on the street—derelicts or revelers—who didn't make it home the night before. The streets, shops, and cafés in the Vieux Carré are crowded with people seven days a week. At night, however, most of the action is located on Bourbon Street. The French Quarter is world famous for its architecture, history, hotels, restaurants, and of course, Bourbon Street. The Quarter is a fascinating place. Natives look upon it with reverence and disgust, but they make regular pilgrimages to the Quarter to keep in touch with their past. They may curse and villify it, but they love it like an errant child.

The contrasts in the Quarter can be mind-boggling. It possesses grace, beauty, and elegance as well as vices that would have made Sodom and Gomorrah look minor league.

The French Quarter's architecture, like its food, is a patois of many cultures tempered by a semitropical climate. Despite the area's name, most of the architecture in the Quarter is a combination of French colonial, West Indian, Spanish, Greek Revival, and Victorian. Most of the Quarter was rebuilt beginning in the late 1790s, after the devastating fires of 1788, 1792, and 1794. Although a few French colonial and a number of Spanish buildings remain, most of the structures in the Quarter were erected after the 1803 Louisiana Purchase.

Directly upriver from the French Quarter and across Canal Street is the **Central Business District (CBD),** the hub of the city's business and commercial community. The CBD also was the city's first suburb, Faubourg (suburb) St. Marie (now anglicized to St. Mary). From 7 A.M. to 6 P.M., Monday through Friday, the CBD is a beehive of business men and women, secretaries, shopkeepers, shoppers, and sales clerks rushing around in the canyonlike streets that run between the high-rise buildings. On Saturdays the workers are elsewhere and the streets are less crowded. The CBD streets are generally empty on Sundays except for tourists walking to and from the French Quarter to their hotels.

One glance at the city's skyline quickly reveals that the CBD is taking on all the trappings of a Sunbelt city. During the last decade, the CBD has experienced phenomenal growth, with more than a dozen new skyscrapers rising above New Orleans's eighteenth-century suburb. Major oil companies have built regional corporate offices here, and big-name hotel chains have constructed luxurious high-rise hotels in the district. The energy is dynamic, and the CBD is experiencing an explosion in construction and development such as it had not seen in over a century. In the mid-1960s with the widening of Poydras Street and later in the early 1970s with the construction of the $160 million plus Louisiana Superdome, despite the controversy surrounding its construction, things began to change.

The CBD runs approximately from Canal Street, called the widest business street in the country, to Howard Avenue and from the Mississippi River to Loyola Avenue in the general vicinity of the Louisiana Superdome. Before the Civil War, this area of the city was known as the American Sector because this was where most Anglo-Americans settled after the 1803 Louisiana Purchase. By the 1830s the area rivaled the Vieux Carré in terms of commerce and population. By the 1850s, the faubourg was unquestionably the dominant commercial and political section of the city, and has remained the city's financial center ever since.

The **Warehouse District** section of the CBD (Poydras to Howard Ave. and St. Charles to river) is becoming one of city's art centers as chic art galleries move in and old warehouses are converted to apartments and offices. It has been dubbed "SoHo of the South."

Uptown New Orleans, upriver from Canal Street, also includes the CBD and several sections of the city: the Garden District, Lower Garden District, the Irish Channel, University Section, Carrollton, and Broadmoor. Each section is connected to the other as the city follows its winding course upriver. The Lower Garden District and Irish Channel are more or less continuations of the CBD. The Garden District is contiguous to the Lower Garden District and Irish Channel, and so on.

Before the Civil War, most of these sections were carved from the sugar plantations that lined the Mississippi River. Today, they include some of the nation's most elegant nineteenth-century neighborhoods (Garden District and Audubon Place). But Uptown also contains impoverished areas that can cause problems for sightseers.

The Garden District, running from Jackson Avenue to Louisiana Avenue and St. Charles Avenue to Magazine Street, is one of the finest residential areas in the country. It was once part of the now-defunct city of Lafayette that was created in 1835 by Americans who were fed up with the Creole-dominated politics of New Orleans. Wealthy American merchants built fine homes here, and it eventually became such a prestigious city that even Creoles moved in, building equally sumptuous houses. Most of the grand homes in the district date from the 1840s to 1870s. Lafayette was annexed to New Orleans in the early 1850s.

One normally visits thc Garden District to see the beautiful homes, architectural styles, lush green lawns, and tree-lined streets. But there are several other points of interest that should not be missed. Magazine Street has hundreds of antique and specialty shops, art galleries, and restaurants.

PRACTICAL INFORMATION

WHEN TO GO. Visiting New Orleans can be fun year-round. The summers are long, hot, and humid, but the winters are usually mild compared with more northern climes. During winter months, one can wear short-sleeved summer wear one day only to watch the temperature drop to freezing by nightfall. Perhaps the best time to visit the city and nearby plantations is in the early spring, when daytime temperatures are in the sixties and seventies. The days are pleasant, except for seasonal cloudbursts, and the nights are cool. The main avenues, parks, private gardens, and plantations are alive with beautiful spring flowers, especially the numerous varieties of azaleas so common in this area. The weather can be intensely hot and humid from mid-June through September, with temperatures in the high eighties and nineties, but that is typical of the Deep South. If you visit New Orleans during the summer, remember that all hotels and restaurants are air-conditioned. Falls are generally pleasant with warm, balmy days and cool evenings.

HOW TO GET THERE. By air. *Moisant International Airport,* located in Kenner, about 17 miles west of the French Quarter, is New Orleans's main airport for visitors. Among the major airlines serving the airport are *American, Delta, Eastern, Republic,* and *Southwest.* Some international airlines serving the New Orleans area are *Aeromexico, Continental, Jet America, Lacsa, Northwest Orient, Pan American, Sahsa, Taca International, USAir,* and *Trans World.* Also serving the New Orleans area are regional airlines that offer many scheduled flights from other southern and midwestern cities.

By bus. *Greyhound-Trailways* bus routes provide a vast array of scheduled trips, allowing travelers from all areas of the U.S. to come closer to their vacation destinations and often reach them directly. Contact a travel agent or a nearby Greyhound-Trailways office for information about special tours to and in the area of New Orleans.

By train. *Amtrak* has three major lines that connect New Orleans with the West and East coasts and the north central states. The *Silver Crescent* makes daily runs from New York to New Orleans by way of Washington, D.C. The *City of New Orleans* runs daily between New Orleans and Chicago. The *Sunset Limited* makes the two-day trip between New Orleans and Los Angeles. It departs New Orleans on Mon., Wed., and Sun. and leaves Los Angeles on Sat., Wed., and Fri. Fares change periodically. Check with Amtrak (800–872–7245) for fares and up-to-date information. The *Union Passenger Terminal,* 1001 Loyola Ave. (528–1600), in the heart of the CBD, is the city's only train station.

By car. Unless you are driving through the Deep South, New Orleans is rather out of the way. Three interstate highways, however, converge in the city. From the northeast, passing through Birmingham, Alabama, comes I-59, and from Chicago and St. Louis comes I-55. I-10 runs east-west through town, connecting Jacksonville, Florida, with Los Angeles.

TELEPHONES. The area code for the New Orleans area is 504. If you are calling within the New Orleans area, you need not use the code number. For information within the New Orleans area, dial 1–411. For information (directory assistance) outside of New Orleans but within southeastern Louisiana, dial 1–555–1212. When direct-dialing a long-distance number from anywhere in New Orleans, you must dial the number 1 before dialing the area code and the number itself. Pay phones cost 25 cents with no time limit.

Emergency Telephone Number. Dial the 911 emergency number anywhere in the immediate New Orleans area for police, fire, ambulance, and paramedics.

ACCOMMODATIONS. New Orleans offers almost every kind of accommodation from simple motel rooms to posh hotels in the French Quarter.

10
30
S. ROBERTSON
CANAL ST.
S. VILLERE
N. VILLERE
CLARA
MAGNOLIA
S. ROBERTSON
FRERET
LA SALLE
TULANE AVE.
MARAIS
S. LIBERTY
TREME
33
GIROD
JULIA
35
SARATOGA
CROZAT
29
26
ELK PLACE
BASIN ST.
5
POYDRAS
PERDIDO
22
31
N. RAMPART
GRAVIER
UNIVERSITY PLACE
BURGUNDY
LOYOLA AVE.
S. RAMPART
BIENVILLE
19
36
O'KEEFE
PENN
DAUPHINE
IBERVILLE
COMMON
BOURBON
S. RAMPART
LAFAYETTE
CARROLL
UNION
ROYAL
BARONNE
COMMERCIAL
CANAL ST.
CHARTRES
HOWARD AVE.
CARONDELET
NORTH
SOUTH
CONTI
ST. CHARLES AVE.
DECATUR
CHURCH
NATCHEZ
CLINTON
CAMP
N. PETERS
MAGAZINE
4
N. FRONT
LEE CIRCLE
ST. JOSEPH
JULIA
GIROD
CARDEVILLE
CONSTANCE
WELLS
B.R. 90
TCHOUPITOULAS
POYDRAS
NOTRE DAME
LAFAYETTE
CALLIOPE
POEYFARRE
HOWARD AVE.
CONSTANCE
S. PETER
39
FULTON
27
COMMERCE
S. FRONT
14
ANNUNCIATION
DIAMOND
N. DIAMOND
S. DIAMOND
TRIANGLE
GAIENNE
World's Fair Site
Mississippi
To Greater New Orleans Bridge
CALLIOPE

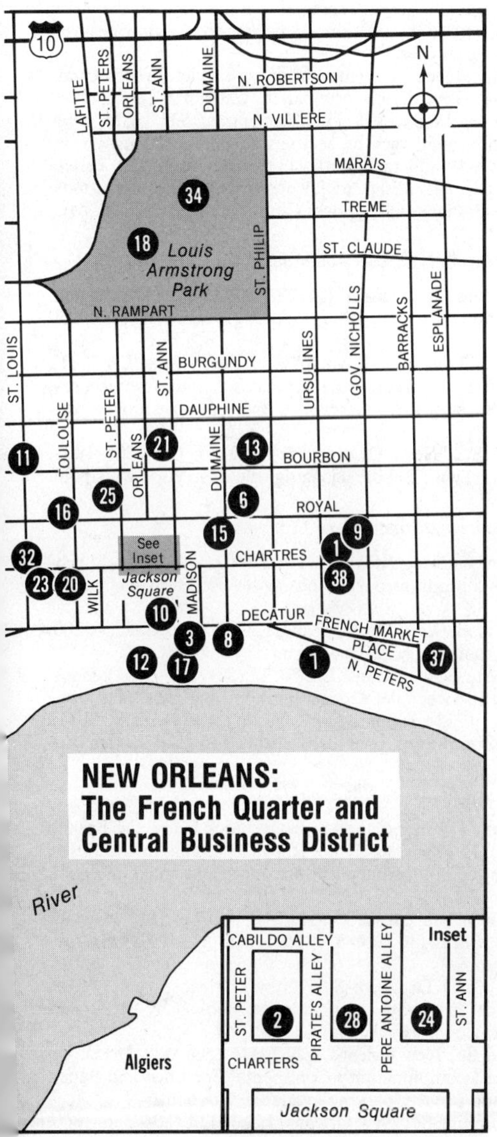

Points of Interest

1) Beauregard House
2) Cabildo
3) Café du Monde
4) Canal Place
5) City Hall
6) Cornstalk-Iron Fence
7) Farmer's Market
8) French Market
9) Gallier House
10) Greater New Orleans Convention and Visitors Bureau
11) Hermann-Grima House
12) Jackson Brewery
13) Lafitte's Blacksmith Shop
14) Louisiana Children's Museum
15) Madame John's Legacy
16) Merieult House
17) Moon Walk
18) Municipal Auditorium
19) Musée Conti Wax Museum
20) Napoleon House
21) New Orleans Spring Fiesta Mid-19th Century Town House
22) Orpheum Theater
23) Pharmacy Museum
24) Presbytere
25) Preservation Hall
26) Public Library
27) Riverwalk
28) St. Louis Cathedral
29) St. Louis Cemetery 1
30) St. Louis Cemetery 2
31) Saenger Performing Arts Center
32) State Wildlife and Fisheries Building
33) Superdome
34) Theatre for the Performing Arts
35) Trailways Station
36) Union Station (Amtrak and Greyhound)
37) U.S. Mint
38) Ursuline Convent
39) World Trade Center

The best known hotels—Windsor Court, the Hilton, Hyatt, Royal Orleans, Marriott, Fairmont, Sheraton, Meridien, Pontchartrain, Westin, and Monteleone—are fashionable and in the center of the city and are generally high-priced, providing a variety of restaurants and services. However, some of them, especially the chain hotels, offer special Christmas, weekend, and summer package vacation rates that are generally lower than their usual tabs.

Hotels are listed by geographical location: central business district, French Quarter, and Uptown. Rates are based on double occupancy. Categories, determined by price, are as follows: *Reasonable,* $60 to $95; *Very Economical,* $35 to $65. Budget motels are $30 to $60. Prices may vary by season and inflate during special events such as Mardi Gras; they do not include the 11 percent room tax. Unless otherwise noted, the hotels and motels accept major credit cards. (Abbreviations: American Express, AE; Carte Blanche, CB; Diners Club, DC; MasterCard, MC; Visa, V.)

Central Business District—Reasonable

Clarion Hotel. 1500 Canal, New Orleans, LA 70112 (504–522–4500). Ballroom, exhibition hall, restaurants, coffee shop, deli, lounges, rooftop swimming pool; 750 rooms.

Downtown Howard Johnson's Motel. 330 Loyola Ave., New Orleans, LA 70112 (800–535–7830, 504–581–1600). Free parking, valet service, baby-sitter service, restaurants, swimming pool, facilities for the handicapped, free in-house movies, restaurants; 300 rooms.

Radisson Inn. 315 Julia St., New Orleans, LA 70130 (504–525–1993, 800–822–2323). An all-suite hotel with wet bars, jogging track, lap pool, whirlpool, pay parking; 351 units.

Central Business District—Very Economical

Bayou Plaza. 4040 Tulane Ave., New Orleans, LA 70119 (504–486–7144). Tennis courts, swimming pools, restaurants, airport limousine service, free parking; 310 rooms.

Best Western Patio. 2820 Tulane Ave., New Orleans, LA 70119 (504–822–0200, 800–528–1234). Free parking, outdoor pools, washerteria; 76 rooms.

LaSalle Hotel. 1113 Canal St., New Orleans, LA 70112 (504–523–5831). Complimentary coffee, baby-sitting service, valet service, laundry machines; 60 rooms.

Rodeway Inn Downtown. 1725 Tulane Ave., New Orleans, LA 70112 (504–529–5411). Free parking, restaurant, pool, baby-sitting and valet services, in-room movies; 94 rooms.

French Quarter—Reasonable

A Hotel . . . The Frenchman. 417 Frenchman Street, a block below the French Quarter, New Orleans, LA 70116 (504–948–2166). Restored Creole town houses, period furnishing, ceiling fans, complimentary full breakfast and cocktails, pool, courtyard, valet service; 25 rooms.

Best Western Landmark Bourbon Street Hotel. 541 Bourbon St., heart of French Quarter, New Orleans, LA 70130 (504–524–7611, 800–535–7891). Restaurants, cabaret, parking; 178 rooms.

Bienville House Hotel. 320 Decatur St., New Orleans, LA 70116 (504–529–2345, 800–535–7836). Free parking, restaurant, pool, baby-sitting service, meeting rooms, valet service; 82 rooms.

Cornstalk Hotel. 915 Royal St., New Orleans, LA 70116 (504–523–1515). On the Register for Historic Places, complimentary Continental breakfast and paper, antique furnishings, baby-sitting service, parking available; 14 rooms.

Dauphine Orleans. 415 Dauphine St., New Orleans, LA 70112 (504–586–1800, 800–251–1962). Free parking, complimentary cocktail and Continental breakfast, baby-sitting service, pool, valet service, laundry service, in-house movies; 110 rooms.

De La Poste Motor Hotel. 316 Chartres, New Orleans, LA 70130 (504–581–1200). Free valet parking, baby-sitting service, restaurant, facilities for the disabled, pool; 100 rooms.

LaMothe House. 621 Esplanade Ave., New Orleans, LA 70116 (504–947–1161, 800–367–5858). Restored to Victorian splendor, courtyard and gardens, free Creole breakfast, free parking, walking distance to French Quarter; 11 rooms.

Le Richelieu Motor Hotel. 1234 Chartres, New Orleans, LA 70116 (504–529–2492, 800–535–9653). Free parking, restaurant, pool, kitchenettes, baby-sitting and valet services; 88 rooms.

Place D'Armes Hotel. 625 St. Ann, New Orleans, LA 70116 (504–524–4531, 800–535–7791). Free Continental breakfast, baby-sitting and valet service, pool, meeting room; 74 rooms.

Prince Conti Hotel. 830 Conti, New Orleans, LA 70112 (504–529–4172, 800–535–4172). Free parking, complimentary Continental breakfast, baby-sitting and valet service, meeting room; 58 rooms.

Provincial Motor Hotel. 1024 Chartres, New Orleans, LA 70116 (504–581–4995, 800–535–7922). Free parking, restaurant, pool, baby-sitting service, complimentary champagne for honeymoon couples; 97 rooms.

French Quarter—Very Economical

A Creole House. 1013 St. Ann St., New Orleans, LA 70116 (504–524–8076, 800–535–7858). Continental breakfast; 20 rooms. No credit cards.

Burgundy Inn—French Quarter. 911 Burgundy St., New Orleans, LA 70116 (504–524–4401, 800–535–7785). Off-street parking, color TV, private bath; 67 rooms. No credit cards.

Chateau Motor Hotel. 1001 Chartres, New Orleans, LA 70116 (504–524–9636). Free parking, sidewalk café, pool, baby-sitting and valet service; 42 rooms.

Hotel Villa Convento. 616 Ursulines St., New Orleans, LA 70116 (504–522–1793). European—style hotel, Continental breakfast, pay parking; 24 rooms.

Nine-O-Five Royal Hotel. 905 Royal St., New Orleans, LA 70116 (504–523–0219). Period furnishings, kitchenettes, balconies, and courtyard.

Noble Arms Inn, Hotel and Guest House. 1006 Royal St., New Orleans, LA 70116 (504–524–2222). Balconies, courtyard, pay parking, kitchenettes; 16 rooms.

Uptown—Very Economical

Columns Hotel. 3811 St. Charles Ave., New Orleans, LA 70115 (504–899–9308). On Register of National Historic Landmarks. Victorian lounge, complimentary Continental breakfast and paper. 20 rooms; shared or private bath.

Old World Inn. 1330 Prytania St., New Orleans, LA 70130 (504–566–1330). European-style guest house, complimentary Continental breakfast. V and MC; 17 rooms.

Parkview Guest House. 7004 St. Charles Ave., New Orleans, LA 70118 (504–861–7564). Old Victorian guest house furnished with antiques, on streetcar line, Continental breakfast; 25 rooms; private or shared baths.

The Prytania Park Hotel. 1525 Prytania St., New Orleans, LA 70130 (504–524–0427). Restored Victorian town house, complimentary Continental breakfast and wine; 13 rooms.

St. Charles Guest House. 1748 Prytania, New Orleans, LA 70130 (504–523–6556). Pool, patio, complimentary Continental breakfast; 26 rooms, 22 with private bath.

St. Charles Inn. 3636 St. Charles Ave., New Orleans, LA 70130 (504–899–8888). Baby-sitting and valet service, complimentary newspaper and Continental breakfast; 40 rooms.

Terrell House. 1441 Magazine St., New Orleans, LA 70130 (504–524–9859, 488–7932). Restored 1850 mansion elegantly furnished with antiques, private baths, color TV, complimentary Continental breakfast; 10 rooms.

Budget Motels. Days Inn—Downtown. 1630 Canal St., New Orleans, LA 70112 (504–586–0110, 800–325–2525). In CBD. Restaurant, pool, meeting rooms, facilities for the disabled, free parking, valet service; 216 rooms.

Days Inn—St. Charles. 2203 St. Charles Ave., New Orleans, LA 70140 (504–566–1200, 800–325–2525). On famous streetcar line in fashionable Uptown. Restaurant; 121 rooms.

Family Inns of New Orleans. 6301 Chef Menteur Hwy., New Orleans, LA 70126 (504–246–2400, 800–251–9752). Kitchenettes, pool, free movies, tours, meeting rooms; 86 rooms.

Holiday Inn East Hi Rise Hotel. 6324 Chef Menteur Hwy., New Orleans, LA 70126 (504–241–2900, 800–238–5400). Restaurant, pool, baby-sitting service, free bus to French Quarter, meeting rooms; 207 rooms.

Howard Johnson's—East. 4200 Old Gentilly Rd., New Orleans, LA 70126 (504–944–0151, 800–654–2000). Restaurant, pool, valet service, meeting rooms, free parking; 160 rooms.

Quality Inn—Midtown. 3900 Tulane Ave., New Orleans, LA 70119 (504–486–5541). In CBD. Meeting rooms, steam-baths, laundry service and machines, free parking, facilities for the disabled; 102 rooms.

The Roadway Inn—Kenner. 1700 I-10 Service Rd., Kenner, LA 70062 (504–467–1300, 800–228–2000). Near the airport. Restaurant, live entertainment, pool, exercise room; 293 rooms.

TraveLodge Airport. 2240 Veterans Blvd., Kenner, LA 70062 (504–469–7341, 800–255–3050). Courtesy airport transportation, restaurant, pool, baby-sitting service, facilities for the disabled, valet service, conference center, free parking.

Bed-and-Breakfast. Bed & Breakfast Inc. 1360 Moss St., Box 52257, New Orleans, LA 70152–2257 (504–525–4640, 800–228–9711–184). Listing of areawide homes offering B&B accommodations, from $35.

New Orleans Bed & Breakfast. 2714 Canal St., New Orleans, LA 70119 (504–949–6705, 822–5038, 822–5046). Extensive listing of area homes offering B&B accommodations as well as private homes and apartments for rent. Tours available. $25 and up.

Lindsay Enterprises. 4431 St. Charles Ave., New Orleans, LA 70115 (504–897–3867). Garden District location near St. Charles streetcar, private bath. $40 to $50. Also offers B&B listings throughout uptown area.

Ys and Hostels. New Orleans offers two hostels, both located in the heart of the city close to many of the attractions.

Marquette House International Hostel. 2253 Carondelet St., New Orleans, LA 70130 (504–523–3014). Not far from the CBD. Member of the International Youth Hostel Association. TV lounge, user's kitchen, dining area, garden, patio. Members, $7; nonmembers, $9.

International Center YMCA. 936 St. Charles Ave., New Orleans, LA 71030 (504–568–9622). Parking, indoor pool, restaurant, health center. Located on streetcar line in central business district, 9 blocks from French Quarter and 5 blocks from Superdome. Male and female, 225 rooms. $20–$22.

HOW TO GET AROUND. From the airport. To get to the French Quarter and CBD from Moisant International Airport by cab costs $18 for the first three people plus $6 for each additional passenger. The *Louisiana Transit* system (737–9611) also runs a bus from the airport to the CBD. The fare is $1.10 one way, but the ride is long (at least an hour) and tedious because the bus makes regular stops to pick up passengers along the way. In the CBD, the airport bus can be caught at the corner of Tulane Ave. and Elks Pl. across the street from the New Orleans Public Library. Limousine service to and from the airport and downtown hotels also is available through *Airport Rhodes* (464–0611, 469–4555) for $7. This is probably the best way to go.

By bus. The *Regional Transit Authority* (RTA) operates a good public transportation system with interconnecting lines throughout the city. The buses generally are clean and on time. Bus fare is 60 cents plus 5 cents for transfers. For route information, call 569–2700.

By streetcar. RTA also operates the St. Charles Avenue streetcar that makes the 5-mile trek from the CBD to Carrollton along picturesque St. Charles Ave. The fare is 60 cents plus 5 cents for transfers.

By taxi. Rates are fairly high in the city, although most rides are relatively short. Cabs are metered: $1.10 minimum plus $1 per mile. Cabs can be secured by telephone, hailed from the sidewalk, or found at the numerous hotel cab stands in the CBD and French Quarter. The larger taxi companies include *Morrison's* (891–5818), *United* (522–9771), and *Yellow-Checker* (943–2411).

On foot. The best way to see much of New Orleans is on foot. The French Quarter and CBD are contiguous, and most tourist sites in those areas are within walking distance. Other sections of the city are accessible by public transit. However, there are certain sections and neighborhoods that should be avoided. See Security for more information.

By car. Most major car rental agencies, including *Avis, American, Budget, Dollar, Econo-Car, Hertz, National, Payless, Sears,* and *Thrifty,* are located at the airport. Many of them rent vans as well. Check your local telephone directory for toll-free reservations. It is often cheaper to rent at the airport. Also ask your travel agent to check the rates of small, locally owned car rental companies such as *Lamarque Ford* (443–2500) and *Toyota Car and Truck Rental* (837–0623, 467–5119 near Airport also, 529–3720 in CBD). Rates and mileage allowances often are cheaper than those of larger companies.

By boat. You can catch the free Canal Street ferry at the foot of Canal St. and the Mississippi River. The half-mile trip from Canal St. to Algiers Point is the best bargain in the city. It gives you a great view of the river, CBD, French Quarter, docks, shipping on the river, and other great sights. The ferry casts off every 12 minutes, and the round trip takes about 40 minutes.

HINTS TO THE MOTORIST. If you plan to drive, get a road map of the city in advance and study it carefully. Driving in New Orleans can be especially challenging. Most of the city's streets are very narrow, and the locals drive through them fast and often with abandon. New Orleanians are not very good drivers. They dart in and out of traffic lanes as though they've never discovered the turn signal device on the steering column. If possible, avoid using a car in the French Quarter and CBD and during rush hour (roughly 5:00–6:30 P.M.). On certain streets, parking is forbidden during rush hours. Look for the warning signs. Illegally parked cars are towed away. There's nothing more frustrating than having to bail your car out of the local police auto pound. Parking violations can cost $20 to $65. Parking lots are not too expensive, but they are usually quite busy with regular daily traffic. Parking meters are available but offer limited-time use, usually no more than 2 hours. Most hotels provide free or paid parking for guests. Curbs painted yellow designate no parking or stopping. Once you have reached the French Quarter or CBD hotel where you will be staying, the best thing to do is to park your car in the lot and walk, depending on the neighborhood, or take some form of public transportation.

Louisiana and New Orleans speed limits comply with federal law: 55 mph. General speed limits for school zones range from 15 to 20 mph. The speed limit on most New Orleans streets is 35 mph unless marked otherwise. Watch the signs; there is no state or city requirement for posting warning signs on radar, mechanical, or electrical speed-checking devices.

TOURIST INFORMATION. The *Greater New Orleans Tourist and Convention Commission* and the *Louisiana Tourist Development Commission,* both at 529 St. Ann St., where there is a visitors information center, (566–5011), publish a number of booklets, brochures, and maps on New Orleans and the surrounding area. In addition, they distribute scores of informational brochures about hotels, sightseeing companies, tours, plantations, shops, and restaurants. The center, in the French Quarter, should be the first stop for visitors to the New Orleans area. There is also a visitors information desk at the New Orleans International Airport near the customs office. Both places have bilingual staffs. Open 9 A.M.–5 P.M. Mon.–Fri. Written requests for information should be addressed to the commission at 1520 Sugar Bowl Dr., New Orleans, LA 70112.

The Louisiana Office of Tourism also has a great deal of information available, including guides, booklets, brochures, and maps. Call toll free 800–231–4730 (outside Louisiana); Louisiana residents call 504–925–3860.

When visiting a city like New Orleans, there are several telephone numbers you should have at your fingertips. For weather forecasts, call 525–8831; marine recreational forecast, 522–2686; passports, 589–6728; for daily information about arts and entertainment, 566–5031.

A number of publications in New Orleans offer extensive up-to-date information and listings for restaurants, museums, shopping, children's activities, theater events, films, dance, art, and music. These publications include *Louisiana Life* magazine, *New Orleans* magazine, *New Orleans Travel Weekly, This Week in New Orleans, Menu, Where* magazine, and *Go* magazine. Most can be obtained at minimal or no cost in hotel rooms. Others can be purchased at newsstands. The city's largest newspaper, *The Times-Picayune/The States-Item,* has daily listings of things to do and see in its calendar of events and its weekly (Friday) entertainment tabloid, "Lagniappe" (pronounced "lan-yap").

Foreign currency exchange. All the major banks in the CBD offer this service. Two of the largest are *Whitney National Bank,* 228 St. Charles Ave. (9 A.M.–2 P.M., Mon.–Fri.) and *Hibernia National Bank,* 313 Carondelet St. (9 A.M.–3 P.M., Mon.–Fri.).

SENIOR-CITIZEN AND STUDENT DISCOUNTS. Some attractions in the New Orleans area offer discounts to senior citizens and students. In most cases, showing a driver's license, passport, or some other proof of age will suffice; senior generally is defined as 65 or over for men and 62 or over for women. Museums often post special senior citizen rates. Places offering student discounts are generally somewhat more stringent in their proof requirements; a high school or college ID, international student traveler card, or evidence of age may be requested.

Many hotels and motels also offer special rates to senior citizens and students. It's best to call ahead to make sure these rates are available at the place of your choice.

Visiting senior citizens 65 or over who have a valid Medicare ID card may ride public transit for only 20 cents 24 hours a day, 7 days a week. For further transit information, call 569–2700.

FREE EVENTS. New Orleans is in itself a free event. The city's unique architecture and neighborhoods have delighted visitors for generations. The French Quarter is known worldwide. On weekends, especially during spring and summer, the Quarter is alive with street musicians, and scores of artists can be found at work around Jackson Square. Ambling through the farmer's market and flea market at the lower end of the French Market is a pleasant way to spend a warm morning or afternoon.

In recent years, festivals have become increasingly popular in New Orleans and nearby communities. Usually there is no admission charge, but you are expected to buy food, refreshments, and other items.

For day-to-day listings of free events and activities in the city, check *The Times-Picayune* daily calendar of events section or call 566–5031.

Unquestionably, the biggest free show on earth is **Mardi Gras.** During the two weeks building up to the celebration, over 60 parades roll through the streets. On Mardi Gras day (Feb. 7, 1989), the delightful and abandoned madness lasts the full 24 hours with over a score of carnival clubs and marching groups parading through the streets. The French Quarter, especially Bourbon St., is packed shoulder to shoulder with revelers, and you will see and experience things that you probably have never seen before and may never see again. Among the best known parades are Bacchus, Zulu, Rex, and Comus. Bacchus parades the Sunday night before Shrove Tuesday, and the other three roll on Mardi Gras day. For information about Mardi Gras schedules, contact the Greater New Orleans Tourist and Convention Commission, 1520 Sugar Bowl Dr., New Orleans, LA 70112 (504–566–5011). Also get a copy of Arthur Hardy's annual *New Orleans Mardi Gras Guide.*

Parades are a big part of the city's history, and New Orleanians look for any excuse to hold one. The descendants of Erin hold their annual **Saint Patrick's Day Parade** on March 17 in the Irish Channel. It is fun, but it is by no means on the same scale as the Saint Patrick's Day Parade in New York. Two days later New Orleanians of Sicilian descent, and there are many, celebrate **Saint Joseph's Day.** This is a carry-over celebration from the Middle Ages, when, as the story goes, a prayer to St. Joseph saved Sicily from a devastating famine. Saint Joseph Day in New Orleans is celebrated in private homes and churches (especially at Saint Joseph's on Tulane Ave.) with Saint Joseph altars stacked high with magnificent Italian and Sicilian pastry. Anyone who has prayed to Saint Joseph for a favor and gotten it erects an altar the next year in his honor. There also is a parade in the French Quarter that night. **Spring Fiesta** is a parade, "A Night in Old New Orleans," held the first Fri. after Easter. The Fiesta continues 19 days. Call 504–581–1367 or write to Spring Fiesta, 826 St. Ann St., New Orleans, LA 70116.

TOURS. Tourism is one of New Orleans's major industries, and practically every type of touring service has popped up. There are bus tours, walking tours, and steamboat tours. There are tours of restaurants and bars, plantations, the French Quarter, the Mississippi River, museums, houses, and graveyards.

River and Bayou cruises. For one-day or half-day excursions on the Mississippi River and connecting waterways, the New Orleans Steamboat Company has the *Steamboat Natchez* (about as authentic a steamboat as one can get), the *Riverboat President* (with moonlight cruises and dance bands), the *Bayou Jean Lafitte* (travels the Mississippi to Bayou Barataria, once the stronghold of the infamous pirate, Jean Lafitte), and the sternwheeler *Cotton Blossom.* The *Natchez* has three trips daily at 11:30 A.M., 2:30 and 6:30 P.M. Adults, $9.75; children 3 to 11, half price; children under 3 free. Prices higher in the evening. The *Bayou Jean Lafitte* makes one trip each day, 10:30 A.M. to 4 P.M.; the charge is $12.50 for adults, half price for children. The *Natchez* has the "Moonlight Dance Cruise," 10 P.M.–midnight Sat. The cost is $9.75, but food (cafeteria-style buffet) and drinks cost extra. The *Natchez* is moored on the river at the foot of St. Peter St. in the French Quarter. Riverboat *President* has a Sat. dinner-dance cruise, 8 P.M.–11 P.M., $19.75; and a Sun. brunch cruise, 11 A.M.–2 P.M., $16.95 (522–3030). The *President, Bayou Jean Lafitte,* and *Cotton Blossom* are tied up at the foot of Canal St. The *Cotton Blossom* also offers a "Zoo Cruise" round-trip from Canal St. upriver to the Audubon Park Zoo. Sailing time each way is about an hour. Round trip. Adults, $7.75; children 2 to 11, $3.75. One way is $5.25 for adults, $3.25 for children 2 to 11. Children 3 and younger may travel free on all cruises. Zoo admission extra. For further information, call 586–8777.

The **Canal Street ferry** crosses the river from the foot of Canal Street to Algiers Point. It's a great ride (about 40 min. round-trip) and it's free.

City and plantation tours. Several of the larger sightseeing companies offer a variety of bus tours in New Orleans and to the plantation houses up and down the Mississippi River. *Gray Line Tours of New Orleans,* for example, offers three daytime tours of the city, including a riverboat ride, the French Quarter, Garden District, cemeteries, lakefront, zoo, and St. Charles Ave. It also offers a tour of plantation houses along the old River Road, after-dark tours of the city's nightlife, swamp and bayou tours. The tours depart from several of the leading hotels; prices range from $16–$32 (add another $20 if you take the dinner tour); tour lengths vary. For reservations, check with the hotel desk or call 587–0861. Several other large sightseeing companies offer similar tours. Sometimes the choice comes down to convenience and price. Others include *Southern Tours Inc. of New Orleans* (486–0604), *New Orleans Tours* (246–1991), and *Dixieland Tours* (283–7318). *Gay 90s Carriage Tours* (482–7013) offers a horse-drawn carriage tour of the French Quarter. Tours are available throughout the day at Jackson Square and other French Quarter locations.

Friends of the Cabildo, a nonprofit volunteer affiliate of the Louisiana State Museum system in the French Quarter, offers a walking tour of the Quarter at 9:30 A.M. and 1:30 P.M. daily, 1:30 P.M. Sun. The $7 charge is tax-deductible. Children under 12, free; senior citizens and ages 13–20, $3.50. For further details, call 523–3939.

National Park Service guides give free walking tours of the French Quarter in the morning and afternoon (times may vary), except New Year's Day, Mardi Gras, and Christmas. They also give tours of St. Louis Cemetery No. 1 at 9:30 A.M. and of the Garden District at 2 P.M. (reservations required). Also available are special-topic tours, such as voodoo, ghost stories, and women of New Orleans. All tours begin at the National Park Service Information Center, 916 N. Peters St. in French Market (589–2636).

The Preservation Resource Center, 604 Julia St. (581–7032), is dedicated to the preservation of old New Orleans. Throughout the year the PRC offers walking tours of New Orleans neighborhoods. The tours are given irregularly during the year, so check with the center for prices (which are quite reasonable) and schedules.

Spring Fiesta begins the first Friday after Easter and continues for 19 days, with tours of French Quarter and Garden District homes, plantations, and patios by candlelight. Call 581–1367 or write Spring Fiesta, 826 St. Ann St., New Orleans, LA 70116.

Louisiana Superdome. Guided tours of the world's largest building of its kind are given 9 A.M.–4 P.M. daily. Adults, $4; senior citizens, $3; children 5 to 12, $3; infants 4 and younger free. Call 587–3810.

For those who do not mind venturing a short way out of the city, the **Chalmette Battlefield** will prove interesting. It is in the town of Chalmette just downriver, and you can get there by driving down St. Claude Ave. from Esplanade Ave.—you can't miss it. It was here that General Andrew Jackson defeated the British in the Battle of New Orleans in January 1815 on the Chalmette plantation. The battle was one of the last dramatic performances in what most American historians call the second war of independence. When the dust and smoke cleared, the Americans counted 13 dead, 39 wounded, and 19 missing. The British reported 858 killed, 2,468 wounded, and many others missing. Ironically, in early February the British and Americans received word that the United States and Great Britain had signed a peace treaty at Ghent, Belgium, on December 24, 1814—two weeks before the Battle of New Orleans had taken place.

FESTIVALS. The Jazz and Heritage Festival, held the last week of April and the first week of May, has become world famous for music (jazz, gospel, folk, popular) and Louisiana food. It takes place at the Fairgrounds Race Track, 1751 Gentilly Blvd. Anything you have heard in the way of New Orleans music is found here, from traditional New Orleans jazz and gospel to early rhythm and blues, rock 'n' roll, and bluegrass. Admission is $8 at gate, $6 advance, children $2, $1.50 advance. There are dozens of acts in a day, at numerous stages outdoors and in tents, and an immense variety of food that is cheap and fabulous. Call 522–4786 or write: New Orleans Jazz and Heritage Festival, Box 53407, New Orleans, LA 70153.

After the jazz festival closes, not much else happens in New Orleans during May and June. But in late June and July two relatively new festivals crank up: **La Fête** and the **New Orleans Food Festival.** They were created in the late 1970s to attract visitors to the city during the hot summer months. The city bills La Fête as an annual family summer festival, featuring special events in the French Market, a fireworks display on the River on July 4, and festivities on Bastille Day (July 14). The Food Festival, held the weekend before the Fourth, where for the price of a reasonable admission charge one gets to sample the best Louisiana food prepared by the best Creole and Cajun chefs. Call 525–4143.

Festa d'Italia, sponsored by the American Italian Federation of the Southeast, is held on Columbus Day (second Mon. in Oct.). Parade, good Italian food, art, and music. Held at the Piazza d'Italia on Poydras and Tchoupitoulas streets in the CBD. Call 891–1904.

PARKS AND GARDENS. Audubon Park and Zoological Garden, 6800 block of St. Charles Ave. (861–2537), is one of the most beautiful urban parks in the nation. It encompasses 400 acres in the fashionable Uptown New Orleans area on St. Charles Ave. across from Tulane and Loyola universities. The land making up the park originally was the Foucher and Bore plantations. The city bought the land from speculators in 1871 and created the Upper City Park. The park was renamed Audubon Park for naturalist John James Audubon around the turn of the century and redesigned partially from plans drawn up earlier by the famed landscape architect Frederick Law Olmstead and Sons, who designed New York's Central Park. It was the site of the 1884–1885 World's Industrial and Cotton Centennial Exhibition—New Orleans's first world's fair—and featured a 31-acre main exhibition hall. All traces of the fair are now gone.

Aside from the 18-hole golf course, Audubon Park offers a public swimming pool, tennis courts, picnicking throughout the park, and jogging paths. There is also a 1¾-mile jogging path with exercise stations along the way. The park is closed to automobile traffic on weekends. There is plenty of parking throughout the park. Mon.–Fri., 9:30 A.M.–5 P.M.; Sat.–Sun., till 6 P.M. The magnificent Audubon Zoo also is located here. See Zoos.

City Park, located in the Midcity area at Esplanade and City Park avenues, about 3 miles from the French Quarter, was once the sugar plantation of Louis Allard. Today the 1500-acre park is the fifth largest urban park in the nation. The park is closed from 10 P.M. until sunrise. The grounds, with their magnificent live oaks and network of man-made lagoons, are well worth seeing. Located in City Park is the New Orleans Museum of Art. On the south side of the museum are the majestic nineteenth-century dueling oaks where many scores were settled and honor upheld. Much of the park was built or improved under the aegis of the Works Progress

Administration during the Depression of the 1930s. Evident everywhere are signs left by the WPA, including the Beaux Arts-style pavilion that stands near the Casino (1914). The Casino has an information office, concessions, and bicycle and boat rentals. The bronze statue of New Orleans-born Confederate General P. G. T. Beauregard stands at the main entrance to the park at Esplanade Ave. (Beauregard's forces fired the first shot opening the Civil War at Fort Sumter, South Carolina.)

City Park also features three 18-hole golf courses, tennis courts, canoes and paddle boats, picnic grounds, horseback riding, fishing, an amusement park, a beautiful carousel (built in 1904), a petting zoo and storyland for children, and a miniature train.

Longue Vue House and Gardens, 7 Bamboo Rd, off Metaire Rd. (488–5488), once was the 8-acre private estate of Edith and Edgar B. Stern. It is now open to the public. The 45-room house and five surrounding English and Spanish gardens are exquisite. The formal English gardens complement the great country house, and the Spanish "water" gardens with their 25 fountains provide a soothing treat for eye and ear. The house was built in the late 1930s in the Classical style. Admission to house and garden: adults, $5; children and students, $3. Tues.–Fri., 10 A.M.–4:30 P.M.; Sat.–Sun., 1–5 P.M. Closed Mon. and holidays.

Louisiana Nature and Science Center, located in eastern New Orleans, 11000 Lake Forest Blvd. (246–9381), is an 86-acre wilderness park in the middle of suburban New Orleans. The center is a nonprofit private institution dedicated to preserving what little is left of the natural environs that once surrounded the city. Contains exhibitions on south Louisiana flora and wildlife, media center, lecture hall, and gift shop. The center also offers woodland trails and bird-watching classes, nighttime canoe trips through swamplands, craft workshops, and field trips. Adults, $3; senior citizens, $2; children 4 to 17, $1; children under 4 free. Open Tues.–Fri., 9 A.M.–5 P.M.; Sat.–Sun., noon–5 P.M. Closed Mon.

ZOOS. The 58-acre **Audubon Zoo,** 6500 Magazine St., is in a state of ongoing expansion, and in recent years it has become one of the finest zoos in the nation. The main entrance is off Magazine St. behind Audubon Park near the river. Visitors can stroll through the picturesque setting and see over a thousand animals kept in natural settings or take the Mombasea Railway ($1) for a guided tour. You catch the train inside the zoo. The zoo is divided into various sections—Asian Domain, World of Primates, African Savannah, North American Grasslands, South American Pampas, Louisiana Swamps, and Australian exhibits—that feature animals native to those parts of the world. Also has a sea lion pool, reptile aquarium, elephant rides, and children's petting zoo.

The zoo is open Mon.–Sun., 9:30 A.M.–5 P.M. Adults, $5.50; children 2–12 and senior citizens, $2.75; children under 2 free. Call 861–2537. You can get there by Magazine bus, St. Charles streetcar (ask driver for transfer at Broadway), by car up St. Charles Ave., or *Steamboat Cotton Blossom.* See Tours.

PARTICIPANT SPORTS. Swimming. A public swimming pool in New Orleans is located at *Audubon Park* (two pools); call 524–8829. Open late May through Aug., 10 A.M.–6 P.M., Tues.–Sun. Admission $1. Almost all motels and hotels have swimming pools for their guests. Swimming in Lake Pontchartrain is not recommended because of high pollution levels.

Tennis. The *River Center Tennis and Racquetball Club* at the New Orleans Hilton Hotel, 2 Poydras St. (587–7242), offers indoor and outdoor tennis, racquetball, gym, saunas, and whirlpools. Prices range from $8 to $24 an hour.

Public tennis courts in New Orleans include: *Wisner Tennis Center* at City Park (483–9383, 488–1142); *Stern Tennis Center,* 4025 Saratoga St. (891–0627); *Joe Brown Park,* Read Blvd. in eastern New Orleans; and *Audubon Park,* off Magazine St. (865–8638). Almost all have day and night tennis; prices range from $4–$5 per hour.

Golf. Four 18-hole public golf courses are at *City Park,* 1046 Filmore (483–9396). Greens fees $7.50–$8.75. *Audubon Park,* 473 Walnut (861–9511), has one 18-hole course. Greens fees: weekdays, $6; weekends, $9.

Jogging. Popular places to jog in New Orleans are *City Park* in Midcity and *Audubon Park* in Uptown. Audubon Park is probably the most popular because the 1¾-mile track winds through lagoons and has exercise stations along the way.

Bicycling. *City Park* rents bicycles for about $5 for 2 hours (482–4888). There also are two commercial bicycle rental shops in town. *Bicycle Michael's*, 618 Frenchman St. near the French Quarter (945–9505), charges $3.50 an hour and $12.50 for a full day. *Joe's Bicycle Shop,* 2501 Tulane Ave. (821–2350), charges $9.95 plus $50 deposit a day. Anyone interested in renting a bike to tour the city neighborhoods should purchase a copy of Louis Alvarez's *New Orleans Bicycle Book* at a local bookstore.

Canoeing. *City Park* (482–4888) offers canoe and paddle boat rentals for the park's network of semitropical lagoons for $5 an hour. The *Canoe and Trail Shop,* 624 Moss St. (488–8528), frequently sponsors canoe trips into nearby swamp and marshlands. Their prices vary but are quite reasonable.

Hiking. *The Canoe and Trail Shop* (488–8528) and the *Louisiana Nature and Science Center* (246–LNSC) frequently sponsor excursions into the prime backpacking and hiking areas in southern Louisiana and Mississippi.

SPECTATOR SPORTS. Although New Orleans does not have a major or minor league **baseball** team, top-flight collegiate baseball is played by Tulane University and the University of New Orleans in the spring. The University of New Orleans also plays NCAA Division I **basketball.** The Louisiana Superdome is the site of the annual *Sugar Bowl Basketball Tournament,* played the week preceding the annual football classic.

The Superdome is the site for a good many **football** games. The New Orleans Saints of the National Football League (tickets, 522–2600) and Tulane University (tickets, 861–3661) play their home games there. Grambling and Southern universities renew their annual rivalry each November in the *Bayou Classic,* also in the Superdome (587–3822). The Superdome is also the site of the Sugar Bowl Classic played in the evening on New Year's Day (525–8603).

The nation's top professional **golfers** compete annually in the *Greater New Orleans U.S.F.&G. Open* at English Turn Golf and Country Club, West Bank, 1 Club House Dr., New Orleans, LA 70131 (529–3343), in April 1989.

Horse racing has been popular in New Orleans for generations. The *Fair Grounds,* 1751 Gentilly Blvd. (944–5515), the nation's third oldest track, is open afternoons Wed.–Sun. from Thanksgiving Day to early April. From April to Nov., night racing is held Wed.–Sun. at *Jefferson Downs,* Williams Blvd. and Lakefront, Kenner (466–8521), about 20 minutes from downtown New Orleans. Both tracks offer clubhouse dining. The 26.2-mile *Mardi Gras Marathon* is held annually on the Sunday preceding Mardi Gras Day. For information, call 246–0001.

CHILDREN'S ACTIVITIES. Kids especially love *Mardi Gras* and its 2 weeks of "Throw me somethin', Mister!" They can scramble on the ground with natives and fellow visitors for the coveted toys and trinkets thrown from the parade floats.

The major historical and art museums have exhibits for children. Of particular interest is the **Musée Conti Wax Museum,** 917 Conti St. in the French Quarter. It has a number of exhibits with life-size wax figures of Jean Lafitte, the Louisiana pirate; Andrew Jackson and the Battle of New Orleans; and Marie Laveau, the Voodoo Queen. Open 10 A.M.–5:30 P.M. daily. Children of all ages will enjoy the Mardi Gras exhibit in the **Old U.S. Mint Building,** 400 Esplanade at the River. Open 9 A.M.–5 P.M. Tues.–Sun. Adults, $2; senior citizens and students, $1; children under 12 and military personnel free. Also popular is the **Pontalba Historical Puppetorium,** facing Jackson Square (522–0344). Open 10 A.M.–6 P.M. daily. Adults, $2; children, $1. **The Louisiana Children's Museum,** 428 Julia St. in the CBD (2nd floor), (523–1357), features hands-on exhibits to help learning. 9:30 A.M.–4:30 P.M. Tues.–Sun. Children and adults, $2.50.

Watching ships of all types ply the Mississippi River is exciting for children. The best place to view them is from the "Moon Walk" in front of Jackson Square. Jackson Square also hosts a number of diversions for children with its carnival of street musicians, clowns, mimes, and sidewalk artists.

HISTORIC SITES AND HOUSES. The Gallier House, 1118–1132 Royal St., in the French Quarter (523–6722), is one of the finest historic houses in the city. It was built around 1858 by James Gallier, Jr., and has been lovingly restored to its state at the time when the notable architect lived there. This house shows how the wealthy lived in middle nineteenth century New Orleans. Adults, $3; students and senior citizens, $2.50; children under 12, $1. Docent tours. Open 10 A.M.–3:45 P.M. Mon.–Sat.

Historic Hermann-Grima House and Courtyard. 820 St. Louis St., in the French Quarter (525–5661). The local headquarters of the Christian Women's Exchange. It was built in 1831 for a wealthy New Orleans merchant. The historic house contains a gift shop, Creole kitchen, and courtyard *par-terre.* The courtyard, one of the largest in the French Quarter, has been replanted in the early nineteenth-century style. Adults, $3; children, students, and senior citizens, $2. Open weekdays and Sat. 10 A.M.–3:30 P.M.

Le Carpentier or Beauregard-Keyes House. 1113 Chartres St., in the French Quarter (523–7257). Built in 1827. During the winter of 1866–67 Civil War General P. G. T. Beauregard rented a room here and then lived here after the war. The house later became the residence of the novelist Frances Parkinson Keyes, who wrote many novels about the region. The historic house boasts lovely French Quarter gardens. Adults, $3; students and senior citizens, $2; children under 12, $1. Open 10 A.M.–3 P.M. Mon.–Sat.

New Orleans Spring Fiesta Mid-19th Century Townhouse. 826 St. Ann St., in the French Quarter (581–1367). Furnished with early nineteenth-century and Victorian pieces and *objets d'art.* Admission $1.50. Group tours arranged. Docent guides. Open 11 A.M.–4 P.M., Mon.–Thurs.

St. Louis Cathedral, on Jackson Square, is the oldest active Roman Catholic cathedral in the U.S. (1793). The present cathedral (built in the 1790s and remodeled in the 1850s) is the third church to occupy this site since New Orleans was founded in 1718. The cathedral was named for Louis IX of France. Free guided tours daily Mon.–Sat., 9 A.M.–5 P.M.; Sun., 1–5 P.M.

Jackson Square, in the heart of the French Quarter, was first established in 1721 as a drill field for soldiers. Known first as the Place D'Armes under the French and then the Plaza de Armas under the Spanish, the square was renamed in honor of General Andrew Jackson in 1851. The focal point of the square is the large bronze equestrian statue of Jackson by Clark Mills. During the summer free concerts are held on Sat. afternoon. The park is open to the public from sunup to sundown.

St. Louis Cemeteries No. 1 and 2. St. Louis No. 1 is located on Basin and St. Louis streets, and No. 2 can be found between St. Louis and Iberville streets along North Claiborne Ave. Both are located behind the French Quarter in Faubourg Tremé. Established in 1796, St. Louis No. 1 is the oldest extant graveyard in the city. These cemeteries, like others in the city, are famous for their ornate aboveground tombs. They have been called cities of the dead. Local legend has it that New Orleans cemeteries are built aboveground because some parts of the city are just at or below sea level, and to dig into the ground would mean coming up with water. It's a nice story, but the city's Mediterranean and southern European heritage probably had more to do with the custom of aboveground tombs. St. Louis No. 2 dates from the 1820s and was laid out in the same general style as its predecessor. New Orleanians from all walks of life were buried here during the nineteenth century; white, black, slave, and free, from the city's most prominent citizens to its lowliest. Some of those buried in these two cemeteries include Voodoo Queen Marie Laveau (notice *gris gris* X's marked on her tomb) and Paul Morphy (renowned nineteenth-century world chess champion from New Orleans). A word of caution: The best and safest way to visit these cemeteries is by guided tour and in large numbers.

MUSEUMS. Because of the city's preoccupation with its past, most New Orleans museums are historical in nature. The two largest, the Louisiana State Museum and the New Orleans Museum of Art, both of which have recently staged major exhibits, have gained impressive national reputations. With the New Orleans Symphony and Mardi Gras, they form the nucleus of the city's cultural life.

Louisiana State Museum. Jackson Square in the French Quarter (568–6985). Has eight historical buildings. Wed.–Sun., 10 A.M.–5 P.M. Adults, $3; students and senior citizens, $1.50; children under 12 free.

New Orleans Museum of Art. City Park (488–2631). The permanent collection ranges from pre-Columbian and Far Eastern to European and African art. Since the 1960s, the museum has been building a special collection devoted to the Arts of the Americas: North, Central, and South. Tues.–Sun., 10 A.M.–5 P.M.; Thurs., 1–9 P.M. Adults, $3, children 6 to 17 and senior citizens, $1.50, children under 6 free. Thursdays free.

Historic New Orleans Collection. 533 Royal St. in the French Quarter (523–4662). Ten galleries featuring the history of New Orleans in maps, charts, paintings, and historical documents. Tues.–Sat., 10 A.M.–3:15 P.M. Docent tour, $2.

Confederate Memorial Museum. 929 Camp St. near Lee Circle (523–4522). Adults, $2; students and senior citizens, $1; children under 12 free. Mon.–Sat., 10 A.M.–4 P.M.

Louisiana Children's Museum. 428 Julia St. (second floor) (523–1357). Hands-on exhibits to stimulate children's imagination. 9:30 A.M.–4:30 P.M. Tues.–Sun. Admission, $2.50.

Pharmacy Museum. 514 Chartres St. in the French Quarter (524–9077). "La Pharmacie Française" resembles a nineteenth-century New Orleans apothecary. Tues.–Sun., 10 A.M.–5 P.M. Admission, $1.

Middle American Research Institute. Fourth floor, Dinwidde Hall, Tulane University, facing St. Charles Ave. (865–5110). Pre-Columbian Mayan artifacts. Mon.–Fri., 8:30 A.M.–4:30 P.M. Admission free.

Musée Conti Wax Museum. 917 Conti St. in the French Quarter (525–2605). New Orleans historical exhibits and people. Adults, $4; senior citizens, $3.50; children 13 to 17, $3; children 6 to 12, $2.50; under 5 free. Open daily 10 A.M.–5:30 P.M.

ARTS AND ENTERTAINMENT. Music. In addition to jazz and rhythm and blues—types of music that New Orleans made famous—the city also has a strong symphony orchestra and opera company. The *New Orleans Philharmonic Symphony* performs in the recently restored Orpheum Theatre, 129 University Pl., in the CBD (525–0500). The season runs from Oct. to May. The *New Orleans Opera Association* now performs at the Theater of the Performing Arts, 801 North Rampart St. (529–2278 or 529–2279), behind the French Quarter in Louis Armstrong Park. The French Market Corporation sponsors *free jazz concerts* every Sun. afternoon during the summer at St. Philip and Decatur streets. The New Orleans Recreation Department also sponsors occasional free Sat. afternoon concerts in Jackson Square. There is no set schedule, so be sure to check the newspapers. The *Jazz and Heritage Festival* takes place annually during the last week of April and the first week of May. (See Festivals.)

Dance. Professional dancing is experiencing its bleakest period in recent New Orleans history. The *New Orleans City Ballet* is the only major professional dance troupe in the city. It performs at the Theater of the Performing Arts, 801 N. Rampart St. (522–0996), during Sept., Dec., March, and May.

Stage. Theater in New Orleans, dating back to the late eighteenth century, is a tradition almost as old as the city itself. For current productions and performances, consult the local newspapers. *Saenger Performing Arts Center,* Canal and N. Rampart streets (524–0876), is the closest thing New Orleans has to big-time theater. Housed in a recently restored Italianate vaudeville and movie palace dating from the 1920s, the Saenger is on the national theater circuit for Broadway revivals and road shows. Seats are reasonably priced. Reservations needed.

There are several other popular but smaller theaters in the city that often give credible performances. They include the *Tulane University Theatre* (865–5106); *Le Petit Theatre Du Vieux Carré,* 616 St. Peter St., in the French Quarter (522–2081), *Theatre Marigny,* 616 Frenchman St., below the French Quarter (944–2653); and the *Contemporary Arts Center,* 900 Camp St., in the CBD (523–1216). The *Rose Dinner Theatre,* located at 201 Robert St. across the River in Gretna (367–5400), offers excellent plays and an all-you-can-eat Creole buffet. Prices, $18–$23. Another popular theater is the *Bayou Dinner Theatre* in the Bayou Plaza Hotel on Tulane and Carrollton aves. (486–4545).

SHOPPING. New Orleans has its *Saks Fifth Avenue, Gucci, Brooks Brothers,* and their pricey local equivalents but also has a number of bargain shopping places with great buys. New Orleans has only two major department stores: *D.H. Holmes* and *Maison Blanche* (closed Sun.). Both are located on Canal St. in the CBD and have good prices. Caroline Rekoff's *The Underground Shopper of New Orleans* is a must for bargain hunters. The 197-page indexed paperback sells for $4.95 at local bookstores; it has a wealth of information on bargain shopping in the New Orleans area. Write to Box 3231, Baton Rouge, LA 70821. The *New Orleans Shopping Guide* can be obtained free at the New Orleans Visitor's Center.

There are legions of swanky shops throughout the French Quarter, CBD, and Uptown areas, but there also are a number of discount and outlet stores with good buys. If you just want to ogle but not buy, don't miss One Canal Place at the foot of Canal St. and the river. It has become the shopping mecca in this part of the country with such stores as Brooks Brothers, Saks Fifth Avenue, and F.A.O. Schwarz. Most shops close about 6 P.M.

Antiques. New Orleans has an excellent selection of antique shops, ranging from the pricey stores on Royal St. to the moderately priced and bargain-hunting spots on Magazine and Chartres streets. The outdoor flea market is held each weekend in the lower French Market near Esplanade Ave. It is a hodgepodge of furniture, bric-a-brac, clothes, appliances, and you name it. The outdoor flea market is held Sat.–Sun., 7 A.M.–7 P.M. Moreover, in the vicinity of the market, at addresses in the 1100 to 1300 blocks of Decatur St., are a number of smaller indoor flea markets and shops with interesting secondhand merchandise. For antique shoppers, there is no better place than Magazine St., which starts at Canal St. and parallels the river to Audubon Park. Along this route you will find almost 5 miles of antique shops, art galleries, clothing shops, a delicatessen, restaurants, and almost anything else. The shops start in about the 2000 block of Magazine. Be careful along Magazine; it's close to high-crime areas.

Fun and Food. The old *Jackson Brewery* (529–1340), near the river facing Jackson Square, is brand-new on the New Orleans shopping scene. Housed in the turn-of-the-century Jax brewing house, it has four floors of shops, restaurants, lounges, art galleries, and refreshment stands. *Central Grocery,* 923 Decatur St. (523–1620), in the French Quarter, has spices, cheese, oils, and imported delicacies from Italy plus great Old World smells. The new Rouse Riverwalk (522–1555), on the former World's Fair site, has become one of the city's top tourist and shopping attractions. Great view of the Mississippi. Open daily.

DINING OUT. Visitors to New Orleans almost immediately fall in love with the area's fabulous food, and they don't have to spend a fortune. There are a number of famous but expensive restaurants in the city, such as Antoine's, Brennan's, Jonathan's, and Broussard's, and then there are those less known, with superb food at a fraction of the cost. If you just want the experience of dining in the famous ones, check their less costly lunch menus.

Restaurant categories, determined by the price of a meal for one, without beverage, tax (9 percent), or tip, are: *Reasonable,* $13 to $19; *Very Economical,* $8 to $12; and *Low Budget,* under $7. Unless otherwise noted, all restaurants listed accept some if not all major credit cards. Every effort has been made to ensure that the list is up to date. Restaurants come and go so quickly, however, that it is always advisable to call ahead. See *Gambit* weekly magazine for great listings.

Reasonable

Casamento's. 4330 Magazine St., Uptown (895–9761). Specializes in oysters, raw at the bar or fried to order on a platter or in a sandwich. An Uptown favorite. Lunch and dinner Wed.–Sun. Closed throughout the summer months. No credit cards.

Charlie's Steak House. 4510 Dryades, Uptown (895–9705). Steaks are brought out sizzling on metal plates in butter sauce, and in the case of the T-bones and strips, they are gargantuan. Great side dishes. Lunch and dinner Mon.–Sat.

Chez Helene. 316 Chartres, French Quarter (in Dela Poste Hotel) (581–1200). Great Creole dishes. Breakfast, lunch, and dinner daily.

Compagno's Fern Restaurant. 7839 St. Charles Ave., Uptown (866–9313). A small neighborhood place with a menu of good seafood and Italian dishes. Lunch and dinner Wed.–Sun. No credit cards.

Delmonico. 1300 St. Charles Ave., Uptown (525–4937). One of the older restaurants in town, founded before the turn of the century. Delmonico still purveys a consistently good and broad selection of old-style Creole cooking in a comfortable, antique-filled, very New Orleans setting. Lunch and dinner every night.

Dooky Chase. 2301 Orleans, Downtown (822–9506). For years this has been the dining-out bastion of the black community as well as one of the most consistently good Creole restaurants in the city. Near the French Quarter and popular among people of all races. However, it is located in a high-crime area, and one would be wise to take a cab to and from the front door. Lunch and dinner every night.

Felix's. 739 Iberville, French Quarter (522–4440). Popular seafood restaurant and oyster bar, especially among tourists. Lunches cost much less than full dinners. Lunch and dinner Mon.–Sat. No credit cards.

Galatoire's. 209 Bourbon St., French Quarter (525–2021). No reservations. The line to get in starts out front at 11 A.M. for lunch and 6 P.M. for dinner. One of the best old-line New Orleans restaurants and a must for the gourmet even on the briefest stop in New Orleans. Lunch and dinner Tues.–Sun. No credit cards.

Kolb's. 125 St. Charles Ave., CBD (522–8278). One of New Orleans's few German restaurants. Over the years, however, it has been heavily influenced by the city's Creole cooking. The atmosphere is great: beer steins, heavy wood, all the trappings of a Munich beer hall. Especially popular lunch spot for businessmen. Lunch and dinner Mon.–Sat.

Mr. B's Bistro. 201 Royal St., French Quarter (523–2078). Run by the same family as famous Brennan's and Commander's Palace. Popular with natives. Lunch and dinner daily.

Patout's. 1319 St. Charles (Quality Inn), CBD (522–0187). Hails from Cajun country with mouth-watering dishes. Breakfast, lunch, and dinner daily.

Very Economical

Copelands of New Orleans. 4338 St. Charles Ave., Uptown (897–2325). Louisiana Cajun cuisine at its finest. Innovative dishes from seafood to steak. Great family restaurant. Lunch and dinner every day. American Express only.

Hard Rock Cafe. 418 N. Peters St., French Quarter (529–5617). This new member of the internationally famous chain is now New Orleans' trendiest eating spot. Broad (but unspectacular) menu includes salads, steaks, and ample burgers. Don't forget to pick up a Hard Rock sweatshirt on your way out. Lunch and dinner daily.

The Jackson Brewery. Decatur St. facing Jackson Square, French Quarter (581–4082). Housed in this recently renovated turn-of-the-century brewhouse are six stories of shops, art galleries, restaurants, and food stalls, featuring practically every conceivable type of New Orleans and Louisiana cuisine from gumbo to meat pies. Try *Trey Yuen,* 620 Decatur in the Brewery (588–9354). Outstanding Chinese food with Louisiana touch and great view of the River. Very popular with locals. Lunch and dinner daily.

The Pearl Restaurant. 119 St. Charles, CBD (525–2901). Great oyster bar and sandwich bar where huge roasts, hams, corned beef, pastrami, and turkeys stand ready to be carved before the customer's eyes. Also good seafood and Creole dishes. Breakfast, lunch, and dinner every day.

Low Budget

Central Grocery. 923 Decatur, French Quarter (523–1620). Serves and originated the great muffuletta, a large Italian sandwich. Also a wonderland of imported spices and delicacies. Great aroma. Mon.–Sat., 9 A.M.–5 P.M. No credit cards.

Camellia Grill. 626 S. Carrollton, Uptown (866–9573). The class act among lunch counters, with linen napkins and a maitre d'. The hamburgers are legendary, as are the deli sandwiches, breakfasts, pecan pie, and cheesecake. Breakfast, lunch, and dinner. No credit cards.

D.H. Holmes Cafeteria. 220 Dauphine, French Quarter (561–6141). Features a wide variety of Creole and American cuisine, seafoods, home-style dishes. Family pricing. Breakfast, lunch, and dinner, Mon.–Sat. V, MC.

Johnny's Po-Boy Restaurant. 511 St. Louis, French Quarter (524–8129). One of the best po-boy restaurants in the French Quarter. A popular spot among locals. Serves all forms of po-boys, from roast beef to seafood, as well as gumbo and seafood dishes. Breakfast and lunch, Mon.–Sat. No credit cards.

Maspero's. 601 Decatur, French Quarter (523–8414). A popular French Quarter sandwich shop with people often queuing up to get in. Sandwiches served on tasty hard bun, stuffed with ham, pastrami, corned beef, roast beef, etc. Lunch and dinner every day. No credit cards.

Mother's. 401 Poydras, Central Business District (523–9658). Mother's is the great po-boy restaurant, serving sandwiches the length of your lower arm on fresh, delicious French bread. They roast all their own meats; the ham is a special treat, but the roast beef, turkey, and other combinations are marvelous. Also serves good breakfasts and rib-sticking plate lunches. Breakfast and lunch, Tues.–Sat. No credit cards.

A good stop for a quick, casual meal or snack is **Riverwalk,** foot of Canal St. facing the River. This mile-long strip of trendy shops and food booths features everything from hot dogs to red beans and rice. Great river views, too.

Recommended Splurge. K-Paul's Louisiana Kitchen. 525 Chartres, French Quarter (524–7394). No reservations. If you are going to splurge on at least one fine restaurant, this is the place to do it. Don't be put off by the external appearance of this hole in the wall. K-Paul's, with its owner-chef Paul Prudhomme, currently is one of the most talked-about restaurants in America. Prudhomme's cookbook has become a best-seller nationwide, and his Cajun-Creole dishes are sumptuous. His most notable dishes include sauteed veal with crawfish (crayfish), crawfish étouffée, blackened prime ribs with brown garlic butter, and blackened redfish. It's a dining delight. Entrees range in price from $22–$26; appetizers cost from $4 to $9. A sign on the door sets the house rules: no reservations, no personal checks: American Express, traveler's checks, or cash only, $15 minimum per person. Open 5:30–10 P.M. Closed weekends.

If the line in front of K-Paul's is too long or if you happen to be in the city over the weekend, there are a number of other fine restaurants in the French Quarter, CBD, and Uptown, including **Antoine's, Moran's,** the **Rib Room, Caribbean Room, Bon Ton,** and **Delmonico. Arnaud's,** 813 Bienville St. in the French Quarter, 523–5433, is an old New Orleans favorite. It is especially known for turning out delicious Louisiana French Creole classics, such as Shrimp Arnaud, pompano en croute, trout meunière, and redfish hollandaise. A four-course à la carte dinner without liquor will average about $26 per person, add another $8 for before dinner drink and wine with main course. Complete lunches range from $9–$12 and Sunday brunch (with many favorite Creole dishes) from $17–$20 per person (about $25 with liquor). Arnaud's has the delightful atmosphere of nineteenth-century New Orleans, including Mardi Gras museum. Reservations suggested.

Cafés and Coffeehouses. Outdoor cafés are few. However, there is one tradition of long standing here: finishing off the evening at the **Café du Monde.** It is still where it's always been, at the uptown extremity of the French Market (Decatur at St. Ann), with a small dining room and a large covered section outside. The coffee is *café au lait,* the famous New Orleans dark-roasted coffee and chicory blend, far too strong to be drunk without the hot milk poured in the cup at the same time the coffee is. The doughnuts are *beignets,* leaden little fried squares of sourdough, served three to the order (65 cents), dusted with powdered sugar that will probably wind up dusting you, too.

Just off Jackson Square is **La Marquise,** 525 Chartres, French Quarter (524–0420), 9 A.M.–5 P.M., Thurs.–Tues., a fine little French pastry shop run by two very talented French chefs. There are a few tables inside and on the patio. A favorite among local artists. Also, **La Madeleine Bakery,** 547 St. Ann St., facing Jackson Square (568–9950).

The new **Jackson Brewery,** Decatur St. facing Jackson Square, is a six-floor shopping and dining palace that features several pastry shops and coffee shops overlooking the Mississippi River. The **Rouse Riverwalk,** starting at the foot of Canal St. and running along the river in the CBD, offers a variety of stops for coffee and snacks.

NIGHTLIFE AND BARS. It has been said that if one drops dead of cirrhosis of the liver in New Orleans, it's considered death by natural causes. Drinking accompanies almost every recreational activity, particularly those which take place after dark. Major events like Mardi Gras or the Jazz Festival take on truly bacchanalian proportions with regard to imbibing.

Of course, the main attraction in the way of nightlife in New Orleans is live music. There is plenty of it, ranging from the very oldest and most authentic Dixieland jazz to new wave rock and modern jazz. The best places tend to be rather old, slightly run-down, and crowded; clubs offering comfortable seating are few and far between.

Everyone winds up on Bourbon St. sooner or later. Although there is a little bit of everything and much of interest, the street is dominated at present by T-shirt stores, porn theaters, bad fast-food places, etc. The strip joints continue in operation, even though the sexual revolution has turned them into a tawdry curiosity, the barkers will still try to get you inside for a peek. There also are several good night spots on Bourbon that feature good jazz and food.

All bars in the New Orleans area are allowed unlimited hours. In the French Quarter, closing is rarely earlier than 2 A.M., with a great many places open 24 hours, 7 days. Prices range from around $5 a drink in the best hotels down to $1.50 or even less in neighborhood bars. In the jazz clubs, it is customary to have a two-drink minimum, but few Quarter bars have a cover charge. The legal drinking age in Louisiana is 21.

For up-to-date information on performers at clubs, the best places to look are the "Lagniappe" section in the Friday *Times-Picayune* or in *Gambit,* a weekly newspaper.

Jazz. The most famous venue is **Preservation Hall,** 726 St. Peter, French Quarter (523–8939). You'll have to line up to pay your pittance to get into this old place, where jazz aficionados from all over the world flock in to listen to the most authentic old New Orleans jazz played by groups who learned and played with the jazz greats. Nightly from 8 P.M. For more information on jazz spots call the New Orleans Jazz Club (455–6847).

There are several other good jazz spots in the French Quarter. **The Famous Door,** 339 Bourbon (522–7626), features jazz, blues, and rock. There is no cover charge but drinks run $3.50 to $7.75. Open nightly. **Duke's Place,** in Mahogany Hall, 309 Bourban St. (525–5595), is home base for the popular Dukes of Dixieland. Cover charge of $13.90 per person gets you two drinks and a great show. Showtimes are at 9, 10:20, and 11:40 P.M. **Storyville Jazz Hall,** 1104 Decatur (525–8199), is a relative newcomer to the scene. In addition to traditional Dixieland Jazz, Storyville also has New Orleans rhythm and blues and a dance floor in case you want to strut along with the music. There's no cover charge (except for weekend special events) but drinks run $2 to $3. Open 7 P.M. **Pete Fountain's,** in the New Orleans Hilton Hotel at 2 Poydras St. (523–4374), is where the internationally famous jazz clarinetist performs 10 months of the year. There is a $16.50 cover charge that comes with the show and one drink. Showtime is 10 P.M. Tues., Wed., Fri., and Sat. Often closed July and Aug. Reservations are sometimes difficult to get, so call ahead well in advance. But for good old, down and dirty New Orleans Jazz, Preservation Hall is the best deal in town.

Blue Room, Fairmont Hotel, University Place, CBD (529–4744). Prices vary at this supper club, so call in advance. One of the last of the big, gilded rooms outside Las Vegas, the Blue Room offers a continually varying lineup of big-name acts, such as Cab Calloway, Lena Horne, and Buddy Greco, performing with the room's standing orchestra. Not cheap.

R&B, Rock, and New Wave *544 Club,* 544 Bourbon, French Quarter, (523–8611). Features soul, rhythm and blues, and a bit of jazz. Music daily from 3 P.M. till late. *Riverboat President,* Canal Street Wharf (586–8777). Night cruises with popular dance bands of all types. Uptown, *The Maple Leaf,* 8316 Oak St. (866–9359), and *Tipitina's,* 501 Napoleon Ave. (895–8477), are the best.

Local Hangouts. *Columns Hotel,* 3811 St. Charles, Uptown (899–9308). Old St. Charles Ave. mansion converted to a small guest house and swanky lounge. It was the setting for Louis Malle's movie *Pretty Baby* and was one of *Esquire* magazine's 100 best lounges in the U.S. *Fat Harry's,* 4330 St. Charles, Uptown (895–9582). Popular haunt for local college students and French Quarter residents. *Jonathan's,* 714 N. Rampart, French Quarter (586–1930). Pricey but elegant art deco restaurant and lounge. *Napoleon House,* 500 Chartres, French Quarter (524–9752). The Napoleon House is a holdover from another age. Its stained and crumbling walls, classical music piped throughout the bar, and musty patio make it one of the most interesting watering holes in the Quarter. It oozes atmosphere. The building is so named because, as legend has it, it was offered to the Emperor Napoleon as a refuge. *Pat O'Brien's,* 718 St. Peter, French Quarter (525–4823). It's always a mob scene in this best known of New Orleans lounges, with a Mardi Gras atmosphere year-round. There are several large rooms here and an even larger patio, with each section having a different form of entertainment. The sing-along rooms are especially popular, as is its best known drink, the Hurricane. It's inexpensive and great fun. *Que Sera,* 3636 St. Charles Ave., Uptown (897–2598). A popular spot among Uptown yuppies, with a large front patio facing the streetcar tracks and the avenue. *Top of the Mart,* World Trade Center, 2 Canal Street, CBD (522–9795). This is a revolving lounge atop one of the taller buildings downtown with a great view of the entire city and the river traffic. The lounge is comfortable, the service is fast and friendly, and there is occasionally a jazz trio playing. Open daily.

SECURITY. New Orleans is a wonderful place to have a good time, but an enjoyable visit to the "Big Easy" can be spoiled by violence and theft. Some sections of the city should be avoided altogether by visitors; other sections should be avoided at certain times of the day and night. Perhaps the best way to see the city is to sign up for a guided bus or walking tour; there's safety in numbers.

The French Quarter is a great place during the day, and it is generally safe for those who simply enjoy strolling about. When visiting the Quarter at night, stick to Royal, Bourbon, and Chartres streets. There are usually a number of people just like yourself milling around enjoying the sights. Avoid the dark side streets and alleys. Many a vacation has been spoiled by a holdup and mugging.

To visit the old colonial St. Louis cemeteries behind the French Quarter, take a guided tour during the day; never go alone, especially at night.

Also avoid walking at night in the central business district, particularly in the area near the Superdome and the Union Passenger Terminal. If you are traveling in and out of these areas at night, take a cab. A good general rule is to avoid walking anywhere at night except in the heart of the French Quarter.

If you are planning a visit to the Irish Channel or Garden District, plan to go by car or guided tour bus. Once there, walking along Magazine Street is generally safe.

As in most other places, don't leave money or valuables in your hotel room. Hotels are magnets for professional thieves. Always be sure to lock your doors, even when you are inside. For valuables, use the safe-deposit boxes offered by hotels; they are usually free. If you are planning to attend crowded events such as Mardi Gras, men should consider putting their wallets in some other pocket than the usual breast pocket or back pocket.

NEW YORK

by
Ira Mayer and JoAnn Greco

Ira Mayer is president of Presentation Consultants, a New York editorial services company specializing in travel and entertainment. He is the author of Fodor's Fun in Montreal *and coauthor of* Fodor's Fun in London *as well as numerous articles. JoAnn Greco is a freelance writer based in New York.*

New York has more of everything you could want in the way of culture, entertainment, food and activities than any other place in the United States. Alas, it also has more of many things you could easily do without, such as crowds, dirt, crime, and a pace that can be staggering. To appreciate New York City it is necessary to accept, at least for the duration of the visit, these contradictions.

Just as the character of New York goes to extremes, so does traveling there on a budget. Compared with other areas of the country, no such thing as inexpensive lodging exists in New York, though we will recommend the most consistently reasonable establishments. But you can eat cheaply and well, use relatively inexpensive public transportation, and see the sights most reasonably. The key to New York on a budget is flexibility or, as New Yorkers might have it, going with the flow.

You can see a show on or off Broadway or an opera, ballet, or concert at half price if you are willing to wait until the day of the performance and select from what is available at specially designated, centrally located box offices.

By choosing carefully among the city's nightclubs, you can save money by going to a club where the minimum can be applied to meals or drinks that are reasonably priced, as at Michael's Pub.

To dine in opulence, select a pretheater fixed-price dinner at such luxurious restaurants as Central Park's Tavern on the Green—for less than a third of what you would pay ordering à la carte. Alternatively, New York offers an enormous selection of ethnic eateries where atmosphere is strong, food freshly prepared, and prices low.

No one can see "all" of New York. Not in a single visit, probably not in a lifetime. It isn't that the city is particularly large, especially considering that most tourists concentrate on the five miles or so of Manhattan between Wall Street at the south and Lincoln Center to the north. It's the density of the city that makes it such a challenge for the visitor and the native alike.

The trick is to be selective and then narrow your choices. Say your interest is art. You couldn't take in the entire Metropolitan Museum of Art in one day, let alone such other outstanding museums as the Modern, the Whitney, and the Guggenheim. Not if you're going to do more than aimlessly stroll corridors. (This ignores the galleries of 57th Street, upper Madison Avenue, and SoHo; the medium-size collections in smaller museums; and the special exhibitions that are placed around town.)

Most visitors want to divide their time among the major sites and attractions: a museum or two, the Statue of Liberty, Wall Street, a Broadway show, the World Trade Center, Chinatown, nightclubs, Greenwich Village, the South Street Seaport, restaurants, Rockefeller Center, and so on. A little planning can make the going easier so that you don't spend the bulk of your time crisscrossing the city on buses and subways. Grouping the attractions that satisfy your interests will save you considerable time as well as transportation costs. It also leaves you feeling less harried.

Some may wish to build their trips around dining. If that is the case and if there are specific restaurants you want to try, make reservations as far ahead as possible, remembering that in order to take advantage of pretheater specials you probably will have to be seated between, say, 5:30 and 6:30 or 7 P.M. (The rules vary from restaurant to restaurant.) Reservations for lunch on weekdays at establishments that cater to business executives and brunch on the weekends are also recommended.

However you organize your sight-seeing, remember to keep your eyes wide open. There are skyscrapers to be appreciated, windows to be gazed at (especially department stores such as Altman's and Lord & Taylor at Christmas), and traffic to watch for (speeding bicycle messengers as well as automobiles, buses, and trucks). Best of all, there are people to watch. The most colorful are probably the street kids in the East Village and the high-fashion artist types in SoHo. By Broadway and Lincoln Center it's the performing artists: young ballet dancers, cellists wheeling their instruments, professorial sorts in their wool sport coats and mufflers. On the Upper East Side, life (and dress) is more formal.

New York is a city of constant change in regard to the skyline, the streets (forever being ripped open), and the people. The character will be different every time you visit, partly as a function of the different sites you choose to see, partly as a reflection of the city's mood swings.

PRACTICAL INFORMATION

WHEN TO GO. Aside from the need to be prepared for temperature extremes at all times, New York offers everything it has year-round. This is a city that's alive 24 hours a day 365 days a year. Spring and fall may be the most pleasant seasons

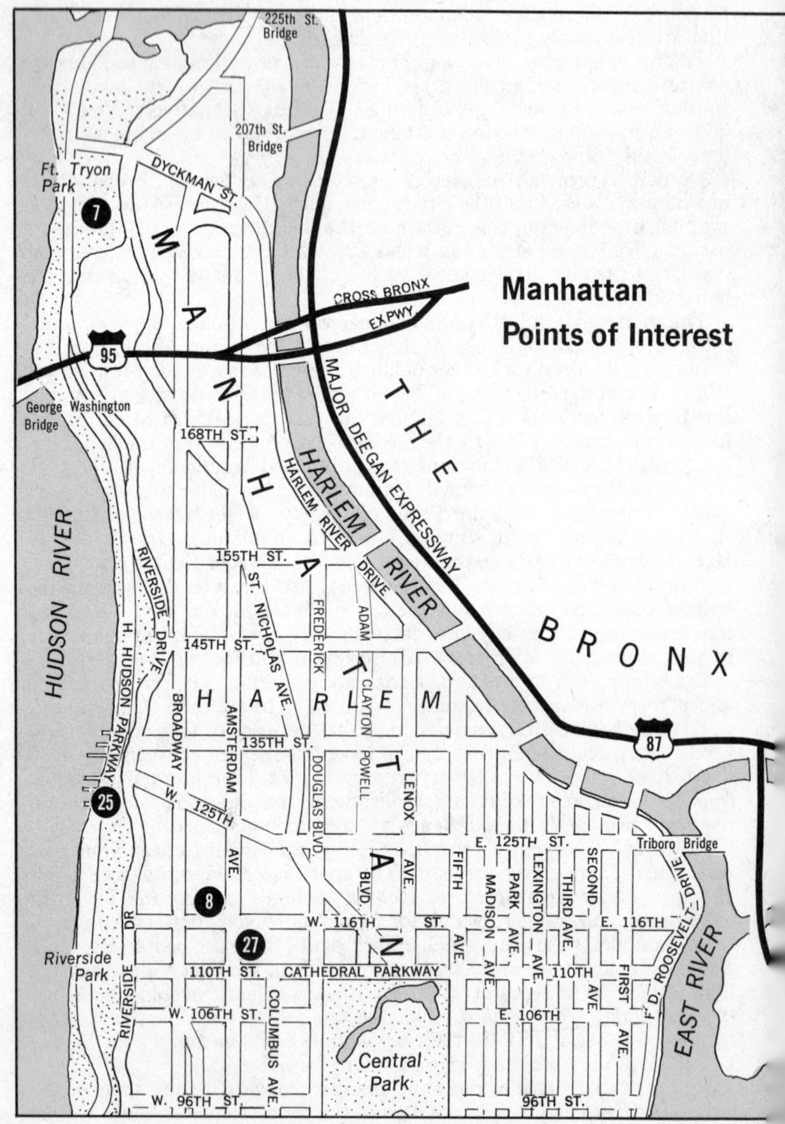

Points of Interest

1) American Museum of Natural History
2) Carnegie Hall
3) Central Park Zoo
4) Chinatown
5) Citicorp Center
6) City Hall
7) Cloisters
8) Columbia University
9) Empire State Building
10) Frick Museum
11) Gracie Mansion
12) Gramercy Park
13) Grand Central Station
14) Guggenheim Museum
15) Hayden Planetarium

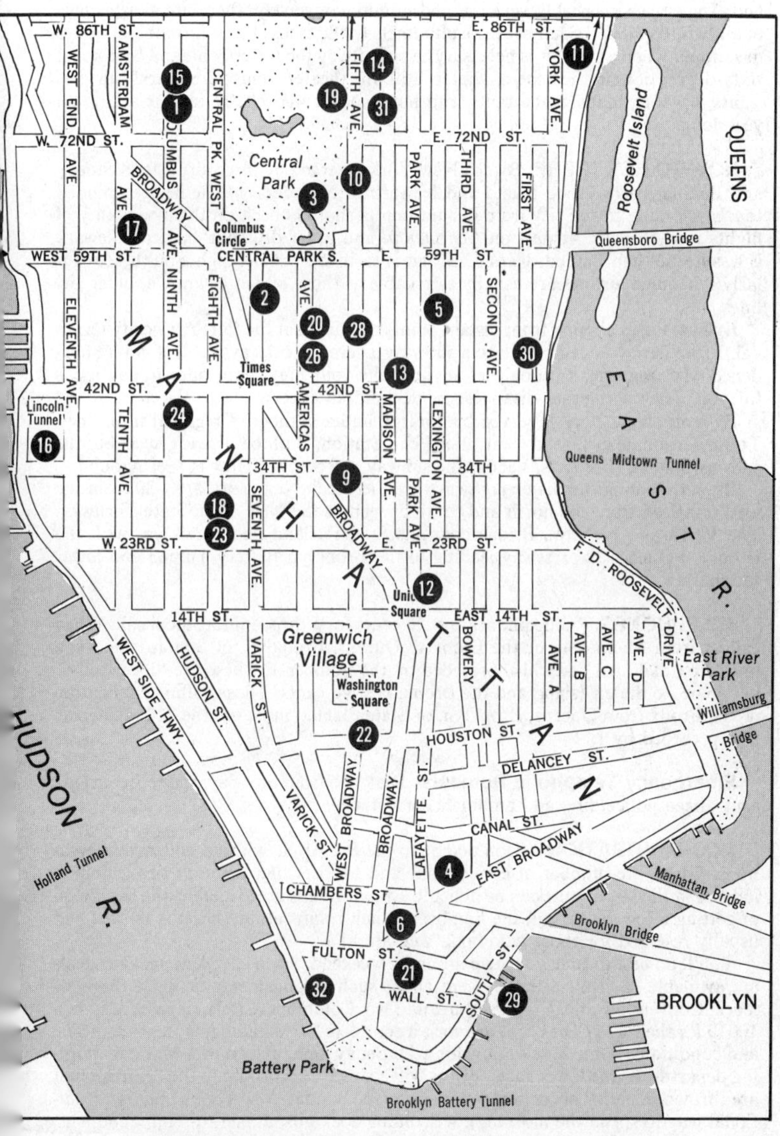

16) Jacob K. Javits Convention Center
17) Lincoln Center
18) Madison Square Garden
19) Metropolitan Museum of Art
20) Museum of Modern Art
21) N.Y. Stock Exchange
22) New York University
23) Pennsylvania Station
24) Port Authority Bus Terminal
25) Riverside Church
26) Rockefeller Center
27) St. John's Episcopal Cathedral
28) St. Patrick's Cathedral
29) South Street Seaport
30) United Nations
31) Whitney Museum
32) World Trade Center

for strolling and sightseeing, but these seasons seem to grow shorter each year. July and August are invariably very hot and humid; conversely, there are always days in midwinter when the temperature plummets to the teens. There are cool, dry days in summer when a sweater is necessary, especially by the waterfront, and occasional sixty-degree days in the dead of winter. Still, the theaters, museums, parks, historic sights, harbors, clubs, restaurants, and hotels of New York are for the asking all year long.

HOW TO GET THERE. By air. New York is served by three airports: Kennedy and LaGuardia on Long Island and Newark in New Jersey. The budget-minded tourists coming to the city from distant points should check on the availability of flights into Newark Airport on *Continental* and other discount carriers. Newark is less hectic than LaGuardia or JFK and is easily accessible; flights on these regularly scheduled airlines are usually as reliable as those on better known, older airlines.

By bus. Buses coming from distant points terminate at the Port Authority terminal. From here you can switch to a subway. There are cabs available if you're burdened with baggage, but don't let anyone take your luggage or offer to hail a cab for you. They will either disappear or demand an excessive tip.

By train. New York is served by Amtrak and a number of regional train lines. Trains terminate at Grand Central or Penn Station. Both offer ready access to the subway system. (For details about the subway, see below, "How to Get Around.")

By car. Among the major highways used to reach New York are I-80 from the west and I-95 from the north and south as well as the New York State Thruway. The Verrazano Narrows Bridge connects Staten Island and Brooklyn, with the Brooklyn-Queens Expressway leading to the Brooklyn Battery Tunnel and lower Manhattan.

TELEPHONES. Public phones cost 25 cents for a three-minute local call. When calling from Manhattan or the Bronx to Queens, Brooklyn, or Staten Island you must first dial area code 718, preceded by the number 1. These are "local calls," but some, to Staten Island and the Bronx, cost 40 cents. Those calling Manhattan or the Bronx from Queens, Brooklyn, or Staten Island must use the 212 area code, also preceded by 1.

Emergency Telephone Numbers. Dial 911 from any pay phone free to get centralized police, fire, and ambulance assistance.

ACCOMMODATIONS. Don't come to the Big Apple without advance reservations. Given the number of conventions and tourists that come to town, finding lodging at the last minute can be difficult. Even if rooms are available, the likelihood of getting a low rate is nil; the number of such rooms at any hotel is limited and usually reserved for those who book well ahead.

You'll do best to time your trip around a weekend, when excellent package deals are available. Consult a travel agent about such arrangements or write the New York Convention and Visitors Bureau, Two Columbus Circle, New York, NY 10019 for their *Tour Package Directory,* a complete list including days, prices, frills, and conditions. Some hotels allow for a Thursday night arrival or a Monday morning departure at the lower rates. Prices will also vary according to the "extras" that are thrown in: fancy brunches, newspapers (the Sunday *New York Times* is a traditional way to spend the morning), welcoming cocktails, dinner, discount coupons, and even limousine service to the theater or financial district. Obviously the more such items included in the package, the higher the price, although sometimes this can still work out cheaper than doing the same things on your own. Some more formally organized tours include theater or concert tickets, some meals, sightseeing, and other attractions. Our suggestion is to do such things on your own, mostly to get a better impression of what the city is about.

Both regular rates and package rates change rapidly depending on the season and how busy the major hotels are. Price wars erupt every so often, though a rule of thumb is that a double room with private bath in a good tourist hotel will run at least $100 a night. Singles aren't much less. As a reference point, the best rooms, with views of the skyline or Central Park, in deluxe or super deluxe hotels typically go for more than twice that amount. Many of the top hotels—the Helmsley Palace, for example—also offer packages, though the rates hardly fall in the budget category.

We've been very selective in the following listing of hotels. We've sought out the best values: places where visitors can feel comfortable, where they stand a chance of getting personalized service, where there might be some sense of atmosphere. In some instances price and location are the primary assets, as in some of the larger chain hotels, where service is almost nonexistent. But you can stay in such establishments, assured of a clean bed, private bath, telephone, and TV, and take advantage of nearby attractions and restaurants. In such cases the savings in transportation and time can more than offset the slightly higher price per night.

Bed and breakfast is a widely popular alternative, offering room and board—and breakfast—to visitors in hosted or unhosted apartments. In New York the choices are rather limited, but two services offer cheap, clean rooms or even entire apartments complete with a hospitable native to provide special insights. Urban Ventures, Box 426, New York, NY 10024 (212–594–5650), offers double rooms beginning at $70 per night and apartments beginning at $80. They also arrange thematic tours for groups of four or more. Bed and Breakfast Network of New York, 134 W. 32d St., Suite 602, New York, NY 10001 (212–645–8134), offers similar services at comparable prices. Both suggest that you reserve at least two weeks in advance.

Hotel rates are based on double occupancy. Categories, determined by price, are as follows: *Reasonable,* $110 to $150; *Very Economical,* $70 to $110;

Reasonable

Algonquin. 59 W. 44th St. (212–840–6800). A must for the literary-minded (it is still the hangout for *The New Yorker* magazine's editorial staff) and perfect for theatergoers. The rooms are slightly tattered, but there's a feeling of old-world tradition unique among New York hostelries.

Bedford. 118 E. 40th St. (212–697–4800). Midsize hotel in the heart of midtown. Rooms are large and unglamorous but are equipped with kitchenettes.

Beekman Tower. 3 Mitchell Place (First Ave. at 49th St.); (212–355–7300). Located in a quiet and uncrowded area across from the United Nations. Prices are a bit higher here—$165 for a studio, $200 for a one-bedroom—but these are apartment suits, with full kitchens. Special weekend, weekly, and monthly rates available. An excellent choice for families, with a taste of luxury thrown in at no extra charge. A word of caution: The charges for using the room telephones are astronomical, including for local calls; use pay phones if possible for outgoing calls.

Beverly. Lexington Ave. at 50th St. (212–753–2700). Quiet clublike hotel near Museum of Modern Art and Rockefeller Center.

Lexington. Lexington Ave. at 48th St. (212–755–4400). Large, standard hotel in center of the city. Convenient to most major stops on a tour itinerary; good for business travelers. Has 800 rooms.

Mayflower. 61st St. and Central Park West (212–265–0060). Excellent views of Central Park, away from the hotel clutter on the park's south end and a fraction the cost. Walking distance to Carnegie Hall and Lincoln Center.

Milford Plaza. 700 Eighth Ave. (212–869–3600, 800–528–1234). In the heart of the theater district; package deals often run half the official $90 to $115 rate. Very popular with tourist groups.

Novotel. 226 W. 52d St. (212–315–0100). A glittering 500-room emporium. Several lounges and restaurants. Convenient to Carnegie Hall and right in the heart of the Broadway theater district. Offers a variety of weekend and "getaway" packages that run considerably less than the regular $115 to $170.

Very Economical

Empire. 63d St. and Broadway (212–265–7400). Across the street from Lincoln Center and popular for tour groups. Clean, simple accommodations.

Excelsior. 45 W. 81st. St. (212–362–9200). A bit removed from most attractions, but across the street from the American Museum of Natural History. You'll never lack for restaurants or singles bars—the fashionable Columbus Ave. strip begins here.

Gorham. 136 W. 55th St. (212–245–1800). Within walking distance of Carnegie Hall and Lincoln Center. Rooms are fairly large, and all include kitchenettes.

Gramercy Park. 2 Lexington Ave. (212–475–4320, 800–221–4083). A little out of the way but situated in one of the city's most untouched neighborhoods. Rooms looking out onto the private park are especially pleasant.

Mansfield. 12 W. 44th St. (212–944–6050). Located on a street filled with the once grand and the still grand (such as the Algonquin); offers no-frills accommodations at very reasonable rates. Has 200 rooms; $44 to $55.

Murray Hill. 42 W. 35th St. (947–0200). Small, serviceable hotel convenient to shopping at Lord & Taylor and B. Altman; near transportation via Penn Station. $80.

Shoreham. 33 W. 55th St. (212–247–6700). Spartan hotel located off stylish Fifth Ave. Near St. Patrick's Cathedral, Rockefeller Center, and Carnegie Hall.

Tudor. 304 E. 42d St. (212–986–8800). Gracious hotel with more personal touches than might be expected at these rates. Central to U.N.; convenient crosstown bus stops are right outside the door.

Wales. 1295 Madison Ave. (212–876–6000). Charming, friendly hotel where everyone seems to know each other. Away from the hustle and bustle, in one of Manhattan's nicest residential neighborhoods. Museum lovers are in luck, with the Cooper-Hewitt, Guggenheim, Metropolitan, and Whitney within easy walking distance. Costs $50 to $100 a day, with suites available from $70 to $100.

Wellington. Seventh Ave. at 55th St. (212–247–3900). Large, cheery hotel close to Broadway district. Some rooms with pantries and kitchenettes.

HOW TO GET AROUND. From the airports. From Newark, New Jersey, Transit Authority buses go to the Port Authority, Eighth Ave. and 42d St., in Manhattan, and Olympic Bus Lines goes to downtown's World Trade Center and to the east side of Manhattan.

Carey buses from LaGuardia and JFK bring passengers to the Grand Central Station vicinity, 42d St. and Lexington Ave. There is also a combination bus and subway ride called Train to the Plane to and from JFK. Although it can be somewhat faster than the bus, it does require switching vehicles, and the trains are not coordinated with the buses, so there may be a wait. The advantage is that the train makes a handful of convenient stops in Manhattan along Sixth Ave.

Fares for all of the above range from $4 to $6, and the rides are almost just as fast as a cab. Cabs between Newark or JFK and Manhattan will run in excess of $25, $15 to $20 between LaGuardia and midtown Manhattan. If you use a cab, be sure the meter is running—never accept "special deals." The dispatcher at JFK and LaGuardia can advise you about how much the fare will be to your destination; remember, though, that waiting time in heavy traffic adds up on the taxi meter, and getting stuck in one of New York's monumental tie-ups can be costly.

By bus. Subway tokens are also good on buses. Buses are a good bet for very short distances during the day, after the business day is over, or on weekends. During high traffic times, they move at a snail's pace, though this is improving somewhat on avenues with special bus lanes. Bus routes, however, are even more confusing than the interlocking subway lines. Only one free transfer is given per passenger, and the buses for which they are good (going east-west if the trip started on a north-south route, or vice versa) are listed on the transfer ticket. Transfers must be requested when paying the fare (on entering the bus). Those not using tokens must have exact change.

By subway. For all the fear and loathing the New York subway system inspires, it is still the fastest, most economical way to get around the city. Used judiciously—observing designated areas where late-night passengers are urged to congregate and avoiding loiterers—the subways are also reasonably safe. Keep wallets in inside pockets and purses securely closed, and don't expose jewelry such as gold chains. At night, ride in a center car, where the conductor is located. For directions on what train (or bus) to take to get to your destination, call 330–1234. This information hotline is available 24 hours a day, though if you're calling from a pay phone be prepared with plenty of change since you'll probably have to wait a while for an operator to answer your question. Subway maps are generally available at token booths, or at the Convention and Visitors' Bureau, 59th St. and Columbus Circle. A handy folding, laminated subway and street-finder map is on sale at many card shops and bookstores; it is easier to cope with than the full subway map.

Transfers from one train to the other are usually free within the subway system, with no formal "transfer" needed, though the lines intersect only at given points.

Local and express trains on the same line run parallel. The fare is $1, and passengers must purchase tokens that are inserted at turnstiles. The lines to buy tokens can be long during rush hours.

By taxi. Cab fares are $1.15 for the first eighth of a mile and 15 cents for each additional eighth. Cabs can be hailed at any curb, though it is illegal for them to stop in the middle of the street. At press time there is talk of doubling the number of yellow cabs on the streets, but at the moment it is next to impossible to get a cab during rush hour (when most serve charge-account customers who phone in their requests and pay an average $4 service charge on top of the meter price) or when the weather is bad. At theaters and airports many people solicit passengers for private limousines or car services; if you are inclined to take advantage of their services, be sure to negotiate a price before you get in the car. Generally these vehicles have no meters, and the drivers try to get as much as they can.

By foot. The best bet, of course, is seeing New York on foot. It is the most leisurely for sightseeing, the least expensive, and in some instances, the fastest. By concentrating on distinct neighborhoods or areas and using the subway to travel between the more distant points on your itinerary, you won't need to use public transportation much at all.

On Manhattan streets. Fifth Avenue is the dividing line between east and west until Fourth Street, where Broadway becomes the demarcation line. Avenues, which head north and south, are numbered First through Twelfth but with a few names thrown in between to keep you on your toes. Starting at the East River at, for purposes of illustration, 42d Street and heading west: First, Second, Third, Lexington (aka Fourth), Park, Madison, Fifth, Avenue of the Americas (aka Sixth), Broadway, Seventh (they intersect at Times Square; to the north, Seventh would come first, then Broadway), Eighth, Ninth, Tenth, Eleventh, Twelfth. Add East End and York avenues on the Upper East Side and West End, Columbus, Amsterdam, and Riverside Drive on the Upper West Side.

Street numbers from 8th Street in Greenwich Village north (north is uptown, with the numbers conveniently ascending; south is downtown) are numbered consecutively. In the Village, Soho, and farther south (especially the financial district), it is best to follow a map. Numbered streets run east and west, with major crosstown routes at 14th, 23d, 34th, 42d, 48th (eastward) and 49th (westward), 57th, 66th, 72d, 79th, and 86th streets.

HINTS TO THE MOTORIST. There are signs along certain main avenues in Manhattan that say "Don't Even Think of It." What they are referring to is parking. Whatever form of transportation you prefer, don't expect to drive around Manhattan for sightseeing. With very few exceptions you simply can't park on the street in midtown, and the cost of parking is prohibitive: as much as $20 for two hours on the Upper East Side or in the garment district. Traffic moves almost not at all during the day, and tow trucks are at the ready if you leave your car in the wrong place even for a few minutes. Retrieving the vehicle will cost in excess of $100, plus a lot of wasted time and aggravation. If you are driving into town, park the car in a lot on the far West Side, say on Tenth Ave. in the Forties, where the daily rate will be $4 to $6.

Be sure to lock all doors and don't leave anything tempting in the car or trunk. Hotels that have parking will charge from $12 up for overnight storage. Pay the extra amount for the hotel or another indoor garage if your vehicle has a radio or tape player. These disappear especially rapidly when cars are parked on the street or in open lots, which is why you'll see some cars around town with signs in the windows proclaiming "No radio!"

TOURIST INFORMATION. Write the *New York State Division of Tourism,* One Commerce Plaza, Albany, NY 12245 (800–225–5697, 212–309–0560), for copies of the latest brochures on the city or state. The *New York Convention and Visitors' Bureau,* on the ground floor of the former Huntington Hartford Museum at Columbus Circle, 59th St. and Eighth Ave. (397–8222), is open for questions about New York City only: Mon.–Fri., 9 A.M.–6 P.M.; weekends and holidays, 10 A.M.–6 P.M. Best listings for current entertainment, museum shows, sports schedules, and the like are the weekly magazines *New York* and *The New Yorker,* the weekly newspaper *Village Voice,* the Sunday Arts and Leisure sections of the *New York Times,* and the Friday editions of the *Times, Post,* and *Daily News.*

SENIOR-CITIZEN AND STUDENT DISCOUNTS. Both senior citizens and students should carry proof of status. Seniors travel on the buses and subways for half price during nonrush hours, can attend movies (including many first-run houses) for $2 or so in the afternoons, and along with students frequently get discounts on museum admissions. Seniors might also wish to have their travel agents check on possible discounts at hotels, though this is rare in New York.

HINTS TO DISABLED TRAVELERS. Some buses have hydraulic lifts for the wheelchair-bound, and crosswalks generally have ramps. The subways are difficult to navigate for those in wheelchairs, as there are few stations with elevators. Many museums offer sign-language interpretation of tours, and theaters are often outfitted with infrared systems to aid the hearing-impaired. Louise Weiss, author of *Access to the World* (Facts on File, $14.95), suggests that theatergoers be sure to consider off-Broadway and off-off-Broadway theaters where the hearing or visually impaired maybe able to sit closer to the stage than at a Broadway house. Check with individual theaters for wheelchair accessibility.

Tours specially designed for the disabled generally parallel those for the disabled traveler but at a more leisurely pace. For a complete list of tour operators who arrange such travel, write to the *Society for the Advancement of Travel for the Handicapped,* 26 Court St., Brooklyn, NY 11242 (718–858–5483).

FREE EVENTS. There are designated days or hours when selected museums that ordinarily charge admission are free; some smaller museums and historic sites (Grant's Tomb) are always free. For example, Tues. evenings are free at the Cooper-Hewitt and Guggenheim museums, and Wed. evenings are free at the New Museum of Contemporary Art. The Museum of Modern Art is pay what you wish on Thurs. evening. The free Washington Square Outdoor Art Exhibit is held each spring and fall for several weeks either side of Memorial Day and Labor Day, with hundreds of artists setting up their work (for sale) along Greenwich Village streets surrounding Washington Square Park.

In the summer there are street fairs galore at which you are free to stroll, though the aromas wafting about from vendors hawking bean sprout pancakes, sausage and pepper heroes, barbecue chicken wings, shish kebob, and the like will no doubt entice you into spending something. Check the weekend newspapers beginning in mid-May for street fair specifics; the kickoff is the Ninth Avenue Festival, which is probably also the most interesting foodwise. Others of particular note are the 52d Street fair, which generally has the best free entertainment (52nd Street having once been home to many jazz clubs) and the May-June Feast of Saint Anthony and the September San Gennaro Festival in Little Italy.

There are parades almost all year long marking various national, ethnic, and patriotic figures and events. The biggest is Macy's annual Thanksgiving Day Parade, which marches from West 77th St. and Central Park West down to the giant department store at 34th St. and Broadway. This is the one with helium-filled balloons of favorite cartoon characters and star-studded floats.

The performing arts go outdoors—and free—in the summer, with the New York Philharmonic performing in city parks June and July, followed by the Metropolitan Opera in August. Bring a blanket, some pillows, and a picnic and get ready to share the evening with 100,000 or so other fans who start gathering in front of the stage by noon for an 8 or 8:30 P.M. performance!

There's free Shakespeare at the Delacorte Theater in Central Park. Tickets, distributed on the day of performance only, are necessary as seating is limited. The line begins to form in midafternoon; tickets are given out at 6 P.M. It is best to bring a picnic and dine alfresco right outside the theater.

In addition, there is a weeks-long outdoor festival in the plaza at Lincoln Center, usually in August, and there are regular free concerts and performances at the Goldman Band Shell in Central Park and the Ninth Street Bandshell in Brooklyn's Prospect Park. The daily papers and local weekly newspapers and magazines list other free performing arts activities all year-round.

Jazzmobile takes live jazz to various neighborhoods, and there are free concerts invariably associated with the late June-early July Kool Jazz Festival and the Aug.-Sept. Dewar's Greenwich Village Jazz Festival. July 4 is always ablaze with a Macy's fireworks display (others have been sponsoring fireworks as well in recent years) viewable from many vantage points. Check the daily papers for this and other special events.

A host of other museums are free at all times. These include the Hispanic Society of America, Broadway at 155th St. (212–690–0743); Library and Museum of the Performing Arts, 111 Amsterdam Ave. (212–870–1630); Fashion Institute of Technology, 27th St. and Seventh Ave. (212–760–7760); Federal Hall National Memorial, 26 Wall St. (212–264–8711); and Urban Center, 457 Madison Ave. (212–935–3960).

TOURS AND SPECIAL-INTEREST SIGHTSEEING. A general tour is always a good idea in an unfamiliar city. It can help orient you and give you a quick feel for what you want to pursue. Probably the best of the lot, available spring through fall, is not through the city streets but on the water: the *Circle Line* around Manhattan Island. Boats leave frequently throughout the day from the Hudson River pier at the foot of West 42d St. The narrated ride takes about two and a half hours: adults, $13; children, $6. As for bus tours, *Gray Line* (212–397–2600), *ShortLine* (212–354–5122), and *Manhattan Sightseeing* (212–869–5005) offer various tours. We recommend a basic two-hour morning tour; anything you want to cover in detail will require a visit on your own anyway.

Other tours of special note:

United Nations. First Ave. at 45th St. (212–964–7713). Hour-long tours leave the main lobby every half-hour between 9:15 A.M. and 4:45 P.M. daily. Tours are normally in English, but people speaking other languages can be accommodated. Adults, $4.50; students, $2.50; children, $2.00.

NBC Studios. 30 Rockefeller Plaza (49th and 50th streets between Fifth and Sixth avenues) (212–664–7174). Tours depart about every 15 min., 9:30 A.M.–4:30 P.M. Mon.–Sat. Stops include the NBC radio and television studios. Admission $6; no children under 6.

Radio City Music Hall. Sixth Ave. at 50th St. (212–246–4600). Schedule varies; the landmark art deco hall is very much worth seeing. Admission $5.

Lincoln Center. Broadway at 64th St. (212–877–1800). Tours meet in Avery Fisher Hall between 10 A.M. and 5 P.M. daily. Visitors explore Avery Fisher, the Metropolitan Opera House, and the New York State Theater. Adults, $6.25; students and senior citizens, $5.25; children, $3.50.

Backstage on Broadway. 228 West 47th St. (212–575–8065). Tours can be arranged to order, but do call ahead for specifics.

PARKS AND GARDENS. First-time visitors to New York are invariably amazed that there's so much green in the city. Most figure that any form of plant life must have been uprooted in the course of constructing the skyscrapers that are the city's trademark. Not necessarily so. Brownstone-inhabited neighborhoods such as Greenwich Village, Chelsea, Gramercy Park, and the Upper West Side have beautiful tree-lined blocks, as do many areas in the other boroughs. And the city's parks offer hundreds of acres of rolling green meadows.

Central Park is the most famous, and despite all the tales of crime in the park, it is a fine place to visit during the day or when there is a special event taking place during summer evenings. Bicycles and rowboats can be rented at the 72d Street boathouse; the park roads are closed to traffic much of the time to enable joggers, walkers, and bicyclers to enjoy this oasis undisturbed by motor vehicles.

On the west side north of 72d St., located between the Hudson River and Riverside Dr., is **Riverside Park,** with a marina at 79th St. This is a less populated park than Central, frequented by those living along Riverside Drive and West End Ave.

Prospect Park and the nearby **Brooklyn Botanic Gardens** (718–622–4433) in Brooklyn are as surprising to New Yorkers as to visitors. Prospect Park, with its Quaker cemetery, lake, historic mansions, bandshell, and rolling hills provides a wonderful respite from the rigors of daily urban life. The Brooklyn Botanic Garden features a Japanese garden (25 cents) complete with a cherry blossom festival each May, a Shakespeare Garden, and an aromatic herb garden.

The refurbished **New York Botanical Garden** (212–220–8700) in the Bronx has a vast set of greenhouses, beautiful grounds, explanatory exhibits, and regular special events such as the springtime Holland tulip celebration.

Gateway National Recreation Area (718–338–3338), taking in the beach at Jacob Riis Park in Queens as well as waterfront areas in Brooklyn, Staten Island, and

New Jersey, is taking an increasingly active role in the city's cultural life. Floyd Bennett Field is the site of numerous ethnic festivals during the summer, and the Gateway Wildlife Sanctuary in Howard Beach is particularly suited for bird watching.

Back in Manhattan, there are so-called vest-pocket parks all over; out of towners may laugh at the notion of these little patches, usually with potted trees, sculpted waterfalls, and the like as being parks, but they offer New Yorkers a pleasant place to relax at lunchtime.

BEACHES. The most famous is no doubt **Coney Island** (take the B, D, F, M, N, or QB trains on the IND subway), a mere shadow of its former glory and not an area for wandering in the evenings. Daytime by the water is fine. Astroland Amusement Park is right along the shore.

The other major beach within city limits is in the **Rockaways,** a peninsula that juts out into the Atlantic. **Jacob Riis Park** is the most popular, with plenty of sports fields and a playground. Take the number 2 or 3 train on the IRT subway to Flatbush Avenue; a Green Line bus ($1) from here will take you directly to the beach.

Just beyond the city is **Jones Beach,** probably the most crowded of all, so get there early. Take the Long Island Railroad-bus combination for $7 round trip, $4.50 one way.

ZOOS. Nothing in these parts rivals the *Bronx Zoo,* Fordham Rd. and Southern Blvd. (212–220–5100), with its natural habitat environments, snazzy Skyfari cablecar, and Bengali Express monorail. Open 10 A.M.–4:30 P.M. (4:00 P.M. Nov.–Jan.). Admission is free Tues., Weds., and Thurs. Parking is $4. Admission: $1.75 adults; 75 cents children; senior citizens free. The children's zoo and rides are extra.

For seafaring creatures, the *New York Aquarium,* Surf Ave. at West 8th St., near Brooklyn's Coney Island (718–268–3400), is the place to go. 10 A.M.–4:45 P.M. daily; $3.75 for adults, $1.50 for children 2–12.

PARTICIPANT SPORTS. Joggers need not fear having to give up their favorite exercise when they venture into Manhattan. In fact, jogging is probably the top participant sport in the city. Although you're welcome to do your stuff in the streets of midtown, you'd be much better off taking to the city's many parks. Areas most frequented include the roads in and around *Central, Riverside,* and *Washington Square parks.*

The parks are also great for **biking,** horseback riding, and even rowing. Bikes can be rented for about $3 per hour; check the Yellow Pages for centrally located outlets. For a little bit of country in the city, **horseback riding** is an unexpected pleasure. Manhattan offers the Claremont Stable, 175 W. 89th St. (212–724–5100), and some stables are also offered in the boroughs. Hourly rates are about $27. **Rowboating** is a real summertime release, and you'll find all you need at the Central Park Lake, just north of 72d St. The Loeb boathouse rents rowboats at $5 per hour. Here, as in all cases where rental is involved, a deposit is required.

Bowling alleys and ice-skating rinks can be found in the yellow pages. Racquetball and tennis are increasingly fashionable energy outlets, but most chain courts such as those at the NY Health & Racquet Club are only open to members. The beautiful Wall St. Racquet Club, Wall St. and East River (212–952–0760); the Village Tennis Courts, 110 University Pl. (212–989–2300); and the Tennis Club, 15 Vanderbilt Ave, in Grand Central Station (212–687–3841), however, all offer hourly court time to the general public. Those wishing to use outdoor tennis courts must obtain a visitor's permit. A pass is $4 and entitles the player to one hour of time on any city-run court. They can be picked up at the Central Park Courts, 93d St. in the park.

SPECTACTOR SPORTS. New York's reign as *the* sports town of America is fast coming to an end as teams leave the city proper for nearby towns. Still, New York does host one of the major **tennis** events, the *U.S. Open,* in September at the USTA Tennis Center (718–592–8000) in Queens. The final **horse race** of the prestigious *Triple Crown* is held at Belmont Raceway (718– 641–4700) in June. Other than that, local teams include **baseball's** *Mets* at Shea Stadium (718–507–8499) and *Yankees* at Yankee Stadium (212–293–6000) and **basketball's** *Knicks* and **hockey's**

Rangers at Madison Square Garden (212- 563-8300). The *Devils* play ice hockey and the *Giants* and *Jets* football at the Meadowlands (201-935-3900) in East Rutherford, New Jersey. Long Island's hockey *Islanders* are at the Nassau Coliseum (516-587-9222).

CHILDREN'S ACTIVITIES. The sights, museums, Bronx Zoo, and street fairs are all perfectly suitable for children. Of more specific interest are the various theatrical efforts that often spring up, particularly around the school holiday seasons (Thanksgiving/Christmas, Easter/Passover, and the summer). Check local papers and *New York* magazine, which lists children's events separately. Also of interest is, of course, the Ringling Bros.-Barnum & Bailey Circus, which romps into town in the late spring. Call Madison Square Garden (212-563-8300) for details.

HISTORIC SITES AND HOUSES. The following is a very selected list of some of New York's sites and buildings of historic, cultural, or architectural interest, arranged by neighborhood, starting all the way downtown with the Statue of Liberty and the financial district.

Lower Manhattan. This area encompasses the earliest settlements of the city and includes roughly everything south of Canal Street. The section is, however, much larger than ever before. Many of the newer skyscrapers crowding the neighborhood sit on landfill, accounting for the current placement of, say, Water Street, which is quite inland. Across the East River lies the borough of Brooklyn, connected to Manhattan by the Brooklyn, Manhattan, and Williamsburg bridges.

The southern tip of Manhattan is known as the financial district because it houses the American Stock Exchange and the New York Stock Exchange as well as numerous trading, insurance, and banking firms. Few of these companies are actually located on Wall Street, which is in fact only a few narrow blocks along which once ran the northernmost wall of the city. This part of Manhattan is also the center of much of the city's official business, including City Hall and the courts.

Fraunces Tavern. 54 Pearl St. (212-269-0144). The restaurant where George Washington bade farewell to his troops before retiring as general. The current building is a rough estimate of the original. Interesting for its upstairs museum.

New York Stock Exchange. 20 Broad St. (212-656-5168). Look down as hundreds of brokers bandy shouts and papers and run around at incredible speed. The third-floor gallery is open 9:20 A.M.-4 P.M. Free.

South Street Seaport. Fulton St. The newly renovated seaport area centers on the three-story Fulton Market Building, which is replete with restaurants (sit-down and fast food), take-out shops, and food boutiques, and Pier Pavilion on Pier 17. Walking around the seaport is a treat in itself, but visitors wanting a sense of the area's history should also stop by the Seaport Museum, 207 Front St. (212-669-9416); Trans-Lux Seaport Theatre, Beekman and Front Streets (212-644-1118); and the five historic ships docked in the harbor at Pier 16.

Statue of Liberty. This gift from the French marked its hundredth anniversary in New York Harbor in 1986—and was spruced up anew for the occasion. The American Museum of Immigration is housed in the statue's base. Admission to this national monument is free, but the round-trip ferry ride from lower Manhattan is $3 for adults and $1.50 for children. Call 363-3200 for information.

Trinity Church. Broadway and Wall streets (212-602-0800). The Gothic Revival structure, designed by Richard Upjohn, that currently occupies the site is the third Trinity Church. The small cemetery is the final resting place of Alexander Hamilton and Robert Fulton.

World Trade Center. Cortlandt and Church streets. Best known for its gigantic twin towers, the complex in fact consists of seven buildings. The 107th floor of building 2 is an enclosed observation deck (212-466-7397) with the highest such vantage point in the world, though the building is second to Chicago's Sears Roebuck Tower in height. Adults, $2.95; children, $1.50.

Little Italy and Chinatown. These areas border each other and play host to two of the city's major ethnic groups. Little Italy is quieter, and you won't find as much of a cultural flavor. Chinatown is always streaming with people and features touches such as pagodalike phone booths. The major attraction of each is its food, but beware: Dessert in Little Italy can easily cost more than dinner in Chinatown.

SoHo. Roughly, the blocks between Canal and Houston streets (hence, SoHo, or *So*uth of *Ho*uston; but pronounced So Ho). A once-bleak neighborhood of warehouses, it has become the premier center for new art and to some extent high (avant-garde) fashion. Most of the cast iron structures are of no historical significance, but the streets above Canal have been designated a landmark district. West Broadway and the side streets are better suited for walking and browsing, with lots of galleries and shops ready for the viewing. Sunday is an especially popular day for gallery hopping.

Greenwich Village. Whatever preconceived notions you have of the Village, as it is familiarly known, you will find verification in your travels. Two of the city's bigger universities are here: New York University and Cooper Union, in the East Village. The Village is constantly subdividing. The East Village is a mecca for punk-rock clubs and boutiques; it's easternmost part (called "alphabet city," because of avenues A, B, C, and D) is the city's *newest* art spot. The West Village is much more placid and is where the *old* Bohemians congregated. Highlighted by twisting, tree-lined streets with nineteenth-century brownstones, the West Village is home to much of the city's gay population. Literary giants such as Edgar Allan Poe, Thomas Wolfe, O. Henry, and Mark Twain have all made the West Village their home.

The twain meet, so to speak, at **Washington Square Park,** whose arch marks the beginning of Fifth Avenue, Manhattan's dividing line between east and west. The park has been used as a burial place for plague victims and for unfortunates who were forced to pay a visit to the gallows. The Greek Revival row houses that stand guard over the park's north side are landmarks. There is more literary history here, with the former dwellings of Edith Wharton, Henry James, William Dean Howells, and John Dos Passos all a part of the "row."

On the Avenue of the Americas, one of the area's main thoroughfares, is the former **Jefferson Market Courthouse,** 475 Ave. of Americas. Built in 1877 and designed in part by Calvert Vaux, the coarchitect of Central Park, the building is an odd assemblage of architectural styles, with the result being a mock-castle. Now used as one of the Village branches of the New York Public Library.

Midtown. Midtown is the city's other major heart of business, with publishing, advertising, and multinational corporations based here. The area is designated as 14th to 59th streets, with most interests centered between Second and Eighth avenues. Within those boundaries rest many pockets and neighborhoods: the Flatiron district, centered on the landmark triangular 1902 building of the same name on the corner of Broadway and 23 St.; the flower district, Ave. of the Americas from 22d to 27th streets; the fur and garment districts, in the West 20s and 30s; the warehouse-art district Chelsea in the West 20s; Gramercy Park, one of the city's most untouched areas, in the East 20s; the Kips Bay and Murray Hill residential neighborhoods in the East 30s; Hell's Kitchen and Herald Square in the West 30s; the Grand Central area in the East 40s, featuring the once stately Grand Central Station and the always lovely Chrysler Building; Rockefeller Center in the West 50s; and the Tudor City-Turtle Bay area in the East 50s.

Some of these are more interesting than others, and you'll probably want to breeze through those areas replete with the spoils of industry, whether they be the crowds of suited folks milling around Grand Central or the legions of blue-collar workers pulling dress racks down Seventh Avenue in the 30s. Other areas, such as Gramercy Park, Tudor City, and some of the "parks" shoehorned between office buildings, can give the welcome gift of quiet and breathing room. Among the specifics worth visiting:

Empire State Building. 350 Fifth Ave. (212–736–3100). This 1931 art deco skyscraper was once the tallest building in the world and a self-proclaimed Eighth Wonder of the World (it's onetime resident King Kong notwithstanding). The lobby is just as beautiful as the celebrated view from the 86th and 102nd floors. The observation deck is open 9:30 A.M. to midnight. Adults, $3.25; senior citizens and children, $1.75.

Grand Central Terminal. 42d St. and Park Ave. Now rather depressing and down on its heels, but the vaulted ceiling is a beautiful tribute to the skies; once thousands of lights decorated it. Free tours meet under the big Kodak ad Weds. at 12:30 P.M. The Oyster Bar is also a major attraction.

Jacob K. Javits Convention Center. 34th–39th sts. between 11th and 12th aves. Completed in 1986, this huge glass-and-steel convention complex has become a West Side landmark. Its sprawling 630,000 square feet of exhibit space attract millions of visitors to the city year-round.

Madison Square Garden. 33rd St. and Seventh Ave. (212–563–8300). Third location for this complex; now used for sports and rock concerts. Connects to Penn Station.

New York Central Public Library. 42d St. and Fifth Ave. (212–930–0501). Gorgeous Beaux Arts structure placed behind the newly refurbished Bryant Park, the site of a former city reservoir. The library is noted for free exhibitions. Free tours meet Mon.–Sat. at 11 A.M. and 2 P.M. in the main library.

United Nations. 1st Ave. and 45th St. (212–964–7713). The world's diplomatic focal point; consists of the skyscraper Secretariat Building and the low domed General Assembly. The outside gardens are graciously inviting, and inside the Assembly building works of art from all nations are displayed. Guided tours: adults, $4.50; children and students, $2. Free tickets to sessions are distributed for those who choose to go it alone.

Fifth Avenue. The ten or so blocks of Fifth Avenue leading up to Central Park are home to some of the world's most exclusive shops. Inside the Trump Tower on 56th St. you'll find dozens of deluxe palaces where only the richest dare do more than window shop. On Fifth itself lie Saks, Gucci, Tiffany's, Mark Cross, F.A.O. Schwarz, and Cartier. None are generally for the budget-minded, though there are occasional sales.

Fifth Avenue also plays host to two of New York's greatest sights, Saint Patrick's Cathedral and Rockefeller Center. Even on Fifth Ave., separate districts are delineated, mainly in the one-block cross streets of 47th St. (diamond retailers) and 57th St. (art galleries).

New York Experience. McGraw Hill Building, 48th St. and Ave. of Americas (212–869–0345). New York's longest-running movie, now entering its twelfth year, a multimedia extravaganza detailing the past and present of the Big Apple. A must for all visitors. Adults, $5; children, $3.

Rockefeller Center. Fifth Ave. at 48th St. The center links 47th through 50th streets and Fifth and Sixth avenues through underground passages. The Art Deco RCA Building, enhanced at night by floodlighting, is capped by the Rainbow Room restaurant. Adults, $3.25; children, $2.75. An hourlong Radio City (212–246–4600) tour is another option at $5. TV fans might be interested in a tour of NBC studios (212–664–4000) at $6.

Saint Patrick's Cathedral. Fifth Ave. and 50th St. This is a soaring French Gothic structure designed by James Renwick, who is also responsible for Grace Church in Greenwich Village. Church fanciers should also pay a visit to the more austere but in many ways lovelier Saint Thomas Church down the avenue at 53d St.

Times Square. The theatrical and film center of the city, Times Square is literally the patch of ground at 42d St. and Seventh Ave. where Broadway crosses. But New Yorkers generally mean the streets between 42d and 49th from Broadway to Eighth Ave. It is within these blocks that most "Broadway" theaters are located, as well as dozens of movie houses (many of thcm X-rated). Be sure to get a nighttime view with all the lights aglow.

Uptown. Away from the noise and confusion of midtown, both the Upper East Side and the Upper West Side, divided by Central Park, are fine places for strolling. Each side retains distinctive characteristics, and those who can afford to live on either end choose to do so for their opposing personalities. The stereotype has it that East Siders are traditional and old rich. That is borne out by the profusion of fashion showrooms, antique stores, and art galleries lining Madison Ave. Westsiders are supposed to be funky but chic, riche but nouveau. The proof is in the boutiques, novelty stores, and nouvelle cuisine restaurants on Columbus Ave. Museum lovers should be on both ends of the park: The American Museum of Natural History straddles the West Side; the East Side is famous for its Museum Mile, including the Metropolitan Museum of Art, the Guggenheim, and nearly a dozen others.

The Abigail Adams Smith Museum. 421 E. 61st St. (212–838–6878). One of Manhattan's last 18th-century buildings. Originally the carriage house for the home the then Vice-President John Adams had built for his daughter Abigail. A gem kept in perfect condition by the Colonial Dames of America. Guide on duty. Mon.–Fri., 10 A.M.–4 P.M. Adults, $2; senior citizens, $1.

The Dyckman House. 204th St. and Broadway (212–304–9422). Built in 1783, this was the farm residence of the wealthy Dyckman family, which once owned most of northern Manhattan. The only remaining Dutch farmhouse in New York City. *To get there:* IND (Eighth Ave.) subway (A) to 207th St. Tues.–Sun., 11 A.M.–4 P.M. Free.

General Grant National Memorial. Riverside Dr. and 122d St. (212–666–1640). The Civil War general and two-term president is buried in the crypt, with photo and other exhibits also housed in the tomb. Open daily, 9 A.M.–5 P.M.; closed Mon.–Tues.

Morris-Jumel Mansion. W. 161st St. and Edgecombe Ave. (212–923–8008). This Georgian colonial hilltop house was built in 1765. A year later, George Washington slept here for a night; his camp bed may still be seen. Here too Aaron Burr married the wealthy Mme. Jumel, then in her sixties, and soon divorced her. *To get there:* Fifth Ave. bus 2 or 3 to 162d St.; or IND Eighth Ave. subway to 163rd St. (AA local). Tues.–Sun., 10 A.M.–4 P.M. Adults, $2; students and senior citizens, $1.

MUSEUMS AND GALLERIES. New York has perhaps the largest concentration of museums anywhere in the world. Although most are art museums, others specialize in fashion, theater, performing arts, dolls, fire engines, coins, architecture, and ethnic cultures. What follows is a baker's dozen of the most popular museums. Make particular note of those offering free or pay-as-you-wish evening admissions (usually on Tuesday evening). Also, most make available substantially discounted student rates; inquire before paying.

American Craft Museum. 40 W. 53rd St. (212–956–3535). Changing exhibitions center on contemporary works of glass, tapestry, metal, and others. Wed.–Sun., 10 A.M.–5 P.M., Tues., 10 A.M.–8 P.M. Adults, $3.50; children, $1.50.

American Museum of Natural History. Central Park West at 79th St. (212–769–5100). The granddaddy of New York museums, the one every school kid loves to visit. As its name implies, the museum is filled with artifacts of the earth's past and present. You'll find representations of every animal species, culture, and life form here. Open daily 10 A.M.–5:45 P.M., to 9 P.M. on Weds., Fri., and Sat. Suggested contribution: adults, $3; children, $1.50. Free Fri. and Sat. evenings. An accompanying attraction is the Hayden Planetarium (212–769–5920), which extends the study to the skies. Separate admission is $3.75 for adults, $2 for children. Fri. and Sat. evenings feature the spectacular rock music-based Laser Concert (212–769–5921) at $6 per seat.

Brooklyn Museum. Eastern Parkway and Washington Ave., Brooklyn (718–638–5000). Its dark rooms and hallways can be rather intimidating and even downright spooky. Its cellarlike atmosphere is suitably mysterious for the extensive collections of Egyptian and primitive arts that make it the seventh largest musuem in the U.S. Also fine collection of American painting. Daily 10 A.M.–5 P.M.; closed Tues. Adults, $3; children $1.50.

The Cloisters. Fort Tryon Park (212–923–3700). A branch of the Metropolitan Museum of Art, this medieval art complex is perched on a hill overlooking the George Washington Bridge and the Hudson River. Constructed from the ruins of five French cloisters, some of the highlights include: 12th- and 13th-century Spanish frescoes; the extraordinary Unicorn tapestries; a complete 12th-century architectural ensemble from a ruined abbey of Gascony; the Bury Saint Edmunds Cross; stained-glass lancets from the Carmelite Church of Boppardam-Rhein; and an arcade from a Benedictine priory of Froville in eastern France. It's well worth the trip uptown to this very peaceful retreat. Can be reached on the M4 bus, which goes up Madison Ave. in midtown. Open Tues.–Sun., 9:30 A.M.–4:45 P.M. Suggested contribution: adults, $5; senior citizens and students, $2; children under 12, free.

Cooper–Hewitt Museum. 2 E. 91st St. (212–860–6868). Again, the setting is almost as important as the work. The building is the former mansion of millionaire Andrew Carnegie, and both its small rooms and its landscaped garden are lovely. The museum houses the decorative arts collection of the Smithsonian Institution. Tues., noon–9 P.M.; Wed.–Sun., noon–5 P.M. Closed Mon. and holidays. Admission, $3. Free Tues. evenings.

Solomon R. Guggenheim Museum. 1071 Fifth Ave. at 88th St. (212–360–3513). The spiraling architecture of Frank Lloyd Wright's handiwork raised eyebrows in 1959 and still does today. Emphasis on twentieth-century art, including Kandinsky, Ernst, and de Kooning. Tues., 11 A.M.–7:45 P.M.; Wed.–Sun. to 4:45 P.M. Closed Mon. Adults, $4; children, $2. Free Tues. evening.

International Center for Photography. 1130 Fifth Ave. (212–860–1777). Devoted exclusively to photography, with changing exhibits unfortunately geared exclusively to the big-time best (Cartier-Bresson, et. al.). Tues., noon–8 P.M.; Wed.–Fri. to 5 P.M.; Sat.–Sun., 11 A.M.–6 P.M. Admission, $2.50; students, $1; free Tues. evening.

Intrepid **Sea-Air-Space Museum.** Pier 86, Hudson River at 46th St. (212–245–0072). A U.S. Naval aircraft transformed into a museum detailing U.S. military history and technology. Wed.–Sun., 10 A.M.–5 P.M. Adults, $4.75; children, $2.50.

Metropolitan Museum of Art. Fifth Ave. at 82d St. (212–535–7710). The emphasis is on pre-twentieth-century painting, though a considerable cache of modern fare is also to be found. The recently added American Wing features an intact reconstruction of the living room from Frank Lloyd Wright's "Little House." Other highlights throughout the museum include the fabulous collection of antique musical instruments, the ever-changing costume gallery downstairs, and the assemblage of Tiffany and other glassworks behind the Egyptian Galleries. Tues. 9:30 A.M.–8:45 P.M., Wed.–Sun. to 5:15 P.M.; closed Mon. Suggested contribution $5, children $2.25.

Museum of Broadcasting. 1 E. 53 St. (212–752–7684). More like a library than anything else. Features an enormous collection of tapes and videos covering the history of radio and television. Be forewarned that what you're most interested in is often the same thing everybody else wants to see (for example, a bored staffer will tell you the exact position of the Beatles performances on an old Ed Sullivan tape), so you may have a long wait ahead of you. Tues., noon–8 P.M.; Weds.–Sat. to 5 P.M. Adults, $4; children, $2.

Museum of Holography. 11 Mercer St. (212–925–0526). Until recently the only, and still the best, museum in the world entirely devoted to holography, the art of creating three-dimensional light images through the use of lasers. Tues.–Sun., noon–6 P.M.; Adults, $3; children, $1.75.

Museum of Modern Art. 11 W. 53d St. (212–708–9400). Recently expanded, the museum now includes new architecture and photography galleries. MOMA's strength still lies in its collection of modern art, stemming from a few representations of late Impressionist works (particularly the huge panels of Monet's *Water Lilies*) to the present. Open daily 11 A.M.–6 P.M., to 9 P.M. on Thurs. Closed Wed. Adults, $5; children free. Pay what you wish Thurs. evening.

Museum of the City of NY. Fifth Ave. at 103d St. (212–534–1672). Everything you always wanted to know about the city. Highlights include dioramas depicting historical scenes, a trolley car, and furnished rooms. Tues.–Sat., 10 A.M.–5 P.M.; Sun. and holidays opens at 1 P.M. Suggested contribution $3 for adults, $1 for children.

Whitney Museum of American Art. 945 Madison Ave. at 75th St. (212–570–3600). One of the best places for seeing the newest alternative art forms around. It was here that Nam Jun Paik foresaw the current video "revolution" with his (literally) video-as-art displays. Tues., 1 P.M.–8 P.M.; Wed.–Sat., 11 A.M.–5 P.M., Sun., noon to 6 P.M. Closed Mon. Adults, $4; children, $2. Free Tues. evening.

FILM. Hundreds of movie houses can be found in Manhattan, but generally speaking, most are congregated around three areas: Times Square, the East 50s and 60s, and Greenwich Village. Movie tickets are higher in Manhattan than in other areas of the country, with prices for first-runs ranging between $4.50 and $7. Reservations are generally not taken, and you should get to the movie house *at least* half an hour early, more if the film is a major hit. You'll be expected to wait on a line to purchase tickets and then to get on a "ticket holders" line. You can avoid all of this by going in the afternoon, when prices are often cheaper as well.

The Upper East Side is especially known for movies that have not opened widely and foreign movies. You'll also find foreign films at the Lincoln Center Triplex (Broadway and 63rd St). The Times Square movies are more populist and populated. The Village sports houses for about a dozen first-runs as well as several "revival houses," such as the Bleecker Street Cinema (Bleecker and LaGuardia Pl.; 212–674–2560), Theatre 80 St. Marks (80 St. Marks Place; 212–254–7400); Cinema Village (22 E. 12 St.; 212–924–3363); and the Thalia SoHo (15 Vandam St.; 212–675–0498). The *Village Voice* has extensive listings of revival house schedules.

MUSIC. New York probably offers more kinds of music more often than anyplace in the world. The two major sites are *Lincoln Center* (Broadway at 64th St.), which consists of Avery Fisher Hall, New York State Theater, Alice Tully Hall, and the Metropolitan Opera, along with the Juilliard School of Music; and *Carnegie Hall* (57th St. and Seventh Ave.). Avery Fisher Hall (212–874–2424) is the home of the New York Philharmonic; Alice Tully (212–362–1911) is the base for the Chamber Music Society of Lincoln Center and also the host for free concerts by Juilliard students. The Metropolitan Opera (212–362–6000), located in the most beautiful building of the complex, is open Sept.–April. Also at Lincoln Center is the New York City Opera (212–870–5570), located in the New York State Theater. Visiting opera companies also perform at Lincoln Center. The legendary Carnegie Hall (212–247–7800) plays host to visiting orchestras and recitalists.

The cheaper tickets to all events at Lincoln Center and Carnegie Hall can run as low as $6. Standing room tickets are also distributed just before the performance at substantial discounts. The Bryant Park TKTS booth, 42d St. between Fifth and Sixth avenues (212–382–2323), sells half-price day-of-performance tickets for music and dance events. Also of interest is the 92d Street Y, 1395 Lexington Ave. (212–427–4410); which features house and visiting orchestras. Symphony Space, Broadway and 95th (212–864–5400); Town Hall, 123 W. 43rd St. (212–840–2824). The Brooklyn Academy of Music, 30 Lafayette Ave., Brooklyn (718–636–4100), is the nation's oldest performing arts center and features a very popular avant-garde festival each winter (see also Free Events).

Popular music is also a major part of the New York music life, with an ever-burgeoning list of clubs playing host to on-the-rise bands. The Ritz, 119 E. 11th St. (212–254–2800), and The Bottom Line, 15 W. 4th St. (212–228–6300), are two of the most popular. Madison Square Garden and Radio City welcome some of the bigger bands. For outdoor music in the summer, the South Street Seaport's Pier 16 and the Miller Time Pier 84 Festival (43d St. on the Hudson River) offer ongoing series. Check local papers for specifics (see also the Nightlife section).

DANCE. New Yorkers are forever on their toes with an incredibly wide choice of dance styles and companies. Ballet can be found at the New York City Ballet, New York State Theater (212–870–5570) under the direction of Peter Martins; the American Ballet Theatre takes up residence at the Metropolitan Opera House (212–362–6000) under the direction of Mikhail Baryshnikov. City Center, 131 W. 55th St. (212–246–8989), is home for the acclaimed black dance group of Alvin Ailey as well as the modern stylings of the Joffrey Ballet. The Joyce Theatre, 175 Eighth Ave. (212–242–0800), is one of the city's newer dance halls. Still other companies perform on various Broadway and off-Broadway stages for limited engagements. The Bryant Park TKTS booth sells half-price tickets to many events (see listing under Music).

STAGE. When it comes to theater, there is no question that New York dominates the country and very often (depending on the season, to some extent) the world. Broadway is virtually synonymous with theater to many (except to Londoners, who regard their theatrical scene as the ultimate). But theater in New York is far more than the 20 or so blockbuster musicals and dramas crowding Broadway. The so-called off-Broadway world is a viable alternative, often providing more serious plays or plays that any day will move to Broadway and slightly lower prices (the difference in cost is not as great as it once was). Off-off-Broadway houses, where the greatest experimentation takes place, are cheaper still, though often located in out-of-the-way and frequently daunting neighborhoods.

An orchestra seat to a Broadway musical will run about $45 on a weekend evening, slightly less during weekdays, and still less for matinees (Weds., Sat., and sometimes Sun.); dramas run slightly less. There is often very little difference in the price of orchestra and balcony seats. Best seats off Broadway are $30.

The TKTS booths (in Times Square and in the World Trade Center) make half-price tickets abundantly available for most of the older plays, new ones that are in preview, and even the occasional hit. Naturally, the earlier you arrive on the lines—and they tend to be very long—the better chance you have of getting what you want. For matinees, the booths open at noon (performances are at 2 P.M. on Wed. and Sat., 3 P.M. on Sun.) and at 3 P.M. for evening performances (which begin at 8 P.M.). Most theaters are dark on Mondays.

Several outstanding theater companies are also in residence, often with inexpensive last-minute "rush tickets" or generally low ticket prices. Joseph Papp's Public Theatre, 425 Lafayette St. (212–598–7150), is in a beautiful building that once housed the Astor Library. Papp has done much to revitalize the off-Broadway scene with his daring and thought-provoking productions. Circle in the Square, 159 Bleecker St. (212–254–6330), manages to attract stars such as Al Pacino to appear in its works. It is at these theaters where playwrights such as Sam Shepard and Peter Nichols get the attention they deserve. You might also want to check some of the newer theaters on W. 42d St. between Ninth and Tenth avenues for other noncommercial alternatives and companies such as the Negro Ensemble and the American Place.

SHOPPING. You can spend more money than you ever dreamed of in New York, but you can find bargains as well. It's all a matter of knowing when and where to look. (Remember that some of the stores advertising going-out-of-business sales have been doing so for years—and they're still in business. Always compare prices at other stores.) New Yorkers are proud of their ability to sniff out the best buys and to "discover" new worthwhile places. Watch for department store holiday sales (Presidents' Day, Easter, Memorial Day, and throughout November and December). You'll want to stop by *Macy's* at Herald Square (34th St. and Broadway; 212–971–6000), *Bloomingdale's* (60th St. and Lexington Ave.; 212–705–2000), and *Saks* (49th St. and Fifth Ave.; 212–753–4000) as tourist attractions quite apart from the shopping itself. Urban malls also feature plenty of shops, some of the more popular atriums including *Trump Tower* (56th St. and Fifth Ave.; prohibitively expensive), *CitiCorp Building* (Lexington Ave. and 53d St.), and *Herald Center* (Herald Square).

For specialty items, there are thousands of smaller retail stores. New York is a haven for electronics stores, and some of them, such as those on 45th St. between Fifth and Sixth avenues and *Trader Horn* at 226 E. 86th St. (212–535–3600), are full of discounted merchandise. The various *Barnes and Noble* outlets and *Strand Books,* 828 Broadway (212–473–1452), are overflowing with discounted and discontinued books. On the Lower East Side, the Canal Street and Delancey Street areas are veritable havens for those seeking bargains on lamps, clothing, white goods, and kitchen wares. This area is particularly well known for prices only slightly above wholesale on designer clothes. Take a subway to the Williamsburg Bridge area. All around town you'll find stores selling odd lots of miscellaneous merchandise, from telephones to dishes to toys. These go by such names as *Odd Lot, Job Lot,* and *Pushcart.* Those traveling through New Jersey, around the George Washington Bridge area, will pass by many outlets offering appliances and electronics at just above wholesale prices.

DINING OUT. Eating out is one of the great New York pastimes. Regardless of the neighborhood, the cuisine, or the price you want to pay, there's always someplace new and exciting to try. And there are plenty of reliable old standbys. The budget traveler can do especially well in New York, particularly if he or she is a tad adventurous. Remember that even many of the most expensive restaurants have inexpensive price-fixed pre- or post-theater dinner menus or reasonable lunches.

Until recently, eating ethnic was synonymous with eating cheap, except where French food was concerned. That isn't the case anymore: there are some very fancy Chinese, Indian, and Italian restaurants, along with some very simple, inexpensive bistrolike French places. Here are descriptions of some of the more common ethnic foods found in New York. The restaurants mentioned in these paragraphs are described in more detail in the geographical and alphabetical lists that follow.

Chinese. Stick to Chinatown. The atmosphere in the streets is as much a part of the meal as the food itself. Best bets for people watching *and* food: Hunan House and Peking Duck House. Don't expect to spend the evening lingering, though; if that's your intention, the pricier (though still reasonable) restaurants on and around Second Avenue in the 40s will have to be substituted.

French. "Inexpensive" and "French food" are believed by many to be mutually exclusive categories. They haven't tried Cafe 58 or Crepes Suzette, where full dinners run well under $20. The latter, representing the peasant tradition, is the friendlier; the former, a classic bistro, is a little haughty and slack on service but still an outstanding value.

German. It's up to 86th Street between Second and Third avenues for serious wiener schnitzel, sauerbraten, and the like. This is the Yorkville, or Germantown, end of the city, where Kleine Konditorei and Cafe Geiger offer best values, fresh food, and *gemütlichkeit.*

Greek. It seems as though every coffee shop in the city is run by Greeks, though that's not what we refer to when discussing Greek *food.* The classic of the genre is the inconveniently located Z, but Acropolis in the theater district, and Delphi near the World Trade Center are equally worthwhile for souvlaki, moussaka, stuffed grape leaves, and baklava.

Indian. Head to Sixth Street between First and Second avenues for a dozen or so of the cheapest restaurants in the city, cheap but with quite respectable menus filled with kabobs and curries. A similar string of places is on Lexington in the upper 20s, while Mitali West in the heart of the Village and India Pavillion West near Carnegie Hall are a little fancier, only a little more expensive (still $10 to $12 per person for a meal), and quite good.

Italian. The storefront restaurants that used to be inexpensive pasta houses are giving way to high-tech, high-price places where maitre d's in tuxedos shun anyone without a reservation or an extra $2 bread-and-butter charge. Go to the old standbys in Greenwich Village: Monte's, Il Ponte Vecchio, and Roccos. Or make it a pizza night at John's or Pizza Piazza.

Japanese. Sushi bars seem to have popped up everywhere, and many offer full dinners in the $10 range. Most also serve beef, chicken, and pork dishes as well as fish and seafood. As for sushi, order a sampler plate or à la carte; individual items usually go for $1.50 to $3, depending on the type of fish. When eating raw foods, always be sure everything is fresh. Favorite near Lincoln Center: Dan Tempura House.

Jewish deli. Unique to New York are its delicatessens, unequaled anywhere else in the world. Corned beef, pastrami, and brisket sandwiches are piled inches high on fresh rye bread. Share a sandwich and a side order of fries or potato salad at the Carnegie in midtown; one of each is more than enough for two eaters and brings the price to within reason ($7 for a sandwich and $2.50 for a side dish is reasonable? Sure, when it's split between two). Or go down to the Second Avenue Deli in the East Village, which is about half the price and just as good, though out of the way. Warning: Plenty of sandwich shops and take-out counters call themselves delicatessens. They are, but for serious deli stick to our suggestions.

Kosher. Try the Second Avenue Deli; Levana, 141 W. 69th St. (877–8457), for fish and vegetarian dishes; Boychiks, 19 W. 45th St. (719–5999), for pizza, sandwiches, and quiches; Bernstein on Essex, 135 Essex (473–3900), for kosher Chinese and deli all on one menu; and Ratner's, 138 Delancey St. (677–5588). Fancier spots such as Lou G. Siegel, 209 W. 38th St. (921–4433), and Moshe Peking, 40 W. 37th St. (594–6500) are quite expensive.

Mexican. Possibly the trendiest category, partly because it's typically inexpensive, partly because the restaurants tend to be colorful, and definitely because of the tequila-based drinks that are so popular. Caramba! in the Village, on the Upper East Side, and near the theater district is the innest of the in—the Village location especially for singles.

Spanish. Different from Mexican, but just as spicy, plentiful, and cheap, with an emphasis on fish and chicken entrees. 23d St. between Seventh and Ninth avenues has become a sort of Spanish town.

The following list of restaurants is arranged first geographically (*Lower Manhattan* includes the financial district, the World Trade Center, and Chinatown) and then alphabetically within price categories. The categories, determined by the price of a meal for one, without beverage, tax, or tip, are as follows: *Reasonable,* $13 to $20; *Very Economical,* $10 to $12. In this chapter, because there are so many fine, expensive restaurants in New York, we are substituting *Special Finds,* which are our recommendations for the best value for the money, for Recommended Splurge.

A word of caution about credit cards: Many inexpensive establishments simply don't take them; others have a minimum amount below which they will not charge a bill. Almost all of our Reasonable listings take major credit cards; the very economical places more often than not don't. Also, New York restaurants aren't as easy about cashing traveler's checks as places in most other cities, so try to carry enough cash to cover yourself.

Lower Manhattan—Very Economical

The Big Kitchen at the World Trade Center and the **Market at the South Street Seaport** offer enormous arrays of quality fast food. The selection is somewhat more exotic at the Seaport, though there are hamburgers and pizza along with sushi, Indian samosas, and deli, and these shops are open from lunch through late evening. The Big Kitchen is best visited weekdays at lunch, for despite the lines, that's when traffic ensures that everything is fresh. Both locales are good for family outings.

The Delphian. 60 Duane St. (267–5463). Good inexpensive Greek food. No credit cards but open till midnight.

Hamburger Harry's. 157 Chambers St. (267–4446); also 145 W. 45th St. (840–2756). Best charcoal and mesquite-fired burgers in the city, served in a stainless steel-cum-deco setting unlike any burger joint you've seen. Try the potato salad, too. Lunchtime the place is overrun, but dinners and weekends are almost calm.

Hunan House. 45 Mott St. (962–0010). Tell them you want it hot, and you'll get it. Typical Chinatown.

Peking Duck House. 22 Mott St. (962–8208). This is the place that inspired a host of imitators (some by the same ownership) to make Peking duck available without ordering 24 hours ahead. The dish is authentic, and the presentation is as exciting as the food.

SoHo—Reasonable

Elephant & Castle. 183 Prince St. (260–3600); also 68 Greenwich Ave. in the Village (212–243–1400). They line up to get into these two. Features interesting sandwiches, some hot dishes, and desserts.

Manhattan Bistro. 129 Spring St. (966–3459). Charming bistro serving cassoulet, blood sausage, *steak frites,* a wonderful warm goat cheese salad, and more. A place to linger and chat (the tables are nicely spaced), but skip the desserts.

New Deal. 152 Spring St. (431–3663). Pretheater dinners run $15 to $18 in this lovely 1930s-style restaurant. But be forewarned that the à la carte menu is two to three times higher. There are shellfish festivals and other rarities periodically highlighted.

Patisserie Lanciani. 177 Prince St. (477–2788). Surely the best desserts in New York—a chocolate fiend's heaven—but breakfast, brunch, and light meals are also featured. Brioche French toast, smoked chicken salad, pasta with multipepper tomato sauce, sandwiches, and omelets are fresh and prepared with a flair for presentation as well as taste. And then, of course, dessert—or, dessert as the main course. You'll understand as soon as you look in the window.

Spring St. 143 Spring St. at West Broadway (219–0157). Appropriately spring-like decor with a nice lineup of Continental fare; strong, too, on salads and omelets.

Tennessee Mountain. 143 Spring St. at Wooster St. (431–3993). Great place for ribs, shrimp, chili, and chicken housed in a clapboard-sided 150-year-old landmark building. Reservations a must, and then expect to wait.

Greenwich Village—Reasonable

Butterfly. 125 Seventh Ave. So. (807–0134). A wonderful place to sit and chat all day. Original entrees tinged with a touch of the Mideast.

Caramba! Three locations: 684 Broadway at 3rd St. (420–9817); 918 Eighth Ave. at 54th St. (245–7910); and 1576 3rd Ave. at 88th St. (876–8838). They hang from the rafters at these Mexican outposts. Prime singles haunts and big favorites for food, too. Very hefty margaritas.

Cornelia Street Café. 29 Cornelia St. (989–9318). Charming romantic spot. Outdoor tables (in season), poetry readings, and guitar players. Simple menu, leisurely place.

The Front. 91 Seventh Ave. S. (691–3430). Nice atmosphere to enjoy wonderfully light pasta entrees and a perfect place for watching the West Village scene.

Il Ponte Vecchio. 206 Thompson St. (228–7701). A longtime Village favorite for Italian food, a bit pricier than Rocco and Monte's but a bit more pleasant to sit as well.

Monte's. 97 MacDougal St. (674–9456). A Village institution that's family-run. Good for standard Italian fare like spaghetti in meat sauce, veal parmigiana, and the like. No credit cards.

Rocco. 181 Thompson St. (677–0590). Northern Italian home-style cooking; mussels in garlic sauce are a favorite, along with veal and pasta dishes. One of the best.

Toon's. 417 Bleecker St. (924–6420). An excellent representation of and exceedingly pleasant spot for Thai food, a cross between Chinese and Indian styles.

Greenwich Village—Very Economical

John's Pizzeria. 278 Bleecker St. (243–1680). A New York institution where people actually line up to get inside. One sample of the delicious house specialty and you'll know why.

Kiev. 117 Second Ave. (674–4040). Open 24 hours and specializing in Russian and Ukrainian entrees. It's dinerish but a must for the colorful clientele, apple pancakes, and hearty meals that run $5 to $7.

Mitali West. 296 Bleecker St. (989–1367). A spruced-up version of the original, which resides on East 6th Street. Particularly good curries.

Olive Tree. 117 MacDougal St. (254–3630). The menu is limited to Middle Eastern fare, but the blackboard tables and constant Charlie Chaplin showings more than make up.

Peacock Caffe. 24 Greenwich Ave. (242–9395). Long, dark room with dawdling daydreamers sitting at oak tables sipping cappuccino, tearing into a string bean salad, or slurping the cream sauce bathing fresh-cooked tortellini.

Pizza Piazza. 785 Broadway (505–0977). Pizza served Chicago-style in individual deep-dish pans. Lovely setting to enjoy America's favorite finger food presented with a touch of class.

Sandolino. 9 Jones St. (255–6669). A college (NYU) hangout that's kind of grown up. Best turkey salad around, great omelets, and something that'll be just right even when you don't know what you want. Caters to those who want to linger.

Second Avenue Deli. 156 Second Ave. (677–0606). Best deli value in the city; great sandwiches, great mushroom barley soup, and if you're still hungry, a half sandwich for dessert.

West Fourth Street Saloon. 174 W. 4th St. (255–0518). The decor—green and summery—is light as the food. Great for omelettes, burgers, etc.

Whole Wheat 'N' Wild Berry's. 57 W. 10th St. (677–3410). A sure bet to change your mind about natural foods forever. You'll be hooked as soon as you walk in and catch the aroma of . . . pasta and red sauce? Yes, and the entire menu is filled with delicious but all-natural surprises. Not a bit of tofu on the premises.

Z. 117 E. 15th St. (254–0960). A favorite for years for all the standard Greek specialties, though vegetables are always overcooked and the service is faster than a speeding bullet. A few outside tables in the back during summer.

Midtown—Reasonable

Beanstalk. 1221 Ave. of the Americas (997–1005). Best for salads, though there are hot entrees, too. Convenient to midtown shopping at Saks and business meetings, and across the street from Radio City Music Hall.

Beubern Cafe. 42 W. 28th St. (725–9280). A quaint red-and-white-checkered tablecloth setting in which to enjoy burgers, chicken, and sandwiches.

Between the Bread. 141 E. 56th St. (888–0449). Good place for lunch or early dinner. Great pasta salads, desserts, and gigantic muffins.

Cabana Carioca. 123 W. 45th St. (581–8088) and 133 W. 45th St. (212–730–8375). Brazilian food in a festive setting (especially at the former location). Wonderfully convenient to the Broadway theaters. Hearty fare and large portions at very low prices. Great for families.

Cafe Madeleine. 405 W. 43rd St. (246–2993). Light, French-accented meals; they'll keep you satisfied, but not uncomfortably stuffed, through an evening's theater.

Century Cafe. 132 W. 43rd St. (398–1988). Mesquite grilled veal chops, filet mignon, and fish; duck and dried fruits; splendid salads and great desserts (especially the sour cream apple pie). Skip the appetizers both because they're not as good as the main courses and because that will keep you under the $20 limit. Perfect for before or after theater, lunch—any time.

Crepes Suzette. 363 W. 46th St. (581–9717 and 974–9002). Excellent for pretheater dinners that run $12 to $18 depending on entree. Friendly and unhurried but timed to get you to the theater on time.

Mike's American Bar & Grill. 650 Tenth Ave., near 46th St. (246–4115). "American" here means Southwest. Don't be put off by the look from the outside. Inside it's bright, cheery, and fun—and that goes for the food, too.

Sapporo. 152 W. 49th St. (869–8972). Excellent Japanese restaurant with the kitchen off to the side for easy access to the wonderful odors permeating the air.

Siam Inn. 916 Eighth Ave. (974–9583). Siam special chicken, crabs (when in season), and basil-based dishes are standouts.

Tenth Ave. Jukebox Cafe. 637 Tenth Ave., at 45th St. (315–4690). A simple, unpretentious but pretty restaurant, great for light meals. Caters to those living and working in the theater district.

Wylie's. 891 First Ave. (751–0700). Ribs and an onion loaf near the United Nations.

Midtown—Very Economical

Acropolis. 767 Eighth Ave. (581–2733). Greek specialties; very friendly.

Beggar's Banquet. 125 W. 43rd St. (212–997–0959). No frills American menu in long, narrow, pleasant restaurant. Good for a light pretheater dinner.

Marvin's Place. 598 Ninth Ave. (246–9454). Superior bar food—pâtés, pastas, burgers, and beautiful salads—and a popular hangout for theater people.

West Bank Cafe. 407 W 42nd St. (695–6909). An interesting mix of Oriental and Continental dishes built around ribs, chicken, and fresh fish. An entree and coffee will probably be enough before or after theater and will keep the bill within the limit.

Around 57th Street—Very Economical

Cafe 57. 312 W. 57th St. (397–8335). Extremely friendly neighborhood eatery with a surprisingly imaginative chef whose seemingly unlikely creations invariably work. Very low prices.

Carnegie Delicatessen. 854 Seventh Ave. (757–2245). A must. Two or three should share the corned beef hash for breakfast. In fact, whatever you order, share. The portions are enormous. And good.

English Pub. 900 Seventh Ave. (265–4360). British fare is featured right across from Carnegie Hall.

Hobeau's. 988 Second Ave. (421–2888). Be prepared for a wait. But be prepared for great fish and seafood, too.

India Pavillion West. 240 W. 56th St. (489–0035). The service is frustrating if you are trying to make a curtain at nearby Carnegie Hall, but the food is first rate—especially the assorted appetizers.

Prego. 1365 Sixth Ave. at 56th St. (307–5775). The setting is jarring—all that white—and service is hurried, but attractive pasta and other Italian dishes run a palatable $5.85.

Lincoln Center—Reasonable

The Saloon. 1920 Broadway (874–1500). Order carefully at this large, noisy, but fun emporium because the menu takes off for the stratosphere. But there are plenty of reasonable selections, and Lincoln Center is just across the street. Reservations a must.

Shun Lee West. 43 W. 65th St. (595–8895). Fancified Chinese across the street from Lincoln Center. Plush, full-service restaurant and less expensive dim sum café.

Lincoln Center—Very Economical

Anita's Chili Parlor. 287 Columbus Ave. (595–4091). Just what the name implies, though other Mexican dishes are available as well. In summer, the sidewalk tables are packed for eating and people-watching along this prime singles' strip.

Dan Tempura. 2018 Broadway (877–4969). At 69th St., Dan is a few blocks north of Lincoln Center but by far the most reliable Japanese restaurant in the area. Those on Columbus Ave. come and go, but Dan is consistently good, with dinner menus a real bargain.

Diane's. 249 Columbus Ave. (799–6750). Small but immensely popular hamburgery. Good shakes and sundaes, too.

Dobson's. 341 Columbus Ave. (362–0100). Best noted for seafood; the salads and burgers are more than respectable as well. Very accommodating staff, and kids are most definitely welcome.

Lincoln Square Coffee Shoppe. 2 Lincoln Sq. (799–4000). It looks like a coffee shop, but the food is several cuts above the expected. Especially noteworthy is the salad bar (about $6), with several varieties of chicken salad, many vegetable and pasta options, tuna, cheese, the works. Always a line right before curtain time.

Perretti. 270 Columbus Ave. (362–3939). Bright, noisy family place for unusual pizzas and excellent pastas.

Also, check out the cafes along Columbus Avenue featuring everything from Mexican food to yogurt concoctions to burgers. Ditto the plethora of Chinese restaurants. Assuming it's mealtime, the presence of a fair number of diners is a good indication that a place is worthwhile.

Upper East Side—Reasonable

Cafe Bonjour. 801 Lexington Ave. (223–2270). Small, bustling café specializing in sandwiches, "les hamburgers," and wonderful desserts.

Cafe Geiger. 206 E. 86th St. (734–4428). First you pass the cakes and pastries on your way to a table, and then you're faced with the decision of which of the German dishes you want as a meal.

Kleine Konditorei. 234 E. 86th St. (737–7130). Skip the appetizers, as entrees come with a variety of side dishes and portions are generous. Besides, you want room for dessert.

Mumbles. 1622 Third Ave. (427–4355). Great little place with the usual club menu: burgers, omelets, salads, quiche.

Serendipity. 225 E. 60th St. (838–3531). For those with kids. Oversize everything: burgers, banana splits, and a boutique all rolled into one. Share everything.

Yellowfingers. 60th St. and Third Ave. (751–8615). Convenient to the East Side movie houses. Lively setting for nibbling on omelets and salads.

Real Finds. Black Sheep. 344 W. 11th St. (242–1010). For a sense of what the Village is like to those who live there, stroll down 11th St. until you hit this double storefront restaurant that offers five-course extraveganzas in the $25 range (including selections priced a little higher). The food is American with a French accent, and the wine list is worth treasuring (and reasonably priced); a place to linger, though earlybirds on weekends get the rush. Still, the evening will be memorable.

Cafe des Artistes. 1 W. 67th St. (877–3500). Get a feel for what the gentry once enjoyed at this (mostly) French enclave right near Lincoln Center. Given the location, service, and cuisine, the prices are quite reasonable; you'll probably stray above the $20 for sampling three courses (not to mention the sampler dessert plate), but you can easily be satisfied on less. Reservations ahead are a must.

Tavern on the Green. Central Park West at 67th St. (873–3200). It's worth planning ahead to ensure a weekday reservation between 5:30 and 6:30 P.M. for the $14.50–$19.50 three-course pretheater dinner. Sit in the heart of Central Park, with a million (literally) tiny light bulbs illuminating the trees. Getting to your table is a hectic affair, as you wind your way through the various dining rooms, waiters with filled trays shoving you to the side. Once at your seat all is forgiven, and the food, at the price, is absolutely unbeatable. After 7, beware: The prices more than double for the exact same fare ordered à la carte. The same policy is in effect for a sister restaurant, Maxwell's Plum, 64th St. and First Ave. (628–2100), which offers California nouvelle cuisine.

Brunches. Numerous restaurants offer huge weekend brunches that can carry you through the day. For about $10, you'll get breakfastlike foods such as eggs, waffles, pancakes, etc., or lunch-dinner eats such as hamburgers or steak. Sometimes a free drink is included, traditional brunch liquor being champagne, mimosa, or bloody Mary.

Many bruncheries supply music with the food, a relatively inexpensive form of entertainment as there is usually no cover charge. Among the best: the **Angry Squire,** 216 Seventh Ave. (242–9066), featuring jazz. Many hotels, including the **Waldorf,** 49th and Park (872–4895), **Grand Hyatt,** near Grand Central Station (883–1234), and **Plaza,** 59th St. and Fifth Ave. (759–3000), also feature dining rooms that serve musical brunches in extravagant surroundings at equally extravagant prices (about $25). This should be considered for a special splurge.

Cafes and Coffeehouses. The streets of Greenwich Village provide several opportunities for weary folk to rest and plan the day's travel itinerary. Many of these cafés serve a variety of coffees and pastries and will allow you to sit and daydream as long as you wish. If you meander along the cross section of Bleecker and MacDougal streets and, further west, Greenwich Ave., you'll find plenty of coffeehouses. Some recommendations: **Caffee Reggio,** 119 MacDougal St. (475–9557) and **Le Figaro** at the corner of Bleecker and MacDougal streets (677–1100). **Patisserie Lanciani,** 177 Prince St. (477–2788), and 275 West Fourth St. (929–0739) are the modern version of the classic coffeehouse. Expect to see neighborhood residents waiting for the doors to open. New York *Times* in hand, for fresh croissant and coffee in the morning. For the showiest of the coffeehouses, though, no place can top **Ferrara's** in Little Italy, at 195 Grand St. (226–6150) even if the pastry—especially the chocolate cheesecake—is better and the atmosphere less harried around the block at **Cafe Biondo,** 141 Mulberry St. (226–9285).

BARS. New York is a big bar town, and to list them all would be an inhuman task. The city is famous for lots of "neighborhood" bars as well as singles haunts and celebrity hangouts. Bar hopping in the Village is exceedingly easy; try University Place, Bleecker St., and the West Village. Of particular note: **Knickerbocker Saloon** (University Place and 9th St.), a jazz "hang" catering to a slightly older crowd; and **McSorley's Old Ale House** (15 E. 7th St.), one of the oldest taverns in the city, great for atmosphere and very popular with college students. On the other side of the Village sits the literary pub **White Horse Tavern** (Hudson St. and 11th St.), once a regular haunt for Dylan Thomas and company. Another onetime literary haunt, and the city's oldest bar, is **Pete's Tavern** (Irving Place and 18th St.), where O. Henry went to down the old suds. The spacious **Century Cafe** (132 W. 43rd St.) is a haven for the theater set. **The Saloon** (Broadway and 64th St.) is known for its picture windows, its heavy-duty bar scene, and the best Buffalo chicken wings in the city. The infamous singles scene on the Upper East Side is still swinging away. **Jim McMullen** (Third Ave. and 76th St.) is named after its owner, a former model who plays host to any number of models, sports figures, and rock stars.

NIGHTLIFE. Let it be said that the new breed of **dance emporiums** are incredible both for their very existence and their indulgences. They are often haughty, exclusive, rude, and expensive to get into—but once inside, they are environments completely devoted to making you want to dance. Expect a $15–$20 admission charge and drinks (including sodas) that start at $4. Sometimes, arriving before 10 P.M. will gain free admission, but don't count on it. Most have "parties" with "invited guests" as many nights as they can, but these are pseudo events with thousands of invitations mailed to those on select lists; the invitations don't even guarantee entry!

The popularity of any given venue waxes and wanes with the celebrity list it attracts, and dance clubs come and go. Be sure to call to make sure the one (or ones) you've set your sights on are still in business. Here are a few suggestions from among the survivors of recent years:

Limelight, Sixth Ave. at 20th St. (807–7850), is probably the most notorious, partly because of its setting—a deconsecrated church, most of its features left untouched. Occasional live music shows start at midnight, but they're nothing compared to the parade of party-goers who frequent the place.

The Palladium, 126 E. 14th St. (212–473–7171), is a massive theater that's been a vaudeville house, movie theater, and rock concert palace. Refurbished by the team that brought you the original Studio 54 (now defunct), the Palladium caters to yuppies from New Jersey and Long Island, and the fashion industry.

Heartbreak, 179 Varick (212–691–2388), is a cafeteria by day for the printing and manufacturing industries in the industrial buildings surrounding it, and a disco for those who like dancing to the music of the '50s and '60s at night. Roll out the sneakers and get the poodle skirt out of mothballs.

For more traditional ballroom or Latin dancing, the venerable **Roseland** is the place: 239 W. 52d St. (212–247–0200). Admission is $8 to $12.

For live **rock and pop,** the best-known venues include **The Bottom Line,** 15 W. 4th St. (212–228–6300), and **The Ritz,** 119 E. 11th St. (212–254–2800), for name acts. **Kenny's Castaways,** 157 Bleecker St. (212–473–9870), offers a *cheap,* relaxed atmosphere for enjoying local and up-and-coming rock and folk acts. **S.O.B.'s,** 204 Varick St. (212–243–4940), stands for Sounds of Brazil, and it's here where you'll find some of the most percussive and persuasive music going—and a great Brazilian menu.

Jazz buffs know of course that New York is home to most of the world's legendary clubs. Few of the 52d Street and Harlem clubs remain, but there are literally dozens elsewhere to choose from. The **Village Vanguard,** 178 Seventh Ave. South (212–242–1785), while the **Knickerbocker,** 33 University Place (212--228–8490) and **Bradleys,** 70 University Place (212–228–6440) are best for piano-bass duos. Admissions run $6 to $15, depending on the act.

Best jazz bargains: **West End Cafe,** 2909 Broadway at 114th St. (212–666–8750), where bebop and mainstream sounds prevail at low cover charges. **Michael's Pub,** 211 E. 55th St. (212–758–2272), is surprisingly reasonable with the usual $10 minimum applied to food or drinks and the menu being both good and a good value.

For **country** and **blues,** the **Lone Star Cafe,** Fifth Ave. and 13th St. (212–242–1664), is home to many Texans-at-heart. It's always easy to get a laugh in the city, with dozens of **comedy clubs** giving over the mike to hardworking young comedians. Among the best for atmosphere and talent: Improvisation, 358 W. 44th St. (212–756–8268), Comic Strip, 1568 Second Ave. (212–861–9386), and Comedy Cellar, 117 MacDougal St. (212–254–3630).

SECURITY. If you exercise care and common sense, you should have a safe visit to New York. Begin by keeping a close eye on your luggage. At the train stations, don't give it to someone to carry to a cab. If you set it down, don't turn your back on it. Keep watch even in hotel lobbies.

Talk to the staff of your hotel about the neighborhood you're staying in and those you want to visit. Some general rules to follow: Carry as little cash as possible; prepay as many expenses as you can. Buy traveler's checks; they're almost as good as cash and safer. Carry only one or two credit cards, and destroy carbons of charge card forms. Use safe deposit boxes at the hotel for valuables rather than carrying them or leaving them in your room. Do not wear expensive jewelry on the streets or public transportation. Women should carry their purses close to the body and not hang them over chairs in restaurants. Men should watch out for pickpockets, especially in crowds. Do not wander around dark streets at night. If you're out late come home in a cab. Subways are pretty safe during the day, but don't get into an empty car.

ORLANDO

by
Pam Parks

Orlando's early beginnings were as a military post, Fort Gatlin, in the Seminole War (1835–1842). The fort was established in 1837, though there was no seaport or major waterway.

Many Florida cities retained the names of the original forts—Fort Pierce, Fort Lauderdale, Fort Meyers—but this city was named for soldier Orlando Reeves, who was killed by an Indian after he saved the hamlet by warning of an impending raid. It was incorporated in 1875 with 85 pioneers on one square mile of land. Many central Florida settlements sprang up in pioneer times, but Orlando grew because of its connection to the South Florida Railroad. By 1900, it had developed into a sophisticated city, thanks to the railroad and citrus. The groves blossomed in all directions.

Orlando was nicknamed "The City Beautiful" in 1908; its treasures then were fragrant orange blossoms and crystal-clear springs and lakes. By its hundredth birthday, Orlando had become the number one tourist destination in the world, thanks to the opening of Walt Disney World in 1971. A phenomenal period of growth followed with the construction of new hotels, condominiums, apartments, and other attractions. Now the boom is on again, thanks in large part to the attractions that provide Central Florida with a strong economy. The lure of Disney has kept tourism king, and its plans to add several new attractions should boost the number of visitors to record highs.

Each year from Easter to September the population of Central Florida swells; 9.5 million visit here annually. For the best bargains and the smallest crowds, come in September through November or January.

The city's fine climate—about 72 degrees year-round, though it's been known to drop to freezing—and beaches that are less than an hour away add to the lure of the man-made attractions. Many come for fishing, sailing, and wind surfing on the city's hundreds of lakes and for canoeing on the waterways that crisscross the area.

The Orlando area is a gold mine for spirited bargain hunters. The many attractions, hotels, campgrounds, and restaurants in the area have cut prices considerably. It's estimated that there are more than 60,000 hotel rooms in the area. Though luxury hotels and restaurants abound, Orlando is a place for travelers on a limited budget, thanks to the local tradition of southern hospitality. Visitors can stretch a vacation from one week to two by checking into simple but comfortable hotels, many locally owned, near the attractions.

Though there is a lot more to Orlando than Mickey Mouse, Walt Disney gave this area an identity. His vision for Central Florida was a new community that would avoid the mistakes made at Disneyland. In 1964 he started buying land at $200 an acre; by 1965 he owned 27,443 acres, and that same year he unveiled plans that would forever change Orlando. Walt Disney World opened in 1971. Epcot Center, the Experimental Prototype Community of Tomorrow, opened in October 1982.

Although admission to the parks may seem a bit steep—it's climbed to $28 a ticket—it is money well spent. Every day is like a giant party in the Magic Kingdom, and Epcot Center is a world of learning and experiencing.

The Magic Kingdom seems old-fashioned compared with Epcot Center, but it's an attraction no one ever seems to tire of, even when the weather is warm and visitors may have to wait more than an hour for admission to some attractions. There are six lands in the 100-acre Magic Kingdom: Main Street USA, Adventureland, Frontierland, Liberty Square, Fantasyland, and Tomorrowland. Main Street runs straight to the soaring spires of Cinderella's Castle, where you'll marvel at the elaborate mosaic of the story of Cinderella, depicted with a million bits of colored Italian glass, silver, and 14-karat gold.

Don't miss the Main Street Electrical Parade, usually presented during Easter, summer, and when the park is open until midnight. Best spot for watching the million twinkling lights, 30 floats, and hundreds of performers is the Main Street railroad depot.

Wear your walking shoes; Epcot Center is twice the size of the Magic Kingdom, a modern version of Walt Disney's dream of a city of tomorrow. Lasers, fiber optics, and the newest ideas in technology and science are exhibited in six pavilions in Future World. Newest to open is the Living Seas, with the world's largest aquarium and undersea studies.

Nestled around a magnificent lagoon, World Showcase is an international exchange of customs, cultures, and ideas from ten countries. You can order tacos and cold Mexican beer streetside and visit Japanese gardens, French cafés, and more. The ultimate extravaganza of lasers, lights, fountains, and fireworks brightens the World Showcase lagoon nightly. The show, accompanied by classical music with a fireworks finale, is dazzling.

Minutes from Disney World, cross over Interstate 4 and visit Shamu's home at Sea World, 12 miles southwest of Orlando. The lovable four-ton killer whale has a new habitat in the $15 million Shamu Stadium where trainers delight the audiences with an educational show starring Shamu and her new offspring. Other shows in the world's largest marine park include performances by sea lions, otters, a walrus, dolphins, and penguins. The park's Shark Encounter is home for 30 sharks; here you travel through an aquatic tunnel surrounded by the predators.

Most visitors stay on nearby International Drive, an overgrown row of restaurants, fast food, hotels, shops, and small attractions, most catering to the budget traveler and to families. The south portion of the street is adding new upscale hotels and eating places. The latest addition here is Mercado, a sophisticated new shopping and food complex. The Mediterranean-style, 100,000-square-foot center houses a dinner theater and Mardi Gras, with spicy Cajun dishes and a colorful, fast-paced cabaret show. The north end of International Drive is fast becoming a mecca for discount shoppers. Factory Outlet Mall paved the way several years back; now there are several new shopping centers, all discount.

Church Street Station, in Orlando's historic **downtown** district, is a renovated complex of bars, restaurants, and shops with everything from cancan dancers to bluegrass music and a disco. A new retail center with upscale shops, the Church Street Exchange, has helped revitalize the area. Renovation continues up Church Street to the Early Victorian railroad depot, now a charming antique shop. Friday mornings the Junior League of Orlando offers a free 45-minute walking tour of historic downtown, starting at Wall Street and Orange Avenue. But if you're on your own, glimpse the Art Deco McCrory's building built in 1906, the La Belle Epoque architecture of the Kress building, and the Classic Egyptian Revival style of the First National Bank building. Cross over a block and stroll around Lake Eola, with its famous fountain, for years Orlando's most noted landmark.

A few minutes north of downtown on Interstate 4 is tree-shaded, brick-paved **Winter Park,** a vacation resort for wealthy northerners with a reverence for tradition long before Walt Disney put Orlando on the map. Catch a glimpse of the elegant homes of the town's wealthy and famous on the Winter Park Boat Tour, 12 miles on the city's lakes winding through narrow canals with a guide who provides commentary on the homes ringing the water.

Park Avenue is a sophisticated street with international boutiques, galleries, museums, and restaurants. You can see Tiffany on display in the tiny Morse Gallery, much of the works rescued from the ruins of Tiffany's New York home, the only art nouveau mansion ever built in this country. At the south end of Park Avenue is **Rollins College,** containing 56 acres with beautiful Spanish Renaissance architecture. Three points of interest here are the Cornell Fine Arts Museum, the Beal-Maltbie Shell Museum, with one of the largest collections of seashells in the world, and the Walk of Fame, with 800 inscribed stones from the birthplaces and homes of famous people.

PRACTICAL INFORMATION

WHEN TO GO. The slowest months for tourists are Jan. and Sept. For the best bargains in hotel prices, go Jan.–Feb. or Sept–Nov., when rooms rates are cut in half at most hotels. The real crowds arrive in April.

Orlando weather is ideal; the average temperature is 72 degrees. The rainy season is June–Sept., with scattered showers almost daily. Temperatures do drop to freezing in the winter months.

HOW TO GET THERE. If you've got the time to drive, bring your car. If not, it's necessary to rent one in Orlando. There are so many attractions that you'll always find yourself on the move, and the beaches are within 50 miles.

By air. Orlando International Airport is served by most commercial carriers. Private airports include Orlando Executive and Kissimmee Airport; both service private and corporate aircraft. Major airlines serving Orlando International are *American, Braniff, British Airways, Continental, Delta, Eastern, Icelandair, Pan Am, Piedmont, TWA, USAir,* and *United.*

By bus. *Greyhound-Trailways* buses serve Orlando.

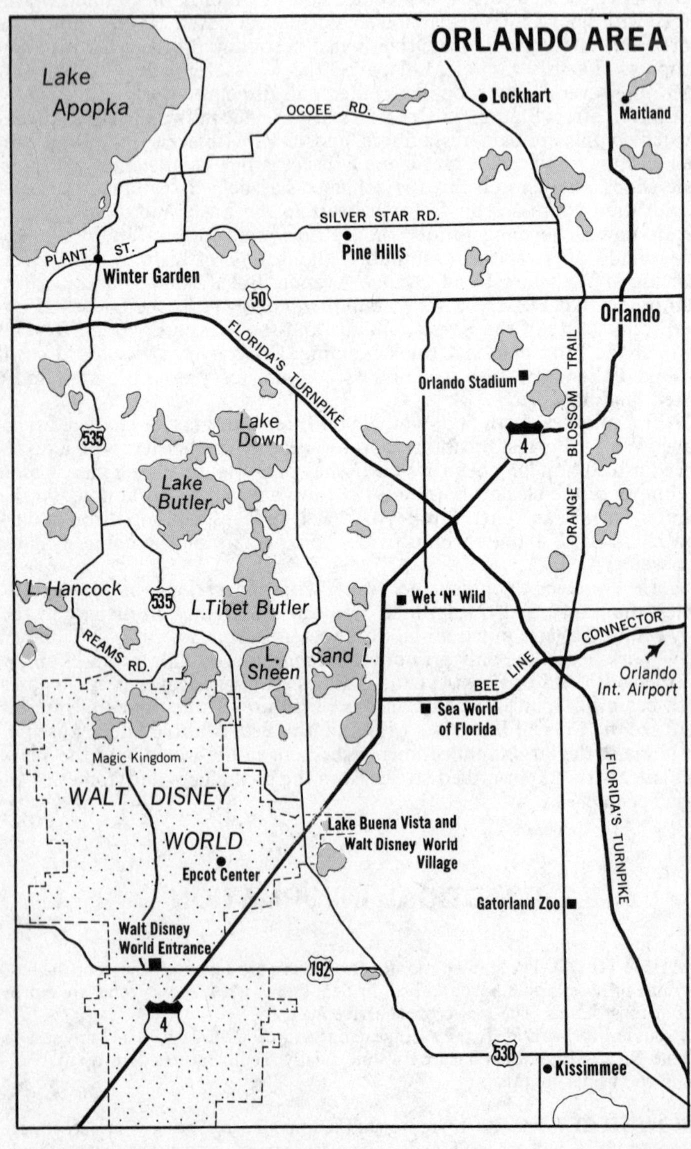
ORLANDO AREA
Lake Apopka
OCOEE RD.
Lockhart
Maitland
SILVER STAR RD.
Pine Hills
PLANT ST.
Winter Garden
50
Orlando
FLORIDA'S TURNPIKE
Orlando Stadium
Lake Down
535
4
Lake Butler
ORANGE BLOSSOM TRAIL
L. Hancock
535
L. Tibet Butler
Wet 'N' Wild
REAMS RD.
CONNECTOR
L. Sheen
Sand L.
BEE LINE
Orlando Int. Airport
Sea World of Florida
Magic Kingdom
WALT DISNEY WORLD
FLORIDA'S TURNPIKE
Lake Buena Vista and Walt Disney World Village
Epcot Center
Gatorland Zoo
Walt Disney World Entrance
192
4
530
Kissimmee

By train. Passenger train service along the Eastern seaboard is provided by *Amtrak* with stops in Orlando, Winter Park, and Sanford. Call 800–872–7245. For visitors who would like to drive their own cars in Florida, Amtrak offers daily service between Sanford 28 miles north of Orlando and Lorton, VA, carrying both cars and people on an overnight trip.

By car. Orlando is served by a number of highways. The Florida Turnpike connects Orlando with the northern and southern parts of the state. The main route through Orlando is Interstate 4, which runs from Daytona Beach to Tampa and intersects most of the area's thoroughfares, including U.S. Highway 17–92, State Road 50, and State Road 436. All major attractions are located at or near an I-4 intersection. Two toll roads run through Orlando: the Bee Line Expressway connecting Kennedy Space Center with Orlando and the East-West Expressway, which runs from the west side of Orlando through downtown to the east side of town.

TELEPHONES. The area code for Orlando is 407. You do not need to dial the area code if it is the same one from which you are dialing. Local directory assistance is 411; long-distance is 800–555–1212. Ask if there is an 800 number for the business you want to reach. An operator will assist if you dial 0 first. Local calls are 25 cents in most places.

Emergency Telephone Numbers. The emergency number for fire, police, ambulance, and paramedics is 911, or dial 0 and ask the operator for help. Poison control is 841–5222. The Chamber of Commerce operates a 24-hour hotline in 56 languages at 828–9200.

ACCOMMODATIONS. Because of a recent boom in hotel building, there are hundreds of hotels in the Orlando area, from world-class resorts to budget mom-and-pops. You'll pay top dollar from Easter through Labor Day and the Christmas holidays through March. The more expensive rooms are found around Walt Disney World and Sea World. But because Orlando is the family fun capital of the world, many offer family rates, free lodging for children under 18, and discounts on meals for children. For convenience to the attractions, the area along U.S. 192 east and west, the Kissimmee area, and International Drive offer the best bargains.

Rates are based on double occupancy. Categories, determined by price, are as follows: *Reasonable,* $40 to $60; *Very Economical,* under $40 (both are lower off-season). Most accept credit cards. Tax on a room is 7 percent.

Reasonable

Best Western Near Boardwalk and Baseball. I-4 and U.S. 27, Davenport, FL 33837 (813–424–2511 or 800–235–5650). Outdoor pool, restaurant, and lounge. No pets. 159 rooms.

Best Western Vacation Lodge. 8600 W. Spacecoast Parkway, Kissimmee, FL 32741 (407–396–0100). Restaurant with buffet and reduced prices for children. Lounge open 5 P.M. to midnight. 300 rooms. No pets. Has game room, gift shop.

Casa Rosa Inn. 4600 W. Hwy. 192, Kissimmee, FL 32741 (407–396–2020). Delicate pink hotel set in a wooded area. Pool, no pets, 56 rooms. Nonsmoking section.

Comfort Inn. 5825 International Dr., Orlando, FL 32819 (800–228–5150). Outdoor pool, restaurant, laundromats. No pets. 160 rooms.

Continental Plaza Hotel. 6825 Visitors Circle, Orlando, FL 32819 (800–241–8955). Located across from Wet 'N Wild. Pool, no pets. 192 rooms.

Delta Hotel. 6301 International Dr., Orlando, FL 32809 (407–351–4430). Heated outdoor pool, Granny's Kitchen restaurant, game room, 258 rooms.

High "Q" Motor Inn. 5905 International Dr., Orlando, FL 32809 (800–228–5151). Restaurant, lounge, adult and children's pools, pool bar in summer. No pets, 298 rooms, game room, sauna.

King's Motel. 4836 W. Hwy. 192, Kissimmee, FL 32741 (407–843–3051). Pool, no pets, 98 rooms. Low season, $34; prime time, $50. Efficiencies available that sleep up to four.

Larson's Lodge. 2009 W. Vine St., Kissimmee, FL 32741 (800–327–9074). Owned and operated by the Larson family. Heated pool, transportation to attractions, Jacuzzi, restaurant and lounge, pets, game room, gift shop.

Palm Motel. 4519 W. Hwy. 192, Kissimmee, FL 32741 (407–396–0744). Pool, no pets. 39 rooms, across from Medieval Times.

Quality Inn West. 3330 W. Colonial Drive, Orlando, FL 32808 (407–296–6710). Pool, restaurant and lounge, no pets. 128 rooms.

Ramada Westgate. Box 1386, Kissimmee, FL 32742–1386 (800–282–2124). Pool, restaurant, lounge, gift shop. No pets, 198 rooms. Kids free.

Rodeway Inn. 9956 Hawaiian Court, Orlando, FL 32819 (800–228–2000). Large pool courtyard, hot tub, game room, guest service desk for attractions. Lounge open 5:30 P.M.–1 A.M. Continental breakfast. No pets. Has 222 rooms, some with in-room Jacuzzis.

1776 Resort Inn. 5858 International Dr., Orlando, FL 32819 (800–327–2115). Heated outdoor pool, lounge, game room, playground. Has 272 rooms; no pets.

Travelers Inn. 4990 W. Spacecoast Pkwy., Kissimmee, FL 32741 (407–396–1668). New inn with beautiful view of Lake Cecile, lounge, game room, pool, elevator service. Has 107 rooms; no pets.

TraveLodge Maingate East. 5711 W. Hwy. 192, Kissimmee, FL 32741 (407–396–4222). 417 rooms, 29 efficiencies. Free shuttle to Disney, game room, lounge, baby sitting service.

Very Economical

Central Motel. 4698 W. Hwy. 192, Kissimmee, FL 32741 (407–396–2333). Pool, cable TV, no pets. Has 50 rooms.

Gemini. 4624 W. Hwy. 192, Kissimmee, FL 32741 (407–396–2151). Pool, 80 rooms. Low season, $24.95; prime time, $49.

Lakeview Inn. 131 N. Orlando Ave., Winter Park, FL 32789 (407–644–1808). On Lake Killarney; pool, shuffleboard. 64 rooms, no pets. Low season, $25; prime time, $32.

Spacecoast Motel. 4125 W. Vine St., Kissimmee, FL 32741 (407–933–5732). Spacecoast has six rooms with Jacuzzis, pool, 50 rooms, no pets.

Budget Chains. **Days Inn.** There are 17 Days Inns in the Orlando area. To reserve a room, you must call the toll-free number (800–325–2525).

Key Motel. 4810 W. Hwy. 192, Kissimmee, FL 32741 (407–396–6200). Next door to Xanadu attraction. 47 rooms, no pets, free shuttle to attractions. Low season $18; prime time $40.

Famous Host. 5859 American Way, Orlando, FL 32809 (407–345–8880). Heated pool, no pets, morning coffee in lobby. Has 192 rooms. Low season, $25; prime time, $49.

Motel 6. 7455 W. Hwy. 192, Kissimmee, FL 32741 (407–396–6422). Single, $22.95, double $28.95. Pool, 140 rooms, small pets. Cable TV. Special rooms for disabled.

Scottish Inn. 4669 W. Hwy. 192, Kissimmee, FL 32741 (407–396–1890). Pool, game room, cable TV. Has 100 rooms; no pets. Low season, $20; prime time, $40. Discount for senior citizens. Attraction tickets available.

Bed-and-Breakfast. A & A of Florida Inc. is a clearinghouse for rate information and room availability for inn and guest houses in the Orlando area. Host homes and establishments are inspected by the company prior to listing. Prices, double occupancy: $35 to $45 standard; $45 to $65 deluxe. Weekly rates usually available. A&A of Florida Inc., Box 1316, Winter Park, FL 32790 (407–628–3233).

Brown's Bed & Breakfast. 529 W. Dartmouth St., Orlando, FL 32804 (407–423–8858). Old-fashioned two-story house with lake view. Small apartment with two rooms, private bath, and small kitchen. Low season, $35; prime time, $45.

The Beaumont House. 206 S. Beaumont Ave., Kissimmee, FL 32741 (407–846–7916). Turn-of-the-century home overlooking Lake Tohopekaliga. Furnished in antiques with original mahogany mantels and fireplaces; formal dining room and country kitchen. Three guest rooms; bath is shared. No pets, no smoking, children under 6 discouraged. Double, $38.

Norment Parry Inn. 211 N. Lucerne Circle, Orlando, FL 32801 (407–648–5188). City's oldest house, recently renovated and reopened with six suites, decorated with antiques. Complimentary bottle of wine, Continental breakfast, fresh flowers. $65.

Houseboats. For a scenic vacation, houseboats are available for rental on the Saint Johns River. Contact *Sunshine Lines* at Holly Bluff Marina near Deland (904–736–9422). Rates are for full or partial week, approximately $125 a day.

HOW TO GET AROUND. From the airport. A taxi to downtown or International Drive averages about $20 plus tip. Most cabs are metered, but check and settle on a price before starting. Call City and Yellow Cab (425–3111), Ace Taxi (859–7514), or White Rose (851–3812). City bus number 11 leaves from the airport for downtown Orlando once an hour on the half hour from the second level at A and B terminals. The cost is 75 cents.

By bus. City buses serve only a limited route and are not adequate for the vacationer's purposes.

By rental car. Driving is the recommended means of getting around Orlando, even if you have to rent a car. Whenever possible, call ahead for a reservation. There are more than 50 rental agencies in the area, but during high season it's sometimes difficult to find a car. All major companies have offices in Orlando International Airport, and many smaller ones are on the airport approach roads. At press time, rates for a subcompact car for one week averaged $79 with unlimited mileage. Many firms allow you to drop a rental car elsewhere in Florida at no extra charge.

The larger car rental firms include *Alamo,* 8200 McCoy Rd., Orlando, FL 32809 (407–855–0210); *Exchange,* 5625 McCoy Rd., Orlando, FL 32809 (407–851–8044); *American International,* 3011 McCoy Rd., Orlando, FL 32812 (407–851–6910); *Avis,* Orlando International Airport (800–331–1212); *Budget Rent-A-Car,* 8855 Rent-a-Car Rd., Orlando, FL 32812 (850–6700); *Enterprise Leasing Co.,* 2901 McCoy Rd., Orlando, FL 32809 (859–2296); *General Rent-A-Car,* 7011 McCoy Rd, Orlando, FL 32812 (859–1340); *Hertz,* Orlando International Airport (800–654–3131); *National Car Rentals,* 3101 McCoy Road, Orlando, FL 32812 (407–857–4848); *National Car Rentals,* 8333 Bear Rd., Orlando, FL 32812 (407–855–4170); and *Superior Rent A Car,* 8000 International Dr., Orlando, FL 32819 (407–352–8171).

Car seats for children are available for rental through K.I.S.S. (407–857–0353). Cost is $15.75 a week; delivery to hotel room is free.

HINTS TO THE MOTORIST. Driving in Orlando can be leisurely or quick. Choose a scenic drive winding through brick-paved streets shaded by oak trees or hop on I-4, which runs from Daytona Beach to Tampa and crosses most of the area's thoroughfares.

Slicing north and south through downtown Orlando is I-4, which runs from Daytona to Tampa. Also in the downtown area is the East-West Expressway, a toll road that carries State Road 50 traffic above the city streets and out of the heavy traffic. Farther south, the Beeline Expressway fronts the airport and connects Cocoa Beach and the east coast areas with I-4. The Florida Turnpike links northwest and central Florida to the southwest and Miami. U.S. 192 runs along the southern edge of the Disney property and passes the main entrance to the Magic Kingdom. Called the Spacecoast Parkway, U.S. 192 has a concentration of motels and campgrounds both east and west of the Disney entrance. It leads east into Kissimmee, crosses the Florida Turnpike, and ends on the beach at Indiatlantic.

Speed limits comply with the federal law (55 mph) and are enforced. Don't park at yellow curbs or in disabled zones. Time limits for airport parking are closely enforced.

TOURIST INFORMATION. For information on the Orlando area and its attractions, the Greater Orlando Chamber of Commerce publishes an annual guide that's free at the chamber's visitors' center at 75 E. Ivanhoe Blvd., Orlando, or $2 on the newsstand. You can write the chamber at Box 1234, Orlando, FL 32802 (407–425–1234).

The Kissimmee/St. Cloud Convention and Visitors Bureau can be reached at Box 2007, Kissimmee, FL 32741 (800–327–9159).

Foreign currency can be exchanged at most major banks including Sun Bank, 200 S. Orange Ave., and most of the Sun Bank branch offices; Barnett Bank, Barnett Plaza, 201 S. Orange Ave., Orlando, and most branch offices; and the foreign currency exchange kiosk in the airport.

HINTS TO DISABLED TRAVELERS. All major Central Florida attractions are equipped for the disabled and have reserved parking. Restrooms and telephones are marked with the international "wheelchair" symbol. *Most* rides have wheelchair acceptability. At Disney World ask for a free pamphlet, "The Disabled Guest."

FREE EVENTS. Three special art festivals are worth a visit: *Winter Park Sidewalk Art Festival* held every March, *Festival of the Masters* at Walt Disney World Shopping Village in November, and the *Autumn Art Festival* on the Rollins College campus in October. A free street fair, *Light Up Orlando,* is held in November, with entertainment, dance programs, food booths, and general merriment after dark. Other free events include:

Recruit Graduation Exercises. A weekly ceremony at the Orlando Naval Training Center featuring a chorus, 50-state flag team, drill team, color guard, and Navy Band. Fri., 9:30 A.M. Take the General Rees Road entrance off Corrine Dr. between Orlando and Winter Park.

Ben White Raceway. Lee Rd. and Edgewater Dr., Orlando. A 125-acre site with two half-mile tracks and a 1-mile track. Horses from as far away as Canada come to trot and pace at the Ben White, known in racing circles as the Colt Capital of the World.

TOURS AND SPECIAL-INTEREST SIGHTSEEING. Downtown walking tour. Starts 10 A.M. every Thurs. in downtown Orlando at the corner of Wall Street Plaza and Orange Ave. Sponsored by Junior League. Free look at historic areas. One hour. Call 843–7463.

Scenic boat tour. One-hour peek into life-style of locally rich and famous on shores of lakes Maitland, Osceola, and Virginia. Launched on Lake Osceola from dock at east end of Morse Boulevard. Historic homes, Rollin College campus, Kraft Azalea Gardens. Tours leave on the half hour 10 A.M.–4:30 P.M. daily except Christmas. Adults, $4.40; children under 12, $2.20; children under 2 free. Call 407–644–4056.

Scenic tour drive. Do-it-yourself tours of historic Orlando and Winter Park. Follow the signs. Both start at Chamber of Commerce. Orlando, 75 E. Ivanhoe Blvd. (425–1234); Winter Park, 150 New York Ave. (644–8281).

Genius drive. Winding dirt road surrounded by orange trees, oaks, and lush foliage. More than 50 peacocks inhabit the 150-acre preserve. Two-mile stretch owned by Winter Park Land Co., open to public noon–6 P.M. Sun. Enter off Osceola Ave. through Henkel Circle or off Lakemont Ave. to Mizell Ave. in Winter Park.

PARKS AND GARDENS. Leu Gardens. Fifty-five-acre botanical garden open 9 A.M.–5 P.M. daily, 1730 N. Forest Ave., Orlando (407–849–2620); adults, $3; children 5 to 11, $1; children 4 and under, free. Hourly guided tours of Leu House, a re-creation of a turn-of-the-century Florida home. Thurs.–Sat., 9 A.M.–3 P.M.; Sun., 1–3:30 P.M.

Wekiva Springs. Swimming in crystal springs, fishing, boating, picnicking, nature trails, canoe rentals. Five miles northeast of Apopka on Wekiva Springs Rd. Open daily 8 A.M.–sunset. $1 driver, 50 cents each additional passenger, under 6 free. Call 407–889–3140.

Kraft Azalea Gardens. Lakeside on Alabama Dr. off Palmer Ave., Winter Park. Thousands of azaleas bloom January through March. Open daylight hours. Free.

Mead Gardens. Subtropical foliage, birds. Off North Mills Ave. at Garden St., Winter Park. Open daylight hours, free.

Turkey Lake Park. About same size as New York City's Central Park. Crisscrossed by 3 miles of bike paths and nature trails. Two white-sand beaches, pool, old Florida-style Cracker farm, five-senses garden paved for wheelchairs with interpretative signs in Braille. Primitive tent camping, $5.35 night; site with water and electricity, $12.84; water, electric, and sewer, $14.98. Off Hiawassee Rd. west of Orlando. Open 9:30 until dusk. Admission, $1 person; under 2 free. Call 407–299–5594.

Lake Fairview Recreational Complex. 23 acres off Lee Rd. and U.S. Highway 441. Boat ramp, dock, picnic tables, grills, concession stand during summer.

BEACHES. Some of the best beaches in Florida are less than an hour away. These include:

Playalinda. One of the state's last unspoiled beaches; the high-water dunes boast more than 700 species of native coastal vegetation. No cars allowed; 20 wooden boardwalks take visitors from parking to the beach. The Florida Park Service offers free programs each summer. Take State Road 50 east to U.S. 1, then State Road 402 east to the ocean.

Daytona. Cars can drive and park on the beach. Lifeguards, fishing pier, boardwalk, concessions, rest rooms, surfing. No alcoholic beverages, glass containers, or pets.

Ponce Inlet. Lifeguards, concessions, and surfing. Alcoholic beverages; no glass containers. Dogs on leash. Driving on beach.

New Smyrna Beach. Lifeguards, rest rooms, concessions, surfing. Alcoholic beverages permitted weekdays only. No pets. Driving on beach permitted.

Cocoa Beach. Surfing, beer only, no pets, no glass containers. Driving on beach prohibited.

PARTICIPANT SPORTS. Central Florida is known as the Bass Fishing Capital of the World. A freshwater fishing license is necessary to take most varieties of fish. Largemouth bass are some of the most famous fish caught in central Florida waters; prime **fishing** months are January through March. Best bass waters include the St. Johns River, Lake Kissimmee, and West Lake Tohopekaliga in Kissimmee.

Tennis. Orlando parks that offer free tennis courts include *Orlando Tennis Center,* downtown at Exposition Park, 15 courts, all lighted (407–849–2161); *Sanlando Park,* Altamonte Springs, 14 courts, all lighted (407–869–5966); and *Red Bug Lake Park,* Casselberry, 10 courts, all lighted (407–695–7113).

Golf. There are 32 courses in the Orlando area. Public courses include *Buena Vista Club,* Lake Buena Vista, 18 holes, 6,273 yards (407–828–3741); *Casselberry Golf Club,* 301 S. Lake Triplet Drive, Casselberry, 18 holes, 6,000 yards (407–699–9310); *Dubsdread Golf & Country Club,* 549 W. Par St., Orlando, 18 holes, 6,917 yards (407–849–2551); *Walt Disney World,* two courses, both approximately 6,500 yards (407–824–2200); and *Winter Park Country Club,* 761 Old England Ave., Winter Park, 9 holes, 2,800 yards (407–644–8195).

Ice skating. *Orlando Ice Skating Palace,* at the corner of John Young Parkway and West Colonial Dr., Parkwood Plaza (407–299–5440) is open year-round. Public skating only at night. Adults, $3.95–$4.95; children 12 and under, $3.45–$4.45. $1.25 skate rental.

Racquetball. Three public facilities offer courts: *Cady Way* in Winter Park (407–644–9860); *Sanlando Park* in Altamonte Springs (407–869–5966); and *Red Bug Lake Park* in Casselberry (407–695–7113).

Sailing and wind surfing. Favorite waters include *Lake Virginia* and the *Butler Chain of Lakes* in Orlando and *Lake Monroe* near Sanford. Sailboat rentals are available at Lake Virginia.

SPECTATOR SPORTS. Football. The annual Citrus Bowl football classic is held each December in Orlando Stadium. For dates and participants, call 849–2107.

Baseball. The *Minnesota Twins* spring training runs from the middle of February through the end of March in Orlando. Beginning the first week of April through August, the *Orlando Twins* play at Tinker Field in Orlando. For ticket information, call 849–6346. The *Kansas City Royals* moved their spring training headquarters to the new Boardwalk and Baseball attraction in 1988. The $8 million baseball complex has a 7,000-seat stadium. Boardwalk and Baseball information, 407–648–5151.

Golf. Orlando hosts several PGA and LPGA events at Disney World courses. Bay Hill Club & Lodge, and the Hyatt Regency Grand Cypress near Lake Buena Vista. For specific dates, call the Chamber of Commerce at 425–1234.

Orlando-Seminole Jai-Alai Fronton, Fern Park on U.S. Highway 17–92, open from September through January, General admission, $1. For a schedule, call 339–9191.

Greyhounds race at two tracks in Orlando: *Sanford-Orlando Kennel Club* in Longwood and *Super Seminole Greyhound Park* in Casselberry. Sanford-Orlando is open December through April; Super Seminole, May through September. General admission to both is $1. Parimutuel betting at both tracks; Sanford-Orlando, (831–1600); Super Seminole, 669–4510.

THEME PARKS. Boardwalk and Baseball. I-4 and U.S. 27 (648–5151). Central Florida's newest attraction. 135-acre park with daily baseball games, amusements, and a memorabilia exhibit in addition to live shows, 30 thrill rides, and a midway. Open 9 A.M.–6 P.M. Mon.–Thurs., 9 A.M.–9 P.M. Fri. and Sun., 9 A.M.–11 P.M. Sat. $16.95 adults; under 48 inches and ages 55 and over, $12.95; under 3, free.

Florida Cypress Gardens. East of Winter Haven off State Road 450 (in Orlando, 813–342–2111). Exotic flowers, waterskiing, ski-ramp jumping, diving and ice-skating shows. Southern Crossroads reproduction of an antebellum town, Animal Forest nature center, Island in the Sky, magic shows, children's rides, hotel, dining facilities, and gift shops. Open 9 A.M.–7 P.M. daily. Ages 12 and over, $15.95; ages 4 to 11, $10.95; ages 3 and under when accompanied by an adult, free.

Gatorland. Just south of Orlando on U.S. 17–92 near Kissimmee. From walkway over lagoon view hundreds of alligators and crocodiles in 35 acres of natural habitat. Wild animals include snakes, flamingos, monkeys, deer, and zebra. Open 8 A.M.–6 P.M. daily with shows at 10:30 A.M., 12:30 P.M., 2:30 P.M., and 4:30 P.M. Age 12 and over, $5; ages 3 to 11, $3.75; age 2 and under, free. Call 407–857–3845.

Sea World. Marine life park featuring Shamu the killer whale, Baby Shamu, dolphin, seal, and walrus shows, feeding pools, World of the Sea Aquarium, Cap'n Kids World playground, and Atlantis Theater waterski show. Open 8:30 A.M.–10 P.M. daily. Located at 7007 Sea World Drive off the Bee Line Expressway at Interstate 4 southwest of Orlando. Admission: $21; children 3–11; $18; children under 3, free. Call 407–351–0021.

SeaEscape. One day cruises off Florida's east coast with meals, entertainment, and casino. Departs 10 A.M. Tues., Wed., and Thurs. from Port Canaveral, returns 10 P.M. $79 adults, $49 ages 12–17, $29 ages 11 and under. Call 800–432–0900; out-of-state call 800–327–7400.

Silver Springs. One mile east of Ocala on State Road 40 (904–236–1212). Glass-bottom boats, deer park, jungle cruise, reptile institute, and antique car collection. Open 9 A.M.–5:30 P.M. daily. Age 12 and over, $12.95; ages 3 to 11, $8.50; age 2 and under free.

Walt Disney World. With the Magic Kingdom's 45 major adventures divided into six lands: Main Street USA, Tomorrowland, Fantasyland, Adventureland, Liberty Square, and Frontierland. Hours change monthly, but park usually opens at 9 A.M. One-day pass: adults, $28; ages 3 to 9, $22; three-day pass: adults, $78; ages 3 to 9, $63; for age 2 and under free. **Epcot Center** is Disney World's showcase of technology and foreign cultures. Usually open 9 A.M.–9 P.M. daily. Ticket prices same as Magic Kingdom (three-day passes good for both parks). Call 407–824–4321.

Wet 'n Wild. 6200 International Dr. (407–351–3200). Twenty-five acres of activities handy for families staying on the International Drive area. Water flumes and slides, whirlpools, swimming, boats, and ski-tow rides. Adults, $13.50; ages 3 to 12, $11.50; age 2 and under free.

Xanadu. Intersection of State Road 535 and U.S. Hwy. 192, Kissimmee (407–396–1992). Dome-shaped prototype home showcasing the latest technological and electronic advancements. Open 10 A.M.–10 P.M. daily. Adults, $4.75; ages 4 to 17, $3.50; ages 3 and under free.

MUSEUMS AND GALLERIES. Many of the area's finest museums and galleries are in suburban Winter Park, but Disney's power has brought some of the world's best traveling collections to Epcot Center's Japanese, Chinese, and Mexican pavilions.

Beal-Maltbie Shell Museum. Rollins College, Winter Park (646–2364). Vast collection of shells from around the world. Open Mon.–Fri., 10 A.M.–4 P.M. Adults, $1; children, 50 cents.

Center Street Gallery. 136 Park Ave., S., Winter Park (644–1545). Works by gallery artists. Mon.–Sat., 9:30 A.M.–5:30 P.M. Free.

Crealde Art Center Gallery. 600 St. Andrews Blvd., Winter Park (671–1886). Gallery and art school. Mon.–Sat., 10 A.M.–4 P.M. Free.

Orlando Museum of Art. Loch Haven Park, off North Mills Rd. at Princeton Ave. (896–4321). Houses permanent collection of pre-Columbian, African, and twentieth-century American art; hosts traveling collections. Admission free except for special exhibits. Gift shop. Tues.–Fri., 10 A.M.–5 P.M.; Sat. and Sun., noon–5 P.M.

Maitland Art Center. 231 W. Packwood Ave., Maitland (645–2181). Center resembles a Mayan temple; exhibits vary throughout the year. Admission $3, $2 seniors and students. Gift shop. Tues.–Fri., 10 A.M.–4 P.M.; Sat.–Sun., 1–4 P.M.

Morse Museum of American Art. 133 E. Welbourne Ave., Winter Park (645–5311). Tiffany windows, pottery, and vases; traveling exhibits. Tues.–Sat. 9:30 A.M.–4 P.M.; Sun., 1–4 P.M. Adults, $2.50; students and children, $1.

Orlando Science Center. Loch Haven Park off North Mills St. at Princeton Ave. (896–7151). A museum and planetarium with exhibits on astronomy, health, science, and history. Adults, $4; children under 18 and seniors, $3. Mon.–Thurs. 9 A.M.–5 P.M.; Fri. 9 A.M.–9 P.M.; Sat. noon–9 P.M.; Sun. noon–5 P.M.

Pine Castle Center of the Arts. 6015 Randolph St., Orlando (407–855–7761). Old Florida exhibits. 10 A.M.–5 P.M. Tues.–Fri., 10 A.M.–2 P.M. Sat.

Elvis Presley Museum. Over 300 items that once belonged to Elvis. Daily, 9 A.M.–10 P.M. 5931 American Way off International Drive, Orlando. Adults, $4; ages 7 to 12, $3; age 6 and under free. Call 407–345–8860.

FILM. Orlando is home of the "dollar movie" theater, where second-runs are shown in a theater with tables and chairs instead of traditional theater seating row by row, and serving beer, wine, and snacks.

Aloma Cinema 'n' Drafthouse. Aloma Shopping Center, half mile west of State Road 436, Winter Park (671–4964).

Conway Movie Pitcher Co. 4446 Curry Ford Road, Orlando (282–3456).

Enzian Theater. 1300 S. Orlando Ave., Maitland (629–1088). Foreign films and American classics. Admission, $3.

MUSIC. Orlando is home for the **Florida Symphony Orchestra,** the state's only full-time professional orchestra. Home for the symphony is the Bob Carr Performing Arts Centre, but its outdoor concerts, usually free to the public, are not to be missed. For times and dates, call the symphony at 896–0331.

Orlando Opera Company. Presents four major operas each season, usually in November, December, January, and March, at the Bob Carr Performing Arts Centre. Ticket prices are steep because most star international operatic talent. For information, call 896–7664.

The Bach Festival of Winter Park is an annual program of choral compositions of Bach and other famous composers. A full week of acclaimed chamber music in February and March at Rollins College. Most events are sold out before tickets are available publicly; in recent years some free events have been added. For information, call 646–2110.

DANCE. Southern Ballet Theatre. Orlando's only professional dance company. Performances, usually three a season, are at the Bob Carr Performing Arts Centre. For information, call 628–0133.

STAGE. Zev Bufman Broadway Theater Series at the Bob Carr Performing Arts Centre brings traveling Broadway shows, many with major talent. Five productions each season beginning in December. Tickets $21.50 to $29.50. For information, call 843–1512.

King Henry's Feast is Medieval entertainment with comedy, musicians, jesters, jugglers, and singing and dancing. Five-course dinner with unlimited beer and wine is served throughout the evening. Dinner shows 8 P.M. daily. 8984 International Drive, Orlando, $22.95 adults, $14.95 children 3–11. For reservations, call 407–351–5151.

It's Louisiana cooking for a four-course, family-style dinner at **Mardi Gras** on International Drive, 7:30 P.M. daily. 8445 International Drive, Orlando. Dinner and show $22.95 adults, $14.95 children 3 to 11. For reservations, call 407–351–5151.

Fort Liberty. 5620 W. Hwy. 192, Kissimmee. Features a Wild West show and dinner with fried chicken, roast pork, and hot apple pie. $22.95 adults, $14.95 children 3 to 11. For reservations call 407–351–5151.

Medieval Times. Knights in armor compete in jousting matches and medieval tournament games while visitors eat a four-course dinner in a European-style castle. Castle opens at 5:45 P.M. for 7 P.M. dinner show daily; dinner and show cost $25 for adults and $17 for ages 3 to 11; free for age 2 and under. U.S. Highway 192, Kissimmee. For information, call 407–239–0214.

SHOPPING. Orlando is a shopper's dream. The choices extend from the unique world-class shopping offered at Walt Disney World Village, to the quaint boutiques of Winter Park, to the new Florida Mall with its own attached hotel or the bargains at the Factory Outlet complex. Although there is no Macy's or Saks, the quality is matched under different names. There is a 5 percent sales tax.

Outlets. *Dansk,* 7000 International Drive, importers of contemporary Danish glassware, stainless steel, teak, and pottery. *Belz Factory Outlet Mall* on West Oakridge Rd. (off International Dr.) is popular with bargain hunters. The same end of the street has several other centers with merchandise from Corning to Mikasa to Pfaltzgraf.

Old Town on U.S. Hwy. 192 in Kissimmee (one mile east of I-4) is a re-creation of an old Florida town with shopping, restaurants, and a great old-fashioned carousel for the kids.

Discount Shopping. Some of the country's leading off-price retailers have opened stores in the Orlando area. *TJ Maxx* is in Interstate Mall on State Road 436 in Altamonte Springs; *Ashby's* is on State Road 436 in Ashby Square; *Marshall's* and *Stein Mart* are on the same busy stretch of highway.

Outdoor markets. For everything from a haircut to house plants, *Flea World* on U.S. 17–92 north of Orlando is the place to bargain. This 33-acre playground is open Friday, Saturday, and Sunday 8 A.M.–5 P.M. Admission and parking are free. The area is covered and paved. If it's fresh produce and baked goods you're looking for, don't miss the *Winter Park Farmer's Market* in the depot at New England and New York streets. Open year-round Saturdays, 8 A.M.–2 P.M.

DINING OUT. To eat cheap in Orlando, the best suggestion is to stick with ethnic foods. International Drive has every fast food imaginable, but if you want cheap eats besides a hamburger, best suggestions are Cuban, barbecue, and fresh seafood.

Categories, based on the price of a meal for one, without beverage, tip, or tax, are as follows: *Reasonable,* $7 to $10; *Very Economical,* $4 to $7; *Low Budget,* under $4. Unless otherwise noted, all restaurants accept some if not all major credit cards. Most accept traveler's checks; few accept personal checks.

Reasonable

Alfredo's. Italy pavilion, Epcot Center, Walt Disney World. Make reservations when you first come into Epcot Center. You'll find the original Fettuccine Alfredo here. Beer and wine.

Beijing. 19 N. Orange Ave., Orlando (423–2522). Mon.–Fri., 11 A.M.–11 P.M.; Sat., noon–11 P.M.; Sun., 1–10 P.M. Chinese restaurant downtown. The lines grow long at lunchtime. Beer and wine.

Buckets. 1825 N. Mills Ave., Orlando (894–5197). 11 A.M.–midnight Sun.–Thurs., 11 A.M.–2 A.M. Fri. and Sat. Great for late-night, up-scale food. Mahogany and brass give this restaurant the feel of a luxurious cruise ship. Full bar.

China Garden. 118 S. Semoran Blvd., Winter Park (671–2120). Mon.–Thurs. 11 A.M.–10 P.M.; Fri.–Sat., 11:30 A.M.–11 P.M.; Sun., 4–10 P.M. Cantonese, Mandarin, and Szechwan in award-winning style.

Ming Garden. Across from the Holiday Inn on International Dr. (352–8044). Open 11 A.M.–11 P.M. seven days a week. Mandarin, Szechwan, Hunan, Shanghai, and Cantonese cooking. The lines get long here. Full bar.

Shells. 852 Lee Rd., Orlando (628–3968). 5–10P.M. Sun.–Thurs., 5–11 P.M. Fri. and Sat. Beer and wine. No credit cards. Fresh seafood, lobster specials on Tues.

South Seas Seafood Restaurant. 3001 Curry Ford Rd., Orlando (898–8331). 11 A.M.–10 P.M. Sun.–Thurs., 11 A.M.–11 P.M. Fri. and Sat. Fresh seafood. Beer and wine.

Very Economical

Chastain's. 23 N. Orange Blossom Trail, Orlando (843–2900). 5:30 A.M.–3 P.M. Mon.–Sat. Down-home cooking. Beer. No credit cards.

Chesapeake Crab House. 1700 N. Orlando Ave., Maitland (831–0442). Open 5:30–10 P.M. daily except Sun. Frequented by local residents who go there for the blue crab and cold beer. No credit cards.

Holiday House. 2037 Lee Road, Orlando (283–4930); 1522 S. Orange Ave., Orlando (425–1521); 2203 Aloma Ave., Winter Park (671–6181). Mon.–Sat., 11 A.M.–2:30 P.M. and 4–9 P.M. Inexpensive dinner buffet.

Lee & Rick's. 5621 Old Winter Garden Road, Orlando (293–3587); and 1601 S. Orlando Ave., Maitland. Hours vary at each location. Raw oysters. Full bar.

Luigi's. 1800 Lee Rd., Orlando (298–3832). Mon.–Thrus., 11 A.M.–11 P.M.; Fri.–Sat., 11 A.M.–midnight, Italian dishes, terrific pizza. Beer and wine.

Olive Garden. General Mills chain with several locations in Central Florida. Check the telephone directory. Homemade pasta. Full bar. Major credit cards.

Po Folks. 440 S. Semoran Blvd., Orlando (281–6696). Open 11 A.M.–10 P.M. daily. Heavy-duty home cooking: fried chicken, country steak and gravy, biscuits. No credit cards.

Spicy Pot. 1442 N. Pine Hills Rd., Orlando (297–8255). 11 A.M.–8 P.M. Tues.–Thurs., 11 A.M.–9 P.M. Fri. and Sat. Caribbean cooking by a family from Trinidad. Beer and wine. No credit cards.

Tandoor Indian Bistro. 7451 International Dr., Orlando (352–7887). Outstanding Indian cuisine.

B's Diner. 1210 Nebraska St., Orlando (896–6746). Excuse the surroundings, because this is the best barbecue in the city. Beer, except Sun. Mon.–Thurs., 6 A.M.–9 P.M.; Fri.–Sat., 6 A.M.–10 P.M.; Sun., 7 A.M.–9 P.M. No credit cards.

Paco's. 1801 W. Fairbanks Ave., Winter Park (629–0149). Mon.–Fri., 11:30 A.M.–3 P.M.; dinner served 5–9:30 P.M. Mon.–Thurs., 5–10 P.M. Fri.–Sat. Orlando's most authentic Mexican food. Beer and wine. No credit cards.

Skeeter's. 1212 Lee Road, Orlando (298–7973). Open 24 hours. The place to go for breakfast. No credit cards.

Cuban Food in Orlando is cheap and reliable. Try the black beans and yellow rice or a Cuban sandwich at almost any restaurant. Six good restaurants follow:

El Bohio Cafe. 5756 Dahlia Drive, Orlando (282–1723). Open 11 A.M.–9 P.M. daily except Mon. No credit cards.

Jose's Sandwich Shop. 517 E. Michigan St., Orlando (423–2451). Open 9 A.M.–6 P.M. daily except Sun. Beer and wine. No credit cards.

La Lechonera. 2420 Curry Ford Road, Orlando (894–6711). Open 11 A.M.–10:30 P.M. daily. Beer and wine. No credit cards.

Medina's Cafe. 2406 E. Washington St., Orlando (894–2206). Open 11 A.M.–10 P.M. daily except Sun. Beer and wine. No credit cards.

Numero Uno. 2499 S. Orange Ave., Orlando (841–3840). Open 11 A.M.–9:30 P.M. daily except Weds. Major credit cards. Beer and wine.

Vega's Cafe. 1835 E. Colonial Drive, Orlando (898–5196). Open 10 A.M.–5 P.M. Mon.–Fri., 10 A.M.–3 P.M. Sat. No credit cards.

Recommended Splurge. If you couldn't get reservations at Alfredo's in the Italy pavilion at Epcot Center, call **Christini's.** Chris Christini opened the Epcot Center restaurant, and his cozy place in the Marketplace on Sand Lake Road serves Continental Italian cuisine, with specialties like fettuccine àla Christini and lobster fra diavolo. If you want something special, call ahead and Mr. Christini will grant your wish. Full bar. Call 407–345–8770. Dinner 6 P.M.–midnight daily.

NIGHTLIFE AND BARS. For most visitors to Orlando, nightlife is secondary because there's an overload of attractions during the daylight hours. Still, there's no shortage of things to do after dark.

If you've promised yourself only one night out, make it at **Church St. Station** in downtown Orlando (at Church St. and I-4). This restored area houses **Rosie O'Grady's Goodtime Emporium,** a restaurant, disco, easy-listening courtyard, and across the street, the **Cheyenne Saloon & Opera House,** with live country bands, clogging, and three stories of memorabilia, and **Bumby Arcade,** with the new Orchid Garden Ballroom, Crackers oyster bar and wine cellar. Admission to the complex is $7.95; it's open 11 A.M.–2 A.M. daily. Before 5 P.M., admission is free.

One of Orlando's best comedy clubs is **Bonkerz** at 4315 N. Orange Blossom Trail (298–2665). Local and national comedians; call for times and performers.

For country-and-western, try **Sullivan's Trailway Lounge,** 1108 S. Orange Blossom Trail, Orlando (843–2934). Live band from 9 P.M. Mon.–Sat. Also, try the **Cheyenne Saloon,** 129 W. Church St., in Church Street Station (422–2434). Live music nightly.

Happy Hours

Sumptuous buffets and discount drinks are regular Happy-Hour fare instead of the old two-for-one rule. Here's a partial listing of some of the best:

Villa Nova. 839 N. Orlando Ave., Winter Park (647–4477). Free hors d'oeuvres and reduced price drinks 5–7 P.M. in the Cheek to Cheek to Lounge.

JJ Whispers. 5100 Adanson St., Orlando (629–4779). Hot and cold hors d'oeuvres, reduced drink prices 4:30–8 P.M. Tues.–Fri. Thursday is Ladies' Night with 75 cent drinks, no cover charge. Tuesday male revue.

Bowties. Altamonte Springs Hilton, 350 S. North Lake Blvd., Altamonte Springs (830–1985). Happy hour 4–7 P.M. seven days a week; sumptuous free buffet 4–8 P.M.

Laughing Kookabura. Buena Vista Palace, Lake Buena Vista (827–3520). Enjoy free hors d'oeuvres 5–8 P.M. Mon.–Fri. in one of Orlando's most elegant hotels.

Bars

Bailey's. 118 W. Fairbanks Ave., Winter Park. This neighborhood bar near the Rollins College campus has a daily Happy Hour 4:30–6:30 when all drinks are discounted; Wednesday night all drinks for women in the bar's Crocodile Club are discounted; Thursday night there's free champagne for women in the Crocodile Club. Dress is casual.

Park Avenue. 4315 N. Orange Blossom Trail (295–3750). This is Orlando's best-known disco, with a powerful sound system and a flair for promotions. Monday and Wednesday are "Spit" nights with New Wave music (and dress). Admission, $3. No blue jeans.

Giraffe Lounge. Hotel Royal Plaza, Lake Buena Vista (828–2828). This is the favorite spot for the younger Disney crowd. Top 40 music seven days a week. From 4–9:30 P.M. drinks are two for one, and there's free hors d'oeuvres. Ladies' Night is Wednesday with two-for-one drinks from 9:30 P.M. till closing. Dress is eclectic but casual.

Live Music

Cheek to Cheek. Villa Nova, 839 N. Orlando Ave., Winter Park (647–4477). From 9 P.M. nightly except Sunday.

Lil Darlin's Rock 'n' Roll Palace. 5770 Space Coast Parkway, Kissimmee (396–6499). Open 11 A.M. daily. Shows Monday through Saturday, 8:30 and 10:30 P.M. with well-known musicians from the '50s, '60s, and '70s.

Village Lounge. Walt Disney World Shopping Village, lake Buena Vista (828–3830). Jazz from 6:30 P.M. nightly.

SECURITY. Orlando and the amusement parks are very safe. The only security problem has been occasional break-ins at hotels. Although most hotels have safes (where you should leave your valuables) and adequate security, it is best not to travel with valuables and never to leave them in your room. Exercise reasonable caution and be sure to lock your car in parking lots.

PHILADELPHIA

by
Joyce Eisenberg

Joyce Eisenberg is a free-lance writer and editor whose travel and feature articles have appeared in local and national publications. She is editor of the Delaware Valley edition of Travelhost *magazine and area editor of* Fodor's Guide to Philadelphia.

Philadelphia is a city of charming contradictions. Its most beloved musical groups are the world-famous Philadelphia Orchestra, which performs at the opulent, dignified Academy of Music on Broad Street, and the sequined and feathered Mummers string bands, which on New Year's Day strut and prance along that same street. It's city nationally known by gourmets for its sophisticated new cuisine and praised by locals for the quality of its "junk" food: cheese steaks, hoagies, and soft pretzels with mustard. The city's residents include descendants of the staid Quaker founding fathers, the self-possessed socialities of the Main Line, and the sports fans who have reportedly booed the Easter Bunny when their teams have failed them.

Although Philadelphia is the fifth largest city in the nation with close to 1.7 million people, it has maintained the feel of a friendly small town. It's a cosmopolitan, exciting, but not overwhelming city, a town that's easy to explore but big enough to keep surprising even those most familiar with it.

City planners have pegged Philadelphia as a very livable city. The same features that keep the native-born in residence—neighborhood spirit, nationally prominent cultural institutions, a respect for its history, excellent restaurants, scenic public parks, and a manageable cost of living—make a vacation here pleasant for the visitor.

There are three aspects of the city that all visitors should sample: its history, its cultural attractions, and its neighborhoods. (There are 109 by one count, but we'll just pick a few.)

Philadelphia was the birthplace of the nation, the home of the first government. The spirit of the early days is palpable along the cobbled streets and in the red-brick Georgian buildings in the city's historic district, which spans from the Delaware River west to about 6th Street.

Most of the sites that played an important role in that history are clustered in Independence National Historical Park, known as America's most historic square mile. Administered by the National Park Service, the park includes 42 acres and close to 40 buildings. If you have just one day to sightsee, put this at the top of your list.

Like most of the city, this area is best explored on foot. The place to orient yourself is at the Visitor Center, 3d and Chestnut streets, where you can get a map of the park's important sites and some tips on what to see if your time is limited. Then hurry over to Independence Hall to get a place at the head of the classes of schoolchildren who've come to tour one of our nation's most precious gems. The hall, built in 1732, was where Thomas Jefferson's eloquent Declaration of Independence was signed and where later the Constitution was adopted.

The Liberty Bell, which hung in the belfry of Independence Hall since 1753, was moved to a glass pavilion on Independence Mall north of the Hall in 1976, during the Bicentennial celebration. The bell fulfilled the words of its inscription when it rang to "proclaim liberty throughout all the land unto all the inhabitants thereof," beckoning Philadelphians to the State House Yard to hear the first reading of the Declaration of Independence. The underground museum at Franklin Court, once the site of Ben Franklin's home, is an imaginative tribute to the Renaissance man. You can dial-a-quote to hear his thoughts and pick up a telephone and call his contemporaries to find out what they really thought of him. (For more information, see Historic Sites.)

Old City, the neighborhood north of Market Street and Independence National Historical Park, was always "the other side of the tracks." Its earliest residents were a strict sect of William Penn's followers called "stiff Quakers." South of Market, in Society Hill, lived the "World's People," the wealthier Anglicans who arrived after Penn and who loved music and dancing—pursuits the Quakers shunned. Society Hill's southern neighbor, Southwark, contained the modest dwellings of artisans and craftsmen. Today, many homes in these three areas have been lovingly restored by young professionals who began moving to the city 15 to 20 years ago, stemming the tide of urban decay. Inspired urban renewal efforts have transformed vast empty spaces into airy lofts; colonial houses have been rehabbed and charming courtyards rediscovered. As a result, these areas are not just showcases for historic churches and mansions but living, breathing neighborhoods.

Seeing some sights in Old City will complete your picture of colonial Philadelphia. Christ Church, an architectural gem, was the only Anglican church in the city for at least half a century; 15 signers of the Declaration of Independence worshiped here, and Ben Franklin lies in its burial ground. Elfreth's Alley, the oldest continuously occupied residential street in the country, offers a glimpse of what much of colonial Philadelphia looked like.

One of the most famous residents of this neighborhood was Betsy Ross, who is credited with sewing the first Stars and Stripes. Her authentically furnished home is a top tourist attraction. Nearby is the Friend's Meeting House, a Quaker building of simple lines, in keeping with their faith. Penn's life and achievements are depicted in exhibits within.

Society Hill was—and still is—Philadelphia's showplace. It is a fashionable residential district where beautifully preserved colonial, Georgian, and Federal homes are interspersed with some historically relevant and just plain fun tourist attractions, such the Powel and Hill-Physick-Keith houses, the Perelman Antique Toy Museum, and numerous old churches. The area is well marked with signs for self-guided tours. On a leisurely stroll here, you'll stumble upon an occasional hitching post, wrought-iron foot scrapers, exquisite ironwork on railings and balconies, and delightful gardens. At 2d and Pine streets is Head House Square, a colonial marketplace that is the site of the Head House Crafts Fair on summer weekends.

Between 6th Street and the Delaware River are three other areas worth exploring. Penn's Landing, the several-block-long riverfront promenade running from Market Street to South Street, is a popular spot for concerts, festivals, and sunning. Permanent attractions include the Port of History Museum, several historic ships turned floating museum, and the Moshulu, a sailing ship that is now a maritime museum and restaurant (have a drink at their topside bar and watch the traffic on the Delaware, one of the world's largest freshwater ports). By 1989 a $50-million waterfront complex of shops, restaurants, outdoor cafés, and movie theaters will be completed.

South Street, the dividing line between Society Hill and Southwark, is where you'll see Philadelphia at its funkiest. The city's Greenwich Village, it is an eclectic, artsy strip (from Front Street to about 8th Street) of antique shops, bookstores, galleries, trendy boutiques, cafés, and many of the restaurants that began the city's restaurant renaissance. One of Philadelphia's liveliest late night spots, South Street is great for people watching.

Across from Independence Mall is the Bourse, a magnificently restored Victorian commodities exchange now filled with the exclusive boutiques of Saint Laurent, Howard Heartsfield, and Cacharel. On the top floor are ethnic eateries.

The mile-long Benjamin Franklin Parkway, which stretches from City Hall to the Philadelphia Museum of Art, is the city's museum row. There may be more cultural attractions per square foot here than along any boulevard in the world. The parkway was designed by French architects to be the city's Champs-Elysées, a broad street lined with fountains, trees, sculpture, and flags of many nations.

To explore the parkway and Fairmount Park just beyond, your best bet is to head to the Visitor Center at 1525 John F. Kennedy Boulevard for a map and to pick up the Fairmount Park Trolley bus, which stops at all the museums and many sites in the park.

Surrounding Logan Circle are the Academy of Natural Sciences, the oldest institution of its kind in America, best known for its displays of stuffed animals in their natural habitats, dinosaurs, birds, and extinct and endangered species, and the Franklin Institute Science Museum and Planetarium. The latter, the national memorial to Ben Franklin, is as stimulating and imaginative as was its namesake. A gigantic walk-through human heart and energy and aviation halls delight children and adults.

Nearby is the Rodin Museum, which houses a priceless collection of the sculptor's originals and castings and the largest exhibition of his works outside the Musée Rodin in Paris. Crowning the parkway, atop a hill, sits the Greco-Roman temple known as the Philadelphia Museum of Art. Ranked among the world's major art museums, it is Philadelphia's cultural highlight. Its collections include American crafts, furniture, and glass; Renaissance treasures; twentieth-century art; and architectural acquisitions such as a Hindu temple, a medieval cloister, and a Chinese Buddhist temple hall.

Beyond the museum is Fairmount Park, the largest landscaped city park in the world. The park offers something for everybody: historic mansions furnished with period pieces, an authentic Japanese house, Victorian boathouses strung along Kelly Drive, the Philadelphia Zoo, hiking and biking trails, picnic areas, and amphitheaters for summer concerts. (The Philadelphia Orchestra performs free in the summer at the Mann Music Center.)

Other important attractions sit in the shadow of City Hall. John Wanamaker's, one of the first of the grand department stores, with Tuscan columns and mosaic walls, offers self-guided walking tours. The Reading Terminal Market is a still-active 19th-century European-style marketplace. A few blocks north is the Pennsylvania Academy of the Fine Arts, housed in a gingerbready Victorian building that is itself a masterpiece, the work of Philadelphia architect Frank Furness. Inside are masterworks by American painters such as Charles Willson Peale, Benjamin West, and Thomas Eakins as well as more contemporary works.

The midtown area, stretching along Broad Street and the blocks east and west, is a mix of residential, business, and cultural institutions. Here are some of the city's finest hotels and restaurants, its most exclusive stores and private clubs, and its theaters. Many performing arts groups proudly call the Academy of Music, known as the Grand Dame of Broad Street, home; the opulent hall was modeled after the La Scala Opera House in Milan.

Rittenhouse Square, near 18th and Walnut, is the city's most fashionable address; accordingly, the city's most fashionable shops decorate the streets surrounding the square. You can peek inside one of the city's grand homes, dating from 1860, when you visit the Rosenbach Museum and Library. The treasures here include antique English furnishings, paintings, silver, and more than 30,000 rare books and manuscripts, including the original of James Joyce's *Ulysses* and Chaucer's *Canterbury Tales.*

Although Philadelphia has hotels that charge $150 a night and restaurants from which you can't escape for less than $100 for two, the vast majority of delights are affordable. Most of the historic attractions are free; museum admission prices are low (free on certain days); free music festivals abound; and strolling and exploring, the best pastimes for tourists, don't cost a cent. At times you can sample even the high-priced pleasures without denting your pocketbook. Luxury hotels dramatically lower their rates when businessmen on expense accounts go home on weekends; car rentals halve their prices at the same time. Restaurants offer greatly reduced early bird specials, and the Philadelphia Orchestra performs free during the summers.

After a few days in town, you'll discover what the residents already know and have kept a secret: Philadelphia is a very pleasant place to live and visit, a city with an impressive past and a promising future.

PRACTICAL INFORMATION

WHEN TO GO. Philadelphia has four distinct seasons, with temperatures ranging from the upper eighties to below freezing. It can be uncomfortably hot and humid in the summer and blustery in the winter, leaving the mild late spring and early fall as the ideal times to visit in terms of weather. But as William Penn noted 300 years ago, the city's weather "often changeth without notice, and is constant almost in its inconstancy."

Ultimately, any time is right for a visit, for there are special pleasures throughout the year. Summer, the most popular tourist season, is highlighted by the July 4 Freedom Festival, which celebrates the nation's birth and Philadelphia's role in it with hot-air balloon races, restaurant extravaganzas, and special ceremonies. The world-renowned Philadelphia Orchestra gives free summer concerts at the Mann Music Center. In winter, the highlight is the spectacular Mummers Parade on New Year's

Day and a calendar of orchestra, theater, and ballet performances. In spring, a city blooming with cherry blossoms and azaleas welcomes visitors at Open House Tours. Fall brings Super Sunday, a giant block party; parades; and the Army-Navy football classic.

HOW TO GET THERE. In the past 10 years, Philadelphia has dramatically improved its airport and train terminals. A new, much-needed international air terminal now under construction should be open by 1989.

By bus. *Greyhound Lines* has acquired *Trailways,* and the combined company now operates out of a sparkling new terminal at 10th and Filbert sts., just north of the Gallery at Market East (215–568–4800). The terminal also serves *N.J. Transit's* Jersey shore buses.

By air. Philadelphia International Airport, in the southwest section of Philadelphia, about eight miles from Center City, is served by many airlines, including *American, Continental, Delta, Eastern, Mexicana, Northwest Orient, Pan American, Piedmont, TWA, USAir,* and *United.*

By train. Philadelphia is served by *Amtrak,* which operates rail service along the busy Northeast Corridor stretching from Boston to Washington. Intercity service is also provided to many points south and west as well as to Montreal. By train, Philadelphia is less than 90 minutes from New York City and 2 hours from Washington, D.C. Amtrak's *Metroliner,* which runs between Washington and New York, costs almost twice what an express train costs and saves very little time.

Amtrak pulls into 30th Street Station at 30th and Market streets. To reach the center of the city, show your Amtrak ticket stub and (for free) board a local train to Suburban Station at 16th St. and John F. Kennedy Blvd. (close to major hotels) or the Market Street East Station at 10th and Market streets (closer to the historical area). Phone 215–824–1600 for Amtrak information.

By car. The major route into Philadelphia from the north or south is I-95. Because there is no Center City exit northbound, motorists coming from the airport should follow 291 north to I-76 west to Vine St. From the west, the Pennsylvania Turnpike runs from Pittsburgh to Valley Forge and enters Philadelphia as the Schuylkill Expressway (I-76), which has several exits in the downtown area. Extensive repairs of the Schuylkill Expressway will drag on until at least Thanksgiving of 1989. To avoid delays, call the expressway hotline at 800–672–7600. From the east, the New Jersey Turnpike and I-295 provide easy access to either U.S. 30 or New Jersey State Road 42, both of which lead to the city's downtown area. For maps and route information, AAA members can call Philadelphia's Keystone Auto Club at 215–569–4321. Their emergency road service number is 215–569–4411.

TELEPHONES. The area code for Philadelphia and the surrounding counties (Bucks, Chester, Delaware, and Montgomery) is 215. You don't need to dial the area code if it is the same as the one from which you are calling. When calling long distance, dial 1 before the area code and 7-digit number. For person-to-person, credit-card, and collect calls, dial 0 for operator assistance. Within the city, directory assistance is 555–1212; from outside the city, dial 215–555–1212. Directory information for toll-free numbers can be obtained by calling 800–555–1212. Pay telephones within the Philadelphia area cost 25 cents.

Emergency Telephone Numbers. In the Philadelphia area, the emergency number for fire, police, ambulance and paramedics is 911, or dial 0 for operator and ask for help in being connected immediately with the appropriate agency. The suicide prevention number is 686–4420. The Poison Information Center can be reached at 386–2100; the Rape Hotline is 922–3434.

ACCOMMODATIONS. Philadelphia has over 10,000 rooms to satisfy a variety of budgets and tastes; unfortunately, the large majority are clustered in the expensive and deluxe categories. What follows are those hotels and motels which offer good value—comfort, cleanliness, and some extra features—for reasonable prices. Some are in Center City, and others are near the airport or at the City Line exit of the Schuylkill Expressway. Although downtown hotels are slightly more expensive, you can save money by not renting a car. Price categories are based on double occupancy, as follows: *Reasonable,* $80 to $100; *Economical,* $65 to $80; *Very Eco-*

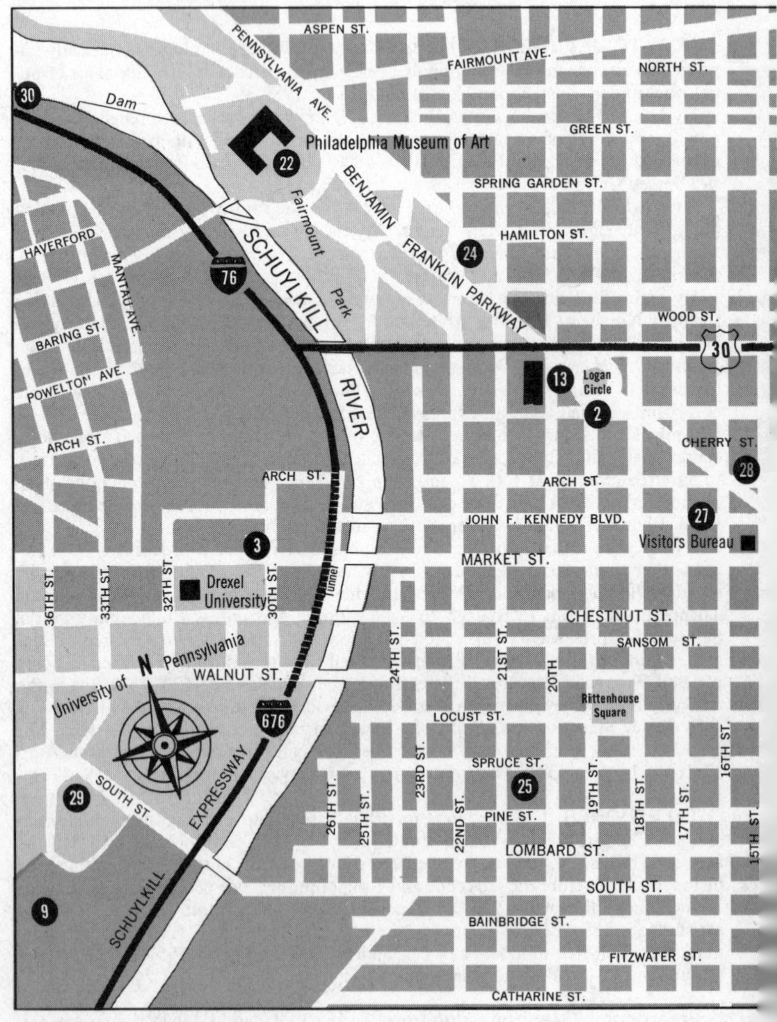

Points of Interest

1) Academy of Music
2) Academy of Natural Sciences
3) Amtrak 30th Street Station
4) Betsy Ross House
5) The Bourse
6) Chinatown
7) City Hall
8) Christ Church
9) Convention Hall/Civic Center
10) Edgar Allan Poe National Historic Site
11) Elfreth's Alley
12) Franklin Court
13) Franklin Institute Science Museum
14) Gallery at Market East/Market Street East Station
15) Greyhound-Trailways Station
16) Independence Hall
17) Independence National Historical Park Visitor Center

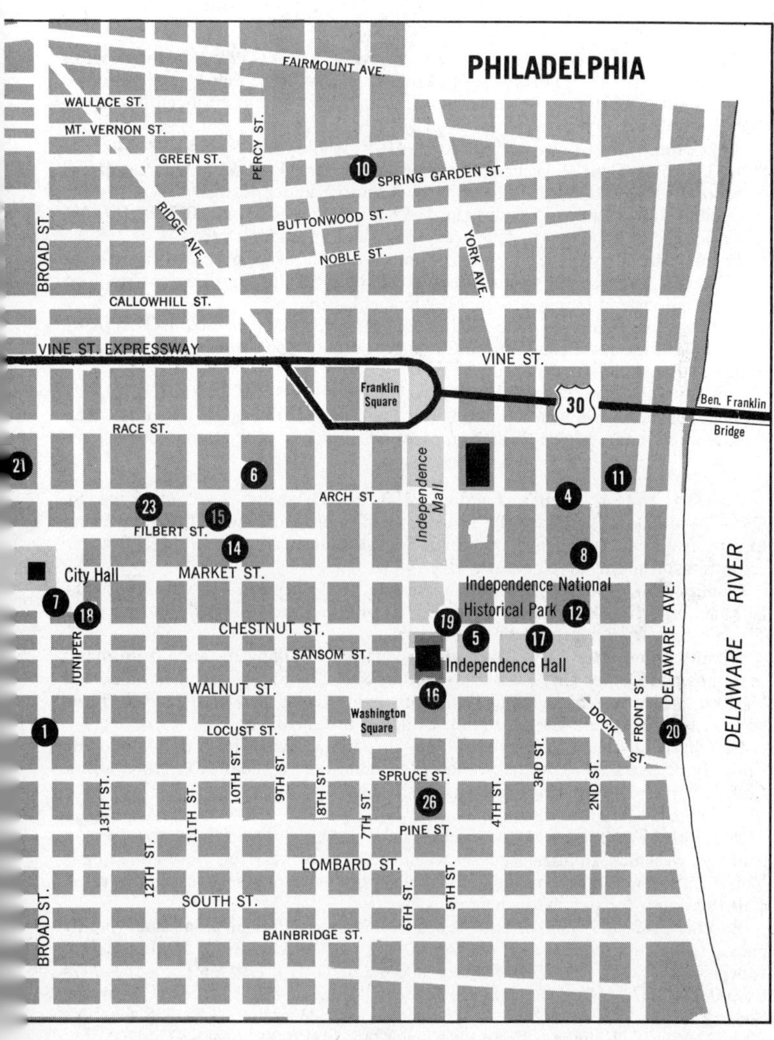

18) John Wanamaker
19) Liberty Bell
20) Penn's Landing
21) Pennsylvania Academy of the Fine Arts
22) Philadelphia Museum of Art
23) Reading Terminal Market
24) Rodin Museum
25) Rosenbach Museum and Library
26) Society Hill
27) Suburban Station
28) Convention and Visitors Bureau's Visitor Center
29) University Museum of Archeology and Anthropology
30) Zoo

nomical, $35 to $65. A 6 percent state sales tax and 5 percent occupancy tax will be added to your bill. When you call for reservations, be sure to ask about special rates.

Reasonable

Chestnut Hill Hotel. 8229 Germantown Ave. (215–242–5905). In the heart of Chestnut Hill, six miles northwest of Center City. 284-cozy, well-appointed rooms in a restored colonial country inn. Charming and comfortable. 18th-century reproduction furniture. Two restaurants.

Days Inn. Two Gateway Center, 4101 Island Ave. (215–492–0400 or 800–325–2525). Four-story property near the airport. Free parking, free airport transportation. Restaurant, outdoor pool. Children under 12 free.

Holiday Inn-Airport. 45 Industrial Hwy. (215–521–2400 or 800–HOLIDAY). DJ in lounge, outdoor pool. Pets accepted. Children under 15 free.

Holiday Inn-City Line. At City Line Ave. exit of I-76 (215–477–0200 or 800–HOLIDAY). Recently refurbished hotel about 5 miles from Center City. Restaurant, indoor/outdoor heated pool, whirlpool, game room.

Holiday Inn-Midtown. 1305 Walnut St. (215–735–9300 or 800–HOLIDAY). Near major theaters. Restaurant and lounge, outdoor pool, free parking, children under 18 free in parents' room.

Holiday Inn-Center City. 1800 Market St. (215–561–7500, 800–HOLIDAY). Popular for its central location and better than usual Holiday Inn amenities. Restaurant and lounge. Movie theater on premises. Outdoor pool, low-priced parking.

Economical

Comfort Inn at Penn's Landing. 100 N. Delaware Ave. at Race St. (215–724–4000, 800–228–5150). Ten-story hotel, opened Nov. '87, is convenient to waterfront and historical attractions. Complimentary continental breakfast. No restaurant on premises. Request a river view.

Quality Inn-Airport. 20th and Penrose Ave. (215–755–6500 or 800–228–5151). Circular high rise. Restaurant, lounge with entertainment. Heated outdoor pool. Three blocks from sports complex.

Quality Inn-Center City. 22d and the Parkway, walking distance from major museums and Center City (215–568–8300 or 800–228–5151). Excellent value and location. Recently remodeled in California style. Restaurant, outdoor café, room service, entertainment, outdoor pool. Children under 18 free.

St. Charles Hotel. 1935 Arch St. (215–567–5651). Across from the Apollo and similarly priced. Private baths available, air-conditioning, color TV. No elevator. Coffee shop and restaurant adjacent. Cash only.

Weekend Packages. Many of the city's deluxe hotels lower their rates dramatically on weekends to attract guests when the business travelers have gone home. You'll get top-notch accommodations and service at surprisingly reasonable rates. Call the hotels for details of their packages.

Barclay (215–545–0300 or 800–421–6662). **Hershey Philadelphia Hotel** (family packages Thurs.–Sun.) (215–893–1600 or 800–533–3131). **Holiday Inn-Independence Mall** (215–923–8660 or 800–HOLIDAY). **Latham** (215–563–7474 or 800–LATHAM–1). **Palace Hotel** (215–963–2222 or 800–225–5843). **Sheraton Society Hill** (215–238–6000 or 800–325–3535). **Warwick** (215–735–6000 or 800–523–4210). **Wyndham Franklin Plaza** (215–448–2000 or 800–822–4200).

Bed-and-Breakfast. **Independence Park Inn.** 235 Chestnut St. (215–922–4443). This 1856 warehouse has been transformed into a cozy, elegant, 36-room hostelry with a five-story atrium and glass-enclosed courtyard, where continental breakfast and afternoon tea are served. Rooms from $80.

Society Hill Hotel. 3rd and Chestnut streets, in the historic area (925–1394). The city's first bed-and-breakfast establishment—an urban inn. Brass double beds, antiques, fresh flowers, private baths. Piano bar and restaurant. Continental breakfast in bed. Rooms from $80.

Thomas Bond House. 129 S. Second St. (215–923–8523). A 12-room inn in a restored Georgian and Federal house which now belongs to the National Park Service. Private baths, library with woodburning fireplace. Continental breakfast weekdays, full brunch on weekends. Innkeepers: John and Peggy Poth. Rooms from $70.

Ys and Hostels. Chamounix Mansion. Chamounix Dr., west Fairmount Park (215–878–3676). A youth hostel in a renovated Quaker farmhouse. Dormstyle; linen rental $2. $7 a night for AYH members, additional $3 fee for guests. Check in between 4:30 and 8 P.M.; lock up at 11 P.M. Kitchen facilities available; bring food with you. No credit cards.

International House. 3701 Chestnut St. (387–5125). Anyone with academic affiliation may reserve a room. A good value, not fancy but fun. Small, pleasant, air-conditioned rooms, some with private baths. Only towels and linens provided. No children allowed. Gourmet cafeteria. Visa and MasterCard accepted; no personal checks. Singles, $38; doubles are rarely available.

HOW TO GET AROUND. From the airport. Allow at least 30 minutes travel time for the 8-mile trip between Center City and Philadelphia International Airport. Cab fare averages $17 without tip. Deluxe Transportation Company (463–8787) travels between the airport and Center City hotels for a $6 fare. Their vans stop regularly outside baggage claim. SEPTA's highspeed rail line concepts the airport to the 30th Street Station and other downtown rail stations. Trains run every half hour between 5:30 A.M. and midnight. Fare: $4 one-way if purchased at ticket booth; $5 if bought on the train. For exact times, call SEPTA (574–7800) or the airport information desk (492–3333).

By bus, trolley, and subway. SEPTA (574–7800) operates an extensive system of buses, trolleys, subways, and commuter trains. During daytime hours, SEPTA provides the easiest and cheapest way of getting around the city. You can pick up timetables, routes, and the official street and transit map at information centers in the underground concourse at 15th and Market streets or at the Market Street East Station, 10th and Market streets. Fares are uniform: $1.25 for the base fare, 25 cents additional for a transfer. Exact change is required. Information centers all sell tokens (10 for $8.50) or a weekly $12 Transpass that entitles you to unlimited rides on most routes. The #76 bus, which runs on Chestnut St. between Independence Mall and 18th St., will drop you off close to shopping and historic attractions.

By commuter train. Philadelphia has a fine commuter rail network serving its suburban regions. These trains are your best bet for reaching attractions in Germantown, Chestnut Hill, and Merion. Trains leave from 30th street, Suburban, and Market Street East stations. Call SEPTA at 574–7800.

By taxi. Taxi fares are competitive, and the cabs are metered. Rates average $2.90 for the first mile, $1.40 for each additional mile. The major cab companies are Yellow Cab (922–8400), United Cab (625–2881) and Quaker City (728–8000).

By foot. Most of the historic and cultural attractions are easy walks from midtown. The Visitor Center at 1525 John F. Kennedy Blvd. has maps to follow for do-it-yourself tours. *AudioWalk & Tour of Historic Philadelphia,* 6th and Sansom streets (925–1234) offers a taped walking tour.

By rental car. The major car rental agencies, including Avis, Budget, Dollar, Hertz, and National, have offices at the airport and at convenient downtown locations. (Call 800–555–1212 for their toll-free numbers.) Reservations are usually necessary. The best savings are on the weekends, when rental rates are half the weekday prices. For super discounts, try Rent-a-Dent (521–2300); the cars aren't wrecks, and the agency is located two and a half miles from the airport.

HINTS TO THE MOTORIST. If your visit to Philadelphia will be focused in Center City, it's best to leave your car at home and depend on public transportation, which services the nearby suburbs as well. Narrow streets and congestion, especially during rush hours (7–9:30 A.M. and 4–6:30 P.M.), make driving difficult. On-street parking is often forbidden during rush hours, but some metered parking is permitted at other times. Parking meters are 25 cents for 20 minutes and 75 cents for an hour, with a 2-hour time limit. Some meters don't need to be fed after 6:30 or on Sundays, but be sure to read the signs as the regulations vary from street to street and the meter maids are vigilant. Parking lots and garages range from about $2.25 to $3.50 an hour to around $7 for 24 hours.

If you drive, avoid driving into and out of the city during rush hours. During the 7–9:30 A.M. morning rush, avoid the major arteries leading into the city, particularly I-95, U.S. 1, and the Schuylkill Expressway (I-76). The traffic pattern reverses during the 4–6:30 P.M. outgoing rush period.

For frequent traffic reports, tune into KYW news radio (1060 AM). For alternative routes and information, AAA members can call 569–4321.

A right turn on red is permitted after a full stop unless prohibited by a sign. In the city, streets generally alternate one way.

There are no on-street parking spaces specifically marked for use by handicapped drivers. However, drivers of cars with disabled plates don't have to feed the meters. Read the warning signs carefully; illegally parked cars will be ticketed or towed.

TOURIST INFORMATION. Before you visit, call or write th *Philadelphia Visitors Center* at 1525 John F. Kennedy Blvd., Phila., PA 19102 (215–636–1666 or 800–523–2004) to request a copy of the *Official Visitors Guide.* When you arrive, drop by their office; it's the round building across the street from Suburban Station. They offer free transit and city maps; hotel, restaurant, an sight-seeing information; and seasonal listings of the city's special attractions. They also offer special services to groups, foreign visitors, and the disabled and discount tickets to various events. Open daily 9 A.M.–5 P.M. (until 6 P.M. in summer).

The Visitor Center at *Independence National Historical Park,* 3rd and Chestnut streets, has information and maps for the most important historic sites. Open daily 9 A.M.–5 P.M.; phone 597–8974 or 627–1776 for a recorded message.

The International Visitors Center of Philadelphia's 24-hour emergency number (879–5248) provides help in 60 languages.

The Greater Philadelphia Cultural Alliance's *Cultural Connection Hotline* (564–4444) provides a detailed, up-to-the-minute taped message of cultural events—theater, museum exhibits, gallery shows, etc. Call the hotline to see if their discount ticket booth has reopened. The *Philly Fun Phone* (568–7255) offers a prerecorded listing of sports, theater, music, dance, and special events 24 hours a day. The two-minute message is updated three times a week.

For current calendar listings, refer to *Philadelphia* magazine, published monthly; the *Welcomat,* published Wednesdays; or the weekend pullout sections (available Friday) of Philadelphia's daily papers—the *Inquirer* and the *Daily News.* The latter three are available for free at the Tourist Center.

Foreign Currency. *American Express Travel Service,* Two Penn Center Plaza (587–2300); *Meridian Bank,* Broad and Walnut streets (854–3703); *Continental Bank,* 1201 Chestnut St. (564–7188); *Fidelity Bank,* Broad and Walnut streets (985–7068/7729); *First Pennsylvania Bank,* 15th and Market streets (786–8865); *Mellon Bank,* Broad and Chestnut streets (553–2145); and *Philadelphia National Bank,* 5th and Market streets (629–4402).

SENIOR-CITIZEN AND STUDENT DISCOUNTS. Many attractions offer considerable discounts to senior citizens and students. Always ask if there are special rates. A Medicare card is the best ID for seniors; students may be asked to show high school or college ID or an international student traveler card.

SEPTA offers free bus, trolley, and subway rides to seniors during off-peak hours and discounted fares of 60 cents from 6 A.M. to 9 A.M. and 3:30 P.M. to 6:30 P.M. Share-a-Ride Services offers a 90 percent discount on Yellow Cab fares to seniors who order a cab at least 48 hours in advance. Call 831–7680 between 8:30 A.M. and 4:30 P.M. for reservations. Cabs run for 8 A.M. to 10 P.M.

Many movie theaters offer seniors a reduced fare of $3. Everyone can save money at the daily bargain matinees (usually $3 before 1 P.M.) offered by many theaters.

HINTS TO DISABLED TRAVELERS. There have been efforts to make Philadelphia more accessible for the disabled. Newer SEPTA buses are equipped with lifts for passengers in wheelchairs. Disabled people are issued license plates allowing special parking privileges.

A pertinent publication is the *Guide to Philadelphia for the Handicapped,* available free of charge from the *Mayor's Commission on People With Disabilities,* Room 143, City Hall, Philadelphia, PA 19107, or order by calling MU6–2798. One of the best sources of information about disabled travel (local and national) is *The Travel Information Service,* Moss Rehabilitation Hospital, 12th St. and Tabor Rd., Philadelphia, PA 19141. They'll send you information about sights, accommodations, transportation, and the names of travel agencies to assist you.

FREE EVENTS. Philadelphia's most precious historical sites are found in Independence National Historical Park; the major attractions here are free. Many of the city's smaller museums are free as well; others have free days. See Museums, below, or the *Official Visitors Guide* available at the Visitor Center.

During the summer, the city is filled with **music,** much of it free. The most remarkable offerings are the free concerts given by the **Philadelphia Orchestra** at the Mann Music Center in Fairmount Park. Tickets are available the day of the concert at the Visitor Center, 1525 John F. Kennedy Blvd. (Be there when it opens to get tickets.) At JFK Plaza, adjacent to the Visitors Center, there's music, dance, tournaments, and entertainment daily from noon to 1 P.M. There's more music, from bluegrass to gospel, at the Great Plaza, a terraced waterfront park at Penn's Landing. In late May, the **Mozart on the Square Festival** celebrates the music of Mozart, Bach, Beethoven, and others at locations around Rittenhouse Square. During the Christmas season, don't miss the **light show and pipe organ concert** in the Grand Court of John Wanamaker's at 13th and Market streets.

It's worth the small price of admission to see the **Philadelphia Flower and Garden Show,** the nation's largest indoor flower show, which transforms the Civic Center in March. In May, Philadelphians open their houses and gardens for tours conducted by the Friends of Independence National Historical Park (928–1188 or 597–7919). **Philadelphia Open House Tours** vary in price, depending whether they are by foot, bus, or trolley.

Philadelphia has a year-round calendar filled with parades, street fairs, and festivals. The excitement kicks off with the **Mummers Parade** on New Year's Day, when more than 30,000 members of string bands, fancy and comic divisions don their feathers and glitter and strut up Broad Street. **Black History Month** is celebrated throughout February; March, April, and May feature **parades** for Saint Patrick's Day, Easter, and Israeli Independence Day.

In June, the work of local artists is shown in America's oldest outdoor exhibit of fine art, the **Rittenhouse Square Fine Arts Annual.** On summer weekends, artisans exhibit jewelry, stained glass, quilts, and other items at the **Head House Crafts Fair** at Head House Square, 2d and Pine streets.

The highlight of the year for Philadelphia, the birthplace of the nation, is the week-long **Freedom Festival** that culminates with a July 4 fireworks spectacular. In the days preceding are free concerts, parades, hot-air balloon races, the **Olde City Restaurant Festival,** and **Independence Day** ceremonies.

October brings **Super Sunday,** a giant block party with rides, entertainment, and food along the Benjamin Franklin Parkway. In October and November, **parades** marking Columbus, Pulaski, and Von Steuben days and Thanksgiving draw large crowds.

TOURS AND SPECIAL-INTEREST SIGHTSEEING. The best way to explore Philadelphia's historic and cultural attractions is on self-guided walking tours, which give you a chance to discover the city's charming nooks and crannies. An 8-minute taped walking tour of Independence National Historical Park is available from *Audio Walk & Tour,* in the Norman Rockwell Museum, 6th and Sansom streets (925–1234). Cassette and players are adaptable for one or two people, $8 per person, $6 per person if two share. Pick up equipment daily, 10 A.M.–1 P.M. If the weather is bleak or your feet are aching, try one of *Gray Line's* (569–3666) daily city tours, which depart from the Visitor's Center, 1525 John F. Kennedy Blvd. The $15 cultural tour takes two hours and 15 minutes; the three-hour historic tour is $13.50. Both provide a good orientation to the city.

The following tours offer particularly good value: The *Fairmount Park Trolley Bus,* a recreation of a Victorian trolley, departs about every 30 minutes from the Visitor Center, 1525 John F. Kennedy Blvd., and from the Independence National Historical Park Visitor Center, 3rd and Chestnut streets, Wed.–Sun., 10 A.M–4 P.M., April–Nov. It stops at the city's top museums and at attractions in Fairmount Park, including historic houses and the zoo. The tour takes 90 minutes and includes on-off privileges. Adults, $3; seniors, $1; children, 50 cents. Daily in the winter, and Monday and Tuesday only the rest of the year, the "Town and Country Tour" takes a 2½-hour narrated trolley bus trip through Society Hill and into Fairmount Park. Adults, $5.50; children, $4.50. For information for either tour, call 879–4044.

From May to October, *Centipede Tours* supplies guides in colonial dress who lead 1½-hour Candlelight Strolls through Colonial City (Friday) and Society Hill

(Wednesday and Saturday). Groups leave at 6:30 P.M. from City Tavern, 2d and Walnut streets. Phone 735–3123. Adults, $4; seniors and children, $3.50.

Delaware River Cruises. The *Spirit of Philadelphia* sails every day, April to December, from Penn's Landing, Delaware Ave. and Spruce St. Lunch, dinner, and Sunday brunch, sight-seeing cruises, all with entertainment, are available. The buffet lunch cruise, at $15 per person, offers the best value. Phone 923–1419 for reservations.

Free Tours

City Hall. Broad and Market streets (567–4476). Guided tour of the seat of Philadelphia's municipal government. It is patterned after the New Louvre in Paris and is splendid inside. Tours Mon.–Fri., 12:30 P.M. Meet in Conversation Hall through the North Broad St. entrance.

The Free Library of Philadelphia. 19th and Vine Streets (686–5322). Half-hour tours of its rare books department (from cuneiform tablets to Dickens's letters) at 11 A.M. weekdays.

Masonic Temple. One N. Broad St. (988–1917). Tour the ornate headquarters of the Pennsylvania Masons, an architectural treasure. Weekdays at 10 and 11 A.M. 1, 2, and 3 P.M.; Saturdays except July and August, 10 and 11 A.M.

Pennsylvania Hospital. 8th and Spruce streets (829–3971). The nation's oldest hospital is full of artwork, early medical instruments, and other items of medical interest. Open weekdays 9 A.M.–3 P.M. for self-guided tours.

Philadelphia Naval Base. South Broad St. (897–8775). This is where our mothball fleet docks. Tour the shipbuilding center and land facilities on their special tour bus. U.S. citizens only; children under 8 not permitted. Reservations required: Fridays and Saturdays at 9 and 11 A.M.

United States Mint. 5th and Arch streets (597–7350). An hour-long self-guided tour with audiovisual assistance that explains how coins are made. Open 9 A.M.–4:30 P.M. daily, May–Sept.; weekdays only Jan.–Mar.; Mon.–Sat. the rest of the year.

PARKS AND GARDENS. Philadelphia is dotted by five **public squares** that were planned by william Penn himself: *Franklin Square,* at 7th and Race streets; the London parklike *Washington Square,* with brightens the southeast section of the city at 6th and Walnut streets; *Rittenhouse Square,* a well-manicured park by 18th and Walnut streets in the southwest; *Logan Circle,* enhanced by Alexander Stirling Calder's Swann Memorial Fountain, at 18th St. and the Benjamin Franklin Pkwy.; and *Centre Square,* which is now occupied by City Hall. The first four squares are scenic spots to relax or eat a picnic lunch during your touring.

Fairmount Park. The largest landscaped city park in the world has more than 8,500 acres containing historic and cultural treasures, along with woods, meadows, flowers, statues, sports facilities, and five particularly scenic acres along the banks of the Schuylkill River. Along Kelly Drive are the Victorian houses of Boat House Row, home to the "Schuylkill Navy" rowing clubs. Tourists are particularly drawn to the park's seven historic, authentically furnished houses dating from the mid-1700's. Phone 787–5449. Another park attraction is the Japanese House, patterned after a seventeenth-century Japanese residence. The Horticultural Center has a 28-acre arboretum and a wonderful greenhouse with thousands of plants and trees used to beautify the city properties. The best way to visit these sites is on the Fairmount Park Trolley Bus (see Tours above).

Also in the park are the Philadelphia Museum of Art (see Museums), the Philadelphia Zoological Gardens (see Zoo, below), and sports facilities (see Participant Sports).

Tinicum National Environmental Center. 86th St. and Lindbergh Blvd. The largest remaining wetland in Pennsylvania; dates back to 1643. Walking trails, an observation tower, and a boardwalk afford a good view of the marshland's abundant birds and wildlife. Fishing, biking, and photography are permitted. Visitor Center open daily 8:30 A.M.–4 P.M. Admission free; call 365–3118.

Bartram's Garden. 54th St. and Lindbergh Blvd. (729–5281). The historic home of colonial botanists John and William Bartram and the nation's first aboretum. Still blooms with exotic flora from all over the "New World." Garden open daily, dawn to dusk. Admission free.

ZOOS. When the **Philadelphia Zoological Gardens** opened in 1874, people flocked there on foot, by horse and carriage, and even by steamboat. They've been showing up in herds ever since. Today, the country's oldest zoo has over 1,600 animals representing more than 540 species, plus more than 500 species of native and exotic plants. The World of Primates shows off apes and monkeys in an outdoor natural habitat. In the Treehouse, children can experience the world from the point of view of a bee or a tree frog. Bear Country is home to polar bears, sloth bears, and spectacled bears. The five-acre African Plain; Jungle Bird Walk, a walk-through aviary; and Wolf Woods are special features. A monorail overlooks all this, treating visitors to a bird's-eye view of the zoo. The Children's Zoo allows visitors to touch and feed the animals and has an hourly animal show. The zoo is at 34th St. and Girard Ave. in West Philadelphia. Open daily 9:30 A.M.–5 P.M., till 6 P.M. April to October, Adults, $4.50; for seniors and children 2 to 11, $3.50, children under 2 free. Phone 243–1100.

PARTICIPANT SPORTS. Fairmount Park is a sportsman's paradise for bikers, hikers, joggers, golfers, and fishermen. **Bicyclists** can rent "wheels" from Fairmount Park Bike Rental, 1 Boat House Row (236–4359). Rental rates are $5 an hour; a $10 deposit is required on all bikes.

Those interested in testing the waters of the Schuylkill can head to the Public Canoe House, Kelly Drive, just south of the Strawberry Mansion Bridge (225–3560). **Canoes** and **rowboats** go for $10 an hour; **sailboats** are $15 an hour. A $10 deposit and picture ID are required.

Several public **golf courses** wind through Fairmount Park. They are open throughout the year and charge between $9 and $12 for 18 holes. *Cobbs Creek,* 7800 Lansdowne Ave. (877–8707); *Karakung,* 7800 Lansdowne Ave. (877–8707); *Juniata,* L and Cayuga streets (743–4060); *Walnut Lane,* Walnut Lane and Henry Ave. (482–3370); and *Franklin D. Roosevelt,* 20th St. and Pattison Ave. (462–8997).

Ice skaters can take to the rink at the *University of Pennsylvania's Class of 1923 Skating Rink,* 3130 Walnut St. (898–1923). October through March, daily except Thurs. Admission $3.75; skate rentals, $1.

You can jog, swim, and play handball, racquetball, and squash indoors at the *Philadelphia Athletic Club,* 314 N. Broad St. (564–2002). Open daily. Guest fee: men, $12; women, $10.

Tennis. *Pier 30,* Delaware Ave. and Bainbridge St. (985–1234), has fine courts available for rental daily. They charge $16 an hour for courts during the day, evening rates rise to $27. Call for hours.

SPECTATOR SPORTS. Philadelphia has become known as a City of Champion's, thanks to winning efforts by its professional teams. The National League Phillies (463–1000) play **Baseball** from April to October at Veterans Stadium. Home games are played mostly at night; prices range from $4 for general admission to $9 for field boxes.

The Philadelphia 76ers (339–7676), the city's pro **basketball** team, shoot the hoops from October to April at the Spectrum. There are 40 home dates, mostly at night. Tickets are $8 to $18. Sharing the Spectrum and the same time span with the Sixers are the Flyers (755–9700), two-time Stanley cup hockey champions. Tickets range from $12 to $23.

The Eagles (463–5500), the city's entry in the National **Football** League, play their games at the Vet on Sunday afternoon from August to December. Tickets are about $20.

Tickets for all pro games are available at the ball park and at city ticket agencies (expect a surcharge of up to $5). Veterans Stadium and the Spectrum are located in the South Philadelphia sports complex at Broad St. and Pattison Ave. They can be reached by subway (the southern end of the Broad Street line), by the C bus, which runs south on Broad Street, or by car. Parking is ample and costs $3.75.

Rowing regattas in which college teams compete on the banks of the Schuylkill take place between March and June. The U.S. Pro Indoor Tennis Championships, set for the Spectrum in February, attract the top men in the game including Ivan Lendl, John McEnroe, and Jimmy Connors. The Penn Relays, a track meet featuring the country's best runners, are held the last weekend in April in Franklin Field. The CoreStates Pro Cycling Championship, the nation's only professional cycling competition, is in mid-June. The Army-Navy football classic is played at Veterans Stadium the weekend following Thanksgiving (subject to change according to TV coverage).

CHILDREN'S ACTIVITIES. For children age 7 and younger, the top attraction is the **Please Touch Museum,** 210 No. 21st St., where kids are invited to climb, explore, dress up, and touch everything. Open 10 A.M.–4:30 P.M. Tues.–Sun. Admission is $3.50 for everyone. Phone 963–0666.

Perelman Antique Toy Museum, 270 S. 2nd St., has three floors of Early American tin and cast iron toys, the world's largest collection of mechanical and still banks, and more. Open daily 9:30 A.M.–5 P.M. Adults, $2; children under 14, 95 cents. Phone 922–1070.

Sesame Place in Langhorne (752–4900), a 25-minute ride north of Center City, is a family play park that takes up where Sesame Street leaves off. For ages 3–13. Open daily May–mid-Sept.; weekends only the rest of the year.

Three of the city's top museums have special programs for kids. In the Fels Planetarium of the **Franklin Institute Science Museum,** there is a special children's show Saturdays at 10:30 A.M. The **Academy of Natural Sciences** offers Outside-In, a hands-on nature center; and the **University Museum of Archaeology and Anthropology** (their mummies are especially popular) has a Children's Film Program on Saturdays at 10:30 A.M. from October to March. See Museums for hours, prices, and times. Check the weekend listings of the daily papers for children's theater events.

HISTORIC SITES AND HOUSES. Philadelphia has more historic buildings associated with early American history than any other city in the United States. The top attractions are listed here.

Betsy Ross House. 239 Arch St. (627–5343). The 13-star "Old Glory" waves from the second floor window of the restored eighteenth-century home of Betsy Ross. Furnished with period pieces. Open daily 9 A.M.–5 P.M. (till 6 P.M. in summer). Free.

Christ Church. 2d St. north of Market St. (922–1695). Many who were instrumental in America's independence worshipped here at the oldest Episcopal church in America. An architectural treasure. Donations welcome. In Christ Church Burial Ground, 5th and Arch streets, five signers of the Declaration of Independence are buried. Its most famous "resident" is Benjamin Franklin. Open June–Sept., call church for hours.

Elfreth's Alley. 2d St. between Arch and Race streets (574–0560). The cobblestone lane and small houses on this, the oldest continuously occupied street in America, offer a glimpse of what much of colonial Philadelphia looked like. No. 126 is a museum, open to the public daily, 10 A.M.–4 P.M. Weekends only in January and February. Free.

Independence National Historical Park. The most historic square mile in America incorporates many of the country's most important sites. More than 4.5 million people visit these attractions each year; all are free. Most of the buildings are open daily 9 A.M.–5 P.M.; later hours in summer. Head first to the Park Visitor Center, 3rd and Chestnut streets (597–8974; 627–1776 for a taped message). The staff here will supply you with a map and outline a tour for you, depending on your interests and time. Information in 12 foreign languages; a 28-minute film, *Independence,* dramatizes the events from 1774 to 1800.

Don't miss these three sites: *Independence Hall,* Chestnut between 5th and 6th streets. America's most historic building is where the Declaration of Independence was signed and the U.S. Constitution adopted. Guided tours leave every 15 or 20 minutes from the East Wing. Lines are long; get in line early. *Liberty Bell Pavilion,* Market St. between 5th and 6th streets. The nation's most hallowed symbol of liberty resides here. *Franklin Court,* Market St. between 3rd and 4th streets. This museum serves as an imaginative tribute to Old Ben. The genius of this statesman, diplomat, scientist, printer, and author are revealed in hands-on exhibits.

Other important sites in the park include *Carpenters' Hall,* where the First Continental Congress met; *Second Bank of the United States,* with its portrait gallery; *Graff House,* the reconstructed house where Thomas Jefferson wrote the Declaration of Independence; *Bishop White House,* home of the first bishop of the Episcopal diocese of Pennsylvania; and the *Todd House,* home of Dolley Payne Todd, who later became Dolley Madison. Free tour tickets for the last two must be picked up at the Visitor Center. Near the park is the *Edgar Allan Poe House,* his only Philadelphia residence still standing.

Penn's Landing. Delaware River waterfront between Chestnut and Spruce streets. The Port of History Museum and several ships turned floating museum, including a World War II sub and Commodore Dewey's flagship, are among the permanent attractions. Ships open daily for tours. Call 922–1898.

MUSEUMS. Philadelphia is a great cultural center with over 50 museums, many of which are world-renowned. Most of the city's major institutions are located on the Benjamin Franklin Parkway, a short walk from Center City. What follows is a sampling of the best:

Academy of Natural Sciences. 19th St. and Benjamin Franklin Pkwy. (299–1000). America's first natural history museum has achieved international fame for its displays of stuffed animals in their natural habitats, extinct and endangered species, birds, and insects. "Discovering Dinosaurs" is a popular multimedia exhibit. Open Mon.–Fri., 10 A.M.–4:30 P.M., Sat.–Sun., 10 A.M.–5 P.M. Adults, $4.50; students and seniors, $4; children 3–12, $3.50.

Barnes Foundation. 300 N. Latche Lane, Merion (667–0290). Call the Visitors Center (636–1666) for directions. One of the world's finest private art collections, it is never lent for exhibit. Impressionists, including Renoir, Cezanne, and Matisse, are well represented. Fri.–Sat., 9:30 A.M.–4:30 P.M.; Sun., 1 P.M.–4:30 P.M. Closed July and August. Admission, $1; children under 12 not admitted.

Franklin Institute Science Museum. 20th St. and Benjamin Franklin Pkwy. (448–1200; 564–3375 for taped message). Imaginative hands-on exhibits bring science and technology to life. New exhibits on astronomy, electronics, and electricity. Aviation Hall and a giant walk-through human heart are favorites. Daily planetarium shows in Fels Planetarium. Open Mon.–Sat., 10 A.M.–5 P.M.; Sunday, noon–5 P.M. Adults, $5; children 4–12, $4; seniors, $3.50.

Mummers Museum. 2nd St. and Washington Ave. (336–3050). The history, costumes, and folklore of the Mummers, one of the city's most colorful and unique traditions, are on display. Open Tues.–Sat. 9:30 A.M.–5 P.M.; Sunday, noon–5 P.M. Adults, $1.50; children and seniors, 75 cents. String Band concerts are held outside the museum on Tuesday evenings, May through September.

Pennsylvania Academy of the Fine Arts. Broad and Cherry streets (972–7600). The country's oldest museum and art school is a National Historic Landmark containing three centuries of American art. Tues.–Sat, 10 A.M.–5 P.M. (till 7 P.M. Wed.); Sun., 11 A.M.–5 P.M. Adults, $3; seniors and students, $2. Free Saturday, 10 A.M.–1 P.M. Tours leave every hour 11 A.M.–3 P.M.

Philadelphia Museum of Art. 26th St. and Benjamin Franklin Pkwy. (763–8100; 787–5488 for tapes message). The city's cultural highlight, a Greco-Roman temple, holds dazzling collections of American crafts, furniture, and glass; Renaissance treasures; twentieth-century art; and a wing of orginial architectural wonders including a Hindu temple hall. Tues.–Sun., 10 A.M.–5 P.M. Adults, $4; students and seniors, $2. Free Sunday until 1 P.M. Tours leave every hour 11 A.M.–3 P.M.

Rodin Museum. 22d St. and Benjamin Franklin Pkwy. (787–5476). A priceless collection of Auguste Rodin's originals and castings—the largest exhibition of his works outside the Musée Rodin in Paris—are on display. Tues.–Sun., 10 A.M.–5 P.M. Donations welcome.

Rosenbach Museum and Library. 2010 Delancey Place (732–1600). Paintings; antiques; Chippendale, Hepplewhite, and Louis XV furniture; thousands of rare books and manuscripts including the original manuscript of James Joyce's *Ulysses;* Maurice Sendak drawings; and more in a nineteenth-century townhouse. Tues.-Sun., 11 A.M.–4 P.M. (closed August). Adults, $2.50; students and seniors, $1.50 for one-hour guided tour.

The University Museum of Archaeology and Anthropology. 33rd and Spruce streets (898–4000; 222–7777 for taped exhibit information). One of the largest U.S. collections of ancient and primitive cultures and one of the world's leading archaeological museums. Tues.–Sat., 10 A.M.–4:30 P.M.; Sun., 1–5 P.M. Closed Sundays in July and August. Tours Saturday and Sunday, October to May, at 1:15 P.M. Adults, $3; students and seniors, $1.50; under 6, free.

FILM. Many of the city's first-run movie theaters are located between Broad and 20th on Chestnut. The *Inquirer* and *Daily News* have daily movie listings indicating which theaters offer reduced rates ($3) for the matinee and the first evening show. Regular prices average $5.

The crown jewel of all local houses is the five-screen **Ritz Five,** 214 Walnut St. (925–7900), with the latest in foreign fare as well as small gems. The **Roxy Screening Rooms I** and **II,** 2021–23 Sansom St. (561–0114), is an "art" house featuring intellectual and esoteric fare.

Independent, small, and art film buffs chose the **Temple Cinematheque,** 1619 Walnut St. (787–1529); **International House,** 3701 Chestnut St. (387–5125); and **University Museum,** 33rd and Spruce streets (898–4025), for their weekend revivals, Oct.–March, and the **Art Museum,** 26th St. and the Parkway (763–8100), for the weekend afternoon film series.

MUSIC. If there is one art that shapes the cultural skyline of Philadelphia, it is music. From the world-famous Philadelphia Orchestra to chamber music groups, the city offers music for myriad moods and interests. **The Philadelphia Orchestra** (893–1930), under the baton of Riccardo Muti, performs its classical concerts from September to May at the Academy of Music, Broad and Locust streets. One hour before each Friday and Saturday performance, tickets for the amphitheater go on sale for $2 each. The line forms two hours before the concert. On weeknights, unsold orchestra tickets can be had for $5 beginning at 7:30 P.M. (student ID required). From mid-June through July, the orchestra gives free open-air concerts at the Mann Music Center in West Fairmount Park. Free tickets are available the day of the concert at the Visitors Center at 1525 John F. Kennedy Blvd. Be there when they open at 9 A.M.

The Emmy Award-winning **Opera Company of Philadelphia** (732–5814) attracts the biggest names in the operatic field; they perform at the Academy of Music from October to April. The **Concerto Soloists** (735–0202) perform classical music under the batons of Marc Mostovoy and Max Rudolf, Sept.–June at the Academy of Music and other locations.

Moe Septee's **All-Star Forum** season runs from October to May at the Academy of Music, offering such classical artists as Itzhak Perlman and Isaac Stern. Phone 735–7506. Septee also presents the Philly Pops, conducted by Peter Nero, in concerts from October to May at the Academy. The new American Music Theater Festival (988–9050) stages its concerts at the Walnut Street Theatre and other sites throughout the year; the Mellon Jazz Festival arrives in June.

Such popular names as Billy Joel, Sting, and Madonna are in town often under the auspices of **Electric Factory Concerts.** For information about who'll be performing where and when and how to get tickets, call 976–HITS. The **Robin Hood Dell East** (477–8810), Ridge Ave. and Dauphin St., stages a series of low-cost concerts in July and August, a mix of rhythm and blues and soul sounds. The **Philadelphia Folk Festival** takes root in August at the Old Poole Farm in Schwenksville (242–0150 or 247–1300).

During the summer, there are numerous free music festivals and concerts. See Free Events above or call the Visitors Center at 636–1666 for information.

DANCE. Robert Weiss and Peter Martins lead the Pennsylvania and Milwaukee Ballet Company, which performs its repertory at the Academy of Music and the Shubert Theatre, Broad and Locust streets, from October to June. Its "Nutcracker" is a Christmastime favorite for old and young audiences alike. Phone 978–1429. The Annenberg Center, 3680 Walnut St., plays host to its annual Dance Celebration series, featuring modern dance talents such as Twyla Tharp and Alvin Ailey. The shows run from November to May. Call 898–6791 for information.

STAGE. The Forrest Theater, 1114 Walnut St. (923–1515), is the top Broadway house in town. The Walnut Street Theatre Company, 9th and Walnut streets (574–3550), offers a schedule of musicals, comedy, and drama in the oldest operating theater in the United States. Their season runs November to March. The Philadelphia Drama Guild (563–7530) favors twentieth-century works; they perform at the Annenberg Center, 3680 Walnut St., from October to May. The Annenberg Center (898–6791) also plays host to visiting theater companies, presenting eclectic fare. The Shubert Theatre, a performing arts center at 250 S. Broad St., is a showcase for ballet, opera, Broadway shows, and headliners.

Both the Wilma Theater, 2030 Sansom St. (963–0345), and the Philadelphia Company of Plays and Players, 1714 Delancey St. (592–8333), offer innovative, offbeat seasons. Also contributing to the theater scene are Society Hill Playhouse, 507 8th St. (923–0210), with contemporary works; and Painted Bride Art Center, 230 Vine St. (925–9914), a gallery and performing arts center which features original theater, jazz, dance, poetry, and folk music.

The Theater of the Living Arts, 334 South St. (922–1010), a midsize theater, features excellent productions of off-Broadway hits, like *Little Shop of Horrors.* On Stage Theater, 2020 Sansom St. (567–0741), fills in with foreign films between productions of shows like Gary Trudeau's *Rap Master Ronnie.*

SHOPPING. From its unique enclosed shopping complexes to its boutique-lined streets, Philadelphia is a treasure trove for shoppers. Although there is not much in the way of outlets and discount shops, the careful shopper can find bargains.

The Gallery at Market East, which spans Market St. between 8th and 11th streets, was the country's first enclosed inner city shopping mall. In addition to J.C. Penney, Strawbridge & Clothier, and Stern's, there are more than 250 mid-priced shops and restaurants, plus Market Fair, with 25 international fast-food counters. **The Bourse,** on 5th between Market and Chestnut, was a commodities exchange in Victorian times. A splendid restoration has given it new life as an elegant shopping center with the latest from Cacharel and Saint Laurent, one-of-a-kind boutiques, and ethnic eateries. It's great for browsing.

Chestnut Street is a pedestrian mall from 18th to 6th streets with assorted shoe, book, and clothing stores. Goods here are more modestly priced than they are just one block south; the boutiques, galleries, and specialty shops on **Walnut Street** between Broad and 19th could just as well flank New York's Fifth Avenue. Among them are Burberry's, Jaeger, Laura Ashley, and Nan Duskin. **South Street** from front to about 8th is the place to find funky fashions, vintage clothing, antiques, hard-to-find books, natural foods, and endless oddities. Careful bargain shoppers can score here. The **Italian Market,** 9th St. between Christian and Federal streets in South Philadelphia, is a fascinating outdoor market. The pushcarts and open stalls are stuffed with produce and meats as well as low-priced handbags and clothing.

The windows sparkle with diamonds, gold, and precious stones on **Jewelers Row** in the vicinity of 8th and Sansom. You'll find a wide selection and good, competitive prices. Although antique shops are scattered throughout the city, dozens of antique dealers and collectors are clustered along Pine Street's **Antique Row,** especially between 9th and 12th.

Sales are held throughout the year, so if you are looking for a special item, check the daily newspapers first. Stores generally open at 9:30 or 10 A.M., Monday through Saturday, and close at 6 P.M. Many shops extend their hours on Wednesday evening; malls and department stores are often open on Sundays. A 6 percent sales tax will be added to the price tag of all items except clothing, which is exempt.

As Bloomingdale's is to New York, **John Wanamaker** is to Philadelphia. The world famous landmark at 13th and Market streets was one of the first great department stores in the country. In the basement is the Automatic Markdown Center, where all kinds of goods are discounted from 20 to 60 percent. Stop at the information desk for a brochure detailing a self-guided tour. Strawbridge & Clothier is another Philadelphia favorite. The main store at 8th and Market streets has a bargain basement and monthly Clover Day sales (check the daily papers for ads) that offer great bargains.

DINING OUT. Philadelphia has garnered national attention for its cuisine, an artful blend of American, French, and Oriental. But it's also known for its junk food: hoagies, cheese steaks, and soft pretzels with mustard. The dining guide below offers ideas on how to sample the sophisticated cuisine at reasonable prices and junk food at low-budget rates. Some additional strategies: (1) Eat early and take advantage of the many early bird specials, often before 6:30 P.M., which offer a full meal for reduced rates. (2) Stick with a fixed-price dinner. This may allow you to eat at a restaurant otherwise beyond your budget. (3) Make lunch your main meal and eat a light dinner. Many restaurants offer the same food at lunch at half the price. Check the daily papers for special deals.

Categories, based on the price of an average three-course dinner for one person, without beverages, tax (6 percent), or tip, are as follows: *Reasonable,* $12–$16; *Very Economical,* $8–$12, *Low Budget,* under $8. Unless otherwise stated, the restaurants listed here accept some if not all major credit cards.

Reasonable

Carolina's. 261 S. 20th St. (545–1000). Something for everyone, from Chinese dumplings to chili chicken, but built on a down-home base. Country bread and sinful desserts. Piano bar, L, Mon.–Fri.; D, nightly; Sunday brunch. Reservations required.

The Commissary. 1710 Sansom St. (569–2240). Gourmet cafeteria with soups, salads, omelets, pâtés, desserts, and daily entree specials. Browse through the cookbook library while you sample wine by the glass. A piano bar is adjacent. B, L, D, daily.

Joe's Peking Duck House. 925 Race St. (922–3277). The best Chinese restaurant in Chinatown. Fresh fish, roast duck, and barbecued pork are specialties. Informal, friendly. Reservations suggested, L, D daily. No cards.

Marabella's. 1420 Locust St. (545–1845). This trendy trattoria offers everything from mesquite-grilled seafood to pizza with goat cheese and sun-dried tomatoes to homemade pastas. Fun, casual, and near the theaters; great for an after-show bite. L, D, daily.

The Restaurant. 2129 Walnut St. (561–3649). A restaurant run by the students and staff of the nationally known Restaurant School. It's on-the-job training for chefs and waiters, and if you're willing to be a guinea pig, you can usually get a very good meal in the attractive Victorian brownstone. Prix fixe $12.50 for appetizer and entree. D, Tues.–Sat. Reservations required.

Sansom Street Oyster House. 1516 Sansom St. (567–7863). The best raw oysters in town are found at this small, informal fish house. L, D Mon.–Sat.

Very Economical

Eden. 1527 Chestnut St. (972–0400); 3701 Chestnut St. (387–2471). A stylish cafeteria that features hamburgers with 12 toppings, stir-fries, salads, quiche, delicious homemade soups, and desserts. Good and quick. No cards.

Saladalley. The Bourse, Independence Mall East (627–2406); 1720 Sansom St. (564–0767). The draw here is the salad bar, with a good selection of greens and goodies, along with soups and a limited number of entrees. Sunday brunch buffet. L, D daily. No cards at the Bourse location.

Silveri's. 315 S. 13th St. (545–5115). A friendly neighborhood bar famous for its Buffalo chicken wings and great hamburgers. L, D Mon.–Fri.; D only, Sat.–Sun.

Triangle Tavern. 10th and Reed streets, South Philadelphia (467–8683). A casual neighborhood spot known for old-style Italian cooking—ravioli, manicotti, mussels, in white or red sauce. D, daily. No cards.

Walt's King of Crabs. 804–6 S. 2d St., South Philadelphia (339–9124). Good fresh seafood in a casual atmosphere; crabs, mussels, and an $8 lobster are specialities. L, D Mon.–Sat.; D only, Sun. No cards.

Low Budget

Corned Beef Academy. 121 S. 16th St. (665–0460); 18th and JFK Blvd. (568–9696). State-of-the-art deli where all is homemade. B, L, Mon.–Fri. 16th St. is also open for L on Sat. No cards.

Italian Market. 9th St. between Christian and Federal. A colorful open-air market where vendors crowd the sidewalks and spill onto the streets. Munch on pizza, olives, cheese, and Italian pastries. Open daily.

Jim's Steaks. 400 South St. (928–1911). Steak sandwiches in an Art Deco decor. L, D daily.

Pat's King of Steaks. 1237 E. Passyunk Ave. (468–1546). The place for a sidewalk steak sandwich with onions, cheese, and peppers. Open 24 hours daily.

Reading Terminal Market. 12th and Filbert streets (922–2317). A nineteenth-century European-style marketplace lined with meat, fish, and produce stands plus more than 20 stalls with ready-to-eat ethnic treats. Eat at least one lunch here and don't miss Bassetts ice cream, the soft pretzels at Fisher's Ice Cream, and the Amish farm-fresh goodies. Mon.–Sat., 8 A.M.–6 P.M.

Recommended Splurge. Le Bec-Fin. 1523 Walnut St. (567–1000). Philadelphia's premier French restaurant (and one of the best French restaurants on the East Coast) offers a classic French setting Louis XVI would feel at home in. Service is impeccable, and the seasonal menu features the best of ingredients imaginatively prepared and beautifully presented. Dinner is astronomically expensive, but a three-course prix-fixe lunch is available for $24, and the menu is just as enticing. Reservations essential. Seatings at 11:30 A.M. and 1:30 P.M. Lunch served Mon.–Fri.

NIGHTLIFE AND BARS. Reports that Philadelphia has no nightlife are greatly exaggerated; you just have to know where to look. Whether you like mellow piano music, jazz favorites, or the light show and pickup scene, you can find it. Certain clubs are members-only, after-hours places that can stay often after the 2 A.M. legal closing time. Usually, anyone can join them on the spot by paying a guest fee. Most of these clubs close at 4 A.M. In the state of Pennsylvania, the legal age for purchase and consumption of alcoholic beverages is 21. Many clubs have strict ideas about proper dress; it's wise to call ahead.

Bars with Something Extra

The following bars offer something special to entice you: maybe an unusual ambience, talented musicians, or elaborate munchies during their happy hours.

Apropos. 211 S. Broad St. (546–4424). A Brazilian band delivers terrific sambas, bossa novas, and slow tunes for dancing on a small dance floor in the middle of this chic eatery. Fri.–Sat., from 11 P.M.

The Bar. Hershey Hotel, Broad and Locust streets (893–1600). Handsome lounge with band, 9 P.M.–1:30 A.M., daily. You can even dance to contemporary and Top 40 music. Some of the city's best Happy Hour munchies, Mon.–Fri., 5–7 P.M.

The Bar at Carolina's. 261 S. 20th St. (545–1000). A homey watering hole open nighly till 2 A.M. You can get a full meal at the bar. Live jazz Sat. nights.

Cafe Royal. Palace Hotel, 18th and the Parkway (963–2244). A great trio delivers classics from Chopin to Gershwin. Only "grownups" in ties and jackets will be happy at this sophisticated lounge. Music Fri.–Sat. from 9 P.M.

Liberties. 705 N. 2nd St., above Fairmount (238–0660). A hot spot with a great old look. This handsome restored Victorian pub features live music—contemporary folk rock and jazz—Wed.–Sat. nights from 9 P.M.

Mirabelle. 1836–40 Callowhill St. (557–9793). A stylish art deco restaurant featuring a piano bar where patrons sing along with show tunes and old favorites. If you like to sing don't miss the experience. Music Mon.–Sat. from 7:30 P.M.; crowd warms up around 10 P.M. Weekend nights are the liveliest.

Not Quite Crickett. 17th and Walnut streets (563–9444). A dark, pleasing lounge with good sound: jazz and top 40 hits, Tues.–Fri., 8:30 P.M.–1:30 A.M.

Top of Center Square. First Pennsylvania Bank Tower, 15th and Market streets (563–9494). Popular meeting place for young single professionals. Hot and cold Happy Hour snacks Mon.–Fri., 4:30–8 P.M., jazzy vocalist and pianist Fri.–Sat. from 9 P.M.

White Dog Cafe. 3420 Sansom St. (386–9224). Live entertainment in a charming café near the University of Pennsylvania. Changing venue of jazz, Dixieland country, '30s tunes, and pop. Mon., Fri., Sat., from 9 P.M.

Music and Dancing

Beverly Hills Bar & Grill. 5th and Ranstead, in the Bourse (627–0778). A restaurant/club serving up tunes from the '50s to the '80s. Happy Hour with free buffet Tues.–Fri. 4:30–8 P.M. DJ Tues.–Sat. till 2 A.M. $5 cover Wed. and weekends.

Chestnut Cabaret. 3801 Chestnut St. (382–1201). This concert hall-dance club by the Penn campus features live music by rock and rhythm and blues musicians as well as music programmed by local disc jockeys. Cover is minimal; popular with college students. Casual, but men's shirts should have collars. Open Tues.–Sat., 8 P.M.–2 A.M.

Equus. 254 S. 12th St. (545–8088). One of Philadelphia's best gay bars draws a 30-and-up professional crowd. Bar open from 4 P.M. daily; disco gets going

Wed.–Sun. at 10 P.M. $3 cover on weekends. Dinner served Mon.–Sat.; Sunday brunch.

Flanigan's. Abbotts Square, Second and South streets (928–9898), Huge, glittery nightspot is a popular young singles club. 18-foot happy hour buffet 5–8 P.M. Tues.–Fri. DJ spins records nightly. $5 cover weekends. Teen dance Sun.

Glitters. 427 South St., upstairs (592–4512). Chrome and mirrors line this nightclub with a mile-long bar and glass encased dance area. DJ programs high-energy dance music. Wed.–Sat. 9–2. No jeans. Weekend cover $5.

Memphis. 2121 Arch St. (569–1123). Located above a bar-café, this roomy, casual dance bar draws an eclectic early-20s crowd. Ancient Egyptian decor with modern touches. Danceable '80s music and light New Wave. Live jazz Wed. nights. Open Tues.–Sat. Weeknight Happy Hour buffet.

Monte Carlo Living Room. 2nd and South streets (925–2220). A romantic disco/cocktail lounge with a DJ manning the turntable with Top 40 hits and slow music for touch dancing. Jackets required. Open Tues.–Sat., 6 P.M.–2 A.M.

PT's. 6 S. Front St. (922–5676). Casual, comfortable club popular with young singles. DJ plays hits Wed.–Sun. Reduced drink prices and complimentary buffet Wed., 9 P.M.–midnight; Happy Hour buffet Wed.–Fri., 5–7:30 P.M. Cover varies.

Polo Bay Club. 17th and Locust streets, in the Warwick Hotel (546–8800). Newly decorated with tropical decor, this club is very popular. In-house dance troupe performs. DJ spins records from 5 P.M.–2 A.M. Tues.–Sat., 7 P.M.–midnight Sun. Cover $3 weeknights, $5 weekends. Great Happy Hour buffet.

The Strand. 1215 Walnut St. (592–7650). After-hours club plays progressive music, Soft lights, fireplace lounge, and loft lounge. Occasional live bands. Wed.–Sun. 10 P.M.–4 A.M. $10 cover.

Trocadero. 10th and Arch streets (592–TROC). A hot rock 'n' roll club in a former burlesque house. Nationally known concert acts weeknights (call for schedule and ticket information). Dance parties Fri. 4 P.M.–2 A.M., and Saturday 7 P.M.–2 P.M. $5 admission after 8 P.M. Fri., 9 P.M. Sat.

Vampire. 2222 Market St. (569–0569). A DJ plays current dance music in this three-story club with perhaps the city's largest dance floor. Game room, sofa lounge with bar, and tropical blender bar. Open Wed.–Thurs. until 2 A.M.., Fri.–Sat. until dawn. Weekend cover of $6 includes one drink.

Jazz

Cafe Borgia. 406 S. 2nd St., downstairs at Lautrec restaurant (574–0414). Voted one of the best 100 bars in America by *Esquire* magazine. Live jazz nightly from 9:30 P.M.

Jewel's Jazz Club. 679 N. Broad St., at Fairmount Ave. (236–1396). The hottest jazz joint in town, re-pioneering jazz in Philadelphia. Past and present greats like Betty Carter and Herbie Mann perform Thurs.–Sat. nights in the 80-seat club. Tickets in advance or at the door.

Si! Ristorante. 212 Walnut St. (238–1628) Northern Italian restaurant features local and big-name artists Wed.–Sat. nights in their lounge. Music begins 869 P.M. Cover varies.

Tivoli. 757 S. Front St. (339–8090). Attractive Danish restaurant features live music—top 40s early in the evening, jazz later—Tues.–Sun. nights. Small dance floor.

T'n'T Monroe's. 1433 Arch St. (567–7385). Big names sit in with Bootsie Barnes' house band Mon.–Wed. nights, 8 P.M.–1 A.M. Periodic weekend performances. No weeknight cover.

Comedy Clubs

Comedy Factory Outlet. 31 Bank (between Market and Chestnut, 2d and 3d) (386–6911). Funny stuff ranging from local comics (open stage night on Thursday) to the young pros. Thurs.–Sat.

Comedy Works. 126 Chestnut St., upstairs (922–5997). The city's original full-time comedy club. Top young comics from both coasts perform Thurs.–Sat. Wednesday is open stage night for aspiring comics.

Going Bananas. 613 S. 2d St. (226–2621). Stand-up comedy with local area and New York talent. Friday and Saturday night shows.

SECURITY. Like all big cities, Philadelphia has its share of crime. But if you exercise common sense, you won't be an easy target. The neighborhoods described in the introduction of this chapter are heavily used and quite safe by day, with the possible exception of the more remote areas of Fairmount Park. At night, some of these areas are sparsely populated and unsavory, particularly the 13th Street "strip" between Spruce and Vine streets. Avoid walking down dark, deserted streets; women should not walk alone at night, except in the busiest areas. If you are uncertain of your route, take a cab. Extra security during rush hours makes the subway safe, but subways should be avoided at night unless you are traveling to the stadium complex for a sports event; then you'll have lots of company.

PHOENIX

by
Dana Cooper

Dana Cooper is a Phoenix-based free-lancer who has written on a variety of topics for Arizona newspapers and magazines. She is financial columnist for Phoenix Home & Garden *and has published several stories in* Arizona Highways. *A Phoenician for seven years, Cooper lives with her husband and daughter in Paradise Valley.*

"The Valley of the Sun." A more appropriate slogan for this desert metropolis could not be found, since it almost never rains in Arizona. With about 300 sunny days per year, and only seven to twelve inches of rainfall, Phoenix is indeed sun country.

No wonder people are coming to the valley in droves. Now the ninth-largest city in the United States, Phoenix today has a population of more than 1.5 million, a figure that is expected to double by the year 2012. Drive along any city street and you're sure to see several construction sites for office buildings. In housing starts, Phoenix is among the top five cities in the nation, and everywhere an energetic atmosphere prevails. Growth is a major topic of discussion here, and the issue seems to weigh more heavily on newcomers who don't want their newly found paradise spoiled.

Sun is the lure, but Phoenix is a community with an appealing life-style. It's a casual, friendly, yet hardworking town, a city filled with professional workers and middle-class families. The emphasis on outdoor living makes Phoenix a perfect place for raising children, catching a quick game of tennis after work, or enjoying a relaxing week in the sun.

Many have an image of Phoenix as a retirement haven, and there are lovely retirement communities, but the average age of Phoenicians is twenty-nine years old. Native Arizonans are rare among the transplanted Californians and Midwesterners, but given the rate of growth of the city, it doesn't take long before a newcomer feels at home.

Phoenix sprawls for 258 square miles on the flat desert at the base of the kneeling dromedary that is Camelback Mountain. It's surrounded on three sides by rocky mountains studded with saguaro cactus. To the south and west are cotton fields, remnants of the city's rural past before the building boom of the mid-1970s turned much of Phoenix into concrete and glass. The east side is bordered by the McDowell Mountains and, visible on most days, the Superstition Mountains, nearly 60 miles away, where the Lost Dutchman's Mine is still hidden.

Phoenix is Arizona's largest and most important city. It is the state capital, home of the state's largest banks and some of the nation's bigger companies: the Greyhound Corporation, Ramada Inns, Best Western International, and divisions of American Express, Motorola, Honeywell, and GTE. The valley is also home to a host of celebrities, including Erma Bombeck, Senator Barry Goldwater, Glen Campbell, rocker Alice Cooper, and heavy-metalist Rob Halford.

Mayor Terry Goddard, an aggressive forty-one-year-old who was reelected in fall 1987, symbolizes the energy of Phoenix. Inherent in rapid expansion are growing pains, and Goddard has embarked on a campaign to reorganize the city government to position Phoenix for the future. Transportation is a controversial issue in a town whose sprawl is much like that of Los Angeles but that has only two freeways to accommodate traffic. Capturing corporate relocations is another priority; Phoenix faces competition from other Sunbelt cities such as San Antonio and Albuquerque and has stepped up efforts to market its availability to attractive industry.

Perhaps the most controversial topic is whether downtown should be the focus for development. Like most major cities, Phoenix experienced urban flight in the late 1950s and 1960s, rendering the already small downtown area useless for anyone except bankers, lawyers, and city and state government workers. The sidewalks were rolled up at night. During the past five years, however, there has been an effort to refurbish and build and create a real people place, a vibrant setting that will be suitable for recreation as well.

Phoenix is a curious mix of sophistication and small-town stability, with the finest in shopping and resorts yet an unpretentious and easygoing pace. The capital city and surrounding communities of Scottsdale, Tempe (home of Arizona State University), Mesa, Chandler, Goodyear, Avondale, Litchfield Park, Glendale, Peoria, Sun City, Cave Creek, and Carefree are clean and modern yet retain a western flavor. Phoenix has a wide range of cultural institutions, from the Phoenix Symphony Orchestra to a variety of theater companies to suit every taste. Art is a big business here, with a concentration of galleries in Scottsdale, and several noted western artists live in the area, including Native American Fritz Scholder. Dining out is a favorite pastime of many Phoenicians. Known for its hearty Mexican food as well as cowboy steaks grilled over mesquite, Phoenix and its environs have equally good French and Continental cuisine.

Phoenix is rooted in ancient Indian cultures, particularly the Hohokam ("ones who are gone"), who settled the area in the 1300s and constructed an elaborate irrigation system that was rediscovered in Civil War times. Darrel Duppa, an Englishman, was among the first of the modern-day settlers and an organizer of the canal company that became the wellspring of the town. He believed that, like the mythical Phoenix bird, a great metropolis would rise from the ashes of the Hohokam ruins—thus Phoenix was born.

By 1870 a townsite had been established, along with the beginnings of the grid street system, shops, saloons, and a jail. Built of adobe to withstand the desert heat, the town drew adventurers from all over the country who sought their fortunes in agriculture, mining, and services. When Arizona became a state in 1912, Phoenix had a population of 25,000.

While in Phoenix, it's worthwhile and easy to take some side trips to experience the contrasts of Arizona. Within a day's drive are Sedona's breathtaking red rock formations; Humphrey's Peak, at 12,670 feet the highest point in Arizona, overlooking Flagstaff; prehistoric Indian ruins at Montezuma's Castle; Paolo Soleri's Arcosanti, an experimental city being built in the middle of the desert; Tucson's Arizona-Sonora Desert Museum; Roosevelt Dam, reached via the Apache Trail; and a handful of ghost towns abandoned after the mines gave out. Marvel at the geographic differences as you move from pine forests, rocky buttes, and sandstone mountains to gently rolling chaparral country and flat desert floor sprinkled with blue-green sage, prickly pear, cholla, and palo verde, the state tree. Arizona is wildly beautiful, and the subtle desert colors can be soothing to the eye.

There's something to satisfy everyone in Phoenix, whether you're looking for a ritzy resort to pamper your body and soul, energetic outdoor activity, or a taste of culture that combines Anglo, native American, and Hispanic.

PRACTICAL INFORMATION

WHEN TO GO. Phoenix is one of the nation's sunniest spots, with 86 percent overall sunshine. That translates into nearly 300 sunny days per year and an annual average of 7 inches of rain. There are two rainy seasons, July and August, which is called "monsoon" season for the moist winds that blow in from the south; and November through January, when there may be a few cloud-filled days.

But warm, sunny and dry is the usual report. In fact, the average temperature for June, July and August is 102 degrees, with 99 percent sunshine. Low humidity makes the summer heat comfortable, and when the sun goes down, you may wish for a sweater if you're poolside, even though temperatures only cool off to about 95 degrees.

Winters are mild, pleasant, and the best time for visitors and residents alike. Daytime temperatures hover right around 70 degrees, with lows of about 40 degrees. You can work on your tan during the day and curl up to a roaring firepit at night.

The tourist season lasts from November until Easter, with the busiest months being January and February. Much of Phoenix is booked during the beginning of the year, and so it is wise to make reservations far in advance. There is no real agreement among hotels and resorts as to when the "season" begins and ends, but with respect to rates there are three general categories: January 1 through April 30, when the highest rates are in effect; May 1 through September 30, when rates are the lowest; and October 1 through December 31, when rates fall in the middle.

HOW TO GET THERE. By air. Phoenix Sky Harbor International Airport is relatively new, has excellent facilities for handicapped persons, and is within a half hour from most points in Phoenix. It has three terminals and is served by all major carriers, including *American, Braniff, Continental, Eastern, Northwest, TWA, United, USAir,* and *Western,* which bring visitors from all over the United States. Regional airlines are *America West,* which is based in Phoenix and flies to a number of major cities; *Southwest;* and *PSA,* a California carrier. *Delta* offers has begun nonstop service from Cincinnati daily.

By bus. Phoenix is on *Greyhound-Trailways'* major routes from Dallas to Los Angeles. Greyhound has a clean and modern terminal and restaurant in the heart of downtown, 5th St. and Washington, within walking distance of the Convention Center, Symphony Hall, and the major downtown hotels. For fares and schedule information, call 602–248–4040.

Points of Interest

1) Arizona Historical Society Museum
2) Arizona Museum
3) Arizona State University
4) Art Museum
5) Capitol Building
6) City-County Complex
7) Civic Plaza
8) Desert Botanical Garden
9) Grady Gammage Memorial Auditorium
10) Greyhound Park (Dog Racing)
11) Heard Museum
12) Mineral Museum
13) Municipal Stadium
14) Pueblo Grande
15) State Fairgrounds
16) Veteran's Memorial Coliseum
17) Phoenix Zoo

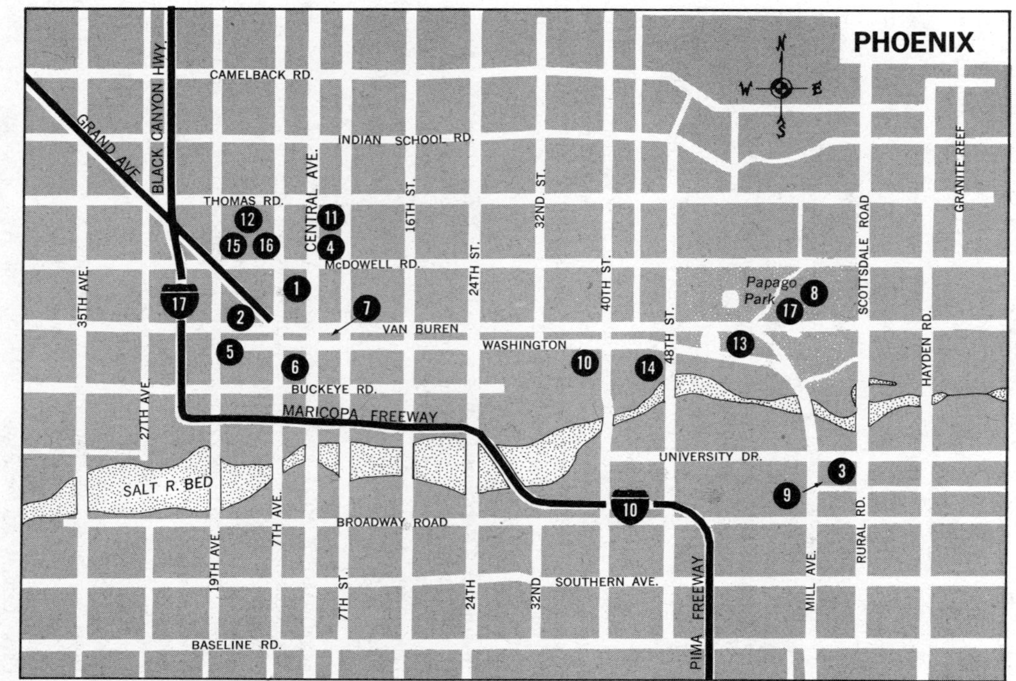

By car. The main east-west route through Arizona is I-10, which runs from Tucson northwest to Phoenix and west from Phoenix to Los Angeles. I-17 runs north to Flagstaff. Another Interstate, I-8, cuts southwest from I-10 south of Phoenix to Yuma and San Diego.

A free illustrated Arizona state road map is available from the Arizona Department of Transportation by writing to *Arizona Highways* magazine, 2039 West Lewis Ave., Phoenix, AZ 85009.

By train. Train travel is time-consuming and often costly, but it can be a great vacation experience and a good way to see the country. *Amtrak* serves Phoenix with a downtown passenger station at 401 W. Harrison (602–253–0121). The toll-free information and reservations phone number is 800–872–7245 (USA–RAIL). Amtrak's Sunset Ltd. route starts in New Orleans and winds its westerly way through Houston, San Antonio, and El Paso, arriving in Phoenix 36 hours later before going on to Yuma and Los Angeles. The Southwest Ltd. takes 28 hours from Chicago through Kansas City, Albuquerque, and Flagstaff, where you must obtain bus tickets for the final stretch into Phoenix (140 miles).

TELEPHONES. The area code for Phoenix and all of Arizona is 602. Long-distance calls within the state can be made by dialing 1 and the number (no area code needed). Directory assistance for the entire state can be reached by dialing 1–411; long distance directory assistance outside Arizona can be reached at 1–area code–555–1212. Pay phones cost 25 cents, with no time limit.

Emergency Telephone Numbers. The Phoenix Police Department number is 911 for life-and-death emergencies. For fire department and paramedics, call 253–1191. Poison control can be reached at 253–3334 or call toll-free 800–362–0101. Other useful numbers are: *Doctor's Referral Service* (258–6461); *Dentists' Referral Service* (264–3575); and *Arizona Automobile Association* (252–7751).

ACCOMMODATIONS. The Valley of the Sun is filled with hotels, motels, and resorts. Amid the famous and sumptuous (there are four Mobil five-star properties in the valley), there are some places to stay that won't break your bank. Hotel rates are based on double occupancy. Categories, determined by price, are as follows: *Reasonable,* $50 to $65; *Very Economical,* under $50. Summer rates are lower.

Reasonable

Days Inn. 502 W. Camelback Rd., Phoenix, AZ 85013 (602–264–9290). Kitchenette, pool, sauna and steam room, restaurant, live entertainment in lounge, free limousine to airport, some wet bars.

Hotel San Carlos. 202 N. Central Ave., Phoenix, AZ 85004 (602–253–4121). Refurbished concierge-style hotel downtown. Pool, restaurant, free airport transportation and parking, free local calls, and Continental breakfast.

Park Central Motor Hotel. 3033 N. 7th Ave., Phoenix, AZ 85013 (602–277–2621). Central location, near shopping. Kitchenettes, pool, restaurant, coin laundry, in-room movies.

TraveLodge Airport Inn. 2901 Sky Harbor Blvd., Phoenix, AZ 85034 (602–275–3634 or 800–325–3535). On airport grounds, 24-hour limousine service, pool, tennis, airport, gift shop.

Very Economical

Arizona Ranch House Inn. 5600 N. Central, Phoenix, AZ 85021 (602–279–3221). Complimentary Continental breakfast, spa, kitchenettes, pool, restaurant, quiet grounds, central location.

Best Western Airport Inn. 2425 S. 24th St., Phoenix, AZ 85034 (602–273–7251, 800–528–1234). Pool, racquetball, restaurant, courtesy airport transportation. Crib free, children under 12 free. Coin laundry.

Best Western St. Francis Inn. 4321 N. Central Ave., Phoenix, AZ 85012 (602–277–6671, 800–528–1234). Located in central corridor; pool, in-room movies, restaurant adjacent, game room, room service, some refrigerators. Crib free; children under 12 free. Free airport and bus depot transportation.

Kon Tiki Hotel. 2364 E. Van Buren St., Phoenix, AZ 85006 (602–244–9361). Near airport. Pool, restaurant, free Continental breakfast, free airport transportation, refrigerators.

Quality Inn Desert Sky. 3541 E. Van Buren, Phoenix, AZ 85008 (602–273–7121, 800–228–5151). Landscaped grounds, pool, restaurant, children under 16 free, senior citizen rates, in-room movies, close to botanical garden and zoo.

Budget Motel Chains. The following national chains are essentially no-frills operations with bargain prices.

Comfort Inn Airport. 4120 E. Van Buren, Phoenix, AZ 85021 (602–275–5746, 800–228–5150). Pool, restaurant, kitchenettes.

Phoenix Sunrise Motel. 3644 E. Van Buren, Phoenix, AZ 85008 (602–275–7661). Free HBO, coffee; family suites, pool, small pets allowed. Near airport.

Bed-and-Breakfast referral services: **Bed & Breakfast in Arizona,** 8433 N. Black Canyon, Suite 160, Phoenix, AZ 85021 (602–995–2831); **Mi Casa Su Casa Bed & Breakfast,** 1456 N. Scottsdale Rd., Suite 110, Tempe, AZ 85281 (602–990–0682).

Ys and Hostels. The **Downtown YMCA,** 350 N. 1st Ave., Phoenix, AZ 85025 (602–253–6181), has apartments for singles only for as little as $55 per week ($11 per night), including use of facilities—pool, weight rooms, and gym. Cafeteria. For youth hostel information, get in touch with **Arizona State Council, AYH, Inc.** 14049 N. 39th Place, Phoenix, AZ 85032 (602–254–9803).

HOW TO GET AROUND. From the airport. A taxi from the airport to downtown Phoenix costs about $12. Phoenix transit bus number 17 runs from the airport to downtown, every 30 minutes after 6 A.M. The last bus leaves the last terminal at 6:40 P.M. The cost is 75 cents. Supershuttle runs from the airport to nearly anywhere in the Phoenix metro area 24 hours a day. They guarantee a maximum of three stops and charge $10. Some hotels and resorts offer complimentary limousine service.

By bus. Phoenix is an automobile city; public transportation is inefficient, and city campaigns to encourage riding the bus and car pooling have had little success. Phoenix Transit is working to upgrade bus service; currently, buses run from 6 A.M. to 7:30 P.M. Mon.–Fri., and 6:30 A.M. to 7:30 P.M. Sat. There is no bus service on Sunday. Adults, 75 cents; senior citizens, handicapped, and children, 35 cents. Exact change required. Route information: 257–8426, 261–8208 for TTY-TDD.

By taxi. Taxis are expensive and not a common method of transport. They do not cruise the streets, so you must call for one. Taxi competition is fierce, and mileage fees and charges for waiting time vary greatly. A reasonably priced company is Air Courier (244–1818); you might also try Yellow Cab (252–5252).

By rental car. Most car rental companies have offices at Sky Harbor airport or nearby. Weeklong packages can be had at *Avis* (273–3222); *Budget* (249–6124), open 24 hours with a discount voucher booklet; *National* (275–4771), which offers special vacation rates; and *Thrifty* (244–0311), with unlimited mileage and 24-hour service.

HINTS TO THE MOTORIST. Phoenix streets are laid out in an uncomplicated grid system, the center of which is Central Avenue (north-south) and Washington (east-west). From there, all roads running north and south are either numbered streets (east of Central) or avenues (west of Central), commencing with 1st Street all the way out to 70th Street. Major east-west arteries are situated at 1-mile intervals; for example, Camelback Road is 5 miles from the heart of the city and is in the 5000 block of North Central Avenue. The only complication in the grid is going around mountains, but streets resume their logical pattern on the other side.

Traffic in Phoenix is getting denser owing to the increasing number of cars and the lack of freeways crossing the valley. Rush hour begins about 4 P.M. You may turn right on a red light, after a *complete* stop, in Arizona unless otherwise noted, but beware: Arizonans have such a propensity for running the long yellow lights that Phoenix launched a "Don't Run Red Lights" campaign with stiff fines. A high number of winter visitors unsure of their way also makes for travel hassles, so drive defensively. The city is also working to institute more left-hand-turn arrows at major intersections to improve the traffic flow.

As with most of the country, Arizona is enforcing stiff drunk driving penalties. Do not drink and drive.

Parking meters downtown are free after 5 P.M. and on Saturday and Sunday, but street parking spaces can be difficult to find during the week. You're usually better off with an office building parking garage; try the First Interstate Plaza parking garage off 1st Avenue just north of Washington. Rates are about $4 per day. Less expensive are uncovered lots, including one at 2d Avenue and Monroe for about $2 per day.

The speed limit is 25 mph unless otherwise posted. Arizona adheres to the federal law of 55 mph on major roads and freeways, 65 mph on rural interstates.

The *Arizona Automobile Association* (AAA) offers emergency road service to members (members of the American Automobile Association included); dial 274–1114. Their travel agency insurance number is 252–7751; for dial-a-trip, call 277–0930.

See the desert-driving tips in the chapter on Tucson.

TOURIST INFORMATION. The *Phoenix and Valley of the Sun Convention and Visitors Bureau* publishes a free *Visitors Guide* with information on attractions and museums, sports, dining, and shopping; a complete map of the Valley of the Sun; listings of accommodations and transportation; and a calendar of events. Write to them at 505 N. Second St., Suite 300, Phoenix, AZ 85004, or call 602–254–6500 from 8:30 A.M. to 5 P.M. Mon.–Fri. The bureau also operates a toll-free reservations number for over 100 hotels, inns, and resorts in the Phoenix-Scottsdale area and for the Grand Canyon. Out-of-state, dial 800–528–0483; within Arizona, call 800–221–5596.

There are recordings with visitor information hotline (252–5588), tourist information (254–6500), and foreign visitors' multilingual information (ask for Visit USA Desk at 800–255–3050).

Foreign Currency. Foreign currency may be exchanged at: *First Interstate Bank of Arizona,* 100 West Washington (271–6000), open Monday through Friday, 9 A.M.–4 P.M.; *Valley National Bank,* Central and Van Buren (261–2900), open Monday through Thursday, 10 A.M.–4 P.M., Friday 10 A.M.–6 P.M.; the *Arizona Bank,* 101 North 1st Avenue, (262–2891), open 9 A.M.–3 P.M., Monday through Friday.

HINTS TO DISABLED TRAVELERS. Much of Phoenix is new and geared to providing easy access to disabled visitors. Office buildings, libraries, and museums generally have wheelchair entries and rest-room facilities. Phoenix Transit has special buses to accommodate wheelchair passengers and a Dial-A-Ride service for the elderly or infirm (257–8426, Sundays 271–4545). The main branch of the Phoenix Public Library, Central and McDowell, has recordings for the blind, and most pay phones have TTY-TDD devices for the hard of hearing. Special parking privileges are extended to the handicapped in most parking lots, and the state issues license plates designating vehicles operated by disabled drivers. For travel tips for the disabled, write Consumer Information Center, Pueblo, CO 81109. It is a good idea when making reservations to inquire about specific accommodations for disabled travelers.

FREE EVENTS. Some of the best free events in Phoenix include driving the area to marvel at the desert topography, the different landscaping techniques and architecture, and Camelback Mountain and Squaw Peak. There is no charge to enjoy the city's collection of parks, such as South Mountain Park with its dramatic view of the city and Encanto Park with its wide range of activities. The city sponsors a **lunchtime lively arts series** at Patriots Park in the heart of downtown; for information call the Phoenix Parks Department (262–6861). Free **evening concerts** are held in the summer at the Encanto Park bandshell; call 262–6861 for details.

Hello, Phoenix! is a festival set up at Civic Plaza that includes food booths, arts and crafts, ethnic dances and entertainment. Usually held the third weekend in April. **Cinco de Mayo** (May 5), Mexican independence day, is the cause for another festival at Civic Plaza featuring Hispanic food, culture, and entertainment. **June-**

teenth, June 19th, is a downtown street fair commemorating the Emancipation Proclamation. **Christmas** officially begins in Phoenix with the lighting of the city tree at Phoenix Art Museum, usually at 5 P.M. on the Wednesday before Christmas.

Parades celebrating a variety of holidays and occasions generally march south on Central from Osborn to Fillmore; most notable is the **Fiesta Bowl** parade on New Year's weekend, which is nationally televised. Other traditional parades are held on **Saint Patrick's Day, Veterans Day,** and the **Phoenix Rodeo.**

Free attractions in Phoenix include:

Arizona Mineral Resource Museum. State Fairgrounds, 19th Ave. and McDowell, Phoenix, AZ 85007 (255–3791). Large collection of minerals and ores from Arizona. Call for hours.

Arizona Museum. 1002 W. Van Buren St., Phoenix, AZ 85007 (253–2734). Two thousand years of Arizona history with Hohokam Indian artifacts in the original adobe building of the first museum in Phoenix. Weds.–Sun., 11 A.M.–4 P.M.

Arizona Capitol Museum. 1700 W. Washington, Phoenix, AZ 85009 (255–4900). Restoration of the turn-of-the-century capitol. Open 8 A.M.–5 P.M., Mon.–Fri.

Arizona Military Museum. 5636 East McDowell, Phoenix, AZ (273–9700). Open 1 P.M.–4 P.M., Sat.–Sun.

Arizona Historical Society Museum. 1242 N. Central Ave., Phoenix, AZ 85004 (255–4479). Exhibits include an old-time general store, pharmacy, mine, toy store, and Phoenix street car. Open 10 A.M.–4 P.M., Tues.–Sat.

Phoenix Art Museum. Central and McDowell, Phoenix, AZ 85004 (257–1222). More than 11,000 works of art; permanent collections and traveling exhibitions. Free Wed. 10 A.M.–9 P.M.

Rawhide. 23023 North Scottsdale Rd., Scottsdale, AZ 85261 (563–5111). An authentic Arizona town of the 1880s, stagecoach rides, cowboy shoot-outs. Open Mon.–Fri., 5 P.M. to midnight; Sat.–Sun., noon to midnight. Free admission.

TOURS AND SPECIAL-INTEREST SIGHTSEEING. Phoenix is the site of a number of unusual tours—among them are jeep tours, horseback journeys, cookouts, even balloon rides—listed in the Convention and Visitors Bureau's *Visitors Guide.* **Walkabout Arizona** offers free neighborhood walks in urban, suburban, and rural environments. For a monthly schedule, send a self-addressed stamped envelope to Walkabout Arizona, Box 17212, Phoenix, AZ 85011. **Gray Line/Sun Valley Bus Lines,** Box 2471, Phoenix, AZ 85002 (254–4550), conducts half-day bus tours of Phoenix and the Valley of the Sun for $15 per person, children $7.50; this is a particularly good way to get oriented.

Arizona Jeep Tours Inc., 12430 N. 65 Pl., Phoenix, AZ 85251 (481–0223), conducts tours of the surrounding Sonoran desert and exotic homes in the town of Carefree. Adults, $45; children $22.50.

The Arizona State Capitol, 1700 W. Washington (255–4581), has informative, free tours at 10 A.M. and 2 P.M., Mon.–Fri. during legislative sessions. The building, completed in 1901, has been renovated and is filled with Arizona state relics. Open weekdays 8 A.M. to 5 P.M.

During the season (November through March), **art walks** take place on Thursday evenings from 7 to 9 P.M. on Scottsdale's "gallery row," Main Street. Most galleries stay open for this festive trek, and many serve complimentary wine. If you hit upon a show's opening night, you'll be able to meet the artist or watch him work.

It costs nothing to drive through the grounds of the **Arizona Biltmore,** 24th St. and Missouri, the famous resort built in 1929 by the Chicago Wrigleys, based on a Frank Lloyd Wright design. The adjoining **Wrigley Mansion,** once the Wrigleys' summer retreat and now a private club operated by Western Savings, is a gracious 25-room Spanish colonial mansion that sits atop a hilly perch with one of the best views in the city. Tours of the mansion are $10 per person, leaving from Western Savings' Mansion Club at 9:30 A.M. Monday through Friday. Reservations are required; call 955–4079.

Worth the drive is **Taliesin West,** 108th St. and Shea Blvd., northeast Scottsdale, Frank Lloyd Wright's redwood and desert facestone residence and architectural school. The famous architect died in 1959, and his former students now carry on his work. Students stay from 3 to 5 years and live behind Taliesin. Tours are conducted every hour, daily, 10 A.M.–4 P.M. from mid-October to mid-May. Adults, $5; children under 12, $2. Tours are limited in the summer; call 860–8810.

PARKS AND GARDENS. The Phoenix Parks, Recreation and Library Department operates 55 community parks and seven desert mountain parks. Many have swimming pools, tennis courts, and golf courses for a minimal charge. For details, call 262–6711.

Encanto Park is the largest of the community parks. With 27 holes of golf, racquetball courts, archery, an Olympic-sized swimming pool, baseball diamonds, lagoon with fishing for children under age 15, canoes and pedal boats, and Kiddieland (an amusement park for children), there is something for everyone. Located at 15th Ave. and Encanto Blvd., the park borders one of the loveliest residential neighborhoods in the city.

The desert mountain parks are open 5:30 A.M.–midnight. Particularly spectacular is **Squaw Peak Park** in north Phoenix at 2701 East Squaw Peak Dr. Hike the 1.2-mile summit trail for a workout and a view that can't be beat. Fire pits, picnic ramadas, and tables are available for picnickers. Off the beaten path is **Echo Canyon Park,** East MacDonald Dr. and Tatum Blvd., tucked into the side of Camelback Mountain, with a wide variety of desert flora.

Desert Botanical Garden, 1201 N. Galvin Parkway, Phoenix, AZ 85008 (941–1225), founded in 1937, is recognized as one of the world's finest collections of desert flora, with more than 8,000 plants on 150 acres. Special events such as bird walks and desert gardening workshops are offered. Open from 9 A.M. to sunset, 7 A.M. to sunset in July and August. Adults, $3; seniors, $2.50; children 5 to 12, 50 cents; children under 5, free. Wheelchairs are available without charge.

ZOOS. The Phoenix Zoo, 5810 East Van Buren St., Phoenix, AZ 85010 (273–1341), is situated among the red buttes of Papago Park, a natural setting with room for many of the animals to roam. There are more than a thousand animals, including rare species such as the Arabian oryx, the New Guinea forest wallaby, and the double-wattled cassowary. An extensive children's zoo has areas for petting the animals, a farm, an animal nursery, and birthday party facilities. Open daily 9 A.M.–5 P.M. (summer hours 8 A.M.–5 P.M.).

PARTICIPANT SPORTS. Joggers can be found everywhere, but a safe and interesting place to run is along the Arizona Canal. Park your car along the canal banks at the corner of 32d St. and Stanford, half a mile north of Camelback Rd. You can jog along the canal for miles, west through the grounds of the Biltmore, past the Wrigley Mansion, and through portions of some of the nicest residential neighborhoods. In summer months start early; the day's intense heat makes 5 or 6 A.M. the best time to jog. Check local newspapers—Arizona *Republic* or Phoenix *Gazette*—for weekend 10K listings.

Many Phoenix hotels have private **tennis** courts open to their guests, but there are also several public, free-of-charge courts available. *Encanto Park,* 15th Ave. and Encanto Blvd., has eight lighted public courts open from dawn to 10 P.M. *Granada Park,* 6505 N. 20th St., has four lighted courts open to the public 6 A.M.–11 P.M. *Phoenix Tennis Center,* 6330 N. 21st Ave. (249–3712), has 22 lighted public courts; $1 per person for 1½ hours of play, $1.80 per court for lights. For reservations, call 249–3712.

Swimming pools are also found at most hotels, but 21 of the city parks have pools open for a minimal charge from Memorial Day–Labor Day. *Encanto Park,* the most centrally located, has an Olympic-sized pool with diving area, children's area, snack bar, and lane for lap swimming. For details on city public pools, call 262–6541.

Public **racquetball** courts are also available at Encanto Park. Call 261–8994 for reservations.

Phoenix and Scottsdale have some of the best golfing weather and **golf courses** in the world; more than 75 tournaments are held each year, including the Phoenix Open, a PGA tradition. *Encanto Park* offers a 9-hole course, 2300 N. 17th Ave. (262–6870); and an 18-hole course, 2705 N. 15th Ave. (262–6870). Both open 6:30 A.M.–6:30 P.M. You'll pay $4 for 9 holes, $2.50 if you're 62 and over. *Papago Golf Course* in Papago Park, 52d St. and E. Van Buren, has 18 holes of golf and is open 6 A.M. until dark. The fee is $13.25, $10 for those 62 and over. For reservations, call 275–8428. *Thunderbird Country Club,* in the South Mountains, 701 E. Thunderbird Trail, has 18 holes of golf for $24.50, on weekdays, including a golf cart. Senior citizens qualify for a $18.75 rate with cart on weekdays. For reservations, call 243–1262.

Stables in Phoenix offer more than just **horseback riding;** you can sign up for desert cookouts, hayrides, or breakfast and twilight rides. *Papago Riding Stables,* featuring rides through Papago Park, 52d St. and East Van Buren (966–9793), charges $10 per person for the first hour and $8 per hour thereafter. *South Mountain Stables,* 10005 S. Central Ave. (276–8131), charges $9 per person for 1 hour and $17 for 2 hours for guided or unescorted rides through South Mountain Park.

Hiking in the city's desert mountain parks is a way to experience the desert clime firsthand. *Squaw Peak Park,* 2701 East Squaw Peak Dr., offers a 1.2-mile summit trail winding up to the top of Squaw Peak, one of the most spectacular views in the city. *Echo Canyon Park,* East MacDonald Dr. and Tatum Blvd., offers access to Camelback Mountain.

Tubing the Salt River is a favorite activity in the summer. You'll need almost an entire day, but it's worth the experience if you've never tried floating down the river in an oversized inner tube. Call *Salt River Raft Trips* (968–1552).

The Arizona Senate authorized a study of bike and foot paths and proposed a $20 million statewide system of biking, hiking, and equestrian trails covering 3,300 miles. Today there are 47 miles of **bike trails** in the valley, running through park and picnic areas, beside desert mountains, and along canal banks. For a detailed map and information on bike rentals, call the Phoenix Parks, Recreation and Library Department (262–6861).

SPECTATOR SPORTS. Phoenix has lots of sporting events to choose from. The valley is a popular **baseball** training spot, even though Phoenix has no major league team. (The Phoenix Giants, farm team for the San Francisco Giants, play in the spring and summer at Phoenix Municipal Stadium, 5999 East Van Buren. Call 275–4488 for ticket information.) The San Francisco Giants play exhibition games at Municipal Stadium, and the Seattle Mariners conduct spring training camp at Arizona State University's Tempe Diablo Stadium. The Oakland Athletics train at Scottsdale Stadium, the Chicago Cubs at Mesa's Hohokam Stadium, and the Milwaukee Brewers at Sun City Stadium. Call each for game times and ticket information.

Scheduled to arrive in Phoenix for the 1988–89 season are the NFL **football** Cardinals, formally of St. Louis.

The NBA Phoenix Suns play **basketball** at Phoenix Memorial Coliseum, 19th Ave. and McDowell, Oct.–March. Tickets are about $12 per person. For details, call the Suns' ticket office at 263–7867.

The **Arizona State University** Sun Devils are continual league contenders in baseball, football, and basketball. For more information about game schedules and tickets, call 965–2381.

Dog racing takes place at Phoenix Greyhound Park, 3801 East Washington (273–7181), Sept.–March, Wed.–Sun. The grandstand is glass-enclosed and air-conditioned. There also is a clubhouse dining room, snack bars and cocktail lounges, and pari-mutuel betting. General admission, $1; for clubhouse admission, $2.

Turf Paradise, 1501 W. Bell Rd. (942–1101), has parimutuel betting on **thoroughbred horses** October through mid–May. General admission, $2.50.

CHILDREN'S ACTIVITIES. Phoenix Children's Theater presents plays four times a year, with a special production slated for Christmas. Acted by children for children on Saturdays and Sundays; reservations highly recommended. Call 263–5770 between 10 A.M. and 2 P.M.; tickets may be purchased at the place of performance, usually the Phoenix Little Theater, 25 East Coronado Rd.

Free to the public is the **Lilliput Pops Concerts Series,** Sundays at 3 P.M. in Phoenix Civic Plaza, 225 E. Adams, downtown Phoenix. Performances have included puppet shows, ballets such as *Peter and the Wolf,* singers, mimes, and symphony music. Call 271–9318 for details.

Encanto Park Kiddieland, 13th Ave. and Encanto Blvd. (254–0410), has rides and a paddlewheeler that cruises the lagoon and picnic areas.

Arizona Museum for Youth, 35 North Robson Street, Mesa (898–9046). This fine-arts center, intended especially for children, presents changing shows emphasizing hands-on activities.

The Hall of Flame, 6101 East Van Buren (275–3473), is a child's dream of shining red fire engines, hook and ladders, badges, helmets, axes, and other fire-fighting equipment. Mon.–Sat., 9 A.M.–5 P.M. Children under 6 free; children 6 to 18, 50 cents.

The brand new **Arizona Museum of Science and Technology** is a hands-on museum designed especially for kids, but adults will enjoy it as well. Located in the heart of downtown at 80 N. 2d St., Phoenix, AZ 85004 (256–9388). Open 9 A.M.–5 P.M., Mon.–Sat.; 1 P.M.–5 P.M., Sun. Adults, $2.50; children, $1.50; families, $5.

Pioneer Arizona Living History Museum, Interstate 17 and Pioneer Rd. (about 15 miles north of downtown), is a nineteenth-century town complete with jail, homestead cabins, and a main street where holdups are staged and horse-drawn carriages roll. Young people in costume act as guides and demonstrate old-fashioned crafts and skills. Picnic grounds are available, and there is a restaurant on the premises. Admission is free for children 5 and under. Open 9 A.M.–4:30 P.M., Tues.–Sun. For details, call 993–0212.

Big Surf, 1500 North Hayden Rd., Tempe (947–2478), is Arizona's answer to the beach. A machine in this huge outdoor pool creates waves large enough for body surfing. The water slide is a kid's dream. Call for hours and admission fees.

HISTORIC SITES AND HOUSES. **Heritage Square,** 7th St. and Monroe (262–5071), is a historical city park with eight restored turn-of-the-century homes, each converted into a museum. The open-air Lath House filled with lush plants is perfect for a picnic lunch from the on-site sandwich café. Featured is the Victorian Rosson House, lovingly restored and furnished. Tours conducted every half hour, Weds.–Sat., 10 A.M.–4 P.M.; Sun., noon–4 P.M. Adults, $1; children 7 to 15, 50 cents.

Pueblo Grande Museum, 4619 E. Washington (275–3452), is a Hohokam archaeological site and ruin believed to have been inhabited from 200 B.C. to A.D. 1400. Open 9 A.M.–4:45 P.M., Mon.–Sat.; 1 P.M.–4:45 P.M., Sun. Admission, 50 cents.

MUSEUMS AND GALLERIES. Phoenix boasts a number of museums that provide insight into the southwestern way of life, Indian culture, and desert clime. The Valley of the Sun is also an art mecca with numerous galleries open free of charge. (See also Free Events.)

The Heard Museum. 22 E. Monte Vista (252–8848). Primitive and contemporary art and culture of the Southwest, including Goldwater Kachina doll collection. Gift shop. Mon.–Sat., 10 A.M.–4:45 P.M., Sun. 1–4:45 P.M. Adults, $1.50; seniors, $1; students, 50 cents; children under 7 free.

Phoenix Art Museum. Central and McDowell (257–1222). Permanent and traveling exhibits, sculpture court, western, contemporary, Mexican, and European galleries. Open Tues.–Sat., 10 A.M.–5 P.M.; Weds., 10 A.M.–9 P.M. (donation); Sun., 1–5 P.M. Disabled facilities, gift shop. Adults, $2; senior citizens 65 and over, $1; students, $1; children 12 and under free.

Arizona History Room. First Interstate Bank Plaza, 1st Ave. and Washington (271–6879). Territorial banking office of 1800s, with changing exhibits illustrating life in early Arizona. Mon.–Fri., excluding holidays, 10 A.M.–3 P.M. Free.

Art galleries are generally open Monday through Saturday and are free. Call each for specific hours, as they change according to the season.

Gallery McGoffin. 902 W. Roosevelt (255–0785). Batik work displayed in a restored Phoenix bungalow; artists' studio adjoining.

The Thompson Gallery. 815 N. Central (258–4412). Original paintings, modern graphics, sculpture, and ceramics by local artists.

John Douglas Cline Gallery. 424 N. Central (252–7213). Works by southwestern artists.

Scottsdale's Main Street and Fifth Avenue Shops are dotted with galleries, many specializing in cowboy art, contemporary native American works, and fiber art. For more complete listings, check the yellow pages under "Art Galleries." (See Tours and Special-Interest Sightseeing for details.)

FILM. First-run movies are shown at *Chris-Town Theaters,* 5707 N. 19th Ave. (249–2843), five theaters in one; *Cine Capri,* 2323 East Camelback Rd. (956–1901); *Tower Plaza Cinemas,* 3841 E. Thomas Rd. (273–7711), two movies under one roof; *Town and Country,* 2087 E. Camelback Rd. (957–3500), six theaters; and *UA Cinemas,* Christown Mall, 15th Ave. and Montebello (242–4525). Matinees at most are half price, with Tuesdays being special low-rate days. The Tower Plaza Cinemas' movies usually are discounted. Call or check newspaper listings for details.

Valley Art Cinema, 509 S. Mill Avenue, Tempe (967–6664), shows classics and cult films. **The Camelview Plaza,** 7001 E. Highland (945–6178), is known for foreign films and revivals.

Worth the half-hour drive to Scottsdale is the **Scottsdale Center for the Arts'** film series, 7383 Scottsdale Mall (994–2301). Classics, travel films, and children's movies are shown at 7 P.M. Thursday through Saturday, with 1 P.M. matinees on Saturday. Reasonably priced tickets are available at the box office before shows. The **Classical Film Society** presents a diverse selection of films at the Unitarian-Universalist Church, 4027 E. Lincoln Dr., Paradise Valley (840–8400). Adults, $1.50; children, 50 cents.

MUSIC. Musical entertainment in Phoenix runs the gamut from symphony and opera to jazz, blues, and rock in the valley's many nightclubs. For more complete listings, check the Arizona *Republic,* the Phoenix *Gazette,* and the *New Times,* a weekly alternative paper.

The **Phoenix Symphony Orchestra,** which has recently achieved major status, plays classical, pops, chamber, and special Christmas concerts at Symphony Hall, 2d St. and Adams, from Oct.–May. For ticket information, call 264–4754; single ticket prices start at $8.

People's Pops Concert Series are performed on a monthly basis year-round at Symphony Hall, 2d St. and Adams (262–4634). For no charge, you can enjoy members of the Phoenix Symphony playing light classics and popular music; concerts also feature aspiring musicians, singers, and dancers. Free tickets are available at Phoenix public libraries.

Arizona State University student recitals and the ASU Symphony Orchestra concerts are also free of charge. For information about these performances, given on the ASU campus at Grady Gammage Auditorium, call 965–3434.

You can get the scoop on **jazz** concerts in the valley by calling a 24-hour hotline at 254–4545. There are a number of clubs around town offering jazz, folk, and rock performances; for show times and cover charges, check local newspapers.

STAGE. Phoenix Little Theater, 25 East Coronado (254–2151), is the nation's longest continuously running theater. Performances include musicals, premieres, and dramas directed and acted by local talent. Matinees are generally less expensive. **Actors Lab Arizona** presents four performances each season at its facility at 7624 E. Indian School Rd. (990–1731). Acting classes and workshops are offered. **Arizona Theater Company** brings professional theater to Phoenix and Tucson. Winter season performances are held at Phoenix College, 15th Ave. and Thomas Rd. (279–0534).

SHOPPING. Most items unique to Phoenix—Indian art and jewelry, fine art, cowboy clothing—are not inexpensive. Be sure to buy from a reputable dealer; unbelievably inexpensive Navajo rugs or Hopi Kachina dolls are more than likely cheap imitations.

Biltmore Fashion Park has 55 elegant shops and restaurants in a lushly landscaped setting at 24th St. and Camelback. **The Borgata of Scottsdale,** 6166 N. Scottsdale Rd., Scottsdale, an Italian Renaissance castle-inspired collection of shops, is strictly off-limits to your pocketbook but worth a browse if you enjoy gasping at $500 blouses. **Tower Plaza,** 3743 E. Thomas Rd., is an entire shopping mall devoted to discount shops. **The Fifth Avenue Shops,** Fifth Ave. at Scottsdale Rd., Scottsdale, are 150 specialty shops and restaurants with everything from Indian crafts to children's clothing.

Goldwaters, Park Central Mall, 3100 N. Central Ave. (248–0061), is Phoenix's most famous department store. The senator's family no longer owns it, but it's worth a visit for the finest in fashions, cosmetics, home furnishings, and special cactus-and-roadrunner-emblemed gift items. *Gilbert Ortega's Indian Arts* features fine sterling silver and 14-karat-gold jewelry plus authentic Indian arts and crafts at several locations, including 1803 E. Camelback Rd. (265–4311), and the downtown Hyatt Regency, 122 N. 2d St. (252–6440).

DINING OUT. Part of the fun of being in Phoenix is having such a wide selection of restaurants. Eating out is a favorite pastime in the valley; the amazing number of eating establishments and variety of ethnic choices is testimony to this fact. Of course, Phoenix is known for good Mexican food and the distinctive cowboy steak grilled over mesquite. But seafood lovers needn't despair—fresh fish is flown to landlocked Phoenix daily, and sushi lovers can belly up to several bars.

Categories, based on the cost of an average three-course dinner for one person, without beverage, tax (6 percent), or tip, are as follows: *Reasonable* $12 to $20; *Very Economical,* $6 to $11; *Low Budget,* $3 to $5. Unless otherwise noted, the restaurants listed below accept some if not all major credit cards.

It is also worth noting that dress in Phoenix is generally casual, yet men won't feel out of place at any of the "Reasonable" restaurants with a jacket and tie. Save your jeans for the "Low Budget" category.

Reasonable.

The Other Place. 7101 E. Lincoln Dr. (948–7910). Cozy, rustic decor. Prime ribs, fresh seafood, and steaks. Open for lunch Mon.–Fri. and dinner nightly. Reservations.

Pasta Segio's. 1904 E. Camelback Rd. (274–2795). Nicely prepared pasta dishes and other northern Italian specialties. Centrally located, open for lunch Mon.–Fri. and dinner daily. Reservations recommended.

Pinnacle Peak Patio. 10426 E. Pinnacle Peak Rd. (949–7311). A 45-minute drive from central Phoenix but well worth the experience. Elevated high over the valley; wonderful views. Family-style cowboy steaks, beans, and salad. Country band entertainment on patio. Don't wear a tie! Dinner 7 days, open at noon Sunday for lunch. Reservations not accepted for parties less than 14.

Oscar Taylor. 2420 E. Camelback Rd. (956–5705). Steaks and seafood in trendy old Chicago-style saloon atmosphere with lots of wood and brass. Extensive beer selection, separate bar. Huge portions, outstanding desserts (carrot cake is heavenly). Very crowded evenings; reservations a must. Lunch and dinner daily.

Salt Cellar. 550 N. Hayden Rd., Scottsdale (947–1963). The freshest in seafood flown in daily from both coasts makes this and its sister restaurant, Salt Cellar's Lobster House, 4900 E. Indian School Rd., Phoenix (840–1843), Valley favorites. For great deals on appetizers check out late-night happy hours.

Very Economical

Cactus Flower Cafe. 5641 E. Lincoln Dr. at Mountain Shadows Resort (948–7111). Pretty restaurant in the gorgeous setting of one of the valley's best resorts. Every evening from 4:30 to 10 P.M. entire dinner—soup or salad, entree, bread, dessert, and beverage—for $5.95 to $7.95; veal Marsala, prime rib, snapper, stuffed chicken.

Lunt Avenue Marble Club. 2 E. Camelback Rd. (265–8997). Pleasant, comfortable atmosphere; extensive menu including crepes, pizza, omelets, salads, specialty sandwiches, and giant burgers. Lunch and dinner daily.

The Spaghetti Company. 1418 N. Central Ave. (257–0380). Interesting antique shop atmosphere, great family meals. Good clam sauce and unusual Mizithra cheese sauce. Dinner daily, lunch Mon.–Fri. No reservations necessary.

Tee Pee. 4144 E. Indian School Rd. (956–0178). Diner-type atmosphere, yuppie crowd hangout evenings. Tasty Mexican food, decidedly less touristy. Try the chile relleno, Mexican pizza deluxe, margaritas. Lunch and dinner Mon.–Sat.; closed Sun.

Willy and Guillermo's. 5600 N. Central Ave. (266–1900). Lovely Spanish colonial building with patio and inside fountain. Bar and dance floor, several dining rooms with Mexican tile, wood tables, and inside fountain. Fun menu loaded with Mexican goodies and American dishes. Lunch and dinner daily.

Low Budget

Café Casino. 4824 N. 24th St. (955–3430). Charming French cafeteria-delicatessen with attractive eating areas. Variety of good French food, including trout almondine, coq au vin, quiche, salad niçoise. Wine and beer, great pastries, cheeses, and bread. Breakfast, lunch, and dinner daily.

Chive's. 1847 E. Camelback Rd. in the Colonnade Mall (234–1915). A 31-foot salad bar with more than 50 items; separate soup and bakery bar, fresh fruits, and dessert. Greenhouse atmosphere; wine and beer available. Lunches and dinner daily.

Downtown YMCA Cafeteria. 350 N. 1st Ave. (253–6181). Home cooking from scratch; huge portions, tiny prices. Country breakfasts, salad bar. Cafeteria atmosphere catering to downtown business types, Y residents, and those catching a quick bite after noontime workout. Breakfast and lunch Mon.–Fri.

Rosita's Place. 1914 E. Buckeye Rd. (262–9372). This is where Phoenicians go to get real Mexican food; Spanish network television is on, and much of the clientele speaks Spanish. The hottest salsa and best beans around; beer and margaritas. Lunch and dinner every day but Monday. No credit cards.

Tokyo Express. 3517 E. Thomas Rd. (955–1051). Japanese fast food; healthful, delicious, unusual. Teriyaki chicken on bed of rice, beef, tofu dishes. No alcoholic beverages. Picnic-style eating, bus your own table. Lunch and dinner Mon.–Sat.; closed Sun. No credit cards.

Note. You can never go wrong with good deli food or pizza. Some recommended places to try with reasonably priced family meals: **Katz Delicatessen,** 5144 N. Central Ave. (277–8814); **Munch A Bagel,** 5111 N. 7th St. (264–1975); **Miracle Mile,** 9 Park Central Mall (277–4783); **Tommy's Pizza,** 518 E. Dunlap (997–7578); and **Pizzafarro's,** 4225 E. Camelback Rd. (840–7990).

Recommended Splurge. The Gold Room at the Arizona Biltmore, 24th St. and Missouri (955–6600). Elegance is redefined in this Frank Lloyd Wright-inspired resort, a Phoenix landmark. The Gold Room offers gracious dining and has one of the most resplendent Sunday brunch buffets in town. Cooked-to-order omelets, papaya and strawberries, salads, cheeses, pastries, desserts, including enormous glass bowls of chocolate mousse. You can relax and dine for hours, looking out over the Biltmore's exquisite gardens. Reservations a must; $17 per person; $12.50 for children ages 3 to 12; free for children under 3.

Brunches. Most of the hotels and resorts in Phoenix have Sunday brunch buffets that vary in price. The most popular are listed below; call, or check the Sunday *Arizona Republic* "Leisure and Arts" section for current prices. Remember, if the fact is pertinent to your idea of the perfect Sunday brunch, that alcohol is not served before noon on Sundays in Arizona. (See also Recommended Splurge.)

Camelback Inn, 5402 E. Lincoln Dr. (948–1700), $13.95. **Hyatt Regency,** 2d St. and Adams (257–1110), $15.50, half price for children under 12. **Mountain Shadows,** 5641 E. Lincoln Dr. (948–7111), $8.50 adults, $5.95 children 6 to 12, free for children under 5. **Scottsdale Hilton,** 6333 N. Scottsdale Rd. (948–7750), $14.95 adults, $7.95 children under 11, 2 and under free.

NIGHTLIFE AND BARS. Phoenix is filled with bars of every kind: sophisticated saloons, college hangouts, bars with jazz bands, rock bands, reggae, and country. Bar hopping is big business here. The drinking age in Arizona is 21 and bars must close at 1 A.M. by law. The recent national crackdown on drunk drivers is very much alive in Phoenix; penalties are stiff, and it is highly recommended that you do not drink and drive.

Central Phoenix bars cater to the young professional business crowd, whereas Tempe has a mixture of blues and jazz clubs and college pubs with live music. The best source to check is the valley's weekly tabloid the *New Times,* which carries a comprehensive listing of hours and entertainment. Also call the Jazz in Arizona Hotline (254–4545) for a recorded message concerning local jazz shows. Recommended are:

Mr. Lucky's. 3660 Grand Ave. (246–0686). Live country music nightly; cowboy crowd. No cover charge Sun.–Thurs., otherwise $3 per person.

Zazoo. 909 E. Camelback Rd. (254–1354). Recorded music and a truly impressive 50-foot Happy Hour buffet draw the young professional singles crowds. Get there early on Friday nights or be ready to stand in line.

Timothy's Pub and Grill. 6335 N. 16th St. (277–7634). Sophistication and charm are a great backdrop for good live jazz nightly.

SECURITY. For the most part, Phoenix is a safe place to visit. The immediate downtown area closes up after workers escape the streets by 6 P.M., with the exception of the major hotels and the Civic Plaza-Symphony Hall complex. As a warm-weather haven, Phoenix is home to an increasing number of homeless transients who wander the streets by day and have been known to sleep in city parks by night. It may be best, therefore, not to walk about downtown unescorted after dark; be sure to lock car doors and hotel doors. Portions of South Phoenix just below downtown are high-crime areas and should be avoided. East Van Buren, dotted with tacky hotels, bars, and pawn shops, is the "red light" district, not a nice area for visitors. (Farther east on Van Buren are such delightful attractions as Papago Park and the Phoenix Zoo.)

PORTLAND

by
Linda Lampman

Linda Lampman is a coauthor of the Portland section of Fodor's Pacific North Coast, The Portland GuideBook, *and* Oregon for All Seasons *and a former reporter for the* Oregonian.

One of the first travelers to strike a bargain in Portland was Asa Lovejoy of Massachusetts, who paid 25 cents for a half interest in the original city site along the west bank of the Willamette River in 1844. He was joined shortly after by his partner, Francis Pettygrove of Maine, a man with no cash but enough store goods to barter for the other half of the claim.

No big spenders, the two later tossed a coin to determine a name for their cluster of log cabins among the stumps (Lovejoy picked Boston after his native state), and the coin has become a recognized asset in Oregon ever since. The state counts tourism as its second largest industry, and for good reason. Visitors continue to receive good value for their investment when they vacation here.

The city of Portland is in the middle of one of its greatest changes in decades. More than a dozen new office and public buildings have risen in the past five years, blocking the snow-capped Cascade Range and often the suburban west hills from a city center view. A cosmopolitan city has emerged from the cluster of cabins in the stumps.

But city planners in this community of 420,144 have kept careful watch on its more than 125 public parks and gardens, adding even more places designed for people. From the floating dock at Waterfront Park where a lucky line can catch a salmon at the city center to more than 5,000 acres of forest with hiking trails, much has been planned for pedestrian pleasure.

Old Town, where Lovejoy and Pettygrove tossed the coin, is a riverside area of rejuvenated Victorian iron fronts stretching from Front and Fifth between N.W. Everett and S.W. Yamhill. The area, which radiates from the restored Skidmore Fountain, dedicated in 1888 to the men, horses, and dogs of the city, is still partially paved in cobblestones that were used as ballast by the nineteenth-century sailing ships that docked in Portland's freshwater harbor. The view up any street here is romantically ornate, with as many nooks and crannies as the queen's sideboard. But watch the streets as well as the crannies here. Those curved tracks, set amid cobblestone swirls, bring MAX, the city's Metropolitan Area Express. The 15-mile light rail connection joining the East County runs a silent, but speedy, schedule daily, and is the first of its kind in the Northwest. Board at any station downtown. The ride is free until you cross the Willamette.

Old Town is Portland's beginning, but national news stories have been written about some of its newer buildings. First-time Portland visitors will want to see the Portland Building by Michael Graves at 1120 S.W. 5th. Dedicated in 1983, this multicolored example of postmodernism housing city offices still proves newsworthy.

South on 3d Avenue at Clay, just across from Civic Auditorium, is the Ira Keller Fountain, which Ada Louise Huxtable, *New York Times* critic, called "perhaps the greatest open space since the Renaissance." The city block of monolithic cement, covered most days with rushing water, has also been dubbed "the people's fountain" since it draws so many splashers and waders on warm days. Lifeguards are on duty during the summer.

Gov. Tom McCall Waterfront Park, a 23-acre strip of Willamette River frontage on the western bank, begins just east at S.W. Front, following the Willamette River north to Old Town at the foot of Ankeny, where it ends with a staging area for outdoor concerts and a floating dock.

The riverside park was a major undertaking begun in 1974 to give the river back to the people, but a similar swath of city greenery known as the Park Blocks has run parallel to this area behind Broadway for more than a century. Stately elms and gardens maintained by the city line this passageway through downtown that was set aside by founding fathers in the late 1840s from portions of their donation land claims. Among the residents of this lane are the Oregon Historical Society and the Oregon Art Institute, which face each other at S.W. Jefferson, as well as some of Portland's most historic churches and oldest art. The statuary, including a fountain donated by a "grateful immigrant," is echoed in sentiment by contemporary Oregon artists on the newer Downtown Mall, S.W. 5th and 6th avenues, where brick-lined sidewalks are spread with fountains, flowers, and sculpture.

The Portland Mall was dedicated in 1978 to bring the people back to the inner city. People were delighted with the downtown area, and the mall soon begat Pioneer Courthouse Square (1984), a public park created from a public parking lot between Broadway and 6th at Morrison and Yamhill, designed with humor and love by Will Martin. The people of Portland literally paid for the ground on which they walk, as the bricks bearing individual names of donors will prove. Excited with the power to shape their own city, Portland voters approved a new Performing Arts Center, a three-building complex on S.W. Broadway at Main. The Arlene Schnitzer Concert Hall, dubbed "the Schnitz" by locals, opened its doors in 1985 almost simultaneously with the adjoining Heathman Hotel, another case of contagious progress that emerged completely renovated and decorated as a new luxury hotel.

Outlying Portland offers other interesting areas. Northwest Portland, beyond W. 23d and Burnside, is full of small shops and restaurants. Both the Sellwood (S.E.) and Multnomah (S.W.) areas attract antique browsers. American history lovers will want to cross the Columbia River at the Washington border (I-5) to spend the better part of a day visiting Fort

Vancouver, the original Hudson's Bay site for fur traders, completely reconstructed by the National Park Bureau and open free of charge. To the south, off I-5, are other historic spots within a half hour's drive. Oregon's beaches and mountains are within an hour and a half of the city as well.

There is so much to do and see in the Portland area for so little that the visitor would do well to emulate Lovejoy and Pettygrove and flip a coin.

PRACTICAL INFORMATION

WHEN TO GO. Tourism is Oregon's second largest industry. With the exception of some coastal and mountain resort areas, there are no off-season rates in the state; skiing and fishing plus moderate temperatures draw tourists year around. Portland's biggest and longest summer celebration is the Rose Festival the second week in June. Bring your umbrella. Historians cannot recall a festival without rain in this city that claims the oldest (1888) and largest rose society in the nation. From mid-June through September the weather is warm and sunny with plenty of free music in the city parks at night. Advance reservations are always a good idea.

HOW TO GET THERE. By air. Major airlines that fly into Portland International Airport are *Alaska, American, America West, Continental, Delta, Eastern, Hawaiian, Northwest, PSA, TWA,* and *United.* Since none of these is a reduced-fare airline, the best deals are generally discount fares. Providing good connections to and from most Pacific Northwest cities are several regional airlines including *Horizon, San Juan,* and *United Express.*

By bus. *Greyhound-Trailways* buses both serve Portland and often offer specials for long-distance travelers.

By train. *Amtrak* connects Portland to all major cities on the West Coast and to points east via Pasco and Spokane or Denver.

By car. Portland is 637 miles north of San Francisco and 172 miles south of Seattle. Oregon maintains an excellent freeway system with frequent, well-maintained rest stops that include picnic facilities and, often, free coffee. The most direct route to Portland from California or Washington is I-5. Travelers from the south who have more time may want to take scenic U.S. 101, which follows the Oregon coast and connects with good roads over the Coast Range to Portland. Highways east and west, while not freeways, include divided highways or frequent passing lanes over mountain routes.

TELEPHONES. The area code for Portland and all of Oregon is 503. All local phone calls are 25 cents. Some areas in the greater Portland area may require an additional toll, and you will need to dial 1 before the number. Information (directory assistance) can be reached at 555–1212. For operator assistance, dial 0.

Emergency Telephone Numbers. In the greater Portland area the emergency number for fire, police, ambulance, and paramedics is 911. Outside the area, dial 0 for operator assistance and ask for the correct agency. Oregon's State Police can be reached at 238–8434.

HOTELS AND MOTELS with moderate prices in the Portland area are friendly and family-oriented with staff particularly helpful with hints for the budget-minded. Hotel rates are based on double occupancy. Categories, determined by price, are *Reasonable,* \$40 to \$65; and *Very Economical,* \$29 to \$39.

The City of Portland levies a 9 percent hotel-motel tax which is generally quoted with the price of a room. It is always a good idea to make reservations in advance, but during Portland's annual Rose Festival, which begins the second week in June, advance reservations in the downtown area are essential. All accommodations listed take major credit cards. Hotels normally considered "deluxe" in the city center have mounted an aggressive program to fill rooms on weekends. Such hotels as the Hil-

Points of Interest

1) Art Institute of Oregon
2) Benson Hotel
3) City Hall
4) Civic Auditorium
5) Civic Theater
6) County Justice Center
7) Hilton Hotel
8) Ira's Fountain
9) Japanese Garden
10) Lownsdale/Chapman Squares
11) Marriott Hotel
12) Memorial Coliseum
13) Multnomah Civic Stadium
14) Multnomah County Courthouse
15) Nordstrom
16) O'Bryant Square
17) Oregon Historical Society
18) Oregon Museum of Science & Industry
19) Performing Arts Center
20) Pioneer Courthouse/Square
21) Portland Building
22) Portland Motor Hotel
23) Portland State University
24) Post Office; Meier & Frank
25) River Place and Alexis Hotel
26) Trailways and Greyhound Bus Depots
27) Tri-Met Customer Service
28) Union Station
29) Waterfront Park
30) Willamette Center (Visitors Info)
31) Yamhill Market
32) Zoo
33) American Advertising Museum
34) New Market Street Theater

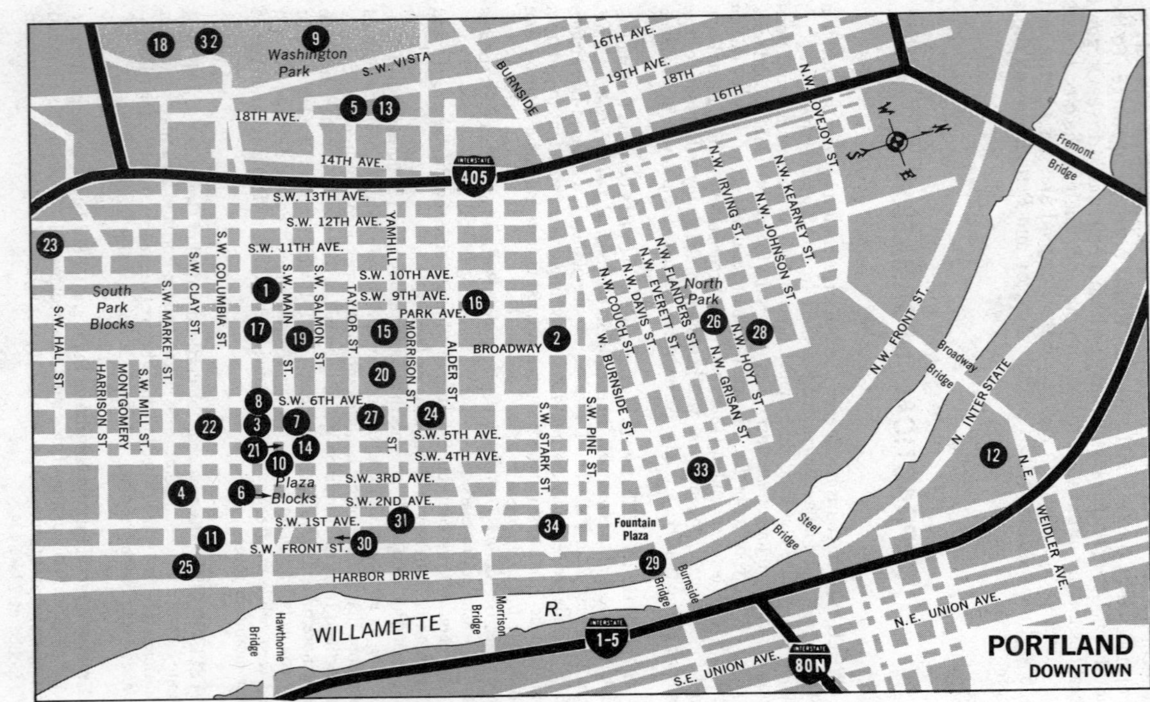

ton, 921 S.W. 6th, Portland, OR 97204 (503–226–1611), lower Fri. and Sat. room rates within budget limits.

Reasonable

Corsun Arms Motor Hotel. 809 S.W. King, Portland, OR 97205 (503–226–6288). 44 rooms, all with kitchens. This older inn, located in Portland's exclusive West Hills residential area, has been totally renovated (1988). Satellite TV, and free parking. Several reasonable restaurants nearby.

Imperial Hotel. 400 SW Broadway, Portland, OR 97205 (503–228–7221). 145 rooms. In the center of downtown Portland, this older hotel offers spacious rooms, twin, double, and queen-size-beds. Restaurant and lounge on premises, air conditioning, TV, Portland Downtowner service to airport, free cribs, and no charge for children in the same room.

Portland Inn. 1414 S.W. 6th, Portland, OR 97201 (503–221–1611). On the city's transit mall, which allows free bus transportation. 175 rooms with color TV. Outdoor swimming pool, free parking. Restaurant and lounge. Children under 12 free in same room as parents.

Riverside Inn. 50 S.W. Morrison, Portland, OR 97204 (503–221–0711). Faces the Willamette River on the edge of the historic Yamhill District. 140 rooms with color TV, restaurant, lounge. Free parking. Children under 16 free in same room as parents.

Super 8 Motel. 11011 N.E. Holman (503–257–8988). Just off I-205 on Airport Way, this new motel offers free 24-hour shuttle service to the airport as well as neighboring restaurants. TV with movie channel, free phones, shower-tub. Free parking.

Very Economical

Capri Motel. 1530 N.E. 82d St., Portland, OR 97220 (503–253–1151). Outdoor pool, free parking, restaurant and lounge. Some rooms air-conditioned.

Cabana Motel. 1707 N.E. 82d, Portland, OR 97220 (503–252–0224). Near airport. Restaurant and lounge nearby, free coffee.

Caravan Motor Hotel. 2401 S.W. 4th St., Portland, OR 97201 (503–226–1121). 40 rooms. Just across the street from a 12-acre park and jogging track, this downtown motel offers family units, direct dial phones, air-conditioning, heated pool, free coffee in rooms, and color TV with movies. Restaurant and lounge. Free parking.

Mallory Motor Hotel. 729 S.W. 15th, Portland, OR 97205 (503–223–6311). 144 rooms. On the perimeter of the downtown area, within easy walking distance, this hotel provides cribs free, with no charge for children 3 years and younger. Air conditioning, free parking, color TV, dining room, and lounge.

Saharan 4th Avenue. 1889 S.W. 4th (503–226–7646). Color TV, direct dial phones, free parking. Close to downtown and adjacent to Portland State University.

Budget Motel Chains. Motel 6. The Portland area has two budget motels with lower rates, both located away from city center. Rate per night is based upon number of people in room. Both offer TV and showers. Both take credit cards.

Motel 6. 3104 SE Powell Blvd., Portland, OR 97202 (503–238–0600). 70 units. Well run, older establishment.

Motel 6. 17950 S.W. McEwan, Tigard, OR 97223 (503–620–2066). 5 minutes south of Portland off I-5.

Bed-and-Breakfast. Northwest Bed and Breakfast, 610 S.W. Broadway, Suite 609, Portland, OR 97205 (503–243–7616), in business since 1979, personally inspects and guarantees more than a dozen bed-and-breakfast homes in Portland, many for $30 to $40, double occupancy. The outlet represents more than 350 homes from British Columbia through Washington and Oregon to California. Portland visitors may wish to have them organize a tour of the Northwest with destinations including other bed-and-breakfast stops. The basic charge for a night's stay includes a full breakfast. No credit cards.

Hostel. Portland International Youth Hostel, 3031 S.E. Hawthorne Blvd. (503–236–3380), is open 365 days a year. Call from 5–9 P.M. to reserve space. The charge is $5 a night for dorm-style accomodations. $1 charge for sheet rental.

HOW TO GET AROUND. From the airport. Travel from the airport to downtown (about 11 miles) by Tri-Met buses requires one transfer, but the price is only $1.10 as of 1988. Catch a number 12 (Sandy Blvd.) at the airport's bus zone to Portland Mall in the city center. More convenient but more expensive is Portland Downtowner, 246–4676, which leaves the airport from 5:30 A.M. to midnight 7 days a week. Adult fare is $5 one-way; children 6–12, $1; those under 6 ride free. Buses stop at downtown hotels and the Greyhound Bus Terminal. Cab fare between the airport and downtown is about $14.

By bus and light rail. The best tourist buy in Portland is *Tri-Met,* the area's public transit system. Before making sight-seeing plans, buy the system's *Transportation Guide and Map* at the Tri-Met Customer Assistance Office, 1 Pioneer Courthouse Square (behind the waterfall) on S.W. 6th between Morrison and Yamhill; call 233–3511. Travel on Tri-Met is free in Fareless Square, both bus and by MAX (Metropolitan Area Express), Portland's new light rail system that links the growing East County population with the urban area which includes downtown Portland and Old Town. For MAX information call 22–TRAIN. To use Tri-Met for sightseeing, riders may purchase an all-day ticket for $3, giving them unlimited miles in the Tri-County area. Other rides, beyond Fareless Square, are by zone. Zone, route, and bus number information is available at kiosks along Portland's Mall, SW 5th and 6th. The minimum fare on "short hop" rides is 65 cents; senior citizens riding during non-rush hours, pay 25 cents. Exact change is required for bus and MAX rides outside Fareless Square. For complete information on Tri-Met fares, call 231–3198; for schedules, call-a-bus at 231–3199.

By taxi. In Portland you don't hail a cab; you phone for one or try to find one at a downtown hotel or major department store. The fare is $2.70 for the first mile and $1.40 each additional mile. The oldest and largest company is *Broadway* (227–1234); others include *Radio* (272–1212). Special telephones for ordering cabs are provided in many busy locations.

By rental car. Car rental agencies with lower rates provide shuttle service to and from the airport but do not have counters there. Major rental agencies, which are more expensive, have in-terminal service. Among the lower priced agencies with shuttle service are *Rent-A-Dent* (503–777–4701, 800–426–5243) and *Car Rental 6* (503–257–9411).

HINTS TO THE MOTORIST. Portland is not a difficult city to navigate. To locate yourself on a map, remember that the Willamette River divides the city from east to west, while Burnside Street bisects the city from north to south. Streets running north from Burnside are in alphabetical order.

The *Automobile Club of Oregon,* 600 S.W. Market, offers 24-hour emergency road service to American Automobile Association members (222–6777) as well as a full line of travel information. They also maintain a 24-hour road-and-weather-condition telephone number (222–6721).

The state of Oregon enforces the 55 mph speed on all freeways passing within city limits. The speed is 65 mph otherwise. Parking designated for the handicapped is strictly enforced; the fine is $500.

Otherwise, parking is relatively easy. Urban parking lots owned by the city offer "park and shop" service by which customers of downtown merchants can have parking tickets validated with a minimum purchase and receive 2 hours of free parking per store.

TOURIST INFORMATION. The *Greater Portland Convention and Visitors' Association, Inc.,* 26 S.W. Salmon St., Portland, 97204 (503–222–2223), is open weekdays 8:30–5 P.M. and offers a wide array of maps and printed information including a free Portland tour map and guide marked with 50 downtown sights and places of interest. A current calendar of events is also available. The state operates a *Travel Information Center* at 12345 N. Union (285–1631) from May to Nov. 1.

HINTS TO DISABLED TRAVELERS. Parks, restaurants, and public places most easily enjoyed by the disabled are listed in the *Oregon Guide to Accessibility.* For a free copy, contact the Spinal Chord Association (257–0706), 10112 N.E. Clackamas, Portland, 97220. Most downtown street corners have been ramped for wheelchairs, and public buildings have been adapted for the disabled. Other special accommodations in regard to disabled parking areas, which are strictly enforced, include a Special Needs Transportation program offered by Tri-Met. Call 238–4952 (weekdays 8:30 A.M.–4:30 P.M.) for information about Tri-Met's services to the disabled and about proof of disability. *Shared Outdoor Adventure Recreation* (SOAR) helps disabled people enjoy outdoor activities. Call 238–1613. For information about the Portland Park Bureau's program for disabled and senior citizens which includes hiking, overnight camping, softball, bowling, and fitness, call 248–4328.

Two outlying recreation areas are designed especially for the disabled. **Oral Hull Park,** off U.S. 26 at Sandy, some 30 miles east of Portland, has carefully built trails, signs in braille, and other facilities for those without sight. Paved paths and rest rooms designed for wheelchairs are available at **Wildwood Recreation Area,** also on U.S. 26, 39 miles southeast of Portland.

FREE EVENTS. Portland's **Rose Festival,** held the second week in June, has been an annual celebration since 1907. Most events are free. Among the parades with floral floats is one especially for and by children and the *Grand Floral Parade* that begins at Memorial Coliseum and winds through downtown streets featuring marching bands and floats from other states as well as Oregon, equestrians, and visiting celebrities. Other rose events include the *International Rose Show,* an award for the best rose garden in the city, the *Golden Rose Ski Classic* at Timberline Lodge on Mt. Hood, and the visitation of U.S. and Canadian naval ships to the downtown seawall. A fun center is located adjacent to the seawall. The CART/PPG Indy Car World Series, part of the festival, has an admission charge. For more information on the festival, write Oregon State Highway Division, Salem, OR 97310.

Other free events in Portland include **Saturday Market,** held Saturdays and Sundays from April through December under the Burnside Bridge on the west side; **Neighbor Fair,** a gathering of the city's neighborhoods for ethnic foods and entertainment at Waterfront Park in July; and music in Portland's parks. Washington Park is the scene, from late July through August, for every kind of **music** from opera to symphony to sounds of the big bands. Call the Bureau of Parks and Recreation (796–5193) for a current schedule of events at all public parks. A ticket to **Washington Park Zoo** will get you in on Wednesday for an evening of live jazz during the annual zoo jazz festival, weekly in July and August. In August and September, the **Oregon Symphony** and the **West Coast Chamber Orchestra** perform the classics at Tom McCall Waterfront Park, just south of Burnside, on warm summer evenings. In cooler weather, free concerts are available at **Reed College Commons** once a month during the school year. Call the college, which is at 3203 S.E. Woodstock (777–7591), for concert times. **Portland State University,** 724 S.W. Harrison (229–4440), offers brown bag concerts at Lincoln Hall Tuesdays and Thursdays at noon. Sack-lunch concerts are also held Wednesdays at noon at the **Old Church,** 1422 S.W. 11th (222–2031). Check the *Oregonian* for other events.

TOURS AND SPECIAL-INTEREST SIGHTSEEING. Take a self-guided tour of Portland's urban art. It's free. The Metropolitan Arts Commission, located in the Portland Building, 1120 S.W. 5th, Room 518, produces a slick map and highlighted tour of 31 pieces of art in the downtown area. Stop by for a copy or call 503–796–5111 to have one mailed to you. Individuals wishing to be part of the audience for "AM Northwest," a live telecast Monday through Friday on KATU, Channel 2, may call to reserve a seat. The station is at 2153 N.E. Sandy Blvd. (231–4610). There is no charge. Reservations are required. KGW-TV produces "On The Spot," a lively game show that offers free admission for the studio audience. Taping is generally Tuesday through Thursdays starting at 7 P.M. Call the station's audience line (503–220–1505) for tickets. Refreshments are served and the audience is in the drawing for free dinners in Portland restaurants. The station is at 1501 S.W. Jefferson.

A free guided tour of Portland's **port area** leaves the parking lot at N.E. 16th and Multnomah, near the Lloyd Center, during summer months. Reservations are necessary. Call 231–5000, ext. 268. Daily 1-hour tours of **Portland International Airport** are also given by the Port of Portland. For reservations, call 231–5000, and ask for "Port Tours."

PARKS AND GARDENS. Portland's parks and gardens are known for diversity. Visitors may spend an entire day hiking through miles of wilderness, all bounded by the city, look at sheer cliffs of lava, or visit formal test gardens or carefully identified arboretums. The public is welcome, and each park listed here is free and offers a different experience.

Among the most unique: The **International Rose Test Garden** at the edge of Washington Park (take Salmon St. west from downtown or follow signs west on Burnside) where 400 varieties, each labeled, of roses bloom year-round; **Forest Park,** with 4,700 acres of wilderness and 30 miles of hiking trails (one entrance is at the extreme end of N.W. Thurman St.); **Pittock Wildlife Sanctuary,** Audubon House, N.W. 53d and Cornell (503–292–6855), with more than 100 acres dedicated to birds and maintained by the Audubon Society; **Crystal Springs Rhododendron Garden,** S.E. 28th near S.E. Woodstock, where more than 2,000 plants are maintained by the American Rhododendron Society; **Laurelhurst Park,** S.E. 39th and Oak, a 33-acre park with tennis courts, play equipment, and large duck pond; **The Grotto,** Sandy Blvd. at 85th, with 58 acres run by the Order of Servants to Mary, outdoor masses offered Sunday at noon May–Sept.; **Mount Tabor Park,** SE 69th and Yamhill, said to be the only volcano within city limits in the U.S.; and **Kelley Point Park,** at the far end of North Portland where the Columbia River and the Willamette River join; beaches, wooded areas and good swimming are found here.

ZOOS. Washington Park Zoo (226–ROAR) is just one of four destinations rimming the large parking lot at 4001 S.W. Canyon Rd. The zoo is open every day of the year, but Christmas, from 9:30 A.M. until dusk and includes the nation's largest bred-in-captivity elephant herd. Adults, $2.50; children 3–11 and seniors, $1.25. Admission is free to everyone Tuesday after 3 P.M. Other attractions included in the admission charge are a night country exhibit where day is turned into night to observe nocturnal creatures, a cascade stream and pond, penguins, and chimpanzees learning sign language. A children's petting zoo adjoins the larger one. Also on the hill is *Oregon Museum of Science and Industry* (OMSI), the *Harry C. Kendall Planetarium* (222–2828), and the *World Forestry Center,* where visitors see the value of lumber to Oregon's economy. Nominal entrance fees. Gift shops. Snack bar at OMSI.

PARTICIPANT SPORTS. Runners get the right-of-way on downtown streets where the businessperson on a lunch hour is often seen heading for Waterfront Park and a 4-mile run between meetings. Downtown hotels issue running maps. Among other energetic experiences in the Portland area are hiking, bicycling, skiing (both Alpine and cross country), water sports including boating and freshwater fishing, golf, and tennis. Call the Bureau of Parks and Recreation *sports line* (796–5150). In most cases the only cost is equipment.

Getting There By Bike is a map covering biking routes in the Portland area. To obtain it write METRO, 2000 SW 1st, Portland, 97201, or go to the Metropolitan Services offices (221–1646) for a copy. The cost of this comprehensive map is $3.50. Canoes may be rented at Brown's Landing on Sauvie Island (227-6283) or at Sportcraft Marina in Oregon City (656–6484). Portland offers excellent opportunities for golfing with many fine public courses. For information on *fishing,* call the recorded information number of Oregon Fish and Wildlife (229–5222). At the end of a line are salmon, trout, catfish, and bass—all in the Portland area. Public racquetball and handball courts are located throughout the city. Hourly rates are quoted by St. Johns Racquet Center, 7519 N. Burlington (248–4200), and YMCA Metro Fitness Center, 2831 S.W. Barbur Blvd. (294–3366). The Portland Park Bureau maintains a number of indoor and outdoor swimming pools. Call 796–5193 for times and locations. More than 100 outdoor tennis courts are available to the public in Portland parks, and the Portland Tennis Center offers municipally owned indoor courts. Most outdoor courts require no reservations. For indoor play call the Tennis Center, 324 N.E. 12th Ave. (233–5959), to reserve a court from 6:30 A.M. until 11:15 P.M.

SPECTATOR SPORTS. Portland supports three professional franchises including one major league sport franchise, the 1977 world champion *Trailblazers* of the NBA. Oct.–Mar. season, with home games at Memorial Coliseum, 1401 N. Wheeler (239–4422). Some seating and standing-room-only tickets, substantially lower in price, are available the night of the game. The *Beavers* (223–2837), one of the oldest

AAA baseball teams, play at Portland's Civic Stadium, 1844 S.W. Morrison, Apr.–Sept. The *Winter Hawks,* a Western Hockey League team (238–6366), play Oct.–Mar. at Memorial Coliseum.

In addition, Portland supports two **race tracks** for pari-mutuel betting. *Portland Meadows Horse Race Track,* 1001 N. Schmeer Rd. (285–9144), operates from early November until late April. The greyhounds race at *Multnomah Kennel Club Dog Race Track,* N.E. 233d, between Halsey and Glisan in Fairview (667–7700), about 15 miles east of the city, May–Sept.

CHILDREN'S ACTIVITIES. Alpenrose Dairy, 6149 S.W. Shattuck Rd. (244–1133), is one of the last family-owned dairies in the area and provides an ideal way for city kids to visit the farm. The barns are open for petting animals. Admission is free, and picnic areas are provided. For the price of a loaf of bread, children can draw hundreds of feathered friends at duck ponds at **Crystal Springs Rhododendron Garden,** S.E. 28th just off Woodstock, or at **Laurelhurst Park,** S.E. 39th and Stark. Laurelhurst also has play equipment, tennis courts, summer roller skate rental, and a wading pool. The **Children's Museum,** 3037 S.W. 2d (248–4587), is especially geared to the young, with two floors of exhibits and activities. Call for a schedule. **Oaks Amusement Park,** S.E. Spokane at the east foot of the Sellwood Bridge (236–5722), offers roller skating year-round, carnival rides (under $1) during the summer months, and picnic facilities. Other merry-go-rounds can be found at **Willamette Center,** S.W. 1st and Salmon, and **Jantzen Beach Center,** off I-5 at the Washington state border.

HISTORIC SITES AND HOUSES. A great deal of Oregon territorial history has been maintained and preserved in the Portland area. Three sites are within city limits. The others require a car but are within a half hour's driving time. In Portland: The **Old Church,** 1422 S.W. 11th (222–2031), is the oldest standing church structure on its original site in Portland. Built in 1882, it is now a popular place for weddings, receptions, and music. Admission is free. **Pioneer Courthouse** (and Post Office), 555 S.W. Yamhill (221–0282), was the first federal office building in the Pacific Northwest and is the oldest public building in the area. The first floor is now a postal station, but visitors may tour the restored Victorian courtroom on the second floor and the judges' chambers on the third. Both floors are still in use for hearings. Admission is free. The **Pittock Mansion,** 3229 NW Pittock Dr. (248–4469), was built at the turn of the century by the founder of the *Oregonian* and now belongs to the city. One of the best views of the skyline and mountains can be seen from the front lawns of this 46-acre estate. Volunteers conduct tours of this French Renaissance mansion, which is open to the public year-around. Adults, $2.50; senior citizens, $2; students, $1; children 6–11, 50 cents.

West of Portland on Sauvie Island is the **Bybee-Howell House,** a pre-Civil War farmhouse administered by the Oregon Historical Society. The house is open free of charge June–Sept.

Fort Vancouver, just across the Columbia River via the Interstate Bridge on the Washington State side, is the center of the Old Oregon country and is a National Historic Site. A full-scale replica of the fort operated by Dr. John McLoughlin for fur traders and the Hudson's Bay Company is open to the public free; it includes a trading store, bakery, blacksmith shop, bastion, dispensary, and the home of the chief factor; all are furnished. Two streets up from the fort is **Officers Row,** which dates back to the days of Indian wars in the West and is believed to be one of three such rows remaining. The oldest house, that of Ulysses S. Grant (206–694–4002), built in 1849, is a museum open to the public. Small admission charge.

South of Portland, less than 15 minutes off I-5, are two historic sites. **Aurora,** a pioneer colony founded by Dr. William Keil, includes the *Ox Barn Museum,* open for a small charge Wed.–Sun., 1–5 P.M., except Jan. Call 678–5754. The town of Aurora is filled with small antique shops. **Champoeg Park** is the spot on the Willamette River where U.S. Marshal Joe Meek called for a provisional government. Among the spots of interest are the *home of Dr. Robert Newell* (small fee), the last remaining structure of the settlement; the *Champoeg Pioneer Mother's Home* (DAR) (small fee); and a visitors information center (free) with sight-and-sound exhibits relating to early Oregon. The Visitor Center is closed weekends in the winter, open 7 days in the summer.

John McLoughlin House, 7th and Center streets, Oregon City (656–5146) is the retirement home of the chief factor of Fort Vancouver. Moved from its original site on the lower level of Oregon City, the house is fully restored with McLoughlin furniture and is open Feb.–Dec., closed Mon. (Small fee.)

MUSEUMS AND GALLERIES. Oregon Historical Society. 1230 S.W. Park (222–1741). Free. Closed Sun. Rotating exhibits about the Northwest on the main floor; Northwest Indian exhibit in panoramas on the second, along with a maritime collection. Library on 3d floor has open stacks for browsing. Gift shop.

Oregon Art Institute. 1219 S.W. Park (226–2811). Permanent collections include outstanding exhibit of Northwest Indian art; paintings by Picasso, Renoir, and Degas; pre-Columbian; Asian; African; and European works. Gift shop. Closed Mon. Adults, $2.75; students, $1.

Oregon Museum of Science and Industry. 4015 S.W. Canyon Rd. (222–2828). Viewer-operated scientific displays, live reptiles, and hatching chicks. Adjacent to Washington Park Zoo, this museum also includes the Kendall Planetarium. Open daily except Christmas. Gift shop and snack bar. Adults, $4; children and seniors, $2.50.

American Advertising Museum. 9 N.W. 2nd (226–0000). The first of its kind in the nation. Exhibits representing early advertising graphics, including a room for television, radio, and store ads. Closed Mon. and Tues. Donation.

Contemporary Crafts Gallery. 3934 S.W. Corbett (223–2654). A nonprofit organization that features the works of more than 1,000 Oregon artists.

ARTS AND ENTERTAINMENT. The Friday "Arts & Entertainment" section of the *Oregonian* will give you a complete rundown of entertainment in the Portland area along with a good idea of which offers the best bargain for the week. Prices for entertainment in Portland range from expensive season ticket rates to free.

Film. Vintage films can been seen at *Clinton Street,* S.E. 26th and Clinton (238–8899); *Roseway Theatre,* 7229 N.E. Sandy (281–5713). *The Movie House,* 1220 S.W. Taylor (222–4595), runs foreign films. Some theaters offer admission for 69 cents. Among them:*Mt. Tabor.* 4811 S.E. Hawthorne Blvd. (238–1646), with three screens. Check Friday entertainment section of *The Oregonian* for other reduced prices. In addition, the *Luxury Theater* group, which shows first-run films, has economy matinees and reduced admission until 6 P.M.

Music. *Oregon Symphony Orchestra,* 813 S.W. Alder (228–1353), is heard in concert at the Arlene Schnitzer Concert Hall, S.W. Broadway and Main. Sunday afternoon concerts, featuring light classical music, are less expensive. *Portland Opera Association,* 1530 S.W. 2d (241–1802), gives four productions a year with three performances of each, fall and spring.

Portland Youth Philharmonic, 1119 S.W. Park (223–5939), is the best buy in classical music. More than 100 young musicians under the direction of Jacob Avshalomov perform at the Arlene Schnitzer Concert Hall four times annually. Ticket prices are under $10. The group, which has toured Europe twice, was heard with the New York Philharmonic in 1984. *Chamber Music Northwest,* 421 S.W. 6th (223–3202), gives a series of summer concerts at Reed College and repeats these in Lincoln Hall on the Portland State University campus.

Concerts in the Parks. the Bureau of Parks and Recreation, 1120 S.W. 5th (796–5193), sponsors more summer music free of charge than any other local organization. Call for a current listing.

Stage. Portland has an active community theater schedule. The oldest is the Portland Civic Theatre, 1530 S.W. Yamhill (226–3048), which runs mainstage productions concurrently with theater in the round. Curtain time for both is 8 P.M. In addition, the theater offers summer repertory and children's plays at Sat. matinees. Tickets are reasonably priced.

SHOPPING. For the budget-minded, the best buy in the downtown area may well be the bus or light rail. Within the confines of Fareless Square (bounded by the Stadium Freeway, N.W. Hoyt, and the Willamette River), all rides on Tri-Met are free. Passengers may get on and off at will as they explore the shopping areas of the city.

Many major outlets offer economy rooms and special sales tables. *Nordstrom's Rack,* 401 S.W. Morrison (243–1492), offers men's, women's, and some children's clothing at close-out prices. *The Big Bang,* 616 S.W. Park (274–1741) imports vintage clothing, from formal wear to funk, at low prices. Men's all-wool overcoats, in mint condition, are $65; sport coats, $25. Italian fashions for men are greatly discounted by *Giovanni's Mens Fashions* at L'Uomo Discount Store, 717 S.W. Alder (227–0109). Suits, sport coats, sportswear.

Outlying neighborhoods offer special shopping areas with lower prices as well. **Antiques** are found in the Sellwood area, S.E. 13th St., just east of the Sellwood Bridge, where more than 35 shops deal in primitives. Some real bargains can still be uncovered. Stop for lunch at *Bread and Ink Cafe.* 3610 S.E. Hawthorne Blvd. (239–4757). Some of the best fresh-baked bread in town is served amply with your meal and you can walk off the calories by shopping used-book, antique, and specialty and gourmet food stores on both sides of the street.

Northwest Portland, beginning at 23d and W. Burnside, is filled with small boutiques, vintage clothing stores, thrift shops, and one-of-a-kind restaurants with inexpensive but excellent entrees. Just west on Burnside is *Powell Books,* 1005 W. Burnside, a new and used book store so vast that the staff provides browsers with a map covering each level and shelf of specialty categories.

Oregon wines by the case can be the best buy; a complete list of vineyards and visiting hours is available by writing to the Oregon Winegrowers Association, Box 2134, Salem, OR 97310.

Another destination for the thrifty is the *Pendleton Woolen Mills'* Mill Ends Store in Washougal, WA. The trip takes less than a half hour using the new I-205 bridge, and the drive up the north side of the Columbia River through Camus is a beautiful way to see the river. The shop is open weekdays until 4 P.M. and sells wool by the yard, flawed merchandise, and overruns. All flaws are noted. Other clothing outlets offering substantial savings include the *Kuppenheimer Factory Store,* 508 S.W. Taylor St., where men's suits, sport coats, and slacks are sold for low prices. Pay 50 percent less for pantyhose and other clothing at *Ross Dress For Less,* outlets in several suburban shopping malls. Check the phone book for locations.

One of the best buys for travelers returning directly home is Oregon **produce,** which can be gathered at great savings from local roadside stands and U-Pick fields June–Sept. Raspberries in the field often cost less than 50 cents a pound. Other good buys include nuts, locally produced honey (under $4 per quart), strings of garlic, and dried flowers. Check the *Oregonian*'s classified section for stands or fields offering choice selections. Two of the best permanent summer-month stands include *The Pumpkin Patch* on Sauvie Island and *Faist's Fruit Stand* on 99E at New Era, just south of Oregon City. Both are open 7 days during the harvest season.

Another seasonal buy is **art** by Oregon artists. Saturday Market (Sat.–Sun., Apr.–Dec., under the west side of the Burnside Bridge), is said to be the oldest continually operating effort of its kind in the U.S. Booths open, rain or shine, in early morning and close at 5 P.M. Work includes pottery, woodworking, photography, jewelry, leatherwork, glass, and folk art.

DINING OUT. Fine dining is available at moderate prices in the Portland area, and some of the kitchens in outlying communities offer exceptional culinary experiences. Restaurant categories, based on the price of a meal for one, without beverage, tax, or tip, are as follows: *Reasonable,* $6 to $12; *Very Economical,* $4 to $6; *Low Budget,* under $4. Unless otherwise noted, all restaurants accept some if not all major credit cards. Every effort has been made to ensure that this list is up to date, but restaurants come and go so often that it is always advisable to call ahead.

Reasonable

Crepe Faire. 133 S.W. 2d (227–3365). Breakfast, lunch, dinner, and after-theater dining in Portland's Old Town. Soups, salads, pasta, and quiche in addition to crepes of all varieties. Liquor.

Harrington's Bar & Grill. S.W. 6th and Main (243–2932). Continental menu in the dining room, long and comfortable bar with a dance floor. A regular gathering place for local bankers and attorneys. Liquor. Closed Sun.

Newport Bay Seafood Broiler. 0425 S.W. Montgomery (227–3474). Floats on the Willamette River at RiverPlace. Open for lunch and dinner, this fresh seafood outlet also sells fish and chips through the window to diners who prefer the great outdoors.

Old Country Kitchen. 10519 S.E. Stark (252–4171) and on Beaverton Hillsdale Hwy. at Griffith Dr., Beaverton (644–1492). These established steak houses offer the best buy around if you know your capacity. Among other cuts, the menu provides a 72-ounce steak. Eat it all, including the trimmings, and your dinner is free. Senior citizens are welcome to order from the children's menu with its smaller portions. Open daily for dinner. Liquor. No reservations.

Very Economical

Abou Karim. 221 S.W. Pine (223–5058). Lebanese menu with weekday lunches, dinners on Mon.–Sat. Roast lamb is the dinner favorite. Liquor.

Alexis Restaurant and Lounge. 215 W. Burnside (224–8577). Authentic Greek food and music including a wide variety of Greek appetizers. Liquor. Closed Sun.

Bread and Ink Cafe. 3610 S.E. Hawthorne Blvd. (239–4756). A Parisian cafe with 40s atmosphere. Rotating daily specials and outstanding bread, served and re-served fresh from the oven. Lunch, dinner, Sun. brunch. Beer, wine. Closed Mon.

Buster's Smokehouse Texas Style Barbecue. 17883 S.E. McLoughlin Blvd., Milwaukie (652–1076). Worth the drive for meats cooked 12 hours over mesquite. Ribs, brisket, beef, ham, and chicken with a choice of side dishes. Lunch and dinner both under $5. Beer.

Dave's Delicatessen. 1110 S.W. 3rd (222–5461). Kosher-style food in the new Justis Center. Wide assortment from blintzes to gefilte fish and fresh lox. Beer.

Fong Chong Restaurant. 301 N.W. 4th (220–0235). Dim sum service makes this a particularly good buy, but other menu items are also economical. Lunch and dinner 7 days. Beer and wine. No credit cards.

Molly Bloom's. 50 S.W. Pine (224–2270). Open for breakfast through dinner, this cozy spot keeps a soup kettle at simmer every day. Food to go and sidewalk dining on sunny days as well. Beer and wine.

Old Spaghetti Factory. 0715 S.W. Bancroft (222–5375). Best buy with a river view is under this great sprawling purple roof where spaghetti with a choice of five sauces is served for lunch and dinner. Liquor. No credit cards.

Papa Haydn. 701 N.W. 23d (228–7317) and 5829 S.E. Milwaukie (232–9440). A good spot for lunch and dinner whether shopping the boutiques along N.W. 23d or the antiques on S.E. 13th St., these delectable outlets have a long and faithful following for fantastic desserts. Sandwiches, pasta, salads, and soups as well. Beer and wine.

Poor Richard's Restaurant. 3907 N.E. Broadway (288–5285). Steak dinner for two for less than $10. Wide menu for other meals as well. Liquor.

Sylvia's Italian Restaurant. 5115 N.E. Sandy Blvd. (288–6828). Open 7 days for full-course Italian dinners. Call for days with family-style spaghetti dinner service, when adults eat abundantly for less than $5 and children for half that price. Liquor.

Low Budget

Dan and Louis Oyster Bar. 208 S.W. Ankeny (227–5906). Fresh seafood is a precious commodity on any menu. This spot, loaded with atmosphere, lets do-it-yourself diners save substantially on fresh oysters by handing them the pliers and directions for opening their own. Other seafood as well, including oyster stew and clam chowder and seafood platters. Open 7 days 11 A.M.–midnight. No liquor.

Escape from New York Pizza. 913 S.W. Alder (226–4129). Offers little except pizza by the slice for $1.25. Pizza orders to go as well, but the price is higher. The thrifty eat on the spot and pace themselves.

King's Table has 5 locations in the Portland area. A buffet service with rates for senior citizens, the two most accessible outlets to the downtown area are at 4006 S.E. 82d at Eastport Plaza shopping center (777–2870) and 11419 S.W. Pacific Hwy., Tigard (246–6126). No credit cards.

Metro On Broadway, S.W. Broadway at Taylor (no phone), is a collection of fine quick-food outlets ranging from a deli to coffees and ice cream. Something for any time of day and excellent for people watching. Open from breakfast through late evening.

New Market Street Theater. S.W. 1st and Ankeny, offers a wide range of fast food outlets. Diners may select from each and any and meet to eat, either in the great hall or outside during sunny weather.

North's Chuck Wagon. An excellent buy in buffet service with some of the best fried chicken in the area. Four outlets serve daily. Those nearest downtown are just off I-5 at the Lake Oswego-Durham exit 290 (639–4313) and at 2875 S.W. Cedar Hills Blvd., Beaverton (646–2500). Do-it-yourself sundaes and senior citizen rates.

Yamhill Market. S.W. 3d and Yamhill. Health- and budget-conscious businessmen have been known to buy a fresh, juicy apple from the produce vendor in front and continue on down the street. Other food outlets on the main floor offer an oyster bar, a slab of fresh-baked Italian bread with plenty of butter for 25 cents, and French breads and pastries. The third floor is a complete circle of exotic food outlets. Beer and wine. No credit cards. Open 7 days.

Recommended Splurge. Live music, lively dining, and one of the prettiest views of the Willamette River make the **Harbor Side Restaurant** and **Shanghai Lounge,** 0309 S.W. Montgomery (220–1865), a best bet for a special night out. Nearly every table has a river view and the menu features the latest food fancies, including Cajun-style blackened sturgeon, smoked salmon pizza, fresh seafood, and steaks. Through the double doors, diners will find live music 7 nights a week and a polished dance floor large enough to burn off all the extra calories. A quiet stroll along the esplanade will take the adventuresome to a nearby informal floating lounge or to the deluxe Alexis Hotel for an after-dinner cordial. All are located along Portland's new RiverPlace development. Validated parking is adjacent to the Harbor Side. Reservations are suggested. Major credit cards.

NIGHTLIFE AND BARS. Happy hours. One of the best ways to sample the more expensive kitchens in Portland is through happy hours when free hors d'oeuvres are served. Three restaurants downtown normally not considered moderately priced tempt diners with excellent free tidbits during cocktail hour. *McCormick & Schmick's Oak St. Restaurant,* 235 S.W. 1st (224–7522), claims a bar with standing room for 200. The area is generally packed at cocktail hour. *Brasserie Montmartre,* 629 S.W. Park (224–5552), offers French decor of the 1920s along with snacks at cocktail time.

Clubs with entertainment. There is plenty of entertainment in the evening in Portland, with the price running from the cost of a single beer to an admission ticket charge. To be sure, call ahead. Friday's "Arts and Entertainment" section of the *Oregonian* contains the latest listings for all entertainment under the heading "nightmusic." Some of the most dependable outlets are: *Key Largo,* 31 N.W. First (223–9919), which books a variety of musicians from the best local to name groups each night of the week; and *The Dakota,* 239 S.W. Broadway at Oak (241–4151), a hot new gathering spot with live and taped music and low drink prices.Live rock on two floors at *Eli's Cafe,* 424 S.W. 4th (223–4241). *Remo's,* 1425 N.W. Glisan (221–1150), with local and national jazz artists seven nights a week; *Starry Night,* 8 N.W. 6th (227–0071), with a variety of touring entertainers including some big names, with tickets varying in price accordingly.

Brewpubs. Don't miss a taste of Portland's newest nightlife passion, German-style ales, lagers, and fruit ales, often served at the brewery site in a brewpub. More than 80 varieties of brew, all produced in the Northwest, are served nightly throughout the city with a special flair. The McMenamin Brewery brewpubs offer such unusual drinks as rasberry and cranberry ales in a number of different establishments. Try the *Blue Moon* (31 taps), 432 N.W. 21st (223–3184); *McMenamin's Tavern & Pool* (30 taps), 1716 N.W. 23rd (227–0929); and the *Mission Street Theater and Pub* (25 taps), 1624 N.W. Glisan (223–4031), where a good second-run or vintage film is offered free with the purchase of a glass of beer in a colorful British theater setting. Other equally entertaining pubs include the *Horse Brass,* 4534 S.E. Belmont (232–2202), which features tap and imported beers and such traditional British pub fare as meat pies and Scotch eggs; and for a touch of Irish blarney, try the *Dublin Pub* (37 taps), 3014 S.E. Belmont (230–8817), with live music, usually Irish in nature, and over 200 varieties of imported beer. For a free copy of the quarterly *Great Northwest Beer,* a newsletter that extolls local breweries and provides information on where to sample their output, write to John Zimmer, Editor, Box 908, Lake Oswego, OR 97034.

SECURITY. Portland, like most rapidly growing cities, has its rough spots. If you keep to well-lighted areas, you will have little trouble after dark. Day and night several urban areas are patrolled by mounted police with extremely calm horses. Old Town, with its excellent restaurants and shopping experiences, is the site of the city's Skid Road, so use nearby available parking lots for dinner parking. These lots are unattended, and the meters at the parking booths take quarters only. Plan to take a minimum of $1.50 in quarters to park and lock your own car, or use a cab.

ST. LOUIS

by
Joan Dames

Joan Dames is the travel editor of the St. Louis Post-Dispatch, *for which she also writes a column. Her researcher was Cecilia M. Dames, a native St. Louisan.*

Not many cities can claim a founding father who was exactly 13 years old at the time or a founding mother who left the comforts of civilized New Orleans for the rigors of the frontier.

St. Louis was founded unofficially in 1763 when Pierre Laclede Liguest selected high ground on the west bank of the Mississippi River downstream from Indian trading grounds. Liguest began the city as a fur-trading post. A year later he was joined by Auguste Chouteau and Chouteau's mother, Therese, whose miller husband, Rene Chouteau, had returned to his native France. Other children who bore the name Chouteau helped build St. Louis.

The city was named for Louis IX, the king of France who led a crusade to the Holy Land and became a saint. It was a noble beginning for a tiny French fur-trading post. From this spot Lewis and Clark set out in 1804 to map the uncharted west that had been acquired by Thomas Jefferson in 1803 in the Louisiana Purchase for $15 million.

The growing nation was on a westward move, and adventurous settlers stocked their wagons in St. Louis for the big push west. St. Louis was the most westward outpost of civilization; it became the gateway to the west.

To commemorate its role in westward expansion, the city completed in 1966 the magnificent Saarinen Arch, a 630-foot bow of stainless steel, the tallest monument in the nation. Located on the riverfront in the Jefferson National Expansion Memorial Park, the arch has become a symbol of the nation's hopes and dreams.

Permanently moored on the riverfront below the arch are several floating restaurants, including a McDonalds hamburger spot, in a paddlewheeler, its golden arches eliminated in reverence to Saarinen's masterpiece.

Just west of wharf street is the Old Cathedral, the Basilica of St. Louis, the King, at 209 Walnut Street. Built in 1834 on the site of the first log cabin chapel dedicated in 1770, the museum holds the original church bell from 1770 and an 800-year-old Spanish crucifix.

West of the cathedral in the heart of a revitalized and booming downtown area on South Broadway is the Old Courthouse. It was here that the famous Dred Scott case was decided. Dred Scott was a slave who had been freed by his master in a state which did not have slavery. On his return to St. Louis, Scott was enslaved again and appealed for freedom in 1846. In an historic decision, the state supreme court decided against Scott and in appeal to the U.S. Supreme Court, the decision that Scott had no rights nine years later increased the tension between North and South directly before the Civil War.

On the northern edge of the downtown area is the Shrine of Saint Joseph, which contains a relic of Saint Peter Claver, a seventeenth-century Spanish Jesuit who devoted his life to the care of slaves in African slave ships. Claver took the slaves food and medicine and tended them himself. A miracle—one of two that led to Claver's canonization in 1888—is alleged to have taken place in this church connected with the relic. To some it is ironic that on the south edge of downtown St. Louis is the place where the courts decided that blacks were not citizens, while on the north side the shrine commemorates a saint who saw poor African slaves as children of God.

Also on the north side of the 12-block downtown area is Laclede's Landing, a redeveloped area with cobblestone streets and many different restaurants and bars ranging from cheap to costly. There is something here for every pocketbook, including in the summer months free sidewalk entertainers, including mimes, jugglers, and magicians. Natives love Laclede's Landing, too.

West of the downtown area is the old Gateway to the West, Union Station. Remodeled and reopened in August 1985, Union Station is a business, entertainment, and recreation center. In the parkway across the street is the beautiful Carl Milles Fountain, the Meeting of the Waters, which represents the marriage of the (male) Mississippi River with the (female) Missouri River.

West of downtown is what St. Louisans refer to as the-Fashionable-Central-West-End, all in one breath. It begins near the St. Louis Cathedral (or the New Cathedral), which houses the largest collection of mosaics in the world. The heart of the **Central West End** is the Chase–Park Plaza Hotel, on the corner of Lindell Boulevard and Kingshighway, catty-corner from Forest Park (where you will find a wealth of free or inexpensive things to do). North, south, and east of the Chase are dozens of fine restaurants, boutiques, and antique and junk shops in a 10-block area that is both trendy and chic and draws a fashionable crowd. But there are good buys here.

In **Forest Park** you will find one of the largest public city parks in the nation. It includes a modestly priced public golf course, handball courts, and tennis courts; one of the nation's finest zoos; a splendid art museum housed in one of the original buildings from the St. Louis World's Fair in 1904; the Missouri Historical Society Museum, housed in the Jefferson Memorial; a combined planetarium and museum of science and industry; and an ice- and roller-skating rink. Much of all this is free. Best of all is the Muny, a huge outdoor theater seating 11,573 and offering 1,456 free seats each night of the ten-week summer season. The Muny is St. Louis's pride and joy. Shows, ranging from top Broadway productions to ballet, change weekly, and many sell out the giant amphitheater. The sound system is so good that some people who can't get in for a show spread a blanket on the grass outside and listen.

About ten minutes south of Forest Park is **the Hill** area, an Italian section that has seen generations of young people who grew up here moving into the old, small houses within minutes after the old people have vacated them. Some of the best food in town is found here in the dozens of restaurants, Italian, naturally, and many modestly priced. The old men play bocce, an Italian bowling game, in a field here on summer nights. Yogi Berra and Joe Garagiola both grew up here.

Some benighted city fathers a long time ago set in legal stone the City Limits, so you will find much of the better parts of St. Louis in St. Louis County. **Clayton,** a five-minute drive west of Forest Park just past the green campus of Washington University, is the county government center, a fine shopping area, and the home of many high-rise corporate headquarters, all nestled within a sleepy residential area. There are good restaurants here.

PRACTICAL INFORMATION

WHEN TO GO. A recent study of the livability of cities put St. Louis in seventh place on the basis of varying factors, including the climate. It is true that the January temperature may dip below zero, with the wind-chill factor intensifying the cold, and that summer can be steamy, its high temperatures aggravated by the wealth of water from the Mississippi and Missouri rivers and the numerous tributaries in our water-rich region. The abysmally bad weather, however, never hangs on too long; usually the weather is mild.

The biggest tourist time is summer, when the baseball season and the Muny make St. Louis particularly appealing. The natives' favorite time is autumn, when Indian summer stretches from September until well into November. There have even been years when St. Louisans picked roses from their own garden for Thanksgiving dinner tables. December is often milder than anyone living in the Midwest has the right to expect.

Spring is a mass of Japanese magnolias, tulips, jonquils, and daffodils, azaleas, hyacinths, and dogwood—the state flower—but warmer than spring elsewhere. In May the great deciduous trees that shade the streets produce leaves of the most delicious shade of green.

HOW TO GET THERE. By air. Twenty-one airlines serve the Lambert-St. Louis International Airport. *TWA* uses St. Louis as its hub and has 308 departures daily. *TWA* also has direct flights to both Frankfurt and London. Its commuter line has 54 flights a day to regional destinations, including a daily flight to the resort area of Lake of the Ozarks. *Northwest Airlines* has a connecting flight from St. Louis to many of the world's capital cities. Among major airlines serving St. Louis are *American, Delta, Eastern, USAir,* and *United Airlines.*

By bus. *Greyhound-Trailways* has a terminal in the downtown area just north of the Arch.

By train. *Amtrak* serves St. Louis with a rather laconic service not known for punctuality, a situation that may be exacerbated in winter when ice freezes train switches.

By car. Most tourists arrive in St. Louis by car. It's cheaper, and it's convenient to have the car once you're here. A number of interstate highways run through St. Louis. I-55 runs north and south from Chicago to Louisiana. I-70 runs east and west, I-64 comes in from the east, and I-44 goes southeast to Oklahoma.

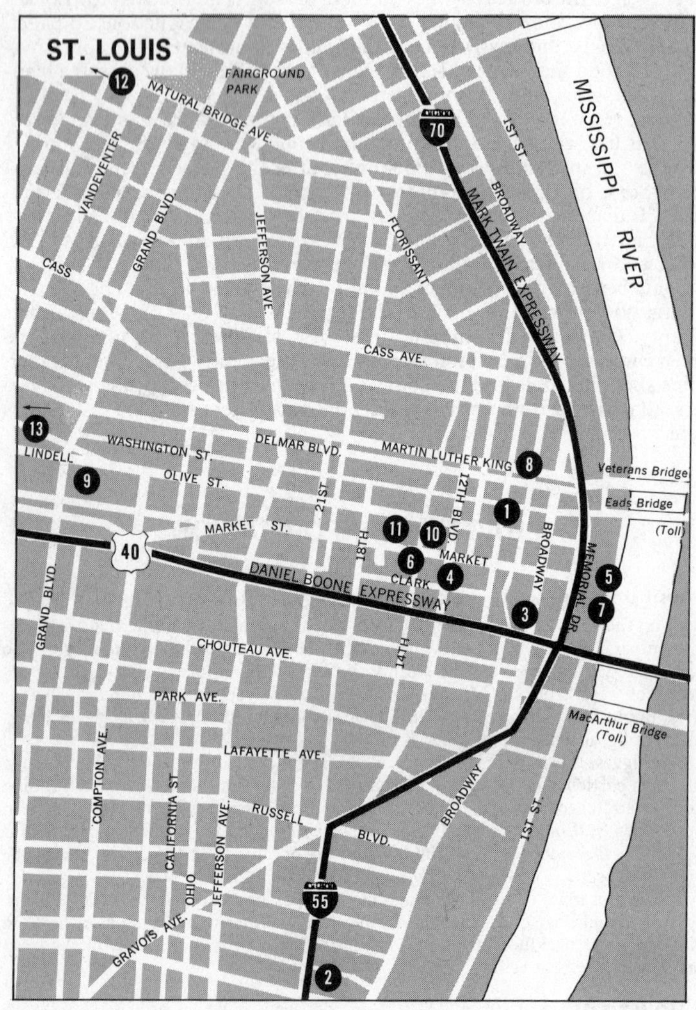

Points of Interest

1) American Theater
2) Anheuser-Busch Brewery
3) Busch Memorial Stadium
4) City Hall
5) Gateway Arch
6) Henry W. Kiel Auditorium
7) Old Cathedral
8) St. Louis Gateway Convention & Exhibition Center
9) St. Louis University
10) Soldiers Memorial Building
11) Union Station
12) University of Missouri
13) Washington University

TELEPHONES. The area code for St. Louis and most of its 92 municipalities is 314. You do not need to dial the area code if it is the same code as the one from which you are dialing. On the east side of the Mississippi River in Illinois, the most common area codes are 271 and 618. To dial most out-of-state regions in Missouri, dial 1 plus the number for a toll call. Information from directory assistance can be obtained by dialing 411 from St. Louis; from out of St. Louis call 314–555–1212, or for 800 numbers, call 800–555–1212. Local directory assistance calls are free from phone booths. A phone call from a pay phone costs 20 cents. Most hotels charge 35 cents for each local phone call made from a room.

Emergency Telephone Numbers. Fire, police, ambulance, and paramedics can be reached by dialing 911. In a hotel, dial O for operator.

ACCOMMODATIONS. It is next to impossible to get a hotel at the last minute any time shortly before, during, and after the Veiled Prophet Fair over the weekend nearest to July 4. If you plan to celebrate July 4 in St. Louis, make your reservation a year in advance for rooms with river views. Remember that this celebration draws a couple of million visitors a year. Rooms may also be difficult to rent during a major convention or when the baseball Cardinals are heading for a pennant. For the best rooms, be sure to reserve when your travel plans are firm.

Hotel rates are based on double occupancy. Categories, determined by price, are as follows: *Reasonable,* $45 to $55; *Very Economical,* under $45. There is a room tax of slightly under 10 percent.

Reasonable

Best Western Executive International. 4530 North Lindbergh Blvd. (Interstate 70 at Highway 67), St. Louis, MO 63044 (314–731–3800, 800–528–1234). Standard rate two beds for two, $49 (for one, $39); children under 11 with parents, free; rollaway, $5; crib, $2.50. Restaurant, pool, sauna, playground, free parking. Senior citizens discount, 10 percent.

Days Inn at the Park. 4630 Lindell Blvd., St. Louis, MO 63108 in Central West End (367–7500). $43 single, $53 double. July 1–4, three-night minimum stay required. Recently renovated. Free underground parking, outdoor pool, sauna. Inexpensive cafeteria with good fried fish and tartar sauce a specialty; open 6:30 A.M.–8 P.M. Coin-operated laundry.

Rodeway Inns. Two locations. 10232 Natural Bridge Rd., St. Louis County, MO 63134 (telephone for both inns, 800–228–2000). $48 double, with cable television. Children under 18, free, plus $6 additional charge of $8 for rollaway bed. Laundry service. At Natural Bridge location, one room specially equipped for disabled, outdoor pool, and video game room, restaurant with Sunday all-you-can-eat brunch at $5.95, half price ages 4–9, under 4 eat free. At 3660 S. Lindbergh Blvd., St. Louis, MO 63127, the cost is $48 double, children under 17 free; $6 charge for rollaway. Outdoor pool and video game room, coin-operated laundry or laundry service, playground. Senior citizen discount of 10 percent.

Quality Inn. 7350 Hanley Rd., St. Louis County, MO 63042 (800–228–5151). $55 for two adults; children under 16 free; $5 charge for each additional adult; $5 charge for rollaway beds. Restaurant, lounge, and outdoor pool, laundry facilities.

Very Economical

Comfort Inn. 3730 South Lindbergh Blvd., St. Louis County, MO 63127 (800–228–5150). Family trade, 100 rooms. $44 for two double beds; children under 16 free; $5 charge for each additional adult; $5 charge for rollaway beds. Outdoor pool; restaurant serves American breakfast and Chinese lunch and dinner. Coin-operated laundry. Two-week advance on reservations advised during summer.

Days Inn. Box 10365, 4545 Woodson Rd., St. Louis County, MO 63145 (800–325–2525). $48 May thru Aug., $41 the rest of the year. $1 for each additional child; ten percent discount for senior citizens. No extra charge for children in rooms with two double beds unless family exceeds occupancy rates. Outdoor pool; restaurant 6 A.M.–10 P.M. No laundry facilities. (800–228–5151).

Howard Johnsons. Several locations. (800–654–2000). Rates vary locally because the motels are franchises; location at 1200 South Kirkwood Rd., St. Louis County, MO 63122 (where Lindberg Boulevard meets Highway I-44), is convenient for motorists and priced at approximately $39 a night for a family of four; about $7 higher

May–Aug. Restaurant lounge, same-day laundry service; children under 18 stay free but extra charge for rollaway beds.

Viking Lodge-Best Western. 10709 Hwy. 366 (314–821–6600, 800–528–1234). Twin beds for two, $40; two full-size beds for family of 4, $44. Video game room, restaurant, lounge with live entertainment, 10 percent senior citizen discount.

Bed-and-Breakfast. The bed-and-breakfast movement is comparatively new to the area. **River Country,** 1 Grandview Heights, St. Louis County, MO 62131 (314–965–4328), prints a *Hostess Directory* of bed and breakfast spots in a two-state area of Missouri and Illinois that includes half a dozen spots in the city of St. Louis and for which reservations are advised several months ahead. **Bed and Breakfast in St. Louis,** 4418 West Pine Blvd., St. Louis, MO 63108 (314–533–9299), offers a reservations service providing "hospitable accommodations in private homes."

Ys and Hostels. Huckleberry Finn Youth Hostel, 1904–06 S. Twelfth St., St. Louis, MO 63104 (314–241–0076). Will pick up guests from bus stations; open April–Sept. $6.25 to $7.25 per night; neighborhood iffy.

HOW TO GET AROUND. From the airport. Taxis from the airport to downtown average about $16; to midtown or Clayton area, about $12.50. Drive time by expressway is about 20 minutes to downtown, 15 minutes to Clayton (except during rush hour). Cabs waiting at the airport taxi stands charge a little more than cabs you phone for, but then there is a 15-minute wait. An airport limousine connects with most of the major hotels (about $6).

By bus. Bi-State Transit (information, 314–231–2345), the bus service, charges 75 cents per ride within a given region plus 10 cents for transfer to another bus or another region. Free shuttle bus in downtown shopping area. St. Louisans generally drive.

By rental car. You will find that a car is the best way to get around St. Louis. Dollar Rent-A-Car (314–434–4004) and Budget Rent-A-Car (314–423–3000) are the cheapest compact cars, and Avis (314–426–7766) is the cheapest for larger cars. All three have airport locations in addition to central offices.

HINTS TO THE MOTORIST. One-way streets downtown can be confusing, so allow time for circling. St. Louis streets don't always run in a north-south east-west grid but radiate like spokes from downtown. Strangers often get lost, so be sure to get a good street map.

Missouri enforces the national 55 mph speed limit. In most of the metropolitan area, the speed limit is 35 mph, occasionally 30 or 40 where marked, but only 25 mph in Forest Park. A right turn on red is permissible through most of the state except where otherwise posted or in the 12-block central business area downtown. Radar detection devices are used in many police cars in the area. Downtown parking is ample, but the meter maids love to write tickets.

In winter cars must have snow tires or chains on specially marked snow routes. Nothing will happen if you don't comply unless you have the misfortune to be stuck in snow or ice and block traffic; then you may be fined.

Existing laws make it mandatory to buckle seat belts for both passenger and driver in front seat; children under four in back seat must be seat-belted, and special infant safety seats are mandatory for the front or back seat. Police are stopping motorists at random to check compliance.

It is also the law that no driver of a vehicle may drink any beverage while driving, not even coffee. Although not generally enforced, drivers have been pulled over for this.

If you plan to tour the surrounding areas, try the Golden Eagle Ferry near Elsah, Illinois, which transports both cars and passengers across the river. Elsah's Landing is a good place to eat.

TOURIST INFORMATION. *Saint Louis Convention and Visitor's Bureau,* 10 S. Broadway, Suite 300, St. Louis, MO 63102 (800–325–7962 or from St. Louis 421–1023). Open Mon.–Fri., 8:30 A.M.–5 P.M. Offers maps and brochures on hotels and attractions, both group and individual guides, and information on driving regulations. The *Levee Branch,* 702 Leonor K. Sullivan Blvd. (formerly Wharf St.)

(421–1799), offers the same information as the main bureau with the addition of a monthly calendar highlighting significant happenings in the area. Calendars are updated every three months and include an area map. Levee Branch is located on a boat next to the Goldenrod Showboat except when displaced by high water (usually in spring); then the location is in the Mansion House Center, 330 N. Fourth St., Suite 211.

Send a self-addressed stamped envelope to *St. Louis County Department of Parks and Recreation,* 41 S. Central Ave., Clayton, MO 63105 (885–2459), for a complete list of events taking place in county parks, such as the St. Louis Symphony Orchestra's summer pops series at Queeny Park, antique and crafts fairs, and sports facilities open to the public. A SASE sent to *St. Louis Department of Parks and Recreation,* 5600 Clayton Rd., St. Louis, MO 63110 (535–1503), will net maps of the major parks in the city of St. Louis, which include Wilmore, Carondelet, O'Fallon, and Forest Park, the latter a 1,300-acre park, one of the largest city parks in the nation, offering many free and low-cost attractions.

SENIOR-CITIZEN AND STUDENT DISCOUNTS. As many stores and shops offer senior citizen discounts with proof of age, it is a good idea to inquire before you buy. Senior citizen discounts at two major movie theater chains (with many locations) result in prices of $2 per person per show for first-run movies at both RKO Mid-America Theaters and Wehrenberg Theaters. Most theaters have rush hour shows around 5 P.M. priced at $1.50 for all, and some movie houses offer discounts to students with valid identification.

Dance St. Louis and the St. Louis Symphony Orchestra offer student rush tickets just before performance time if you have a valid ID. The Tivoli theater on Delmar in University City and the Hi-Pointe theater on McCausland in Richmond Heights run golden oldies, film classics, and art films; both offer student discounts. Because these policies change from time to time and are often extended to senior citizens and students on an occasional basis, it is wise to check. Missouri Botanical Garden is free at all times to those over 65 years who offer proof of age.

HINTS TO DISABLED TRAVELERS. Specially marked parking spaces for the disabled can be recognized by blue-and-white signs and often a wheelchair symbol in white paint at the parking spot. When renting a car in St. Louis, you must bring your own disabled sign, but if that is not removable, you may obtain such a sign for use during your visit at any of the state auto licensing agencies (listed in the Blue Pages of the center section of the telephone book) on presenting proof of disability.

The Missouri Tourist Information Center, Highway 270 and Riverview Dr., St. Louis, MO 63138, offers information on the accessibility of parks. The St. Louis Convention and Visitors Bureau and the Levee Branch (see Tourist Information) offer a group guide called "St. Louis: The Meeting Place," which includes information on a particular attraction's accessibility to the disabled. Paraquad, a nonprofit organization founded by a local paraplegic, offers telephone directory service and information to the disabled; call 314–531–3050.

FREE EVENTS. **The Muny** is the largest outdoor theater in the world. Each summer during a 10-week season, it offers everything from light rock concert stars such as James Taylor to live musicals and Broadway shows with big stars. Over 1,456 free seats are available to first arrivals at the theater each night.

The Muny is involved in a joint venture during the winter with the restored Fox Theater on Grand Avenue in midtown. For those shows at the Fox in which the Muny has an interest, free seats are available shortly before showtime to those standing in line at the box office. This is not commonly known to St. Louisans because it has not been publicized since the renovated Fox opened a few years ago. The Fox does not have as many free seats as the Muny.

Check the "Calendar" section of the St. Louis *Post-Dispatch* on Thursday for free events coming up within the following 10-day period. Many regional and neighborhood fairs and ethnic events are held each year, most clustered between April and October.

The **Saint Patrick's Day Parade** downtown on the Saturday closest to March 17 is getting bigger every year as the Irish and would-be Irish use the occasion for a big party. The **Shriners** host a parade downtown before their annual "Circus with a Purpose" in early June that raises money for the free Shriners Hospital for Crippled Children in St. Louis County. There is a charge for the circus at Busch Stadium.

Other free events include **Black History Month** in Feb. at the Gateway Arch with theater, exhibits, and music, and the **Annual Storytelling Festival,** the first week in May on the grounds of the Gateway Arch, in which professional and traditional storytellers and visitors participate.

International Festival, last weekend in May, Steinberg Rink, Forest Park. Authentic music, dance and crafts of 35 nationalities. Admission free; ethnic food for sale. For information, call 314–432–4013.

Japanese Festival at Missouri Botanical Garden is free from 9 A.M. till noon on Wed. and Sat. of the two-week-long festival held in late August and early September, a celebration of Japanese culture through dance, music, food, and crafts with charges for buying food or craft items. At other times admission is $1 for adults, 50 cents for children ages 13 to 15. For information, call 314–577–5100.

Great Meramec River Raft Race and Festival is a wacky parade and race of homemade rafts that starts at Unger Park and ends at George Winter Park in Fenton, MO (on the outskirts of St. Louis County) and is always held on the last Saturday in June. Race and entertainment are free, but there is a charge to enter a raft for judging. Telephone Gloria Rogers (889–2863).

Veiled Prophet Fair is held on the grounds of the Gateway Arch but often spills out through the downtown area. A stupendous three- or four-day festival that includes July 4 and is preceded by a downtown parade. It offers live entertainment by nationally known performers and local groups; river race by the Mississippi *River Queen* and the *Delta Queen;* water shows; aerial shows, ethnic dance, and food (the food is not free) and crafts. Each night ends with brilliant fireworks over the river reflected in the water and the shimmering Saarinen Arch. Telephone VP Fair (367-FAIR). The VP organization is a civic group of men who like to have fun.

St. Louis Strassenfest is held in the last weekend in July in an area downtown bounded by Eleventh, Thirteenth, Pine, and Clark streets. German food, dancing, arts and crafts, bratwurst, pails of beer, and oom-pah-pah bands. Telephone Mrs. Lee Toberman (721–7454). Admission is free; charge for food and beer.

Great Forest Park Balloon Race. Brilliantly colored hot-air balloons take off from Forest Park and fly where the prevailing winds take them in a bright spectacle against vivid blue September skies. Held the second weekend following Saturday of Labor Day weekend. For information, call 962–4981.

TOURS AND SPECIAL-INTEREST SIGHTSEEING. Anheuser-Busch Brewery Tour departs from the Bevo Plant at the corner of South Broadway and Pestalozzi St., St. Louis, MO 63118 (577–2626). Tour takes 1 hour and 10 minutes and includes the brew house, the bottling plant, a stable with several Clydesdale horses, and a hospitality room for sampling the product. Admission free; no reservation required. Tours are continuous Mon.–Fri. (except for company holidays), 9:30 A.M.–3:30 P.M., starting on the half hour.

Gray Line Sightseeing Tours. Box 14464, St. Louis, MO 63178 (241–1224). Tour begins at Laclede's Landing and covers the riverfront, including the Old Cathedral, Anheuser-Busch Brewery, the Missouri Botanical Garden, and Forest Park. Lecture alternates stop-offs between the New Cathedral and Jefferson Memorial. Adults, $13.50; children under 12, $6.75; children under 6, free; senior citizens, $12.50. Air-conditioned motor coaches.

River Cruises on the *Huck Finn* and *Tom Sawyer.* 319 N. Fourth St. (621–4040). Located on Leonor K. Sullivan Blvd. below the Gateway Arch; day trips run every hour during the summer from 10 A.M. to 8 P.M. Narrated. Adults, $5.25; children under 12, $2.75. In spring and fall, there are four departures daily. In summer a dinner-dance cruise departs at 7:30 P.M. and returns to dock at 10 P.M.; $27.50 for adults, $14.50 for children.

The St. Louis Cathedral (or New Cathedral) on the corner of Lindell Blvd. at North Newstead Ave. Guided tour after noon mass on Sunday; telephone 533–2824.

St. Louis Tram Tours. Tram Tours Depot, 516 Cerre St., St. Louis, MO 63102 (241–1400). Weekends in April, daily from May through mid-November; 9 A.M.–4

P.M. weekdays; 9 A.M.–6 P.M. Sat.; 11 A.M.–6 P.M. Sun. Trams depart every half hour and offer unlimited stop-offs covering almost every major sight in downtown St. Louis plus the antique and junk area of Cherokee St. The tram stops at all major hotels downtown; passes for one day: adults, $13.95; children under 12, $5; children under 5, free; senior citizens, 10 percent discount. Trams are open air with bright awnings.

PARKS AND GARDENS. Faust Park. Olive Street Road at Arrowhead Estates (532–7298). Restored home and granary of Missouri's second governor, Frederick Bates; most charming feature is the bright Dentzel carousel made in Philadelphia in the early 1920s with four rows deep of 64 carved and painted wooden animals and two chariots, all German style. Park is free, but there is a charge for carousel rides (carousel open Wed.–Sun., noon–5 P.M., call 537–0222 for information).

Forest Park. Located on the west end of the city, its 1,300 acres are bounded from Kingshighway at the west to the city limits at Skinker Blvd. at the east; on the north by Lindell Blvd. and on the south by Highway 40.

Jefferson Barracks County Park. At the end of South Broadway at Grant Rd. Park offers reenactments from Indian days, the Civil War, and World War II; restored barracks and museums.

Laumeier Sculpture Park. 12580 Rott Rd., St. Louis County. 96-acre outdoor park built in 1976; works of over 50 major sculptors displayed in natural settings. Admission free, donation requested for indoor gallery. Park hours 8 A.M. to ½ hour after sunset. Gallery hours Wed.–Sat., 10 A.M.–5 P.M. Picnicking in the park is encouraged.

Lone Elk Park. Juncture of Highway 141 where the North Outer Road of Interstate Highway 44 joins. 405 acres stocked with elk, buffalo, sheep, and white-tailed deer roaming freely. Picnic areas are fenced in; lookout tower offers fine view of wild-life. Open from dawn until ½ hour after dusk. Telephone 889–3305 (ask for the Lone Elk Park ranger's office).

Missouri Botanical Garden. 2101 Tower Grove Ave. (577–5100). Begun in 1859 by Henry Shaw, it is ranked second only to London's Kew Gardens and is classed as a National Historic Landmark. Seventy-nine acres house the Climatron, a tropical greenhouse geodesic dome in the manner of Buckminister Fuller; houses for both cacti and orchids; prize-winning rose gardens lush from May through September; splendid Japanese garden and delicate English woodlands area; Ridgway Center for indoor displays and events; and Tower Grove House, the restored home of Henry Shaw. Open daily and holidays except Christmas until dusk. Adults, $1; children ages 13 to 15, 50 cents; senior citizens free.

Queeny Park. 550 Weidman Rd., St. Louis County, MO 63011 (391–0900). Built on land donated by the late Edgar M. Queeny, who founded Monsanto Company. Outdoor Olympic-size swimming pool, tennis courts, hiking trails, and playground; hiking trails are full of edible blackberries in August. Charge for use of pool: $2 adults, $1 children; see Participant Sports for information on tennis courts.

ZOOS. Grant's Farm. 10501 Gravois Rd., St. Louis, MO 63123 (843–1700). Ulysses S. Grant once farmed part of this 281-acre estate now owned by beer baron Gussie Busch, who has filled the grounds with over 200 species of animals in a vast game preserve that is privately owned but open to the public free with reservations 1 week in advance required. Bird shows and trackless train tour of the wildlife area, viewing of Clydesdale horses. Grant's cabin, the actual log cabin home of the Civil War general who became the eighteenth president.

St. Louis Zoo. Forest Park. Eighty-three acres shelter 2,500 animal inhabitants, many seemingly roaming free, such as the lions and tigers and leopards of Big Cat Country. Shows in summer and hands-on children's zoo year-round. Regular admission is free; train rides through the zoo cost $1, and admission to the children's zoo is 45 cents. Telephone 781–0900.

Wolf Sanctuary. Box 760, Eureka, MO 63025 (938–5900). Located at Tyson Valley Research Center of Washington University on the outskirts of St. Louis County. The project of Carole and Marlin Perkins (of Mutual of Omaha's *Wild Kingdom*) and is devoted to the preservation of wolves, including Mexican and red wolves, both species in danger of extinction; wolves roam freely in packs. Morning tours only July–Jan.; no tours during the spring breeding and whelping season.

PARTICIPANT SPORTS. Bicycling. *Forest Park* has a 7-mile-long bike trail and various other routes through the park. Please note that bicycle theft has been a problem in the past, and although the situation now seems to be under control it is not advisable to leave bikes unattended in the park. The biggest bicycling event is the *Moonlight Ramble* held the last weekend in August, beginning 2 A.M. downtown and continuing for 22 miles. Entrance fee covers free emergency towing service for broken-down bikes or broken-down cyclists; for information, call American Youth Hostel (314–421–2044). It is the nation's largest scheduled nighttime bicycling event.

Boating. April through October you may rent canoes, rowboats, and electric boats at the *Post-Dispatch Lake* in Forest Park; $3 per hour for electric boats, $2 per hour for canoes and rowboats.

Bowling. Most of the bowling arenas cater to league bowling, but keep Saturday and Sunday nights open for individual bowling; call ahead for reservations. *Tropicana Bowling Center,* 7960 Clayton Road (314–781–0282), has open play Sat. 9 A.M.–11:30 P.M. and Sun. 9 A.M.–10:30 P.M. Shoe rental, 85 cents; games, $1.35 until 6 P.M., $1.85 after 6 P.M. Lane reservations suggested. *Red Bird Lanes* offers 32 lanes, 7339 Gravois Rd. (314–352–1515). Red Bird has open lanes from 4:30 P.M. Sat. all night until closing time Sunday evening; shoe rental is 75 cents, lane rental $1.25 until 5 P.M., $1.75 after 5 P.M.

Disc golf. If you have not heard of it, it's just like golf only played with Frisbees; weather permitting, a year-round sport of 18 holes. *White Birch Park,* 1186 Tesson Rd., Hazelwood (314–731–0980). Price is $1 for age 16 and over; 50 cents under 16 years. Mon.–Sat., 11 A.M. to dusk, Sun., 12:30 P.M. to dusk; season runs April–Oct.

Floating. The rivers in Missouri are beautiful and serene in summer and fall for novice floaters but can be dangerous in early spring and summer for those who don't know how to read water. River grades one and two on the Eastern Grading Scale are best for novice floaters and can be found into mid-summer on the Meramec River, the Huzzah, the Courtois, the Current River, and Jacks Fork, with many canoe rental services offered. For lists of floats and fishing outfitters on major streams, call or write to the *Missouri Conservation Commission,* 1221 South Brentwood Blvd., Clayton, MO 63105 (314–726–6800). Missouri is famous for floating.

Golf. There are 23 public golf courses in the St. Louis area; one of the most centrally located courses is the 18- and 9-hole course in *Forest Park;* open year-round 7 A.M.–5 P.M. Nov.–March and 5:30 A.M.–9 P.M. April–Oct. there is cart rental but you must bring your own clubs. The 9-hole greens fee are $8; 18-hole fee is $12. Weekends the greens fee are $11.65 for both 9 and 18 holes. Telephone 314–652–2433; senior citizen discount rate applies Mon., Tues., and Fri.

Horseback riding. Two state parks rent horses in all except the winter months. *Babler State Park* reserves horses for those over age 8 (under 8 rides a pony), at a cost of $10 per hour for guided tours. Telephone 314–458–3088 for reservations.

Jogging. Most of the city and county parks have jogging trails. The two most used in the city are in *Tower Grove Park* and *Forest Park.* It is not recommended that women use these trails alone. Both jogging courses have a Parcourse. The *Y.M.C.A.,* 1528 Locust St. (downtown), has an indoor track open Mon.–Fri. from 6 A.M.–8:30 P.M. and 9 A.M.–5 P.M. Sat. Open to men and women. Fees are $2 for card holders; $5 for nonmembers; $3.50 for visitors showing hotel key. The *St. Louis Track Club* offers a listing of weekly track events throughout the year to those who call the recorded message at 314–727–7582.

Roller skating. *Steinberg Rink* in Forest Park (361–5103) offers roller skating May–Sept. (in winter ice skating is offered at irregular hours) at low cost. *Aloha Roller Rink,* 12080 Pattern Rd., Spanish Lake, MO 63138 (314–355–1744), has rates that vary; family night special on Thursday with entrance fee for family of 6 at $4 (maximum 2 persons over age 17), with skate rental at 75 cents per person. *Saint's Olivette Family Roller Skating Center,* 1168 North Warson Rd., St. Louis, MO 63132 (314–991–4116 or 991–4117); skate rental included, lowest rate of $2.75 available 6:30–9:00 P.M. Sun.

Sledding. All parks in the city and county allow sledding when it snows, except for Lone Elk Park. The city builds bonfires for sledders. The favorite place for families is at the top of *Art Hill* (in front of the Art Museum marked by the Statue of St. Louis, king of France). If you didn't bring a sled, it's okay to grab an inner tube from a local gas station. Away from the bonfire at the top of the hill near Forsyth and Skinker roads is the spot for the more daring; it is called Suicide Hill.

Tennis. The *Dwight F. Davis Tennis Center* in Forest Park is open 8 A.M.–4:30 P.M. all year, weather permitting, and from dawn to dusk March–Oct. $2 per day with permits required during the season of April–Oct. Call 367–2292. Open 8 A.M.–4:30 P.M. *Queeny Park* has nine year-round outdoor courts open from dawn to dusk at no charge, first come, first served (391–0900). *Tower Grove Park* in the city of St. Louis charges a daily fee of $3, $5 on weekends. Open dawn until 10 P.M. with metered lights (which invariably go out during your best shot) priced at 25 cents for 21 minutes (776–8722).

SPECTATOR SPORTS. St. Louis Cardinals, **baseball;** Busch Stadium, St. Louis, MO 63102 (421–3060), Apr.–Oct. Box seats are $10.50, reserved seats $8, general admission $5, bleachers $4. To purchase tickets through mail, write: Baseball Cardinal Ticket Office, Box 8787, St. Louis, MO 63102. Discount rates for senior citizens and on certain days for families and women.

St. Louis Blues **hockey** team, 5700 Oakland Ave., St. Louis, MO 63110 (781–5300). An NHL professional hockey team; season runs from mid-October through early May. There are no discounts, with tickets priced from $9 to $17. Additional $1 is charged for each ticket sent through the mail.

St. Louis **Soccer** Steamers, 5700 Oakland Ave., St. Louis, MO 63110 (781–4030). Western Division of the Major Indoor Soccer League; season Oct. through April. Ticket prices are $4, $6, $8, and $10.

HISTORIC SITES AND HOUSES. Bissel House. 10225 Bellefontaine Rd., St. Louis, MO 63137 (314–868–0973). Former home of General Daniel Bissel, who commanded Fort Bellefontaine from 1809 to 1912; restored. Hours Wed.–Sun., 12–5. Adults, $1; children, 50 cents. Guided tours only; last one leaves at 4 P.M.; closed Jan. and Feb.

Campbell House. 1508 Locust St., St. Louis, MO 63103 (314–421–0325). Built in 1851 by fur trader Robert Campbell, furnished with Campbell family's hand-carved rosewood pieces. Open 10 A.M.–4 P.M. Tues.–Sat.; from noon–5 P.M. Sun.; closed Mon. Adults, $2; children under 12, 50 cents. Guided tours of varying lengths. Closed Jan. and Feb.

Chatillon-DeMenil Mansion. 3552 DeMenil Place, St. Louis, MO 63118 (314–771–5828). Original farmhouse built in 1848 with major alterations and expansion in 1856. Guided tours Tues.–Sat., 10 A.M.–3:30 P.M.; Sun., noon–4:30 P.M. Adults, $1.50; children, 50 cents. The DeMenil Carriage House restaurant open for lunch from 11:30 A.M.–2 P.M., Tues.–Sat., closed Jan.

Cupples House. 3673 West Pine, St. Louis, MO 63108 (314–658–3025). On mall at center of St. Louis University campus. Built in 1890, house is famous for intricate wood carving and parquet floors; restored recently. Admission $1 adults, 50 cents senior citizens and children under 12. Guided tours on request, open 10 A.M.–3 P.M., Mon.–Fri.; closed Sat.; open Sun. 2–4 P.M. Art gallery in basement houses unusual collections and is site for changing art collections and offbeat exhibitions.

Eugene Field House. 6334 South Broadway, St. Louis, MO 63103 (314–421–4689). Poet Eugene Field created "Wynken, Blynken and Nod" from memories of his early years spent in this house. Contains Field's original manuscripts, antique toy collection, and memorabilia. Restored to the time of its building in 1845. Open 10 A.M.–4 P.M. Tues.–Sat.; noon–5 P.M. Sun. Adults, $1.50; children, 50 cents.

Hanley House. 7600 Westmoreland Ave., Clayton, MO 63105 (727–8100), Mon.–Fri. Ask to be connected to Hanley House. Built in mid-nineteenth century, house's rooms are papered with unmatched designs which was the custom in early days; old tree used as a whipping post for slaves is a grim reminder of an unjust era. Open Fri.–Sun., 1 P.M.–5 P.M. Adults, $1; children under 13, 50¢.

St. Louis Carousel. Olive Street Rd. at Arrowhead Estates in St. Louis County (889–3356). This ornate carousel was made by the Dentzel Company of Philadelphia in 1920 for a St. Louis park and features 64 hand-carved, carefully restored wooden animals. Rides offered Wed.–Sun. Adults, $1; children, 50 cents. Open noon–5 P.M.

Sappington House. 1015 South Sappington Rd., Crestwood, MO 63126 (314–957–4785). Two-story farmhouse built in 1818 is one of the oldest brick houses west of the Mississippi River; barn converted to a tearoom for luncheons served 11 A.M.–3 P.M. Tues.–Fri. and noon–3 P.M. Sat. Guided tours of house, open from 11 A.M.–3 P.M. Tues.–Fri.; noon–3 P.M. Sat. Adults, $1; children, 50 cents.

MUSEUMS AND GALLERIES. Mercantile Money Museum. Mercantile Bank's Eighth and Locust street Building, downtown (314–425–8199). Assembled by one of the country's leading numismatists; the focus is on the history of the development of money and ranges from coins to all kinds of paper currency. Open 9 A.M.–4 P.M. Closed Sat. and Sun. Admission free.

Museum of Westward Expansion. Ground floor of the Gateway Arch, 702 N. First St. (425–4465). Overview of pioneer days. Rides up to the Arch's observation room. Daily, Memorial Day–Labor Day, 8 A.M.–10 P.M.; other seasons, 9 A.M.–6 P.M. Museum, free; rides to the top of the Arch, $1.50 adults, 50 cents children under 12; under 3 ride free.

National Bowling Hall of Fame. 111 Stadium Plaza, St. Louis, MO 63102 (314–231–6340). Traces origins of bowling from 5200 B.C. child's game in Egypt to present day. Open daily, Memorial Day–Labor Day, 9 A.M.–4 P.M. Adults, $3; senior citizens, $2; children, $1.50.

National Museum of Transport. 3015 Barrett Station Rd. (314–965–7998). An outdoor museum with 159 years of railroad history, including trains of all varieties, spread over 39 acres and the finest collection of trains and train equipment in the nation; kids love it because they can play on some of the trains. Adults, $2; children 5–13, $1; under 5, free; senior citizens, $1.

St. Louis Art Museum. Forest Park (314–721–0067). Known for its eclectic collection of great art of the world through all times with exceptionally fine pre-Columbian art and the most complete collection of German born painter Max Beckmann's work. Closed Mon.; open 10 A.M.–5 P.M. every other day except Tues., when the hours are 1:30 P.M.–8:30 P.M. Free except for occasional special exhibits, when a donation is requested every day except Tues.

Sports Hall of Fame. 100 Stadium Plaza, St. Louis, MO 63102 (314–421–6790). Located in Busch Stadium, contains over a century of St. Louis sports in the form of trophies, uniforms, and sports equipment; recently remodeled with new exhibits. Open 7 days a week mid-Mar. through mid-Dec., closed weekends mid-Dec. through mid-March. 10 A.M.–5 P.M. and until 11 P.M. on nights of Cardinal baseball team home games. Museum and stadium, adults, $3.50; children, $1.50. Museum only or stadium only, adults, $2; children $1.

FILM. St. Louis Art Museum Film Series. Top of Art Hill, Forest Park (314–721–0067). Friday nights they show American film classics such as Cary Grant, Judy Garland, or Fred Astaire movies; Tuesday nights internationally acclaimed films are shown, often coinciding with current museum exhibitions, but sometimes featuring one nation such as Chinese or Japanese films. Sometimes free; other times cost is minimal.

Webster College Film Series. 470 East Lockwood Blvd., Webster Groves, MO 63119 (314–968–7487). Regular series vary among film classics, box office hits, children's film series, to documentaries of special interest and fine art premiers. Adults, $2; children and senior citizens $1.50 except for premieres when cost is $3 and $2, respectively. Season runs Sept.–May, with premieres on Fri. and Sat. night; all other films Thurs.–Sun. nights; children's series on Sat. and Sun. afternoon.

One-time-only film series are offered in varying locations; see the "Calendar" section in Thursday's St. Louis *Post-Dispatch* and the listings in the *Riverfront Times,* a free paper available in restaurants and hotels downtown.

MUSIC. The St. Louis Symphony Orchestra, under maestro Leonard Slatkin, performs twice weekly during the season, which runs from September through April, and then picks up in a summer pops season in Queeny Park. The symphony's home is at Powell Hall, 718 North Grand (533–2500); the box office number for single performance tickets is 534–1700. See DISCOUNTS and FREE EVENTS.

The Ethical Society. 9001 Clayton Rd. (991–0955). Runs a series of musical evenings whose offerings range from jazz and folk to classical and avant-garde. Ticket prices vary by performance but usually range between $5 and $10. Check it out on arrival.

Opera Theatre of St. Louis, # 1 Kirthom Ln., Webster Groves (314–961–0171), is not exactly a budget offering but a Recommended Splurge. Tickets are priced from $9 to $40 for the nearly six week season running from mid-May through June and are hard to come by. Four different offerings make up this regional opera company's season each year. Opera Theatre of St. Louis has won raves internationally and attracted favorable critiques from *The New Yorker* and the *New York Times.*

Rock and pop concert tickets may be purchased by calling Dialtix (314–421–1400), which handles performances for most major concerts.

DANCE. Dance St. Louis, 149 Edgar Rd. (314–968–3770), has a winter season with performances held in several locations. It offers both experimental and classical dance and is always stimulating. Tickets range in price from $12 to $22; students with ID get tickets half price, senior citizens get a 20 percent discount.

STAGE. American Theater. 416 North Ninth St., St. Louis, MO 63101 (314–231–7000). Offers performances by road companies of Broadway hits; when given in conjunction with the Muny, there are 74 free seats available 1 hour before each performance; otherwise ticket prices run $20.90 to $24.90 with $2 off at weekend matinees.

Repertory Theater of St. Louis. 130 Edgar Road, Webster Groves, MO (314–968–4925). Everything from Shakespeare to avant-garde plays from early September to mid-April. Tickets as low as $16.50 during weeknights to $19.50 for the best seat in the house on Friday or Saturday night. An offbeat Studio Theatre has less frequently produced offerings and innovative interpretations of standard fare. The Studio Theatre seats are priced at $12.

Theater Project Company. New City School, 5209 Waterman Ave., Central West End (314–531–1301). A repertory company; season from Sept. to May. Tickets $8 to $13; discounts for students, seniors, and groups of 10 or more.

DINING OUT. You can get a good meal for a very reasonable price in St. Louis. Restaurant categories, based on the price of a meal for one, without beverage, tax, or tip, are as follows: *Reasonable,* $8 to $24; *Very Economical,* $6 to $8; and *Low Budget,* under $6. We've made every effort to ensure that this list is up to date, but, because restaurants come and go so quickly, it is always advisable to call ahead.

Reasonable

Nantucket Cove. 40 North Kingshighway, in the fashionable Central West End (361–0625). An excellent seafood restaurant with pleasant ambience offers a pricefixe menu between 5:30 and 6:30 P.M. starting at $8.95 for a platter of scrod; $12.95 for shrimp and clams.

Riddles Restaurant. 6307 Delmar (725–6985). American cuisine with lots of pasta, steak, and chicken entrees to choose from. Extensive wine list featuring 167 Californian and European wines. Desserts and ice cream made fresh daily.

Very Economical

Hacienda Restaurant. 2435 Woodson Rd. (426–4569). Family-style Mexican restaurant where it is possible to eat as cheaply as $3.40 per person, exclusive of beverage (75¢ extra). Large dinner entrees range in price from $6.95 to $10.25; lunch menu is cheaper. Open 4–10 P.M. Sun.; 11 A.M.–12 P.M. Mon.–Sat.

Old Spaghetti Factory. 727 North First St. (621–0276). Located in Laclede's Landing. Pasta prices range from $3.50 to $6.50, depending on the sauce; portions are huge. Children's plates $2.90. Open 5 P.M.–10 P.M. Mon.–Thurs.; 5 P.M.–11:30 P.M. Fri.; 4 P.M.–11:30 P.M. Sat.; 3:30 P.M.–10 P.M. Sun. Be ready for a wait of an hour or longer during summer months.

The Pasta House Company. 11 locations to choose from, consult the phone directory. The Pasta House Company offers a wide variety of pastas and sandwiches ranging in price from $4 to $15. Children's menu ranges from $1 to $2.55.

Low Budget

Amighettis Bakery. Two locations: 101 Broadway (downtown), and 5141 Wilson Ave. (on the Hill, the traditional Italian section of town) (968–0333). Amighettis' sandwiches are a local version of the poor boy, Italian bread thickly laid with Italian sausages and meats, cheeses, and antipasto big enough to feed two adults and priced at $4.10 to carry out or eat in; outdoor wine and beer garden in warm weather. Wilson Ave. hours: Tues.–Fri. 8:30 A.M.–8 P.M., Sat. 8:30 A.M.–5 P.M.; Broadway hours: Mon.–Sat. 10 A.M.–6:30 P.M., open until 8 P.M. if there's an evening baseball game.

Grones Cafeteria. Two locations: 1269 S. Laclede Station Rd. (776–2855) and 4409 Woodson Rd., Woodson Terrace (314–423–7880). Family-run restaurant with an "elderly ambience" but first-rate food bargains with choice of four or five full meals daily in price range of $2.50 to $5 for complete meal. Open 11 A.M.–8 P.M. Sun.–Fri.

Miss Hulling's Cafeteria. 1103 Locust St., St. Louis, MO 63101 (436–0840). Best cafeteria in town with sumptuous desserts and home-style cooking. Offers a special that is a buy; for about $5.85, a complete meal with salad, entree, dessert, bread, and butter and sometimes beverage. Special changes daily. Open 6 A.M.–8:15 P.M. Mon.–Sat.

Brunches. Casa Gallardo. Seven locations; brunch 11 A.M.–2 P.M. Sun. of both Mexican and American dishes with dessert bar and complimentary champagne served after noon. Adults, $5.95; children under 12, $2.95.

Cheshire Inn. 63106 Clayton Rd., Clayton, MO 63105 (647–7300). Brunch seven days a week. Open 7 A.M.–10 A.M. Mon.–Sat. at $5.95, adults, $3.45, children 5 to 10, and $1.65 children 2 to 5; Sat.–Sun. 7:30 A.M.–11:30 A.M., $8.95 adults, $4.50 children 5 to 10, and $2.25 children 2 to 5. All you can eat from scrumptious choice of standard breakfast fare to chicken Cantonese, fruit or cheese crepes, English muffins, and fabulous pastries. A Recommended Splurge.

Magic Pan. Plaza Frontenac, at the corner of Clayton Rd. and Lindbergh Blvd., next to Saks Fifth Avenue (569–1810). Sunday brunch 10:30 A.M. to 2 P.M. caters chiefly to local after-church crowd; menu from standard breakfast fare. Crêpes, steak and eggs, and salmon Florentine. Adults $7.95 to $8.95; children under age 12, $2.95.

Cafes and Coffeehouses. There are no real coffeehouses in the Viennese sense in St. Louis, but there are a number of places where guests are welcome to drop in and linger over a good cup of coffee.

Andre's Swiss Confiserie and Tea Room. 1026 South Brentwood Blvd., Richmond Heights (727–9928). Swiss pastries and other delicacies, also continental breakfast and light lunch. Lunch prices moderate to expensive. Mon.–Sat. 7:30 A.M.–5 P.M.

La Patisserie. 6269 Delmar Blvd., University City (725–4902). Great croissants and soups; have a cup of coffee and a pastry and listen to classical music.

Zimfel's. 238 North Euclid Ave., St. Louis (Central West End) (367–3155). Café and specialty store selling good wines and cheese. In summer, both indoor and outdoor seating.

NIGHTLIFE AND BARS. Bars in St. Louis are relatively inexpensive. Even those with live entertainment generally have small cover charges of only a dollar or two. Several areas are considered entertainment centers.

The Central West End in midtown is about 10 city blocks long and grouped primarily along Euclid Ave. one block east of Kingshighway, a main north-south artery. A fashionable crowd but some modestly priced places.

Laclede's Landing is located near the riverfront just north of Washington Avenue and east of Third Street, above which is an elevated highway that circles the downtown area. Over 50 bars and restaurants with entertainment from jazz to disco to rock 'n' roll. Cover charges can vary here, so shop carefully. Street entertainers during the summer.

West Port Plaza is a large mall with many shops and restaurants, some economical. Shops stay open late. Special attractions include the Comedy Theatre (Funny Bones), West Port Playhouse, and West Port Cinema. Attracts young professionals.

Soulard District is just south of downtown. Two specially popular bars here are Mike & Mins for great bands but little room to dance and McGurk's, an Irish bar with authentic Irish music.

SECURITY. Tourists would be wise to avoid the north side of the city and use Lindell Boulevard or Highway 40 as an east-west axis. Staying roughly south of

Delmar Avenue in the suburbs immediately west of the city is also wise for strangers. Downtown is deserted at night except on nights when there is sports activity. Avoid Grand Avenue at night when the Fox and Symphony are both dark. The Central West End is safe only on the main, more crowded streets. Unaccompanied women are asking for trouble if they walk alone here at night. Laclede's Landing is well policed, but it too is not recommended for women alone after dark.

The East Side, or East St. Louis, IL, is best avoided entirely by out-of-towners unfamiliar with this region of high unemployment. When traveling east on one of the connecting highways, be sure to exit before crossing the bridge to the East Side inadvertently.

As in every big city, there is a certain amount of crime and people who prey on strangers. As a rule, stay to the main arteries and avoid out-of-the-way places and strangers who offer unusual buys. The city is relatively safe, but no place is safe for those travelers who lack prudence or common sense.

SALT LAKE CITY

by
Harry E. Fuller, Jr.

Harry Fuller has lived in Salt Lake City for 23 years. He is an editorial writer for the Salt Lake City Tribune.

The capital of Utah, Salt Lake City, is a genuinely unique Rocky Mountain municipality. No other metropolis in the western state nestles close to adjacent mountains. The Wasatch Range rises 9,000 feet from the back door of 172,000 urban residents. The setting—of mountainsides, foot hills, and plains, sloping to a large inland sea, the Great Salt Lake—is duplicated nowhere else in the United States. That was part of the plan of the city's original settlers.

Salt Lake City's most notable distinction is that it is the headquarters of an international Christian denomination—the 3-million-member Church of Jesus Christ of Latter-day Saints, commonly referred to as the Mormon Church. The Jordan Valley, in which Salt Lake City sits, was chosen by the church's second president, Brigham Young, as a place sufficiently isolated at the time—mid-1840s—to protect the congregation from persecution and harassment.

With irrigation systems built to deliver snowmelt from the nearby mountains, the Mormon pioneers converted an otherwise arid desert into flourishing farmlands, which gradually gave way to residential neighborhoods of green lawns, leafy shade trees, and vividly-hued gardens. Today the city is for the most part a community of homeowners. Well maintained even in advanced age, most of the neighborhoods, beginning at the very perimeter of the downtown commercial districts, have a clean and snug appearance.

The wide downtown streets, common to all Utah Mormon communities, were part of Brigham Young's original city design. He wanted a 20-mule team to be able to change directions—by making a U-turn—without going around the block. Most of the city's entertainment and cultural centers cluster downtown, although some athletic and performing arts events occur 14 blocks to the east, on the University of Utah campus. Of course, the famed Temple Square is at the heart of downtown. It encloses the first Utah Mormon temple, the renowned Tabernacle, a new visitors center, and other associated buildings. Temple Square is also distinctive for the 15-foot-high masonry wall embracing it.

As a gateway to winter skiing and with a full inventory of state and national parks farther south, Salt Lake City commands a prominent place among the nation's metropolitan areas—conducive to both strenuous and relaxing outdoor recreation. In the city itself, this is a characteristic revealed by several public golf courses, tennis courts, and parks. The arts also are well represented; the city has a first-rate symphony orchestra, a ballet, and a budding opera company. An array of museums beckons visitors and residents alike.

Salt Lake City's religious heritage and its location on westward immigrant trails and transcontinental railways invest it with a historical quality as matchless as its natural surroundings. The city is so conscious of its distinctive origins that when a part of the town was rejuvenated and the Triad Center, with modern office buildings, high rise hotels, and shops, was built, it was deliberately situated around a former territorial-era home, the Devereaux House, and adjacent to the once-bustling Union Pacific depot. In early summer, it is the site of the city's arts festival, further emphasizing the variety and vivacity found in Utah's capital.

PRACTICAL INFORMATION

WHEN TO GO. Although framed by mountains, Salt Lake City's climate is more typical of the high desert. July and August are the hottest, driest months, with extremes in the 90s and even above 100 degrees. Because of the mile-high altitude, summer evenings in Salt Lake City are always refreshed by mountain breezes, no matter how torrid the day. January and February can be the coldest, lows occasionally near zero. Of course, the wintry conditions assure magnificent skiing in the same nearby mountains. Although spring, late summer, and fall may be the most comfortable time to enjoy Salt Lake City, the history, scenery, and programmed events of the metropolitan area make it a fascinating stopping place any time.

HOW TO GET THERE. Selected by the Mormon pioneers for its remoteness, Salt Lake City remains hundreds, often thousands, of miles from other U.S. population centers. Nonetheless, it sits astride two interstate highways and the confluence for three Amtrak trains, and has a first-rate, modernized international airport.

By air. *Delta* is the largest carrier serving Salt Lake City. Other carriers include *American, Continental, Eastern, PSA, TWA,* and *United.* Deregulation has caused brisk competition in air fares to and from Salt Lake City. Prices change frequently, but it is not unusual to find a San Francisco to Salt Lake City flight for $99 one-way; a Dallas–Fort Worth one-way flight for $119; or a New York to Salt Lake City flight, one-way, for $139. But the prices fluctuate, depending on time of day, time of week, and seasons.

By bus. *Greyhound-Trailways* is the only transcontinental service operating through Salt Lake City. *Pacific Trailways* connects the city to Oregon, Washington, Idaho, and Northern California.

By train. A transfer point on the *Amtrak* system, Salt Lake City can be reached from Oakland on the *Zephyr,* from Seattle on the *Pioneer,* and from Los Angeles on the *Desert Wind.* The latter two connect with the *California Zephyr* as it operates between Salt Lake City and Chicago. Fares fluctuate seasonally.

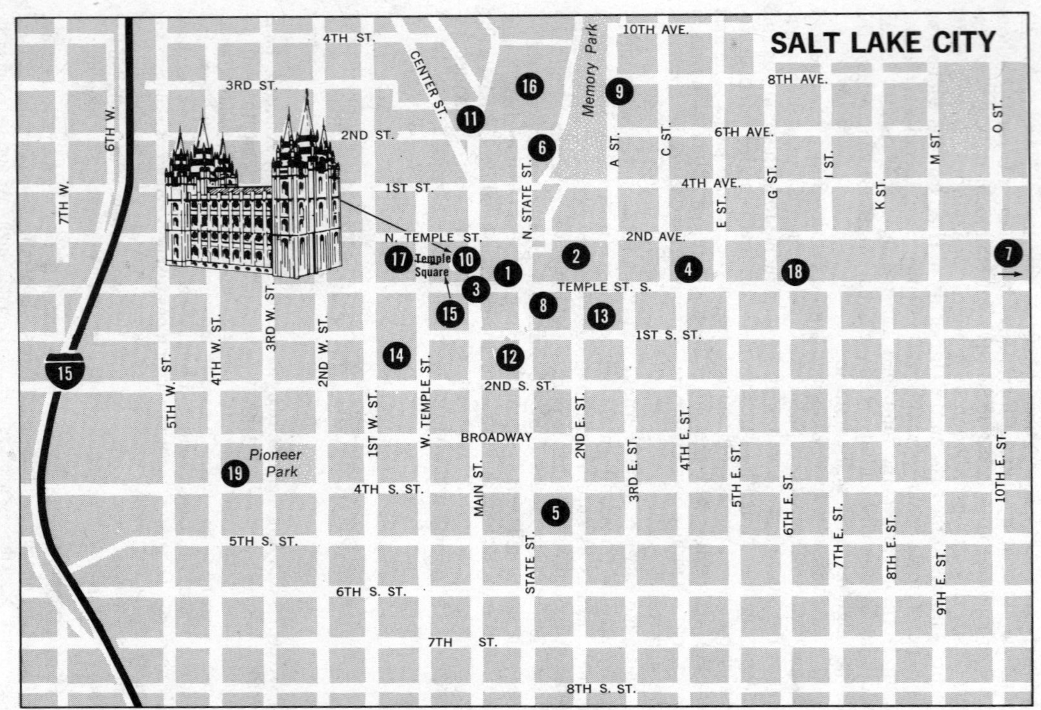

Points of Interest

1) Beehive House
2) Brigham Young's Grave
3) Brigham Young Statue
4) Cathedral of the Madeleine
5) City Hall
6) Council Hall
7) University of Utah and Museum of Natural History
8) Hansen Planetarium
9) Memory Grove
10) Mormon Temple
11) Pioneer Museum
12) Promised Valley Theater
13) Saint Mark's Cathedral
14) Salt Palace and Concert Hall
15) Seagull Monument
16) State Capitol
17) Tabernacle & Assembly Hall
18) Utah Governor's Mansion
19) Utah State Historical Society

TELEPHONES. The area code for Salt Lake City and all of Utah is 801. Dial 1 before Utah numbers out of Salt Lake City and 1 + area code outside the state. Directory assistance number is 555–1212. Person-to-person and credit card calls are placed by dialing the operator (0). Pay-phone price for local calls is 25 cents, with no time limit.

Emergency Telephone Numbers. In Salt Lake City the emergency phone number for police and sheriff departments, fire and paramedic departments are 911. The poison control center is 581–2151; highway conditions, 964–6000.

ACCOMMODATIONS. Salt Lake City is not known for its low-priced hotels. Some of the newer, finer hotels, however, do offer certain discounts during weekends or off-peak seasons. Since it's impossible to know precisely when these will appear, contacting a travel agent is probably the most reliable procedure. Peak season, because of local ski attractions, is mid-winter, Christmas through mid-March. The city room tax is 9.75 percent. Hotel rates are based on double occupancy. Categories, determined by price, are: *Reasonable,* $45 to $60; and *Very Economical,* $35 to $44.

Howard Johnsons. 122 W. South Temple, Salt Lake City, UT 84101 (801–521–0130). In the heart of town, directly west of Temple Square and directly north of the Salt Palace and symphony hall. Has a swimming pool and 24-hour cafe.

Orleans Inn. 352 South 300 East, Salt Lake City, UT 84111 (801–521–3790). Three blocks east of downtown. Swimming pool year-round, underground parking, complimentary Continental breakfast, full kitchens, separate living and dining rooms.

Shilo Inn. 206 S. West Temple, Salt Lake City, UT 84101 (801–521–9500). Downtown, directly south of the Salt Palace and symphony hall, just one block south of Temple Square. Summer swimming pool and restaurant.

Very Economical

Temple Square Hotel. 75 W. South Temple, Salt Lake City, UT 84101 (801–355–2961). In the heart of town, directly south of Temple Square, a few doors directly east of the Salt Palace and symphony hall. An old but recently remodelled hotel, comfortable and unpretentious, with a cafe-restaurant.

Budget Motels. Decent, economical motels are available close-in to downtown Salt Lake City. Rates for these range from $20 to $40 per night, plus the usual 9.75 percent room tax.

Aquarius Motel. 325 N. 300 West, Salt Lake City, UT 84103 (801–521–9525). Nothing fancy, some units feature kitchens.

Colonial Village. 1530 S. Main St., Salt Lake City, UT 84115 (801–486–8171). Next to a popular German restaurant, a summertime pool and coin-operated laundry three blocks away.

Covered Wagon. 230 W. North Temple, Salt Lake City, UT 84116 (801–533–9100). Just off I–80, and across the street from an all-night restaurant. Within short distance of downtown.

Desert Inn. 50 W. 5th South, Salt Lake City, UT 84101 (801–532–2900). Swimming pool with adjacent sun deck. Suites are available and a third of the rooms have extra-large beds.

Super 8. 616 S. 200 West, Salt Lake City, UT 84101 (801–534–0808). One and two-bed double occupancy, near I–15, underground parking and cable-TV.

Thrifty-Scot. 1970 W. North Temple, Salt Lake City, UT 84116 (801–539–8538). Continental breakfast included in nightly rate, near restaurants and on bus line to downtown.

Bed-and-Breakfast. There is only one "budget" B&B in Salt Lake City. Known as the **Saltair Bed and Breakfast** and listed on the National Historic Register, it is a 1903 home offering five bedrooms complete with antiques and homemade bedspreads. Continental breakfast is offered. The double occupancy rate is $39 for a shared bath, $49–$59 for a private bath. Write: Saltair Bed and Breakfast, 164 South 9th East, Salt Lake City, UT 84102 (801–533–8184).

HOW TO GET AROUND. Salt Lake City has an excellent bus service. Three cab companies are also available, reasonably punctual—but at 90 cents per mile—not cheap for long distances. In the downtown area, all rides on the bus, called the UTA, are free. Another service, between the old commercial district and Trolley Square shopping mall, is provided by the *Brigham Street Trolley.* These buses resemble old-time trolley cars.

From the airport. Downtown Salt Lake City is 4 ½ miles from the airport. The public bus line serves the route for 50 cents. The cab fare is about $8. Certain hotels and motels provide van pick-up. Limousine service is mostly to the ski resorts, Ogden and Provo.

By bus. *Utah Transit Authority (UTA)* offers reasonably priced, well-dispersed service throughout metropolitan Salt Lake City. Buses are free in the downtown zone; outside, the fare is 50 cents. For route information, call 287–4636.

By taxi. The three major cab companies in Salt Lake City are Yellow (521–2100), City (363–5014), and Ute (359–7788). The rate is $1.20 a mile.

By rental car. The Salt Lake City telephone directory carries ten pages of car rental outlets. They range from nationwide to strictly local. Many have airport pick-up service, others downtown. It is advisable to reserve in advance. Among the majors are *Budget* (airport, 801–363–1500; downtown, 801–322–5581; or 800–527–0700), *Hertz* (airport, 801–539–2683; downtown, 801–521–4100; or 800–654–3131), *National* (airport, 801–539–0200; downtown, 801–328–3221; or 800–227–7368), *Avis* (airport, 801–539–1117; downtown, 801–539–2177; or 800–331–1212), *Thrifty* (801–328–2545; or 800–367–2277), and *Rent-A-Wreck* (801–486–7501; or 800–421–7253).

HINTS TO THE MOTORIST. Car travel is reasonably simple in Salt Lake City. Although the geography tends to undulate, streets are laid out in an uncomplicated grid system. Since mountains on both sides of the valley run north and south, it's virtually impossible to lose direction. But if a landmark is necessary, always remember the State Capitol, looming on foot hills above the city, is north from downtown.

Rush hours are the usual, between 7 and 8 A.M. and between 4 and 6 P.M. Curbside parking downtown is always scarce, but numerous parking lots and ramps are available. Pedestrians have the right-of-way. Some lots have stalls for the handicapped, but no such provision is made at curbsides.

Right turns on red lights are permitted by state law. Both city and state police are tough on drunk driving, so it is advisable to be particularly careful when leaving a nightclub or lounge parking lot. In the hilly sections of the city, use low gear and remember to turn the front wheels in the proper safety position. Because Utah drivers are used to wide streets, they tend to swing wide when turning at an intersection. Be warned. Lane changing can also sometimes be abrupt. Curbside parking is always at a premium in downtown Salt Lake City, but most stores and shopping malls validate for parking lots. All curbside parking is metered and patrolled.

TOURIST INFORMATION. The *Salt Lake Convention and Visitors Bureau,* 180 S. West Temple, Salt Lake City, UT 84101 (801–521–2822), offers brochures and guide material at no cost, a detailed city map for $1, and, usually, posters at reasonable prices. A walking and driving tour guide of the city is printed in German, Spanish, French, and Japanese. Mon.–Fri., 7:30 A.M.–5:30 P.M.; Sat., 9 A.M.–6 P.M.; Sun., 10 A.M.–4 P.M.

HINTS TO DISABLED TRAVELERS. Salt Lake City has made some progress in accommodating the disabled, with curb cuts and specially marked parking areas. The best information on hotels, motels, restaurants, and shopping malls that are most convenient for the disabled is in the booklet *Accessibility Guide to Salt Lake.* It can be obtained free by writing to the Utah Division of Rehabilitation Services, 250 E. 500 South St., Salt Lake City, Utah 84111. Additional information can be obtained from the Utah Travel Council, at the Council Hall, Capitol Hill, Salt Lake City, Utah 84114.

FREE EVENTS. Local jazz ensembles perform every Saturday night, June through August, from 7 P.M. to 9:30 P.M. at Trolley Square, 7th East and 5th South. Ethnic festivals open to the public are normally held throughout the summer in

Liberty Park, 5th East and 12th South. The **Utah Scottish Festival and Highland Games** are also held in the city during June. The world famous **Mormon Tabernacle Choir** (information: 531–2534) can be heard in the Tabernacle in Temple Square during its Thursday evening rehearsals (8–10 P.M.) and regular Sunday performances (9:30–10 A.M.—you must be in your seat by 9:15). On July 24, one of the nation's largest parades is held in Salt Lake City as part of **Pioneer Days** celebration, commemorating the first Mormon settlers' arrival in Utah. Fireworks at public parks on July 4 and July 24 can be watched without charge. The July 24 **Desert News Marathon** is routed down Salt Lake City's Main Street just prior to the parade's start.

The Mormon Church maintains one of the largest **genealogical libraries** in the world. Located on the west side of West Temple St., between North and South Temple streets, these records are available to the public. It can be fascinating to trace family lines back several generations. Mon., 7:30 A.M.–6 P.M.; Tues.–Fri., 7:30 A.M.–10 P.M.; Sat., 7:30 A.M.–5 P.M.

TOURS. Using Salt Lake City's public bus system, UTA, it's possible to conduct your own inexpensive tours. The fare is 50 cents one way, and buses will take you just about anywhere you choose to go. For instance, the Route 4 bus runs to the University of Utah, Fort Douglas, Hogle Zoological Gardens, and This is the Place Monument, traveling along the South Temple Street historic homes district. Route 23 goes to Capitol Hill and the State Capitol; Route 27, to 700 East St. and then Liberty Park. Ride it all the way and see southern suburbs of Salt Lake City. Route 32 also runs past Liberty Park, winding through an eastern suburb of the city. All these buses can be caught on Main Street in downtown Salt Lake City. Helping to simplify bus use is UTA's *route guide and system map.* A copy can be obtained free at the information booth in the ZCMI shopping mall's interior courtyard, downtown. 15 S. Main St. Mon.–Fri., 10 A.M.–9 P.M. Sat. 10 A.M.–6 P.M. The booth also has route schedules available.

More formal, guided, and expensive tours are offered by *Gray Line of Salt Lake* (521–7060) and *Lewis Bros.* (359–8677). Lewis Bros. provides a 90-minute mini-tour of the city aboard its "Old Salty," an open-air, simulated tour train driven around downtown city streets. It departs from the north side of Temple Square daily during the summer at 9 and 11 A.M., 1, 3, 6, and 7:30 P.M. Spring and fall departures are at 11 A.M., 1, 3, and 6 P.M. The charge is around $5.

PARKS AND GARDENS. Salt Lake City has two large public parks; both are handsomely planted in spring, summer, and fall and are always open. **Liberty Park,** at 5th East and 12th South streets, was originally a Brigham Young farm. Full of activity in decent weather, it offers a well-stocked aviary, exotic birds and animals, a pond large enough for rented paddle boats, a swimming pool and a small midway for children, with merry-go-round, ferris wheel, and kiddy cars. **Sugar House Park,** at 21 South and 13 East streets, on the former site of Utah State Prison, also has a large pond. Winter snow permits sledding on a long, steep hill groomed for that purpose.

This is the Place Monument and **Park,** at Sunnyside Ave., off Foothill Blvd., is a collection of old homes and farm houses, arranged to resemble a pioneer community. Complete with statuary and information center, it commemorates the Mormon Pioneers' journey westward and arrival at what became Salt Lake City.

ZOO. Hogle Zoological Garden, 2600 Sunnyside Ave. (582–1631), has long been a Salt Lake City treasure. Displaying more than 1,000 mammals, birds, and reptiles from around the world, it features a petting zoo for children and a ride on a miniature train pulled by a replica 1869 steam engine. Hours are: summer, 9 A.M.–6 P.M.; spring and fall, 9 A.M.–5 P.M.; winter, 9 A.M.–4:30 P.M. Admission: $4 adults, $2 children 5–16 and senior citizens, under 4 free.

PARTICIPANT SPORTS. Joggers and runners are a common sight on Salt Lake City's downtown streets. The most popular place for this exercise, however, is Liberty Park, Salt Lake City's largest, most centrally located park, at 5th East and 12th South streets.

Liberty Park has 12 **tennis** courts. Fees are: $1 an hour 5 P.M.–10 P.M. daily and 8 A.M.–1 P.M. weekends. All courts are open from April 1 to Oct. 31, four have nets year-round. During summer months, it is advisable to call for reservations, which can be done a day ahead (535–7994). Other public courts can be found at school grounds and parks around the city. All are heavily used in morning and evening hours during the summer.

The city operates six **golf courses.** Again, it is advisable to call ahead for tee times and exact information on green fees. The courses are: *Bonneville,* 954 Connor (582–0497); *Forest Dale,* 2375 S. 900 East (467–1765); *Glendale,* 1630 W. 2100 South, 972–5690; *Mountain Dell,* Porleys Canyon, which is outside the city, off I–15, about 14 miles from downtown (582–3812); *Nibley Park,* 2780 S. 700 East (467–3930); *Rose Park,* 1386 Redwood Rd. (322–3495).

Of course, in winter, **skiing** is conveniently nearby, up adjacent canyons. Rates run from $12 to $30 daily, but some resorts offer special prices during the week, or, depending on the apparent current promotional need. Such information is available at the Council House on Capitol Hill (521–8102).

Raging Waters, at 1200 W. 1700 South, is a slightly different desert-area recreation facility. Considered a water theme park, it has 11 swimming pools, 15 water slides and 13 other aquatic attractions. The park's major attraction is an 18,000-square-foot pool featuring mechanically produced waves. The swells are five feet high, the cresting waves, three feet. Wave action runs for 10 minutes, followed by 10 minutes of quiet water. Lockers are available for $1, along with food and drink outlets. Inflated rubber rafts, for the wave pool, can be rented for $2. A parking lot holds 700 vehicles and there is a gift shop. Admission is $8.50 all day, ages 8 and older; 4–7, $7.50. The nighttime rate, 5 P.M.–dark, $5.55, children under 3, free.

SPECTATOR SPORTS. A full schedule of professional and collegiate athletics is on display from fall through spring, at the Salt Palace, 100 S. West Temple St. (363–7681), and the University of Utah (561–6641). The university offers first-rate football, basketball, swimming, and women's gymnastics. The N.B.A. *Utah Jazz* basketball team and the IHL Salt Lake *Golden Eagles* hockey team play at the Salt Palace. Sometimes, local merchants sell discounted tickets to the professional basketball and hockey games as promotionals. A minor league baseball team is expected to appear once again soon at Derks Field. Bonneville Raceway, 6555 W. 2100 South (250–4560), west of Salt Lake City, stages various kinds of auto competitions during the summer.

HISTORIC SITES AND HOUSES. **The Alta Club,** at the southeast corner of State and South Temple, is the home of Utah's oldest club for local high-rollers.

The Beehive House, on the northwest corner of State and South Temple streets, is one of several houses built and used by Brigham Young. It is furnished as it might have been during his lifetime and can be viewed on a free guided tour.

Capitol Hill includes the Capitol Building and the restored Council House, 300 N. State St. (533–5681), originally the territorial governing office.

The Eagle Gate, spanning State Street just east of the Beehive House, is the replica of one that originally guarded the entrance to woodlands where Brigham Young permitted people to scavenge for firewood at a price.

Fort Douglas Military Reservation, just above the University of Utah campus, has been a U.S. Army installation since soldiers were led into the valley to help enforce territorial laws 100 years ago. Open to the public.

South Temple Street, between the university campus and downtown, is lined on both sides with homes built with money earned by the state's first mining barons. In fact, this street is a historic district, preserved by city ordinance against excessive redevelopment.

Temple Square. At the heart of downtown Salt Lake City, historic Temple Square is contained within a square block formed by Main St., South Temple St., North Temple St., and West Temple St. It contains five principal buildings: The Temple itself, two visitor centers, the Assembly Hall and the Tabernacle. All are open to the public except the temple, in which sacred devotional work, including marriages, is performed by church members in good standing. Admittance is gained to the temple by members only on a recommendation from their bishop, equivalent to a minister in other Christian denominations. Half-hour tours are conducted through the public buildings daily, from 8 A.M.–7:30 P.M., Jun.–Aug., and 9 A.M.–7:30 P.M. the rest of the year. The south visitor center is interesting for its model of a baptismal font, the north visitor center features artistic depictions of the life of Jesus Christ. The Tabernacle houses the famed Temple Square pipe organ and is where the Sunday Mormon Tabernacle Choir broadcasts its Sunday concerts. The Assembly Hall is significant for having been the gathering place for worship before other church buildings were constructed in the Jordan Valley and on Temple Square. No admission charge to Temple Square or any buildings open to the public. For information call 531–2534.

Washington Square, at State and Fifth S. streets, on which now sits the sandstone City Hall, a replica of London's Victoria station, is where early pioneer arrivals camped.

ZCMI Center, a leading downtown shopping mall at 15 S. Main St., encloses what was once the initial ZCMI, said to be the first department store in the United States, and certainly the first west of the Mississippi.

Churches. The ward houses and stake centers, in which Mormons gather for worship and other church-related work, are found throughout Salt Lake City neighborhoods. Architecture varies, depending on period influences at the time they were constructed. The first Catholic church building, the Cathedral of the Madeleine, is at 331 E. South Temple, an impressive edifice. Another interesting church is the Holy Trinity Greek Orthodox Church, at 279 S. 300 West.

MUSEUMS AND GALLERIES. Chase Home, in Liberty Park (533–5757). Run by the Utah Arts Council, this gallery concentrates on work by Utah artists in painting, drawing, photography, prints, sculpture, fiber, and crafts. Open Tues.–Fri., 10 A.M.–7 P.M., weekends noon–5 P.M.

Fort Douglas Military Museum, at Fort Douglas, directly east of the University of Utah, main gate on Wasatch Dr. (524–4154). Features displays on founding of Fort Douglas, history of the U.S. Army in Utah, and military exploration of the Utah Territory. Open 10 A.M.–noon, and 1–4 P.M. Tues.–Sat. Closed Sun., Mon., and holidays. Free.

Hansen Planetarium, 15 South State St. (538–2098). Everything a planetarium should be, with star shows, exhibits, an "astroshop" and educational services. Star shows Mon.–Sat. 11 A.M., 2 P.M., 4:30 P.M. and 7 P.M.; Sun., 2 P.M. and 4:30 P.M. Admission: $4 adults, $3 senior citizens and children under 12.

The Museum of Church History and Art, 45 N. West Temple (531–3310) is the newest Salt Lake City museum, devoted to Mormon history. It contains 60,000 items related to the church's origins and background. Some of the exhibits were displayed in the former visitors center on Temple Square. Others have been organized since the move to new galleries in 1984. The museum is open from April through Dec. from 9 A.M.–9 P.M., Mon.–Fri.; 10 A.M.–7 P.M. weekends and holidays; Jan.–March, 10 A.M.–7 P.M. Mon. and Thurs. Closed Thanksgiving, Christmas, New Year's Day and Easter. Free.

Pioneer Museum, 300 N. Main (533–5759), established and maintained by the Daughters of the Utah Pioneers, loaded with collections from the earliest settlement days of Utah. Open 9 A.M.–5 P.M. Mon.–Sat. In summer months, also open Sun. from 1 P.M.–5 P.M. No admission charge, ample parking at State Capitol grounds to the east.

Salt Lake Art Center, Salt Palace complex, 20 S. West Temple (328–4201). A showcase for regional artists, but also features guest and traveling exhibits. Open 10 A.M.–5 P.M. Tues.–Thurs.; 10 A.M.–9 P.M. Fri.; 1–5 P.M. weekends.

Utah Museum of Fine Arts, also located on the University of Utah campus (581–7332), features French, Dutch, Flemish, Chinese, Italian, Egyptian, British, and pre-Columbian artwork as well as collections from India and Southeast Asia, eighteenth- and nineteenth-century American artists, and Utah and American West painters. Open Mon.–Fri., 10 A.M.–5 P.M.; Sat. and Sun., 2 P.M.–5 P.M. Admission free; parking off South Campus Drive.

Utah Museum of Natural History, at the University of Utah campus, five minutes from downtown, features the state's varied geology, biology, and human habitation for the past 10,000 years. One feature is a simulated underground mine. Listening stations with recorded commentary are provided. Open 9:30 A.M.–5:30 P.M. Mon.–Sat. and noon–5 P.M. Sun. Closed New Year's Day, Thanksgiving and Christmas. Adults, $1; children, 50 cents. Gift shop.

The Utah State History Museum is located in the former Denver and Rio Grande Depot, 400 West and 300 South, the main gallery occupying the lobby. Exhibiting collections related to Utah history, the museum is the responsibility of the Utah State Historical Society. Open 8 A.M.–5 P.M. Mon.–Fri. Free. For information, 533–7037.

ARTS AND ENTERTAINMENT. Films. Standard contemporary is the usual fare in **film** in Salt Lake City. Downtown, the major theaters are the *Utah,* 148 S. Main (328–2681); the *Centre,* Broadway and State (328–2691); *Crossroads Cinema,* 50 S. Main (355–3883); and the *Elks Cinema,* 139 E. South Temple (364–0199). Outside downtown, try the *Trolley Theaters,* at Trolley Square, 515 S. 700 East (521–8181). Except for the Crossroads and Elks Cinema, downtown theaters don't provide parking. Trolley theaters do.

Music. Everything from cowboy to opera is available in Salt Lake City. *The Utah Symphony* (533–6407) performs during fall, winter and early spring in the Bicentennial Symphony Hall on the Salt Palace Block. Opera is performed at the Capitol Theater, 50 W. 200 South (533–5555). *Snowbird Resort,* up Little Cottonwood Canyon, east of Salt Lake City, hosts musical events ranging from symphony to jazz on its outdoor plaza throughout the summer months. Some have an admission charge, some are free. The mountain setting is magnificent.

Dance. The Capitol Theater is home for *Ballet West.* It also features programs by visiting and local dance groups. The University of Utah, known for its dance instruction, produces programs fall, winter and spring months. The Nutcracker, staged by Ballet West at Christmastime, is an annual event.

Stage. Most live theater is presented at the University of Utah's *Pioneer Memorial Theater* (581-6961), on the campus. Musical comedies and operettas are frequently performed at *Promised Valley Playhouse,* a renovated and restored theater, 132 S. State St., 364-5677.

SHOPPING. Salt Lake City is not a manufacturing center, nor is it close to shipping points. Consequently, it is not a bargain-hunter's dream. The cost of living in the area, however, is considerably below that found in the nation's larger metropolitan centers, so prices tend to be lower. Two large malls dominate downtown Salt Lake City on upper Main Street, the Crossroads Plaza and ZCMI Center. Department stores and speciality stores can be found in both. A cluster of antique shops are gathered at 251 South State Street, where objects peculiar to early Rocky Mountain living are available to the discriminating buyer. *Otanez Imports,* 780 W. North Temple, specializes in Mexican, Philippine and Guatemalan products at reasonable prices. The *Cosmic Airplane,* 258 E. 100 South, is a good source of used books and magazines. It also stocks a full variety of the latest paperbacks. Comfortable place to browse, providing a small coffee shop, too. Open Mon.–Sat., 10 A.M.–9 P.M.; Sun., 1–7 P.M. *Trolley Square* is the city's leading boutique center. Worth a visit for the occasional sale items and a look at the surroundings: converted from a trolley barn and bus garages. Located at 7th East and 5th South. Sales tax is 5.25 percent.

DINING OUT. There's really no such thing as "Mormon cooking." So, in Salt Lake City, the normal bill of fare is about what would be found in most cities. It ranges from American meat and potatoes to ethnic foods. Restaurant categories, based on the price of a meal for one, without beverage, 5¼ percent tax, or tip, are: *Reasonable,* $10 to $20; *Very Economical,* $5 to $10; and *Low Budget,* under $5. Unless otherwise stated, the restaurants listed below take some, if not all, major credit cards. Every effort has been made to ensure that the list is up-to-date, but restaurants come and go so quickly that it is always advisable to call ahead.

Reasonable

Cedars of Lebanon. 154 E. 200 South (364–4096). A small downtown eatery specializing in authentic Armenian, Lebanese and Moroccan dishes. From falafel with sesame seed sauce to stuffed grape leaves. Reservations advisable.

King Joy Cafe. 264 S. Main (355–5243). A downtown mainstay, featuring traditional Chinese selections. No reservations necessary.

Lambs Restaurant. 169 S. Main (364–7166). One of the city's most enduring downtown restaurants. Standard fare, carefully prepared. During breakfast and lunch hours, customers normally include some of the town's more prominent professionals and business people. No reservations necessary.

The Panda. 1701 South State St. (485–3226). Billed as Salt Lake City's "only Mongolian barbecue restaurant," this effort at uniqueness features tasty stir-fry and a selection of other good entrees. Senior citizen discounts are offered.

Spaghetti Factory. 189 Trolley Square. Great family dining in antique surroundings. No reservations necessary.

Very Economical

Bill and Nada's Cafe. 479 S. 600 South. Every inch the cafe, just north of Trolley Square. American menu, choice of some University of Utah students. Open 24 hours, no reservations necessary.

Crossroads Plaza. Upper Main St. A downtown shopping mall chock full of fast-food outlets on the first floor, especially convenient at lunch time.

Howard Johnson's Coffee Shop. 102 W. South Temple (322–3327). Standard hotel coffee shop, open 24 hours. No reservations necessary.

Plaza Restaurant. At the Utah State Capitol. American cafeteria selections. Convenient at lunch time while visiting the capitol. No reservations necessary, but busy with state government workers between noon and 1 P.M.

Low Budget

Assembly Line. 142 South Main St. Typical hot dog, coke, and coffee drop-in place, in the heart of downtown. Convenient for lunch or early evening quick bite.

Chuck A-Rama. 744 E. 400 South (531–1123). Cafeteria-style with all you can eat specials. Daily, lunch, 11 A.M.–3:30 P.M.; dinner, 4–9 P.M. No reservations necessary.

Recommended Splurge. Max Mercier's La Parisien. 417 S. 300 East (364–5223). French named, owned, and operated, featuring elegant French and Italian food, carefully prepared. When summer weather permits, outdoor service is an attraction of this popular midtown dining place. Reservations recommended.

NIGHTLIFE AND BARS. Because of Utah's restrictive liquor laws, Salt Lake City is not much of a nightclub city. All liquor sales are through state-licensed outlets, either package stores or restaurants authorized to offer mini-bottles or splits of wine. The legal drinking age is 21. All package agencies are closed on Sundays and holidays. Liquor bought at a restaurant must be consumed on the premises with a meal. Setups, the mix of your choice, served in the appropriately sized cocktail or highball glass, with or without ice (you provide the alcohol), are available at most public lounges and taverns. Alcohol is available, even on Sunday, in private clubs located throughout Salt Lake City. Many such clubs will sell a temporary membership (up to two weeks) for as little as $5. Beer, the 3.2 variety, is obtainable at most restaurants, grocery, and drug stores seven days a week. Drunken driving is considered a major offense in Utah. The Salt Lake County Visitors and Convention Bureau has a "Guide to Alcoholic Beverages" which lists addresses and phone numbers of local state liquor stores, restaurants with liquor outlets, private clubs, lounges and taverns. We recommend:

Bongo Lounge, 2965 Highland Drive (466–0057). About five miles from downtown. Beer and setups, mostly younger crowd, recorded pop music.

Brownstone Ltd., 22 East 1st South (322–1031). A walk up lounge-and-lunch only restaurant located in an historic downtown office building. Features live jazz Wednesday through Sunday, from 7 P.M. to 1 A.M. Beer only, but setups for cocktails and highballs are available.

Dead Goat, 90 Arrow Press Square. Downstairs saloon across West Temple Street from the Salt Palace. Live music, everything from jazz to new wave. Beer and setups, $3 cover charge on weekends. Open until 1 A.M., 2 A.M. daylight saving time. Favorite for some Golden Eagle hockey players during winter.

The Foundation, 401 E. 200 South (328–8471). Located in the basement of an old church, now remodeled, with a savings bank upstairs. Features live music Tues.–Sat., rock, reggae, modern, and traditional jazz. $2–$3 cover charge, depending on performing group. Beer and setups. No cover and free beer for women on Ladies' Night, usually Thurs.

Peery Pub and Cafe, 110 W. 300 South (521–8919). A small, comfortable bar and dining room, located downtown in the restored Peery Hotel. Serves delicious sandwiches in a modern saloon atmosphere. Popular with college students and young professionals.

The Pub, Trolley Square, 7th East and 5th South (521–8917). In the midst of one of Salt Lake City's shopping malls, this is a beer and setup watering hole popular with University of Utah students and a generally younger crowd. 11:30 A.M. to 1 A.M. (kitchen closes at 11 P.M.). Closed Sun.

The Westerner, 3360 S. Redwood Rd. (972–9708). Five miles west of downtown, a country-western bar, complete with live music and sizable dance floor. Beer and setups. $2 cover charge Fri. and Sat., $1 Wed., when all drinks are 50 cents. Space to park 500 cars, open until 1 A.M. Occasionally, name country-western groups and performers appear.

SECURITY. Salt Lake City is a comparatively safe place, where people need not fear being on the streets any time of the day or night. There are no neighborhoods considered too dangerous to wander in alone. Take normal precaution with children—keep an eye on them—and try to explore unfamiliar surroundings in groups of twos or more. Don't leave valuables lying around in hotel and motel rooms and lock car, hotel and motel room doors as ordinary protection policies.

SAN ANTONIO

by
Nancy Haston Foster

Nancy Haston Foster writes on Texas topics for regional and national magazines. She is the author of The Alamo and Other Texas Missions to Remember *and coauthor of* San Antonio, *a* Texas Monthly *guidebook.*

Mosey into San Antonio, even if you have to ride a 737 airline jet to do so.

Why mosey? Well, because somehow it suits the city's parlance. If any city of plate glass, looped freeways, and 936,000 urbanites can ever be said to mosey, surely San Antonio qualifies. At least remnants and pockets of a laissez-faire life-style do still exist in San Antonio, where a smaller town atmosphere prevails in its gregarious mentality. The city has its share of rush hour traffic, but it's a lot less hectic than Houston's roller derby.

Somehow San Antonio grew up differently from other Texas municipalities. It was spawned as a Spanish mission outpost (the Alamo), grew progressively into a cattle town and military fort, and still has a bit of saloon-town ambience.

Mix that with the Mexican culture and you have a city that is fond of festivals, Mexican music, country and western dances, German oompah (German families surged on the Texas continent in a later wave of settlement), football, and even polo and the arts. In short, this is a place to have a sporting good time. Evidence of that can be seen in the teeming tourist trade. Out-of-towners come to San Antonio to party and for a change-of-pace, whether it's in convention herds or as independent stragglers. And with the giant Sea World of Texas recently opening in northwest San Antonio, tourism should burgeon.

It's also an economical spot, probably cheaper than other large Texas cities. Hotel room costs have skyrocketed as in other cities, but there are still a few older inns with lower overhead and rates, and many motel rooms can be rented for a moderate cost. But the best news is what you can get for your entertainment and restaurant dollar. Nonhotel meals are still fairly reasonable, and many entertainment and sight-seeing events are free or next to it if you know where to search.

In terms of climate, San Antonio is again a bargain, because you can visit out of peak season and still get mild and usually sunny weather. In fact, if you don't cotton to 90-degree heat, you might not want to visit in the summer anyway.

From the air, San Antonio is a typical sprawling metropolis ringed with freeways and with a downtown of tall structures. The land is generally flat with plenty of trees and low-slung hills. A tiny, scraggly river meanders through downtown. It's naturally called the San Antonio River and is the reason for San Antonio's existence, because the Spanish originally settled on it when exploring Texas. It may not look like much now, but it was much larger in 1718 when the Spaniards first used the site as a mission way station to earlier settlements in east Texas. San Antonio was established just a tad after New Orleans, so antiquity is another of its assets.

A whole chain of missions were built here in the early 1700s, five to be exact, with the Alamo being the first. San Antonio is the only city in the United States to claim that many of the weather-beaten Spanish churches still standing. It was the provincial capital for many years and later played a famous part in Texas history with the ill-fated stand at the Alamo mission turned fort in 1836. The John Wayne movie on the Alamo wasn't entirely accurate, but it gives one an idea how Texans feel about the Alamo.

In the twentieth century, San Antonio became the biggest city in Texas. But soon manufacturing complexes began converging on urban areas, and San Antonio snorted at this dirty industry and "progress" and so got left a little behind by Houston and Dallas. These two have never quite comprehended San Antonio's concern for historical preservation (the San Antonio Conservation Society is a leader in the field and an active, vocal force in the community) and quality of life. Many restored buildings and small shops dot downtown, giving it a human feel not found in its plastic counterparts.

Of course, the ninth largest city in the nation has not ignored progress. Not in the sun belt, and not with its highly visible mayor, Henry Cisneros, who presides over a city populated by a Mexican-American majority-minority. In the past, the military (five bases) and agribusiness, plus tourism, have been the dominant industries. But now there's a South Texas Medical Center complex and oil, computer, and insurance companies, with a growing bio-tech center, the Texas Research Park, in the building stage.

The people of San Antonio are a mixed bag, from the rising political star Cisneros and retired generals to weather-beaten ranchers, rednecks, and intellectuals. There is also a creative contingent of artists and writers attracted by the town's laid-back fiesta life-style. The city's largest festival celebration is appropriately tagged Fiesta. It's a 10-day bash of parades, balls, ethnic food and dance, and arts and sports events that falls around April 21 every year.

Exploring the City

You can practically do downtown on foot. The well-worn Alamo anchors down the central business district, and the popular River Walk meanders through. Unlike many urban areas, San Antonio's downtown is alive and well at night, particularly the River Walk with its shops, restaurants, and bars.

For day exploring, numerous historical sites and museums lie within a mile radius. Or take the VIA streetcar (only 10 cents), which stops at various sights. The rest of the city is easily accessible by bus or car (the older streets sometimes wind unpredictably, so it's wise to carry a map). If you don't want to use your own car, take one of the many city bus tours that leave from in front of the Alamo.

Downtown

Even without a car, you can imbibe most of San Antonio's attractions by confining yourself to the mile radius of the hotel where you're staying downtown.

First, concentrate on the River Walk. The Alamo simply doesn't offer the variety of things to do. You may want to use this River Walk and its sidewalk cafés, stores, and entertainment spots as a base to return to intermittently between other sight-seeing ventures.

It's the soul of the town, with an emphasis on the Mexican culture, such as enchilada fare and mariachi music, but with plenty other ethnic food and entertainment thrown in. It's good, cheap entertainment just to stroll up and down or order a cool one at a sidewalk table and people watch. There is often free entertainment at the open-air Arneson River Theater, or you can freeload by listening to music wafting out of various bistros.

The Alamo is only about two blocks east of the River Walk. It's on Alamo Plaza, and there's a helpful Visitor Information Center just across the street. The Alamo is hard to miss. It's that big rock structure shaped like an Alamo (surely everyone is familiar with the postcard curvilinear shape) with a Texas flag waving over it. There is no admission fee for the Alamo's exhibits or immaculately landscaped grounds.

Two other main attractions are HemisFair Plaza and Market Square. HemisFair Plaza, which contains museums (Institute of Texan Cultures), a few restaurants, melodrama theater, and high-rise tower, is just a couple of blocks south of the Alamo. You can't miss the revolving tower in the skyline, and it's a popular spot from which to view the city's panorama day or night (small fee).

Market Square anchors the western side of downtown and gives the tourist a chance to see a Mexican market. The market is a motley of shops hawking reasonably priced Mexican imports (dresses, men's shirts, toys, clay pots, etc.). Plan to have lunch or a taco break at one of the several restaurants and take in the frequent free entertainment in the promenade.

Between HemisFair Plaza and Market Square, history buffs can stop by to see La Villita, a historic village of shops and artisans, San Fernando Cathedral, the Spanish Governor's Palace, and the Navarro State Historic Site. The picturesque Old Ursuline Academy (Southwest Craft Center) is on the fringe of downtown, as is the San Antonio Museum of Art, though it's a little too far for walking.

Historic South San Antonio

To the south of downtown is older San Antonio. Immediately south is the restored King William District, full of the Victorian homes of the early German aristocracy. (See horse 'n' carriage ride tours, but they're not cheap.) The other four historic missions are sprinkled along the river among the predominantly working-class neighborhoods. See at least Mission San Jose, one of the largest and most charming in the United States, if you have limited time.

PRACTICAL INFORMATION

WHEN TO GO. Almost any time is fine. Even the winters are usually mild (40 to 50 degrees daytime), and rainfall is moderate. Summers are warm to hot (90 degrees). Peak tourist time is summer, but look for hotel packages then and in December. Dress casual and cool for the summertime.

HOW TO GET THERE. There are plenty of air and bus routes, but many Texans travel by car because of the fine freeway system and roadside parks.

By air. *American, American Eagle, Braniff, Continental, Delta, Eastern, Executive Express, Mexicana, Pan Am, Southwest, Texas National, TWA, USAir, and United* airlines fly to San Antonio. Regular limousine service to downtown. Check out *Southwest* for frequent bargain fares.

By bus. *Greyhound-Trailways* runs buses frequently into San Antonio. Check for current special discounts.

By train. Limited *Amtrak* service from Los Angeles, New Orleans, and Chicago (all three times weekly). Look for special discount travel plans.

By car. Driving times to San Antonio are: from Austin, 1½ hours; Corpus Christi, 3 hours; Dallas–Fort Worth, 5½ hours; El Paso, 12 hours; Houston, 4 hours; Laredo, 3 hours. Take I–10 from Houston, I–35 from Dallas and Austin.

TELEPHONES. The area code for San Antonio and surrounding counties is 512. If calling from outside San Antonio for directory assistance, dial 512–555–1212. If in San Antonio, call 1411. Pay phones cost 25 cents.

Emergency Telephone Numbers. Call 911 for fire, police, and ambulance emergencies. For the poison control center, dial 713–654–1701.

ACCOMMODATIONS. Tourists migrate here especially in the summer, but look for special family-plan hotel-motel packages at this time and also in December and January, when the convention trade is slow. Contact the Convention and Visitors Bureau for brochures on current special plans. Even some of the more expensive and deluxe hotels not mentioned here may occasionally offer weekend or holiday specials, but you have to ferret them out. Hotel and motel rates are based on double occupancy. Categories, determined by price, are as follows: *Reasonable,* $45 to $65; *Very Economical,* $35 to $45; *Budget Motels,* $35 and under.

Reasonable

Courtyard by Marriot. 8585 Marriott Dr. (512–696–7100, 800–321–2211). Located near Medical Center. Landscaped courtyard, pool, restaurant.

Drury Inn. 143 N.E. Loop 410, San Antonio, TX 78216 (512–366–4300, 800–325–8300). North. Children free, Continental breakfast.

Executive Guesthouse. 12828 Hwy. 281 North, San Antonio, TX 78216 (512–494–7600). Special weekend rates. Includes breakfast and cocktails.

Holiday Inn Market Square. 318 W. Durango, San Antonio, TX 78207, downtown (225–3211). Close to Mexican Market. Free parking.

La Quinta Motor Inns. *La Quinta Convention Center,* 1001 E. Commerce, San Antonio, TX 78205 (512–222–9181). Downtown. *La Quinta Market Square,* 900 Dolorosa, San Antonio, TX 78207 (512–271–0001). Downtown. *La Quinta Airport East,* 333 Northeast Loop 410, San Antonio, TX 78216 (512–828–0781, 800–531–5900).

Menger Hotel. 204 Alamo Plaza, San Antonio, TX 78205 (512–223–4361, 800–241–3848). Downtown. Probably your best bet for price and location. You can't get much closer to the Alamo than this historic old hotel, which has added on motel section and pool. Comfortable, with restaurant-bar.

Ramada Inn Airport. 1111 Northeast Loop 410, San Antonio, TX 78209 (512–828–9031). Modern high-rise motor hotel near airport.

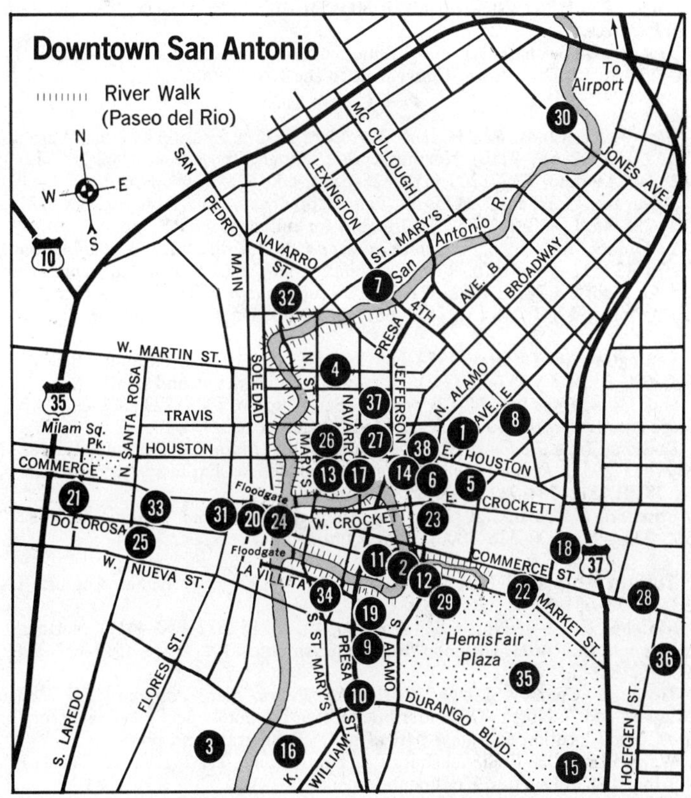

Points of Interest

1) Alamo
2) Arneson River Theater
3) Arsenal/H.E.B. Headquarters
4) Bus Station
5) Crockett Hotel
6) Dillard's (formerly Joske's)
7) El Tropicano Hotel
8) Emily Morgan Hotel
9) Fairmount Hotel
10) Four Seasons Hotel
11) Hertzberg Circus Collection
12) Hilton Palacio Hotel
13) Holiday Inn River Walk
14) Hyatt Regency Hotel
15) Institute of Texas Cultures
16) King William Historic Area
17) La Mansion del Rio Hotel
18) La Quinta Downtown
19) La Villita
20) Main Plaza
21) Market Square
22) Marriott Hotel
23) Menger Hotel
24) MBank-Alamo Building
25) Navarro State Historic Site
26) Radisson Gunter Hotel
27) St. Anthony Inter-Continental Hotel
28) St. Paul Square
29) San Antonio Convention Center and Visitors Bureau
30) San Antonio Museum of Art
31) San Fernando Cathedral
32) Southwest Craft Center
33) Spanish Governor's Palace
34) Tower Life Building
35) Tower of the Americas
36) Train Station
37) Travis Park
38) Visitor Information Center

Seven Oaks. 1400 Austin Hwy., San Antonio, TX 78209 (512–824–5371). Includes a 21-acre conference center with pools, tennis courts, and 9-hole golf course.

Texian Inns. *Texian Inn Market Square,* 211 North Pecos, San Antonio, TX 78207 (512–225–1111). Downtown. *Texian Inn Northwest,* 9400 Wurzbach, San Antonio, TX 78240 (512–690–8000, 800–531–1000). Northwest. New, modern. Children free.

TraveLodge on the River. 100 Villita, San Antonio, TX 78205 (512–226–2271, 800–255–3050). Downtown. Convenient to the River Walk.

Very Economical

Best Western Inns. *Best Western Northport,* 2635 N.E. Loop 410, San Antonio, TX 78217 (512–653–9110). Northeast. *Best Western Town House,* 942 N.E. Loop 410, San Antonio, TX 78209 (512–826–6311, 800–528–1234). North.

Days Inn Northeast. 3443 N. Pan Expressway, San Antonio, TX 78219 (512–225–4521, 800–325–2525). Discount for military, AARP, etc.

La Quinta Motor Inns. *La Quinta Lackland,* 6511 Military Dr. W., San Antonio, TX 78242 (512–674–3200). West. *La Quinta South,* 7202 S. Pan Am Expressway, San Antonio, TX 78231 (512–922–2111). *La Quinta Windsor Park,* 6410 I-35 N., San Antonio, TX 78218 (512–653–6619 or 800–531–5900). Chain's headquarters here.

Lexington Hotel Suites. 4934 Northwest Loop 410, San Antonio, TX 78229 (512–680–3351, 800–53–SUITE). Northwest. Kitchenettes and pool.

Oak Hills Motor Inn. 7401 Wurzbach, San Antonio, TX 78229 (512–696–9900). Large complex in the South Texas Medical Center area.

Rodeway Inns. *Rodeway Inn Downtown,* 900 N. Main, San Antonio, TX 78212 (512–223–2951). *Rodeway Inn Wonderland,* 6804 N.W. Expressway, San Antonio, TX 78201 (512–734–7111, 800–228–2000).

Stratford House Inn. 3911 N. Pan Am Expressway, San Antonio, TX 78219 (512–224–4944, 800–336–8000). Pool, Continental breakfast.

Budget Motels. All Star Inn. 5522 N. Pan Am Expressway, San Antonio, TX 78221 (512–661–8791). Northeast.

Motel 6. 9503 I–35 North, San Antonio, TX 78218 (512–650–4419). Northeast.

Regal 8 Inn. 4621 Rittiman Rd., San Antonio, TX 78218 (512–653–8088, 800–851–8888).

Town & Country Lodge. 6901 San Pedro, San Antonio, TX 78216 (512–344–4511). North. This older but substantial motel offers good value for the price. Good location and good part of town. Restaurant and pools.

Warren Inn. 5050 Fredericksburg Rd., San Antonio, TX 78229 (512–342–1179). Northwest. Kitchenettes. Continental breakfast.

Bed-and-Breakfast. Bed and Breakfast Hosts of San Antonio. 166 Rockhill, San Antonio, TX 78209 (512–824–8036). Contact this service for list of homes available. Double occupancy rates in the $40–$80 range.

Rische House House Bed & Breakfast. 210 E. Rische, San Antonio, TX 78204 (512–227–1190). Victorian homes in King William historic district, range $40–$100.

Ys and Hostels. No lodging accommodations at local Ys, but there is the **San Antonio International Hostel,** 621 Pierce, San Antonio, TX 78208 (512–223–9426).

HOW TO GET AROUND. Most people opt to drive a car if they want to see more of the city than downtown. But downtown has many sites and diversions within walking distance, or take the cheap (10 cents) VIA motorized streetcar. To get to your downtown hotel or motel from the airport (about a 15-minute ride), there are several choices. VIA limousine service costs $6; a taxi, about $12. A VIA express bus runs in the peak mornings and evenings for 75 cents. For visiting the rest of the city, regular public bus (VIA) fares are 40 cents within Loop 410 and 75 cents for express service. Taxi fares are $2.45 for the first mile, $1 for each additional mile. Rental car agencies have offices at the airport.

HINTS TO THE MOTORIST. Traffic is a shade less hectic than in most metropolises, with free parking available except downtown (from $1.50 to $4 per day). But take a street map along, since some of the streets still amble aimlessly or change names abruptly.

TOURIST INFORMATION. Write *San Antonio Convention & Visitors Bureau,* Box 2277, San Antonio, TX 78298 (512–270–8700; 800–531–5700; in Texas, 800–292–1010), for free brochures and information on sites and accommodations. When visiting the city, stop at the *Visitor Information Center,* 317 Alamo Plaza, just across from the Alamo (299–8155). Open daily.

HINTS TO DISABLED TRAVELERS. Write the *San Antonio Handicapped Access Office,* Box 9066, San Antonio, TX 78285, for downtown ramp map and information. Or refer to San Antonio *Express-News* Weekender supplement on Fridays for access symbols.

FREE EVENTS. San Antonio has many freebie entertainment events and low-cost festivals. Check the Friday special supplements of the local newspapers for a calendar of events. There's usually something free going on, particularly downtown on the River Walk or at Market Square. Also free entertainment at noon in the parks weekly during the spring and summer called **Brown Bag Days.** In February, catch the outdoor **Great Country River Festival** on the River Walk for three days of continual free live country and western music. Also in February, visit the **Stock Show and Rodeo** (admission) and see the real thing. Then look for the 10-day festival **Fiesta** in April. One of the largest such city events in the nation, Fiesta has something for everybody, including free parades, music, and Mexican rodeos. More Mexican events can be experienced at two ethnic holidays, **Cinco de Mayo** in May and **Diez y Seis** in September. And two festivals, the **San Antonio Festival** (arts) in June and **Texas Folklife Festival** (admission) in August, provide some freebie entertainment. But perhaps the best bet is at **Christmastime** when the River Walk is lit up with lights and caroling and Market Square comes alive with **Fiesta Navidena,** all free. During the summertime, there is weekly low-cost Mexican entertainment at the outdoor **Arneson River Theater.**

TOURS AND SPECIAL-INTEREST SIGHTSEEING. The tour choice is either bus, streetcar, horse 'n' carriage, or river barge. City tours: *VIA Gray Line* (227–5251) offers several bus tours of the city, ranging from 2¼ to 7¼ hours long, costing around $9 to $24. Like most of the other tours listed below, these leave daily from in front of the Alamo. Other city tours offered by *San Antonio Trolley* (533–3992) and various horse 'n' carriage services (fairly expensive at $10 per person per half hour). The *river tours* leave daily every 15 minutes at the Paseo del Rio Boat dock (222–1701) across from the Hilton Hotel at Market Street; $1.50.

Special Sightseeing. Downtown there are three areas not to miss. First, the **River Walk** (Paseo del Rio). This is the heart of downtown, where 2 miles of landscaped parkland lines the San Antonio River with sidewalk restaurants, shops, bars, and hotels. Alive 24 hours for sauntering, people watching, and nightlife. Many step-down entrances downtown, one at Commerce and Losoya. Nearby at 200 South Alamo is **HemisFair Plaza,** a 92-acre complex of museums, restaurants, and convention center. The 750-foot Tower of the Americas is a popular high place to view the city; open daily, $1.50. On the west side of downtown at 514 W. Commerce is **Market Square,** a colorful mishmash of restaurants, shops, and a north-of-the-border Mexican market selling imports. You might check out the five military bases (Fort Sam Houston, Lackland, Randolph, Brooks, and Kelly) to see military installations and museums.

Sea World of Texas. Elsewhere in northwest San Antonio is the city's newest attraction, the huge 250-acre Sea World complex. Spend the day seeing shows of killer whales, dolphins, and sea lions, plus marine-life exhibits and gardens. 10500 Sea World Dr. (call 225–4903 or 800–422–7989). Open daily 9 A.M.–7 P.M., later in summer. Adults, $19; children, $16.

PARKS AND GARDENS. The largest of the parks with the most diversified recreational facilities is **Brackenridge,** 3800 Broadway (821–3000), with 343 acres that are open all the time. Located not very far north of downtown, it has picnic tables, bridle and hiking paths, a golf course, miniature train ride, stables, and an aerial sky ride. The zoo and Witte Museum are there too. There are many other city parks to choose from, but for unspoiled wilderness try the 230-acre **Friedrich Park,** a few miles north of town off I–10 on Milsa Road (821–3000). Open during the day Wed.–Sun. The rustic 33-acre **San Antonio Botanical Center** (admission fee) is located at 555 Funston Place (821–5115). Or visit the lush **Japanese Tea Gardens** in Brackenridge Park at 3800 N. St. Mary's. Open daily; free.

ZOO. The **San Antonio Zoo** is a cozy, nationally renowned zoo with natural terrain and streams. Located in Brackenridge Park at 3903 N. Saint Mary's (734–7183), it is open daily from 9:30 A.M.–5 P.M. (till 6:30 P.M. in summer). Adults, $4; children, $2.

PARTICIPANT SPORTS. With plenty of sun and an abundance of land, Texans can afford to indulge in a variety of outdoor sports. There are numerous city parks with golf courses, jogging trails, swimming pools, and tennis courts. *Brackenridge Park* offers a municipal golf course (226–5612), as does *Riverside Park* (533–8371). Look in the Yellow Pages under "Golf Courses–Public" for additional locations. Most tennis courts are free, but the largest, *McFarlin,* at 1503 San Pedro (732–1223), has a fee. Swimming pools are available in various city parks, with the indoor *San Antonio Natatorium* being a fine facility at 1430 W. Durango (226–8541). For jogging try Brackenridge and McAllister Parks, and the stables at Brackenridge for horseback riding (732–8881).

SPECTATOR SPORTS. Basketball is the main pro sport here, with the San Antonio Spurs (NBA) playing October through April in the Convention Center Arena. There is a minor league baseball team, the San Antonio Dodgers. The PGA Texas Open golf tournament is in October.

CHILDREN'S ACTIVITIES. Best bet is **Brackenridge Park** with its varied activities: zoo, miniature train ride, aerial skyride, horseback riding stables, and natural history museum. Other possibilities include the **Buckhorn Hall of Horns** at Lone Star Brewery (226–8301) and two caves about 15 miles north: **Natural Bridge Caverns** (651–6101) near I–35 and **Cascade Caverns** (512–755–9285) near I–10. And, of course, **Sea World of Texas** (see Tours) has enough activities to occupy the kiddies all day.

HISTORIC SITES. Alamo. Alamo Plaza and Houston St., downtown. This is where the city began as Mission San Antonio de Valero in 1718 when the Spanish settled Texas. Famous site of Texas's battle for independence in 1836. Landscaped grounds and museum. Mon.–Sat., 9 A.M.–5:30 P.M.; Sun., 10 A.M.–5:30 P.M. Free. Call 225–1391.

Fort Sam Houston and Quadrangle. Main gate at New Braunfels and Grayson (221–1211). This historic old fort makes an interesting drive-through. Several military museums. Fort area open daily.

King William Historic Area. South of downtown, this elegant Victorian neighborhood has been restored. One house, the Steves Homestead at 509 King William, is open to the public for a fee. Call 225–5924.

La Villita. At Alamo and Nueva streets, downtown. This restored "little village" dates back to the mid-1700s. Old houses and buildings now harbor shops, artisans, and restaurants. No admission. Open daily. Call 299–8614.

Old Ursuline Academy (now Southwest Craft Center). 300 Augusta, downtown. These picturesque French buildings, built in 1851, now house artisans. Good informal lunchroom open weekdays. Whole complex open also on Saturday. No admission. Call 224–1848.

San Antonio Missions National Historical Park. Includes four different mission sites scattered on the San Antonio River in the southern part of town. To tour these unusual Spanish churches (built from 1720 to 1731), follow the *Mission Trail* signs by going south on S. Alamo at Market St. All open daily 8 A.M.–5 P.M. in winter and 9 A.M.–6 P.M. in summer. Free. Call 229–6000. **Mission Concepción.** First on the Trail at 807 Mission Rd. **Mission San José.** At 3200 block of Roosevelt Ave. and Mission Rd. (229–4770). If your time is limited, see this one; it's the largest and most beautiful of the restored Texas missions. Whole walled-in compound is intact. **Mission San Juan Capistrano.** 9101 Graf. Quaint, rustic square remains. **Mission Espada.** 10040 Espada. Last of the missions on the Trail at the edge of the city limits.

San Fernando Cathedral. 114 Military Plaza, downtown. Centuries-old church founded by original colonists. Still in use. Open daily.

Spanish Governor's Palace. 105 Plaza de Armas, downtown. Restored with period furnishings. Open daily. Small fee.

MUSEUMS AND GALLERIES. The city museum association runs two museums. Buy a ticket to one and you're entitled to get into the other half-price over a 3-day period. Adults, $3; children, $1. Hours are same for both museums listed below: Mon.–Sat., 10 A.M.–5 P.M. (6 P.M. in summer); Tues., till 9 P.M.; Sunday, noon–5 P.M. Same phone: 226–5544.

San Antonio Museum of Art. 200 W. Jones Ave. Renovated old Lone Star Brewery building (with its award-winning architecture) houses big traveling exhibits, plus Mexican folk art, eighteenth- and nineteenth-century paintings, and pre-Columbian, Texan, and Spanish colonial art. Gift shop.

Witte Museum. In Brackenridge Park at 3801 Broadway. Natural science and history exhibits, dinosaurs to Indian art. Take the kids.

Other Museums

Hertzberg Circus Collection. At S. Presa and Market streets. Mon.–Sat., 9 A.M.–5:30 P.M. (Sunday, 1 P.M.–5 P.M. during summer). Free. Call 299–7810.

Institute of Texan Cultures. In HemisFair Plaza at Bowie and Durango streets. Colorful exhibits of ethnic groups that settled Texas. Open 9 A.M.–5 P.M. Tues.–Sun. Free. Call 226–7651.

McNay Art Museum. 6000 N. New Braunfels (824–5368). Spacious old estate and grounds. An excellent postimpressionist collection plus others. Open 9 A.M.–5 P.M. Tues.–Sat.; 2–5 P.M. Sun. Free.

ARTS AND ENTERTAINMENT. The Alamo city is full of freebie or low-cost entertainment. Refer to "FREE EVENTS" and pay special attention to holidays when the River Walk and Market Square feature ongoing free entertainment. During the summer there are low-cost Mexican shows at the outdoor **Arneson River Theater** and free concerts in the parks. Look for the **San Antonio Festival** in June with many art events, some free, or the **Carver Jazz Festival** in August. The **San Antonio Symphony** (223–5591) has a September-May season, and the **San Antonio Little Theatre** (735–6922) performs year-round. If you prefer corn, try the **Melodrama Playhouse and Saloon** (271–0300) at HemisFair Plaza. The **San Antonio Performing Arts Association** (224–8187) brings in top-name musicians, while the **Majestic Performing Arts Center** (226–2626) has traveling Broadway shows.

SHOPPING. Your best bargain for shopping is Mexican imports at *El Mercado* in the downtown Market Square at 514 W. Commerce. But check out competing prices before buying. This pot-luck Mexican market has everything from clay pots and clothing to handmade toys and fine jewelry. *Los Patios,* 2015 NE Loop 410, is more upscale but worth the trip to enjoy the rustic setting of 32 acres with shops and restaurants. For a classy shopping mall downtown, buzz into the new *Rivercenter* at Commerce and Bowie streets.

DINING OUT. Compared with other places, food in San Antonio is reasonably priced. Look for some of the best in the unlikeliest places, the converted Dairy Queens and storefronts, particularly in the cultural staple here, Mexican cuisine. But always sample the hot sauce warily at first to determine its alarm equivalent! Categories, based on the price of a dinner for one, without beverage, tip, or tax, are as follows: *Reasonable,* $7 to $15; *Very Economical,* $3 to $7; *Low Budget,* $3 and under. Some credit cards are accepted, if not stated otherwise.

Reasonable

Cadillac Bar. 212 South Flores, downtown (223–5533). Classy, restored old 1870's building, with outside patio tables. Steaks, Mexican food. Informal.

Cappy's. 5011 Broadway, northeast (828–9669). A pleasant wood and greenery restaurant in uptown Alamo Heights. Casually formal, with southwestern and fish dishes.

Crumpets. 5800 Broadway, northeast (821–5454). European cuisine in a chic atmosphere. Also sidewalk tables and bakery. Try the croissants.

L'Etoile. 6106 Broadway, northeast (826–4551). Traditional French food in an informal but uptown suburban setting.

Niki's Tokyo Inn. 819 W. Hildebrand, north (736–5471). Japanese dishes such as shrimp tempura.

Paesano's. 1715 McCullough, north (226–9541). Routine decor, but a lot of high rollers frequent this Italian restaurant.

Los Patios. 2015 N.E. Loop 410, northeast (655–6190). Shop at this specialty shop center on rustic acreage with three restaurants (crêpes, Mexican, steaks). Lunch only.

Pearl's Oyster Company. 3011 N. St. Mary's, north (734–0058). Seafood in a cozy renovated gas station. Happy Hour: 25 cents for oysters and shrimp.

Settlement Inn. On I–10 about 12 miles north of Loop 410 (698–2580). All-you-can-eat barbecue platters in a restored country building setting.

Sze-Chuen. 5443 Walzem, northeast (653–4142); 8637 Fredericksburg Rd., Northwest (641–6408). Chinese restaurants featuring Mandarin food.

Very Economical

Big Bend. 511 River Walk, downtown (225–4098). Sidewalk café ideal for people watching on the River Walk. Sandwiches, etc.

Calico Cat Tea Room. 304 N. Presa, downtown near River Walk (226–4925). Casual with homemade soups, quiches, and sandwiches. Lunch only. No credit cards.

Copper Kitchen. 300 Augusta, downtown in the Southwest Craft Center (224–0123). Soups and sandwiches in this delightful renovated Catholic school. No credit cards. Open only on weekdays for lunch.

La Fogata. 2427 Vance Jackson, northwest (341–9930). Expect crowds. This no-frills spot with some outdoor seating is a favorite for Mexican food.

Four Ten Diner. 8315 Broadway, northeast (822–6246). Vegetable plates and chicken fried steak.

Hickory Hut Bar-B-Q. 3731 Colony Dr., northwest (696–9134). Tasty barbecue in a self-serve setup. No credit cards.

Jim's Coffee Shops. Numerous locations in town; see the telephone directory.

Liberty Bar. 328 E. Josephine, near downtown (227–1187). Homey in old wooden structure. Sandwiches, entrees, homemade bread.

Little Red Barn. 1836 S. Hackberry, south (532–4235). They literally sell hundreds of steaks a day in this down-home setting.

Luby's Cafeterias. See the telephone directory for many locations of this excellent cafeteria chain. Best value for quality food. There is a special of entree and vegetables, around $3. No credit cards.

Mi Tierra Cafe and Bakery. 218 Produce Row, downtown at Market Square (225–1262). Mexican, not fancy, but open 24 hours. Tourist crowds and mariachi music.

Twin Sisters Bakery & Cafe. 6322 N. New Braunfels, northeast (822–2265). Quiche, soup, and sandwiches in this comfy uptown café frequented by Junior Leaguers and clerks alike. Breakfast and lunch.

Schilo's Delicatessen. 424 E. Commerce, downtown near River Walk (223–6692). Genuine old-time deli. No credit cards. Lunch only.

Viet Nam. 3244 Broadway, northeast (822–7461). Plain decor hides good Vietnamese food.

Low Budget

Adelante. 21 Brees, northeast (822–7681). Mexican food to take out or eat in this, suburban, self-serve eatery. No credit cards.

Picnic Court at North Star Mall. At San Pedro and Loop 410. Group of assorted ethnic fast-food shops with tables in the middle. No credit.

Taco Cabana. 3310 San Pedro, north (733–9332); 5630 Wurzbach, northwest (681–8242). Fast food Mexican-style. Numerous other locations.

Whataburgers. See the telephone directory for many locations of this burger chain.

Recommended Splurge. Las Canarias. At La Mansion del Rio Hotel, 112 College, downtown on the River Walk (225–2581). Dine in a Spanish formal setting on southwestern cuisine. Live Spanish entertainment, usually on weekends only. Reservations.

Brunches. There are many Sunday brunches in town, but probably the best deal is an all-you-can-eat breakfast buffet that is offered every day at **Aunt Julie's Kitchen,** 11827 San Pedro, north (496–5223). Lasts till 11 A.M. Adults, around $4; kids, about $2.

Cafes. Sidewalk cafés abound on the River Walk for people watching, and one of the more amenable is **Kangaroo Court,** 512 River Walk (224–6821), an informal English pub. Serves sandwiches and seafood. Another place to see a cross section of locals is the **Beauregard Cafe & Bar,** 320 Beauregard (223–1388), a casual place with burgers and occasional live rock music.

NIGHTLIFE AND BARS. No need to go to sleep early in San Antonio, as there is plenty of low-cover entertainment and Happy Hour buffets, but limited space permits us to list only a few representative night spots. Call ahead about live music times.

Bayous Oyster Bar Cabaret. 517 N. Presa, downtown on the River Walk (223–6403). A quiet touch of Casablanca with piano music on weekends.

Bluebonnet Palace. 16842 IH 35N. a few miles northeast of San Antonio in Selma (651–6702). Country-western dancing in warehouse setting. Live bull-riding events on weekends.

Cold River Cattle Co. 5500 Babcock, northwest (699–0908). Country-western night spot with nightly Happy Hour buffet, theme nights, and lots of special events.

Durty Nellie's Pub. Hilton Palacio del Rio, 200 S. Alamo, downtown (222–2481). Informal Irish pub on the River Walk. Piano player and sing-along.

Esquire Bar. 155 E. Commerce, downtown (222–2521). An old shoe neighborhood bar downtown, where blue-collar and exec meet to drink. Mariachi music.

Floore Country Store. About 12 miles northwest in Helotes, just off Hwy. 16 (695–8827). Old country-western dance hall. Also outdoor area.

Joe's Kantina. 102 Produce Row, downtown (225–0445). Uptown watering hole at Market Square.

Landing. Hyatt Regency Hotel, 123 Losoya, downtown (222–1234). Looking for classic jazz? Follow the music in from the River Walk.

TGI Friday. I-10 at Callaghan, northwest (340–8401). Bar and restaurant catering to the young working set.

SECURITY. The crime rate is probably average here, but parts of downtown are safer than most other cities at night. The River Walk, Market Square, and convention center areas are well patrolled. However, it is still wise to exercise caution when exploring at night. Try to travel on well lit streets. Women should not walk alone at night except along the busiest streets. At night it is best to always use the deadbolt and chain on your hotel room door.

SAN DIEGO

by
Maribeth Mellin

Maribeth Mellin is a contributor to San Diego *magazine, the Los Angeles* Times, *and other publications.*

The temperature averages 70 degrees; the annual rainfall, less than ten inches. Meteorologists call it the only area in the United States with perfect weather. Its western border contains 70 miles of Pacific Ocean beaches; its southern border is the busiest international crossing in the world. Just north lie Disneyland and Los Angeles; to the east, the Cuyumaca Mountains and Cleveland National Forest provide vistas from desert to sea.

No wonder San Diego claims the title America's Finest City.

For the budget traveler, San Diego provides unlimited free pleasures. There's no charge to swim, sun, and surf at the miles of sandy beaches or walk, bike, or roller skate through Mission Bay. The climate and terrain are conducive to leisurely sight-seeing on foot or in a car—in fact, the only unavoidable expense is transportation. San Diego is far from compact, and public transportation is expensive and time-consuming; it is better to splurge on car rental and drive the designated 52-mile scenic drive from the tip of Point Loma to La Jolla. Along the way you'll pass miles of ocean where giant gray whales spout offshore on their way to southern spawning grounds in the winter and dolphins and sea lions mingle with brazen bathers in the summer months. Even the highways look like botanical gardens, with median strips and hillsides filled with fields of blooming yellow, pink, and blue ice plant edging towering palms. It would take weeks to see all the city has to offer, but by plotting your sight-seeing to include nearby attractions, you can cover a lot of territory in just a few days.

At the southern point of central San Diego sits Coronado, one of the city's oldest and most charming communities. Coronado is an island connected to the mainland by the blue 2.2-mile Coronado Bridge and a long narrow sandbar called the Silver Strand. The town's major landmark is the grand Hotel del Coronado, a massive gingerbread house facing the ocean. The rooms are far from inexpensive, but there is no charge to mingle with dignitaries in the magnificent red-carpeted lobby and wander the basement shops and hallways, past photographic exhibits of the hotel's history.

At the northeast end of the Coronado Bridge lies Seaport Village, a popular shopping and restaurant center with 14 acres of bayfront park, dozens of specialty shops, and an antique Broadway Flying Horses Carousel. The village has three major restaurants, but for bargain hunters the best meals are found in the cluster of ethnic take-out shops at the north end, with picnic tables overlooking the harbor. The towering mirrored San Diego Marriott borders the village at the south, near the historic San Diego Rowing Club, now a Chart House restaurant.

From Seaport Village to the southern end of downtown, San Diego Harbor is filled with navy ships, commercial freighters, tuna seiners, cruise ships, and thousands of pleasure craft. The Maritime Museum provides tours of three vintage ships, and harbor cruises leave every hour from the foot of Broadway Pier. This Embarcadero area contains some of downtown's premier hotels and restaurants, but for low-cost fresh seafood visit Anthony's Fish Grotto and outdoor café.

Downtown San Diego is an area in transition. Massive redevelopment has resulted in the renovation of the beautifully tiled Santa Fe Amtrak station, the construction of the bright red Tijuana Trolley, running through downtown to the Mexico border, and the reconstruction of the Gaslamp Quarter, a national historic district with ornate turn-of-the-century buildings housing restaurants, offices, and shops. The quarter bustles with office workers and tourists during the day; at night it tends to return to its former status as a hangout for street people and transients and is best avoided unless you are visiting a restaurant with valet parking, such as the historic Golden Lion Tavern. Walking tours of the district's brick-lined streets are available through the Gaslamp Quarter Association.

San Diego's major airport, Lindbergh Field, is just a few blocks north of downtown, near Harbor and Shelter islands. Major hotels line the waterfront on both islands, with private marinas and restaurants hosting prominent nightclub talent.

Looming over downtown is Balboa Park's 1,400 acres of lush landscaping and indigenous canyon terrain. The park, one of the most diverse in the country, includes the internationally acclaimed San Diego Zoo, with the world's largest collection of wild animals and landscaping that rivals any tropical paradise. The zoo also operates the spectacular Wild Animal Park east of the city in the rocky terrain of Escondido. Although the park is some 30 miles from downtown, it is well worth a day trip. Those wishing to spend the night can find lodging in Escondido, where the Lawrence Welk Village and Museum is a popular resort for golfers and those wishing to get closer to "Mr. Bubbles."

At the park, the zoo represents only the beginning of a major sightseeing expedition. The park's center is the Prado, constructed for the 1915 Panama-California Exposition. Intricately carved and domed Spanish-Moorish buildings house art, natural history, anthropology, and photographic museums (many of which are free on the first Tuesday of every month); near the main fountain, the Reuben H. Fleet Space Theater features a dome-screened planetarium and a science center with fascinating gadgets and gizmos. On a stroll from the fountain to the park's Laurel Street Bridge tourists pass by mimes, jugglers, and musicians performing before the lattice-work Botanical Building and lily pond and the Organ

Pavilion, where free concerts are given on the outdoor 5,000-pipe Spreckles organ.

Balboa Park could be called San Diego's cultural center. Besides the museums, it includes the nationally known professional repertory Old Globe Theater and Cassius Carter Stage and the outdoor Starlight Bowl.

Other performing arts centers are located downtown, at the Civic Center's Golden Hall, and the California, Fox, and Spreckle's Theaters. The San Diego Opera offers a winter season featuring well-known stars and a summer Verdi festival. Various ballet, jazz, and modern dance companies perform throughout the year and sponsor appearances by internationally recognized dance troupes.

Completing the downtown, Balboa Park triangle is Old Town, a state historic park highlighting San Diego's Mexican-American history with original adobe buildings housing museums and shops. The Bazaar del Mundo, a major shopping area in the park, has outdoor cafés serving gigantic margaritas and free chips and salsa; on weekends there are often free performances by flamenco dancers and musicians. Presidio Park, high above Old Town, offers a panoramic view of the city and mountains and houses the Junipero Serra Museum and San Diego Historical Society. On the other side of the hill lies Hotel Circle and Mission Valley, once San Diego's fertile riverbed farming district. Now the valley is filled with hotels, restaurants, and major shopping centers, providing a central headquarters easily accessible from all major freeways.

Looking northeast from Presidio you see Mission Bay, a 4,600-acre aquatic playground with 27 miles of bayfront beaches, a championship golf course, miniature golf, a campground, bicycle and roller skating trails, boat rentals, sport fishing and whale watching charters, and five major resort hotels. A central information center distributes maps and directories to the park's many services, but the best way to see it all is to rent a bike and tour the park slowly, watching out for picnickers, kite flyers, and amateur athletes. Mission Bay's top attraction is Sea World, the world's largest marine-life park. Shamu, the three-ton killer whale, is the park's mascot and leading star, but the new Penguin Encounter, exhibiting hundreds of penguins in their natural habitat, is stealing some of Shamu's glory. Cap'n' Kids World is a must-see for children, who delight in the nautical-theme play equipment; another must is the California tidepool exhibit, where visitors can examine starfish and sea urchins.

Although the bay is popular for land and water sports, the ocean is where the action really begins. Small beach communities line San Diego's coastline, starting with Ocean Beach, a popular spot for surfers and navy personnel and their families. Ocean Beach merges into Sunset Cliffs, where viewers line the edge on spectacular sunset evenings, and Point Loma, an old and affluent community with military bases lining its edges. Point Loma's waterfront is filled with private marinas and centers that offer exciting sport fishing excursions. At the tip of Point Loma, Cabrillo National Monument provides an unequaled view past downtown to Mexico. This is the most frequently visited national monument in the country and gets particularly crowded during the winter months, when the whales swim by below.

Traveling north up the coast from Ocean Beach, you pass Mission Bay's most popular picnic grounds and enter Mission Beach, a classic slice of southern California. The Mission Beach boardwalk runs from south Mission Beach through Pacific Beach, past the ruins of the old Belmont Park roller coaster. In the summer the boardwalk is filled with nearly nude nubile roller skaters with blaring tape decks, hulking volleyball players battling for daily scores, and surfers strutting their stuff across the waves. There's also an odd assortment of wanderers, watchers, and police officers who eye the activities from their beach bikes. The boardwalk undergoes major destruction during winter storms and major construction at the beginning of the summer, when ice cream stands, restaurants, and outdoor cafés pop up as if they'd been hibernating under the sand.

The boardwalk ends at the north end of Pacific Beach, where the sand and streets are less cluttered and serious body surfers and swimmers enjoy the long uninterrupted waves. Throughout Mission and Pacific beaches the cross streets and main boulevards boast a proliferation of hotels, motels, bars, restaurants, and shops, each with a distinct breed of clientele.

At the other end of the beach spectrum is La Jolla, "the Jewel." Easily the most scenic and elegant of San Diego's beach communities, La Jolla is often compared with Monte Carlo, where screen stars and international luminaries summer in luxurious oceanfront villas. The village's main promenade, Prospect Street, includes rows of high-caliber shops, gourmet restaurants, and hotels overlooking La Jolla Cove. The cove has an underwater marine park where bright orange garabaldi dodge enormous lobsters and crabs, putting on quite a show for snorkelers and divers. Scripps Park, above the beach, is lined for blocks with stately palms and wind-bowed Torrey pines, with grassy lawns where sunbathers lounge and locals celebrate special events with elaborate picnics and parties. At the park's south end, just under the glass walls of the La Jolla Museum of Contemporary Art, the Children's Pool natural cove forms a calm, safe pool for neophyte swimmers and snorkelers. Beaches both north and south of the cove, including Windansea and La Jolla Shores, have some of the best surfing waves in southern California as well as lots of rocky outcroppings and caves where sea creatures gather during low tide.

La Jolla is also the home of the Scripps Institute of Oceanography Aquarium, where those same creatures are on display in a man-made tidal pool. The world-famous Salk Institute and the Torrey Pines Gliderport overlook the northern end of La Jolla Shores; on windy days, colorful hang gliders soar overhead.

San Diego's North County cities have yet to garner their share of the tourist trade, but more hotels and resorts are being built there each year. Del Mar, first stop on the San Diego-Los Angeles Amtrak line, is a quaint little town whose main attraction is the Del Mar Racetrack, where "the surf meets the turf." Similar towns dot the coastline: Cardiff by the Sea, with its row of seaside restaurants, and Encinitas, Leucadia, and Carlsbad, all laid back yet exclusive, with miles of more private beaches backed by towering cliffs and magnificent oceanfront homes. At the farthest point north in the county, Oceanside borders the Marine Camp Pendleton, a natural green belt separating San Diego from the spreading megalopolis of Orange and Los Angeles counties.

No trip to San Diego is complete without a visit south of the border, to Tijuana, only a half-hour drive on Interstate 5 from downtown. If you drive to Tijuana, be sure to get Mexican car insurance (about $7) at one of the many stands in San Ysidro, the last stop before the border crossing. Driving in Mexico can be confusing, hazardous, and frustrating; if you're planning on just touring Tijuana, it's best to leave your car in one of the large lots on the U.S. side of the border and walk or take a cab into town. The Tijuana trolley has a stop and parking lot right by the downtown San Diego Amtrak station; for $1.50 each way you can relax and enjoy the sights on the way to the border.

Once in Mexico, the place to shop and dine is Avenida Revolución, the main tourist strip. The Mexican government has worked hard at improving this area in the past few years, and now it is relatively safe and enjoyable. Most shop proprietors speak some English, and bartering is definitely encouraged and expected. There is a wide array of Mexican crafts available at the shops, with good bargains on leather goods, silver jewelry, hand-embroidered clothing, and pottery. There are quite a few good restaurants along Revolución, particularly nearby the Jai Alai Palace at the intersection with Calle 4.

The new Tijuana Cultural Center, or Centro Cultural Fonapas, has a fine anthropological museum with exhibits of many of Mexico's indigenous cultures as well as an omnimax theater and concert hall. The museum is not within easy walking distance of downtown, but a cab ride shouldn't cost more than a couple of dollars. Whether you visit Tijuana in your car or on foot, be prepared for a wait at the border, where you must pass through customs and declare your purchases. The tourist center just inside the border entrance has information on what you may and may not bring back into the United States.

PRACTICAL INFORMATION

WHEN TO GO. Meteorologists repeatedly vote San Diego one of the most livable cities in the world. Almost any time during the year there are clear sunny days and comfortable evenings. Summertime—when the sand warms your toes and the surf is at its glorious best—is the peak of the tourist season, so be prepared for larger crowds.

Traveling through San Diego in the off season can be pleasant in a different way. Attractions are less crowded, rates are lower, and the weather remains mild, although ocean temperatures drop below 60 degrees. Winter days can be rainy; middle to late spring can bring a series of overcast days. And there is always the possibility of fog right at the coast, especially in the morning.

From January to December there is always something happening in San Diego, and the weather encourages sightseeing year-round. It's no wonder both natives and visitors have nicknamed San Diego America's Finest City.

HOW TO GET THERE. By air. Most major airlines and some low-cost regional ones serve San Diego, with frequent special fares available. San Diego International Airport is near the downtown area; transportation from the airport is available via taxi, city bus, hotel limo, and rental car.

By bus. The main *Greyhound-Trailways* bus station is located at 120 W. Broadway downtown, and has daily arrivals and departures to most major cities in the U.S. Check on special fares and packages that may be available. For information in San Diego call 239–9171.

By train. Long-distance *Amtrak* routes reach San Diego through interchanges in Los Angeles and arrive at the downtown Santa Fe station. Daily trains serve San Diego and Los Angeles with stops along the coast and inland. Promotional fares are sometimes available during the winter. The toll-free number for fares and information is 800–872–7245.

By car. The major routes into San Diego are Interstate Highway 5, running north-south through most of California; Interstate 8/U.S. 80, running east-west to the coast; Highways 163 and 15, the inland north-south route; and U.S. 94, from the eastern desert. Interstate 805 intersects with Highway 163 and Interstate 5 north of San Diego and provides an alternative route to the Mexican Border.

TELEPHONES. The area code for San Diego County is 619; Orange County is 714; most of Los Angeles is 213; Burbank and Pasadena are 818. Dial 1 before long-distance numbers. For operator assistance with collect, person to person, and credit card calls, dial 0 before the number; the operator will come on. Local information is available by dialing 411; outside San Diego, dial 619–555–1212 for information. Pay telephones cost 20 cents, and many public phones in the area are set up for credit card calls.

Emergency Telephone Numbers. The emergency number for fire and rescue, police, sheriff, and ambulance is 911. The Coast Guard emergency number is 295–3121. The number for the poison control center is 294–6000.

ACCOMMODATIONS. There is a "peak" season during June, July, and August. January and February are also considered "peak" season at many hotels. During these months, hotel and motel rates increase, sometimes by a large amount. This varies from hotel to hotel. To assure yourself of accommodations, reserve early. In general, San Diego is not as expensive as many other cities. The guest pays more for a view of the ocean or the bay than for room appointments.

Hotel rates are based on double occupancy. Categories, determined by price, are as follows: *Reasonable,* $45 to $70; *Very Economical,* under $45. There is a 7 percent tax on all hotel and motel rooms. It is worth asking about various discounts, such as senior citizen and government employee, because they are often unadvertised.

Reasonable

Andrea Villa Inn. 2402 Torrey Pines Rd., La Jolla, CA 92037 (619–459–3311, 800–367–6467). A medium-sized attractive La Jolla motel. It has a swimming pool and restaurant.

Catamaran Hotel. 3999 Mission Blvd., Pacific Beach, CA 92109 (619–488–1081, 800–821–3619). In Mission Beach, not far from the ocean, Mission Bay Park, Sea World, and other attractions. The rooms are large, airy and pleasant. There is a coffee shop and a restaurant-bar with live entertainment and dancing.

Circle 8 Motor Inn. 543 Hotel Circle S., San Diego, CA 92108 (619–297–8800, 800–227–4743). A large complex located in Mission Valley, with pool, coffee shop, and small refrigerators in all rooms. Weekly rates available.

Ebb Tide Hitching Post. 5082 West Point Loma Blvd., Ocean Beach, CA 92107 (619–224–9339). Only a block from the ocean and a half block to the bay. Some units have kitchens. Weekly rates available.

Fabulous Inns of America. 2485 Hotel Circle Pl., San Diego, CA 92108 (619–291–7700, 800–824–0950). A family-oriented Mission Valley motel with swimming pool and game room. Golf course and tennis courts adjacent.

Harbor View Holiday Inn. 1617 First Ave., San Diego, CA 92101 (619–239–6171, 800–HOL–IDAY). This Holiday Inn is located between downtown and Balboa Park, near the airport and the ocean. The view from the bar and restaurant at the top is one of the best downtown.

Holiday Inn Mission Valley. 595 Hotel Circle S., San Diego, CA 92108 (619–291–5720, 800–HOL–IDAY). This nondescript hotel is a pleasant, predictable, reliable place to stay.

Hotel San Diego. 339 West Broadway, San Diego, CA 92101 (619–234–0221, 800–621–5380). This old hotel has been restored tastefully, giving it the glitter it enjoyed when it opened in 1912. The rooms are nicely done; the dining is average. Senior citizen and government discounts available.

Mission Valley Inn. 875 Hotel Circle S., San Diego, CA 92108 (619–298–8281, 800–854–2608). A comfortable low-rise facility offering the convenience of proximity by car to practically everything in town. Liquor store, coffee shop, and deluxe Mexican restaurant on the premises. Senior citizen and government discounts offered.

Outrigger Motel. 1370 Scott St., Shelter Island, CA 92106 (619–223–7105). Just across from sport fishing docks, 2 miles from the airport. All units have full kitchens. Shops and restaurants within walking distance. Swimming pool.

Pacific Shores Inn. 4802 Mission Blvd., San Diego, CA 92109 (619–483–6300, 800–367–6467). A large motel for this area, a half block from the beach. Nicely decorated with most amenities, including a pool. Accepts pets; $50 deposit required.

Surfer Motor Lodge. 711 Pacific Beach Dr., Pacific Beach, CA 92109 (619–483–7070). Right on the beach; has a restaurant and cocktail lounge as well as a swimming pool and kitchens. Senior citizen and government discounts available.

Tradewinds Motel. 4305 Mission Bay Dr., San Diego, CA 92109 (619–273–4616). Near Mission Bay Park; motel offers a view of the bay as well as the golf course. Weekly and monthly rates.

TraveLodge–Balboa Park. 840 Ash St., San Diego, CA 92101 (619–234–8277, 800–255–3050). Convenient downtown location for walking to the park and zoo; has swimming pool and kitchens.

TraveLodge–Civic Center. 1505 Pacific Hwy., San Diego, CA 92101 (619–239–9185, 800–255–3050). A small motel with no restaurant or bar. Senior citizen and government discounts available.

TraveLodge–La Jolla. 1141 Silverado St., La Jolla, CA 92307 (619–454–0791, 800–255–3050). Its best feature is the location, right in the heart of La Jolla's shop-

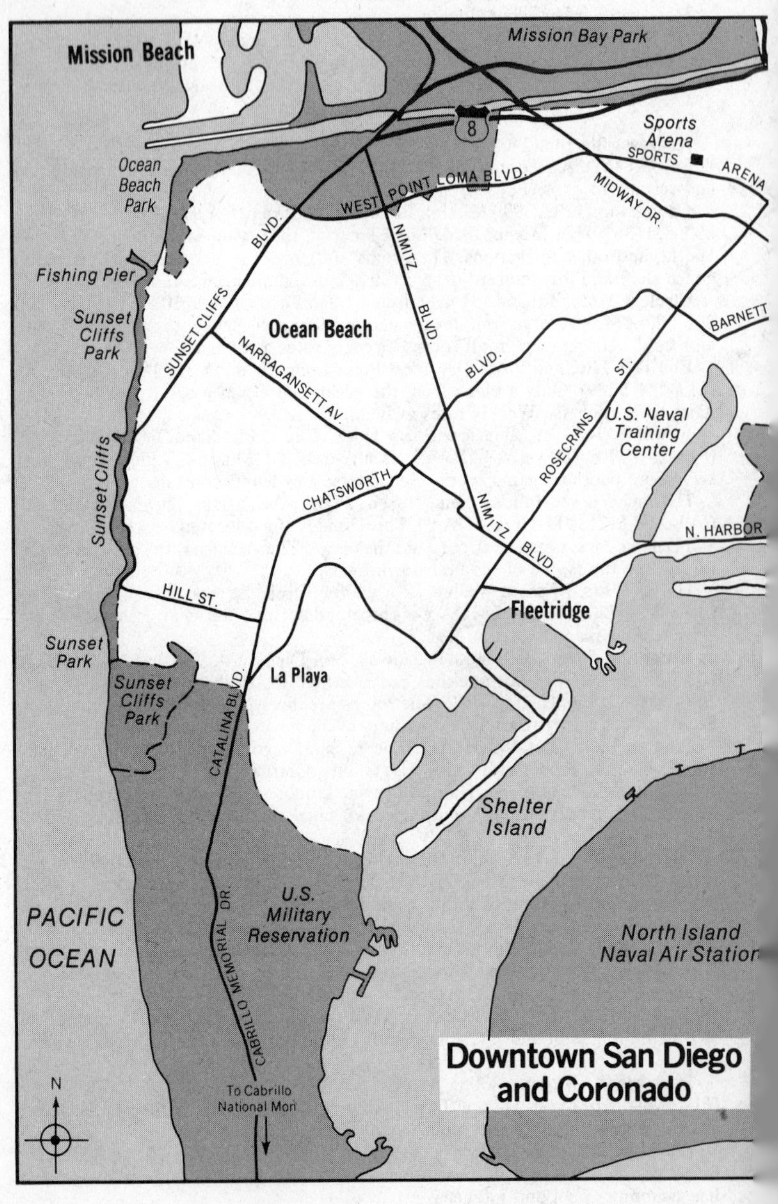
Mission Beach
Mission Bay Park
8
Sports Arena
SPORTS ARENA
Ocean Beach Park
WEST POINT LOMA BLVD.
MIDWAY DR.
Fishing Pier
SUNSET CLIFFS BLVD.
NIMITZ BLVD.
Sunset Cliffs Park
Ocean Beach
BARNETT
NARRAGANSETT AV.
BLVD.
ROSECRANS ST.
U.S. Naval Training Center
Sunset Cliffs
CHATSWORTH
NIMITZ BLVD.
N. HARBOR
HILL ST.
Fleetridge
Sunset Park
Sunset Cliffs Park
CATALINA BLVD.
La Playa
Shelter Island
PACIFIC OCEAN
U.S. Military Reservation
CABRILLO MEMORIAL DR.
North Island Naval Air Station
Downtown San Diego and Coronado
N
To Cabrillo National Mon

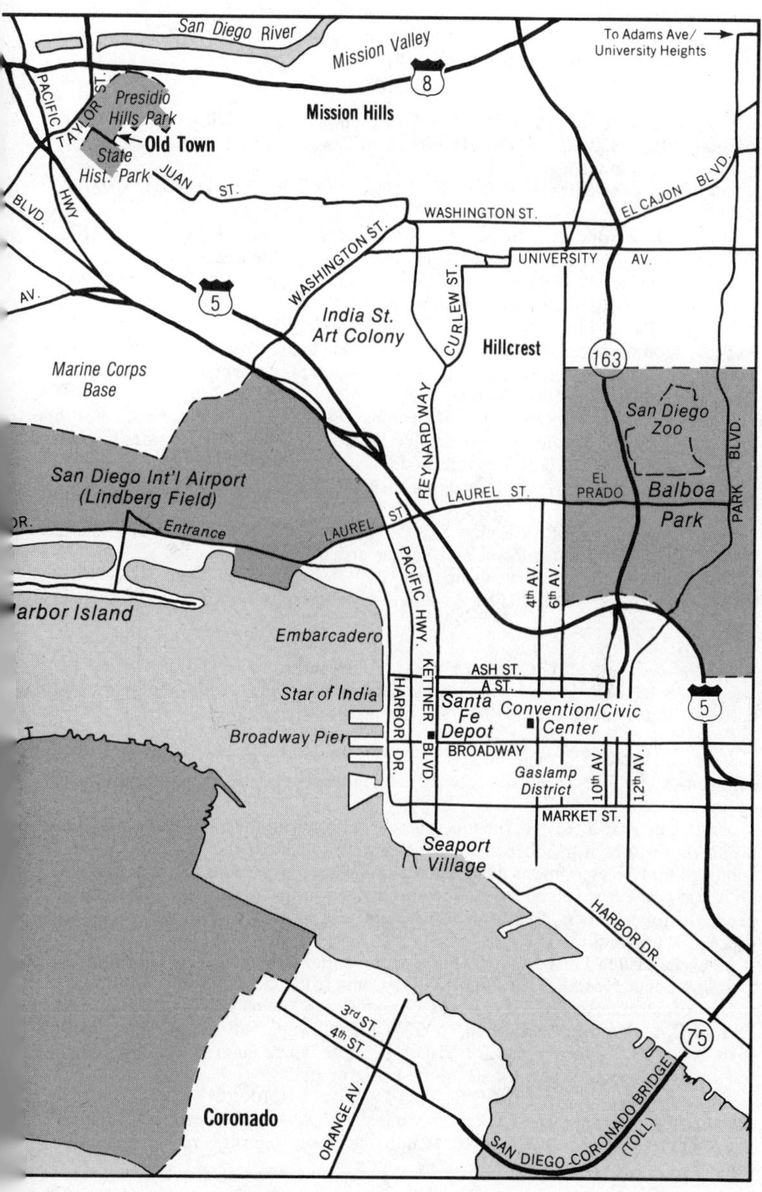
San Diego River
Mission Valley
8
To Adams Ave/ University Heights
PACIFIC
TAYLOR ST.
Presidio Hills Park
State Hist. Park
Old Town
Mission Hills
JUAN ST.
BLVD.
HWY
WASHINGTON ST.
EL CAJON BLVD.
WASHINGTON ST.
UNIVERSITY AV.
CURLEW ST.
AV.
5
India St. Art Colony
Hillcrest
163
Marine Corps Base
San Diego Zoo
REYNARD WAY
PARK BLVD.
San Diego Int'l Airport (Lindberg Field)
EL PRADO
Balboa Park
LAUREL ST.
LAUREL ST.
Entrance
PACIFIC HWY.
4th AV.
6th AV.
Harbor Island
Embarcadero
KETTINER
ASH ST.
A ST.
Star of India
HARBOR DR.
Santa Fe Depot
Convention/Civic Center
5
Broadway Pier
BLVD.
BROADWAY
Gaslamp District
10th AV.
12th AV.
MARKET ST.
Seaport Village
HARBOR DR.
3rd ST.
4th ST.
75
ORANGE AV.
Coronado
SAN DIEGO-CORONADO BRIDGE (TOLL)

ping and restaurant district. Kitchens are available; senior citizen and government discounts.

TraveLodge–San Diego Downtown. 1345 Tenth Ave., San Diego, CA 92101 (619–234–6344, 800–255–3050). Basic motel with a pool; kitchens available.

Vagabond Motor Hotel. 625 Hotel Circle S., San Diego, CA 92108 (619–297–1691, 800–522–1555). Rooms are clean, neat, and comfortable. No restaurant or bar on the premises but several close by.

Very Economical

Budget Motel of America. 1835 Columbia, San Diego, CA 92101 (619–544–0164, 800–824–5317). New motel in downtown with large, clean rooms and a good restaurant.

E-Z 8 Motel of Mission Valley. 2484 Hotel Circle Pl., San Diego, CA 92108. (619–291–8252). Central location, clean rooms; no restaurant.

Hotel Circle Budget Motel. 445 Hotel Circle S., San Diego, CA 92108. (619–692–1288). Air-conditioned rooms, color TV, laundromat.

La Jolla Motel. 4540 Mission Bay Dr., San Diego, CA 92109 (619–273–7515). Modest but near the bay; has a swimming pool.

La Jolla Palms Inn. 6705 La Jolla Blvd., La Jolla, CA 92037 (619–454–7101). Friendly atomosphere, attractive landscaping. One block from beach and walking distance from nearby restaurants. Has a pool, restaurant, cocktail lounge, kitchen units, weekly rentals. Accepts pets.

Loma Manor Motel. 1518 Rosecrans St., Point Loma, CA 92106 (619–223–8391). Centrally located, not too far from beaches. Weekly rates offered.

Mission Bay Motel. 4221 Mission Blvd., San Diego, CA 92109 (619–483–6440). Close to ocean and bay, within walking distance of restaurants. Swimming pool, kitchens available.

Point Loma Inn. 2933 Fenelon St., Point Loma, CA 92106 (619–226–9333). Near Shelter Island, downtown, and harbor areas.

Townhouse Lodge–A Friendship Inn. 810 Ash St., San Diego, CA 92101 (619–233–8826, 800–982–2020). A basic two-story motel with a pool. Central downtown location.

Bed-and-Breakfast. Carolyn's Bed and Breakfast Homes. Box 84776, San Diego, CA 92138 (619–435–5009). Finds accommodations in private homes and cottages. Rates range from $40 to $75 per night.

Ys and Hostels. Ys and hostels are very inexpensive accommodations if they suit your style. They are usually set up dormitory-style and rarely have private rooms.

American Youth Hostels Inc. operates three hostels in the San Diego area. You do not have to be a member of the organization to stay at the hostels, and there is no age limit. Reservations can be made in advance; otherwise, space is available on a first-come first-served basis. They are busy during the summer. Rates are $7 per night for members, $10 for nonmembers. For information on all hostels call the AYH Travel Shop (619–239–2644).

Imperial Beach Hostel. 170 Palm Ave., Imperial Beach (619–423–8039).

Point Loma Hostel. 3790 Udall, Point Loma (619–223–4778 or 234–3330).

San Clemente Hostel. 233 Avenue Granada, San Clemente (714–692–2428).

Y.M.C.A. Downtown Branch, 500 W. Broadway, San Diego, CA 92101 (619–232–1133), offers rooms for $16.05 per night for a single room and $26.75 for a double room. Reservations can be made by mail.

Downtown Y.W.C.A., 1012 C St., San Diego, CA 92101 (619–239–0355), also rents rooms; reservations are taken only one day in advance. Rates are $13 for singles, $12.50 to share a double room; refundable $5 key deposit is required in either case.

HOW TO GET AROUND. From the airport. San Diego International Airport is located very near the downtown area. Transportation from the airport is available via taxis, city buses, hotel limos, and rental cars.

By bus. San Diego Transit operates buses throughout the county, but schedules and transfers can be complicated unless you are staying downtown or at the Hotel

Circle. Many hotels, train and bus stations, and tourist information centers have bus schedules and route maps. Call 233–3004 for specific route information or schedules, but be prepared to redial often. The fare is 80 cents (exact change only) for regular routes and $1 (exact change only, no bills) for express routes, and transfers are usable for only a half hour or until the next available bus. Senior citizen fares are 40 cents during nonpeak hours. Some buses have bike racks; 20 are equipped for handicapped riders.

By trolley. The San Diego Trolley's bright red electric cars travel south through downtown to the Mexican border. The trolley doesn't reach any of the major tourist attractions but is an inexpensive way to reach the border; from there, Tijuana is a short walk or taxi ride away. Each stop has a map and ticket machines, which take only quarters for the $1.50 fare from downtown to the border. Some major stops have change machines. Call 231–1466.

By taxi. The average taxi fare in San Diego is $2 for the first mile and $1 for each additional mile. Since the mileage between attractions can be considerable (15 miles from downtown to La Jolla, for example), it is best to use cabs only for short jumps. Cab companies are listed in the Yellow Pages; be sure to ask about fares and whether the company serves only a particular area.

By rental car. Car rental companies abound in San Diego, and the rates are competitive, some as low as $8 per day. Most companies will not allow you to take cars into Mexico; ask when you call. Since the mileage can add up, particularly if you plan on driving to Los Angeles or Disneyland, it is best to get some kind of mileage deal. Most major companies have offices at the airport, downtown, and in Hotel Circle; the less-expensive ones are grouped near the airport, along Pacific Highway and Kettner Blvd., and usually have shuttle services to and from the airport. Some budget agencies are: *Alamo* (800–327–9633), *Budget* (800–527–0700), *Getaway* (619–233–3777), *Rent-A-Car Cheap* (619–238–1012), and *Thrifty* (800–367–2277).

HINTS TO THE MOTORIST. California motorists are notorious for ruthless freeway driving; we suggest that you study road maps before heading for your first on-ramp. The *Automobile Club of Southern California* (AAA) has good city and county road maps and has nine offices in the county. The downtown office is at 815 Date St. (233–1000). Three major freeways serve central San Diego: I-5, running north-south along the coast; I-8, running east-west; and I-805, which runs north-south inland. The posted speed limit is 55 mph, but despite the proliferation of Highway Patrol cars and no state regulations regarding posting signs for radar and mechanical or electric speed-checking devices, only the slowest lane is safe at that speed. Drivers tend to speed up at major freeway intersections, and so it is best to plan your exits in advance. There are no call boxes for emergencies, and roadside businesses are scarce along some stretches in the northern and eastern sections of the county.

Scenic drives and bicycle routes are marked and provide a more leisurely way of getting through the coastal towns. A right turn after stopping at a red light is legal. Parking regulations are enforced strictly; in the downtown area, most meters are good for 2 hours only; in some beach areas, the meters last only 1 hour. It doesn't pay to just keep putting more money in the meter; the space itself is good only for the allotted time, and you can be ticketed if you exceed that time even if you have put more money in the meter.

TOURIST INFORMATION. The *San Diego Convention and Visitors Bureau* publishes a general brochure on San Diego available in English, Japanese, Spanish, French, and German along with maps and pamphlets on various vacation pamphlets, including a monthly publication *What's Doing in San Diego,* listing special activities and information on all major tourist attractions. Write or call the bureau for free information at 1200 Third Ave., Suite 824, San Diego, CA 92101; for a 24-hour information recording, call 239–9696; for a 24-hour arts and entertainment hotline, call 234–ARTS.

The *International Visitors Information Center,* Horton Plaza, First and F streets, San Diego, CA 92101 (236–1212). The center is open daily from 8:30 A.M. to 5:30 P.M. and offers brochures, maps, and tourist information.

The *Mission Bay Visitors Information Center,* 2688 East Mission Bay Drive, San Diego, CA 92109 (276–8200,) located in Mission Bay off Interstate 5 at the Clairemont Drive exit, is open from 9 A.M. until dark and offers a full range of tourist services including hotel reservations, information and maps for all tourist attractions, bus schedules, and information on Mexico.

The *Mission Bay Harbor Patrol* has a telephone recording of current beach and weather conditions for surfers, sailors, snorkelers, and swimmers. Call 225–9492.

San Diego magazine, the San Diego *Union, Evening Tribune,* San Diego edition of the Los Angeles *Times,* and the free weekly *Reader* all carry listings of current events. Many hotels and motels supply free tourist publications, and some carry Tele-Vu, a televised overview of San Diego attractions.

HINTS TO DISABLED TRAVELERS. The *Community Service Center for the Disabled,* 1295 University Ave., San Diego, CA 92103 (293–3500), has information on hotels, motels, and attractions with access for the disabled. San Diego does not have any wheelchair-accessible beaches, but most have cement walkways bordering the beach. Disabled parking spaces are available at all attractions and are closely policed by parking patrols.

FREE EVENTS. There is no charge to play on San Diego's 70 miles of beaches, bays, and harbors, stroll through Balboa Park and Old Town, or drive through the mountains and desert. During the summer, the beach areas become a huge playground, with free kite flying, sand castle building, volleyball, body surfing, wind surfing, and speedboat and crew racing contests. **Fourth of July** picnics, parades, and fireworks displays take place in nearly every county community. August's **America's Finest City Week,** usually held in the middle of the month, features parades, fireworks, concerts, marathons, and other free events. December is packed with free holiday events, including Old Town's **Las Posadas** procession and pinata party, downtown's **Christmas in the City** parade, Balboa Park's **Christmas on the Prado,** with displays at all the museums and a tree-lighting ceremony, and neighborhood parades and celebrations throughout the county. January is **Maple Leaf Month,** with various celebrations to honor Canadian visitors. March brings the **Saint Patrick's Day Parade,** usually held around Balboa Park, and on May 5 San Diego's large Mexican population celebrates **Cinco de Mayo** with ethnic performances and feasts at Old Town and other locations.

On the first Tuesday of each month, the museums at Balboa Park have free admission, and the zoo celebrates Founders Day with free admission to all on October 1.

TOURS AND SPECIAL-INTEREST SIGHTSEEING. Walking. *Walkabout International* (223–9255) offers free imaginative walks through San Diego's neighborhoods at all hours of the day and night, led by volunteers with ample information on the area. *Elegant Ambles* (222–2224) charges a small fee for their tours, which are usually more in-depth and exotic. The *Gaslamp Quarter Association* (233–5227) has tours of downtown's renovated Gaslamp Quarter, and the *Natural History Museum* (232–3821) has hikes through nearby canyons.

Boating. A variety of boats leave the downtown Embarcadero for narrated tours of the harbor, including the *Harbor Excursions* (234–4111) and the *Invader* sailing schooner and *Showboat* paddlewheeler (234–8687), with fees ranging around $8 for an hour. The winter migration of the California gray whales is particularly popular from December through February; the tour boats above offer special **whale-watching trips,** as do *H&M Landing* (222–1144) and *Islandia Sportfishing* (222–1164). The *Bahia Belle* paddlewheeler offers moonlight cruises through Mission Bay during the summer months (488–0551).

Bus. *Gray Line Sightseeing Tours* (231–9922) has half-day tours throughout the city for about $10 and longer tours to Tijuana and Disneyland. *Mexicoach* (232–5049) offers tours to Tijuana and Baja. *San Diego Mini Tours* (234–9044) charges $10 to $20 for trips to local attractions. The *Molly Trolley*'s (233–9177) open-air cars travel along the waterfront from Shelter Island to Seaport Village and through downtown to Balboa Park. The 25-cent fare is a real bargain, and the cars stop at hotels along the route.

PARKS AND GARDENS. There is no shortage of parkland in San Diego, starting with **Cabrillo National Monument,** the most frequently visited monument in the country. Located on a high cliff at the tip of Point Loma, this is a prime whale watching spot and offers a remarkable view of the San Diego Harbor and the Coronado Islands. The Visitor's Center offers a museum, theater, gift shop, and narrated tours of the monument, including the old Point Loma Lighthouse, built in 1854. A small paved road right before the entrance leads down to marine research labs with dolphins and seals swimming in enormous tanks. Cabrillo Monument is open daily year-round, and there is no admission fee. Call 293–5450 for information.

Closer to sea level there's the 4,600-acre **Mission Bay Park,** a waterfront wonderland that is overrun by bicyclists, roller skaters, joggers, picnickers, kite flyers, Frisbee throwers, and all sorts of outdoor enthusiasts. Sections of the bay are partitioned for swimming and wading, waterskiing, and sailing. Within the park there are miniature and professional golf courses, tennis courts, resort hotels, a campground, boat rentals, sport fishing charters, a jogger's courses, restaurants, all sorts of seasonal events, and plenty of free parking.

Balboa Park's 1,400 acres were first designated as a city park in 1835, but it took the Panama-California Exposition of 1915 and the California Pacific International Exposition of 1935 to transform the park into the city's cultural and recreational center. Many of the museums and theaters listed elsewhere are located in the park, along with the world's largest outdoor pipe organ at the Spreckels Organ Pavilion, where free Sunday afternoon concerts are held during the summer. Musicians, mimes, jugglers, and other performers appear on most of the park's grassy lawns; restaurants and outdoor vendors provide nourishment to keep you going. One can easily spend an inexpensive day or two roaming the park; there's plenty of space for impromptu picnicking and enough free sights to please everyone.

Presidio Park above Old Town, off I-8 is the site of the founding of San Diego and the headquarters of the San Diego Historical Society at the Serra Museum. The park, with its steep grassy hills and panoramic view of much of central San Diego, is a popular spot for grass skiing, San Diego's remedy for the lack of snow, and weddings held under the rose arbor.

Many smaller parks, such as **La Jolla Cove** and the **Embarcadero** (the waterfront downtown), offer recreational opportunities, and there's always the beaches.

BEACHES. With 70 miles of coastline, San Diego offers almost every ocean pleasure possible, from skin diving to midnight campfires. Ocean temperatures average around 62 degrees, with lows in the fifties during winter months and highs in the seventies usually by the middle of July. Some of the most popular beaches have lifeguards year-round; many have rest rooms, showers, and changing rooms. Camping, pets, and glass containers and dishes are prohibited on all beaches, and ticket writers bearing coolers concealing their official papers wander the sand in the summer. Police officers patrol the boardwalks on bicyles and the beaches in jeeps. Picnicking is allowed on all beaches, but fires are prohibited except in established fire pits, which dot the coastline. On almost any beach you'll find surfing (body, board, and wind), swimming, and the most popular pastime of all, sunbathing. You'll also find crowds and a scarcity of parking spaces during the summer.

Different types tend to gather at different beaches, though the trends vary from year to year. *Imperial Beach, Coronado, Ocean Beach, Mission Beach,* and *Pacific Beach* all have long stretches of sand for volleyball games, sunbathing, and people watching; plenty of waves for surfers and swimmers; and crowds as varied as the general population. Small neighborhood beaches favored by locals curve into the coastline along *Sunset Cliffs* and the rocky strip between *Pacific Beach* and La Jolla. *La Jolla Cove*'s underwater preserve is the place for snorkeling, diving, and wave-free swimming; its narrow cliffside beaches fill up quickly on sunny summer weekends.

North of the cove, *La Jolla Shores* has a long stretch of uninterrupted beach sectioned off for swimmers, body surfers, boogie boarders, and surfers; its northern end leads past spectacular oceanfront homes to the Torrey Pines Glider Port atop the rising cliffside. The beach gets very narrow here and is passable only during the lowest of tides, and the cliffs are highly unstable. The area just under the glider port was once a popular "swimwear optional" beach called *Black's Beach,* but the cliffside paths down to it have eroded with time, making it dangerous to reach; once there, you may be cited if not dressed. Black's can be reached more safely by walking (almost an hour) south from *Torrey Pines State Beach,* another good sunning, swimming, and surfing beach beneath the cliffs of vegetation of the state reserve. North County's beaches are as popular as the rest, but it is possible to roam far enough away from the crowds to find your own cliffside niche.

San Diego's waves are said to rival those of Hawaii, and they draw scores of surfers who prefer *Windansea* in La Jolla, *La Jolla Shores,* and *Pacific, Mission,* and *Ocean* beaches.

ZOOS. The 100-acre **San Diego Zoo,** in Balboa Park (234–3153), is a botanist's delight, with lush tropical vegetation that is as unusual and fascinating as the 5,000 animals that inhabit the park. The quickest way to tour the zoo is on a double-decker guided tour bus, but it is much more rewarding to wander the winding paths over bridges, past waterfalls, and through the junglelike terrain filled with all sorts of exotic species. The Children's Zoo has a nursery where baby chimps play with educational toys and goats and sheep roam freely, helping themselves to any edibles you may be carrying. The zoo is open daily 9 A.M.–dusk.Adults, $8.50; children, $2.50; military in uniform free.

The Zoo's **San Diego Wild Animal Park** (619–234–6541) is a 1,800-acre animal preserve designed to allow endangered and nearly extinct breeds of animals to roam and reproduce. The park's highlight is the electric monorail safari through exhibits that recreate the terrain of north, south, and East Africa and the Asian plains and swamps, where giraffes, gazelles, antelope, and other animals gallop, graze, and mingle as they would in the wild. The ride is particularly impressive during the early evening feeding times. Within the park there are impressive, informative animal shows, a fascinating children's zoo, and a hiking trail through an east African setting. On summer evenings, bluegrass, jazz, and rock concerts are held in the park's outdoor amphitheater. The Wild Animal Park is about 30 miles northeast of downtown but well worth the drive if you prefer seeing animals allowed to roam free. The park is open from 9 A.M. until dusk during the winter and until 11 P.M. in the summer. Adults, $12.95; children, $6.25. Parking is $1.

The **Scripps Institute of Oceanography Aquarium** is filled with fish tanks displaying an incredible array of freshwater and saltwater inhabitants. An outdoor man-made tidal pool displays many of the sea creatures found off San Diego's coastline, including sea anemones, starfish, octopus, and garabaldi. The aquarium is located at 8602 La Jolla Shores Dr.; a donation is requested for admission. Call 534–6933 for information.

At the south end of Mission Bay lies **Sea World,** Sea World Dr., off I-5, a 100-acre marine park with exhibits, shows, petting pools, and Cap'n Kid's World, a wonderful self-contained playground. The park's new Penguin Encounter contains hundreds of penguins in a simulated Arctic environment, and Shamu the whale puts on a great show. The PSA Sky Tower rises 320 feet into the air for a full-circle view of San Diego, and the Sky Ride Tram joins Sea World and the Atlantis restaurant across Mission Bay. Sea World's newest exhibit, City Streets, resembles an inner-city neighborhood with musical shows featuring skateboard and bicycle stunts. Allow at least half a day to tour the park, longer if you're interested in browsing through the many good gift shops. The park is open daily year-round from 9:00 A.M. until dusk. Full admission to Sea World including rides is $17.95 for adults and $11.95 for children ages 3 to 11. Discounts are available for seniors and active military personnel. Call 226–3901 for information.

PARTICIPANT SPORTS. Because of San Diego's consistently excellent weather, the city is alive with sporting enthusiasts and sporting opportunities. With more than 70 distinctive courses in the county, it's little wonder **golf** is popular. Green fees range from $11 to $14 at the frequently used municipal courses. A few courses are: *Balboa Park Municipal* 9-hole course, Golf Course Drive (232–2717); *Balboa Park Municipal* 18-hole course, Golf Course Drive (232–2470); *Coronado Golf Course,* 2000 Visalia Row (435–3121); *Mission Bay Golf Course,* 2702 N. Mission Bay Dr. (273–1221); and *Torrey Pines Municipal Golf Course,* 11480 N. Torrey Pines Rd. (453–0380).

Jogging. The pathways along the beaches and through all of the parks as well as the beaches themselves are great for jogging. *Fiesta Island* in Mission Bay is also a runners' and bike riders' favorite.

Tennis. There are numerous public tennis courts maintained by the city of San Diego that are available free or for a minimal fee. Courts at local colleges or high schools are usually open to the public when classes are not in session. Here are just a few: *Robb Field,* 2525 Bacon St. (224–7581); *Mission Bay Youth Field,* 2639 Grand Ave. (273–9177); *La Jolla Recreation Center,* 615 Prospect St. (454–2071) (free); and *Morley Field-Love Tennis Center,* in Balboa Park (295–9278).

Bicycling. The parks and beach areas all have paths that are wonderful for bicycle riding. There are rentals available along the beach areas.

Sailing, wind surfing, and rowboating. Mission Bay is the most popular boating place, but both Shelter and Harbor islands are crowded with marinas. Instruction and rentals are available. Prices vary, but you should be able to find windsurfers for around $10 and Hobie Cats for $16 per hour. *California Pacific Catamaran Rental and Inc.,* 2211 Pacific Beach Dr., Pacific Beach (270–3211). *Harbor Sailboats,* 2040 Harbor Island Dr. (291–9568). *Mission Bay Sports Center,* 1010 Santa Clara Pl., Mission Beach (488–1004).

Scuba diving and snorkeling. *La Jolla Shores, La Jolla Cove,* and *Scripps Pier* are good spots for both scuba and snorkeling. These areas are all within the *La Jolla Shores Ecological Reserve* and are closed to hunting and fishing. For further information about the reserve and other diving areas, call local dive shops: *The Diving Locker,* 1020 Grand Ave., Pacific Beach (272–1120); *New England Divers,* 3860 Rosecrans St. (298–0531); and *San Diego Divers Supply,* 7522 La Jolla Blvd. (459–3439).

Fishing. San Diego is a haven for sport fishers. Boats set off for all types of fishing trips. In the summer, the catch includes marlin, bonito, barracuda, and tuna; in the winter, ling cod, black fish, and rock cod. Naturally, fishermen must have the proper license, which is sold at bait shops, boat landings, the Department of Fish and Game Offices, and many sporting goods stores. Half-day and full-day trips are offered by *Seaforth Sportfishing,* 1717 Quivira Rd. (224–3383); *H&M Landing,* 2803 Emerson St. (222–1144); and *Islandia Sportfishing,* 1551 West Mission Bay Dr. (222–1164).

Horseback riding. San Diego, especially the hilly outlying areas, has many stables and lovely riding areas. For information and rates, call one of these listed numbers or check the phone book for others: *Hilltop Stables,* 2671 Monument Rd., San Diego (428–5441); *Smith Ranch,* 4673 Dehesa Rd., El Cajon (442–9095); and *Rancho San Diego Stables,* 11990 Campo Rd., Spring Valley (463–2836).

Raquetball. Racquetball has always been a favorite in San Diego, and there is a choice of court space around town. *San Diego State University* has courts that are available for less than those at most other clubs; for court times and reservations, call 265–6492. A partial listing of San Diego's public courts follows: *Standley Park and Recreation Center,* 3585 Governor Dr. (452–8556); *Family Fitness Centers,* three locations (292–7079); *YMCA of San Diego,* Copely Family Branch, 3901 Landis (283–2251); and Northwest Family Branch, 8355 Cliffridge Ave. (453–2144).

Swimming. There are all of the fabulous beaches for swimming with water temperatures up to 73 degrees in the summer, but there are also a number of pools run by the city of San Diego's Park and Recreation Department: Allied Gardens, 6707 Glenroy St. (265–9930); Clairmont, 3600 Clairmont Dr. (273–9540); and Mission Beach Plunge, 3102 Mission Blvd. (488–2087).

SPECTATOR SPORTS. Football. The *San Diego Chargers* evoke a blue-and-gold fever that pervades the town during football season, and tickets are hard to get. Some 11 home games (regular and preseason) are played at Jack Murphy Stadium, held the *1988 Super Bowl.* Tickets cost $8 to $19; information is available by calling 280–2111. If you do get tickets, plan to tailgate at the parking lot before the game like the locals do—it saves some of the aggravation of sitting in a line of cars as the game begins and gives you the chance to see how Charger fans party. On the college level, the *San Diego State Aztecs* also play their games at the stadium, which hosts the annual December *Holiday Bowl,* pitting the Western Athletic Conference Champion against one of the best teams in the country chosen at large. The Holiday Bowl has become an integral part of the holiday social season, and tickets move fast. Call 238–5808 for information.

Baseball. The National League *Padres* have rallied forth in the past few years to win the 1984 Western Division championship, and tickets are not as easy to come by as they once were. The Padres play at Jack Murphy Stadium from April through September; tickets cost $4 to $6.50, and information is available by calling 283–4494.

Horse racing. The *Del Mar Thoroughbred Club* brings legal betting to the Del Mar Fairgrounds for the 43-day season beginning in late July. Nine races are run daily except Tuesday, with gates opening at noon. Opening day at Del Mar is always a San Diego summer highlight, with celebrity fans mingling with the local elite in a high society show. Admission is $2 to $5; call 299–1340 or 755–1141 for information.

Golf. The *Isuzu Andy Williams San Diego Open* puts golf in the forefront the last weekend in January at the Torrey Pines Gold Course; call 272–0851 for information. In April, the *MONY Tournament of Champions* brings together tour champions at the La Costa Hotel and Spa; call 438–9111 for information.

Other major sporting events include the July *La Jolla Tennis Tournament* (454–4434), the September *Miller High Life Thunderboat Regatta* at Mission Bay (232–1289), and the April *San Diego Crew Classic* at Mission Bay (488–1039). San Diego is home of the *U.S.A. Men's Olympic Volleyball Team* training center, and matches are held periodically with visiting teams (692–4192).

HISTORICAL SITES. The **San Diego Historical Society** operates the **Serra Museum** in Presidio Park, housing a collection of maps, documents, and records from San Diego's early days. The museum is open daily; for information, contact the historical society at 297–3258.

The Gaslamp Quarter, along Fourth and Fifth avenues downtown, contains many of San Diego's historic buildings; the Gaslamp Quarter Association offers guided tours of the area and historical information. Call 233–5227.

Old Town State Historic Park contains much of San Diego's original settlement, with historical buildings and displays, new shops, and an abundance of Mexican restaurants lining San Diego Ave. to the Bazaar Del Mundo, a popular dining and shopping square. **Heritage Park,** a collection of historic Victorian buildings, and other shopping complexes line the side streets, and there are plenty of grassy park areas for picnics and people watching.

Missions. San Diego must be the mission capital of the nation, starting with the **Mission San Diego de Alcala,** established by Padre Junipero Serra in 1769. The mission is located at 10818 San Diego Mission Road, near Mission Valley, and is open 9 A.M.–5 P.M. daily; services are held every Sunday in the original mission chapel. The Father Luis Jayme Museum features relics of early mission days and is the only permanent ecclesiastical art museum in southern California. Call 281–8449 for information.

Mission San Luis Rey, 4050 Mission Ave., San Luis Rey (757–3651), is the largest of the 21 Franciscan California missions and was once the home of 3,000 Indians. On the 50-cent self-guided tour you can explore the Spanish, Mexican, and Moorish architecture and the cloister garden, Indian cemetery, archaeological excavations, and a large collection of Spanish vestments. The mission is located about 40 miles from downtown, east of Oceanside. Call 757–3651 for information.

The Assistencia de San Antonio de Pala (Pala Mission) is located in the back country of North County and is still used as a school and church by the Indians. Call 742–3317 for information. Mission Santa Ysabel, an original assistencia to San Diego de Alcala, is located 50 miles outside the city and is best reached during a drive through the mountains. Call 765–0810 for information.

MUSEUMS AND GALLERIES. Most of San Diego's museums are gathered along Balboa Park's El Prado. All have free admission on the first Tuesday of each month and discounts for seniors, students, and military personnel. The gift shops can be visited without paying the admission fee, and they carry an unusual collection of gift items. Starting at the Laurel Street Bridge end of El Prado, the museums are the following:

The Hall of Champions and Hall of Fame honors the country's great athletes and is popular with sports fans. Open daily 10 A.M.–4:30 P.M. except major holidays; admission is $2 for adults, 50 cents for children.

The Museum of Man (239–2001) is housed under the California Tower and includes exhibits of the anthropology and archaeology of man in the western Americas and artifacts from Indian and Mexican cultures. The "Wonder of Life" exhibition housed across the street is a multimedia presentation of human reproduction and birth. Adults, $2, with discounts for students, seniors, and military personnel; children under 16, 25 cents. Open 10 A.M.–4:30 P.M. except on major holidays.

The Museum of Natural History (232–3821) contains permanent collections on the Southwest, Baja, and the desert and an excellent scientific library. The museum holds nature walks throughout the county, whale-watching trips, weekly films, children's classes, and mineralogy displays. Open 10 A.M.–5 P.M. daily except major holidays. Adults, $3; children 6–18, $1.

Museum of Photographic Arts (239–5262) presents various photography exhibits. Admission is $2, and the museum is open daily 10 A.M.–5 P.M.

The Reuben H. Fleet Space Theater and Science Center (238–1168) has the largest projection dome in the country, where films on space and nature are shown throughout the day. The Science Center contains hands-on exhibits that explain scientific principles. Admission to the theater and science center is $4 for adults and $2.50 for juniors (5 to 15) and seniors. Open daily 9:45 A.M.–9:30 P.M.

The San Diego Aerospace Museum (234–2544) is south of El Prado in the renovated Ford building, an impressive circular structure with neon outlining. The museum houses old military planes, Lindbergh's *Spirit of St. Louis,* and an Aerospace Hall of Fame. Open daily 10 A.M.–4:30 P.M. Adults, $2; children under 17, $1.

San Diego Art Institute (234–5946) sponsors monthly shows covering nearly every medium. Open Tues.–Sun. 10 A.M.–4:30 P.M.; admission free.

The San Diego Museum of Art (232–7931) features a permanent collection of Old Master paintings and American and Asian arts and popular traveling shows including the Muppet exhibit and the Golden Treasures of Peru. Adjacent to the museum is the outdoor Sculpture Garden and Cafe, serving French specialties. Open 10 A.M.–4:30 P.M. Tues.–Sun.

The Timken Art Gallery (239–5548) houses a collection of American and European art including paintings by Rembrandt and Cézanne. Open 10 A.M.–4:30 P.M. Tues.–Sat.; admission free.

Other Museums

The Firehouse Museum, 1572 Columbia St., downtown, an exhibit of early fire-fighting equipment housed in a 1915 fire station. Open weekends 10 A.M.–4 P.M.; admission free.

La Jolla Museum of Contemporary Art, 700 Prospect St., La Jolla (454–0267), has a permanent collection of post-1950s art and design and rotating exhibitions by major modern artists. The museum holds an annual International Film Festival in the fall and films and concerts by visiting artists. Call for hours and special shows.

The Maritime Museum (234–9153) consists of the 1863 *Star of India* sailing ship, the 1898 *Berkeley Ferry,* and the 1904 *Medea* coal-burning yacht from Scotland, each containing nautical exhibits. Admission is $4 for adults; $3 for ages 3–17 and senior citizens. Open daily 9 A.M.–8 P.M. The ships are located in the San Diego Harbor at 1306 North Harbor Dr., downtown.

The Mingel International Museum of World Folk Art features historical and contemporary arts and crafts exhibits; it is located in University Towne Center, 4405 La Jolla Village Dr. (453–5300).

FILM. There are plenty of small multiplex theaters in San Diego with $1 to $2 bargain shows in the early evening. The older, larger theaters offer more pleasurable viewing but usually don't have bargain rates. Some of the nicer theaters are: the *Cinerama,* 5889 University Ave. (583–6201); *Cinema 21,* 1140 Hotel Circle N. (291–2121); and *Valley Circle,* Mission Valley Center West (297–3931).

Older neighborhood theaters that show current and classic American and foreign films include the *Ken,* 4061 Adams Ave., Kensington (283–5909); the *Guild,* 3827 Fifth Ave., Hillcrest (296–2000); the *Cove,* 7730 Girard Ave., La Jolla (459–5404); the *Village,* 820 Orange Ave., Coronado (435–6161); the *Strand,* 4950 Newport Ave., Ocean Beach (223–3141); and *La Paloma,* 471 First St., Encinitas (436–7469).

There are many foreign-language theaters that serve San Diego's large Mexican and Asian communities. Most universities and art museums have occasional screenings, which are usually listed in the *Reader, San Diego* magazine, and the daily papers.

MUSIC. The **San Diego Opera** (232–7636) season runs from mid-October until May, with the annual June Verdi Festival a particularly popular event. Most performances are at the Civic Center. The **San Diego Civic Light Opera Association** (280–9111) presents a series of outdoor musicals in the outdoor Starlight Bowl in Balboa Park during the summer.

San Diego State's **Open Air Theater** (265–6947) offers summer concerts by popular classical, jazz, and rock performers. At times it is possible to sit on the grass outside the theater and hear the performances, though sometimes the sprinklers are turned on and the free show is cancelled.

The **Mandeville Center Auditorium** at the University of California San Diego (452–4559) hosts appearances by international musicians throughout the year. Other musical events are held throughout the county and are listed in *San Diego* magazine, the *Reader,* and the daily papers.

STAGE. The most celebrated theater in San Diego is the **Old Globe Theater** in Balboa Park, a replica of the Shakespearean Theater at Stratford-on-Avon. The Old Globe is part of three interconnected stages known as the Simon Edison Centre for the Performing Arts. The popular summer Shakespearean festival takes place on the outdoor Festival Stage, and the Old Globe and Cassius Carter stages host major productions throughout the year. Call 239–2255 for ticket information.

The **San Diego Repertory Theatre** (231–3585), a local production company, performs year-round in their new theater in Horton Plaza, downtown. The **Marquis Theaters** (298–8111) are three stages that hold contemporary, experimental, and original plays at 3717 India St., near downtown. The **Gaslamp Quarter Theatre** (234–9583) holds contemporary plays in an intimate 90-seat historical site at 547 Fourth Ave., downtown. The **Coronado Playhouse** (435–4856), located near the historic Hotel Del Coronado, presents about five plays a year in a charming small theater. The **Old Town Theater** (298–0082) at 4040 Twiggs St. in Old Town presents plays and performances by comedians and musicians, often low-priced to attract tourists in the park.

SHOPPING. San Diego is filled with shopping centers, theme specialty shop areas, and boutiques, with a sales tax of 6 percent. The true bargain hunters head for the **swap meets,** which are mobbed on weekends. The most popular is the *Kobey Swap Meet* at the Sports Arena parking lot, 3500 Sports Arena Blvd. (226–0650). You can find new and used versions of nearly anything you'd ever want, from plants and paintings to ethnic clothing and automotive supplies. Other swap meets and flea markets come and go and are usually advertised in the daily papers.

There are more than half a dozen major **shopping malls** in San Diego; because of the pleasant climate, few are enclosed. Among the biggest, with major department stores, restaurants, and boutiques, are *Fashion Valley* and *Mission Valley,* both along I-8 by Hotel Circle; *University Towne Center* and *La Jolla Village Square* in La Jolla; and the new *Horton Plaza* center downtown, with department stores, restaurants, and theaters.

Specialty shopping centers where **tourist souvenirs** and **southwestern arts and crafts** are available abound in *Old Town,* particularly in the *Bazaar Del Mundo,* a Mexican marketplace with jewelry, ethnic clothing, pottery, and imports. On weekends, *San Diego Avenue* is lined with artisans selling blankets, pottery, jewelry, and Mexican crafts, usually priced lower than in the shops. *Pottery Village,* 4009 Taylor, carries Mexican pottery and glassware and Franciscan dinnerware at discount prices.

There aren't many bargains to be found at **Seaport Village,** but it is a scenic spot at the end of the San Diego Harbor downtown. The village is a reproduction of an early California fishing town and wharf, with seafood restaurants perched on the waterfront and specialty shops carrying kites, clown supplies, T-shirts, fine art, books, toys, and music boxes. A good place to find unusual souvenirs.

DINING OUT. The dining-out scene in San Diego is less sophisticated than in other cities of comparable size, and dress codes tend to be casual except in the most exclusive spots. Theme and chain restaurants proliferate; for unusual dining experiences it is best to stick to the small neighborhood spots. Ethnic restaurants (other than Mexican) are finally beginning to appear but still tend to Americanize their cooking. San Diego is not a late-night city, and many places close by 9 or 10 P.M.

Restaurant categories, based on the price of a meal for one, without beverage, tip, or tax (6 percent), are as follows: *Reasonable,* \$10 to \$15; *Very Economical,*

$5 to $10; *Low Budget,* under $5. Many restaurants accept credit cards, but the cheaper takeouts do not. Every effort has been made to ensure that this list is up to date, but restaurants come and go quickly, so it is always advisable to call ahead.

Reasonable

Bully's. Two locations: 5755 La Jolla Blvd., La Jolla (459–2768); and Bully's East, 2401 Camino del Rio S., Mission Valley (291–2665). Possibly the best hamburgers in town, steaks, seafood, prime ribs, and hearty drinks. The singles scene hits its peak here, with many local sports stars hanging out with their fans. Dinner served until midnight.

Calliope's. 3958 Fifth Ave., Hillcrest (291–5588). Pretty Greek café with unusual dishes prepared by Greek cooks. Wine bar and deli and extensive wine list.

Doc Master's. 2051 Shelter Island Dr. (223–2572). Singing waiters, live entertainment, and a terrific view of the marina accompany fresh fish and Maine lobster dinners.

Fat City and China Camp. 2137 Pacific Coast Hwy. (232–0686 and 232–1367). The first is a European café decorated in pink neon, serving good fish, pasta, and salads; the second is supposed to resemble a California gold-mining settlement and serves fair Chinese specialties. The large bar is a popular Happy Hour spot.

French Gourmet. 713 Pearl St., La Jolla (454–6736). The pastries are incomparable, and the main dishes are pretty good and lower priced than at most French restaurants. Late dining on weekends.

Harbor House. Seaport Village, 831 W. Harbor Dr. (232–1141). A nice view of the downtown harbor and great fish specialities. Oyster bar and live music.

Very Economical

Albie's 'n' Adam's. 1201 Hotel Circle S., Mission Valley (291–1103). Specializes in grilled steaks and chicken for lunch and dinner. Adam's, open until noon, serves one of the best breakfasts in town, including excellent corn fritters, steak and eggs, and Mexican huevos rancheros.

Alfonso's. 1251 Prospect St., La Jolla (454–2232). The wonderful margaritas are served by the pitcher or half pitcher, and the free chips, hot salsa, and marinated carrots and peppers are delicious. The sidewalk café is one of the few along La Jolla's main drag, where the elite stroll by on their way to the beach. Alfonso's menu features Mexican recipes that are family secrets well worth discovering.

Casa de Pico and Casa de Bandini. Bazaar del Mundo, Old Town (296–3267 or 297–8211). Great margaritas and good Americanized Mexican dishes in lovely surroundings with lush tropical plants, colorful surroundings, and mariachi music. For inexpensive dining, order from the à la carte menu.

City Deli. 535 University Ave., Hillcrest (295–2747). The closest San Diego comes to a real New York deli, with lox, whitefish, and other hard-to-find deli dishes. Campy Art Deco decor; late night dining.

Diego's Cafe y Cantina. 860 Garnet Ave., Pacific Beach (272–1241). This is the hottest of the hot spots, constantly packed with beachgoers and singles eying each other at the restaurant before going upstairs to the dance floor. The food is decent and plentiful; the outdoor patio is especially nice on warm summer evenings.

Firehouse Beach Cafe. 722 Grand Ave., Pacific Beach (272–1999). Oceanfront café with upstairs outdoor deck is particularly popular for breakfast omelets and homemade rolls but serves lunch and dinner as well right on the boardwalk.

Golden Lion Tavern. 801 Fourth Ave., downtown (233–1131). This restored early 1900s tavern with a spectacular 50-foot bar and gorgeous stained glass dome attracts the downtown lunch and after-work drinking crowd. The food is okay but not great; best to stick with the burgers and salads. Oyster bar open for late munchies.

Hamburguesa. Bazaar Del Mundo, Old Town (295–3413). With 22 burger variations, this spot is popular with the kids but not the place to try real Mexican food. The outdoor café is particularly popular.

Old Town Mexican Cafe. 2489 San Diego Ave. (297–4330). Wonderful Mexican food including carnitas, fresh tortillas, and shredded beef tacos. Outdoor patio and gigantic dining room; long wait during peak hours, but the margaritas are great and the food is worth the wait.

Point Loma Sea Foods. 2805 Emerson St., Pt. Loma (223–1109). No credit cards. A large fish market with take-out sandwiches, fish dinners, and seafood salads. The sourdough bread is the best in town, and the tuna and crab sandwiches are delicious. Open until dusk.

San Diego Museum of Art Sculpture Garden Cafe. Prado area, Balboa Park (232–7931). Pastries, croissant sandwiches, salads, and soups served in this delightful outdoor café. Beer and wine available; open for lunch and dinner, later on nights when major events are happening in the park's museums and theaters.

Low Budget

Aztec. 2811 San Diego Ave., Old Town (295–2965). Authentic Sonoran-style Mexican food, including sopapillas and huge tostados. Quick service, large dining rooms slightly off the beaten track, so the wait might not be as long as at other Old Town favorites.

Cornucopia. 112 W. Washington St. (299–4174). A homey storefront restaurant serving vegetarian food with a Mexican twist. Giant omelets and fresh-baked healthy desserts.

El Indio. 3695 India St. (299–0333). Some of the best take-out Mexican food in the city, with fresh tortillas and chips and enormous burritos and quesadillas. There are a few tables in an outdoor patio across the street; many people get their food and then stop in the market next door for a beer.

Greektown. 431 E St., downtown (232–0461). One of the best Greek menus in town, with gyros sandwiches and giant Greek salads the best bargains.

Kung Food. 2949 Fifth Ave. (298–7302). Vegetarian restaurants specializing in tofu dishes and great healthy salads.

Sportsmen's Sea Foods. 1617 Quivira Rd., Mission Bay (224–3551). No credit cards. Informal self-serve café on the shores of Mission Bay, with outdoor and indoor tables. Fresh seafood specialties including inexpensive fish and chips and cioppino.

Recommended Splurge. Cafe Pacifica, 2414 San Diego Ave. (291–6666), in Old Town, and **Pacifica Grill,** 1202 Kettner Blvd. (696–9226), downtown. Fresh fish grilled over mesquite wood and Cajun specialties are presented at these two innovative restaurants.

Cafés and Coffeehouses. For a relaxing break between sightseeing trips, nothing beats a cup of fresh-brewed coffee and stimulating conversation. **Pannikin of La Jolla,** 7467 Girard Ave., La Jolla, has a delightful front-porch patio popular with armchair philosophers and idle gossipers. The Pannikin also has coffeehouses in Encinitas and Del Mar and stores in downtown and Point Loma, where a fresh pot of coffee is always ready for the customers. **La Jolla Spice Company,** 7556 Fay Ave., La Jolla, carries coffees, teas, and gourmet sweets from around the world and serves fresh-baked muffins and full breakfasts to enjoy at their indoor and outdoor tables. **Quel Fromage,** 523 University Ave., Hillcrest, is a favorite with the after-theater crowd and neighborhood residents who catch up on the local news in the gallerylike setting with refreshments from the espresso bar.

Upstart, Crow & Company, 835 W. Harbor Dr., Seaport Village, combines a fine bookstore with coffeehouses serving light meals, decadent desserts, and coffee drinks. **D.G. Wills Books & Coffeehouse,** 7527 La Jolla Blvd., La Jolla, is a tiny espresso bar in a lovely bookstore where poetry readings and performances by local actors are a frequent occurrence.

NIGHTLIFE AND BARS. Since San Diego's major attractions are the sun and sea, the town appears to shut down at night. But the city is gaining a cosmopolitan flair, and more bars and clubs are opening. Downtown, the nightlife is still struggling to emerge; for now, most of the action takes place in the hotels. La Jolla probably has the largest selection of high-class clubs, and discos and dance spots abound in Hotel Circle. The beach areas have everything from dive bars to members-only clubs, and the dress codes are usually casual.

You must be 21 or older to buy or drink alcoholic beverages in California, and this law is strictly enforced. Bars stop serving and attempt to close at 2 A.M.; coffee is usually served at closing time. The police are clamping down on drunk driving and on occasion set up roadblocks in areas where the most popular bars are located to catch drivers who have been drinking.

The *margarita* is probably the most popular drink in San Diego. Unfortunately, the drink has undergone the same Americanization as Mexican food and typically consists of a glass filled with crushed ice and a taste of tequila. If you want the real thing, order it on the rocks. Tropical drinks topped with cherries and pineapple are available, but the locals tend to stick with beer or white wine.

Happy hours. Since San Diegans tend to turn in early, happy hours are popular with the after-work crowd. From 4 until 7 P.M. parking lots at local watering holes are packed, particularly if free munchies are offered. Bars tend to use happy hours as promotional events, offering two-for-one drink specials, and may change their special prices and free food once they've gained a good following. The *Reader* has a full section on entertainment events and is the best place to check for up-to-date information.

Many of the most popular happy hour spots are in Hotel Circle and Mission Valley. **La Hacienda,** 875 Hotel Circle S., has free chips and salsa and fresh seafood at low, low prices. **El Torito,** 445 Camino del Rio S., gets packed with singles chowing down on free Mexican appetizers.

Near the water, you can watch the sunset at **Humphrey's,** 2241 Shelter Island Dr., which has a rotating Happy Hour menu and special margarita prices. **The Boat House,** 2040 Harbor Island Dr., has a good view of the harbor and a relaxed atmosphere with special drink prices. Seaport Village, **Papagayo,** 861 W. Harbor Dr., and **Harbor House,** 831 W. Harbor Dr., both have free hors d'oeuvres.

In Old Town, **Casa Vallarta,** 2467 Juan, serves mini tacos, burritos, and tostadas and reduced-price margaritas. Many other bars have Happy Hour specials; if you're there in the early evening, be sure to ask.

Jazz

Chuck's Steak House. 1250 Prospect St., La Jolla (454–5325). This small club is nearly always packed with jazz fans who come to hear outstanding local and visiting jazz artists. No cover charge.

Old Pacific Beach Cafe. 4287 Mission Blvd. Huge bar and beer drinker's hall of fame with live jazz on weekend nights. Late-night dining.

Pop and Rock

Anthony's Harborside. 1355 N. Harbor Dr. (232–6358). Large lounge with dance floor, view of the harbor, and contemporary live music. Happy Hour with low-cost drinks and good munchies. No cover charge.

Jose Murphy's. 4302 Mission Blvd., Pacific Beach (270–3220). A rowdy singles spot with live rock. Cover charge.

Mandolin Wind. 308 University Ave., Hillcrest. The house band, the King Biscuit Blues Band, has been rocking this bar for years, appearing Thurs.–Sat. Jazz, rock, and blues bands play on the other nights. Cover charge.

Reflections. Sheraton Harbor Island Hotel, 1380 Harbor Island Dr. (291–2900). Contemporary bands and a nice harbor view.

Country Music

Abilene. Town & Country Hotel, 500 Hotel Circle N., Mission Valley (291–7131). Good dance floor and live music. Country dance lessons on weeknights.

Top 40 Dancing

Club Diego's. 860 Garnet Ave., Pacific Beach (272–5171). This popular nightclub features top 40 and new-wave video dancing and seems to always be packed with young singles. Cover charge.

Confetti. 5373 Mission Center Rd., Mission Valley (291–8635). Wild, noisy, and popular, with long lines on weekends. Cover charge.

Rio's. 4258 W. Point Loma Blvd. (225–9559). Premier singles spot with live rock 'n' roll.

Comedy

The Comedy Store South. 916 Pearl St., La Jolla (454–9176). Live comedy shows with well-known performers, amateur nights, and audience participation.

The Improv. 832 Garnet Ave., Pacific Beach (483–4520). Sister club to the original Improv in New York, this club offers performances by popular comedians, amateur nights, and comical dinner menu.

Hotel and Piano Bars

Hilton Hotel Cargo Bar. 1775 E. Mission Bay Dr. (276–4010). Great bay view from the large lounge, where live groups play contemporary and mellow music. No cover charge.

Humphrey's. 2241 Shelter Island Dr. (224–3577). Contemporary hits and golden oldies in the piano bar nightly; live jazz in the restaurant on Sun.

Kelly's Steak House. 248 Hotel Circle (296–2131). Golden oldies piano bar with steady crowd of regulars.

Westgate Hotel. 1055 Second Ave., downtown (238–1818). Elegant, classy hotel with one of the most popular piano bars in town—the Plaza Bar.

SECURITY. Despite its size, San Diego is relatively safe, particularly in the tourist areas. Downtown has its rough sections south of Market Street and along lower Broadway. The Gaslamp Quarter area is in a transitional stage from being one of the scruffier sections of downtown to becoming a central tourist area and is patrolled by private police, called Clancy Cops. The canyons of Balboa Park are not safe at night, but the central El Prado area is usually fairly busy when evening shows are scheduled at the museums and theaters. Use the same precautions you would in any large city. Carry most of your money in traveler's checks, with the numbers recorded in a separate place. Lock all valuables in your hotel's safe and always lock your car, particularly in the beach areas.

SAN FRANCISCO

by
Robert Taylor

Robert Taylor, a San Francisco resident for more than 20 years, is the film and theater critic for the Oakland Tribune.

President Taft, honoring San Francisco's rebuilding after the 1906 earthquake and fire, called it "the city that knows how." Columnist Herb Caen, surveying its diversity, described it as "Baghdad by the Bay." Writer George Sterling called it "the cool, grey city of love." Shocked conservatives claim it is "the kook capital of the world." Observant San Franciscans would conclude that all these notions are true—and might describe a day's activity in a single neighborhood. Beautiful views of the hills and San Francisco Bay make it America's most photogenic city, and the sights can be breathtaking even to long-time residents. But San Francisco's diversity within compact borders, sense of history, and legendary tolerance are what make it the city that knows how to live. The variety of its attractions have inspired indelible sights and sounds in popular culture: Jeanette MacDonald singing in a Barbary Coast saloon and triumphantly surviving the earthquake with her co-stars in the movie *San Francisco.* Director Alfred Hitchcock exploring the city's mysteries and awesome heights in *Vertigo.* Tony Bennett crooning about little cable cars climbing halfway to the stars in the song that became the city's ballad, "I Left My Heart in San Francisco." Steve McQueen climbing into his car for a chase that became a terrifying classic in the movie *Bullitt.* Clint Eastwood uncovering jagged edges of contemporary life as the stoic police detective Dirty Harry.

San Francisco's diversity was established when it was founded by the Spanish army and the Catholic church in 1776. The Spanish, Chinese, and

Russians were involved in early maritime trade, followed by whalers of all nationalities, Italian fishermen, and Scandinavians shipping lumber from the Northern California coast. It was the California Gold Rush, beginning in 1848, that set the precedent for the city's future images of financial promise, ethnic and cultural diversity, and vigorous pursuit of pleasure. (Gambling dens were among the first permanent buildings among the miners' and shopkeepers' tents.) By 1854, city maps indicated Chinatown as well as a "Sydney Town" of Australians at the base of Telegraph Hill, and "Little Chile" to identify Chilean miners who had sailed to California. San Francisco's population is now slightly more than 700,000; one out of every three persons comes from a home where a language other than English is spoken. The Chinese, Hispanic and black populations are about 80,000 each. There are sizable groups of Filipinos, Vietnamese, Japanese, Laotians, and Samoans, along with Europeans. Other groups that cross ethnic lines have made their mark in San Francisco: the artists and writers dubbed "beatniks" in the 1950s and 1960s, the hippie counterculture movement of the Haight-Ashbury in the 1960s and 1970s, and the gay community that began to flourish in the 1970s.

San Francisco is a compact 46.6 square miles at the tip of a 32-mile-long, hilly peninsula between San Francisco Bay and the Pacific Ocean. It is only 7.5 miles wide at the widest point, but it was not until the 1940s that housing filled all the residential blocks from downtown westward to the ocean. Many neighborhood centers were established over a century ago. Union Square has been the city's downtown hub for at least that long, and it was quickly rebuilt after the 1906 earthquake and fire, which swept as far west as Van Ness Avenue. Because the city's past has been fragile, and because its location has set it slightly apart from the rest of California, San Franciscans have been fiercely protective of their history. They have preserved it not only for themselves, but to display proudly to international visitors. Of the 48,000 Victorian houses built in the city, 14,000 remain, and no project is as heartfelt as restoration of a dilapidated nineteenth-century home to its former glory.

If there is a "San Francisco style," it is the retaining of a human scale amidst the urban development of the late twentieth century. The office towers of the Golden Gateway Center in the financial district are across the street from Jackson Square, the only group of commercial buildings to survive as the 1906 fire swept the area. The charming, small-scale brick buildings have been restored for offices and designers' shops. The pyramid-shaped Transamerica Building is adjoined by a grove of young redwood trees in a mini-park setting. The Bank of America headquarters building, the largest structure on the city's skyline, is fronted by a plaza with a flower stand and a polished stone sculpture that has been dubbed "banker's heart." One of the city's most-photographed sites is a row of Victorian homes on Steiner Street at Alamo Square, with the high-rise towers of the downtown office district rising behind their peaked roofs.

Many of the city's most popular attractions for visitors cost nothing to visit, and offer tributes to San Francisco's colorful history, its visionaries, romantics, and eccentrics. Golden Gate Park is now 1,017 acres of lush greenery, but when the city proposed development in the 1860s, one newspaper described it as "a dreary waste of shifting sandhills where a blade of grass cannot be raised without four posts to keep it from blowing away." It was the ingenuity of park superintendant John McLaren that tamed the sand dunes. Another "folly" that found success was the cable car system invented by Andrew S. Hallidie, who was at the controls when the first car made its maiden run on Nob Hill in 1873. Several generations of San Franciscans have protected the system from abandonment, and a $60 million overhauling of the system was completed in 1984. They are still the most pleasant way to climb Nob Hill. The Palace of Fine Arts near the approach to the Golden Gate Bridge is the last remaining "palace" from the 1915 Panama-Pacific International Exposition. The picturesque colonnade, made of lath and plaster, was crumbling to dust by the 1960s, when a generous civic benefactor helped pay for the $8-million restoration.

Another landmark is Coit Tower on Telegraph Hill, a legacy from Lillie Hitchcock Coit, an honorary member of the volunteer fire brigade when fire fighting equipment was pulled by teams of horses. Not far away, the Italian settlement of North Beach is still dotted with delicatessens and cafes serving espresso, and farther downtown, Chinatown has not been abandoned by the Chinese despite the waves of visitors. Along the bay's waterfront, Ghirardelli Square was the first to refurbish historic factory buildings for a retail shopping center, followed by The Cannery (once a fruit-packing plant) nearby. The newer Pier 39 development was built with wood siding from demolished Embarcadero warehouses.

San Francisco's accessible landmarks, preserved and restored historical sites, ethnic enclaves, and revitalized neighborhoods provide a wealth of attractions for budget-minded visitors. It is possible, of course, to spend $2,000 a night on a hotel suite and $75 for dinner, but the lifestyle of the wealthy is far removed from most San Franciscans. They are far more likely to spend an afternoon in Golden Gate Park, have dinner in an inexpensive Chinese or Italian (or Vietnamese or Basque) restaurant, sip an espresso in a neighborhood café, buy a serving of house-made ice cream in a paper cup, and finish the evening in a cabaret far from Nob Hill.

One way to take advantage of the city's diversity and lower prices is to explore the neighborhoods on the extensive San Francisco Municipal Railroad bus lines. Even faster are the Muni Metro trains which run underground on Market Street downtown, then fan out on routes into residential areas. The N-Judah line reaches the Haight-Ashbury and the edge of Golden Gate Park; the L-Taraval goes as far as the San Francisco Zoo at the Pacific Ocean; the J- Church line serves the area near Mission Dolores and Noe Valley, with its mixtures of shops and restaurants along 24th Street that reflects the city's heritage as well as its thriving, youthful neighborhoods.

PRACTICAL INFORMATION

WHEN TO GO. A day's weather cycle in San Francisco can be unpredictable, but in the long run the climate is mild and temperate. Daytime temperatures in the summer usually range from the mid-sixties to 70 degrees Fahrenheit. In the winter, daytime temperatures are usually in the mid-fifties, nighttime lows in the mid-forties. It is rare for temperatures to drop below 40 degrees, and when they reach 80, front-page newspaper headlines proclaim a heat wave. San Franciscans consider the ideal seasons the weeks in May and June, between spring rains and the summer fog, and the "Indian summer" that can extend from Sept. into Nov.

The fog, so picturesque on postcards, can be a shock to unsuspecting summer visitors. It rolls in from the Pacific Ocean when California's hot interior valleys create a convection current, and it lingers from late afternoon through the night, usually burning off by mid-morning. When sight-seeing, pack or carry a sweater or jacket, no matter how bright and sunny the day may appear.

HOW TO GET THERE. Maps don't always suggest the great driving distances along the West Coast. It takes 8–9 hours, for instance, to drive between Los Angeles and San Francisco. Long-distance travel from the East Coast or Midwest is cheaper by plane, but there can be bargain fares on trains and buses within the western states.

By air. San Francisco International Airport, located 15 miles south of the city on San Francisco Bay, logs more than 1,000 flights a day and is served by 34 major

Points of Interest

1) Alcoa Building
2) Balclutha
3) Bank of America
4) Cannery
5) City Hall
6) Civic Center
7) Coit Tower
8) Curran Theater
9) Embarcadero Center
10) Ferry Building
11) Fisherman's Wharf
12) Flood Building
13) Geary Theater
14) George R. Moscone Convention Center
15) Golden Gateway Center
16) Grace Cathedral
17) Hilton Hotel
18) Hyatt Regency Hotel
19) Hyde Street Pier
20) Lotta's Fountain
21) Maritime Museum
22) Municipal Pier
23) Museum of Modern Art
24) Old U.S. Mint
25) Opera House
26) Pier 39
27) St. Mary's Cathedral
28) St. Patrick's Church
29) Stock Exchange
30) Transamerica Pyramid
31) Victorian Park/Aquatic Park
32) Visitor Information Center

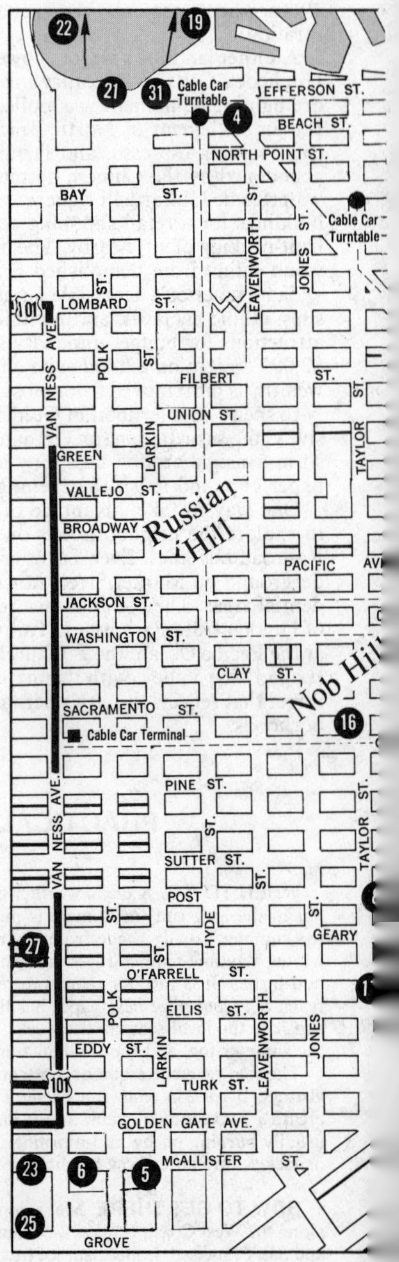

Downtown San Francisco
SAN FRANCISCO BAY
N
W
E
S
BAY ST.
FRANCISCO ST.
CHESTNUT ST.
LOMBARD ST.
GREENWICH ST.
STOCKTON ST.
North Beach
Telegraph Hill
Washington Square
UNION ST.
GREEN ST.
VALLEJO ST.
BROADWAY
POWELL ST.
COLUMBUS AVE.
KEARNY ST.
SANSOME ST.
BATTERY ST.
THE EMBARCADERO
FRONT
DAVIS ST.
JACKSON ST.
Jackson Square
Cable Car Barn
Chinatown
CLAY ST.
SACRAMENTO ST.
DRUMM
CALIFORNIA ST.
Cable Car Terminal
MASON ST.
GRANT AVE.
BUSH ST.
MONTGOMERY ST.
MAIN ST.
FREMONT ST.
BEALE ST.
1ST ST.
Standard Oil Plaza
Union Square
NEW MONTGOMERY ST.
2ND ST.
HOWARD ST.
EMBARCADERO FREEWAY
MARKET ST.
3RD ST.
Cable Car Turntable
MISSION ST.
4TH ST.
5TH ST.
FOLSOM ST.
HARRISON ST.
480
80
SAN FRANCISCO-OAKLAND BAY BRIDGE
1
2
3
7
9
10
11
12
13
14
15
18
20
24
26
28
29
30
32

airlines. *Continental Airlines* has promoted the lowest discount fares, but other lines have matched prices from major U.S. cities to San Francisco and Oakland International Airport, 10 miles east of San Francisco International on the opposite side of San Francisco Bay.

By bus. While airlines and passenger trains have cut back service to smaller towns across the U.S., the network of bus routes remains. The two major lines that reach San Francisco are Greyhound and Trailways. The *Greyhound* terminal is at 50 7th Street between Market and Mission streets. *Trailways* buses pull into the Transbay terminal at First and Mission. The two lines serve virtually the same cities for the same fares, but exact routes vary.

By car. San Francisco is a compact 47 square miles at the northern tip of the San Francisco Peninsula, with only a few major routes into the city. The most famous, of course, is the Golden Gate Bridge, which carries traffic from U.S. 101 from the north. The major route from the east is I-80 across the San Francisco–Oakland Bay Bridge. Both bridges are toll crossings heading into the city. Major routes from the south are U.S. 101 and I-280, which cuts off from 101 in San Jose and follows a more scenic course northward along the peninsula. Because of a celebrated revolt in the 1960s against further destruction of residential neighborhoods and parks, freeway construction was curtailed. Major routes abruptly funnel traffic onto intersections downtown and along the northern waterfront near Fisherman's Wharf.

By train. *Amtrak's California Zephyr* serves San Francisco daily from Chicago, via Denver and Salt Lake City. Accommodations include an economy bedroom for two and a family bedroom for two adults and three children. The *Coast Starlight* links San Francisco daily with Portland and Seattle to the north and Los Angeles and San Diego to the south. Major rail service terminates in Oakland at the 16th and Wood Street station. Shuttle buses transport passengers to the Transbay Terminal at First and Mission streets in San Francisco, where the Amtrak ticket office is located. Fare and schedule information is available toll free by telephoning 800-USA-RAIL.

TELEPHONES. The area code for San Francisco as well as for Marin County, Oakland, Berkeley, and the San Francisco Peninsula as far south as Palo Alto is 415. It is not necessary to dial the area code on calls to other numbers within the area. For operator assistance on person-to-person, collect, and credit-card calls, dial 0 first, then the number. Pay phones cost 20 cents for the first three minutes. Many hotels add service charges to outgoing calls from guests' rooms; calling from a lobby pay phone can be less expensive. The number for directory assistance is 411. From outside the area, dial toll free 415–555–1212.

Emergency Telephone Numbers. In San Francisco and some other nearby communities, the emergency number for fire, police, ambulance, and paramedics is 911. This can also alert the Coast Guard for search and rescue emergencies. The emergency number can be dialed from most pay phones without depositing coins. To report emergencies to the California Highway Patrol from all localities, dial 0 and ask operator for Zenith 1–2000. The number for the San Francisco Bay Area Poison Control Center is 666–2845. The Care-Line for urgent medical information is 333–3333. San Francisco Police Department, routine nonemergency business, 553–0123. For cars that have been towed from city streets, 553–1235.

ACCOMMODATIONS. The boom in construction of high-rise, high-priced hotels has been matched by a thriving industry remodeling older hotels for plush but moderately priced accommodations. Rooms comparable to the ones on Nob Hill, just a few blocks away, can cost 1/3–1/2 less. The rooms, and the hotels, may be smaller, but the staff is professional and often more friendly. There are also many new bed-and-breakfast inns, but most are in the expensive and deluxe price categories. Summer is the peak season for tourism, but because of convention business and the city's year-round appeal, few hotels have seasonal rates.

Hotel rates are based on double occupancy. Most of the hotels listed have comparable accommodations and a range of prices. Categories, determined by the price of a double room, are: *Reasonable,* \$60 to \$75; and *Very Economical,* \$45 to \$60. In addition, there is a 9.75 percent transient occupant tax.

Reasonable

Abigail. 246 Mc Allister St., San Francisco, CA 94102 (415–861–9728, 800–243–6510 nationwide). A cozy British-owned hotel near the Civic Center, two blocks from the Museum of Modern Art and Opera House. Free Continental breakfast.

Carlton. 1075 Sutter St., San Francisco, CA 94109 (415–673–0242, 800–227–4496 nationwide, 800–792–0958 in California). A large, recently upgraded hotel a few blocks from the Union Square congestion. Wine bar in the lobby.

Cartwright. 524 Sutter, San Francisco, CA 94102 (415–421–2865, 800–227–3844 nationwide, 800–652–1858 in California). Redecorated, comfortable hotel amid art galleries a block from Union Square.

Grosvenor Inn. 1050 Van Ness Ave., San Francisco, CA 94109 (415–673–4711, 800–227–3154 nationwide, 800–345–0111 in California). This big, busy hotel north of the Civic Center has been redecorated in a turn-of-the-century style. Complimentary newspaper and Continental breakfast. Free parking upon availability.

Savoy. 580 Geary, San Francisco, CA 94102 (415–441–2700, 800–227–4223 nationwide, 800–622–0553 in California). Charming and comfortable, with antique reproductions and fresh flowers in rooms. Near theaters and Union Square.

Very Economical

Amsterdam. 749 Taylor St., San Francisco, CA 94108 (415–673–3277 or 441–9014). A remarkably inexpensive discovery on the slope of Nob Hill. European ambience. There are less expensive rooms sharing baths.

Beresford. 635 Sutter St., San Francisco, CA 94102 (415–673–9900, 800–227–4048 nationwide, 800–652–1244 in California). Small, European-style hotel known for friendly service, three blocks from Union Square.

Beresford Arms. 701 Post St., San Francisco, CA 94109 (415–673–2600, 800–227–4048 nationwide; 800–652–1414 in California). A sister hotel to the Beresford, this features an elegant lobby and large rooms. Modestly priced suites have kitchens or wet bars.

Beverly Plaza. 342 Grant Ave., San Francisco, CA 94108 (781–3566, 800–227–3818 nationwide, 800–652–1535 in California). Directly opposite the Chinatown Gate, this is a pleasantly redecorated discovery, favored by Japanese tour groups.

Mark Twain. 345 Taylor, San Francisco, CA 94102 (415–673–2332, 800–227–4074 nationwide, 800–622–0873 in California). Friendly staff, redecorated rooms and one of the city's best values, a half block from the downtown airline terminal.

Olympic. 140 Mason, San Francisco, CA 94102 (415–982–5010). Basic accommodations, but neat, clean, and rock-bottom rates as low as $30. Next door to the posh new Ramada Renaissance.

Willows Inn. 710 14th St., San Francisco, CA 94114 (415–431–4770). A charming, comfortable oasis in a busy neighborhood at Market and Church St. Willow furniture, Laura Ashley fabrics, and Continental breakfast. Across the street from the Muni Metro Church Street underground station.

Budget Motel Chains. Motels in San Francisco are often on busy, noisy streets, but budget chains such as **Best Western** (800–528–1234) and **Friendship Inns** (800–453–4511) offer nationwide toll-free reservations. The following very economical to reasonable motels are recommended for their locations:

Beck's. 2222 Market St., San Francisco, CA 94114 (415–621–8212, 800–227–4368 nationwide, 800–622–0797 in California). Near Muni Metro Church Street station.

Capri. 2015 Greenwich St., San Francisco, CA 94123 (415–346–4667). A block from busy Lombard.

Laurel. 445 Presidio Ave., San Francisco, CA 94115 (415–567–8467, 800–552–8735). Near Sacramento Street.

Nob Hill. 1630 Pacific, San Francisco, CA 94109 (415–775–8160, 800–343–6900 in California). Between Van Ness and Polk.

Vagabond Inn. 2250 Van Ness Ave., San Francisco, CA 94109 (415–776–7500, 800–552–1555 nationwide). At Filbert St.

Bed-and-Breakfast. Most of the city's bed-and-breakfast inns are in higher price categories. Note, however, the Willows Inn, above, and smaller hotels that serve complimentary Continental breakfasts. **Bed & Breakfast International,** 151 Ardmore Road, Kensington, CA 94707 (415–525–4569 or 527–8836), is the major agency for accommodations in private homes, at rates in the Very Economical range. Credit cards accepted for deposit only.

Ys and Hostels. The Embarcadero YMCA, 166 Embarcadero at Mission St. (415–392–2191, 800–622–9622) has a variety of rates for rooms with shared baths, with doubles at about $35. **The Central YMCA,** 220 Golden Gate Ave. near the Civic Center (415–885–0460) has plain but pleasant doubles at about $30 without bath. Both YMCAs offer rooms to men, women, and couples. Rates include use of pools and other health facilities. The **YWCA Hotel,** 620 Sutter Street near Union Square (415–775–6500) has 32 rooms, some sharing baths, at inexpensive rates, for women only.

San Francisco International Hostel is in Building 240 on the landscaped heights of Fort Mason Center, Bay and Franklin streets (415–771–7277). It offers the city's least expensive accommodations, in dormitories and a few family rooms.

HOW TO GET AROUND. From the airport. Cab fare from *San Francisco International Airport* to the downtown area is about $25, plus tip. There are many less expensive alternatives, departing from the street level of the connecting North, Central, and South terminals. *Airporter* buses (673–2433) offer the most frequent service, from 6:15 A.M. to 3:30 A.M., between the airport and the downtown terminal at the corner of Taylor and Ellis streets, three blocks from Union Square. Direct service is also provided to major downtown hotels. One-way fare is $6; children 5–11, $3; under 5, free. *San Mateo County Transit* buses (SamTrans) are the least expensive transportation into San Francisco, picking up passengers on the airport's upper (departure) level at the North and South terminals only. From the city **to the airport,** the choices include Airporter and SamTrans buses, and door-to-door vans from the Supershuttle (558–8500), *Yellow Cab* (861–7291), and *Luxor* (552–4166). Fare is $6 to $7. Call for reservations a day before departure.

Oakland International Airport, where the discount fare airline *America West* and many charter flights arrive, is served by *BART* (see below) and a shuttle bus link. "Air-BART" buses run between the terminal's main entrance and BART's Coliseum station.

San Francisco Municipal Railway. "The Muni" was considered an experiment in socialism when it began operation in 1912 as the nation's first publicly-owned transit system. Today it is a network of 80 routes with more than 1,000 vehicles serving 900,000 weekday passengers. It boasts that more than 95 percent of the city's addresses are within two blocks of a Muni stop. Diesel and electric trolley buses serve most of the routes on city streets. The Muni Metro system was added in 1980, high-speed trains that operate underground along Market Street downtown, and on the streets in the outer neighborhoods.

The basic fare is 75 cents for adults 18–64, 15 cents for persons 65 and older, 25 cents for youngsters 5–17, free for children under 5. Exact change is necessary; drivers carry no change. Transfers good for 90 minutes are issued free when fare is paid. Single-day passes for unlimited travel on the Muni system are $5, available only from self-service fare machines. The machines are located at all cable car terminals (Market and Powell streets, Beach and Hyde, Bay and Taylor, Market and California, Van Ness and California,) and also along the lines at California and Powell, and California and Grant Avenue. The Muni has a helpful information line, and will give details for getting from any point in the city to any other. The telephone number is 673–MUNI. Basic transit maps are available at the Visitor Information Center, Powell and Market streets.

Cable cars. San Francisco's rolling landmark first clattered into service in 1873, not as picturesque entertainment for visitors but for the simple purpose of hauling passengers up the steep east slope of Nob Hill. While only three lines remain, they have survived repeated attempts to replace them with more modern transportation. When "modernization" came in 1982–84, it was a $60 million project to replace cables, tracks, turntables, and gears, making the cars as safe as possible while restoring their quaint nineteenth-century appearance.

Two lines begin at Powell and Market streets. The Powell-Hyde line, the most spectacular ride, climbs over Nob Hill and Russian Hill to its turntable in Victorian Park on the Northern Waterfront. The Powell-Mason line also climbs Nob Hill, then runs to Fisherman's Wharf. The third line, which is less crowded and seldom has a waiting line, runs along California Street from the intersection of Market and Drumm streets to Van Ness Avenue. The cable car lines run from 6 A.M.–1 A.M. Adult fare, $1.50; children 5–17, 75 cents.

BART. The Bay Area Rapid Transit regional system links eight San Francisco stations with Daly City to the south and 25 stations in the East Bay. It's the fastest of the Bay Area's rapid transit systems, with trains reaching speeds up to 80 miles per hour in the tunnel beneath the bay. Underground stations in downtown San Francisco are at the Embarcadero, Montgomery Street, Powell Street and the Civic Center. Minimum adult fare is 80 cents, increasing with the distance traveled; the fare from downtown San Francisco to Berkeley is $1.80. Children 4 and under ride free. For a regular $2.60 fare, passengers can explore the entire 71-mile BART system, as long as they return to the point of entry and do not exit the computerized gates at any other station. BART trains run from 6 A.M.–midnight Mon.–Sat., 9 A.M.–midnight Sun. Information: 788–BART. For significant discounts for senior citizens, call 464–7133.

Golden Gate Transit. This bus service links San Francisco to Marin and Sonoma Counties, including the communities of Sausalito, Tiburon, Stinson Beach, Inverness, and Santa Rosa. Buses depart from the Transbay Terminal, First and Mission streets, and follow routes through the financial district and Civic Center, then cross the Golden Gate Bridge. Information: 332–6600.

Ferries. *Golden Gate Transit* ferries depart from the south end of the Ferry Building at the foot of Market Street for Sausalito and Larkspur in Marin County. The fare for the 30-minute crossing to Sausalito is $3.50. High-speed service for the 15-minute commute to Larkspur is $2.20 for adults on weekdays, $3 weekends and holidays. Persons 65 and older or handicapped persons, half price any time; children 6–12, 25 percent discount; under 5, free. Information: 332–6600.

Red and White Fleet. Ferries depart from Pier 41 at Fisherman's Wharf for Sausalito daily, and from the Ferry Building weekdays only during commute hours. Fares to Sausalito are $3.50 for adults, $1.75 for children 5–11. All fares to Tiburon, $3.50. Ferries to Marine World Africa USA in Vallejo depart from Pier 41. Fare is $19–$29 including park admission. Ferries depart from Pier 43 ½ for Angel Island State Park. Information, 546–2896. Red and White ferries also transport visitors to Alcatraz; information, 546–2805.

Taxis. Rates are high, approximately $3 for the first mile, $1.50 for each additional mile, but most trips within the city are only a few miles. Cabs are difficult to hail downtown, easier to find waiting outside major hotels. Major companies: *Yellow* (626–2345), *De Soto* (673–1414), *Luxor* (282–4141), and *Veterans* (552–1300).

By rental car. All the major car rental agencies and about two dozen others serve San Francisco International Airport. Most have offices downtown near Union Square and in major hotels. Agencies include *Hertz, Avis, Budget, National, Thrifty, Ajax, Dollar,* and such rock-bottom outfits as *Rent-a-Heap-Cheap* and *Rent-a-Wreck.* Reservations are usually necessary, and the major agencies have nationwide, toll-free 800 telephone numbers. Lowest daily rates seem to be at downtown offices on weekends, when demand by business travelers is low. Since a car really isn't necessary within the city, weekend rental is a good idea for jaunts to Muir Woods in Marin County, the wineries around Napa and Sonoma, or the Monterey Peninsula and Carmel.

HINTS TO THE MOTORIST. Driving in San Francisco is complicated by 40 hills, the density of the downtown financial and retail districts, and commuters whose cars clog the relatively limited access routes from the north, east, and south. On weekdays and Saturdays, it is wise to avoid the areas around Union Square and Chinatown; Saturdays and Sundays bring additional traffic to the Northern Waterfront attractions such as Ghirardelli Square, the Cannery and Fisherman's Wharf.

In spite of the high-speed movie chase images in *Bullitt* and *Dirty Harry,* driving in San Francisco is not a reckless sport. It does require some confidence, and good brakes. A car with an automatic transmission is preferable, since dealing with clutch, brake, and gearshift when stopped in traffic at the crest of a hill can be nerve-wracking, even for native San Franciscans. Parking requires as much care as driving in the city. Always curb your wheels—turn the tires toward the street when facing uphill, and toward the curb when facing downhill, to use the curb as a block. San Francisco conforms to most California state driving regulations, which set a maximum highway speed of 55 miles per hour. The usual limit in residential and commercial districts is 25, unless otherwise posted. Right turns are permitted after stopping at a red light, unless prohibited by another posted sign.

Painted curbs indicate these **parking** restrictions: red for no stopping or parking, yellow loading zone for vehicles with commercial license plates only, green for 10-min. parking, white for 5-min. parking during the adjacent business's hours of operation. Blue-painted zones are for handicapped parking, but only with a license or placard issued by the state Motor Vehicles Department (557–1191). Other curbside parking restrictions: parking lanes must be cleared for traffic on many major streets during rush hours, in residential neighborhoods for street sweeping once a week, and there are time restrictions in some neighborhoods to discourage parking by commuters from the suburbs. Tow-away regulations, especially downtown during morning and evening rush hours, are relentlessly enforced.

TOURIST INFORMATION. The *San Francisco Convention & Visitors Bureau* publishes a colorful variety of free guides and maps of "everybody's favorite city." They may be requested, along with the comprehensive quarterly *San Francisco Book,* in advance from the bureau at 201 Third St., San Francisco, CA 94105. The bureau's primary *Visitor Information Center* is on the lower level of Hallidie Plaza at Market and Powell streets. It is open weekdays from 9 A.M.–5:30 P.M., Sat. 9 A.M.–3 P.M., and Sun. 10 A.M.–2 P.M. Closed Thanksgiving, Christmas, and New Year's Day. A multi-lingual staff is available to answer questions. The telephone number is 974–6900. A recorded message lists daily events and activities at 391–2001.

The *Redwood Empire Association* is the source for information about exploring the California coast from San Francisco north to the Oregon border, including the wine country, the old Russian trading post of Fort Ross, and the rustic mecca of Mendocino. The office is at One Market Plaza, Spear Street Tower, Suite 1001, San Francisco, CA 94105. Open Mon.–Fri., 9 A.M.–5 P.M. Telephone 543–8334.

Updated listings of arts and entertainment events and other activities can be found in the "Datebook" section of the Sunday San Francisco *Examiner and Chronicle.* The weekly, independent *Bay Guardian* offers a guide to more offbeat events, as well as budget-priced shopping and dining. *San Francisco Focus* magazine, available at newsstands, lists a full month's best bets.

Foreign Currency Exchanges. *Bank of America,* Central Terminal, San Francisco Airport, 7 A.M.–11 P.M. daily; *International Banking office,* 345 Montgomery St., 9 A.M.–3 P.M. Mon.–Fri. (622–2451). and Powell at Market streets, 10 A.M.–3 P.M. Mon.–Thurs., 10 A.M.–5 P.M. Fri. (662–4498). *Citicorp* office, Central Terminal, second floor, San Francisco Airport. *Foreign Exchange Ltd.,* 415 Stockton St. at Union Square, 8:30 A.M.–5 P.M. Mon.–Fri., and 9 A.M.–1:30 P.M. Sat. (397–4700). *Macy's,* Geary Street at Union Square, fourth floor cashier's office, 9:30 A.M.–8 P.M. Mon.–Fri., 9:30 A.M.–6:30 P.M. Sat., and noon–5 P.M. Sun. (397–3333).

SENIOR-CITIZEN AND STUDENT DISCOUNTS. Transportation, musical and theatrical events, and museums frequently offer discounts to senior citizens, less often to students. Discounts to young people are usually based on age rather than school attendance. Identification showing age may be required. San Francisco's Muni transit fare is 25 cents for youngsters 5–17, 15 cents for persons 65 and older. BART offers a $12 train ticket to persons 65 and older for $1.20; for sale locations, telephone 464–7133. Golden Gate ferries to Sausalito and Larkspur are half-price for persons 65 and older. The American Conservatory Theatre, 415 Geary Street, sells tickets to students for half-price, and persons 62 and older can buy any available matinee tickets for $5. All the major museums offer discount admission on certain days; see Museum listings.

HINTS TO DISABLED TRAVELERS. Community activists in San Francisco and nearby Berkeley have pushed the area into the forefront in making public facilities and transportation accessible to the disabled. In 1982, San Francisco created a Mayor's Council on Disabilities Concerns, which with the help of volunteers published a *Guide to San Francisco for the Person Who Is Disabled.* It lists stores and shopping centers, civic buildings, health facilities, parks, museums and transportation. It is available free by writing the council at the San Francisco Council of Churches, 942 Market Street, Room 408, San Francisco, CA 94102. The office is near the intersection of Fifth Street and the Civic Center BART and Muni Metro stations (433–4890). The city's hills and old buildings can create difficulties for the disabled, but all major civic buildings, museums, and theaters are wheelchair-accessible.

The entire BART system is accessible, with elevators at every station as well as accessible rest rooms. The high-speed Muni Metro trains are accessible at these stations: Embarcadero, Montgomery, Powell, Civic Center, Van Ness, Church, Castro, Forest Hill and West Portal. There are ramps for access to the Muni Metro L-Taraval line at the zoo, the M-Ocean View line at San Francisco State University, the end of the N-Judah line at Ocean Beach. In addition, nearly 300 new buses provide access on other major routes. They have ramps that extend from entrance doors for passengers in wheelchairs, and fronts of the buses can "kneel" to a position eight inches from the ground for passengers who have difficulty with steps.

FREE EVENTS. San Francisco's mild weather and diverse population stimulate a variety of ethnic and neighborhood celebrations, street fairs and parades year-round. Check with the Convention and Visitors Bureau (974–6900) for specific dates of seasonal events. The year begins with the city's most famous celebration, **Chinese New Year,** with more than a week of festivities climaxing with the **Golden Dragon Parade** in late February or early March, depending on the lunar calendar. Japantown is transformed in April for **Cherry Blossom Festival,** two weekends of demonstrations of everything from martial arts to origami, culminating in a colorful parade. An "only in San Francisco" event is the **Fair and Exposition** at Moscone Center in late summer or early fall, with such events as regional gourmet food bake-offs and foghorn-calling contests.

Free musical events include classical, jazz, and pop concerts and dance performances Sundays at 2 P.M. from mid-June to mid-August in **Stern Grove** amphitheater, Sloat Blvd. at 19th Ave. Free band concerts are held in the **Golden Gate Park concourse** between the de Young Museum and Academy of Sciences, Sundays at 2 P.M. during fair weather.

Points of interest that are free at all times: the **Golden Gate Bridge,** free for pedestrians; **Fort Point,** the 1861 fortification in the Presidio near the Golden Gate Bridge anchorage; the **Cable Car Barn and Museum,** Clay and Washington streets; **Mission Dolores,** 16th St. at Dolores (donation suggested); **Kong Chow Temple** in Chinatown, 855 Stockton St. See "Museums" below for a number of other free attractions; major museums are free certain days of the week.

TOURS AND SPECIAL-INTEREST SIGHTSEEING. Bay cruises. *Blue and Gold Fleet* offers daily 1 ¼-hour narrated cruises which take passengers beneath the Golden Gate Bridge and Bay Bridge, and past Alcatraz and Angel Island State Park. They leave frequently, beginning at 10 A.M. from Pier 39's west marina, near the intersection of The Embarcadero and Powell Street. Fare is $10 for adults, $5 for youngsters 5–18 and seniors. Children under 5 ride free with an adult. Three-hour dinner cruise with live music is scheduled at 7:30 P.M. Fridays and Saturdays, spring through fall. Validated parking in the Pier 39 garage. Information: 781–7877. *Red and White Fleet* offers 45-minute narrated cruises, departing daily at 10 A.M. from Pier 43 ½ near Fisherman's Wharf. Adults, $8–$10; children, $5–$7. Information: 546–2810. Red and White ferries also serve Angel Island, a 740-acre state park and wildlife refuge, April–Oct. Information: 546–2815.

Alcatraz ferries depart every 45 minutes from 8:45 A.M. to 2:45 P.M. from Pier 41 near Fisherman's Wharf. The two-hour round-trip journey includes a tour by National Park Service guides of the abandoned maximum-security prison, once the home of Al Capone, "Machine Gun" Kelly and Robert Stroud, the "Birdman of Alcatraz." Dress warmly and wear comfortable walking or hiking shoes. Tickets are available on a daily basis beginning at 8:30 A.M. Information: 546–2805. During the summer, the boat trip can be sold out two weeks in advance. Reservations can be made through Ticketron outlets or by writing Ticketron, Box 26430, San Francisco, CA 94126. The price is $5 for adults, $3.50 for children 5–11.

Walking tours. There is no better way to see the city, and no better bargain than the free tours conducted by volunteers from the **Friends of the San Francisco Public Library.** Tours last about 1 ½ hours. No reservations are needed; just appear at the starting point and look for the person wearing the "City Guide" badge. *City Hall tour,* Thurs., noon, leaves from San Francisco Room, third floor, Main Library, Larkin at McAllister streets. *Coit Tower,* Sat., 11 A.M., from door of tower atop Telegraph Hill. *Fire Department Museum,* Fri.–Sun., 1–4 P.M., 655 Presidio Ave. at Pine. *Gold Rush City,* Portsmouth Square and Jackson Square, Wed. at noon and Sun. at 2 P.M., from Clay and Montgomery sts. *Historic Market Street,* Tuesday at noon, from One Market Plaza, Southern Pacific Building. *North Beach,* Sat. at 10 A.M. from the steps of Sts. Peter and Paul Church, 666 Filbert Street. *Pacific Heights Victorian architecture,* Sat. at 2 P.M., Sun. at 2 P.M., Bush and Octavia sts. *Cathedral Hill-Japantown,* Sat. at 2 P.M. from the St. Mary's church plaza, Geary and Gough sts. Additional free neighborhood walks are held in May and Oct.; phone 558–3981 for updated information.

The **Foundation for San Francisco's Architectural Heritage** (441–3004) offers a 2-hour Pacific Heights walk, Sundays at 12:30 P.M. from the historic Haas-Lilienthal House, 2007 Franklin Street. No reservations, $3. Tours of the house, a grand survivor of the 1906 earthquake and fire, are held Wed. noon–4 P.M., Sun. 11 A.M.–4:30 P.M. No reservations; adults $3, seniors and children $1. The Foundation also sponsors 1 ½-hour tours of the Northern Waterfront, including historic wharves, restored ships, and Ft. Mason. Saturdays at 10:30 A.M. from Hyde and Beach sts. Fee is $3.

Dashiell Hammett tours, following the "real-life" setting of the novelist's *Maltese Falcon,* begin Sat. at noon on the steps of the Main Library, Larkin and McAllister streets. The fee is $5; phone 564–7021 for information. Hammett buff Don Herron leads this as well as other literary tours through the city.

The Chinese Culture Foundation, 750 Kearny St., third floor of Holiday Inn (986–1822) offers **Chinatown heritage walks,** Sat. at 2 P.M. Adults $9, children under 12, $2; and culinary walks with a dim sum lunch, $18. Reservations are necessary.

From Jan. to Apr., thousands of gray whales migrate south along the Pacific Coast to Baja California. **Whale-watching** boat trips and flights are sponsored by the Oceanic Society, San Francisco (441–1106); and the Whale Center, Oakland (654–6621).

PARKS AND GARDENS. Golden Gate Park. From Stanyan Street in the Haight-Ashbury neighborhood west to the Pacific Ocean, and from Fulton Street on the north to Lincoln way on the south. The attractions include 11 lakes, a buffalo paddock, the Victorian glass palace of the Conservatory of Flowers, a children's playground with a 1912 carousel, the Japanese Tea Garden, two windmills, and the de Young Museum, Asian Art Museum and California Academy of Sciences. The Tea Garden, built for an 1894 international fair, is open daily, 8:30 A.M.–5:30 P.M. Admission $1, children 6–12, 50 cents. The Conservatory is open 9 A.M.–5 P.M. (9–6 during daylight saving time), admission for adults $1, children 6–12, 50 cents. Maps are posted at major park entrances, and are available at headquarters in McLaren Lodge, Kennedy Drive near Stanyan Street. The portion of Kennedy Drive in the busiest area of the park is closed to auto traffic on Sunday. Free walking tours are offered weekends; information, 221–1311.

Golden Gate National Recreation Area. Established in 1972, this is the largest urban park in the world, covering 72,815 acres and 28 miles of California coastline. In San Francisco, it includes the Cliff House, ruins of Sutro Baths, China and Baker beaches, the 1861 Fort Point beneath the Golden Gate Bridge, and the Maritime Museum on the Northern Waterfront. Park headquarters is inside Fort Mason, entrance at Franklin and Bay streets. It is open weekdays 7:30 A.M.–5 P.M. Information: 556–0560.

ZOOS. Founded in 1889 with the gift of a single grizzly bear, the **San Francisco Zoo** (661–4844) now houses more than 1,000 animals, among them more than 130 designated as endangered species. Main entrance is on Sloat Boulevard near the Great Highway, overlooking Ocean Beach. The zoo's latest achievement is a $6 million Primate Discovery Center, the first of its kind in the world, the size of a football field and five stories high. It houses 16 endangered or threatened species, from the tree shrew to the black and white colobus, in a series of atrium-like habitats. Another recent addition is "Gorilla World," which offers eight separate viewing areas. The zoo is open daily from 10 A.M.–to 5 P.M. Admission, $3.50 for adults and children without an adult; children 15 and under with an adult, free; seniors, $1. Children's Zoo, 11 A.M.–4 P.M. daily, admission $1.

Marine World Africa USA, in Vallejo 30 miles northeast of San Francisco on I-80 (707–644–4000), features more than 1,000 animals including performing sea lions and killer whales. Admission is $10–$15. There is ferry service to the park from Fisherman's Wharf; 546–2815.

PARTICIPANT SPORTS. Jogging. Contrary to San Francisco's popular image, the city does offer flat areas for running. The busiest as well as the most scenic are Kennedy Drive through Golden Gate Park; the Marina Green, along Marina Boulevard near the Golden Gate Bridge approach; the Embarcadero; and Lake Merced in the southwest corner of the city. *City Sports* magazine, available free at most sporting goods stores, carries the most complete calendar of running events.

Two marked, scenic **bike routes** wind through the city. One tours Golden Gate Park to Lake Merced, the other stretches from the south end of the city north across the Golden Gate Bridge to Marin County. Caltrans, a state agency, offers Bay Area bike maps at 150 Oak Street, San Francisco, CA 94102 (923–4444). Bikes are available for rent on Stanyan Street facing Golden Gate Park.

Fitness centers have sprung up in all the city's neighborhoods, but the YMCA and YWCA may be most easily available to visitors, at day rates of only a few dollars. The **YMCA** at 166 the Embarcadero (392–2191) has Nautilus and aerobics centers, free weights, racquetball courts, and a pool. The **YMCA** at 220 Golden Gate Avenue (885–0460) has similar facilities and an indoor track. Both are also open to women. The **YWCA** main center is at 620 Sutter Street (775–6500). **Kabuki Hot Springs** in the Japan Center, 1750 Geary Boulevard (922–6000) is a notable spa, with shiatsu massage.

Sailing on San Francisco Bay offers spectacular views of the city, but tricky currents and unpredictable weather can make it hazardous for inexperienced navigators. Available rentals are listed under "Boats-Charter" in the San Francisco yellow pages. Fishing can be as simple as casting a line from the Municipal Pier at the foot of Van Ness Avenue, the adjacent Aquatic Park, Fisherman's Wharf or Lake Merced, or as involved as charter sportsfishing for salmon and bass. Many boats depart daily from Fisherman's Wharf. They are listed under "Fishing Parties" in the yellow pages.

Horseback riding within the city begins with rentals from Golden Gate Park Stables, Kennedy Dr. at 36th Ave. (668–7360). There are miles of trails through the park.

The Recreation and Parks Department maintains more than 100 **tennis** courts throughout the city. All are free and available on a first-come, first-served basis, with the exception of 21 courts in Golden Gate Park, which charge a small fee. Tennis information: 558–4054. Golden Gate Park reservations: 478–9500. Racquetball is available at the YMCA branches, 220 Golden Gate Ave. (885–0460) and 166 the Embarcadero (392–2191).

Swimming is recommended in the bay at Aquatic Park on the Northern Waterfront, in the ocean at China Beach near Seacliff Avenue and El Camino del Mar. Swimming from other ocean beaches can be dangerous. The YMCA and YWCA pools are open to visitors with daily memberships. The city maintains nine other pools, with locations convenient to visitors at Geary Boulevard and Steiner Street, Lombard and Mason streets, Arguello and Mason streets. Information, 558–3643.

The city maintains five municipal **golf courses:** *Lincoln Park,* with vistas of the Golden Gate, 18 holes, Clement St. at 34th Ave. (221–9911); *Harding Park,* 18 holes, Harding Rd. off Skyline Blvd. (664–4690); *Golden Gate Park,* 9 holes, 47th Ave. and Kennedy Dr. (751–8987); *Fleming Golf Course,* 9 holes, Harding Rd. off Skyline Blvd. (661–1865); *Sharp Park,* 18 holes, in the suburb of Pacifica (355–2862). Check with each course regarding nonresident fees and rental equipment.

SPECTATOR SPORTS. Candlestick Park at the southeastern edge of the city, and the Oakland Coliseum and Arena across the bay are the major sites for professional events. The San Francisco Giants **baseball** team plays at Candlestick in the spring, and has a ticket office downtown at 170 Grant Avenue (467–8000). The 49ers **football** games at Candlestick have been sold out before the season begins; call 468–2249 for information or check the classified ads in the San Francisco newspapers for tickets to individual games. The Oakland A's **baseball** team (638–0500) plays at the Coliseum in the spring, the Golden State Warriors **basketball** team (638–6000) in the Coliseum Arena Oct.–April. Ticketron and BASS agencies handle ticket orders by telephone. Depending on the season, there is **horse racing** at either Golden Gate Fields in Albany, north of Oakland (526–3020), or Bay Meadows in San Mateo (574–7223). The Grand National Rodeo, Horse Show and Livestock Expo is held in Oct. or Nov. at the Cow Palace (469–6065).

CHILDREN'S ACTIVITIES. Nothing in the city—or elsewhere—matches the fascination of the **Exploratorium,** a "hands-on" science museum in the Palace of Fine Arts near the approach to the Golden Gate Bridge, at Marina Blvd. and Baker St. (563–7337). Founded in 1969 by physicist Frank Oppenheimer, it is a center for adults and children to touch, hear, see, and explore in the fields of science, art, and technology. There are 500 exhibits, including a distorted room with no right angles, a momentum machine, and a tactile cavelike dome. Located in the north end of the building at Bay and Lyon streets. Hours, Wed., 1–9:30 P.M.; Thurs., Fri., 1–5 P.M.; Sat. and Sun., 10 A.M.–5 P.M. Admission free for everyone under 18; $4 for adults, $2 seniors.

The Josephine D. Randall Junior Museum. 199 Museum Way near Roosevelt Way (863–1399). Includes a petting corral, mineral and dinosaur exhibits, and Saturday morning nature walks. For other attractions, see the Zoo section, Parks, and Museum listings for the National Maritime Museum with six historic ships, the Wells Fargo History Room, and the Cable Car Museum, Power House and Car Barn.

Shopping and browsing excursions beyond the usual toy stores: *Robinson's* pet store, 135 Maiden Lane near Union Square; the *Nature Company,* with an array of science projects, Ghirardelli Square, Four Embarcadero Center (Sacramento and Drumm streets), and in the California Academy of Sciences, Golden Gate Park; *Star Magic,* full of space-age books, puzzles and star charts, 4026–A 24th Street near Noe Street; *Banana Republic,* which might be a Tarzan movie set, 224 Grant Avenue. Another downtown attraction is the Transamerica Pyramid building. There is an express elevator to the 27th floor observation deck; open 9 A.M.–4 P.M. Mon.–Fri. (free).

HISTORIC SITES AND HOUSES. Mission Dolores. 1321 Dolores St. near 16th St. (621–8203). The city's most venerable building is the sixth of 21 missions established by the Franciscans. Moorish, Mission, and Corinthian styles are combined in the church, founded in 1776 in the sunniest and most sheltered area of the northern peninsula. Open daily 9 A.M.–4:30 P.M. May 1–Oct. 31, and until 4 P.M. the rest of the year; closed Thanksgiving and Christmas.

The Presidio. In the same year Mission Dolores was founded, Col. Juan Bautista de Anza chose this site for the Spanish military fortification to protect the bay. It is now headquarters for the U.S. Sixth Army, and the 1,500 acres of wooded hills, cliffs and beaches are open to the public. Fort Point at the base of the Golden Gate Bridge was built 1853–1861. It is accessible from Long Avenue, open daily 10 A.M.–5 P.M., and there are guided tours and a museum (556–1693). The early commandant's house, circa 1782, has been remodeled into the Officer's Club, at Moraga and Graham streets.

Portsmouth Square, Kearny between Clay and Washington streets, was the city's first plaza, where Capt. John Montgomery and his troops from the USS *Portsmouth* raised the American flag and claimed San Francisco for the United States on July 9, 1846. What he "claimed" amounted to about 50 adobe and frame buildings and about 200 people, with another 100 living at Mission Dolores.

Chinatown was established in the area around Grant Avenue (then Dupont Street) in the 1850s. Quickly rebuilt after the 1906 earthquake and fire, it now extends from the gateway spanning Grant at Bush Street to Broadway. Sing Lee Co. at 560 Grant is one of the few shops not remodeled. Waverly Place, paralleling Grant from Sacramento to Washington, retains Chinatown's historic appearance.

Kong Chow Temple, 855 Stockton Street, is the oldest Chinese family association in America. It is open, daily 11 A.M.–4 P.M. Free.

Jackson Square, originally the infamous Barbary Coast, is the only group of commercial buildings to survive the earthquake and fire. Later renamed the "International Settlement of rowdy night clubs," the brick buildings bounded by Pacific, Sansome, Washington streets, and Columbus Avenue have been restored for offices and decorator showrooms.

Telegraph Hill was once crowned by a semaphore signaling the approach of ships through the Golden Gate. It has been marked since 1933 by Coit Tower (362–8037), bequeathed by Lillian Hitchcock Coit to honor volunteer firemen. Located at the end of Lombard Street it is open daily 10 A.M.–5 P.M. except Jan. 1, Thanksgiving and Christmas. Admission is $1.50, children 50 cents, seniors $1. Another Telegraph landmark: the charming Filbert Street steps that pass wooded gardens and Victorian cottages from Montgomery Street to the eastern base of the hill.

The Embarcadero. Although shadowed by a freeway, the 1896 Ferry Building at the foot of Market Street retains a scale suggesting the 50 million passengers it served in peak years before the Golden Gate and Bay Bridges were built. Murals from the 1939 World's Fair on Treasure Island are now installed in the building's World Trade Center. Nearby, at Mission Street and the Embarcadero, is the 1889 Audiffred Building, meticulously restored to its nostalgic French style.

The Palace of Fine Arts, Marina Blvd. at Baker St., is the last remaining structure from the 1915 Panama-Pacific International Exposition. Designed by Bernard Maybeck, the crescent-shaped building houses the Exploratorium and a theater; the Greco-Romanesque rotunda with Corinthian colonnades was recast in concrete in 1962. Swans and ducks swim in the lagoon of the pleasant neighborhood park.

The Cliff House, at the end of Point Lobos Ave., is the fifth structure to occupy the bluff overlooking the Pacific and Seal Rocks since 1863. The building houses restaurants, a Musée Mechanique arcade, a history-oriented gift shop. Ruins of the Sutro Baths, once three acres of indoor fresh and salt water swimming pools, are nearby.

The Haas-Lilienthal House, 2007 Franklin St. at Washington (441–3004). Built in 1886, it is the only fully furnished Victorian mansion open to the public. Open noon–4 P.M. Wed., 11 A.M.–4:30 P.M. Sun.; admission $3 for adults, $1 for students under 18 and seniors. Includes tour. A map of other Victorian homes in the city is available at the Visitor Information Center, Powell and Market streets.

MUSEUMS AND GALLERIES. The Asian Art Museum adjoins the de Young Museum in Golden Gate Park (668–8921). It was established in the 1960s with the collection of Avery Brundage, and it is the only museum in the country devoted entirely to Asian art. It contains nearly 10,000 objects representing China, Japan, India, Southeast Asia, Nepal, Tibet, Korea, and Iran. Only 10 percent of the objects can be displayed at one time. They range from tiny netsuke and ivory carvings to massive sculpture and dramatic samurai armor. Open 10 A.M.–5 P.M. Wed.–Sun. Joint admission with de Young Museum (see listing below), adults, $4; seniors, $2; children, free; first Wed. of the month and Sat. 10 A.M.–noon, free.

The California Academy of Sciences is San Francisco's natural history museum and aquarium in Golden Gate Park (221–5100). It includes Morrison Planetarium, a hands-on exhibit of tidepool life, a fish roundabout viewed from the center, and a "Safe-Quake" vibrating platform (with hand rails) that simulates an earthquake. Open daily, 10 A.M.–5 P.M.; July 4–Labor Day until 7 P.M. Admission $3; youths 12–17 and seniors, $1.50; children 6–11, 75 cents; first Wed., free. Morrison Planetarium offers one-hour sky shows throughout the day; admission is $2 for adults, $1 for seniors and ages 17 and under. There is an extensive Nature Company store at the museum and a cafeteria. The science-oriented Exploratorium is listed under Children's Activities.

The California Palace of the Legion of Honor (221–4811), on a spectacular hilltop in Lincoln Park (entrance at 35th Ave. and Clement St.), was designed to resemble the Palace of the Legion of Honor in Paris, and dedicated to the memory of California servicemen who died in World War I. Its collection is primarily French—notable for Rodin sculptures, an opulent Louis XVI period room from Paris, and paintings by Fragonard, Corot, Manet, Monet, Degas, and Seurat. The Achenbach Foundation for Graphic Arts contains more than 100,000 items. Open

Wed.–Sun., 10 A.M.–5 P.M. Admission $4; seniors, $2; children, free; free to all first Wed. and Sat. 10 A.M.–noon. There is a modest bookshop and an indoor-outdoor cafe.

The M. H. de Young Memorial Museum, on the Music Concourse in Golden Gate Park (221–4811). Is the city's most popular, with masterpieces by Rubens, El Greco, Titian, Goya, and Rembrandt, and an expanded American collection including Eakins, Sargent, Homer, and Bierstadt. Period rooms are the settings for much of the collection. Major touring exhibitions are frequently housed at the de Young. Open 10 A.M.–5 P.M. Wed.–Sun. Admission, $4; seniors, $2; children, free; first Wed. of the month and Sat. until noon, free. One admission charge admits visitors to the de Young, Asian Art, and Legion of Honor museums on the same day. There is an extensive bookshop and a cafe.

The Oakland Museum. 1000 Oak St. near Lake Merritt BART station (273–3401). Offers an introduction to the Bay Area that none of the San Francisco museums can match; it is "the museum of California." The Ecology Hall simulates a walk across the state's environmental zones; the Art Gallery documents the state's visual heritage; and the Hall of California History contains artifacts from the Indian era, through the Gold Rush and earthquake, and on to the "California dream" of the 1950s, 1960s and 1970s. Open 10 A.M.–5 P.M. Wed.–Sat.; noon–7 P.M. Sun. Free admission.

The San Francisco Museum of Modern Art, founded in 1935, occupies two floors of the Veterans Building in Civic Center at Van Ness at McAllister streets (863–8800). It displays a permanent collection including Matisse, Dali, Rivera, Orozco, Albers, Stella, and Diebenkorn. It is also well known for originating touring exhibitions, and it recently added a department of architecture and design. Open Tues., Wed. and Fri., 10 A.M.–5 P.M.; Thurs. until 9 P.M.; Sat. and Sun., 11 A.M.–5 P.M. Admission $3.50; under 16 and seniors, $1.50; free Tues. The convenient, street-level bookshop stocks 5,000 titles, and the excellent cafe can be patronized without paying museum admission.

Historical Museums: *The Cable Car Museum.* Powerhouse and Car Barn displays the system's workings at Washington and Mason streets (474–1887). Open daily 10 A.M.–5 P.M., free admission. *National Maritime Museum,* Aquatic Park at the foot of Polk Street (556–8177). Includes a sidewheel ferry boat and other ships afloat at the Hyde Street Pier; daily except Christmas, 10 A.M.–5 P.M., free. *Old Mint,* Fifth and Mission streets (974–0788). A restored 1874 building with gold nuggets and bars; Mon.–Fri. 10 A.M.–4 P.M., free. *Wells Fargo History Room,* 420 Montgomery St. (396–2619). A stage coach and other artifacts are on display; Mon.–Fri. 9 A.M.–5 P.M., free.

Art Galleries are clustered around Union Square, usually above street level, on Grant, Post, Sutter, and California streets, with more contemporary galleries in the area south of Market Street. Other groups of galleries are on Hayes Street just west of the Performing Arts Center, and along the shopping areas of Union and Sacramento streets. The free *Gallery Guide* and *Artweek* magazine, available at most galleries, lists current schedules. Most galleries are open Tues.–Sat. 10 or 11 A.M.–5 or 6 P.M.

FILMS. In addition to major international films, popular attractions at local theaters include political documentaries, experimental works, and revivals of Hollywood classics. The **San Francisco International Film Festival** (221–9055) runs for two weeks in April at the Palace of Fine Arts Theater, Bay and Lyon streets, and at a second theater, offering a number of free screenings. First-run theaters are scattered throughout the city, with new ones opening recently on Van Ness Avenue, convenient to Muni buses. All are listed in the daily newspapers. Busy revival houses, with modest prices, are the *Strand,* Market between 7th and 8th streets (552–5990); *Red Victorian,* 1659 Haight St. (863–3994); and the grandly restored *Castro* at Castro and Market streets (621–6120). Avant-garde alternatives, with lower prices: *Cinematheque* at the San Francisco Art Institute, 800 Chestnut St. (558–8129); *Video Free America,* 442 Shotwell St. (648–9040).

MUSIC. San Francisco began touting itself as a cultural capital not long after the Gold Rush, and it now supports a wide range of musical groups giving dozens of performances each week. Although composers living in the area produce contemporary works, "new" music on concert and operatic programs tends to be rediscovered works of the past. Tickets to many events are available at the STBS box office on the Stockton Street side of Union Square; Downtown Center box office, 325 Mason St.; and Ticketron in Emporium-Capwell, Market and Powell sts.

San Francisco Symphony, Davies Hall, Civic Center (431–5400), performs Sept.–May under conductor Herbert Blomstedt, with guest soloists. The symphony also sponsors visiting soloists and orchestras, a Mozart series in February, Beethoven festival in June-July, and modestly priced pops concerts in July and August in Civic Auditorium. Low-priced tickets to Davies Hall are sold just before concerts, for seating at the sides of and behind the orchestra.

San Francisco Opera, War Memorial Opera House, Civic Center, is the largest company west of New York, featuring such stars as Pavarotti and Horne during a 13-week season beginning in September, with Wagner's *Ring* performed every fifth summer, next in 1990. Prices range from $10 to over $50 and most performances are sold out, but standing room tickets are always sold (431–1210). Patrons often sell tickets on the Opera House steps just before curtain time. The Opera presents the "Fol de Rol," an informal, wide-ranging vocal concert in Civic Auditorium in November, at budget prices.

The Lamplighters, Presentation Theater, 2350 Turk Blvd. (752–7755) is the nation's oldest Gilbert and Sullivan repertory troupe, with local singers and full orchestra.

Pocket Opera, performing at the Waterfront Theatre in Ghirardelli Square (398–2220), is the sprightly, modestly priced answer to grand opera. Donald Pippin's highly regarded company has 50 operas in its repertory, notably rediscovered operettas by Offenbach. The season runs February through April and July-August, with most performances in English.

There are also free or modestly priced concerts throughout the year at **Grace Cathedral** (Nob Hill), **St. Mary's Cathedral** (Gough and Geary), the **de Young Museum** (Golden Gate Park) and **Palace of the Legion of Honor** (Lincoln Park).

DANCE. San Francisco Ballet, Opera House, Civic Center (621–3838), offers two seasons: an opulent production of *The Nutcracker* in November and December, and a repertory season January through April, with premieres as well as such full-length favorites as *Cinderella, Romeo and Juliet,* and *The Tempest.* Tickets range from $5 to $37.50, with standing room available.

There are innumerable modern and experimental dance groups in the city. The most prestigious are the **Margaret Jenkins Dance Co.,** which works in abstract movement, often with "sound scores" instead of music; **Oberlin Dance Collective,** one of the most purely entertaining troupes; and **San Francisco Moving Co.,** a modern ballet group oriented to storytelling and emotion. All three, and many smaller groups, may be seen at the **New Performance Gallery,** 3153 17th St. (863–9834).

STAGE. Half-price tickets to many local and touring productions are sold at the STBS booth on the Stockton Street side of Union Square. Similar to New York City's TKTS booth, it is open Tuesday through Saturday, noon to 7:30 P.M., and offers tickets at half price (plus a small service charge) for otherwise unsold seats on the day of performance. STBS is also a full-service box office for theater and other events throughout the Bay Area.

The **American Conservatory Theatre** (ACT), 415 Geary St. (672–6440), is the major resident theater, with a November-May season of approximately eight contemporary and classic plays, in rotating repertory. Half-price tickets are available to students with identification cards for any performance; $5 tickets for seniors 62 and over to matinees. The major commercial theaters for touring shows are the **Curran,** 445 Geary St. (673–4400); **Golden Gate,** Golden Gate Ave. at Taylor St. (474–3800); **Orpheum,** 1192 Market St. (474–3800); and the smaller **Marines Memorial Theater,** Sutter at Mason (441–7444); and **Theatre on the Square,** 450 Post St. (433–9500). *Beach Blanket Babylon,* the colorful, zany musical revue unique to San Francisco, performs at **Club Fugazi,** 678 Green (421–4222).

A number of theaters produce new plays and experimental works. Ticket prices are usually modest. Among the most reliable groups: **Magic Theater,** Building D, Fort Mason Center (441–8822); **Eureka Theater,** 2730 16th St. (558–9898); **Theatre Artaud,** 450 Florida St. (621–7797); the **One-Act Theater,** 430 Mason St. (421–6162); and the touring **Mime Troupe** (285–1717).

SHOPPING. Union Square, bounded by Geary, Stockton, Sutter, and Powell streets, has been the city's retail center for nearly a century. It remains the prime source for luxury goods and designer imports. Self-contained retail centers have opened in recent years beyond the downtown core: **Ghirardelli Square,** Northpoint and Larkin St.; **The Cannery,** Beach and Leavenworth Sts.; **Embarcadero Center,** at the foot of Market St.; and **Pier 39** on The Embarcadero at Beach St. All offer specialty shops for fashion, crafts and housewares, bookstores, restaurants, and musicians performing in protected plazas and courtyards. An additional attraction at Pier 39 is *The San Francisco Experience,* an evocative 30-minute film and slide show, presented daily from 10 A.M. to 6:30 P.M. The chic newcomer among the shopping centers is **The Galleria,** Post and Kearny streets, with exclusive designer boutiques, a few less expensive shops, and an international cafe beneath the soaring, arched skylight.

The first stop for downtown shoppers is usually the Emporium or Macy's, the department stores with competitive sales events that seem to be perennial, especially on clothing. The *Emporium*'s landmark building, Market St. between Fourth and Fifth streets (764–2222), is open Mon.–Fri., 9:30 A.M.–8 P.M.; Sat., 9:30 A.M.–6 P.M.; Sun., noon–6 P.M. The store accepts American Express, MasterCard, and Visa. *Macy's,* Stockton at O'Farrell streets (397–3333), has taken over a second building across the street for men's and children's wear and electronics. Both stores are open Mon.–Fri., 9:30 A.M.–9 P.M.; Sat., 9:30 A.M.–6:30 P.M.; Sun., noon–5 P.M. Holders of Visa, Mastercard, and American Express cards can obtain instant credit. Surrounding Union Square are the impressive, but not entirely expensive, *Saks Fifth Avenue* (Powell and Sutter streets), *Neiman-Marcus,* and *I. Magnin* (both Geary and Stockton streets).

Neighborhood shopping provides a wide selection in a more relaxed setting, featuring ethnic specialties, imports, moderately priced cafes and a more accurate sense of San Franciscans' own lifestyles. Major shopping areas include: Japantown around Sutter and Buchanan streets (for crafts, antiques, art books, unusual housewares); Hayes St. between Franklin and Gough (antiques, crafts, art galleries); Fillmore St. between Sutter and Sacramento (clothes, books, gourmet foods); Union St. between Laguna and Steiner (antiques, boutiques, traditional clothing); Sacramento St. between Baker and Spruce (antiques, housewares, clothing boutiques); the revitalized Haight Street between Masonic and Stanyan (imports, vintage clothing and housewares); and the neighborly 24th Street between Church and Diamond (clothes, imports, books, gourmet foods).

In addition to the major downtown stores, these **specialty shops** offer good value, extensive selection, or unusual items:

Women's clothing. *Susan Mathews,* 3505 California St., better contemporary fashions collected by off-price buyers. *Bio,* 432 Castro St., tasteful, casual natural fiber clothing. *Loehmann's,* John Daly Blvd. at Lake Merced Blvd. in Daly City (755–2424), the queen of designer discounters. *The Gap,* at 934 Market St., Columbus and Chestnut St., and Polk and California sts., colorful sportswear. *ACA Joe,* Geary at Powell streets, has youthful and colorful casual wear.

Men's clothing. *Clothing Clearance Center,* 695 Bryant St. at Fifth St., has manufacturers' and retailers' overstock in huge quantities. *Executive Clothes,* 520 Washington St., private label menswear, heavy discounts. *Johnson Leather Mfg. Co.,* 1808 Polk St., leather jackets, vests, pants at substantial savings. Menswear is also at *The Gap, Bio,* and *ACA Joe,* listed above. *Banana Republic,* 224 Grant Ave., and *Eddie Bauer,* 220 Post St., have a wide selection of outdoor wear for both men and women.

Vintage clothing. Major sources for fashion revivals, especially from the 1940s and 1950s: *American Rag Cie.,* the major selection, 1355 Bush St.; *The Way We Wore,* 2238 Fillmore St.; *LaRosa,* 722 Columbus Ave. and 1711 Haight.

Factory outlets. Many are located in the blocks south of Market St. Most carry women's apparel only. Hours and days can be irregular; be sure to telephone in advance. Resources for the serious discount shopper are the book *Bargain Hunting in the Bay Area* by Sally Socolich (published by Wingbow Press, Berkeley) and *Share the Wealth* outlet newsletter, available for $2 and a self addressed, stamped envelope from 3216 Geary Blvd., San Francisco, CA 94118.

The **outlets** include: *Banana Republic,* 135 Bluxome St. (243–0362), trendy outdoor wear. *Coat Factory Outlet,* 1350 Folsom St. (864–5050), coats and furs. *Esprit,* 16th St. at Illinois (821–2000), the most dynamic outlet for colorful, youthful separates. *Gunne Sax Ltd.,* 634 Second St. (495–3326), lacy, feminine dresses and separates from a trend-setting junior designer. *Lili Ann,* 2701 16th St. (863–2720), elegant, sophisticated dresses, suits, and coats. *San Francisco Mercantile Co.,* 2915 Sacramento St. (563–0113), nostalgic dresses and sleepwear from Eileen West and Queen Ann's Lace.

Bargains around town. *Cost Plus,* now consolidated into a huge store at Bay and Taylor streets, is the venerable importer of bargain housewares, clothing, ethnic arts. *Williams-Sonoma,* 576 Sutter St., and *Forrest Jones,* 151 Jackson St., 3274 Sacramento St., are the kitchenware emporiums with excellent selections in the lower price range. Reasonably priced antiques and collectibles are available at *Beaver Bros.,* 1637 Market St.; *Great American Collective,* 1736 Lombard St.; *Grand Central Antiques,* 1676 Market St.; *Luminescence,* an Art Deco specialist, 1415 Green St.; *Naomi's Antiques to Go,* ceramics and kitchenware, 1207 Sutter St.; *The Ritz,* an extensive selection, 1157 Masonic St.

In **North Beach,** don't miss *City Lights* bookstore, a bohemian landmark, 261 Columbus Ave.; *Postermat,* 401 Columbus, with psychedelic rock relics of the original Fillmore ballroom; and *Quantity Postcards,* an astonishing collection of bizarre new and nostalgic old cards, 1441 Grant Ave.

DINING OUT. There are few regional or international cuisines that cannot be found among the city's 4,000 restaurants. Seafood has always been a specialty, influenced by successive French, Italian and Asian cooks. Recent years have seen a burgeoning of regional Chinese, Korean, Vietnamese, Thai and Burmese restaurants and, of course, "California cuisine" with lightly grilled meats, fresh seasonal foods, and innovative combinations of ingredients. Ethnic restaurants offer such inexpensive fare that there is no reason to settle for fast food franchises. The best bakeries provide tables, chairs, and bargain-priced Continental breakfasts. Take-out sandwich shops, especially in the financial district, offer a modest brown-bag lunch for as little as $3.

Good areas for inexpensive dining are: the side streets off Grant Ave. in Chinatown; North Beach; Castro St. between Market and 19th St.; the restaurant mall in the Kintetsu building of Japan Center; Union St. between Laguna and Steiner. The most thriving "restaurant row" is Clement Street between Arguello and 10th Avenue. Recommended on Clement: the Fook and New Ocean, Chinese; Mai's and the Garden House, Vietnamese; Giorgio's Pizza; Firehouse Barbeque; and Anna's California cooking.

Restaurant categories, based on the price of an average three-course dinner for one, without beverage, tax (6½ percent), or tip: *Reasonable,* $12 to $18; *Very Economical,* $8 to $12; and *Low Budget,* $6 to $8. Unless otherwise noted, all accept some, if not all, major credit cards. Abbreviations for meals: B, breakfast or brunch; L, lunch; D, dinner. All neighborhood restaurants listed are easily reached on Muni bus lines. Every effort has been made to ensure that the list is up-to-date, but restaurants come and go so quickly that it is always advisable to call ahead.

Reasonable

Ironwood Cafe. 901 Cole St., Upper Haight-Ashbury (664–0224). Traditional American cooking in a setting that might be the Midwest in the 1920s. Hearty, reliable, fresh food with an emphasis on chicken and fish. Comforting desserts. L, Mon.–Fri.; D, Mon.–Sat. Weekend reservations recommended.

Kuleto's. 221 Powell St. (397–7720). Italian-Tuscan cuisine, with a wide variety of appetizers that could make a meal, and grilled meats and seafood. Casually elegant atmosphere. B, L, D, daily.

Les Joulins. 44 Ellis St. near Union Square (397–5397). A friendly, unpretentious French bistro with authentic cuisine. Fish, shellfish, chicken, steak, pasta. L, Mon.–Fri.; D, Tues.–Sat. A sampling of the menu, plus sandwiches, salads, and pastries are available in adjacent café, B, L, Mon.–Sat.

Vivande. 2125 Fillmore St., Lower Pacific Heights (346–4430). Traditional pasta dishes, innovative salads and colorful tarts and omelets. The combination cold plates delight the eye as well as the palate, and nearly everything is available to take out. L, daily until 4 P.M.; cold dishes available until 6:30 P.M.

Very Economical

Anchor Oyster Bar. 579 Castro St. (431–3990). A tiny neighborhood cafe with a marble-topped counter, a few tables and a surprising variety of fresh seafood. Oysters and clams in the shell; bountiful crab and shrimp Louis; broiled fish and pasta-shellfish dishes. L, Mon.–Sat.; D, daily.

Billboard Cafe. 299 9th St., South of Market (558–9500). A young, trendy, flashy crowd with waiters and waitresses to match. The food is unusually good considering the price: Grilled chicken, fish and beef kabob; burgers and steaks; pasta and salads. Careful ordering can make this a "Low Budget" alternative. L, daily; D (late), Mon.–Sat. No credit cards.

The Deli. 1980 Union St., Cow Hollow (563–7274). Hearty roasts, sandwiches, salads, along with cheese blintzes and potato pancakes, in large portions. Ask to sit in the flower-filled greenhouse. L, D (late) daily.

Green Valley. 510 Green St., North Beach (788–9384). One of the few remaining Italian family-style restaurants with a fixed-price, five-course dinner and neighborhood character. A remarkable selection of entrees, including tender roast chicken and some of the best fried calamari in the city. L, D, Tues.–Sun.

La Mediterranee. 288 Noe St., Upper Market St. area (431–7210); and 2210 Fillmore, Lower Pacific Heights (921–2956). Middle Eastern specialties such as chicken pomegranate, ground lamb patties, with several vegetarian versions. Combination plates provide a sampling. B, Sat.–Sun. L, D, Tues.–Sun., Noe St.; Mon.–Sat., Fillmore St. No credit cards.

Max's Diner. 311 3d St. near Moscone Convention Center (546–6297). A grand version of a 1950s roadside diner, with upgraded hamburgers, milk shakes, pies, and cakes. Breakfast and the entire menu is served all hours. Mid-morning to at least 11 P.M. daily.

Original Joe's. 144 Taylor St., downtown (775–4877). When they say original, they mean it: waiters in tuxedos, a line of cooks behind the counter grilling and sauteing mammoth portions of Italian food. Hearty hamburgers, roasts, pastas; no larger portions in the city. L, D (late) daily.

The Plum. Stockton and O'Farrell sts. in Macy's men's store (984–7463). A popular, lively café with a variety of fresh soups, salads, sandwiches, desserts. L, daily; D (to 8 P.M.), Mon.–Fri.

Schroeder's. 240 Front St., financial district (421–4778). This amiable German restaurant, with dark wood beams and collection of beer steins, has been an institution since 1893. Wide selection of daily specials, from fish and duck through Sauerbrauten, always in sizable portions with a stack of whole-grain bread. L, D, Mon.–Fri.

Low Budget

Brother Juniper's. 1065 Sutter St. near Polk St. (771–8929). Probably the city's least expensive good food, in a pleasant and friendly cafe operated by a religious order; the proceeds support a family shelter. A variety of appealing sandwiches, soups, omelets, in large portions. B, L, D until 7 P.M. Mon.–Fri.; B, L to 3 P.M. Sat. No credit cards.

Mifune. 1737 Post St., second floor of Kintetsu Bldg., Japan Center (922–0337). The Japanese version of fast food: wheat or buckwheat noodles in broth, with egg, seafood, vegetable toppings. Rice and tempura, too; children seem to enjoy this eating adventure. L, D, daily.

Salmagundi. 1236 Market St., Civic Center (431–7337); Two Embarcadero Center (982–5603). The city's classic soup restaurants, with three selections daily, as well as quiche, salad, excellent house-made desserts. L, D, daily at Market St.; Mon.–Sat. at Embarcadero Center.

Tempura House. 529 Powell St., Union Square (392–3269). A familiar variety of tempura, sukyaki, teryaki, with family dinner specials, and a view of cable cars climbing Nob Hill. L, D, daily.

Vicolo. Ghirardelli Square (776–1331) and 201 Ivy St. off Franklin between Hayes and Grove, Civic Center (863–2382). Innovative pizza in "new wave" settings, with the freshest ingredients and careful preparation. There is real flavor to the variety of cheese, herb, vegetable, and sausage toppings, and the salads are crisp and fresh. L, D, daily. No credit cards.

Yuet Lee. 1300 Stockton, Chinatown (982–6020). Impeccable fresh clams, oysters, squid and lobster; ask about the specialties, which may not be on the menu. A late-night favorite; don't be put off by the plastic-looking exterior. L, D (until 3 A.M.), Wed.–Mon.

Recommended Splurge. Zuni Cafe. 1658 Market St., Civic Center (552–2522). A crisp, Southwestern setting and an innovative menu distinguish this restaurant, which specializes in a variety of fresh shellfish, grilled fish, chicken, and meat, and pasta with shellfish and herbs. A variety of salads, and rich house-made pastries and ice cream completes the menu. B, Tues.–Sat.; L, Tues.–Fri.; Sun. brunch; D, Tues.–Sun. The average meal, without beverage, tax, or tip, will cost $16 to $20. Reservations recommended.

Brunches. Sunday, and to a lesser extent, Saturday brunch is a major social gathering in San Francisco. Recommended restaurants are **The Deli** and **La Mediterranee** (see above). Others: **Sears Fine Foods,** 439 Powell St. (986–1160), arrive early for the popular pancakes and fruit; **Doidge's,** 2217 Union St. (921–2149), grandma-style country cooking; **Hilton Hotel,** Henri's Room at the Top, Mason and O'Farrell sts. (771–1400), the best of the "skyroom" brunches; **Pauli's Cafe,** 2500 Washington at Fillmore (921–5159), a busy, friendly, neighborhood favorite.

Cafés. The city's Italian heritage and new bakeries have provided a wealth of cafés for relaxing, sipping a coffee drink, and making conversation. Among the favorites: **Caffe Trieste** (609 Vallejo St.), which roasts its own coffee; **Caffe Roma** (414 Columbus Ave.) with world-class cappuccino; **Caffe Puccini** (411 Columbus) across the street; **Just Desserts** (248 Church St. and 3735 Buchanan in the Marina District), with some of the city's best pies and cakes; **Port Deli** (3499 16th St.), bountiful meals near Mission Dolores; **Spuntino** (524 Van Ness Ave.) near Civic Center.

NIGHTLIFE AND BARS. Visitors are often disappointed to discover nothing happening at night downtown around Union Square. Except for the major hotels and piano bars in the theater district, the area can be deserted. That doesn't mean San Francisco has lost its reputation as a hard-drinking, fun-loving town. The action has simply moved elsewhere. Right after work, bars are packed in the financial district around Montgomery Street, and in Embarcadero Center. Later, crowds shift to these neighborhoods: Union Street between Laguna and Fillmore, and Fillmore between Union and Lombard, the center for singles bars; Castro Street between Market and 19th Street, heart of the gay neighborhood; the Inner Sunset area around 9th Avenue and Judah Street, popular with students from the nearby University of California medical center; North Beach just off tawdry Broadway. For informal entertainment, simply head for these neighborhoods and follow the crowds. The pink "Datebook" section of the Sunday paper runs a comprehensive list of club soloists, concerts and dancing. Minimum age for drinking is 21; drink service ends at 2 A.M. This is a selection of some of the city's notable nightspots.

Music clubs. *Kimball's,* just behind the Opera House at 300 Grove St. (861–5585), is the most reliable jazz club. *Milestones,* 376 5th St., in the developing south of Market St. district (777–9997) is an elegant jazz club. *Last Day Saloon,* 406 Clement St. (387–6343), presents country, blues, rock, and folk acts with some "name" performers. *The Jazz Workshop,* 473 Broadway (398–9700), is one of the few music clubs along this flashy strip. *Plough & Stars,* 116 Clement St. (751–1122), is the local Irish bar with the thickest brogues, and Irish music from local and touring groups. Singing waiters entertain at the glittering *Max's Opera Cafe,* 601 Van Ness Ave. (771–7300).

Music halls and supper clubs. *Great American Music Hall,* 850 O'Farrell St. (885–0750), is a grand old-world setting for jazz, folk, fusion performers, often big-name singers. *The Venetian Room* at the Fairmont Hotel, California and Mason sts. (772–5000) is one of the few glamorous supper clubs remaining in the country, the place to see Tony Bennett, Joel Grey, Ella Fitzgerald, Carmen McRae. Substantial entertainment charge; skip the dinner and see the later cocktail show.

Cabarets. *The Plush Room* in the York Hotel, 940 Sutter St. (885–6800) is the premiere cabaret, with revues or name singers. *The City Cabaret,* 401 Mason St.

at Geary (441–7787) and *Teddy Bear's* (621–6766) 131 Gough St. near the Civic Center (552–8177) are new, reliable alternatives.

Piano bars. All the big-name hotels have rooms in this category, without a cover charge but with expensive drinks. Worth a visit is the warm and elegant old *Redwood Room* in the Clift, Geary at Taylor streets (775–4700). Alternatives are *Bentley's,* in the financial district at 185 Sutter St. (989–6895), and the *Washington Square Bar & Grill,* a crowded, clubby hangout at 1707 Powell St. in North Beach (982–8123).

Comedy. Everyone from Lenny Bruce to Phyllis Diller to Robin Williams developed in San Francisco; *who's next?* The already-popular are usually at the *Punchline,* 444 Battery St. in the financial district (474–3801), or *Cobb's Comedy Club,* 280 Leavenworth St. in The Cannery (928–4320). Up-and-coming comics, and lower prices, at *Holy City Zoo,* 408 Clement St. (386–4242), and the *Other Cafe,* Carl at Cole St. (681–0748), a neighborhood favorite in the Haight-Ashbury.

Basic bars, with some extras. *The Buena Vista,* 2765 Hyde St. on the Northern Waterfront (474–5044), claims to have introduced Irish coffee to America; huge crowds are still testing. *The Carnelian Room,* 555 California St. (433–7500), on the 55th floor of the Bank ofAmerica Building, has the most breathtaking view; it's a dressy place. *Edinburgh Castle,* 950 Geary St. (885–4074) offers beer, ale, liquor, darts, fish and chips, and bagpipe music. *Happy Valley Bar* in the Sheraton Palace Hotel, Market and New Montgomery St. (392–8600) is the home of Maxfield Parrish's huge painting, *The Pied Piper. Penny Farthing Pub,* 679 Sutter St. above Union Square (771–5155), has an authentic British feel. *Specs'* at 12 Adler Place, below Broadway and Columbus (421–4112), is a cozy, unchanged corner of North Beach. *Tosca,* 255 Columbus in North Beach (986–9651) is another nostalgic bar, with espresso as well as alcohol, and a juke box full of opera records.

Singles bars. The financial district is busy just after work, with free hors d'oeuvres in many bars. Among the most popular are *The Holding Company,* Two Embarcadero Center (986–0797); the *Royal Exchange,* 301 Sacramento St. (956–1710); *MacArthur Park,* 607 Front St. (398–5700). One of the original "fern bars" is *Lord Jim's,* 1500 Broadway at Polk (928–3015). *Perry's,* 1944 Union St. (922–9022) is the temple of successful preppies; *Pierce St. Annex,* 3138 Fillmore (567–1400) caters to the neighborhood's more boisterous crowd.

Dancing. All the major hotels provide music for dancing, usually for a mature crowd. The notable rooms: free tea dancing early Friday evening in the atrium lobby of the *Hyatt Regency,* Market at Drumm St. (788–1234); dancing to a jazz combo in the *New Orleans Room* of the Fairmont, California at Mason sts. (722–5259). At the other end of the spectrum, the liveliest young dancers head for the *I-Beam,* 1748 Haight St. (668–6006) for disco, music videos and some live bands; the *Oasis,* 278 11th St. south of Market (621–8119), which also has live bands, and a heated outdoor pool; the *DNA Lounge,* 375 11th St. (626–1409), is an expansive dance club nearby.

SECURITY. San Francisco is a disarming place, and looks safer than it really is. The Union Square area, with its world-famous hotels, is bounded on the west and south by some seamy areas—and the hotels here and elsewhere in the city are magnets for professional thieves. As in most places in the world these days, don't leave money or valuables in your hotel room. Always lock your door, even when you are inside. (This goes for your car too: keep it locked even when you are in it.) Keep valuables in the safe-deposit boxes offered by hotels; they are usually free.

Avoid walking along Market Street outside the downtown area, or in the nearby Tenderloin District or south of Market. Also avoid Polk and Larkin streets in the evening or at night and the Mission District, all of which have a reputation for street crime. Broadway at night, east of Columbus, is also to be avoided, if only because of the sleazy porno shops centered there.

Stay away especially from the Western Addition, an area roughly bounded by Geary Boulevard on the north, Hayes Street on the south, Gough Street on the east, and Steiner Street on the west, which, although within minutes of popular Japantown or St. Mary's Cathedral, is unsafe for outsiders.

It isn't hard to have a safe vacation in San Francisco, and it is a pity to let a little carelessness spoil it.

SEATTLE

by
Archie Satterfield

Archie Satterfield is the editor of the magazine Northwest Edition *and has written several regional travel guides, including* The Seattle Guidebook.

The best way to get an idea of Seattle's setting is to invest $3.75 in a ride to the top of the Space Needle, from which you can see the entire region. Clockwise from Queen Anne Hill to the north are the marinas, ship repair yards, houseboats, and sailboats of Lake Union with the University District behind; Capitol Hill and Beacon Hill to the east; the central business district, Elliott Bay, and its shipping activity to the south; and to the west, Puget Sound and its islands with the Olympic Mountains as the backdrop. To the east is Lake Washington (24 miles long), a city boundary, and, in the distance, the Cascade Range where Seattleites ski in the winter, and backpack and fish in the summer.

On a clear day—and they do exist in Seattle in spite of what you might have heard—you can see 10,778-foot Mount Baker, which is near the Canadian border; 14,410-foot Mount Rainier to the south, the state's highest mountain; 12,307-foot Mount Adams to the southeast; and, 65 miles away, Mount Saint Helens, which used to be more than 9,000 feet high but is now 1,300 feet shorter due to the volcanic eruption on May 18, 1980, the Northwest's biggest blast.

Pioneer Square, at First and Yesler, gives its name to the district around the park and giant totem pole and south to the Kingdome, which is where the Mariners (baseball) and Seahawks (football) play. Seattle had its beginnings in this area in the 1850s. The first sawmill on Puget Sound was started there and Henry Yesler, the owner, skidded logs down a hill to the mill. The route became known as Skid Road, and that is how the term *skid row* began. Over the years the local businesses moved northward, and the area became a haven for down-and-outers, cheap hotels, missions, taverns, and inexpensive cafés. Now the area is protected by preservation ordinances, and the Pioneer Square Historic District is laden with small shops, galleries, theaters, restaurants, and open spaces—where, it should be noted, the transients and street people still roam.

East of Pioneer Square, in an area bound roughly by Fourth and Eighth avenues and Main and Lane streets, is the International District. It is sometimes called Chinatown, but many Japanese, Filipinos, Southeast Asians, and others from the Pacific Rim nations have settled here. You will find excellent Oriental foods, many "Benevolent Societies," ornate buildings, and tours of the area. The Bon Odori festival is held in August, with street dancers in costumes and streets filled with booths and tables laden with exotic foods and clothing.

The downtown waterfront, which runs some 20 blocks, is one of Seattle's major tourist attractions and one of the best places to shop for imported bargains and inexpensive seafoods. From Pier 70, on the far north end of the shopping district, to Pier 52, southward where the Washington State Ferries dock, you will find some of the most interesting shopping areas in Seattle, as well as the most reasonable. Nearly every pier is used for some public purpose. Just south of Pier 59, for example, is the Waterfront Park, where you can fish from the piers or sit peacefully and eat lunch.

Just above the waterfront, built along the edge of a steep hill, is the Pike Place Market, a covered warren of stalls heaped with fresh fish, fruits, and vegetables; delis; import shops; spice shops; and dozens of artisans. During the weekends and summer months, street musicians, with the inevitable upturned hat for donations, perform for the shoppers. The market was started in 1907 and has undergone several renovation campaigns, and at least twice bureaucrats have tried to turn it into a shopping mall. But Seattle likes its market, winos and all.

A short distance from midcity lies Lake Union, with its marinas, boat moorings, and very large houseboat community that like the Pike Place Market, have managed to survive all the attempts to change them. Lake Union is connected to both Lake Washington and the ship canal leading to Hiram M. Chittenden Locks that permits boats and ships to enter from the sea. The locks are Seattle's most popular visitor attraction, and have consistently drawn more visitors than any other attraction in the city. The addition in recent years of the fish ladder on the south side has increased the visitor count. And it's all free.

Lake Washington, the largest of the metropolitan lakes, is spanned by two long floating bridges. On the east side of the lake are residential suburbs, the largest of which is Bellevue with a population of some 100,000. The west side is dotted with moorings, playgrounds, beaches, and parks. The biggest is Seward Park; a new park at Sand Point, where a naval base formerly stood, is named in honor of the former longtime U.S. Senator, Warren G. Magnuson. The lake's entire character changes in August when the hydroplane races are held as a part of Seafair, a city-wide celebration.

Seattle remains one of the few cities whose core district has not only remained viable as a place to work, shop, and play, but has also continually improved itself. Urban renewal of the most positive kind (meaning that neighborhoods and business districts are renovated, not demolished) has made Seattle's downtown a continually interesting place to visit. This, along with some imaginative and practical programs, such as free bus rides in the core district, have made visitors feel welcome in Seattle.

PRACTICAL INFORMATION

WHEN TO GO. Seattle is noted for its overcast weather and frequent rain, which leads to the inevitable jokes: "Our annual drought is the last weekend of July." "If summer comes on a weekend this year, we'll have a picnic." But the truth is that the city doesn't have all that much rainfall. The 36 to 38 annual inches compare favorably with many cities that have more rainfall but hot summers and cold winters. Seattle has a gentle, marine climate with summer highs seldom in the nineties, and winter lows infrequently below 20 degrees. The annual rainfall makes Seattle green almost year-round.

For those who insist on clear, sunny weather, July and August are usually the sunniest months. For more than two decades, the Bellevue Arts and Crafts Fair has been held the last weekend of July in both indoor and outdoor sites, and it has never rained then since the fair began. Because the weather is so mild for a place so far north (Seattle is at about the same latitude as Maine), sailors are out on Puget Sound every month of the year. Skiing is 50 miles away in the Cascades, and that season usually runs Dec.–March. Like most cities, hotels that advertise seasonal rates usually have higher-priced summer rates running from Memorial Day to mid-Sept.

HOW TO GET THERE. By air. Because Seattle is the closest city in the lower 48 states to Alaska and Japan, it is served by airlines that use Seattle-Tacoma International Airport (Sea-Tac) as a port of entry. Some of the airlines listed are in the process of merging with other carriers and their corporate identity may change this year: *Alaska, American, America West, Braniff, British Airways, Canadian, Continental, Delta, Eastern, Finnair, Hawaiian, Japan, Mexicana, Northwest Orient, Pan Am, Piedmont, SAS, Thai, TWA, United* and *USAir.* Commuter airlines include *Air BC, Coastal Airways, Harbor, Horizon, San Juan,* and *United Express.*

By bus. As with most cities, *Greyhound-Trailways* is the major bus company. Buses serve cities along the I-5 corridor between Seattle and Portland.

By train. *Amtrak* connects Seattle with eastern, midwest, and western cities. From the east come the *Empire Builder* (from Chicago via St. Paul, Spokane, and Portland), *The Pioneer* (from Salt Lake City, Ogden, Boise, and Portland); from the south, the *Coast Starlight* (from Los Angeles), and *Mount Rainier* (daily service between Seattle and Portland).

By car. The two major corridors to Seattle from everywhere else are I-5, which runs from the Canadian border to the Mexican border; and I-90, which begins at Seattle (or ends there, depending on the direction you are traveling) and heads east toward the Atlantic. I-5 gets you to Vancouver, British Columbia, and Portland, Oregon. I-90, which points east, takes you skiing at Snoqualmie Summit, and to Spokane.

By boat. Sitmar Cruises' *Fairsea* home ports in Seattle on its Inside Passage cruises to Alaska in summer months. Seattle is also the southern terminus for ferries from the Alaska Marine Highway System.

TELEPHONES. The area code for all telephones west of the Cascades is 206. You do not need to dial the area code if you are calling within the area. Seattle is served by the Bell system, which means you can make local calls to most of the outlying communities. But if you are calling from some of the towns that are served by General Telephone, you will pay long distance rates. Pay phones cost 25 cents, but all emergency calls can be made free of charge.

Emergency Telephone Numbers. All emergency calls, whether police, fire, or medical, go through the one emergency number: 911. Emergency calls can be made free from a pay phone.

ACCOMMODATIONS. Since Seattle is not a resort city, hotel rates, which have been going steadily upward, do not change during the year. A few good buys re-

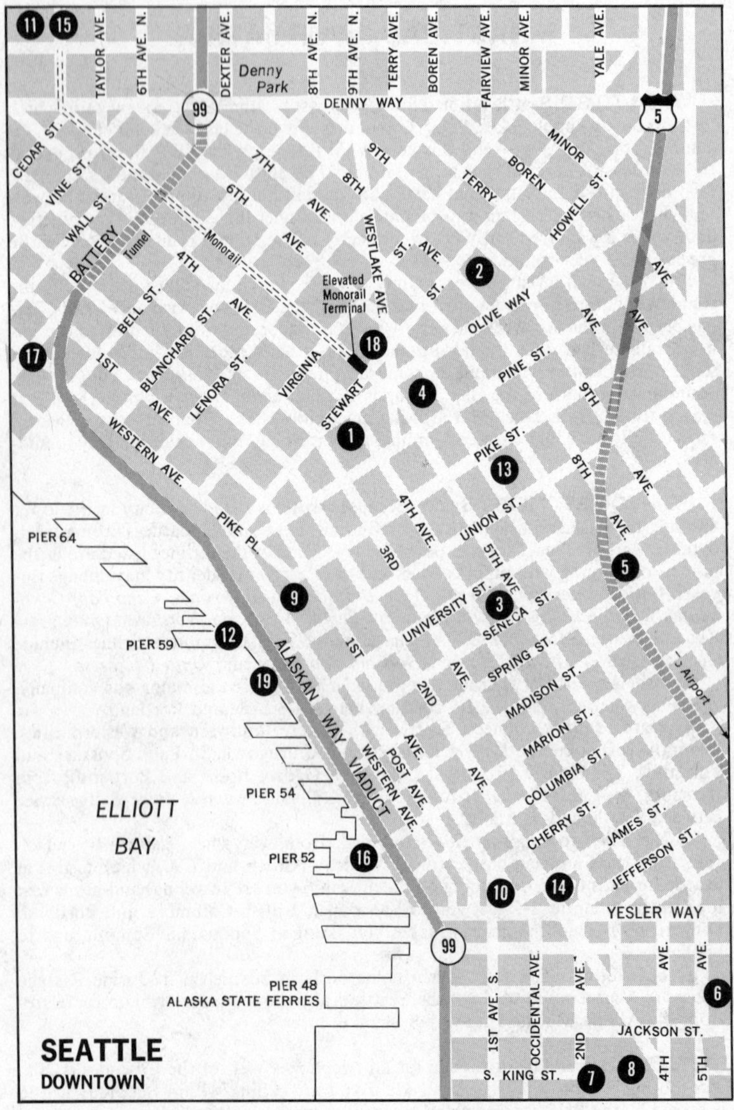

Points of Interest:

1) The Bon
2) Central Bus Terminal
3) Four Seasons Olympic Hotel
4) Frederick & Nelson
5) Freeway Park
6) International District
7) Kingdome
8) King Street Station (Amtrak)
9) Pike Place Market
10) Pioneer Square
11) Seattle Center
12) Seattle Public Aquarium
13) Seattle Sheraton
14) Smith Tower
15) Space Needle
16) State Ferry Terminal
17) Waterfront Terminal
18) Westin Hotel
19) Waterfront Park

main, however, and some inexpensive hotels and motels on the fringes of the city are clean and convenient. Rates are based on double occupancy, EP. Categories, determined by price, are: *Reasonable,* $45 to $60; and *Very Economical,* $25 to $40.

Reasonable

Airport Plaza. 18601 Pacific Highway S., Seattle, WA 98188 (206–433–0400). 125 rooms. Undergoing renovation at press time, should be complete by beginning of 1989. Located across the street from the beautiful Red Lion hotel. Jacuzzi and hot tub, weight room, and sun deck. Airport transportation.

Best Western–Continental Plaza. 2500 Aurora Ave. N., Seattle, WA 98109 (206–284–1900, 800–528–1234). 94 rooms. Some great views of Lake Union and the mountains. Outdoor pool, coffee shop on premises.

Best Western-Landmark Inn. 4300 200th S.W., Lynnwood, Seattle, WA 98036 (206–775–7447, 800–528–1234). 102 rooms. Indoor pool and Jacuzzi. Restaurant, coffee shop, and lounge on premises. Convenient to airport transportation.

Quality Inn at Sea-Tac. 3000 S. 176th St., Seattle, WA 98188 (206–246–9110, 800–228–5151). 214 rooms. Indoor pool, coffee shop. Shuttle to airport.

Sandstone Town & Country Inn. 19225 Pacific Highway S., Seattle, WA 98188 (206–824–1350). 98 rooms. 24-hour restaurant on premises, lounge with big-screen TV. Walking distance to a small lake and golf course.

Seattle Downtown TraveLodge. 2213 8th Ave., Seattle, WA 98121 (206–624–6300, 800–255–3050). 72 rooms. Complete renovation just finished. No restaurant on premises but several within walking distance. Convenient to airport transportation.

Sixth Avenue Inn. 2000 6th Ave., Seattle, WA 98121 (206–441–8300, 800–648–6440). 166 rooms. Coffee shop and lounge on premises. Located in downtown area, walking distance to shopping and monorail. Express bus to airport across the street.

Town Center Inn. 2205 7th Ave., Seattle, WA 98155 (206–448–3434, 800–325–2525). 93 rooms. Coffee shop and lounge on premises. Near free bus to downtown, walking distance to the Bon and major shopping areas. Express bus to airport stops at the door.

TraveLodge by the Space Needle. 200 6th Ave., Seattle, WA 98109 (206–441–7878, 800–255–3050). 87 rooms. Recently renovated. No restaurant on premises, but free coffee and tea offered 24 hours. Outdoor pool. Convenient to Grayline airport shuttle buses.

Very Economical

Airport Motel. 4006 S. 139th, Seattle, WA 98168 (206–244–0810). 50 rooms. Jacuzzi, weight room, no restaurant on the premises, but room service (except breakfast); restaurant a block away. Located 8 miles north of airport, free shuttle bus.

Airporter Inn. 14845 Pacific Highway S., Seattle, WA 98188 (206–248–1061). 72 rooms. Restaurant and coffee shop on premises. 1 mile from the airport, free shuttle buses. Jacuzzi and recreation room should be completed by late 1988.

Aloha Motor Inn. 1911 Aurora Ave. N., Seattle, WA 98109 (206–283–6070). 55 rooms. Restaurant on premises. Two saunas. Located near downtown, Space Needle, and Seattle Center. Free van to airport.

Black Angus Motor Inn. 125th & Aurora, Seattle, WA 98133 (206–363–3035). 53 rooms. Restaurant on premises, nearby coffee shop. Outdoor pool. Located off I-5, 10 miles from downtown.

Casabel Motel. 3938 Whitman N., Seattle, WA 98103 (206–632–8200). 17 rooms. Cable TV in rooms. Located 3 miles from downtown, nice view of Seattle skyline.

Cosmopolitan Motel. 2106 5th Ave., Seattle, WA 98121 (206–441–8833). 70 rooms. Basic accommodations; some rooms with VCRs. Located in downtown.

Imperial Inn. 17108 Pacific Highway S., Seattle, WA 98188 (206–244–1230, 800–368–4400). 73 rooms. Recently renovated. Restaurant next door. Free coffee, morning paper, and airport shuttle. Located 2 miles from airport and 14 miles from downtown.

Park Plaza Motel. 4401 Aurora Ave. N., Seattle, WA 98103 (206–632–2101). 14 rooms. Popular motel with basic but clean, quiet, comfortable rooms. Cable TV, in-room coffee. Located near the zoo and the University, 5 miles from downtown. Shuttle service to airport (1 hour away).

Bed-and-Breakfasts. The number of B&Bs continues to grow in the Seattle area, and the rates range from roughly $35 to $70 for a double room, with breakfast. Major booking associations in the Seattle area are:

Pacific Bed & Breakfast. 701 N.W. 60th, Seattle, WA 98107 (206–784–0539).

Seattle Bed & Breakfast Inn Association. Box 95853, Seattle, WA 98145 (206–547–1020).

Travellers' Bed & Breakfast. Box 492, Mercer Island, WA 98040 (206–232–2345).

Whidbey Island Bed & Breakfast Association. 2388 E. Sunlight Beach Road, Clinton, WA 98236 (206–221–2964).

Ys and Hostels. The **Y.M.C.A.,** 909 Fourth Ave., Seattle, WA 98101 (206–382–5000), has 236 rooms (including coed rooms), a pool and barbershop. $24.77–$66.21 per night. American Youth Hostel members stay for $13.78. The **Y.W.C.A.,** 1118 Fifth Ave., Seattle, WA 98101 (206–447–4888), with rooms only for women over 18, also has a pool. $21 to $26 per night. In the summer, write ahead for reservations, three weeks in advance. Enclose first night's deposit.

HOW TO GET AROUND. From the airport. The Airport Express leaves every 30 minutes from several downtown hotels: Sheraton, Four Seasons Olympic, Holiday Inn Crowne Plaza, Stouffer Madison, the Warwick, and the Westin. Fare each way is $5 adult, $3.50 child. Taxicabs have been deregulated by the county government, resulting in a caveat-emptor situation: you must shop for the best prices at the airport cab stand. Distance between Sea Tac and downtown is approximately 15 miles, and the trip takes roughly 30 minutes by airporter bus.

By bus. Seattle has a widely praised public transportation system called Metro; buses run all over King County and into surrounding counties. The Magic Carpet service provides free bus rides at all times of the day and night in the downtown area between Battery and Jackson streets, and Sixth Avenue and the waterfront. Fares are 65 cents during peak hours, and 55 cents at other times. Senior-citizen fares are 20 cents. On weekends and holidays, an all-day pass is available for $1. Call 447–4800 for information.

By rental car. All the major rental agencies, including *Hertz* (800–654–3131), *Avis* (800–331–1212), and *National* (800–328–4567), are represented at the airport and various downtown and suburban locations. Also, *Rent-a-Dent* (824–7878) and other discount agencies are scattered around the area.

HINTS TO THE MOTORIST. Driving in Seattle is no different than in most cities, except that there are a few hills that give nervous or overly cautious drivers white knuckles when the light changes and the car must be stopped at a steep angle. But these hills are in only a small portion of the downtown area, between University Street and James, and from the waterfront to Sixth Avenue.

Right turns are permitted on a red light after stopping. The speed limit in the city is 25 mph, unless otherwise posted. Rush hours are 6–9 A.M. and 3:30–6:30 P.M. Most shopping centers and parking lots outside public buildings have designated disabled parking.

Parking can be a problem downtown. The busier the street, the shorter the time permitted at metered parking. On-street parking in the downtown area is virtually nonexistent during weekdays because it has remained a viable urban area popular with shoppers. Several parking garages are available. A good alternative, if you are coming in from a hotel or motel on the outskirts, is to use a free "park-and-ride" and take a bus into the city. Information: 447–4800.

TOURIST INFORMATION. The Seattle-King County Convention and Visitors Bureau is the basic source of information for the area, and the organization's storefront information center, at the corner of Seventh Avenue and Stewart Street, has brochures and schedules from all over the state. Address: 1815 Seventh Ave., Seattle, WA 98101 (447–4200).

The bureau publishes a brochure several times a year that lists not only the coming events, but also basic information for visitors that includes: foreign consulates, important phone numbers; airline reservation numbers; shopping information, including major shopping centers around the area; and numerous sightseeing tips.

Foreign currency exchange. Money can be changed at the airport, where booths are set up at convenient locations. Otherwise, three banks—*First Interstate,* 999 Third Ave. (343–8311); *Rainier Bank,* 1301 Fifth Ave. (621–5621); and *Seafirst Bank,* 800 Fifth Ave. (583–3131)—and five hotels—*Four Seasons Olympic,* 411 University; *Seattle Hilton,* Sixth and University; *Seattle Airport Hilton,* 17620 Pacific Hwy S.; *Seattle Sheraton,* Sixth and Pike; and the *Westin,* Fifth and Westlake—all offer exchange services.

SENIOR-CITIZEN DISCOUNTS. Seattle was one of the first cities to establish a commission on aging. As a result, senior citizens enjoy a number of discounted prices for transportation, meals, entertainment, and other expenditures. For information, call 386–1274.

FREE EVENTS. The Seattle Center, site of the 1962 World's Fair, is a mecca for free entertainment that ranges from concerts by local talent to square dancing in the Center House. The biggest events outdoors are the annual **Folklife Festival** in May, and the **Bumbershoot Festival** in September. The city's biggest celebration of all is the **Seafair** summer series of events. These events, nearly all of which are free, include a milk carton derby on Green Lake, several ethnic festivals in various neighborhoods, community parades, the Seafair unlimited hydroplane race in August, and the annual salmon derby with major cash prizes for the person who catches a tagged salmon.

Another notable city event is the annual **parade of boats** that marks the opening of the boating season in early May. Thousands of boats cruise through lakes Washington and Union, and people crowd the shores of the canal (Montlake Cut, in local parlance) between the two lakes to get a closer look at the boats.

The most popular place to visit (free!) is the **Hiram Chittenden Locks,** N.W. 45th and Ballard, better known as the Ballard Locks. Allow plenty of time to watch boats go up and down between saltwater Shilsole Bay and the freshwater lakes. From a viewing room, you can also see fish go up the ladder. There are neatly landscaped grounds and an information center, where you can learn how the locks work.

During the summer months, **free concerts**—classical, jazz, and others—are offered at several city parks, especially Freeway Park in the heart of downtown, and sometimes on the Seattle Public Library's patio. Some shopping areas, such as the Ranier Square, engage musicians who perform during the day and into the evenings. There's always something free going on in Seattle Center, particularly in the Center House. Also, the giant fountain is a wonderful spot to pass an hour or two.

Another popular form of free entertainment is walking through the **Pike Place Market** to people-watch the entire spectrum of Seattle residents. There's no admission charged, but it is virtually impossible to wander through the markets without buying *something.*

TOURS AND SPECIAL-INTEREST SIGHTSEEING. Puget Sound Cruises. The most popular sightseeing voyage remains the trip to Victoria Island (in British Columbia, Canada). The *Princess Marguerite* and the *Vancouver Island Princess* make the trip daily, May–Oct., from Pier 69. Round-trip fare $32, children $16. For further information call 441–5560. The 300-passenger catamaran *Victoria Clipper,* new in 1986, makes twice-daily trips in summer, once a day the rest of the year. Call 447–8000 for further information.

Tillicum Village. This is the most popular meal stop on the Sound, and offers the most authentic Indian-style salmon available. The village is a longhouse on Blake Island, and is the only structure there. It houses carvers, who produce totems and other artwork, and provides storage for the alder-smoked salmon. During meals, dancers perform traditional Pacific North Coast Indian dances. Seattle Harbor Tours boats provide transportation to and from the island (329–5700).

Lake Union Air Service (284–0300). One of the best ways to see the beauty of Puget Sound, and the cities and mountains that ring the area, is aboard small seaplanes that fly out of Lake Union and Lake Washington. You can take ½-hour scenic flights around Seattle ($25 per person), or you can charter flights to surrounding towns. They also provide regularly scheduled service to the San Juan Islands, Vancouver Island, and Vancouver.

For more traditional city tours, by coach and by boat, call *Gray Line* (624–5813); *American Sightseeing* (624–5813); or *Seattle Harbor Tours* (623–1445).

PARKS AND GARDENS. Since moisture for grass has never been a problem in Seattle, the town has always had several first-rate parks. It came as no great surprise when it recently adopted the nickname "The Emerald City" in honor of its year-round greenery. Here are some special parks, all free, that you may want to see:

Freeway Park, built over I-5 in the downtown area between Boren and Sixth Ave.

Discovery Park, formerly an army base (Fort Lawton), now a touch of wilderness in the city with two miles of beach. It includes an Indian cultural center. The Visitors Center, 3801 W. Government Way (386–4236) is open daily, 8:30 A.M.–5 P.M.; the park is open until dark.

Green Lake, in the center of town, is perhaps the city's most popular park. Its 2.8-mile path is used by runners, skaters, bicyclists, and walkers. The lake is popular with canoeists, kayakers, and rowers.

Seattle Marine Aquarium, Pier 59 (625–4357), is one of Seattle's most popular spots, and one of which the city is especially proud. It is literally built in Puget Sound, so that many of the fish you see are those that happened to be swimming by. The aquarium even developed its own salmon run.

University of Washington Arboretum, Lake Washington Blvd. (543–8800), is one of Seattle's beauty spots. It has plants from all over the world, lots of playing fields, and paths for jogging and bicycling, plus a Japanese garden given by Seattle's sister city, Kobe.

ZOOS. Woodland Park Zoo, N. 59th St. and Aurora Ave. (789–7919), has gone to great lengths to develop imaginative and humane exhibits. One is the Nocturnal House, which reverses day and night; others are swamps and marshes for the animals that live in them, and an African Savannah to house the zoo's growing collection of African animals. Daily, in summer, 8:30 A.M.–6 P.M.; in winter, 8:30 A.M.–4 P.M. Adults, $3; children, senior citizens, and disabled visitors, $1.50; under 6 free.

PARTICIPANT SPORTS. Because of its mild climate, Seattle's playing fields are in constant use the year-round. Taking the sports in alphabetical order: **Archery.** One public range in the south end of Magnuson Park at Sand Point Way N.E. and 65th Ave. Another is at *Marymoor Park* in Redmond.

Bicycling. In addition to the more obvious bicycle rides (around *Green Lake,* along *Burke Gilman Trail* from the University of Washington to Kenmore), there are several popular routes for bicyclists. Most bike rentals are around the Green Lake area. Check with the Seattle Parks Department (684–4075) on best routes. Bicycle Sunday is the third Sunday every month from May through Sept. Lake Washington Blvd. S. is closed off for the event. Good rides include: *West Seattle Beach Ride,* along Harbor and Alki Aves.; *Queen Anne Hill,* around the rim of the hill with views of the ship canal, downtown Seattle, and Puget Sound; and *Lake Washington Ride,* from the Arboretum to Seward Park.

Curling. The *Granite Curling Club,* 1440 N. 128th (362–2446), has competitions Oct.–Apr.

Fishing. Seattle has several public fishing piers, one on Waterfront Park at Pier 57. Other spots include Pier 70's seawall, Myrtle Edwards Park north of Pier 70, and the freshwater sites at Green Lake, Lake Washington, and the ship canal that drains Lake Union into Salmon Bay.

Golf. Seattle has three municipal courses (18–27 holes): *Jackson Park,* 100 N.E. 135th St. (363–4747); *Jefferson Park,* 4101 Beacon Ave. S. (762–4513); and *West Seattle Golf Course,* 4470 S.W. 35th St. (932–9792). There are a dozen public 18-hole courses in the immediate suburbs, some 9-hole courses, and private clubs with exchange privileges for visiting members of other clubs.

Hiking. There are many trails in and around the city. *Myrtle Edwards Park* is a two-mile path along Elliott Bay. *Foster Island Nature Walk* is on a paved trail over marshland beside Lake Washington, leading from the Museum of History and Industry to Foster Island. Other trails are in *Seward Park,* a small peninsula on the south end of Lake Washington; *Schmitz Park,* a small, wooded area in west

Seattle; and *Discovery Park,* a former military base on the tip of Magnolia Bluff in Northwest Seattle. Burke-Gilman Trail runs 12½ miles from north side of Lake Union to Kenmore, north end of Lake Washington. *The Mountaineers,* 300 Third Ave. W, Seattle, WA 98119 (284–6310), publishes guides to hiking trails in the Northwest and offers guided trips for a range of outdoor activities.

Jogging. The most popular spots are around Green Lake, along the waterfront strip from Pier 70 to Pier 92, through the Seattle Center before the lunchtime crowds arrive, and along any of the numbered avenues downtown from Second to Sixth.

Tennis. It is available, free, at dozens of locations around the city, including high schools and, of course, community centers. For information on reservations, covered courts, etc., call the Seattle Tennis Center at 324–2980 for information. Call 684–4075 for information on outside courts.

SPECTATOR SPORTS. The city has its quota of professional teams: The *Seahawks* (827–9766) is the NFL team. The basketball team is the *Supersonics* (281–5850). The baseball team is the *Mariners* (628–3300). The Seahawks and the Mariners play in the Kingdome; the Supersonics play in the Coliseum at the Seattle Center. The hockey team, also professional, is the Thunderbirds (728–9121) and they play in the Arena in the Seattle Center.

The University of Washington has always had good football teams (the *Huskies*), and recently developed good basketball teams, both men and women. Call 543–2200 for all the university tickets.

CHILDREN'S ACTIVITIES. In addition to the rides at the **Seattle Center,** there are many things for families with young children to do in Seattle. One of the first is to take a ride up the elevator to the top of the **Space Needle** ($3.75; children 5–12, $2), which gives an orientation to the area and an opportunity to see many of Seattle's skyscrapers at eye level.

Enchanted Village. South of Seattle just off I-5 at Federal Way, at 36201 Kit Corner Rd. S. (838–1700). This is a family park with the usual rides, but also with pet sheep, goats, and other animals. Open Apr.–Sept., 10 A.M.–7 P.M. daily.

Pizza and Pipes, several locations sprinkled around the area, are a popular places for kids. Three different birthday party plans. Check the yellow pages for nearest location.

Seattle Children's Museum, Center House at the Seattle Center (441–1768). This unusual museum has a combination of hands-on participatory exhibits and fascinating child-oriented collections and curios all specifically designed to involve children and adults in meaningful discovery.

MUSEUMS AND GALLERIES. Seattle has a long tradition of regional art, thanks to the presence during the 1920s and 1930s of Mark Tobey, Kenneth Callahan, Guy Anderson, Morris Graves, and others of what became the Northwest School. Their presence created an awareness of art that has survived, and this awareness was nurtured by the creation of the Seattle Art Museum. The museum opened in 1933 under the financial sponsorship of the Fuller family, which remained a potent force in the museum's policies and collections for four decades.

Frye Art Museum. 704 Terry Ave. (622–9250). The museum has an extensive European collection from nineteenth- and early twentieth-century artists, and sponsors special exhibitions for regional and Alaskan artists. No admission. Mon.–Sat., 10 A.M.–5 P.M., Sun., noon–5 P.M., except Thanksgiving and Christmas.

Henry Art Gallery. University of Washington Campus (543–2280). Contemporary northwest artists along with nineteenth- and twentieth-century European and American artists. Tues.–Fri., 10 A.M.–5 P.M. (7 P.M. on Thurs.); Sat.–Sun., 11 A.M.–5 P.M. $2; $1 for members, students, and seniors.

Museum of Flight. 9404 E. Marginal Way S. (767–7373). Traces the history of aviation in the northwest, Alaska, and the Orient. Gift shop. Daily, 10 A.M.–5 P.M. Adults, $4; 13–18, $3; 6–12, $2.

Museum of History and Industry. 2161 E. Hamlin (324–1125). The region's history is represented here with an emphasis, as the name indicates, on the industrial-business side of life. Mon.–Sat., 10 A.M.–5 P.M. Gift shop. $3 adults, $1.50 children 6–12 and seniors.

Nordic Heritage Museum. 3014 N.W. 67th (789–5707). Collection of Scandinavian memorabilia from early settlers in the region. Tues.–Sat., 10 A.M.–4 P.M.; Sun., noon–4 P.M. $2.50 adults, $1.50 seniors, $1 children 6–16.

Seattle Art Museum. 14th St. E. and Prospect, in Volunteer Park (625–8900). This is the bellweather of the art community. Tues.–Sat., 10 A.M.–5 P.M. (Thurs. till 9 P.M.), Sun., noon–5 P.M. Adults $2, students and seniors $1; free Thurs. In addition, a new Seattle Art Museum will rise in downtown Seattle at First and University, with a scheduled completion date of fall 1990.

Galleries. Most of Seattle's galleries are in Pioneer Square and are open from around noon to 6 P.M. The big gallery event is the first Thurs. evening of the month, when many galleries have their openings and art buffs wander from gallery to gallery. Some of the best known are: *Davidson Galleries,* 313 Occidental Ave. S. (624–7684); *Foster-White Gallery,* 311½ Occidental Ave. S. (622–2833); *Linda Farris Gallery,* 320 Second Ave. S. (623–1110); *Silver Image Gallery,* (Photos), 318 Occidental Ave. S. (623–8116); and *Stonington Gallery,* 2030 First Ave. (443–1108).

ARTS AND ENTERTAINMENT. Film. Seattle has always been an excellent city for film and stage, and many Hollywood studios test films on Seattle markets because national audiences usually go in the direction of Seattle audiences. Seattle also has a tradition of great movie theaters, due in part to an architect from Seattle, B. Marcus Priteca, who designed many elegant theaters dating from the golden age of Hollywood. Three of these—the *Fifth Avenue,* 1301 Fifth; *Paramount,* 901 Pine; and *Coliseum,* Fifth and Pike—still are used for either films or stage plays.

Today, the most imaginative film presentations are by the Seven Gables Corporation, owner of a chain that includes the *Seven Gables,* at Northeast 50th and Roosevelt Way, 632–8820; the *Guild 45th* on Northeast 45th near University Way, 633–3353; the *Crest Cinemas,* a four-screen complex at Northeast 165th and 5th Avenue Northeast, 363–6338; the *Ridgemont,* 78th Avenue and Greenwood, 782–7337; the *Broadway,* 201 Broadway, 323–1085; the *Varsity,* 4329 University Way N.E., 632–3131; the *Egyptian,* 801 E. Pine, 323–4978; the newly opened 10-screen *Metro Cinemas,* 4500 9th Ave. N.E., 633–0055; and the new 4-screen *Capitol Hill* in the Broadway Market.

Music. Three major groups reside in Seattle: The *Seattle Symphony,* conducted by Gerald Schwarz, performs Oct.–May at the Seattle Opera House in the Seattle Center. Performances are on Sun. afternoons, and Mon. and Tues. evenings. Under Schwartz's direction, the orchestra has been taking more artistic risks, mixing Beethoven freely with newer and lesser known composers. Tickets, 443–4747; $8 to $35. The *Seattle Opera Association* (443–4711) presents five operas from Sept. to May. $11 to $55. Performance of Wagner's *Ring Cycle* each summer since the mid-'70s, cancelled for the 1988 season with plans to resume in summer 1989. *Northwest Chamber Orchestra* (343–0445) presents concerts at the Intiman Theater and Nippon Kan Theater Oct.–Mar. $12–$17.50.

Dance. The *Pacific Northwest Ballet* (447–4751), is Seattle's major resident **ballet** company and it performs in the Opera House Oct.–May, with an annual *Nutcracker* performed in December. $8–$24.

Stage. When the 1984 Obie Awards were handed out in New York, four of the winning shows were plays that had premiered in Seattle. Apparently 1984 wasn't a fluke, because other plays that were hatched in Seattle have also worked their way to that great Mecca of theater, downtown New York. Some major theaters are:

Seattle Repertory Theater (443–2222) presents six plays each season in the new Bagley Wright Theater in the Seattle Center. The major equity theater in town. $8.50–$19.50.

A Contemporary Theater (ACT), 100 W. Roy St. (285–5110). Experimental contemporary plays plus a children's theater. $10.50–$18.50.

The Pioneer Square Theater, 512 Second (622–2016). More world premieres have been presented here than anywhere else in town, and the most successful of them all is the punk-rock satire, *Angry Housewives.* $9–$14.

Intiman Theater, Seattle Center Playhouse (624–2992). Classics are the main fare. June–Oct. $7–$17.

The Empty Space, First and Jackson (467–6000), offers experimental works, revised classics, and translations. $11–$18.

The Bathhouse Theater, 7312 Greenlake Dr. N. (524–9110). Adaptations of classics, such as staging Shakespearean plays in modern dress, are a mainstay of this respected, small theater on the shore of Green Lake. Mar.–Dec. $8–$12.

SHOPPING. Since Seattle is closer to Japan than any other major American city, oriental imports are very common. For a similar reason, Native Alaskan artwork is also common. This is the home of a number of outdoor-clothing companies (*Eddie Bauer, Inc.,* and *Recreational Equipment, Inc. [REI]*), and a few national brands of clothing as well. Each major clothing firm has seconds stores. *Eddie Bauer's* seconds are in the basement of the main store at Fifth and Union, in the Ranier Square underground shopping mall. *Mountain Products,* 160 S. Jackson (624–2748), a ski-clothing firm, has its seconds outlet at the same address. The downtown *Nordstrom Rack* at Second and Pine is the place to shop for bargains in clothing and shoes. There's also a *Rack* at Bellevue Square and the *Pavilion* at Southcenter.

The "off-price mall" is a first for the Seattle area: The Pavilion Outlet Center, in Tukwila, at S. 180th and Southcenter Blvd., is the first shopping center devoted entirely to discount prices. It has nearly 50 stores in the mall, all offering substantial discounts and nearly all stocking name brands. The Pavilion is open during normal shopping hours seven days a week, throughout the year, and remains open until nearly midnight during the Christmas season.

DINING OUT. Seattle is noted for its seafood because it is on the Puget Sound and because it is so close to Alaska, the prime source of king crab, halibut, bottom fish, salmon, steelhead trout, clams, oysters, and geoducks.

We've used the following restaurant categories, based on the price of a meal for one without beverage or tip. *Reasonable,* $10 to $15; and *Very Economical,* $10 and under. Unless otherwise noted, all the restaurants accept some, if not all, major credit cards. Every effort has been made to ensure that the list is up-to-date, but restaurants come and go so rapidly that it is always advisable to call ahead.

Reasonable

Andy's Dinner. 2963 4th S. (624–4097). Long-standing railroad theme restaurant in old passenger cars. Specializes in steaks and seafood. Open Mon.–Sat., 11:30 A.M.–11 P.M. Closed Sun.

Ivar's Acres of Clams. On Pier 52 (624–6852), where the Harbor Tours boats are docked and where boats leave for Tillicum Village and other destinations around the Sound. This is probably the best value in seafood. 11 A.M.–10 P.M., Fri.–Sat. to 11 P.M. All major credit cards.

Very Economical

The Old Spaghetti Factory. Elliott and Broad (441–7724). One of Seattle's oldest and most popular budget eateries. It is very popular with large groups—families, groups of friends, or small organizations. Mon.–Thurs., 5–10 P.M.; Fri., till 11 P.M.; Sat., 4:30–11 P.M. No credit cards.

King's Table. 16549 Aurora N. (542–5665). This is one of several locations around the Seattle suburbs, and specializes in family fare. They charge 30 cents per year for children through the age of 15, meaning an eight-year-old pays $2.40 for all he or she can eat. 11 A.M.–8:30 P.M., Mon.–Thurs.; Fri. and Sat., till 9 P.M.; Sun., 8 A.M.–8 P.M.

Sizzler. 1827 Broadway (324–3593), is one of a chain of steak, seafood, and salad restaurants with prices below $10 per person. Others in Burien, Factoria, Federal Way, Northgate, and Southcenter.

Guadalajara Cafe. 1429 Fourth Ave. (622–8722), is one of three. Authentic and inexpensive Mexican food. Others are on N. 45th and in West Seattle. Mon.–Sat., 11 A.M.–9 P.M.; closed Sun.

International District. Nearly all restaurants here are inexpensive, and they range from Chinese and Japanese to Korean and Vietnamese. Among the best of the Chinese restaurants are: *Hong Kong,* 507 Maynard S. (622–0366); *Four Seas Restaurant,* 714 S. King (682–4900); *Tai Tung,* 659 S. King (622–7372).

Hakata. 3306 N.E. 130th (363–8643). One of Seattle's best, and least expensive, Japanese restaurants. Mon.–Fri., 11 A.M.–9 P.M.; Sat.–Sun., 4–9 P.M.

Han Il. 409 Maynard S. (587–0464). A moderately priced Korean restaurant in the International District.

Cafe Loc. 407 Broad (441–6883). This is one of the best of the Vietnamese restaurants that have become popular around the area, and it is one of the least expensive.

Recommended Splurge. Fuller's. Seattle Sheraton, 1400 Sixth Ave. (621–9000). Female chefs, first Kathy Casey and now Caprial Pence, have won a basketful of awards for their culinary excellence and imaginative presentation. Fuller's menu concentrates on Northwest cuisine—fresh local seafood, meats, fruits, and vegetables. The Sheraton has devoted more than $1 million to its art collection; the best of the Northwest pieces are displayed in Fuller's. Be sure to take a look at the splendid display of Pilchuck glass in the adjacent Pilchuck Room. Hours: Lunch, Mon.–Fri., 11:30 A.M.–2 P.M.; dinner, Mon.–Sat., 5:30–9:30 P.M. Closed Sun. All major credit cards.

NIGHTLIFE AND BARS. It took a while after the blue laws were lifted for Seattle to become comfortable with nightlife. But now it is acceptable for people to go out after work or on weekends.

Jazz

Dimitriou's Jazz Alley. 6th and Lenora (441–9729), where nationally known musicians play.

Rock

Pier 70 Restaurant. Alaskan Way and Broad St. (624–8090). Local and regional bands.

Bluegrass

The New Melody. 5213 Ballard Ave. N.W. (782–3480). *The* place to go in Seattle for bluegrass.

Folk and Ethnic

La Esquina Tavern. 5000 Rainier Ave. S. (721–0380). Mexican and Latin music on weekends.

Comedy

Comedy Underground. 222 S. Main (628–0303). Stand-up comics seven nights a week.

Giggles Comedy Nite Club. 5220 Roosevelt Way NE (526–5653).

Bars with Views

Hiram's at the Locks. 5300 34th N.W. (784–1733). Great view of the activity in the Ballard (Hiram Chittenden) Locks. Grassy patio area outside.

At the Lakeside. 2501 N. Northlake Way (634–0823). You can either tie up your boat at the Lake Union dock or drive in for a view across Lake Union toward the city.

Mirabeau. 46th floor, Sea-First Building, 4th and Madison (624–4550). The highest spot in the city for a drink, with a stunning view across the Sound and to the Cascades.

Ray's Boathouse. 6049 Seaview Ave. N.W. (789–3770). At the entrance to the Lake Washington Ship Canal with vistas of Puget Sound and the Olympic Mountains.

The Space Needle. Seattle Center (443–2100). This slowly revolving restaurant gives you the full 360-degree view of the region.

SECURITY. Although Seattle is one of the safest cities in the country, it still has the usual problems that occur wherever people gather.

Generally speaking, the area to exercise the most caution in are Pioneer Square and along First Avenue after dark. Sometimes the Seattle Center is overrun with teenagers, and there have been some isolated incidents involving teenage gangs, but the Center is still relatively safe.

Most of the panhandlers in Pioneer Square and along First Avenue, and in the Pike Place Market for that matter, are relatively harmless. Seattle has a reputation of concern for the street people who are being evicted by various urban renewal projects.

In general, you should exercise the same caution you would anywhere else. Park in lighted areas and, if you are going to be spending an evening on the town, then try to park in a hotel lot or one with valet parking and ride in a cab instead.

TAMPA–ST. PETERSBURG

by
Fred. W. Wright, Jr.

Fred W. Wright, Jr., lives on Florida's west coast and writes for numerous publications, including the St. Petersburg Times.

Forgotten as it was by the initial influx of homesteaders and tourists, Florida's west coast, and its central metropolitan hub, Tampa and St. Petersburg, for decades have played country cousin to the more developed east coast.

Now that's changing. Unprecedented growth and fresh vistas have made the Tampa Bay area a new mecca for tourists, developers, and businesses alike. The untouched and unnoticed quality that once permeated much of the west coast—dubbed by promoters years ago the Suncoast—is disappearing fast. There are still fewer people on the west coast than the east coast, but the Tampa Bay area, with 2 million year-round residents, now ranks twenty-fourth among the nation's metropolitan markets. The Suncoast still offers cheaper land prices and more room to grow than the Gold Coast, the Miami-Dade County megalopolis, but the skyline of Tampa changes yearly with new high-rise office buildings and upscale, downtown hotels, and St. Petersburg's beach communities are altered yearly by new condominiums and more development.

Separated by Tampa Bay and connected by three jam-packed commuter bridges, Tampa and St. Petersburg complement each other in dozens of ways. They share a common future: change is coming; growth is inevitable.

Even so, there's still a piece of paradise to be found here. The ethnic flavor of Tampa's Spanish-Cuban heritage lingers and the leisurely pace that draws tens of thousands of visitors yearly to St. Petersburg survives. The Tampa Bay area is still a bargain and still a place where guests are received with respect and warmth.

Tampa

Tampa was settled first, simply because it was more accessible, as first the Indians and later the farmers and other settlers worked their way west and south into Florida. The Spanish explorers fairly ignored Tampa in their quest for rumored gold and the Fountain of Youth. It wasn't until 1824 that Tampa became a true settlement, with the founding of Fort Brooke.

The Cuban cigar-makers, and generations of refugees from Spanish-ruled Cuba, came to Tampa in the mid-1800s, establishing a still-going cigar industry as well as an ethnic quarter, Ybor City. They came seeking freedom from the Spanish rulers of their homeland.

Today Ybor City, a two-mile-square Spanish city in east Tampa, offers Spanish and Cuban cafes, business houses and clubs, and Spanish theaters. Ybor Square, at Eighth Avenue and 13th Street, features arts-and-crafts shows, free musical performances on most weekends, antique marts, a nostalgia market, and more. Restaurants in the area stay open from 11 A.M. to midnight or later.

In the late 1800s, tourists began to come from all over the world, to stay in the Tampa Bay Hotel, then called "the world's most elegant hotel." Teddy Roosevelt set up headquarters at the hotel in 1898, and 30,000 U.S. troops were encamped in Tampa to train for the Spanish-American War.

The Tampa of today is emerging as a financial and business city. Tampa International Airport provides easy access and exit for residents and visitors alike. The downtown is developing quickly, yet there are plenty of lush areas on the city's edges. Residential neighborhoods such as Carrollwood and Davis Island offer plush homes and up-scale lifestyles, while older sections of town, such as oak-lined Hyde Park, are being restored for families and small businesses. Joggers can pace along the world's largest continuous sidewalk—3.8 miles in all—that borders Bayshore Boulevard, with an open-air view of Tampa Bay.

For tourists tuned to attractions, Busch Gardens, in north Tampa, is one of the most popular spots in Florida, second only to Walt Disney World. Here, more than 3,300 exotic birds await visiting eyes and cameras.

St. Petersburg

Just south of Tampa sprawls St. Petersburg, technically an island unto itself connected by three bridges to Tampa, and by another to Bradenton and Sarasota to the south. Johnny Carson occasionally jokes about the sleepy, senior-citizen reputation of St. Petersburg. Yet the growing influx of high-tech industry, the rise in median income and drop in median age, and the tenacious quest of community and business leaders for an identity separate from Tampa all belie Johnny's quips.

St. Petersburg's distinctive downtown is dominated by a waterfront rich in views and sights. The city's Museum of Fine Arts rests next to Vinoy Basin, and at the city marina the masts of scores of boats and yachts line the sky. The city's main entertainment complex, Bayfront Center, is downtown, as is the St. Petersburg campus of the University of South Florida (which has its main campus in Tampa).

The waterfront has several distinctive features. One is the city's municipal pier, topped by The Pier, an upside-down pyramid that houses a restaurant, lounge, observation deck, and information center. At its base, people and pelicans alike line up for the fishing. The view from here is one of the best in St. Petersburg.

Twenty-eight miles of public beaches line the Gulf of Mexico along St. Petersburg's west side. This is *the* place people come to relax and let go. For the more active, there's fishing—in the surf, off bridges, or out on the Gulf.

A popular activity in and around St. Petersburg is eating out. Restaurants abound in Pinellas County, with a heavy but by no means exclusive emphasis on seafood. Indeed, dining is possibly the most popular "tourist" thing to do here, next to simply lounging pool-side or on the beaches.

The sun, sand and surf, a cliche for promoters, really is here in abundance. Strolling along Gulf Boulevard, which links the string of Gulf-front communities up and down the coast, is one of the major delights on long, late summer evenings when daylight lasts past 8 o'clock.

PRACTICAL INFORMATION

WHEN TO GO. The Tampa Bay area offers a year-round supply of sunshine. Fewer than five days a year have no sunshine whatsoever. There are two tourist seasons for Tampa and St. Petersburg. The biggest is the winter season (Nov.–Mar.), when northern visitors traditionally flee the bleak cold. Many of these visitors are retired senior citizens who spend summers in the north and winters in the south. The second tourist season is during the hot, often humid months of the summer (June–Aug.), when families with children out of school can hit the road on a budget.

Rates are lower during the summer months, although major tourist attractions such as Busch Gardens (and Walt Disney World in Orlando) often fill their parking lots to the limit during the summer.

HOW TO GET THERE. By air. More than a dozen major airlines serve Tampa International Airport, including *Air Canada, American, Continental, Delta, Eastern, Northwest, Pan Am, Republic, Trans World, United,* and *USAir.* In addition, a growing number of commuter airlines as well as *American* serve the smaller St. Petersburg/Clearwater International Airport in northern Pinellas County. Virtually all of the commercial airlines offer special reduced rates into and out of Florida during the winter tourist season. Look for "air wars" between major carriers during the peak tourist months of January and February.

By bus. *Greyhound-Trailways* has regular service into Hillsborough (Tampa) and Pinellas (St. Petersburg) counties. Some competitive fares are offered during the winter months, but not often. Check with your local Greyhound reservation offices, or with your travel agent, for information and ticket prices or call 800–531–5332.

By train. You can get to Tampa and St. Petersburg by train, sort of. *Amtrak* has daily service into Florida aboard the *Silver Meteor* out of Washington, D.C., with connections along the way. The *Silver Meteor* then splits at Jacksonville, where it continues down the east coast of Florida to Miami, Ft. Lauderdale, and the area known as the Gold Coast, while the other section heads through Orlando to Tampa and the Suncoast. There is connecting charter bus service from the Tampa Amtrak station to St. Petersburg and Clearwater, which is included in the train fare. The *Autotrain* is back in business as well. It runs between Lorton, Virginia, which is about 7½ miles south of Washington, to Sanford, Florida, which is just north of Orlando. For specific fare information and reservations, call Amtrak, 800–872–7245.

By car. Driving to the west coast of Florida couldn't be easier. The old highways—U.S. 19 down the edge of the Gulf of Mexico, or U.S. 41, which parallels the coast a few miles inland—are still there and still offer an alternative to the high-speed billboard blur of the interstates. But I-75 runs down the west third of the state, also roughly parallel to the Gulf of Mexico, changing temporarily to I-275 for its run through St. Petersburg. At St. Petersburg's southern tip, I-75 picks up at the stunning new Sunshine Skyway Bridge and feeds traffic south to Bradenton, Sarasota, and beyond.

Points of Interest

Tampa
1) Al Lopez Field (baseball)
2) Greyhound Track
3) Jai Alai Fronton
4) Municipal Beach
5) Shrimp Fleet
6) Tampa Stadium
7) University of South Florida
8) University of Tampa
9) Busch Gardens

St. Petersburg
10) Bayfront Center
11) Big Pier 60
12) Al Lang Stadium
13) Derby Lane (dog racing)
14) Jack Russell Stadium
15) Salvador Dali Museum
16) London Wax Museum
17) Museum of Fine Arts
18) Payson Field (baseball)
19) Sunken Gardens
20) The Pier
21) Tiki Gardens

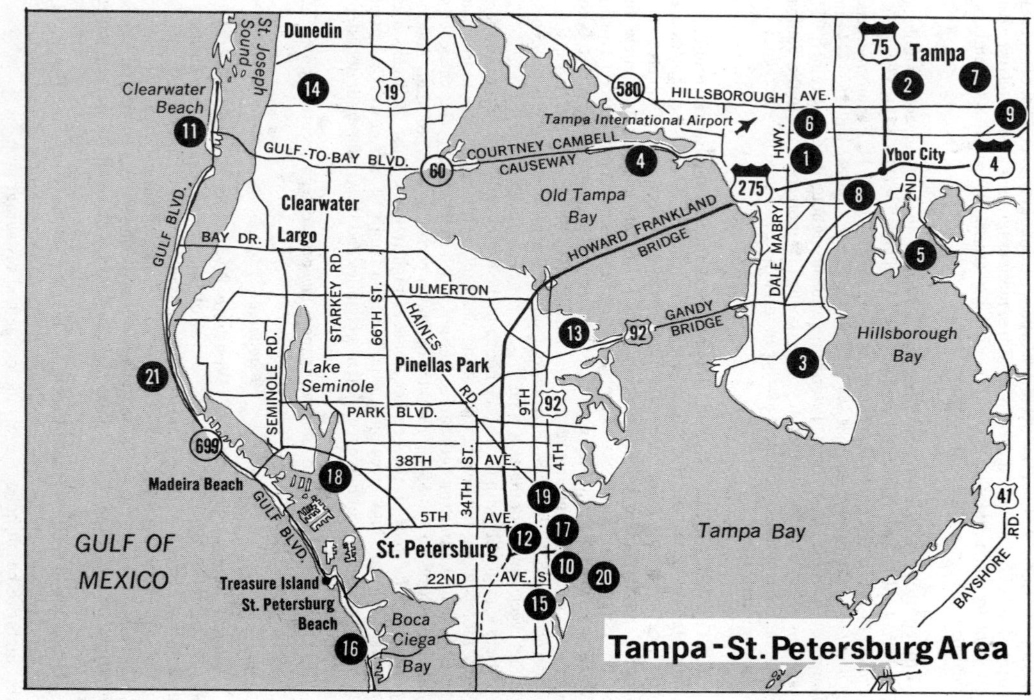

TELEPHONES. The area code for all of the west coast of Florida, including Tampa and St. Petersburg, is 813. Information (directory assistance) is 555–1212. Locally, information is 1411. Directory assistance from outside the west coast area is 813–555–1212. To check if there is a toll-free number for the motel, hotel or resort you want to reach, dial 800–555–1212, directory assistance for all 800 numbers. Local pay phones are 25 cents.

Emergency Telephone Numbers. In Tampa, these emergency numbers should be kept handy: *Police* and *paramedics,* 223–1112; *fire,* 223–4211. The *Hillsborough (Tampa) County Sheriff's* emergency number is 224–9911. For an emergency *ambulance* in Tampa, call 681–4422. And for *Poison Control,* call 253–4444 in Tampa or 800–282–3171. In St. Petersburg, and throughout Pinellas County, 911 serves for *all* emergency services. If you're staying at a motel or hotel in the Tampa Bay area, the front desk is almost always an immediate resource for emergency information and help.

ACCOMMODATIONS. With the heavy influx of tourists almost year-round, accommodations in the Tampa Bay area are abundant. In Tampa, the choices are largely between luxury high-rise hotels downtown, and more modest motels along some of the city's older arteries, many catering to military and family clientele. In St. Petersburg, the less expensive motels can be found along Fourth Street North, which once was the main entrance into St. Petersburg, and along 34th Street, both north and south of Central Avenue: incidentally, 34th Street is also U.S. 19, since bypassed by I-75. Hotels in St. Petersburg tend to cater toward long-term residents, staying weeks and months at a time.

Prices vary greatly with the season: higher in the winter and lower in the summer. Many motels along the beaches bordering the Gulf of Mexico charge more than those on Fourth Street or 34th Street, but not much more. Many offer efficiencies and charge little—$3 to $5—for a third or fourth person in a room. Many condominiums are for rent on the beaches, some at nightly rates, most for weeks and months. Prices are high, even off-season, but for a family of four, a week's rent at an off-season condo, complete with kitchen facilities and the Gulf at your doorstep, isn't unreasonable.

Hotel rates are based on double occupancy. The price categories are *Reasonable,* $35 to $75; and *Very Economical,* under $35.

Reasonable

Admiral Benbow Inn. 1200 N. Westshore Blvd., Tampa, FL 33607 (813–879–1750 or 800–237–7535). Accessible to all of Tampa, and popular with businessmen. Good seafood in the restaurant, and pleasant, comfortable rooms.

Colonial Gateway Inn. 6300 Gulf Blvd., St. Petersburg Beach, FL 33706 (813–367–2711). On the beach and close to lots of shops, restaurants and places to stroll. Has a restaurant and lounge on the premises, with an all-you-can-eat buffet seven nights a week.

Hilton Inn of St. Petersburg Beach. 5250 Gulf Blvd., St. Petersburg Beach, FL 33706 (813–360–1811 or 800–445–8667). Every room has a view and a balcony in this high-rise beach hotel. Revolving lounge and restaurant atop.

Inn on the Point. 7627 Courtney Campbell Parkway, Tampa, FL 33607 (813–884–2000). Sauna and sunning beach around an Olympic-size pool. Restaurant, lounge, tennis courts, putting green.

Tampa Airport Hilton. 2225 N. Lois Ave., Tampa, FL 33607 (813–877–6688 or 800–445–8667). New, with 240 rooms and convenient to Tampa Stadium and the interstate. Outdoor heated pool, whirlpool, color TV (with Home Box Office).

Tierra Verde Island Resort. 200 Madonna Blvd., Tierra Verde, St. Petersburg, FL 33715 (813–867–8611). Opened in 1962 by band leader Guy Lombardo, this resort has five interconnected two-story buildings and more than 60 condo units for rent, plus color TV, radio, phones, pools, bike rentals and docks.

Very Economical

Americana Motel. 3314 S. Dale Mabry Hwy., Tampa, FL 33629 (813–837–9510). Efficiencies, pool, TV and phones. Three miles south of Tampa Stadium.

Buccaneer Resort Motel. 10800 Gulf Blvd., Treasure Island, FL 33706 (813–367–1908). Rooms and apartments on private beach. Heated pool.

Econo Lodge. 321 E. Fletcher Ave., Tampa, FL 33612 (813–933–4545 or 813–933–7831). One-bedroom units with kitchenettes. Near Busch Gardens, with cable TV, free in-room movies, pool. Offers weekly or monthly rates as well.

La Mark Charles Motel. 6200 34th St. N., St. Petersburg, FL 33710 (813–527–7334). Centrally located; phones, rental refrigerators, heated pool.

Rodeway Inn. 34th St. North, St. Petersburg, FL 33713 (813–327–5647). Smartly kept downtown motel, convenient to St. Petersburg and the Gulf beach communities. Reasonable and reliable.

Safari Resort Inn. 4139 E. Busch Blvd., Tampa, FL 33614 (813–988–9191, 800–282–6291). Almost at the gate to Busch Gardens theme park. Shuttle to park, sauna, whirlpool, in-room VCR players.

Budget Motel Chains. Because of the high volume of tourist traffic through the Tampa Bay area, the motel chains are well represented. Many are located on the Gulf of Mexico, which means their prices tend to be higher than those located elsewhere in Tampa and St. Petersburg. While prices vary, generally you pay for the view. Virtually all motel chains offer a generic room—bed, bath, color TV, and phone. Pools are usually available, and many have an on-premises restaurant; if not, there's surely one nearby.

Budget motel chains with outlets in the Tampa-St. Petersburg area include: **Best Western** (800–528–1234); **Days Inns** (800–325–2525); **Holiday Inn** (800–465–4329); **Howard Johnson's** (800–654–2000); **La Quinta Motor Inn** (800–531–5900); **Omni/Dumfey Hotels** (800–228–2121); **Quality Inns** (800–228–5151); **Ramada** (800–272–6232); **TraveLodge** (800–255–3050).

Bed-and-Breakfast. For information on B&B's in the Tampa-St. Petersburg area, contact **B&B Suncoast Accommodations,** 8690 Gulf Blvd., St. Petersburg Beach, FL 33708 (813–360–1753), or **A Specialties Accommodations,** Indian Shores, 813–596–5424.

HOW TO GET AROUND. From the airport. There is no bus service out of Tampa International Airport. Shuttle van service (known locally as "limousine service") to downtown Tampa averages $7.50; to St. Petersburg, the Gulf beach communities, and the rest of Pinellas County, $8.25 to $10, depending on the company. The vans pick up outside the baggage claim area. Agencies include *Central Florida Limousine* (276–3730), serving only Hillsborough County; *The Limo* (822–3333); and *Airport Transport of Pinellas* (541–5600). Taxi fares range from $10 for most of Hillsborough County to $20 or more for most of Pinellas County.

St. Petersburg/Clearwater International Airport is served by several local taxi companies; rates into other parts of Pinellas start at $1.50. Also, a handful of rental car agencies operate out of this airport, including *Alamo* (800–327–9633).

For pickup and transportation to either airport, but especially to Tampa International Airport, reservations are required and should be made, when possible, 24 hours in advance.

By bus. There is no municipal bus service between Tampa and St. Petersburg. Check with *Greyhound-Trailways* for information and fares for trans-city runs. There is a complex and not always efficient municipal bus system in each county. Around Tampa: The Hillsborough Area Regional Transit (254–4278) serves most of the county, except Plant City. The fare is 60 cents all day, and children under 5 ride free. Around St. Petersburg: Pinellas County Transit Authority (530–9911) serves the entire county. The fare is 60 cents and transfers are 10 cents, with discounts for those over 65 and the handicapped. After 6:30 P.M., PCTA buses operate only on a Dial-a-Bus schedule; call for information.

By trolley. In St. Petersburg, a free shuttle runs along The Pier approach, from a free parking area at the foot of the structure to the upside-down, pyramid-shaped building at the end.

By taxi. Nearly a hundred major and minor taxi companies serve Tampa and St. Petersburg, and nearly every community has its own taxi company. Rates vary according to the size of the community, but remain competitive in the larger areas. Some cab companies to keep in mind: *Bay City Cab,* St. Petersburg (397–0949);

Beach Taxi and Airport Service, Clearwater Beach (797–2230); *Dart Handicapped Transportation* (for those in wheelchairs), St. Petersburg (895–5571); *United Cab,* Tampa (253–2424); *Yellow Cab,* St. Petersburg (821–7777). *Yellow Cab,* Tampa (253–0121) accepts American Express cards.

By rental car. More than fifty local and national rental car agencies operate on the west coast of Florida. Quite a choice. Rates vary with the season and with the day—and even with the tides, it seems. Many of the major agencies operating in this area have toll-free information and reservation numbers, including: *Ajax* (800–654–2529); *Alamo* (800–327–9633); *Avis* (800–331–1212); *Budget* (800–527–0700); *Dollar* (800–421–6868); *Enterprise* (800–325–8007); *General* (800–327–7607); *Hertz* (800–654–3131); *National* (800–328–4567); *Sears* (800–527–0770); and *Value* (800–327–2501). Budget rental agencies (charging about 1/3 what the others do) include *Rent-a-Wreck* (800–421–7253); *Rent-a-Relic* (239–3825 or 623–3741), in Tampa; *Ugly Duckling Rent-a-Car* (800–528–1584) in Tampa; *Rent-A-Heap* (581–4805), Clearwater.

HINTS TO THE MOTORIST. Interstate driving is not much different here than anywhere else. The three major bridges connecting Tampa and St. Petersburg—Howard Franklin Bridge, which is an extension of I-75, and Gandy Bridge and the Courtney Campbell Bridge, linking Tampa and Clearwater—are almost always crowded, and always awful during rush hour (7 A.M.–9 A.M., 4 P.M.–6 P.M.). Check your gas especially before heading onto Howard Franklin.

Right-on-red is the rule in Florida, and most streets in St. Petersburg and Tampa are controlled by a stoplight or a stop sign. Tampa has a number of one-way streets downtown that require getting used to and some major arteries are one-way as well. St. Petersburg is very easy to get oriented to: streets run north-south, avenues east-west, and the city is gridded for the most part in sequentially numbered streets and avenues, with Central Avenue as the main dividing line. U.S. 19 is an older link between St. Petersburg and northern Pinellas County, and it is congested virtually all the time.

Florida speed limits conform to federal law—55 mph on the interstates, 30 to 35 in the city. There are special speed zones for some residential areas, schools, and some older and narrowed innercity streets. While bicycling is not a major means of transportation in either city, adult tricycles are popular with many retired people in St. Petersburg, and they travel in the regular traffic lanes. One final caution: Florida no longer has a mandatory vehicle-inspection program, so it is not unusual to see cars at night with only one headlight, or faulty taillights.

TOURIST INFORMATION. For information on the Tampa Bay area, there are three primary sources. Nearly every little community has its own chamber of commerce to promote its own merchants and businesses. There is also, for first-hand information, the *Suncoast Welcome Center* (813–573–1449), just off I-275 as you come into St. Petersburg, on the Ulmerton Road exit, just east of the Showboat Dinner Theater. Open 9 A.M. to 5 P.M. daily, the staff is well-armed with brochures and answers. There is also a pair of rest rooms here. There are two other information centers operated by the *St. Petersburg Area Chamber of Commerce.* One is in the lobby at the The Pier, staffed from 10 A.M. to 4 P.M. daily. Finally, the downtown chamber office (100 Second Avenue North, St. Petersburg, 33701) is open 9 A.M. to 5 P.M. Mon.–Fri., and has information on tourist attractions, hotels, motels, restaurants, service clubs, and activities of all kinds. For visitor information, call 813–821–4715. In Tampa, call 813–228–7777, or write: *Tampa Chamber of Commerce,* Box 420, Tampa, FL 33601.

Foreign Currency Exchange. Most downtown banks in both cities will exchange some foreign currencies, generally Canadian and British. A handful, including *Landmark Union Trust,* Central Avenue and Ninth Street North, St. Petersburg, handle all foreign currencies. A modest currency exchange booth is staffed during peak hours at Tampa International Airport, in the mid-lobby area between airline ticket counters, near the escalators.

SENIOR-CITIZEN DISCOUNTS. Some attractions and activities offer a senior citizen discount. In St. Petersburg particularly, reduced prices for senior citizens—people over 65—can be found with a little effort. Some movie theaters, particularly those in the American Multi-Cinema chain, offer reduced rates for seniors with a theater card. Busch Gardens in Tampa offers senior citizens 55 or older unlimited admission to the theme park and the use of its attractions with a discounted annual pass. Also, during "Senior Safari Days" (offered during the peak winter tourist months), senior citizens receive special discount coupons for $3.50 which are good throughout the park.

There are two centers in St. Petersburg tailored for seniors—the *Sunshine Center,* 330 Fifth Street North, and the *Enoch Davis Center,* 111 18th Avenue South—that come alive daily, and sometimes nightly, with activities and special events, including political forums, wellness seminars, musical entertainment and classes. They are also good resources for information on citywide activities for seniors. Call 813–893–7101, the city's Office on Aging, for more information.

HINTS TO DISABLED TRAVELERS. The City of St. Petersburg has long been "landscaped" for individuals with limited mobility. Many downtown curbs slope at intersections, allowing for easy maneuvering by someone in a wheelchair or with a walker. Green benches, once the trademark of the city, aren't as plentiful anymore, but there are still a few choice ones to be found, usually courtesy of a nearby merchant. There is special parking, marked by signs at most public buildings, malls, shopping centers, supermarkets and so forth. Unfortunately, many able-bodied motorists use these parking spaces, but they are there nonetheless.

In St. Petersburg, programs for the disabled are coordinated through the city's *Special Populations Program* (893–7899), which provides recreation and other events for people who are mentally or physically disabled. *The Social Club* (893–7899) for disabled youth and adults (ages 13 and older) meets first and third Saturday of every month at Northwest Community Center, 7–9 P.M.

FREE EVENTS. Since so many of the leisure activities in Tampa and St. Petersburg are oriented to the outdoors, there are events year-round geared to the tourist and resident alike, many of them free. **Parades** lead the list, what with the abundance of sunshine and good weather. In Tampa, each February, pirates come to town: **The Gasparilla Invasion and Parade.** Everybody dresses up in pirate costumes, "invades" downtown Tampa, and in general gets crazy in a tourist-oriented celebration of a once-upon-a-time invasion of Tampa by a mythical Jose Gaspar and friends. Across Tampa Bay, St. Petersburg has its own annual celebration, the **Festival of States,** each March. It's one of the oldest festivals in Florida, dating back to 1896, and a yearly salute to springtime. There are band competitions and no fewer than three parades.

Seafood festivals are also very popular in the area. Treasure Island, one of the beach communities along St. Petersburg's western shoulder, turns pirate sanctuary (pirates are very big in these parts) each June during its **Pirate Days.** In November, another beach community, Madeira Beach, celebrates the start of the winter tourist season with its annual **Johns Pass Seafood Festival.** The food is local, fresh and bountiful, and there are fireworks, free fish chowder, and so on. The event is kicked off with a blessing of the fishing fleet that uses Johns Pass as its home base.

In Tampa's Riverview Park—the river is the Alafia, and the view is just fine—each July is the occasion for a **Bluegrass Festival.** There's continuous bluegrass pickin' and singin' by both professionals and local amateur groups, as well as camping, canoeing, and workshops. In October, Tampa's Latin Quarter, Ybor City, offers a **Latin Festival** on Broadway, with all the music, food, dancing, and atmosphere of an Old World celebration.

In December, the annual **Santa Parade** brings out Saint Nick in St. Petersburg, as well as thousands of youngsters, and more than 25 of Florida's best bands, marching in a parade of more than 100 units. And what would Christmas on the Gulf of Mexico be without a **boatacade?** Madeira Beach has one—a night parade of a colorfully lit line of boats cruising in and out of the fingers and inlets along the intercoastal waterway.

TOURS. Several guided tours are available in **Tampa.** *Around the Town, Inc.,* 14009 N. Dale Mabry, Tampa, FL 33618 (813–961–4120), takes groups of 25 or more on customized tours to anywhere in the Tampa Bay area. One of the most popular is the Historic Tour, through Ybor City, downtown Tampa, the residential areas, universities, museums, Port of Tampa, and Davis Islands. Reservations are suggested a month in advance. *Gray Line Sightseeing Tours,* 921 3rd St. S., St. Petersburg (822–3577, 822–0845 in Tampa), has a variety of tours available throughout the area. *Travel Is Fun,* One Day Motor Coach Tours, 157 3rd St. N., St. Petersburg (813–821–9479), offers full-day tours of sights and attractions in the area. Call ahead for scheduled tours and prices.

By boat. The *Baytowne Belle,* docked at Harbour Island, south of downtown Tampa (813–229–5380). A modest-sized tour boat, holding 49 people on two decks, the bottom one enclosed, the upper one open. Luncheon and cocktail tours last about two hours. Also available for charters around Tampa Bay and on the Hillsborough River. Other sightseeing cruises, combined with dinner and dancing, are available on several *Captain Anderson ships,* including one docked behind the Dolphin Village Shopping Center, St. Petersburg Beach (367–7804).

By foot. A walk through downtown St. Petersburg gives visitors a pigeon's eye view of the city and its waterfront. Guides are available free from the St. Petersburg Area Chamber of Commerce (821–4069 or 821–4715).

PARKS AND GARDENS. If St. Petersburg has the beaches, Tampa has the parks. Two of the best are Lowery Park and Riverfront Park. **Lowery Park,** on the corner of North Boulevard and Sligh Avenue in Tampa (935–5503), offers a fun day for the whole family, including children. It holds the only traditional zoo, though modest in offering, on the west coast of Florida, as well as fairyland creatures to play among. Open during daylight hours. **Riverfront Park,** 900 North Blvd. (251–3742), offers beautifully landscaped walkways on the banks of the Hillsborough River. There are also courts for tennis, racquetball, handball, shuffleboard and a theater-in-the-round. Open dawn to dusk.

In St. Petersburg, there's a bit of nature almost downtown. **Boyd Hill Nature Trail** and **Lake Maggiore Park,** on 9th St. South, near 36th Ave., offer boardwalks, picnic areas, family activities, a children's playground and nature center in an unspoiled tropical setting. Open daily 9 A.M. to 5 P.M. Admission is 75 cents for adults and 35 cents for children. Call 813–893–7326 for more details. **Fort De Soto Park,** just south of St. Petersburg's city limits, is located off the U.S. Bayway (54th Avenue South). It offers acres and acres of undisturbed areas for walking, resting, hiking, camping, eating, sunning, whatever-ing. The Spanish-American War ended before the fort on Mullet Key was finished, but the rusting cannons there are still menacing. Great fishing as well. For information, call 866–2484.

War Veterans Memorial Park, Bay Pines Boulevard N., Alt. U.S. 19, St. Petersburg (392–9575), presents well-kept picnic grounds, playground, open-air shelters and quiet. A World War II tank is there for children to play on, and there are boat ramps, rest rooms, eagles' nests in a fenced-in area. Open 7 A.M.–dark. Call for picnic table reservations.

THEME PARKS. Busch Gardens, 3000 E. Busch Blvd., Tampa (988–5171), is the second largest theme park in the state, next to Walt Disney World. The African theme of "The Dark Continent" is carried throughout, and the animals are spectacular. They are allowed, for the most part, to run loose in a manmade "veldt." Also to see: a Moroccan village, orangutan and bird show, African Bazaar, Timbuktu theme area, Dwarf Village and much more. There's a breeding colony of rare white Bengal tigers that are wonderful to watch and, of course, plenty of rides. Shows in Stanleyville offered at least three times a day. General admission is pricy—$19.95. Children under two admitted free. (Parking is another $2, although some nearby entrepreneurs offer a parking space for less.) Admission includes all rides, shows, and attractions. Open daily, 9:30 A.M.–6 P.M.

PARTICIPANT SPORTS. Joggers have the easiest route; there's little required for a lope down the beach or around the block, and the weather generally cooperates. When running in the street, remember to run "against" the traffic, but obey all traffic lights. On the beach, jogging demands a bit more of the runner because of the softer surface, but with most of Pinellas County's 28 miles of beaches accessible (during low tide at least), there's lots of scenic choices.

There are no municipal **bike** paths in the Tampa Bay area, although several parks do offer smaller bike paths. It's best to ask when planning to visit a state park, or when arriving. For bike rentals, try *The Beach Cyclist,* St. Petersburg Beach, (813–367–5001).

Sailing equipment is readily available. Try the *Annapolis Sailing School* in St. Petersburg (867–8102); the *La Gringa Sailing Services,* also in St. Petersburg (822–4323); and *Suncoast Sailing Center,* Clearwater Beach Marina (462–6954), with boats 17 to 65 feet long. If you say you can sail, most places will rent to you. The only exception are those flippy one-man sailboards; many sailboard rental shops along the beaches will ask for proof of skill first.

Powerboat rentals are possible, too. Try: *American Boat Rentals,* St. Petersburg (578–1661); or *Budget Boat Rentals,* Madeira Beach (397–6400). **Canoeing** fans who want to go slow and on their own power can find rentals, and a car rack, at *Art's Swap Shop* in Tampa (935–4011).

Fishing is free in salt water; a license is needed only for freshwater angling. Bridge fishing is very popular in this part of Florida; there are lots of bridges, and the water, and fish, tend to run deep under them. Others like to wade out into the low flats near shore; waders and some skill are required for this.

For those who want to go out **deep sea fishing** on the Gulf for prey such as grouper and snapper, numerous party boats are available for half-day or all-day trips. Prices run $10 for a half day, and about $18 for all day. Some boats also go out all night. Some suggested places to try: *Hubbard's Pass Port Marina,* Madeira Beach (393–1947); *Dolphin Landings,* St. Petersburg Beach (360–7411); *Florida Sports Fishing Center,* St. Petersburg (393–0407); and *Miss Pass-a-Grille,* St. Petersburg Beach (360–2082).

Golfers have dozens of courses to choose from, including the *Apollo Beach Club,* Tampa (645–6212); the *Babe Zaharis Golf Course,* Tampa (932–4401); the *Rocky Point Golf Course,* Tampa (884–5141); the *Pasadena Golf Club,* St. Petersburg (345–9329). Many golf shops rent equipment and it's a good idea to scan the sports sections of local newspapers for discount coupons for green's fees and golf-cart rental.

Swimmers have numerous municipal pools to choose from and, of course, the Gulf of Mexico is free, although treacherous in spots. For Gulf and Bay swimming, it's a good idea to ask the natives what's safe and what isn't. Johns Pass on Madeira Beach is definitely *not* safe. Tampa offers 12 municipal pools (call 223–8615 for more information), and St. Petersburg operates eight swimming pools, one of which is heated and open year-round (call 893–7441 for details). If you're a member of a YMCA or YWCA anywhere in the country, you can swim at the "Y" pools in Tampa (839–0210) or St. Petersburg (822–3911) for free. If you're not a member, there's a usage fee of $5 and $3.50, respectively.

There are dozens of tennis courts in both communities, particularly in St. Petersburg. Tampa has 78 courts (call 253–3782 for details); St. Petersburg has 77—free, lighted and open to the public until 11 P.M. (call 893–7900 for details). **Racquetball** courts are also available for a usage fee. Check the yellow pages in the telephone directory for names.

SPECTATOR SPORTS. Florida is the home base for spring training in professional baseball. Most major league teams arrive for conditioning in March and early April. For information on all teams, call 904–488–9377. In the Tampa Bay area, teams and cities include: Clearwater, Philadelphia *Phillies* (442–8496) Dunedin, Toronto *Blue Jays* (733–9302); St. Petersburg, the St. Louis *Cardinals* (421–4510); and in Tampa, the Cincinnati Reds (873–8617).

Pro-football fans can catch the home games of the NFL Tampa Bay *Buccanneers* (800–282–0683 or 813–461–2700). Professional **soccer** in the form of the Tampa Bay Rowdies (877–7800) also calls Tampa Stadium home.

Various forms of betting are legal in Florida. **Horse racing** is at *Tampa Bay Downs,* Race Track Road off State Road 580, in Oldsmar, just north of Tampa (855–4401), Dec.–Mar. **Dog racing** is available most of the year: at *Derby Lane,* 10490 Gandy Blvd., St. Petersburg (576–1361), Jan.–May, and at *Tampa Greyhound Track,* 8300 N. Nebraska Ave. (932–4313), Sept.–Jan. Admission is just $1.00 at both dog tracks; no minors allowed. The ancient Spanish sport **jai alai** is offered at the *Tampa Jai-Alai Fronton,* S. Dale Mabry and Gandy Blvd., Tampa, Jan.–mid-June, 831–1411.

And for people who like sedate gambling, **bingo** abounds as well. There are numerous small **bingo** games—$1.50 and up to play; jackpots of $25 to $100—offered every night of the week; check the local community centers and free shopper newspapers distributed at supermarkets and malls. For the big-spending bingo player, the one-of-a-kind **Seminole Bingo Hall,** run by Seminole Indians, is at 5221 Orient Road, Tampa (800–282–7016). It has 1,400 seats and jackpots of $60,000 or more.

Finally, **stock-car racing** can be seen, Feb.–Nov., at *Sunshine Speedway,* 4550 State Road 688, St. Petersburg (577–4598).

HISTORIC SITES AND HOUSES. Ybor City in Tampa has history and ethnic charm. It not only holds many of Tampa's finest and most popular Spanish restaurants, but it was funds raised in Ybor City in the 1890s that enabled Jose Marti to lead the successful invasion that freed Cuba from the Spanish, an event that culminated in the Spanish-American War. Ybor City is also the home for the cigar industry, which began in 1885, when cigar-makers migrated from Havana via Key West. In St. Petersburg's **Heritage Park,** 11909 125th St., Largo, there are old, early-Florida homes restored to their original look. These homes date back to Pinellas County's pioneer days, and include Seven Gables, a 17-room home built in 1907. There's also a log house dating back to the 1850s, and a small Florida museum. Open 10 A.M. to 4 P.M. Tues.–Sun., it's free, and guided tours are available.

MUSEUMS. Haas Historical Museum, 3511 2nd Ave. S., St. Petersburg (327–1437), is actually a series of houses and buildings, including two homes built in the 1850s, a historical and preserved railroad station, blacksmith shop, eagle's nest (without eagle), treehouse, and more. Open 10 A.M.–5 P.M. daily except Monday. Admission: $2 for adults, 25 cents for children 12 and under.

Museum of Fine Arts, 255 Beach Drive NE, St. Petersburg (896–2667), has a small but special collection displayed in a Mediterranean-style villa. Numerous traveling exhibitions visit here, and there is some fine pre-Columbian art, black-and-white photographs, and oils by Monet, Renoir, and others in the permanent collection. The museum also has a stylish but reasonable gift shop, especially at Christmas, and a small but respected art library. Open 10 A.M.–5 P.M. Tues.–Sat., 1 P.M.–5 P.M. Sun. Free.

Museum of Science and Industry, 4801 E. Fowler Ave, Tampa (985–5531). Clearly one of the most innovative museums in the Southeast. It's fun! There are hands-on exhibits dealing with the weather, physical science, botany and related sciences. The most popular is the Gulf Coast Hurricane, a wind tunnel that creates 75 mph winds that you can actually lean into. Open 10 A.M.–4:30 P.M. daily. Admission: $2 adults, $1 children up to age 15; children under 5 free.

Salvador Dali Museum, 1000 3rd St. S., St. Petersburg (823–3767). Truly a must-see museum for any Florida visit, it's the world's largest collection of works by the Spanish master, including 93 oils, 200 watercolors, and 1,000 graphics and three-dimensional objects. Valued at more than $35 million, the collection is a surrealistic tour through a one-room gallery that allows visitors to view the giant Dali works from every angle. The gift shop sells Dali memorabilia. Open 10 A.M.–5 P.M. Tues. through Sat., noon to 5 P.M. Sun. Admission: $3.25 adults, $2.25 senior citizens.

The Tampa Museum, 601 Doyle Carlton Dr., in downtown Tampa, behind the easy-to-find Curtis Hixon Conventional Hall (223–8130). This is the city's major museum, young but impressive, with a permanent collection of sculpture, ancient artifacts and nineteenth-century oil paintings. The museum has a strong hands-on program for children. The gift shop is inexpensive. Open 10 A.M.–6 P.M. Tues., Thurs., Fri.; 10 A.M.–9 P.M. Wed.; 9 A.M.–5 P.M. Sat.; 1–6 P.M. Sun. Admission free.

FILMS. Most first-run movies are found in malls and shopping centers, often in multi-plex theaters, where three or more screens are under the same roof. Check the local daily newspapers for show times and places. The best buy is before 6:00 every day, when reduced prices—often $2.25 to $2.75—are charged for the same film you'd pay $4.75 or more for at night. Second-run houses are fewer in number—the *Twin Bay Theatres* in Tampa, the *Seminole II Theatres* in north St. Petersburg, the *Beach Theatre* on St. Petersburg Beach—where tickets cost $1.50 or less.

For **art films** and **foreign films,** the choices are much fewer. The *University of South Florida in Tampa* (974–2141) offers a film series open to the public during the school sessions. *Tampa Theatre,* at the Franklin Street Mall in downtown Tampa (223–8981), has a film series, usually Thurs.–Sun. A month's membership is $2.50; individual films cost $2.50 for adults, $1 for children 13 and under. In St. Petersburg, the only established art-film house is the rustic *Beaux Arts Gallery,* 7711 60th St. N., in Pinellas Park (544–7087), which offers a film or two in a very casual atmosphere, Thurs.–Sun.

MUSIC. One of the finest orchestras in the Southeast, the **Florida Orchestra** (221–2365, Tampa; 447–4210, St. Petersburg), under the baton of leading guest conductors, performs a concert series of 10 or more programs throughout the Tampa Bay area each fall and winter, September through May. The 88-piece orchestra performs at McKay Auditorium (on the University of Tampa campus) in Tampa and at the Bayfront Center, 400 First Street, S., in St. Petersburg. The orchestra offers music from baroque to twentieth century, and also performs numerous outdoor concerts, pop concerts conducted under guest batons and has an extensive in-school program.

The Tampa Bay Chamber Orchestra (875–6476), formed in 1983, has a 35-member ensemble that performs in both cities, usually during the Florida Orchestra's off-season.

The **Tampa Oratorio Society** (988–2165) performs free concerts, mostly masses and oratorios, in the fall, winter and spring throughout the Tampa area. Finally, the **Florida Opera Inc.** (874–7667) holds performances at the Bayfront Center in St. Petersburg and in Tampa, featuring major operatic works with guest artists.

STAGE. Most local theater, professional or amateur, is geared to the nonsummer months. But there are stage productions available year-round. When in town, check out **The Playmakers,** who perform at the Cuban Club in Ybor City (248–6933), the **Tampa Players** (229–1505) and the **American Stage Company,** (822–8814), which uses a downtown movie theater for its productions in St. Petersburg.

Also very popular in the Tampa Bay area are **dinner theaters.** Patrons eat buffet-style and view a stage production, usually a comedy or musical, from the same seat. There are three in St. Petersburg: *Showboat Dinner Theater,* 3405 Ulmerton Road (576–3818); the *Country Dinner Playhouse,* Gateway Mall, 7951 9th St. N. (577–5515), and the *Encore Dinner Theater,* 1850 Central Ave. (821–6676).

DINING OUT. With a tremendous variety of restaurants to choose from and the availability of fresh seafood (grouper is the local favorite), dining out is *the* big tourist attraction in the Tampa Bay area. There are enough restaurants to go around, but seats may be hard to find during the peak dining rush, 5–8 P.M. Although many restaurants do not take reservations, it's a good idea to call ahead and try. Dress is always casual. Ties are not required even at the more expensive restaurants, but the shorts and sandals that were acceptable at lunch may not be at dinner.

Prices do differ: downtown St. Petersburg is cheaper than downtown Tampa, and the Gulf beaches are a little more expensive. Some restaurants offer newspaper coupons for reduced prices. Many restaurants offer senior citizens "early bird" specials from 4–6 P.M. weekdays, with reduced prices and reduced choices. Good prices also abound for breakfast, for everyone at downtown restaurants in both cities. On the Gulf beaches, recurring breakfast price wars bring tabs down below $1.75.

Tipping is still by choice in most restaurants, but with the increase in foreign tourists some are now adding a service charge of 12–15 percent to the bill. Tax is five percent.

Restaurant categories, based on the price of an average three-course meal for one, without beverage, tax, or tip, are: *Reasonable,* $13 to $15; *Very Economical,* $8 to $13; and *Low Budget,* under $8. Unless otherwise indicated, the restaurants all accept some, if not all, major credit cards. Every effort has been made to ensure that this list is up-to-date, but restaurants come and go so quickly that it is always advisable to call ahead.

Reasonable

Basta's Cantina D'Italia. 1625 Fourth St. S., St. Petersburg (894–7880). A full range of Italian-style dishes, including six chicken choices and as many filet mignon items.

Chavez at the Royal. 2901 Bayshore Blvd., Tampa (251–6986). Dozens of appetizers, including a shrimp souffle, sets the menu in competition with the scenic view. Nice setting for fine food from chicken to veal to duck.

Feinschmecker's. 2525 S. Pasadena Ave. S., St. Petersburg (367–7105). Offers the best of Northern European food. Out of the way and unassuming, but a treasure.

Selena's. 1623 Snow St., Tampa (251–2116). Located in rustic and tree-lined Hyde Park residential section, this is a very popular restaurant and lounge. Great salads and New Orleans and Sicilian "home cooking."

Very Economical

Friendly Inn Restaurant. 17807 Gulf Blvd., Redington Shores (397–3883). Seafood and spaghetti, plus a salad bar. Good specials as well.

Giacone's. 15229 Gulf Blvd., Madeira Beach (397–6116). Great pizza, with possibly the best crust in town, and very rich fettuccine Alfredo. Take-out service as well.

Golden Phoenix Restaurant. 107th Ave. and Gulf Blvd., Treasure Island (360–6296). Unassuming Chinese restaurant serves delicious egg drop soup and snow peas that are always fresh.

Ilona's. 2721 Gulf Blvd., Indian Rocks Beach (596–5008). A great variety of ethnic dishes on one menu—German, French, Bohemian, Hungarian—at domestic prices.

Jasmine Thai Restaurant. 13248 N. Dale Mabry, Tampa (968–1501). This Thai food is nicely mixed and spiced, with attention to subtle flavors.

Mac Dinton's. 405 S. Howard Ave., Tampa (254–1661). Seafood and more seafood, featuring shrimp and grouper fritters. Entrees come with homemade muffins and lots of extras.

Valencia Gardens. 811 W. Kennedy Blvd., Tampa (253–3773). The interior has been spruced up a bit in recent years, but the food remains as Cuban as ever. The Spanish bean soup here is renowned.

Low Budget

Adam's Rib. 213 Gulf Blvd., Indian Rocks Beach (595–4400). Great ribs, as you might expect, but there are many other tasty items on a simple menu. Ask about the Platter on the Beach.

Chattaway's. 358 22nd Ave. S., St. Petersburg (823–1594). One of the few outdoor eateries in St. Petersburg. Not much of a view, but great "chattaburgers" for $2.25.

The Frog Pond. 7380 Gulf Blvd., St. Petersburg Beach (367–6076). Breakfast and lunch are the specialties here, with huge portions.

The Greek Village. 3501 Central Ave., St. Petersburg (321–9683). Great prices for a lot of food. Features include roast leg of lamb, a revolving dessert showcase, and huge cheese pie slices.

Jack the Ribber Barbeque. 1212 W. Fletcher Ave., Tampa (969–2325). Top barbecued ribs and chicken, plus seafood. Everything's cooked fresh—baked beans, veggies, and more.

The Silver Ring Cafe. 17471 Gulf Blvd., Redington Shores (393–1460). A touch of Tampa's ethnic flavor on the Gulf Beaches. Fine Cuban sandwiches and soups, and very casual atmosphere.

Recommended Splurge. Peter's Place International Cafe. 208 Beach Drive SE, St. Petersburg (822–8436). Exquisite cuisine and service, with attention to every detail. Fixed, five-course meals with a set price of $27.50. Pre-theater and pre-concert dinners offered with 20 and 10 percent discounts with membership card from an area arts organization. House specialty is couscous, a spicy Moroccan dish of capon or filet.

NIGHTLIFE AND BARS. No, the sidewalks do not roll up at night in the Tampa Bay area, although nightlife on the west coast tends to concentrate itself. In Tampa, there is more activity around Ybor City's restaurants and lounges, and at some of the more upscale, high-rise hotel lounges. In St. Petersburg, aside from neighborhood bars and a few trendy spots, most nightlife and live entertainment is found on the beaches.

Dress is casual for most of the smaller places, trendy for some of the "in" clubs offering dancing. Drinking age is 21 in Florida, and while happy hours still abound, they're becoming less popular.

Brothers, Too. 1408 N. West Shore Blvd., Tampa (879–1962). Long popular with the music crowd; live guest bands often featured.

Clancy's. 4055 Tyrone Blvd., St. Petersburg (381–6585). Long a landmark, this lounge has an Irish flavor, huge-screen TVs for sports fans, and frequent guest groups.

Coliseum Ballroom. 535 4th Ave. N., St. Petersburg (894–1812). Not exactly a nightclub, but dancing each and every Wednesday and Saturday night—ballroom dancing, mostly to live music. Increasingly popular with younger people. Customers bring their own booze and buy setups.

Friendly Fisherman Waterfront Lounge. 150 128th Ave., W. John's Pass, Madeira Beach (391–6025). Nightly ballads to waterfront aromas. No cover, no minimum.

Hurricane Restaurant and Lounge. 807 Gulf Way, Pass-a-Grille Beach (360–9558). Good food, easy listening, and a stunning sunset view. Some jazz, some rock.

Mr. Joe's Lounge. 50 153d Ave., Madeira Beach (392–1044). Live entertainment nightly. Men's night Mon., ladies night Wed. Happy hours daily. Cover $1 Fri. and Sat.

The Stadium Lounge. 5016 N. Dale Mabry, Tampa (879–3699). Just north of Tampa Stadium; live bands, special promotional evenings, guest DJs, and plenty of rock 'n' roll.

Ten Beach Drive. 10 Beach Drive, St. Petersburg (823–0629). Downtown tradition. Near the waterfront, with a piano bar and comfortable seating.

Yesterday's Lounge. 7651 W. Waters, Tampa. (886–0666). Rock club with live bands Tues. through Sat., juke box music Sun. and Mon.

SECURITY. Common sense helps ensure safety and security when visiting any city. The local police departments will gladly help with advice and tips, as will the local chambers of commerce. The Tampa Bay can be disarming. Everything is so open and casual, it's easy to forget to lock the sliding glass door on your motel room when you go to the beach, or to leave extra cash and jewelry with the front desk of your hotel. Traveler's checks are the safest way to carry cash; be sure to leave a copy of the check numbers home with a friend, just in case.

Drive with doors locked, and windows rolled up, if that's practical. Nearly every rental car in Florida has air-conditioning. There are many areas that are fairly deserted after business hours. Some popular areas, such as Ybor City with its restaurants and lounges, are best visited with friends after 9:00 P.M. Downtown St. Petersburg is virtually abandoned after dark, except for the few theaters and restaurants.

Areas to avoid on foot after dark: In Tampa, Nebraska Avenue and some sections downtown. In St. Petersburg, avoid areas west of Ninth St. after dark, and south of Central Avenue. On the other hand, the long, long stretch of Gulf Boulevard, the thoroughfare up and down the Gulf beaches, is full of strollers until midnight, and most of it is safe and secure. Ask at the front desk of your motel or hotel, or call the local police department for more information.

TUCSON

by
Robert J. Farrell

Robert J. Farrell is an editor for an Arizona travel magazine and a free-lance writer living in Phoenix.

Spanish colonial outpost. Burgeoning high-tech center. Dude Ranch capital of the Southwest. University town. Luxury resort haven. Jumping off place for Mexico and the Gulf of California. Desert city surrounded by snow-capped mountains. Tucson has the variety to entertain and intrigue everyone.

Sprawling across a high desert valley surrounded by mountains soaring to 9,000 feet, Tucson is the sparkling jewel of southern Arizona. In the heart of the Sonoran Desert at 2,410 feet above sea level, the vegetation grows surprisingly lush with an enormous variety of arid land vegetation. Two of the world's finest stands of saguaro cactus border the city limits at Saguaro National Monument.

A short drive to the surrounding mountains takes Tucsonans another 5,000 feet higher where they can hike the cool, pine-covered slopes in summer, and snow ski in winter. Beyond the mountains to the south and east, large ranches and farms dot the rolling grasslands, and miners tear copper ore from the earth. Ghost towns, deserted when the gold and silver booms of the late 1800s played out, bask silently in the warm desert sun.

Less than 150 miles southwest, the warm sparkling blue waters of Mexico's Gulf of California beckon sport fishermen, sailors and those who just like to loll on glimmering white sand beaches.

The close proximity of Mexico gives Tucson an exotic Latin American flavor. The city began as a Spanish "presidio," or fort in 1776 (although the Hohokam Indians inhabited the area as early as A.D. 900), and remained a sleepy frontier outpost through the Mexican Revolution of 1821. The United States purchased Southern Arizona in 1854, and Tucson became an American city.

Through the latter half of the nineteenth century Anglo pioneers immigrated to Tucson and married into the leading Mexican families, forging the strong Anglo-Mexican cultural mix Tucson enjoys today.

The town grew slowly through the late nineteenth and early twentieth centuries, becoming a major stop on the Southern Pacific Railroad and the site for Arizona's first university. Tucson maintained a small college town status until World War II when military air bases near the town brought an influx of servicemen from all over the United States. They discovered Tucson was a terrific place and after the war returned to live here. They spread the word to friends and family back home, and Tucson has been growing by leaps and bounds ever since.

The major economic influences in Tucson today are the air bases and the thousands of military personnel and their families; the University of Arizona, its faculty and large student population; the astronomical observatories, scientists, and support employees; tourism and resorts, which have experienced a dramatic increase in the last few years; and high-tech industry, which could turn Tucson into another Silicon Valley within the next decade.

Tucson's character is influenced by a number of factors. First and foremost is its natural setting. The beauty of the desert, clean air, and a relaxed lifestyle create a superior "quality of life," a phrase near and dear to most Tucsonans. The cultural mix also strongly affects Tucson: architecture, style of dress, and cuisine all reflect the charm and grace found only in an Anglo-Mexican city. And the great things about Tucson that prompted so many to move here in recent years are especially great for travelers on a budget; the beauty of southern Arizona, sunshine, clean air, and the relaxed friendly people all are free.

Since Tucson developed from a small Mexican town surrounding a fort, Tucsonans decided to preserve that heritage by protecting and restoring those downtown neighborhoods as historic districts. These feature houses built in the Sonoran style—with high, two-feet-thick walls of mud adobe, small windows, and nearly flat roofs. Most of these homes were built right on the street and had an enclosed patio and garden. The cool, cavelike interiors were a welcome relief from the hot summer sun in the days before air conditioning. Historic highlights of the downtown neighborhood include the John C. Fremont House, El Adobe Mexican Restaurant, The Samaniego House, and the Cushing Street Bar. Also in the downtown area, visit the Tucson Community Center complex, the Metropolitan Tucson Convention and Visitors Bureau, and check out La Placita Village for some shopping. The juxtaposition of century-old houses with the glass and steel highrises of modern Tucson emphasizes how fast this city has grown.

Tucson is a desert city and most of it is buff colored, because many homes and businesses feature native landscaping. The central city and the University of Arizona were built before the importance of water conservation was realized and appear as a large green oasis in the desert. Points of interest on the campus include the Arizona State Museum with its comprehensive archeological exhibits; the Student Memorial Union Building, housing the bronze bell of the USS *Arizona* (sunk in the attack on Pearl Harbor); the University Art Gallery which features the Kress collection of Renaissance Art; the Grace H. Flandrau Planetarium with star shows projected on the ceiling; the Mineral Museum with a collection of specimens from all over the world. Across from the campus, the Arizona Historical Society warrants the attention of anyone seeking a complete Southwestern research library and pioneer museum. Nearby is the Center for

Creative Photography with important collections of famed photographers' work and memorabilia, including the complete works of Ansel Adams.

To really see Tucson, you need to get out and explore around the fringes of the city for the hidden jewels that delight residents and visitors alike. The Catalina Mountains tower 9,157 feet above sea level and their foothills hold a wealth of outdoor vacation pursuits. The mountain itself includes a pine-covered recreation area where there's snow skiing from January through March, and hiking and camping the rest of the year. Both the Hitchcock Highway on the south face and the road down the north face provide stunning scenic panoramas and beautiful roadside flora and fauna. The drive takes you from the Sonoran desert life-zone up to the Canadian life-zone in less than two hours. About a half hour's drive up the mountain from downtown brings you to Sabino Canyon, a wonderland of cactus, trees, trout pools, gurgling streams, picnic sites, and nature trails that give you an intimate look at the lower reaches of the Catalina Mountains.

In the northern part of Tucson near the foothills rests the evocative remains of Fort Lowell, now a museum. Once a defense position during the Apache wars of the 1880s, Fort Lowell is now partially restored and you can still see the original adobe walls that protected the soldiers. Another point of interest in north Tucson is the Gallery in the Sun, gallery of the late artist Ted De Grazia whose colorful portrayals of Indians, children, bullfighters and madonnas delighted millions worldwide. The rambling structure is unique and attractive, designed and built by De Grazia and his Yaqui Indian friends. The gallery displays bronzes, stone lithographs, etchings, serigraphs, and paintings. Also there are less expensive reproductions of De Grazia's works. Next to the Gallery is the Mission in the Sun, also built by De Grazia and dedicated to honor Our Lady of Guadalupe.

On Tucson's west side Tucson Mountain Park rolls across 17,000 acres of rugged peaks and thick desert growth such as saguaro cactus, mesquite, and ocotillo cactus providing panoramic views of the open desert, downtown Tucson and the spectacular sunsets for which the area is famous. Within the Tucson Mountains you'll find the Arizona-Sonora Desert Museum, the world famous living museum of desert animals, plants, and geology. Here, animals are kept in enclosures similar to their natural habitat. The museum also features an excellent botanical garden of desert plants, exceptional underground replicas of wet and dry desert caves, and burrowing animals. Other exhibits from fish to minerals are also here.

The next stop in the Tucson Mountains should be Old Tucson, the movie set originally built in 1940 for the western, *Arizona.* It is supposed to resemble what Tucson looked like in 1860. Old Tucson now serves as a television set–amusement area with stuntmen performing gunfights, stagecoach, pony and train rides, and an assortment of typical frontier-style buildings.

Also available in the Tucson Mountains is the 35-mile scenic drive, 17 miles of hiking and bridle trails to such destinations as pictographs, abandoned mines, and the Saguaro National Monument.

South of the mountains rests the "White Dove of the Desert," Mission San Xavier del Bac, a monument to the strong spirituality of the missionary priests. Established around 1700 by Father Kino, it represents a major breakthrough in early Spanish missionary work and has remained important to the Southwest since its founding. The present structure, completed in 1797, reigns as the queen of Spanish colonial architecture with carved stone portals, Indian murals, and elaborate altar. It fell into an era of neglect, but has been fully restored and is a fully functioning religious center for the Tohono O'odham Indians. San Xavier annually hosts fiestas on the eves of October 4th and December 2d, in honor of the two St. Francises, and also the San Xavier Pageant and Fiesta the first Friday after Easter.

Swinging east of Tucson on I-10, take the Vail exit to the Spanish Trail where the Apaches and pioneers often fought. You'll wind through the Rincon Mountains on your way west back toward Tucson, and find Colossal Cave, a huge limestone cavern with unusual formations carved by nature. Never fully explored, the cave has several openings, and bandits pursued to the cave's depths escaped a sheriff's posse here. This so-called dry cave is a constant 72 degrees Fahrenheit. It has lighted paths for easier touring.

Closer to Tucson you'll find the other half of Saguaro National Monument protecting some of the most magnificent stands of the huge saguaro cacti in the world. Saguaros grow almost exclusively in southern Arizona and in Sonora, Mexico, with only a few scattered across the border into California. They often reach 30–40 feet in height and can weigh tons. Saguaros grow very slowly, and some of the larger ones are 200 years old. The curving, twisting, looping, and pointing arms provide endless delights for photographers. The monument's Forest Loop Drive, nature trails, and the visitor center guide you through more than two dozen varieties of cacti, plus an array of desert birds, wildlife, and geology.

PRACTICAL INFORMATION

WHEN TO GO. Let's face it. Tucson emphatically is a desert town. Summer temperatures commonly exceed 100 degrees Fahrenheit. Because of a major seasonal shift in regional weather patterns, July, August, and September days may also be humid. This combination of solar radiation and moist, unstable air generates thunderstorms—characterized by winds blowing dust—and occasional downpours.

But on the bright side, even in the warmest summers, temperatures tend to plunge after sundown, and following afternoon squalls, nights on the desert usually become comfortable. But the one saving grace for Tucson and the rest of the modern American Southwest is air conditioning. The cost of cooling is built into the price of everything—but the alternative (no relief from the heat) seems unacceptable to all but the hardiest of travelers.

Another Arizona rainy season may occur from November through March. But at its latitude Tucson often is bypassed by eastward-bound Pacific storm systems. In some years Tucson gets little rain, with the yearly average just a drop or two above eleven inches. Within 40 minutes of downtown Tucson motorists may climb a mile to the ridges of the Santa Catalina Mountains, where temperatures generally are 15 to 20 degrees cooler than those of the desert floor. Likewise, in winter snow skiers revel atop nearby Mount Lemmon while water-skiers bask at Tucson's artificial lakes.

HOW TO GET THERE. By air. The only Arizona city of size south of Phoenix, Tucson enjoys air service exceeding that of other cities of similar size. Among major airlines operating to and through Tucson: *America West, American, TWA, PSA, Eastern, USAir, Delta, Northwest,* and *Aeromexico.* Several commuter lines extend scheduled service to counties and states adjoining the Tucson area.

By bus. *Greyhound-Trailways* buses service Tucson, it being a logical cross-country stopover and connection to other Southwestern cities and northern Mexico.

By train. Passenger rail service by *Amtrak* makes three stops a week in Tucson between El Paso and Los Angeles. Toll-free information: 800–USA–RAIL.

By car. A splendid highway system follows and augments America's historical Southern Route (now I-10). Also I-19 runs south from Tucson to the Arizona-Mexico border.

TELEPHONES. The area code for all of Arizona is 602. You do not need to dial the area code for a number in the same area as the one from which you are calling. Information for Tucson and all Arizona is 1–411; out-of-state call 602–555–1212. For operator assistance on person-to-person, credit card, and collect

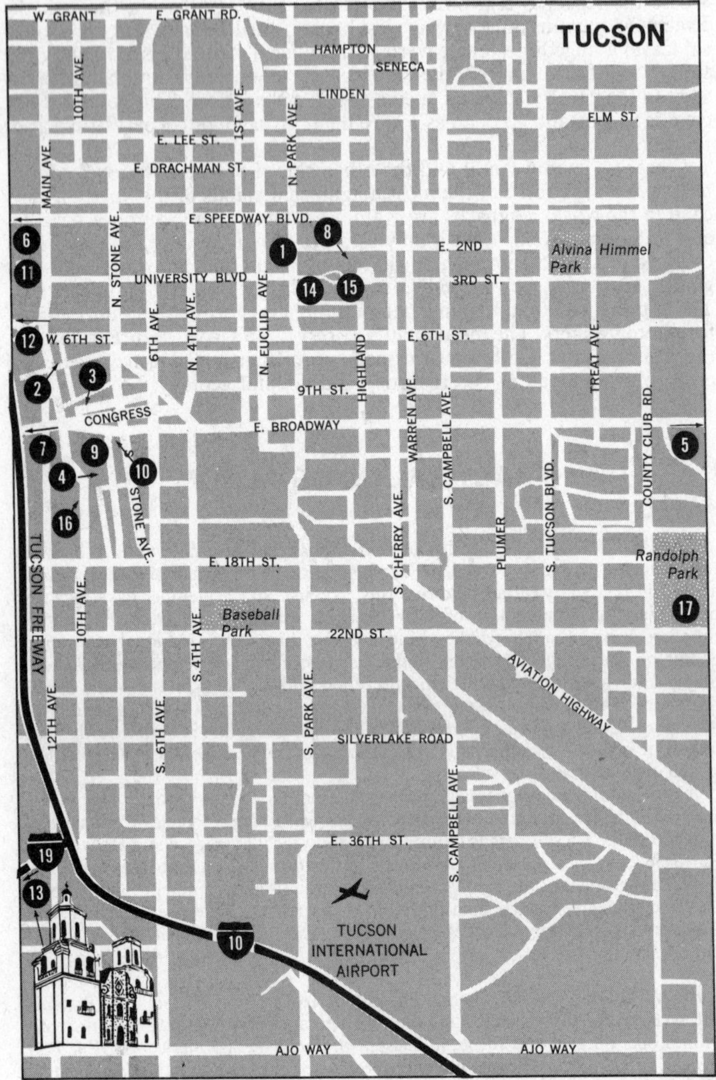

Points of Interest

1) Arizona Historical Society
2) Art Center
3) City Hall
4) Community Center
5) Colossal Cave
6) Desert Museum
7) Garden of Gethsemane
8) Mineral Museum
9) Music Hall
10) Old Adobe
11) Old Tucson
12) Pima College
13) San Xavier Mission
14) Arizona State Museum
15) University of Arizona
16) Wishing Well
17) Zoo

calls, dial an 0 first instead of 1. For telephone service to Mexico, consult the "International Calling" section at the front of the Tucson-and-vicinity telephone directory.

Emergency Telephone Numbers. In Tucson and surrounding communities the emergency number for fire, police, ambulance, police or sheriff rescue, and the highway patrol is 911. Or, dial 0 for Operator and ask for immediate connection with the appropriate agency.

ACCOMMODATIONS. Once Tucson and other warm climate communities experienced a relatively brief "tourist high," Christmas through Easter. The tourist high now begins so early and lasts so long, in effect it meets in the middle. August is Arizona's heaviest season for visitors who drive their own cars. Yet some hotels, motels, and resorts attract business with special summer rates, and it is wise to check around. Hotel rates are based on double occupancy. Categories, determined by price, are: *Reasonable,* $40 to $60; and *Very Economical,* $25 to $40.

Reasonable

Best Western Ghost Ranch Lodge. 801 W. Miracle Mile, Tucson, AZ 85706 (602–791–7565). Pool, guest laundry, sauna, Jacuzzi.

Cliff Manor Motor Inn. 5900 N. Oracle Rd., Tucson, AZ 85704 (602–887–4000). Spa, golf, tennis, coffee shop.

Desert Inn. 1 N. Freeway, Tucson, AZ 85745 (602–624–8151). Pool, dining room, 24-hour coffee shop.

La Quinta Motor Inn. 665 N. Freeway, Tucson, AZ 85705 (602–622–6491). Pool, in-room movies, complimentary coffee.

La Siesta Motel. 1602 N. Oracle Rd., Tucson, AZ 85705 (602–624–1192). Color TV, HBO, pool.

Wayward Winds Lodge. 707 W. Miracle Mile, Tucson, AZ 85705 (602–791–7526). Kitchenettes, pool, shuffleboard.

Very Economical

Franciscan Inn. 1165 N. Stone Ave., Tucson, AZ 85705 (602–622–7763). Pool, and pets.

Lamp Post Motel and Apts. 5451 E. 30th St., Tucson, AZ 85711 (602–790–6021). Kitchenettes, pool; daily, weekly, and monthly rates.

Lazy 8 Motel. 314 E. Benson Highway, Tucson, AZ 85743 (602–622–3336). Handicapped facilities, pool, airport transportation.

Quail Inn. 1650 N. Oracle Rd., Tucson, AZ 85705 (602–622–8757). Kitchens, color TV, pool, queen and king size beds, close to downtown and University of Arizona.

Tucson Inn Motor Hotel. 127 W. Drachman, Tucson, AZ 85705 (602–624–8531). Color TV, HBO, pool, free local calls, weekly and commercial rates, summer rates, near University of Arizona and downtown.

Vista Del Sol Motel. 1458 W. Miracle Mile, Tucson, AZ 85705 (602–293–9270). Pool, near shopping and restaurants.

Budget Motel Chains. Tucson seems to have at least its share of familiar chain motels. The normal range for double occupancy for these accommodations is $20 to $35 per night. Some advertise summer rates. In many instances commercial and off-season rates are negotiable.

Executive Inn. 333 W. Drachman, Tucson, AZ 85705 (602–791–7551).

Motel 6. 1031 E. Benson Highway, Tucson, AZ 85713 (602–628–1264). Pool, color TV available, dependable no frills budget chain, always clean and comfortable.

Regal 8 Inn. 1222 S. Freeway, Tucson, AZ 85705 (602–624–2516). Pool, color TV, in-room coffee, close to shopping and golf course, handicapped facilities. This chain is usually quite luxurious for a budget rate. Nationwide reservations call 1–800–851–8888.

Rodeway Inn. 810 E. Benson Hwy., Tucson, AZ 85713 (602–884–5800). Pool, in-room movies, restaurant adjacent.

Bed-and-Breakfast. An up-to-date listing of some 250 homes, ranches, and guest houses (clean, comfortable, and charming) is available through **Bed & Break-**

fast in Arizona, Inc., Box 8628, Scottsdale, AZ 85252 (602–995–2831). Another service is **Mi Casa, Su Casa Bed & Breakfast,** Box 950, Tempe, AZ 85281 (602–990–0682). For reasonable accommodations in Tucson, try **Barbara's Bed and Breakfast,** Box 13603, Tucson, AZ 85732 (602–790–2399).

Campgrounds and Rv Parks. These range from simple hookups to elaborate resorts. The following are some of Tucson's offerings: *Cactus Country RV Park,* Rte. 7, Box 840, Tucson, AZ 85747 (602–298–8428); *Crazy Horse Campgrounds,* 6660 S. Craycroft Rd., Tucson, AZ 85706 (602–574–0157); *Justin's RV Park,* 3551 San Joaquin Rd., Tucson, AZ 85746 (602–883–8340).

HOW TO GET AROUND. From the airport. Tucson International Airport is located about seven miles south of the city's center, and a taxicab ride costs $16 plus tip. Travelers should establish the approximate fee at the beginning of the trip. More reasonable is the bus limo service from and to the airport, making stops at many of the Tucson area hotels and motels.

By bus. Sun Tran operates a citywide bus service, from 6 A.M. to 7 P.M., with a few buses running until 9 P.M. The fare is 60 cents and passes are available to seniors and students. Call 792–9222 for information; a map is available from Sun Tran, 4220 S. Park, Tucson, AZ 85714.

By taxi. The cheapest way to get from the airport to almost anywhere in town is *The Arizona Stagecoach* (889–9681) which offers 24-hour service to hotels, resorts, and residences. They also feature custom tours and charter van services. The rate from the airport to downtown is $9 per person. Regular taxi fare to downtown is about $20. Companies are *Allstate Cab Company* (881–2227), *Yellow Cab* (624–6611), and *Checker Cab* (623–1133).

By rental car. As is the case in so many new western cities, Tucson sprawls; a car is the most convenient way to get around. Several agencies rent used cars. At this writing one agency, *Ugly Duckling Rent-A-Car* (602–747–3825), with three locations in Tucson, was offering a daily rate of $18.95 with 200 free miles; also weekly rates. *Budget Rent-A-Car* (602–889–8800), locations all over Tucson, offers a daily rate of $29.99, unlimited mileage; also weekly rates. *Alamo Rent-A-Car* (602–746–0196) has rates from $19.99 per day, unlimited mileage, and very low weekly rates.

HINTS TO THE MOTORIST. Tucson is a relatively easy town in which to find your way around. The streets are set up in a grid system running north–south, east–west, with few winding streets or confusing intersections. Some of the main east–west arteries running off the freeway (I-10) are Ina, Orange Grove, Prince, Grant, Speedway, 6th Street, and Broadway. North-south arteries include Thornydale, Shannon, Oracle, Stone, Kino, Country Club, Alvernon, Swan, Craycroft, Wilmot, and Kolb.

As a city without a freeway system (I-10 swings through the west and south parts of town), most driving is stop-and-go all day downtown and on main arteries during rush hours (7–9 A.M. and 4–6 P.M.). But a traffic jam in Tucson is mild in comparison with other cities. The outlying areas of the city are easy to get around in and make for delightful scenic drives. The foothills areas north and east of town are prime examples.

Parking is ample in all but the downtown and university areas. Most malls and businesses have parking. Downtown and the university have parking, but spaces are usually at a premium and restricted hours are enforced.

Technically, Arizona authorities are in full compliance with the national 55 mph speed limit. In practice, traffic officers seem to wink at 60 mph and slower. But this is no guarantee. Speed limits less than 55 mph are posted. These are strictly enforced in some urban neighborhoods and smaller municipalities. The speed limit in a school zone is 15 mph. Equally important, do not pass another car which is going slower or is stopped in a school zone. Right turns on red lights, after a full stop, are allowed unless otherwise posted. Radar zones and aircraft surveillance areas generally are posted. Penalties for driving while intoxicated can be severe—including time in jail.

DESERT DRIVING TIPS. Whatever your mode of travel *to* the desert, you should heed basic advice for motoring *through* desert country. Hot climate imposes a double burden upon equipment: the cooling system of a water-cooled engine must be in good condition to cope with desert temperatures; and air conditioning in warm weather requires extra capacity to get rid of heat. Knowing this, desert-wise motorists closely watch temperature gauges. Should engine temperature exceed normal (as in long uphill pulls or long waits in traffic) it may be best to switch off the air conditioner to reduce the engine's work load. Other desert driving tips:

• Midsummer road temperatures may reach 160 degrees. Tires should be in good condition and properly inflated.

• Watch the weather. Dust storms generated by squalls are so dangerous that, some freeways in southern Arizona are equipped with solar-powered warning signs.

• Some secondary routes have dips that flood during heavy rain. In wet weather, negotiate dips with extreme caution.

• In the highlands a swing of 40 degrees between a day's high and low temperatures is not uncommon. Water-cooled engines require both antifreeze and coolant; in colder months it's wise to pack a set of tire chains for mountain driving. At the highest elevations snow may fall as early as October and as late as June, and north-facing roadways and open bridges may be sheathed in ice.

• Remember, Arizona is the sixth-largest of the United States. For strangers, distances can be deceptively long. Carry enough fuel and allow ample time. Toward Yuma lies a stretch of 37 miles with *no* facilities. None.

• Monitor fuel supply carefully in the mountains. Uphill driving can double fuel consumption.

• Heed "open range" and "deer crossing" signs. Where rangelands are unfenced, livestock wander the roadsides. Especially after dark, deer may linger in thoroughfares.

TOURIST INFORMATION. The **Metropolitan Tucson Convention and Visitors Bureau** biannually publishes *The Official Visitors Guide to Metropolitan Tucson* which can be picked up during the center's working hours or be mailed to you upon request. Also available at the Visitors Bureau are pamphlets published by their various members. For more information write, call, or drop by: 450 West Paseo Redondo, Suite 110, Tucson, AZ 85701 (602–624–1817). Hours: Mon.–Fri., 8 A.M.–5 P.M. All brochures are free.

You may also write the **Arizona Office of Tourism,** 1480 E. Bethany Home Rd., Phoenix, AZ 85014.

SENIOR-CITIZEN AND STUDENT DISCOUNTS. Senior citizen discounts are common throughout Arizona, but there are no set standards. Some discounts are available to people over 55, others to people over 65, others range somewhere in between. Some businesses require you to fill out a card and register, others only request proof of age. The best way to find out about discounts is, simply, to ask. Most common places to find these discounts are restaurants, transportation, lodging, and drug stores. Most municipal, county, state, and federal agencies—such as national and state parks, city bus lines, and state hunting and fishing license bureaus, offer some sort of price break to the elderly, but requirements vary.

For student discounts, the same hints apply. Ask if the business or agency offers them, and have valid proof of age such as school identification. Most movie theaters offer these discounts.

HINTS TO THE DISABLED. In 1964 Congress authorized the Land and Water Conservation Fund, which channels money to state and local governments, as well as to Indian tribes, to expand and enhance outdoor recreation areas. These projects are fairly flexible as long as they provide something people can enjoy outdoors. As far as the disabled are concerned, this law mandates *access.* Many outdoor places built recently with L&WCF money are designed for handicap accessibility. The Arizona State Parks can provide more information on such areas; call or write *Arizona State Parks,* 1688 West Adams, Phoenix, AZ 85007 (602–255–4174).

Access books for major areas of the state with detailed guides for the disabled are free from the *Easter Seals Society,* 903 N. 2d St., Phoenix, AZ 85004 (602–252–6061) and 920 North Swan Road, Tucson, AZ 85710 (602–795–7542). The *Arizona-Sonora Desert Museum,* near Tucson, hosts many programs for the blind and disabled. For further information contact the museum, Route 9, Box 900, Tucson, AZ, 85704 (602–883–1380).

FREE EVENTS. For further information about the following and other events contact the Tucson Chamber of Commerce (602–792–1212). **La Fiesta de los Vaqueros Parade** in downtown Tucson occurs in late February or early March and kicks off America's largest outdoor mid-winter rodeo. Hundreds of horses, floats, handsome cowboys, and pretty cowgirls all decked out in the finest in western wear make for a colorful morning. The parade starts at 9 A.M. but be there by 8 to get a good seat.

Tucson Festival. A six-week celebration in March and April with events reflecting the Indian, Spanish, and pioneer-American phases of Tucson's development. Over 1,000 volunteers and 100 organizations take part to make this one of the top festivals in the nation. Highlights include: orchestral, choral, and ensemble music from classical to jazz; Mexican fiesta with authentic music, costumes, refreshments, and games; chuckwagon barbecue; Indian crafts, foods, and dances; cavalry and artillery in full historic uniforms.

Yaqui Easter Ceremonials. The Yaqui Indians, originally from Mexico, interpret the Easter events of Crucifixion and Resurrection in a colorful yet solemn and impressive ceremony combining Catholic ritual with tribal traditions. Ceremonies are held at Pascua Village, just south of Grant Road on Calle Central.

Tucson Pops Orchestra performs under the stars Sundays in early summer at Reid Park Bandshell. Take a picnic dinner, a blanket, and a friend. For exact dates call the Tucson Parks and Recreation Department (791–4873).

Tucson Meet Yourself. A unique three-day festival held each October at El Presidio Park to celebrate the diverse cultures that make up Tucson. Musical presentations, ethnic traditions, food, dance, and crafts. A great place to learn about the various cultures—Anglo, Spanish, Indian, black, Armenian, Norwegian, Scottish, Vietnamese, Chinese and more—that make Tucson the fascinating city it is.

TOURS AND SPECIAL-INTEREST SIGHTSEEING. Colossal Cave. On Old Spanish Trail Rd., 20 miles southeast of Tucson (791–7677). One of the world's largest dry caverns, formerly home to Indians, desperados, and explorers. In addition to stalactites, stalagmites, and calcite columns, a system of hidden lights illuminates formations such as the Frozen Waterfall, Kingdom of the Elves, Madonna, and Praying Nuns. Daily: 8 A.M.–6 P.M., summer; 9 A.M.–5 P.M., winter; open one hour later on Sun. Admission: Adults, $4; ages 11–16, $3; ages 6–10, $1.50; Includes guided tour.

Old Tucson. 201 S. Kinney Rd., 12 miles west of Tucson (883–0100). Main streets, stagecoaches, and cowboys, set on famous movie locations. An assortment of nostalgic rides, entertainment, food, and shopping. Hours: daily, 9 A.M.–5 P.M. Admission: Adults, $6.95; children 4–12, $4; under 4, free.

Sabino Canyon. 17 miles east of Tucson, via Tanque Verde Rd. and Sabino Canyon Rd. Closed to automobiles, this preserve allows you to enjoy nature at its best. Wildflowers, rushing water, trees, cacti, birds, and howling coyotes. Ride the open-air shuttle buses through the canyon, stop for picnics or short hikes, and continue your ride later. The Visitor Center displays educational exhibits, and National Forest Service naturalists are on duty to give information and offer assistance. The canyon is free to visitors, and the shuttles are offered at a reasonable price. You may enter the park on foot, bicycle, or horseback, and parking is available. Visitor Center is open 8 A.M.–4:30 P.M. daily. For information call 749–3223 (Visitor Center) or 749–2861 (shuttle bus).

Walking Tours of Tucson. The Metropolitan Tucson Convention and Visitors Bureau, 450 West Paseo Redondo, Suite 110 (624–1817), provides free brochures and detailed maps that outline places of interest. Open Mon.–Fri., 8 A.M.–5 P.M. Guided tours of the downtown historic district leave every Saturday at 10 A.M., Nov.–Apr., from the John C. Fremont House; $3 per person. Call 622–0966 for reservations.

R. W. Webb Winery. 13605 E. Benson Hwy., Vail (629–9911). Arizona's largest commercial winery gives Tucson visitors an extensive tour of their operations, demonstrations of the fascinating process of wine making. The winery produces 25,000 cases of Arizona wine annually. For a $1 admission charge, refundable upon the purchase of a bottle of wine, enjoy a sample of wine, served with bread and cheese. Tours and tastings are conducted daily, noon–5 P.M. It is recommended that you call in advance.

PARKS AND GARDENS. Saguaro National Monument, Box 17210, Tucson, AZ 85731 (629–6680). Offers a view of some of the most diverse flora of North America, including saguaro cacti (sometimes as tall as 40 ft.) which appear in enormous numbers *only* in the state of Arizona. In May and June, if the Sonoran has had ample rainfall, saguaros by the thousands put out creamy colored blossoms, which are the official state flower of Arizona. There are two units, both very close to Tucson:

Rincon Mountain Unit (296–8576) immediately east of Tucson (via E. Broadway and the Old Spanish Trail) embraces a stand of mature-to-aging saguaros. Picnicking. Winter hours, 7:30 A.M.–5 P.M.; summer hours, 6 A.M.–7 P.M. Visitors center open 8 A.M.–5 P.M. $1 per car.

Tucson Mountain Unit (883–6366) preserves a thriving forest of growing giant cacti, in 11,000 acres of typical Sonoran desert. Picnicking. The park, on Kinney Rd., is reached via AZ Route 86 or Gates Pass Road from West Speedway. Visitors center open 8 A.M.–5 P.M. Free.

Tucson Botanical Gardens. 2150 N. Alvernon Way (326–9255). Arid, semi-tropical, and tropical plants are displayed as a pleasant landscape for an adobe home. Weekdays, 9 A.M.–4 P.M.; Sat., 10 A.M.–4 P.M.; Sun., noon–4 P.M. Call for summer hours. Admission, $1.

Randolph Park. Between Broadway and E. 22nd St., west of Alvernon Way. Fun for family recreation. Offering golf courses, tennis courts, a zoo, and swimming pool.

ZOOS. "World Class" properly describes the **Arizona-Sonora Desert Museum,** 2021 N. Kinney Road (883–1380). When BBC filmed a documentary in this unique arid reserve it was named one of the world's seven top zoos, and best in America after the San Diego Zoo. Reached by a lovely fourteen-mile drive west from downtown Tucson, the museum presents some 500 species of the animals and plants of the Sonoran desert region of Arizona, Sonora, Mexico, and the Gulf of California in natural settings. Among the unusual attractions: a walk-in aviary, home of adaptive desert birds; an earth-sciences center within a maze of artificial but realistic limestone caves, and windows into the dark world of nocturnal desert life. Daily, 8:30 A.M.–sundown, winter; 7 A.M.–sundown, June–Sept. Adults, $5; children 6–12, $1. Wheelchairs and strollers provided free. All exhibits may be reached by wheelchair. Call for special tour information, including group rates. The museum may be reached via AZ Route 86 and Kinney Road, or via Speedway, Anklam Road, and Gates Pass.

A considerably less expensive zoo experience in Tucson is the **Reid Park Zoo,** Randolph Way and E. 22nd St. (791–3170), whose emphasis is on natural habitat, be it for African cats or Arctic bears. Daily, 9:30 A.M.–5 P.M., winter; 8 A.M.–4 P.M., summer; open until 6 P.M. weekends. Closed Christmas. Adults, $1.50; seniors and ages 5–14, 50 cents. Strollers available at extra cost.

PARTICIPANT SPORTS. Golf. With Tucson's climate you can golf every day of the year. Public courses are crowded during the cooler seasons, so be sure to make reservations well in advance. Greens fees are $7 and up. Public courses include: *Randolph North and Randolph South Courses,* 702 S. Alvernon Way (791–4336); *El Rio Golf Course,* 1400 W. Speedway (791–4336); *Dorado Public Golf Course,* 6601 E. Speedway (885–6751); *Cliff Valley Golf Course,* 5910 N. Oracle Rd. (887–6161); *Silverbell Golf Course,* 3600 N. Silverbell (791–4336); *Arthur Pack Golf Course,* 7101 N. Thornydale Rd. (744–3322); and *Santa Rita Country Club,* 22000 S. Houghton Rd. (629–9717). *Golf 'N Stuff,* 6503 E. Tanque Verde Rd. (296–2366); has two 18-hole miniature golf courses, hardball and softball batting cages, bumper boats, Indy carts. Open daily, all year.

Horseback riding. Miles of beautiful open desert surround Tucson and horseback is a delightful way to see it. A number of stables offer instruction, guided trail rides, hay rides, steak rides, and moonlit rides. Rates for hourly rentals start at around $10, hayrides are $5 per person. Good stables include: *Pusch Ridge Stables,* 11220 N. Oracle Rd. (297–6908); *Slim's Horseback Outfitter & Guide Service,* (825–3506); and *Tucson Mountain Stables,* 6501 W. Ina Rd. (744–4407).

Bicycling. Although Tucson has one of the largest bicycles per capita ratios in the nation, the city is surprisingly devoid of bike paths. So pay close attention when riding in traffic. *Broadway Bicycles,* 140 S. Sarnoff (296–7819), rents bikes for $10 per day, or $45 per week.

Swimming. Most hotels in Tucson offer cool pools where you can avoid the summer heat. If yours doesn't, there are numerous public pools open June–Sept. For information on rates and schedules call the Pima County Park and Recreation office at 882–2680.

Justin's Water World, 3551 San Joaquin Rd. (883–8340), is a water-fun park equipped with giant slides, swimming pools and other aquatic facilities. Open late May–Labor Day. Admission, $5.95; seniors and children under 5, free.

Tennis. For $1 you can purchase a lifetime reservation identification card from the city allowing you to make reservations at any city court that charges a fee. The fees range from 50 cents to $3 for 1½ hours. For information and reservations call 791–4873. There are courts at the following city parks: *Fort Lowell Park,* 2900 N. Craycroft Rd. (791–2584); *Himmel Park,* 1000 N. Tucson Blvd. (791–3276); *Randolph Tennis Center,* 100 S. Randolph Way (791–4896).

Hiking. *The Phone Line Trail,* the route of an old telephone line that climbs up the mountain to the Palisade ranger station, gives sightseers a view of Sabino Canyon rarely seen by the average visitor. The trail is 4½ miles long and rises 400 feet above the canyon floor. Information at Sabino Canyon Visitors Center. A shuttle will take you to this or other trails.

Snow skiing. You can be swimming, golfing, or playing tennis in the morning and still run up for an afternoon on the slopes only 35 miles from downtown Tucson in Coronado National Forest. *Mt. Lemmon Ski Valley,* Box 612, Mt. Lemmon, AZ 85619 (recorded ski report, 576–1400). The many slopes, at 8,200–9,100 ft. elevation, range in difficulty from beginner to expert, and in length from a couple of hundred yards to ¾ mile through pines and aspens. The season usually starts in late Dec. and runs through early Apr. Adult, all-day lift tickets on weekends and holidays are $20; other tickets are less. Write or call 576–1321 for further information.

Snow sledding. Lots of people have as much fun sliding down a snow-covered mountain on a sled or inner tube as skiing. Drive up the Catalina Highway, where you'll join the others. Just park your car and take a slide.

SPECTATOR SPORTS. Baseball. The Cleveland Indians conduct spring training in Tucson at Hi Corbett Field, 900 S. Randolph Way. Ticket office; 791–4096. The Tucson Toros, a Houston Astros farm team, also play at Hi Corbett Field. Ticket office: 325–2621. Tickets are $5 for box seats, $3.50 for grandstand, and $2.50 for bleachers.

University of Arizona teams play baseball, basketball, and football. Information, 621–4163; tickets, 621–2411.

Tucson Greyhound Park. S. Fourth Ave. at 36th St. (884–7576). Greyhound racing, pari-mutuel wagering, and clubhouse dining. Fully enclosed, racing rain or shine. Closed ten days at Christmas. General admission, $1.25; children under 12, free. Clubhouse admission $2.25 (no children under 12 allowed in clubhouse). Thursday ladies are free. Betting starts at $2. Wed.–Sun., 7:45 P.M. Matinees: Wed., Sat. and Sun., at 3 P.M.

Pima County Fairgrounds. 11300 S. Houghton (624–1013). Over 40 events yearly. Various horse shows, rodeos, carnivals, and livestock shows take place in exhibit halls, two covered arenas, three polo fields, jumping fields, two practice arenas, and stage. Prices generally $2.50 for adults and $1.50 for children under 12. Special days are offered for senior citizens.

HISTORIC SITES AND HOUSES. Armory Park. West of Stone Ave. A residential district, featuring homes built in the late 1880s, with styles ranging from Queen Anne to Spanish Colonial. For information call the Tucson-Pima County Historical Commission at 791–4121.

Charles O. Brown House-The Old Adobe Patio. 40 W. Broadway. This building once belonged to saloon owner, Charles O. Brown, is now the property of the Arizona Historical Society, and is one of the best examples of the Arizona Sonora style of architecture.

Casa del Gobernador. (John C. Fremont House) 151 South Granada Ave. (622–0956). This adobe structure, built in 1858, served as the home of the Arizona

Territory's most famous military governor. Luxury furnishings circa 1880. Open Wed.–Sat., 10 A.M.–4 P.M. Closed holidays. Free.

El Presidio. North of Almeda St. Tucson's original neighborhood, built around the Spanish presidio (or "fort"), established in 1775. There is a walking tour of the district and various other Tucson landmarks including the Presidio itself. For information call the Tucson-Prima County Historical Commission at 791–4121.

Fort Lowell Park and Museum. 2900 N. Craycroft Rd. (885–3832). Established in 1873, this fort was the regimental headquarters of the Sixth United States Cavalry and was the site where the Apache leader Geronimo surrendered after years of battle. Wed.–Sat., 10 A.M.–4 P.M. Closed holidays. Free.

Garden of Gethsemane. On W. Congress St. and I-10 (791–4873). Statues depicting the Last Supper, the Nativity, the Crucifixion and Christ's tomb. Created because of a vow made by an artist when his life was spared in World War I. Open daily. Free.

Mission San Xavier del Bac. Nine miles SW of Tucson, on San Xavier Rd. exit off L-19 (294–2624). Considered the finest example of mission architecture in the United States, the site was established by Father Eusebio Francisco Kino. The original structure was destroyed and today's mission was begun in 1783, and completed in 1797. Called the "White Dove of the Desert," this magnificent stark white church stands amid the brown desert and purple mountains, and combines Spanish, Byzantine, and Moorish architecture. It is the spiritual center of the Papago Indian Reservation. Masses held daily at 8 and 10:30 A.M., and 12:30 P.M. Taped lectures Mon.–Sat. hourly from 9:30 A.M.–4:30 P.M. Free.

MUSEUMS AND GALLERIES. Arizona Heritage Center. 949 E. Second St. (628–5774). Exhibition of pioneer materials. Books. Research facilities. Mon.–Sat., 10 A.M.–4 P.M.; Sun., noon–4 P.M. Closed holidays. Free.

Arizona State Museum. Campus of the University of Arizona (621–6302). Exhibits on prehistoric and modern Indians of the Southwest, including northern Mexico. Mon.–Sat., 9 A.M.–5 P.M.; Sun., 2 P.M.–5 P.M. Free.

Center for Creative Photography. 843 E. University (621–7968). The late Ansel Adams elected to place his priceless master prints of black and white photography at this center. Adding to this treasure are the works of other great American twentieth-century photographers. Mon.–Fri. 9 A.M.–5 P.M.; Sun., noon–5 P.M. Free.

De Grazia Gallery in the Sun. 6300 N. Swan Rd. (299–9191). Despite his death in 1982, Ted De Grazia's works remain popular, and his adobe studio, surrounded by his beloved desert, sponsors the creations of lesser known local artists as well. Daily, 10 A.M.–4 P.M.

Grace H. Flandrau Planetarium. University Blvd. and Cherry Ave. (621–4556). Features a 16-inch public telescope, exhibit halls devoted to space science and optics, and a gift shop. Also offered are theater performances on astronomy and space exploration. Mon.–Fri., 10 A.M.–5 P.M.; Tues.–Sat., 7–9 P.M.; weekends, 1–5 P.M. Admission charge for theater *only.*

Kitts Peak National Observatory. State Route 86 to Kitts Peak turn-off (325–9204). The world's largest astronomical facility. The Visitor Center and three telescopes are open to the public. Tours begin 10:30 A.M. and 1:30 P.M. on weekends and holidays. Free.

Mineral Museum. University of Arizona Campus (621–6024). An extraordinary display from a highly mineralized region. Included are exhibits of fine gem stones and fossils. Weekdays, 8 A.M.–12 P.M. Closed holidays. Free.

Old West Wax Museum. 205 S. Kinney Rd. (883–4203). Features scenes from movies filmed at Old Tucson and re-creations of historical figures in authentic scenes. Every day of the year, 9 A.M.–5:30 P.M. Adults, $2.75; ages 4–14, $1.50.

Pima Air Museum. Wilmot Road exit off I-10 (574–9658). More than a hundred vintage aircraft, some rare, many in flying condition. From the full scale model of the Wright Brothers' 1903 *Wright Flyer* to a mock-up of the world's fastest aircraft, the X-15. Daily, 9 A.M.–5 P.M. Adults, $4; seniors, groups, military, $3; ages 10–17, $2.

Tucson Museum of Art (TMA). 140 N. Main Ave. at Alameda (624–2333). The museum block consists of the contemporary Museum of Art, five historic buildings, and the Plaza of the Pioneers sculpture courtyard. It is designed with ramps and elevator for handicapped visitors. Tues.–Sat., 10 A.M.–5 P.M.; Sun., 1–5 P.M. Adults, $2; children, $1.

University of Arizona Museum of Art. University of Arizona Campus (621–7567). Presents special exhibits throughout the academic year in addition to its permanent collections from the Middle Ages through the twentieth century. Mon.–Sat., 9 A.M.–5 P.M. Sun., 12–5 P.M. Seasonal hours. Free.

ARTS AND ENTERTAINMENT. Film. One theater in Tucson that offers classic and foreign art films at $3 is *New Loft Theatre,* 504 N. Fremont (624–4981). Chain theaters present first-run films at around $5 admission. Possibilities include *Catalina Theater* (881–0616), *Cineworld 4 Cinemas* (745–6059), *Foothills Cinemas* (742–6174), *Mann's Park Mall Theatres* (747–0487). Others can be found under "theaters" in the Tucson "Yellow Pages." Many theaters in the area offer dollar movie night on Tuesdays.

Music. *Arizona Opera Company.* 3501 N. Mountain Ave. (293–4336). The opera presents four major productions each season, Oct.–Mar. Concerts are also presented at the *Main Auditorium,* University of Arizona, 843 E. University Blvd. (621–1111).

Dance. *The Arizona Ballet.* Music Hall, Tucson Community Center Complex, 260 S. Church Ave. (628–7446). A varied season of classical ballets.

Stage. *Arizona Theatre Company.* Little Theater, Tucson Community Center Complex, 260 S. Church Ave. (884–8210; box office, 622–2823). Offers a balance of classic and contemporary plays.

Gaslight Theatre. Gaslight Square, 7000 E. Tanque Verde Rd. (886–9428). Melodrama provides fun family entertainment with lots of audience participation including hisses and boos for the villains, and cheers for the heroes and heroines. Most shows are originals. Tickets run about $10 each. A 1950s restaurant adjoins the theater.

SHOPPING. Adobe Trading Post. 4036 East Grant Rd. (327–3845). Authentic Indian arts and crafts. Authentic, handmade jewelry, baskets, pottery, rugs, kachina dolls, sandpaintings. Hours: Mon.–Sat., 9:30 A.M.–5:30 P.M.

Downtown Mercado. Between Stone and Church Aves., off Pennington. An open-air market selling ethnic foods, fresh produce, and handmade local crafts. Open Fri. and Sat., 9 A.M.–3 P.M.

Foothills Center, 4500 North LaCholla Blvd. (742–7191). Desert sun streams through skylights and highlights the ornate columns of the tiled concourse. Chain stores, as well as specialty boutiques, restaurants, and four movie theaters. Weekdays, 10 A.M.–6 P.M.; Sat., until 6 P.M.; Sun., noon–5 P.M.

Old Town Artisans. 186 N. Meyer Ave. (623–6024). Located in Tucson's historic El Presidio neighborhood, this unique adobe structure fills an entire city block. Restored in 1978, and recognized as a historic landmark, it hosts a cafe, bake shop, and Old Town Artisans, where over 150 local artists exhibit their work. Mon.–Sat., 10 A.M.–5 P.M. Sun., noon–8 P.M.

Tanque Verde Swap Meet. Tanque Verde and Grant roads. Treasures, junque, and bargains galore can be found at this flea market. Open Wed.–Fri., 3 P.M.–11 P.M.; Sat. and Sun., 7 A.M.–11 P.M.

Tepopa Trading Co. 1628 E. Broadway (622–3063). Features an exciting and complete selection of authentic, handmade Indian items for the advanced and beginning collector. Mon.–Sat., 9:30 A.M.–5:30 P.M.

The Tucson Mall. 4500 N. Oracle Road (293–7330). Shop indoors in a cool air conditioned and lushly landscaped mall, housing 160 shops, boutiques, restaurant and picnic place as well as franchised department stores. Weekdays, 10 A.M.–9 P.M.; until 6 P.M. on Sat., until 5 P.M. on Sun.

United Nations Center – UNICEF. 2911 E. Grant Rd. at Country Club Rd. (881–7060). This non-profit store offers shoppers a variety of unique and unusual gifts from around the world. Aside from jewelry, trinkets, and original clothing, the store also carries UNICEF cards, educational materials, posters, and flags. Weekdays, 10 A.M.– 5:30 P.M.; Sat., 10 A.M.–5 P.M.; closed Sun.

DINING OUT. Perhaps the best food bargains in Tucson are the Mexican restaurants. Savory spicy food served up in huge quantities in charming surroundings, usually for less than $7 per plate. The city is famous for the vast number of these restaurants and for the high quality and variety of menus.

Other good deals include oriental food, all-you-can-eat smorgasbords, and a number of cheap-eats restaurants found around the university, where everyone is on a perpetual budget.

Restaurant categories determined by the price of a meal for one without beverages, tax, or tip are: *Reasonable*, $10 to $15; *Very Economical*, $5 to $10; and *Low Budget*, under $5. Major credit cards at least accepted unless noted otherwise. Traveler's checks are accepted nearly everywhere with identification.

Reasonable

Blue Willow Restaurant and Poster Gallery. 2616 N. Campbell Ave. (795–8736). Omelettes, quiches, salads, and soups served in a cozy renovated house. Beer and wine. Breakfast, lunch and dinner daily. No credit cards.

The Courtyard Café. 186 N. Meyer (in the Old Town Artisan's Patio) (622–0351). Healthful well-prepared soups, salads, sandwiches, and quiches. Sit inside or outside under numerous shade trees. Beer and wine. Lunch only, Mon.–Sat. No credit cards.

Lunt Avenue Marble Club. 60 N. Alvernon Way (325–4536). Varied menu from pizza to fresh fruit to steak, served in a light airy wood, glass, and plant filled atmosphere. Lunch and dinner daily. Cocktails.

Pinnacle Peak. 6541 E. Tanque Verde Rd. (296–0911). Huge steaks cooked over an open fire, barbecue ribs, salads and beans come with the meal. Old West atmosphere; if you wear a tie they'll cut it off and hang it on the wall with thousands of others. Dinner only, cocktails.

Very Economical

Bum Steer. 1910 N. Stone Ave. (884–7377). Great burgers, hot dogs, steaks and fried vegetables, plus cocktails, and an electric atmosphere with thousands of antiques, memorabilia, and junk suspended from the ceilings and walls, make for a fun place to eat and party. Cocktails. Lunch and dinner. No credit cards.

Café Magritte. 254 E. Congress St. (884–8004). Imaginative meals are served in this stylish downtown eatery. Lunch and dinner daily. Beer and wine.

Delectables. 533 N. 4th Ave. (884–9289). Step back in time for elegant, simple deli-type imported cheeses, marinated beef, salads, soups, and terrific fresh breads. Beer and wine. Lunch and dinner Mon.–Sat.

The Electric Café. 7053 E. Tanque Verde Rd. (885–2842). Truly an electric menu, including soups, crepes, quiches, sandwiches, vegetarian curry, and a selection of Mexican dishes, all freshly prepared. Beer and wine. Breakfast, lunch, and dinner daily.

Sir George's Royal Buffet. 4343 E. 22d (745–2266). All you can eat. Breakfast, lunch, and dinner. No credit cards.

Low Budget

Gordo's Mexicateria. 6940 E. Broadway (886–5386). All-you-can-eat Mexican buffet. Lunch and dinner daily. Beer, margaritas. No credit cards.

Michas. 2908 S. 4th Ave. (623–5307). Authentic Mexican food in a charming atmosphere that even includes strolling mariachis. Cocktails. Lunch and dinner daily.

Millie's West Pancake Haus. 6530 E. Tanque Verde Rd. (298–4250). Pancakes, blintzes, Belgian waffles, omelets. Breakfast and lunch daily. Closed Mon. No credit cards.

Mi Nidito. 1813 S. 4th Ave. (622–5081). A Tucson favorite for 30 years, serving great chimichangas and topopos. Cocktails. Lunch and dinner Wed.–Sun.

NIGHTLIFE AND BARS. Alcoholic beverages may be legally consumed in any licensed bar, restaurant, hotel, or inn from 6 A.M.–1 A.M. weekdays and from noon–1 A.M. on Sundays. Most open about 9 or 10 A.M. Personal supplies may be obtained from regular package stores, drugstores, or markets, most of which close about 9–11 P.M. There are no state liquor stores. Drinking age is 21.

Tucson has an eclectic mix of night spots from the typical college bars around the university, and country-western dance joints in the outlying areas, to bars where professionals hang out after a hard day at the office. The music scene is also varied, with western swing, jazz, blues, rock, new wave, easy listening—anything you could possibly want. Here is just a partial listing. For a more complete selection, check the local papers' entertainment section.

Bobby McGee's Restaurant. 6464 E. Tanque Verde Rd. (886–5551). A DJ plays Top 40s for the dance crowd every night. No cover except on Thurs.

Cushing Street Bar. 343 S. Meyer Ave. (622–7984). Great conversational atmosphere in this historic adobe. Acoustic guitar Tues.–Sat., closed Sun.

Ft. Lowell Depot. 3501 E. Ft. Lowell Rd. (795–8110). Country-western entertainment Tues.–Sat., 8:30–1 A.M. No cover charge.

Carlos Murphy's. 419 W. Congress St. (628–1956). A remodeled train station filled to the ceiling with antiques and stuff. Live dance music most nights. No cover.

The Shanty. 401 E. Ninth St. (622–9210). The attraction here is beer from all over the world, and the show is the clientele—students, professors, and local philosophers. No bands, no dancing, no cover.

SECURITY. Tucson is as safe as most major cities in the United States. If you stay out of the really bad parts of town and watch your step, you will probably have a pleasant stay in Tucson. The part of town to avoid, especially after dark, is the eastern end of downtown—specifically the neighborhood around 6th Avenue and Congress. This is the neighborhood near the bus station, where transients tend to congregate in and around skid-row bars. The rest of the town is fairly safe from this element and the only thing you have to watch out for is the vacation thief who preys on unsuspecting travelers.

WASHINGTON, D.C.

by
Judy Liberson

Judy Liberson has reviewed restaurants for the Washington Post *and contributes regularly to* USA Today, *WAMU-FM's "Morning Edition," and* Country *magazine.*

Washington is not like any other city anywhere else in the country or even the world. Referred to as the "Capital City" in slogans and bumper stickers, it is in many ways a real city-state. Thousands from the surrounding areas come to work here and depart its boundaries nightly for the trek back to the suburbs. Just recently it has experienced a kind of rebirth—the beginning of a nightlife as more downtown places attract suburbanites as well as tourists. Much of this "new" Washington is a classic restoration story: the old has been given a new lease on life, and the once deteriorating areas are receiving recognition.

Washington's popularity is indisputable. Tourism ranks as the city's second largest industry. Just stand among the crowds of eager camera-toting visitors on a bright spring morning, and you'll feel the charisma of Washington. As a symbol of democracy it seems to cast a charm with its tourist attractions, which double as actual work places. Nearly 18 million annual visitors line up to visit the U.S. Capitol, the presidential memorials, and monuments.

Yet, Washington is more than just historical monuments and buildings. It's a tableau of history at work. Visitors can spend several days or weeks uncovering all the diverse personalities of the Smithsonian museums or touring the city's unique neighborhoods. Just walking the city's streets provides excitement and an opportunity to relive American history.

Washington is a difficult city to explore. First-time visitors are often heard to remark "there is so much we haven't seen yet." Maybe that is Washington's charm. You can never tire of it, nor see it all. Prepare for your visit. Otherwise, you have to move here to see it all!

For many, a visit to Washington could not begin without first seeing the Capitol Hill section of the city. Here, after all, are the laws and the lawmakers. You'll be able to visit the Capitol Building and walk its hallowed corridors. Plan for your visit in advance and contact your senator or congressman for tickets to the chambers and the sessions. You may be lucky enough to sit in on an important committee or subcommittee hearing. Schedules are frequently published in the local newspapers and congressional offices can provide greater detail. Congressmen can also provide you with tickets for special "VIP" tours to some important city buildings. Each congressman has a limited number of these tickets, so you need to write away for these as far in advance as possible. Your one-stop "Hill" tour can include visits to congressional offices, the Senate dining room, the nearby Library of Congress, and the Supreme Court—all popular visitor attractions, all free.

Unfortunately, lodging and dining costs are quite different from the city's more than 70 free attractions; they tend to fall under "expensive" and "very expensive" categories. A budget tour of the city is not impossible, but requires logical, well-mapped plans to keep costs in the "economical" and "reasonable" ranges. Many of the bars and restaurants in the Capitol Hill area qualify for budget-conscious travelers; they also cater to Hill staff members who are more comfortable with these less-pricey establishments.

Another neighborhood that attracts record numbers is the area around the White House. As every school-age youngster knows, the White House sits at 1600 Pennsylvania Ave., N.W., but its views extend across Lafayette Park on one side, and to the Washington Monument on the other. Flanked by the gargantuan structures of the Old Executive Office Building and the Department of Treasury, the White House transmits all the feelings of governmental importance.

The White House is open for tours Tuesday through Saturday from 10 A.M. to noon. If you write your member of Congress, you may be able to get tickets for one of the longer, more detailed "VIP" tours that begin earlier in the morning. You'll probably not see any members of the First Family, but you'll catch a "postcard view" of the elegant interior rooms and furnishings and learn how each of the Presidents and their First Ladies lived and entertained. You'll also see where visiting dignitaries are met, where the President's helicopter lands, and how the significant buildings of the city are grouped for viewing.

Across from the White House, on the Mall side, is the Washington Monument, the tallest building in the city. Nothing may be built higher; no modern edifice may obstruct the view of this 555-foot-high masonry obelisk encircled by its 50 flagpoles. You can ride an elevator to the top for magnificent, unobstructed views of the city and the surrounding areas just across the Potomac River. Your trip back down is also by elevator, as the 897 steps have been closed to visitors. In summer there are occasional guided tours down to view the many memorial stones, donated by states and foreign countries, that are embedded into the walls. The monument is open daily (except December 25) from 9 A.M.–5 P.M. with summer hours from 8 A.M. until midnight. It is not surprising to find crowds lining up from early morning until late at night.

The rest of Washington's memorials and monuments are easily accessible by foot from the grounds of the Washington Monument. The nearest and newest, the Vietnam Veterans Memorial, dedicated in 1982, recently unveiled its life-size bronze servicemen sculptures. The black granite, V-shaped walls of the memorial are lined with nearly 60,000 names (listed chronologically from 1959 to 1975) from the Vietnam casualty list.

Another memorial few visitors miss is across the Reflecting Pool from the Washington Monument, the Lincoln Memorial. Its white marble evokes the Greek Parthenon and classicists can find both Doric (its outer) and Ionic (the inner) columns celebrating its Old-World architecture. The 36 columns that surround the walls represent the 36 states that were in the Union at the time of Lincoln's death. The interior walls are inscribed with the words from two of his most famous speeches, his Second Inaugural Address and the more well-known, often memorized Gettysburg Address. Foremost is the marble 19-foot-high statue of a benevolent-looking President Lincoln. This memorial is always open, except Christmas Day, and a park ranger is on duty from 8 A.M. to midnight.

On the south bank of the Tidal Basin is the pantheon-like structure of the Jefferson Memorial. Inside, Jefferson stands atop a pedestal of black granite, with four panels of his writings on freedom—most significantly the Declaration of Independence.

On the steps of the Capitol and the grounds of the Washington Monument, visitors can sit and relax during spring and summer while enjoying nightly entertainment. The most well-known celebration is the fireworks extravaganza on the monument grounds on the Fourth of July.

As you've traversed the Mall, you've been within walking distance of the Smithsonian. The areas of the Smithsonian do not really comprise a neighborhood per se, but a collection of buildings housing the nation's treasures. Each of the 10 museums on the Mall—all part of the world's largest museum complex—has a singular dedication, and an independent feel. Even if you confine your Smithsonian visits to those structures specifically on the Mall, you'll need lots of time. Each building is brimming with collection rooms. The Americana buff will become immersed within "A Nation of Nations" at the National Museum of American History, while the natural historian will be enthralled by the more than 81 million objects at the National Museum of Natural History. Of course, there is the popular, most visited museum in the world, the National Air and Space Museum. Just across 7th Street is the modern art collection at the Hirshhorn Museum and Sculpture Garden. Other art periods are housed within the east and west buildings of the National Gallery of Art.

You've really limited your wanderings through the city into a tight, almost 16-block corridor, concentrating on the Capitol area, the Mall with its museums, and the White House neighborhood. If you're planning a walk along Pennsylvania Avenue, you'll be quite surprised by its new look. Once fashionable and regarded as the legislative thoroughfare, connecting the Capitol and the White House, its prominence waned, and its buildings deteriorated. However, within recent years and under the auspices of the Pennsylvania Avenue Development Corporation (PADC), new life has been breathed into its wide streets and historic structures. Visitors strolling through the Old Post Office Building at 1100 Pennsylvania Ave., N.W., will witness architectural achievement and triumph—and have an opportunity to experience the city's new downtown life of entertainment and dining in the Pavilion, a complex of shops and restaurants located there.

To balance history with near-history, you need to take a bus up Pennsylvania Avenue into the famed Georgetown section of the city, an area that reached its heyday during the Kennedy administration when all the charm of its Federal-styled buildings and cobblestone streets matched the glitter of the White House. Since then, it has experienced several periods of alternating roller coaster popularity and downward slide. More than any other time in the past 25 years, it has become primarily a day area. Its nighttime activities are generally restricted to restaurant visits, and less for casual walks along the famed M St. or Wisconsin Ave. corridor. Its popularity with young, suburban kids and neighboring university students has made it a traffic-clogged artery whose sidewalks overflow with celebrants, yet many shopkeepers are feeling the pinch of high rents and fewer serious shoppers. Still, Georgetown remains home to a variety of first-class restaurants and cafes, and new restaurants often make their debut here.

The greatest explosion in city restaurants has taken place in the Adams-Morgan neighborhood, centered at 18th Street and Columbia Road. Here are the local ethnic restaurants and the smaller, less decorative cafés. In Washington, there are so many restaurants representing so many different ethnic groups that the standard restaurant refrain is "We've got one from every emerging country." How many cities can you name that have four Ethiopian and as many Spanish or Cuban restaurants on the same block? Adams-Morgan is a daytime walk-around area, and an evening taxi-to-the-front-door neighborhood. It's not specifically unsafe, but requires forewarning and caution.

Visitors to Washington who have more time will want to travel to the surrounding countryside for day trips to battlefields, historical properties, and the magnificence of a less hectic lifestyle. In less than an hour, you're in Annapolis or Baltimore, in the mountains of Maryland, or deep within Virginia "hunt country." As for transportation, the car you felt unsure of within the city will give you the freedom to shop and explore the countryside.

For a traveler, Washington is a hard city to forego. Few will come and visit only once, as there are so many fine, free activities to make it a year-round modern, historic destination. Its inherent magic may be due to its aura of history intertwined with its commitment to the future.

PRACTICAL INFORMATION

WHEN TO GO. Although the Japanese cherry trees do not bloom on a specific week each year, their colorful display in late March or early April along the banks of the Tidal Basin traditionally heralds the opening of tourist season and the beginning of spring. The city is at its most beautiful then, with the cherry blossoms and the thousands of tulips and daffodils that fill parks and line highways. However, for pure, natural beauty, fall rivals spring with leaf colors and optimal weather conditions for sight-seeing. For an uncrowded weekend, visit on a snowy, cold one in the middle of January!

HOW TO GET THERE. Washington exemplifies accessibility. You can travel here easily from almost anywhere, nationally or internationally. Fares are not necessarily competitive, due to the city's popularity.

By air. There are three major airports serving the city, *National, Dulles International,* and *Baltimore-Washington International.* National Airport is the closest, less than four miles from the center of the city. There are a few discount fares available, usually on off-peak weekend flights. Check with your airline since airfares are constantly changing.

By train. *Amtrak,* the national railway passenger system, offers regular, frequent rail travel along the Northeast corridor. (Hourly—except on Sat. and Sun. mornings—Metroliner Service trains that operate over this same corridor are faster and more expensive.) Trains arrive at *Union Station* which is near the Capitol and adjacent to a Metro subway stop. Call Amtrak (800–USA–RAIL) for information on special fares from other parts of the country.

By bus. *Greyhound-Trailways* operates bus service into the city. The terminal is located at 1st and L streets NE (737–5800), 4 blocks from the Union Station Metro.

By car. Washington is easily accessible by automobile but is a difficult city for many to drive in. Laid out by a Frenchman, Pierre L'Enfant, it is a city of ceremonial circles and diagonal streets making the traffic flow difficult for the novice and significantly harder for the resident who must come to a grinding halt as a visitor takes out his road map. The AAA advises out-of-town visitors to park their cars and take mass transit.

TELEPHONES. The area code for all of Washington, D.C. is 202. You do not need to dial the area code when calling from nearby Virginia (area code 703) or close-in Maryland (area code 301). Long-distance calls now require a 1 before you dial the area code, and all 800 numbers also require a 1. Pay telephones cost 25 cents. From pay telephones there is no charge for directory assistance, 411. From out of the area, dial Washington area information (202–555–1212). Many hotels and businesses have toll-free 800 numbers (call 800–555–1212 for specific information).

Emergency Telephone Numbers. For police, fire, and ambulance emergencies in the city, dial 911. Or dial 0 for "Operator" and have that person place the call. The nonemergency police number is 727–4326; nonemergency fire is 462–1762.

ACCOMMODATIONS. Washington has seldom been recognized as a budget city. Lodging within the areas near the monuments and other important tourist sites seldom falls below $100 per night. For budget-minded visitors, it means looking at weekend package plans or asking about holiday plans for the best rates. Unfortunately, from April until mid-September many establishments have their highest rates. If you are a member of a major travel club or traveling as part of a large association, you may qualify for a low, unpublicized rate—you have to ask. Look in major out-of-town Sunday newspaper travel sections for some of the best offers. Chances for securing lower rates are more easily available outside of the center of the city and in the nearby surrounding areas. Some downtown "hot" spots do run occasional, short-term specials; again, you have to ask. Be certain to phone ahead for reservations. Call the *Washington D.C. Accommodations* (800–554–2220). Or call *Capital Reservations* (1–800–VISIT–DC), a free one-stop discount reservation service for travelers to the D.C. area.

Hotel rates are based on double occupancy. District hotel tax is 10 percent, Virginia is 6.5 percent, and Maryland is 5 percent, plus D.C. has a $1 per day occupancy charge. Categories, determined by price, are: *Reasonable,* $50 to $70; and *Very Economical,* under $50.

D.C.–Reasonable

Carlyle Suites. 1731 New Hampshire Ave. NW, Washington, DC 20009 (202–234–3200). Converted former apartment building with larger than normal-size rooms. An all-suite hotel near Connecticut Ave. and Dupont Circle. Restaurant on premises. $69 to $99 with special weekend rates.

Connecticut Avenue Days Inn. 4400 Connecticut Ave. NW, Washington, DC 20008 (202–244–5600, 800–325–2525). Former independent hotel that has been completely renovated. There's no restaurant yet, but a number within walking distance. 155 rooms. Complimentary Continental breakfast served daily in lobby. Free parking available. On Metrobus line and near Red Line. $70 to $85.

Days Inn. 2700 New York Ave. NE, Washington, DC 20002 (202–832–5800). Across from the National Arboretum just off Route 50. 195 rooms. Restaurant on premises. Parking at your door. $52.

Envoy-Best Western. 501 New York Ave. NE, Washington, DC 20002 (202–543–7400, 800–528–1234). On crowded thoroughfare with parking available and restaurant on property. 78 rooms. $52.

Farragut West Hotel. 1808 I St. NW, Washington, DC 20006 (202–393–2400). Nothing fancy in a smaller, older building with an ideal downtown location. 76 rooms. Restaurants nearby. $69.

Gralyn Hotel. 1745 N St. NW, Washington, DC 20036 (202–785–1515). English-style, older hotel within 6 blocks of the White House. 38 rooms. Breakfast available. Popular with returning visitors. Shared and private bath rooms. $50 to $60 with private bath, $35 to $45 with shared bath.

Harrington Hotel. 11th and E streets NW, Washington, DC 20004 (202–628–8140, 800–424–8532). Rooms refurbished in one of city's largest, older properties. 310 rooms. Within walking distance of the majority of sights. Full-service cafeteria, the Kitcheteria. $55 to $65.

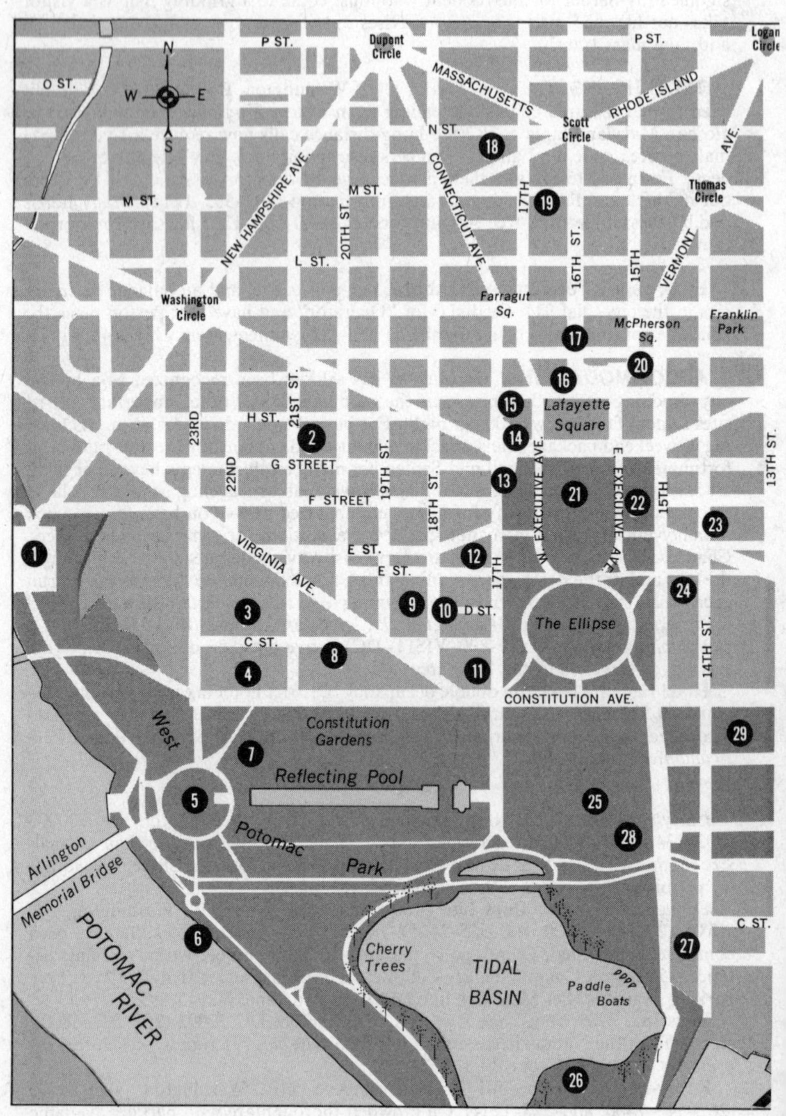

Points of Interest

Arthur M. Sackler Gallery **54**
Blair House **14**
Botanical Gardens **45**
Bureau of Printing and Engraving **27**
Capitol **47**
Constitution Hall **10**
Corcoran Art Gallery **12**
Commerce Dept. Building (Aquarium & Visitor's Center) **24**
Dept. of Energy **52**
Dept. of Interior **9**
Dept. of Justice **36**
Dept. of State **3**
Executive Office Building (former) **13**
FBI (J.E. Hoover Building) **35**
Federal Reserve Board **8**
Ford's Theater **34**
Freer Gallery of Art **40**
George Washington University **2**
Government Printing Office **53**
Hirshhorn Museum & Sculpture Garden **41**
House Office Buildings **46**
Jefferson Memorial **26**
John F. Kennedy Center **1**
Library of Congress **48**
Lincoln Memorial **5**
Metro Center **31**
National Academy of Sciences **4**
National Air & Space Museum **42**

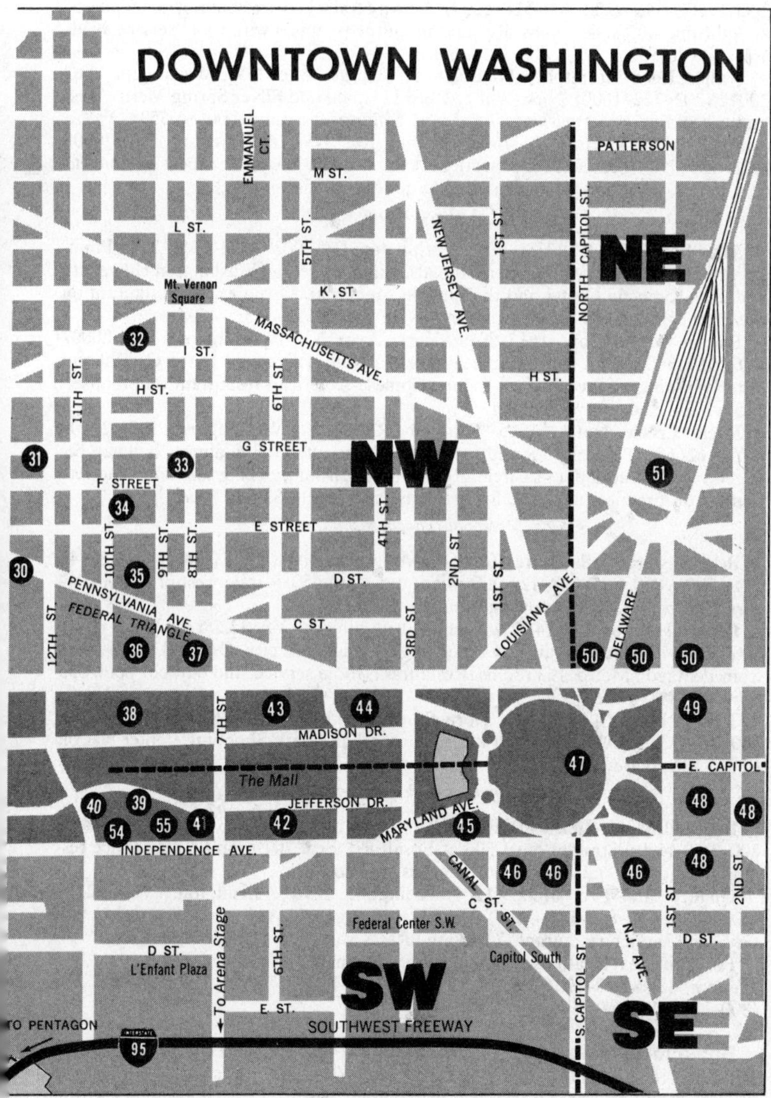

National Archives **37**
National Gallery of Art (East Building) **44**
National Gallery of Art (West Building) **43**
National Geographic Society **19**
National Museum of African Art **55**
National Museum of American Art & Portrait Gallery **33**
National Museum of American History **29**
National Natural History Museum **38**
National Theater **23**
Organization of American States **11**
The Pavilion at the Old Post Office **30**
Potomac Boat Tour Dock **6**
Renwick Gallery **15**
St. John's Church **16**
St. Matthew's Cathedral **18**
Senate Office Buildings **50**
Smithsonian Institution **39**
Supreme Court **49**
Sylvan Theater **28**
Treasury Dept. **22**
Union Station **51**
Veterans' Administration **20**
Vietnam Veterans Memorial **7**
Washington Convention & Visitors Assn. **17**
Washington D.C. Convention Center **32**
Washington Monument **25**
White House **21**

Regency Congress Inn–Best Western. 600 New York Ave. NE, Washington DC 20002 (202–546–9200, 800–528–1234). Heavily trafficked area but not one for casual nighttime walks. 49 rooms. Restaurant on the premises with room service available. $48 to $52.

Walter Reed Hospitality House. 6711 Georgia Ave. NW, Washington, DC 20012 (202–722–1600). Near Walter Reed Hospital and Silver Spring Metro. Restaurant and off-street parking. 70 rooms. Military discounts. $49 to $59.

Windsor Park Hotel. 2116 Kalorama Rd. NW, Washington DC 20008 (202–483–7700). Right off Connecticut Ave., near major, more expensive convention hotels. 43 rooms. No restaurant on premises. $54.

D.C.—Very Economical

Allen Lee Hotel. 2224 F St. NW, Washington, DC 20037 (202–331–1224). Popular with students and young internationals. Right at George Washington University and near Kennedy Center and the Lincoln Memorial. 84 rooms. No restaurant on the premises. Rooms with shared or private baths. $25–$45.

Budget Motor Inn. 1615 New York Ave. NE, Washington, DC 20002 (202–529–3900). Not a strolling neighborhood, but convenient to the Capitol and other Washington favorites. 52 rooms. Chinese-American restaurant on premises. $45 winter, $50 spring/summer.

Rock Creek Hotel. 1925 Belmont Rd. NW, Washington, DC 20009 (202–462–6007). Ideally located just off Connecticut Avenue almost halfway between the zoo and Dupont Circle. Rooms (54) constantly being upgraded and restaurant on premises available for breakfast and lunch. $38 to $46.

Metropolitan—Reasonable

Best Western–Falls Church Inn. 6633 Arlington Blvd., Falls Church, VA 22042 (703–532–9000, 800–528–1234). Straight out Route 50, ½ mile west of Seven Corners. 106 rooms. Restaurant and lounge. $50 to $60.

Imperial Motor Inn. 2485 S. Glebe Rd., Arlington, VA 22206 (703–979–4100, 800–368–4400). Just off an easy access highway into the city. One and a half miles from Pentagon Metro. 163 rooms. Restaurant, room service, and outdoor pool. $55 summer, $48 winter.

Towers Hotel. 420 N. Van Dorn St., Alexandria, VA 22304 (703–370–1000, 800–368–3339). All suites with kitchens near Landmark Shopping Center just off I-395. 186 rooms. $49 to $60.

Metropolitan—Very Economical

Imperial Motor Inn. 6461 Edsall Rd., Alexandria, VA 22312 (703–354–4400; 800–368–4400). Straight out I-395 at Edsall Rd. exit. 207 rooms. Full-service restaurant with cocktail lounge on premises. $44 to $49.

Quality Inn–Iwo Jima. 1501 Arlington Blvd., Arlington, VA 22209 (703–524–5000, 800–228–5151). Near Key Bridge and Arlington National Cemetery. Full-service restaurant. 73 rooms. Rates vary. $45 to $75.

For additional locations in outlying areas, phone the following 800 numbers. *Best Western* (800–528–1234), *Holiday Inn* (800–HOLIDAY), and *Quality Inn* (800–228–5151).

Bed-and-Breakfasts. As the concept of bed-and-breakfast inns established itself across the nation it was no wonder that the Washington area would offer quaint properties and reservation service organizations that list a variety of homes within the city's finer neighborhoods. Each property is quite different, and not all offer guests private-bath facilities. Many provide a quick cup of coffee or morning tea with a sweet roll while others get into more elaborate food arrangements. **Bed 'n' Breakfast Ltd. of Washington, D.C.,** Box 12011, Washington, DC 20005 (202–328–3510), is a reservation center that has homes in Capitol Hill, Georgetown, Logan Circle, and Dupont Circle. **Sweet Dreams & Toast, Inc.,** Box 4835–0035, Washington, DC 20008 (202–483–9191), publishes a yearly directory ($3) for other reservation services throughout the country in addition to having listings in Annapolis, and Washington, D.C. neighborhoods like Georgetown and Cleveland Park, and nearby Chevy Chase and Bethesda. Both agencies have singles from $38 and doubles from $53. Separate bed-and-breakfast properties in Adams-Morgan include the **Kalorama Guest House,** 1854 Mintwood Place NW, Washington, DC 20009

(202–667–6369), a turn-of-the-century 31-room Victorian with rates from $35 to $95 a night. Also, there's the **Adams Inn,** 1744 Lanier Place NW, Washington, DC 20009, (202–745–3600), an 11-room Victorian former townhouse with rates from $35 for a single to $70 for a room with a small kitchen. The newest property, **The Kalorama Guest House at Woodley Park,** 2700 Cathedral Ave., NW, Washington, DC 20008 (202–328–0860), near the zoo, has 19 rooms—12 with private baths—and rates from $35.

Ys and Hostels. The only Y in the metropolitan area that accepts visitors is at 420 E. Monroe Ave., Alexandria, VA 22301 (703–549–0850). They have 44 rooms that are usually filled during peak seasons. All rooms have private baths and some have television. Visa, MasterCard, and cash are accepted but no personal checks. Rates are from $22 daily for a single and from $24 for a double. Weekly rates are also available. *American Youth Hostels, Inc.,* Box 37613, Washington, DC 20003–7613 (202–783–6161), publishes a yearly handbook for its members (membership is available from $20 a year) that details properties which accept hostel members. American Youth Hostels will also refer people to the relocated **Washington International Hostel** at 1009 11th St. NW, DC 20001 (202–737–2333).

HOW TO GET AROUND. From the airport. The taxi fare from National Airport to the 16th and K St., downtown corridor should be $7.40; additional passengers pay $1 and there's a 50-cent gate fee. The fares are based on zones, not meters. Take a Virginia metered cab from the airport to Arlington ($6.80 to the Key Bridge area) or to Bethesda ($13.40 to Wisconsin Ave., East-West Highway area). Or take *Metrorail;* fares range from 80 cents and upward, depending on the time of day and your destination. The *Washington Flyer,* an airport limousine shuttle (202–685–1400), serves National, Dulles, and BWI airports and downtown on a regular schedule. Rates are $5 from National, and $12 from Dulles, and $12 from BWI.

By bus. *Metrobus* (637–7000) services all jurisdictions in the metropolitan areas. The basic fare in D.C. is 75 cents; in Maryland and Virginia, 80 cents. Buses link to subway trains for a coordinated mass transit system, and passengers planning on a subway-to-bus trip can obtain a transfer at the entering subway station for a free connecting bus ride in D.C. and as partial payment in Maryland and Virginia.

By subway. Getting around Washington and its nearby suburbs is easier than ever with Metrorail service (637–7000) available from downtown D.C. to numerous points in suburban Maryland and Virginia. Stations are easily recognized by the "M," a tall brown-colored column that has color strips (red, orange, blue, or yellow) to indicate specific lines. Inside the station there are well-detailed direction maps and each subway car has an easy-to-follow destination guide. Already nearly 70 miles of Metro have been completed with 64 stations in operation. It is far easier and more economical to travel by subway (fares range from 80 cents to $2.40) than to maneuver the streets and compete for limited parking meters. On most every line, trains run every six minutes during off-peak periods and every three minutes during rush hour. Hours of operation are from 6 A.M. to midnight, Monday through Friday, 8 A.M. to midnight Saturday, and 10 A.M. to midnight on Sundays. Holiday schedules are posted in the stations and listed in the daily newspapers.

By taxi. In the city itself, taxicab fares are also based on the unmetered zone system with the minimum ride $2.10 and additional zones charged at 90 cents per zone. Cabs are required to post the current, basic rates. Inquire in advance how many zones your ride will be so you appear in-the-know and can tabulate the fare—and ask for a receipt. Complaints in writing (with the driver's number and name and distance receipts) should be reported to Public Vehicle Services, 2041 Martin Luther King Jr. Ave. SE, 2nd floor, DC 20020 (637–1328).

Complaints about taxi fares from Virginia or Maryland into Washington (e.g., from the airports) should be addressed, in writing, with copies of receipts, to the Washington Metropolitan Area Transit Commission at 1625 I St., NW, Washington, DC 20006 (331–1671).

By rental car. Every major car rental company has offices in the Washington area, most with branches at the airports. Ask for weekend rates, weekly rates, and promotional plans. There are also a number of companies that rent older models for more moderate, less expensive rates. Two companies with very reasonable rates that will pick you up at National Airport are *Arcoa Rent A Car* (703–683–6400) and *USA/MPG Car Rental* (703–892–2088). Check with your automobile insurance company to determine if your plan covers you in a rental car or if you need additional coverage.

HINTS TO THE MOTORIST. Driving in Washington is quite difficult with the city's elaborate diagonal streets making intersections confusing and roads often merging into monument-lined circles. Basically, it's a grid system with four quadrants: N.E., N.W., S.E., and S.W. AAA (the Washington chapter's number is 331–3000) advises its members and all visitors to take mass transit because of the city's confusing traffic patterns and the shortage of parking spaces. Parking lots frequently charge $7 to $8 for several hours.

Most major thoroughfares observe special rush-hour driving rules from 7 A.M.–9:30 A.M. and from 4 P.M.–6:30 P.M. with some jurisdictions having different starting and concluding times. No parking is allowed on rush-hour designated streets during posted times; those who ignore such signs are likely to have their vehicles towed to some far-off city lot. Most city meter spaces cost a quarter for 20 minutes and meter enforcement crews speedily issue tickets for expired meters.

The highway speed limit is 55 mph but most of the parkways that surround the city have a maximum of 40 mph posted speed. Right turns on red are permitted only after a full stop and at intersections that do not have posted restrictive turn signs; most downtown intersections do not allow right turns on red at any time or until after 7 P.M. During snow emergencies, no parking is allowed on designated snow emergency routes. Drivers with radar detectors are not allowed to use them in Virginia.

TOURIST INFORMATION. The *Washington Convention and Visitors Association* (WCVA) publishes maps and booklets to make a visit to Washington fun. A general tourist brochure, "Washington DC: A Capital City" and specific brochures on dining, accommodations, attractions, and a seasonal calendar of events are available by writing WCVA, 1575 I St. NW, Suite 250, Washington, DC 20005 (202–789–7000). To find out exactly what's happening while you are in town, there's WCVA's *Dial-an-Event* line (202–737–8866). They also operate the *Washington Tourist Information Center* at the Department of Commerce building on the main floor in the Great Hall, where visitors can stop by for maps, booklets, or general information. Hours are Mon.–Sat. 9 A.M.–5 P.M. and Sun. 9 A.M.–5 P.M. from April until the end of September.

Nearby Alexandria operates the *Alexandria Tourist Council* at 221 King St., Alexandria, VA 22314 (703–549–0205) for information about events in this mid-1700s styled seaport town. They publish a calendar, booklets that list historic properties, restaurant and accommodation guides.

Foreign currency exchange. Many Washington banks offer currency exchange services. The larger, downtown branches, with two-day notice, can get most currency, even if it's not normally available. Banks are open 9 A.M.–3 P.M. Mon.–Fri., often with later closing hours Fri. Both Dulles International (703–661–8864) and Washington National (979–8383) have Service Centers where currency can be exchanged.

SENIOR-CITIZEN AND STUDENT DISCOUNTS. Most programs, except Saturday evenings, at the John F. Kennedy Center for the Performing Arts offer half-price discounts, subject to availability, for senior citizens and students with appropriate identification. Contact the Friends of the Kennedy Center, a membership auxiliary of the Kennedy Center, in the Hall of States for ticket coupons that can be used with cash purchase at the box office. Many movie theaters and college productions also have reduced price tickets. Senior citizens, with the appropriate card, can ride Metrobus for a reduced fare and can purchase special Metrorail cards for half-fare discounts. Only D.C. public school students riding to school or to a school activity received reduced bus transit. Call Metro (637–7000) for details.

HINTS TO DISABLED TRAVELERS. Many major restaurants and most hotels have ramps to make disabled accessibility a reality. It is always a good idea to telephone ahead to make any advance reservations that may help eliminate last-minute concerns. Most sidewalks have curb ramps and most parking lots and street parking areas have well-marked reserved spaces for cars that are identified by license plate or special sticker as disabled. If you are traveling to the city by rail, air, or bus notify the carrier so that any needs can be accommodated prior to arrival. While in Washington, if your plans include a Tourmobile ride, telephone (554–7020) to make advance plans for their hydraulic-lift van. The WCVA publishes an "attractions" brochure that details facilities readily available for disabled persons and those that need advance notice to make arrangements. Likewise, the **Information, Protection and Advocacy Center for Handicapped Individuals,** 300 I St., NE, Suite 202, Washington, DC 20002 (547–8081) has a set of six brochures called "Access Washington: For Handicapped Individuals." Write for price information.

FREE EVENTS. The beauty of Washington is enhanced by the large number of free events and activities that are open to everyone. The National Park Service operates all the **monuments** and there are no charges, although visitors may experience long waits at the Washington Monument, especially in the summer months. The Washington Convention and Visitors Association publishes a quarterly "Calendar of Events," a seasonal look at things going on, many of which are free. You can't miss with a visit to Washington, something is always going on. **Inaugural festivities** that include parades, concerts, and films kick off the winter season every fourth year. Annually, in February there's the parade festivities surrounding **Chinese New Year** with firecrackers and dragon dancers winding through Chinatown (between 6th and 8th streets from G to H). Also, the annual **Saint Patrick's Day Parade,** which has the "wearers of the green" marching down Constitution Ave.

The **Cherry Blossom Festival,** held in early April, has fireworks, princesses, and floats celebrating the beginning of spring. During that same period there's the **White House Easter Egg Roll.** There's also a number of free events at the John F. Kennedy Center's **Imagination Celebration.**

For a zany homemade costume parade, there's the mid-April **Gross National Parade,** sponsored by radio station WMAL to benefit the Police Boys and Girls clubs of D.C. The route begins at 18th and M streets and winds up at Wisconsin and M streets in Georgetown. Late April and early May inaugurate the **international school and church fairs.** Different ones are held almost every weekend.

Memorial Day Weekend traditionally marks the beginning of the free **outdoor concerts** at the memorials and monuments sponsored by the nation's military bands. The **National Symphony Orchestra** also has outdoor presentations on Memorial Day, the Fourth of July, and Labor Day. In late June and early July, there is the Smithsonian-sponsored **Festival of American Folklife** (357–2700), the fireworks and concert celebration at the Washington Monument for the Fourth of July, and the July 14 **Bastille Day Waiters' Race,** which runs for 12 blocks beginning at Dominique's Restaurant at 20th and Pennsylvania Ave. NW.

Fall seems as festive a season as any other, with an International Children's Festival at **Wolf Trap Farm Park** (Vienna, VA) over the Labor Day weekend (255–1900), a weekend ethnic neighborhood celebration, **Adams-Morgan Day** in mid-September, and **Rock Creek Park Day** at the end of the month (426–6832). The big November event that attracts participant runners from all over the country is the **Marine Corps Marathon** which begins at the Iwo Jima Memorial in Arlington.

Christmas in the Washington area includes candlelighting celebrations in Old Town and at the Pageant of Peace on the Ellipse and Mall grounds with nightly choral performances at the national Christmas tree. The John F. Kennedy Center for the Performing Arts has an annual holiday celebration with many free events and the Smithsonian has a week-long, end-of-December special event program (357–2700). Washington also has a magnificent New Year's Eve Festival at the Old Post Office.

Besides the seasonal yearly events, Washington offers its bounty of free attractions at the **Smithsonian museums,** including the **National Zoo,** the **Corcoran Gallery of Art,** the historic buildings and monuments, the **U.S. National Aboretum,** and **Kenilworth Gardens.**

TOURS AND SPECIAL-INTEREST SIGHTSEEING. Tourmobile Sightseeing, 1000 Ohio Dr. SW (554–7950). This privately owned company is a concessionaire of the National Park Service and provides narrated shuttle service to 18 historic sites including Arlington National Cemetery. From April until October, 9:30 A.M. to 4:30 P.M. daily, they offer separate tours to Mount Vernon. Same-day reboarding tickets (available at one of the well-marked kiosks or directly from the driver) are $7 for adults and $3.50 for children. You can take a separate tour of Arlington Cemetery 8:30 A.M. to 4:30 P.M. daily; $2.25 adults, $1 child which includes stops at the Kennedy grave sites, the Tomb of the Unknown Soldier with the changing of the Guard, and a stop at Arlington House, home of Robert E. Lee. Disabled visitors are advised to notify the offices in advance for information about the hydraulic lift vans. If you want to include a tour of Mount Vernon, you can purchase a two-day pass for $20 for adults, $10 for children, available Apr.–Oct.

Sightseeing companies offer tours of the city by night, but most of these fall into a more expensive category than our budget guide. To see Washington by night economically, take the elevator to the top of the 315-foot clock tower at the **Old Post Office,** Pennsylvania Ave. and 12th St. NW (523–5691) open daily 10 A.M.–5:45 P.M. and in summer from 8 A.M.–11 P.M., or ride to the top of the **Washington Monument,** daily 9 A.M.–5 P.M.; 8 A.M.–midnight, Apr. 1–Labor Day.

There are two ways for the general public to see the White House, by **Congressional ticket** (VIP pass), or in a first-come, first-serve line. Contact your appropriate Congressional office (House zip code is 20515; Senate zip is 20510) and ask for VIP tickets; specify the date and the number of people. These tickets are free, but each Senator and Congressman has a monthly quota so visitors are advised to contact the Congressional offices as soon as possible. When you arrive in town, go to your appropriate Congressional office and also get **Senate and House gallery passes,** required for Visitor Gallery admission, and a Congressional letter that lets you dine in the Senate dining room during specified luncheon hours. Call the general Congressional switchboard (202–224–3121) and ask for your member's direct-dial number. Congressional offices can also make reservations and get tickets for tours of the FBI, the State Department, the Capitol and the John F. Kennedy Center for the Performing Arts.

FBI. 9th St. and Pennsylvania Ave. NW (324–3447). Free hour-long tours are available Monday–Friday 8:45 A.M.–4:15 P.M. Visitors see crime labs, photos of the ten most-wanted criminals, and watch a life firearms target demonstration.

The John F. Kennedy Center for the Performing Arts. New Hampshire Ave. at Rock Creek Pkwy. (202–254–3643). Free tours are conducted by the Friends of the Kennedy Center and held daily except Christmas, New Year's and Thanksgiving. The first public tour begins at 10 A.M. with the last 60-minute tour leaving at 1 P.M. Participants will see each of the four theaters and will learn about the center's history.

State Department Reception Room. 2001 C St. NW (647–3241). Tours are available by reservation. The tours last approximately 45 minutes and include the diplomatic reception rooms on the eighth floor, with their detailed collection of eighteenth-century Americana. Young children are discouraged from taking this tour. Mon.–Fri., 9:30 A.M., 10:30 A.M., and 3 P.M.

U.S. Capitol. National Mall, East End (225–6827). Free half-hour tours depart almost continuously from the Rotunda. Visitors see Statutary Hall, the Crypt that was designed to hold George Washington's remains, and hear a history of the building. In winter they also get to see either the House or Senate chamber. To watch a session from the Visitor's Gallery, you need a special pass available directly from your Senator or Congressman's office. Tours are available daily except Thanksgiving, Christmas, and New Years, 9 A.M.–3:45 P.M.

Voice of America. 330 Independence Ave. SW; visitors entrance on C St. SW, between Third and Fourth streets (485–6231). The VOA, which broadcasts in 42 languages, has tours daily at 8:30 A.M., 9:30 A.M., 10:40 A.M., 1:40 P.M., and 2:40 P.M. with reservations preferred. They last approximately 30 minutes and include visits to the master control room, the news room, the technical operations center, and transmitting broadcast studios.

White House. 1600 Pennsylvania Ave. NW (456–7041). VIP visitors see a little more of the White House than those on the general tours. Basically, the five mansion rooms that all groups see are the celebrated East Room, the Green, Blue, and Red Rooms, and the State Dining Room. The White House is open to the public free of charge, with admission through the East Gate, Tues.–Sat., 10 A.M.–noon. From Memorial Day to Labor Day specific time-designated admission tickets are available at a booth on the Ellipse from 8 A.M.–noon.

PARKS AND GARDENS. If you want to see some of the city's private gardens, there's the Georgetown Garden Tour in mid-April (333–4953), the Old Town House and Garden Tour in late April, and Chevy Chase and Cleveland Park house and garden tours in late spring. *The Washington Post* Weekend section lists such events. Most of these have admission fees.

Dumbarton Oaks, 1703 32nd St. NW (342–3200), sits in the heart of Georgetown. The nineteenth-century mansion with ten acres of formal gardens, houses a Byzantine and pre-Columbian art collection. The museum is open Tues.–Sun. 2–5 P.M. free, but there is a garden admission fee of $2 Apr.–Oct. Guided garden tours are available.

Hillwood, 4155 Linnean Ave. NW (686–5807), sits almost squarely in the middle of the city. Visitors see the gardens (Japanese Gardens, French Gardens, Rhododendron Walk, and Rose Garden) and the well-furnished rooms of what was the Marjorie Merriweather Post mansion. The gardens and museum are closed Tues. and Sun., open the rest of the week, 11 A.M.–4 P.M. Two-hour tours of the mansion, advance reservations required, start at 9 A.M., 10:30 A.M., noon, and 1:30 P.M. $7. Garden visit only, $2. No one under 12 admitted.

Kenilworth Aquatic Gardens, Kenilworth Ave. and Douglas St. NE (426–6905) are home to water plants including lotuses and bamboo that grow in ponds along the Anacostia River. Flowers are in bloom from late May to early fall. Open daily 7 A.M.–dark. Free tours daily during the summer at 9 A.M., 11 A.M., and 1 P.M. on weekends.

Rock Creek Park, one of the country's largest urban parks, with over 1,700 acres and miles of biking, hiking, and jogging trails, is a thing of beauty that almost everyone comments on after a visit to Washington. Some roads (Beach Drive at Broad Branch Road up to the Maryland line) are closed from 7 A.M.–7 P.M. Sat. and Sun., so that recreational pursuits can continue without the annoyance of motorized vehicles. There are picnic tables and fields, exercise courses, a Nature Center with a planetarium (5200 Glover Rd. NW, 426–6829), tennis courts, and a working mill. The National Zoological Park (3000 Connecticut Ave. NW, 673–4717) sits inside its perimeter.

U.S. Botanic Garden, Maryland Ave. at First St. SW (225–8333). When you're visiting Capitol Hill, you're a grassy area away from an in-town garden with Easter lily, azalea, cacti, and palm tree collections. Open daily 9 A.M.–5P.M., until 9 P.M., June–Aug. Free.

U.S. National Arboretum, 3501 New York Ave. NE (475–4815). For the city's largest azalea display, you'll have to join the springtime crowds lining up on the park's 444 acres complete with a bonsai collection and a National Herb Garden. Open Mon.–Fri. 8 A.M.–5 P.M. and weekends from 10 A.M. Free. The Bonsai Collection is open 10 A.M.–2:30 P.M.

ZOOS. The National Zoological Park in the 3000 block of Connecticut Ave. NW (673–4800) is also part of the Smithsonian Institution. Over the last several years, it has been undergoing an almost continual modernization program. Now, there's a new home for the white Bengal tigers, a giant walk-through aviary, and fun-filled Monkey Island. The giant pandas (a gift from China) are the zoo's most famous residents. The zoo can be quite a hilly outing for some, but there are plenty of benches and quick food stops to regain strength. Admission is free but parking, which can fill up quickly on a bright sunny day, is $3. Or you can arrive by Connecticut Ave. bus or Metro's Red Line (Woodley Park–Zoo stop). The grounds are open daily 8 A.M.–6 P.M.; buildings open 9 A.M.–4:30 P.M. From May 1–Sept. 15 the grounds are open until 8 P.M. and the buildings until 6 P.M.

PARTICIPANT SPORTS. With the abundance of public land afforded by both Rock Creek Park and the national Mall, almost every imaginable sport has its fair share of enthusiasts. It's not unusual to see a volleyball game in one corner of the Mall and a polo match in another. Joggers seem to favor all seasons as they trade three-piece suits for shorts and tennis shoes. Each Friday the *Washington Post* Weekend section publishes a list of sporting events.

Jogging and running are especially popular around the memorials and monuments, and along the paths of Rock Creek Park. The big event for racers is the annual November *Marine Marathon.*

Tennis. D.C. Department of Recreation tennis courts are available on a first-come, first-serve basis or by permit (673–7646). Pay courts are available at Hains Point, 16th and Kennedy streets NW, and near Rock Creek Park at Peirce Mill. Call 554–5962 for information for all three.

Bicycling. There are paths all the way from Mount Vernon, VA, to Rockville, MD, and along the C° Canal. Hour or day bike rentals are available at Fletcher's Boat House, Reservoir and Canal roads NW (244–0461) and at Thompson Boat Center, Rock Creek Pkwy. at Virginia Ave. NW (333–4861).

Boating. One of the prettiest water settings is by the Jefferson Memorial where visitors can rent a paddleboat. If water sports along the Potomac or the canal sound even more romantic, there are three places that have boat and canoe rentals, Jack's Boats at 3500 K St. NW (337–9642), Thompson's, and Fletcher's (see under bicycling).

Fishing. One of the most popular springtime sports along the banks of the Potomac is fishing for the otherwise expensive but popular catch, the shad. The rocky stretch below Chain Bridge in Virginia, where enthusiasts hike down the rocks to the water's edge, is filled with fishermen.

Horseback riding. You can rent a horse for a guided tour right within Rock Creek Park at Rock Creek Stables, Military and Glover Rds. NW (362–0117), for $11 daily except Mon.

Golf. In East Potomac Park there are two 9-hole and one 18-hole courses (863–9007) and an 18-hole course within Rock Creek Park (723–9832) at 16th and Rittenhouse NW. Rates are $3.50 for 9 holes and $6 for 18 with higher holiday and weekend rates.

Swimming. Several public pools are available (576–6436). Also, members of the YMCA from others parts of the country can pay $5 and use the new recreational facilities at the Y at 1711 Rhode Island Ave. NW (862–9650) during off-peak hours.

Ice skating. During well-frozen, solid periods of winter, skaters can travel along designated areas of the C° Canal (299–3613) from Georgetown up to Maryland along posted areas of the park. Those who need skates and want more of a central location can enjoy the National Sculpture Garden Rink (289–7560) on Constitution Ave. between 7th and 9th sts. Admission and skate charge.

SPECTATOR SPORTS. Except for professional baseball, the Washington area has a spectator sport for every season. For **football,** there's the *Washington Redskins* who play home games at RFK Stadium at E. Capitol and 22nd streets SE, but have tickets available only for pre-season events. **Basketball** fans have the *Washington Bullets* who play at Capitol Centre (350–3400) in Landover, Maryland. The same field becomes transformed within hours to meet the needs of the **hockey** team, the *Washington Capitals* (350–3400). There's **horse racing** for almost every season and every type of racing enthusiast with tracks at *Laurel* for six months out of the year. As for university games, there are outstanding competitive teams in football at the University of Maryland, and basketball at Georgetown University. All summer there are Sunday afternoon **polo** matches on the fields of the Lincoln Memorial. **Tennis** fans will enjoy world-class names at the *Virginia Slims Event* in January and the *D.C. National Bank* tourney in July. **Golfers** will see the big names in June at the *Kemper Open* at Congressional Country Club.

CHILDREN'S ACTIVITIES. What better way for a child to unwind from the demands of sightseeing than a romp on the grass of the **National Mall!** All the museums and monuments that surround the Mall are child-oriented as well as filled with adult pleasures; there's plenty for everyone. Some of the **Smithsonian** highlights include The Insect Zoo, a live collection with an actual beehive and the Discovery Room, a hands-on young person's science lab (need advance, free tickets from the information booth), in the National Museum of Natural History. Nearby at the National Museum of American History is Ford's original Model T, gowns worn by the first ladies, and antique musical instruments. *Discovery Theater,* Baird Auditorium, National Museum of Natural History (357–1500), gives children's music, dance, mime, and puppet presentations. Weekday morning schedule; weekend afternoons. Reservations needed. Children $2.50, adults $3. Discounts for groups.

Or take the kids over to the **Tidal Basin Boat House** (484–3475) at 15th St. and Maine Ave. SW, and exercise those legs with a paddle boat rental. Rentals ($5.50

an hour at press time) are available, depending on the weather, from 10 A.M.–dark. If you want someone else to do the work, then you can take a narrated **mule-drawn barge** ride from mid-April to mid-October along the C&O Canal aboard *The Georgetown* from 30th and Thomas Jefferson streets NW, at $4 for adults, $3 for seniors, and $2 for children. Call (472–4376) for exact Wed.–Sun. schedule. Or grab a frisbee, pack a picnic, and enjoy the Mall grounds and Rock Creek Parkway.

What child could resist "The Spirit of St. Louis," the "Wright Flyer," a walk-through Skylab, or a touchable Moon Rock in the **National Air and Space Museum?** This museum also holds some of the city's most popular continuously-running movies (on a 5-story screen). *To Fly, The Dream Is Alive,* and *On the Wing.* $2 adults, $1 children, seniors and students. Food is available. Before you leave the Mall area, young children will enjoy a photo-opportunity climb aboard "Uncle Beazley," a statute of a triceratops dinosaur on the Mall side of Natural History or a springtime ride (Apr.–Sept., weather permitting) aboard an old-fashioned beautifully maintained late 1940's carousel near the Arts and Industries Building.

The Capital Children's Museum, 800 Third St., at H St. NE (543–8600), is just as its name implies. A young person's hands-on museum with a working Mexican village, a metric room, a Future Center complete with computers, and additional city "touch and go" exhibits in every nook and cranny of the building. Parking is $2 and there is an admission charge of $4 for adults and children. Open daily, 10 A.M.–5 P.M.

Children won't want to miss the **Bureau of Printing and Engraving** at 14th and C streets SW (447–1380) where they'll be able to join a free self-guided tour and watch real money being made. The Gift Shop does a brisk business in selling souvenir sacks of shredded money! Mon.–Fri., 9 A.M.–2 P.M.

HISTORIC SITES AND HOUSES. It's hard to talk about historic sites in Washington as almost everything seems to qualify. We'll just list a couple of different ones not mentioned elsewhere in this chapter.

Decatur House, 748 Jackson Pl. NW (673–4030), is the nineteenth-century former home of Naval officer Stephen Decatur. Convenient to the White House, it was the first private residence at Lafayette Square. Visitors see both Victorian- and Federal-style period rooms in the designated National Historic Landmark. Open Tues.–Fri., 10 A.M.–2 P.M. and on weekends from noon–4 P.M. Adults, $2.50; students and senior citizens, $1.25; children under 7, free.

Old Stone House, 3051 M St. NW (426–6851), is the oldest surviving house in Washington, built in 1765. Its six rooms have been restored and furnished in colonial American decor. Open Wed.–Sun., 9:30 A.M.–5 P.M. Closed on all holidays. Free.

MUSEUMS AND GALLERIES. How can you miss learning about our nation in a city so totally devoted to the cultural enrichment of its residents and visitors? The Smithsonian Institution, founded in 1846, now has 13 local museums and the National Zoo under its domain. There are over 78 million collected artifacts, with about 1 percent of that total on display at any one time. There's never an admission charge and visitors have no difficulty spending days within each building or touring some of the temporary special exhibits. The only word of caution for first-timers is that you probably can't see it all or do it all, so plan your time carefully and visit the special exhibit or museum that caters to your particular interests. For recorded information, call Dial-A-Museum (357–2020). Buildings are open daily except Christmas from 10 A.M.–5:30 P.M. with extended summer hours. 357–1300 is the information number for museums, unless noted.

National Museum of American History at 14th St. and Constitution Ave. NW, is home to Americana collections, with everything from George Washington's teeth to the original "star spangled banner." At 10th and Constitution Ave. NW, dinosaurs, giant meteorites, and a living coral reef are at the **National Museum of Natural History.** The **Freer Gallery of Art** at 12th St. and Jefferson Dr. SW, is home to a large collection of Oriental art and some late 19th- and 20th-century American art. New on the Mall are the **Arthur M. Sackler Gallery,** filled with art from Asia and the Near East; and the brand new **National Museum of African Art,** the only museum in the country that houses exclusively African art and artifacts. Both museums are underground with above-ground entrance pavilions in the Victorian Garden behind the Smithsonian Castle. Modern art followers will delight to the indoor and outdoor collections at the **Hirshhorn Museum and Sculpture Garden** at 7th St. and Independence Ave. SW. In the summertime you can enjoy lunch at the outdoor terrace restaurant. Next door is the museum world's most popular attraction, the **National Air and Space Museum,** with its 23 galleries that trace the contributions of aviation. The **National Gallery of Art** at 4th St. and Constitution Ave. NW (737–4215), houses European and American paintings and sculpture from the thirteenth century to the present day in its East and West Wings. The **Arts and Industries Building** at 900 Jefferson St. SW, is the second oldest Smithsonian building on the Mall, and home of the "1876 Centenial Exhibition." Away from the Mall area are the **National Museum of American Art** at 8th and G streets NW, home of the **National Portrait Gallery** and site of Abraham Lincoln's second inaugural reception. Across from the White House at 17th and Pennsylvania Ave. NW, is the **Renwick Gallery,** which is devoted to contemporary and historic American crafts and decorative arts.

The **Corcoran Gallery of Art,** 17th St. and New York Ave. NW (638–3211), is the city's largest private gallery with a major emphasis on American paintings and sculpture from the eighteenth century to the present day. Photography exhibits are frequent and local Washington artists receive particular attention. Open Tues.–Sun. 10 A.M.–4:30 P.M. Thurs. until 9 P.M. Free to gallery, admission fee to select exhibits.

The **National Archives** at 8th St. and Constitution Ave. NW (523–3000), house the original documents upon which our nation is based—the Declaration of Independence, the Constitution, and the Bill of Rights. Open daily except December 25 from 10 A.M.–5:30 P.M. with longer summer hours. Those who want to trace family histories should enter through the 8th St. and Pennsylvania Ave. NW, entrance for the upstairs Microfilm and Research Rooms open Mon.–Fri. from 8:45 A.M.–10 P.M. and Sat. 9 A.M.–5 P.M. The Nixon Presidential Materials Project, the well-known Watergate tapes, are available at 845 S. Pickett St. in Alexandria. A shuttle runs from the 7th and Pennsylvania Ave. Archive entrance. Call for schedule.

ARTS AND ENTERTAINMENT. Even in this high-priced city, there are numerous opportunities to see a variety of cultural productions for reduced prices. *Ticketplace* on F Street Plaza, between 12th and 13th sts., NW (TIC-KETS), operates a same-day half-price ticket window and sells full-price (future performances) tickets. Open Mon., noon–2 P.M.; Tues.–Sat., 11 A.M.–6 P.M. Most events at the Kennedy Center are included under the Friends of the Kennedy Center format, which offers half-price tickets for senior citizens, students, disabled individuals, and certain members of the military.

FILMS. There is no shortage of movies houses in the city and surrounding suburbs; it seems each month announces the opening of a new theater, many with three or four smaller screens under one roof. The only city theater with first-run features that has remained intact, complete with balcony, without being subdivided, is the *Circle Uptown* at 3426 Connecticut Ave. NW (966–5400). The **American Film Institute** (Kennedy Center Hall of States entrance) emphasizes theme-oriented festivals. The box office is open 5 to 9 P.M., Mon.–Fri.; weekends, one hour before showtime. Shows usually scheduled twice a day, at 6:30 P.M. and 8:30 or 9 P.M. Non-member tickets are $4.50 (785–4600). The major theater chains in the city that specialize in first-run productions are the *K-B* and the *Circle* chains. The *Biograph* at 2819 M St. NW (333–2696), focuses on foreign and avant-garde films and offers moderate weekend shows. $4.50, $2 senior citizens and children under 12.

MUSIC. The weekly music scene in Washington is discussed in detail in the local newspapers and specifically the Friday *Washington Post* Weekend tabloid and the Sunday Show section. Some highlights to plan for are free summer outdoor events by the military bands and orchestras and performances by the National Symphony Orchestra on major holidays.

The National Symphony performs at the John F. Kennedy Center for the Performing Arts (800–424–8504 or 785–8100) from Sept.–June in the Concert Hall. Mstislav Rostropovich is the music director.

The Barns of Wolf Trap. Wolf Trap Park, Vienna, VA (703–938–2404). Wide variety of weekend music and dance programs. Oct. to May season. Reasonable prices.

The Washington Opera is the resident opera company of the John F. Kennedy Center for the Performing Arts with a full calendar from early November until early February. Depending on production, they use both the 2,200-seat Opera House and the smaller, 1,100-seat Eisenhower Theater for their ensemble opera productions. Standing-room is available for all performances at $8.50 (at press time) in the Opera House and $8 in the Eisenhower Theater whether the event is sold out or not. Call (800–424–8504 or 822–4757) for ticket information.

Wolf Trap Farm Park, Vienna, VA (703–255–1900) is an easy drive from downtown on I-66 and the Dulles Toll Road. The nation's only national park for the performing arts has been rebuilt after a tragic fire several years ago. Events are classified in a range of ticket prices, and a few programs, especially on Sundays and holidays, are free. Lawn seats (gourmet picnics have become the blanket rage) are available at reduced prices.

Washington Performing Arts Society (WPAS) (393–3600) is the nonprofit organization that sponsors orchestra, recital, and dance-company productions at the Kennedy Center and other theaters.

DANCE. Dance production in Washington runs the range from full-scale university production to those sponsored by the WPAS and held at the Kennedy Center. The height of the season is in December when two companies present *The Nutcracker.* **Washington Ballet** (362–1683) has a box office at George Washington University's Lisner Auditorium.

Arena Stage at the Old Vat Room (488–3300) has played host to Stephen Wade's "Banjo Dancing" for over 7 years now. He clogs and jigs and spins his yarns as he makes history come alive on the small stage.

STAGE. There are no shortages of theater productions in the Washington area, between those at the Kennedy Center to smaller productions at college theaters around town. Most of these groups use Ticketplace for their unsold seats.

Theater in Washington literally begins at the **Kennedy Center** with dramatic plays and musical productions in the Eisenhower Theater. Each year for two weeks in the spring the **American College Theater,** the best in college productions chosen from 12 regional festival competitions throughout the country, gives free performances in the Terrace Theater. Free productions are often available in spring at Imagination Celebration, in the summertime and at the December Holiday Festival. For all information, call (800–424–8504 or 254–3600) daily from 10 A.M.–9 P.M., Sunday noon–9.

National Theater, 1321 Pennsylvania Ave., NW (628–6161), is the oldest cultural institution in Washington, dating back to 1835. It has undergone a major $6-million renovation, restoring its original prominence as the "Theater of Presidents." There is a special patron ticket half-price program for senior citizens, full-time students, handicapped persons, economically disadvantaged, and certain grades of the military. There are also special free Saturday and Monday amateur theater programs.

Arena Stage, 6th and Maine Ave. SW (488–3300), houses the Arena, the Kreeger, and the Old Vat Room theaters. Productions range from new works to foreign productions, including a number of revivals. Student and senior citizen discounts available.

Ford's Theater, 511–10th St. NW 20004 (347–4833), represents a tour into history, as it has been restored to its appearance, at the time of Abraham Lincoln's assassination in April, 1865. Seniors can participate in the reduced price Matinee Club.

Warner Theater, 13th St. between E and F sts. (626–1050), is a former movie house that now holds concerts and other stage productions.

As for university theater productions, the most elaborate ones are in the **Hartke Theater** at Catholic University (635–5367). There are discounts for senior citizens and students.

Other productions of interest include those at the *Folger Theater* (546–4000), *Source Theater* (462–1073), the *Olney Theater* (924–3400), and the *Woolly Mammoth Theater* (393–3939).

SHOPPING. Washington has become a trendy center of high-priced, high fashion shopping. At the same time, its off-price emphasis has spread into outlying outlet centers. If you have designer taste but a limited budget for shopping, you should have no difficulty making the two match.

In Washington the sales tax is 6 percent (although restaurant meals are taxed 8 percent), in Virginia 4.5 percent, and in Maryland 5 percent. The following stores all offer discounted merchandise and are arranged by categories: women, men and family. Check with each store for its specific return policy. Also, phone numbers listed below are for one store in the chain. Call for other locations in the area.

Women

Loehmann's. (703–573–1510). The famous New York-born women's off-price retailer has large, unprivate dressing rooms and merchandise with the labels clipped off, but the crowds don't seem to mind. Not all merchandise is in perfect condition. No charge cards accepted. All sales are final.

Sassafras. (301–469–8500). What was once a single local discounter has grown into a competitive discount sportswear chain, with prices at least 25 percent off.

T.H. Mandy. (202–659–0024). The emphasis here is contemporary first-quality sportswear with large selections of slacks, sweaters, and skirts. They have a minimum 20 percent off policy.

Men

Dash's Designer. (202–296–4470). A men's discount clothing center that looks like a regular retail store, but has a 45 to 50 percent off policy.

Jos. A. Bank Clothiers. (202–466–2282). One of the oldest local discounters, with an extensive mail order business. They design and manufacture their own merchandise and have expanded their women's department over the last several years.

Kuppenheimer. (301–984–3765). As a manufacturer, they have developed a large range of quality clothing at below-retail prices.

Wall Street Clothing. (301–770–4984). They carry men's clothing in hard-to-find large sizes. Discounts average 40 percent.

Family

Burlington Coat Factory Outlet. (301–736–6685). Lost of famous brand name items available at 25 to 60 percent off. Household goods, too.

Marshall's. (301–345–0660). Their approach to discounting is to carry a large number of products, some of which are from this season and others that represent manufacturer's overstocks. Also, stocks household items such as glassware and linens, and jewelry.

Syms. (703–241–8500). Primarily a men's and women's discounter, it has a large inventory of big name designers. They are especially strong in the men's suit department and offer continual markdowns on merchandise that does not sell quickly.

Regular Department Stores and Specialty Shops. For well-heeled shoppers there are two main department stores: *Woodward and Lathrop* and *Hecht's* with downtown locations and in area shopping centers. *Neiman Marcus, Garfinckel's, Saks Fifth Avenue, Bloomingdale's,* and *Lord and Taylor* offer more specialty shopping with fewer locations (Saks and Neiman's each have one store in the area) and high-fashion full-service shopping.

For a present for a friend back home, you'll enjoy the varied boutiques at the elegantly restored Victorian mall *Georgetown Park* 3222 M St. NW. Next door to the National Theater are *The Shops at National Place* 1331 Pennsylvania Ave. NW that offer boutiques and dining relaxation. Also downtown is the *Pavillion at the Old Post Office* 1100 Pennsylvania Ave. NW with shops, restaurants, and entertainment on weekends and holidays.

DINING OUT. Almost before a country becomes headline news, there's a restaurant serving that country's ethnic cooking style. However, many restaurants close almost as soon as they open; it is a good idea to call before setting out. Many other restaurants have very pricey menus. Because Washington is regarded as the premier expense account town, it is no wonder that there is an almost unending proliferation of "expensive" places where lunch can exceed $30 per person. It's often challenging to find "reasonable" and "very economical" places where you feel you get quality at affordable prices. When practical, consider brunch, especially an all-you-can-eat brunch and make it the day's main meal. Or opt for a late lunch, when menu prices are often more reasonable than at dinner.

Restaurant categories, based on a three-course dinner for one person, without beverage, tax, or tip, are: *Reasonable,* $10 to $15; *Very Economical,* $6 to $10; and *Low Budget,* under $6. Unless otherwise noted, all restaurants accept some, if not all, major credit cards.

Reasonable

American Cafe. Georgetown: 1211 Wisconsin Ave. NW (337–3600); Capitol Hill: 227 Massachusetts Ave. NE (547–8500); and other suburban locations. Intriguing American cuisine and regional specialties; imaginative soups, salads, and sandwiches; yummy desserts. Great for brunch, lunch, dinner, or late-night snack. Trendy decor.

The Armadillo. 4912 Wisconsin Ave. NW (244–3961). Neighborhood Southwest-styled Mexican restaurant with weekday two-for-one Happy Hour and fresh fruit margaritas. Rice and beans accompany the dinners. No reservation policy.

Bamiyan. 3320 M St. NW (338–1896); also 300 King. St., Alexandria (548–9006). For your introduction to Afghan food there are stews and curries to tickle your tastebuds as well as Kabobs or vegetarian dishes.

Brasil Tropical. 2519 Pennsylvania Ave. NW (293–1773). If you're willing to keep trying different dishes, the stew and specialty fish items will please your palate. Weekend samba music.

Chadwick's. 3205 K St. NW (333–2565). Sandwiches, salads, burgers, and soups with nightly dinner specials. Happy Hour appetizer menu. Several locations. No reservations.

Hamburger Hamlet. 3125 M St. NW, Georgetown (965–6970). Stay with the hamburger portion of the menu, and save room for the ultimate fudge cake.

Hunan Gourmet. 726 7th St. NW (783–6268). Here's a chance to experience both Hunan- and Szechuan-style dishes.

Matuba. 2915 Columbia Pike, Arlington (703–521–2811); and 4918 Cordell Ave., Bethesda (301–652–7449). A pretty neighborhood setting to sample sushi and other Japanese specialties. Everything prepared with an eye for detail.

New Orleans Cafe. 1790 Columbia Rd. NW (234–5111). Here you can try a creole, a gumbo, or a jambalaya. Brunch served daily at all hours. Happy Hour two-for-one drinks.

Omega. 1858 Columbia Rd. NW (462–1732). One of the original neighborhood restaurants in Adams-Morgan. Black beans and white rice accompany the generous Cuban and South American dishes. Good place to try paella.

Suzanne's. 1735 Connecticut Ave. NW (483–4633); and at the Phillips Collection, 600–21st St. NW (483–7779). Popular caterer with a wine bar and intimate second-floor, light menu restaurant, daily except Sunday. At the museum location there are morning and teatime options in addition to lunch, daily except Mon.

Thai Room. 5037 Connecticut Ave. NW (244–5933). Lots of appetizers and your choice of spicy seasonings. Easy way to sample satays.

The Tombs. 1226–36th St. NW, Georgetown (965–1789). University favorite for burgers and pizza. Late night dining and no reservations.

Tout Va Bien. 1063–31st St. NW (965–1212). A chance to visit Georgetown in a pretty, unharried, French town house cafe. Daily specials complement unusual dishes like avocado-topped calf's liver.

Very Economical

Armand's Chicago Pizzeria. 4231 Wisconsin Ave. NW (686–9450), plus 3 other locations in the area. Popular with nearby college students for its deep-dish pies and 6-foot subs. Long lines often, but it's open late and has carry-out.

Astor. 1813 M St. NW (331–7994). If it's a Greek dish you've never tried then start with a salad and add a moussaka. Save room for baklava. Upstairs entertainment.

Big Wong. 610 H St. NW (638–0116). Noisy and crowded, and for a good reason: the prices are very low and the quality of the largely Cantonese fare is consistent at this basic basement eatery.

Booeymonger. 5252 Wisconsin Ave. NW (686–5805) and a small shop corner deli in Georgetown, 3265 Prospect St. NW (333–4810). Primarily a salad, sandwich and sub menu. Vegetarian possibilities. No credit cards.

China Inn. 629 H St. NW (842–0910). Cantonese and Szechuan restaurant in the heart of Chinatown. Carry-out menu also available.

Curtain Call Cafe. Rooftop Terrace level, Kennedy Center (833–8870). No hassle pre-theater dining. Food timed to performance schedules. Open 5–8 P.M., Tues.–Sat.

El Torito. 700 Water St. SW (554–5302). Large number of dishes under $5 in this festive atmosphere with a number of suburban locations. Popular for Happy Hour and extra-sized frozen margaritas.

Encore Cafeteria. Kennedy Center (833–8870). Perfect after the tour or anytime you're in the neighborhood. Soups, salads, and hot entrees. Classic view of D.C. skyline. Open 11 A.M.–7 P.M., seven days a week. No credit cards.

Hawk 'n Dove. 329 Pennsylvania Ave. SE (543–3300). A long-time Hill favorite for burgers and deli-type sandwiches. Homemade soups and chili.

Kalorama Cafe. 228 18th St. NW (667–1022). A natural foods vegetarian restaurant in Adams-Morgan with an eclectic menu. Pastas, tempura, and spiced shrimp. Popular Sunday brunch. No credit cards.

Kramerbooks & Afterwords. 1517 Connecticut Ave. NW (387–1462). If you've always wanted to eat in a library, this is for you. Homemade soups, pastas, and desserts. Perfect for a leisurely cappuccino breakfast.

Luigi's. 1132 19th St. NW (331–7574). Midtown pizza location. Popular at lunch and with university crowd in the evenings.

Mr. L's & Sun Delicatessen. 5018 Connecticut Ave. NW (244–4343). Two menus—deli and Chinese—in one setting. Leanest corned beef around.

Red Sea. 2463–18th St. NW (483–5000). Try the platter—a taste of the house specialties, chicken, lamb, and beef stews. Some vegetarian dishes.

Timberlake's. 1726 Connecticut Ave. NW (483–2266). What started as a neighborhood bar has developed into more than just another burger place. Daily specials, specialty soups and desserts. Late night stop for burgers.

Tom Sarris Orleans House. 1213 Wilson Blvd., Arlington (703–524–2929). All-you-can-eat riverboat salad bar. Famous for reasonably priced prime rib dinners. No reservations. Often long lines.

Vie de France. 1990 K St. NW (659–0055) and three other locations in D.C. Bakery-turned-cafe. Indulge yourself with croissant or brioche dishes. Also, soups, quiches, burgers, and daily specials. Popular for weekend brunches.

Low Budget

Adams-Morgan Spaghetti Garden. 2317 18th St. NW (265–6665). No less crowded than its international neighbors with consistently high quality and reasonably priced pasta performances.

Connecticut Connection. Farragut North Metro Stop, 1001 Connecticut Ave. NW (783–1101). Eclectic group of fast food possibilities. No credit cards.

Hard Times Cafe. 1404 King St., Alexandria (703–683–5340) and Rockville. Here's your chance to do a spice test—try Cincinnati, Texas, or vegetarian chili.

Kitcheteria Cafeteria. Harrington Hotel, 11th and E St. NW (628–8140). Downtown popular spot for busy tourist schedules. Nothing fancy, but all hearty and homemade.

Le Souperb. 1221 Connecticut Ave. NW (347–7600). Over 50 varieties of soup for any season's mood. Also, lots of homemade desserts. If a salad bar is more appealing, there is one available. No credit cards.

National Gallery of Art Buffet. In concourse between east and west buildings (737–4215). One of the prettier museum cafeteria spots. Avoid the hot-steamed burgers and fries and select a salad or freshly made sandwich. Adjacent to table service restaurant. No credit cards.

Reeves Bakery. 1209 F St. NW (347–3781). Well loved, down-to-earth landmark bakery/restaurant convenient to Metro Center. Famous for strawberry pie in season and an all-you-can-eat brunch (served 6:30–11:30 A.M. Mon. to Fri., until 12 P.M. Sat.). Counter service and tables. Closed Sun.

Sholl's Colonial Cafeteria. 1990 K St. NW (296–3065). Long regarded as Washington's premier cafeteria with homemade pies and fresh vegetables. Crowds line up early. Closed Sun. No credit cards.

Sholl's New Cafeteria. 1735 N. Lynn St., Rosslyn (703–528–8841). Originally opened by the original Sholl's, this establishment is under new management and draws a good luncheon crowd. Near Rosslyn Metro station. Closed Sat. and Sun.

Recommended Splurge. Dominique's. 1900 Pennsylvania Ave. NW (452–1126). What fun to dine in the atmosphere of the stars and the local power brokers! Or maybe it's the endangered species menu with rattlesnake and buffalo catching your eye. Make reservations and eat early (5:30–6:30 P.M.) or late (after 10:30 P.M.) for the reduced prix-fixe menu ($14.95). Afterwards, you can go home and tell your friends how you mingled with the gossip column names that want Dominique himself or the affable hostesses to sit and share an anecdote. Reservations are a must!

Brunches. Many of the prior listings indicate daily or weekend brunches. More elaborate, detailed, and often more expensive productions are at the hotels. Plan on dining late and stretching your budget by making this the main meal of the day. You'll have no shortage of items nor need any excuses to start your day with a Continental breakfast and have only the brunch. Most of these are under $20 per person. Some charge extra for coffee and juice; others include beverage and offer complimentary champagne.

Hyatt Hotels (various locations). Sunday brunches run the gamut with everything from ice sculptures to soft ice cream machines.

Marriott Hotels. Most hotels in the area have some form of Sunday brunch or dinner buffet. Also, many have an all-you-can-eat weekday buffet.

Cafes and Coffeehouses. When spring comes, restaurants in the city move outdoors. Even if it's only a few tables bordering a traffic-clogged intersection, outdoor cafes attract a loyal following. There are often blocks of next door restaurant tables. Connecticut Avenue, M St. downtown, upper Wisconsin Avenue, and Dupont Circle areas head the list. Other cafes are listed by price range in the main dining guide.

Dinner Theaters. A show and a meal make dinner theaters an almost unbeatable price combination. If you don't mind a heavy lunch, they're even more reasonable for matinee performances. Menus are often keyed to the production. Reservations are strongly recommended and visitors should allow for travel time as few of these establishments are near the main downtown corridor.

d.c. Space. 443–7th St. NW (347–1445). Avant-garde cabaret-dinner theater and nightly dinner specials in the city's new arts section. Downtown location near the Portrait Gallery. From $8, food additional. Also open for regular luncheon and dinner menu.

Harlequin. 1330 E. Gude Dr., Rockville (301–340–8515). Lively musical productions and theme-laden buffets. Nonsmoking performance and special children's priced matinees. Open Tues.–Sun. evenings with Wed. and Sun. matinees. From $30 to $31.75.

Hayloft. 10501 Balls Ford Rd., Manassas (703–631–0230). Equity performers and ice-sculptured buffets. Open Tues.–Sun. with some Thurs. and Sun. matinees. $22.50–$28.

Lazy Susan. U.S. 1, Woodbridge (703–494–6311). Pennsylvania Dutch buffet served Tues.–Sun. $24 to $26.

Toby's. South Entrance to Village of Columbia at Route 29, Columbia, MD (301–596–6161). Continental buffet and performers from the theater's own acting school. Performances Tues.–Sun. evenings at 8 P.M. Also matinees on occasional Wed., and every Sun. $21.95–$26.50.

West End Dinner Theater. 4615 Duke St., Alexandria, VA (703–370–2500). The area's newest facility complete with an elaborate buffet. Attractive setting with evening performances Tues.–Sat., and Wed. and Sun. matinees. $24.25–$30.25.

NIGHTLIFE AND BARS. There is no shortage of lively clubs and bars throughout town. The downtown professional corridor, Georgetown, Capitol Hill, and Dupont Circle house the most spots. Some partygoers get started with happy hour prices and stay until closing. All areas, even popular ones, can become a little suspect late at night. Security is a definite concern; after all this is a big city and it's easy to have problems.

Hard liquor drinks can easily top $3 in the majority of the establishments with wine and beer near $2. The legal drinking age in D.C. is 18 for beer and wine, 21 for hard liquor and picture identification is an acceptable form of proof of age. In Maryland and in Virginia the legal drinking age is 21.

Clubs are constantly changing. Call ahead to see who's in town or read the Friday Weekend section, the *Washington Post.*

Comedy

Comedy Cafe. 1520 K St. NW (638–JOKE).

Garvin's Comedy Club. 1335 Green Ct. NW (near 13th and L) (726–1334).

Country

Birchmere. 3901 Mt. Vernon Ave., Alexandria, VA (703–549–5919). Weekly schedule of country and bluegrass entertainers including the Seldom Scene on Thurs. Limited food.

Dinner Cruises

Potomac party cruises on the *Dandy,* Zero Prince St., Old Town, Alexandria, VA (683–6076). Four-course dinner or luncheon buffet. Music and dance floor with L $25, D $40. Luncheon and dinner cruises aboard the 600–passenger *Spirit of Washington.* Departures from Pier 4, 6th and Water sts., SW. L from $15.95, D from $24.95, mid-Mar. to the end of Dec. (554–8000).

Jazz

Blues Alley. 1073 Wisconsin Ave. NW, Georgetown (337–4141). The city's oldest jazz supper club with a New Orleans-style menu and big name performers. Shows at 8:30 A.M. and 10:30 P.M. plus midnight shows on Fri. and Sat. Cover charge from $8–$25.

One Step Down. 2517 Pennsylvania Ave. NW (331–8863). Live music Thur.–Mon. nights. Workshop jam sessions at Sat. and Sun. afternoons. Cover charge for evening shows.

Rock

9:30 Club. 930 F St. NW (393–0930). New wave bar with videos, live music, and dancing. A Happy Hour video cabaret on Wed., Thurs., and Fri. from 4–9 P.M.

SECURITY. Washington has had a reputation for being dangerous, which it has been working hard to change. It is a big city with its share of big city problems. The 14th Street corridor has drug and prostitution problems and some downtown areas have a deserted feel after the theaters close.

Common sense prevails. Lock your car doors. Do not walk around in neighborhoods you're unfamiliar with, or in crowded noon hour districts that become deserted at night. Hold tight to your purse and protect your wallet from pickpockets. Leave valuables locked up in a hotel safe-deposit box and hide packages in car trunks. Use taxicabs for door-to-door service, and protect yourself by using traveler's checks.

Index

Fodor's Travel Guides

U.S. Guides

Alaska
American Cities
The American South
Arizona
Atlantic City & the New Jersey Shore
Boston
California
Cape Cod
Carolinas & the Georgia Coast
Chesapeake
Chicago
Colorado
Dallas & Fort Worth
Disney World & the Orlando Area
The Far West
Florida
Greater Miami, Fort Lauderdale, Palm Beach
Hawaii
Hawaii *(Great Travel Values)*
Houston & Galveston
I-10: California to Florida
I-55: Chicago to New Orleans
I-75: Michigan to Florida
I-80: San Francisco to New York
I-95: Maine to Miami
Las Vegas
Los Angeles, Orange County, Palm Springs
Maui
New England
New Mexico
New Orleans
New Orleans *(Pocket Guide)*
New York City
New York City *(Pocket Guide)*
New York State
Pacific North Coast
Philadelphia
Puerto Rico *(Fun in)*
Rockies
San Diego
San Francisco
San Francisco *(Pocket Guide)*
Texas
United States of America
Virgin Islands *(U.S. & British)*
Virginia
Waikiki
Washington, DC
Williamsburg, Jamestown & Yorktown

Foreign Guides

Acapulco
Amsterdam
Australia, New Zealand & the South Pacific
Austria
The Bahamas
The Bahamas *(Pocket Guide)*
Barbados *(Fun in)*
Beijing, Guangzhou & Shanghai
Belgium & Luxembourg
Bermuda
Brazil
Britain *(Great Travel Values)*
Canada
Canada *(Great Travel Values)*
Canada's Maritime Provinces
Cancún, Cozumel, Mérida, The Yucatán
Caribbean
Caribbean *(Great Travel Values)*
Central America
Copenhagen, Stockholm, Oslo, Helsinki, Reykjavik
Eastern Europe
Egypt
Europe
Europe *(Budget)*
Florence & Venice
France
France *(Great Travel Values)*
Germany
Germany *(Great Travel Values)*
Great Britain
Greece
Holland
Hong Kong & Macau
Hungary
India
Ireland
Israel
Italy
Italy *(Great Travel Values)*
Jamaica *(Fun in)*
Japan
Japan *(Great Travel Values)*
Jordan & the Holy Land
Kenya
Korea
Lisbon
Loire Valley
London
London *(Pocket Guide)*
London *(Great Travel Values)*
Madrid
Mexico
Mexico *(Great Travel Values)*
Mexico City & Acapulco
Mexico's Baja & Puerto Vallarta, Mazatlán, Manzanillo, Copper Canyon
Montreal
Munich
New Zealand
North Africa
Paris
Paris *(Pocket Guide)*
People's Republic of China
Portugal
Province of Quebec
Rio de Janeiro
The Riviera *(Fun on)*
Rome
St. Martin/St. Maarten
Scandinavia
Scotland
Singapore
South America
South Pacific
Southeast Asia
Soviet Union
Spain
Spain *(Great Travel Values)*
Sweden
Switzerland
Sydney
Tokyo
Toronto
Turkey
Vienna
Yugoslavia

Special-Interest Guides

Bed & Breakfast Guide: North America
1936...On the Continent
Royalty Watching
Selected Hotels of Europe
Selected Resorts and Hotels of the U.S.
Ski Resorts of North America
Views to Dine by around the World